Lecture Notes in Computer Science 10403

Commenced Publication in 1973
Founding and Former Series Editors:
Gerhard Goos, Juris Hartmanis, and Jan van Leeuwen

More information about this series at http://www.springer.com/series/7410

Jonathan Katz · Hovav Shacham (Eds.)

Advances in Cryptology – CRYPTO 2017

37th Annual International Cryptology Conference Santa Barbara, CA, USA, August 20–24, 2017 Proceedings, Part III

Springer

Editors
Jonathan Katz
University of Maryland
College Park, MD
USA

Hovav Shacham
UC San Diego
La Jolla, CA
USA

ISSN 0302-9743 ISSN 1611-3349 (electronic)
Lecture Notes in Computer Science
ISBN 978-3-319-63696-2 ISBN 978-3-319-63697-9 (eBook)
DOI 10.1007/978-3-319-63697-9

Library of Congress Control Number: 2017947035

LNCS Sublibrary: SL4 – Security and Cryptology

Printed on acid-free paper

This Springer imprint is published by Springer Nature
The registered company is Springer International Publishing AG
The registered company address is: Gewerbestrasse 11, 6330 Cham, Switzerland

Preface

The 37th International Cryptology Conference (Crypto 2017) was held at the University of California, Santa Barbara, USA, during August 20–24, 2017, sponsored by the International Association for Cryptologic Research.

There were 311 submissions to Crypto 2017, a substantial increase from previous years. The Program Committee, aided by nearly 350 external reviewers, selected 72 papers to appear in the program. We are indebted to all the reviewers for their service. Their reviews and discussions, if printed out, would consume about a thousand pages.

Two papers—"Identity-Based Encryption from the Diffie-Hellman Assumption," by Nico Döttling and Sanjam Garg, and "The first Collision for Full SHA-1," by Marc Stevens, Elie Bursztein, Pierre Karpman, Ange Albertini, and Yarik Markov—were honored as best papers. A third paper—"Watermarking Cryptographic Functionalities from Standard Lattice Assumptions," by Sam Kim and David J. Wu—was honored as best paper authored exclusively by young researchers.

Crypto was the venue for the 2017 IACR Distinguished Lecture, delivered by Shafi Goldwasser. Crypto also shared an invited speaker, Cédric Fournet, with the 30th IEEE Computer Security Foundations Symposium (CSF 2017), which was held jointly with Crypto.

We are grateful to Steven Myers, the Crypto general chair; to Shai Halevi, author of the IACR Web Submission and Review system; to Alfred Hofmann, Anna Kramer, and their colleagues at Springer; to Sally Vito of UCSB Conference Services; and, of course, everyone who submitted a paper to Crypto and everyone who attended the conference.

August 2017

Jonathan Katz
Hovav Shacham

Crypto 2017

The 37th IACR International Cryptology Conference

University of California, Santa Barbara, CA, USA
August 20–24, 2017

Sponsored by the *International Association for Cryptologic Research*

General Chair

Steven Myers	Indiana University, USA

Program Chairs

Jonathan Katz	University of Maryland, USA
Hovav Shacham	UC San Diego, USA

Program Committee

Masayuki Abe	NTT Secure Platform Laboratories, Japan
Shweta Agrawal	IIT Madras, India
Adi Akavia	The Academic College of Tel Aviv-Yaffo, Israel
Elena Andreeva	KU Leuven, Belgium
Mihir Bellare	UC San Diego, USA
Dan Boneh	Stanford University, USA
Elette Boyle	IDC Herzliya, Israel
Ran Canetti	Boston University, USA, and Tel Aviv University, Israel
Jung Hee Cheon	Seoul National University, Korea
Dana Dachman-Soled	University of Maryland, USA
Ivan Damgård	Aarhus University, Denmark
Nico Döttling	UC Berkeley, USA
Orr Dunkelman	University of Haifa, Israel
Eiichiro Fujisaki	NTT Secure Platform Laboratories, Japan
Sergey Gorbunov	University of Waterloo, Canada
Vipul Goyal	Carnegie Mellon University, USA
Matthew Green	Johns Hopkins University, USA
Nadia Heninger	University of Pennsylvania, USA
Viet Tung Hoang	Florida State University, USA
Dennis Hofheinz	Karlsruhe Institute of Technology, Germany
Sorina Ionica	Université de Picardie, France

Tetsu Iwata	Nagoya University, Japan
Seny Kamara	Brown University, USA
Gaëtan Leurent	Inria, France
Rachel Lin	UC Santa Barbara, USA
Stefan Lucks	Bauhaus-Universität Weimar, Germany
Vadim Lyubashevsky	IBM Zurich, Switzerland
Mohammad Mahmoody	University of Virginia, USA
Payman Mohassel	Visa Research, USA
Claudio Orlandi	Aarhus University, Denmark
Elisabeth Oswald	University of Bristol, UK
Rafael Pass	Cornell University, USA
Gregory G. Rose	TargetProof LLC, USA
Christian Schaffner	University of Amsterdam and CWI and QuSoft, The Netherlands
Gil Segev	Hebrew University, Israel
Yannick Seurin	ANSSI, France
Douglas Stebila	McMaster University, Canada
Stefano Tessaro	UC Santa Barbara, USA
Mehdi Tibouchi	NTT Secure Platform Laboratories, Japan
Eran Tromer	Tel Aviv University, Israel, and Columbia University, USA
Dominique Unruh	University of Tartu, Estonia
Vassilis Zikas	Rensselaer Polytechnic Institute, USA

Additional Reviewers

Aysajan Abidin
Shashank Agrawal
Thomas Agrikola
Ali Akhavi
Gorjan Alagic
Martin Albrecht
Jacob Alperin-Sheriff
Joel Alwen
Joran van Apeldoorn
Daniel Apon
Gilad Asharov
Tomer Ashur
Nuttapong Attrapadung
Christian Badertscher
Saikrishna Badrinarayanan
Shi Bai
Foteini Baldimtsi
Marshall Ball
Achiya Bar-On
Razvan Barbulescu
Guy Barwell
Carsten Baum
Amin Baumeler
Fabrice Benhamouda
Daniel J. Bernstein
Jean-François Biasse
Alex Biryukov
Nir Bitansky
Olivier Blazy
Jeremiah Blocki
Andrej Bogdanov
Xavier Bonnetain
Charlotte Bonte
Carl Bootland
Christina Boura
Zvika Brakerski
Brandon Broadnax
Leon Groot Bruinderink
Benedikt Bunz
Anne Canteaut
Angelo de Caro
Ignacio Cascudo
David Cash
Wouter Castryck
Nishanth Chandran
Eshan Chattopadhyay
Binyi Chen
Jie Chen
Yilei Chen
Alessandro Chiesa
Chongwon Cho
Arka Rai Chouduhri
Heewon Chung
Kai-Min Chung
Benoit Cogliati
Aloni Cohen

Ran Cohen
Katriel Cohn-Gordon
Henry Corrigan-Gibbs
Geoffroy Couteau
Alain Couvreur
Cas Cremers
Jan Czajkowski
Wei Dai
Bernardo David
Jean Paul Degabriele
Jeroen Delvaux
Apoorvaa Deshpande
Bogdan Adrian Dina
Itai Dinur
Yevgeniy Dodis
Benjamin Dowling
Rafael Dowsley
Leo Ducas
Yfke Dulek
Tuyet Duong
Tuyet Thi Anh Duong
Fred Dupuis
Frédéric Dupuis
Alfredo Rial Duran
Sébastien Duval
Aner Moshe Ben Efraim
Maria Eichlseder
Keita Emura
Naomi Ephraim
Saba Eskandarian
Thomas Espitau
Oriol Farràs
Pooya Farshim
Sebastian Faust
Prastudy Fauzi
Nelly Fazio
Serge Fehr
Houda Ferradi
Manuel Fersch
Dario Fiore
Ben Fisch
Joseph Fitzsimons
Nils Fleischhacker
Tore Frederiksen
Rotem Arnon Friedman
Georg Fuchsbauer
Marc Fyrbiak
Tommaso Gagliardoni
Nicolas Gama
Juan Garay
Sanjam Garg
Christina Garman
Romain Gay
Peter Gazi
Alexandre Gelin
Daniel Genkin
Marios Georgiou
Benoit Gerard
Essam Ghadafi
Niv Gilboa
Dov Gordon
Rishab Goyal
Vincent Grosso
Jens Groth
Paul Grubbs
Siyao Guo
Helene Haag
Helene Haagh
Kyoohyung Han
Marcella Hastings
Carmit Hazay
Ethan Heilman
Brett Hemenway
Minki Hhan
Justin Holmgren
Akinori Hosoyamada
Yan Huang
Pavel Hubacek
Ilia Iliashenko
Vincenzo Iovino
Yuval Ishai
Joseph Jaeger
Zahra Jafragholi
Tibor Jager
Aayush Jain
Abhishek Jain
Chethan Kamath
Bhavana Kanukurthi
Angshuman Karmakar
Pierre Karpman
Stefan Katzenbeisser
Xagawa Keita
Marcel Keller
Nathan Keller
Iordanis Kerenidis
Dakshita Khurana
Andrey Kim
Dongwoo Kim
Duhyeong Kim
Eunkyung Kim
Jae-yun Kim
Jihye Kim
Jinsu Kim
Jiseung Kim
Sam Kim
Taechan Kim
Fuyuki Kitagawa
Susumu Kiyoshima
Dima Kogan
Vlad Kolesnikov
Ilan Komargodski
Venkata Koppula
Venkata Kopulla
Evgenios Kornaropoulos
Juliane Kraemer
Mukul Kulkarni
Ashutosh Kumar
Ranjit Kumaresan
Alptekin Küpçü
Lakshmi Kuppusamy
Thijs Laarhoven
Changmin Lee
Joohee Lee
Younho Lee
Nikos Leonardos
Tancrède Lepoint
Baiyu Li
Benoit Libert
Eik List
Yi-Kai Liu
Steve Lu
Yun Lu
Atul Luykx
Saeed Mahloujifar
Giulio Malavolta
Alex Malozemoff
Antonio Marcedone
Daniel P. Martin

Marco Martinoli
Daniel Masny
Takahiro Matsuda
Florian Mendel
Bart Mennink
Peihan Miao
Daniele Micciancio
Gabrielle De Micheli
Ian Miers
Andrew Miller
Kazuhiko Minematsu
Tarik Moataz
Ameer Mohammed
Hart Montgomery
Andrew Morgan
Nicky Mouha
Pratyay Mukherjee
Muhammad Naveed
María Naya-Plasencia
Kartik Nayak
Gregory Neven
Ruth Ng
Michael Nielsen
Tobias Nilges
Ryo Nishimaki
Ariel Nof
Kaisa Nyberg
Adam O'Neill
Maciej Obremski
Sabine Oechsner
Miyako Ohkubo
Rafail Ostrovsky
Daniel Page
Jiaxin Pan
Omer Paneth
Dimitris Papadopoulos
Sunno Park
Anat Paskin-Cherniavsky
Kenny Paterson
Arpita Patra
Filip Pawlega
Chris Peikert
Josef Pieprzyk
Cécile Pierrot
Krzysztof Pietrzak
Benny Pinkas
Rafael del Pino
Oxana Poburinnaya
David Pointcheval
Antigoni Polychroniadou
Raluca Ada Popa
Bart Preneel
Thomas Prest
Emmanuel Prouff
Carla Rafols
Srinivasan Raghuraman
Samuel Ranellucci
Mariana Raykova
Oded Regev
Ling Ren
Oscar Reparaz
Leo Reyzin
Silas Richelson
Matt Robshaw
Mike Rosulek
Yann Rotella
Lior Rotem
Ron Rothblum
Arnab Roy
Sujoy Sinha Roy
Olivier Ruatta
Ulrich Rührmair
Yusuke Sakai
Olivier Sanders
Yu Sasaki
Sajin Sasy
Alessandra Scafuro
Patrick Schaumont
Thomas Schneider
Peter Scholl
Gregor Seiler
Ido Shahaf
abhi shelat
Timothy Sherwood
Kyoji Shibutani
Sina Shiehian
Mark Simkin
Leonie Simpson
Maciej Skorski
Nigel Smart
Yongha Son
Fang Song
Yongsoo Song
Pratik Soni
Florian Speelman
Akshayaram Srinivasan
Martijn Stam
François-Xavier Standaert
John Steinberger
Igors Stepanovs
Noah Stephens-Davidowitz
Valentin Suder
Koutarou Suzuki
Björn Tackmann
Alain Tapp
Isamu Teranishi
Benjamin Terner
Aishwarya Thiruvengadam
Sri Aravinda Krishnan Thyagarajan
Yosuke Todo
Junichi Tomida
Luca Trevisan
Roberto Trifiletti
Daniel Tschudi
Nik Unger
Salil Vadhan
Margarita Vald
Luke Valenta
Kerem Varici
Srinivas Vivek Venkatesh
Muthuramakrishnan Venkitasubramaniam
Daniele Venturi
Damien Vergnaud
Jorge Villar
Dhinakaran Vinayagamurthy
Ivan Visconti
Damian Vizar
Christine van Vreedendal
Michael Walter
Mingyuan Wang
Xiao Wang
Yuyu Wang
Yohei Watanabe

Hoeteck Wee
Avi Weinstock
Mor Weiss
Jakob Wenzel
Daniel Wichs
David Wu
Keita Xagawa
Sophia Yakoubov
Avishay Yanay
Kan Yasuda
Donggeon Yhee
Chen Yilei
Eylon Yogev
Kazuki Yoneyama
Lanqing Yu
Thomas Zacharias
Samee Zahur
Greg Zaverucha
Mark Zhandry
Ren Zhang
Yupeng Zhang
Hong-Sheng Zhou

Platinum Sponsor

NSF

Silver Sponsors

moz://a

FUJITSU

Western Digital.

Contents – Part III

Authenticated Encryption

Boosting Authenticated Encryption Robustness with Minimal Modifications

Tomer Ashur[1(✉)], Orr Dunkelman[2], and Atul Luykx[1,3]

[1] imec-COSIC, KU Leuven, Leuven, Belgium
{tashur,atul.luykx}@esat.kuleuven.be
[2] University of Haifa, Haifa, Israel
orrd@cs.haifa.ac.il
[3] Department of Computer Science, University of California, Davis,
One Shields Ave, Davis, CA 95616, USA

Abstract. Secure and highly efficient authenticated encryption (AE) algorithms which achieve data confidentiality and authenticity in the symmetric-key setting have existed for well over a decade. By all conventional measures, AES-OCB seems to be the AE algorithm of choice on any platform with AES-NI: it has a proof showing it is secure assuming AES is, and it is one of the fastest out of all such algorithms. However, algorithms such as AES-GCM and ChaCha20+Poly1305 have seen more widespread adoption, even though they will likely never outperform AES-OCB on platforms with AES-NI. Given the fact that changing algorithms is a long and costly process, some have set out to maximize the security that can be achieved with the already deployed algorithms, without sacrificing efficiency: ChaCha20+Poly1305 already improves over GCM in how it authenticates, GCM-SIV uses GCM's underlying components to provide nonce misuse resistance, and TLS1.3 introduces a randomized nonce in order to improve GCM's multi-user security. We continue this line of work by looking more closely at GCM and ChaCha20+Poly1305 to see what robustness they already provide over algorithms such as OCB, and whether minor variants of the algorithms can be used for applications where defense in depth is critical. We formalize and illustrate how GCM and ChaCha20+Poly1305 offer varying degrees of resilience to nonce misuse, as they can recover quickly from repeated nonces, as opposed to OCB, which loses all security. More surprisingly, by introducing minor tweaks such as an additional XOR, we can create a GCM variant which provides security even when unverified plaintext is released.

Keywords: Authenticated encryption · Robust · AES · OCB · ChaCha20 · Poly1305 GCM · RUP

1 Introduction

Authenticated encryption (AE) is well established within the research community as the method to achieve confidentiality and authenticity using symmetric

J. Katz and H. Shacham (Eds.): CRYPTO 2017, Part III, LNCS 10403, pp. 3–33, 2017.
DOI: 10.1007/978-3-319-63697-9_1

keys. Initially introduced as a response to a need in practice [6,7], it has caught on in recent years. As a result, AE is used in many different environments, each with their own security and efficiency requirements. For this reason, the ongoing CAESAR competition [20], which aims to identify the next generation of authenticated encryption schemes, drafted three use cases as guides to what AE schemes should target: lightweight, high-performance, and defense in depth.

Within the high-performance category, OCB [43,64,65] is one of the most competitive AE schemes. Over ten years old, it is well known for its speed, and theoretically achieves the best performance when measured in block cipher calls. Although OCB has been standardized [1,44], adoption has remained limited, for which its patents are usually assumed to be the main cause.

Instead, GCM [49] was chosen as the baseline algorithm with which to compare in the CAESAR competition. GCM is widely adopted and standardized [1,24], and although it remains slower than OCB due to the additional universal hash on the output, it is getting more competitive as a result of improved hardware support [30]. ChaCha20+Poly1305 [12,13,56] is a popular alternative for settings where AES-NI is not implemented.

OCB, GCM, and ChaCha20+Poly1305 all target the high-performance category. Other than the fact that GCM and ChaCha20+Poly1305 are already widely adopted, and setting aside differences between using AES versus ChaCha20, from a conventional point of view there seems to be little reason to prefer them over OCB.

1.1 Robust Algorithms

The increased adoption of AE has been accompanied by an improved understanding of the limits of AE security within the research community. Even though OCB, GCM, and ChaCha20+Poly1305 are secure as proved in the conventional models (relative to their underlying primitives), questions often arise as to how robust they are once one of the assumptions in those models no longer holds. Already in 2002, Ferguson [25] pointed out that with a birthday bound attack on OCB one can mount forgeries, and Joux [42] illustrated with his "forbidden attack" how one can similarly construct forgeries for GCM after a repeated nonce. Furthermore, many have expressed concerns with the improved effectiveness of multi-key brute-force attacks [14,16,17,21,28] when applied to widely deployed algorithms.

Given the fact that modifying and deploying algorithms requires significant effort, and that the longer algorithms are used, the more their components are optimized, there has been interest in finding minimal modifications to deployed algorithms so that they are robust to settings which break one of the assumptions of the conventional security definitions. For example, TLS added extra nonce randomization to combat easier key-recovery attacks in the multi-key setting, which was later analyzed by Bellare and Tackmann [11]. The combination of ChaCha20+Poly1305 is neither a direct application of Encrypt-then-MAC [6] nor a copy of GCM: the authentication key used for Poly1305 is changed for *every* message, thereby preventing attacks which make GCM fragile. Going a step further, worries about nonce misuse in GCM have led Gueron and Lindell to use the components underlying GCM in order to create GCM-SIV [31], an algorithm that provides best possible security even when nonces are repeated. The common theme among these modifications is to squeeze as much security out of the schemes without sacrificing efficiency.

1.2 Release of Unverified Plaintext

Previous modifications have focused on providing additional security in the multi-key setting, or when nonces are repeated. However, other robust security properties, such as security with variable-length tags [63], under distinguishable decryption failures [19], or under release of unverified plaintext [3] are equally desirable. The CAESAR competition's use case describing defense in depth lists authenticity and limited confidentiality damage from release of unverified plaintexts (RUP) as desirable properties [15].

One of the advantages of schemes secure under release of unverified plaintext is that they provide another line of defense with faulty implementations: if an implementation for whatever reason fails to check authenticity, then RUP-confidentiality guarantees that if the ciphertext did not originate from the sender or was modified en route, the resulting decrypted plaintext will look like garbage. Furthermore, there are settings where a RUP-secure AE scheme provides desirable properties beyond confidentiality and authenticity; in Appendix C we explain informally how our construction can be used to efficiently prevent the crypto-tagging attack in Tor, which is an attack on user anonymity.

State-of-the-art research might give the impression that achieving RUP security by minimally modifying existing schemes is out of reach: all designs providing such security either require significant changes, a completely new design, or an additional pass, making the schemes slower and adding design complexity. This is because so far the only solutions provided are essentially variable-input-length (VIL) ciphers [8], which can be viewed as block ciphers that can process arbitrarily long messages. However, VIL ciphers are "heavy" constructions, requiring often three or more passes over the plaintext in order to ensure sufficient mixing, or relying on subtle design choices to achieve security.

1.3 Contributions

We continue the line of research on robust AE design by exploring properties and variants of OCB, GCM, and ChaCha20+Poly1305 which go beyond the conventional view of AE.

Our first contribution focuses on analyzing the difference in nonce robustness provided by OCB, GCM, and ChaCha20+Poly1305, to provide a framework complementing the work of others [18,25,42,53]. The conventional nonce misuse models are very black and white about security: GCM and ChaCha20+Poly1305 do not provide security under nonce misuse since an adversary can determine the XOR of two plaintexts when both are encrypted under the same nonce.

However, what the conventional security models do not capture is that this insecurity affects only the involved plaintexts and does not "spill" onto others. If, for example, a faulty implementation repeats a nonce for a pair of plaintexts and then changes it correctly, confidentiality is only compromised for the plaintexts in the pair, and not for future plaintexts. In some sense, GCM (with 96 bit nonces) and ChaCha20+Poly1305 allow one to gracefully recover from re-used nonces by making them unique again, leading us to formalize such a definition, *nonce-misuse resilience*: plaintexts encrypted under unique nonces remain compartmentalized even when other plaintexts are compromised.

Within this model we establish that OCB is not resilient to nonce misuse, confirm that GCM with 96 bit nonces only provides confidentiality resilience, and that ChaCha20+Poly1305 provides both authenticity and confidentiality resilience, thereby formally showing that ChaCha20+Poly1305's choice to depart from both the Encrypt-then-MAC and GCM designs boosts robustness to nonce misuse. Inspired by this result, one can also tweak GCM to achieve the same level of nonce misuse resilience by applying Minematsu and Iwata's composition [53].

Our second, more surprising contribution is a minor modification to GCM which achieves both RUP confidentiality and authenticity, which neither OCB, GCM, nor ChaCha20+Poly1305 currently provide. Our design approach is generic, meaning it can add RUP security to a general class of encryption schemes. The core idea is to use a digest of the ciphertext to "hide" the nonce in such a way that recovering it properly requires that no change was made to the ciphertext. As a result, if a change *did* occur, it would affect the nonce, which, when used by the decryption algorithm, would decrypt the ciphertext into meaningless data.

2 Related Work

Our approach to analyzing nonce misuse differs from the line of research on *online* nonce misuse resistance [4,27,36], which seeks to analyze schemes which are not able to provide the best possible robustness to nonce misuse [66], but are able to guarantee more than nonce misuse resilience. Böck, Zauner, Devlin, Somorovsky, and Jovanovic [18] investigate the practical applicability of nonce-misusing attacks in TLS by searching for servers which repeat nonces with GCM.

Besides nonce misuse, another extension to the basic AE security model considers what happens when decryption algorithms may output multiple decryption errors [19]. Further research explored the security of known AE schemes when their decryption algorithms release partially decrypted plaintext before verification is complete [3], also known as the *release of unverified plaintext* (RUP) model. Both the multiple decryption error and RUP models were unified by Barwell, Page, and Stam [5] in the *subtle AE* framework, by using a "leakage" function which captures information leaked via a side channel. The "leakage" function represents any information that can be received through additional channels. Hoang, Krovetz, and Rogaway introduce the concept of "Robust AE" (RAE) [35] which formalizes one of the strongest types of security that an AE scheme can satisfy. Our use of the term "robust" describes a gradient, in which RAE represents the most robust form of AE, and conventional definitions the most basic form.

Imamura, Minematsu, and Iwata [37] show that ChaCha20+Poly1305 maintains authenticity in the RUP setting.

We follow Shrimpton and Terashima [71] in taking a modular approach to the problem of adding RUP security to encryption schemes, by first providing a solution in the most general form possible, and then providing an instantiation. Furthermore, our construction is similar to the lower half of Shrimpton and Terashima's PIV construction. However, their goal is to achieve something similar to a VIL cipher, which we argue might be overkill in some scenarios. Note that combining SIV [66] with our construction would result in a solution very similar to PIV. RIV [2] is another construction which takes a modular approach in designing a robust AE scheme.

For a survey on ways to construct VIL ciphers, see Shrimpton and Terashima's paper [71]. All the previous methods are generic approaches to designing VIL ciphers, although there are dedicated approaches as well, such as AEZ [35], which in fact aims for RAE.

Hirose, Sasaki, and Yasuda [33] presented a construction similar to ours. However, their construction only accounts for changes over the tag, rather than the entire ciphertext, hence their solution only provides limited robustness and would, for example, not prevent the Tor crypto-tagging attack described in Appendix C. In recent work, Hirose, Sasaki, and Yasuda [34] introduce constructions which do account for changes over the entire ciphertext, and focus on formalizing how such AE constructions make verification unskippable.

3 Preliminaries

3.1 Notation

The set of strings of length not greater than x bits is $\{0,1\}^{\leq x}$, and the set of strings of arbitrary length is $\{0,1\}^*$. Unless specified otherwise, all sets are subsets of $\{0,1\}^*$. If $X, Y \in \{0,1\}^*$, then $|X|$ is the length of X, and $X \parallel Y$ and XY denote the concatenation of X and Y.

Let ε denote the empty string, and let 0^n denote the n-bit string consisting of only zeros. Given a block size n, the function $\mathsf{len}_n(X)$ represents the length of X modulo 2^n as an n-bit string, and $X0^{*n}$ is X padded on the right with 0-bits to get a string of length a multiple of n. If $X \in \{0,1\}^*$, then $|X|_n = \lceil |X|/n \rceil$ is X's length in n-bit blocks. The operation

$$X[1]X[2]\cdots X[x] \xleftarrow{n} X \tag{1}$$

denotes splitting X into substrings such that $|X[i]| = n$ for $i = 1,\ldots,x-1$, $0 < |X[x]| \leq n$, and $X[1] \| X[2] \| \cdots \| X[x] = X$.

The set of n-bit strings is also viewed as the finite field $GF(2^n)$, by mapping $a_{n-1}\ldots a_1 a_0$ to the polynomial $a(\mathtt{x}) = a_{n-1} + a_{n-2}\mathtt{x} + \cdots + a_1\mathtt{x}^{n-1} + a_0\mathtt{x}^{n-1} \in$

$GF(2)[\mathrm{x}]$, and fixing an irreducible polynomial which defines multiplication in the field. For $n = 128$, the irreducible polynomial is $1 + \mathrm{x} + \mathrm{x}^2 + \mathrm{x}^7 + \mathrm{x}^{128}$, the one used for GCM.

The function $\mathsf{int}(Y)$ maps the j bit string $Y = a_{j-1} \ldots a_1 a_0$ to the integer $i = a_{j-1}2^{j-1} + \cdots + a_1 2 + a_0$, and $\mathsf{str}_j(i)$ maps the integer $i = a_{j-1}2^{j-1} + \cdots + a_1 2 + a_0 < 2^j$ to the j bit string $a_{j-1} \ldots a_1 a_0$. Let $\mathsf{inc}_m(X)$ denote the function which adds one modulo 2^m to X when viewed as an integer:

$$\mathsf{inc}_m(X) := \mathsf{str}_m(\mathsf{int}(X) + 1 \bmod 2^m)\,.$$

Define $\mathsf{msb}_j(X)$ to be the function that returns the j most significant bits of X, and $\mathsf{lsb}_j(X)$ the j least significant bits.

For a keyed function defined on a domain $\mathsf{K} \times \mathsf{X}$, we write $F(K, X)$ and $F_K(X)$ interchangeably. If the function has three inputs, $\mathsf{K} \times \mathsf{N} \times \mathsf{X}$, then the second input will often be written as a superscript, $F(K, N, X) = F_K^N(X)$. If $E : \{0,1\}^n \to \{0,1\}^m$ is a function, then the notation

$$F \leftarrow E(C \parallel \cdot) \tag{2}$$

defines F to be the function from $\{0,1\}^{n-|C|}$ to $\{0,1\}^m$ which maps an element $X \in \{0,1\}^{n-|C|}$ to $E(C \parallel X)$.

The expression $a \stackrel{?}{=} b$ evaluates to $\top$ if a equals b, and $\bot$ otherwise.

3.2 Adversaries and Advantages

An adversary $\mathbf{A}$ is an algorithm which interacts with an oracle O. Let $\mathbf{A}^O = 1$ be the event that $\mathbf{A}$ outputs 1 when interacting with O, then define

$$\underset{\mathbf{A}}{\Delta}(f\,;\,g) := \left|\mathbf{P}\left[\mathbf{A}^f = 1\right] - \mathbf{P}\left[\mathbf{A}^g = 1\right]\right|, \tag{3}$$

which is the advantage of $\mathbf{A}$ in distinguishing f from g, where f and g are viewed as random variables. The notation can be extended to multiple oracles by setting $O = (O_1, \ldots, O_\ell)$.

We assume that all keyed functions do not change their output length under different keys, that is, $|F_K(X)|$ is the same for all $K \in \mathsf{K}$. Given a keyed function F, define $\$_F$ to be the algorithm which, given X as input, outputs a string chosen uniformly at random from the set of strings of length $|F_K(X)|$ for any key K. When given the same input, $\$_F$ returns the same output. Often $\$_F$ is called a *random oracle*.

3.3 Authenticated Encryption Schemes

The syntax for conventional authenticated encryption (AE) schemes specifies an encryption and decryption algorithm, where the decryption algorithm may output either plaintext or a single, pre-defined error symbol. Formally, an AE scheme is a tuple of functions — encryption Enc and decryption Dec — where

$$\mathsf{Enc} : \mathsf{K} \times \mathsf{N} \times \mathsf{M} \to \mathsf{C}, \tag{4}$$
$$\mathsf{Dec} : \mathsf{K} \times \mathsf{N} \times \mathsf{C} \to \mathsf{M} \cup \{\bot\}, \tag{5}$$

with K the keys, N the nonces, M the messages, C the ciphertexts, and $\bot$ an error symbol not contained in M, which represents verification failure. It must be the case that for all $K \in \mathsf{K}$, $N \in \mathsf{N}$, and $M \in \mathsf{M}$,

$$\mathsf{Dec}_K^N(\mathsf{Enc}_K^N(M)) = M \quad . \tag{6}$$

AE schemes must provide both chosen-ciphertext confidentiality and authenticity. The AE advantage of adversary $\mathbf{A}$ against $\Pi = (\mathsf{Enc}, \mathsf{Dec})$ is

$$\mathsf{AE}_\Pi(\mathbf{A}) := \underset{\mathbf{A}}{\Delta} \left(\mathsf{Enc}_K, \mathsf{Dec}_K \,;\, \$_{\mathsf{Enc}}, \bot\right) , \tag{7}$$

where $\mathbf{A}$ is *nonce-respecting*, meaning the same nonce is never queried twice to Enc. Nonces may be repeated with Dec. Furthermore, $\mathbf{A}$ cannot use the output of an O_1^N query as the input to an O_2^N with the same nonce N, otherwise such queries result in trivial wins.

4 Resilience to Nonce Misuse

Rogaway and Shrimpton [66,67] formalize the best possible security when adversaries may re-use nonces. They illustrate how such *nonce misuse resistance* can be achieved using the construction SIV, which was later the inspiration for GCM-SIV [31].

Finding attacks against OCB, GCM, and ChaCha20+Poly1305 which exploit repeated nonces is relatively straightforward. When nonces are repeated, OCB is not much better than ECB mode [57] since one can easily identify when plaintext blocks are repeated across messages in the same block position. In GCM, keystreams are tied to nonces, hence all messages encrypted with the same nonce will use the same keystream, allowing one to recover the XOR of plaintexts; furthermore, authenticity is broken using Joux's forbidden attack [42]. ChaCha20+Poly1305 suffers from similar attacks as GCM. However, looking more closely at the nonce misusing attacks, one can see that the three algorithms behave very differently.

For a description of OCB, GCM, and ChaCha20+Poly1305, and the notation we use see Appendices A.1, A.2, and A.3, respectively.

4.1 OCB Attacks

OCB computes two intermediate keys L and R, which it uses to mask the block cipher inputs and outputs. The value L is computed as the output of the block cipher when given 0^n as input, $L := E_K(0^n)$, and remains fixed per key.

The value R changes per nonce, and is computed by encrypting $L \oplus N$ under the block cipher. Finally, the masks are computed as $\gamma_i \cdot L \oplus R$.

Ferguson [25] illustrates how to recover the intermediate key L by finding a collision using a birthday-bound attack, and subsequently shows how to perform forgeries with L for any nonce. In fact, a chosen-plaintext confidentiality attack can be performed as well, by XORing the sequence $(\gamma_1 \cdot L, \gamma_2 \cdot L, \ldots, \gamma_m \cdot L)$ to the plaintext and ciphertext in order to remove dependence on L. This compromises OCB's confidentiality under any nonce N since repeated plaintext blocks in the same message will encrypt to the same ciphertext block. Below we show how to recover L using a nonce-repeating attack.

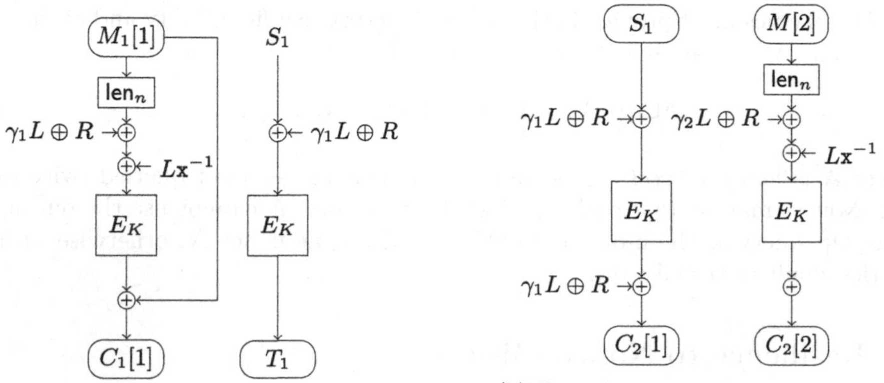

(a) First query with message M_1 of length one block, which can be chosen arbitrarily.

(b) Second query with message $M_2 = S_1 \| M_2[2]$, where $M_2[2]$ can be arbitrarily chosen. Computation of the tag is not included in the figure.

Fig. 1. An illustration of two queries which would form the first step of the OCB attack. In both cases $R = E_K(L \oplus N)$.

Our attack needs to repeat a particular nonce four times, and works best when $\tau = n$. First, encrypt an arbitrary full-block message M_1 of block length m under nonce N. Receive the corresponding tag T_1 and let S_1 denote the checksum used to generate T_1, so that $T_1 = E_K(S_1 \oplus Z[m])$, where $Z[m] = \gamma_m L \oplus R$. Encrypt another message M_2 of length greater than m blocks under the same nonce N, with the mth block of M_2 equal to $M_2[m] = S_1$. The two queries are depicted in Fig. 1. Note that the corresponding ciphertext block $C_2[m]$ equals

$$E_K(S_1 \oplus Z[m]) \oplus Z[m], \tag{8}$$

and so

$$C_2[m] \oplus T_1 = Z[m] = \gamma_m L \oplus R. \tag{9}$$

Encrypt another two messages M_1' and M_2' under nonce N where M_1' has length $m' \neq m$, performing the same steps as above to receive T_1' and $C_2[m']$ such that

$$C_2[m'] \oplus T_1' = Z[m'] = \gamma_{m'} L \oplus R. \tag{10}$$

Then L can be recovered from

$$C_2[m] \oplus T_1 \oplus C_2[m'] \oplus T_1' = (\gamma_m \oplus \gamma_{m'})L\,. \tag{11}$$

4.2 Chosen-Plaintext Confidentiality

Although the above attack against OCB requires a nonce to be repeated four times, once those repetitions have occurred, OCB can no longer guarantee security. As already observed by Joux [42], one cannot apply a similar confidentiality attack to GCM, since every new nonce generates a new, roughly independent keystream, and no information can be determined from the plaintext without knowing anything about the keystream. The intuition that no information about the plaintext can be determined from other keystreams can be formalized with the following definition.

Definition 1. *Let* **A** *be an adversary and* (Enc, Dec) *an AE scheme, then the CPA resilience advantage of* **A** *against* (Enc, Dec) *is defined as*

$$\underset{\mathbf{A}}{\Delta}\left(\mathsf{Enc}_K, \mathsf{Enc}_K\,;\, \$_{\mathsf{Enc}}, \mathsf{Enc}_K\right)\,, \tag{12}$$

where **A** *may re-use nonces with* O_2*, but it may not re-use nonces with* O_1*, nor may it use a nonce already queried to* O_2 *for an* O_1*-query and vice versa.*

The above definition allows adversaries to perform nonce-reusing attacks with Enc_K, but forces the adversary to win by distinguishing Enc_K from $\$_{\mathsf{Enc}}$ using a nonce-respecting attack, thereby capturing the intuition that a scheme which provides confidentiality resilience to nonce misuse must maintain confidentiality for properly generated nonces, even if the attacker is given the power to re-use other nonces. Note that the form of our definition follows the framework of Barwell, Page, and Stam [5], by separately providing oracles representing the adversary's goal (Enc_K versus $\$_{\mathsf{Enc}}$), as well as oracles representing the adversary's power (the second Enc_K).

In order for schemes to be secure according to the above definition, they must ensure that encryption under one nonce is roughly independent from encryption under another, even if adversaries may gain information by re-using nonces with the encryption oracle. Proving that GCM with 96 bit nonces satisfies this definition up to the birthday bound is straightforward. First note that adversaries which only have access to GCM encryption are essentially interacting with a stream cipher, CTR mode, since unless a nonce is repeated, no two block cipher calls are ever the same. This fact holds even if $E_K(0^n)$ is released to the adversary, since this value is never output by the underlying CTR mode. Then, after applying a PRP-PRF switch, the keystreams generated by the underlying CTR mode under different nonces are independent of each other and uniformly distributed. Therefore interacting with $(\mathsf{Enc}_K, \mathsf{Enc}_K)$ is indistinguishable from interacting with $(\$_{\mathsf{Enc}}, \mathsf{Enc}_K)$. Similar reasoning applies to ChaCha20, assuming the underlying ChaCha20 block function is a good PRF.

Furthermore, OCB does not provide security according to the above definition, because an adversary can make nonce-repeating queries to Enc_K via its O_2 oracle to recover L, and can then perform a confidentiality attack with its other oracle. Similarly, GCM with non-96 bit nonces does not provide nonce resilient confidentiality: since adversaries can recover $E_K(0^n) = L$ (e.g. using Joux's forbidden attack [42]), they can manipulate the counters used in the underlying CTR mode to perform a confidentiality attack, since GHASH_L is applied to the nonce before using it in CTR mode (see e.g. Fig. 5).

4.3 Authenticity

Unlike confidentiality, if a nonce is repeated with GCM, then attackers can recover the authentication key, allowing one to construct forgeries for arbitrary nonces, as illustrated by Joux [42]. Therefore, even though 96-bit-nonce GCM is resilient to nonce misuse when considering chosen plaintext confidentiality attacks, it is not resilient with respect to authenticity. Similarly, OCB is not resilient to nonce misuse with respect to authenticity.

With ChaCha20+Poly1305, authentication keys are changed with every nonce, hence even if a nonce is repeated and the authentication key recovered, an adversary will only be able to forge ciphertexts under the compromised nonce. Such authentication resilience can be formalized as follows.

Definition 2. *Let* $\mathbf{A}$ *be an adversary and* $(\mathsf{Enc}, \mathsf{Dec})$ *an AE scheme, then the authenticity resilience advantage of* $\mathbf{A}$ *against* $(\mathsf{Enc}, \mathsf{Dec})$ *is*

$$\underset{\mathbf{A}}{\Delta} \left(\mathsf{Enc}_K, \mathsf{Dec}_K \, ; \, \mathsf{Enc}_K, \perp\right) , \tag{13}$$

where if a nonce is used twice with O_1*, then it cannot be used in an* O_2 *query, and adversaries may not query* $O_1^N(M) = C$ *followed by* $O_2^N(C)$*.*

Here the Enc_K oracle is the adversary's power, since it may repeat nonces with that oracle. The challenge of the adversary is to distinguish Dec_K and $\perp$, by constructing a forgery with a nonce which has not been repeated to Enc_K.

The only difference between the above definition and the conventional definition of authenticity is in the restrictions on the adversary: in the conventional definition adversaries must be nonce-respecting, whereas in this definition they may repeat nonces, but may not use repeated nonces to construct forgeries.

One way for schemes to provide authenticity resilience is to ensure that tags verified during decryption under one nonce are independent of verification under another. For example, assuming that the ChaCha20 block function behaves as a PRF, each keystream generated by ChaCha20 under one nonce is independent of the keystreams generated under different nonces, since, as was the case with 96-bit-nonce GCM, no two block function calls are the same. Furthermore, Poly1305 is keyed using the output of the keystream. This means that, after replacing the ChaCha20 block function by a uniformly random function, each nonce picks a different, independently distributed instance of ChaCha20+Poly1305. In particular, tag production and verification under one nonce is independent of other nonces. Say that an adversary submits a decryption query (N, C). If N was never queried to any previous Enc_K query, then tag verification is independent of all previous Enc_K queries, and it is unlikely that a forgery will be successful. Even if N was queried previously to Enc_K, then it could have only been queried once to Enc_K, and tag verification will be independent of all other Enc_K queries, meaning the adversary will have no better chance of attacking the scheme than if it had been nonce-respecting.

OCB and GCM do not satisfy the above definition because an adversary can use the Enc_K oracle to recover intermediate keys, and perform forgeries. However, there is an easy way for 96-bit-nonce GCM to mimic ChaCha20+Poly1305 such that it does become resilient to nonce re-use: produce an additional keystream block with its underlying CTR mode, and use the output of that block as the authentication key for each nonce. Minematsu and Iwata [53] consider a general version of this construction written in terms of a variable-output-length PRF and a MAC, and by replacing the PRF with CTR mode and the MAC with GHASH, one can construct a variant of GCM which provides authenticity resilience under nonce misuse, with security justification following along the lines of ChaCha20+Poly1305.

4.4 Chosen-Ciphertext Confidentiality

Much like in the conventional settings, schemes which achieve both chosen-plaintext confidentiality and authenticity resilience, achieve chosen-ciphertext confidentiality resilience, as defined below.

Definition 3. *The CCA confidentiality resilience advantage of* $\mathbf{A}$ *against* $(\mathsf{Enc}, \mathsf{Dec})$ *is*

$$\underset{\mathbf{A}}{\Delta}\left(\mathsf{Enc}_K, \mathsf{Enc}_K, \mathsf{Dec}_K\,;\, \$, \mathsf{Enc}_K, \bot\right), \tag{14}$$

where nonces may not be repeated with queries to O_1*, a nonce used twice with* O_2 *cannot be used for an* O_3 *query, a query* $O_1^N(M) = C$ *or* $O_2^N(M) = C$ *may not be followed by* $O_3^N(C)$*, and finally a nonce* N *used to query* O_1^N *may not be re-used to query* O_2^N*, and vice versa.*

The fact that CPA confidentiality and authenticity resilience imply the above definition follows from a straightforward application of the triangle inequality:

$$\underset{\mathbf{A}}{\Delta}\left(\mathsf{Enc}_K, \mathsf{Enc}_K, \mathsf{Dec}_K\,;\, \$, \mathsf{Enc}_K, \bot\right) \le \underset{\mathbf{A}}{\Delta}\left(\mathsf{Enc}_K, \mathsf{Enc}_K, \mathsf{Dec}_K\,;\, \mathsf{Enc}_K, \mathsf{Enc}_K, \bot\right) \tag{15}$$

$$+ \underset{\mathbf{A}}{\Delta}\left(\mathsf{Enc}_K, \mathsf{Enc}_K, \bot\,;\, \$, \mathsf{Enc}_K, \bot\right) \tag{16}$$

The first term on the right hand side can be bounded above by authenticity of $(\mathsf{Enc}, \mathsf{Dec})$, and the second term by confidentiality.

5 Adding RUP Security to Encryption Schemes

In this section we introduce our generic method of adding RUP security to a class of encryption schemes. Following Shrimpton and Terashima [71], we take a modular approach in designing our construction. We start by describing the generic components from which the construction will be made, namely tweakable block ciphers and encryption schemes, and the security requirements they must satisfy, SPRP and SRND [32], respectively. The advantage of this approach is that the sufficient conditions to achieve security under release of unverified plaintext are made explicit, and then, depending upon the available primitives, different instantiations of the construction can be considered without resorting to new proofs.

Following a discussion of the components, we describe the construction, and discuss informally why it enhances the security of the underlying encryption scheme. The generic construction achieves RUPAE, meaning it provides both authenticity and confidentiality even if unverified plaintext is released. A formal security argument for the construction is given in Appendix B. Finally we complete the section by discussing an instantiation, GCM-RUP, which uses GCM's components to create a scheme which provides RUP-security.

5.1 Definitions

Following the RUP-model [3], we focus on designing **separated AE schemes**, where the decryption algorithm is split into plaintext computation and verification algorithms, to ensure that the decryption algorithm does not "hide" weaknesses behind the error symbol. Furthermore, our construction will communicate nonces in-band, meaning it will encrypt them and consider them as part of the ciphertext. As a result, the nonce no longer needs to be synchronized or communicated explicitly, as sufficient information is contained in the value S. This changes the syntax slightly, since now the decryption and verification algorithms no longer accept an explicit nonce input.

Formally, a separated AE scheme which communicates nonces in-band is a triplet of functions — encryption SEnc, decryption SDec, and verification SVer — where

$$\mathsf{SEnc} : \mathsf{K} \times \mathsf{N} \times \mathsf{M} \to \mathsf{C}\,, \tag{17}$$

$$\mathsf{SDec} : \mathsf{K} \times \mathsf{C} \to \mathsf{M}\,, \tag{18}$$

$$\mathsf{SVer} : \mathsf{K} \times \mathsf{C} \to \{\bot, \top\}\,. \tag{19}$$

with K the keys, N the nonces, M the messages, and C the ciphertexts. Recall that the symbols $\top$ and $\bot$ represent success and failure of verification, respectively, and we assume that neither are elements of M. It must be the case that for all $K \in \mathsf{K}$, $N \in \mathsf{N}$, and $M \in \mathsf{M}$,

$$\mathsf{SDec}_K(\mathsf{SEnc}_K^N(M)) = M \quad \text{and} \quad \mathsf{SVer}_K(\mathsf{SEnc}_K^N(M)) = \top\,. \tag{20}$$

From a separated AE scheme (SEnc, SDec, SVer) one can reconstruct the following conventional AE scheme (AEnc, ADec):

$$\mathsf{AEnc}_K^N(M) := \mathsf{SEnc}_K^N(M) \tag{21}$$

$$\mathsf{ADec}_K(C) := \begin{cases} \mathsf{SDec}_K(C) & \text{if } \mathsf{SVer}_K(C) = \top \\ \bot & \text{otherwise} \end{cases}, \tag{22}$$

where we assume that the AE scheme communicates nonces in-band as well.

Separated AE schemes must provide both chosen-ciphertext confidentiality and authenticity. Both of these security aspects are captured in the **RUPAE** measure of Barwell, Page, and Stam [5]. We adopt a stronger version of their definition, by requiring the decryption algorithm to look "random" as well. Let Π denote a separated AE scheme (SEnc, SDec, SVer), then the *RUPAE*-advantage of adversary **A** against Π is

$$\mathsf{RUPAE}_{\Pi}(\mathbf{A}) := \underset{\mathbf{A}}{\Delta}\left(\mathsf{SEnc}_K, \mathsf{SDec}_K, \mathsf{SVer}_K\,;\, \$_{\mathsf{SEnc}}, \$_{\mathsf{SDec}}, \bot\right), \tag{23}$$

where **A** is *nonce-respecting*, meaning the same nonce is never queried twice to SEnc. Nonces may be repeated with SDec and SVer. Furthermore, **A** cannot use the output of an O_1^N query as the input to an O_2^N or O_3^N query with the same nonce N, otherwise such queries result in trivial wins.

5.2 Generic Construction

Components. A *tweakable block cipher* [47] is a pair of functions (E, D), with

$$\mathsf{E} : \mathsf{K} \times \mathsf{T} \times \mathsf{X} \to \mathsf{X} \tag{24}$$

$$\mathsf{D} : \mathsf{K} \times \mathsf{T} \times \mathsf{X} \to \mathsf{X}, \tag{25}$$

where K is the key space, T the tweak space, and X the domain, where $\mathsf{X} = \{0,1\}^x$ is a set of strings of a particular length. For all $K \in \mathsf{K}$ and $T \in \mathsf{T}$ it must be the case that E_K^T is a permutation with D_K^T as inverse. We will need to measure the SPRP quality of the tweakable block cipher, which is defined as

$$\mathsf{SPRP}(\mathbf{A}) := \underset{\mathbf{A}}{\Delta}\left(\mathsf{E}_K, \mathsf{D}_K\,;\, \pi, \pi^{-1}\right), \tag{26}$$

where K is chosen uniformly at random from K, and (π, π^{-1}) is a family of independent, uniformly distributed random permutations over X indexed by T.

Although Liskov, Rivest, and Wagner [47] introduced the concept of finite-tweak-length (FTL) block ciphers, for our construction we need tweakable block ciphers that can process variable tweak lengths (VTL). Starting from an FTL block cipher, one can construct a VTL block cipher by compressing the tweak using a universal hash function, and using the resulting output as the tweak for the FTL block cipher, as explained by Coron et al. [22]. Minematsu and Iwata [54] introduce the XTX construction which extends tweak length while minimizing security loss.

There are a few dedicated constructions of FTL block ciphers: the hash function SKEIN [26] contains an underlying tweakable block cipher, the CAESAR competition candidates Joltik [41] and Deoxys [40] also developed new tweakable block ciphers, and the TWEAKEY framework [39] tackles the problem of designing tweakable block ciphers in general. Besides dedicated constructions, there are also constructions of tweakable block ciphers using regular block ciphers; see for example Rogaway's XE and XEX constructions [64], Minematsu's beyond-birthday bound construction [52], Landecker, Shrimpton, and Terashima's CLRW2 construction [45], and Mennink's beyond-birthday bound constructions [51].

An *encryption scheme* $(\mathsf{Enc}, \mathsf{Dec})$ is a separated AE scheme without SVer. The basic security requirement for encryption schemes is chosen-plaintext confidentiality, but this is not sufficient for our purpose. In particular, a mode like CBC [55] will not work, since during decryption a change in the nonce will only affect the first decrypted plaintext block. We need encryption schemes where during decryption a change in the nonce will result in the entire plaintext changing. Modes such as CTR [55], OFB [55], and the encryption of OCB [43,64,65] suffice. In particular, it is necessary that both encryption and decryption algorithms give uniform random output when distinct nonces are input across both encryption *and* decryption. For example, with CTR mode, decryption is the same as encryption, and if nonces are never repeated across both algorithms then its output will always look uniformly random.

We use Shrimpton and Terashima's [71] SRND measure for encryption schemes, which was introduced by Halevi and Rogaway [32]:

$$\mathsf{SRND}(\mathbf{A}) := \underset{\mathbf{A}}{\Delta}\left(\mathsf{Enc}_K, \mathsf{Dec}_K\, ;\, \$_{\mathsf{Enc}}, \$_{\mathsf{Dec}}\right), \tag{27}$$

where K is chosen uniformly at random from K, and $\mathbf{A}$ must use a different nonce for *every* query it makes, to both of its oracles.

Description. Let $(\mathsf{Enc}, \mathsf{Dec})$ be an encryption scheme with key space K, nonce space N, message space M, and ciphertext space C. Let (E, D) be a tweakable block cipher with $\mathsf{T} = \mathsf{N} \times \mathsf{C}$, $\mathsf{X} = \mathsf{N}$, and key space K. Let $\alpha \in \{0,1\}^\tau$ be some pre-defined constant. Then define the separated AE scheme $(\mathsf{SEnc}, \mathsf{SDec}, \mathsf{SVer})$ as follows. The key space is K^2, with keys denoted by (K, L), the nonce space is N, the message space is M, and the ciphertext space is $\mathsf{N} \times \mathsf{C}$:

$$\mathsf{SEnc}^N_{K,L}(M) := \left(\mathsf{E}^C_L(N), C\right) \tag{28}$$

$$\text{with } C := \mathsf{Enc}^N_K(\alpha \parallel M) \tag{29}$$

$$\mathsf{SDec}_{K,L}(S, C) := \mathsf{lsb}_{|C|-\tau}\left(\mathsf{Dec}^{N'}_K(C)\right) \tag{30}$$

$$\text{with } N' := \mathsf{D}^C_L(S) \tag{31}$$

$$\mathsf{SVer}_{K,L}(S, C) := \left(\mathsf{msb}_\tau\left(\mathsf{Dec}^{N'}_K(C)\right) \stackrel{?}{=} \alpha\right). \tag{32}$$

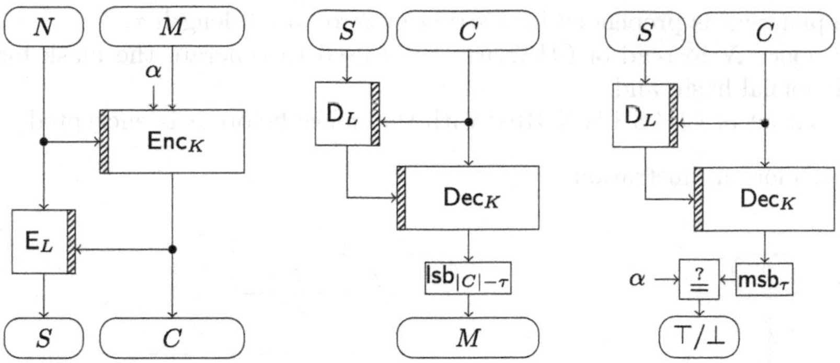

(a) Encryption (b) Decryption (c) Verification

Fig. 2. Adding RUP security to an existing encryption scheme. The circles indicate duplication of the value.

The construction is depicted in Fig. 2.

The construction adds robustness to the encryption scheme (Enc, Dec) by compressing the ciphertext via the tweak of the tweakable block cipher, and using that information to encrypt the nonce. As a result, during decryption, if any bit of the ciphertext is modified, then the ciphertext will result in a different tweak with essentially probability one, and the tweakable block cipher will decrypt the nonce into some random value, which is used as the new nonce for Dec. By assumption, Dec will output garbage, or more precisely, plaintext which is unrelated to any other plaintext queried.

Similarly, if the ciphertext is kept the same, and the encrypted nonce, S, is modified, then the tweakable block cipher will be queried on an input for which it has not been queried on before with the given tweak computed from the ciphertext. As a result, the decryption of S will be random, and Dec's output will look random as well.

With respect to authenticity, our construction follows the encode-then-encipher paradigm [9], which uses redundancy in the plaintext in order to guarantee authenticity. The level of authenticity is determined by the length of the constant α: if verification can be removed, then α's length is set to zero. However, the only requirement from α is to be known to both sides, and users may use any predictable bits already present in the plaintext.

5.3 GCM-RUP

We illustrate an instantiation of the construction using familiar primitives, namely those used to construct GCM [49,50]. The resulting instantiation uses three independent keys, but only makes three minor modifications to AES-GCM in order to achieve RUP security:

1. the plaintext is prepended by a string of zero bits of length τ,
2. the nonce N instead of $\mathsf{GHASH}(\varepsilon, N)$ is used to generate the mask for the polynomial hash, and
3. the output of GHASH is XORed with the nonce before it is encrypted.

See Fig. 3 for an illustration.

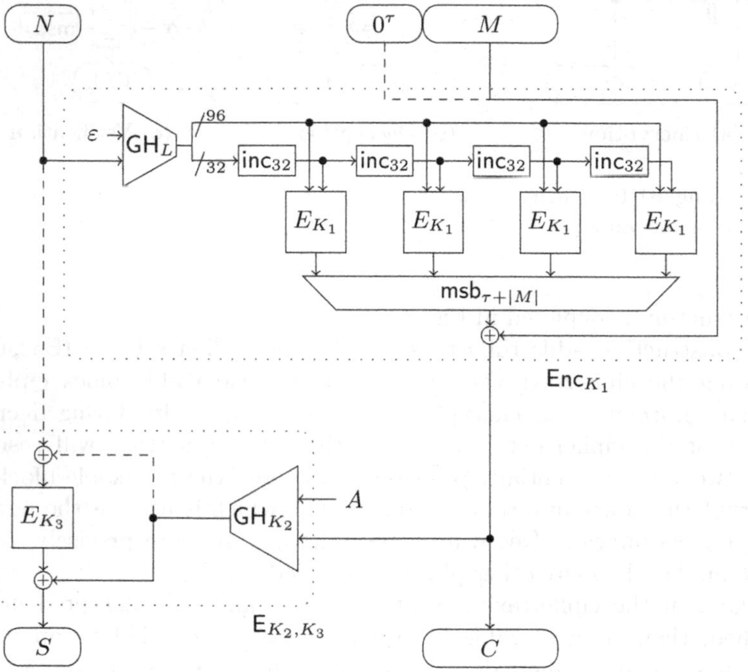

Fig. 3. Instantiation of our construction using GCM's components. Changes from GCM are indicated using a dashed pattern, and the dotted boxes point out the underlying encryption scheme and tweakable block cipher. Filled circles indicate duplication of the values. GH is GHASH, and $/_m$ indicates the number of bits on a wire. The value L is $E_{K_1}(0^n)$, and A represents associated data.

Appendix A.2 contains a description of the GCM components that we use to describe the instantiation, including the function GHASH, defined in Algorithm 3, and CTR mode, defined in Algorithm 4. Note that our formalization above did not include associated data, whereas GCM-RUP does, however it is straightforward to extend the definitions and generic construction to include it.

Since the generic construction's security relies on generating random nonce input during decryption, in order to maintain security up to the birthday bound on the block size, as is the case with GCM, the nonce size in the instantiation is fixed to be the same as the block size. The encryption scheme underlying the

Algorithm 1. $\mathsf{GCM\text{-}RUP}_{K_1K_2K_3}(A, M)$

Input: $K_1K_2K_3 \in \{0,1\}^{3n}$, $A \in \{0,1\}^{\leq n2^{32}}$, $M \in \{0,1\}^{\leq n2^{32}}$
Output: $(S, C) \in \{0,1\}^n \times \{0,1\}^{\tau+|M|}$

$M \leftarrow 0^\tau \parallel M$
$L \leftarrow E_{K_1}(0^n)$
$I \leftarrow \mathsf{GHASH}_L(\varepsilon, N)$
$m \leftarrow |M|_n$
$F \leftarrow E_{K_1}(\mathsf{msb}_{96}(I) \parallel \cdot)$
$S \leftarrow \mathsf{CTR}[F](\mathsf{inc}_{32}(\mathsf{lsb}_{32}(I)), m)$
$C \leftarrow M \oplus \mathsf{msb}_{|M|}(S)$
$T \leftarrow \mathsf{GHASH}_{K_2}(N \| A, C)$
$S \leftarrow E_{K_3}(I \oplus T) \oplus T$
return (S, C)

instantiation, (Enc, Dec), is the same as GCM without authentication, or in other words CTR mode, therefore Enc and Dec are identical, and so the SRND quality of (Enc, Dec) can be measured by looking only at Enc-queries. This allows us to use the GCM confidentiality result of Niwa et al. [58,59], which gives (Enc, Dec) an SRND-bound of

$$\frac{0.5(\sigma + q + d + 1)^2}{2^n} + \frac{64 \cdot q(\sigma + q + d)}{2^n}, \tag{33}$$

where σ is the total number of blocks queried, q the number of Enc queries, d the number of Dec queries, and the nonce length is n bits, which is the block size as well.

Security of the underlying tweakable block cipher follows from the XTX construction of Minematsu and Iwata [54], where we extend the tweak space of a block cipher to arbitrary tweak size by XORing GHASH to both the input and output of the block cipher. Hence the SPRP-quality of the underlying tweakable block cipher is

$$\frac{q^2(\ell + 1)}{2^n}, \tag{34}$$

where q is the total number of queries made to the tweakable block cipher, and ℓ is the maximal tweak length, or in other words, the maximal ciphertext and associated data length in blocks.

Putting together the results along with the result of Appendix B, we get the following bound for the instantiation.

Theorem 1. *Let* **A** *be a RUPAE-adversary against the instantiation making at most q* SEnc *queries, and v* SDec *and* SVer *queries. Say that at most σ blocks are queried, with ℓ the maximum ciphertext and associated data block length of any query, then* **A***'s advantage is at most*

$$\frac{0.5(\sigma + q + v + 1)^2}{2^n} + \frac{64 \cdot q(\sigma + q + v)}{2^n} + \frac{(q + v)^2(\ell + 1)}{2^n} + 2\frac{v(q + v + 1)}{2^n - q - v}. \tag{35}$$

If $q + v \leq 2^{n-1}$, then since $q + v \leq \sigma$, the bound can be simplified to

$$\frac{3 \cdot 64 \cdot \sigma^2}{2^n} + \frac{\sigma^2(\ell + 1)}{2^n}, \tag{36}$$

which is similar to GCM's security bounds [38,58].

Acknowledgments. The authors would like to thank Günes Acar, Roger Dingledine, Ian Goldberg, Mark Juarez, Bart Mennink, and Vincent Rijmen, as well as the anonymous reviewers. This work was supported in part by the Research Council KU Leuven: GOA TENSE (GOA/11/007). Tomer Ashur was supported in part by the Research Fund KU Leuven, OT/13/071. Orr Dunkelman was supported in part by the Israeli Science Foundation through grant No. 827/12 and by the Commission of the European Communities through the Horizon 2020 program under project number 645622 PQCRYPTO. Atul Luykx is supported by a Fellowship from the Institute for the Promotion of Innovation through Science and Technology in Flanders (IWT-Vlaanderen). This article is based upon work from COST Action IC1403 CRYPTACUS, supported by COST (European Cooperation in Science and Technology).

A Algorithm Descriptions

In this section we provide descriptions of OCB, GCM, and ChaCha20+Poly1305. The descriptions are only given to the level of detail sufficient for the paper. The notation is borrowed various sources: the description of OCB by Rogaway, Bellare, and Black [65], the description of GCM by Iwata, Ohashi, and Minematsu [38], and the documents by Procter analyzing ChaCha20+Poly1305 [61,62].

A.1 OCB

In this section we describe the OCB mode of operation [43,64,65]. We focus on OCB version 1 [65], however our results extend to all versions of OCB. We do not include associated data as we do not need it for the OCB attacks. The reference used for the figure, pseudocode, and notation below is from [65]. Let $E : \mathsf{K} \times \{0,1\}^n \to \{0,1\}^n$ be a block cipher and let τ denote the tag length, which is an integer between 0 and n. Let $\gamma_1, \gamma_2, \ldots$ be constants, whose values depend on the version of OCB used; for example, in OCB1 [65] these are Gray codes. Then Algorithm 2 gives pseudocode describing OCB encryption, and Fig. 4 provides an accompanying diagram.

A.2 GCM

In this section we describe the GCM mode of operation [49,50] with nonces of 128 bit length. We let $E : \{0,1\}^{128} \times \{0,1\}^{128} \to \{0,1\}^{128}$ denote a block cipher. The function GHASH is defined in Algorithm 3. Algorithm 5 provides pseudocode for GCM encryption, which also uses the keystream generator CTR mode in Algorithm 4. See Fig. 5 for an illustration.

Algorithm 2. $\mathsf{OCB}_K(N, M)$

Input: $K \in \{0,1\}^n$, $M \in \{0,1\}^*$
Output: $C \in \{0,1\}^*$

$M[1]M[2]\cdots M[m] \xleftarrow{n} M$
$L \leftarrow E_K(0^n)$
$R \leftarrow E_K(N \oplus L)$
for $i = 1$ **to** m **do**
  $Z[i] = \gamma_i \cdot L \oplus R$
end
for $i = 1$ **to** m **do**
  $C[i] \leftarrow E_K(M[i] \oplus Z[i]) \oplus Z[i]$
end
$X[m] \leftarrow \mathsf{len}_n(M[m]) \oplus L \cdot \mathtt{x}^{-1} \oplus Z[m]$
$Y[m] \leftarrow E_K(X[m])$
$C[m] \leftarrow Y[m] \oplus M[m]$
$\text{Checksum} \leftarrow M[1] \oplus \cdots \oplus M[m-1] \oplus C[m]0^{*n} \oplus Y[m]$
$T \leftarrow \mathsf{msb}_\tau\Big(E_K(\text{Checksum} \oplus Z[m])\Big)$
return $C[1]\cdots C[m]T$

Algorithm 3. $\mathsf{GHASH}_L(A, C)$

Input: $L \in \{0,1\}^n$, $A \in \{0,1\}^{\leq n(2^{n/2}-1)}$, $C \in \{0,1\}^{\leq n(2^{n/2}-1)}$
Output: $Y \in \{0,1\}^n$

$X \leftarrow A0^{*n} \parallel C0^{*n} \parallel \mathsf{str}_{n/2}(|A|) \parallel \mathsf{str}_{n/2}(|C|)$
$X[1]X[2]\cdots X[x] \xleftarrow{n} X$
$Y \leftarrow 0^n$
for $j = 1$ **to** x **do**
  $Y \leftarrow L \cdot (Y \oplus X[j])$
end
return Y

Algorithm 4. $\mathsf{CTR}[F](X, m)$

Input: $F : \{0,1\}^x \rightarrow \{0,1\}^n$, $X \in \{0,1\}^x$, $m \in \mathbb{N}$
Output: $S \in \{0,1\}^{mn}$

$I \leftarrow X$
for $j = 1$ **to** m **do**
  $S[j] \leftarrow F(I)$
  $I \leftarrow \mathsf{inc}_x(I)$
end
$S \leftarrow S[1]S[2]\cdots S[m]$
return S

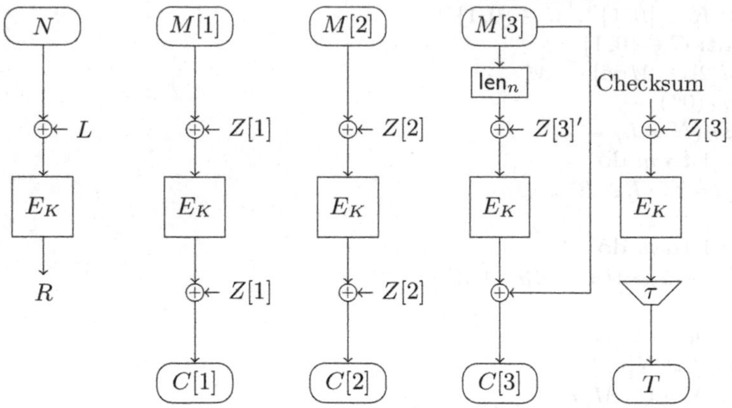

Fig. 4. The OCB mode of operation applied to a plaintext of length at most three blocks. The value L is $E_K(0^n)$ and $Z[3]' = Z[3] \oplus L \cdot \mathbf{x}^{-1}$.

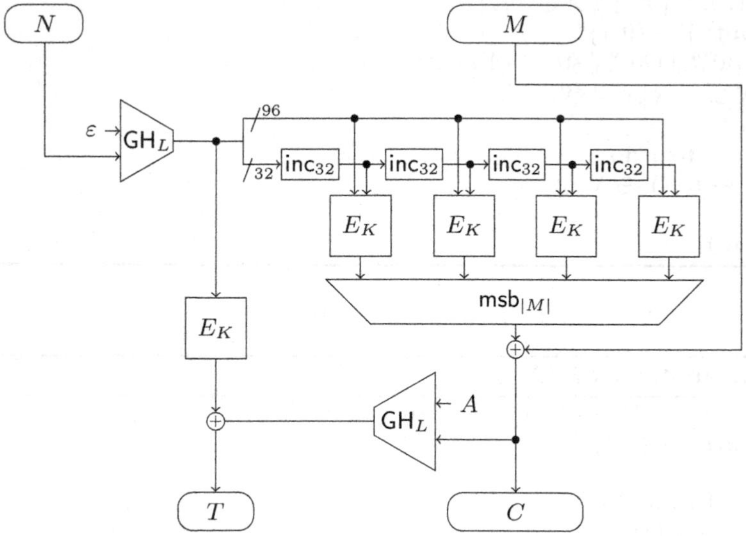

Fig. 5. The GCM mode of operation with 128 bit nonces. GH is GHASH and $/_m$ indicates the number of bits on a wire. The value L is $E_K(\mathsf{str}_n(0))$.

Algorithm 5. $\mathsf{GCM}_K(N, A, M)$

Input: $K \in \{0,1\}^{128}$, $N \in \{0,1\}^{128}$, $A \in \{0,1\}^{\leq 128 \cdot 2^{32}}$, $M \in \{0,1\}^{\leq 128 \cdot 2^{32}}$
Output: $(C, T) \in \{0,1\}^{\leq 128 \cdot 2^{32}} \times \{0,1\}^{128}$

```
L ← E_K(str_128(0))
I ← GHASH_L(ε, N)
m ← |M|_128
F ← E_K(msb_96(I) || ·)
C ← M ⊕ msb_|M|(CTR[F](inc_32(lsb_32(I)), m))
T ← E_K(I) ⊕ GHASH_L(A, C)
return (C, T)
```

A.3 ChaCha20+Poly1305

Our description of ChaCha20+Poly1305 is taken from the RFC [56] describing it, as well as Procter's analysis [61,62]. The combination of ChaCha20 [13] and Poly1305 [12] is similar to that of GCM, with the main differences being the fact that block cipher calls are replaced by ChaCha20's block function calls, and the key for Poly1305 is generated differently.

The ChaCha20 block function is denoted by

$$\mathsf{CC} : \{0,1\}^{256} \times \{0,1\}^{32} \times \{0,1\}^{96} \to \{0,1\}^{512}, \tag{37}$$

which operates on keys of length 256 bits, a block number of length 32 bits, a nonce of length 96 bits, and with an output of size 512 bits. The Poly1305 universal hash function is denoted by

$$\mathsf{Poly} : \{0,1\}^{128} \times \{0,1\}^{*} \to \{0,1\}^{128}. \tag{38}$$

The description of ChaCha20+Poly1305 encryption is given in Algorithm 6.

Algorithm 6. $\mathsf{CC\&Poly}_K(N, A, M)$

Input: $K \in \{0,1\}^{256}$, $N \in \{0,1\}^{96}$, $A \in \{0,1\}^{\leq 8 \cdot (2^{64}-1)}$, $M \in \{0,1\}^{\leq 512 \cdot (2^{32}-1)}$
Output: $(C, T) \in \{0,1\}^{|M|} \times \{0,1\}^{128}$

```
F ← CC_K(·, N)
C ← M ⊕ msb_|M|(CTR[F](str_32(1), |M|_512))
L ← msb_256(F(str_32(0)))
T ← lsb_128(L) ⊕ Poly_msb_128(L)(A0^{*128} || C0^{*128} || str_64(|A|_8) || str_64(|C|_8))
return (C, T)
```

B Formal Security Argument For The Generic Construction

We start by defining two reductions which use an adversary $\mathbf{A}$ playing the RUPAE game against the construction $\mathbb{S} = (\mathsf{SEnc}, \mathsf{SDec}, \mathsf{SVer})$. Let $\mathbb{B} = (\mathsf{E}, \mathsf{D})$ denote the tweakable block cipher and $\mathbb{E} = (\mathsf{Enc}, \mathsf{Dec})$ the encryption scheme. Furthermore, let $\$_{\mathbb{S}} = (\$_{\mathsf{SEnc}}, \$_{\mathsf{SDec}}, \bot)$, $\$_{\mathbb{B}} := (\pi, \pi^{-1})$, where (π, π^{-1}) is from the definition of SPRP security in Eq. (26), and $\$_{\mathbb{E}} := (\$_{\mathsf{Enc}}, \$_{\mathsf{Dec}})$. Then we define the following two reductions:

1. A reduction $\mathbf{B}\langle\mathbf{A}\rangle$ to the SPRP quality of the tweakable block cipher $\mathbb{B}$, meaning $\mathbf{B}\langle\mathbf{A}\rangle$ will attempt to distinguish $\mathbb{B}$ from $\$_{\mathbb{B}}$, using $\mathbf{A}$, an algorithm which is expecting either $\mathbb{S}$ or $\$_{\mathbb{S}}$. The reduction $\mathbf{B}$ generates a key K independently, and uses K to simulate the encryption scheme $\mathbb{E}$. Then, $\mathbf{B}$ runs $\mathbf{A}$, and responds to $\mathbf{A}$'s queries by reconstructing $\mathbb{S}$ using its own oracles, either $\mathbb{B}$ or $\$_{\mathbb{B}}$, and the simulated $\mathbb{E}$.
2. A reduction $\mathbf{C}\langle\mathbf{A}\rangle$ to the SRND quality of the encryption scheme $\mathbb{E}$. In contrast with $\mathbf{B}$, the reduction $\mathbf{C}$ simulates $\$_{\mathbb{B}}$ instead of $\mathbb{B}$. Then using its own oracles, either $\mathbb{E}$ or $\$_{\mathbb{E}}$, and $\$_{\mathbb{B}}$, $\mathbf{C}$ reconstructs $\mathbb{S}$.

Theorem 2. *The advantage of any nonce-respecting RUPAE adversary* $\mathbf{A}$ *attempting to distinguish* $\mathbb{S}$ *from* $\$_{\mathbb{S}}$*, making at most* q SEnc *queries, and at most* v SDec *and* SVer *queries, is bounded above by*

$$2\frac{v(q+v)}{|\mathsf{N}|-q-v} + \frac{v}{2^{\tau}} + \mathsf{SPRP}_{\mathbb{B}}(\mathbf{B}\langle\mathbf{A}\rangle) + \mathsf{SRND}_{\mathbb{E}}(\mathbf{C}\langle\mathbf{A}\rangle)\,. \tag{39}$$

Proof. Let $\mathbb{S}[\Pi, \Sigma]$ denote $\mathbb{S}$ using Π as tweakable block cipher and Σ as encryption scheme. By definition, we seek to bound

$$\mathsf{RUPAE}(\mathbf{A}) = \underset{\mathbf{A}}{\Delta}\left(\mathbb{S}[\mathbb{B},\mathbb{E}]\,;\,\$_{\mathbb{S}}\right)\,. \tag{40}$$

Applying the triangle inequality, we get

$$\underset{\mathbf{A}}{\Delta}\left(\mathbb{S}[\mathbb{B},\mathbb{E}]\,;\,\$_{\mathbb{S}}\right) \le \underset{\mathbf{A}}{\Delta}\left(\mathbb{S}[\mathbb{B},\mathbb{E}]\,;\,\mathbb{S}[\$_{\mathbb{B}},\mathbb{E}]\right) + \underset{\mathbf{A}}{\Delta}\left(\mathbb{S}[\$_{\mathbb{B}},\mathbb{E}]\,;\,\$_{\mathbb{S}}\right) \tag{41}$$

Using reduction $\mathbf{B}\langle\mathbf{A}\rangle$, we know that

$$\underset{\mathbf{A}}{\Delta}\left(\mathbb{S}[\mathbb{B},\mathbb{E}]\,;\,\mathbb{S}[\$_{\mathbb{B}},\mathbb{E}]\right) \le \underset{\mathbf{B}\langle\mathbf{A}\rangle}{\Delta}\left(\mathbb{B}\,;\,\$_{\mathbb{B}}\right)\,. \tag{42}$$

Therefore we can focus on

$$\underset{\mathbf{A}}{\Delta}\left(\mathbb{S}[\$_{\mathbb{B}},\mathbb{E}]\,;\,\$_{\mathbb{S}}\right) \tag{43}$$

which in turn is bounded above by

$$\underset{\mathbf{A}}{\Delta}\left(\mathbb{S}[\$_{\mathbb{B}},\mathbb{E}]\,;\,\mathbb{S}[\$_{\mathbb{B}},\$_{\mathbb{E}}]\right) + \underset{\mathbf{A}}{\Delta}\left(\mathbb{S}[\$_{\mathbb{B}},\$_{\mathbb{E}}]\,;\,\$_{\mathbb{S}}\right)\,. \tag{44}$$

The analysis of these two remaining terms relies on computing the probability that $\mathbf{A}$ makes a query which results in a nonce collision during a decryption query, thereby violating the SRND game's requirement. In the analysis below, we find that the probability of such an occurence is at most

$$\varepsilon := \frac{v(q+v)}{|\mathsf{N}| - q - v}\,. \tag{45}$$

Therefore, using the reduction $\mathbf{C}\langle\mathbf{A}\rangle$ we know that the first term of Eq. (44) is bounded by

$$\varepsilon + \underset{\mathbf{C}\langle\mathbf{A}\rangle}{\Delta}\left(\mathbb{E}\,;\,\$_{\mathbb{E}}\right), \tag{46}$$

and the bound for

$$\underset{\mathbf{A}}{\Delta}\left(\mathbb{S}[\$_{\mathbb{B}},\$_{\mathbb{E}}]\,;\,\$_{\mathbb{S}}\right) \tag{47}$$

is given below.

Say that $\mathbf{A}$ generates SEnc inputs (N_1, M_1), (N_2, M_2), $\ldots$, (N_q, M_q), and SDec and SVer inputs (S_1, C_1), (S_2, C_2), $\ldots$, (S_v, C_v), where (S_i, C_i) could be the input to either an SDec or SVer query. Let N_i^* denote the nonce input to $\$_{\mathsf{Dec}}$ resulting from the query (S_i, C_i), that is

$$N_i^* = \pi^{-1,C_i}(S_i)\,. \tag{48}$$

Similarly, define M_i^* and α_i^* such that

$$\alpha_i^* \| M_i^* = \$_{\mathsf{Dec}}^{N_i^*}(C_i)\,. \tag{49}$$

We call N_i^*, M_i^*, and α_i^* the "decrypted" nonces, plaintexts, and constants, respectively.

If the nonces N_i and N_j^* are distinct from each other then the SRND game's requirement is respected, hence $\$_{\mathbb{E}}$ will always give uniformly distributed and independent output. Let event denote the event that either $N_i = N_j$ for $1 \le i < j \le q$, or $N_i^* = N_j^*$ for $1 \le i < j \le v$, or $N_i = N_j^*$ for $1 \le i \le q$ and $1 \le j \le v$. Then, by the fundamental lemma of game playing [10], Eq. (47) can be bounded by

$$\mathbf{P}\left[\mathsf{event}\right] + \mathbf{P}\left[\exists i \text{ s.t. } \alpha_i^* = \alpha \;\middle|\; \overline{\mathsf{event}}\right], \tag{50}$$

where $\overline{\mathsf{event}}$ is the negation of event. Given $\overline{\mathsf{event}}$, the nonce input to $\$_{\mathsf{Dec}}$ will always be distinct, hence the α_i^* are independent and uniformly distributed, which means the quantity on the right is bounded above by $v/2^\tau$.

Therefore we focus on the probability of event, i.e. that there is a collision in the N_i and N_j^*. By hypothesis, $\mathbf{A}$ is nonce-respecting, hence we know that $N_i \neq N_j$ for $1 \le i < j \le q$. Therefore we focus on the case that a decrypted nonce collides with some N_i, or another decrypted nonce.

Consider the query (S_i, C_i) associated to the ith decrypted nonce N_i^*, and say that event has not yet been triggered. Let (N_j, M_j) be a previous SEnc query, and (S_j, C_j) its corresponding output. By hypothesis, $(S_j, C_j) \neq (S_i, C_i)$.

If $C_j \neq C_i$, then the tweak input to (π, π^{-1}) will be different for the SEnc and SDec or SVer queries, hence the probability that N_i^* collides with N_j is at most $1/|\mathsf{N}|$. If $C_j = C_i$, then $S_j \neq S_i$, which means that (π, π^{-1}) is queried under the same tweak for both the SEnc and SDec or SVer queries. However, the probability that

$$N_j = \pi^{-1,C_j}(S_j) = \pi^{-1,C_i}(S_i) = N_i^* \tag{51}$$

is at most $1/(|\mathsf{N}| - q - v)$.

Now consider the probability that an SEnc query (N_i, M_i) is such that N_i equals N_j^* for some previous SDec or SVer query. Since the adversary's view is independent of N_j^*, it can guess N_j^* with probability at most $1/(|\mathsf{N}| - q - v)$. Therefore, the probability that a decrypted nonce collides with some nonce N_j is at most

$$\frac{qv}{|\mathsf{N}| - q - v} . \tag{52}$$

Given that no decrypted nonces collide with any nonce N_j, we are left with the event that two decrypted nonces collide with each other. However, similar reasoning as above shows that this probability is bounded above by

$$\frac{v^2}{|\mathsf{N}| - q - v} , \tag{53}$$

Putting the above computations together, if **A** makes q SEnc queries, and v SDec and SVer queries, then Eq. (47) is bounded above by

$$\frac{v(q+v)}{|\mathsf{N}| - q - v} + \frac{v}{2^\tau} . \tag{54}$$

□

C Application to Tor

The advantage in coming up with new, robust AE schemes is that they can then be used for applications which go beyond the traditional goals of ensuring data confidentiality and authenticity between two communicating parties. Consider for example Tor [23], which uses CTR mode [55] to ensure anonymity. CTR mode is a basic encryption scheme which provides data confidentiality, and no authenticity. In particular, its decryption algorithm provides no robustness to changes in its ciphertext: a change in the ith bit of ciphertext will result in the same change to the ith bit of the resulting plaintext. This property enables the crypto-tagging attack [73] against Tor, which breaches anonymity. Using an RAE [35] or encode-then-encipher [9,71] scheme prevents the crypto-tagging attack, and potentially introduces a new level of robustness to Tor's anonymity. Hence, the Tor community has initiated a search for replacements for CTR mode [48].

However, replacing CTR mode with known robust solutions not only comes at an efficiency cost, but also increased design, and hence implementation, complexity. This is because so far the only solutions provided for full robustness are essentially variable-input-length (VIL) ciphers [8], which can be viewed as block ciphers that can process arbitrarily long messages. However, VIL ciphers are "heavy" constructions, requiring often three or more passes over the plaintext in order to ensure sufficient mixing, or relying on subtle design choices to achieve security.

We now outline how our construction can be used in Tor to avoid the crypto-tagging attack [73]. Our intention is not to provide a detailed description, but to give a high-level overview.

C.1 Tor

Tor [23] is a circuit-based low-latency anonymous communication service. The core idea underlying Tor is *onion routing*, a distributed overlay network designed to anonymize TCP-based applications, presented by Syverson, Reed and Goldschlag in [72].

Generally speaking, Tor communication is encrypted and relayed by nodes in the Tor-network via *circuits*. When building circuits, clients exchange keys with several nodes, usually 3, where each node only knows its predecessor and successor.

Clients prepare messages using multiple layers of encryption. First, the message is encrypted using the key and nonce shared with the circuit's last node. The resulting ciphertext is then encrypted again with the keys and nonce of the one-before-last node. This process is repeated for each node, until the first node's key is used.

The output of the multi-layered encryption is then sent from the client to the first node, which decrypts one layer, and forwards the result to the next node. In every step, another layer of encryption is removed, and the message is passed forward, until it reaches the last node. The last node authenticates and forwards the message to the intended recipient outside of the Tor network.

C.2 The Crypto-tagging Attack

By design, the Tor protocol offers an end-to-end integrity check, which the exit node does by computing a SHA-1 digest of the decrypted message. Such a check prevents e.g., attacks by rogue nodes which "tag" the encrypted message, and then search outbound communication for the corresponding corrupted traffic.

In 2012, an anonymous email was sent to the Tor developers mailing list describing the *crypto-tagging attack* [73]. In this attack, two nodes, the entry and exit nodes, collude by tagging and untagging messages upon entry and exit to the network, respectively, thereby making the changes transparent to all other parties.[1] Due to the mode of operation used for encryption, CTR mode, the location of corrupt bits introduced at the entry to the network are maintained

[1] Tagging can be done in several ways. We mention here only one: the entry node XORs an identifing string to the message they are passing. Untagging is done by XORing the same identifier by the exit node.

through all decryptions, and can be removed by the exit node by just knowing their location. Furthermore, since the integrity check is only performed by the exit node, the corruption cannot be detected by intermediate nodes in the circuit. Moreover, the attack is amplified by the fact that if only one of the nodes (i.e., either the entry node or the exit node) is malicious, the tagged message cannot be verified, and the circuit is destroyed. Any new circuit where only one of the nodes is malicious will also be destroyed, thus biasing the set of possible circuits towards compromised ones.

An obvious solution to this problem is to add an authentication tag to each layer of the encryption, allowing intermediate nodes to verify the data passed through them and act according to some policy. However, in the discussion following the attack, such a solution was ruled out due to two main problems: (i) by adding authentication tags, the available bandwidth for sending messages is reduced, and (ii) the circuit's length could be revealed, an undesirable property in such systems.

C.3 Avoiding the Attack

We propose a different approach allowing intermediate nodes to release unverified plaintext, using the generic construction proposed in Sect. 5. The only change from the above procedure for preparing the message is how the nonces are chosen.

As before, clients start by encrypting the plaintext with the key and nonce of the last node using CTR mode. Then, the ciphertext is compressed and used as a tweak for the encryption of the nonce as per Fig. 2. Afterwards, the encrypted nonce, S, is used as the nonce for the next layer of encryption, i.e., with the keys of the one-before last node. This is repeated for each node of the circuit all the way to the first one. The result is a multi-layered application of our construction where the first layer receives the nonce and the plaintext as input, and each subsequent layer receives the previous layer's output. The new RUP secure layered encryption mode of operation is presented in Fig. 6, where each layer can be realized using e.g., the robust version of GCM presented in Sect. 5.3 with $|\alpha| = 0$.

When the message is ready, the client sends the ciphertext, along with the 3-times encrypted nonce to the first node. The first node uses the decryption algorithm as per Fig. 2 to remove the outermost encryption, and forwards the result, as well as the now 2-times encrypted nonce, to the next node. After the last layer of encryption has been removed by the last node, it authenticates the message and sends it to the intended recipient.

The security against an adversary trying to mount the crypto-tagging attack comes from the fact that any change to the ciphertext will affect the entire message, effectively decrypting it to garbage. In other words, once decrypted by a non-colluding node, the crypto-tag corrupts the nonce, which will then be used to decrypt the message into garbage. Using the Tor terminology, by the time the message reaches the exit node, the crypto-tag can no longer be removed and the message is unrecognizable and should thus be dropped and the circuit is torn down.

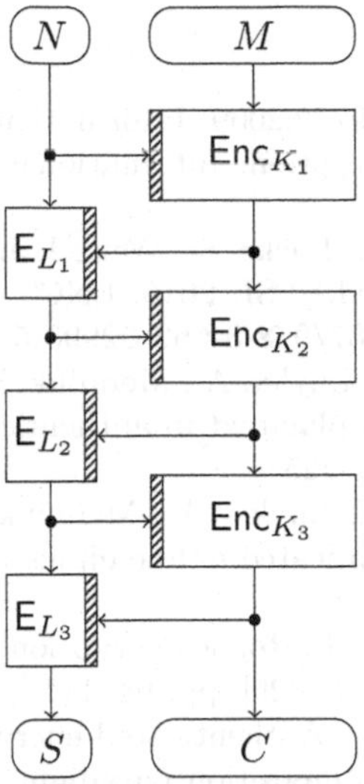

Fig. 6. A RUP secure 3-node layered encryption. The three layers are distinguished by their keys: $(K_1, L_1), (K_2, L_2)$, and (K_3, L_3).

For example, consider a circuit with three nodes, and say that (S_1, C_1), (S_2, C_2), and (S_3, C_3) are the outputs of the first, second, and third layers of encryption, respectively. In particular, the client uses (N, P) to produce (S_1, C_1), then (S_1, C_1) to produce (S_2, C_2), and (S_2, C_2) to produce (S_3, C_3). Finally, (S_3, C_3) is sent to the first node. Say that the first node is malicious, namely it decrypts (S_3, C_3) and obtains (S_2, C_2), then proceeds to tag (S_2, C_2) and passes (S_2', C_2') instead of (S_2, C_2) as it is supposed to do. Then, assuming the second node is honest, it will follow the protocol and decrypt (S_2', C_2'). However, by the properties of our construction, we know that the decryption will be random since $(S_2, C_2) \neq (S_2', C_2')$, and in particular, the first node will not be able to predict anything about (S_1', C_1'), i.e., the decryption of (S_2', C_2'). As a result, the second node will pass (S_1', C_1') to the third node, and the third node will not be able to conclude anything, regardless of whether it shares information with the first node or not. In particular, it would not be able to conclude the source and the destination of the message.

The disadvantage to our approach is that 16 extra bytes must be expropriated to send the encrypted nonce S. However, unlike adding per-hop authentication tags, the reduction in available bandwidth to send messages is fixed, and does not change according to the circuit length. Furthermore, the solution can be built efficiently using familiar components, and is simple enough to allow for fast deployment.

References

1. ISO/IEC JTC 1/SC 27 19772:2009 Information technology – Security techniques – Authenticated encryption. International Organization for Standardization, Geneva, Switzerland
2. Abed, F., Forler, C., List, E., Lucks, S., Wenzel, J.: RIV for robust authenticated encryption. In: Peyrin, T. (ed.) FSE 2016. LNCS, vol. 9783, pp. 23–42. Springer, Heidelberg (2016). doi:10.1007/978-3-662-52993-5_2
3. Andreeva, E., Bogdanov, A., Luykx, A., Mennink, B., Mouha, N., Yasuda K.: How to securely release unverified plaintext in authenticated encryption. In: Sarkar, P., Iwata, T. (eds.) [70], pp. 105–125
4. Andreeva, E., Bogdanov, A., Luykx, A., Mennink, B., Tischhauser, E., Yasuda, K.: Parallelizable and authenticated online ciphers. In: Sako, K., Sarkar, P. (eds.) [69], pp. 424–443
5. Barwell, G., Page, D., Stam, M.: Rogue decryption failures: reconciling AE robustness notions. In: Groth, J. (ed.) [29], pp. 94–111
6. Bellare, M., Namprempre, C.: Authenticated encryption: relations among notions and analysis of the generic composition paradigm. In: Okamoto, T. (ed.) [60], pp. 531–545
7. Bellare, M., Namprempre, C.: Authenticated encryption: relations among notions and analysis of the generic composition paradigm. J. Cryptol. **21**(4), 469–491 (2008)
8. Bellare, M., Rogaway, P.: On the construction of variable-input-length ciphers. In: Knudsen, L.R. (ed.) FSE 1999. LNCS, vol. 1636, pp. 231–244. Springer, Heidelberg (1999). doi:10.1007/3-540-48519-8_17
9. Bellare, M., Rogaway, P.: Encode-then-encipher encryption: how to exploit nonces or redundancy in plaintexts for efficient cryptography. In: Okamoto, T. (ed.) [60], pp. 317–330
10. Bellare, M., Rogaway, P.: The security of triple encryption and a framework for code-based game-playing proofs. In: Vaudenay, S. (ed.) [74], pp. 409–426
11. Bellare, M., Tackmann, B.: The multi-user security of authenticated encryption: AES-GCM in TLS 1.3. In: Robshaw, M., Katz, J. (eds.) CRYPTO 2016. LNCS, vol. 9814, pp. 247–276. Springer, Heidelberg (2016). doi:10.1007/978-3-662-53018-4_10
12. Bernstein, D.J.: The Poly1305-AES message-authentication code. In: Gilbert, H., Handschuh, H. (eds.) FSE 2005. LNCS, vol. 3557, pp. 32–49. Springer, Heidelberg (2005). doi:10.1007/11502760_3
13. Bernstein, D.J.: ChaCha, a variant of Salsa20 (2008). http://cr.yp.to/papers.html#chacha
14. Bernstein, D.J.: 2015.11.20: break a dozen secret keys, get a million more for free. The cr.yp.to blog (2015). https://blog.cr.yp.to/20151120-batchattacks.html
15. Bernstein, D.J.: CAESAR use cases. In: Google Groups: Cryptographic Competitions (2016). https://groups.google.com/forum/#!topic/crypto-competitions/DLv193SPSDc
16. Biham, E.: How to decrypt or even substitute des-encrypted messages in 2^{28} steps. Inf. Process. Lett. **84**(3), 117–124 (2002)
17. Biryukov, A., Mukhopadhyay, S., Sarkar, P.: Improved time-memory trade-offs with multiple data. In: Preneel, B., Tavares, S.E. (eds.) SAC 2005. LNCS, vol. 3897, pp. 110–127. Springer, Heidelberg (2006). doi:10.1007/11693383_8

18. Böck, H., Zauner, A., Devlin, S., Somorovsky, J., Jovanovic, P.: Nonce-disrespecting adversaries: practical forgery attacks on GCM in TLS. In: 10th USENIX Workshop on Offensive Technologies, WOOT 16, Austin, TX, 8–9 August 2016. USENIX Association (2016)
19. Boldyreva, A., Degabriele, J.P., Paterson, K.G., Stam, M.: On symmetric encryption with distinguishable decryption failures. In: Moriai, S. (ed.) FSE 2013. LNCS, vol. 8424, pp. 367–390. Springer, Heidelberg (2014). doi:10.1007/978-3-662-43933-3_19
20. CAESAR: Competition for authenticated encryption: security, applicability, and robustness, May 2014. http://competitions.cr.yp.to/caesar.html
21. Chatterjee, S., Menezes, A., Sarkar, P.: Another look at tightness. In: Miri, A., Vaudenay, S. (eds.) SAC 2011. LNCS, vol. 7118, pp. 293–319. Springer, Heidelberg (2012). doi:10.1007/978-3-642-28496-0_18
22. Coron, J.-S., Dodis, Y., Mandal, A., Seurin, Y.: A domain extender for the ideal cipher. In: Micciancio, D. (ed.) TCC 2010. LNCS, vol. 5978, pp. 273–289. Springer, Heidelberg (2010). doi:10.1007/978-3-642-11799-2_17
23. Dingledine, R., Mathewson, N., Syverson, P.F.: Tor: the second-generation onion router. In: Blaze, M. (ed.) Proceedings of the 13th USENIX Security Symposium, 9–13 August 2004, San Diego, CA, USA, pp. 303–320. USENIX (2004)
24. Dworkin, M.J.: Sp 800–38d. recommendation for block cipher modes of operation: galois/counter mode (gcm) and gmac (2007)
25. Ferguson, N.: Collision attacks on OCB. http://csrc.nist.gov/groups/ST/toolkit/BCM/documents/comments/General_Comments/papers/Ferguson.pdf
26. Ferguson, N., Lucks, S., Schneier, B., Whiting, D., Bellare, M., Kohno, T., Callas, J., Walker, J.: The skein hash function family. http://skein-hash.info/
27. Fleischmann, E., Forler, C., Lucks, S.: McOE: a family of almost foolproof on-line authenticated encryption schemes. In: Canteaut, A. (ed.) FSE 2012. LNCS, vol. 7549, pp. 196–215. Springer, Heidelberg (2012). doi:10.1007/978-3-642-34047-5_12
28. Fouque, P., Joux, A., Mavromati, C.: Multi-user collisions: applications to discrete logarithm, even-mansour and PRINCE. In: Sarkar, P., Iwata, T. (eds.) [70], pp. 420–438
29. Groth, J. (ed.): IMACC 2015. LNCS, vol. 9496. Springer, Cham (2015)
30. Gueron, S.: AES-GCM software performance on the current high end CPUs as a performance baseline for CAESAR competition. Directions in Authenticated Ciphers (DIAC) (2013)
31. Gueron, S., Lindell, Y.: GCM-SIV: full nonce misuse-resistant authenticated encryption at under one cycle per byte. In: Ray, I., Li, N., Kruegel, C. (eds.) Proceedings of the 22nd ACM SIGSAC Conference on Computer and Communications Security, Denver, CO, USA, 12–16 October 2015, pp. 109–119. ACM (2015)
32. Halevi, S., Rogaway, P.: A parallelizable enciphering mode. In: Okamoto, T. (ed.) CT-RSA 2004. LNCS, vol. 2964, pp. 292–304. Springer, Heidelberg (2004). doi:10.1007/978-3-540-24660-2_23
33. Hirose, S., Sasaki, Y., Yasuda, K.: Iv-fv authenticated encryption and triplet-robust decryption. In: Early Symmetric Crypto, ESC 2015, Clervaux, Luxembourg, 12–16 January 2015
34. Hirose, S., Sasaki, Y., Yasuda, K.: Message-recovery macs and verification-unskippable AE. IACR Cryptol. ePrint Arch. **2017**, 260 (2017)
35. Hoang, V.T., Krovetz, T., Rogaway, P.: Robust authenticated-encryption AEZ and the problem that it solves. In: Oswald, E., Fischlin, M. (eds.) EUROCRYPT 2015. LNCS, vol. 9056, pp. 15–44. Springer, Heidelberg (2015). doi:10.1007/978-3-662-46800-5_2

36. Hoang, V.T., Reyhanitabar, R., Rogaway, P., Vizár, D.: Online authenticated-encryption and its nonce-reuse misuse-resistance. In: Gennaro, R., Robshaw, M. (eds.) CRYPTO 2015. LNCS, vol. 9215, pp. 493–517. Springer, Heidelberg (2015). doi:10.1007/978-3-662-47989-6_24
37. Imamura, K., Minematsu, K., Iwata, T.: Integrity analysis of authenticated encryption based on stream ciphers. In: Chen, L., Han, J. (eds.) ProvSec 2016. LNCS, vol. 10005, pp. 257–276. Springer, Cham (2016). doi:10.1007/978-3-319-47422-9_15
38. Iwata, T., Ohashi, K., Minematsu, K.: Breaking and repairing GCM security proofs. In: Safavi-Naini, R., Canetti, R. (eds.) [68], pp. 31–49
39. Jean, J., Nikolić, I., Peyrin, T.: Tweaks and keys for block ciphers: the TWEAKEY framework. In: Sarkar, P., Iwata, T. (eds.) ASIACRYPT 2014. LNCS, vol. 8874, pp. 274–288. Springer, Heidelberg (2014). doi:10.1007/978-3-662-45608-8_15
40. Jean, J., Nikolić, I., Peyrin, T.: Deoxys v1.3. CAESAR submissions (2015). http://competitions.cr.yp.to/round2/deoxysv13.pdf
41. Jean, J., Nikolić, I., Peyrin, T.: Joltik v1.3. CAESAR submissions (2015). http://competitions.cr.yp.to/round2/joltikv13.pdf
42. Joux, A.: Comments on the draft GCM specification – authentication failuresin NIST version of GCM. http://csrc.nist.gov/groups/ST/toolkit/BCM/documents/comments/800-38_Series-Drafts/GCM/Joux_comments.pdf
43. Krovetz, T., Rogaway, P.: The OCB authenticated-encryption algorithm, June 2013. http://datatracker.ietf.org/doc/draft-irtf-cfrg-ocb
44. Krovetz, T., Rogaway, P.: The OCB authenticated-encryption algorithm. RFC 7253, May 2014
45. Landecker, W., Shrimpton, T., Terashima, R.S.: Tweakable blockciphers with beyond birthday-bound security. In: Safavi-Naini, R., Canetti, R. (ed.) [68], pp. 14–30
46. Leander, G. (ed.): FSE 2015. LNCS, vol. 9054. Springer, Heidelberg (2015)
47. Liskov, M., Rivest, R.L., Wagner, D.: Tweakable block ciphers. J. Cryptol. **24**(3), 588–613 (2011)
48. Mathewson, N.: Cryptographic directions in Tor: past and future. In: Real World Cryptography Conference (2016)
49. McGrew, D.A., Viega, J.: The security and performance of the galois/counter mode (GCM) of operation. In: Canteaut, A., Viswanathan, K. (eds.) INDOCRYPT 2004. LNCS, vol. 3348, pp. 343–355. Springer, Heidelberg (2004). doi:10.1007/978-3-540-30556-9_27
50. McGrew, D.A., Viega, J.: The security and performance of the galois/counter mode of operation (full version). IACR Cryptol. ePrint Arch. **2004**, 193 (2004)
51. Mennink, B.: Optimally secure tweakable blockciphers. In: Leander, G. (ed.) [46], pp. 428–448
52. Minematsu, K.: Beyond-birthday-bound security based on tweakable block cipher. In: Dunkelman, O. (ed.) FSE 2009. LNCS, vol. 5665, pp. 308–326. Springer, Heidelberg (2009). doi:10.1007/978-3-642-03317-9_19
53. Minematsu, K., Iwata, T.: More on generic composition. In: Early Symmetric Crypto (ESC) 2015, pp. 69–71 (2015)
54. Minematsu, K., Iwata, T.: Tweak-length extension for tweakable blockciphers. In: Groth, J. (ed.) [29], pp. 77–93
55. National Institute of Standards and Technology: DES Modes of Operation. FIPS 81, December 1980
56. Nir, Y., Langley, A.: ChaCha20 and Poly1305 for IETF protocols. RFC 7539, May 2015

57. NIST Special Publication 800–38A: Recommendation for block cipher modes of operation - Modes and techniques. National Institute of Standards and Technology (2001)
58. Niwa, Y., Ohashi, K., Minematsu, K., Iwata, T.: GCM security bounds reconsidered. In: Leander, G. (ed.) [46], pp. 385–407
59. Niwa, Y., Ohashi, K., Minematsu, K., Iwata, T.: GCM security bounds reconsidered. IACR Cryptol. ePrint Arch. **2015**, 214 (2015)
60. Okamoto, T. (ed.): ASIACRYPT 2000. LNCS, vol. 1976. Springer, Heidelberg (2000)
61. Procter, G.: A security analysis of the composition of chacha20 and poly1305. IACR Cryptol. ePrint Arch. **2014**, 613 (2014)
62. Procter, G.: The design and analysis of symmetric cryptosystems. Ph.D. thesis (2015)
63. Reyhanitabar, R., Vaudenay, S., Vizár, D.: Authenticated encryption with variable stretch. In: Cheon, J.H., Takagi, T. (eds.) ASIACRYPT 2016. LNCS, vol. 10031, pp. 396–425. Springer, Heidelberg (2016). doi:10.1007/978-3-662-53887-6_15
64. Rogaway, P.: Efficient instantiations of tweakable blockciphers and refinements to modes OCB and PMAC. In: Lee, P.J. (ed.) ASIACRYPT 2004. LNCS, vol. 3329, pp. 16–31. Springer, Heidelberg (2004). doi:10.1007/978-3-540-30539-2_2
65. Rogaway, P., Bellare, M., Black, J.: OCB: a block-cipher mode of operation for efficient authenticated encryption. ACM Trans. Inf. Syst. Secur. **6**(3), 365–403 (2003)
66. Rogaway, P., Shrimpton, T.: A provable-security treatment of the key-wrap problem. In: Vaudenay, S. (ed.) [74], pp. 373–390
67. Rogaway, P., Shrimpton, T.: Deterministic authenticated-encryption: a provable-security treatment of the key-wrap problem. IACR Cryptol. ePrint Arch. **2006**, 221 (2006)
68. Safavi-Naini, R., Canetti, R. (eds.): CRYPTO 2012. LNCS, vol. 7417. Springer, Heidelberg (2012)
69. Sako, K., Sarkar, P. (eds.): ASIACRYPT 2013. LNCS, vol. 8269. Springer, Heidelberg (2013)
70. Sarkar, P., Iwata, T. (eds.): ASIACRYPT 2014. LNCS, vol. 8873. Springer, Heidelberg (2014)
71. Shrimpton, T., Terashima, R.S.: A modular framework for building variable-input-length tweakable ciphers. In: Sako, K., Sarkar,P. (eds.) [69], pp. 405–423
72. Syverson, P.F., Goldschlag, D.M., Reed, M.G.: Anonymous connections and onion routing. In: 1997 IEEE Symposium on Security and Privacy, 4–7 May 1997, Oakland, CA, USA, pp. 44–54. IEEE Computer Society (1997)
73. The 23 Raccoons. Analysis of the Relative Severity of Tagging Attacks, March 2012. Email to the Tor developers mailing list https://lists.torproject.org/pipermail/tor-dev/2012-March/003347.html
74. Vaudenay, S. (ed.): EUROCRYPT 2006. LNCS, vol. 4004. Springer, Heidelberg (2006)

ZMAC: A Fast Tweakable Block Cipher Mode for Highly Secure Message Authentication

Tetsu Iwata[1], Kazuhiko Minematsu[2(✉)], Thomas Peyrin[3,4,5], and Yannick Seurin[6]

[1] Nagoya University, Nagoya, Japan
tetsu.iwata@nagoya-u.jp
[2] NEC Corporation, Kawasaki, Japan
k-minematsu@ah.jp.nec.com
[3] School of Physical and Mathematical Sciences, Nanyang Technological University, Singapore, Singapore
[4] School of Computer Science and Engineering, Nanyang Technological University, Singapore, Singapore
[5] Temasek Laboratories, Nanyang Technological University, Singapore, Singapore
thomas.peyrin@ntu.edu.sg
[6] ANSSI, Paris, France
yannick.seurin@m4x.org

Abstract. We propose a new mode of operation called ZMAC allowing to construct a (stateless and deterministic) message authentication code (MAC) from a tweakable block cipher (TBC). When using a TBC with n-bit blocks and t-bit tweaks, our construction provides security (as a variable-input-length PRF) beyond the birthday bound with respect to the block-length n and allows to process $n + t$ bits of inputs per TBC call. In comparison, previous TBC-based modes such as PMAC1, the TBC-based generalization of the seminal PMAC mode (Black and Rogaway, EUROCRYPT 2002) or PMAC_TBC1k (Naito, ProvSec 2015) only process n bits of input per TBC call. Since an n-bit block, t-bit tweak TBC can process at most $n + t$ bits of input per call, the efficiency of our construction is essentially optimal, while achieving beyond-birthday-bound security. The ZMAC mode is fully parallelizable and can be directly instantiated with several concrete TBC proposals, such as Deoxys and SKINNY. We also use ZMAC to construct a stateless and deterministic Authenticated Encryption scheme called ZAE which is very efficient and secure beyond the birthday bound.

Keywords: MAC · Tweakable block cipher · Authenticated encryption

1 Introduction

Block Cipher-Based MACs. A Message Authentication Code (MAC) is a symmetric-key cryptographic function that ensures the authenticity of messages. A large family of MACs (such as CBC-MAC [BKR00] or OMAC [IK03]) are constructed as modes of operation of some underlying block cipher. They are often

J. Katz and H. Shacham (Eds.): CRYPTO 2017, Part III, LNCS 10403, pp. 34–65, 2017.
DOI: 10.1007/978-3-319-63697-9_2

provably secure and reasonably efficient, however, they also have inherent limitations with respect to speed and security. First, such modes cannot process more than n bits of input per block cipher call, where n is the block-length (in bits) of the underlying block cipher. Second, most block cipher-based modes are secure only up to the so-called birthday bound (i.e., up to $2^{n/2}$ message blocks), and very few proposals, such as PMAC_Plus [Yas11], achieve security *beyond the birthday bound* (BBB), often at the cost of efficiency. For block ciphers with block-length 128, birthday-bound security can be deemed to low in many situations.

For these reasons, a recent popular trend has been to design modes of operation for a stronger primitive, namely *tweakable* block ciphers (TBCs). In comparison to traditional block ciphers, TBCs take an extra t-bit input called the *tweak*, and should behave as a family of 2^t independent block ciphers indexed by the tweak. This primitive was formalized by Liskov *et al.* [LRW02] (even though the informal idea surfaced in several papers before), and turns out to be surprisingly flexible for building various cryptographic functionalities. A TBC can be either constructed in a generic way from a block cipher through a mode of operation such as XEX [Rog04], or as a dedicated design such as Threefish [FLS+10], SCREAM [GLS+14], Deoxys-BC [JNP14a], Joltik-BC [JNP14b], KIASU-BC [JNP14c], and SKINNY [BJK+16], these last four examples following the so-called TWEAKEY framework [JNP14d].

The first construction of a parallelizable[1] MAC from a TBC is PMAC1 [Rog04], derived from the block cipher-based construction PMAC [BR02] by abstracting the block cipher-based TBC implicitly used in PMAC. Assuming that the underlying TBC has n-bit blocks and t-bit tweaks, PMAC1 processes n bits of inputs per TBC call, handles messages of length up to (roughly) 2^t n-bit blocks, and is secure up to the birthday bound (i.e., up to roughly $2^{n/2}$ message blocks). This scheme is simple, efficient and fully parallelizable (all calls to the TBC except the final one can be made in parallel). For these reasons, it has been adopted for example by multiple TBC-based submissions to the CAESAR competition for Authenticated Encryption (AE), e.g. SCREAM [GLS+14], Deoxys [JNP14a], Joltik [JNP14b], or KIASU [JNP14c].

Several authors have proposed schemes that push security beyond the birthday bound. Naito [Nai15] proposed two constructions called PMAC_TBC1k and PMAC_TBC3k which are reminiscent from PMAC_Plus [Yas11]. As PMAC1, they allow to process only n bits of inputs per TBC call, but their security is significantly higher than for PMAC1: they are secure up to roughly 2^n message blocks. Recently, List and Nandi [LN17] proposed PMAC2x which extends the output size of Naito's PMAC_TBC1k scheme from n to $2n$ bits without harming efficiency nor security. (They also proposed a minor modification of PMAC_TBC1k with n-bit outputs called PMACx.) We remark that Minematsu and Iwata [MI17] recently reported severe flaws in [LN17] (the ePrint version of [LN17] was subsequently updated in order to fix these flaws).

[1] Liskov *et al.* [LRW02] suggested a MAC construction from a TBC called TBC-MAC, but the construction is serial.

Our Contribution. We propose a new TBC-based MAC called ZMAC. As PMAC_TBC1k [Nai15] or PMAC2x/PMACx [LN17], it achieves BBB-security (as a variable-input-length PRF) and it is fully parallelizable. However, our proposal is more efficient than any of the previous schemes. Specifically, ZMAC processes $n+t$ bits of inputs per TBC call when using an n-bit block and t-bit tweak TBC, whereas previous schemes are limited to n bits of inputs per TBC call, independently of the tweak size (see Table 1 for a comparison with existing schemes). To the best of our knowledge, this is the first TBC-based MAC that exploits the full power of the tweak input of the underlying TBC. Note that an n-bit block, t-bit tweak TBC cannot handle more than $n+t$ bits of public input per call, hence the efficiency of our construction is essentially optimal (a few tweak bits are reserved for domain separation but the impact is very limited). The tweak-length t of the TBC used in ZMAC can be arbitrary, which is important since existing dedicated TBCs have various tweak-length, smaller (e.g. Threefish or KIASU-BC) or larger (e.g. Deoxys-BC or SKINNY) than the block-length n.

Main Ideas of Our Design. Our construction follows the traditional "UHF-then-PRF" paradigm: first, the message is hashed with a universal hash function (UHF), and the resulting output is given to a fixed-input-length PRF. Building a BBB-secure fixed-input-length PRF from a TBC is more or less straightforward (one can simply use the "XOR of permutations" construction, which has been extensively analyzed [Luc00, Pat08, Pat13, CLP14]). The most innovative part of our work lies in the design of our TBC-based UHF, which we call ZHASH. The structure of our proposal is reminiscent of Naito's PMAC_TBC1k (and thus of PMAC_Plus) combined with the XTX tweak extension construction by Minematsu and Iwata [MI15]. We note that a TBC is often used to abstract a block cipher-based construction to simplify the security proof, for example in the case of PMAC and OCB [Rog04], where one can prove the security of TBC-based abstraction and the construction of TBC itself separately. The TBC-based abstraction eliminates the handling of masks, which simplifies the security proof. That is, it is often the case that TBC-based constructions do not have masks, where the masks are treated as tweaks. With ZMAC, we take the opposite direction to the common approach. We restore the masks in the construction, and our scheme explicitly relies on the use of masks together with a TBC.

Application to Deterministic Authenticated Encryption. Following List and Nandi [LN17], we use ZMAC to construct a (stateless) Deterministic Authenticated Encryption (DAE) scheme (i.e., a scheme whose security does not rely on the use of random IVs or nonces[2] [RS06]). The resulting scheme, called ZAE, is BBB-secure and very efficient: it processes on average $n(n+t)/(2n+t)$ input bits per TBC call (this complex form comes from the fact that the MAC, resp. encryption part processes $n+t$, resp. n input bits per TBC call). Note that when $t=0$, this is (unsurprisingly) similar to standard double-pass block cipher-based DAE schemes ($n/2$ bits per block cipher call), but as t grows,

[2] DAE implies resistance against nonce-misuse by incorporating the nonce into the associated data, and thus is also called Misuse-Resistant AE (MRAE).

Table 1. Comparison of our designs ZMAC and ZAE with other MAC and DAE (a.k.a MRAE) schemes. Column "# bits per call" refers to the number of bits of input processed per primitive call. Notation: n is the block-length of the underlying BC/TBC, t is the tweak-length of the underlying TBC. NR denotes the nonce-respecting scenario.

Scheme	Prim.	# bits per call	Parallel	Security	Ref.
Message Authentication Code					
CMAC	BC	n	N	$n/2$	[IK03]
PMAC	BC	n	Y	$n/2$	[BR02]
SUM-ECBC	BC	$n/2$	N	$2n/3$	[Yas10]
PMAC_Plus	BC	n	Y	$2n/3$	[Yas11]
PMAC1	TBC	n	Y	$n/2$	[Rog04]
PMAC_TBC1k	TBC	n	Y	n	[Nai15]
PMACx/PMAC2x	TBC	n	Y	n	[LN17]
ZMAC	TBC	$n+t$	Y	$\min\{n, (n+t)/2\}$	Sect. 3
Deterministic Authenticated Encryption					
SIV	BC	$n/2$	Y	$n/2$	[RS06]
SCT	TBC	$n/2$	Y	$n/2$ (n for NR)	[PS16]
SIVx	TBC	$n/2$	Y	n	[LN17]
ZAE	TBC	$n(n+t)/(2n+t)$	Y	$\min\{n, (n+t)/2\}$	Sect. 5

efficiency approaches n bits per TBC calls, i.e., the efficiency of an *online* block cipher-based scheme (which cannot be secure in the DAE sense). We provide a comparison with other DAE schemes in Table 1. We emphasize that ZAE is a mere combination of ZMAC with a TBC-based encryption mode called IVCTRT previously proposed in [PS16] through the SIV composition method [RS06]. Nevertheless, we think the proposal of a concrete DAE scheme based on ZMAC is quite relevant here, and helps further illustrate the performance gains allowed by ZMAC (see Table 3 in Sect. 6).

FUTURE WORKS. ZMAC achieves optimal efficiency while providing full n-bit security (assuming $t \geq n$). For this reason, it seems that this mode cannot be substantially improved. However, it would be very interesting to study how ZMAC's design can influence ad-hoc TBC constructions: if one could construct an efficient, BBB-secure n-bit block TBC with a very large tweak (something which has not been studied much yet), this would lead to extremely efficient MAC algorithms.

ORGANIZATION. We give useful definitions in Sect. 2. Our new mode ZMAC is defined in Sect. 3, and its security is analyzed in Sect. 4. Applications to Authenticated Encryption are presented in Sect. 5. Finally, a performance estimation for ZMAC and ZAE when Deoxys-BC or SKINNY are used to instantiate the TBC is provided in Sect. 6.

2 Preliminaries

Basic Notation. Let $\{0,1\}^*$ be the set of all finite bit strings. For an integer $n \geq 0$, let $\{0,1\}^n$ be the set of all bit strings of length n, and $(\{0,1\}^n)^+$ be the set of all bit strings of length a (non-zero) positive multiple of n. For $X \in \{0,1\}^*$, $|X|$ is its length in bits, and for $n \geq 1$, $|X|_n = \lceil |X|/n \rceil$ is its length in n-bit blocks. The string of n zeros is denoted 0^n. The concatenation of two bit strings X and Y is written $X \| Y$, or XY when no confusion is possible. For any $X \in \{0,1\}^n$ and $i \leq n$, let $\mathtt{msb}_i(X)$, resp. $\mathtt{lsb}_i(X)$ be the first, resp. last i bits of X. For non-negative integers a and d with $a \leq 2^d - 1$, let $\mathtt{str}_d(a)$ be the d-bit binary representation of a.

Given a bit string $X \in \{0,1\}^{i+j}$, we write

$$(X[1], X[2]) \xleftarrow{i,j} X$$

where $X[1] = \mathtt{msb}_i(X)$ and $X[2] = \mathtt{lsb}_j(X)$. For $X \in \{0,1\}^*$, we also define the parsing into fixed-length subsequences of length n, denoted

$$(X[1], X[2], \ldots, X[m]) \xleftarrow{n} X,$$

where $m = |X|_n$, $X[1] \| X[2] \| \ldots \| X[m] = X$, $|X[i]| = n$ for $1 \leq i < m$ and $0 \leq |X[m]| \leq n$ when $|X| > 0$. When $|X| = 0$, we let $X[1] \xleftarrow{n} X$, where $X[1]$ is the empty string.

Let n and t be positive integers. For any $X \in \{0,1\}^*$, we define the "one-zero padding" $\mathtt{ozp}(X)$ to be X if $|X|$ is a positive multiple of $(n+t)$ and $X \| 10^c$ for $c = |X| \bmod (n+t) - 1$ otherwise. We stress that $\mathtt{ozp}(\cdot)$ is defined with respect to $(n+t)$-bit blocks rather than n-bit blocks, and that the empty string is padded to 10^{n+t-1}.

For any $X \in \{0,1\}^n$ and $Y \in \{0,1\}^t$, we define

$$X \oplus_t Y \stackrel{\text{def}}{=} \begin{cases} \mathtt{msb}_t(X) \oplus Y & \text{if } t \leq n, \\ (X \| 0^{t-n}) \oplus Y & \text{if } t > n. \end{cases}$$

Hence, $|X \oplus_t Y| = t$ in both cases and if $t = n$ then $X \oplus_t Y = X \oplus Y$.

Given a non-empty set $\mathcal{X}$, we let $X \xleftarrow{\$} \mathcal{X}$ denote the draw of an element X uniformly at random in $\mathcal{X}$.

Galois Field. An element a in the Galois field $\mathrm{GF}(2^n)$ will be interchangeably represented as an n-bit string $a_{n-1} \ldots a_1 a_0$, a formal polynomial $a_{n-1}\mathtt{x}^{n-1} + \cdots + a_1\mathtt{x} + a_0$, or an integer $\sum_{i=0}^{n-1} a_i 2^i$. Hence, by writing $2 \cdot a$ or $2a$ when no confusion is possible, we mean the multiplication of a by $2 = \mathtt{x}$. This operation is called *doubling*. For $n = 128$, we define the field $\mathrm{GF}(2^n)$ (as is standard) by the primitive polynomial $\mathtt{x}^{128} + \mathtt{x}^7 + \mathtt{x}^2 + \mathtt{x} + 1$. The doubling $2a$ over this field is $(a \ll 1)$ if $\mathtt{msb}_1(a) = 0$ and $(a \ll 1) \oplus (0^{120}10000111)$ if $\mathtt{msb}_1(a) = 1$, where $(a \ll 1)$ denotes the left-shift of a by one bit.

Keyed Functions and Modes. A keyed function with key space $\mathcal{K}$, domain $\mathcal{X}$, and range $\mathcal{Y}$ is a function $F : \mathcal{K} \times \mathcal{X} \to \mathcal{Y}$. We write $F_K(X)$ for $F(K, X)$.

If Mode is a mode of operation for F using a single key $K \in \mathcal{K}$ for F, we write $\mathsf{Mode}[F_K]$ instead of $\mathsf{Mode}[F]_K$.

For any keyed function $F : \mathcal{K} \times (\{0,1\}^n)^+ \to \{0,1\}^a$ for some a, we define the collision probability of F as

$$\mathsf{Coll}_F(n, m, m') \stackrel{\text{def}}{=} \max_{\substack{M \in (\{0,1\}^n)^m \\ M' \in (\{0,1\}^n)^{m'} \\ M \neq M'}} \Pr[K \stackrel{\$}{\leftarrow} \mathcal{K} : F_K(M) = F_K(M')].$$

Tweakable Blockciphers. A tweakable blockcipher (TBC) is a keyed function $\widetilde{E} : \mathcal{K} \times \mathcal{T} \times \mathcal{M} \to \mathcal{M}$ such that for each $(K, T) \in \mathcal{K} \times \mathcal{T}$, $\widetilde{E}(K, T, \cdot)$ is a permutation over $\mathcal{M}$. Here, K is the key and T is a public value called tweak. Note that a conventional block cipher is a TBC such that the tweak space $\mathcal{T}$ is a singleton. The output $\widetilde{E}(K, T, X)$ of the encryption of $X \in \mathcal{M}$ under key $K \in \mathcal{K}$ and tweak $T \in \mathcal{T}$ may also be written $\widetilde{E}_K(T, X)$ or $\widetilde{E}_K^T(X)$. Following [PS16], when the tweak space of $\widetilde{E}$ is $\mathcal{T}_\mathcal{I} = \mathcal{T} \times \mathcal{I}$ for some $\mathcal{I} \subset \mathbb{N}$ and for some set $\mathcal{T}$, we call $\mathcal{T}$ the *effective* tweak space of $\widetilde{E}$, and we write $\widetilde{E}^i(K, T, X)$ to mean $\widetilde{E}(K, (T, i), X)$. By convention we also write $\widetilde{E}_K^i(T, X)$ or $\widetilde{E}_K^{i,T}(X)$. The set $\mathcal{I}$ is typically a small set used to generate a small number of distinct TBC instances in the scheme, something we call domain separation. For $T' = (T, i) \in \mathcal{T}_\mathcal{I}$, we call $i \in \mathcal{I}$ the domain separation integer of tweak T'.

Random Primitives. Let $\mathcal{X}$, $\mathcal{Y}$ and $\mathcal{T}$ be non-empty finite sets. Let $\mathrm{Func}(\mathcal{X}, \mathcal{Y})$ be the set of all functions from $\mathcal{X}$ to $\mathcal{Y}$, and let $\mathrm{Perm}(\mathcal{X})$ be the set of all permutations over $\mathcal{X}$. Moreover, let $\mathrm{Perm}^\mathcal{T}(\mathcal{X})$ be the set of all functions $f : \mathcal{T} \times \mathcal{X} \to \mathcal{X}$ such that for any $T \in \mathcal{T}$, $f(T, \cdot)$ is a permutation over $\mathcal{X}$.

A uniform random function (URF) with domain $\mathcal{X}$ and range $\mathcal{Y}$, denoted $\mathsf{R} : \mathcal{X} \to \mathcal{Y}$, is a random function with uniform distribution over $\mathrm{Func}(\mathcal{X}, \mathcal{Y})$. Similarly, a uniform random permutation (URP) over $\mathcal{X}$, denoted $\mathsf{P} : \mathcal{X} \to \mathcal{X}$, is a random permutation with uniform distribution over $\mathrm{Perm}(\mathcal{X})$. An n-bit URP is a URP over $\{0,1\}^n$. Finally, a tweakable URP (TURP) with tweak space $\mathcal{T}$ and message space $\mathcal{X}$, denoted $\widetilde{\mathsf{P}} : \mathcal{T} \times \mathcal{X} \to \mathcal{X}$, is a random tweakable permutation with uniform distribution over $\mathrm{Perm}^\mathcal{T}(\mathcal{X})$.

Security Notions. We recall standard security notions for (tweakable) block ciphers and keyed functions.

Definition 1. *Let $\widetilde{E} : \mathcal{K} \times \mathcal{T} \times \mathcal{X} \to \mathcal{X}$ be a TBC, and let $\mathcal{A}$ be an adversary with oracle access to a tweakable permutation whose goal is to distinguish $\widetilde{E}$ and a TURP $\widetilde{\mathsf{P}} : \mathcal{T} \times \mathcal{X} \to \mathcal{X}$ by oracle access. The advantage of $\mathcal{A}$ against the Tweakable Pseudorandom Permutation-security (or TPRP-security) of $\widetilde{E}$ is defined as*

$$\mathtt{Adv}_{\widetilde{E}}^{\mathtt{tprp}}(\mathcal{A}) \stackrel{\text{def}}{=} \left| \Pr[K \stackrel{\$}{\leftarrow} \mathcal{K} : \mathcal{A}^{\widetilde{E}_K} \Rightarrow 1] - \Pr[\widetilde{\mathsf{P}} \stackrel{\$}{\leftarrow} \mathrm{Perm}^\mathcal{T}(\mathcal{X}) : \mathcal{A}^{\widetilde{\mathsf{P}}} \Rightarrow 1] \right|,$$

where $\mathcal{A}^{\widetilde{E}_K} \Rightarrow 1$ denotes the event that the final binary decision by $\mathcal{A}$ is 1.

We remark that the above definition only allows $\mathcal{A}$ to make encryption queries. If decryption queries are allowed, the corresponding notion is called Strong TPRP (or STPRP) security. In this paper, we only use TPRP-security for the TBC underlying our constructions. The standard PRP-security notion for conventional block ciphers is recovered by letting the tweak space $\mathcal{T}$ be a singleton.

Definition 2. *For $F : \mathcal{K} \times \mathcal{X} \to \mathcal{Y}$, let $\mathcal{A}$ be an adversary whose goal is to distinguish F_K and a URF $\mathsf{R} : \mathcal{X} \to \mathcal{Y}$ by oracle access. The advantage of $\mathcal{A}$ against the PRF-security of F is defined as*

$$\mathtt{Adv}_F^{\mathtt{prf}}(\mathcal{A}) \overset{\text{def}}{=} \left| \Pr[K \overset{\$}{\leftarrow} \mathcal{K} : \mathcal{A}^{F_K} \Rightarrow 1] - \Pr[\mathsf{R} \overset{\$}{\leftarrow} \mathrm{Func}(\mathcal{X}, \mathcal{Y}) : \mathcal{A}^{\mathsf{R}} \Rightarrow 1] \right| .$$

Moreover, for any $F : \mathcal{K} \times \mathcal{X} \to \mathcal{Y}$ and $G : \mathcal{K}' \times \mathcal{X} \to \mathcal{Y}$, the advantage of $\mathcal{A}$ in distinguishing F and G is defined as

$$\mathtt{Adv}_{F,G}^{\mathtt{dist}}(\mathcal{A}) \overset{\text{def}}{=} \left| \Pr[K \overset{\$}{\leftarrow} \mathcal{K} : \mathcal{A}^{F_K} \Rightarrow 1] - \Pr[K' \overset{\$}{\leftarrow} \mathcal{K}' : \mathcal{A}^{G_{K'}} \Rightarrow 1] \right| .$$

When a cryptographic scheme (or a mode of operation) Mode uses a (T)BC of block-length n bits, the security bound (i.e., the best advantage for any adversary with fixed resources) is typically a function of the query complexity of the adversary (in terms of number q of queries or total number σ of queried blocks) and n. When this function reaches 1 for query complexity $2^{n/2}$, we say that Mode is secure up to the birthday bound, since this typically arises from the birthday paradox on the block input of the (T)BC. Conversely, if the advantage is negligibly small for any adversary of query complexity $2^{n/2}$, we say that Mode is secure beyond the birthday bound (BBB-secure).

3 Specification of ZMAC

3.1 Overview

Let $\widetilde{E} : \mathcal{K} \times \mathcal{T}_\mathcal{I} \times \{0,1\}^n \to \{0,1\}^n$ be a TBC with tweak space $\mathcal{T}_\mathcal{I} = \mathcal{T} \times \mathcal{I}$, where $\mathcal{T} = \{0,1\}^t$ for some $t > 0$ and $\mathcal{I} \supseteq \{0, 1, \ldots, 9\}$. We present a construction of a PRF $\mathsf{ZMAC}[\widetilde{E}] : \mathcal{K} \times \{0,1\}^* \to \{0,1\}^{2n}$ with variable-input-length and $2n$-bit outputs based on $\widetilde{E}$.

The ZMAC mode has the following properties, holding for any effective tweak size $t > 0$:

1. it uses a single key for calls to $\widetilde{E}$;
2. the calls to $\widetilde{E}$ are parallelizable;
3. it processes on average $n + t$ input bits per TBC call;
4. it is provably secure as long as the total length σ of queries in $(n + t)$-bit blocks is small compared with $2^{\min\{n,(n+t)/2\}}$.

ZMAC is more efficient than any previous TBC-based MAC, which process at most n bits per TBC call (e.g., when $t = n$, ZMAC is twice faster than PMAC1). We emphasize that any mode based on an n-bit block, t-bit tweak TBC can process at most $n + t$ input bits per TBC call, thus ZMAC's efficiency is essentially optimal if one wants to achieve any meaningful provable security, since otherwise there must be some part of the input which is not processed by the TBC.[3]

Property 4 shows that the security of ZMAC is beyond the birthday bound with respect to n. In particular, it is n-bit secure when $t \geq n$. These properties demonstrate that ZMAC is the first TBC-based MAC to fully use the power of the underlying TBC.

We specify ZMAC with $2n$-bit outputs, which will be useful for defining our BBB-secure DAE scheme in Sect. 5. However, if one simply wants an n-bit-secure MAC, one can truncate the output of ZMAC to n bits (which saves two TBC calls in the finalization).

DESIGN RATIONALE. The structure of ZMAC has some similarities with previous BBB-secure TBC-based PRF constructions [Nai15,LN17]. However, there are several innovative features that make ZMAC faster and n-bit secure.

The core idea of [Nai15,LN17] is to start from a TBC-based instantiation of PHASH, the UHF underlying PMAC [Rog04]. PHASH is quite simple: it simply XORs together the encryptions $\widetilde{E}_K(i, M_i)$ of message blocks with the index i of the block as tweak. In order to obtain a $2n$-bit output, some linear layer is applied to all encrypted blocks, as originally introduced by Yasuda [Yas11] in his PMAC_Plus block cipher-based PRF. This yields a $2n$-bit message hash, to which some finalization function (a fixed-input-length PRF) is applied to obtain the final output.

Whereas the t-bit tweak in the previous schemes takes as input the index of each message block, we crucially use both the message space and the tweak space of the TBC to process $n + t$ input bits in order to improve efficiency. The block index is incorporated via (a variant of) a tweak extension scheme called XTX [MI15], which allows to efficiently update the block index with only two field doublings, somehow similarly to XEX [Rog04].

The above trick, however, is not enough to achieve BBB-security. Since we process each $(n + t)$-bit input block by one call to an n-bit output TBC, the input block and the output block are no longer in one-to-one correspondence. Yet the BBB-security of previous schemes (where each input block is n-bit) crucially relies on this fact (otherwise, one can find a collision with complexity $2^{n/2}$, resulting in $n/2$-bit security). Fortunately, this problem can be solved by processing each $(n + t)$-bit input block with a Feistel-like permutation involving one TBC call, and applying the linear layer to the output of this $(n + t)$-bit permutation.

[3] Alternatively, one can combine another large non-linear component such as a field multiplication with an extra key, however this increases the implementation size.

Algorithm $\mathsf{ZHASH}[\widetilde{E}_K](X)$

$U \leftarrow 0^n, V \leftarrow 0^t$
$L_\ell \leftarrow \widetilde{E}^9_K(0^t, 0^n)$
$L_r \leftarrow \widetilde{E}^9_K(0^{t-1}1, 0^n)$
$(X[1], \dots, X[m]) \xleftarrow{n+t} X$
for $i = 1$ **to** m **do**
  $(X_\ell, X_r) \xleftarrow{n,t} X[i]$
  $S_\ell \leftarrow L_\ell \oplus X_\ell$
  $S_r \leftarrow L_r \oplus_t X_r$
  $C_\ell \leftarrow \widetilde{E}^8_K(S_r, S_\ell)$
  $C_r \leftarrow C_\ell \oplus_t X_r$
  $U \leftarrow 2(U \oplus C_\ell)$
  $V \leftarrow V \oplus C_r$
  $(L_\ell, L_r) \leftarrow (2L_\ell, 2L_r)$
return (U, V)

Algorithm $\mathsf{ZFIN}[\widetilde{E}_K](i, U, V)$

$Y[1] \leftarrow \widetilde{E}^i_K(V, U) \oplus \widetilde{E}^{i+1}_K(V, U)$
$Y[2] \leftarrow \widetilde{E}^{i+2}_K(V, U) \oplus \widetilde{E}^{i+3}_K(V, U)$
$Y \leftarrow Y[1] \parallel Y[2]$
return Y

Algorithm $\mathsf{ZMAC}[\widetilde{E}_K](M)$

$X \leftarrow \mathsf{ozp}(M)$
$(U, V) \leftarrow \mathsf{ZHASH}[\widetilde{E}_K](X)$
if $M \in (\{0,1\}^{n+t})^+$
  $Y \leftarrow \mathsf{ZFIN}[\widetilde{E}_K](0, U, V)$
else
  $Y \leftarrow \mathsf{ZFIN}[\widetilde{E}_K](4, U, V)$
return Y

Fig. 1. Specification of ZMAC.

HIGH-LEVEL STRUCTURE OF ZMAC. ZMAC consists of a hashing part

$$\mathsf{ZHASH}[\widetilde{E}] : \mathcal{K} \times (\{0,1\}^{n+t})^+ \to \{0,1\}^{n+t}$$

and a finalization part

$$\mathsf{ZFIN}[\widetilde{E}] : \mathcal{K} \times \{0,1\}^{n+t} \to \{0,1\}^{2n}.$$

Then, ZMAC is defined as the composition of ZHASH and ZFIN. When the input-length is not a positive multiple of $(n+t)$ bits, one-zero padding (into $(n+t)$-bit blocks) is applied first. To separate inputs whose length is a positive multiple of $(n+t)$ bits or not, we use distinct domain separation integers in ZFIN.

The pseudocode for ZHASH, ZFIN, and ZMAC is shown in Fig. 1. See Fig. 2 and Fig. 3 illustrating ZHASH and ZFIN. Fig. 1 gives a unified specification that covers both cases $t \le n$ and $t > n$ (note that the only operation which differs in the two cases is the $\oplus_t$ operation). We describe more informally ZHASH separately for $t \le n$ and $t > n$, as well as ZFIN in the following sections.

3.2 Specification of ZHASH for the Case $t \le N$

We first define $\mathsf{ZHASH}[\widetilde{E}]$ when $t \le n$. For simplicity, we assume $n + t$ is even. Before processing the input, $\mathsf{ZHASH}[\widetilde{E}]$ computes two n-bit initial mask values $L_\ell = \widetilde{E}^9_K(0^t, 0^n)$ and $L_r = \widetilde{E}^9_K(0^{t-1}1, 0^n)$.

Given input $X \in (\{0,1\}^{n+t})^+$, $\mathsf{ZHASH}[\widetilde{E}]$ parses X into $(n+t)$-bit blocks $(X[1], \dots, X[m])$, parses each block $X[i]$ as $X_\ell[i] = \mathtt{msb}_n(X[i])$ and $X_r[i] =$

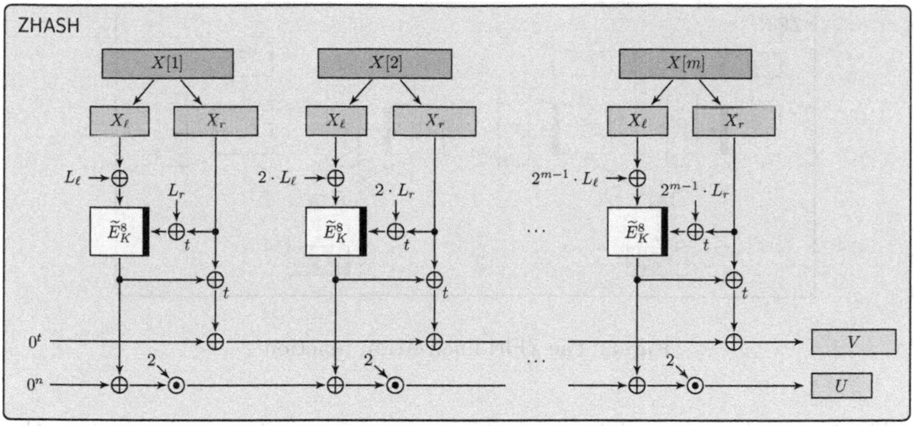

Fig. 2. The ZHASH hash function.

$\texttt{lsb}_t(X[i])$, and computes, for $i = 1$ to m,

$$C_\ell[i] = \widetilde{E}^8_K(2^{i-1}L_r \oplus_t X_r[i], 2^{i-1}L_\ell \oplus X_\ell[i]), \quad (1)$$
$$C_r[i] = C_\ell[i] \oplus_t X_r[i]. \quad (2)$$

Then ZHASH$[\widetilde{E}]$ computes two chaining values, $U \in \{0,1\}^n$ and $V \in \{0,1\}^t$ defined as

$$U = \bigoplus_{i=1}^{m} 2^{m-i+1} C_\ell[i],$$
$$V = \bigoplus_{i=1}^{m} C_r[i].$$

The final output is (U, V).

As shown in Fig. 1, the field doublings are computed in an incremental manner. Specifically, ZHASH$[\widetilde{E}]$ needs one call to $\widetilde{E}$ and three GF(2^n) doublings to process an $(n+t)$-bit block, plus two pre-processing calls to $\widetilde{E}$. Obviously, the calls to $\widetilde{E}$ are parallelizable.

3.3 Specification of ZHASH for the Case $t > n$

The hashing scheme ZHASH$[\widetilde{E}]$ for the case $t > n$ is defined as follows (the two internal masks L_ℓ and L_r are derived and incremented in the same way as in the case $t \leq n$).

- The input X is parsed into $(n+t)$-bit blocks as in the case $t \leq n$, and each block is further parsed into n, n, and $t - n$ bit-blocks;

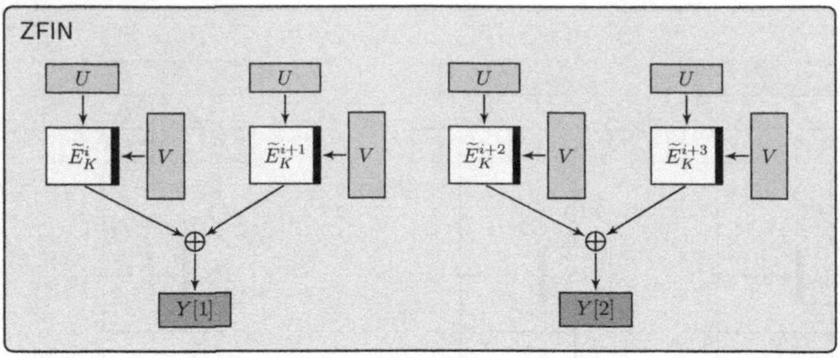

Fig. 3. The ZFIN finalization function.

- The first and second n-bit sub-blocks are processed in the same way as in the case $t = n$. The third $(t - n)$-bit sub-block is directly fed to the tweak input of the TBC as the last $(t - n)$ bits of effective tweak;
- The output consists of two checksums, $U \in \{0,1\}^n$ and $V \in \{0,1\}^t$, where $(U, \mathtt{msb}_n(V))$ corresponds to the output for the case $t = n$, and $\mathtt{lsb}_{t-n}(V)$ corresponds to the sum of all third $(t - n)$-bit sub-blocks.

Hence, the computation of V is just written as the sum of all C_r blocks in the unified specification of Fig. 1, since the last $(t-n)$ bits of $C_r[i]$ only contains the last $(t - n)$ bits of the input block $X[i]$.

3.4 Finalization

The finalization function, denoted by $\mathsf{ZFIN}[\widetilde{E}]$, takes the output of $\mathsf{ZHASH}[\widetilde{E}]$, $(U, V) \in \{0,1\}^n \times \{0,1\}^t$, and generates a $2n$-bit output. It is defined as

$$\mathsf{ZFIN}[\widetilde{E}_K](i, U, V) = (\widetilde{E}_K^i(U, V) \oplus \widetilde{E}_K^{i+1}(U, V) \,\|\, \widetilde{E}_K^{i+2}(U, V) \oplus \widetilde{E}_K^{i+3}(U, V)),$$

where the first argument i is a non-negative integer used for domain separation. Note that if $|i - j| \geq 4$, domain separation integers used for TBC calls in $\mathsf{ZFIN}[\widetilde{E}_K](i, \cdot, \cdot)$ and in $\mathsf{ZFIN}[\widetilde{E}_K](j, \cdot, \cdot)$ are distinct. We use $i = 0$ when no padding is applied, i.e., when $M \in (\{0,1\}^{n+t})^+$, and $i = 4$ otherwise.

We remark that ZFIN is close but not identical to finalization functions used in previous works [Nai15, LN17]. For example, Naito [Nai15] employed $\widetilde{E}_K^i(U, V) \oplus \widetilde{E}_K^{i+1}(V, U)$ for building a PRF with n-bit outputs. One potential advantage of ZFIN over using two independent instances of Naito's construction is that ZFIN can be faster if the algorithm of $\widetilde{E}$ allows to leverage on the similarity of inputs for computing $\widetilde{E}_K^i(U, V)$ and $\widetilde{E}_K^{i+1}(U, V)$.

4 The PRF Security of ZMAC

4.1 XT Tweak Extension

Our first step is to recast the use of masks $2^{i-1}L_\ell$ and $2^{i-1}L_r$ as a way to extend the tweak space of $\widetilde{E}$. More specifically, we observe that the "core" construction of ZHASH in Eq. (1),

$$((T,i),X) \mapsto \widetilde{E}_K^8(2^{i-1}L_r \oplus_t T, 2^{i-1}L_\ell \oplus X), \tag{3}$$

keyed by $(K,(L_\ell,L_r))$, is an instantiation of a CPA-secure variant of a tweak extension scheme called XTX proposed in [MI15], which allows to extend the tweak space of $\widetilde{E}^8$ from $\mathcal{T} = \{0,1\}^t$ to $\mathcal{T}_J = \mathcal{T} \times \mathcal{J}$ with $\mathcal{J} = \{1,\dots,2^n-1\}$. Following the naming convention for XE and XEX by Rogaway [Rog04] which defines CPA- and CCA-secure TBCs based on a block cipher, we use XT to denote the CPA-secure variant of XTX without output mask.

In order to describe the XT construction, we need the notion of partial AXU hash function introduced by [MI15].

Definition 3. *Let $H : \mathcal{L} \times \mathcal{X} \to \mathcal{Y}$ be a keyed function with key space $\mathcal{L}$, domain $\mathcal{X}$, and range $\mathcal{Y} = \{0,1\}^n \times \{0,1\}^t$. We say that H is (n,t,ϵ)-partial almost-XOR-universal ((n,t,ϵ)-pAXU) if for any $X \neq X'$, one has*

$$\max_{\delta \in \{0,1\}^n} \Pr[L \xleftarrow{\$} \mathcal{L} : H_L(X) \oplus H_L(X') = (\delta, 0^t)] \leq \epsilon.$$

Now define the XT tweak extension scheme. Let $\widetilde{E} : \mathcal{K} \times \mathcal{T} \times \{0,1\}^n \to \{0,1\}^n$ be a TBC with tweak space $\mathcal{T} = \{0,1\}^t$ and let $H : \mathcal{L} \times \mathcal{T}' \to \mathcal{Y}$ be a keyed function with range $\mathcal{Y} = \{0,1\}^n \times \{0,1\}^t$. Let $\mathsf{XT}[\widetilde{E},H]$ be the TBC with key space $\mathcal{K} \times \mathcal{L}$, tweak space $\mathcal{T}'$, and message space $\{0,1\}^n$ defined as

$$\mathsf{XT}[\widetilde{E},H]_{K,L}(T',X) = \widetilde{E}_K(Z_r, Z_\ell \oplus X) \text{ where } H_L(T') = (Z_\ell, Z_r). \tag{4}$$

The following lemma characterizes the security of $\mathsf{XT}[\widetilde{\mathsf{P}},H]$ where $\widetilde{E}$ is replaced by a TURP $\widetilde{\mathsf{P}}$. It is similar to [MI15, Theorem 1] and its proof is deferred to the full version of the paper.

Lemma 1. *Let $\mathsf{XT}[\widetilde{\mathsf{P}},H]$ be defined as above, where $\widetilde{\mathsf{P}} : \mathcal{T} \times \{0,1\}^n \to \{0,1\}^n$ is a TURP and H is (n,t,ϵ)-pAXU. Then, for any adversary $\mathcal{A}$ making at most q queries, one has*

$$\mathsf{Adv}^{\mathtt{tprp}}_{\mathsf{XT}[\widetilde{\mathsf{P}},H]}(\mathcal{A}) \leq \frac{q^2\epsilon}{2}.$$

Assume for a moment that $L_\ell = \widetilde{E}_K^9(0^t, 0^n)$ and $L_r = \widetilde{E}_K^9(0^{t-1}1, 0^n)$ are uniformly random (this will hold once the TBC underlying ZMAC has been replaced by a TURP later in the security proof). Consider the function H with key space $\{0,1\}^n \times \{0,1\}^n$, domain $\mathcal{T}_J = \mathcal{T} \times \mathcal{J}$ with $\mathcal{J} = \{1,\dots,2^n-1\}$, and range $\{0,1\}^n \times \{0,1\}^t$ defined as

$$H_{(L_\ell,L_r)}(T,i) = (2^{i-1}L_\ell, 2^{i-1}L_r \oplus_t T). \tag{5}$$

Then observe that the construction of Eq. (3) is exactly $\mathsf{XT}[\widetilde{E}^8,H]$ with H defined as above. We prove that H is pAXU in the following lemma.

Lemma 2. *Let H be defined as in Eq.* (5)*. Then H is $(n, t, 1/2^{n+\min\{n,t\}})$-pAXU.*

Proof. Assume first that $t \leq n$. Then, by definition of $\oplus_t$, one has

$$H_{(L_\ell,L_r)}(T,i) = (2^{i-1}L_\ell, \mathtt{msb}_t(2^{i-1}L_r) \oplus T).$$

Hence, we must upper bound

$$p \stackrel{\text{def}}{=} \Pr_{(L_\ell,L_r)}\left[\left((2^{i-1}+2^{j-1})L_\ell, \mathtt{msb}_t((2^{i-1}+2^{j-1})L_r) \oplus T \oplus T'\right) = (\delta, 0^t)\right]$$

for any distinct inputs $(T,i),(T',j) \in \mathcal{T}_J$ and any $\delta \in \{0,1\}^n$.

If $i = j$, then necessarily $T \neq T'$, and hence

$$\mathtt{msb}_t((2^{i-1}+2^{j-1})L_r) \oplus T \oplus T' = T \oplus T' \neq 0^t.$$

Thus the probability p is zero.

If $i \neq j$, then $2^{i-1} \neq 2^{j-1}$. Therefore, $2^{i-1}+2^{j-1}$ is a non-zero element over $\mathrm{GF}(2^n)$ and thus

$$\begin{aligned} p &= \Pr_{(L_\ell,L_r)}[(2^{i-1}+2^{j-1})L_\ell = \delta, \mathtt{msb}_t((2^{i-1}+2^{j-1})L_r) \oplus T \oplus T' = 0^t] \\ &= \Pr_{(L_\ell,L_r)}[(2^{i-1}+2^{j-1})L_\ell = \delta, \mathtt{msb}_t((2^{i-1}+2^{j-1})L_r) = T \oplus T'] \\ &= \frac{1}{2^n} \cdot \frac{1}{2^t} = \frac{1}{2^{n+t}}. \end{aligned}$$

For the case $t > n$, observe that by definition of $\oplus_t$,

$$H_{(L_\ell,L_r)}(T,i) = (2^{i-1}L_\ell, (2^{i-1}L_r \,\|\, 0^{t-n}) \oplus T).$$

Hence, we can use the previous analysis for the special case $t = n$, so that p is at most $1/2^{2n}$. In all cases, p is at most $1/2^{n+\min\{n,t\}}$. □

Combining Lemmas 1 and 2, we obtain the following for the construction of Eq. (3) when $\widetilde{E}_K^8$ is replaced by a TURP.

Lemma 3. *Let $\mathsf{XT}[\widetilde{\mathsf{P}}, H]$ be defined as in Eq.* (4) *where $\widetilde{\mathsf{P}} : \mathcal{T} \times \{0,1\}^n \to \{0,1\}^n$ is a TURP and H is defined as in Eq.* (5)*. Then, for any adversary making at most q queries,*

$$\mathtt{Adv}^{\mathtt{tprp}}_{\mathsf{XT}[\widetilde{\mathsf{P}},H]}(\mathcal{A}) \leq \frac{q^2}{2^{n+\min\{n,t\}+1}}.$$

4.2 Collision Probability of ZHASH

Let $\widetilde{E}' : \mathcal{K}' \times \mathcal{T}_J \times \{0,1\}^n \to \{0,1\}^n$ be a TBC with tweak space $\mathcal{T}_J = \mathcal{T} \times \mathcal{J}$ where $\mathcal{T} = \{0,1\}^t$ and $\mathcal{J} = \{1, \ldots, 2^n - 1\}$ as before. We define $\mathbb{ZHASH}[\widetilde{E}']$ as shown in Fig. 4 and depicted in Fig. 5. Note that, assuming that masking keys L_ℓ and L_r are uniformly random rather than derived through $\widetilde{E}_K^9$, $\mathsf{ZHASH}[\widetilde{E}]$ is exactly $\mathbb{ZHASH}[\mathsf{XT}[\widetilde{E}^8, H]]$, with H defined as in Eq. (5).

Let $\widetilde{\mathsf{P}}_J : \mathcal{T}_J \times \{0,1\}^n \to \{0,1\}^n$ be a TURP. The following lemma plays a central role in our security proof.

Algorithm $\mathbb{ZHASH}[\widetilde{E}'_{K'}](X)$
($|X|$ is a positive multiple of $n+t$)

1. $U \leftarrow 0^n, V \leftarrow 0^t$
2. $(X[1], \ldots, X[m]) \xleftarrow{n+t} X$
3. **for** $i = 1$ **to** m **do**
4. $\quad (X_\ell, X_r) \xleftarrow{n,t} X[i]$
5. $\quad C_\ell \leftarrow \widetilde{E}'_{K'}((X_r, i), X_\ell)$
6. $\quad C_r \leftarrow C_\ell \oplus_t X_r$
7. $\quad U \leftarrow 2(U \oplus C_\ell)$
8. $\quad V \leftarrow V \oplus C_r$
9. **return** (U, V)

Fig. 4. Pseudocode for the $\mathbb{ZHASH}$ construction using $\widetilde{E}' : \mathcal{K}' \times \mathcal{T}_J \times \{0,1\}^n \to \{0,1\}^n$ with $\mathcal{T}_J = \{0,1\}^t \times \{1, 2, \ldots, 2^n - 1\}$.

Lemma 4. *For any $m, m' \leq 2^{\min\{n,(n+t)/2\}}$, we have*

$$\mathsf{Coll}_{\mathbb{ZHASH}[\widetilde{\mathsf{P}}_J]}(n+t, m, m') \leq \frac{4}{2^{n+\min\{n,t\}}}.$$

Proof. Without loss of generality, we assume $m \leq m'$. Let $X = (X[1], \ldots, X[m])$ and $X' = (X'[1], \ldots, X'[m'])$ be two distinct messages of $(n+t)$-bit blocks. Let $(U, V) = \mathbb{ZHASH}[\widetilde{\mathsf{P}}_J](X)$ and $(U', V') = \mathbb{ZHASH}[\widetilde{\mathsf{P}}_J](X')$ be the outputs. We define $X_r[i]$, $X_\ell[i]$, $C_\ell[i]$, and $C_r[i]$ following Fig. 4 augmented with the loop index i. Let $\Delta U = U \oplus U'$, $\Delta V = V \oplus V'$, etc. A collision of $\mathbb{ZHASH}[\widetilde{\mathsf{P}}_J]$ outputs is equivalent to $(\Delta U, \Delta V) = (0^n, 0^t)$.

We perform a case analysis. We first focus on the case $t \leq n$, and consider four sub-cases.

Case 1: $m = m'$, $\exists h \in \{1, \ldots, m\}$, $X[h] \neq X'[h]$, $X[i] = X'[i]$ for $\forall i \neq h$. Then we have

$$\Delta U = \bigoplus_{1 \leq i \leq m} 2^{m-i+1} \Delta C_\ell[i] = 2^{m-h+1} \Delta C_\ell[h],$$

$$\Delta V = \bigoplus_{1 \leq j \leq m} \Delta C_r[j] = \Delta C_r[h].$$

Since the mapping $(X_\ell[i], X_r[i]) \mapsto (C_\ell[i], C_r[i])$ is a permutation, we have $(C_\ell[h], C_r[h]) \neq (C'_\ell[h], C'_r[h])$ and thus we have either $\Delta C_\ell[h] \neq 0^n$ or $\Delta C_r[h] \neq 0^t$. This implies $\Delta U \neq 0^n$ or $\Delta V \neq 0^t$.

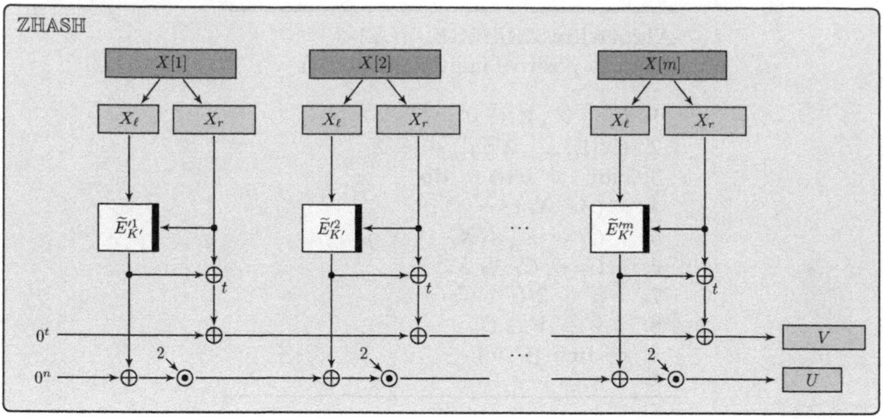

Fig. 5. The ZHASH hash function.

Case 2: $m = m'$, $\exists h, s \in \{1, \ldots, m\}$, $h \neq s$, $X[h] \neq X'[h]$, $X[s] \neq X'[s]$. Then we have

$$\Delta U = 2^{m-h+1} \Delta C_\ell[h] \oplus 2^{m-s+1} \Delta C_\ell[s] \oplus \underbrace{\bigoplus_{\substack{1 \le i \le m \\ i \neq h,s}} 2^{m-i+1} \Delta C_\ell[i]}_{\Delta_1},$$

$$\Delta V = \Delta C_r[h] \oplus \Delta C_r[s] \oplus \underbrace{\bigoplus_{\substack{1 \le i \le m \\ i \neq h,s}} \Delta C_r[i]}_{\Delta_2}.$$

Observe that Δ_1 and Δ_2 are functions of variables of the form $\widetilde{\mathsf{P}}_J((T, i), X'')$ where $i \notin \{h, s\}$ and T and X'' are determined by X and X'. In particular, by definition of a TURP, they are independent (as random variables) from the other terms in the two right-hand sides. Hence, letting $\lambda_h = 2^{m-h+1}$ and $\lambda_s = 2^{m-s+1}$, and using that since $t \le n$, $C_r[i] = \mathtt{msb}_t(C_\ell[i]) \oplus X_r[i]$, we have

$$\begin{cases} \Delta U = 0^n \\ \Delta V = 0^t \end{cases} \iff \begin{cases} \lambda_h \Delta C_\ell[h] \oplus \lambda_s \Delta C_\ell[s] = \Delta_1 \\ \Delta C_r[h] \oplus \Delta C_r[s] = \Delta_2 \end{cases}$$
$$\iff \begin{cases} \lambda_h \Delta C_\ell[h] \oplus \lambda_s \Delta C_\ell[s] = \Delta_1 \\ \mathtt{msb}_t(\Delta C_\ell[h]) \oplus \Delta X_r[h] \oplus \mathtt{msb}_t(\Delta C_\ell[s]) \oplus \Delta X_r[s] = \Delta_2 \end{cases}$$
$$\iff \begin{cases} \lambda_h \Delta C_\ell[h] \oplus \lambda_s \Delta C_\ell[s] = \Delta_1 \\ \mathtt{msb}_t(\Delta C_\ell[h] \oplus \Delta C_\ell[s]) = \Delta_2 \oplus \Delta X_r[h] \oplus \Delta X_r[s]. \end{cases}$$

Hence, it follows that

$$\Pr\begin{bmatrix}\Delta U = 0^n \\ \Delta V = 0^t\end{bmatrix} \leq \max_{\substack{\delta_1\in\{0,1\}^n \\ \delta_2\in\{0,1\}^t}} \Pr\begin{bmatrix}\lambda_h \Delta C_\ell[h] \oplus \lambda_s \Delta C_\ell[s] = \delta_1 \\ \mathtt{msb}_t(\Delta C_\ell[h] \oplus \Delta C_\ell[s]) = \delta_2\end{bmatrix}$$
$$\leq \max_{\substack{\delta_1\in\{0,1\}^n \\ \delta_2\in\{0,1\}^t}} \sum_{\substack{\delta_3\in\{0,1\}^n \\ \mathtt{msb}_t(\delta_3)=\delta_2}} \Pr\begin{bmatrix}\lambda_h \Delta C_\ell[h] \oplus \lambda_s \Delta C_\ell[s] = \delta_1 \\ \Delta C_\ell[h] \oplus \Delta C_\ell[s] = \delta_3\end{bmatrix}.$$

Observe that since $h \neq s$, $\lambda_h \oplus \lambda_s \neq 0$ and the linear system inside the last probability above has a unique solution for any pair (δ_1, δ_3), namely

$$\Delta C_\ell[h] = (\lambda_s\delta_3 \oplus \delta_1)/(\lambda_h \oplus \lambda_s)$$
$$\Delta C_\ell[s] = \delta_3 \oplus (\lambda_s\delta_3 \oplus \delta_1)/(\lambda_h \oplus \lambda_s).$$

Moreover, the random variables $\Delta C_\ell[h]$ and $\Delta C_\ell[s]$ are independent (as they involve distinct tweaks) and their probability distributions are uniform over either $\{0,1\}^n$ or $\{0,1\}^n \setminus \{0^n\}$, implying that their point probabilities are at most $1/(2^n - 1)$. Hence,

$$\Pr\begin{bmatrix}\Delta U = 0^n \\ \Delta V = 0^t\end{bmatrix} \leq \max_{\substack{\delta_1\in\{0,1\}^n \\ \delta_2\in\{0,1\}^t}} \sum_{\substack{\delta_3\in\{0,1\}^n \\ \mathtt{msb}_t(\delta_3)=\delta_2}} \frac{1}{(2^n-1)^2}$$
$$\leq \frac{2^{n-t}}{(2^n-1)^2} \leq \frac{4\cdot 2^{n-t}}{2^{2n}} \leq \frac{4}{2^{n+t}}.$$

Case 3: $m' = m + 1$. Then, isolating the terms corresponding to block indices m and $m + 1$, we have

$$\Delta U = \bigoplus_{1\leq i\leq m} 2^{m-i+1} C_\ell[i] \oplus \bigoplus_{1\leq i\leq m+1} 2^{m+1-i+1} C'_\ell[i]$$
$$= 2(C_\ell[m] + 2C'_\ell[m] + C'_\ell[m+1] \oplus \Delta_1)$$

and

$$\Delta V = \bigoplus_{1\leq \leq m} C_r[i] \oplus \bigoplus_{1\leq i\leq m+1} C'_r[i]$$
$$= \mathtt{msb}_t(C_\ell[m] + C'_\ell[m] + C'_\ell[m+1]) \oplus \Delta_2,$$

where Δ_1 and Δ_2 are independent (as random variables) from $C_\ell[m]$, $C'_\ell[m]$, and $C'_\ell[m+1]$. Hence, exactly as for Case 2, the probability that $\Delta U = 0^n$ and $\Delta V = 0^t$ is at most

$$\max_{\substack{\delta_1\in\{0,1\}^n \\ \delta_2\in\{0,1\}^t}} \sum_{\substack{\delta_3\in\{0,1\}^n \\ \mathtt{msb}_t(\delta_3)=\delta_2}} \Pr\begin{bmatrix}C_\ell[m] + 2C'_\ell[m] + C'_\ell[m+1] = \delta_1 \\ C_\ell[m] + C'_\ell[m] + C'_\ell[m+1] = \delta_3\end{bmatrix}.$$

Letting $Y = C_\ell[m] + C'_\ell[m+1]$ and $Z = C'_\ell[m]$, the linear system in the probability above becomes

$$\begin{cases} Y + 2Z = \delta_1 \\ Y + Z = \delta_3, \end{cases}$$

which has a unique solution over $\mathrm{GF}(2^n)$ for any pair (δ_1, δ_3). Note that Y and Z are uniformly random and independent (since Y involves domain separation integer $m+1$ but Z does not) and hence, the system is satisfied with probability $1/2^{2n}$. Therefore,

$$\Pr\begin{bmatrix} \Delta U = 0^n \\ \Delta V = 0^t \end{bmatrix} \le \max_{\substack{\delta_1 \in \{0,1\}^n \\ \delta_2 \in \{0,1\}^t}} \sum_{\substack{\delta_3 \in \{0,1\}^n \\ \mathtt{msb}_t(\delta_3) = \delta_2}} \frac{1}{2^{2n}} = \frac{1}{2^{n+t}}.$$

Case 4: $m' \ge m+2$. Then, isolating terms corresponding to block indices m' and $m'-1$, we have

$$\Delta U = 2(2C'_\ell[m'-1] \oplus C'_\ell[m'] \oplus \Delta_1),$$
$$\Delta V = \mathtt{msb}_t(C'_\ell[m'-1] \oplus C'_\ell[m']) \oplus \Delta_2,$$

where Δ_1 and Δ_2 are independent of $C'_\ell[m'-1]$ and $C'_\ell[m']$. Moreover, $C'_\ell[m'-1]$ and $C'_\ell[m']$ are independent and uniformly random. Letting $Y = C'_\ell[m']$ and $Z = C'_\ell[m'-1]$, we can apply the same analysis as for Case 3, and therefore, the collision probability is at most $1/2^{n+t}$.

In the above analysis, the collision probability is bounded by $4/2^{n+t}$ for all cases, which proves the lemma for the case $t \le n$.

We next consider the case $t > n$. We let $\overline{X}_w[i] = \mathtt{lsb}_{t-n}(X[i])$ and $\overline{X}_r[i] = \mathtt{lsb}_n(\mathtt{msb}_{2n}(X[i]))$, i.e., the $(n+1)$-th to $2n$-th bits of $X[i]$. For $V \in \{0,1\}^t$, let $\overline{V} = \mathtt{msb}_n(V)$ and $\overline{W} = \mathtt{lsb}_{t-n}(V)$, thus $V = (\overline{V} \,\|\, \overline{W})$. The corresponding variables are also defined for X'.

We first focus on the case $m = m'$. When $\overline{X}_w[i] = \overline{X}'_w[i]$ for all $1 \le i \le m$, the analysis is the same as the case $t \le n$, since for each i-th input block, $\widetilde{\mathsf{P}}_J$ takes exactly the same values (between X and X') for the last $(t-n)$-bit of $\mathcal{T}$. Thus the output collision probability (in particular, the first $2n$-bit of output (U, V)) is at most $4/2^{2n}$.

If there exists an index i such that $\overline{X}_w[i] \ne \overline{X}'_w[i]$ and $\overline{X}_w[j] = \overline{X}'_w[j]$ for all $j \ne i$, we have $\Delta\overline{W} \ne 0^{t-n}$, that is, the non-zero difference in the last $(t-n)$ bits of ΔV. Hence the collision probability is zero.

If there exist two (or more) distinct indices i, j such that $\overline{X}_w[i] \ne \overline{X}'_w[i]$ and $\overline{X}_w[j] \ne \overline{X}'_w[j]$, the analysis is almost the same as (the Case 2 of) the case $t \le n$. The collision probability of (U, V) is at most $1/2^{2n}$.

Finally, we consider the case $m < m'$. For both $m' = m+1$ and $m' \ge m+2$, we can apply the same arguments as the corresponding cases for $t \le n$ and the collision probability of (U, V) is at most $1/2^{2n}$. Summarizing, the collision probability of (U, V) is at most $4/2^{2n}$. □

We remark that because of Case 1 when $t \leq n$, $\mathbb{ZHASH}[\widetilde{\mathsf{P}}_J]$ is not almost XOR universal (i.e., the output differential probability is not guaranteed to be small).

4.3 PRF Security of Finalization

We prove that ZFIN is a fixed-input-length PRF with n-bit security. The key observation is that, given $V \in \{0,1\}^t$, ZFIN is reduced to a pair of independent instances of the sum of two independent random permutations, also called SUM2 by Lucks [Luc00]. More precisely, let SUM2 be a function that maps n-bit input to n-bit output, such that $\mathsf{SUM2}(X) \stackrel{\text{def}}{=} \mathsf{P}_1(X) \oplus \mathsf{P}_2(X)$ for $X \in \{0,1\}^n$, using two independent n-bit URPs P_1 and P_2.

On input (U, V), each n-bit output in ZFIN is equivalent to $\mathsf{SUM2}(U)$ for two independent n-bit URPs P_1 and P_2, and the sampling of the pair of these URPs is independent for each $V \in \{0,1\}^t$ and for the output blocks, thanks to the domain separation.

SUM2 has been actively studied and BBB bounds have been proved [Luc00, BI99]. Among them, Patarin [Pat08, Pat13] has proved that

$$\mathtt{Adv}^{\mathtt{prf}}_{\mathsf{SUM2}}(\mathcal{A}) \leq O\left(\frac{q}{2^n}\right),$$

for any adversary $\mathcal{A}$ using q queries. However, the constant is not known in the literature. Here, following [PS16], we propose a well-accepted conjecture that SUM2 is an n-bit secure PRF with a small constant.

Conjecture 1. For any adversary with q queries, $\mathtt{Adv}^{\mathtt{prf}}_{\mathsf{SUM2}}(\mathcal{A}) \leq Cq/2^n$ holds for some small constant $C > 0$.

For $i \in \{0, 4\}$, we let $\mathsf{ZFIN}_i[\widetilde{E}_K](U, V) = \mathsf{ZFIN}[\widetilde{E}_K](i, U, V)$. Based on Conjecture 1, the following lemma gives the PRF security of ZFIN_i in the information-theoretic setting, i.e., when $\widetilde{E}_K$ is replaced by a TURP $\widetilde{\mathsf{P}}_I : \mathcal{T}_I \times \{0,1\}^n \to \{0,1\}^n$.

Lemma 5. *Let $\mathcal{A}$ be an adversary against the PRF-security of $\mathsf{ZFIN}_i[\widetilde{\mathsf{P}}_I]$ making at most q queries. Then, for $i \in \{0, 4\}$, we have*

$$\mathtt{Adv}^{\mathtt{prf}}_{\mathsf{ZFIN}_i[\widetilde{\mathsf{P}}_I]}(\mathcal{A}) \leq \sum_{T \in \{0,1\}^t} \frac{2Cq_T}{2^n} \leq \frac{2Cq}{2^n},$$

where q_T denotes the number of queries with $V = T$.

The proof is obtained by the standard hybrid argument and an observation that adaptive choice of q_T's does not help. Lemma 5 shows that ZFIN is a parallelizable and n-bit secure PRF with $(n+t)$-bit inputs using a TBC with n-bit blocks and t-bit tweaks.

Alternative Constructions. We could build the finalization function from [CDMS10, Min09]. Coron *et al.* [CDMS10] proposed a $2n$-bit SPRP construction using 3 TBC calls of n-bit block and tweak, and Minematsu [Min09] proposed a $2n$-bit SPRP construction using 2 TBC calls with two $GF(2^n)$ multiplications. Both constructions achieve n-bit security with small constants. As they are also n-bit secure $2n$-bit PRFs (via standard PRP-PRF switching), we could use them. However, they are totally serial, hence if input to MAC is short (say 64 bytes) and we have a parallel TBC computation unit, this choice of finalization will be quite slower than ZFIN.

We could also use CENC by Iwata [Iwa06]. In a recent work by Iwata *et al.* [IMV16], it is shown that $\mathsf{P}(X \,\|\, 0) \oplus \mathsf{P}(X \,\|\, 1)$ for $X \in \{0,1\}^{n-1}$, called XORP[1], achieves n-bit PRF-security with constant 1, by making explicit that this was in fact already proved by Patarin [Pat10]. However, we think the finalization based on this construction would be slightly more complex than ours.

4.4 PRF Security of ZMAC

We are now ready to state and prove the security result for ZMAC.

Theorem 1. *Let $\mathcal{A}$ be an adversary against* $\mathsf{ZMAC}[\widetilde{E}]$ *making at most q queries of total length (in number of $(n+t)$-bit blocks) at most σ and running in time at most* $\mathtt{time}$. *Then there exists an adversary $\mathcal{B}$ against $\widetilde{E}$ making at most $\sigma + 4q + 2$ queries and running in time at most $\mathtt{time} + O(\sigma)$ such that*

$$\mathtt{Adv}^{\mathtt{prf}}_{\mathsf{ZMAC}[\widetilde{E}]}(\mathcal{A}) \leq \mathtt{Adv}^{\mathtt{tprp}}_{\widetilde{E}}(\mathcal{B}) + \frac{2.5\sigma^2}{2^{n+\min\{n,t\}}} + \frac{4Cq}{2^n},$$

where the constant $C > 0$ is as specified in Conjecture 1.

Proof. Since ZMAC calls the underlying TBC $\widetilde{E}$ with a single key K, we can replace $\widetilde{E}_K$ by a TURP $\widetilde{\mathsf{P}}_I : \mathcal{T}_I \times \{0,1\}^n \to \{0,1\}^n$ and focus on the information-theoretic security of $\mathsf{ZMAC}[\widetilde{\mathsf{P}}_I]$. Derivation of the computational counterpart is standard.

Let $G : \mathcal{K}_G \times (\{0,1\}^{n+t})^+ \to \{0,1\}^{n+t}$ and $F : \mathcal{K}_F \times \{0,1\}^{n+t} \to \{0,1\}^{2n}$. Let $\mathsf{CW3}[G_{K_1}, F_{K_2}, F_{K_3}]$ be the three-key Carter-Wegman construction with independent keys (K_1, K_2, K_3) as defined by Black and Rogaway [BR05], i.e.,

$$\mathsf{CW3}[G_{K_1}, F_{K_2}, F_{K_3}](M) = \begin{cases} F_{K_2}(G_{K_1}(\mathtt{ozp}(M))) & \text{if } M \in (\{0,1\}^{n+t})^+, \\ F_{K_3}(G_{K_1}(\mathtt{ozp}(M))) & \text{otherwise.} \end{cases}$$

It is easy to see that $\mathsf{ZMAC}[\widetilde{\mathsf{P}}_I]$ is a instantiation of CW3. Indeed,

$$\mathsf{ZMAC}[\widetilde{\mathsf{P}}_I] = \mathsf{CW3}\big[\mathsf{ZHASH}[\widetilde{\mathsf{P}}_I], \mathsf{ZFIN}_0[\widetilde{\mathsf{P}}_I], \mathsf{ZFIN}_4[\widetilde{\mathsf{P}}_I]\big],$$

and independence between the three components follows from domain separation of tweaks which implies that for distinct integers $i, j \in \mathcal{I}$, $\widetilde{\mathsf{P}}^i_I$ and $\widetilde{\mathsf{P}}^j_I$ are independent TURPs with tweak space $\mathcal{T} = \{0,1\}^t$. Besides, as already observed in Sect. 4.2, since the masking keys $L_\ell = \widetilde{\mathsf{P}}_I^9(0^t, 0^n)$ and $L_r = \widetilde{\mathsf{P}}_I^9(0^{t-1}1, 0^n)$ are uniformly random, one has

$$\mathsf{ZHASH}[\widetilde{\mathsf{P}}_I] = \mathbb{ZHASH}[\mathsf{XT}[\widetilde{\mathsf{P}}_I^8, H]],$$

with H as defined by Eq. (5). Hence, by replacing $\mathsf{XT}[\widetilde{\mathsf{P}}_I^8, H]$ by a TURP $\widetilde{\mathsf{P}}_J : \mathcal{T}_J \times \{0,1\}^n \to \{0,1\}^n$ and ZFIN_0, resp. ZFIN_4 by independent random functions R_0, resp. R_1 from $\{0,1\}^{n+t}$ to $\{0,1\}^n$, we have that there exists an adversary $\mathcal{B}'$ against $\mathsf{XT}[\widetilde{\mathsf{P}}_I^8, H]$ making at most σ queries and an adversary $\mathcal{B}''$ against $\mathsf{ZFIN}_{0/4}[\widetilde{\mathsf{P}}_I]$ making at most q queries such that

$$\begin{aligned}
\mathsf{Adv}^{\mathrm{prf}}_{\mathsf{ZMAC}[\widetilde{\mathsf{P}}_I]}(\mathcal{A}) &= \mathsf{Adv}^{\mathrm{prf}}_{\mathsf{CW3}[\mathbb{ZHASH}[\mathsf{XT}[\widetilde{\mathsf{P}}_I^8,H]],\mathsf{ZFIN}_0[\widetilde{\mathsf{P}}_I],\mathsf{ZFIN}_4[\widetilde{\mathsf{P}}_I]]}(\mathcal{A}) \\
&\le \mathsf{Adv}^{\mathrm{prf}}_{\mathsf{CW3}[\mathbb{ZHASH}[\widetilde{\mathsf{P}}_J],\mathsf{R}_0,\mathsf{R}_1]}(\mathcal{A}) + \mathsf{Adv}^{\mathrm{tprp}}_{\mathsf{XT}[\widetilde{\mathsf{P}}_I^8,H]}(\mathcal{B}') \\
&\quad + \mathsf{Adv}^{\mathrm{prf}}_{\mathsf{ZFIN}_0[\widetilde{\mathsf{P}}_I]}(\mathcal{B}'') + \mathsf{Adv}^{\mathrm{prf}}_{\mathsf{ZFIN}_4[\widetilde{\mathsf{P}}_I]}(\mathcal{B}'') \\
&\le \mathsf{Adv}^{\mathrm{prf}}_{\mathsf{CW3}[\mathbb{ZHASH}[\widetilde{\mathsf{P}}_J],\mathsf{R}_0,\mathsf{R}_1]}(\mathcal{A}) + \frac{\sigma^2}{2^{n+\min\{n,t\}+1}} + \frac{4Cq}{2^n}, \qquad (6)
\end{aligned}$$

where the last inequality follows from Lemmas 3 and 5.

From Lemma 2 of [BR05] and Lemma 4, we have

$$\begin{aligned}
\mathsf{Adv}^{\mathrm{prf}}_{\mathsf{CW3}[\mathbb{ZHASH}[\widetilde{\mathsf{P}}_J],\mathsf{R}_0,\mathsf{R}_1]}(\mathcal{A}) &\le \max_{m_1,\dots,m_q} \sum_{i \ne j} \mathsf{Coll}_{\mathbb{ZHASH}[\widetilde{\mathsf{P}}_J]}(n+t, m_i, m_j) \\
&\le \max_{m_1,\dots,m_q} \sum_{i \ne j} \frac{4}{2^{n+\min\{n,t\}}} \\
&\le \frac{2q^2}{2^{n+\min\{n,t\}}}, \qquad (7)
\end{aligned}$$

where the maximum is taken over all $m_1, \dots, m_q$ such that $\sum_i m_i = \sigma$. Combining (6) and (7), we obtain the information-theoretic bound. □

4.5 Other Variants of ZMAC

ZMAC has a wide range of variants, depending on the required level of security. We briefly discuss some of them.

ELIMINATING THE INPUT-LENGTH EFFECT. ZMAC ensures security as long as the total number of $(n+t)$-bit blocks σ throughout queries is small compared to $2^{\min\{n,(n+t)/2\}}$. If one wants to completely remove the effect of the input length as in [Nai15,LN17] (i.e., to get security as long as the number of *queries* q is small compared to $2^{\min\{n,(n+t)/2\}}$), we suggest to use $\mathbb{ZHASH}$. The underlying TBC $\widetilde{E}$ needs to have a tweak space of the form $\{0,1\}^t \times \mathcal{J} \times \mathcal{I}$, where $\mathcal{J} = \{1, 2, \dots, B\}$ for some $B > 0$ and $\mathcal{I}$ is a set of domain separation integers. Here, the effective tweak space of $\widetilde{E}$ is $\{0,1\}^t \times \mathcal{J}$ and the effective tweak-length is $t' = t + \log_2 B$ bits.

For finalization, we can use $\mathsf{ZFIN}[\widetilde{E}]$ with an adequate domain separation. From Lemma 4, the message hashing has a constant collision probability of $4/2^{n+\min\{n,t\}}$ for both cases of $t \leq n$ and $t > n$. The security bounds (for both $t \leq n$ and $t > n$) are $O(q^2/2^{n+\min\{n,t\}})$ plus the PRF bound of $\mathsf{ZFIN}[\widetilde{E}]$, thus, security does not degrade with the total input length.

On the downside, since we waste $\log_2 B$ effective tweak bits to process the input block index, this mode processes only $n+t$ input bits per TBC call rather than the optimal amount $n+t'$. This is a trade-off between efficiency and security.

Birthday Security. If we only require up-to-birthday bound security, then we could simply use $\mathsf{XT}[\widetilde{E}]$ in the same manner to PMAC, that is, the message hashing is mostly the same as ZHASH, however we XOR all TBC outputs C_ℓ in Fig. 1 to form the final n-bit output. The finalization is done by a single TBC call with an adequate domain separation, and hashing and finalization are composed by CW3.

From Lemma 3 and the security proof for (TBC-based) PMAC1 found in [Rog04], this variant has PRF advantage $O(\sigma^2/2^{n+\min\{n,t\}} + q^2/2^n)$, which is slightly better than "standard" birthday bound $O(\sigma^2/2^n)$. Efficiency is optimal since $n+t$ input bits are processed per TBC call for any $\widetilde{E}$ having effective tweak space of t bits, for any $t > 0$.

5 Application to Authenticated Encryption: ZAE

As an application of ZMAC, we provide an efficient construction of a Deterministic Authenticated Encryption (DAE) scheme [RS06] from a TBC called ZAE.

Let us briefly recall the syntax and the security definition for a DAE scheme (see [RS06] for details). A DAE scheme DAE is a tuple $(\mathcal{K}, \mathcal{AD}, \mathcal{M}, \mathcal{C}, \mathsf{DAE.Enc}, \mathsf{DAE.Dec})$, where $\mathcal{K}$, $\mathcal{AD}$, $\mathcal{M}$, and $\mathcal{C}$ are non-empty sets and DAE.Enc and DAE.Dec are deterministic algorithms. The encryption algorithm DAE.Enc takes as input a key $K \in \mathcal{K}$, associated data $AD \in \mathcal{AD}$, and a plaintext $M \in \mathcal{M}$, and returns a ciphertext $C \in \mathcal{C}$. The decryption algorithm DAE.Dec takes as input a key $K \in \mathcal{K}$, associated data $AD \in \mathcal{AD}$, and a ciphertext $C \in \mathcal{C}$, and returns either a message $M \in \mathcal{M}$ or the special symbol $\perp$ indicating that the ciphertext is invalid. We write $\mathsf{DAE.Enc}_K(AD, M)$, resp. $\mathsf{DAE.Dec}_K(AD, C)$ for $\mathsf{DAE.Enc}(K, AD, M)$, resp. $\mathsf{DAE.Dec}(K, AD, C)$. As usual, we require that for any tuple $(K, AD, M) \in \mathcal{K} \times \mathcal{AD} \times \mathcal{M}$, one has

$$\mathsf{DAE.Dec}(K, AD, \mathsf{DAE.Enc}(K, AD, M)) = M.$$

The associated data AD is authenticated but not encrypted, and may include a nonce, which is why DAE is sometimes called nonce-misuse resistant authenticated encryption (MRAE), since for such a scheme the repetition of a nonce does not hurt authenticity and only allows the adversary to detect repetitions of inputs (AD, M) to the encryption algorithm.

Definition 4. *Let* DAE *be a DAE scheme. The advantage of an adversary* $\mathcal{A}$ *in breaking the DAE-security of* DAE *is defined as*

$$\mathsf{Adv}^{\mathsf{dae}}_{\mathsf{DAE}}(\mathcal{A}) \stackrel{\text{def}}{=} \left|\Pr[K \xleftarrow{\$} \mathcal{K} : \mathcal{A}^{\mathsf{DAE.Enc}_K, \mathsf{DAE.Dec}_K} \Rightarrow 1] - \Pr[\mathcal{A}^{\$,\perp} \Rightarrow 1]\right|,$$

where oracle $\$(\cdot,\cdot)$*, on input* (AD, M)*, returns a random bit string of length*[4] $|\mathsf{DAE.Enc}_K(AD, M)|$*, and oracle* $\perp(\cdot,\cdot)$ *always returns* $\perp$*. The adversary* $\mathcal{A}$ *is not allowed to repeat an encryption query or to submit a decryption query* (AD, C) *if a previous encryption query* (AD, M) *returned* C*.*

In addition to ZMAC, our construction will rely on a (random) IV-based encryption (ivE) scheme IVE. Such a scheme consists of a tuple $(\mathcal{K}, \mathcal{IV}, \mathcal{M}, \mathcal{C}, \mathsf{IVE.Enc}, \mathsf{IVE.Dec})$, where $\mathcal{K}$, $\mathcal{IV}$, $\mathcal{M}$, and $\mathcal{C}$ are non-empty sets and IVE.Enc and IVE.Dec are deterministic algorithms. The encryption algorithm IVE.Enc takes as input a key $K \in \mathcal{K}$, an initialization value $IV \in \mathcal{IV}$, and a plaintext $M \in \mathcal{M}$, and returns a ciphertext $C \in \mathcal{C}$. The decryption algorithm IVE.Dec takes as input a key $K \in \mathcal{K}$, an IV $IV \in \mathcal{IV}$, and a ciphertext $C \in \mathcal{C}$, and returns a message $M \in \mathcal{M}$. Given $K \in \mathcal{K}$, we let $\mathsf{IVE.Enc}^{\$}_K$ denote the randomized algorithm which takes as input $M \in \mathcal{M}$, draws $IV \xleftarrow{\$} \mathcal{IV}$, computes $C = \mathsf{IVE.Enc}(K, IV, M)$, and returns (IV, C).

Definition 5. *Let* IVE *be an IV-based encryption scheme. The advantage of an adversary* $\mathcal{A}$ *in breaking the ivE-security of* IVE *is defined as*

$$\mathsf{Adv}^{\mathsf{ive}}_{\mathsf{IVE}}(\mathcal{A}) \stackrel{\text{def}}{=} \left|\Pr[K \xleftarrow{\$} \mathcal{K} : \mathcal{A}^{\mathsf{IVE.Enc}^{\$}_K} \Rightarrow 1] - \Pr[\mathcal{A}^{\$} \Rightarrow 1]\right|,$$

where oracle $\$(\cdot)$*, on input* $M \in \mathcal{M}$*, returns a random bit string of length* $|\mathsf{IVE.Enc}^{\$}_K(M)|$*.*

For our purposes, we consider the IV-based encryption mode IVCTRT proposed in [PS16, Appendix B]. This mode uses a TBC $\widetilde{E}$ with tweak space $\mathcal{T}' = \{0,1\}^t \times \mathcal{I}$ and message space $\{0,1\}^n$, and has $2n$-bit IVs. We assume $10 \in \mathcal{I}$ as all calls to $\widetilde{E}$ in IVCTRT will use domain separation integer 10 which is distinct from all those used in ZMAC. The encryption $\mathsf{IVCTRT}[\widetilde{E}_K].\mathsf{Enc}(IV, M)$ of a message M with initialization value IV under key K is defined as follows. The IV and the message are parsed as

$$(IV[1], IV[2]) \xleftarrow{n,n} IV$$
$$(M[1], \ldots, M[m]) \xleftarrow{n} M.$$

Let $IV'[1] = IV[1] \oplus_t 0^t$, i.e., $IV[1]$ is either padded with zeros up to t bits when $t > n$ or truncated to t bits when $t \leq n$. Then, the ciphertext is $C = (C[1], \ldots, C[m])$ where $X \boxplus Y$ denotes t-bit modular addition,

$$C[i] = M[i] \oplus \widetilde{E}^{10}_K(IV'[1] \boxplus i, IV[2]) \qquad \text{for } i = 1, \ldots, m-1,$$
$$C[m] = M[m] \oplus \mathtt{msb}_{|M[m]|}(\widetilde{E}^{10}_K(IV'[1] \boxplus m, IV[2])).$$

[4] We assume that the length of $\mathsf{DAE.Enc}_K(AD, M)$ is independent from the key K.

Algorithm $\mathsf{IVCTRT}[\widetilde{E}_K].\mathsf{Enc}(IV, M)$

$(IV[1], IV[2]) \xleftarrow{n,n} IV$
$IV[1] \leftarrow IV[1] \oplus_t 0^t$
$(M[1], \ldots, M[m]) \xleftarrow{n} M$
for $i = 1$ **to** $m - 1$ **do**
  $C[i] \leftarrow M[i] \oplus \widetilde{E}_K^{10}(IV[1] \boxplus i, IV[2])$
$S \leftarrow \mathtt{msb}_{|M[m]|}(\widetilde{E}_K^{10}(IV[1] \boxplus m, IV[2]))$
$C[m] \leftarrow M[m] \oplus S$
$C \leftarrow (C[1] \| \ldots \| C[m])$
return C

Algorithm $\mathtt{encode}(AD, M)$

$\mathtt{Len} \leftarrow \mathtt{str}_{n/2}(|AD|) \| \mathtt{str}_{n/2}(|M|)$
$X \leftarrow (\mathtt{ozp}(AD) \| \mathtt{ozp}(M) \| \mathtt{Len})$
return X

Algorithm $\mathsf{ZAE}[\widetilde{E}_K].\mathsf{Enc}(AD, M)$

$X \leftarrow \mathtt{encode}(AD, M)$
$IV \leftarrow \mathsf{ZMAC}[\widetilde{E}_K](X)$
$C \leftarrow \mathsf{IVCTRT}[\widetilde{E}_K].\mathsf{Enc}(IV, M)$
return $C' = (IV, C)$

Algorithm $\mathsf{ZAE}[\widetilde{E}_K].\mathsf{Dec}(AD, C')$

$(IV, C) \xleftarrow{2n, |C'|-2n} C'$
$M \leftarrow \mathsf{IVCTRT}[\widetilde{E}_K].\mathsf{Dec}(IV, C)$
$X \leftarrow \mathtt{encode}(AD, M)$
$IV' = \mathsf{ZMAC}[\widetilde{E}_K](X)$
if $IV' = IV$ **then return** M
else return $\bot$

Fig. 6. Pseudocode for the ZAE deterministic authenticated encryption scheme. Algorithm $\mathsf{IVCTRT}[\widetilde{E}_K].\mathsf{Dec}$ is similar to $\mathsf{IVCTRT}[\widetilde{E}_K].\mathsf{Enc}$ and hence omitted.

Our TBC-based BBB-secure DAE mode proposal ZAE follows the generic[5] SIV construction [RS06], where the PRF is instantiated with ZMAC and the IV-based encryption mode is instantiated with IVCTRT.

Let $\widetilde{E}$ be a TBC with tweak space $\mathcal{T}' = \{0,1\}^t \times \mathcal{I}$ where $\mathcal{I} \supseteq \{0, 1, \ldots, 10\}$ and message space $\{0,1\}^n$. The encryption $\mathsf{ZAE}[\widetilde{E}_K].\mathsf{Enc}(AD, M)$ of a message M with associated data AD under key K is the pair $C' = (IV, C)$ where

$$IV = \mathsf{ZMAC}[\widetilde{E}_K](\mathtt{encode}(AD, M))$$
$$C = \mathsf{IVCTRT}[\widetilde{E}_K].\mathsf{Enc}(IV, M).$$

The $\mathtt{encode}$ function is an injective mapping which pads AD and M independently using the $\mathtt{ozp}()$ function, so that the bit length of the resulting strings are multiples of $(n + t)$. Then, it concatenates these two strings and appends the $n/2$-bit representations of the lengths of AD and M (an n-bit representation can naturally be used if more than $2^{n/2}$ AD and M blocks are possible). The tag (synthetic IV) is $2n$ bits, which is inevitable for n-bit security of the SIV construction, since a collision of two tags would immediately break the scheme. See Fig. 6 for the pseudocode and Fig. 7 for a graphical representation of ZAE.

The security bound for ZAE is given in the following theorem. Here, we let the length of a query (encryption or decryption) be the block length of $\mathtt{encode}(AD, M)$, where $(IV, C) \xleftarrow{2n, |C'|-2n} C'$ and $M \leftarrow \mathsf{IVCTRT}[\widetilde{E}_K].\mathsf{Dec}(IV, C)$ for a decryption query (AD, C').

[5] The name SIV is used in [RS06] to denote either a generic construction of a DAE scheme from a PRF and an IV-based encryption scheme, or the block cipher mode of operation resulting from instantiating the PRF with (a variant of) CMAC and the encryption scheme with the counter mode.

Theorem 2. *Let $\widetilde{E}$ be a TBC with tweak space $\mathcal{T}' = \{0,1\}^t \times \mathcal{I}$ and message space $\{0,1\}^n$. Let $\mathcal{A}$ be an adversary attacking $\mathsf{ZAE}[\widetilde{E}]$ making at most q (encryption or decryption) queries, such that the total length of all its queries is at most σ blocks of n bits*[6]*, and running in time at most* $\mathtt{time}$. *Then there exists an adversary $\mathcal{B}$ against $\widetilde{E}$ making at most $2\sigma + 4q + 2$ chosen-plaintext queries and running in time at most $\mathtt{time} + O(\sigma)$ such that*

$$\mathtt{Adv}^{\mathtt{dae}}_{\mathsf{ZAE}[\widetilde{E}]}(\mathcal{A}) \leq \mathtt{Adv}^{\mathtt{tprp}}_{\widetilde{E}}(\mathcal{B}) + \frac{3.5\sigma^2}{2^{n+\min\{n,t\}}} + \frac{4Cq}{2^n} + \frac{q}{2^{2n}},$$

where the constant C is from Conjecture 1.

Proof. We prove the information-theoretic security of $\mathsf{ZAE}[\widetilde{\mathsf{P}}]$ where $\widetilde{\mathsf{P}}$ is a TURP (the computational counterpart is standard). By Theorem 2 of [RS06], there exists an adversary $\mathcal{A}'$ attacking $\mathsf{ZMAC}[\widetilde{\mathsf{P}}]$ and an adversary $\mathcal{A}''$ attacking $\mathsf{IVCTRT}[\widetilde{\mathsf{P}}]$, both making at most q queries of total length σ, such that

$$\mathtt{Adv}^{\mathtt{dae}}_{\mathsf{ZAE}[\widetilde{\mathsf{P}}]}(\mathcal{A}) \leq \mathtt{Adv}^{\mathtt{prf}}_{\mathsf{ZMAC}[\widetilde{\mathsf{P}}]}(\mathcal{A}') + \mathtt{Adv}^{\mathtt{ive}}_{\mathsf{IVCTRT}[\widetilde{\mathsf{P}}]}(\mathcal{A}'') + \frac{q}{2^{2n}}. \quad (8)$$

According to [PS16, Appendix B], we have

$$\mathtt{Adv}^{\mathtt{ive}}_{\mathsf{IVCTRT}[\widetilde{\mathsf{P}}]}(\mathcal{A}'') \leq \frac{\sigma^2}{2^{n+\min\{n,t\}}}.$$

(In more details, the security bound from [PS16, Appendix B] is $\sigma^2/2^{n+t}$ assuming $IV'[1]$ is uniform in $\{0,1\}^t$, which is the case here only when $t \leq n$. When $t > n$, the security bound caps at $\sigma^2/2^{2n}$ since only the first n bits of $IV'[1]$ are random.) The result follows by combining these two equations with Theorem 1. The query complexity of $\mathcal{B}$ follows from the fact that ZAE makes at most 2 TBC calls per n-bit block of input and the complexity of ZFIN and masks. □

It is to be noted that for the encryption part IVCTRT there is no specific efficiency benefit in having access to a TBC with a larger tweak input than n bits. In contrary, for the ZMAC part, there is a direct gain in having a large tweak if this is not too costly (say much smaller than a factor of two), since this increases the amount of input bits per TBC call. In order to optimize performance, one can thus use a TBC with $t = n$ for the encryption part, but switch to a TBC with $t > n$ for the MAC part of the scheme, since building a TBC with a large tweak usually leads to (slightly) slower performances than a TBC with a small tweak [JNP14d].

Another direction to further increase performance of ZAE in practice, without reducing its security, is to use a counter addition on only $\min\{n,t\}$ bits instead of t bits, i.e. by redefining $X \boxplus Y$ for $Y \in \{1,\ldots,2^{\min\{n,t\}}\}$ to denote

$$\mathtt{msb}_{\min\{n,t\}}(X) + Y \bmod 2^{\min\{n,t\}} \,\|\, \mathtt{lsb}_{t-\min\{n,t\}}(X),$$

[6] Note that, for simplicity, the lengths are counted in n-bit blocks.

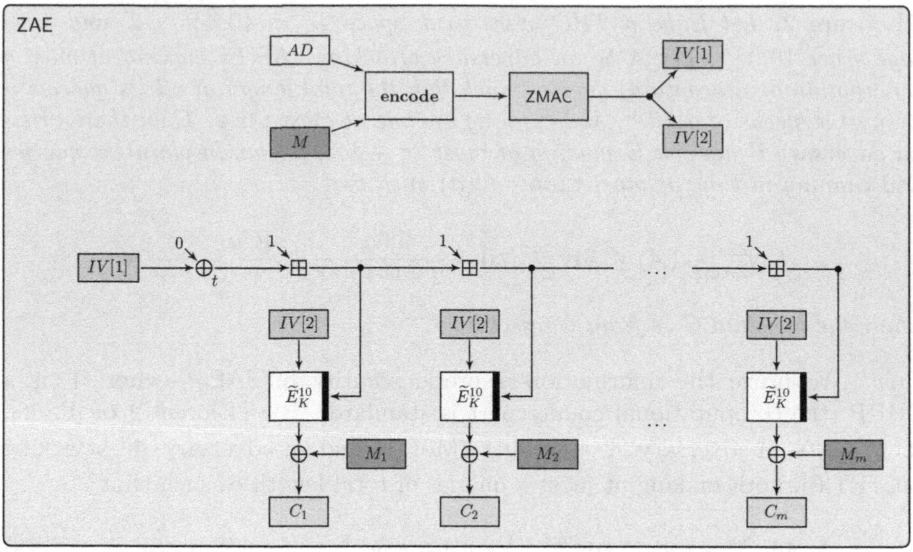

Fig. 7. The ZAE deterministic authenticated encryption scheme with associated data. Note that the n-bit value $IV[1]$ is mapped to the t-bit value $IV[1] \oplus_t 0^t$ to obtain the initial t-bit counter.

that is, addition over the first $\min\{n, t\}$ bits and the remaining bits intact. One could even consider having a LFSR-based counter instead of a modular addition based counter to improve hardware implementations. We have not used these improvements in ZAE specifications in order to simplify its description.

ZAE compares very favorably with existing TBC-based MRAE solutions both in terms of efficiency and security. Indeed, it can process $n + t$ message bits per TBC call for the MAC part, and n bits per TBC call for the encryption part. Other schemes such as SIV [RS06], SCT [PS16], or SIVx [LN17] can only handle n message bits per TBC call in the MAC part. Moreover, ZAE is secure beyond the birthday bound and hence provides better security than SIV (only birthday security) or SCT (only birthday security in the nonce-misuse setting) while leading to better performances.

We remark that ZMAC could also be used to improve OCB-like (more precisely its TBC-based generalization ΘCB [KR11]) or SCT-like designs: by changing the PMAC-like part that handles the associated data for ZMAC, one would fully benefit from the efficiency improvement provided by our design.

6 MAC and AE Instances

In this section, we give instantiation examples of ZMAC and ZAE. There are many possible ways to build a TBC, but in practice block cipher-based constructions are generally less efficient than ad-hoc TBCs. Since our design leverages heavily the possibilities offered by a large tweak, a candidate such as Threefish [FLS+10] is not very interesting as it handles only 128 bits of tweak input for a block size of 256/512/1024 bits. The effective efficiency gain would be limited (and Threefish is much slower than AES on current platforms, due to AES-NI instruction sets).

One could also consider using block ciphers with large keys (in comparison to their block size), but as remarked in [JNP14d], it remains unclear if one can generally use the key input of a TBC as tweak input. For example, using AES-256 while allocating half of its key input as tweak is a very bad idea, considering the related-key attacks against AES-256, such as [BKN09].

Recently, Jean *et al.* [JNP14d] proposed a framework called TWEAKEY and a generic construction STK for building ad-hoc tweakable Substitution-Permutation Network (SPN) ciphers. The authors proposed three TBCs based on the STK framework, Deoxys-BC [JNP14a], Joltik-BC [JNP14b], and KIASU-BC [JNP14c], as part of three candidates for CAESAR authenticated encryption competition [CAE]. In particular, Deoxys-BC is the TBC used in the Deoxys CAESAR candidate (together with the SCT authenticated encryption mode), selected for the third round of the competition. Later, SKINNY [BJK+16], a lightweight family of TBCs based on similar ideas was proposed.

We will study here the performances of ZMAC and ZAE when instantiated with Deoxys-BC and the 128-bit block versions of SKINNY. Note that for a key size of 128 bits, both these ciphers offer versions with 128 or 256 bits of tweak input (respectively Deoxys-BC-256/SKINNY-128-256 and Deoxys-BC-384/SKINNY-128-384). It is interesting to compare the respective number of rounds (and thus efficiencies) of these different versions (see Table 2).

Table 2. Number of rounds of Deoxys-BC-256/Deoxys-BC-384, and SKINNY-128-128/SKINNY-128-256/SKINNY-128-384.

TBC	$t=0$	$t=n$	$t=2n$
Deoxys-BC	–	14	16
SKINNY	40	48	56

This shows the strength of the ZMAC general design: for practical ad-hoc TBC constructions, it seems that adding twice more input to the TBC slows down the primitive by a much smaller factor than 2. Thus, we can expect the efficiency to improve with the tweak-length.

6.1 Handling the Domain Separation of TBC Instances

In ZMAC and ZAE, we use several independent TBC instances through domain separation integers. In detail, for ZMAC, one needs one TBC instance ($\widetilde{E}_K^9$) for the generating the masking keys L_ℓ and L_r, one instance ($\widetilde{E}_K^8$) for the hashing part, 4 instances ($\widetilde{E}_K^0$, $\widetilde{E}_K^1$, $\widetilde{E}_K^2$, $\widetilde{E}_K^3$) for the finalization function when the message is a positive multiple of $(n+t)$ bits, and 4 instances

$(\widetilde{E}_K^4, \widetilde{E}_K^5, \widetilde{E}_K^6, \widetilde{E}_K^7)$ for the finalization function when the message is not a positive multiple of $(n+t)$ bits. This sums up to 10 instances. Moreover, ZAE requires one more instance $(\widetilde{E}_K^{10})$ for the encryption part.

For all instances, encoding can be achieved by simply reserving 4 bits of the tweak input of the TBC. This has the advantage of being very simple and elegant, but it also means that in practice the message block size of ZMAC will be a little unusual (as the tweak-length is usually a multiple of the block-length).

Another solution is to separate the instances using distinct field multiplications. This allows the message block size of ZMAC to be a multiple of the TBC block size. However, the number of distinct multiplications is non-negligible and will render the implementation much more complex.

Finally, a last solution could be to XOR into the state distinct words that are dependent of the secret key (for example generated just like the masks L_ℓ and L_r, but with different plaintext inputs). The advantage is that the implementation is simple and it allows the message block size of ZMAC to be a multiple of the TBC block size. However, more precomputations will be needed.

All these solutions represent different possible tradeoffs, and we note that this issue is present for most TBC-based MAC or AE schemes.

6.2 Efficiency Comparisons

In this subsection, we report the efficiency estimates of our operating modes ZMAC and ZAE, when the TBC is instantiated with Deoxys-BC and SKINNY, while comparing with existing MAC and AE schemes.

We do not perform a comprehensive comparison with schemes combining a (T)BC and a $2n$-bit algebraic UHFs, such as a 256-bit variant of GMAC [MV04]. In principle such schemes can achieve n-bit security. However, the additional implementation of an algebraic UHF would require more resources (memory for software and gates for hardware) than pure (T)BC modes, which is not desirable for the performance across multiple devices. Moreover, the existence of weak-key class for the popular polynomial hash functions, such as [HP08, PC15], can be an issue.

We will consider two scenarios: (1) long messages and (2) long messages with equally long associated data (AD). For these two scenarios, the cost of the precomputations or finalizations can be considered negligible (for benchmarking, we used 65536 bytes for long messages or AD). Moreover, we note that in ZMAC, the two calls for precomputation can be done in parallel, while the calls in the finalization function ZFIN can also all be done in parallel. For modern processors, where parallel encryptions (for bitslice implementations) or pipelined encryptions (for implementations using the AES-NI instructions set) are by far the most efficient strategy, having a finalization composed of four parallel encryption calls (like in ZMAC) or a single one (like in SCT) will not make a big difference in terms of efficiency.

On an Intel Skylake processor Intel Core i5-6600, we measure that for long messages AES-128 runs at 0.65 c/B (cycles/Byte), while Deoxys-BC-256 runs at

Table 3. Estimated efficiencies (in c/B) of various MAC and AE primitives (for (1) long messages and (2) long message with equally long AD) on a Intel Skylake processor. For (2), the input bytes are the sum of message and AD bytes. NR denotes the nonce-respecting scenario. GCM-SIV is proposed by [GL15]. (*) Performances are reported for SIV instantiated with a fully parallelizable PRF (e.g., PMAC), while the specifications from [RS06] use a PRF based on CMAC which has a limited parallelizability.

Mode	Cipher	Long M	Long M Long AD	Security
Message Authentication Code				
CMAC	AES-128	2.68	–	64
PMAC	AES-128	0.65	–	64
PMAC1	Deoxys-BC-256	0.87	–	64
PMAC_TBC1k	Deoxys-BC-256	0.87	–	128
ZMAC	Deoxys-BC-256	0.61	–	128
ZMAC	Deoxys-BC-384	0.52	–	128
ZMAC	SKINNY-128-256	2.06	–	128
ZMAC	SKINNY-128-384	1.60	–	128
(Deterministic) Authenticated Encryption				
OCB	AES-128	0.65	0.65	64 (NR)
GCM	AES-128	0.65	0.65	64 (NR)
ΘCB	Deoxys-BC-256	0.87	0.87	128 (NR)
SIV	AES-128	1.30*	0.97*	64
GCM-SIV	AES-128	0.95	0.80	64
SCT	Deoxys-BC-256	1.74	1.30	64 (128 for NR)
SIVx	Deoxys-BC-256	1.74	1.30	128
ZAE	Deoxys-BC-256	1.48	1.04	128
ZAE	Deoxys-BC-384	1.58	1.09	128
ZAE	Deoxys-BC-256/Deoxys-BC-384	1.46	1.03	128
ZAE	SKINNY-128-256	6.18	4.12	128
ZAE	SKINNY-128-256	6.38	3.98	128
ZAE	SKINNY-128-256/SKINNY-128-384	5.70	3.64	128

0.87 c/B, Deoxys-BC-384 runs at 0.99 c/B, SKINNY-128-256 at 4.12 c/B and SKINNY-128-384 at 4.8 c/B. However, these numbers assume that the tweak input of the ciphers is being used as a counter (as in SCT or SIVx). This can make an important difference depending on the TBC considered, especially for ciphers with a heavy key schedule. One can observe [BJK+16] that when the tweak input is considered random (in opposition to being a counter), there is not much efficiency penalty for SKINNY (probably due to the fact that the best SKINNY implementations use high-parallelism bitslice strategy). For Deoxys-BC, we have implemented a random tweak version and compared it with the case where the tweak is used as a counter. We could observe that in the case of

AES-NI implementations a penalty factor on efficiency of 1.4 must be taken in account for Deoxys-BC-256, and a factor 1.8 for Deoxys-BC-384. We emphasize that these penalties will probably not appear for other types of implementations (table or bitslice implementations).

Taking into account all these considerations, we compare ZMAC and ZAE efficiencies with its competitors[7] in Table 3. One can see that ZMAC is the fastest MAC, while providing n-bit security. Moreover, ZAE offers better performances when compared to misuse-resistant competitors, while providing optimal n-bit security, even in nonce-misuse scenario.

It is interesting to note that, as foreseen in previous section, for ZAE the maximum speed might be achieved by using a TBC version with a large tweak for the MAC part, and a TBC version with a small tweak for the encryption part (typically Deoxys-BC-384 for the MAC part and Deoxys-BC-256 for the encryption part). This is because ZMAC really benefits from using a TBC with a large tweak, while the encryption part is not faster when using a TBC with a large tweak (and a TBC with a large tweak is supposed to be slightly slower).

Acknowledgements. The authors would like to thank the anonymous reviewers of CRYPTO 2017 for their helpful comments. The first author is supported by JSPS KAKENHI, Grant-in-Aid for Scientific Research (B), Grant Number 26280045, and the work was carried out in part while visiting Nanyang Technological University, Singapore. The third author is supported by the Singapore National Research Foundation Fellowship 2012 (NRF-NRFF2012-06) and Temasek Labs (DSOCL16194). The fourth author has been partially supported by the French Agence Nationale de la Recherche through the BRUTUS project under Contract ANR-14-CE28-0015.

References

[BI99] Bellare, M., Impagliazzo, R.: A tool for obtaining tighter security analyses of pseudorandom function based constructions, with applications to PRP to PRF conversion. IACR Cryptology ePrint Archive, Report 1999/024 (1999). http://eprint.iacr.org/1999/024

[BJK+16] Beierle, C., Jean, J., Kölbl, S., Leander, G., Moradi, A., Peyrin, T., Sasaki, Y., Sasdrich, P., Sim, S.M.: The SKINNY family of block ciphers and its low-latency variant MANTIS. In: Robshaw, M., Katz, J. (eds.) CRYPTO 2016. LNCS, vol. 9815, pp. 123–153. Springer, Heidelberg (2016). doi:10.1007/978-3-662-53008-5_5

[BKN09] Biryukov, A., Khovratovich, D., Nikolić, I.: Distinguisher and related-key attack on the full AES-256. In: Halevi, S. (ed.) CRYPTO 2009. LNCS, vol. 5677, pp. 231–249. Springer, Heidelberg (2009). doi:10.1007/978-3-642-03356-8_14

[7] We can mention that algebraic UHFs such as GHASH would probably perform twice slower for a $2n$-bit output and current best implementation on latest processors show that GHASH costs about 1/2 of an AES call. Therefore, we can estimate that ZHASH instantiated with Deoxys-BC-256 or Deoxys-BC-384 would require a bit more clock cycles than a $2n$-bit version of GHASH, while processing much more data at the same time (ZHASH can handle $n + t$ bit per TBC call).

[BKR00] Bellare, M., Kilian, J., Rogaway, P.: The security of the cipher block chaining message authentication code. J. Comput. Syst. Sci. **61**(3), 362–399 (2000)

[BR02] Black, J., Rogaway, P.: A block-cipher mode of operation for parallelizable message authentication. In: Knudsen, L.R. (ed.) EUROCRYPT 2002. LNCS, vol. 2332, pp. 384–397. Springer, Heidelberg (2002). doi:10.1007/3-540-46035-7_25

[BR05] Black, J., Rogaway, P.: CBC MACs for arbitrary-length messages: the three-key constructions. J. Cryptology **18**(2), 111–131 (2005)

[CAE] CAESAR: Competition for Authenticated Encryption: Security, Applicability, and Robustness. http://competitions.cr.yp.to/caesar.html

[CDMS10] Coron, J.-S., Dodis, Y., Mandal, A., Seurin, Y.: A domain extender for the ideal cipher. In: Micciancio, D. (ed.) TCC 2010. LNCS, vol. 5978, pp. 273–289. Springer, Heidelberg (2010). doi:10.1007/978-3-642-11799-2_17

[CLP14] Cogliati, B., Lampe, R., Patarin, J.: The indistinguishability of the XOR of k permutations. In: Cid, C., Rechberger, C. (eds.) FSE 2014. LNCS, vol. 8540, pp. 285–302. Springer, Heidelberg (2015). doi:10.1007/978-3-662-46706-0_15

[FLS+10] Ferguson, N., Lucks, S., Schneier, B., Whiting, D., Bellare, M., Kohno, T., Callas, J., Walker, J.: The Skein Hash Function Family. SHA3 Submission to NIST (Round 3) (2010)

[GL15] Gueron, S., Lindell, Y.: GCM-SIV: full nonce misuse-resistant authenticated encryption at under one cycle per byte. In: Ray, I., Li, N., Kruegel, C. (eds.) ACM Conference on Computer and Communications Security - CCS 2015, pp. 109–119. ACM (2015)

[GLS+14] Grosso, V., Leurent, G., Standaert, F.-X., Varici, K., Durvaux, F., Gaspar, L., Kerckhof, S.: SCREAM and iSCREAM. Submitted to the CAESAR competition (2014)

[HP08] Handschuh, H., Preneel, B.: Key-recovery attacks on universal hash function based MAC algorithms. In: Wagner, D. (ed.) CRYPTO 2008. LNCS, vol. 5157, pp. 144–161. Springer, Heidelberg (2008). doi:10.1007/978-3-540-85174-5_9

[IK03] Iwata, T., Kurosawa, K.: OMAC: one-key CBC MAC. In: Johansson, T. (ed.) FSE 2003. LNCS, vol. 2887, pp. 129–153. Springer, Heidelberg (2003). doi:10.1007/978-3-540-39887-5_11

[IMV16] Iwata, T., Mennink, B., Vizár, D.: CENC is Optimally Secure (2016). http://eprint.iacr.org/2016/1087

[Iwa06] Iwata, T.: New blockcipher modes of operation with beyond the birthday bound security. In: Robshaw, M. (ed.) FSE 2006. LNCS, vol. 4047, pp. 310–327. Springer, Heidelberg (2006). doi:10.1007/11799313_20

[JNP14a] Jean, J., Nikolić, I., Peyrin, T.: Deoxys v1. Submitted to the CAESAR competition (2014)

[JNP14b] Jean, J., Nikolić, I., Peyrin, T.: Joltik v1. Submitted to the CAESAR competition (2014)

[JNP14c] Jean, J., Nikolić, I., Peyrin, T.: KIASU v1. Submitted to the CAESAR competition (2014)

[JNP14d] Jean, J., Nikolić, I., Peyrin, T.: Tweaks and keys for block ciphers: the TWEAKEY framework. In: Sarkar, P., Iwata, T. (eds.) ASIACRYPT 2014. LNCS, vol. 8874, pp. 274–288. Springer, Heidelberg (2014). doi:10.1007/978-3-662-45608-8_15

[KR11] Krovetz, T., Rogaway, P.: The software performance of authenticated-encryption modes. In: Joux, A. (ed.) FSE 2011. LNCS, vol. 6733, pp. 306–327. Springer, Heidelberg (2011). doi:10.1007/978-3-642-21702-9_18

[LN17] List, E., Nandi, M.: Revisiting full-PRF-secure PMAC and using it for beyond-birthday authenticated encryption. In: Handschuh, H. (ed.) CT-RSA 2017. LNCS, vol. 10159, pp. 258–274. Springer, Cham (2017). doi:10.1007/978-3-319-52153-4_15

[LRW02] Liskov, M., Rivest, R.L., Wagner, D.: Tweakable block ciphers. In: Yung, M. (ed.) CRYPTO 2002. LNCS, vol. 2442, pp. 31–46. Springer, Heidelberg (2002). doi:10.1007/3-540-45708-9_3

[Luc00] Lucks, S.: The sum of PRPs is a secure PRF. In: Preneel, B. (ed.) EUROCRYPT 2000. LNCS, vol. 1807, pp. 470–484. Springer, Heidelberg (2000). doi:10.1007/3-540-45539-6_34

[MI15] Minematsu, K., Iwata, T.: Tweak-length extension for tweakable blockciphers. In: Groth, J. (ed.) IMACC 2015. LNCS, vol. 9496, pp. 77–93. Springer, Cham (2015). doi:10.1007/978-3-319-27239-9_5

[MI17] Minematsu, K., Iwata, T.: Cryptanalysis of PMACx, PMAC2x, and SIVx. IACR Trans. Symmetric Cryptol. **2017**(2) (2017)

[Min09] Minematsu, K.: Beyond-birthday-bound security based on tweakable block cipher. In: Dunkelman, O. (ed.) FSE 2009. LNCS, vol. 5665, pp. 308–326. Springer, Heidelberg (2009). doi:10.1007/978-3-642-03317-9_19

[MV04] McGrew, D.A., Viega, J.: The security and performance of the galois/counter mode (GCM) of operation. In: Canteaut, A., Viswanathan, K. (eds.) INDOCRYPT 2004. LNCS, vol. 3348, pp. 343–355. Springer, Heidelberg (2004). doi:10.1007/978-3-540-30556-9_27

[Nai15] Naito, Y.: Full PRF-secure message authentication code based on tweakable block cipher. In: Au, M.-H., Miyaji, A. (eds.) ProvSec 2015. LNCS, vol. 9451, pp. 167–182. Springer, Cham (2015). doi:10.1007/978-3-319-26059-4_9

[Pat08] Patarin, J.: A proof of security in $O(2^n)$ for the xor of two random permutations. In: Safavi-Naini, R. (ed.) ICITS 2008. LNCS, vol. 5155, pp. 232–248. Springer, Heidelberg (2008). doi:10.1007/978-3-540-85093-9_22

[Pat10] Patarin, J.: Introduction to Mirror Theory: Analysis of Systems of Linear Equalities and Linear Non Equalities for Cryptography (2010). http://eprint.iacr.org/2010/287

[Pat13] Patarin, J.: Security in $O(2^n)$ for the Xor of Two Random Permutations: Proof with the Standard H Technique. IACR Cryptology ePrint Archive, Report 2013/368 (2013). http://eprint.iacr.org/2013/368

[PC15] Procter, G., Cid, C.: On weak keys and forgery attacks against polynomial-based MAC schemes. J. Cryptology **28**(4), 769–795 (2015)

[PS16] Peyrin, T., Seurin, Y.: Counter-in-tweak: authenticated encryption modes for tweakable block ciphers. In: Robshaw, M., Katz, J. (eds.) CRYPTO 2016. LNCS, vol. 9814, pp. 33–63. Springer, Heidelberg (2016). doi:10.1007/978-3-662-53018-4_2

[Rog04] Rogaway, P.: Efficient instantiations of tweakable blockciphers and refinements to modes OCB and PMAC. In: Lee, P.J. (ed.) ASIACRYPT 2004. LNCS, vol. 3329, pp. 16–31. Springer, Heidelberg (2004). doi:10.1007/978-3-540-30539-2_2

[RS06] Rogaway, P., Shrimpton, T.: A provable-security treatment of the key-wrap problem. In: Vaudenay, S. (ed.) EUROCRYPT 2006. LNCS, vol. 4004, pp. 373–390. Springer, Heidelberg (2006). doi:10.1007/11761679_23

[Yas10] Yasuda, K.: The sum of CBC MACs is a secure PRF. In: Pieprzyk, J. (ed.) CT-RSA 2010. LNCS, vol. 5985, pp. 366–381. Springer, Heidelberg (2010). doi:10.1007/978-3-642-11925-5_25

[Yas11] Yasuda, K.: A new variant of PMAC: beyond the birthday bound. In: Rogaway, P. (ed.) CRYPTO 2011. LNCS, vol. 6841, pp. 596–609. Springer, Heidelberg (2011). doi:10.1007/978-3-642-22792-9_34

Message Franking via Committing Authenticated Encryption

Paul Grubbs[1](✉), Jiahui Lu[2], and Thomas Ristenpart[1]

[1] Cornell Tech, New York, USA
pag225@cornell.edu
[2] Shanghai Jiao Tong University, Shanghai, China

Abstract. We initiate the study of message franking, recently introduced in Facebook's end-to-end encrypted message system. It targets verifiable reporting of abusive messages to Facebook without compromising security guarantees. We capture the goals of message franking via a new cryptographic primitive: compactly committing authenticated encryption with associated data (AEAD). This is an AEAD scheme for which a small part of the ciphertext can be used as a cryptographic commitment to the message contents. Decryption provides, in addition to the message, a value that can be used to open the commitment. Security for franking mandates more than that required of traditional notions associated with commitment. Nevertheless, and despite the fact that AEAD schemes are in general not committing (compactly or otherwise), we prove that many in-use AEAD schemes can be used for message franking by using secret keys as openings. An implication of our results is the first proofs that several in-use symmetric encryption schemes are committing in the traditional sense. We also propose and analyze schemes that retain security even after openings are revealed to an adversary. One is a generalization of the scheme implicitly underlying Facebook's message franking protocol, and another is a new construction that offers improved performance.

Keywords: Authenticated encryption · Encrypted messaging

1 Introduction

Encrypted messaging systems are now used by more than a billion people, due to the introduction of popular, industry-promoted products including WhatsApp [60], Signal [61], and Facebook Messenger [30]. These use specialized (non-interactive) key exchange protocols, in conjunction with authenticated encryption, to protect messages. Many tools are based off the Signal protocol [44], which itself was inspired by elements of the off-the-record (OTR) messaging protocol [20]. A primary design goal is end-to-end security: intermediaries including the messaging service providers, or those with access to their systems, should not be able to violate confidentiality or integrity of user messages.

J. Katz and H. Shacham (Eds.): CRYPTO 2017, Part III, LNCS 10403, pp. 66–97, 2017.
DOI: 10.1007/978-3-319-63697-9_3

Scheme	MO security	Sender binding	Rec. binding	Enc	Dec	Ver
Encode-then-Encipher (Ideal)		✓	✓	–	–	–
Encrypt-then-HMAC (one key)		✓	✓	2+1	2+1	2+1
HMAC-then-CBC		✓	✓	2+1	2+1	2+1
CtE1	✓	✓	✓	3+1	3+1	1+1
CtE2 (Facebook)	✓	✓	✓	3+2	3+2	1+1
CEP	✓	✓	✓	2+1	2+1	1+1

Fig. 1. Summary of schemes investigated in this work. The columns indicate whether the scheme meets multiple-opening (MO) security, sender binding, and receiver binding. The last three columns indicate the number of cryptographic passes over a bit string of length equal to the message plus the number of passes needed to handle the associated data, for each of the three main operations. We omit comparisons with concrete encode-then-encipher constructions, which vary in the number of passes required.

End-to-end security can be at odds with other security goals. A well known example is dealing with filtering and reporting spam in the context of encrypted email [39,56]. Similar issues arise in modern encrypted messaging systems. For example, in Facebook's system when one user sends harassing messages, phishing links, malware attachments, etc., the recipient should be able to report the malicious behavior so that Facebook can block or otherwise penalize the sender. But end-to-end confidentiality means that Facebook must rely on users sending examples of malicious messages. How can the provider know that the reported message was the one sent? Reports could, in turn, become a vector for abuse should they allow a malicious reporter to fabricate a message and convince the provider it was the one sent [39].

Facebook messenger recently introduced a seeming solution for verifiable abuse reporting that they refer to as *message franking* [31,47]. The idea is to include in the report a cryptographic proof that the reported message was the one sent, encrypted, by the particular sender. They offer a protocol (discussed below) and a sensible, but informal and vague, discussion of security goals. At present it is ultimately not clear what message franking provides, whether their approach is secure, and if there exist better constructions. Given the critical role message franking will play for most messaging services moving forward, more study is clearly needed.

We therefore initiate the formal study of message franking. We introduce the notion of compactly committing authenticated encryption with associated data (AEAD) as the cryptographic primitive of merit that serves as the basis for message franking. We provide security definitions, show how several widely used existing AEAD schemes can already serve as compactly committing AEAD, give an analysis of (a generalization of) the scheme underlying Facebook's protocol, and design a new scheme that has superior performance. A summary of schemes treated in this work, and their efficiency, is shown in Fig. 1.

Facebook's message franking protocol. Facebook's protocol works as follows, modulo a few details (see Sect. 3). A sender first generates a fresh key for HMAC [3], and applies HMAC to the message. It then encrypts the HMAC key and message using a conventional AEAD scheme with a symmetric key shared with (just) the recipient, and sends along the resulting ciphertext and the hash value to Facebook's servers. Facebook signs the hash and forwards on the whole package — signature, HMAC hash, and ciphertext — to the recipient, who decrypts and checks the validity of the HMAC output using the recovered HMAC key. Should the recipient want to report abuse, their software client sends the signature, message, HMAC hash, and HMAC key to Facebook who can now verify the signature and hash.

While descriptions of Facebook's protocol do not use the term commitment, intuitively that is the role played by HMAC. This may suggest viewing message franking as simply a construction of committing encryption [23]. But committing encryption views the entire ciphertext as the commitment and opens ciphertexts by revealing the secret key. Neither is true of the Facebook scheme.

A new primitive: compactly committing AEAD. We introduce a new cryptographic primitive that captures the properties targeted in verifiable abuse reporting. We refer to it as compactly committing AEAD. This is an AEAD scheme for which a small portion of the ciphertext can be used as a commitment to the message. Decryption reveals an opening for the message, and the scheme comes equipped with an additional verification algorithm that can check the commitment. This formalization has some similarity to one for non-AEAD symmetric encryption due to Gertner and Herzberg [36], but differs in important ways and, in short, their treatment does not suffice for message franking (see Sect. 9 for more detailed comparisons).

Formalizing security for committing AEAD schemes requires care. Informally we want confidentiality, ciphertext integrity, and that the ciphertexts are binding commitments to their underlying plaintexts. While seemingly a straightforward adaptation of real-or-random style confidentiality and ciphertext integrity notions would suffice [52,54,55], this turns out to provide only a weaker form of security in which reporting abuse may invalidate security of the encryption moving forward. In short, this is because the opening might reveal cryptographic key material, e.g., if the secret key is itself used as the opening. We refer to this as single-opening (SO) security. We formalize also multiple-opening (MO) security notions which, in addition to the usual challenge oracles, gives the adversary the ability to obtain regular encryptions and decryptions (which, by our syntax, reveals the opening should a ciphertext be valid) under the target key. Analogously to previous AEAD treatments [55], we formalize this both via an all-in-one security game that simultaneously establishes confidentiality and integrity, and as separate notions for confidentiality and integrity. We prove them equivalent.

Standard integrity notions like INT-CTXT do not by themselves imply that the ciphertext is a binding commitment to the underlying message. We introduce a notion called receiver binding, which is similar to the binding notions from the commitment literature, notions from the robust encryption literature [1,32,33], and the prior notion of binding for committing encryption due to Gertner and Herzberg. Importantly, we deal with the fact that only a portion of the ciphertext is committing, and other details such as associated data. Achieving receiver binding means that no computationally limited adversary can find two opening, message pairs that verify for the same committing portion of a ciphertext.

At first glance this seemed like the end of the story with regards to binding security. But in the message franking setting, schemes that are only receiver binding may spectacularly fail to ensure verifiable abuse reporting. In particular, we show how schemes that are receiver binding still allow the following attack: a sender carefully chooses a ciphertext so that an abusive message is correctly decrypted by the receiver, but verification with the resulting opening of that message fails. Such an attack is devastating and arises quickly without careful design. We give an example of a natural performance improvement for the Facebook scheme that provably enjoys confidentiality, ciphertext integrity, and receiver binding, yet subtly falls to this attack. We therefore formalize and target meeting a *sender* binding property that rules out such attacks.

Legacy schemes. With formal notions in place, we start by investigating whether existing, in-use AEAD schemes are compactly committing. For these legacy schemes the opening is taken to be the secret key and per-message randomness used, and in each case we identify a small portion of the ciphertext to take as the committing portion. In this context proving receiver binding also proves the scheme to be committing in the more traditional sense.

As mentioned, AEAD schemes are not in general binding via simple counterexamples. We therefore analyze specific constructions, focusing on three important schemes. The first, Encode-then-Encipher [12], uses a variable-input-length tweakable block cipher to build an authenticated encryption scheme by padding messages with randomness and redundancy information (zero bits). We show that, modeling the underlying tweakable cipher as ideal, one can show that taking a security-parameter number of bits of the ciphertext as the commitment is both receiver and sender binding. Verification re-encrypts the message and checks that the resulting ciphertext properly matches the commitment value.

We next investigate Encrypt-then-MAC constructions [9], which are particularly relevant here given that Signal [44], and in turn Facebook messenger, uses AES-CBC followed by HMAC for authenticated encryption of messages. In practice, one uses a key-derivation function to derive an encryption key and a MAC key. Interestingly, if one uses as opening those two separate keys, then a simple attack shows that this scheme is *not* receiver binding. If, however, one uses the input to the KDF as the opening, we can prove receiver binding assuming the KDF and MAC are collision resistant. Notably this rules out using CMAC [41], PMAC [18], and Carter-Wegman MACs [59], but Encrypt-then-HMAC suffices.

This means that in Facebook messenger the underlying encryption already suffices as a single-opening-secure committing AEAD scheme. Moreover, due to ratcheting [14,26,45] Signal never reuses a symmetric key. Thus Facebook could have avoided the dedicated HMAC commitment. Admittedly they may be uncomfortable — for reason of psychological acceptability — with an architecture that sends decryption keys to Facebook despite the fact that this represents no harm to future or past communications.

We finally investigate MAC-then-Encrypt, the mode of operation underlying TLS 1.2 and before. The binding properties of MAC-then-Encrypt were briefly investigated in a recent paper that used TLS 1.2 records as commitments [58], including a brief proof sketch of receiver binding when taking the entire ciphertext as the commitment. We expand on their proof sketch and provide a full proof for the scheme instantiated with CBC-mode and HMAC (the instantiation used in TLS), taking a small constant number of ciphertext blocks as the committing portion. Interestingly this proof, unlike that of Encrypt-then-MAC, required modeling the block cipher underlying CBC-mode as an ideal cipher and HMAC as a random oracle [28].

Commit-then-Encrypt constructions. We next turn to analyzing generic constructions that combine a commitment with an existing AE scheme. We provide a generalization of the Facebook scheme, and show that it is multiple-opening secure and both sender and receiver binding, assuming only that the underlying AEAD scheme is sound and the commitment is unique. HMAC is a unique commitment, thereby giving us the first formal security analysis of Facebook's message franking scheme. One can also use a non-malleable commitment [29]. If one instead uses a malleable commitment, then the scheme will not achieve ciphertext integrity.

We also offer an alternative composition that removes the need for non-malleable commitments, and also can improve performance in the case that associated data is relatively long. Briefly, we use a commitment to the associated data and message as the associated data for the underlying AEAD scheme. This indirectly binds the encryption ciphertext to the associated data, without paying the cost of twice processing it.

Both these constructions are multiple-opening secure, since the commitment opening is independent of the underlying AE keys. This is intuitively simple but the proof requires care — commitments play a role in achieving CTXT and so we must take care to show that unopened encryptions, despite using the same keys as opened encryptions, retain ciphertext integrity. See the body for details.

The Committing Encrypt-and-PRF (CEP) scheme. The generic constructions that meet multiple-opening security are slower than existing (single-opening secure) AEAD schemes, since they require an additional cryptographic pass over the message. This represents approximately a 1.5x slowdown both for encryption and decryption. For the expected workload in messaging applications that consists primarily of relatively short plaintexts, this may not matter, but if one wants to use committing AEAD for large plaintexts such as image and video attachments or in streaming settings (e.g., a committing version of TLS) the overhead will add up quickly.

We therefore offer a new AEAD scheme, called Committing Encrypt-and-PRF (CEP) that simultaneously enjoys multiple-opening security while also retaining the two-pass performance of standard AEAD schemes. As an additional bonus we make the scheme nonce-based [54], meaning that it is derandomized and only needs to be used with non-repeating nonces. (We formalize nonce-based committing AEAD in the body; it is largely similar as the randomized variant.)

The basic idea is to adapt an Encrypt-and-PRF style construction to be compactly committing and multiple-opening. To do so we derive one-time use PRF keys from the nonce, and compute a tag that is two-part. The commitment value for the ciphertext is the output of a keyed hash that is simultaneously a PRF when the key is private and collision resistant when it is adversarially chosen. The latter is critical since receiver binding requires, in this context, a collision-resistance property. If one stopped here, then the scheme would not be secure, since openings reveal the PRF's key, rendering it only CR, and CR is not enough to prevent future ciphertext forgeries. We therefore additionally run a one-time PRF (with key that is never opened) over this commitment value to generate a tag that is also checked during decryption. Ultimately we prove that the scheme achieves our notions of sender binding, receiver binding, and multiple-opening confidentiality and ciphertext integrity.

We strove to make the scheme simple and fast. Instantiated with a stream cipher such as AES-CTR-mode or ChaCha20, we require just a single secret key and use the stream cipher to generate not only the one-time keys for the PRFs but also a pad for encrypting the message. Because we need a collision-resistant PRF, our suggested instantiation is HMAC, though other multi-property hash functions [10] would work as well.

Future directions. Our work has focused on the symmetric encryption portion of messaging protocols, but one can also ask how the landscape changes if one holistically investigates the public-key protocols or key exchange in particular. Another important direction is to understand the potential tension between committing AEAD and security in the face of selective opening attacks (SOA) [7,8]. Our current definitions do not model SOAs. (An SOA would allow, for example, a compromise of the full cryptographic key, not just the ability to get openings.) While it may seem that committing encryption and SOA security are at odds, we actually conjecture that this is not fundamental (particularly in the random oracle model), and future work will be able to show SOA-secure compactly committing AEAD.

2 Preliminaries

We fix some alphabet Σ, e.g., $\Sigma = \{0, 1\}$. For any $x \in \Sigma^*$ let $|x|$ denote its length. We write $x \leftarrow\!\!\$\; X$ to denote uniformly sampling from a set X. We write $X \parallel Y$ to denote concatenation of two strings. For a string X of n bits, we will write $X[i, \ldots, j]$ for $i < j \leq n$ to mean the substring of X beginning at index i and ending at index j. For notational simplicity, we assume that one can unambiguously parse $Z = X \parallel Y$ into its two parts, even for strings of varying length. For strings $X, Y \in \{0, 1\}^*$ we write $X \oplus Y$ to denote taking the XOR of $X[1, \ldots, \min\{|X|, |Y|\}] \oplus Y[1, \ldots, \min\{|X|, |Y|\}]$.

We use code-based games [13] to formalize security notions. A game G is a sequence of pseudocode statements, with variables whose type will be clear from context. Variables are implicitly initialized to appropriate defaults for their type (zero for integers, empty set for sets, etc.). Each variable is a random variable in the probability distribution defined by the random coins used to execute the game. We write $\Pr[G \Rightarrow y]$ to denote the event that the game outputs a value y. Associated to this pseudocode is some fixed RAM model of computation where most operations are unit cost. We will use "big-O" notation $\mathcal{O}(\cdot)$ to hide only small constants that do not materially impact the interpretation of our results.

We will work in the random oracle model (ROM) [11] and the ideal cipher model (ICM). In the ROM, algorithms and adversaries are equipped with an oracle that associates to each input a random output of some length that will vary by, and be clear from, context. In the ICM, algorithms and adversaries are equipped with a pair of oracles. The first takes input a key, a tweak, and a message, all bit strings of some lengths k, t, and n, respectively. Each key, tweak pair selects a random permutation on $\{0,1\}^n$. The second oracle takes as input a key, a tweak, and an n-bit value, and returns the inverse of the permutation selected by the key and tweak applied to the value.

Below, we will only discuss the time complexity of a reduction if bounding it is non-trivial. Otherwise we will omit discussions of time complexity.

Symmetric encryption. A nonce-based authenticated encryption (AE) scheme $\mathsf{SE} = (\mathsf{Kg}, \mathsf{enc}, \mathsf{dec})$ consists of a triple of algorithms. Associated to it are a key space $\mathcal{K} \subseteq \Sigma^*$, nonce space $\mathcal{N} \subseteq \Sigma^*$, header space $\mathcal{H} \subseteq \Sigma^*$, message space $\mathcal{M} \subseteq \Sigma^*$, and ciphertext space $\mathcal{C} \subseteq \Sigma^*$. The randomized key generation algorithm Kg outputs a secret key $K \in \mathcal{K}$. Canonically Kg selects $K \leftarrow\!\!\$\, \mathcal{K}$ and outputs K. Encryption enc is deterministic and takes as input a four-tuple $(K, N, H, M) \in (\Sigma^*)^4$ and outputs a ciphertext C or a distinguished error symbol $\perp$. We require that $\mathsf{enc}(K, N, H, M) \neq \perp$ if $(K, N, H, M) \in \mathcal{K} \times \mathcal{N} \times \mathcal{H} \times \mathcal{M}$. Decryption dec is deterministic and takes as input a tuple $(K, N, H, C) \in (\Sigma^*)^4$ and outputs a message M or $\perp$.

An SE scheme is correct if for any $(K, N, H, M) \in \mathcal{K} \times \mathcal{N} \times \mathcal{H} \times \mathcal{M}$ it holds that $\mathsf{dec}(K, N, H, \mathsf{enc}(K, N, H, M)) = M$.

Some schemes that we will analyze predate the viewpoint of nonce-based encryption, including generic compositions that utilize CTR or CBC mode. A randomized SE scheme $\mathsf{SE} = (\mathsf{Kg}, \mathsf{enc}, \mathsf{dec})$ is the same as a nonce-based SE scheme except that we omit nonces everywhere, and have enc take an additional input, the coins, that are assumed to be drawn from some coin space $\mathcal{R} \subseteq \sigma^*$. Correctness now is met if for any $(K, H, M, R) \in \mathcal{K} \times \mathcal{H} \times \mathcal{M} \times \mathcal{R}$ it holds that $\mathsf{dec}(K, H, \mathsf{enc}(K, H, M; R)) = M$. We will focus on schemes that are public-coin, meaning the ciphertext includes R explicitly. This is true, for example, of CTR or CBC mode encryption. For notational simplicity, we will assume for such schemes that enc outputs R concatenated with the remainder of the ciphertext.

Pseudorandom functions. For a function $F : \mathcal{K} \times \{0,1\}^* \to \{0,1\}^n$ and adversary $\mathcal{A}$ we define the *pseudorandom function* (PRF) advantage of $\mathcal{A}$ to be

$$\mathbf{Adv}_F^{\mathrm{prf}}(\mathcal{A}) = \left| \Pr\left[K \leftarrow\!\!\$\, \mathcal{K} \colon \mathcal{A}^{F(K,\cdot)} = 1 \right] - \Pr\left[R \leftarrow\!\!\$\, \mathbf{Func} \colon \mathcal{A}^{R(\cdot)} = 1 \right] \right| .$$

We define **Func** to be the space of all functions that output n bits.[1] Informally, we say the function F is a PRF if $\mathbf{Adv}_F^{\mathrm{prf}}()$ is small for all efficient adversaries. Below we will sometimes refer to the left-hand experiment as the "real world" and the other as the "ideal world".

In proofs it will be convenient to use multi-user PRF security [4]. We define the MU-PRF advantage of an adversary $\mathcal{A}$ to be

$$\mathbf{Adv}_F^{\mathrm{mu\text{-}prf}}(\mathcal{A}) = \left| \Pr\left[\mathcal{A}^{\overline{F}(\cdot,\cdot)} \Rightarrow 1 \right] - \Pr\left[\mathcal{A}^{\overline{R}(\cdot,\cdot)} \Rightarrow 1 \right] \right| .$$

where $\overline{F}$ on input a key identifier $S \in \{0,1\}^*$ and a message M, checks if there is a key associated to S, and if not chooses a fresh one $K[S] \leftarrow\!\!\$ \{0,1\}^k$. It then returns $F(K[S], M)$. The oracle $\overline{R}$ on input a key identifier $S \in \{0,1\}^*$ and a message M, checks if there is a random function associated to S, and if not chooses a fresh one $R[S] \leftarrow\!\!\$$ Func. It returns $R[S](M)$. Note that MU-PRF security is implied by PRF security via a standard argument.

Collision-resistance. For a function $F : \{0,1\}^* \times \{0,1\}^* \to \{0,1\}^n$ and adversary $\mathcal{A}$, define the *collision-resistance* (CR) advantage as

$$\mathbf{Adv}_F^{\mathrm{cr}}(\mathcal{A}) = \Pr\left[((x_1,x_2),(x_1',x_2')) \leftarrow\!\!\$\ \mathcal{A} \colon \begin{array}{c} F(x_1,x_2) = F(x_1',x_2'), \\ (x_1,x_2) \neq (x_1',x_2') \end{array} \right] .$$

Informally, we say F is collision-resistant if $\mathbf{Adv}_F^{\mathrm{cr}}()$ is small for all efficient adversaries.

Commitment schemes with verification. A commitment scheme with verification $\mathsf{CS} = (\mathsf{Com}, \mathsf{VerC})$ consists of two algorithms. Associated to any commitment scheme is an opening space $\mathcal{K}_f \subseteq \Sigma^*$, a message space $\mathcal{M} \subseteq \Sigma^*$, and a commitment space $\mathcal{C} \subseteq \Sigma^*$. The algorithm Com is randomized and takes as input a $M \in \Sigma^*$ and outputs a pair $(K, C) \in \mathcal{K}_f \times \mathcal{C}$ or an error symbol $\perp$. We assume that Com returns $\perp$ with probability one if $M \notin \mathcal{M}$. The algorithm VerC is deterministic. It takes input a tuple $(K, C, M) \in \Sigma^*$ and outputs a bit. We assume that VerC returns 0 if its input $(K, C, M) \notin \mathcal{K}_f \times \mathcal{C} \times \mathcal{M}$. We assume that the commitment values C are of some fixed length (typically denoted by t).

A commitment scheme (with verification) is correct if for all $M \in \mathcal{M}$ it holds that $\Pr[\mathsf{VerC}(\mathsf{Com}(M), M) = 1] = 1$ where the probability is over the coins used by Com. We will not use the alternate definition of commitments with opening [21]. We can formalize the binding security notion of our commitment scheme as a game. Formally, the game $\mathrm{vBIND}_{\mathsf{CS},\mathcal{A}}$ first runs the adversary $\mathcal{A}$ who outputs a tuple (K_c, M, K_c', M', C). The game then runs $b \leftarrow \mathsf{VerC}(K_c, C, M)$ and $b' \leftarrow \mathsf{VerC}(K_c', C, M')$. The game outputs true if $M \neq M'$ and $b = b' = 1$ and false otherwise. To a commitment scheme CS and adversary $\mathcal{A}$ we associate the vBIND advantage

$$\mathbf{Adv}_{\mathsf{CS}}^{\mathrm{v\text{-}bind}}(\mathcal{A}) = \Pr\left[\, \mathrm{vBIND}_{\mathsf{CS},\mathcal{A}} \Rightarrow \mathsf{true} \,\right] .$$

[1] We are abusing the formalism here by sampling R from an infinite set; we do so for notational consistency and simplicity.

The probability is over the coins used by the game.

Commitment schemes should enjoy a hiding property as well. Traditionally this is formalized as a left-or-right indistinguishability notion (q.v., [6]). For our purposes we will target a stronger notion, analogous to real-or-random (ROR) security for symmetric encryption. It asks that a commitment be indistinguishable from a random bit string while the opening remaining secret. Game $\mathrm{ROR1}_{\mathsf{CS},\mathcal{A}}$ runs an adversary $\mathcal{A}$ and gives it access to an oracle **Com** to which it can query messages. The oracle computes $(K_c, C) \leftarrow_\$ \mathsf{Com}(M)$ and returns C. The adversary outputs a bit, and the game outputs true if the bit is one. Game $\mathrm{ROR0}_{\mathsf{CS},\mathcal{A}}$ is similar except that the oracle returns a string of random bits of length $|C|$ and the game outputs true if the adversary outputs zero. We define the advantage by $\mathbf{Adv}^{\text{cs-ror}}_{\mathsf{CS}}(\mathcal{A}) = |\Pr[\,\mathrm{ROR1}_{\mathsf{CS},\mathcal{A}} \Rightarrow \mathsf{true}\,] - \Pr[\,\mathrm{ROR0}_{\mathsf{CS},\mathcal{A}} \Rightarrow \mathsf{false}\,]|$.

HMAC is a good commitment. Any PRF that is also collision-resistant meets our security goals for commitments. In particular, one can build a commitment scheme $\mathsf{CS}[F] = (\mathsf{Com}, \mathsf{VerC})$ works from any function $F \colon \mathcal{K} \times \{0,1\}^* \to \{0,1\}^n$ as follows. Commitment $\mathsf{Com}(M)$ chooses a fresh value $K \leftarrow_\$ \mathcal{K}$, computes $C \leftarrow F(K, M)$ and outputs (K, C). Verification $\mathsf{VerC}(K, C, M)$ outputs one if $F(K, M) = C$ and zero otherwise. Then the following theorem captures the security of this commitment scheme, which rests on the collision resistance and PRF security of F. A proof of this theorem appears in the full version of the paper.

Theorem 1. *Let F be a function and $\mathsf{CS}[F]$ be the commitment scheme built from it as described above. Then for any efficient adversaries $\mathcal{A}$ making at most q queries in game ROR and $\mathcal{A}'$ in game* vBIND *respectively, there exists a pair of adversaries $\mathcal{B}, \mathcal{B}'$ so that*

$$\mathbf{Adv}^{\text{cs-ror}}_{\mathsf{CS}[F]}(\mathcal{A}) \leq q \cdot \mathbf{Adv}^{\text{prf}}_{F}(\mathcal{B}) \quad \textit{and} \quad \mathbf{Adv}^{\text{v-bind}}_{\mathsf{CS}[F]}(\mathcal{A}') \leq \mathbf{Adv}^{\text{cr}}_{F}(\mathcal{B}') \,.$$

The adversary $\mathcal{B}$ runs in time that of $\mathcal{A}$ and makes the same number of oracle queries as $\mathcal{A}$. Adversary $\mathcal{B}'$ runs in time that of $\mathcal{A}'$.

As the underyling function needs to be both CR and a good PRF, a suitable candidate would be HMAC [5], i.e., $F(K, M) = \mathsf{HMAC}(K, M)$. Other multi-property hash functions [10] could be used as well. The Facebook franking scheme (discussed in Sect. 3) uses a non-standard HMAC-based commitment based on $F(K, M) = \mathsf{HMAC}(K, M \parallel K)$. We will assume HMAC remains a PRF when used in this non-standard way. One can substantiate this assumption directly in the random oracle model, or using techniques from the key-dependent message literature [19,37].

3 Message Franking and End-to-End Encryption

In end-to-end encrypted messaging services there exists a tension between message privacy and reporting abusive message contents to service providers.

The latter is important to flag abusive accounts, but reports need to be verifiable, meaning that the provider can check the contents of the allegedly abusive message *and* be certain that it was the message sent. Otherwise abuse-reporting mechanisms could themselves be abused to make false accusations.

A recipient can send the allegedly abusive plaintext to the service provider, but message privacy guarantees that the provider does not know whether the alleged message was in fact the one sent.[2] A seeming solution would be for the service to log ciphertexts, and have the recipient disclose the secret key to allow the provider to decrypt the ciphertext. Not only is this impractical due to the storage requirements, but it also does *not* guarantee that the decrypted message is correct. It could be that the recipient chose a key that somehow decrypts the (legitimate) ciphertext to a fake message. Ultimately what is required for this to work is for the encryption to be committing: no computationally efficient adversary can find a secret key that decrypts the ciphertext to anything but the originally encrypted message.

Facebook's approach. Facebook recently detailed a new cryptographic mechanism [31,47] targeting verifiable abuse reporting on Facebook messenger, which uses end-to-end encryption based on Signal [61]. The basic idea is to force the sender to provide a commitment, sent in the clear, to the plaintext message. A diagram of Facebook's protocol, that they call "message franking" (as in "speaking frankly"), is shown in Fig. 2. The sender first applies HMAC with a fresh key K_f to the concatenation of the message and K_f to produce a value C_2, and then encrypts using an AEAD scheme the message and K_f to produce a ciphertext C_1 using a key K_r shared with the recipient. Then (C_1, C_2) is sent to Facebook. Facebook applies HMAC with its own secret key K_{FB} to C_2 to get a tag a, and sends to the recipient (C_1, C_2, a). The recipient decrypts C_1, recovers the message M and key K_f and checks the value $C_2 = \mathsf{HMAC}(K_f, M \parallel K_f)$. To report abuse, the recipient sends M, K_f, and a to Facebook. Facebook recomputes $\mathsf{HMAC}(K_f, M \parallel K_f)$ and checks the tag a.

It is clear that the sender is using HMAC as a cryptographic commitment to the message. (This terminology is not used in their technical specifications.) The use of HMAC by Facebook to generate the tag a is simply to forego having to store commitments, instead signing them so that they can be outsourced to recipients for storage and verified should an abuse report come in.

There are interesting security issues that could arise with Facebook's scheme, and cryptographic abuse reporting in general, that are orthogonal to the ones discussed here. In particular, binding Facebook's tag to the communicating parties seems crucial: otherwise a malicious party could create a sock-puppet (i.e. fake) account, send itself an abusive message, then accuse a victim of having sent it.

While the design looks reasonable, and the Facebook white paper provides some informal discussion about security, there has been no formal analysis to

[2] Of course, if the recipient is running a trusted client, then this assertion could be trusted. We are concerned with the case that the client is subverted.

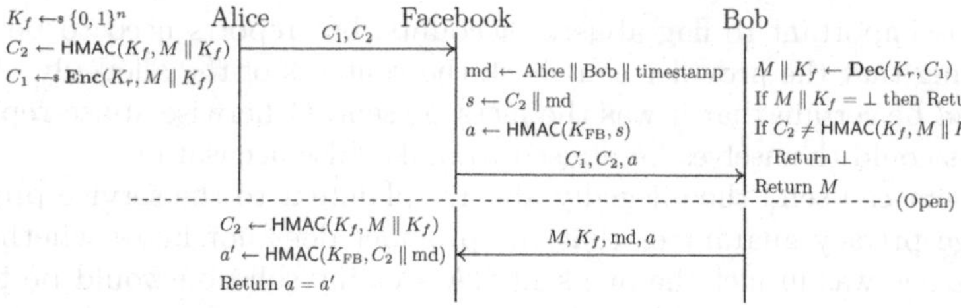

Fig. 2. Facebook's message franking protocol [47]. The key K_r is a one-time-use symmetric key derived as part of the record layer protocol. The top portion is the sending of an encrypted message to the recipient. The bottom portion is the abuse reporting protocol.

date. It is also not clear what security properties the main cryptographic construction — combining a commitment with AEAD — should satisfy. We rectify this by introducing, in the following section, the notion of committing AEAD. This will allow us not only to analyze Facebook's franking scheme, but to suggest alternative designs, including ones that are legacy-compatible with existing deployed AEAD schemes and do not, in particular, require adding an additional dedicated commitment.

4 Committing AEAD

Formally, a committing AEAD scheme $\mathsf{CE} = (\mathsf{Kg}, \mathsf{Enc}, \mathsf{Dec}, \mathsf{Ver})$ is a four-tuple of algorithms. Associated to a scheme is a key space $\mathcal{K} \subseteq \Sigma^*$, header space $\mathcal{H} \subseteq \Sigma^*$, message space $\mathcal{M} \subseteq \Sigma^*$, ciphertext space $\mathcal{C} \subseteq \Sigma^*$, opening space $\mathcal{K}_f \subseteq \Sigma^*$, and franking tag space $\mathcal{T} \subseteq \Sigma^*$.

- ***Key generation:*** The randomized key generation algorithm Kg outputs a secret key $K \in \mathcal{K}$. We write $K \leftarrow_\$ \mathsf{Kg}$ to denote executing key generation.
- ***Encryption:*** Encryption Enc is randomized. The input to encryption is a triple $(K, H, M) \in (\Sigma^*)^3$ and the output is a pair $(C_1, C_2) \in \mathcal{C} \times \mathcal{T}$ or a distinguished error symbol $\bot$. Unlike with regular symmetric encryption, the output includes two components: a ciphertext C_1 and a franking tag C_2. We also refer to C_2 as the commitment. We require that $\mathsf{Enc}(K, H, M) \neq \bot$ if $(K, H, M) \in \mathcal{K} \times \mathcal{H} \times \mathcal{M}$. We write $(C_1, C_2) \leftarrow_\$ \mathsf{Enc}(K, H, M)$ to denote executing encryption.
- ***Decryption:*** Decryption, which is deterministic, takes as input a tuple $(K, H, C_1, C_2) \in (\Sigma^*)^4$ and outputs a message, opening value pair $(M, K_f) \in \mathcal{M} \times \mathcal{K}_f$ or $\bot$. We write $(M, K_f) \leftarrow \mathsf{Dec}(K, H, C_1, C_2)$ to denote executing decryption.
- ***Verification:*** Verification, which is deterministic, takes as input a tuple $(H, M, K_f, C_2) \in (\Sigma^*)^4$ and outputs a bit. For $(H, M, K_f, C_2) \notin \mathcal{H} \times \mathcal{M} \times \mathcal{K}_f \times \mathcal{T}$, we assume that Ver outputs 0. We write $b \leftarrow \mathsf{Ver}(H, M, K_f, C_2)$ to denote executing verification.

We will often place K in the subscript of relevant algorithms. For example, $\mathsf{Enc}_K(H, M) = \mathsf{Enc}(K, H, M)$ and $\mathsf{Dec}_K(H, C_1, C_2) = \mathsf{Dec}(K, H, C_1, C_2)$.

We require that CE schemes output ciphertexts whose lengths are determined solely by the length of the header and message. Formally this means that there exists a function $\mathsf{clen} : \mathbb{N} \times \mathbb{N} \to \mathbb{N} \times \mathbb{N}$ such that for all $(K, H, M) \in \mathcal{K} \times \mathcal{H} \times \mathcal{M}$ it holds that $\Pr[(|C_1|, |C_2|) = \mathsf{clen}(|H|, |M|)] = 1$ where $(C_1, C_2) \leftarrow\!\!\$\ \mathsf{Enc}_K(H, M)$ and the probability is over the coins used by encryption.

We say a CE scheme has *decryption correctness* if for all $(K, H, M) \in \mathcal{K} \times \mathcal{H} \times \mathcal{M}$ it holds that $\Pr[\mathsf{Dec}(K, H, C_1, C_2) = M] = 1$ where the probability is taken over the coins used to compute $(C_1, C_2) \leftarrow\!\!\$\ \mathsf{Enc}(K, H, M)$.

We say that a scheme has *commitment correctness* if for all $(K, H, M) \in \mathcal{K} \times \mathcal{H} \times \mathcal{M}$ it holds that $\Pr[\mathsf{Ver}(H, M, K_f, C_2) = 1] = 1$ where the probability is taken over the random variables used in the experiment

$$(C_1, C_2) \leftarrow\!\!\$\ \mathsf{Enc}_K(H, M)\ ;\ (M, K_f) \leftarrow \mathsf{Dec}_K(H, C_1, C_2)\ ;\ \text{Return } (K_f, C_2)$$

Our formulation of CE schemes is a generalization of that for conventional (randomized) AE schemes in the following sense. One can consider an AE scheme as a CE scheme that has encryption output the entire ciphertext as C_2, decryption output an empty string for the opening value, and has verify always return one.

Compactly committing AEAD. In our formalism, a ciphertext has two components. A scheme may output $C_1 = \varepsilon$ and a C_2 value that therefore consists of the entire ciphertext. This embodies the traditional viewpoint on committing AEAD, in which the entire ciphertext is viewed as the commitment. But we are more general, and in particular our formalism allows schemes with *compact* commitments, by which we mean schemes for which $|C_2|$ is small. In particular we will want $|C_2|$ to be linear in the security-parameter, rather than linear in the message length. One can make any CE scheme compact by hashing the ciphertext with a collision-resistant (CR) hash function, as we show formally in a moment. But we will also show compact schemes that have better performance.

Single versus multiple openings. In some protocols, we may wish to use a CE scheme so that multiple different ciphertexts, encrypted under the same secret key, can be opened without endangering the privacy or integrity of other unopened ciphertexts. In other contexts, the CE scheme's opening need only be "single-use" — the secret key will not continue to be used after an opening. An example of the latter is Signal, which due to ratcheting effectively has a fresh secret key per message. As we will now discuss, whether one wants single-opening or multiple-opening CE must be reflected in the security definitions.

Confidentiality. We want our CE schemes to provide message confidentiality. We will in fact adapt the stronger real-or-random notion from the AE literature (q.v., [55]) to CE. At a high level we ask that no adversary can distinguish between legitimate CE encryptions and (pairs of) random bit strings. A complexity arises in the multi-opening case, where we want confidentiality to hold even after openings occur. We handle this by giving the attacker an additional pair of oracles, one for encryption and decryption. We must take care to avoid trivial

MO-REAL$_{\mathsf{CE},\mathcal{A}}$:
$K \leftarrow\!\$\ \mathsf{Kg}$
$b' \leftarrow\!\$\ \mathcal{A}^{\mathbf{Enc},\mathbf{Dec},\mathbf{ChalEnc}}$
Return b'

Enc(H, M)
$(C_1, C_2) \leftarrow\!\$\ \mathsf{Enc}_K(H, M)$
$\mathcal{Y}_1 \leftarrow \mathcal{Y}_1 \cup \{(H, C_1, C_2)\}$
Return (C_1, C_2)

Dec(H, C_1, C_2)
If $(H, C_1, C_2) \notin \mathcal{Y}_1$ then
  Return $\perp$
$(M, K_f) \leftarrow \mathsf{Dec}_K(H, C_1, C_2)$
Return (M, K_f)

ChalEnc(H, M)
$(C_1, C_2) \leftarrow\!\$\ \mathsf{Enc}_K(H, M)$
Return (C_1, C_2)

MO-RAND$_{\mathsf{CE},\mathcal{A}}$:
$K \leftarrow\!\$\ \mathsf{Kg}$
$b' \leftarrow\!\$\ \mathcal{A}^{\mathbf{Enc},\mathbf{Dec},\mathbf{ChalEnc}}$
Return b'

Enc(H, M)
$(C_1, C_2) \leftarrow\!\$\ \mathsf{Enc}_K(H, M)$
$\mathcal{Y}_1 \leftarrow \mathcal{Y}_1 \cup \{(H, C_1, C_2)\}$
Return (C_1, C_2)

Dec(H, C_1, C_2)
If $(H, C_1, C_2) \notin \mathcal{Y}_1$ then
  Return $\perp$
$(M, K_f) \leftarrow \mathsf{Dec}_K(H, C_1, C_2)$
Return (M, K_f)

ChalEnc(H, M)
$(\ell_1, \ell_2) \leftarrow \mathsf{clen}(|H|, |M|)$
$(C_1, C_2) \leftarrow\!\$\ \{0,1\}^{\ell_1} \times \{0,1\}^{\ell_2}$
Return (C_1, C_2)

MO-CTXT$_{\mathsf{CE},\mathcal{A}}$:
$K \leftarrow\!\$\ \mathsf{Kg}$; $\mathsf{win} \leftarrow \mathsf{false}$
$\mathcal{A}^{\mathbf{Enc},\mathbf{Dec},\mathbf{ChalDec}}$
Return win

Enc(H, M)
$(C_1, C_2) \leftarrow\!\$\ \mathsf{Enc}_K(H, M)$
$\mathcal{Y} \leftarrow \mathcal{Y} \cup \{(H, C_1, C_2)\}$
Return (C_1, C_2)

Dec(H, C_1, C_2)
Return $\mathsf{Dec}_K(H, C_1, C_2)$

ChalDec(H, C_1, C_2)
If $(H, C_1, C_2) \in \mathcal{Y}$ then
  Return $\perp$
$(M, K_f) \leftarrow \mathsf{Dec}_K(H, C_1, C_2)$
If $M \neq \perp$ then
  $\mathsf{win} \leftarrow \mathsf{true}$
Return (M, K_f)

Fig. 3. Confidentiality (left two games) and ciphertext integrity (rightmost) games for committing AEAD.

wins, of course, separating use of the real oracles from the challenge ones. We also additionally require that the adversary can only query its decryption oracle on valid ciphertexts returned from the encryption oracle. This all is formalized in the games MO-REAL$_{\mathsf{CE},\mathcal{A}}$ and MO-RAND$_{\mathsf{CE},\mathcal{A}}$ shown in Fig. 3. We measure the multiple-openings real-or-random (MO-ROR) advantage of an adversary $\mathcal{A}$ against a scheme CE by

$$\mathbf{Adv}^{\text{mo-ror}}_{\mathsf{CE}}(\mathcal{A}) = |\Pr[\,\text{MO-REAL}_{\mathsf{CE},\mathcal{A}} \Rightarrow 1\,] - \Pr[\,\text{MO-RAND}_{\mathsf{CE},\mathcal{A}} \Rightarrow 1\,]|\ .$$

The single-opening ROR (SO-ROR) games REAL$_{\mathsf{CE},\mathcal{A}}$ and RAND$_{\mathsf{CE},\mathcal{A}}$ are identical to MO-REAL$_{\mathsf{CE},\mathcal{A}}$ and MO-RAND$_{\mathsf{CE},\mathcal{A}}$ in Fig. 3 except that we omit the **Enc** and **Dec** oracles. We measure the single-openings real-or-random (ROR) advantage of an adversary $\mathcal{A}$ against a scheme CE by

$$\mathbf{Adv}^{\text{ror}}_{\mathsf{CE}}(\mathcal{A}) = |\Pr[\,\text{REAL}_{\mathsf{CE},\mathcal{A}} \Rightarrow 1\,] - \Pr[\,\text{RAND}_{\mathsf{CE},\mathcal{A}} \Rightarrow 1\,]|\ .$$

Ciphertext integrity. We also want our CE schemes to enjoy ciphertext integrity. As with confidentiality, we will lift the standard (randomized) AEAD security notions to the multiple-opening and single-opening CE settings. The game MO-CTXT$_{\mathsf{CE},\mathcal{A}}$ is shown in Fig. 3. The adversary can obtain encryptions and decryptions under the secret key, and its goal is to query a valid ciphertext to a challenge decryption oracle. That ciphertext must not have been returned by the encryption oracle. We measure the multiple-openings ciphertext integrity (MO-CTXT) advantage of an adversary $\mathcal{A}$ against a scheme CE by

$$\mathbf{Adv}^{\text{mo-ctxt}}_{\mathsf{CE}}(\mathcal{A}) = \Pr[\,\text{MO-CTXT}_{\mathsf{CE},\mathcal{A}} \Rightarrow \mathsf{true}\,]\ .$$

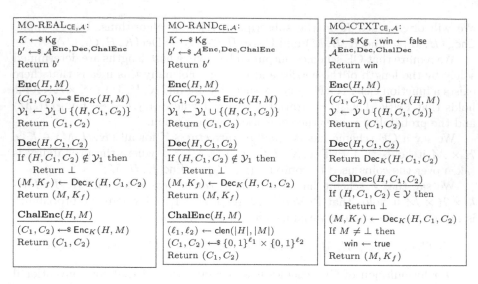

s-BIND$^{\mathcal{A}}_{\mathsf{CE}}$:	r-BIND$^{\mathcal{A}}_{\mathsf{CE}}$:

$(K, H, C_1, C_2) \leftarrow\$ \mathcal{A}$
$(M', K_f) \leftarrow \mathsf{Dec}(K, H, C_1, C_2)$
If $M' = \bot$ then Return false
$b \leftarrow \mathsf{Ver}(H, M', K_f, C_2)$
If $b = 0$ then
  Return true
Return false
	$((H, M, K_f), (H', M', K'_f), C_2) \leftarrow\$ \mathcal{A}$
	$b \leftarrow \mathsf{Ver}(H, M, K_f, C_2)$
	$b' \leftarrow \mathsf{Ver}(H', M', K'_f, C_2)$
	If $(H, M) = (H', M')$ then
	  Return false
	Return $(b = b' = 1)$

Fig. 4. Binding security games for committing AEAD. Sender binding (left game) models a setting where a malicious sender wants to send a message, but prevent commitment opening from succeeding. Receiver binding (right game) models a setting where a sender and recipient collude to open a ciphertext to different messages.

As with confidentiality, we can also specify a single-opening version of security by removing the decryption oracle **Dec** from game MO-CTXT$_{\mathsf{CE},\mathcal{A}}$. Let the resulting game be CTXT$_{\mathsf{CE},\mathcal{A}}$. We measure the single-openings ciphertext integrity (CTXT) advantage of an adversary $\mathcal{A}$ against a scheme CE by

$$\mathbf{Adv}^{\mathrm{ctxt}}_{\mathsf{CE}}(\mathcal{A}) = \Pr[\,\mathrm{CTXT}_{\mathsf{CE},\mathcal{A}} \Rightarrow \mathsf{true}\,]\,.$$

All-in-one notions. We have given separate confidentiality and ciphertext integrity notions. As with traditional AEAD security, however, we can alternatively give an all-in-one notion that simultaneously captures confidentiality and integrity goals. We defer the details to the full version of this work.

Security for AEAD. Given the fact that CE schemes encompass (randomized) AEAD schemes as well (see our comments above), we note that the RORand CTXTnotions apply to standard (randomized) AE schemes. As a slight abuse of notation, we will therefore use RORand CTXTand their associated games and advantage measures for the security of traditional AE schemes.

Binding security notions. We introduce two security notions for binding: *sender binding* and *receiver binding.* Sender binding ensures the sender of a message is bound to the message it actually sent. In abuse-reporting scenarios, this prevents the sender of an abusive message from generating a bogus commitment that does not give the receiver the ability to report the message. The pseudocode game s-BINDon the left-hand-side of Fig. 4 formalizes this requirement. To an adversary $\mathcal{A}$ and CE scheme CE we associate the "sender binding" advantage

$$\mathbf{Adv}^{\mathrm{s\text{-}bind}}_{\mathsf{CE}}(\mathcal{A}) = \Pr[\,\mathrm{s\text{-}BIND}_{\mathsf{CE},\mathcal{A}} \Rightarrow \mathsf{true}\,]\ .$$

The probability is over the coins used in the game.

A CE scheme can generically meet sender binding by running Ver during Dec and having Dec return $\bot$ if Ver returns 0. We omit the proof of this, which follows by inspection. But legacy AEAD schemes do not do this, and one needs to check sender binding. For new schemes we will see more efficient ways to achieve sender binding.

The second security notion, receiver binding, is a lifting of the more traditional binding notion from commitment schemes (see Sect. 2). This definition is important in abuse reporting, where it formalizes the intuition that a malicious receiver should not be able to accuse a non-abusive sender of having said something abusive. A malicious receiver could do this by opening one of the sender's ciphertexts to an abusive message instead of the one the sender intended.

The pseudocode game r-BIND is shown on the right in Fig. 4. It has an adversary output a pair of triples containing associated data, a message, and an opening. The adversary outputs a franking tag C_2 as well. The adversary wins if verification succeeds on both triples with C_2 and the header/message pairs differ. To a CE scheme CE and adversary $\mathcal{A}$ we associate the "receiver binding" advantage

$$\mathbf{Adv}^{\text{r-bind}}_{\mathsf{CE}}(\mathcal{A}) = \Pr\left[\,\text{r-BIND}_{\mathsf{CE},\mathcal{A}} \Rightarrow \mathsf{true}\,\right] \ .$$

The probability is over the coins used in the game.

It is important to note that r-BIND security does not imply s-BIND security. These notions are, in fact, orthogonal. Moreover, our MO-RORand MO-CTXTnotions do not generically imply either of the binding notions.

Discussion. Our definitions also allow associated data, sometimes referred to as headers. This puts committing AEAD on equal footing with modern authenticated encryption with associated data (AEAD) schemes [52], which require it. That said, modern AEAD schemes are most often formalized as nonce-based, meaning that instead of allowing internal randomness, a non-repeating value (the nonce) is an explicit input and encryption is deterministic. Existing systems relevant to abuse complaints use randomized AEAD (e.g., Signal [44]) that do not meet nonce-based AEAD security. That said, we will explore nonce-based committing AEAD in Sect. 7.

5 Are Existing AEAD Schemes Committing?

In this section we will study whether existing AEAD schemes meet our security goals for CE. We believe it is important to study legacy schemes for several reasons. If existing AEAD schemes are also committing, it will have important positive and negative implications for deployed protocols (such as OTR or Facebook's franking scheme) that implicitly rely on binding (or non-binding) properties of symmetric encryption. It is also helpful for protocol designers who may want to build a protocol on top of existing legacy encryption. If well-tested, mature implementations of AEAD can be used as CE schemes without code changes, the attack surface of new protocol implementations is minimized.

In this section we only examine the binding properties of schemes, since past work has shown they meet standard definitions for confidentiality and integrity. We will prove that encode-then-encipher and encrypt-then-MAC (EtM) satisfy our binding notions in the ideal cipher model, with the additional requirement that the MAC used in EtM is a collision-resistant PRF. We will prove MAC-then-encrypt meets our binding notions in the random oracle and ideal cipher

$\mathsf{Enc}(K, H, M)$:	$\mathsf{Dec}(K, H, C_1, C_2)$:	$\mathsf{Ver}(H, M, K_f, C_2)$:
$R \leftarrow\!\!\$ \{0,1\}^r$	$M' \parallel R' \parallel Z \leftarrow \widetilde{D}^H_K(C_1 \parallel C_2)$	$R \parallel K \leftarrow K_f$
$C \leftarrow \widetilde{E}^H_K(M \parallel R \parallel 0^s)$	If $Z \neq 0^s$ then	$\ell \leftarrow l+r+s-t$
$\ell \leftarrow l+r+s-t$	Return $\perp$	$C \leftarrow \widetilde{E}^H_K(M \parallel R \parallel 0^s)$
$C_1 \leftarrow C[1,\ldots,\ell]$	Return $(M', (R', K))$	Return $C[\ell+1,\ldots,l+r+s] = C_2$
$C_2 \leftarrow C[\ell+1,\ldots,l+r+s]$		
Return (C_1, C_2)		

Fig. 5. Encode-then-encipher as a committing AEAD scheme where the commitment is the final t bits of the ciphertext. $\widetilde{E}^H$ and $\widetilde{D}^H$ refer to encryption and decryption for a tweakable blockcipher where the header H is the tweak.

model. We will also show simple attacks that break binding for real-world modes using Carter-Wegman MACs (GCM and ChaCha20/Poly1305).

5.1 Committing Encode-then-Encipher

The Encode-then-Encipher (EtE) construction of Bellare and Rogaway shows how to achieve AE security for messages given only a variable-input-length PRP [12]. Their construction is quite simple: given a key $K \in \mathcal{K}$, encrypt a message $M \in \mathcal{M}$ ($|\mathcal{M}| = 2^l$) with header $H \in \mathcal{H}$ by first drawing a random string $R \leftarrow\!\!\$ \{0,1\}^r$ and computing $c = \widetilde{E}^H_K(M \parallel R \parallel 0^s)$ where $\widetilde{E}^H$ is a tweakable, variable-input length cipher with the header as the tweak. Decrypting a ciphertext M works by first running $M' = \widetilde{D}^H_K(C)$ and checking whether the last s bits of M' are all zero. If they are, we call the message "valid" and output M, else we output $\perp$. For compactness, we commit to only the last t bits of the ciphertext. We must include the randomness used to encrypt in the opening of the commitment. Detailed pseudocode is given in Fig. 5. We will assume that E is an ideal tweakable cipher in our proof of r-BIND security.

Theorem 2. *Let* EtE[E] *be the scheme defined above using an ideal tweakable cipher E and parameters $s, t > 0$. Let $\mathcal{A}$ be any adversary making at most q queries to its ideal cipher oracles. Then* $\mathbf{Adv}^{\text{r-bind}}_{\text{EtE}}(\mathcal{A}) \leq \frac{q+1}{2^s} + \frac{q^2}{2^t}$.

The proof will appear in the full version of this work. The scheme achieves perfect s-BIND security: the advantage of any adversary for is zero because the output of decryption is simply re-computed in Ver.

5.2 Encrypt-then-MAC

The classic Encrypt-then-MAC (EtM) construction composes a symmetric encryption scheme and a message authentication code (MAC), by first encrypting the message, then computing the MAC over the ciphertext and any associated data.

Committing EtM. We analyze EtM as a committing AEAD scheme in the case that the encryption and authentication keys are derived via a key derivation function (KDF) that is a collision-resistant pseudorandom function. The scheme $\mathsf{EtM}[\mathsf{KDF}, F, \mathsf{SE}]$ is detailed in Fig. 6. Beyond the functions F and KDF, the scheme also makes use of a public-coin randomized symmetric encryption algorithm $\mathsf{SE} = (\mathsf{Kg}, \mathsf{enc}, \mathsf{dec})$ that does not use associated data and whose key generation is a random selection of some fixed-length bit string. It is important that the scheme is public coin, as we require the randomness to be recoverable during decryption to be included in the opening.

$\mathsf{Enc}(K, H, M)$:
$K^e \leftarrow \mathsf{KDF}_K(0)$
$K^m \leftarrow \mathsf{KDF}_K(1)$
$R \leftarrow\!\!\$\ \mathcal{R}$
$R \,\|\, C \leftarrow \mathsf{enc}_{K^e}(M\ ;\ R)$
$T \leftarrow F_{K^m}(H \,\|\, R \,\|\, C)$
Return $(R \,\|\, C, T)$

$\mathsf{Dec}(K, H, C_1, C_2)$:
$R \,\|\, C \leftarrow C_1$
$K^e \leftarrow \mathsf{KDF}_K(0)$
$K^m \leftarrow \mathsf{KDF}_K(1)$
$T' \leftarrow F_{K^m}(H \,\|\, R \,\|\, C_1)$
If $T' \neq C_2$ then Return $\bot$
$M \leftarrow \mathsf{dec}_{K^e}(C_1)$
If $M = \bot$ then Return $\bot$
Return $(M, (R, K))$

$\mathsf{Ver}(H, M, (R, K), C_2)$:
$K^e \leftarrow \mathsf{KDF}_K(0)$
$K^m \leftarrow \mathsf{KDF}_K(1)$
$C \leftarrow \mathsf{enc}_{K^e}(M\ ;\ R)$
$T \leftarrow F_{K^m}(H \,\|\, R \,\|\, C)$
Return $T = C_2$

Fig. 6. Committing AEAD scheme $\mathsf{EtM}[\mathsf{KDF}, F, \mathsf{SE}]$ that composes an encryption scheme $\mathsf{SE} = (\mathsf{Kg}, \mathsf{enc}, \mathsf{dec})$ using random coins from $\mathcal{R}$, a MAC F, and that derives keys via a function KDF.

This scheme arises in practice. The Signal protocol [44], for example, uses HKDF to derive keys for use with CTR mode encryption combined with HMAC. The following theorem proves the committing EtM construction in Fig. 6 meets r-BIND if the MAC and key derivation function are both collision-resistant PRFs.

Theorem 3. *Let* $\mathsf{EtM} = \mathsf{EtM}[\mathsf{KDF}, F, \mathsf{SE}]$ *be the EtM construction using functions* F *and* KDF *as well as encryption scheme* SE. *Let* $\mathcal{A}$ *be any* r-BIND$_{\mathsf{EtM}}$ *adversary. Then there exist adversaries* $\mathcal{B}$ *and* $\mathcal{C}$, *each that run in time that of* $\mathcal{A}$, *such that* $\mathbf{Adv}^{\text{r-bind}}_{\mathsf{EtM}}(\mathcal{A}) < \mathbf{Adv}^{\text{cr}}_{F}(\mathcal{B}) + \mathbf{Adv}^{\text{cr}}_{\mathsf{KDF}}(\mathcal{C})$.

The proof of this theorem will appear in the full version of this work. The s-BIND security of $\mathsf{EtM}[\mathsf{KDF}, F, \mathsf{SE}]$ is perfect because verification re-encrypts the plaintext to check the tag.

Two-key EtM is not binding. The use of a KDF to derive the encryption and MAC keys above is requisite to achieve receiver binding security. Consider omitting the KDF steps, and instead letting keys be a pair (K^e, K^m) where each component is chosen randomly. The opening output by encryption and used by verification is instead $(R, (K^e, K^m))$. The rest of the scheme remains the same as that in Fig. 6. But it is easy to break the receiver binding for this two-key variant: simply have an adversary $\mathcal{A}$ that chooses an arbitrary header H, message M, keys (K^e, K^m), and randomness R, and computes $R \,\|\, C \leftarrow \mathsf{enc}_{K^e}(M\ ;\ R)$ and then

$\mathsf{Enc}(K, H, M)$:	$\mathsf{Dec}(K, H, C_1, C_2)$:	$\mathsf{Ver}(H, M, K_f, C_2)$:
$K^e, K^m \leftarrow K$	$K^e, K^m \leftarrow K$	$K^e, K^m \leftarrow K_f$
$IV \leftarrow\!\$\ \{0,1\}^n$	$IV \parallel C_{\ell-2} \parallel C_{\ell-1} \parallel C_\ell \leftarrow C_2$	$IV \parallel C'_{\ell-2} \parallel C'_{\ell-1} \parallel C'_\ell \leftarrow C_2$
$T \leftarrow \mathrm{RO}_{K^m}(H \parallel M)$	$C_f \leftarrow C_{\ell-2} \parallel C_{\ell-1} \parallel C_\ell$	$T \leftarrow \mathrm{RO}_{K^m}(H \parallel M)$
$C \leftarrow \mathrm{CBC}_{K^e}(\mathrm{Pad}_n(M \parallel T)\,;\, IV)$	$M \parallel T \leftarrow \mathrm{CBC}^{-1}_{K^e}(C_1 \parallel C_f\,;\, IV)$	$P \leftarrow \mathrm{Pad}_n(M \parallel T)$
$\ell \leftarrow \mathrm{Pad}_n(M \parallel T)/n$	$T' \leftarrow \mathrm{RO}_{K^m}(H \parallel M)$	$C \leftarrow \mathrm{CBC}_{K^e}(P\,;\, IV)$
$C' \parallel C_{\ell-2} \parallel C_{\ell-1} \parallel C_\ell \leftarrow C$	If $T \neq T'$ then Return $\perp$	$C' \parallel C''_{\ell-2} \parallel C''_{\ell-1} \parallel C''_\ell \leftarrow C$
Return $(C', IV \parallel C_{\ell-2} \parallel C_{\ell-1} \parallel C_\ell)$	Return $(M, (K^e, K^m))$	Return $\bigwedge_{i=\ell-2}^{\ell} (C''_i = C'_i)$

Fig. 7. Committing authenticated encryption based on MtE composition of CBC mode and a MAC modeled as a random oracle. The length ℓ is defined to be $\mathrm{Pad}_n(M \parallel T)/n$. The function Pad is the standard PKCS#7 padding used in TLS. The notation $\mathrm{CBC}_K(\cdot\,;\, IV)$ and $\mathrm{CBC}_K^{-1}(\cdot\,;\, IV)$ means CBC mode encryption and decryption with key K and initialization vector IV.

$T \leftarrow F_{K^m}(H \parallel R \parallel C)$. It then chooses another key $\widetilde{K}^e \neq K^e$, and computes $\widetilde{M} \leftarrow \mathsf{dec}_{\widetilde{K}^e}(R \parallel C)$. Finally, it outputs $(H, (R, (K^e, K^m))), (H, (R, (\widetilde{K}^e, K^m))), T)$. It is easy to check that this adversary will win the r-BIND game with probability close to one, assuming SE is such that decrypting the same ciphertext under different keys yields distinct plaintexts with overwhelming probability.

5.3 MAC-then-Encrypt

The MAC-then-encrypt mode generically composes a MAC and an encryption scheme by first computing the MAC of the header and message, then appending the MAC to the message and encrypting them both. The pseudcode in Fig. 7 uses for concreteness CBC mode encryption and we refer to this committing AEAD scheme as MtE. We will also assume the MAC is suitable to be modeled as a keyed random oracle; HMAC-SHA256 is one such [28]. CBC with HMAC in an MtE mode is a common cipher suite for modern TLS connections, which motivated these choices. Prior work has investigated the security of MtE in the sense of CTXT [42,51] and its ROR security is inherited directly from the encryption mode. Below we will assume that the block size of n bits for the cipher underlying CBC mode, and that our MACs have output length $2n$ bits.

Unlike with Encrypt-then-MAC, we are able to prove the two-key version of MtE secure in the sense of receiver binding. The binding security of MtE in the case where keys are derived via a KDF follows as a corollary, though we believe better bounds can be achieved in this case.

A sketch of an argument that MtE is binding (in the traditional sense where the entire ciphertext is the commitment) appeared in [58]. Their approach, which only relied on modeling the MAC as a RO and made no assumptions about CBC mode, led to a rather loose bound. We instead additionally model the cipher underlying CBC as ideal. This results in a simpler and tighter proof. Our proof, given in the full version of the paper, can also be readily adapted to when CTR mode is used instead of CBC.

Theorem 4. *Let* MtE *be the scheme defined above using a random oracle and an ideal cipher within CBC mode. For any* r-BIND$_{\mathsf{MtE}}$ *adversary* $\mathcal{A}$ *making at most* q_i *queries to its ideal cipher and* q_r *queries to its random oracle, it holds that* $\mathbf{Adv}^{\text{r-bind}}_{\mathsf{MtE}}(\mathcal{A}) < q_i q_r / 2^{2n}$.

The s-BIND advantage against compactly-committing MtE is zero, since the commitment along with the output of a successful call to Dec uniquely defines the inputs to Ver. Thus, no other ciphertext can be computed in Ver other than the one previously decrypted in Dec, because the inputs to Ver are fixed by Dec.

5.4 Some Non-binding AEAD Schemes

In this section we will briefly detail attacks which break the receiver binding security of some deployed AEAD schemes. In particular, typical schemes that use MACs which are not collision resistant, such as Carter-Wegman MACs, do not suffice. For completeness we spell out an example of breaking the receiver binding of GCM [46], an encrypt-then-MAC style construction that uses a Carter-Wegman MAC.

A slight simplification of the GCM MAC is the function F shown in Fig. 8 applied to a ciphertext. (We ignore associated data for simplicity.) It uses a key K for a block cipher E with block size n, as well as a nonce N. An initial point $P_0 \leftarrow E_K(0^n)$ and a pad $R \leftarrow E_K(N)$ are computed. GCM uses an ϵ-almost XOR universal (ϵ-AXU) [57] hash function computed by considering a ciphertext of m encrypted message blocks an m-degree polynomial defined over a finite field $\mathbb{F}$. The field is a particular representation of GF(2^{128}). This polynomial is evaluated at the encryption point P_0 and the result is XOR'd with the pad R. The GCM AEAD scheme encrypts the message using CTR mode encryption using E_K and a random 96-bit IV concatenated with a 32-bit counter initially set at one, and then MACs the resulting ciphertext $C = C_1, \ldots, C_m$ to generate a tag $T = F(K, IV \parallel 0^{32}, C_1, \ldots, C_m)$.

A straightforward way to consider GCM as a compactly committing AEAD is to have encryption output as the commitment portion C_2 the tag T, and the rest of the ciphertext as the first portion C_1. Decryption works as usual for GCM, but additionally outputs (IV, K) as the opening. Verification works by recomputing encryption and checking that the resulting tag matches the commitment value C_2. We denote this scheme simply by $\mathsf{GCM} = (\mathsf{Kg}, \mathsf{Enc}, \mathsf{Dec}, \mathsf{Ver})$ below.

$F(K, N, (C_1, \ldots, C_m))$:
$P_0 \leftarrow E_K(0^n)$
$R \leftarrow E_K(N)$
$S \leftarrow \sum_{i=1}^{m} C_i P_0^{m-i}$
$T \leftarrow R \oplus S$
Return T

Fig. 8. A simplified description of the CW MAC used in GCM.

We now give an r-BIND$_{\mathsf{GCM}}$ adversary $\mathcal{A}$. We ignore associated data for simplicity. To win, $\mathcal{A}$ must output $((M, (IV, K), (M', (IV', K'), T)$ so that $\mathsf{Ver}(M, (IV, K), T) = \mathsf{Ver}(M', (IV', K'), T) = 1$. We will build an $\mathcal{A}$ that chooses messages such that $|M| = |M'|$. The adversary $\mathcal{A}$ will start by choosing a ciphertext $C_1, \ldots, C_m$ such that

$$F(K, IV, C_1, \ldots, C_m) = F(K', IV', C_1, \ldots, C_m) \quad (1)$$

CtE1-Enc(K, H, M)	CtE1-Dec(K, H, C_1, C_2)	CtE2-Dec(K, H, C_1, C_2)
$(K_f, C_2) \leftarrow\!\$\ \mathsf{Com}(H \parallel M)$ $C_1 \leftarrow\!\$\ \mathsf{enc}_K(C_2, M \parallel K_f)$ Return (C_1, C_2)	$(M \parallel K_f) \leftarrow \mathsf{dec}_K(C_2, C_1)$ If $M = \bot$ then Return $\bot$ $b \leftarrow \mathsf{VerC}(K_f, C_2, H \parallel M)$ If $b = 0$ then Return $\bot$ Return (M, K_f)	$(M \parallel K_f) \leftarrow \mathsf{dec}_K(H, C_1)$ If $M = \bot$ then Return $\bot$ $b \leftarrow \mathsf{VerC}(K_f, C_2, H \parallel M)$ If $b = 0$ then Return $\bot$ Return (M, K_f)
CtE2-Enc(K, H, M)		
$(K_f, C_2) \leftarrow\!\$\ \mathsf{Com}(H \parallel M)$ $C_1 \leftarrow\!\$\ \mathsf{enc}_K(H, M \parallel K_f)$ Return (C_1, C_2)		

Fig. 9. Algorithms for two Commit-then-Encrypt variants. Facebook's scheme uses CtE2 with an HMAC-based commitment. CtE1-Ver and CtE2-Ver both just output $\mathsf{VerC}(H, M, K_f, C_2)$.

and letting M (resp. M') be the CTR-mode decryption of $C_1, \ldots, C_m$ under IV, K (resp. IV', K'). Choosing the ciphertext such that condition 1 holds is straightforward, as plugging in for the definition of F and rearranging, the adversary must solve the equation

$$\left[\sum_{i=1}^{m} C_i(P^{m-i} + (P')^{m-i})\right] + (E_K(N) + E_{K'}(N')) = 0$$

where $P \leftarrow E_K(0^n)$ and $P' \leftarrow E_{K'}(0^n)$. For example, pick arbitrary $C_1, \ldots, C_{m-1}$ and solve for the C_m that satisfies the equation.

This attack works even if associated data is used, or if the whole ciphertext is used as the commitment. A very similar attack works on ChaCha20/Poly1305 [15]; a small tweak is required to handle the fact that not every member of $\mathbb{F}_{2^{130}-5}$ is a valid ciphertext block.

6 Composing Commitment and AEAD

In the last section we saw that existing AEAD schemes already realize (compactly) committing AEAD in some cases. These schemes, however, only realize single-opening security as the opening includes the secret key. We now turn to schemes that achieve multi-opening committing AEAD, and focus specifically on schemes that generically compose AEAD with a commitment scheme.

Commit-then-Encrypt. We start with a simple general construction, what we call the Commit-then-Encrypt scheme.[3] It combines a commitment scheme $\mathsf{CS} = (\mathsf{Com}, \mathsf{VerC})$ with an AEAD scheme $\mathsf{SE} = (\mathsf{Kg}, \mathsf{enc}, \mathsf{dec})$. Formally the scheme CtE1[CS, SE] = (Kg, CtE1-Enc, CtE1-Dec, CtE1-Ver) works as shown in Fig. 9.

The CtE1 scheme produces a commitment value to the message and associated data H, and then encrypts the message along with the opening of the commitment. It uses as associated data during encryption the commitment value,

[3] This name was also used in [36], but the scheme is distinct. See Sect. 9.

but not H. This nevertheless binds the underlying AEAD ciphertext to H as well as C_2 — as we will show tampering with either will be detected and rejected during decryption. One could additionally include H in the associated data for enc, but this would be less efficient. Should a protocol want H to not be in the commitment scope, one can instead include H only as associated data within enc and omit it from the commitment.

The proofs of the next two theorems will appear in the full version.

Theorem 5 (CtE1 confidentiality). *Let* $\mathrm{CtE1} = \mathrm{CtE1}[\mathsf{CS}, \mathsf{SE}]$. *Let* $\mathcal{A}$ *be an* $\mathrm{MO\text{-}ROR}_{\mathrm{CtE1}}$ *adversary making at most* q *queries to its oracles. Then we give adversaries* $\mathcal{B}_1$, $\mathcal{B}_2$, $\mathcal{C}$ *such that*

$$\mathbf{Adv}^{\text{mo-ror}}_{\mathrm{CtE1}}(\mathcal{A}) \le \mathbf{Adv}^{\text{ror}}_{\mathsf{SE}}(\mathcal{B}_1) + \mathbf{Adv}^{\text{ror}}_{\mathsf{SE}}(\mathcal{B}_2) + \mathbf{Adv}^{\text{cs-ror}}_{\mathsf{CS}}(\mathcal{C}) .$$

The adversaries $\mathcal{B}_1$, $\mathcal{B}_2$, *and* $\mathcal{C}$ *all make the same number of queries as* $\mathcal{A}$ *and all run in time that of* $\mathcal{A}$ *plus at most* $\mathcal{O}(q)$ *overhead.*

Theorem 6 (CtE1 ciphertext integrity). *Let* $\mathrm{CtE1} = \mathrm{CtE1}[\mathsf{CS}, \mathsf{SE}]$. *Let* $\mathcal{A}$ *be an* $\mathrm{MO\text{-}CTXT}_{\mathrm{CtE1}}$ *adversary making at most* q *queries to its oracles. Then we give adversaries* $\mathcal{B}$, $\mathcal{C}$ *such that*

$$\mathbf{Adv}^{\text{mo-ctxt}}_{\mathrm{CtE1}}(\mathcal{A}) \le \mathbf{Adv}^{\text{ctxt}}_{\mathsf{SE}}(\mathcal{B}) + \mathbf{Adv}^{\text{v-bind}}_{\mathsf{CS}}(\mathcal{C}) .$$

Adversary $\mathcal{B}$ *makes the same number of queries as* $\mathcal{A}$ *and runs in time that of* $\mathcal{A}$ *plus at most* $\mathcal{O}(q)$ *overhead. Adversary* $\mathcal{C}$ *runs in time that of* $\mathcal{A}$.

The receiver binding security of CtE1 is trivially implied by the security of the underlying commitment scheme, as captured by the next theorem.

Theorem 7 (CtE1 receiver binding). *Let* $\mathrm{CtE1} = \mathrm{CtE1}[\mathsf{CS}, \mathsf{SE}]$. *Let* $\mathcal{A}$ *be an* $\mathrm{r\text{-}BIND}_{\mathrm{CtE1}}$ *adversary. Then* $\mathbf{Adv}^{\text{r-bind}}_{\mathrm{CtE1}}(\mathcal{A}) = \mathbf{Adv}^{\text{v-bind}}_{\mathsf{CS}}(\mathcal{A})$.

We conclude the section by noting CtE1 meets s-BIND security, since it runs Ver during decryption.

Facebook's scheme. The Facebook franking scheme (Sect. 3) is almost, but not quite, an instantiation of CtE1 using HMAC as the commitment scheme CS. One difference is that their franking scheme does not bind C_2 to C_1 by including C_2 in the associated data during encryption. The other difference is that the Facebook scheme builds a commitment from HMAC by first generating a random secret key, then using it to evaluate HMAC on the concatenation of the message and the key itself (see Fig. 2 for a diagram). Assuming HMAC remains a collision-resistant PRF when evaluated on its own key, we can prove Facebook's non-standard construction is a secure commitment (see Theorem 1).

To analyze Facebook's scheme, then, we introduce the scheme $\mathrm{CtE2}[\mathsf{SE}, \mathsf{CS}] = (\mathsf{Kg}, \mathrm{CtE2\text{-}Enc}, \mathrm{CtE2\text{-}Dec}, \mathrm{CtE2\text{-}Ver})$ that works as shown in Fig. 9. Note that Facebook does not discuss how to handle associated data, and so their scheme is CtE2 using CS instantiated with HMAC and requiring $H = \varepsilon$.

There are two benefits to the approach of CtE1: (1) proving ciphertext integrity does not require any special properties of the commitment scheme, and (2) it is more efficient because associated data is cryptographically processed once, rather than twice. We therefore advocate CtE1, but analyze CtE2 here since it is already in use.

CtE2 is *not* secure assuming just that CS is hiding and binding. The reason is that such commitments can be malleable and this allows easy violation of ciphertext integrity. Specifically, consider a commitment scheme $\mathsf{CSBad} = (\mathsf{ComBad}, \mathsf{VerBad})$ built using a standard commitment scheme $\mathsf{CS} = (\mathsf{Com}, \mathsf{VerC})$. Algorithm $\mathsf{ComBad}(M)$ runs $(K_c, C) \leftarrow\!\!\$\ \mathsf{Com}(M)$ and then outputs $(K_c, C \parallel 1)$. Algorithm $\mathsf{VerBad}(M, K_f, C \parallel b)$ runs $\mathsf{VerC}(M, K_f, C)$ and outputs the result. An easy reduction shows that CSBad is both hiding and binding, assuming CS is too. But it's clear that CtE2[SE, CSBad] does *not* enjoy ciphertext integrity. The adversary simply obtains one ciphertext, flips the last bit, and submits to the challenge decryption oracle to win.

This shows that standard commitments with hiding and binding properties are insufficient to instantiate CtE2. But if a scheme CS has unique commitments, then we can in fact show security of CtE2. A scheme has *unique commitments* if for any pair $(K_c, M) \in \mathcal{K}_f \times \mathcal{M}$ it holds that there is a single commitment value $C \in \mathcal{C}$ for which $\mathsf{Ver}(K_c, C, M) = 1$. All hash-based CS schemes, including the HMAC one used by Facebook's franking scheme, have unique commitments. If one wanted to use a scheme that does not have unique commitments, then one would need the commitment to satisfy a form of non-malleability [29].

The following sequence of theorems captures the security of CtE2 assuming a unique commitment scheme. Proofs appear in the full version.

Theorem 8 (**CtE2 confidentiality**). *Let* CtE2 = CtE2[CS, SE]. *Let* $\mathcal{A}$ *be an* MO-ROR$_{\text{CtE2}}$ *adversary making at most* q *oracle queries. Then we give adversaries* $\mathcal{B}_1, \mathcal{B}_2$, $\mathcal{C}$ *such that*

$$\mathbf{Adv}^{\text{mo-ror}}_{\text{CtE2}[\mathsf{CS},\mathsf{SE}]}(\mathcal{A}) \leq \mathbf{Adv}^{\text{ror}}_{\mathsf{SE}}(\mathcal{B}_1) + \mathbf{Adv}^{\text{ror}}_{\mathsf{SE}}(\mathcal{B}_2) + \mathbf{Adv}^{\text{cs-ror}}_{\mathsf{CS}}(\mathcal{C})$$

Adversaries $\mathcal{B}_1$, $\mathcal{B}_2$, *and* $\mathcal{C}$ *all run in time that of* $\mathcal{A}$ *plus at most* $\mathcal{O}(q)$ *overhead and make at most* q *queries.*

Theorem 9 (**CtE2 ciphertext integrity**). *Let* CtE2 = CtE2[CS, SE] *and assume* CS *has unique commitments. Let* $\mathcal{A}$ *be an* MO-CTXT$_{\text{CtE2}}$ *adversary making at most* q *queries. Then we give adversaries* $\mathcal{B}$, $\mathcal{C}$ *such that*

$$\mathbf{Adv}^{\text{mo-ctxt}}_{\text{CtE2}[\mathsf{CS},\mathsf{SE}]}(\mathcal{A}) \leq \mathbf{Adv}^{\text{ctxt}}_{\mathsf{SE}}(\mathcal{B}) + \mathbf{Adv}^{\text{v-bind}}_{\mathsf{CS}}(\mathcal{C}).$$

Adversaries $\mathcal{B}$ *and* $\mathcal{C}$ *both run in time that of as* $\mathcal{A}$ *plus at most* $\mathcal{O}(q)$ *overhead. Adversary* $\mathcal{B}$ *makes at most* q *queries to its oracles.*

Theorem 10 (**CtE2 receiver binding**). *Let* CtE2 = CtE2[CS, SE]. *Let* $\mathcal{A}$ *be an* r-BIND$_{\text{CtE2}}$ *adversary. Then we give an adversary* $\mathcal{B}$ *such that*

$$\mathbf{Adv}^{\text{r-bind}}_{\text{CtE1}[\mathsf{CS},\mathsf{SE}]}(\mathcal{A}) \leq \mathbf{Adv}^{\text{v-bind}}_{\mathsf{CS}}(\mathcal{B}).$$

Adversary $\mathcal{B}$ *runs time that of* $\mathcal{A}$.

Finally, note that CtE2 achieves s-BIND security because it verifies the commitment during decryption.

7 Nonce-Based Committing AEAD and the CEP Construction

The committing AEAD schemes thus far have all been randomized. Cryptographers have advocated that modern AEAD schemes, however, be designed to be nonce-based. Here one replaces internal randomness during encryption with an input, called the nonce. Security should hold as long as the nonce never repeats throughout the course of encrypting messages with a particular key.

We formalize nonce-based committing AEAD and provide a construction of it that additionally achieves a number of valuable properties. It will achieve a multiple-opening security notion suitably modified to the nonce-based setting. It is faster than the other multiple-opening schemes, requiring only two cryptographic passes during encryption and decryption, and a single one during verification. It also reduces ciphertext stretch compared to the schemes of Sect. 6, since the opening will be recomputed in the course of decryption and so does not need to be sent in the encryption.

Nonce-based committing AEAD. A nonce-based CE scheme is a tuple of algorithms $\mathrm{nCE} = (\mathrm{Kg}, \mathrm{Enc}, \mathrm{Dec}, \mathrm{Ver})$. We define it exactly like CE schemes (Sect. 4) except for the following differences. In addition to the other sets, we associate to any nCE scheme a nonce space $\mathcal{N} \subseteq \Sigma^*$. Encryption and decryption are now defined as follows:

- *Encryption*: Encryption Enc is deterministic and takes as input a tuple $(K, N, H, M) \in (\Sigma^*)^4$ and outputs a pair $(C_1, C_2) \in \mathcal{C} \times \mathcal{T}$ or a distinguished error symbol $\bot$. We require that for any $(K, N, H, M) \in \mathcal{K} \times \mathcal{N} \times \mathcal{H} \times \mathcal{M}$ it is the case that $\mathrm{Enc}(K, N, H, M) \neq \bot$.
- *Decryption*: Decryption Dec is deterministic. It takes as input a quintuple $(K, N, H, C_1, C_2) \in (\Sigma^*)^5$ and outputs a message, opening value pair $(M, K_f) \in \mathcal{M} \times \mathcal{K}_f$ or $\bot$.

Key generation and verification are unchanged relative to randomized CE schemes. As for randomized schemes, we assume that the length of ciphertexts are dictated only by the lengths of the header and message. We will often write $\mathrm{Enc}_K^N(H, M)$ for $\mathrm{Enc}(K, N, H, M)$ and $\mathrm{Dec}_K^N(H, C_1, C_2)$ for $\mathrm{Dec}(K, N, H, C_1, C_2)$.

Nonce-based security. We adapt the confidentiality and integrity security notions from Sect. 4 to the nonce-based setting. Let game $\text{MO-nREAL}_{\mathrm{nCE}}^{\mathcal{A}}$ be the same as the game $\text{MO-RAND}_{\mathrm{nCE}}^{\mathcal{A}}$ (Fig. 3), except that all oracles take an additional input N, Enc and Dec executions use that value N as the nonce, the sets $\mathcal{Y}_1, \mathcal{Y}_2$ are instead updated with (N, H, C_1, C_2), and the decryption oracle checks if $(N, H, C_1, C_2) \in \mathcal{Y}_1$. Similarly let game $\text{MO-nRAND}_{\mathrm{nCE}}^{\mathcal{A}}$ be the same as $\text{MO-RAND}_{\mathrm{nCE}}^{\mathcal{A}}$ (Fig. 3), except that all oracles take an additional input N, and Enc and Dec use that value N as the nonce, and $\mathcal{Y}_2$ is updated with (N, H, C_1, C_2). For a scheme nCE, we measure the nonce-based multiple-openings real-or-random MO-nROR$_{\rm nCE}$ advantage of an adversary $\mathcal{A}$ by

$$\mathbf{Adv}^{\rm mo\text{-}nror}_{\rm nCE}(\mathcal{A}) = \left|\Pr\left[\,\text{MO-nREAL}^{\mathcal{A}}_{\rm nCE} \Rightarrow 1\,\right] - \Pr\left[\,\text{MO-nRAND}^{\mathcal{A}}_{\rm nCE} \Rightarrow 1\,\right]\right|.$$

An adversary is *nonce-respecting* if its queries never repeat the same N across a pair of encryption queries (two queries to **Enc**, two to **ChalEnc**, or one to each). We will assume nonce-respecting MO-nRAND$_{\rm nCE}$ adversaries.

Let MO-nCTXT$^{\mathcal{A}}_{\rm nCE}$ be the same as the game MO-CTXT$^{\mathcal{A}}_{\rm nCE}$ (Fig. 3), except that all oracles take an additional input N, **Enc** and **Dec** executions use that value N as the nonce, and the set $\mathcal{Y}$ is instead updated with (N, H, C_1, C_2). For a scheme nCE, we measure the nonce-based multiple-openings real-or-random MO-nCTXT$_{\rm nCE}$ advantage of an adversary $\mathcal{A}$ by

$$\mathbf{Adv}^{\rm mo\text{-}nctxt}_{\rm nCE}(\mathcal{A}) = \Pr\left[\,\text{MO-nCTXT}^{\mathcal{A}}_{\rm nCE} \Rightarrow 1\,\right].$$

As with randomized committing AEAD, we can provide single-opening versions of the above definitions, and can give an all-in-one version of nonce-based MO and SO security. We omit the details for the sake of brevity.

The sender binding notion s-BIND for nonce-based schemes is the same as for randomized schemes except that the adversary also outputs a nonce N, which is used with Dec. Because verification is unchanged, receiver binding security is formalized exactly the same for randomized and nonce-based committing AEAD.

The Committing Encrypt-and-PRF scheme. One can analyze some traditional nonce-based AEAD schemes to show they are compactly committing. As one example, it is easy to see that the EtE construction (Sect. 5.1) works just as well with non-repeating nonces, but with only single-opening security. The other schemes in Sect. 5 do not, but can be easily modified to by replacing IV with $E_K(N)$. Here we focus on a new scheme that will have better overall performance and security than previous ones. Unlike the legacy schemes studied in Sect. 5 it will be provably secure for multiple openings. At the same time, it will be more efficient than the schemes in Sect. 6.

The scheme $\text{CEP}[\text{G}[\text{K}], \text{F}, \text{F}^{\rm cr}] = (\text{Kg}, \text{CEP-Enc}, \text{CEP-Dec}, \text{CEP-Ver})$ is in the style of an Encrypt-and-PRF construction. It uses an underlying stream cipher $G[E]$ built from a block cipher $E\colon \{0,1\}^k \times \{0,1\}^n \times \{0,1\}^n$ and functions $F, F^{\rm cr}\colon \{0,1\}^n \times \{0,1\}^t \to \{0,1\}^t$. The key space is $\mathcal{K} = \{0,1\}^k$ and key generation simply outputs a random draw from it. Encryption starts by using the nonce with the key K to derive one-time keys for the keyed cryptographic hash $F^{\rm cr}$ and a PRF F, as well as to generate an encryption pad to XOR with the message. We use a block cipher E in CTR mode to generate these values. Finally it computes a binding value for H, M and applies F to that commitment value to generate a tag. Detailed pseudocode is given in Fig. 10.

We will need $F^{\rm cr}$ to both be CR (for binding) as well as secure as a one-time PRF (for confidentiality). This rules out some otherwise desirable choices such as CMAC [41], PMAC [53] and Carter-Wegman-style PRFs such as Poly1305 [16]

$\text{CEP-Enc}_K^N(H, M)$:	$\text{CEP-Dec}_K^N(H, C_1 \parallel T, C_2)$:	$\text{CEP-Ver}(H, M, K_f, C_2)$:
$IV \leftarrow E_K(N)$	$m \leftarrow \lceil \lvert C_1 \rvert / n \rceil$	$C_2' \leftarrow F^{\text{cr}}_{K_f}(H \parallel M)$
$m \leftarrow \lceil \lvert M \rvert / n \rceil$	For $i = 0$ to $m+1$ do	If $C_2' \neq C_2$ then Return 0
For $i = 0$ to $m+1$ do	$\quad P_i \leftarrow E_K(IV + i)$	Return 1
$\quad P_i \leftarrow E_K(IV + i)$	$M \parallel \leftarrow (P_2 \parallel \cdots \parallel P_{m+1}) \oplus C_1$	
$C_1 \leftarrow (P_2 \parallel \cdots \parallel P_{m+1}) \oplus M$	$C_2' \leftarrow F^{\text{cr}}_{P_0}(H \parallel M)$	
$C_2 \leftarrow F^{\text{cr}}_{P_0}(H \parallel M)$	$T' \leftarrow F_{P_1}(C_2')$	
$T \leftarrow F_{P_1}(C_2)$	If $T \neq T' \vee C_2' \neq C_2$ then	
Return $(C_1 \parallel T, C_2)$	$\quad$ Return $\perp$	
	Return (M, P_0)	

Fig. 10. A nonce-based committing AEAD.

and UMAC [17]. These PRFs are some of the fastest available, but would make CEP vulnerable to binding attacks. (See also the discussion in Sect. 5.4.)

The most obvious choice is HMAC, for which formal analyses support it being a secure PRF for a key secret [2,3] and CR for adversarially chosen keys of the same length (assuming the underlying hash function is CR). Other multi-property hash functions [10] would also suffice.

The reason we use E_K both for CTR mode and for key derivation is speed. This ensures that we need ever only use a single key with E; in some environments rekeying can be almost as expensive as another invocation of E. In fact we are simply using E_K to build a stream cipher, and any nonce-based secure stream cipher would do, e.g., ChaCha-20 [15].

One might wonder why have a tag T as well as the commitment value C_2. The reason is that to achieve multi-opening security, we must disclose the key used with F^{cr}, rendering the unforgeability of C_2 values moot. If one instead omitted T and only checked $C_2' = C_2$ to attempt to achieve unforgeability, then there exists a straightforward MO-nCTXT attack that obtains a ciphertext for a nonce N, queries it to **Dec** to get the key for F^{cr}, and then uses that to forge a new ciphertext to be submitted to **ChalDec**. The application of F under a distinct key provides ciphertext integrity even after an adversary obtains openings (keys for F^{cr}). Similarly, dropping the check during decryption that $C_2' = C_2$ also leads to an attack, but this time on sender binding.

Comparisons. Before getting into the formal security analysis in the next section, we first compare CEP to the generic composition constructions that also achieve multiple-opening security. The first benefit over other schemes is that it is nonce-based, making it suitable for stateful as well as randomized settings (see also Rogaway's discussion of the benefits of nonce-based encryption [54]).

The second is that ciphertext expansion is reduced by a security parameter number of bits compared to the generic composition constructions, because in CEP we do not need to transport an explicit opening — the recipient recomputes it pseudorandomly from the secret key. Consequently, CEP ciphertexts are shorter than Facebook's by 256 bits.

The third is that encryption and decryption both save an entire cryptographic pass over the associated data and message. For Facebook's chosen algorithms (HMAC for the commitment, plus Encrypt-then-MAC using AES-CBC and HMAC), this means that CEP offers more than a 50% speed-up for both algorithms.[4] While in some messaging settings encryption and decryption may not be particularly performance-sensitive operations, any cost savings is desirable. In other contexts, such as if one starts using committing encryption on larger files (images, videos) sent over messaging applications or if one wants abuse reporting for streaming communications, performance will be very important.

CEP achieves the stronger multiple-opening security goal, setting it apart from the legacy committing AEAD schemes from Sect. 5. At the same time, CEP has equivalent or better performance than those schemes. With respect to EtM and MtE, verification is reduced from two cryptographic passes to one.

8 Analysis of CEP

Useful abstractions. We will introduce some intermediate abstractions of the underlying primitives. First, a nonce-based stream cipher G takes as input a key K, a nonce N, and an output length ℓ. It outputs a string of length ℓ bits. The second abstraction is of the implicit MAC used within CEP. It is the composition $F \circ F^{\mathrm{cr}}(P_1, P_0, H \,\|\, M) = F_{P_1}(F^{\mathrm{cr}}_{P_0}(H \,\|\, M))$ for random keys P_0, P_1 and any strings H, M. The output is a t-bit string. We defer a discussion of the security properties required from these abstractions to the full version of this work. There, we define a nonce-based pseudorandom generator (PRG) security notion that mandates attackers cannot distinguish between G's output and random bit strings, as well as a multi-user unforgeability notion MU-UF-CMA$_{F \circ F^{\mathrm{cr}}}$ that captures the unforgeability of $F \circ F^{\mathrm{cr}}$ when adversaries can attack it under multiple keys.

Security of CEP. We are now in position to formally analyze the confidentiality, ciphertext integrity, and binding of CEP. We give theorems for each in turn, with proofs deferred to the full version of the paper.

Theorem 11 (CEP confidentiality). *Let* CEP = CEP[G, F]. *Let $\mathcal{A}$ be an* MO-nROR$_{\mathrm{CEP}}$ *adversary making at most q queries and whose queried messages total at most σ bits. Then we give adversaries $\mathcal{B}, \mathcal{C}, \mathcal{D}$ such that*

$$\mathbf{Adv}^{\text{mo-nror}}_{\mathrm{CEP}}(\mathcal{A}) \leq 2 \cdot \mathbf{Adv}^{\mathrm{prg}}_{G}(\mathcal{B}) + 2 \cdot \mathbf{Adv}^{\mathrm{prf}}_{F}(\mathcal{C}) + \cdot \mathbf{Adv}^{\mathrm{prf}}_{F^{\mathrm{cr}}}(\mathcal{D})$$

Adversary $\mathcal{B}$ makes at most q queries to its oracle, the sum of its total outputs requested is σ bits. Adversary $\mathcal{C}$ makes at most q queries to its oracle, and never repeats a key identifier. Adversary $\mathcal{D}$ make at most q queries to its oracle and never repeats a key identifier. All adversaries run in time at most that of $\mathcal{A}$ plus an overhead of at most $\mathcal{O}(q)$.

---

[4] HMAC is slower than AES. If AES-NI is available, then the speed-up will be even larger, since the HMAC passes will be the performance bottleneck.

Theorem 12 (CEP ciphertext integrity). *Let* CEP = CEP[*G*, *F*]. *Let* $\mathcal{A}$ *be an* MO-nCTXT$_{\text{CEP}}$ *adversary making at most* q *queries with query inputs totalling at most* σn *bits. Let* F^2 *be the tagging scheme described earlier. Then we give adversaries* $\mathcal{B}, \mathcal{C}$ *such that*

$$\mathbf{Adv}^{\text{mo-nctxt}}_{\text{CEP}}(\mathcal{A}) \leq \mathbf{Adv}^{\text{prg}}_{G}(\mathcal{B}) + \mathbf{Adv}^{\text{mu-uf-cma}}_{F^2}(\mathcal{C}) \,.$$

Adversary $\mathcal{B}$ *runs in time that of* $\mathcal{A}$ *plus at most* $\mathcal{O}(q)$ *overhead and makes* q *queries totaling at most* σn *bits. Adversary* $\mathcal{C}$ *makes at most* q *queries and runs in time that of* $\mathcal{A}$ *plus at most* $\mathcal{O}(q)$ *overhead.*

Finally we turn to binding. Recall that any scheme that effectively runs commitment verification during decryption achieves sender binding. The check that $C_2' = C_2$ during decryption accomplishes this, and so the scheme is perfectly sender binding. For receiver binding, a simple reduction gives the following theorem showing that the CR of F^{cr} implies binding of CEP.

Theorem 13 (CEP receiver binding). *Let* CEP = CEP[*G*, *F*]. *Let* $\mathcal{A}$ *be any* r-BIND$_{\text{CEP}}$ *adversary. Then we give an adversary* $\mathcal{B}$ *such that* $\mathbf{Adv}^{\text{r-bind}}_{\text{CEP}}(\mathcal{A}) \leq \mathbf{Adv}^{\text{cr}}_{F^{\text{cr}}}(\mathcal{B})$ *and* $\mathcal{B}$ *runs in time that of* $\mathcal{A}$.

9 Related Work

The primary viewpoint in the literature has been that committing encryption is undesirable either because one wants deniability [20,22,50] or due to the theoretical challenges associated with proving encryption confidentiality in the face of adaptive compromises [23]. Thus while *non*-committing encryption has received significant attention (q.v., [22–25,27,34,35,40,43,49,50,62–65]), there is a dearth of literature on building purposefully committing encryption.

We are aware of only one previous work on building committing encryption schemes, due to Gertner and Herzberg [36]. They give definitions that are insufficient for the message franking setting (in particular they do not capture server binding or multiple opening security). They do not analyze AE schemes, and focus only on building asymmetric primitives.

Our receiver binding security property is related to the concept of robust encryption, introduced by Abdalla et al. [1]. They give two security notions for public-key encryption (PKE). The stronger, called strong robustness, asks that an adversarially-chosen ciphertext should only correctly decrypt under at most one legitimate secret key. Mohassel [48] showed efficient ways of adapting existing PKE schemes to be robust. Farshim et al. [32] subsequently pointed out that some applications require robustness to adversarially generated secret keys, and introduced a notion called complete robustness. In a later work, Farshim, Orlandi, and Rosie [33] adapt these robustness definitions to the setting of authenticated encryption, message authentication codes (MACs), and pseudorandom functions (PRFs). They show that in this context, the simpler full robustness notion of [32] is the strongest of those considered.

These prior notions, in particular the full robustness for AE notion from [33], do not suffice for formalizing binding for AEAD. First, it does not capture sender binding. Second, for receiver binding, it turns out that the most straightforward adaptation of full robustness to handle associated data fails to imply receiver binding. We defer a more detailed explanation to the full version of this work.

Abdalla et al. [1] propose a generic composition of a commitment scheme and PKE scheme to achieve robustness and Farshim et al. [33] show a variant of this for the symmetric encryption setting. The latter construction commits to the key, not the message, and could not be used to achieve the multiple opening security targeted by our generic composition constructions.

Selective-opening security allows an adversary to adaptively choose to corrupt some senders that sent (correlated) encrypted messages [8] or to compromise the keys of a subset of receivers [38]. Bellare et al. [8] gave the first constructions of schemes secure against selective-opening attacks for sender corruptions. Non-committing encryption can be used to realize security for receiver corruptions. Our definitions do not model selective-opening attacks, and as mentioned in the introduction, assessing the viability of committing AEAD in selective-opening settings is an interesting open problem.

Acknowledgments. The authors would like to thank the anonymous reviewers of Crypto 2017 for their thoughtful comments, as well as Mihir Bellare for discussions about robust encryption and its relation to binding. This work was funded in part by NSF grant CNS-1330308.

References

1. Abdalla, M., Bellare, M., Neven, G.: Robust encryption. In: Micciancio, D. (ed.) TCC 2010. LNCS, vol. 5978, pp. 480–497. Springer, Heidelberg (2010). doi:10.1007/978-3-642-11799-2_28
2. Bellare, M.: New proofs for NMAC and HMAC: security without collision-resistance. In: Dwork, C. (ed.) CRYPTO 2006. LNCS, vol. 4117, pp. 602–619. Springer, Heidelberg (2006). doi:10.1007/11818175_36
3. Bellare, M., Canetti, R., Krawczyk, H.: Keying hash functions for message authentication. In: Koblitz, N. (ed.) CRYPTO 1996. LNCS, vol. 1109, pp. 1–15. Springer, Heidelberg (1996). doi:10.1007/3-540-68697-5_1
4. Bellare, M., Canetti, R., Krawczyk, H.: Pseudorandom functions revisited: The cascade construction and its concrete security. In: Proceedings of the 37th Annual Symposium on Foundations of Computer Science, 1996, pp. 514–523. IEEE (1996)
5. Bellare, M., Canetti, R., Krawczyk, H.: HMAC: Keyed-hashing for message authentication. Internet Request for Comment RFC, 2104 (1997)
6. Bellare, M., Desai, A., Jokipii, E., Rogaway, P.: A concrete security treatment of symmetric encryption. In: Foundations of Computer Science (FOCS) (1997)
7. Bellare, M., Dowsley, R., Waters, B., Yilek, S.: Standard security does not imply security against selective-opening. In: Pointcheval, D., Johansson, T. (eds.) EUROCRYPT 2012. LNCS, vol. 7237, pp. 645–662. Springer, Heidelberg (2012). doi:10.1007/978-3-642-29011-4_38

8. Bellare, M., Hofheinz, D., Yilek, S.: Possibility and impossibility results for encryption and commitment secure under selective opening. In: Joux, A. (ed.) EUROCRYPT 2009. LNCS, vol. 5479, pp. 1–35. Springer, Heidelberg (2009). doi:10.1007/978-3-642-01001-9_1
9. Bellare, M., Namprempre, C.: Authenticated encryption: relations among notions and analysis of the generic composition paradigm. In: Okamoto, T. (ed.) ASIACRYPT 2000. LNCS, vol. 1976, pp. 531–545. Springer, Heidelberg (2000). doi:10.1007/3-540-44448-3_41
10. Bellare, M., Ristenpart, T.: Multi-property-preserving hash domain extension and the EMD transform. In: Lai, X., Chen, K. (eds.) ASIACRYPT 2006. LNCS, vol. 4284, pp. 299–314. Springer, Heidelberg (2006). doi:10.1007/11935230_20
11. Bellare, M., Rogaway, P.: Random oracles are practical: a paradigm for designing efficient protocols. In: ACM CCS (1993)
12. Bellare, M., Rogaway, P.: Encode-then-encipher encryption: how to exploit nonces or redundancy in plaintexts for efficient cryptography. In: Okamoto, T. (ed.) ASIACRYPT 2000. LNCS, vol. 1976, pp. 317–330. Springer, Heidelberg (2000). doi:10.1007/3-540-44448-3_24
13. Bellare, M., Rogaway, P.: The security of triple encryption and a framework for code-based game-playing proofs. In: EUROCRYPT (2006)
14. Bellare, M., Singh, A.C., Jaeger, J., Nyayapati, M., Stepanovs, I.: Ratcheted encryption and key exchange: The security of messaging. Cryptology ePrint Archive, Report 2016/1028 (2016). http://eprint.iacr.org/2016/1028
15. Bernstein, D.J.: ChaCha, a variant of Salsa20. https://cr.yp.to/chacha/chacha-20080128.pdf
16. Bernstein, D.J.: The Poly1305-AES message-authentication code. In: Gilbert, H., Handschuh, H. (eds.) FSE 2005. LNCS, vol. 3557, pp. 32–49. Springer, Heidelberg (2005). doi:10.1007/11502760_3
17. Black, J., Halevi, S., Krawczyk, H., Krovetz, T., Rogaway, P.: UMAC: fast and secure message authentication. In: Wiener, M. (ed.) CRYPTO 1999. LNCS, vol. 1666, pp. 216–233. Springer, Heidelberg (1999). doi:10.1007/3-540-48405-1_14
18. Black, J., Rogaway, P.: A block-cipher mode of operation for parallelizable message authentication. In: Knudsen, L.R. (ed.) EUROCRYPT 2002. LNCS, vol. 2332, pp. 384–397. Springer, Heidelberg (2002). doi:10.1007/3-540-46035-7_25
19. Black, J., Rogaway, P., Shrimpton, T.: Encryption-scheme security in the presence of key-dependent messages. In: Nyberg, K., Heys, H. (eds.) SAC 2002. LNCS, vol. 2595, pp. 62–75. Springer, Heidelberg (2003). doi:10.1007/3-540-36492-7_6
20. Borisov, N., Goldberg, I., Brewer, E.: Off-the-record communication, or, why not to use PGP. In: ACM Workshop on Privacy in the Electronic Society (2004)
21. Brassard, G., Chaum, D., Crépeau, C.: Minimum disclosure proofs of knowledge. J. Comput. Syst. Sci. **37**, 156–189 (1988)
22. Canetti, R., Dwork, C., Naor, M., Ostrovsky, R.: Deniable encryption. In: Kaliski, B.S. (ed.) CRYPTO 1997. LNCS, vol. 1294, pp. 90–104. Springer, Heidelberg (1997). doi:10.1007/BFb0052229
23. Canetti, R., Feige, U., Goldreich, O., Naor, M.: Adaptively secure multi-party computation. In: STOC (1996)
24. Canetti, R., Poburinnaya, O., Raykova, M.: Optimal-rate non-committing encryption in a CRS model. IACR Cryptology ePrint Archive (2016)
25. Choi, S.G., Dachman-Soled, D., Malkin, T., Wee, H.: Improved non-committing encryption with applications to adaptively secure protocols. In: Matsui, M. (ed.) ASIACRYPT 2009. LNCS, vol. 5912, pp. 287–302. Springer, Heidelberg (2009). doi:10.1007/978-3-642-10366-7_17

26. Cohn-Gordon, K., Cremers, C., Dowling, B., Garratt, L., Stebila, D.: A formal security analysis of the signal messaging protocol. IACR ePrint Archive (2016)
27. Damgård, I., Nielsen, J.B.: Improved non-committing encryption schemes based on a general complexity assumption. In: Bellare, M. (ed.) CRYPTO 2000. LNCS, vol. 1880, pp. 432–450. Springer, Heidelberg (2000). doi:10.1007/3-540-44598-6_27
28. Dodis, Y., Ristenpart, T., Steinberger, J., Tessaro, S.: To hash or not to hash again? (in)differentiability results for H^2 and HMAC. In: Safavi-Naini, R., Canetti, R. (eds.) CRYPTO 2012. LNCS, vol. 7417, pp. 348–366. Springer, Heidelberg (2012). doi:10.1007/978-3-642-32009-5_21
29. Dolev, D., Dwork, C., Naor, M.: Nonmalleable cryptography. SIAM Review (2003)
30. Facebook. Facebook Messenger app (2016). https://www.messenger.com/
31. Facebook. Messenger Secret Conversations technical whitepaper (2016). https://fbnewsroomus.files.wordpress.com/2016/07/secret_conversations_whitepaper-1.pdf
32. Farshim, P., Libert, B., Paterson, K.G., Quaglia, E.A.: Robust encryption, revisited. In: Kurosawa, K., Hanaoka, G. (eds.) PKC 2013. LNCS, vol. 7778, pp. 352–368. Springer, Heidelberg (2013). doi:10.1007/978-3-642-36362-7_22
33. Farshim, P., Orlandi, C., Rosie, R.: Security of symmetric primitives under incorrect usage of keys. IACR Trans. Symmetric Cryptology **2017**(1), 449–473 (2017)
34. Garay, J.A., Wichs, D., Zhou, H.-S.: Somewhat non-committing encryption and efficient adaptively secure oblivious transfer. IACR Cryptology ePrint Archive (2008)
35. Garay, J.A., Wichs, D., Zhou, H.-S.: Somewhat non-committing encryption and efficient adaptively secure oblivious transfer. In: Halevi, S. (ed.) CRYPTO 2009. LNCS, vol. 5677, pp. 505–523. Springer, Heidelberg (2009). doi:10.1007/978-3-642-03356-8_30
36. Gertner, Y., Herzberg, A.: Committing encryption and publicly-verifiable signcryption. IACR Cryptology ePrint Archive (2003)
37. Halevi, S., Krawczyk, H.: Security under key-dependent inputs. In: ACM CCS (2007)
38. Hazay, C., Patra, A., Warinschi, B.: Selective opening security for receivers. In: Iwata, T., Cheon, J.H. (eds.) ASIACRYPT 2015. LNCS, vol. 9452, pp. 443–469. Springer, Heidelberg (2015). doi:10.1007/978-3-662-48797-6_19
39. Hearn, M.: Modern anti-spam and E2E crypto. https://moderncrypto.org/mail-archive/messaging/2014/000780.html
40. Hemenway, B., Ostrovsky, R., Rosen, A.: Non-committing encryption from Φ-hiding. In: Dodis, Y., Nielsen, J.B. (eds.) TCC 2015. LNCS, vol. 9014, pp. 591–608. Springer, Heidelberg (2015). doi:10.1007/978-3-662-46494-6_24
41. Iwata, T., Kurosawa, K.: OMAC: one-key CBC MAC. In: Johansson, T. (ed.) FSE 2003. LNCS, vol. 2887, pp. 129–153. Springer, Heidelberg (2003). doi:10.1007/978-3-540-39887-5_11
42. Krawczyk, H.: The order of encryption and authentication for protecting communications (or: How Secure Is SSL?). In: Kilian, J. (ed.) CRYPTO 2001. LNCS, vol. 2139, pp. 310–331. Springer, Heidelberg (2001). doi:10.1007/3-540-44647-8_19
43. Lei, F., Chen, W., Chen, K.: A non-committing encryption scheme based on quadratic residue. In: Levi, A., Savaş, E., Yenigün, H., Balcısoy, S., Saygın, Y. (eds.) ISCIS 2006. LNCS, vol. 4263, pp. 972–980. Springer, Heidelberg (2006). doi:10.1007/11902140_101
44. Marlinspike, M.: libsignal protocol (Java) (2016). https://github.com/WhisperSystems/libsignal-protocol-java

45. Marlinspike, M., Perrin, T.: The Double Ratchet algorithm. https://whispersystems.org/docs/specifications/doubleratchet/doubleratchet.pdf
46. McGrew, D., Viega, J.: The galois/counter mode of operation (gcm). Submission to NIST Modes of Operation Process 20 (2004)
47. Millican, J.: Challenges of E2E Encryption in Facebook Messenger. Real World Cryptography Conference (2017). https://www.realworldcrypto.com/rwc2017/program
48. Mohassel, P.: A closer look at anonymity and robustness in encryption schemes. In: Abe, M. (ed.) ASIACRYPT 2010. LNCS, vol. 6477, pp. 501–518. Springer, Heidelberg (2010). doi:10.1007/978-3-642-17373-8_29
49. Nielsen, J.B.: Separating random oracle proofs from complexity theoretic proofs: the non-committing encryption case. In: Yung, M. (ed.) CRYPTO 2002. LNCS, vol. 2442, pp. 111–126. Springer, Heidelberg (2002). doi:10.1007/3-540-45708-9_8
50. O'Neill, A., Peikert, C., Waters, B.: Bi-deniable public-key encryption. In: Rogaway, P. (ed.) CRYPTO 2011. LNCS, vol. 6841, pp. 525–542. Springer, Heidelberg (2011). doi:10.1007/978-3-642-22792-9_30
51. Paterson, K.G., Ristenpart, T., Shrimpton, T.: Tag Size *Does* matter: attacks and proofs for the TLS record protocol. In: Lee, D.H., Wang, X. (eds.) ASIACRYPT 2011. LNCS, vol. 7073, pp. 372–389. Springer, Heidelberg (2011). doi:10.1007/978-3-642-25385-0_20
52. Rogaway, P.: Authenticated-encryption with associated-data. In: ACM CCS (2002)
53. Rogaway, P.: Efficient instantiations of tweakable blockciphers and refinements to modes OCB and PMAC. In: Lee, P.J. (ed.) ASIACRYPT 2004. LNCS, vol. 3329, pp. 16–31. Springer, Heidelberg (2004). doi:10.1007/978-3-540-30539-2_2
54. Rogaway, P.: Nonce-based symmetric encryption. In: Roy, B., Meier, W. (eds.) FSE 2004. LNCS, vol. 3017, pp. 348–358. Springer, Heidelberg (2004). doi:10.1007/978-3-540-25937-4_22
55. Rogaway, P., Shrimpton, T.: A provable-security treatment of the key-wrap problem. In: Vaudenay, S. (ed.) EUROCRYPT 2006. LNCS, vol. 4004, pp. 373–390. Springer, Heidelberg (2006). doi:10.1007/11761679_23
56. Ryan, M.D.: Enhanced certificate transparency and end-to-end encrypted mail. In: NDSS. The Internet Society (2014)
57. Stinson, D.R.: Universal hashing and authentication codes. Designs, Codes and Cryptography (1994)
58. Wang, L., Pass, R., Shelat, A., Ristenpart, T.: Secure channel injection and anonymous proofs of account ownership. Cryptology ePrint Archive, Report 2016/925 (2016). http://eprint.iacr.org/2016/925
59. Wegman, M.N., Lawrence Carter, J.: New hash functions and their use in authentication and set equality. Journal of computer and system sciences (1981)
60. Whatsapp. Whatsapp (2016). https://www.whatsapp.com/
61. Wikipedia. Signal (software) (2016). https://en.wikipedia.org/wiki/Signal_(software)
62. Zhu, H., Araragi, T., Nishide, T., Sakurai, K.: Adaptive and composable non-committing encryptions. In: Steinfeld, R., Hawkes, P. (eds.) ACISP 2010. LNCS, vol. 6168, pp. 135–144. Springer, Heidelberg (2010). doi:10.1007/978-3-642-14081-5_9
63. Zhu, H., Araragi, T., Nishide, T., Sakurai, K.: Universally composable non-committing encryptions in the presence of adaptive adversaries. In: SECRYPT (2010)

64. Zhu, H., Bao, F.: Non-committing encryptions based on oblivious naor-pinkas cryptosystems. In: Roy, B., Sendrier, N. (eds.) INDOCRYPT 2009. LNCS, vol. 5922, pp. 418–429. Springer, Heidelberg (2009). doi:10.1007/978-3-642-10628-6_27
65. Zhu, H., Bao, F.: Error-free, multi-bit non-committing encryption with constant round complexity. In: Lai, X., Yung, M., Lin, D. (eds.) Inscrypt 2010. LNCS, vol. 6584, pp. 52–61. Springer, Heidelberg (2011). doi:10.1007/978-3-642-21518-6_4

Key Rotation for Authenticated Encryption

Adam Everspaugh[1(✉)], Kenneth Paterson[2], Thomas Ristenpart[3], and Sam Scott[3]

[1] University of Wisconsin–Madison, Madison, USA
adam.everspaugh@gmail.com
[2] Royal Holloway, University of London, Egham, UK
[3] Cornell Tech, New York, USA

Abstract. A common requirement in practice is to periodically rotate the keys used to encrypt stored data. Systems used by Amazon and Google do so using a hybrid encryption technique which is eminently practical but has questionable security in the face of key compromises and does not provide full key rotation. Meanwhile, symmetric updatable encryption schemes (introduced by Boneh *et al.* CRYPTO 2013) support full key rotation without performing decryption: ciphertexts created under one key can be rotated to ciphertexts created under a different key with the help of a re-encryption token. By design, the tokens do not leak information about keys or plaintexts and so can be given to storage providers without compromising security. But the prior work of Boneh *et al.* addresses relatively weak confidentiality goals and does not consider integrity at all. Moreover, as we show, a subtle issue with their concrete scheme obviates a security proof even for confidentiality against passive attacks.

This paper presents a systematic study of *updatable Authenticated Encryption (AE)*. We provide a set of security notions that strengthen those in prior work. These notions enable us to tease out real-world security requirements of different strengths and build schemes that satisfy them efficiently. We show that the hybrid approach currently used in industry achieves relatively weak forms of confidentiality and integrity, but can be modified at low cost to meet our stronger confidentiality and integrity goals. This leads to a practical scheme that has negligible overhead beyond conventional AE. We then introduce *re-encryption indistinguishability*, a security notion that formally captures the idea of fully refreshing keys upon rotation. We show how to repair the scheme of Boneh *et al.*, attaining our stronger confidentiality notion. We also show how to extend the scheme to provide integrity, and we prove that it meets our re-encryption indistinguishability notion. Finally, we discuss how to instantiate our scheme efficiently using off-the-shelf cryptographic components (AE, hashing, elliptic curves). We report on the performance of a prototype implementation, showing that fully secure key rotations can be performed at a throughput of approximately 116 kB/s.

J. Katz and H. Shacham (Eds.): CRYPTO 2017, Part III, LNCS 10403, pp. 98–129, 2017.
DOI: 10.1007/978-3-319-63697-9_4

1 Introduction

To cryptographically protect data while stored, systems use authenticated encryption (AE) schemes that provide strong message confidentiality as well as ciphertext integrity. The latter allows detection of active attackers who manipulate ciphertexts. When data is stored for long periods of time, good key management practice dictates that systems must support key rotation: moving encrypted data from an old key to a fresh one. Indeed, key rotation is mandated by regulation in some contexts, such as the payment card industry data security standard (PCI DSS) that dictates how credit card data must be secured [PCI16]. Key rotation can also be used to revoke old keys that are comprised, or to effect data access revocation.

Deployed approaches to key rotation. Systems used in practice typically support a type of key rotation using a symmetric key hierarchy. Amazon's Key Management Service [AWS], for example, enables users to encrypt a plaintext M under a fresh data encapsulation key via $C_{dem} = \mathsf{Enc}(K_d, M)$ and then wrap K_d via $C_{kem} = \mathsf{Enc}(K, K_d)$ under a long-term key K owned by the client. Here Enc is an authenticated encryption (AE) scheme. By analogy with the use of hybrid encryption in the asymmetric setting, we refer to such a scheme as a KEM/DEM construction, with KEM and DEM standing for key and data encapsulation mechanisms, respectively; we refer to the specific scheme as AE-hybrid.

The AE-hybrid scheme then allows a simple form of key rotation: the client picks a fresh K' and re-encrypts K_d as $C'_{kem} = \mathsf{Enc}(K', \mathsf{Dec}(K, C_{kem}))$. Note that the DEM key K_d does not change during key rotation. When deployed in a remote storage system, a client can perform key rotation just by fetching from the server the small, constant-sized ciphertext C_{kem}, operating locally on it to produce C'_{kem}, and then sending C'_{kem} back to the server. Performance is independent of the actual message length. The Google Cloud Platform [Goo] uses a similar approach to enable key rotation.

To our knowledge, the level of security provided by this widely deployed AE-hybrid scheme has never been investigated, let alone formally defined in a security model motivated by real-world security considerations. It is even arguable whether AE-hybrid truly rotates keys, since the DEM key does not change. Certainly it is unclear what security is provided if key compromises occur, one of the main motivations for using such an approach in the first place. On the other hand, the scheme is fast and requires only limited data transfer between the client and the data store, and appears to be sufficient to meet current regulatory requirements.

Updatable encryption. Boneh, Lewi, Montgomery, and Raghunathan (BLMR) [BLMR15] (the full version of [BLMR13]) introduced another approach to enabling key rotation that they call *updatable encryption*. An updatable encryption scheme is a symmetric encryption scheme that, in addition to the usual triple of $(\mathsf{KeyGen}, \mathsf{Enc}, \mathsf{Dec})$ algorithms, comes with a pair of algorithms $\mathsf{ReKeyGen}$ and ReEnc. The first, $\mathsf{ReKeyGen}$, generates a compact rekey token given the old and new secret keys and a target ciphertext, while the second, ReEnc, uses a rekey token output by the first to rotate the ciphertext without performing decryption. For example, AE-hybrid can be seen as an instance of an updatable encryption scheme in which the rekey token output by ReKeyGen is C'_{kem} and where ReEnc simply replaces C_{kem} with C'_{kem}. BLMR introduced an IND-CPA-style security notion in which adversaries can additionally obtain some rekey tokens. Their definition is inspired by, but different from, those used for CCA-secure proxy re-encryption schemes [CH07]. Given its obvious limitations when it comes to key rotation, it is perhaps surprising that the AE-hybrid construction provably meets the BLMR confidentiality notion for updatable encryption schemes.

BLMR also introduced and targeted a second security notion for updatable encryption, called ciphertext independence. It demands that a ciphertext and its rotation to another key are identically distributed to a ciphertext and a rotation of another ciphertext (for the same message). The intuition is that this captures the idea that true key rotation should refresh all randomness used during encryption. This definition is *not* met by the AE-hybrid construction above. But it is both unclear what attacks meeting their definition would prevent, and, relatedly, whether more intuitive definitions exist.

BLMR gave a construction for an updatable encryption scheme and claimed that it provably meets their two security definitions. Their construction cleverly combines an IND-CPA KEM with a DEM that uses a key-homomorphic PRF [NPR99,BLMR15] to realize a stream cipher. This enables rotation of both the KEM and the DEM keys, though the latter requires a number of operations that is linear in the plaintext length. Looking ahead, their proof sketch has a bug and we provide strong evidence that it is unlikely to be fixable. Moreover, BLMR do not yet target or achieve any kind of authenticated encryption goal, a must for practical use.

Our contributions. We provide a systematic treatment of AE schemes that support key rotation without decryption, a.k.a. updatable AE.

Specifically, we provide a new security notion for confidentiality, UP-IND, that is strictly stronger than that of BLMR [BLMR15], a corresponding notion for integrity, UP-INT (missing entirely from BLMR but essential for practice), and a new notion called re-encryption indistinguishability (UP-REENC) that is strictly stronger and more natural in capturing the spirit of "true key rotation" than the ciphertext indistinguishability notion of BLMR.

Achieving our UP-REENC notion means that an attacker, having access to both a ciphertext and the secret key used to generate it, should not be able to derive any information that helps it attack a rotation of that ciphertext. Thus, for example, an insider with access to the encryption keys at some point in time but who is then excluded from the system cannot make use of the old keys to learn anything useful once key rotation has been carried out on the AE ciphertexts. Teasing out the correct form of this notion turns out to be a significant challenge in our work.

Armed with this set of security notions, we go on to make better sense of the landscape of constructions for updatable AE schemes. Table 1 summarises the security properties of the different schemes that we consider. Referring to this table, our security notions highlight the limitations of the AE-hybrid scheme: while it meets the confidentiality notion of BLMR, it only satisfies our UP-IND and UP-INT notions when considering a severely weakened adversary who has no access to any compromised keys. We propose an improved construction, KSS, that satisfies both notions for any number of compromised keys and which is easily deployable via small adjustments to AE-hybrid. KSS uses a form of secret sharing to embed key shares in the KEM and DEM components to avoid the issue of leaking the DEM key in the updating process, and adds a cryptographic hash binding the KEM and DEM components to prevent mauling attacks. These changes could easily be adopted by practitioners with virtually no impact on performance, while concretely improving security.

However, the improved scheme KSS cannot satisfy our UP-REENC notion, because it still uses a KEM/DEM-style approach in which the DEM key is never rotated. The BLMR scheme might provide UP-REENC security, but, as noted above, its security proof contains a bug which we consider unlikely to be fixable. Indeed, we show that proving the BLMR scheme confidential would imply that one could also prove circular security [BRS03, CL01] for a particular type of hybrid encryption scheme assuming only the key encapsulation is IND-CPA secure. Existing counter-examples of IND-CPA secure, but circular insecure, schemes [ABBC10, CGH12] do not quite rule out such a result. But the link to the very strong notion of circular security casts doubt on the security of this scheme. One can easily modify the BLMR scheme to avoid this issue, but even having done so the resulting encryption scheme is still trivially malleable and so cannot meet our UP-INT integrity notion.

We therefore provide another new scheme, ReCrypt, meeting all three of our security notions: UP-IND, UP-INT and UP-REENC. We take inspiration from the previous constructions, especially that of BLMR: key-homomorphic PRFs provide the ability to fully rotate encryption keys; the KEM/DEM approach with secret sharing avoids the issue of leaking the DEM key in the updating process; and finally, adding a cryptographic hash to the KEM tightly binds the KEM and DEM portions and prevents ciphertext manipulation. We go on to instantiate the scheme using the Random Oracle Model (ROM) key-homomorphic PRF from [NPR99], having the form $H(M)^k$, where H is a hash function into a group in which DDH is hard. This yields a construction of an updatable AE scheme meeting all three of our security notions in the ROM under the DDH assumption. We report on the performance of an implementation of ReCrypt using elliptic curve groups, concluding that it is performant enough for practical use with short plaintexts. However, because of its reliance on exponentiation, ReCrypt is still orders of magnitude slower than our KSS scheme (achieving only UP-IND and UP-INT security). This, currently, is the price that must be paid for true key rotation in updatable encryption.

Summary. In summary, the main contributions of this paper are:

Table 1. Summary of schemes studied. †In-use by practitioners today. *Introduced in this work.

Scheme	Section	UP-IND	UP-INT	UP-REENC
AE-hybrid†	4.1	✗	✗	✗
KSS*	4.3	✓	✓	✗
BLMR	6	✗	✗	✗
ReCrypt*	7	✓	✓	✓

- To provide the first definitions of security for AE supporting key rotation without exposing plaintext.
- To explain the gap between existing, deployed schemes using the KEM/DEM approach and "full" refreshing of ciphertexts.
- To provide the first proofs of security for AE schemes using the KEM/DEM approach, namely AE-hybrid and KSS.
- To detail the first updatable AE scheme, ReCrypt, that fully and securely refreshes ciphertexts by way of key rotations without ever exposing plaintext data. We implement a prototype and report on microbenchmarks, showing that rotations can be performed in less than 9 µs per byte.

2 Updatable AE

We turn to formalizing the syntax and semantics of AE schemes supporting key rotation. Our approach extends that of Boneh et al. [BLMR15] (BLMR), the main syntactical difference being that we allow rekey token generation, re-encryption, and decryption to all return a distinguished error symbol $\perp$. This is required to enable us to later cater for integrity notions. We also modify the syntax so that ciphertexts include two portions, a header and a body. In our formulation, only the former is used during generation of rekey tokens (while in BLMR the full ciphertext is formally required).

Definition 1 (Updatable AE). *An* updatable AE scheme *is a tuple of algorithms* $\Pi = (\mathsf{KeyGen}, \mathsf{Enc}, \mathsf{ReKeyGen}, \mathsf{ReEnc}, \mathsf{Dec})$ *with the following properties:*

- $\mathsf{KeyGen}() \to k$. *Outputs a secret key* k.
- $\mathsf{Enc}(k, m) \to C$. *On input a secret key* k *and message* m, *outputs a ciphertext* $C = (\tilde{C}, \overline{C})$ *consisting of a ciphertext header* $\tilde{C}$ *and ciphertext body* $\overline{C}$.
- $\mathsf{ReKeyGen}(k_1, k_2, \tilde{C}) \to \Delta_{1,2,\tilde{C}}$. *On input two secret keys,* k_1 *and* k_2, *and a ciphertext header* $\tilde{C}$, *outputs a rekey token or* $\perp$.
- $\mathsf{ReEnc}(\Delta_{1,2,\tilde{C}}, (\tilde{C}, \overline{C})) \to C_2$. *On input a rekey token and ciphertext, outputs a new ciphertext or* $\perp$. *We require that* ReEnc *is deterministic.*
- $\mathsf{Dec}(k, C) \to m$. *On input a secret key* k *and ciphertext* C *outputs either a message or* $\perp$.

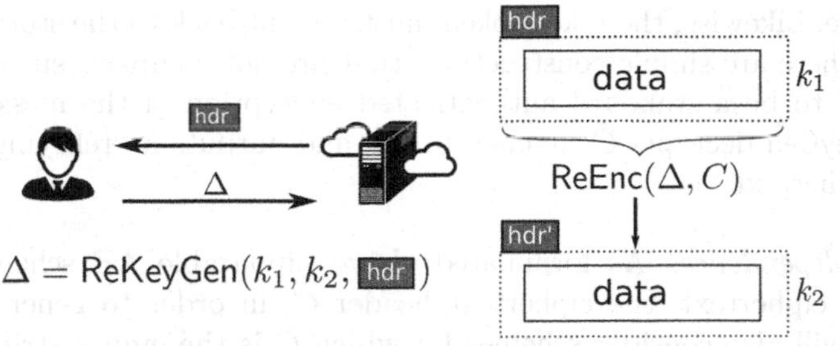

Fig. 1. Interaction between client and cloud during a ciphertext-dependent update. Client retrieves a small ciphertext header, and runs ReKeyGen to produce a compact rekey token Δ. The cloud uses this token to re-encrypt the data. At the end of the update, the data is encrypted using k_2, and cannot be recovered using only k_1.

Of course we require that all algorithms are efficiently computable. Note that, in common with [BLMR15], our definition is *not* in the nonce-based setting that is widely used for AE. Rather, we will assume that Enc is randomised. We consider this sufficient for a first treatment of updatable AE; it also reflects common industry practice as per the schemes currently used by Amazon [AWS] and Google [Goo]. We relegate the important problem of developing a parallel formulation in the nonce-based setting to future work. Similarly, we assume that all our AE schemes have single decryption errors, cf. [BDPS14], and we do not consider issues such as release of unverified plaintext, cf. [ABL+14], tidiness, cf. [NRS14] and length-hiding, cf. [PRS11].

Correctness. An updatable AE scheme is *correct* if decrypting a legitimately generated ciphertext reproduces the original message. Of course, legitimate ciphertexts may be rotated through many keys, complicating the formalization of this notion.

Definition 2 (Correctness). *Fix an updatable AE scheme Π. For any message m and any sequence of secret keys $k_1, \ldots k_T$ output by running KeyGen T times, let $C_1 = (\tilde{C}_1, \overline{C}_1) = \mathsf{Enc}(k_1, m)$ and recursively define for $1 \leq t < T$*

$$C_{t+1} = \mathsf{ReEnc}(\mathsf{ReKeyGen}(k_t, k_{t+1}, \tilde{C}_t), C_t).$$

Then Π is correct if $\mathsf{Dec}(k_T, C_T) = m$ with probability 1.

Compactness. We say that an updatable AE scheme is compact if the size of both ciphertext headers and rekeying tokens are independent of the length of the plaintext. In practice the sizes should be as small as possible, and for the constructions we consider these are typically a small constant multiple of the key length.

Compactness is important for efficiency of key rotation. Considering the abstract architecture in Fig. 1, header values must be available to the key server when rekey tokens are generated. Typically this will mean having to fetch them from storage. Likewise, the rekey token must be sent back to the storage system. Note that there are simple constructions that are not compact, such as the one that sets $\tilde{C}$ to be a standard authenticated encryption of the message and in which ReKeyGen decrypts $\tilde{C}$, re-encrypts it, and outputs a "rekeying token" as the new ciphertext.

Ciphertext-dependence. As formulated above, updatable AE schemes require part of the ciphertext, the ciphertext header $\tilde{C}$, in order to generate a rekey token. We will also consider schemes for which $\tilde{C}$ is the empty string, denoted ε. We will restrict attention to schemes for which encryption either always outputs $\tilde{C} = \varepsilon$ or never does. In the former case we call the scheme ciphertext-independent and, in the latter case, ciphertext-dependent. When discussing ciphertext-independent schemes, we will drop $\tilde{C}$ from notation, e.g., writing $\Delta_{i,j}$ instead of $\Delta_{i,j,\tilde{C}}$.

However, we primarily focus on ciphertext-dependent schemes which appear to offer more flexibility and achieve stronger security guarantees (though it is an open question whether a ciphertext-independent scheme can achieve our strongest security notion). We do propose a very lightweight ciphertext-independent scheme included in Appendix A.1, but we show it achieves strictly weaker confidentiality and integrity notions. One can generically convert a ciphertext-independent scheme into a ciphertext-dependent one, simply by deriving a ciphertext-specific key using some unique identifier for the ciphertext. We omit the formal treatment of this trivial approach.

Directionality of rotations. Some updatable AE schemes are bidirectional, meaning rekey tokens can be used to go forwards or backwards.

We only consider bi-directionality to be a feature of ciphertext-independent schemes. Formally, we say that a scheme is *bidirectional* if there exists an efficient algorithm Invert(·) that produces a valid rekey token $\Delta_{j,i}$ when given $\Delta_{i,j}$ as input.

Schemes that are not bidirectional might be able to ensure that an adversary cannot use rekey tokens to "undo" a rotation of a ciphertext. We will see that ciphertext-dependence can help in building such unidirectional schemes, whereas ciphertext-independent schemes seem harder to make unidirectional. This latter difficulty is related to the long-standing problem of constructing unidirectional proxy re-encryption schemes in the public key setting.

Relationship to proxy re-encryption. Proxy re-encryption targets a different setting than updatable encryption (or AE): the functional ability to allow a ciphertext encrypted under one key to be converted to a ciphertext decryptable by another key. The conversion should not leak plaintext data, but, unlike key rotation, it is not necessarily a goal of proxy re-encryption to remove all dependency on the original key, formalised as indistinguishability of re-encryptions (UP-REENC security) in our work. For example, previous work [CK05, ID03] suggests twice encrypting plaintexts under different keys. To rotate, the previous outer key and a freshly generated outer key is sent to the proxy to perform conversion, but the inner key is never modified. Such an approach does not satisfy the goals of key rotation.

That said, any bidirectional, ciphertext-independent updatable AE ends up also being usable as a symmetric proxy re-encryption scheme (at least as formalized by [BLMR15]).

3 Confidentiality and Integrity for Updatable Encryption

Updatable AE should provide confidentiality for messages as well as integrity of ciphertexts, even in the face of adversaries that obtain rekey tokens and re-encryptions, and that can corrupt some number of secret keys. Finding definitions that rule out trivial wins—e.g., rotating a challenge ciphertext to a compromised key, or obtaining sequences of rekey tokens that allow such rotations — is delicate. We provide a framework for doing so.

Our starting point will be a confidentiality notion which improves significantly upon the previous notion of BLMR by including additional attack vectors, and strengthening existing ones.

For ciphertext integrity, we develop a new definition, building on the usual INT-CTXT notion for standard AE [BN00]. Looking ahead, we will target unidirectional schemes that simultaneously achieve both UP-IND and UP-INT security.

We will follow a concrete security approach in which we do not strictly define security, but rather measure advantage as a function of the resources (running time and number of queries) made by an adversary. Informally, schemes are secure if no adversary with reasonable resources can achieve advantage far from zero.

3.1 Message Confidentiality

The confidentiality game UP-IND is shown in the leftmost column of Fig. 2. The adversary's goal is to guess the bit b. Success implies that a scheme leaks partial information about plaintexts. We paramaterise the game by two values t and κ. The game initialises $t+\kappa$ secret keys, κ of which are given to the adversary, and t are kept secret for use in the oracles. We label the keys by $k_1, \ldots, k_t$ for the uncompromised keys, and by $k_{t+1}, \ldots k_{t+\kappa}$ for the compromised keys. We require at least one uncompromised key, but do not necessarily require any compromised keys, i.e. $t \geq 1$ and $\kappa \geq 0$. We leave consideration of equivalences between models with many keys and few keys and between models with active and static key compromises as interesting problems for future work.

The game relies on two subroutines $\mathsf{Invalid}_{\mathsf{RK}}$ and $\mathsf{Invalid}_{\mathsf{RE}}$ to determine if a re-keygen and re-encryption query, respectively, should be allowed. These procedures are efficiently computed by the game as a function of the adversarial queries and responses. This reliance on the transcript we leave implicit in the notation to avoid clutter. Different choices of invalidity procedures gives rise to distinct definitions of security, and we explain two interesting ones in turn. Note

UP-IND	UP-INT
$b \leftarrow\!\$\ \{0,1\}$ $k_1,\ldots,k_{t+\kappa} \leftarrow\!\$\ \mathsf{KeyGen}()$ $b' \leftarrow\!\$\ \mathcal{A}^{O}(k_{t+1},\ldots,k_{t+\kappa})$ **return** $(b' = b)$	$\mathsf{win} \leftarrow \mathsf{false}$ $k_1,\ldots,k_{t+\kappa} \leftarrow\!\$\ \mathsf{KeyGen}()$ $\mathcal{A}^{O}(k_{t+1},\ldots,k_{t+\kappa})$ **return** win
Enc(i,m)	**Enc(i,m)**
return $\mathsf{Enc}(k_i,m)$	**return** $\mathsf{Enc}(k_i,m)$
ReKeyGen$(i,j,\tilde{C})$	**ReKeyGen$(i,j,\tilde{C})$**
if $\mathsf{Invalid}_{\mathsf{RK}}(i,j,\tilde{C})$ **then return** $\perp$ $\Delta_{i,j,\tilde{C}} \leftarrow\!\$\ \mathsf{ReKeyGen}(k_i,k_j,\tilde{C})$ **return** $\Delta_{i,j,\tilde{C}}$	**return** $\mathsf{ReKeyGen}(k_i,k_j,\tilde{C})$
ReEnc$(i,j,(\tilde{C},\overline{C}))$	**ReEnc$(i,j,(\tilde{C},\overline{C}))$**
$\Delta_{i,j,\tilde{C}} \leftarrow\!\$\ \mathsf{ReKeyGen}(k_i,k_j,\tilde{C})$ $C' = (\tilde{C}',\overline{C}') \leftarrow \mathsf{ReEnc}(\Delta_{i,j,\tilde{C}},(\tilde{C},\overline{C}))$ **if** $\mathsf{Invalid}_{\mathsf{RE}}(i,j,\tilde{C})$ **then return** $\tilde{C}'$ **else return** C'	$\Delta_{i,j,\tilde{C}} \leftarrow\!\$\ \mathsf{ReKeyGen}(k_i,k_j,\tilde{C})$ $C' \leftarrow \mathsf{ReEnc}(\Delta_{i,j,\tilde{C}},(\tilde{C},\overline{C}))$ **return** C'
LR(i,m_0,m_1)	**Try(i,C)**
if $i > t$ **then return** $\perp$ $C \leftarrow\!\$\ \mathsf{Enc}(k_i,m_b)$ **return** C	**if** $\mathsf{InvalidCTXT}(i,C)$ **then return** $\perp$ $M \leftarrow \mathsf{Dec}(k_i,C)$ **if** $M = \perp$ **then return** $\perp$ $\mathsf{win} \leftarrow \mathsf{true}$ **return** M

Fig. 2. Confidentiality and integrity games for updatable encryption security.

that an invalid query (as determined by $\mathsf{Invalid}_{\mathsf{RE}}$) still results in the adversary learning the ciphertext header, giving greater power to the adversary. We believe this to be an important improvement both in practice and theoretically over previous models, which consider only a partial compromise. The full compromise of a client results in the adversary playing the role of the client in the key update procedure, during which the server will return the ciphertext header. In practice, it is likely that an adversary who has initially breached the client would use this access to query related services.

Invalidity procedures. For the invalidity constraints used in UP-IND, we target a strong definition, while preventing the adversary from trivially receiving a challenge ciphertext re-encrypted to a compromised key.

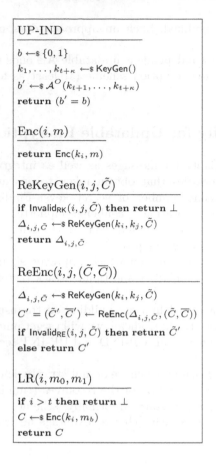

We use the ciphertext headers to determine whether a ciphertext has been derived from a challenge ciphertext. It is natural to use only the headers since these will be processed by the client when performing an update. We define a procedure $\mathsf{Derived}_{\mathsf{LR}}(i, \tilde{C})$ that outputs true should $\tilde{C}$ have been derived from the ciphertext header returned by an LR query.

Definition 3 (LR-derived headers). *We recursively define function* $\mathsf{Derived}_{\mathsf{LR}}(i, \tilde{C})$ *to output* true *iff any of the following conditions hold:*

- $\tilde{C}$ *was the ciphertext header output in response to a query* $LR(i, m_0, m_1)$
- $\tilde{C}$ *was the ciphertext header output in response to a query* $ReEnc(j, i, C')$ *and* $\mathsf{Derived}_{\mathsf{LR}}(j, \tilde{C}') = \mathsf{true}$
- $\tilde{C}$ *is the ciphertext header output by running* $\mathsf{ReEnc}(\Delta_{j,i,\tilde{C}'}, C')$ *where* $\Delta_{j,i,\tilde{C}'}$ *is the result of a query* $ReKeyGen(j, i, \tilde{C}')$ *for which* $\mathsf{Derived}_{\mathsf{LR}}(j, \tilde{C}') = \mathsf{true}$.

The predicate $\mathsf{Derived}_{\mathsf{LR}}(i, \tilde{C})$ is efficient to compute and can be computed locally by the adversary. The most efficient way to implement it is to grow a look-up table $\mathtt{T}$ indexed by a key identifier and a ciphertext header and whose entries are sets of ciphertexts. Any query to $\mathrm{LR}(i, m_0, m_1)$ updates the table by adding the returned ciphertext to the set $\mathtt{T}[i, \tilde{C}]$ where $\tilde{C}$ is the oracle's returned ciphertext header value. For a query $\mathrm{ReEnc}(j, i, C')$, if $\mathtt{T}[j, \tilde{C}']$ is not empty, then it adds the returned ciphertext to the set $\mathtt{T}[i, \tilde{C}^*]$ for $\tilde{C}^*$ the returned ciphertext header. For a query $\mathrm{ReKeyGen}(j, i, \tilde{C}')$ with return value $\Delta_{j,i,\tilde{C}'}$, apply $\mathsf{ReEnc}(\Delta_{j,i,\tilde{C}'}, C)$ for all ciphertexts C found in entry $\mathtt{T}[j, \tilde{C}']$ and add appropriate new entries to the table. In this way, one can maintain the table in worst-case time that is quadratic in the number of queries, and compute in constant time $\mathsf{Derived}_{\mathsf{LR}}(i, \tilde{C})$ by simply checking if $\mathtt{T}[i, \tilde{C}]$ is non-empty. If any call to $\mathsf{ReKeyGen}$ or ReEnc in $\mathsf{Derived}_{\mathsf{LR}}$ or the main oracle procedure returns $\bot$, then the entire procedure returns $\bot$.

Note that $\mathsf{Derived}_{\mathsf{LR}}$ relies on ReEnc being deterministic, a restriction we made in Sect. 2. To complete the definition, we specify the invalidity procedures that use $\mathsf{Derived}_{\mathsf{LR}}$ as a subroutine:

- $\mathsf{Invalid}_{\mathsf{RK}}(i, j, \tilde{C})$ outputs true if $j > t$ and $\mathsf{Derived}_{\mathsf{LR}}(i, \tilde{C}) = \mathsf{true}$. In words, the target key is compromised and $i, \tilde{C}$ derives from an LR query.
- $\mathsf{Invalid}_{\mathsf{RE}}(i, j, \tilde{C})$ outputs true if $j > t$ and $\mathsf{Derived}_{\mathsf{LR}}(i, \tilde{C}) = \mathsf{true}$. In words, the target key is compromised and $i, \tilde{C}$ derives from an LR query.

We denote the game defined by using these invalidity procedures by UP-IND. We associate to an UP-IND adversary $\mathcal{A}$ and scheme Π the advantage measure:

$$\mathbf{Adv}^{\text{up-ind}}_{\Pi,\kappa,t}(\mathcal{A}) = 2 \cdot \Pr\left[\text{UP-IND}^{\mathcal{A}}_{\Pi,\kappa,t} \Rightarrow \mathsf{true}\right] - 1.$$

This notion is very strong and bidirectional schemes cannot meet it.

Theorem 1. *Let Π be a bidirectional updatable encryption scheme. Then there exists an* UP-IND *adversary $\mathcal{A}$ that makes* 2 *queries and for which*

$$\boldsymbol{Adv}^{\textit{up-ind}}_{\Pi,\kappa,t}(\mathcal{A}) = 1$$

for any $\kappa \geq 1$ and $t \geq 1$.

Proof. We explicitly define the adversary $\mathcal{A}$. It makes a query to $C_1 = \mathrm{LR}(1, m_0, m_1)$ for arbitrary messages $m_0 \neq m_1$ and computes locally $C_{t+1} = \mathsf{Enc}(k_{t+1}, m_1)$. It then makes a query $\Delta_{t+1,1,\tilde{C}_{t+1}} = \mathrm{ReKeyGen}(t+1, 1, \tilde{C}_{t+1})$. It runs $C' = \mathsf{ReEnc}(\mathsf{Invert}(\Delta_{t+1,1,\tilde{C}_{t+1}}, C_{t+1}, C_1), C_1)$ locally and then decrypts C' using k_{t+1}. It checks whether the result is m_0 or m_1 and returns the appropriate bit. □

BLMR confidentiality. In comparison, we define invalidity procedures corresponding to those in BLMR's security notion.

- $\mathsf{InvalidBLMR_{RK}}(i, j, \tilde{C})$ outputs true if $i \leq t < j$ or $j \leq t < i$ and outputs false otherwise. In words, the query is not allowed if exactly one of the two keys is compromised.
- $\mathsf{InvalidBLMR_{RE}}(i, j, \tilde{C})$ outputs true if $j > t$ and false otherwise. In words, the query is not allowed if the target key k_j is compromised.

We denote the game defined by using these invalidity procedures by UP-IND-BI (the naming will become clear presently). We associate to an UP-IND-BI adversary $\mathcal{A}$, scheme Π, and parameters κ, t the advantage measure:

$$\mathbf{Adv}^{\text{up-ind-bi}}_{\Pi,\kappa,t}(\mathcal{A}) = 2 \cdot \Pr\left[\text{UP-IND-BI}^{\mathcal{A}}_{\Pi,\kappa,t} \Rightarrow \mathsf{true}\right] - 1\,.$$

A few observations are in order. First, it is apparent that the invalidity procedures for the BLMR notion are significantly stronger than ours, leading to a weaker security notion: the BLMR procedures are not ciphertext-specific but instead depend only on the compromise status of keys. We will show that this difference is significant. In addition, the corresponding BLMR definition did not consider leakage of the ciphertext header when $\mathsf{InvalidBLMR_{RE}}$ returns true. Second, for ciphertext-independent schemes in which $\tilde{C} = \varepsilon$ always, the BLMR definition coincides with symmetric proxy re-encryption security (as also introduced in their paper [BLMR15]). Third, the BLMR confidentiality notion does not require unidirectional security of rekey tokens because it has the strong restriction of disallowing attackers from obtaining rekey tokens $\Delta_{i,j,\tilde{C}}$ with $i > t$ (so the corresponding key is compromised), but with $j < t$ (for an uncompromised key). Thus, in principle, bidirectional schemes could meet this notion, explaining our naming convention for the notion. Finally, the BLMR notion does not require ciphertext-specific rekey tokens because the invalidity conditions are based only on keys and not on the target ciphertext.

Detailed in Appendix A.1 is a bidirectional scheme that is secure in the sense of UP-IND-BI. This result and the negative result that no bidirectional scheme can achieve UP-IND given above (Theorem 1) yields as a corollary that UP-IND-BI security is strictly weaker than UP-IND security. This illustrates the enhanced strength of our UP-IND security notion compared to the corresponding BLMR notion, UP-IND-BI.

Given that bidirectional, ciphertext-independent schemes have certain advantages in terms of performance and deployment simplicity, practitioners may prefer them in some cases. For that flexibility, one trades off control over the specificity of rekey tokens, which could be dangerous to confidentiality in some compromise scenarios.

3.2 Ciphertext Integrity

We now turn to a notion of integrity captured by the game UP-INT shown in Fig. 2. The adversary's goal is to submit a ciphertext to the Try oracle that decrypts properly. Of course, we must exclude the adversary from simply resubmitting valid ciphertexts produced by the encryption oracle, or derived from such an encryption by way of re-encryption queries or rekey tokens.

In a bit more detail, in the Try oracle, we define a predicate $\mathsf{InvalidCTXT}$ which captures whether the adversary has produced a trivial derivation of a ciphertext obtained from the encryption oracle. This fulfills a similar role to that of the $\mathsf{Invalid_{RE}}$ and $\mathsf{Invalid_{RK}}$ subroutines in the UP-IND game.

For the unidirectional security game UP-INT, we define $\mathsf{InvalidCTXT}(i, C = (\tilde{C}, \overline{C}))$ inductively, outputting true if any of the following conditions hold:

- $i > t$, i.e. k_i is known to the adversary
- $(\tilde{C}, \overline{C})$ was output in response to a query $\text{Enc}(i, m)$
- $(\tilde{C}, \overline{C})$ was output in response to a query $\text{ReEnc}(j, i, C')$ and $\mathsf{InvalidCTXT}(j, C') = \mathsf{true}$
- $(\tilde{C}, \overline{C})$ is the ciphertext output by running $\mathsf{ReEnc}(\Delta_{j,i,\tilde{C}'}, C')$ for $C' = (\tilde{C}', \overline{C}')$ where $\Delta_{j,i,\tilde{C}'}$ was the result of a query $\text{ReKeyGen}(j, i, \tilde{C}')$ and $\mathsf{InvalidCTXT}(j, C')) = \mathsf{true}$.

This predicate requires the transcript of queries thus far; to avoid clutter we leave the required transcript implicit in our notation. The definition of $\mathsf{InvalidCTXT}$ is quite permissive: it defines invalid ciphertexts as narrowly as possible, making our security notion stronger. Notably, the adversary can produce any ciphertext (valid or otherwise) using a corrupted key k_i, and use the ReKeyGen oracle to learn a token to update this ciphertext to a non-compromised key. Only the direct re-encryption of the submitted ciphertext is forbidden.

We associate to an updatable encryption scheme Π, an UP-INT adversary $\mathcal{A}$, and parameters κ, t the advantage measure:

$$\mathbf{Adv}^{\text{up-int}}_{\Pi,\kappa,t}(\mathcal{A}) = \Pr\left[\text{UP-INT}^{\mathcal{A}}_{\Pi,\kappa,t} \Rightarrow \mathsf{true}\right].$$

4 Practical Updatable AE Schemes

We first investigate the security of updatable AE schemes built using the KEM/DEM approach sketched in the introduction. Such schemes are in widespread use at present, for example in AWS's and Google's cloud storage systems, yet have received no formal analysis to date. We produce the AE-hybrid construction as a formalism of this common practice.

Using the confidentiality and integrity definitions from the previous section, we discover that this construction offers very weak security against an adversary capable of compromising keys. Indeed, we are only able to prove security when the number of compromised keys κ is equal to 0. Given the intention of key rotation this is a somewhat troubling result.

On a positive note, we show a couple of simple tweaks to the AE-hybrid which fix these issues. The resultant scheme, named KSS, offers improved security at little additional cost.

We leave to the appendix our bidirectional, ciphertext-independent scheme XOR-KEM which does not offer strong integrity guarantees but may be of interest for other applications.

4.1 Authenticated Encryption

In the following constructions we make use of authenticated encryption (AE) schemes which we define here.

Definition 4 (Authenticated encryption). *An authenticated encryption scheme π is a tuple of algorithms $(\mathcal{K}, \mathcal{E}, \mathcal{D})$. $\mathcal{K}$ is a randomised algorithm outputting keys. We denote by $\mathcal{E}_k(\cdot)$ the randomised algorithm for encryption by key k, and by $\mathcal{D}_k(\cdot)$ decryption. Decryption is a deterministic algorithm and outputs the distinguished symbol $\perp$ to denote a failed decryption.*

In keeping with our definitional choices for updatable AE, we consider randomised AE schemes rather than nonce-based ones.

We use the all-in-one authenticated encryption security definition from [RS06].

Definition 5 (Authenticated Encryption Security). *Let $\pi = (\mathcal{K}, \mathcal{E}, \mathcal{D})$ be an authenticated encryption scheme. Let Enc, Dec be oracles whose behaviors depends on hidden values $b \in \{0,1\}$ and key $k \leftarrow\!\!\$\, \mathcal{K}$. Enc takes as input a bit string m and produces $\mathcal{E}_k(m)$ when $b = 0$, and produces a random string of the same length otherwise. Dec takes as input a bit string C and produces $\mathcal{D}_k(C)$ when $b = 0$, and produces $\perp$ otherwise.*

Let $\text{AE-ROR}_\pi^\mathcal{A}$ be the game in which an adversary $\mathcal{A}$ interacts with the Enc and Dec oracles and must output a bit b'. The game outputs true *when $b = b'$. We require that the adversary not submit outputs from the Enc oracle to the Dec oracle.*

We define the advantage of $\mathcal{A}$ in the AE-ROR security game for π as:

$$\mathbf{Adv}_\pi^{\text{ae}}(\mathcal{A}) = 2 \cdot \Pr\left[\text{AE-ROR}_\pi^\mathcal{A} \Rightarrow \mathsf{true}\right] - 1.$$

Unless otherwise stated, our AE schemes will be length-regular, so that the lengths of ciphertexts depend only on the lengths of plaintexts. This ensures that the above definition also implies a standard "left-or-right" security definition.

4.2 (In-)Security of AE-Hybrid Construction

Figure 3 defines an updatable AE scheme, AE-hybrid, for any AE scheme $\pi = (\mathcal{K}, \mathcal{E}, \mathcal{D})$. This is a natural key-wrapping scheme that one might create in the absence of security definitions. It is preferred by practitioners because key rotation is straightforward and performant. Using this scheme means re-keying requires constant time and communication, independent of the length of the plaintext. In fact, we note that this scheme sees widening deployment for encrypted cloud storage services. Both Amazon Web Services [AWS] and Google Cloud Platform [Goo] use AE-hybrid to perform key rotations over encrypted customer data.

We demonstrate severe limits of AE-hybrid: when keys are compromised confidentiality and integrity cannot be recovered through re-encryption. Later we will demonstrate straightforward modifications to AE-hybrid that allow it to recover both confidentiality and integrity without impacting performance.

$\mathsf{Enc}(k, m)$	$\mathsf{ReKeyGen}(k_1, k_2, \tilde{C})$	$\mathsf{Dec}(k, (\tilde{C}, \overline{C}))$
$x \leftarrow_\$ \mathcal{K}$	$x = \mathcal{D}(k_1, \tilde{C})$	$x = \mathcal{D}(k, \tilde{C})$
$\tilde{C} \leftarrow_\$ \mathcal{E}(k, x)$	**if** $x = \perp$ **return** $\perp$	**if** $x = \perp$ **return** $\perp$
$\overline{C} \leftarrow_\$ \mathcal{E}(x, m)$	$\Delta_{1,2,\tilde{C}} \leftarrow_\$ \mathcal{E}(k_2, x)$	$m = \mathcal{D}(x, \overline{C})$
return $(\tilde{C}, \overline{C})$	**return** $\Delta_{1,2,\tilde{C}}$	**return** m

KeyGen : **return** $\mathcal{K}$
$\mathsf{ReEnc}(\Delta_{1,2,\tilde{C}}, (\tilde{C}, \overline{C}))$: **return** $(\Delta_{1,2,\tilde{C}}, \overline{C})$

Fig. 3. Algorithms for the AE-hybrid updatable AE scheme.

Theorem 2 (AE-hybrid insecurity in the UP-IND sense). *Let $\pi = (\mathcal{K}, \mathcal{E}, \mathcal{D})$ be a symmetric encryption scheme and Π be the updatable AE scheme AE-hybrid built using π as defined in Fig. 3.*

Then there exists an adversary $\mathcal{A}$ making 2 queries such that $\mathbf{Adv}^{up\text{-}ind}_{\Pi,\kappa,t}(\mathcal{A}) = 1$ for all $\kappa \geq 1$ and $t \geq 1$.

Proof. We construct a concrete adversary $\mathcal{A}$ satisfying the theorem statement.

$\mathcal{A}$ makes an initial query to $\mathrm{LR}(1, m_0, m_1)$ for distinct messages $m_0 \neq m_1$ and receives challenge ciphertext $C^* = (\mathcal{E}(k_1, x), \mathcal{E}(x, m_b))$. $\mathcal{A}$ subsequently calls $\mathrm{ReKeyGen}(1, t+1, C^*)$. k_{t+1} is corrupted and thus $\mathsf{Invalid}_{\mathsf{RK}}$ returns true, so the adversary receives the re-encrypted ciphertext header $\tilde{C}' = \mathcal{E}(k_{t+1}, x)$.

The adversary decrypts $x = \mathcal{D}(k_{t_1}, \tilde{C}')$, computes $m_b = \mathcal{D}(x, \overline{C}^*)$ and checks whether $m_b = m_0$ or m_1. □

The best one can achieve with this scheme is to prove security when $\kappa = 0$, that is, security is not degraded beyond the underlying AE scheme when the adversary does not obtain any compromised keys. However, such a weak security notion is not particularly interesting, since the intention of key rotation is to provide enhanced security in the face of key compromises. We give proofs for the weak security of the AE-hybrid scheme in the full version.

Similarly, AE-hybrid is trivially insecure in the UP-INT sense when $\kappa \geq 1$.

Theorem 3 (AE-hybrid insecurity in the UP-INT sense). *Let $\pi = (\mathcal{K}, \mathcal{E}, \mathcal{D})$ be a symmetric encryption scheme and Π be the updatable AE scheme AE-hybrid built using π as defined in Fig. 3.*

Then there exists an adversary $\mathcal{A}$ making 2 queries and one Try query such that $\mathbf{Adv}^{up\text{-}int}_{\Pi,\kappa,t}(\mathcal{A}) = 1$ for all $\kappa \geq 1$ and $t \geq 1$.

Proof. We construct a concrete adversary $\mathcal{A}$ satisfying the theorem statement.

$\mathcal{A}$ first queries $\text{Enc}(1, m)$ to obtain an encryption $C = (\mathcal{E}(k_1, x), \mathcal{E}(x, m))$, and subsequently queries $\text{ReEnc}(1, t+1, C)$, receiving the re-encryption $C' = (\mathcal{E}(k_{t+1}, x), \mathcal{E}(x, m))$. Since $\mathcal{A}$ has key k_{t+1}, $\mathcal{A}$ recovers $x = \mathcal{D}(k_{t+1}, \tilde{C}')$ by performing the decryption locally.

Finally, $\mathcal{A}$ constructs the ciphertext $C^* = (\tilde{C}, \mathcal{E}(x, m'))$ for some $m' \neq m$ and queries $\text{Try}(1, C^*)$. Since C^* is not derived from C and k_1 is not compromised, UP-INT outputs true. □

4.3 Improving AE-Hybrid

We make small modifications to the AE-hybrid construction and show that the resulting construction has both UP-IND and UP-INT security. These modifications include masking the DEM key stored inside the ciphertext header (to gain UP-IND security), and including an encrypted hash of the message (for UP-INT). We note that these modifications are straightforward to implement on top of the AE-hybrid scheme and have only minimal impact on the scheme's performance in practice.

Let $(\mathcal{K}, \mathcal{E}, \mathcal{D})$ be an AE scheme and h a hash function with ℓ_h output bits. Then we define KSS (KEM/DEM with Secret Sharing) as in Fig. 4.

Theorem 4 (UP-IND Security of KSS). *Let $\pi = (\mathcal{K}, \mathcal{E}, \mathcal{D})$ be a symmetric encryption scheme and Π be the updatable AE scheme* KSS *built using π as defined in Fig. 4. Then for any adversary $\mathcal{A}$ for the game* UP-IND*, making at most q queries to the LR oracle, there exists an adversary $\mathcal{B}$ for the AE security game where:*

$$\mathbf{Adv}^{up\text{-}ind}_{\Pi,\kappa,t}(\mathcal{A}) \leq 2(t+q) \cdot \mathbf{Adv}^{ae}_{\pi}(\mathcal{B})$$

for all $\kappa \geq 0, t \geq 1$.

For brevity, we leave the full proof to the full version, but we briefly outline the proof here. The proof proceeds in two phases. In the first phase, we use a series of t game-hops to replace ciphertext headers produced by Enc under each of t keys with random strings of the same length. We bound the difference between each game with an AE adversary. In the second phase, we use q game-hops (one for each LR query): each hop replacing encryption of the DEM with

$\mathsf{Enc}(k, m)$

$x, y \leftarrow_\$ \mathcal{K}$
$\chi = x \oplus y$
$\overline{C}^1 \leftarrow_\$ \mathcal{E}(x, m)$
$\tau = \mathcal{E}(x, h(m))$
$\tilde{C} \leftarrow_\$ \mathcal{E}(k, \chi \parallel \tau)$
return $(\tilde{C}, (y, \overline{C}^1))$

$\mathsf{ReKeyGen}(k_1, k_2, \tilde{C})$

$(\chi \parallel \tau) = \mathcal{D}(k_1, \tilde{C})$
if $(\chi \parallel \tau) = \perp$ **return** $\perp$
$y' \leftarrow_\$ \mathcal{K}$
return $(y', \mathcal{E}(k_2, (\chi \oplus y') \parallel \tau))$

$\mathsf{Dec}(k, (\tilde{C}, \overline{C}))$

$(\chi \parallel \tau) = \mathcal{D}(k, \tilde{C})$
if $(\chi \parallel \tau) = \perp$ **return** $\perp$
$x = \chi \oplus \overline{C}^0$
$m = \mathcal{D}(x, \overline{C}^1)$
if $\mathcal{D}(x, \tau) \neq h(m)$ **then**
  return $\perp$
return m

$\mathsf{KeyGen}()$: **return** $k \leftarrow \mathcal{K}$
$\mathsf{ReEnc}(\Delta_{1,2,\tilde{C}}, (\tilde{C}, \overline{C}))$: **return** $(\Delta^1_{1,2,\tilde{C}}, (\overline{C}^0 \oplus \Delta^0_{1,2,\tilde{C}}, \overline{C}^1))$

Fig. 4. Algorithms for the KSS updatable AE scheme.

a call to an AE encryption oracle. Again, we bound the difference between each game with an AE adversary and in the end we get the stated result.

Our modification to include an encrypted hash of the ciphertext is in order to provide a measure of integrity protection. As we will see in the following theorem, collision resistance of the hash function is sufficient to provide UP-INT security, since the hash itself is integrity-protected by the AE encryption of the KEM. The hash itself is encrypted in order to avoid compromise of the ciphertext header being sufficient to distinguish messages.

We achieve collision resistance by assuming h to be a random oracle. However, this assumption could be avoided by either re-using the DEM key x to additionally key the hash function.

We note that this combination of hash function and AE encryption is used to provide an additional integrity mechanism that works for any AE scheme. However, some schemes may be able to avoid this additional computation by re-using components of the AE encryption. For example, if an encrypt-then-MAC scheme is used such that the encryption and MAC keys are both uniquely derived from the DEM key x, then we conjecture that the MAC itself can be used in place of the encrypted hash.

Theorem 5 (UP-INT **Security of** KSS)**.** *Let* $\pi = (\mathcal{K}, \mathcal{E}, \mathcal{D})$ *be a symmetric encryption scheme,* h *be a cryptographic hash function modelled as a random oracle with output length* ℓ_h*, and* Π *be the updatable AE scheme* KSS *built using* π *and* h *as defined in Fig. 4. Then for any polynomial-time adversary* $\mathcal{A}$*, making at most* q_h *queries to the random oracle* h*, there exists an adversary* $\mathcal{B}$ *for the AE security game where:*

$$\boldsymbol{Adv}^{up\text{-}int}_{\Pi,\kappa,t}(\mathcal{A}) \leq t \cdot \boldsymbol{Adv}^{ae}_{\pi}(\mathcal{B}) + \frac{q_h^2}{2^{\ell_h}}$$

for all $\kappa \geq 0, t \geq 1$.

This proof follows a similar format to the previous one: after t game hops to establish the integrity of the ciphertext headers using t AE adversaries, the adversary's success depends on finding two ciphertexts which produce a collision in h. We leave the full proof to the full version.

5 Indistinguishability of Re-encryptions

The KSS scheme in the previous section achieves message confidentiality and ciphertext integrity, even though the actual DEM key is not modified in the course of performing a rotation. Modifying the scheme to ensure the DEM key is also rotated is non-trivial, requiring either significant communication complexity (linear in the length of the encrypted message) between the key server and storage, or the introduction of more advanced primitives such as key- homomorphic PRFs. The question that arises is whether or not changing DEM keys leaves KSS vulnerable to attacks not captured by the definitions introduced thus far.

BLMR's brief treatment of updatable encryption attempts to speak to this issue by requiring that all randomness be refreshed during a rotation. Intuitively this would seem to improve security, but the goal they formalize for this, detailed below, is effectively a correctness condition (i.e., it does not seem to account for adversarial behaviors). It doesn't help clarify what attacks would be ruled out by changing DEM keys.

Exfiltration attacks. We identify an issue with our KSS scheme (and the other schemes in the preceding section) in the form of an attack that is not captured by the confidentiality definitions introduced so far. Consider our simple KSS scheme in the context of our motivating key server and storage service application (described in Sect. 2). Suppose an attacker compromises for some limited time both the key server and the storage service. Then for each ciphertext $(\tilde{C}, \overline{C})$ encrypted under a key k_1, the attacker can compute the DEM key $y \oplus \chi = x$ and exfiltrate it.

Suppose the compromise is cleaned up, and the service immediately generates new keys and rotates all ciphertexts to new secret keys. For the KSS scheme, the resulting ciphertexts will still be later decryptable using the previously exfiltrated DEM keys.

Although a confidentiality issue—the attacker later obtains access to plaintext data they should not have—our UP-IND security notion (and, by implication, the weaker BLMR confidentiality notion) do not capture these attacks. Technically this is because the security game does not allow a challenge ciphertext to be encrypted to a compromised key (or rotated to one). Intuitively, the UP-IND notion gives up on protecting the plaintexts underlying such ciphertexts, as the attacker in the above scenario already had access to the plaintext in the first phase of the attack.

One might therefore argue that this attack is not very important. All of the plaintext data eventually at risk of later decryption was already exposed to the adversary in the first time period because she had access to both the key and ciphertexts. But quantitatively there is a difference: for a given ciphertext an adversary in the first time period can exfiltrate just $|x|$ bits per ciphertext to later recover as much plaintext as she likes, whereas the trivial attack may require exfiltrating the entire plaintext.

The chosen-message attack game of UP-IND does not capture different time periods in which the adversary knows plaintexts in the first time period but "forgets them" in the next. One could explicitly model this, perhaps via a two-stage game with distinct adversaries in each stage, but such games are complex and often difficult to reason about (cf., [RSS11]). We instead develop what we believe is a more intuitive route that asks that the re-encryption of a ciphertext should leak nothing about the *ciphertext* that was re-encrypted. We use an indistinguishability-style definition to model this. The interpretation of our definition is that any information derivable from a ciphertext (and its secret key) before a re-encryption isn't helpful in attacking the re-encrypted version.

Re-encryption indistinguishability. We formalize this idea via the game shown in Fig. 5. The adversary is provided with a left-or-right *re-encryption* oracle, ReLR, instead of the usual left-or-right encryption oracle, in addition to the usual collection of compromised keys, a re-encryption oracle, encryption oracle, and rekey token generation oracle. We assume that the adversary always submits ciphertext pairs such that $|C_0| = |C_1|$.

UP-REENC

$b \leftarrow\$ \{0,1\}$
$k_1, \ldots, k_{t+\kappa} \leftarrow\$ \mathsf{KeyGen}()$
$b' \leftarrow\$ \mathcal{A}^{O}(k_{t+1}, \ldots, k_{t+\kappa})$
return $(b' = b)$

$\text{Enc}(i, m)$

return $\mathsf{Enc}(k_i, m)$

$\text{ReKeyGen}(i, j, \tilde{C})$

if $\mathsf{Invalid_{RK}}(i, j, \tilde{C})$ **then return** $\perp$
$\Delta_{i,j,\tilde{C}} \leftarrow\$ \mathsf{ReKeyGen}(k_i, k_j, \tilde{C})$
return $\Delta_{i,j,\tilde{C}}$

$\text{ReEnc}(i, j, (\tilde{C}, \overline{C}))$

$\Delta_{i,j,\tilde{C}} \leftarrow\$ \mathsf{ReKeyGen}(k_i, k_j, \tilde{C})$
$C' = (\tilde{C}', \overline{C}') \leftarrow \mathsf{ReEnc}(\Delta_{i,j,\tilde{C}}, (\tilde{C}, \overline{C}))$
if $\mathsf{Invalid_{RE}}(i, j, \tilde{C})$ **then return** $\tilde{C}'$
else return C'

$\text{ReLR}(i, j, C_0, C_1)$

if $j > t$ **or** $|C_0| \neq |C_1|$ **then return** $\perp$
for $\beta \in \{0,1\}$ **do**
  $\Delta_{i,j,\tilde{C}_\beta} \leftarrow\$ \mathsf{ReKeyGen}(k_i, k_j, \tilde{C}_\beta)$
  $C'_\beta \leftarrow \mathsf{ReEnc}(\Delta_{i,j,\tilde{C}_\beta}, C_\beta)$
  if $C'_\beta = \perp$ **then return** $\perp$
return C'_b

Fig. 5. The game used to define re-encryption indistinguishability.

To avoid trivial wins, the game must disallow the adversary from simply re-encrypting the challenge to a corrupted key. Hence we define a $\mathsf{Derived_{ReLR}}$ predicate, which is identical to the $\mathsf{Derived_{LR}}$ predicated defined in Sect. 3 for

UP-IND security, except that it uses the ReLR challenge oracle. We give it in full detail in the next definition.

Definition 6 (ReLR-derived headers). *We recursively define the function* $\mathsf{Derived}_{\mathsf{ReLR}}(i, \tilde{C})$ *to output* true *iff* $\tilde{C} \neq \varepsilon$ *and any of the following conditions hold:*

- $\tilde{C}$ *was the ciphertext header output in response to a query* $ReLR(i, C_0, C_1)$*.*
- $\tilde{C}$ *was the ciphertext header output in response to a query* $ReEnc(j, i, C')$ *and* $\mathsf{Derived}_{\mathsf{ReLR}}(j, \tilde{C}') = \mathsf{true}$.
- $\tilde{C}$ *is the ciphertext header output by running* $\mathsf{ReEnc}(\Delta_{j,i,\tilde{C}'}, C')$ *where* $\Delta_{j,i,\tilde{C}'}$ *is the result of a query* $ReKeyGen(j, i, C')$ *for which* $\mathsf{Derived}_{\mathsf{ReLR}}(j, \tilde{C}') = \mathsf{true}$.

Then the subroutines $\mathsf{Invalid}_{\mathsf{RK}}, \mathsf{Invalid}_{\mathsf{RE}}$ used in the game output true if $\mathsf{Derived}_{\mathsf{ReLR}}(i, \tilde{C})$ outputs true and $j > t$. We associate to an updatable encryption scheme Π, UP-REENC adversary $\mathcal{A}$, and parameters κ, t the advantage measure:

$$\mathbf{Adv}^{\text{up-reenc}}_{\Pi,\kappa,t}(\mathcal{A}) = 2 \cdot \Pr\left[\text{UP-REENC}^{\mathcal{A}}_{\Pi,\kappa,t} \Rightarrow \mathsf{true}\right] - 1\,.$$

Informally, an updatable encryption scheme is UP-REENC secure if no adversary can achieve advantage far from zero given reasonable resources (run time, queries, and number of target keys).

Notice that exfiltration attacks as discussed informally above would not apply to a scheme that meets UP-REENC security. Suppose otherwise, that the exfiltration still worked. Then one could build an UP-REENC adversary that worked as follows. It obtains two encryptions of different messages under a compromised key, calculates the DEM key (or whatever other information is useful for later decryption) and then submits the ciphertexts to the ReLR oracle, choosing as target a non-compromised key ($j \leq t$). Upon retrieving the ciphertext, it uses the DEM key to decrypt, and checks which message was encrypted. Of course our notion covers many other kinds of attacks, ruling out even re-encryption that allows a single bit of information to leak.

BLMR re-encryption security. BLMR introduced a security goal that we will call basic re-encryption indistinguishability.[1] In words, it asks that the distribution of a ciphertext and its re-encryption should be identical to the distribution of a ciphertext and a re-encryption of a distinct ciphertext of the same message. More formally we have the following experiment, parameterized by a bit b and message m.

[1] BLMR called this ciphertext independence, but we reserve that terminology for schemes that do not require ciphertexts during token generation as per Sect. 2.

$\underline{\text{UP-REENC0}_{b,m}}$

$k_0, k_1 \leftarrow\!\!\$\ \mathsf{KeyGen}()$
for $i \in [0,1]$ **do**
  $C_i \leftarrow\!\!\$\ \mathsf{Enc}(k_i, m)$
  $\Delta_{0,1,\tilde{C}_i} \leftarrow\!\!\$\ \mathsf{ReKeyGen}(k_0, k_1, \tilde{C}_i)$
  $C'_i \leftarrow\!\!\$\ \mathsf{ReEnc}(\Delta_{1,0,\tilde{C}_i}, C_i)$
return (C_1, C'_b)

Then BLMR require that for all m and all ciphertext pairs (C, C')

$$|\Pr[\text{UP-REENC0}_{0,m} \Rightarrow (C, C')] - \Pr[\text{UP-REENC0}_{1,m} \Rightarrow (C, C')]| = 0$$

where the probabilities are over the coins used in the experiments.

This goal misses a number of subtleties which are captured by our definition. Our definition permits the adversary, for example, to submit *any* pair of ciphertexts to the ReLR oracle. This includes ciphertexts which are encryptions of distinct messages, and even maliciously formed ciphertexts which may not even decrypt correctly. It is simple to exhibit a scheme that meets the BLMR notion but trivially is insecure under ours.[2]

On the other hand, suppose a distinguisher exists that can with some probability ϵ distinguish between the outputs of UP-REENC0$_{1,m}$ and UP-REENC0$_{0,m}$ for some m. Then there exists an adversary against our UP-REENC notion which achieves advantage ϵ. This can be seen by the following simple argument. The adversary gets $C \leftarrow\!\!\$\ \mathsf{Enc}(1,m)$, $C' \leftarrow\!\!\$\ \mathsf{Enc}(1,m)$ and submits the tuple $(1, 2, C, C')$ to its ReLR oracle and receives a re-encryption of one of the ciphertexts, C^*. The adversary then runs the distinguisher on (C, C^*) and outputs whatever the distinguisher guesses. If the distinguisher is computationally efficient, then so too is the UP-REENC adversary.

6 Revisiting the BLMR Scheme

The fact that the simple KEM/DEM schemes of Sect. 4 fail to meet re-encryption security begs the question of finding new schemes that achieve it, as well as UP-IND and UP-INT security. Our starting point is the BLMR construction of an updatable encryption from key-homomorphic PRFs. Their scheme does not (nor did it attempt to) provide integrity guarantees, and so trivially does not meet UP-INT. But before seeing how to adapt it to become suitable as an updatable AE scheme, including whether it meets our stronger notions of UP-IND and UP-REENC security, we first revisit the claims of UP-IND-BI security from [BLMR15].

As mentioned in the introduction, BLMR claim that the scheme can be shown secure, and sketch a proof of UP-IND-BI security. Unfortunately the proof sketch

[2] Such a scheme can be constructed by adding a redundant ciphertext bit to an existing UP-IND-secure scheme, with the redundant bit being randomly generated during encryption and preserved across re-encryptions.

contains a bug, as we explain below. Interestingly revelation of this bug does not lead to a direct attack on the scheme, and at the same time we could not determine if the proof could be easily repaired. Instead we are able to show that a proof is unlikely to exist.

Our main result of this section is the following: giving a proof showing the BLMR UP-IND-BI security would imply the existence of a reduction showing that (standard) IND-CPA security implies circular security [BRS03, CL01] for a simple KEM/DEM style symmetric encryption scheme. The latter seems quite unlikely given the known negative results about circular security [ABBC10, CGH12], suggesting that the BLMR scheme is not likely to be provably secure.

First we recall some basic tools that BLMR use to build their scheme.

Definition 7 (Key-homomorphic PRF [BLMR15]). *Consider an efficiently computable function $F : \mathcal{K} \times \mathcal{X} \rightarrow \mathcal{Y}$ such that $(\mathcal{K}, \oplus)$ and $(\mathcal{Y}, \otimes)$ are both groups. We say that the tuple $(F, \oplus, \otimes)$ is a* key-homomorphic PRF *if the following properties hold:*

1. *F is a secure pseudorandom function.*
2. *For every $k_1, k_2 \in \mathcal{K}$ and every $x \in \mathcal{X}$, $F(k_1, x) \otimes F(k_2, x) = F(k_1 \oplus k_2, x)$.*

A simple example in the ROM is the function $F(k, x) = H(x)^k$ where $\mathcal{Y} = \mathbb{G}$ is a group in which the decisional Diffie–Hellman assumption holds.

As an application of key-homomorphic PRFs, BLMR proposed the following construction. The construction follows a similar approach to the AE-hybrid scheme, but by using a key-homomorphic PRF in place of regular encryption the data encryption key can also be rotated.

Definition 8 (BLMR scheme). *Let π be a symmetric-key IND-CPA encryption scheme $\pi = (\mathcal{KG}, \mathcal{E}, \mathcal{D})$. Furthermore, let $F : \mathcal{K} \times \mathcal{X} \rightarrow \mathcal{Y}$ be a key-homomorphic PRF where $(\mathcal{K}, +)$ and $(\mathcal{Y}, +)$ are groups.*

The BLMR scheme is the tuple of algorithms (KeyGen, Enc, ReKeyGen, ReEnc, Dec) defined as follows:

- $\mathsf{KeyGen}()$: returns $k \leftarrow \mathcal{KG}()$.
- $\mathsf{Enc}(k, m)$: samples a random $x \leftarrow_{\$} \mathcal{K}$ and returns $\tilde{C} = \mathcal{E}(k, x)$, and $\overline{C} = (m_1 + F(x, 1), \ldots, m_\ell + F(x, \ell))$.
- $\mathsf{ReKeyGen}(k_1, k_2, \tilde{C})$: computes $x = \mathcal{D}(k_1, \tilde{C})$, samples a random $x' \leftarrow_{\$} \mathcal{K}$ and returns $\Delta_{1,2,\tilde{C}} = (\tilde{C}' = \mathcal{E}(k_2, x'), x' - x)$.
- $\mathsf{ReEnc}(\Delta_{1,2,\tilde{C}}, (\tilde{C}, \overline{C}))$: parses token as $\Delta_{1,2,\tilde{C}} = (\tilde{C}', y)$, computes $\overline{C}' = (\overline{C}_1 + F(y, 1), \ldots \overline{C}_\ell + F(y, l))$ and returns $(\tilde{C}' \overline{C}')$.
- $\mathsf{Dec}(k, (\tilde{C}, \overline{C}))$: computes $x = \mathcal{D}(\tilde{C})$ and returns $m = (\overline{C}_1 - F(x, 1), \ldots \overline{C}_\ell - F(x, l))$.

Note that encryption here essentially performs a key wrapping step followed by CTR mode encryption using the wrapped key x and PRF F.

6.1 Negative Result About Provable UP-IND Security of BLMR

BLMR sketch a proof for the security of this construction in the UP-IND-BI model (as we refer to it). However, the proof misses a subtle point: the interaction with the ReKeyGen oracle behaves similarly to a decryption oracle and the informal argument given that the IND-CPA security of the KEM is sufficient to argue security is wrong. In fact, the ReCrypt scheme seems unlikely to be provably secure even in our basic security model. To argue this, we show that proving security of the BLMR scheme implies the 1-circular security of a specific KEM/DEM construction. Figure 6 depicts the security game capturing a simple form of 1-circular security for an encryption scheme $\pi = (\mathcal{KG}, \mathcal{E}, \mathcal{D})$.

While our main result here (Theorem 6), can be stated for the BLMR scheme as described earlier, for the sake of simplicity we instead give the result for the special case of using a simple one-time pad DEM instead of the key-homomorphic PRF. This is a trivial example of what BLMR call a key-homomorphic PRG, and their theorem statement covers this construction as well. We will show that proving security for this special case is already problematic, and this therefore suffices to call into question their (more general) theorem. Thus encryption becomes $\mathsf{Enc}(k, m) = \mathcal{E}(k, r), r \oplus m$ where $\mathcal{E}$ is an IND-CPA secure KEM. We assume $|m| = n$. We then have $\mathsf{ReKeyGen}(k_1, k_2, \tilde{C}) = (\mathcal{E}(k_2, r'), r' \oplus \mathcal{D}(k_1, \tilde{C}))$. We have the following theorem:

Theorem 6. *If one can reduce the* ReCrypt UP-IND-BI-*security to the IND-CPA security of $\mathcal{E}$, then one can show a reduction that* Enc *is 1-circular secure assuming $\mathcal{E}$ is IND-CPA.*

Proof. We start by introducing a slight variant of $\mathcal{E}$, denoted $\overline{\mathcal{E}}$, shown in Fig. 6. It adds a bit to the ciphertext[3] that is read during decryption: if the bit is 1

Game 1-circular	$\overline{\mathcal{E}}(k, m)$

$b \leftarrow\$ \{0, 1\}$
$k \leftarrow\$ \mathcal{KG}()$
if $b = 1$ **then**
  $C \leftarrow\$ \mathsf{Enc}(k, k)$
else
  $U \leftarrow\$ \{0, 1\}^n$
  $C \leftarrow\$ \mathsf{Enc}(k, U)$
$b' \leftarrow\$ \mathcal{A}(C)$
return $(b = b')$
	return $\mathcal{E}(k, m) \| 0$
	
	$\overline{\mathcal{D}}(k, C \| b)$
	if $(b = 0)$ **then**
	  return $\mathcal{D}(k, C)$
	else
	  return $k \oplus \mathcal{D}(k, C)$

Fig. 6. Left: The 1-circular security game. Right: Definition of $\overline{\mathcal{E}}, \overline{\mathcal{D}}$ used in the proof of Theorem 6.

[3] Notice that this scheme is not tidy in the sense of [NRS14]. While that doesn't affect the implications of our analysis—BLMR make no assumptions about tidiness—finding a tidy counter-example is an interesting open question.

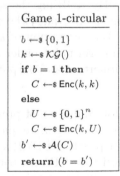

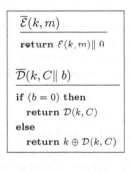

$\mathcal{B}^{\mathrm{LR,ReKeyGen}}$

$U \leftarrow_{\$} \{0,1\}^n$
$(\tilde{C}\|0, \overline{C}) \leftarrow_{\$} \mathrm{LR}(1, U, 0^n)$
$(\tilde{C}'\|0, \overline{C}') \leftarrow_{\$} \mathsf{ReKeyGen}(1, 1, \tilde{C}\|\, 1)$
$b' \leftarrow_{\$} \mathcal{A}(\tilde{C}'\|0, \overline{C} + \overline{C}')$
return b'

Fig. 7. Adversary $\mathcal{B}$ for UP-IND using as a subroutine the adversary $\mathcal{A}$ attacking 1-circular security of EncBad.

then decryption outputs the secret key xor'd with the plaintext. Let EncBad be the same as Enc above but using $\overline{\mathcal{E}}$, i.e., $\mathsf{EncBad}(k, m) = \overline{\mathcal{E}}(k, r), r \oplus m$ and $\mathsf{ReKeyGenBad}(k_1, k_2, C) = \overline{\mathcal{E}}(k_2, r'), r' \oplus \overline{\mathcal{D}}(k_1, C)$.

If $\mathcal{E}$ is IND-CPA then $\overline{\mathcal{E}}$ is as well. Thus if $\overline{\mathcal{E}}$ is IND-CPA, then the security claim of BLMR implies that EncBad is UP-IND-BI. We will now show that UP-IND-BI security of EncBad implies the 1-circular security of EncBad. In turn it's easy to see that if EncBad is 1-circular secure then so too is Enc, and, putting it all together, the claim of BLMR implies a proof that IND-CPA of $\mathcal{E}$ gives 1-circular security of Enc.

It remains to show that UP-IND-BI security implies EncBad 1-circular security. Let $\mathcal{A}$ be a 1-circular adversary against EncBad. Then we build an adversary $\mathcal{B}$ against the UP-IND security of EncBad. It is shown in Fig. 7. The adversary makes an LR query on a uniform message and the message 0^n. If the UP-IND-BI challenge bit is 1 then it gets back a ciphertext $C_1 = (\overline{\mathcal{E}}(k_1, r)\|0, r \oplus U)$ and if it is 0 then $C_0 = (\overline{\mathcal{E}}(k_1, r)\|0, r)$. Next it queries ReKeyGen oracle on the first component of the returned ciphertext but with the trailing bit switched to 1. It asks for a rekey token for rotating from k_1 back to k_1. The value returned by this query is equal to $\overline{\mathcal{E}}(k_1, r')\|0, r' \oplus k_1 \oplus r$. By XOR'ing the second component with the second component returned from the LR query the adversary gets finally a ciphertext that is, in the left world, the encryption of k_1 under itself and, in the right world, the encryption of a uniform point under k_1. Adversary $\mathcal{B}$ runs a 1-circular adversary $\mathcal{A}$ on the final ciphertext and outputs whatever $\mathcal{A}$ outputs. □

The above result uses 1-circular security for simplicity of presentation, but one can generalize the result to longer cycles by making more queries.

The result is relative, only showing that a proof of BLMR's claim implies another reduction between circular security and IND-CPA security for the particular KEM/DEM scheme Enc above. It is possible that this reduction exists, however it seems unlikely. Existing counter-examples show IND-CPA schemes that are not circular-secure [KRW15]. While these counter-examples do not have the same form as the specific scheme under consideration, it may be that one can build a suitable counter-example with additional effort.

7 An Updatable AE Scheme with Re-encryption Indistinguishability

We first point out that one can avoid the issues raised in Sect. 6 by replacing the IND-CPA KEM with a proper AE scheme. This does not yet, however, address integrity of the full encryption scheme. To provide integrity overall, we can include a hash of the message in the ciphertext header. However, to prevent this from compromising confidentiality during re-keying, we further mask the hash by an extra PRF output.

This amended construction—which we refer to as ReCrypt—is detailed in Fig. 8. It uses an AE scheme $\pi = (\mathcal{KG}, \mathcal{E}, \mathcal{D})$, a key-homomorphic PRF $F : \mathcal{K} \times \mathcal{X} \rightarrow \mathcal{Y}$, and a hash function $h : \{0,1\}^* \rightarrow \mathcal{Y}$.

In the remainder of this section we show that the new scheme meets our strongest security notions for updatable encryption. We then assess the viability of using this scheme in practice, discussing how to instantiate F for high performance and reporting on performance of the full scheme.

7.1 Security of ReCrypt

We state three security theorems for ReCrypt: UP-IND, UP-INT, and UP-REENC notions (proofs found in the full version). The proof of UP-INT relies on the collision resistance of the hash h, while the other two proofs

KeyGen()

$k \leftarrow\$ \mathcal{KG}()$
return k

Enc(k, m)

$x, y \leftarrow\$ \mathcal{K}$
$\chi = x + y$
$\tau = h(m) + F(x, 0)$
$\tilde{C} = \mathcal{E}(k, (\chi, \tau))$
for $1 \leq l \leq \ell$
  $\overline{C}_l = m_l + F(x, l)$
return $(\tilde{C}, \overline{C} = (y, \overline{C}_1, \ldots, \overline{C}_\ell))$

ReKeyGen$(k_i, k_j, \tilde{C})$

$(\chi, \tau) = \mathcal{D}(k_i, \tilde{C})$
if $(\chi, \tau) = \perp$ **return** $\perp$
$x', y' \leftarrow\$ \mathcal{K}$
$\chi' = \chi + x' + y'$
$\tau' = \tau + F(x', 0)$
$\tilde{C}' \leftarrow\$ \mathcal{E}(k_j, (\chi', \tau'))$
return $\Delta_{i,j,\tilde{C}} = (\tilde{C}', x', y')$

ReEnc$(\Delta_{i,j,\tilde{C}}, (\tilde{C}, \overline{C}))$

$(\tilde{C}', x', y') = \Delta_{i,j,\tilde{C}}$
$y = \overline{C}_0$
for $1 \leq l \leq \ell$
  $\overline{C}'_l = \overline{C}_l + F(x', l)$
return $(\tilde{C}', \overline{C}' = (y + y', \ldots, \overline{C}'_\ell))$

Dec$(k, (\tilde{C}, \overline{C}))$

$(\chi, \tau) \leftarrow\$ \mathcal{D}(k, \tilde{C})$
if $(\chi, \tau) = \perp$ **return** $\perp$
$y = \overline{C}_0$
for $1 \leq l \leq \ell$
  $m_l = \overline{C}_l - F(\chi - y, l)$
if $h(m) + F(\chi - y, 0) = \tau$ **then**
  return $m = (m_1, \ldots, m_\ell)$
else
  return $\perp$

Fig. 8. The ReCrypt scheme.

do not. For simplicity, and because we will later instantiate the PRF F in the Random Oracle Model (ROM), we model h as a random oracle throughout our analysis. This modelling of h could be avoided using the approach of Rogaway [Rog06], since concrete collision-producing adversaries can be be extracted from our proofs. Note also that the *almost* key-homomorphic PRF construction in the standard model presented by BLMR would not achieve UP-REENC since the number of re-encryptions is leaked by the ciphertext, allowing an adversary to distinguish two re-encryptions.

Theorem 7 (**UP-IND security of** ReCrypt)**.** *Let* $\pi = (\mathcal{KG}, \mathcal{E}, \mathcal{D})$ *be an AE scheme,* $F : \mathcal{K} \times \mathcal{X} \to \mathcal{Y}$ *be a key-homomorphic PRF, and let* Π *be the* ReCrypt *scheme as depicted in Fig. 8.*

Then for any adversary $\mathcal{A}$ *against* Π*, there exist adversaries* $\mathcal{B}$*,* $\mathcal{C}$ *such that*

$$\mathbf{Adv}^{\text{up-ind}}_{\Pi,\kappa,t}(\mathcal{A}) \leq 2t \cdot \mathbf{Adv}^{\text{ae}}_{\pi}(\mathcal{B}) + 2 \cdot \mathbf{Adv}^{\text{prf}}_{F}(\mathcal{C})$$

for all $\kappa \geq 0, t \geq 1$.

Theorem 8 (**UP-INT security of** ReCrypt)**.** *Let* $\pi = (\mathcal{KG}, \mathcal{E}, \mathcal{D})$ *be an AE scheme,* $F : \mathcal{K} \times \mathcal{X} \to \mathcal{Y}$ *be a key-homomorphic PRF,* h *be a cryptographic hash function modelled as a random oracle with outputs in* $\mathcal{Y}$*, and let* Π *be the* ReCrypt *scheme as depicted in Fig. 8.*

Then for any adversary $\mathcal{A}$ *against* Π*, there exists an adversary* $\mathcal{B}$ *such that*

$$\mathbf{Adv}^{\text{up-int}}_{\Pi,\kappa,t}(\mathcal{A}) \leq 2t \cdot \mathbf{Adv}^{\text{ae}}_{\pi}(\mathcal{B}) + \frac{q^2 + q_h^2}{|\mathcal{Y}|} + \frac{q^2}{|\mathcal{X}| \cdot |\mathcal{Y}|}$$

for all $\kappa \geq 0, t \geq 1$*, where the adversary makes* q_h *queries to* h*, and* q *oracle queries.*

Theorem 9 (**UP-REENC security of** ReCrypt)**.** *Let* $\pi = (\mathcal{KG}, \mathcal{E}, \mathcal{D})$ *be an AE scheme,* $F : \mathcal{K} \times \mathcal{X} \to \mathcal{Y}$ *be a key-homomorphic PRF, and let* Π *be the* ReCrypt *scheme as depicted in Fig. 8.*

Then for any adversary $\mathcal{A}$ *against* Π*, there exist adversaries* $\mathcal{B}$*,* $\mathcal{C}$ *such that*

$$\mathbf{Adv}^{\text{up-reenc}}_{\Pi,\kappa,t}(\mathcal{A}) \leq 2t \cdot \mathbf{Adv}^{\text{ae}}_{\pi}(\mathcal{B}) + 2 \cdot \mathbf{Adv}^{\text{prf}}_{F}(\mathcal{C})$$

for all $\kappa \geq 0, t \geq 1$.

The proofs for UP-IND, UP-INT and UP-REENC follow a similar structure, proceeding in two phases. In the first phase, the AE security of π is used to show that the value of x is hidden from an adversary. In the second phase, the PRF security of F is used to show that outputs are indistinguishable to an adversary with no knowledge of x. Full proofs are found in the full version.

7.2 Instantiating the Key-Homomorphic PRF

We dedicate the remainder of this section to analysis of ReCrypt for use in practical scenarios. We delve into the implementation details of the key-homomorphic

PRF in order to further explore some of the subtle security issues that arise when instantiating our scheme in practice.

While BLMR construct key-homomorphic PRFs in the standard model, a more efficient route is to use the classic ROM construction due originally to Naor, Pinkas, and Reingold [NPR99] in which $F(k, x) = k \cdot H(x)$ where H is modelled as a random oracle $H : \mathcal{X} \to \mathbb{G}$ and $\mathbb{G}$ is a group (now written **additively**, since we shall shortly move to the elliptic curve setting) in which the decisional Diffie–Hellman (DDH) assumption holds.

Instantiation details. We will use (a subgroup of) $\mathbb{G} = E(\mathbb{F}_p)$, an elliptic curve over a prime order finite field. However, recall that encryption is done block-wise as $\overline{C}_l = m_l + F(x, l)$. Implicitly, it is assumed that messages m are already in the group $\mathbb{G}$. To make a practical scheme for encrypting data represented as bitstrings, we additionally require an encoding function $\sigma : \{0,1\}^n \to \mathbb{G}$.

Additionally, the existence of such a function proves useful in the construction of the PRF: we show how to instantiate the random oracle H using a regular cryptographic hash function $h : \{0,1\}^* \to \{0,1\}^n$, modelled as a random oracle, together with the encoding function. We also use this definition of H for the instantiation of the random oracle used in the computation of the ciphertext header, which was needed to provide integrity. However, we add a unique prefix to inputs to either computation of H to provide separation.

For a suitable message encoding function, we of course require the function and its inverse to be efficiently computable. However, in addition we also require the inverse to be uniquely defined. Suppose σ^{-1} is defined for all $P \in \mathbb{G}$; then there is the possibility of creating a conflict with the integrity requirements. For example, suppose we have two points P, P' such that $\sigma^{-1}(P) = \sigma^{-1}(P') = m$. Then an adversary can potentially exploit this collision in σ^{-1} to construct a forged ciphertext. While this might not threaten the integrity of the plaintext, it would become problematic for ciphertext integrity.

One solution to this is to add a check to σ to verify that $\sigma(\sigma^{-1}(P)) = P$, and return $\perp$ if not.

In the following theorem, we prove the security of the ReCrypt scheme when instantiated with a carefully chosen encoding function, and the Naor-Pinkas-Reingold PRF.

Theorem 10. *Let $\mathbb{G} = E(\mathbb{F}_p)$ be an elliptic curve of prime order in which the DDH assumption holds. For $n \in \mathcal{O}(\log \#\mathbb{G})$ let the encoding function $\sigma : \{0,1\}^n \to \mathbb{G}$ be an injective mapping such that for any point P outside of the range, i.e. $P \notin \{\sigma(x) : x \in \{0,1\}^n\}$, then $\sigma^{-1}(P) = \perp$.*

Let $H : \{0,1\}^n \to \mathbb{G}$ be defined as $H(x) = \sigma(h(x))$ for a cryptographic hash function h modelled as a random oracle.

Then $F(k, x) = k \cdot H(x)$ is a key-homomorphic PRF.

By rejecting encoded messages outside of the range of σ, we effectively restrict σ to be a bijection from $\{0,1\}^n$ to a subset of $\mathbb{G}$. Given this, it is easy to see instantiating ReCrypt with this message encoding and key-homomorphic PRF results in a secure updatable AE scheme as proven above.

We identified two candidates for the message encoding function. The first uses rejection sampling, in which a bitstring is first treated as an element of $\mathbb{F}_p$, with some redundancy, and subsequently mapped to the elliptic curve. If a matching point cannot be found on the curve, the value is incremented (using the redundancy) and another attempt is made. Repeating this process results in a probabilistic method.

Corollary 1. *Define the encoding function $\sigma : x \mapsto E(\mathbb{F}_p)$ mapping bitstrings of length n to group elements by first equating the bitstring as an element $x \in \mathbb{F}_p$. Let $\bar{x}$ be the minimum value of the set $\{x + i \cdot 2^n \;:\; 0 \leq i < \lfloor \frac{p}{2^n} \rfloor\}$ such that $(\bar{x}, y) \in E(\mathbb{F}_p)$ for some y. Then define $\sigma(x)$ to be the point $(\bar{x}, \bar{y})$ where $\bar{y} = \min\{y, p - y\}$.*

The inverse mapping $\sigma^{-1}(P)$ is computed by taking the x-coordinate and reducing mod 2^n. I.e. set $x' = x(P) \mod 2^n$ and verify $P \neq \sigma(x')$, otherwise return $\perp$.

Then σ satisfies the requirements of Theorem 10.

See the full version Theorem 10 and Corollary 1.

As an alternative to rejection sampling, an injective mapping can be used directly, again first treating the bitstring as an element of $\mathbb{F}_p$. Some examples include the SWU algorithm [SvdW06], Icart's function [Ica09], and the Elligator encoding [BHKL13].

Corollary 2. *For a compatible elliptic curve $E(\mathbb{F}_p)$, the Elligator function as defined in [BHKL13] satisfies the requirement of Theorem 10 for all $m \in \{0,1\}^{\lfloor \log(p-1) \rfloor - 1}$.*

Proof. The Elligator function maps injectively from $\{1, \ldots, \frac{p-1}{2}\}$ to $E(\mathbb{F}_p)$. For the inverse map, if the returned value is greater than $\frac{p-1}{2}$, we return $\perp$. □

7.3 Implementation and Performance

We now provide a concrete instantiation of the ReCrypt scheme using the method described in Sect. 7.2 and report on the performance of our prototype implementation. Our goal is assess the performance gap between in-use schemes that do not meet UP-REENC security, and ReCrypt, which does.

Implementation. We built our reference implementation using the Rust [MKI14] programming language. This implementation uses Relic [AG], a cryptographic library written in C, and the GNU multi-precision arithmetic library (GMP). Our implementation is single-threaded and we measured performance on an Intel CPU (Haswell), running at 3.8 GHz in turbo mode.

We use `secp256k1` [Cer00] for the curve and SHA256 as the hash function h. The plaintext block length is 31 bytes. We use AES128-GCM for the AE scheme π.

The Relic toolkit provided a number of different curve options, as well as access to the low level elliptic curve operations which was essential in our early prototyping and testing. However, Relic does not at the time of writing support curves in Montgomery form, and therefore has an inefficient implementation of scalar multiplication on Curve25519. Therefore, we choose `secp256k1` because it was the most performant among all curve implementations at our disposal with (approximately) 128 bits of security. We project that Curve25519 would offer comparable efficiency, whereas a hand-tuned, optimised variant of a specific curve would result in a significant speedup.

We use a 31-byte block size with the random sampling encoding algorithm, resulting in a probability of $1-2^{-256}$ to find a valid encoding for each block.

We also experimented with the injective encodings such as the Elligator encoding [BHKL13]. The mapping did not appear to improve performance, and moreover is incompatible with `secp256k1`. Additionally, we do not require ciphertexts to be indistinguishable from random, one of the key benefits offered by the Elligator encoding.

When a curve point is serialized, only the x coordinate and the sign of the y coordinate (1-bit) needs to be recorded (using point compression). Since the x coordinate requires strictly less than the full 32 bytes, we can serialize points as 32 byte values. Each 32 byte serialized value represents 31 bytes of plaintext giving a ciphertext expansion of 3%. Upon deserialization, the y coordinate must be recomputed. This requires computing a square root, taking approximately 20 µs. Of course this cost can be avoided by instead serializing both x and y coordinates. This creates a 64 byte ciphertext for each 31 bytes of plaintext which is an expansion of 106%. We consider that to be unacceptable.

Microbenchmarks. Figure 9 shows wall clock times for ReCrypt operations over various plaintext sizes. As might be expected given the nature of the cryptographic operations involved, performance is far from competitive with conventional AE schemes. For comparison, AES-GCM on the same hardware platform encrypts 1 block, 1 KB, 1 MB and 1 GB of plaintext in 15 µs, 24 µs, 9 ms, and 11 s, respectively. KSS has performance determined by that of AES-GCM, while the performance of the ReCrypt scheme is largely determined by the scalar multiplications required to evaluate the PRF. Across all block sizes there is a 1000x performance cost to achieve our strongest notion of security.

ReCrypt Operation	Time per CPU 1 block	1 KB	1 MB	1 GB	cycles/byte
Encrypt	663 µs	10.0 ms	9.2 s	2.6 hours	32.4 K
ReEnc	302 µs	8.8 ms	8.7 s	2.4 hours	30.7 K
Decrypt	611 µs	9.1 ms	8.6 s	2.4 hours	30.6 K
ReKeyGen (total)		450 µs			1.96 M

Fig. 9. Processing times for ReCrypt operations measured on a 3.8 GHz CPU. 1 block represents any plaintext ≤31 bytes. Number of iterations: 1000 (for 1 block, 1 KB), 100 (for 1 MB) and 1 (for 1 GB). Cycles per byte given for 1MB ciphertexts.

Discussion. Given this large performance difference, ReCrypt is best suited to very small or very valuable plaintexts (ideally, both). Compact and high-value plaintexts such as payment card information, personally identifiable information, and sensitive financial information are likely targets for ReCrypt. If the plaintext corpus is moderately or very large, cost and performance may prohibit practitioners from using ReCrypt over more performant schemes like KSS that give strictly weaker security.

8 Conclusion and Open Problems

We have given a systematic study of updatable AE, providing a hierarchy of security notions meeting different real-world security requirements and schemes that satisfy them efficiently. Along the way, we showed the limitations of currently deployed approach, as represented by AE-hybrid, improved it at low cost to obtain the KSS scheme meeting our UP-IND and UP-INT notions, identified a flaw in the BLMR scheme, repaired it, and showed how to instantiate the repaired scheme in the ROM. Through this, we arrived at ReCrypt, a scheme that is secure in our strongest security models (UP-IND, UP-INT and UP-REENC). We implemented ReCrypt and presented basic speed benchmarks for our prototype. The scheme is slow compared to the hybrid approaches but offers true key rotation.

Our work puts updatable AE on a firm theoretical foundation and brings schemes with improved security closer to industrial application. While there is a rich array of different security models for practitioners to chose from, it is clear that achieving strong security (currently) comes at a substantial price. Meanwhile weaker but still useful security notions can be achieved at almost zero cost over conventional AE. It is an important challenge to find constructions which lower the cost compared to ReCrypt without reducing security. But it seems that fundamentally new ideas will be needed here, since what are essentially public key operations are intrinsic to our construction.

From a more theoretical perspective, it would also be of interest to study the exact relations between our security notions, in particular whether UP-REENC is strong enough to imply UP-IND and UP-INT. There is also the question of whether a scheme that is UP-REENC is necessarily ciphertext-dependent. Finally, we reiterate the possibility of formulating updatable AE in the nonce-based setting.

Acknowledgements. We thank the anonymous Crypto reviewers for their feedback and discussion relating to a bug in our initial KSS construction, and for their additional comments and suggestions. This work was supported in part by NSF grant CNS-1330308, EPSRC grants EP/K035584/1 and EP/M013472/1, by a research programme funded by Huawei Technologies and delivered through the Institute for Cyber Security Innovation at Royal Holloway, University of London, and a gift from Microsoft.

A Bidirectional Updatable AE

A.1 XOR-KEM: A Bidirectional Updatable AE Scheme

The AE-hybrid and KSS schemes are unidirectional and ciphertext-dependent. This means that in practice the client must fetch from storage ciphertext headers in order to compute the rekey tokens needed to update individual ciphertexts. It could be simpler to utilize a ciphertext-independent scheme that has rekey tokens that work for any ciphertext encrypted with a particular key. This would make the re-encryption process "non-interactive", requiring that the key holder only push a single rekey token to the place where ciphertexts are stored. Given the obvious performance benefits that such a scheme would have, we also provide such a scheme, called XOR-KEM. This scheme is exceptionally fast, and is built from a (non-updatable) AE scheme that is assumed to be secure against a restricted form of related-key attack (RKA). This latter notion adapts the Bellare-Kohno RKA-security notions for block ciphers [BK03] to the setting of AE schemes. To the best of our knowledge, this definition is novel, and RKA secure AE may itself be of independent interest as a primitive. However, the XOR-KEM scheme cannot meet our integrity notions against an attacker in possession of compromised keys. (And because of its bidirectionality, XOR-KEM also provides the counter-example that we used to separate UP-IND-BI and UP-IND security in Sect. 3.1.)

Let $(\mathcal{K}, \mathcal{E}, \mathcal{D})$ be an AE scheme. Then we define the ciphertext-independent scheme, XOR-KEM, as follows:

- $\mathsf{KeyGen}()$: return $k \leftarrow \mathcal{K}$
- $\mathsf{Enc}(k, m)$: $x \leftarrow \mathcal{K}$; $C \leftarrow (x \oplus k, \mathcal{E}(x, M))$; return C
- $\mathsf{ReKeyGen}(k_1, k_2)$: return $\Delta_{1,2} = k_1 \oplus k_2$
- $\mathsf{ReEnc}(\Delta_{1,2}, C = (C_0, C_1))$: $C' \leftarrow (\Delta_{1,2} \oplus C_0, C_1)$; return C'
- $\mathsf{Dec}(k, C = (C_0, C_1))$: return $\mathcal{D}(C_0 \oplus k, C_1)$

The XOR-KEM scheme has a similar format to the AE-hybrid scheme above. However, instead of protecting the DEM key x by encrypting it, we instead XOR it with the secret key k. The resulting scheme becomes a bidirectional, ciphertext-independent scheme, and one that has extremely high performance and deployability.

Note that although the value $x \oplus k$ fulfils a similar purpose as the ciphertext header in AE-hybrid, since this value is not needed in re-keying, it resides in the ciphertext body.

We provide proofs in the full version that this scheme achieves UP-IND-BI, and UP-INT-BI. However, the latter only holds when the adversary does not have access to any corrupted keys, and relies on the AE scheme being secure against a class of related-key attacks.

References

[ABBC10] Acar, T., Belenkiy, M., Bellare, M., Cash, D.: Cryptographic agility and its relation to circular encryption. In: Gilbert, H. (ed.) EUROCRYPT 2010. LNCS, vol. 6110, pp. 403–422. Springer, Heidelberg (2010). doi:10.1007/978-3-642-13190-5_21

[ABL+14] Andreeva, E., Bogdanov, A., Luykx, A., Mennink, B., Mouha, N., Yasuda, K.: How to securely release unverified plaintext in authenticated encryption. In: Sarkar, P., Iwata, T. (eds.) ASIACRYPT 2014. LNCS, vol. 8873, pp. 105–125. Springer, Heidelberg (2014). doi:10.1007/978-3-662-45611-8_6

[AG] Aranha, D.F., Gouvêa, C.P.L.: RELIC is an efficient library for cryptography. https://github.com/relic-toolkit/relic

[AWS] AWS: Protecting data using client-side encryption. http://docs.aws.amazon.com/AmazonS3/latest/dev/UsingClientSideEncryption.html

[BDPS14] Boldyreva, A., Degabriele, J.P., Paterson, K.G., Stam, M.: On symmetric encryption with distinguishable decryption failures. In: Moriai, S. (ed.) FSE 2013. LNCS, vol. 8424, pp. 367–390. Springer, Heidelberg (2014). doi:10.1007/978-3-662-43933-3_19

[BHKL13] Bernstein, D.J., Hamburg, M., Krasnova, A., Lange, T.: Elligator: elliptic-curve points indistinguishable from uniform random strings. In: Sadeghi, A.-R., Gligor, V.D., Yung, M. (eds.) ACM CCS 2013, pp. 967–980. ACM Press, November 2013

[BK03] Bellare, M., Kohno, T.: A theoretical treatment of related-key attacks: RKA-PRPs, RKA-PRFs, and applications. In: Biham, E. (ed.) EUROCRYPT 2003. LNCS, vol. 2656, pp. 491–506. Springer, Heidelberg (2003). doi:10.1007/3-540-39200-9_31

[BLMR13] Boneh, D., Lewi, K., Montgomery, H., Raghunathan, A.: Key homomorphic PRFs and their applications. In: Canetti, R., Garay, J.A. (eds.) CRYPTO 2013. LNCS, vol. 8042, pp. 410–428. Springer, Heidelberg (2013). doi:10.1007/978-3-642-40041-4_23

[BLMR15] Boneh, D., Lewi, K., Montgomery, H., Raghunathan, A.: Key homomorphic PRFs and their applications. Cryptology ePrint Archive, Report 2015/220 (2015). http://eprint.iacr.org/2015/220

[BN00] Bellare, M., Namprempre, C.: Authenticated encryption: relations among notions and analysis of the generic composition paradigm. In: Okamoto, T. (ed.) ASIACRYPT 2000. LNCS, vol. 1976, pp. 531–545. Springer, Heidelberg (2000). doi:10.1007/3-540-44448-3_41

[BRS03] Black, J., Rogaway, P., Shrimpton, T.: Encryption-scheme security in the presence of key-dependent messages. In: Nyberg, K., Heys, H. (eds.) SAC 2002. LNCS, vol. 2595, pp. 62–75. Springer, Heidelberg (2003). doi:10.1007/3-540-36492-7_6

[Cer00] SEC Certicom: Sec 2: Recommended elliptic curve domain parameters. In: Proceeding of Standards for Efficient Cryptography, Version 1 (2000)

[CGH12] Cash, D., Green, M., Hohenberger, S.: New definitions and separations for circular security. In: Fischlin, M., Buchmann, J., Manulis, M. (eds.) PKC 2012. LNCS, vol. 7293, pp. 540–557. Springer, Heidelberg (2012). doi:10.1007/978-3-642-30057-8_32

[CH07] Canetti, R., Hohenberger, S.: Chosen-ciphertext secure proxy re-encryption. In: Ning, P., De Capitani di Vimercati, S., Syverson, P.F. (eds.) ACM CCS 2007, pp. 185–194. ACM Press, October 2007

[CK05] Cool, D.L., Keromytis, A.D.: Conversion and proxy functions for symmetric key ciphers. In: International Conference on Information Technology: Coding and Computing, ITCC 2005, vol. 1, pp. 662–667. IEEE (2005)

[CL01] Camenisch, J., Lysyanskaya, A.: An efficient system for non-transferable anonymous credentials with optional anonymity revocation. In: Pfitzmann, B. (ed.) EUROCRYPT 2001. LNCS, vol. 2045, pp. 93–118. Springer, Heidelberg (2001). doi:10.1007/3-540-44987-6_7

[Goo] Google: Managing data encryption. https://cloud.google.com/storage/docs/encryption

[Ica09] Icart, T.: How to hash into elliptic curves. In: Halevi, S. (ed.) CRYPTO 2009. LNCS, vol. 5677, pp. 303–316. Springer, Heidelberg (2009). doi:10.1007/978-3-642-03356-8_18

[ID03] Ivan, A., Dodis, Y.: Proxy cryptography revisited. In: NDSS 2003. The Internet Society, February 2003

[KRW15] Koppula, V., Ramchen, K., Waters, B.: Separations in circular security for arbitrary length key cycles. In: Dodis, Y., Nielsen, J.B. (eds.) TCC 2015. LNCS, vol. 9015, pp. 378–400. Springer, Heidelberg (2015). doi:10.1007/978-3-662-46497-7_15

[MKI14] Matsakis, N.D., Klock II, F.S.: The rust language. ACM SIGAda Ada Lett. **34**(3), 103–104 (2014)

[NPR99] Naor, M., Pinkas, B., Reingold, O.: Distributed pseudo-random functions and KDCs. In: Stern, J. (ed.) EUROCRYPT 1999. LNCS, vol. 1592, pp. 327–346. Springer, Heidelberg (1999). doi:10.1007/3-540-48910-X_23

[NRS14] Namprempre, C., Rogaway, P., Shrimpton, T.: Reconsidering generic composition. In: Nguyen, P.Q., Oswald, E. (eds.) EUROCRYPT 2014. LNCS, vol. 8441, pp. 257–274. Springer, Heidelberg (2014). doi:10.1007/978-3-642-55220-5_15

[PCI16] PCI Security Standards Council: Requirements and security assessment procedures. In: PCI DSS v3.2 (2016)

[PRS11] Paterson, K.G., Ristenpart, T., Shrimpton, T.: Tag size *Does* matter: attacks and proofs for the TLS record protocol. In: Lee, D.H., Wang, X. (eds.) ASIACRYPT 2011. LNCS, vol. 7073, pp. 372–389. Springer, Heidelberg (2011). doi:10.1007/978-3-642-25385-0_20

[Rog06] Rogaway, P.: Formalizing human ignorance. In: Nguyen, P.Q. (ed.) VIETCRYPT 2006. LNCS, vol. 4341, pp. 211–228. Springer, Heidelberg (2006). doi:10.1007/11958239_14

[RS06] Rogaway, P., Shrimpton, T.: Deterministic authenticated-encryption: a provable-security treatment of the key-wrap problem. Cryptology ePrint Archive, Report 2006/221 (2006). http://eprint.iacr.org/2006/221

[RSS11] Ristenpart, T., Shacham, H., Shrimpton, T.: Careful with composition: limitations of the indifferentiability framework. In: Paterson, K.G. (ed.) EUROCRYPT 2011. LNCS, vol. 6632, pp. 487–506. Springer, Heidelberg (2011). doi:10.1007/978-3-642-20465-4_27

[SvdW06] Edixhoven, B.: On the computation of the coefficients of a modular form. In: Hess, F., Pauli, S., Pohst, M. (eds.) ANTS 2006. LNCS, vol. 4076, pp. 30–39. Springer, Heidelberg (2006). doi:10.1007/11792086_3

Public-Key Encryption

Kurosawa-Desmedt Meets Tight Security

Romain Gay[1,2(✉)], Dennis Hofheinz[3], and Lisa Kohl[3]

[1] Département d'informatique de l'ENS École normale supérieure, CNRS, PSL Research University, 75005 Paris, France
rgay@di.ens.fr
[2] INRIA, Paris, France
[3] Karlsruhe Institute of Technology, Karlsruhe, Germany
{Dennis.Hofheinz,Lisa.Kohl}@kit.edu

Abstract. At EUROCRYPT 2016, Gay et al. presented the first pairing-free public-key encryption (PKE) scheme with an almost tight security reduction to a standard assumption. Their scheme is competitive in efficiency with state-of-the art PKE schemes and has very compact ciphertexts (of three group elements), but suffers from a large public key (of about 200 group elements).

In this work, we present an improved pairing-free PKE scheme with an almost tight security reduction to the Decisional Diffie-Hellman assumption, small ciphertexts (of three group elements), *and* small public keys (of six group elements). Compared to the work of Gay et al., our scheme thus has a considerably smaller public key and comparable other characteristics, although our encryption and decryption algorithms are somewhat less efficient.

Technically, our scheme borrows ideas both from the work of Gay et al. and from a recent work of Hofheinz (EUROCRYPT, 2017). The core technical novelty of our work is an efficient and compact designated-verifier proof system for an OR-like language. We show that adding such an OR-proof to the ciphertext of the state-of-the-art PKE scheme from Kurosawa and Desmedt enables a tight security reduction.

Keywords: Public key encryption · Tight security

1 Introduction

Tight security reductions. We are usually interested in cryptographic schemes that come with a *security reduction* to a computational assumption. A security reduction shows that every attack on the scheme can be translated into an attack on a computational assumption. Thus, the only way to break the scheme is to solve an underlying mathematical problem. We are most interested in reductions to well-investigated, "standard" assumptions, and in reductions

R. Gay—Supported by ERC Project aSCEND (639554).
D. Hofheinz—Supported by DFG grants HO 4534/4-1 and HO 4534/2-2.
L. Kohl—Supported by DFG grant HO 4534/2-2.

J. Katz and H. Shacham (Eds.): CRYPTO 2017, Part III, LNCS 10403, pp. 133–160, 2017.
DOI: 10.1007/978-3-319-63697-9_5

that are "tight". A tight security reduction ensures that the reduction translates attacks on the scheme into attacks on the assumption that are of similar complexity and success probability. In other words, the difficulty of breaking the scheme is quantitatively not lower than the difficulty of breaking the investigated assumption.

Tight security reductions are also beneficial from a practical point of view. Indeed, assume that we choose the keylength of a scheme so as to guarantee that the only way to break that scheme is to break a computational assumption on currently secure parameters.[1] Then, a tight reduction enables smaller keylength recommendations (than with a non-tight reduction in which, say, the attack on the assumption is much more complex than the attack on the scheme).

Tightly secure PKE schemes. The focus of this paper are public-key encryption (PKE) schemes with a tight security reduction. The investigation of this topic was initiated already in 2000 by Bellare, Boldyreva, and Micali [3]. However, the first tightly secure encryption scheme based on a standard assumption was presented only in 2012 [13], and was far from practical. Many more efficient schemes were proposed [1,2,4,5,10–12,15,19,20] subsequently, but Gay et al. [9] (henceforth GHKW) were the first to present a pairing-free tightly secure PKE scheme from a standard assumption. Their PKE scheme has short ciphertexts (of three group elements), and its efficiency compares favorably with the popular Cramer-Shoup encryption scheme. Still, the GHKW construction suffers from a large public key (of about 200 group elements). Figure 1 summarizes relevant features of selected existing PKE schemes.

Reference	$\|pk\|$	$\|c\| - \|m\|$	sec. loss	assumption	pairing
CS98 [6]	3	3	$\mathcal{O}(Q)$	1-LIN = DDH	no
KD04, HK07 [17, 14]	$k+1$	$k+1$	$\mathcal{O}(Q)$	k-LIN ($k \geq 1$)	no
HJ12 [13]	$O(1)$	$O(\lambda)$	$\mathcal{O}(1)$	2-LIN	yes
LPJY15 [19, 20]	$\mathcal{O}(\lambda)$	47	$\mathcal{O}(\lambda)$	2-LIN	yes
AHY15 [2]	$\mathcal{O}(\lambda)$	12	$\mathcal{O}(\lambda)$	2-LIN	yes
GCDCT15 [10, 15]	$\mathcal{O}(\lambda)$	$6k$	$\mathcal{O}(\lambda)$	k-LIN ($k \geq 1$)	yes
GHKW16 [9]	$2\lambda k$	$3k$	$\mathcal{O}(\lambda)$	k-LIN ($k \geq 1$)	no
H16 [11]	$2k(k+5)$	$k+4$	$\mathcal{O}(\lambda)$	k-LIN ($k \geq 2$)	yes
H16 [11]	20	28	$\mathcal{O}(\lambda)$	DCR	—
Ours	6	3	$\mathcal{O}(\lambda)$	1-LIN = DDH	no
	$2k(k+4)$	$4k$	$\mathcal{O}(\lambda)$	k-LIN ($k \geq 2$)	no

Fig. 1. Comparison amongst CCA-secure encryption schemes, where Q is the number of ciphertexts, $|pk|$ denotes the size (in groups elements) of the public key, and $|c| - |m|$ denotes the ciphertext overhead, ignoring smaller contributions from symmetric-key encryption.

[1] This is unfortunately different from current practice, which does not take into account security reductions at all: practical keylength recommendations are such that known attacks on the *scheme itself* are infeasible [18].

Our contribution. In this work, we construct a pairing-free PKE scheme with an almost[2] tight security reduction to a standard assumption (the Decisional Diffie-Hellman assumption), and with short ciphertexts and keys. Our scheme improves upon GHKW in that it removes its main disadvantage (of large public keys), although our encryption and decryption algorithms are somewhat less efficient than those of GHKW.

Our construction can be seen as a variant of the state-of-the-art Kurosawa-Desmedt PKE scheme [17] with an additional consistency proof. This consistency proof ensures that ciphertexts are of a special form, and is in fact very efficient (in that it only occupies one additional group element in the ciphertext). This proof is the main technical novelty of our scheme, and is the key ingredient to enable an almost tight security reduction.

Technical overview. The starting point of our scheme is the Kurosawa-Desmedt PKE scheme from [17]. In this scheme, public parameters, public keys, and ciphertexts are of the following form:[3]

$$\begin{aligned} \mathit{pars} &= [\mathbf{A}] \in \mathbb{G}^{2\times 1} && \text{for random } \mathbf{A} \in \mathbb{Z}_{|\mathbb{G}|}^{2\times 1} \\ \mathit{pk} &= [\mathbf{k}_0^\top \mathbf{A}, \mathbf{k}_1^\top \mathbf{A}] \in \mathbb{G}\times\mathbb{G} && \text{for random } \mathbf{k}_0, \mathbf{k}_1 \in \mathbb{Z}_{|\mathbb{G}|}^{2} \\ C &= \big([\mathbf{c} = \mathbf{A}\mathbf{r}],\, \mathbf{E}_K(M)\big) && \text{for random } \mathbf{r} \in \mathbb{Z}_{|\mathbb{G}|}, \\ & && K = [(\mathbf{k}_0 + \tau\mathbf{k}_1)^\top \mathbf{A}\mathbf{r}], \\ & && \text{and } \tau = H([\mathbf{c}]). \end{aligned} \tag{1}$$

Here, $\mathbf{E}$ is the encryption algorithm of a symmetric authenticated encryption scheme, and H is a collision-resistant hash function.

In their (game-based) proof of IND-CCA security (with one scheme instance and one challenge ciphertext), Kurosawa and Desmedt proceed as follows: first, they use the secret key $\mathbf{k}_0, \mathbf{k}_1$ to generate the value K in the challenge ciphertext from a given $[\mathbf{c}] = [\mathbf{A}\mathbf{r}]$ (through $K = [(\mathbf{k}_0+\tau\mathbf{k}_1)^\top \mathbf{c}]$). This enables the reduction to forget the witness $\mathbf{r}$, and thus to modify the distribution of $\mathbf{c}$. Next, Kurosawa and Desmedt use the Decisional Diffie-Hellman (DDH) assumption to modify the setup of $\mathbf{c}$ to a random vector not in the span of $\mathbf{A}$. Finally, they argue that this change effectively randomizes the value K from the challenge ciphertext (which then enables a reduction to the security of $\mathbf{E}$).

To see that K is indeed randomized, note that once $\mathbf{c} \notin \mathrm{span}(\mathbf{A})$, the value $K = [(\mathbf{k}_0 + \tau\mathbf{k}_1)^\top \mathbf{c}]$ depends on entropy in $\mathbf{k}_0, \mathbf{k}_1$ that is not leaked through pk. Furthermore, Kurosawa and Desmedt show that even a decryption oracle leaks no information about that entropy. (Intuitively, this holds since any decryption query with $\mathbf{c} \in \mathrm{span}(\mathbf{A})$ only reveals information about $\mathbf{k}_0, \mathbf{k}_1$ that is already contained in pk. On the other hand, any decryption query with $\mathbf{c} \notin \mathrm{span}(\mathbf{A})$

[2] Like [5], we call our reduction *almost* tight, since its loss (of λ) is independent of the number of challenges and users, but not constant.

[3] In this paper, we use an implicit notation for group elements. That is, we write $[\mathbf{x}] := g^{\mathbf{x}} \in \mathbb{G}^n$ for a fixed group generator $g \in \mathbb{G}$ and a vector $\mathbf{x} \in \mathbb{Z}_{|\mathbb{G}|}^n$, see [8]. We also use the shorthand notation $[\mathbf{x}, \mathbf{y}] := ([\mathbf{x}], [\mathbf{y}])$.

results in a computed key K that is independently random, and thus will lead the symmetric authenticated encryption scheme to reject the whole ciphertext.)

An argument of Bellare, Boldyreva, and Micali [3] (which is applied in [3] to the related Cramer-Shoup encryption scheme) shows that the security proof for the Kurosawa-Desmedt scheme carries over to a setting with many users. Due to the re-randomizability properties of the DDH assumption, the quality of the corresponding security reduction does not degrade in the multi-user scenario. The security proof of Kurosawa and Desmedt does however not immediately scale to a larger number of *ciphertexts*. Indeed, observe that the final argument to randomize K relies on the entropy in $\mathbf{k}_0, \mathbf{k}_1$. Since this entropy is limited, only a limited number of ciphertexts (per user) can be randomized at a time.[4]

First trick: randomize $\mathbf{k}_0$. In our scheme, we adapt two existing techniques for achieving tight security. The first trick, which we borrow from GHKW [9] (who in turn build upon [5,15]), consists in modifying the secret key $\mathbf{k}_0, \mathbf{k}_1$ first, before randomizing the values K from challenge ciphertexts. Like the original Kurosawa-Desmedt proof, our argument starts out by first using $\mathbf{k}_0, \mathbf{k}_1$ to generate challenge ciphertexts, and then simultaneously randomizing all values $\mathbf{c}$ from challenges (using the re-randomizability of DDH). But then we use another reduction to DDH, with the DDH challenges embedded into $\mathbf{k}_0$ *and* in all challenge $\mathbf{c}$, to simultaneously randomize all challenge K at once.

During this last reduction, we will (implicitly) set up $\mathbf{k}_0 = \mathbf{k}'_0 + \alpha \mathbf{A}^\perp$ for a known $\mathbf{k}'_0$, a known $\mathbf{A}^\perp \in \mathbb{Z}_{|\mathbb{G}|}^{2\times 1}$ with $(\mathbf{A}^\perp)^\top \mathbf{A} = \mathbf{0}$, and an unknown $\alpha \in \mathbb{Z}_{|\mathbb{G}|}$ from the DDH challenge $[\alpha, \beta, \gamma]$. We can thus decrypt all ciphertexts with $\mathbf{c} \in \mathrm{span}(\mathbf{A})$ (since $\mathbf{k}_0^\top \mathbf{A}\mathbf{r} = \mathbf{k}_0'^\top \mathbf{A}\mathbf{r}$), and randomize all challenge ciphertexts (since their $\mathbf{c}$ satisfies $\mathbf{c} \notin \mathrm{span}(\mathbf{A})$ and thus allows to embed β and γ into $\mathbf{c}$ and K, respectively). However, we will not be able to answer decryption queries with $\mathbf{c} \notin \mathrm{span}(\mathbf{A})$. Hence, before applying this trick, we will need to make sure that any such decryption query will be rejected anyway.

Second trick: the consistency proof. We do not know how to argue (with a tight reduction) that such decryption queries are rejected in the original Kurosawa-Desmedt scheme from (1). Instead, we introduce an additional consistency proof in the ciphertext, so ciphertexts in our scheme now look as follows:

$$C = \big([\mathbf{c} = \mathbf{A}\mathbf{r}],\ \pi,\ \mathbf{E}_K(M)\big) \quad \begin{array}{l} \text{for random } \mathbf{r} \in \mathbb{Z}_{|\mathbb{G}|}, \\ K = [(\mathbf{k}_0 + \tau \mathbf{k}_1)^\top \mathbf{A}\mathbf{r}], \\ \text{and } \tau = H([\mathbf{c}]). \end{array} \tag{2}$$

Here, π is a proof (yet to be described) that shows the following statement:

$$\mathbf{c} \in \mathrm{span}(\mathbf{A}) \ \vee\ \mathbf{c} \in \mathrm{span}(\mathbf{A}_0) \ \vee\ \mathbf{c} \in \mathrm{span}(\mathbf{A}_1), \tag{3}$$

[4] We note that a generic hybrid argument shows the security of the Kurosawa-Desmedt scheme in a multi-ciphertext setting. However, the corresponding security reduction loses a factor of Q in success probability, where Q is the number of challenge ciphertexts.

where $\mathbf{A}_0, \mathbf{A}_1 \in \mathbb{Z}_{|\mathbb{G}|}^{2\times 1}$ are different (random but fixed) matrices. Our challenge ciphertexts will satisfy (3) at all times, even after their randomization.

We will then show that all "inconsistent" decryption queries (with $\mathbf{c} \notin \mathrm{span}(\mathbf{A})$) are rejected with a combination of arguments from GHKW [9] and Hofheinz [11]. We will proceed in a number of hybrids. In the i-th hybrid, all challenge ciphertexts are prepared with a value of $\mathbf{k}_0 + \mathbf{F}_i(\tau_{|i})$ instead of $\mathbf{k}_0$, where $\mathbf{F}_i(\tau_{|i})$ is a random function applied to the first i bits of τ. Likewise, in all decryption queries with inconsistent $\mathbf{c}$ (i.e., with $\mathbf{c} \notin \mathrm{span}(\mathbf{A})$), we use $\mathbf{k}_0 + \mathbf{F}_i(\tau_{|i})$. Going from the i-th to the $(i+1)$-th hybrid proceeds in a way that is very similar to the one from GHKW: First, we set up the $\mathbf{c}$ value in each challenge ciphertext to be in $\mathrm{span}(\mathbf{A}_{\tau_{i+1}})$, where τ_{i+1} is the $(i+1)$-th bit of the respective τ.

Next, we add a dependency of the used $\mathbf{k}_0$ on the $(i+1)$-th bit of τ. (That is, depending on τ_{i+1}, we will use two different values of $\mathbf{k}_0$ both for preparing challenge ciphertexts, and for answering decryption queries.) This is accomplished by adding random values $\mathbf{k}_\Delta$ with $\mathbf{k}_\Delta^\top \mathbf{A}_{\tau_{i+1}} = 0$ to $\mathbf{k}_0$. Indeed, for challenge ciphertexts, adding such $\mathbf{k}_\Delta$ values results in the same computed keys K, and thus cannot be detected. We note however that at this point, we run into a complication: since decryption queries need not have $\mathbf{c} \in \mathrm{span}(\mathbf{A}_{\tau_{i+1}})$, we cannot simply add random values $\mathbf{k}_\Delta$ with $\mathbf{k}_\Delta^\top \mathbf{A}_{\tau_{i+1}} = 0$ to $\mathbf{k}_0$. (This could be detected in case $\mathbf{c} \notin \mathrm{span}(\mathbf{A}_{\tau_{i+1}})$.) Instead, here we rely on a trick from [11], and use that even adversarial $\mathbf{c}$ values must lie in $\mathrm{span}(\mathbf{A})$ or $\mathrm{span}(\mathbf{A}_b)$ for $b \in \{0,1\}$. (This is also the reason why we will eventually have to modify and use $\mathbf{k}_1$. We give more details on this step inside.)

Once $\mathbf{k}_0$ is fully randomized, the resulting K computed upon decryption queries with $\mathbf{c} \notin \mathrm{span}(\mathbf{A})$ will also be random, and thus any such decryption query will be rejected. Hence, using the first trick above, security of our scheme follows.

We finally mention that our complete scheme generalizes to weaker assumptions, including the k-Linear family of assumptions (see Fig. 1).

Relation to existing techniques. We borrow techniques from both GHKW [9] and Hofheinz [11], but we need to modify and adapt them for our strategy in several important respects. While the argument from [9] also relies on a consistency proof that a given ciphertext lies in one of three linear subspaces ($\mathrm{span}(\mathbf{A})$ or $\mathrm{span}(\mathbf{A}_b)$), their consistency proof is very different from ours. Namely, their consistency proof is realized entirely through a combination of different *linear* hash proof systems, and requires *orthogonal* subspaces $\mathrm{span}(\mathbf{A}_b)$. This requires a large number (i.e., 2λ) of hash proof systems, and results in large public keys to accommodate their public information. Furthermore, the ciphertexts in GHKW require a larger $[\mathbf{c}] \in \mathbb{G}^{3k}$ (compared to the Kurosawa-Desmedt scheme), but no explicit proof π in C This results in ciphertexts of the same size as ours.

On the other hand, [11] presents a scheme with an explicit consistency proof π for a statement similar to ours (and also deals with the arising technical complications sketched above similarly). But his construction and proof are aimed at a more generic setting which also accommodates the DCR assumption (both for the PKE and consistency proof constructions). As a consequence, his construction does not modify the equivalent of our secret key $\mathbf{k}_0, \mathbf{k}_1$ at all, but instead modifies ciphertexts directly. This makes larger public keys and ciphertexts with more "randomization slots" necessary (see Fig. 1), and in fact also leads to a more complicated proof. Furthermore, in the discrete-log setting, the necessary "OR"-style proofs from [11] require pairings, and thus his PKE scheme does as well. In contrast, our scheme requires only a weaker notion of "OR"-proofs, and we show how to instantiate this notion without pairings.

Crucial ingredient: efficient pairing-free OR-proofs. In the above argument, a crucial component is of course a proof π for (3). We present a designated-verifier proof π that only occupies one group element (in the DDH case) in C. While the proof nicely serves its purpose in our scheme, we also remark that our construction is not as general as one would perhaps like: in particular, honest proofs (generated with public information and a witness) can only be generated for $\mathbf{c} \in \mathrm{span}(\mathbf{A})$ (but not for $\mathbf{c} \in \mathrm{span}(\mathbf{A}_0)$ or $\mathbf{c} \in \mathrm{span}(\mathbf{A}_1)$).

Our proof system is perhaps best described as a randomized hash proof system. We will outline a slightly simpler version of the system which only proves $\mathbf{c} \in \mathrm{span}(\mathbf{A}) \vee \mathbf{c} \in \mathrm{span}(\mathbf{A}_0)$. In that scheme, the public key contains a value $[\mathbf{k}_y^\top \mathbf{A}]$, just like in a linear hash proof system (with secret key $\mathbf{k}_y$) for showing $\mathbf{c} \in \mathrm{span}(\mathbf{A})$ (see, e.g., [7]). Now given either the secret key $\mathbf{k}_y$ or a witness $\mathbf{r}$ to the fact that $\mathbf{c} = \mathbf{A}\mathbf{r}$, we can compute $[\mathbf{k}_y^\top \mathbf{c}]$. The idea of our system is to encrypt this value $[\mathbf{k}_y^\top \mathbf{c}]$ using a special encryption scheme that is parameterized over $\mathbf{c}$ (and whose public key is also part of the proof system's public key). The crucial feature of that encryption scheme is that it becomes lossy if and only if $\mathbf{c} \in \mathrm{span}(\mathbf{A}_0)$.

We briefly sketch the soundness of our proof system: we claim that even in a setting in which an adversary has access to many simulated proofs for *valid* statements (with $\mathbf{c} \in \mathrm{span}(\mathbf{A}) \cup \mathrm{span}(\mathbf{A}_0)$), it cannot forge proofs for *invalid* statements. Indeed, proofs with $\mathbf{c} \in \mathrm{span}(\mathbf{A})$ only depend on (and thus only reveal) the public key $[\mathbf{k}_y^\top \mathbf{A}]$. Moreover, by the special lossiness of our encryption scheme, proofs with $\mathbf{c} \in \mathrm{span}(\mathbf{A}_0)$ do not reveal anything about $\mathbf{k}_y$. Hence, an adversary will not gain any information about $\mathbf{k}_y$ beyond $\mathbf{k}_y^\top \mathbf{A}$. However, any valid proof for $\mathbf{c} \notin \mathrm{span}(\mathbf{A}) \cup \mathrm{span}(\mathbf{A}_0)$ would reveal the full value of $\mathbf{k}_y$, and thus cannot be forged by an adversary that sees only proofs for valid statements.

We remark that our proof system has additional nice properties, including a form of on-the-fly extensibility to more general statements (and in particular to more than two "OR branches". We formalize this type of proof systems as "qualified proof systems" inside.

Roadmap. After recalling some preliminaries in Sect. 2, we introduce the notion of designated-verifier proof systems in Sect. 3, along with an instantiation in Sect. 4. Finally, in Sect. 5, we present our encryption scheme (in form of a key encapsulation mechanism).

2 Preliminaries

2.1 Notations

We start by introducing some notation used throughout this paper. First we denote by $\lambda \in \mathbb{N}$ the security parameter. By $\mathsf{negl}\colon \mathbb{N} \to \mathbb{R}_{\geq 0}$ we denote a negligible function. For an arbitrary set $\mathcal{B}$, by $x \leftarrow_R \mathcal{B}$ we denote the process of sampling an element x from $\mathcal{B}$ uniformly at random. For any bit string $\tau \in \{0,1\}^*$, we denote by τ_i the i-th bit of τ and by $\tau_{|i} \in \{0,1\}^i$ the bit string comprising the first i bits of τ.

Let p be a prime, and $k, \ell \in \mathbb{N}$ such that $\ell > k$. Then for any matrix $\mathbf{A} \in \mathbb{Z}_p^{\ell \times k}$, we write $\overline{\mathbf{A}} \in \mathbb{Z}_p^{k \times k}$ for the upper square matrix of $\mathbf{A}$, and $\underline{\mathbf{A}} \in \mathbb{Z}_p^{(\ell-k)\times k}$ for the lower $\ell - k$ rows of $\mathbf{A}$. With

$$\mathrm{span}(\mathbf{A}) := \{\mathbf{Ar} \mid \mathbf{r} \in \mathbb{Z}_p^k\} \subset \mathbb{Z}_p^\ell,$$

we denote the *span* of $\mathbf{A}$.

For vectors $\mathbf{v} \in \mathbb{Z}_p^{2k}$, by $\overline{\mathbf{v}} \in \mathbb{Z}_p^k$ we denote the vector consisting of the upper k entries of $\mathbf{v}$ and accordingly by $\underline{\mathbf{v}} \in \mathbb{Z}_p^k$ we denote the vector consisting of the lower k entries of $\mathbf{v}$.

As usual by $\mathbf{A}^\top \in \mathbb{Z}_p^{k \times \ell}$ we denote the *transpose* of $\mathbf{A}$ and if $\ell = k$ and $\mathbf{A}$ is invertible by $\mathbf{A}^{-1} \in \mathbb{Z}_p^{\ell \times \ell}$ we denote the *inverse* of $\mathbf{A}$.

For $\ell \geq k$ by $\mathbf{A}^\perp$ we denote a matrix in $\mathbb{Z}_p^{\ell \times (\ell - k)}$ with $\mathbf{A}^\top \mathbf{A}^\perp = \mathbf{0}$ and rank $\ell - k$. We denote the set of all matrices with these properties as

$$\mathsf{orth}(\mathbf{A}) := \{\mathbf{A}^\perp \in \mathbb{Z}_p^{\ell \times (\ell - k)} \mid \mathbf{A}^\top \mathbf{A}^\perp = \mathbf{0} \text{ and } \mathbf{A}^\perp \text{ has rank } \ell - k\}.$$

2.2 Hash Functions

A hash function generator is a probabilistic polynomial time algorithm $\mathcal{H}$ that, on input 1^λ, outputs an efficiently computable function $\mathsf{H} : \{0,1\}^* \to \{0,1\}^\lambda$, unless domain and co-domain are explicitly specified.

Definition 1 (Collision Resistance). *We say that a hash function generator* $\mathcal{H}$ *outputs* collision-resistant functions H, *if for all PPT adversaries* $\mathcal{A}$ *and* $\mathsf{H} \leftarrow_R \mathcal{H}(1^\lambda)$ *it holds*

$$\mathrm{Adv}_{\mathcal{H},\mathcal{A}}^{\mathrm{CR}}(\lambda) := \Pr\left[x \neq x' \wedge \mathsf{H}(x) = \mathsf{H}(x') \mid (x, x') \leftarrow \mathcal{A}(1^\lambda, \mathsf{H})\right] \leq \mathsf{negl}(\lambda).$$

We say a hash function is collision resistant *if it is sampled from a collision resistant hash function generator.*

Definition 2 (Universality). *We say a hash function generator* $\mathcal{H}$ *is* universal, *if for every* $x, x' \in \{0,1\}^*$ *with* $x \neq x'$ *it holds*

$$\Pr\left[\mathsf{h}(x) = \mathsf{h}(x') \mid \mathsf{h} \leftarrow_R \mathcal{H}(1^\lambda)\right] = \frac{1}{2^\lambda}.$$

We say a hash function is universal *if it is sampled from a universal hash function generator.*

Lemma 1 (Leftover Hash Lemma [16]). *Let $\mathcal{X}, \mathcal{Y}$ be sets, $\ell \in \mathbb{N}$ and $\mathsf{h}\colon \mathcal{X} \to \mathcal{Y}$ be a universal hash function. Then for all $X \leftarrow_R \mathcal{X}$, $U \leftarrow_R \mathcal{Y}$ and $\varepsilon > 0$ with $\log|\mathcal{X}| \geq \log|\mathcal{Y}| + 2\log\varepsilon$ we have*

$$\Delta((\mathsf{h}, \mathsf{h}(X)), (\mathsf{h}, U)) \leq \frac{1}{\varepsilon},$$

where Δ denotes the statistical distance.

2.3 Prime-Order Groups

Let **GGen** be a PPT algorithm that on input 1^λ returns a description $\mathcal{G} = (\mathbb{G}, p, P)$ of an additive cyclic group $\mathbb{G}$ of order p for a 2λ-bit prime p, whose generator is P.

We use the representation of group elements introduced in [8]. Namely, for $a \in \mathbb{Z}_p$, define $[a] = aP \in \mathbb{G}$ as the *implicit representation* of a in $\mathbb{G}$. More generally, for a matrix $\mathbf{A} = (a_{ij}) \in \mathbb{Z}_p^{\ell \times k}$ we define $[\mathbf{A}]$ as the implicit representation of $\mathbf{A}$ in $\mathbb{G}$:

$$[\mathbf{A}] := \begin{pmatrix} a_{11}P \ldots a_{1k}P \\ \\ a_{\ell 1}P \ldots a_{\ell k}P \end{pmatrix} \in \mathbb{G}^{\ell \times k}$$

Note that from $[a] \in \mathbb{G}$ it is hard to compute the value a if the discrete logarithm assumption holds in $\mathbb{G}$. Obviously, given $[a], [b] \in \mathbb{G}$ and a scalar $x \in \mathbb{Z}_p$, one can efficiently compute $[ax] \in \mathbb{G}$ and $[a + b] \in \mathbb{G}$.

We recall the definitions of the Matrix Decision Diffie-Hellman (MDDH) assumption from [8].

Definition 3 (Matrix Distribution). *Let $k, \ell \in \mathbb{N}$, with $\ell > k$ and p be a 2λ-bit prime. We call $\mathcal{D}_{\ell,k}$ a* matrix distribution *if it outputs matrices in $\mathbb{Z}_p^{\ell \times k}$ of full rank k in polynomial time.*

In the following we only consider matrix distributions $\mathcal{D}_{\ell,k}$, where for all $\mathbf{A} \leftarrow_R \mathcal{D}_{\ell,k}$ the first k rows of $\mathbf{A}$ form an invertible matrix.

The $\mathcal{D}_{\ell,k}$-Matrix Diffie-Hellman problem is, for a randomly chosen $\mathbf{A} \leftarrow_R \mathcal{D}_{\ell,k}$, to distinguish the between tuples of the form $([\mathbf{A}], [\mathbf{Aw}])$ and $([\mathbf{A}], [\mathbf{u}])$, where $\mathbf{w} \leftarrow_R \mathbb{Z}_p^k$ and $\mathbf{u} \leftarrow_R \mathbb{Z}_p^\ell$.

Definition 4 ($\mathcal{D}_{\ell,k}$-Matrix Diffie-Hellman $\mathcal{D}_{\ell,k}$-MDDH). *Let $\mathcal{D}_{\ell,k}$ be a matrix distribution. We say that the $\mathcal{D}_{\ell,k}$-*Matrix Diffie-Hellman *($\mathcal{D}_{\ell,k}$-*MDDH*)* assumption *holds relative to a prime order group $\mathbb{G}$ if for all PPT adversaries $\mathcal{A}$,*

$$\begin{aligned} \mathrm{Adv}^{\mathrm{mddh}}_{\mathbb{G},\mathcal{D}_{\ell,k},\mathcal{A}}(\lambda) : &= |\Pr[\mathcal{A}(\mathcal{G}, [\mathbf{A}], [\mathbf{Aw}]) = 1] - \Pr[\mathcal{A}(\mathcal{G}, [\mathbf{A}], [\mathbf{u}]) = 1]| \\ &\leq \mathsf{negl}(\lambda), \end{aligned}$$

*where the probabilities are taken over $\mathcal{G} := (\mathbb{G}, p, P) \leftarrow_R$ **GGen**(1^λ), $\mathbf{A} \leftarrow_R \mathcal{D}_{\ell,k}$, $\mathbf{w} \leftarrow_R \mathbb{Z}_p^k$, $\mathbf{u} \leftarrow_R \mathbb{Z}_p^\ell$.*

For $Q \in \mathbb{N}$, $\mathbf{W} \leftarrow_R \mathbb{Z}_p^{k\times Q}$ and $\mathbf{U} \leftarrow_R \mathbb{Z}_p^{\ell\times Q}$, we consider the Q-fold $\mathcal{D}_{\ell,k}$-MDDH assumption, which states that distinguishing tuples of the form $([\mathbf{A}],[\mathbf{AW}])$ from $([\mathbf{A}],[\mathbf{U}])$ is hard. That is, a challenge for the Q-fold $\mathcal{D}_{\ell,k}$-MDDH assumption consists of Q independent challenges of the $\mathcal{D}_{\ell,k}$-MDDH Assumption (with the same $\mathbf{A}$ but different randomness $\mathbf{w}$). In [8] it is shown that the two problems are equivalent, where the reduction loses at most a factor $\ell - k$.

Lemma 2 (Random self-reducibility of $\mathcal{D}_{\ell,k}$-MDDH, [8]). *Let $\ell, k, Q \in \mathbb{N}$ with $\ell > k$ and $Q > \ell - k$. For any PPT adversary $\mathcal{A}$, there exists an adversary $\mathcal{B}$ such that $T(\mathcal{B}) \approx T(\mathcal{A}) + Q \cdot \mathsf{poly}(\lambda)$ with $\mathsf{poly}(\lambda)$ independent of $T(\mathcal{A})$, and*

$$\mathrm{Adv}^{Q\text{-mddh}}_{\mathbb{G},\mathcal{D}_{\ell,k},\mathcal{A}}(\lambda) \leq (\ell-k)\cdot \mathrm{Adv}^{\mathrm{mddh}}_{\mathbb{G},\mathcal{D}_{\ell,k},\mathcal{B}}(\lambda) + \frac{1}{p-1}.$$

Here

$$\mathrm{Adv}^{Q\text{-mddh}}_{\mathbb{G},\mathcal{D}_{\ell,k},\mathcal{A}}(\lambda) := |\Pr[\mathcal{A}(\mathcal{G},[\mathbf{A}],[\mathbf{AW}])=1] - \Pr[\mathcal{A}(\mathcal{G},[\mathbf{A}],[\mathbf{U}])=1]|,$$

where the probability is over $\mathcal{G} := (\mathbb{G}, p, P) \leftarrow_R \mathbf{GGen}(1^\lambda)$, $\mathbf{A} \leftarrow_R \mathcal{U}_{\ell,k}$, $\mathbf{W} \leftarrow_R \mathbb{Z}_p^{k\times Q}$ and $\mathbf{U} \leftarrow_R \mathbb{Z}_p^{\ell\times Q}$.

The uniform distribution is a particular matrix distribution that deserves special attention, as an adversary breaking the $\mathcal{U}_{\ell,k}$-MDDH assumption can also distinguish between real MDDH tuples and random tuples for all other possible matrix distributions.

Definition 5 (Uniform distribution). *Let $\ell, k \in \mathbb{N}$, with $\ell \geq k$, and a prime p. We denote by $\mathcal{U}_{\ell,k}$ the* uniform distribution *over all full-rank $\ell \times k$ matrices over $\mathbb{Z}_p$. Let $\mathcal{U}_k := \mathcal{U}_{k+1,k}$.*

Lemma 3 ($\mathcal{D}_{\ell,k}$*-MDDH* $\Rightarrow$ $\mathcal{U}_{\ell,k}$*-MDDH*, [8])**.** *Let $\mathcal{D}_{\ell,k}$ be a matrix distribution. For any adversary $\mathcal{A}$ on the $\mathcal{U}_{\ell,k}$-distribution, there exists an adversary $\mathcal{B}$ on the $\mathcal{D}_{\ell,k}$-assumption such that $T(\mathcal{B}) \approx T(\mathcal{A})$ and $\mathrm{Adv}^{\mathrm{mddh}}_{\mathbb{G},\mathcal{U}_{\ell,k},\mathcal{A}}(\lambda) = \mathrm{Adv}^{\mathrm{mddh}}_{\mathbb{G},\mathcal{D}_{\ell,k},\mathcal{B}}(\lambda)$.*

We state a tighter random-self reducibility property for case of the uniform distribution.

Lemma 4 (Random self-reducibility of $\mathcal{U}_{\ell,k}$-MDDH, [8]). *Let $\ell, k, Q \in \mathbb{N}$ with $\ell > k$. For any PPT adversary $\mathcal{A}$, there exists an adversary $\mathcal{B}$ such that $T(\mathcal{B}) \approx T(\mathcal{A}) + Q \cdot \mathsf{poly}(\lambda)$ with $\mathsf{poly}(\lambda)$ independent of $T(\mathcal{A})$, and*

$$\mathrm{Adv}^{Q\text{-mddh}}_{\mathbb{G},\mathcal{U}_{\ell,k},\mathcal{A}}(\lambda) \leq \mathrm{Adv}^{\mathrm{mddh}}_{\mathbb{G},\mathcal{U}_{\ell,k},\mathcal{B}}(\lambda) + \frac{1}{p-1}.$$

We also recall this property of the uniform distribution, stated in [9].

Lemma 5 ($\mathcal{U}_k$-MDDH $\Leftrightarrow$ $\mathcal{U}_{\ell,k}$-MDDH). *Let $\ell, k \in \mathbb{N}$, with $\ell > k$. For any adversary $\mathcal{A}$, there exists an adversary $\mathcal{B}$ (and vice versa) such that $T(\mathcal{B}) \approx T(\mathcal{A})$ and $\mathrm{Adv}^{\mathrm{mddh}}_{\mathbb{G},\mathcal{U}_{\ell,k},\mathcal{A}}(\lambda) = \mathrm{Adv}^{\mathrm{mddh}}_{\mathbb{G},\mathcal{U}_{k},\mathcal{B}}(\lambda)$.*

In this paper, for efficiency considerations, and to simplify the presentation of the proof systems in Sect. 3, we are particularly interested in the case $k = 1$, which corresponds to the DDH assumption, that we recall here.

Definition 6 (DDH). *We say that the DDH assumption holds relative to a prime order group* $\mathbb{G}$ *if for all PPT adversaries* $\mathcal{A}$,

$$\mathrm{Adv}^{\mathrm{ddh}}_{\mathbb{G},\mathcal{A}}(\lambda) := |\Pr[\mathcal{A}(\mathcal{G},[a],[r],[ar]) = 1] - \Pr[\mathcal{A}(\mathcal{G},[a],[r],[b]| \leq \mathsf{negl}(\lambda),$$

where the probabilities are taken over $\mathcal{G} := (\mathbb{G}, p, P) \leftarrow_R \mathbf{GGen}(1^\lambda)$, $a, b, r \leftarrow_R \mathbb{Z}_p$.

Note that the DDH assumption is equivalent to $\mathcal{D}_{2,1}$*-MDDH, where* $\mathcal{D}_{2,1}$ *is the distribution that outputs matrices* $\binom{1}{a}$, *for* $a \leftarrow_R \mathbb{Z}_p$ *chosen uniformly at random.*

2.4 Public-Key Encryption

Definition 7 (Public-Key Encryption). *A public-key encryption scheme is a tuple of three PPT algorithms* (**Gen**, **Enc**, **Dec**) *such that:*

- **Gen**(1^λ): *returns a pair* (pk, sk) *of a public and a secret key.*
- **Enc**(pk, M): *given a public key* pk *and a message* $M \in \mathcal{M}(\lambda)$, *returns a ciphertext* C.
- **Dec**(pk, sk, C): *deterministically decrypts the ciphertext* C *to obtain a message* M *or a special rejection symbol* $\perp$.

We say $\mathbf{PKE} := (\mathbf{Gen}, \mathbf{Enc}, \mathbf{Dec})$ *is* ***perfectly correct****, if for all* $\lambda \in \mathbb{N}$,

$$\Pr[\mathbf{Dec}(pk, sk, \mathbf{Enc}(pk, M)) = M] = 1,$$

where the probability is over $(pk, sk) \leftarrow_R \mathbf{Gen}(1^\lambda)$, $C \leftarrow_R \mathbf{Enc}(pk, M)$.

Definition 8 (Multi-ciphertext CCA security). *For any public-key encryption scheme* $\mathbf{PKE} = (\mathbf{Gen}, \mathbf{Enc}, \mathbf{Dec})$ *and any stateful adversary* $\mathcal{A}$, *we define the following security experiment:*

$\mathrm{Exp}^{\mathrm{cca}}_{\mathbf{PKE},\mathcal{A}}(\lambda)$:	$\mathcal{O}_{\mathbf{enc}}(M_0, M_1)$:	$\mathcal{O}_{\mathbf{dec}}(C)$:
$(pk, sk) \leftarrow_R \mathbf{Gen}(1^\lambda)$ $b \leftarrow_R \{0,1\}$ $\mathcal{C}_{\mathbf{enc}} := \emptyset$ $b' \leftarrow_R \mathcal{A}^{\mathcal{O}_{\mathbf{enc}}(\cdot,\cdot),\mathcal{O}_{\mathbf{dec}}(\cdot)}(pk)$ *if* $b = b'$ ***return*** 1 ***else return*** 0	*if* $\lvert M_0\rvert = \lvert M_1\rvert$ $C \leftarrow_R \mathbf{Enc}(pk, M_b)$ $\mathcal{C}_{\mathbf{enc}} := \mathcal{C}_{\mathbf{enc}} \cup \{C\}$ ***return*** C	*if* $C \notin \mathcal{C}_{\mathbf{enc}}$ $M := \mathbf{Dec}(pk, sk, C)$ ***return*** M ***else return*** $\perp$

We say **PKE** *is IND-CCA secure, if for all PPT adversaries* $\mathcal{A}$, *the advantage*

$$\mathrm{Adv}^{\mathrm{cca}}_{\mathbf{PKE},\mathcal{A}}(\lambda) := \left|\Pr[\mathrm{Exp}^{\mathrm{cca}}_{\mathbf{PKE},\mathcal{A}}(\lambda) = 1] - \frac{1}{2}\right| \leq \mathsf{negl}(\lambda).$$

2.5 Key Encapsulation Mechanism

Instead of presenting an IND-CCA secure encryption scheme directly, we construct a key encapsulation mechanism (KEM) and prove that it satisfies the security notion of *indistinguishability against constrained chosen-ciphertext attacks* (IND-CCCA) [14]. By the results of [14], together with an arbitrary authenticated symmetric encryption scheme, this yields an IND-CCA secure hybrid encryption.[5] Roughly speaking, the CCCA security experiment, in contrast to the CCA experiment, makes an additional requirement on decryption queries. Namely, in addition to the ciphertext, the adversary has to provide a predicate implying some partial knowledge about the key to be decrypted. The idea of hybrid encryption and the notion of a KEM was first formalized in [6].

Definition 9 (Key Encapsulation Mechanism). *A* key encapsulation mechanism *is a tuple of PPT algorithms* (**KGen**, **KEnc**, **KDec**) *such that:*

KGen(1^λ)*: generates a pair* (pk, sk) *of keys.*
KEnc(pk)*: on input* pk*, returns a ciphertext* C *and a symmetric key* $K \in \mathcal{K}(\lambda)$*, where* $\mathcal{K}(\lambda)$ *is the key-space.*
KDec(pk, sk, C)*: deterministically decrypts the ciphertext* C *to obtain a key* $K \in \mathcal{K}(\lambda)$ *or a special rejection symbol bot.*

We say (**Gen**, **Enc**, **Dec**) *is* ***perfectly correct****, if for all* $\lambda \in \mathbb{N}$,

$$\Pr[\mathbf{KDec}(pk, sk, C) = K] = 1,$$

where $(pk, sk) \leftarrow_R \mathbf{Gen}(1^\lambda)$, $(K, C) \leftarrow_R \mathbf{KEnc}(pk)$ *and the probability is taken over the random coins of* **Gen** *and* **KEnc**.

As mentioned above, for *constrained* chosen ciphertext security, the adversary has to have some knowledge about the key up front in order to make a decryption query. As in [14] we will use a measure for the uncertainty left and require it to be negligible for every query, thereby only allowing decryption queries where the adversary has a high prior knowledge of the corresponding key. We now provide a formal definition.

Definition 10 (Multi-ciphertext IND-CCCA security). *For any key encapsulation mechanism* $\mathbf{KEM} = (\mathbf{KGen}, \mathbf{KEnc}, \mathbf{KDec})$ *and any stateful adversary* $\mathcal{A}$*, we define the following experiment:*

$\mathrm{Exp}^{\mathrm{ccca}}_{\mathbf{KEM},\mathcal{A}}(\lambda)$:	$\mathcal{O}_{\mathbf{enc}}$:	$\mathcal{O}_{\mathbf{dec}}(\mathsf{pred}_i, C_i)$:
$(pk, sk) \leftarrow_R \mathbf{KGen}(1^\lambda)$ $b \leftarrow_R \{0,1\}$ $\mathcal{C}_{\mathbf{enc}} := \emptyset$ $b' \leftarrow_R \mathcal{A}^{\mathcal{O}_{\mathbf{enc}}, \mathcal{O}_{\mathbf{dec}}(\cdot,\cdot)}(pk)$ *if* $b = b'$ ***return*** 1 ***else return*** 0	$K_0 \leftarrow_R \mathcal{K}(\lambda)$ $(C, K_1) \leftarrow_R \mathbf{KEnc}(pk)$ $\mathcal{C}_{\mathbf{enc}} := \mathcal{C}_{\mathbf{enc}} \cup \{C\}$ ***return*** (C, K_b)	$K_i := \mathbf{KDec}(pk, sk, C_i)$ *if* $C_i \notin \mathcal{C}_{\mathbf{enc}}$ ***and*** *if* $\mathsf{pred}_i(K_i) = 1$ ***return*** K_i ***else return*** $\perp$

[5] The corresponding reduction is tight also in the multi-user and multi-ciphertext setting. Suitable (one-time) secure symmetric encryption schemes exist even unconditionally [14].

Here $\mathsf{pred}_i \colon \mathcal{K}(\lambda) \mapsto \{0,1\}$ *denotes the predicate sent in the i-th decryption query, which is required to be provided as the description of a polynomial time algorithm (which can be enforced for instance by requiring it to be given in form of a circuit). Let further* $Q_{\mathbf{dec}}$ *be the number of total decryption queries made by* $\mathcal{A}$ *during the experiment, which are independent of the environment (hereby we refer to the environment the adversary runs in) without loss of generality. The uncertainty of knowledge about the keys corresponding to decryption queries is defined as*

$$\mathrm{uncert}_{\mathcal{A}}(\lambda) := \frac{1}{Q_{\mathbf{dec}}} \sum_{i=1}^{Q_{\mathbf{dec}}} \Pr_{K \leftarrow_R \mathcal{K}(\lambda)}[\mathsf{pred}_i(K) = 1].$$

We say that the key encapsulation mechanism **KEM** *is* IND-CCCA *secure, if for all PPT adversaries with negligible* $\mathrm{uncert}_{\mathcal{A}}(\lambda)$*, for the advantage we have*

$$\mathrm{Adv}^{\mathrm{ccca}}_{\mathbf{KEM},\mathcal{A}}(\lambda) := \left| \Pr[\mathrm{Exp}^{\mathrm{ccca}}_{\mathbf{KEM},\mathcal{A}}(\lambda) = 1] - \frac{1}{2} \right| \leq \mathsf{negl}(\lambda).$$

Note that the term $\mathrm{uncert}_{\mathcal{A}}(\lambda)$ in the final reduction (proving IND-CCA security of the hybrid encryption scheme consisting of an unconditionally one-time secure authenticated encryption scheme and an IND-CCCA secure KEM) is statistically small (due to the fact that the symmetric building block is unconditionally secure). Thus we are able obtain a tight security reduction even if the term $\mathrm{uncert}_{\mathcal{A}}(\lambda)$ is multiplied by the number of encryption and decryption queries in the security loss (as it will be the case for our construction).

3 Qualified Proof Systems

The following notion of a *proof system* is a combination of a non-interactive designated verifier proof system and a hash proof system. Our combined proofs consist of a proof Π and a key K, where the key K can be recovered by the verifier with a secret key and the proof Π. The key K can be part of the key in the key encapsulation mechanism presented later and thus will not enlarge the ciphertext size.

Definition 11 (Proof system). *Let* $\mathcal{L} = \{\mathcal{L}_{pars}\}$ *be a family of languages indexed by the public parameters pars, with* $\mathcal{L}_{pars} \subseteq \mathcal{X}_{pars}$ *and an efficiently computable witness relation* $\mathcal{R}$*. A* proof system *for* $\mathcal{L}$ *is a tuple of PPT algorithms* $(\mathbf{PGen}, \mathbf{PPrv}, \mathbf{PVer}, \mathbf{PSim})$ *such that:*

PGen(1^λ)*: generates a public key ppk and a secret key psk.*
PPrv(ppk, x, w)*: given a word* $x \in \mathcal{L}$ *and a witness* w *with* $\mathcal{R}(x,w) = 1$*, deterministically outputs a proof* Π *and a key* K*.*
PVer(ppk, psk, x, Π)*: on input ppk, psk,* $x \in \mathcal{X}$ *and* Π*, deterministically outputs a verdict* $b \in \{0,1\}$ *and in case* $b = 1$ *additionally a key* K*, else* $\perp$*.*
PSim(ppk, psk, x)*: given the keys ppk, psk and a word* $x \in \mathcal{X}$*, deterministically outputs a proof* Π *and a key* K*.*

The following definition of a qualified proof system is a variant of "benign proof systems" as defined in [11] tailored to our purposes. Compared to benign proof systems, our proof systems feature an additional "key derivation" stage, and satisfy a weaker soundness requirement (that is of course still sufficient for our purpose). We need to weaken the soundness condition (compared to benign proof systems) in order to prove soundness of our instantiation.

We will consider soundness relative to a language $\mathcal{L}^{\mathrm{snd}} \supseteq \mathcal{L}$. An adversary trying to break soundness has access to an oracle simulating proofs and keys for statements randomly chosen from $\mathcal{L}^{\mathrm{snd}} \setminus \mathcal{L}$ and a verification oracle, which only replies other than $\perp$ if the adversary provides a valid proof and has a high a-priori knowledge of the corresponding key. The adversary wins if it can provide a valid verification query outside $\mathcal{L}^{\mathrm{snd}}$. The adversary loses immediately if it provides a valid verification query in $\mathcal{L}^{\mathrm{snd}} \setminus \mathcal{L}$. This slightly weird condition is necessitated by our concrete instantiation which we do not know how to prove sound otherwise. We will give more details in the corresponding proof in Sect. 4.2. The weaker notion of soundness still suffices to prove our KEM secure, because we employ soundness at a point where valid decryption queries in $\mathcal{L}^{\mathrm{snd}} \setminus \mathcal{L}$ end the security experiment anyway.

Definition 12 (Qualified Proof System). *Let* $\mathbf{PS} = (\mathbf{PGen}, \mathbf{PPrv}, \mathbf{PVer}, \mathbf{PSim})$ *be a proof system for a family of languages* $\mathcal{L} = \{\mathcal{L}_{pars}\}$. *Let* $\mathcal{L}^{\mathrm{snd}} = \{\mathcal{L}^{\mathrm{snd}}_{pars}\}$ *be a family of languages, such that* $\mathcal{L}_{pars} \subseteq \mathcal{L}^{\mathrm{snd}}_{pars}$. *We say that* $\mathbf{PS}$ *is* $\mathcal{L}^{\mathrm{snd}}$-qualified, *if the following properties hold:*

Completeness: *For all possible public parameters pars, for all words* $x \in \mathcal{L}$, *and all witnesses* w *such that* $\mathcal{R}(x, w) = 1$, *we have*

$$\Pr[\mathbf{PVer}(ppk, psk, x, \Pi) = (1, K)] = 1,$$

where the probability is taken over $(ppk, psk) \leftarrow_R \mathbf{PGen}\,(1^\lambda)$ *and* $(\Pi, K) := \mathbf{PPrv}(ppk, x, w)$.

Uniqueness of the proofs: *For all possible public parameters pars, all key pairs* (ppk, psk) *in the output space of* $\mathbf{PGen}\,(1^\lambda)$, *and all words* $x \in \mathcal{L}$, *there exists* at most one Π *such that* $\mathbf{PVer}(ppk, psk, x, \Pi)$ *outputs the verdict* 1.

Perfect zero-knowledge: *For all public parameters pars, all key pairs* (ppk, psk) *in the range of* $\mathbf{PGen}(1^\lambda)$, *all words* $x \in \mathcal{L}$, *and all witnesses* w *with* $\mathcal{R}(x, w) = 1$, *we have*

$$\mathbf{PPrv}(ppk, x, w) = \mathbf{PSim}(ppk, psk, x).$$

Constrained $\mathcal{L}^{\mathrm{snd}}$-soundness: *For any stateful PPT adversary* $\mathcal{A}$, *we consider the following soundness game (where* $\mathbf{PSim}$ *and* $\mathbf{PVer}$ *are implicitly assumed to have access to ppk):*

$\mathrm{Exp}^{\mathrm{csnd}}_{\mathbf{PS},\mathcal{A}}(\lambda)$:	$\mathcal{O}_{\mathbf{sim}}$:	$\mathcal{O}_{\mathbf{ver}}(x, \Pi, \mathsf{pred})$:
$(ppk, psk) \leftarrow_R \mathbf{PGen}(1^\lambda)$	$x \leftarrow_R \mathcal{L}^{\mathrm{snd}} \backslash \mathcal{L}$	$(v, K) := \mathbf{PVer}(psk, x, \Pi)$
$\mathcal{A}^{\mathcal{O}_{\mathbf{sim}}, \mathcal{O}_{\mathbf{ver}}(\cdot,\cdot,\cdot)}(1^\lambda, ppk)$	$(\Pi, K) \leftarrow \mathbf{PSim}(psk, x)$	***if*** $v = 1$ ***and*** $\mathsf{pred}(K) = 1$
if $\mathcal{O}_{\mathbf{ver}}$ ***returned*** lose	***return*** (x, Π, K)	***if*** $x \in \mathcal{L}$
return 0		***return*** K
if $\mathcal{O}_{\mathbf{ver}}$ ***returned*** win		***else if*** $x \in \mathcal{L}^{\mathrm{snd}}$
return 1		***return*** lose ***and abort***
return 0		***else return*** win ***and abort***
		else return $\bot$

Let $Q_{\mathbf{ver}}$ be the total number of oracle queries to $\mathcal{O}_{\mathbf{ver}}$ and pred_i be the predicate submitted by $\mathcal{A}$ on the i-th query. The adversary $\mathcal{A}$ loses and the experiment aborts if the verification oracle answers lose *on some query of $\mathcal{A}$. The adversary $\mathcal{A}$ wins, if the oracle $\mathcal{O}_{\mathbf{ver}}$ returns* win *on some query (x, Π, pred) of $\mathcal{A}$ with $x \notin \mathcal{L}^{\mathrm{snd}}$ and the following conditions hold:*

- *The predicate corresponding to the i-th query is of the form $\mathsf{pred}_i \colon \mathcal{K} \cup \{\bot\} \rightarrow \{0, 1\}$ with $\mathsf{pred}_i(\bot) = 0$ for all $i \in \{1, \ldots, Q_{\mathbf{ver}}\}$.*
- *For all environments $\mathcal{E}$ having at most running time of the described constrained soundness experiment, we require that*

$$\mathrm{uncert}^{\mathrm{snd}}_{\mathcal{A}}(\lambda) := \frac{1}{Q_{\mathbf{ver}}} \sum_{i=1}^{Q_{\mathbf{ver}}} \Pr_{K \in \mathcal{K}}[\mathsf{pred}_i(K) = 1 \textit{ when } \mathcal{A} \textit{ runs in } \mathcal{E}]$$

is negligible in λ.
Note that in particular the adversary cannot win anymore after the verification oracle replied lose *on one of its queries, as in this case the experiment directly aborts and outputs 0. Let $\mathrm{Adv}^{\mathrm{csnd}}_{\mathcal{L}^{\mathrm{snd}},\mathbf{PS},\mathcal{A}}(\lambda) := \Pr[\mathrm{Exp}^{\mathrm{csnd}}_{\mathbf{PS},\mathcal{A}}(\lambda) = 1]$, where the probability is taken over the random coins of $\mathcal{A}$ and $\mathrm{Exp}^{\mathrm{csnd}}_{\mathbf{PS},\mathcal{A}}$. Then we say* constrained $\mathcal{L}^{\mathrm{snd}}$-soundness *holds for* **PS**, *if for every PPT adversary $\mathcal{A}$, $\mathrm{Adv}^{\mathrm{csnd}}_{\mathcal{L}^{\mathrm{snd}},\mathbf{PS},\mathcal{A}}(\lambda) = \mathsf{negl}(\lambda)$.*

To prove security of the key encapsulation mechanism later, we need to switch between two proof systems. Intuitively this provides an additional degree of freedom, allowing to randomize the keys of the challenge ciphertexts gradually. To justify this transition, we introduce the following notion of indistinguishable proof systems.

Definition 13 ($\mathcal{L}^{\mathrm{snd}}$-indistinguishability of two proof systems). *Let $\mathcal{L} \subseteq \mathcal{L}^{\mathrm{snd}}$ be (families of) languages. Let $\mathbf{PS}_0 := (\mathbf{PGen}_0, \mathbf{PPrv}_0, \mathbf{PVer}_0, \mathbf{PSim}_0)$ and $\mathbf{PS}_1 := (\mathbf{PGen}_1, \mathbf{PPrv}_1, \mathbf{PVer}_1, \mathbf{PSim}_1)$ proof systems for $\mathcal{L}$. For every adversary $\mathcal{A}$, we define the following experiment (where $\mathbf{PSim}_b$ and $\mathbf{PVer}_b$ are implicitly assumed to have access to ppk):*

$\mathrm{Exp}^{\mathrm{PS-ind}}_{\mathcal{L}^{\mathrm{snd}},\mathbf{PS}_0,\mathbf{PS}_1,\mathcal{A}}(\lambda)$:	$\mathcal{O}^b_{\mathbf{sim}}$:	$\mathcal{O}^b_{\mathbf{ver}}(x, \Pi, \mathsf{pred})$:
$b \leftarrow_R \{0,1\}$	$x \leftarrow_R \mathcal{L}^{\mathrm{snd}} \setminus \mathcal{L}$	$(v, K) := \mathbf{PVer}_b(psk, x, \Pi)$
$(ppk, psk) \leftarrow \mathbf{PGen}_b(1^\lambda)$	$(\Pi, K) \leftarrow \mathbf{PSim}_b(psk, x)$	***if*** $v = 1$ ***and*** $\mathsf{pred}(K) = 1$
$b' \leftarrow \mathcal{A}^{\mathcal{O}^b_{\mathbf{sim}}, \mathcal{O}^b_{\mathbf{ver}}(\cdot,\cdot)}(ppk)$	***return*** (x, Π, K)	***and*** $x \in \mathcal{L}^{\mathrm{snd}}$
if $b = b'$ ***return*** 1		***return*** K
else return 0		***else return*** $\perp$

As soon as $\mathcal{A}$ has submitted one query which is replied with lose *by the verification oracle, the experiment aborts and outputs* 0.

We define the advantage function

$$\mathrm{Adv}^{\mathrm{PS\text{-}ind}}_{\mathcal{L}^{\mathrm{snd}},\mathbf{PS}_0,\mathbf{PS}_1,\mathcal{A}}(\lambda) := \left| \Pr\left[\mathrm{Exp}^{\mathrm{PS-ind}}_{\mathcal{L}^{\mathrm{snd}},\mathbf{PS}_0,\mathbf{PS}_1,\mathcal{A}}(\lambda) = 1\right] - \frac{1}{2} \right|.$$

We say $\mathbf{PS}_0$ *and* $\mathbf{PS}_1$ *are* $\mathcal{L}^{\mathrm{snd}}$-indistinguishable, *if for all (unbounded) algorithms* $\mathcal{A}$ *the advantage* $\mathrm{Adv}^{\mathrm{PS\text{-}ind}}_{\mathcal{L},\mathbf{PS}_0,\mathbf{PS}_1,\mathcal{A}}(\lambda)$ *is negligible in* λ.

Note that we adopt a different (and simpler) definition for the verification oracle in the indistinguishability game than in the soundness game, in particular it leaks more information about the keys. We can afford this additional leakage for indistinguishability, but not for soundness.

In order to prove security of the key encapsulation mechanism presented in Sect. 5, we will require one proof system and the existence of a second proof system it can be extended to. We capture this property in the following definition.

Definition 14 ($\widetilde{\mathcal{L}^{\mathrm{snd}}}$-extensibility of a proof system). *Let* $\mathcal{L} \subseteq \mathcal{L}^{\mathrm{snd}} \subseteq \widetilde{\mathcal{L}^{\mathrm{snd}}}$ *be three (families of) languages. An* $\mathcal{L}^{\mathrm{snd}}$*-qualified proof system* $\mathbf{PS}$ *for language* $\mathcal{L}$ *is said to be* $\widetilde{\mathcal{L}^{\mathrm{snd}}}$-extensible *if there exists a proof system* $\widetilde{\mathbf{PS}}$ *for* $\mathcal{L}$ *that complies with* $\widetilde{\mathcal{L}^{\mathrm{snd}}}$*-constrained soundness and such that* $\mathbf{PS}$ *and* $\widetilde{\mathbf{PS}}$ *are* $\mathcal{L}^{\mathrm{snd}}$*-indistinguishable.*

4 The OR-Proof

In the following sections we explain how the public parameters $pars_{\mathbf{PS}}$ are sampled, how our system of OR-languages is defined and how to construct a qualified proof system complying with constrained soundness respective to these languages.

4.1 Public Parameters and the OR-Languages

First we need to choose a $k \in \mathbb{N}$ depending on the assumption we use to prove security of our constructions. We invoke $\mathbf{GGen}(1^\lambda)$ to obtain a group description $\mathcal{G} = (\mathbb{G}, p, P)$ with $|\mathbb{G}| \geq 2^{2\lambda}$. Next we sample matrices $\mathbf{A} \leftarrow_R \mathcal{D}_{2k,k}$ and $\mathbf{A}_0 \leftarrow_R \mathcal{U}_{2k,k}$, where we assume without loss of generality that $\overline{\mathbf{A}}_0$ is full rank. Let $\mathcal{H}_0$ and $\mathcal{H}_1$ be *universal* hash function generators returning functions of the form $\mathsf{h}_0 \colon \mathbb{G}^{k+1} \to \mathbb{Z}_p^k$ and $\mathsf{h}_1 \colon \mathbb{G}^2 \to \mathbb{Z}_p$ respectively. Let $\mathsf{h}_0 \leftarrow_R \mathcal{H}_0$ and $\mathsf{h}_1 \leftarrow_R \mathcal{H}_1$.

Altogether we define the public parameters for our proof system to comprise

$$pars_{\mathbf{PS}} := (k, \mathcal{G}, [\mathbf{A}], [\mathbf{A}_0], \mathsf{h}_0, \mathsf{h}_1).$$

We assume from now that all algorithms have access to $pars_{\mathbf{PS}}$ without explicitly stating it as input.

Additionally let $\mathbf{A}_1 \in \mathbb{Z}_p^{2k \times k}$ be a matrix distributed according to $\mathcal{U}_{2k,k}$ with the restriction $\overline{\mathbf{A}}_0 = \overline{\mathbf{A}}_1$. Then we define the languages

$$\begin{aligned} \mathcal{L} &: = \mathrm{span}([\mathbf{A}]), \\ \mathcal{L}_{\mathrm{snd}} &: = \mathrm{span}([\mathbf{A}]) \cup \mathrm{span}([\mathbf{A}_0]), \\ \widetilde{\mathcal{L}_{\mathrm{snd}}} &: = \mathrm{span}([\mathbf{A}]) \cup \mathrm{span}([\mathbf{A}_0]) \cup \mathrm{span}([\mathbf{A}_1]). \end{aligned}$$

A crucial building block for the key encapsulation mechanism will be a proof system **PS** that is $\mathcal{L}_{\mathrm{snd}}$-qualified and $\widetilde{\mathcal{L}_{\mathrm{snd}}}$-extensible. We give a construction based on $\mathcal{D}_{2k,k}$-MDDH in the following section.

4.2 A Construction Based on MDDH

The goal of this section is to construct an $\mathcal{L}_{\mathrm{snd}}$-qualified proof system for $\mathcal{L}$ based on $\mathcal{D}_{2k,k}$-MDDH for any matrix distribution $\mathcal{D}_{2k,k}$ (see Definition 3). To this aim we give a proof system *Pre***PS** := (*Pre***PGen**, *Pre***PPrv**, *Pre***PVer**, *Pre***PSim**) for $\mathcal{L}$ in Fig. 2.

In case $k = 1$ this is sufficient, namely setting **PGen** := *Pre***PGen**, **PPrv** := *Pre***PPrv**, **PVer** := *Pre***PVer** and **PSim** := *Pre***PSim**, we can prove that **PS** : = (**PGen**, **PPrv**, **PVer**, **PSim**) is $\mathcal{L}_{\mathrm{snd}}$-qualified under the DDH assumption. For the case $k > 1$ we give the construction of **PS** in the full version.

As a compromise between generality and readability, we decided to give the proof in full detail for $k = 1$ (i.e. the DDH case), while sticking to the general matrix notation. As for $k = 1$ a vector in $\mathbb{Z}_p^k = \mathbb{Z}_p^1$ is merely a single element, we do not use bold letters to denote for instance x and r in $\mathbb{Z}_p$ (other than in Fig. 2).

Theorem 1. *If the DDH assumption holds in* $\mathbb{G}$, *and* h_0, h_1 *are universal hash functions, then for* $k = 1$ *the proof system* **PS** := *Pre***PS** *described in Fig. 2 is* $\mathcal{L}^{\mathrm{snd}}$*-qualified. Further, the proof system* **PS** *is* $\widetilde{\mathcal{L}_{\mathrm{snd}}}$*-extensible.*

Proof. Completeness and *perfect zero-knowledge* follow straightforwardly from the fact that for all $r \in \mathbb{Z}_p$, $[\mathbf{K}_x\mathbf{A}]r = \mathbf{K}_x[\mathbf{A}r]$ and $[\mathbf{K}_y\mathbf{A}]r = \mathbf{K}_y[\mathbf{A}r]$.

Uniqueness of the keys follows from the fact that the verification algorithm computes exactly one proof $[\pi]$ (plus the corresponding key $[\kappa]$), and aborts if $[\pi] \neq [\pi^\star]$.

We prove in Lemm 6 that **PS** satisfies constrained $\mathcal{L}^{\mathrm{snd}}$-soundness.

In the full version we prove that **PS** is $\widetilde{\mathcal{L}^{\mathrm{snd}}}$-extensible. □

$Pre\mathbf{PGen}(1^\lambda)$: $\mathbf{K_x} \leftarrow_R \mathbb{Z}_p^{(k+1)\times 2k}$ $\mathbf{K}_y \leftarrow_R \mathbb{Z}_p^{2\times 2k}$ **return** $ppk := ([\mathbf{K_x A}], [\mathbf{K}_y \mathbf{A}])$ $psk := (\mathbf{K_x}, \mathbf{K}_y)$	$Pre\mathbf{PPrv}(ppk, [\mathbf{c}], \mathbf{r})$: $\mathbf{x} := \mathsf{h}_0([\mathbf{K_x A}]\mathbf{r}) \in \mathbb{Z}_p^k$ $y := \mathsf{h}_1([\mathbf{K}_y \mathbf{A}]\mathbf{r}) \in \mathbb{Z}_p$ **return** $[\pi] := \overline{[\mathbf{A}_0]} \cdot \mathbf{x} + \overline{[\mathbf{c}]} \cdot y$ $[\kappa] := \underline{[\mathbf{A}_0]} \cdot \mathbf{x} + \underline{[\mathbf{c}]} \cdot y$
$Pre\mathbf{PVer}(ppk, psk, [\mathbf{c}], [\pi^\star])$: $\mathbf{x} := \mathsf{h}_0(\mathbf{K_x}[\mathbf{c}]) \in \mathbb{Z}_p^k$ $y := \mathsf{h}_1(\mathbf{K}_y[\mathbf{c}]) \in \mathbb{Z}_p$ $[\pi] := \overline{[\mathbf{A}_0]} \cdot \mathbf{x} + \overline{[\mathbf{c}]} \cdot y \in \mathbb{Z}_p^k$ $[\kappa] := \underline{[\mathbf{A}_0]} \cdot \mathbf{x} + \underline{[\mathbf{c}]} \cdot y \in \mathbb{Z}_p^k$ **if** $[\pi] = [\pi^\star]$ **return** $(1, [\kappa])$ **else return** $(0, \perp)$	$Pre\mathbf{PSim}(ppk, psk, [\mathbf{c}])$: $\mathbf{x} := \mathsf{h}_0(\mathbf{K_x}[\mathbf{c}]) \in \mathbb{Z}_p^k$ $y := \mathsf{h}_1(\mathbf{K}_y[\mathbf{c}]) \in \mathbb{Z}_p$ **return** $[\pi] := \overline{[\mathbf{A}_0]} \cdot \mathbf{x} + \overline{[\mathbf{c}]} \cdot y$ $[\kappa] := \underline{[\mathbf{A}_0]} \cdot \mathbf{x} + \underline{[\mathbf{c}]} \cdot y$

Fig. 2. Proof System $Pre\mathbf{PS}$ for $\mathcal{L}$. For $k = 1$ the proof system $\mathbf{PS} := Pre\mathbf{PS}$ is $\mathcal{L}_{\mathsf{snd}}$-qualified based on DDH.

Lemma 6 (Constrained $\mathcal{L}^{\mathsf{snd}}$-soundness of PS). *If the DDH assumption holds in $\mathbb{G}$, and h_0, h_1 are universal hash functions, then the proof system* $\mathbf{PS}$ *described in Fig. 2 (for $k = 1$) complies with constrained $\mathcal{L}^{\mathsf{snd}}$-soundness. More precisely, for every adversary $\mathcal{A}$, there exists an adversary $\mathcal{B}$ such that $T(\mathcal{B}) \approx T(\mathcal{A}) + (Q_{\mathbf{sim}} + Q_{\mathbf{ver}}) \cdot \mathsf{poly}(\lambda)$ and*

$$\mathrm{Adv}^{\mathrm{csnd}}_{\mathbf{PS},\mathcal{A}}(\lambda) \leq \mathrm{Adv}^{\mathrm{ddh}}_{\mathbb{G},\mathcal{B}}(\lambda) + Q_{\mathbf{ver}} \cdot \mathrm{uncert}^{\mathrm{snd}}_{\mathcal{A}}(\lambda) + (Q_{\mathbf{sim}} + Q_{\mathbf{ver}}) \cdot 2^{-\Omega(\lambda)},$$

where $Q_{\mathbf{ver}}$, $Q_{\mathbf{sim}}$ are the number of calls to $\mathcal{O}_{\mathbf{ver}}$ and $\mathcal{O}_{\mathbf{sim}}$ respectively, $\mathrm{uncert}^{\mathrm{snd}}_{\mathcal{A}}(\lambda)$ *describes the uncertainty of the predicates provided by $\mathcal{A}$ (see Definition 12) and* poly *is a polynomial function independent of $T(\mathcal{A})$.*

Note that, as explained in Sect. 2.5, in the proof of IND-CCA security of the final hybrid encryption scheme (where we will employ constrained $\mathcal{L}_{\mathsf{snd}}$-soundness of $\mathbf{PS}$ to prove IND-CCCA security of our KEM), the term $\mathrm{uncert}^{\mathrm{snd}}_{\mathcal{A}}(\lambda)$ will be statistically small, so we can afford to get a security loss of $Q_{\mathbf{ver}} \cdot \mathrm{uncert}^{\mathrm{snd}}_{\mathcal{A}}(\lambda)$ without compromising tightness.

Proof. We prove $\mathcal{L}_{\mathsf{snd}}$-*soundness* of $\mathbf{PS}$ via a series of games, described in Fig. 3. We start by giving a short overview of the proof.

The idea is to first randomize x used in simulated proofs of statements $[\mathbf{c}] \in \mathcal{L}_{\mathsf{snd}} \setminus \mathcal{L}$, using the DDH assumption and the Leftover Hash Lemma (Lemma 1). This makes $[\pi, \kappa]$ an encryption of y that becomes lossy if and only if $[\mathbf{c}] \in \mathrm{span}([\mathbf{A}_0])$. For the final proof step, let $([\mathbf{c}], [\pi], [\kappa])$ be an honestly generated combined proof (with randomized x) with $[\mathbf{c}] \in \mathcal{L}_{\mathsf{snd}}$, that is there exists an $r \in \mathbb{Z}_p$ such that either $[\mathbf{c}] = [\mathbf{A}r]$ or $[\mathbf{c}] = [\mathbf{A}_0 r]$. In the former case, we have $y = \mathsf{h}_1(\mathbf{K}_y^\top [\mathbf{c}]) = \mathsf{h}_1([\mathbf{K}_y \mathbf{A}]r)$, thus no information about $\mathbf{K}_y$ is leaked apart from what is already contained in the public key. In the latter case, we have

#	sim. x for $[\mathbf{c}] \in \mathcal{L}_{\text{snd}} \backslash \mathcal{L}$	ver. $[\kappa]$ for $[\mathbf{c}] \notin \mathcal{L}$	game knows	remark
$\mathbf{G}_0$	$x := \mathsf{h}_0(\mathbf{K}_x[\mathbf{c}])$	$\underline{[\mathbf{A}_0]} \cdot \mathbf{x} + \underline{[\mathbf{c}]} \cdot y$		$\mathcal{L}_{\text{snd}}$-soundn. game w/o *lose*
$\mathbf{G}_1$	$x := \mathsf{h}_0(\mathbf{K}_x[\mathbf{c}])$	$\underline{\mathbf{A}}_0\overline{\mathbf{A}_0}^{-1}\left([\pi^\star] - \overline{[\mathbf{c}]} \cdot y\right) + \underline{[\mathbf{c}]} \cdot y$	$\mathbf{A}, \mathbf{A}_0$	win. chances increase
$\mathbf{G}_2$	$\mathbf{u} \leftarrow_R \mathbb{Z}_p^2$ $x := \mathsf{h}_0([\mathbf{u}])$	$\underline{\mathbf{A}}_0\overline{\mathbf{A}_0}^{-1}\left([\pi^\star] - \overline{[\mathbf{c}]} \cdot y\right) + \underline{[\mathbf{c}]} \cdot y$	$\mathbf{A}, \mathbf{A}_0$	DDH
$\mathbf{G}_3$	$x \leftarrow_R \mathbb{Z}_p$	$\underline{\mathbf{A}}_0\overline{\mathbf{A}_0}^{-1}\left([\pi^\star] - \overline{[\mathbf{c}]} \cdot y\right) + \underline{[\mathbf{c}]} \cdot y$	$\mathbf{A}, \mathbf{A}_0$	Lemma 1 (LOHL)

Fig. 3. Overview of the proof of $\mathcal{L}_{\text{snd}}$-constrained soundness of **PS**. The first column shows how x is computed for queries to $\mathcal{O}_{\mathbf{sim}}$. The second column shows how the key $[\kappa]$ is computed by the verifier in queries to $\mathcal{O}_{\mathbf{ver}}$ when $[\mathbf{c}] \notin \mathcal{L}$.

$[\pi, \kappa] = [\mathbf{A}_0] \cdot x + [\mathbf{c}] \cdot y = [\mathbf{A}_0](x + r \cdot y)$, thus y, and in particular $\mathbf{K}_y$, are completely hidden by the randomized x. This implies that even knowing many sound tuples $([\mathbf{c}], [\pi], [\kappa])$ for $[\mathbf{c}] \in \mathcal{L}_{\text{snd}}$, an adversary cannot do better than guessing y to produce a valid key for a statement outside $\mathcal{L}_{\text{snd}}$, and therefore, only has negligible winning chances.

We start with the constrained $\mathcal{L}_{\text{snd}}$-soundness game, which we refer to as game $\mathbf{G}$. In the following we want to bound the probability

$$\varepsilon := \mathrm{Adv}^{\mathrm{csnd}}_{\mathbf{PS},\mathcal{A}}(\lambda).$$

We denote the probability that the adversary $\mathcal{A}$ wins the game $\mathbf{G}_i$ by

$$\varepsilon_i := \mathrm{Adv}_{\mathbf{G}_i,\mathcal{A}}(\lambda).$$

$\mathbf{G} \rightsquigarrow \mathbf{G}_0$: From game $\mathbf{G}_0$ on, on a valid verification query $([\mathbf{c}], \Pi, \mathsf{pred})$ the verification oracle will not return *lose* and abort anymore, but instead simply return $\perp$. This can only increase the winning chances of an adversary $\mathcal{A}$. Thus we obtain

$$\varepsilon \leq \varepsilon_0.$$

$\mathbf{G}_0 \rightsquigarrow \mathbf{G}_1$**:** We show that $\varepsilon_1 \geq \varepsilon_0$. The difference between $\mathbf{G}_0$ and $\mathbf{G}_1$ is that from game $\mathbf{G}_1$ on the oracle $\mathcal{O}_{\mathbf{ver}}$, on input $([\mathbf{c}], \Pi, \mathsf{pred})$, first checks if $[\mathbf{c}] \in \mathrm{span}([\mathbf{A}])$. If this is the case, $\mathcal{O}_{\mathbf{ver}}$ behaves as in game $\mathbf{G}_0$. Otherwise, it does not check if $[\pi^\star] = [\pi]$ anymore, and it computes

$$[\kappa] = \underline{\mathbf{A}}_0\overline{\mathbf{A}_0}^{-1}\left([\pi^\star] - \overline{[\mathbf{c}]} \cdot y\right) + \underline{[\mathbf{c}]} \cdot y,$$

where y is computed as in $\mathbf{G}_0$. Note that this computation requires to know $\mathbf{A}_0$, but not $\mathbf{K}_x$, since x is not computed explicitly. This will be crucial for the transition to game $\mathbf{G}_2$.

We again have to show that this can only increase the winning chances of the adversary, in particular we have to show that this change does not affect the adversaries view on non-winning queries.

First, from game $\mathbf{G}_0$ on the verification oracle $\mathcal{O}_{\mathbf{ver}}$ always returns $\perp$ on queries from $\mathcal{L}_{\mathsf{snd}} \backslash \mathcal{L}$, and thus games $\mathbf{G}_0$ and $\mathbf{G}_1$ only differ when $\mathcal{O}_{\mathbf{ver}}$ is queried on statements with $[\mathbf{c}] \notin \mathcal{L}_{\mathsf{snd}}$. Therefore it remains to show that for any query $([\mathbf{c}], [\pi^\star], \mathsf{pred})$ to $\mathcal{O}_{\mathbf{ver}}$ with $[\mathbf{c}] \notin \mathcal{L}_{\mathsf{snd}}$, we have that if the query is winning in $\mathbf{G}_0$, then it is also winning in $\mathbf{G}_1$. Suppose $([\mathbf{c}], [\pi^\star], \mathsf{pred})$ satisfies the winning condition in $\mathbf{G}_0$. Then, it must hold true that $[\pi^\star] = [\overline{\mathbf{A}_0}] \cdot \mathbf{x} + [\overline{\mathbf{c}}] \cdot y$ and $\mathsf{pred}\Big([\underline{\mathbf{A}_0}] \cdot \mathbf{x} + [\underline{\mathbf{c}}] \cdot y\Big) = 1$. In $\mathbf{G}_1$, the key is computed as

$$\underline{\mathbf{A}_0}\overline{\mathbf{A}_0}^{-1}\Big([\pi^\star] - [\overline{\mathbf{c}}] \cdot y\Big) + [\underline{\mathbf{c}}] \cdot y = [\underline{\mathbf{A}_0}] \cdot \mathbf{x} + [\underline{\mathbf{c}}] \cdot y,$$

and thus the query is also winning in $\mathbf{G}_1$.

Note that for this step it is crucial that we only require a weakened soundness condition of our proof systems (compared to benign proof systems [11]). Namely, if instead the verification oracle in the soundness experiment $\mathcal{O}_{\mathbf{ver}}$ returned the key $[\kappa]$ for valid statements $x \in \mathcal{L}^{\mathsf{snd}} \backslash \mathcal{L}$, we could not argue that the proof transition does necessarily at most increase the winning chances of an adversary. This holds true as in game $\mathbf{G}_1$ on a statement $x \in \mathcal{L}^{\mathsf{snd}} \backslash \mathcal{L}$ with non-valid proof (but with valid predicate respective to the proof) the key would be returned, whereas in game $\mathbf{G}_0$ "$\perp$" would be returned.

$\mathbf{G}_1 \rightsquigarrow \mathbf{G}_2$: In this transition, we use the DDH assumption to change the way x is computed in simulated proofs. More precisely, we build an adversary $\mathcal{B}$ such that $T(\mathcal{B}) \approx T(\mathcal{A}) + (Q_{\mathbf{ver}} + Q_{\mathbf{sim}}) \cdot \mathsf{poly}(\lambda)$ and

$$|\varepsilon_2 - \varepsilon_1| \leq \mathrm{Adv}^{\mathrm{ddh}}_{\mathbb{G},\mathcal{B}}(\lambda) + 2^{-\Omega(\lambda)}.$$

Let $([\mathbf{B}], [\mathbf{h}_1, \ldots, \mathbf{h}_{Q_{\mathbf{sim}}}])$ be a $Q_{\mathbf{sim}}$-fold DDH challenge. We build the adversary $\mathcal{B}$ as follows. First $\mathcal{B}$ picks $\mathbf{A}, \mathbf{A}_0, \mathbf{A}_1$ as described in Sect. 4.1. Further $\mathcal{B}$ chooses $\mathbf{K}'_x \leftarrow_R \mathbb{Z}_p^{2\times 2}$ and $\mathbf{K}_y \leftarrow_R \mathbb{Z}_p^{2\times 2}$ and implicitely sets $\mathbf{K}_x = \mathbf{K}'_x + \mathbf{U}(\mathbf{A}^\perp)^\top$ for some $\mathbf{A}^\perp \in \mathsf{orth}(\mathbf{A})$, where $\mathbf{U} \in \mathbb{Z}_p^{2\times 1}$ depends on the $Q_{\mathbf{sim}}$-fold DDH challenge (and cannot be computed by $\mathcal{B}$). This will allow $\mathcal{B}$ to embed the $Q_{\mathbf{sim}}$-fold DDH challenge into simulation queries. Note that even though $\mathcal{B}$ does not know $\mathbf{K}_x$ explicitly, the special form of $\mathbf{K}_x$ still allows $\mathcal{B}$ to compute the public parameters $[\mathbf{K}_x\mathbf{A}] = [\mathbf{K}'_x\mathbf{A}]$ and $[\mathbf{K}_y\mathbf{A}]$.

For queries to $\mathcal{O}_{\mathbf{ver}}$ containing $[\mathbf{c}] \in \mathcal{L}$, in order to compute x, $\mathcal{B}$ computes $\mathbf{K}_x[\mathbf{c}] = \mathbf{K}'_x[\mathbf{c}]$ using $\mathbf{K}'_x$ (note that $\mathcal{B}$ can check if $[\mathbf{c}] \in \mathcal{L}$ since it knows $\mathbf{A}$). Answering queries to $\mathcal{O}_{\mathbf{ver}}$ for $\mathbf{c} \notin \mathcal{L}$ does not require knowledge of x. Both cases can thus be handled without concrete knowledge of $\mathbf{K}_x$.

The adversary $\mathcal{B}$ prepares for queries to the simulation oracle $\mathcal{O}_{\mathbf{sim}}$ as follows. First it chooses $w \leftarrow \mathbb{Z}_p$ and defines $[\mathbf{V}] := w \cdot [\mathbf{B}]$. Note that with overwhelming probability over the choices of $\mathbf{A}$ and $\mathbf{A}_0$, the matrix $(\mathbf{A}^\perp)^\top \mathbf{A}_0$ is full rank and thus $(\mathbf{K}'_x + \mathbf{U}(\mathbf{A}^\perp)^\top)\mathbf{A}_0$ is distributed statistically close to uniform over $\mathbb{Z}_p$. Therefore replacing $[(\mathbf{K}'_x + \mathbf{U}(\mathbf{A}^\perp)^\top)\mathbf{A}_0]$ by $[\mathbf{V}]$ is statistically indistinguishable for the adversary $\mathcal{A}$.

On the i-th query to $\mathcal{O}_{\mathbf{sim}}$, for all $i \in [Q_{\mathbf{sim}}]$, the adversary $\mathcal{B}$ defines $[\mathbf{c}_i] := \mathbf{A}_0[\mathbf{h}_i]$ and computes $x := \mathsf{h}_0(w \cdot [\mathbf{h}_i])$. Further $\mathcal{B}$ can compute $y := \mathsf{h}_1(\mathbf{K}_y[\mathbf{c}_i])$ as before. In case of a real DDH challenge, we have $\mathbf{h}_i = \mathbf{B}r_i$ for $r_i \leftarrow_R \mathbb{Z}_p$ and thus we have $[\mathbf{c}_i] = [\mathbf{A}_0 r_i]$ and $x = \mathsf{h}_0(w \cdot [\mathbf{B}r_i]) = \mathsf{h}_0([\mathbf{V}r_i])$. By our previous considerations $[\mathbf{V}r_i]$ is statistically close to $\mathbf{K}_x[\mathbf{c}_i]$ and thus adversary $\mathcal{B}$ simulates game $\mathbf{G}_1$. In case the adversary was given a random challenge, the $\mathbf{h}_i$ are distributed uniformly at random and the adversary simulates game $\mathbf{G}_2$. Now we can employ the random self-reducibility of DDH (Lemma 2) to obtain an adversary as claimed.

Note that in order to prove this transition we require that in the definition of constrained soundness the simulation oracle returns random challenges (otherwise we would not be able to embedd the DDH challenge into simulation queries). This is another reason why we cannot directly employ the notion of benign proof systems [11].

$\mathbf{G}_2 \rightsquigarrow \mathbf{G}_3$: As h_0 is universal, we can employ the Leftover Hash Lemma (Lemma 1) to switch $(\mathsf{h}_0, \mathsf{h}_0([\mathbf{v}]))$ to $(\mathsf{h}_0, \mathbf{u})$ in all simulation queries, where $\mathbf{u} \leftarrow_R \mathbb{Z}_p$. A hybrid argument yields

$$|\varepsilon_2 - \varepsilon_3| \leq Q_{\mathbf{sim}}/p.$$

Game $\mathbf{G}_3$: We show that $\varepsilon_3 \leq Q_{\mathbf{ver}} \cdot \mathrm{uncert}^{\mathrm{snd}}_{\mathcal{A}}(\lambda)$, where $Q_{\mathbf{ver}}$ is the number of queries to $\mathcal{O}_{\mathbf{ver}}$ and $\mathrm{uncert}^{\mathrm{snd}}_{\mathcal{A}}(\lambda)$ describes the uncertainty of the predicates provided by the adversary as described in Definition 12.

We use a hybrid argument over the $Q_{\mathbf{ver}}$ queries to $\mathcal{O}_{\mathbf{ver}}$. To that end, we introduce games $\mathbf{G}_{3.i}$ for $i = 0, \ldots, Q_{\mathbf{ver}}$, defined as $\mathbf{G}_3$ except that for its first i queries $\mathcal{O}_{\mathbf{ver}}$ answers $\perp$ on any query $([\mathbf{c}], [\pi], \mathsf{pred})$ with $[\mathbf{c}] \notin \mathcal{L}_{\mathrm{snd}}$. We have $\varepsilon_3 = \varepsilon_{3.0}$, $\varepsilon_{3.Q_{\mathbf{ver}}} = 0$ and we show that for all $i = 0, \ldots, Q_{\mathbf{ver}} - 1$ it holds

$$|\varepsilon_{3.i} - \varepsilon_{3.(i+1)}| \leq \Pr_{K \in \mathcal{K}}[\mathsf{pred}_{i+1}(K) = 1] + 2^{-\Omega(\lambda)},$$

where pred_{i+1} is the predicate contained in the $i+1$-th query to $\mathcal{O}_{\mathbf{ver}}$.

Games $\mathbf{G}_{3.i}$ and $\mathbf{G}_{3.(i+1)}$ behave identically on the first i queries to $\mathcal{O}_{\mathbf{ver}}$. An adversary can only distinguish between the two, if it manages to provide a valid $(i+1)$-st query $([\mathbf{c}], [\pi], \mathsf{pred})$ to $\mathcal{O}_{\mathbf{ver}}$ with $[\mathbf{c}] \notin \mathcal{L}_{\mathrm{snd}}$. In the following we bound the probability of this happening.

From queries to $\mathcal{O}_{\mathbf{sim}}$ and the first i queries to $\mathcal{O}_{\mathbf{ver}}$ the adversary can only learn valid tuples $([\mathbf{c}], [\pi], [\kappa])$ with $[\mathbf{c}] \in \mathcal{L}_{\mathrm{snd}}$. As explained in the beginning, such combined proofs reveal nothing about $\mathbf{K}_y$ beyond what is already revealed in the public key, as either $[\mathbf{c}] = [\mathbf{A}r]$ for an $r \in \mathbb{Z}_p$ and $y = \mathsf{h}_1([\mathbf{K}_y\mathbf{c}]) = \mathsf{h}_1([\mathbf{K}_y\mathbf{A}]r)$ or $[\mathbf{c}] = [\mathbf{A}_0 r]$ and $[\pi, \kappa] = [\mathbf{A}_0](x + r \cdot y)$. In the former case y itself reveals no more about $\mathbf{K}_y$ than the public key, while in the latter case y is hidden by the fully randomized x.

For any $[\mathbf{c}] \notin \mathcal{L}_{\mathrm{snd}}$, $y = \mathsf{h}_1[\mathbf{K}_y\mathbf{c}]$ computed by $\mathcal{O}_{\mathbf{ver}}$ is distributed statistically close to uniform from the adversary's point of view because of the following. First we can replace $\mathbf{K}_y$ by $\mathbf{K}_y + \mathbf{U}(\mathbf{A}^{\perp})^{\top}$ for $\mathbf{U} \leftarrow_R \mathbb{Z}_p^{2\times 1}$ and $\mathbf{A}^{\perp} \in \mathsf{orth}(\mathbf{A})$

as both are distributed identically. By our considerations, this extra term is neither revealed through the public key, nor through the previous queries to $\mathcal{O}_{\mathbf{sim}}$ and $\mathcal{O}_{\mathbf{ver}}$.

Now Lemma 1 (Leftover Hash Lemma) implies that the distribution of y is statistically close to uniform as desired. Since $[\mathbf{c}] \notin \mathrm{span}([\mathbf{A}_0])$ we have $\underline{[\mathbf{c}]} - \underline{[\mathbf{A}_0]}\overline{\mathbf{A}_0}^{-1}\overline{[\mathbf{c}]} \neq 0$, thus the key

$$[\kappa] := \underline{\mathbf{A}}_0\overline{\mathbf{A}_0}^{-1}[\pi^\star] + \underbrace{\left(\underline{[\mathbf{c}]} - \underline{\mathbf{A}}_0\overline{\mathbf{A}_0}^{-1}\overline{[\mathbf{c}]}\right)}_{\neq 0} \cdot y$$

computed by $\mathcal{O}_{\mathbf{ver}}$ is statistically close to uniform over $\mathbb{Z}_p$. Altogether we obtain:

$$\varepsilon_3 \leq Q_{\mathbf{ver}} \cdot \mathrm{uncert}^{\mathrm{snd}}_{\mathcal{A}}(\lambda) + Q_{\mathbf{ver}} \cdot 2^{-\Omega(\lambda)}.$$

5 Key Encapsulation Mechanism

In this section we present our CCCA-secure KEM that builds upon a qualified proof system for the OR-language as presented in Sect. 4.

Ingredients. Let $pars_{\mathbf{PS}}$ be the public parameters for the underlying qualified proof system comprising $\mathcal{G} = (\mathbb{G}, p, P)$ and $\mathbf{A}, \mathbf{A}_0 \in \mathbb{Z}_p^{2k\times k}$ (as defined in Sect. 4.1). Recall that $\mathcal{L} = \mathrm{span}([\mathbf{A}])$, $\mathcal{L}_{\mathrm{snd}} = \mathrm{span}([\mathbf{A}]) \cup \mathrm{span}([\mathbf{A}_0])$ and $\widetilde{\mathcal{L}_{\mathrm{snd}}} = \mathrm{span}([\mathbf{A}]) \cup \mathrm{span}([\mathbf{A}_0]) \cup \mathrm{span}([\mathbf{A}_1])$ (for $\mathbf{A}_1 \in \mathbb{Z}_p^{2k\times k}$ as in Sect. 4.1). Let further $\mathcal{H}$ be a collosion resistant hash function generator returning functions of the form $\mathsf{H}\colon \mathbb{G}^k \to \{0,1\}^\lambda$ and let $\mathsf{H} \leftarrow_R \mathcal{H}$. We will sometimes interpret values $\tau \in \{0,1\}^\lambda$ in the image of H as elements in $\mathbb{Z}_p$ via the map $\tau \mapsto \sum_{i=1}^{\lambda} \tau_i \cdot 2^{i-1}$.

In the following we assume that all algorithms implicitly have access to the public parameters $pars_{\mathbf{KEM}} := (pars_{\mathbf{PS}}, \mathsf{H})$.

Proof systems. We employ an $\mathcal{L}_{\mathrm{snd}}$-qualified and $\widetilde{\mathcal{L}_{\mathrm{snd}}}$-extensible proof system $\mathbf{PS} := (\mathbf{PGen}, \mathbf{PPrv}, \mathbf{PVer}, \mathbf{PSim})$ for the language $\mathcal{L}$ as provided in Fig. 2 (respectively for $k > 1$ as provided in the full version). We additionally require that the key space is a subset of $\mathbb{G}$, which is satisfied by our construction in Sect. 4.

Construction. The construction of the KEM is given in Fig. 4.

Efficiency. When using our qualified proof system from Sect. 4 (respectively for $k > 1$ from the full version) to instantiate $\mathbf{PS}$, the public parameters comprise $4k^2$ group elements (plus the descriptions of the group itself and four hash functions). Further public keys and ciphertexts of our KEM contain $8k + 2k^2$, resp. $4k$ group elements for $k > 1$.

We stress that our scheme does not require pairings and can be implemented with $k = 1$, resulting in a tight security reduction to the DDH assumption in $\mathbb{G}$. As in this case the upper entries of the matrix $\mathbf{A}$ is 1, we get by with 3 group elements in the public parameters. Further, we can save one hash function due to

KGen(1^λ):
$(ppk, psk) \leftarrow_R \mathbf{PGen}(1^\lambda)$
$\mathbf{k}_0, \mathbf{k}_1 \leftarrow_R \mathbb{Z}_p^{2k}$
return
$\quad pk := (ppk, [\mathbf{k}_0^\top \mathbf{A}], [\mathbf{k}_1^\top \mathbf{A}])$
$\quad sk := (psk, \mathbf{k}_0, \mathbf{k}_1)$

KEnc(pk):
$\mathbf{r} \leftarrow_R \mathbb{Z}_p^k$
$[\mathbf{c}] := [\mathbf{A}]\mathbf{r}$
$(\Pi, [\kappa]) := \mathbf{PPrv}(ppk, [\mathbf{c}], \mathbf{r})$
$\tau := \mathsf{H}(\overline{[\mathbf{c}]})$
return
$\quad C := ([\mathbf{c}], \Pi)$
$\quad K := ([\mathbf{k}_0^\top \mathbf{A}] + \tau[\mathbf{k}_1^\top \mathbf{A}])\mathbf{r} + [\kappa]$

KDec(pk, sk, C) :
parse $C := ([\mathbf{c}], \Pi)$
$(b, [\kappa]) := \mathbf{PVer}(psk, [\mathbf{c}], \Pi)$
if $b = 0$ **return** $\perp$
$\tau := \mathsf{H}(\overline{[\mathbf{c}]})$
return $K := (\mathbf{k}_0 + \tau \mathbf{k}_1)^\top [\mathbf{c}] + [\kappa]$

Fig. 4. Construction of the KEM

the simpler underlying proof system. For the same reason, in case $k = 1$ public keys and ciphertexts contain 6, resp. 3 group elements. Compared to the GHKW scheme [9], our scheme thus has ciphertexts of the same size, but significantly smaller public keys.

Without any optimizations, encryption and decryption take $8k^2 + 12k$, resp. $6k^2 + 14k$ exponentiations for $k > 1$. For DDH we have 11 for both cases (again due to the simpler proof system and the distribution). Since most of these are multi-exponentiations, however, there is room for optimizations. In comparison, encryption and decyption in the GHKW scheme take $3k^2 + k$, resp. $3k$ exponentiations (plus about λk group operations for encryption, and again with room for optimizations). The main reason for our somewhat less efficient operations is the used qualified proof system. We explicitly leave open the construction of a more efficient proof system.

To turn the KEM into a IND-CCA secure hybrid encryption scheme, we require a quantitatively stronger security of the symmetric building block than [9]. Namely, the uncertainty $\text{uncert}_{\mathcal{A}}(\lambda)$ in our scheme has a stronger dependency on the number of queries ($Q_{\mathbf{enc}} \cdot Q_{\mathbf{dec}}$ instead of $Q_{\mathbf{enc}} + Q_{\mathbf{dec}}$). This necessitates to increase the key size of the authenticated encryption scheme compared to [9]. Note though that one-time secure authenticated encryption schemes even exist unconditionally and therefore in the reduction proving security of the hybrid encryption scheme, the uncertainty $\text{uncert}_{\mathcal{A}}(\lambda)$ will be statistically small.

Theorem 2. (Security of the KEM). *If* **PS** *is* $\mathcal{L}_{\text{snd}}$*-qualified and* $\widetilde{\mathcal{L}_{\text{snd}}}$*-extensible to* $\widetilde{\mathbf{PS}}$*, if* H *is a collision resistant hash function and if the* $\mathcal{D}_{2k,k}$*-MDDH assumption holds in* $\mathbb{G}$*, then the key encapsulation mechanism* **KEM** *described in Fig. 4 is perfectly correct and IND-CCCA secure. More precisely, for every IND-CCCA adversary* $\mathcal{A}$ *that makes at most* $Q_{\mathbf{enc}}$ *encryption* *and $Q_{\mathbf{dec}}$ decryption queries, there exist adversaries $\mathcal{B}^{\mathrm{mddh}}$, $\mathcal{B}^{\mathrm{csnd}}$, $\mathcal{B}^{\mathrm{ind}}$, $\mathcal{B}^{\widetilde{\mathrm{csnd}}}$ and $\mathcal{B}^{\mathrm{cr}}$ with running time $T(\mathcal{B}^{\mathrm{mddh}}) \approx T(\mathcal{B}^{\mathrm{csnd}}) \approx T(\mathcal{B}^{\mathrm{ind}}) \approx T(\mathcal{B}^{\mathrm{csnd}}) \approx T(\mathcal{B}^{\mathrm{cr}}) \approx T(\mathcal{A}) + (Q_{\mathbf{enc}} + Q_{\mathbf{dec}}) \cdot \mathsf{poly}(\lambda)$ respectively $T(\mathcal{B}^{\widetilde{\mathrm{csnd}}}) \approx T(\mathcal{A}) + (Q_{\mathbf{enc}} + Q_{\mathbf{enc}} \cdot Q_{\mathbf{dec}}) \cdot \mathsf{poly}(\lambda)$ where poly is a polynomial independent of $T(\mathcal{A})$, and such that*

$$\begin{aligned}\mathrm{Adv}^{\mathrm{ccca}}_{\mathbf{KEM},\mathcal{A}}(\lambda) \leq &\frac{1}{2} \cdot \mathrm{Adv}^{\mathrm{csnd}}_{\mathcal{L}_{\mathrm{snd}},\mathbf{PS},\mathcal{B}^{\mathrm{csnd}}}(\lambda) + \frac{1}{2} \cdot \mathrm{Adv}^{\mathrm{ind}}_{\mathcal{L}_{\mathrm{snd}},\mathbf{PS},\widetilde{\mathbf{PS}},\mathcal{B}^{\mathrm{ind}}}(\lambda)\\ &+ (2\lambda + 2 + k) \cdot \mathrm{Adv}^{\mathrm{mddh}}_{\mathbb{G},\mathcal{D}_{2k,k},\mathcal{B}^{\mathrm{mddh}}}(\lambda)\\ &+ \frac{\lambda}{2} \cdot \mathrm{Adv}^{\mathrm{csnd}}_{\widetilde{\mathcal{L}_{\mathrm{snd}}},\widetilde{\mathbf{PS}},\mathcal{B}^{\widetilde{\mathrm{csnd}}}}(\lambda)\\ &+ \frac{\lambda + 2}{2} \cdot Q_{\mathbf{enc}} \cdot Q_{\mathbf{dec}} \cdot \mathrm{uncert}_{\mathcal{A}}(\lambda)\\ &+ \mathrm{Adv}^{\mathrm{cr}}_{\mathsf{H},\mathcal{B}^{\mathrm{cr}}}(\lambda) + Q_{\mathbf{enc}} \cdot 2^{-\Omega(\lambda)}.\end{aligned}$$

Proof. We use a series of games to prove the claim. We denote the probability that the adversary $\mathcal{A}$ wins the i-th Game $\mathbf{G}_i$ by ε_i. An overview of all games is given in Fig. 5.

The goal is to randomize the keys of all challenge ciphertexts and thereby reducing the advantage of the adversary to 0. The methods employed here for a tight security reduction require us to ensure that $\mathcal{O}_{\mathbf{dec}}$ aborts on ciphertexts which are not in the span of $[\mathbf{A}]$, as we will no longer be able to answer those. The justification of this step relies crucially on the additional consistency proof Π and can be found in the full version.

Game $\mathbf{G}_0$: This game is the IND-CCCA security game (Definition 10).

$\mathbf{G}_0 \rightsquigarrow \mathbf{G}_1$: From game $\mathbf{G}_1$ on, we restrict the adversary to decryption queries with a fresh tag, that is, a tag which has not shown up in any previous encryption query. There are two conceivable bad events, where the adversary reuses a tag.

The first event is due to a collision of the hash function. That is, $\mathcal{A}$ provides a decryption query $([\mathbf{c}], \Pi)$, such that there exists a challenge ciphertext $[\mathbf{c}']$ from a previous encryption query with $\overline{[\mathbf{c}]} \neq \overline{[\mathbf{c}']}$, but $\mathsf{H}(\overline{[\mathbf{c}]}) = \mathsf{H}(\overline{[\mathbf{c}']})$. In that case we can straightforwardly employ $\mathcal{A}$ to obtain an adversary $\mathcal{B}$ attacking the collision resistance of H in time $T(\mathcal{B}) \approx T(\mathcal{A}) + (Q_{\mathbf{enc}} + Q_{\mathbf{dec}}) \cdot \mathsf{poly}(\lambda)$ for a polynomial poly independent of $T(\mathcal{A})$. Thereby we obtain an upper bound on the described event of $\mathrm{Adv}^{\mathrm{cr}}_{\mathsf{H},\mathcal{B}}(\lambda)$.

In the second event, $\mathcal{A}$ provides a valid decryption query $([\mathbf{c}], \Pi)$, such that $\overline{[\mathbf{c}]} = \overline{[\mathbf{c}']}$ for a previous challenge ciphertext $[\mathbf{c}'] \neq [\mathbf{c}]$. By the properties of **PS**, the proof corresponding to a ciphertext $[\mathbf{c}]$ is unique, which in particular implies $[\mathbf{c}] \notin \mathrm{span}([\mathbf{A}])$. We bound the probability that $\mathcal{A}$ submits a valid decryption query $([\mathbf{c}], \Pi)$ such that $[\mathbf{c}] \notin \mathrm{span}([\mathbf{A}])$ by $Q_{\mathbf{dec}} \cdot \mathrm{uncert}_{\mathcal{A}}(\lambda)$, using a series of hybrids: For $i = 0, \ldots, Q_{\mathbf{dec}}$ let $\mathbf{G}_{0.i}$ be defined like $\mathbf{G}_0$, except $\mathcal{O}_{\mathbf{dec}}$ checks the freshness of τ for the first i queries and operates as in game $\mathbf{G}_0$ from the $(i+1)$-st query on. Note that game $\mathbf{G}_{0.0}$ equals $\mathbf{G}_0$ and game $\mathbf{G}_{0.Q_{\mathbf{dec}}}$ equals $\mathbf{G}_1$. We show that for all $i \in \{0, \ldots, Q_{\mathbf{dec}} - 1\}$:

$$|\varepsilon_{0.i} - \varepsilon_{0.(i+1)}| \leq \Pr_{K \leftarrow_R \mathcal{K}}[\mathsf{pred}_{i+1}(K) = 1].$$

#	ch. c	ch. $[\kappa]$	$\mathcal{O}_{\text{dec}}$ **checks**	**remark**
$\mathbf{G}_0$	$\mathbf{A}$	**PPrv**		IND-CCCA
$\mathbf{G}_1$	$\mathbf{A}$	**PPrv**	τ fresh	coll. resist. of H
$\mathbf{G}_2$	$\mathbf{A}$	**PSim**	τ fresh	ZK of **PS**
$\mathbf{G}_3$	$\mathbf{A}_0$	**PSim**	τ fresh	$\mathcal{D}_{2k,k}$-MDDH
$\mathbf{G}_4$	$\mathbf{A}_0$	**PSim**	τ fresh, $[\mathbf{c}] \in \text{span}([\mathbf{A}])$	see full version
$\mathbf{G}_5$	$\mathbf{A}_0$	rand	τ fresh, $[\mathbf{c}] \in \text{span}([\mathbf{A}])$	$\mathcal{D}_{2k,k}$-MDDH

Fig. 5. Security of the KEM. Here column "**ch. c**" refers to the vector computed by $\mathcal{O}_{\mathbf{enc}}$ as part of the challenge ciphertexts, where $\mathbf{A}$ indicates that $[\mathbf{c}] \leftarrow_R \text{span}([\mathbf{A}])$, for instance. Column "**ch.** $[\kappa]$" refers to the key computed by $\mathcal{O}_{\mathbf{enc}}$ as part of the key K. In the column "$\mathcal{O}_{\text{dec}}$ **checks**" we describe what $\mathcal{O}_{\text{dec}}$ checks on input $C = (\mathsf{pred}, ([\mathbf{c}], \Pi))$ additionally to $C \notin \mathcal{C}_{\text{enc}}$ and $\text{pred}(K) = 1$. By a *fresh* tag $\tau := \mathsf{H}(\overline{[\mathbf{c}]})$ we denote a tag not previously used in any encryption query. In case the check fails, the decryption oracle outputs $\perp$.

Game $\mathbf{G}_{0.i}$ and game $\mathbf{G}_{0.(i+1)}$ only differ when the $(i+1)$-st query to $\mathcal{O}_{\mathbf{dec}}$ is valid with $\overline{[\mathbf{c}]} = \overline{[\mathbf{c}']}$ for a previous challenge ciphertext $[\mathbf{c}'] \neq [\mathbf{c}]$. As all challenge ciphertexts are in span($[\mathbf{A}]$), they do not reveal anything about $\mathbf{k}_0$ beyond the public key $[\mathbf{k}_0^\top \mathbf{A}]$. Thus, for $[\mathbf{c}] \notin \text{span}([\mathbf{A}])$, the value $\mathbf{k}_0^\top [\mathbf{c}]$ looks uniformly random from the adversary's point of view, proving the claimed distance between game $\mathbf{G}_{0.i}$ and game $\mathbf{G}_{0.(i+1)}$. Altogether we obtain

$$|\varepsilon_0 - \varepsilon_1| \leq \text{Adv}^{\text{cr}}_{\mathsf{H},\mathcal{B}}(\lambda) + Q_{\mathbf{dec}} \cdot \text{uncert}_{\mathcal{A}}(\lambda).$$

$\mathbf{G}_1 \rightsquigarrow \mathbf{G}_2$**:** From $\mathbf{G}_2$ on, the way challenge ciphertexts are computed is changed. Namely, the simulation algorithmen **PSim**$(psk, [\mathbf{c}])$ is used instead of **PPrv**$(ppk, [\mathbf{c}], \mathbf{r})$ to compute $(\Pi, [\kappa])$. Since for all challenge ciphertexts we have $[\mathbf{c}] \in \mathcal{L}$, the proofs and keys are equal by the perfect zero-knowledge property of **PS**, and thus we have

$$\varepsilon_1 = \varepsilon_2.$$

$\mathbf{G}_2 \rightsquigarrow \mathbf{G}_3$**:** Game $\mathbf{G}_3$ is like $\mathbf{G}_2$ except the vectors $[\mathbf{c}]$ in the challenge ciphertexts are chosen randomly in the span of $[\mathbf{A}_0]$.

We first employ the $Q_{\mathbf{enc}}$-fold $\mathcal{D}_{2k,k}$-MDDH assumption to tightly switch the vectors in the challenge ciphertexts from span($[\mathbf{A}]$) to uniformly random vectors over $\mathbb{G}^{2k}$. Next we use the $Q_{\mathbf{enc}}$-fold $\mathcal{U}_{2k,k}$-MDDH assumption to switch these vectors from random to $[\mathbf{A}_0\mathbf{r}]$.

To be specific, we build adversaries $\mathcal{B}$, $\mathcal{B}'$ such that for a polynomial poly independent of $T(\mathcal{A})$ we have $T(\mathcal{B}) \approx T(\mathcal{B}') \approx T(\mathcal{A}) + (Q_{\mathbf{enc}} + Q_{\mathbf{dec}}) \cdot \mathsf{poly}(\lambda)$ and

$$|\varepsilon_2 - \varepsilon_3| \leq \mathrm{Adv}^{Q_{\mathbf{enc}}\text{-mddh}}_{\mathbb{G},\mathcal{D}_{2k,k},\mathcal{B}}(\lambda) + \mathrm{Adv}^{Q_{\mathbf{enc}}\text{-mddh}}_{\mathbb{G},\mathcal{U}_{2k,k},\mathcal{B}'}(\lambda).$$

Let $([\mathbf{A}], [\mathbf{v}_1|\ldots|\mathbf{v}_{Q_{\mathbf{enc}}}])$ with $[\mathbf{A}] \in \mathbb{G}^{2k\times k}$ and $[\mathbf{V}] := [\mathbf{v}_1|\ldots|\mathbf{v}_{Q_{\mathbf{enc}}}] \in \mathbb{G}^{2k\times Q_{\mathbf{enc}}}$ be the $Q_{\mathbf{enc}}$-fold $\mathcal{D}_{2k,k}$-MDDH challenge received by $\mathcal{B}$. Then $\mathcal{B}$ samples $(ppk, psk) \leftarrow_R \mathbf{PGen}(1^\lambda)$, $\mathbf{k}_0, \mathbf{k}_1 \leftarrow_R \mathbb{Z}_p^{2k}$, $b \leftarrow_R \{0,1\}$ and sends the public key $pk := (ppk, [\mathbf{k}_0^\top \mathbf{A}], [\mathbf{k}_1^\top \mathbf{A}])$ to $\mathcal{A}$.

On the i-th query to $\mathcal{O}_{\mathbf{enc}}$, $\mathcal{B}$ sets the challenge ciphertext to $[\mathbf{c}] := [\mathbf{v}_i]$, next computes $\tau := \mathsf{H}([\mathbf{c}])$, $(\Pi, [\kappa]) := \mathbf{PSim}(psk, [\mathbf{v}_i])$ and finally $K_1 := (\mathbf{k}_0^\top + \tau\mathbf{k}_1^\top)[\mathbf{c}]$ (and $K_0 \leftarrow_R \mathcal{K}(\lambda)$ as usual). As $\mathcal{B}$ has generated the secret key itself, for decryption queries it can simply follow $\mathbf{KDec}(pk, sk, C)$.

In case $[\mathbf{V}] = [\mathbf{AR}]$, $\mathcal{B}$ perfectly simulates game $\mathbf{G}_2$. In case $[\mathbf{V}]$ is uniformly random over $\mathbb{G}^{2k\times Q_{\mathbf{enc}}}$, $\mathcal{B}$ simulates an intermediary game $\mathbf{H}$, where the challenge ciphertexts are chosen uniformly at random. Analogously we construct an adversary $\mathcal{B}'$ on the $Q_{\mathbf{enc}}$-fold $\mathcal{U}_{2k,k}$-MDDH assumption, who simulates game $\mathbf{H}$ if $[\mathbf{V}]$ is uniformly at random over $\mathbb{G}^{2k\times Q_{\mathbf{enc}}}$, and game $\mathbf{G}_3$, if $[\mathbf{V}] = [\mathbf{A}_0\mathbf{R}]$. Altogether this proves the claim stated above.

Finally, from Lemma 4 (random self-reducibility of $\mathcal{U}_{2k,k}$-MDDH), Lemma 3 ($\mathcal{D}_{2k,k}$-MDDH $\Rightarrow$ $\mathcal{U}_{2k,k}$-MDDH), and Lemma 2 (random self-reducibility of $\mathcal{D}_{2k,k}$-MDDH), we obtain an adversary $\mathcal{B}''$ such that $T(\mathcal{B}'') \approx T(\mathcal{A}) + (Q_{\mathbf{enc}} + Q_{\mathbf{dec}}) \cdot \mathsf{poly}(\lambda)$ where poly is independent of $T(\mathcal{A})$ and

$$|\varepsilon_2 - \varepsilon_3| \leq (1 + k) \cdot \mathrm{Adv}^{\mathrm{mddh}}_{\mathbb{G},\mathcal{D}_{2k,k},\mathcal{B}''}(\lambda) + \frac{2}{p-1}.$$

$\mathbf{G}_3 \rightsquigarrow \mathbf{G}_4$**:** We now restrict the adversary to decryption queries with $[\mathbf{c}] \in \mathrm{span}([\mathbf{A}])$. For the justification we refer to the full version.

$\mathbf{G}_4 \rightsquigarrow \mathbf{G}_5$**:** In game $\mathbf{G}_5$, we change the keys $[\kappa]$ computed by $\mathcal{O}_{\mathbf{enc}}$ to random over $\mathbb{G}$. This is justified as follows.

Firstly, we can replace $\mathbf{k}_0$ by $\mathbf{k}_0 + \mathbf{A}^\perp\mathbf{u}$ with $\mathbf{u} \leftarrow_R \mathbb{Z}_p^k$ and $\mathbf{A}^\perp \in \mathsf{orth}(\mathbf{A})$, as those are identically distributed. Note that this change does neither affect the public key, nor the decryption queries, since for all $\mathbf{c} \in \mathrm{span}(\mathbf{A})$, $\mathbf{c}^\top(\mathbf{k}_0 + \mathbf{A}^\perp\mathbf{u}) = \mathbf{c}^\top\mathbf{k}_0$. Thus, the term $\mathbf{A}^\perp\mathbf{u}$ only shows up when $\mathcal{O}_{\mathbf{enc}}$ computes the value $[(\mathbf{A}^\perp\mathbf{u})^\top\mathbf{A}_0\mathbf{r}]$ for $\mathbf{r} \leftarrow_R \mathbb{Z}_p^k$ as part of the key K_1 (the key that is not chosen at random by the security experiment).

Secondly, the distributions $(\mathbf{A}^\perp\mathbf{u})^\top\mathbf{A}_0$ and $\mathbf{v}^\top \leftarrow_R \mathbb{Z}_p^{1\times k}$ are $1-2^{-\Omega(\lambda)}$-close.

Altogether, we obtain that $\mathcal{O}_{\mathbf{enc}}$, on its j-th query for each $j \in [Q_{\mathbf{enc}}]$, can compute key K_1 for $\mathbf{r}_j \leftarrow_R \mathbb{Z}_p^k$, and $\mathbf{v} \leftarrow_R \mathbb{Z}_p^k$ as

$$K_1 := \left[(\mathbf{k}_0 + \tau\mathbf{k}_1)^\top \mathbf{A}_0\mathbf{r}_j\right] + \left[\mathbf{v}^\top\mathbf{r}_j\right] + [\kappa].$$

We then switch from $([\mathbf{r}_j], [\mathbf{v}^\top\mathbf{r}_j])$ to $([\mathbf{r}_j], [z_j])$, where z_j is a uniformly random value over $\mathbb{G}$, using the $Q_{\mathbf{enc}}$-fold $\mathcal{U}_k$-MDDH assumption as follows. On input $([\mathbf{B}], [\mathbf{h}_1|\ldots|\mathbf{h}_{Q_{\mathbf{enc}}}])$ with $\mathbf{B} \leftarrow_R \mathcal{U}_k$ (that is $\mathbf{B} \in \mathbb{Z}_p^{(k+1)\times k}$) and $\mathbf{h}_1, \ldots, \mathbf{h}_{Q_{\mathbf{enc}}} \in \mathbb{Z}_p^{k+1}$, $\mathcal{B}$ samples $(ppk, psk) \leftarrow_R \mathbf{PGen}(1^\lambda)$, $\mathbf{k}_0, \mathbf{k}_1 \leftarrow_R \mathbb{Z}_p^{2k}$, $b \leftarrow_R \{0,1\}$ and sends the public key $pk := (ppk, [\mathbf{k}_0^\top \mathbf{A}], [\mathbf{k}_1^\top \mathbf{A}])$ to $\mathcal{A}$. In the following for all $j \in Q_{\mathbf{enc}}$ let $\overline{[\mathbf{h}_j]} \in \mathbb{G}^k$ comprise the upper k entries and $\underline{[\mathbf{h}_j]} \in \mathbb{G}$ the $(k+1)$-st entry of $[\mathbf{h}_j]$ and similar for $[\mathbf{B}]$ let $\overline{[\mathbf{B}]} \in \mathbb{G}^{k\times k}$ be the upper square matrix of $[\mathbf{B}]$ and $\underline{[\mathbf{B}]} \in \mathbb{G}^{1\times k}$ comprise the last row.

On the j-th encryption query, $\mathcal{B}$ sets $[\mathbf{c}] := \mathbf{A}_0\overline{[\mathbf{h}_j]}$ (and thus $[\mathbf{r}_j] := \overline{[\mathbf{h}_j]}$) and computes the key as

$$K_1 := \left[(\mathbf{k}_0 + \tau\mathbf{k}_1)^\top \mathbf{c}\right] + \underline{[\mathbf{h}_j]} + [\kappa].$$

The adversary $\mathcal{B}$ can answer decryption queries as usual using $\mathbf{k}_0$, as decryption queries outside $\mathcal{L}$ are rejected.

Now if $([\mathbf{B}], [\mathbf{h}_1| \dots |\mathbf{h}_{Q_{\mathbf{enc}}}])$ was a real $\mathcal{U}_k$-MDDH challenge, we have $\mathbf{h}_j = \mathbf{B}\mathbf{s}_j$ for a $\mathbf{s}_j \leftarrow_R \mathbb{Z}_p^k$ and thus we have $\mathbf{r}_j = \overline{\mathbf{B}}\mathbf{s}_j$ and $\underline{[\mathbf{h}_j]} = \underline{[\mathbf{B}]}\mathbf{s}_j = \underline{[\mathbf{B}]}\overline{\mathbf{B}}^{-1}\mathbf{r}_j$. Note that the distribution of $\underline{[\mathbf{B}]}\overline{\mathbf{B}}^{-1}$ is statistically close to the distribution of $\mathbf{v}^\top$ and therefore $\mathcal{B}$ simulates game $\mathbf{G}_4$. In case $\mathbf{h}_j$ was chosen uniformly at random from $\mathbb{Z}_p^{k+1}$, the adversary $\mathcal{B}$ simulates game $\mathbf{G}_5$ instead. In the end adversary $\mathcal{B}$ can thus forward the output of $\mathcal{A}$ to its own experiment.

Finally, Lemmas 3, 4 and 5 yield the existence of an adversary $\mathcal{B}'$ such that $T(\mathcal{B}') \approx T(\mathcal{A}) + (Q_{\mathbf{enc}} + Q_{\mathbf{dec}}) \cdot \mathsf{poly}(\lambda)$ where poly is a polynomial independent of $T(\mathcal{A})$, and

$$|\varepsilon_4 - \varepsilon_5| \leq \mathrm{Adv}^{\mathrm{mddh}}_{\mathbb{G},\mathcal{D}_{2k,k},\mathcal{B}'}(\lambda) + 2^{-\Omega(\lambda)}.$$

Game $\mathbf{G}_5$: In this game, the keys K_1 computed by $\mathcal{O}_{\mathbf{enc}}$ are uniformly random, since the value $[\kappa]$ which shows up in $K_1 := [(\mathbf{k}_0 + \tau\mathbf{k}_1)^\top\mathbf{c}] + [\kappa]$ is uniformly random for each call to $\mathcal{O}_{\mathbf{enc}}$. The same holds true for the keys K_0 which are chosen at random from $\mathcal{K}(\lambda)$ throughout all games. Therefore, the output of $\mathcal{O}_{\mathbf{enc}}$ is now independent of the bit b chosen in $\mathrm{Exp}^{\mathrm{ccca}}_{\mathbf{KEM},\mathcal{A}}(\lambda)$. This yields

$$\varepsilon_5 = 0.$$

□

References

1. Abe, M., David, B., Kohlweiss, M., Nishimaki, R., Ohkubo, M.: Tagged one-time signatures: tight security and optimal tag size. In: Kurosawa, K., Hanaoka, G. (eds.) PKC 2013. LNCS, vol. 7778, pp. 312–331. Springer, Heidelberg (2013). doi:10.1007/978-3-642-36362-7_20
2. Attrapadung, N., Hanaoka, G., Yamada, S.: A framework for identity-based encryption with almost tight security. In: Iwata, T., Cheon, J.H. (eds.) ASIACRYPT 2015. LNCS, vol. 9452, pp. 521–549. Springer, Heidelberg (2015). doi:10.1007/978-3-662-48797-6_22
3. Bellare, M., Boldyreva, A., Micali, S.: Public-key encryption in a multi-user setting: security proofs and improvements. In: Preneel, B. (ed.) EUROCRYPT 2000. LNCS, vol. 1807, pp. 259–274. Springer, Heidelberg (2000). doi:10.1007/3-540-45539-6_18
4. Blazy, O., Kiltz, E., Pan, J.: (Hierarchical) identity-based encryption from affine message authentication. In: Garay, J.A., Gennaro, R. (eds.) CRYPTO 2014. LNCS, vol. 8616, pp. 408–425. Springer, Heidelberg (2014). doi:10.1007/978-3-662-44371-2_23

5. Chen, J., Wee, H.: Fully, (almost) tightly secure IBE and dual system groups. In: Canetti, R., Garay, J.A. (eds.) CRYPTO 2013. LNCS, vol. 8043, pp. 435–460. Springer, Heidelberg (2013). doi:10.1007/978-3-642-40084-1_25
6. Cramer, R., Shoup, V.: Design and analysis of practical public-key encryption schemes secure against adaptive chosen ciphertext attack. SIAM J. Comput. **33**(1), 167–226 (2003)
7. Cramer, R., Shoup, V.: Universal hash proofs and a paradigm for adaptive chosen ciphertext secure public-key encryption. In: Knudsen, L.R. (ed.) EUROCRYPT 2002. LNCS, vol. 2332, pp. 45–64. Springer, Heidelberg (2002). doi:10.1007/3-540-46035-7_4
8. Escala, A., Herold, G., Kiltz, E., Ràfols, C., Villar, J.: An algebraic framework for Diffie-Hellman assumptions. In: Canetti, R., Garay, J.A. (eds.) CRYPTO 2013. LNCS, vol. 8043, pp. 129–147. Springer, Heidelberg (2013). doi:10.1007/978-3-642-40084-1_8
9. Gay, R., Hofheinz, D., Kiltz, E., Wee, H.: Tightly CCA-secure encryption without pairings. In: Fischlin, M., Coron, J.-S. (eds.) EUROCRYPT 2016. LNCS, vol. 9665, pp. 1–27. Springer, Heidelberg (2016). doi:10.1007/978-3-662-49890-3_1
10. Gong, J., Chen, J., Dong, X., Cao, Z., Tang, S.: Extended nested dual system groups, revisited. In: Cheng, C.-M., Chung, K.-M., Persiano, G., Yang, B.-Y. (eds.) PKC 2016. LNCS, vol. 9614, pp. 133–163. Springer, Heidelberg (2016). doi:10.1007/978-3-662-49384-7_6
11. Hofheinz, D.: Adaptive partitioning. In: Coron, J.-S., Nielsen, J.B. (eds.) EUROCRYPT 2017. LNCS, vol. 10212, pp. 489–518. Springer, Cham (2017). doi:10.1007/978-3-319-56617-7_17
12. Hofheinz, D.: Algebraic partitioning: fully compact and (almost) tightly secure cryptography. In: Kushilevitz, E., Malkin, T. (eds.) TCC 2016. LNCS, vol. 9562, pp. 251–281. Springer, Heidelberg (2016). doi:10.1007/978-3-662-49096-9_11
13. Hofheinz, D., Jager, T.: Tightly secure signatures and public-key encryption. In: Safavi-Naini, R., Canetti, R. (eds.) CRYPTO 2012. LNCS, vol. 7417, pp. 590–607. Springer, Heidelberg (2012). doi:10.1007/978-3-642-32009-5_35
14. Hofheinz, D., Kiltz, E.: Secure hybrid encryption from weakened key encapsulation. In: Menezes, A. (ed.) CRYPTO 2007. LNCS, vol. 4622, pp. 553–571. Springer, Heidelberg (2007). doi:10.1007/978-3-540-74143-5_31
15. Hofheinz, D., Koch, J., Striecks, C.: Identity-based encryption with (almost) tight security in the multi-instance, multi-ciphertext setting. In: Katz, J. (ed.) PKC 2015. LNCS, vol. 9020, pp. 799–822. Springer, Heidelberg (2015). doi:10.1007/978-3-662-46447-2_36
16. Impagliazzo, R., Levin, L.A., Luby, M.: Pseudo-random generation from one-way functions (extended abstracts). In: 21st ACM STOC, pp. 12–24. ACM Press, May 1989
17. Kurosawa, K., Desmedt, Y.: A new paradigm of hybrid encryption scheme. In: Franklin, M. (ed.) CRYPTO 2004. LNCS, vol. 3152, pp. 426–442. Springer, Heidelberg (2004). doi:10.1007/978-3-540-28628-8_26
18. Lenstra, A.K., Verheul, E.R.: Selecting cryptographic key sizes. J. Cryptol. **14**(4), 255–293 (2001)

19. Libert, B., Joye, M., Yung, M., Peters, T.: Concise multi-challenge CCA-secure encryption and signatures with almost tight security. In: Sarkar, P., Iwata, T. (eds.) ASIACRYPT 2014. LNCS, vol. 8874, pp. 1–21. Springer, Heidelberg (2014). doi:10.1007/978-3-662-45608-8_1
20. Libert, B., Peters, T., Joye, M., Yung, M.: Compactly hiding linear spans. In: Iwata, T., Cheon, J.H. (eds.) ASIACRYPT 2015. LNCS, vol. 9452, pp. 681–707. Springer, Heidelberg (2015). doi:10.1007/978-3-662-48797-6_28

Asymptotically Compact Adaptively Secure Lattice IBEs and Verifiable Random Functions via Generalized Partitioning Techniques

Shota Yamada(✉)

National Institute of Advanced Industrial Science and Technology (AIST), Tokyo, Japan
yamada-shota@aist.go.jp

Abstract. In this paper, we focus on the constructions of adaptively secure identity-based encryption (IBE) from lattices and verifiable random function (VRF) with large input spaces. Existing constructions of these primitives suffer from low efficiency, whereas their counterparts with weaker guarantees (IBEs with selective security and VRFs with small input spaces) are reasonably efficient. We try to fill these gaps by developing new partitioning techniques that can be performed with compact parameters and proposing new schemes based on the idea.

- We propose new lattice IBEs with poly-logarithmic master public key sizes, where we count the number of the basic matrices to measure the size. Our constructions are proven secure under the LWE assumption with polynomial approximation factors. They achieve the best asymptotic space efficiency among existing schemes that depend on the same assumption and achieve the same level of security.
- We also propose several new VRFs on bilinear groups. In our first scheme, the size of the proofs is poly-logarithmic in the security parameter, which is the smallest among all the existing schemes with similar properties. On the other hand, the verification keys are long. In our second scheme, the size of the verification keys is poly-logarithmic, which is the smallest among all the existing schemes. The size of the proofs is sub-linear, which is larger than our first scheme, but still smaller than all the previous schemes.

1 Introduction

1.1 Background

In cryptography, we define appropriate security notions for cryptographic primitives, in order to capture real world attacks. For a cryptographic scheme to be useful, it is desirable that the scheme achieves security notions as realistic as possible. However, since natural and realistic security notions are hard to achieve in general, we sometimes are only able to prove ad-hoc and unrealistic security notions. Even when proving the former is possible, it sometimes comes with the

J. Katz and H. Shacham (Eds.): CRYPTO 2017, Part III, LNCS 10403, pp. 161–193, 2017.
DOI: 10.1007/978-3-319-63697-9_6

cost of longer parameters or stronger assumptions. In this paper, we focus on two such primitives: identity-based encryption (IBE) and verifiable random function (VRF).

Identity-Based Encryption. IBE [Sha85] is a generalization of public key encryption where the public key of a user can be any arbitrary string such as an e-mail address. The first realizations of IBE are given by [SOK00, BF01] on groups equipped with bilinear maps. Since then, realizations from bilinear maps [BB04a, BB04b, Wat05, Gen06, Wat09], from quadratic residues modulo composite [Coc01, BGH07], and from lattices [GPV08, CHKP10, ABB10a, Boy10] have been proposed.

Among the existing lattice IBE schemes in the standard model, the most efficient one is in [ABB10a]. However, the scheme only satisfies selective security, where an adversary must declare at the start of the game which identity it intends to target. Although schemes with a much more realistic adaptive security (or equivalently, full security) are known [CHKP10, ABB10a, Boy10], they are not as efficient as the aforementioned selectively secure scheme. In particular, all these schemes require master public keys longer by a factor $O(\lambda)$ than the selectively secure one, where λ is the security parameter. This stands in sharp contrast to pairing-based settings, in which we have adaptively secure IBE schemes [Wat09, CLL+12, JR13] that are as efficient as selectively secure ones [BB04a], up to a small constant factor.

There have been several studies that aim at reducing the sizes of the parameters in adaptively secure lattice IBEs [Yam16, AFL16, ZCZ16, KY16]. However, current state of affairs are not satisfactory. These schemes are either based on stronger assumptions [Yam16, KY16], or require still long public parameters [Yam16, KY16, AFL16], or only achieves weaker security guarantee [ZCZ16].

Verifiable Random Function. The notion of VRF was introduced by Micali, Rabin, and Vadhan [MRV99]. A VRF $\mathsf{V}_{\mathsf{sk}}(\cdot)$ is a pseudorandom function with the additional property that it is possible to create a non-interactive and publicly verifiable proof π that a given function value Y was computed correctly as $Y = \mathsf{V}_{\mathsf{sk}}(X)$. Since the introduction of this notion, several realizations have been proposed [MRV99, Lys02, Dod03, DY05, ACF09]. All these constructions only allow a polynomially bounded input space, or do not achieve full adaptive security without complexity leveraging, or are based on an interactive complexity assumption. Following [HJ16], in the sequel, we will say that a VRF has *all the desired properties*, if it has an exponential-sized input space and a proof of full adaptive security under a non-interactive complexity assumption.

The first VRF scheme with all the desired properties was proposed by Hohenberger and Waters [HW10]. Later, constructions from weaker assumptions have been studied [BMR10, ACF14, Jag15, HJ16]. Notably, the scheme in [HJ16] is secure under the standard decisional linear assumption. On the other hand, there has not been improvement on the efficiency since [HW10]. Namely, all existing VRF schemes with all the desired properties require $O(\lambda)$ group elements both in the verification keys and proofs. This is much more inefficient than the scheme with a polynomial-size input space [DY05], which only requires $O(1)$ group elements for both.

The Gaps in Efficiency. As we have seen, there is a distinct gap in efficiency between the state of the art schemes and the desired schemes. Namely, both in lattice IBEs and VRFs, we loose efficiency when we want to achieve stronger security notions. This loss in efficiency is an artifact of the security proofs. Most of the schemes use the partitioning technique based on (an analogue of) Waters' hash [Wat05] or admissible hash functions [BB04b] to achieve adaptive security. However, these techniques typically require long parameters. The powerful framework of dual system encryption methodology, which was introduced by Waters [Wat09], does not seem to be applicable for these settings. In particular, we do not have lattice analogue of the dual system approach yet. Furthermore, the uniqueness property required for VRF seems to contradict the algebraic structure required to apply the dual system approach, as pointed out in [Jag15, HJ16].

1.2 Our Contributions

In this paper, we try to fill the above gaps by generalizing the partitioning technique and proposing new schemes with improved (asymptotic) efficiency. To do so, we first introduce the notion of *partitioning functions*, which can be thought of as a generalization of the standard admissible hash functions [BB04b, CHKP10, FHPS13, Jag15]. The notion of partitioning functions abstracts out the information theoretic properties that are required to perform the partitioning technique in the security proofs for IBE and VRF. Then, we propose two new partitioning functions that can be constructed by much more compact parameters than prior admissible hash functions. Our first construction is obtained by compressing the expression of the existing admissible hash functions by introducing a novel encoding technique, whereas the second construction is based on affine functions over a random modulus. We call the first partitioning function $\mathsf{F}_{\mathsf{MAH}}$ and the second $\mathsf{F}_{\mathsf{AFF}}$, where MAH and AFF stand for modified admissible hash function and affine function respectively. These functions provide us a framework to perform the security proofs in a more space efficient manner than previous ones.

One thing to note is that in order to use them to construct IBE and VRF schemes, we need a certain level of homomorphic capability on the underlying algebraic structures. In the lattice setting, we can implement the idea by carefully applying the powerful fully key homomorphic techniques of [BGG+14, GV15]. On the other hand, in the bilinear group setting, this technique may be inapplicable since we only have very limited amount of homomorphic capabilities. Namely, given group elements, which can be seen as encodings of the corresponding discrete logarithms, we can only compute encodings corresponding to quadratic multi-variate polynomials on them. However, in the special case of VRF, since the evaluator has full access to the secret key, it can evaluate any homomorphism on them to compute the function value. Based on this observation, we can implement the idea in this setting as well.

Table 1. Comparison of adaptively secure lattice IBE schemes

Schemes	$\|\mathsf{mpk}\|$ # of $\mathbb{Z}_q^{n\times m}$ mat.	$\|\mathsf{ct}\|$, $\|\mathsf{sk}\|$ # of $\mathbb{Z}_q^m$ vec.	LWE param $1/\alpha$	Reduction cost	Remarks
[CHKP10]	$O(\lambda)$	$O(\lambda)$	$\tilde{O}(n^{1.5})$	$O(\epsilon^{\nu+1}/Q^{\nu})^{\mathrm{b}}$	
[ABB10a]+[Boy10]	$O(\lambda)$	$O(1)$	$\tilde{O}(n^{5.5})$	$O(\epsilon^2/qQ)$	
[Yam16]	$O(\lambda^{1/\mu})^{\mathrm{a}}$	$O(1)$	$n^{\omega(1)}$	$O(\epsilon^{\mu+1}/kQ^{\mu})^{\mathrm{a}}$	
[ZCZ16]	$O(\log Q)$	$O(1)$	$\tilde{O}(Q^2 \cdot n^{6.5})$	$O(\epsilon/kQ^2)$	Q-bounded
[AFL16][c]	$O(\lambda/\log^2\lambda)$	$O(1)$	$\tilde{O}(n^6)$	$O(\epsilon^2/qQ)$	
[BL16]	$O(\lambda)$	$O(1)$	superpoly(n)	$O(\lambda)$	
[KY16][d]	$O(\lambda^{1/\mu})^{\mathrm{a,d}}$	$O(1)$	$O(n^{2.5+2\mu})^{\mathrm{a}}$	$O((\lambda^{\mu-1}\epsilon^{\mu}/Q^{\mu})^{\mu+1})^{\mathrm{a}}$	Ring-based
Sect. 5.2 + $\mathsf{F}_{\mathsf{MAH}}$	$O(\log^3\lambda)$	$O(1)$	$\tilde{O}(n^{11})$	$O(\epsilon^{\nu+1}/Q^{\nu})^{\mathrm{b}}$	
Sect. 5.2 + $\mathsf{F}_{\mathsf{AFF}}$[e]	$O(\log^2\lambda)$	$O(1)$	$\mathsf{poly}(n)$	$O(\epsilon^2/k^2Q)$	Need [BCH86, Bar89]

We compare with adaptively secure IBE schemes under the LWE assumption in the standard model. $|\mathsf{mpk}|$, $|\mathsf{ct}|$, and $|\mathsf{sk}_{\mathsf{ID}}|$ show the size of the master public keys, ciphertexts, and private keys, respectively. For both our schemes, we set $\eta = \log^2\lambda$. To measure the space efficiency, we count the number of basic components. Q and ϵ denote the number of key extraction queries and the advantage, respectively. $\mathsf{poly}(n)$ (resp. $\mathsf{superpoly}(n)$) represents fixed but large polynomial (super-polynomial) that does not depend Q and ϵ. To measure the reduction cost, we show the advantage of the LWE algorithm constructed from the adversary against the corresponding IBE scheme. To be fair, we calculate the reduction cost by employing the technique of Bellare and Ristenpart [BR09] for all schemes.

[a] $\mu \in \mathbb{N}$ is a constant number that can be chosen arbitrary. Since the reduction cost degrades exponentially as μ grows, we would typically set μ very small (e.g., $\mu = 2$ or 3).

[b] $\nu > 1$ is the constant satisfying $c = 1 - 2^{-1/\nu}$, where c is the relative distance of the underlying error correcting code $C : \{0,1\}^k \to \{0,1\}^\ell$. We can take ν as close to 1 as one wants, by choosing $c < 1/2$ appropriately and make ℓ large enough (See Appendix E.1 of [Gol08]).

[c] They also propose a variant of the scheme with constant-size master public key assuming the exponentially secure collision resistant hash function. Since the use of the exponential assumption can be considered as a certain kind of the complexity leveraging, we do not include the variant in the table.

[d] The scheme can only be instantiated over the rings $R_q = \mathbb{Z}_q[X]/(X^n + 1)$. To measure the size of mpk we count the number of the basic vectors, instead of the basic matrices.

[e] The key generation and encryption algorithm of the scheme involves the heavy step of computing the description of the division circuit in NC^1 using the result of [BCH86] and converting it into a branching program by invoking the Barrington's theorem [Bar89].

New Lattice IBE Schemes. Based on the new partitioning functions, we propose two new adaptively secure lattice IBE schemes. For the overview and comparison, we refer to Table 1. Both our schemes achieve the best asymptotic space efficiency among existing schemes with the same assumption and security notion. In particular, the number of basic matrices in the master public keys are only polylogarithmic. Furthermore, the sizes of the ciphertexts and private keys are optimal, in the sense that they match those of the selectively secure schemes [ABB10a, Boy10] up to a constant factor.

- In our first scheme, the master public key consists of $\omega(\log^2\lambda)$ basic matrices[1], which is the smallest among all the previous schemes. The security of the scheme can be shown from the LWE assumption with approximation factor $\tilde{O}(n^{11})$, where n is the dimension of the lattices.

[1] In our paper, when we say that the size of a parameters is $\omega(f(\lambda))$, it means that the parameter can be set to be *any* (polynomially bounded) function that grows faster than $f(\lambda)$. The parameter can be as small as one wants, as long as it does not violate the lower-bound given by the ω-notation. In this case, we can choose the number of the matrices to be $\Theta(\log^3\lambda)$ or even $\Theta(\log^2\lambda \cdot \log\log\log\lambda)$ for instance.

- In our second scheme, the master public key consists of only $\omega(\log \lambda)$ basic matrices, which is even smaller than the one above. The security of the scheme can be shown from the LWE assumption with approximation factors $\mathsf{poly}(n)$, where $\mathsf{poly}(n)$ is some fixed polynomial that is determined by the depth of the circuit computing a certain function.

We constructed the above schemes in a modular way. We first define the notion of *compatible algorithms* for partitioning functions. Then, we propose a generic construction of an IBE scheme from a partitioning function with its associating compatible algorithms. We obtain our first scheme by instantiating this framework with $\mathsf{F}_{\mathsf{MAH}}$ and its compatible algorithms. We obtain our second scheme by instantiating it with $\mathsf{F}_{\mathsf{AFF}}$.

New VRF Schemes. We also obtain the following three new VRF schemes with all the desired properties. For the overview and comparison, we refer to Table 2. All our schemes are constructed on bilinear groups and proven secure under the L-DDH assumption,[2] as is the same as most of the previous schemes [ACF14, BMR10, Jag15]. In the following, to measure the sizes of the proofs and verification keys, we count the number of group elements. Note that in all existing VRF schemes with all the desired properties [HW10, ACF14, BMR10, Jag15, HJ16], the sizes of the verification keys and proofs are $O(\lambda)$.

- Our first scheme is based on $\mathsf{F}_{\mathsf{MAH}}$, and is parametrized by several parameters, which control the tradeoffs of the efficiency. In certain parameter settings, the scheme achieves the smallest proof-size among all existing VRF schemes that satisfy all the desired properties. The size of the proofs is $\omega(\log \lambda)$, whereas the size of the verification keys is $\omega(\lambda \log \lambda)$. The security is proven from the L-DDH assumption with $L = \tilde{O}(\lambda)$.
- Our second scheme is obtained by setting the parameters appropriately in our first scheme and modifying it slightly. The scheme achieves the smallest verification-key-size among all existing schemes with all the desired properties. The size of the verification keys is $\omega(\log \lambda)$, whereas the size of the proofs is $\omega(\sqrt{\lambda} \log \lambda)$. The size of the proofs is larger than our first scheme, but still smaller than all the previous schemes. The security is proven from the L-DDH assumption with $L = \tilde{O}(\lambda)$.
- Our third scheme is based on $\mathsf{F}_{\mathsf{AFF}}$. The size of the verification keys and the proofs are $\omega(\log \lambda)$ and $\mathsf{poly}(\lambda)$, respectively. The security of the scheme is proven from the L-DDH assumption with $L = \mathsf{poly}(\lambda)$. Here, $\mathsf{poly}(\lambda)$ is some fixed polynomial that is determined by the depth of the circuit computing a certain function.

Note that the main advantage of the third scheme over our first and second schemes is that the security reduction is tighter.

Finally, we note that even though our lattice IBE schemes achieve the best asymptotic space efficiency, it might not outperform [ABB10a, Boy10] in practical parameter settings, due to the large poly-logarithmic factors and the heavy

[2] The L-DDH assumption says that given elements g, h, $g^{\alpha}, \ldots, g^{\alpha^L}$ in a bilinear group, $e(g,h)^{1/\alpha}$ is pseudorandom for any PPT adversary.

Table 2. Comparison of VRF schemes with all the desired properties

Schemes	$\|vk\|$ (# of $\mathbb{G}$)	$\|\pi\|$ (# of $\mathbb{G}$)	Assumption	Reduction cost
[ACF14]	$O(\lambda)$	$O(\lambda)$	$O(\lambda)$-DDH	$O(\epsilon^{\nu+1}/Q^{\nu})$[a]
[BMR10]	$O(\lambda)$	$O(\lambda)$	$O(\lambda)$-DDH	$O(\epsilon/\lambda)$
[HW10]	$O(\lambda)$	$O(\lambda)$	$O(Q\lambda/\epsilon)$-DDHE	$O(\epsilon^2/\lambda Q)$
[Jag15]	$O(\lambda)$	$O(\lambda)$	$O(\log(Q/\epsilon))$-DDH	$O(\epsilon^{\nu+1}/Q^{\nu})$[a]
[HJ16]	$O(\lambda)$	$O(\lambda)$	DLIN	$O(\epsilon^{\nu+1}/\lambda Q^{\nu})$[a]
Sect. 6.1 ($\ell_1 = \ell, \ell_2 = 1, \eta = \log^2 \lambda$).	$O(\lambda \log^2 \lambda)$	$O(\log^2 \lambda)$	$\tilde{O}(\lambda)$-DDH	$O(\epsilon^{\nu+1}/Q^{\nu})$[a]
Sect. 6.2 ($\ell_1 = \ell_2 = \sqrt{\ell}, \eta = \log^2 \lambda$)	$O(\log^2 \lambda)$	$O(\sqrt{\lambda}\log^2 \lambda)$	$\tilde{O}(\lambda)$-DDH	$O(\epsilon^{\nu+1}/Q^{\nu})$[a]
App. C of the full version	$O(\log^2 \lambda)$	$\mathsf{poly}(\lambda)$	$\mathsf{poly}(\lambda)$-DDH	$O(\epsilon^2/\lambda^2 Q)$

We compare VRF schemes with all the desired properties. $|vk|$ and $|\pi|$ show the size of the verification keys and proofs, respectively. To measure $|vk|$ and $|\pi|$, we count the number of group elements. Q and ϵ denote the number of evaluation queries and the advantage, respectively. $\mathsf{poly}(\lambda)$ represents fixed polynomial that does not depend Q and ϵ. To measure the reduction cost, we show the advantage of the algorithm that solves the problem (which is L-DDH for some L except for [HJ16]) constructed from the adversary against the corresponding VRF scheme. To be fair, we measure the reduction cost by employing the technique of Bellare and Ristenpart [BR09] for all schemes.
[a] ν is the constant satisfying $c = 1 - 2^{-1/\nu}$, where c is the relative distance of the underlying error correcting code $C : \{0,1\}^k \to \{0,1\}^\ell$. We can take ν as close to 1 as one wants, by choosing $c < 1/2$ appropriately and make ℓ large enough (See Appendix E.1 of [Gol08]).

encryption algorithm. The construction of truly efficient adaptively secure lattice IBE still remains open.

Comparison with the Dual System Encryption Methodology. The dual system encryption methodology [Wat09, LW10] is a very powerful tool to prove the adaptive security of IBE and even advanced cryptographic primitives such as attribute-based encryption [LOS+10]. However, currently, the technique is not available in several settings. These include lattice-based cryptography and the construction of VRF. We notice that relatively high level of homomorphic capabilities are available in these settings and show that the partitioning technique can be performed more compactly by exploiting this fact. Our technique is somewhat limited in the sense that it requires some homomorphic capabilities and may not be available without them. However, in the settings where our technique does not apply, the dual system encryption methodology may apply. In this sense, they have mutual complementary relationship.

1.3 Related Works

Related Works on Lattice IBE. Yamada [Yam16] used the fully key homomorphic technique of [BGG+14] and asymptotically reduced the size of the master public key. However, it required super-polynomial size modulus. The subsequent work by Katsumata et al. [KY16] showed that for the ring version of Yamada's scheme, it is possible to prove the security for polynomial-size modulus. The scheme by Apon et al. [AFL16] also proposed a scheme with shorter master public keys using a different technique. These schemes require larger number of matrices in the master public keys than ours. The scheme by Zhang et al. [ZCZ16] achieved shorter master public key size than ours, however at the cost of a weaker security guarantee. In particular, their scheme only achieves Q-bounded security, i.e., that the security of the scheme is not guaranteed any more if the number of key extraction queries that the adversary makes exceeds Q, where Q is a parameter that must be *determined at the setup phase* of the scheme. This restriction cannot be removed by just making Q super-polynomial, since the encryption algorithm of the scheme runs in time proportional to Q. Finally, Boyen and Li [BL16] proposed the first lattice IBE schemes with tight security reductions, where the schemes require long master public keys.

Related Works on VRF. Very recently, several works showed generic constructions of VRF from simpler cryptographic primitives [GHKW17,Bit17,BGJS17]. These constructions lead to VRF schemes from various assumptions, including schemes without bilinear maps. However, they cannot be efficiently instantiated because they require general NIWI and constrained PRF (for admissible hash). On the other hand, we focus on the efficient constructions of VRF from the specific number theoretic assumption. While our results are orthogonal to theirs, our definition of partitioning function is very similar to that of the "partitioning scheme" in the independent and concurrent work by Bitansky [Bit17].

2 Technical Overview

2.1 A Twist on the Admissible Hash

We first start with the review of the adaptively secure IBE schemes that use the admissible hash function [BB04b,CHKP10]. The security proofs of these schemes are based on the partitioning technique, a proof methodology that allows to secretly partition the identity space into two sets of exponential size, the uncontrolled set and the controlled set, so that there is a noticeable probability that the adversary's key extraction queries fall in the controlled set and the challenge identity falls in the uncontrolled set. Whether the identity is controlled or uncontrolled is determined by a function $\mathsf{F}_{\mathsf{ADH}}$ that on input a secret randomness K chosen during the simulation and an identity ID outputs 0 or 1. Here, 0 (resp. 1) indicates that ID is in the uncontrolled set (resp. controlled set). Concretely, the partitioning is made by the following specific function:

$$\mathsf{F}_{\mathsf{ADH}}(K, \mathsf{ID}) = \begin{cases} 0, & \text{if } \forall i \in [\ell]: \ C(\mathsf{ID})_i = K_i \quad \vee \quad K_i = \perp \\ 1, & \text{otherwise} \end{cases}$$

where $C(\cdot)$ is a public function that maps an identity to a bit string in $\{0,1\}^\ell$ and K is a string in $\{0,1,\perp\}^\ell$. $C(\mathsf{ID})_i$ and K_i represent the i-th bit of $C(\mathsf{ID})$ and the i-th component of K, respectively. In [BB04b,CHKP10], the master public keys are sufficiently long so that we can embed the secret randomness K into them in a component-wise manner in the security proof. Since $\ell = \Theta(\lambda)$, where λ is the security parameter, this results in large master public keys containing $O(\lambda)$ basic components. Due to the similar reasons, all constructions of VRFs using admissible hash functions [ACF14,BMR10,Jag15,HJ16] also suffer from large public parameters. Our first step to address the problem is to observe that K is very "sparse" in the sense that it conveys only a small amount of information compared to its length. In the simulation, K is chosen uniformly at random from $\{0, 1, \perp\}^\ell$, with $O(\log(Q/\epsilon))$ components being not $\perp$, where Q and ϵ are the number of key extraction queries and the advantage of the adversary, respectively. Since we assume an adversary that makes polynomial number of key extraction queries and has non-negligible advantage in the security proof, we have $O(\log(Q/\epsilon)) = O(\log\lambda)$. This means that $K_i = \perp$ for most $i \in [\ell]$.

$K =$	$\perp$	$\perp$	1	$\perp$	0	$\perp$	$\perp$
	1	3	⑤	7	9	11	13
	2	4	6	8	⑩	12	14
$\mathsf{T} = \{$			5,		10,		$\}$

$C(X) =$	0	1	1	0	0	1	0
	1	③	⑤	7	9	⑪	13
	②	4	6	⑧	⑩	12	⑭
$\mathsf{S}(X) = \{$	2,	3,	5,	8,	10,	11,	14$\}$

Fig. 1. Pictorial explanation of the definition of S and T.

Our key idea is to encode K into a much shorter bit-string. For $K \in \{0, 1, \perp\}^\ell$, let us consider a set $\mathsf{T} \subseteq \{1, 2, \ldots, 2\ell\}$ as

$$\mathsf{T} := \{\ 2i - K_i \mid i \in [\ell],\ K_i \neq \perp\ \}. \tag{1}$$

See Fig. 1 for the illustrative example. Since an element in $\{1, 2, \ldots, 2\ell\}$ can be represented by a bit-string with length $\log 2\ell = O(\log\lambda)$ and T only consists of $O(\log\lambda)$ components, T can be represented by a bit-string with length $O(\log^2\lambda)$, which is much shorter than $\ell = \Theta(\lambda)$.

In the next step, we introduce a modified admissible hash function $\mathsf{F_{MAH}}$ as

$$\mathsf{F_{MAH}}(\mathsf{T}, \mathsf{ID}) = \begin{cases} 0, & \text{if } \mathsf{T} \subseteq \mathsf{S}(\mathsf{ID}) \\ 1, & \text{otherwise} \end{cases} \qquad \text{where} \qquad \mathsf{S}(\mathsf{ID}) = \{\ 2i - C(\mathsf{ID})_i \mid i \in [\ell]\ \}.$$

Again, see Fig. 1 for the illustrative example. For T defined as above, we have

$$\mathsf{F_{ADH}}(K, \mathsf{ID}) = \mathsf{F_{MAH}}(\mathsf{T}, \mathsf{ID}).$$

Namely, $\mathsf{F_{ADH}}$ and $\mathsf{F_{MAH}}$ are essentially the same functions, but they take different forms of inputs. The former takes K as the input, whereas the latter takes T, an encoded form of K, as the input. This fact suggests the possibility of the partitioning technique based on $\mathsf{F_{MAH}}$, rather than $\mathsf{F_{ADH}}$. Namely, we first choose $K \in \{0, 1, \perp\}^\ell$ as specified, then set T as Eq. (1). The identity space is partitioned into two sets by $\mathsf{F_{MAH}}(\mathsf{T}, \cdot)$, which in turn is exactly the same partitioning made by $\mathsf{F_{ADH}}(K, \cdot)$. Since the simulation strategy based on the function $\mathsf{F_{MAH}}$ uses a much shorter secret randomness (i.e. T) than $\mathsf{F_{ADH}}$, this opens up the possibility of constructing a much more compact IBE scheme.

Even given the above idea, the constructions of our IBE and VRF are not straightforward. Although the change is only in the encoding of the secret randomness, it might be the case that the construction of the function is incompatible with the underlying algebraic structures. In particular, $\mathsf{F}_{\mathsf{MAH}}$ seems to require more homomorphic capability than $\mathsf{F}_{\mathsf{ADH}}$. Indeed, even though we know how to construct IBE from bilinear maps using $\mathsf{F}_{\mathsf{ADH}}$ [BB04b], we do *not* know how to do it for $\mathsf{F}_{\mathsf{MAH}}$. In our lattice IBE, we can realize the idea by employing the fully key homomorphic technique introduced by [BGG+14]. However, we have to be careful when applying the technique, otherwise we will end up with a super polynomial LWE as in [Yam16], which is undesirable both from the security and efficiency perspectives. For our VRF based on bilinear maps, we employ the fact that we can compute the function value by highly non-linear operations in the exponent.

2.2 Our First Lattice IBE

Our proposed IBE scheme follows the general framework for constructing a lattice IBE scheme [CHKP10, ABB10a, Yam16, ZCZ16] that associates to each identity ID the matrix $[\mathbf{A}\|\mathbf{B}_{\mathsf{ID}}] \in \mathbb{Z}_q^{n\times 2m}$. In the template construction, the main part of the ciphertext for ID contains $\mathbf{s}^\top[\mathbf{A}\|\mathbf{B}_{\mathsf{ID}}]+\mathbf{x}^\top$, where $\mathbf{s} \stackrel{\$}{\leftarrow} \mathbb{Z}_q^n$ and $\mathbf{x}$ is a small noise term. On the other hand, a private key for ID is a short vector $\mathbf{e}$ satisfying $[\mathbf{A}\|\mathbf{B}_{\mathsf{ID}}]\mathbf{e} = \mathbf{u}$ for a random public vector $\mathbf{u}$.

We compute the matrix $\mathbf{B}_{\mathsf{ID}}$ using the fully key homomorphic technique of [BGG+14]. Informally they showed that there exist algorithms $\mathsf{PubEval}$ and $\mathsf{TrapEval}$ that satisfy

$$\mathsf{PubEval}\left(\mathsf{F}, \{\mathbf{A}\mathbf{R}_i + y_i\mathbf{G}\}_{i\in[u]}\right) = \mathbf{A}\mathbf{R}_{\mathsf{F}} + \mathsf{F}(y)\cdot\mathbf{G}$$
$$\text{where } \mathbf{R}_{\mathsf{F}} = \mathsf{TrapEval}\left(\mathsf{F}, \mathbf{A}, \{\mathbf{R}_i, y_i\}_{i\in[u]}\right).$$

Here, $\mathsf{F} : \{0,1\}^u \to \{0,1\}$ is some function, $\mathbf{R}_i$ is a matrix with small coefficients, and y_i is the i-th bit of the bit-string y. Furthermore, $\mathbf{R}_{\mathsf{F}}$ has small coefficients.

For our construction, we prepare random matrices $\mathbf{A}, \mathbf{B}_1, \ldots, \mathbf{B}_u$ in the master public key, where $u = \omega(\log^2\lambda)$. Then, we set

$$\mathbf{B}_{\mathsf{ID}} = \mathsf{PubEval}(\ \mathsf{F}_{\mathsf{MAH}}(\ \cdot\ , \mathsf{ID}),\ \{\mathbf{B}_i\}_{i\in[u]}\ ).$$

Here, we consider $\mathsf{F}_{\mathsf{MAH}}(\cdot, \mathsf{ID})$ as a function that takes an *binary string* representing T as an input. This is necessary to apply the result of [BGG+14] without using the super-polynomial modulus. The security of the scheme is reduced to the LWE assumption, which says that given $\mathbf{A} \in \mathbb{Z}_q^{n\times m}$ and $\mathbf{w} \in \mathbb{Z}_q^m$, it is hard to distinguish whether $\mathbf{w} \stackrel{\$}{\leftarrow} \mathbb{Z}_q^m$ or $\mathbf{w}^\top = \mathbf{s}^\top\mathbf{A} + {\mathbf{x}'}^\top$ for some noise term $\mathbf{x}'$. To prove security, we set the matrices $\{\mathbf{B}_i\}$ in the master public key as

$$\mathbf{B}_i = \mathbf{A}\mathbf{R}_i + \mathsf{T}_i\cdot\mathbf{G}$$

where $\mathbf{A}$ is from the problem instance of the LWE, $\mathbf{R}_i$ is a random matrix with small coefficients, and $\mathsf{T}_i \in \{0,1\}$ is the i-th bit of the binary representation of T.

Due to the leftover hash lemma, the master public key is correctly distributed. By the properties of PubEval and TrapEval, we have

$$\mathbf{B}_{\mathsf{ID}} = \mathbf{A}\mathbf{R}_{\mathsf{ID}} + \mathsf{F}_{\mathsf{MAH}}(\mathsf{T}, \mathsf{ID}) \cdot \mathbf{G}$$
$$\text{where } \mathbf{R}_{\mathsf{ID}} = \mathsf{TrapEval}\left(\mathsf{F}_{\mathsf{MAH}}(\ \cdot\ , \mathsf{ID}), \mathbf{A}, \{\mathbf{R}_i, \mathsf{T}_i\}_{i\in[u]}\right).$$

Furthermore, by the property of $\mathsf{F}_{\mathsf{MAH}}$, we have

$$\mathsf{F}_{\mathsf{MAH}}(\mathsf{T}, \mathsf{ID}^{(1)}) = \cdots = \mathsf{F}_{\mathsf{MAH}}(\mathsf{T}, \mathsf{ID}^{(Q)}) = 1 \ \wedge\ \mathsf{F}_{\mathsf{MAH}}(\mathsf{T}, \mathsf{ID}^{\star}) = 0 \qquad (2)$$

with noticeable probability, where $\mathsf{ID}^{\star}$ is the challenge identity, and $\mathsf{ID}^{(1)}, \ldots, \mathsf{ID}^{(Q)}$ are identities for which the adversary has made key extraction queries. If this condition holds, the simulation will be successful. The key extraction queries for $\mathsf{ID} \in \{\mathsf{ID}^{(1)}, \ldots, \mathsf{ID}^{(Q)}\}$ can be handled by using $\mathbf{R}_{\mathsf{ID}}$ as a $\mathbf{G}$-trapdoor [MP12] for the matrix $[\mathbf{A}\|\mathbf{B}_{\mathsf{ID}}] = [\mathbf{A}\|\mathbf{A}\mathbf{R}_{\mathsf{ID}} + \mathbf{G}]$. The generation of the challenge ciphertext is also possible by computing

$$\mathbf{w}^{\top}[\mathbf{I}\|\mathbf{R}_{\mathsf{ID}^{\star}}] = \left(\mathbf{s}^{\top}\mathbf{A} + \mathbf{x}'^{\top}\right) \cdot [\mathbf{I}\|\mathbf{R}_{\mathsf{ID}^{\star}}] = \mathbf{s}^{\top}[\mathbf{A}\|\mathbf{B}_{\mathsf{ID}^{\star}}] + \underbrace{\mathbf{x}'^{\top}[\mathbf{I}\|\mathbf{R}_{\mathsf{ID}^{\star}}]}_{\text{noise term}}.$$

A subtle point here is that the noise term above is not correctly distributed. However, this problem can be resolved by the technique in [KY16].

Finally, we remark that our actual construction is different from the above in two points. First, we do not use the (general) fully key homomorphic algorithm of [BGG+14] to compute $\mathbf{B}_{\mathsf{ID}}$ and $\mathbf{R}_{\mathsf{ID}}$. If we use the algorithm in a naive way, the coefficients of $\mathbf{R}_{\mathsf{ID}}$ will become super-polynomial, which somewhat nullifies the merit of having smaller number of matrices. Instead, we show a direct algorithm to compute $\mathbf{B}_{\mathsf{ID}}$ and $\mathbf{R}_{\mathsf{ID}}$ using the technique of [GV15], such that the coefficients of $\mathbf{R}_{\mathsf{ID}}$ are polynomially bounded. The second difference is that we add a matrix $\mathbf{B}_0$ to the master public key and use the matrix $[\mathbf{A}\|\mathbf{B}_0 + \mathbf{B}_{\mathsf{ID}}]$ in the encryption and the key generation, instead of $[\mathbf{A}\|\mathbf{B}_{\mathsf{ID}}]$. This change is introduced because of a subtle technical reason to make the security proof easier.

2.3 Our First VRF

Our VRF is constructed on bilinear maps and obtained by incorporating our technique with the previous inversion-based VRF schemes [DY05, BMR10]. In the scheme, we set the function as

$$\mathsf{V}_{\mathsf{sk}}(X) = e(g, h)^{1/\theta_X}, \qquad (3)$$

where the value $\theta_X = \mathbb{Z}_p^*$ is deterministically computed by the input X. Let us ignore the problem of how we add the verifiability to the scheme for the time being and start with the overview of the security proof for the scheme as a (plain) PRF. The security will be proven under the L-DDH assumption, which says that given $(h, \hat{g}, \hat{g}^{\alpha}, \ldots \hat{g}^{\alpha^L}, \Psi)$, it is infeasible to distinguish whether

$\Psi \xleftarrow{\$} \mathbb{G}_T$ or $\Psi = e(\hat{g}, h)^{1/\alpha}$. As before, we sample T and partition the input space into two sets by $\mathsf{F}_{\mathsf{MAH}}$. By the property and definition of $\mathsf{F}_{\mathsf{MAH}}$, we have

$$\mathsf{T} \not\subseteq \mathsf{S}(X^{(1)}) \wedge \cdots \wedge \mathsf{T} \not\subseteq \mathsf{S}(X^{(Q)}) \wedge \mathsf{T} \subseteq \mathsf{S}(X^{\star})$$

with noticeable probability, where $X^{\star}$ is the challenge input and $X^{(1)}, \ldots, X^{(Q)}$ are the inputs for which the adversary has made evaluation queries. Our strategy to prove the security is to embed the problem instance and T into the parameters of the scheme so that we have

$$\theta_X = \mathsf{P}_X(\alpha) \qquad \text{and} \qquad g = \hat{g}^{\mathsf{Q}(\alpha)}.$$

Here, $\mathsf{P}_X(\mathsf{Z})$ is a polynomial in $\mathbb{Z}_p[\mathsf{Z}]$ that depends on X and $\mathsf{Q}(\mathsf{Z}) \in \mathbb{Z}_p[\mathsf{Z}]$ is some fixed polynomial. We want $\mathsf{P}_X(\mathsf{Z})$ and $\mathsf{Q}(\mathsf{Z})$ to satisfy the following property: There exist $\xi_X \in \mathbb{Z}_p^*$ and $\mathsf{R}_X(\mathsf{Z}) \in \mathbb{Z}_p[\mathsf{Z}]$ such that

$$\frac{\mathsf{Q}(\mathsf{Z})}{\mathsf{P}_X(\mathsf{Z})} = \begin{cases} \frac{\xi_X}{\mathsf{Z}} + \mathsf{R}_X(\mathsf{Z}) & \text{if} \quad \mathsf{T} \subseteq \mathsf{S}(X) \\ \mathsf{R}_X(\mathsf{Z}) & \text{if} \quad \mathsf{T} \not\subseteq \mathsf{S}(X) \end{cases}. \tag{4}$$

If the above holds, the simulation will be successful. To answer the evaluation query on input $X \in \{X^{(1)}, \ldots, X^{(Q)}\}$, we compute $e(\hat{g}^{\mathsf{R}_X(\alpha)}, h)$. This is a valid answer, since we have $\mathsf{T} \not\subseteq \mathsf{S}(X)$ and thus

$$e(\hat{g}^{\mathsf{R}_X(\alpha)}, h) = e(\hat{g}^{\mathsf{Q}(\alpha)/\mathsf{P}_X(\alpha)}, h) = e(g^{1/\mathsf{P}_X(\alpha)}, h) = e(g, h)^{1/\theta_X}.$$

To answer the challenge query, we compute $\Psi^{\xi_{X^\star}} \cdot e\left(\hat{g}^{\mathsf{R}_{X^\star}(\alpha)}, h\right)$. If $\Psi \xleftarrow{\$} \mathbb{G}_T$, it is a random element in $\mathbb{G}_T$, as desired. On the other hand, if $\Psi = e(\hat{g}, h)^{1/\alpha}$, we have

$$\Psi^{\xi_{X^\star}} \cdot e\left(\hat{g}^{\mathsf{R}_{X^\star}(\alpha)}, h\right) = e\left(\hat{g}^{\mathsf{Q}(\alpha)/\mathsf{P}_{X^\star}(\alpha)}, h\right) = e\left(g^{1/\mathsf{P}_{X^\star}(\alpha)}, h\right) = e(g, h)^{1/\theta_{X^\star}}$$

which is the correct value. Now we have to find the polynomials with the desired property (namely, Eq. (4)). Let us take $\mathsf{P}_X(\mathsf{Z})$ to be the following form:[3]

$$\mathsf{P}_X(\mathsf{Z}) = \prod_{i \in [\eta], j \in [\ell]} (\mathsf{Z} - t_i + s_j) \quad \text{where} \quad \mathsf{T} = \{t_1, \ldots, t_\eta\},\ \mathsf{S}(X) = \{s_1, \ldots, s_\ell\}.$$

In some sense, $\mathsf{P}_X(\mathsf{Z})$ checks $(t_i \stackrel{?}{=} s_j)$ in a brute-force manner. We can see that $\mathsf{P}_X(\mathsf{Z})$ can be divided by Z exactly $|\mathsf{T} \cap \mathsf{S}(X)|$ times. Furthermore, we have $|\mathsf{T} \cap \mathsf{S}(X)| = |\mathsf{T}| = \eta \Leftrightarrow \mathsf{T} \subseteq \mathsf{S}(X)$. This motivates us to define $\mathsf{Q}(\mathsf{Z})$ as follows:

$$\mathsf{Q}(\mathsf{Z}) = \mathsf{Z}^{\eta - 1} \cdot \prod_{a \neq 0} (\mathsf{Z} + a), \tag{5}$$

where the product is taken for sufficiently many $a \neq 0$, so that the latter part of $\mathsf{Q}(\mathsf{Z})$ can be divided by any factor of $\mathsf{P}_X(\mathsf{Z})$ except for Z. It is easy to see that

[3] For simplicity, we use a polynomial that is slightly different from the actual proof.

$\mathsf{Q}(\mathsf{Z})$ can be divided by Z exactly $\eta - 1$ times. These imply that $\mathsf{Q}(\mathsf{Z})$ can be divided by $\mathsf{P}_X(\mathsf{Z})$, if and only if the multiplicity of Z in $\mathsf{P}_X(\mathsf{Z})$ is at most $\eta - 1$. This fact allows us to prove Eq. (4).

Finally, we go back and see how our actual construction works. We set the verification key as $\mathsf{vk} = (g, h, \{W_i = g^{w_i}\}_{i\in[\eta]})$ and choose θ_X as

$$\theta_X = \prod_{(i,j)\in[\eta]\times[\ell]} \underbrace{(w_i + s_j)}_{:=\theta_{i,j}} = \prod_{i\in[\eta]} \underbrace{\left(\prod_{j\in[\ell]} (w_i + s_j) \right)}_{\phi_i} \tag{6}$$

and set the function value as $\mathsf{V}_{\mathsf{sk}}(X) = e(g,h)^{1/\theta_X}$. The form of θ_X reflects the "brute-force structure" that has appeared in $\mathsf{P}_X(\mathsf{Z})$. To generate a proof for the function value, we take the "step ladder approach" [Lys02, ACF09, HW10]. Namely, we publish values of the form $g^{1/\theta_{1,1}}, g^{1/\theta_{1,1}\theta_{1,2}}, \ldots, g^{1/\theta_{1,1}\cdots\theta_{\eta,\ell}} = g^{1/\theta_X}$. The correctness of the function value can be verified by the pairing computations using these terms. While this scheme achieves very short verification key, the proofs for the function values are very long. We can make the proofs much shorter by a simple trick. We introduce additional helper components $\{g^{w_i^j}\}_{(i,j)\in[\eta]\times[\ell]}$ to the verification key. Instead of publishing the proof above, we publish $g^{1/\phi_1}, g^{1/\phi_1\phi_2}, \ldots, g^{1/\phi_1\cdots\phi_\eta} = g^{1/\theta_X}$ as a proof. Thanks to the helper components, we can verify whether the function value is correct using the proof.

2.4 Other Constructions

Partitioning with Yet Another Function. We propose another function $\mathsf{F}_{\mathsf{AFF}}$, which is also useful to perform the partitioning technique. The main advantage of the function over $\mathsf{F}_{\mathsf{MAH}}$ is that it achieves even shorter secret randomness K of length $\omega(\log \lambda)$. Here, we begin by reviewing $\mathsf{F}_{\mathsf{WAT}}$, a slight variant of the celebrated Waters' hash [Wat05], and then gradually modify it to our $\mathsf{F}_{\mathsf{AFF}}$. Let the identity space of IBE (or input space of VRF) be $\{0,1\}^k$. The function $\mathsf{F}_{\mathsf{WAT}}$ is defined as

$$\mathsf{F}_{\mathsf{WAT}}(K = (\{\alpha_i\}_{i\in[k]}, \beta), \mathsf{ID}) = \begin{cases} 0, & \text{if } (\sum_{i\in[k]} \alpha_i \mathsf{ID}_i) + \beta = 0 \\ 1, & \text{otherwise} \end{cases}$$
$$\text{where } \alpha_i, \beta \in \mathbb{Z},\ \mathsf{ID} \in \{0,1\}^k$$

Here, ID_i is the i-th bit of ID. In order for the function to be useful, we should choose the random secret K so that

$$\Pr_K\left[\mathsf{F}_{\mathsf{WAT}}(K, \mathsf{ID}^{(1)}) = 1 \ \wedge \ \cdots \ \wedge \ \mathsf{F}_{\mathsf{WAT}}(K, \mathsf{ID}^{(Q)}) = 1 \ \wedge \ \mathsf{F}_{\mathsf{WAT}}(K, \mathsf{ID}^\star) = 0\right]$$

is noticeable. By a standard analysis, one can show that it suffices to satisfy the following two requirements:

(A) $\Pr_K[\mathsf{F}_{\mathsf{WAT}}(K, \mathsf{ID}^\star) = 0]$ is noticeable.
(B) $\Pr_K[\mathsf{F}_{\mathsf{WAT}}(K, \mathsf{ID}^{(i)}) = 0 \mid \mathsf{F}_{\mathsf{WAT}}(K, \mathsf{ID}^\star) = 0]$ is sufficiently small for all $i \in [Q]$.

In order to satisfy the requirements, one way to choose is $\alpha_1, \ldots, \alpha_k \xleftarrow{\$} [1, 4Q]$ and $\beta \xleftarrow{\$} [-4kQ, 0]$. As for requirement (A), we have

$$\Pr_K[\mathsf{F}_{\mathsf{WAT}}(K, \mathsf{ID}^\star) = 0] = \Pr_{\alpha,\beta}\left[\beta = -\sum_{i\in[k]} \alpha_i \mathsf{ID}_i^\star\right] = \frac{1}{4kQ+1}$$

where the second equality follows from $-4kQ \leq \sum_{i\in[k]} \alpha_i \mathsf{ID}_i^\star \leq 0$. We can see that the probability is noticeable as desired. The main observation here is that since the value of each α_i is polynomially bounded and $\mathsf{ID}_i^\star \in \{0,1\}$, the total sum is also confined within the polynomially bounded range and thus can be guessed with noticeable probability. Requirement (B) can be proven by exploiting a certain kind of pairwise independence of $\mathsf{F}_{\mathsf{WAT}}(K, \cdot)$.

The problem of the above function is that it requires long secret randomness K, whose length is linear in k. As the first attempt to shorten this, we could consider a modified function $\mathsf{F}'_{\mathsf{WAT}}$ defined as

$$\mathsf{F}'_{\mathsf{WAT}}(K = (\alpha, \beta), \mathsf{ID}) = \begin{cases} 0, & \text{if } \alpha\mathsf{ID} + \beta = 0 \\ 1, & \text{otherwise} \end{cases} \quad \text{where} \quad \alpha, \beta \in \mathbb{Z}, \mathsf{ID} \in [2^k - 1]$$

where we interpret $\mathsf{ID} \in \{0,1\}^k$ as an integer in $[2^k - 1]$ by the natural bijection. While it is easy to satisfy requirement (B), we no longer know how to satisfy requirement (A) at the same time. Even if the size of α is polynomially bounded, $\alpha \cdot \mathsf{ID}$ can be very large, and we can not guess the value better than with exponentially small probability.

To resolve the problem, we further modify the function and obtain our final function $\mathsf{F}_{\mathsf{AFF}}$ defined as follows:

$$\mathsf{F}_{\mathsf{AFF}}(K = (\alpha, \beta, \rho), \mathsf{ID}) = \begin{cases} 0, & \text{if } \alpha\mathsf{ID} + \beta \equiv 0 \mod \rho \\ 1, & \text{otherwise} \end{cases}$$
$$\text{where } \alpha, \beta, \rho \in \mathbb{Z}, \ \mathsf{ID} \in [2^k - 1].$$

Here, we choose ρ to be a random polynomial-size prime. Now, we can satisfy requirement (A), since we only have to guess $(\alpha \cdot \mathsf{ID} \mod \rho)$, for which there are only a polynomial number of candidates. However, making the size of ρ polynomial causes a subtle problem regarding requirement (B). Let us consider the case where an adversary makes queries such that $\mathsf{ID}^\star = \mathsf{ID}^{(1)} + \rho$. In such a case, we have $\mathsf{F}_{\mathsf{AFF}}(K, \mathsf{ID}^\star) = \mathsf{F}_{\mathsf{AFF}}(K, \mathsf{ID}^{(1)})$ and the simulation fails with probability 1, no matter how we choose α and β. Such queries can be made with noticeable probability, since ρ is polynomial-size and the adversary can guess the value with noticeable probability. However a small subtlety is that the probability does not need to be negligible in order to satisfy requirement (B).

Due to this observation, by choosing ρ randomly from a large enough domain (concretely, from $[kQ^2/\epsilon, 4kQ^2/\epsilon]$), we can make the probability of such queries being made sufficiently small, hence satisfying requirement (A) and (B).

New IBE and VRF Based on the Function. Based on the function $\mathsf{F}_{\mathsf{AFF}}$, we propose a lattice based IBE scheme and a VRF scheme on bilinear groups. To construct a lattice based IBE scheme, we follow the same template as the case of $\mathsf{F}_{\mathsf{MAH}}$ and set $\mathbf{B}_{\mathsf{ID}} = \mathsf{PubEval}(\mathsf{F}_{\mathsf{AFF}}(\cdot\,, \mathsf{ID}), \{\mathbf{B}_i\}_{i\in[u]})$. Again, if we use the fully key homomorphic algorithm of [BGG+14] naively, the scheme will require super polynomial modulus q. To avoid this, to compute $\mathbf{B}_{\mathsf{ID}}$, we first compute a description of a log-depth circuit corresponding to $\mathsf{F}_{\mathsf{AFF}}$. Such a circuit exists by the classical result of Beam, Cook, and Hoover [BCH86], who showed that the computation of division can be performed in $\mathbf{NC}^1$, since division implies modulo ρ arithmetic. Then, we convert the log-depth circuit into a branching program using the Barrington's theorem [Bar89]. Finally, we use the key homomorphic algorithm for branching programs in [GV15]. Note that similar approach was also taken in [BL16] to homomorphically evaluate a PRF. To construct a VRF based on bilinear groups, we again take advantage of the fact that $\mathsf{F}_{\mathsf{AFF}}$ can be computed by a log-depth circuit. This fact is necessary for our VRF to be proven secure under a polynomial-size assumption, since our security proof requires 2^d-DDH assumption, where d is the depth of the circuit.

3 Preliminaries

Due to the space limitation, we omit most of the proofs for the lemmas presented in the paper. They can be found in the full version [Yam17].

Notation. We denote by $[a]$ a set $\{1, 2, \ldots, a\}$ for any integer $a \in \mathbb{N}$. For a set S, $|S|$ denotes its size. We treat a vector as a column vector. If $\mathbf{A}_1$ is an $n \times m$ and $\mathbf{A}_2$ is an $n \times m'$ matrix, then $[\mathbf{A}_1 \| \mathbf{A}_2]$ denotes the $n \times (m + m')$ matrix formed by concatenating $\mathbf{A}_1$ and $\mathbf{A}_2$. We use similar notation for vectors. For a vector $\mathbf{u} \in \mathbb{Z}^n$, $\|\mathbf{u}\|$ and $\|\mathbf{u}\|_\infty$ denote its ℓ_2 and ℓ_∞ norm respectively. Similarly, for a matrix $\mathbf{R}$, $\|\mathbf{R}\|_\infty$ denotes its infinity norm. $\|\mathbf{R}\|_2$ is the operator norm of $\mathbf{R}$. Namely, $\|\mathbf{R}\|_2 := \sup_{\|\mathbf{x}\|=1} \|\mathbf{R}\mathbf{x}\|$. For a function $f(\cdot) : \mathbb{N} \to \mathbb{R}_{\geq 0}$, we say that the function is negligible when for every polynomial $g(\cdot)$ and all sufficiently large λ we have $f(\lambda) < |1/g(\lambda)|$. We say that the function is noticeable when there exists a polynomial $g(\cdot)$ such that we have $f(\lambda) \geq |1/g(\lambda)|$ for all λ.

3.1 Cryptographic Primitives

IBE and VRF. We use the standard syntax of IBE [BF01] and VRF with large input spaces [HW10]. We require standard notion of the correctness for both. For VRF, we also require unique provability. As for the security, we require adaptive anonymity for IBE and pseudorandomness for VRF. We refer to the full version for the formal definitions. These security notions are defined by games between the challenger and the adversary. In the games, we use two random variables coin

and $\widehat{\mathsf{coin}}$ in $\{0,1\}$ for defining the security. coin refers to the random value chosen by the challenger and $\widehat{\mathsf{coin}}$ refers to the guess for coin output by the adversary. We have the following general statement concerning coin and $\widehat{\mathsf{coin}}$.

Lemma 1 (Lemma 8 in [KY16], See also Lemma 28 in [ABB10a]). *Let us consider an IBE (resp. VRF) scheme and an adversary $\mathcal{A}$ that breaks the adaptively-anonymous security (resp. pseudorandomness) with advantage ϵ. Let the identity space (resp. input space) be $\mathcal{X}$ and consider a map γ that maps a sequence of elements in $\mathcal{X}$ to a value in $[0,1]$. We consider the following experiment. We first execute the security game for $\mathcal{A}$. Let $X^\star$ be the challenge identity (resp. challenge input) and $X_1,\ldots,X_Q$ be the identities (resp. inputs) for which key extraction queries (resp. evaluation queries) were made. We denote $\mathbb{X} = (X^\star, X_1,\ldots,X_Q)$. At the end of the game, we set $\mathsf{coin}' \in \{0,1\}$ as $\mathsf{coin}' = \widehat{\mathsf{coin}}$ with probability $\gamma(\mathbb{X})$ and $\mathsf{coin}' \overset{\$}{\leftarrow} \{0,1\}$ with probability $1-\gamma(\mathbb{X})$. Then, the following holds.*

$$\left|\Pr[\mathsf{coin}' = \mathsf{coin}] - \frac{1}{2}\right| \geq \gamma_{\min} \cdot \epsilon - \frac{\gamma_{\max} - \gamma_{\min}}{2}$$

where $\gamma_{\min}$ and $\gamma_{\max}$ are the maximum and the minimum of $\gamma(\mathbb{X})$ taken over all possible $\mathbb{X}$, respectively.

Though the lemma was proven only for IBE in [KY16], the same proof works also for VRF.

3.2 Preliminaries on Lattices and Bilinear Maps

For an integer $m > 0$, let $D_{\mathbb{Z}^m,\sigma}$ be the discrete Gaussian distribution over $\mathbb{Z}^m$ with parameter $\sigma > 0$.

Learning with Errors (LWE) Assumption. We define the learning with errors (LWE) problem, which was introduced by Regev [Reg05].

Definition 1 (LWE). *For an integers $n = n(\lambda)$, $m = m(n)$, a prime integer $q = q(n) > 2$, a real number $\alpha \in (0,1)$, and a PPT algorithm $\mathcal{A}$, an advantage for the learning with errors problem $\mathsf{dLWE}_{n,m,q,\alpha}$ of $\mathcal{A}$ is defined as follows:*

$$\mathsf{Adv}_{\mathcal{A}}^{\mathsf{dLWE}_{n,m,q,\alpha}} = \left|\Pr\left[\mathcal{A}(\mathbf{A}, \mathbf{s}^\top \mathbf{A} + \mathbf{x}^\top) \to 1\right] - \Pr\left[\mathcal{A}(\mathbf{A}, \mathbf{w}^\top + \mathbf{x}^\top) \to 1\right]\right|$$

where $\mathbf{A} \overset{\$}{\leftarrow} \mathbb{Z}_q^{n\times m}$, $\mathbf{s} \overset{\$}{\leftarrow} \mathbb{Z}_q^n$, $\mathbf{x} \overset{\$}{\leftarrow} D_{\mathbb{Z}^m,\alpha q}$, $\mathbf{w} \overset{\$}{\leftarrow} \mathbb{Z}_q^m$. We say that $\mathsf{dLWE}_{n,m,q,\alpha}$ assumption holds if $\mathsf{Adv}_{\mathcal{A}}^{\mathsf{dLWE}_{n,m,q,\alpha}}$ is negligible for all PPT $\mathcal{A}$.

Regev [Reg05] (see also [GKV10]) showed that solving $\mathsf{dLWE}_{n,m,q,\alpha}$ for $\alpha q > 2\sqrt{2n}$ is (quantumly) as hard as approximating the SIVP and GapSVP problems to within $\tilde{O}(n/\alpha)$ factors in the ℓ_2 norm, in the worst case. In the subsequent works, (partial) dequantumization of the Regev's reduction were achieved [Pei09, BLP+13].

Gadget Matrix. Let $m > n\lceil \log q \rceil$. There is a fixed full-rank matrix $\mathbf{G} \in \mathbb{Z}_q^{n\times m}$ such that there exists a deterministic polynomial-time algorithm $\mathbf{G}^{-1}$ which takes the input $\mathbf{U} \in \mathbb{Z}_q^{n\times m}$ and outputs $\mathbf{V} = \mathbf{G}^{-1}(\mathbf{U})$ such that $\mathbf{V} \in \{0,1\}^{m\times m}$ and $\mathbf{GV} = \mathbf{U}$.

Trapdoors. Here, we follow the presentation of [BV16]. Let $n, m, q \in \mathbb{N}$ and consider a matrix $\mathbf{A} \in \mathbb{Z}_q^{n\times m}$. For all $\mathbf{V} \in \mathbb{Z}_q^{n\times m'}$, we let $\mathbf{A}_\sigma^{-1}(\mathbf{V})$ be a distribution that is a Gaussian $(D_{\mathbb{Z}^m,\sigma})^{m'}$ conditioned on $\mathbf{A} \cdot \mathbf{A}_\sigma^{-1}(\mathbf{V}) = \mathbf{V}$. A σ-trapdoor for $\mathbf{A}$ is a procedure that can sample from the distribution $\mathbf{A}_\sigma^{-1}(\mathbf{V})$ in time $\mathsf{poly}(n, m, m', \log q)$, for any $\mathbf{V}$. We slightly overload notation and denote a σ-trapdoor for $\mathbf{A}$ by $\mathbf{A}_\sigma^{-1}$. The following properties had been established in a long sequence of works [GPV08, ABB10a, CHKP10, ABB10b, MP12, BLP+13].

Lemma 2 (Properties of Trapdoors). *Lattice trapdoors exhibit the following properties.*

1. *Given* $\mathbf{A}_\sigma^{-1}$, *one can obtain* $\mathbf{A}_{\sigma'}^{-1}$ *for any* $\sigma' \geq \sigma$.
2. *Given* $\mathbf{A}_\sigma^{-1}$, *one can obtain* $[\mathbf{A}\|\mathbf{B}]_\sigma^{-1}$ *and* $[\mathbf{B}\|\mathbf{A}]_\sigma^{-1}$ *for any* $\mathbf{B}$.
3. *For all* $\mathbf{A} \in \mathbb{Z}_q^{n\times m}$ *and* $\mathbf{R} \in \mathbb{Z}^{m\times m}$, *with* $m \geq n\lceil \log q \rceil$, *one can obtain* $[\mathbf{AR} + \mathbf{G}\|\mathbf{A}]_\sigma^{-1}$ *for* $\sigma = m \cdot \|\mathbf{R}\|_\infty \cdot \omega(\sqrt{\log m})$.
4. *There exists an efficient procedure* $\mathsf{TrapGen}(1^n, 1^m, q)$ *that outputs* $(\mathbf{A}, \mathbf{A}_{\sigma_0}^{-1})$ *where* $\mathbf{A} \in \mathbb{Z}_q^{n\times m}$ *for some* $m = O(n \log q)$ *and is* 2^{-n}*-close to uniform, where* $\sigma_0 = \omega(\sqrt{n \log q \log m})$.
5. *For* $\mathbf{A}_\sigma^{-1}$ *and* $\mathbf{u} \in \mathbb{Z}_q^n$, *it follows* $\Pr[\ \|\mathbf{A}_\sigma^{-1}(\mathbf{u})\| > \sqrt{m}\sigma\ ] = \mathsf{negl}(n)$.

Certified Bilinear Group Generators. We define certified bilinear group generators following [HJ16]. We require that there is an efficient bilinear group generator algorithm GrpGen that on input 1^λ and outputs a description Π of bilinear groups $\mathbb{G}, \mathbb{G}_T$ with prime order p and a map $e : \mathbb{G} \times \mathbb{G} \to \mathbb{G}_T$. We also require that GrpGen is certified, in the sense that there is an efficient algorithm GrpVfy that on input a (possibly incorrectly generated) description of the bilinear groups and outputs whether the description is valid or not. Furthermore, we require that each group element has unique encoding, which can be efficiently recognized. For the precise definitions, we refer to [HJ16] and the full version.

L-Diffie-Hellman Assumptions

Definition 2 (L-Diffie-Hellman Assumptions). *For a PPT algorithm $\mathcal{A}$, an advantage for the decisional L-Diffie Hellman problem L-DDH of $\mathcal{A}$ with respect to* GrpGen *is defined as follows:*

$$\begin{aligned}\mathsf{Adv}_{\mathcal{A}}^{L\text{-}\mathsf{DDH}} = |\Pr[&\mathcal{A}(\Pi, \hat{g}, h, \hat{g}^{\alpha}, \hat{g}^{\alpha^2}, \ldots \hat{g}^{\alpha^L}, \Psi_0) \to 1] \\ -\Pr[&\mathcal{A}(\Pi, \hat{g}, h, \hat{g}^{\alpha}, \hat{g}^{\alpha^2}, \ldots \hat{g}^{\alpha^L}, \Psi_1) \to 1]|\end{aligned}$$

where $\Pi \stackrel{\$}{\leftarrow} \mathsf{GrpGen}(1^\lambda)$, $\alpha \stackrel{\$}{\leftarrow} \mathbb{Z}_p^*$, $\hat{g}, h \stackrel{\$}{\leftarrow} \mathbb{G}$, $\Psi_0 = e(\hat{g}, h)^{1/\alpha}$, *and* $\Psi_1 \stackrel{\$}{\leftarrow} \mathbb{G}_T$. *We say that L-*DDH *assumption holds if* $\mathsf{Adv}_{\mathcal{A}}^{L\text{-}\mathsf{DDH}}$ *is negligible for all PPT $\mathcal{A}$.*

4 Partitioning Functions

In this section, we introduce the notion of *partitioning functions*. The notion abstracts out the information theoretic properties that are useful in the security proofs based on the partitioning techniques. Then, we proceed to recap the specific partitioning function that was given by [Jag15]. Then, we propose two new constructions of partitioning functions. The first one is obtained by introducing a simple but novel twist to the construction by [Jag15]. The second one is based on the affine-functions on random modulus. In the later sections, we will construct new lattice IBEs and VRFs based on these partitioning functions.

4.1 Definition

In the security proofs based on the partitioning technique [BB04b, Wat05], the simulations are successful only with noticeable probabilities. As observed by Waters [Wat05], this causes a subtle problem when considering the reduction to the decisional assumptions (such as the L-DDH). He resolved the problem by introducing the artificial abort step, where the simulator intentionally aborts with certain probability even when the simulation is successful. Later, Bellare and Ristenpart [BR09] showed that by requiring reasonable *upper bound* on the probability that the simulation is successful in addition to the *lower bound*, this step can be removed. In the subsequent work, Jager [Jag15] incorporated the idea of [BR09] into the notion of the admissible hash function [BB04b, CHKP10, FHPS13] to define *balanced admissible hash function*. The notion is a useful tool to perform the security proofs based on the partitioning technique. In addition, it is compatible with the decisional assumptions in the sense that it does not require the artificial abort step. Here, we define the notion of the partitioning function by slightly generalizing the balanced admissible hash function [Jag15].

Definition 3. *Let* $\mathsf{F} = \{\mathsf{F}_\lambda : \mathcal{K}_\lambda \times \mathcal{X}_\lambda \to \{0,1\}\}$ *be an ensemble of function families. We say that* F *is a partitioning function, if there exists an efficient algorithm* $\mathsf{PrtSmp}(1^\lambda, Q, \epsilon)$*, which takes as input polynomially bounded* $Q = Q(\lambda) \in \mathbb{N}$ *and noticeable* $\epsilon = \epsilon(\lambda) \in (0, 1/2]$ *and outputs* K *such that:*

1. *There exists* $\lambda_0 \in \mathbb{N}$ *such that*
$$\Pr\left[K \in \mathcal{K}_\lambda \ : \ K \stackrel{\$}{\leftarrow} \mathsf{PrtSmp}\left(1^\lambda, Q(\lambda), \epsilon(\lambda)\right)\right] = 1$$
for all $\lambda > \lambda_0$*. Here,* λ_0 *may depend on functions* $Q(\lambda)$ *and* $\epsilon(\lambda)$*.*
2. *For* $\lambda > \lambda_0$*, there exists* $\gamma_{\max}(\lambda)$ *and* $\gamma_{\min}(\lambda)$ *that depend on* $Q(\lambda)$ *and* $\epsilon(\lambda)$ *such that for all* $X^{(1)}, \dots, X^{(Q)}, X^\star \in \mathcal{X}_\lambda$ *with* $X^\star \notin \{X^{(1)}, \dots, X^{(Q)}\}$*,*
$$\gamma_{\max}(\lambda) \geq \gamma(X^{(1)}, \dots, X^{(Q)}) \geq \gamma_{\min}(\lambda) \tag{7}$$
holds where
$$\gamma(X^{(1)}, \dots, X^{(Q)}) = \Pr\left[\left(\mathsf{F}(K, X^{(j)}) = 1 \quad \forall j \in [Q]\right) \wedge \ \mathsf{F}(K, X^\star) = 0\right]$$

and the function $\tau(\lambda)$ defined as

$$\tau(\lambda) := \gamma_{\min}(\lambda) \cdot \epsilon(\lambda) - \frac{\gamma_{\max}(\lambda) - \gamma_{\min}(\lambda)}{2} \tag{8}$$

is noticeable. We note that the probability above is taken over the choice of $K \xleftarrow{\$} \mathsf{PrtSmp}(1^\lambda, Q(\lambda), \epsilon(\lambda))$.

We call K the partitioning key and $\tau(\lambda)$ the quality of the partitioning function.

In the following, we often drop the subscript λ and denote F, $\mathcal{K}$, and $\mathcal{X}$ for the sake of simplicity. We remark that the term $\tau(\lambda)$ above, which may seem very specific, is inherited from [Jag15]. As explained in [Jag15], such a term appears typically in security analyses that follows the approach of Bellare and Ristenpart [BR09] (See also Lemma 1). Looking ahead, the quantity $\tau(\lambda)$ will directly affect the reduction cost of our IBEs and VRFs. The length of (the binary representation of) the partitioning key K will affect the efficiency of the resulting schemes. Therefore, we want the partitioning function F for the largest possible $\tau(\lambda)$ and the shortest possible partitioning key.

There are two main differences from the definition of [Jag15]. Firstly, we consider *any* function F, whereas they only considered a specific function (namely, $\mathsf{F}_{\mathsf{ADH}}$ in Sect. 4.2). Secondly, we explicitly add the condition regarding the domain correctness of the output of PrtSmp (the first condition), which was implicit in [Jag15].

Comparison with Programmable Hash Functions. Our notion of the partitioning function is similar to the programmable hash function [HK08, ZCZ16]. The main difference is that whereas the notion of the programmable hash function is defined on specific algebraic structures such as (bilinear) groups [HK08] and lattices [ZCZ16], our definition is irrelevant to them. Since the security proofs of our IBEs and VRFs have the same information theoretic structure in common, we choose to decouple them from the underlying algebraic structures.

4.2 Construction from Admissible Hash Function

Here, we recap the result of Jager [Jag15] who constructed a specific partitioning function that he calls balanced admissible hash function. The result will be used in the next subsection to construct our first partitioning function. Let $k(\lambda) = \Theta(\lambda)$ and $\ell(\lambda) = \Theta(\lambda)$ be integers and let $\{C_k : \{0,1\}^k \to \{0,1\}^\ell\}_{k \in \mathbb{N}}$ be a family of error correcting codes with minimal distance ℓc for a constant $c \in (0, 1/2)$. Explicit constructions of such codes are given in [SS96, Zém01, Gol08] for instance. Let us define

$$\mathcal{K}_{\mathsf{ADH}} = \{0, 1, \perp\}^\ell \qquad \text{and} \qquad \mathcal{X}_{\mathsf{ADH}} = \{0, 1\}^k.$$

We define $\mathsf{F}_{\mathsf{ADH}}$ as

$$\mathsf{F}_{\mathsf{ADH}}(K, X) = \begin{cases} 0, & \text{if } \forall i \in [\ell] : \ C(X)_i = K_i \quad \vee \quad K_i = \perp \\ 1, & \text{otherwise} \end{cases}$$

where $C(X)_i$ and K_i are the i-th significant bit of $C(X)$ and K, respectively. Jager [Jag15] showed the following theorem.

Theorem 1 (Adapted from Theorem 1 in [Jag15]). *There exists an efficient algorithm* $\mathsf{AdmSmp}(1^\lambda, Q, \epsilon)$, *which takes as input* $Q \in \mathbb{N}$ *and* $\epsilon \in (0, 1/2]$ *and outputs* K *with exactly* η' *components not equal to* $\perp$, *where*

$$\eta' := \left\lfloor \frac{\log(2Q + Q/\epsilon)}{-\log(1-c)} \right\rfloor,$$

such that Eqs. (7) *and* (8) *hold with respect to* $\mathsf{F} := \mathsf{F}_{\mathsf{ADH}}$, $\mathsf{PrtSmp} := \mathsf{AdmSmp}$, *and* $\tau(\lambda) = 2^{-\eta'-1} \cdot \epsilon$. *In particular,* $\mathsf{F}_{\mathsf{ADH}}$ *is a partitioning function.*

4.3 Our Construction Based on Modified Admissible Hash Function

Here, we propose our first construction of the partitioning function $\mathsf{F}_{\mathsf{MAH}}$, which is obtained by modifying $\mathsf{F}_{\mathsf{ADH}}$ in the previous subsection. The advantage of $\mathsf{F}_{\mathsf{MAH}}$ is that it achieves much shorter partitioning keys compared with $\mathsf{F}_{\mathsf{ADH}}$. In particular, the length is $\omega(\log^2 \lambda)$ in $\mathsf{F}_{\mathsf{MAH}}$, whereas $\Theta(\lambda)$ in $\mathsf{F}_{\mathsf{ADH}}$. We will use the same notation as in Sect. 4.2. Let us introduce an integer $\eta(\lambda) = \omega(\log \lambda)$. $\eta(\lambda)$ can be set arbitrarily as long as it grows faster than $\log \lambda$. (See footnote in Sect. 1.) For our construction, we set

$$\mathcal{K}_{\mathsf{MAH}} = \{\mathsf{T} \subseteq [2\ell] \quad | \quad |\mathsf{T}| < \eta\} \qquad \text{and} \qquad \mathcal{X}_{\mathsf{MAH}} = \{0,1\}^k.$$

We define $\mathsf{F}_{\mathsf{MAH}}$ as

$$\mathsf{F}_{\mathsf{MAH}}(\mathsf{T}, X) = \begin{cases} 0, & \text{if } \mathsf{T} \subseteq \mathsf{S}(X) \\ 1, & \text{otherwise} \end{cases} \qquad \text{where} \quad \mathsf{S}(X) = \{\, 2i - C(X)_i \mid i \in [\ell] \,\}.$$

In the above, $C(X)_i$ is the i-th bit of $C(X) \in \{0,1\}^\ell$. See Fig. 1 in Sect. 2.1 for an illustrative example of S.

Lemma 3. *The function* $\mathsf{F}_{\mathsf{MAH}}$ *defined above is a partitioning function.*

Proof. To prove the lemma, we define $\mathsf{PrtSmp}_{\mathsf{MAH}}$ as follows. It uses the algorithm AdmSmp from the previous subsection as a subroutine.

$\mathsf{PrtSmp}_{\mathsf{MAH}}(1^\lambda, Q, \epsilon)$: It runs $\mathsf{AdmSmp}(1^\lambda, Q, \epsilon) \to K$ and sets

$$\mathsf{T} = \{2i - K_i \mid i \in [\ell],\ K_i \neq \perp\} \subseteq [2\ell],$$

where K_i is the i-th bit of K. It finally outputs T.

See Fig. 1 in Sect. 2.1 for an illustrative example of T. We first show that $\mathsf{PrtSmp}_{\mathsf{MAH}}$ satisfies the first property of Definition 3. By Theorem 1, $|\mathsf{T}| = \eta' = \lceil \log(2Q + Q/\epsilon)/\log(1-c) \rceil$. To show $\mathsf{T} \in \mathcal{K}_{\mathsf{MAH}}$ for all sufficiently large λ, it suffices to show $\eta'(\lambda) < \eta(\lambda)$ for all sufficiently large λ. This follows since

$$\eta'(\lambda) = \left\lfloor \frac{\log(2Q + Q/\epsilon)}{-\log(1-c)} \right\rfloor = O(\log(\mathsf{poly}(\lambda))) = O(\log \lambda) \quad \text{and} \quad \eta(\lambda) = \omega(\log \lambda)$$

when $Q(\lambda)$ is polynomially bounded and ϵ is noticeable for constant c. We next prove the second property. This follows from Theorem 1 and by the following observation:

$$\begin{aligned} \mathsf{F}_{\mathsf{ADH}}(K, X) = 0 \quad &\Leftrightarrow C(X)_i = K_i \quad \forall i \in [\ell] \text{ such that } K_i \neq \perp \\ &\Leftrightarrow \mathsf{T} \subseteq \mathsf{S}(X) \\ &\Leftrightarrow \mathsf{F}_{\mathsf{MAH}}(\mathsf{T}, X) = 0. \end{aligned}$$

This completes the proof of Lemma 3.

4.4 Our Construction Based on Affine Functions

Here, we propose our second construction of the partitioning function $\mathsf{F}_{\mathsf{AFF}}$. Compared to $\mathsf{F}_{\mathsf{MAH}}$, the function achieves an even shorter length of $\omega(\log \lambda)$ for the partitioning keys. Let $k(\lambda) = \Theta(\lambda)$ and $\eta(\lambda) = \omega(\log \lambda)$ be integers. For our construction, we set

$$\mathcal{K}_{\mathsf{AFF}} = \{0,1\}^{3\eta}, \qquad \mathcal{X}_{\mathsf{AFF}} = \{0,1\}^{k}$$

$\mathsf{F}_{\mathsf{AFF}}(K, X)$ is defined as

$$\mathsf{F}_{\mathsf{AFF}}(K = (\alpha, \beta, \rho),\ X) = \begin{cases} 0, & \text{if } \rho \neq 0 \quad \wedge \quad \alpha X + \beta \equiv 0 \mod \rho \\ 1, & \text{otherwise} \end{cases},$$

where $\alpha, \beta, \rho \in \{0,1\}^{\eta}$. Here, we slightly abuse the notation and identify a bit-string in $\{0,1\}^{\eta}$ with an integer in $[0, 2^{\eta} - 1]$ by its binary representation. Similarly, a bit-string in $\{0,1\}^{k}$ is identified with an integer in $[0, 2^{k} - 1]$.

Theorem 2. $\mathsf{F}_{\mathsf{AFF}}$ *defined above is a partitioning function.*

5 Our IBE Schemes

In this section, we give a generic construction of an adaptively secure lattice based IBE from a partitioning function. Our generic construction requires the underlying partitioning function to be compatible (in some sense) with the structure of lattices. In the following, we first formalize the requirement by giving the definition of compatibility. Then, we show that $\mathsf{F}_{\mathsf{MAH}}$ and $\mathsf{F}_{\mathsf{AFF}}$ are compatible in this sense. Finally, we show the generic construction of IBE.

5.1 Compatible Algorithms for Partitioning Functions

The following definition gives a sufficient condition for partitioning functions to be useful for constructing adaptively secure IBE schemes.

Definition 4. *We say that the* deterministic *algorithms* (Encode, PubEval, TrapEval) *are δ-compatible with a function family* $\{\mathsf{F} : \mathcal{K} \times \mathcal{X} \to \{0,1\}\}$ *if they are efficient and satisfy the following properties:*

- $\mathsf{Encode}(K \in \mathcal{K}) \rightarrow \kappa \in \{0,1\}^u$
- $\mathsf{PubEval}\left(X \in \mathcal{X}, \{\mathbf{B}_i \in \mathbb{Z}_q^{n\times m}\}_{i\in[u]}\ \right) \rightarrow \mathbf{B}_X \in \mathbb{Z}_q^{n\times m}$
- $\mathsf{TrapEval}\left(K \in \mathcal{K},\ X \in \mathcal{X},\ \mathbf{A} \in \mathbb{Z}_q^{n\times m},\ \{\mathbf{R}_i \in \mathbb{Z}^{m\times m}\}_{i\in[u]}\right) \rightarrow \mathbf{R}_X \in \mathbb{Z}^{m\times m}$

We require that the following holds:

$$\mathsf{PubEval}\left(X, \{\mathbf{A}\mathbf{R}_i + \kappa_i \mathbf{G}\}_{i\in[u]}\right) = \mathbf{A}\mathbf{R}_X + \mathsf{F}(K,X)\cdot\mathbf{G}$$

where $\kappa_i \in \{0,1\}$ *is the i-th bit of* $\kappa = \mathsf{Encode}(K) \in \{0,1\}^u$. *Furthermore, if* $\mathbf{R}_i \in \{-1,0,1\}^{m\times m}$ *for all* $i \in [u]$, *we have* $\|\mathbf{R}_X\|_\infty \leq \delta$.

It is possible to obtain compatible algorithms for any partitioning functions, including ours, by directly leveraging the fully key homomorphic algorithm in [BGG+14]. However, if we apply the algorithm naively, it will end up with super-polynomial δ, which is undesirable. By carefully applying the idea from [GV15], we can provide δ-compatible algorithms for $\mathsf{F}_{\mathsf{MAH}}$ and $\mathsf{F}_{\mathsf{AFF}}$ with polynomial δ. In particular, we have following lemmas.

Lemma 4. *For* $u = \eta\cdot\lceil\log(2\ell+1)\rceil$, *there are* $m^3u(\ell+1)$*-compatible algorithms for* $\mathsf{F}_{\mathsf{MAH}}$.

Lemma 5. *For* $u = 3\eta$, *there are* $\mathsf{poly}(n)$*-compatible algorithm for* $\mathsf{F}_{\mathsf{AFF}}$, *where* $\mathsf{poly}(n)$ *denotes some fixed polynomial in* n.

5.2 Construction

Here, we construct an IBE scheme based on a partitioning function $\mathsf{F} : \mathcal{K}\times\mathcal{X} \rightarrow \{0,1\}$ with associating δ-compatible algorithms ($\mathsf{Encode}, \mathsf{PubEval}, \mathsf{TrapEval}$). We assume $\mathcal{X} = \mathcal{ID} = \{0,1\}^k$, where $\mathcal{ID}$ is the identity space of the scheme. If a collision resistant hash $\mathsf{CRH} : \{0,1\}^* \rightarrow \{0,1\}^k$ is available, we can use any bit-string as an identity. For simplicity, we let the message space of the scheme be $\{0,1\}$. For the multi-bit variant, we refer to Sect. 5.3. Our scheme can be instantiated with $\mathsf{F}_{\mathsf{MAH}}$ and $\mathsf{F}_{\mathsf{AFF}}$, which would lead to schemes with efficiency and security trade-offs. We compare the resulting schemes with existing schemes in Sect. 7. (See also Table 1 in Sect. 1.)

$\mathsf{Setup}(1^\lambda)$: On input 1^λ, it sets the parameters n, m, q, σ, α, and α' as specified later in this section, where q is a prime number. Then, it picks random matrices $\mathbf{B}_0, \mathbf{B}_i \overset{\$}{\leftarrow} \mathbb{Z}_q^{n\times m}$ for $i \in [u]$ and a vector $\mathbf{u} \overset{\$}{\leftarrow} \mathbb{Z}_q^n$. It also picks $(\mathbf{A}, \mathbf{A}_{\sigma_0}^{-1}) \overset{\$}{\leftarrow} \mathsf{TrapGen}(1^n, 1^m, q)$ such that $\mathbf{A} \in \mathbb{Z}_q^{n\times m}$ and $\sigma_0 = \omega(\sqrt{n\log q\log m})$. It finally outputs

$$\mathsf{mpk} = \left(\ \mathbf{A},\ \mathbf{B}_0,\ \{\mathbf{B}_i\}_{i\in[u]},\ \mathbf{u}\ \right) \qquad \text{and} \qquad \mathsf{msk} = \mathbf{A}_{\sigma_0}^{-1}.$$

$\mathsf{KeyGen}(\mathsf{mpk}, \mathsf{msk}, \mathsf{ID})$: Given an identity ID, it first computes

$$\mathsf{PubEval}\left(\mathsf{ID},\ \{\mathbf{B}_i\}_{i\in[u]}\ \right) \rightarrow \mathbf{B}_{\mathsf{ID}} \in \mathbb{Z}_q^{n\times m}.$$

It then computes $[\mathbf{A}\|\mathbf{B}_0+\mathbf{B}_{\mathsf{ID}}]_\sigma^{-1}$ from $\mathbf{A}_{\sigma_0}^{-1}$ and samples

$$\mathbf{e} \stackrel{\$}{\leftarrow} [\mathbf{A}\|\mathbf{B}_0+\mathbf{B}_{\mathsf{ID}}]_\sigma^{-1}(\mathbf{u}).$$

Then, it returns $\mathsf{sk}_{\mathsf{ID}} = \mathbf{e} \in \mathbb{Z}^{2m}$. Note that we have $[\mathbf{A}\|\mathbf{B}_0+\mathbf{B}_{\mathsf{ID}}]\cdot\mathbf{e} = \mathbf{u} \mod q$.

$\mathsf{Encrypt}(\mathsf{mpk}, \mathsf{ID}, \mathsf{M})$: To encrypt a message $\mathsf{M} \in \{0,1\}$ for an identity ID, it first computes $\mathsf{PubEval}(\mathsf{ID}, \{\mathbf{B}_i\}_{i\in[u]}) \to \mathbf{B}_{\mathsf{ID}}$. It then picks $\mathbf{s} \stackrel{\$}{\leftarrow} \mathbb{Z}_q^n$, $x_0 \stackrel{\$}{\leftarrow} D_{\mathbb{Z},\alpha q}$, $\mathbf{x}_1, \mathbf{x}_2 \stackrel{\$}{\leftarrow} D_{\mathbb{Z}^m,\alpha' q}$ and computes

$$c_0 = \mathbf{s}^\top\mathbf{u} + x_0 + \mathsf{M}\cdot\lceil q/2\rceil, \qquad \mathbf{c}_1^\top = \mathbf{s}^\top[\mathbf{A}\|\mathbf{B}_0+\mathbf{B}_{\mathsf{ID}}] + [\mathbf{x}_1^\top\|\mathbf{x}_2^\top].$$

Finally, it returns the ciphertext $\mathsf{ct} = (c_0, \mathbf{c}_1) \in \mathbb{Z}_q \times \mathbb{Z}_q^{2m}$.

$\mathsf{Decrypt}(\mathsf{mpk}, \mathsf{sk}_{\mathsf{ID}}, \mathsf{ct})$: To decrypt a ciphertext $\mathsf{ct} = (c_0, \mathbf{c}_1)$ using a private key $\mathsf{sk}_{\mathsf{ID}} := \mathbf{e}$, it first computes

$$w = c_0 - \mathbf{c}_1^\top \cdot \mathbf{e} \in \mathbb{Z}_q.$$

Then it returns 1 if $|w - \lceil q/2\rceil| < \lceil q/4\rceil$ and 0 otherwise.

We claim that the correctness and security of the scheme can be proven under the following parameter selection. We refer full version to the justification.

$$m = O(n\log q), \qquad q = n^{7/2}\cdot\delta^2\cdot\omega(\log^{7/2} n), \qquad \sigma = m\cdot\delta\cdot\omega(\sqrt{\log m})$$
$$\alpha q = 3\sqrt{n}, \qquad \alpha' q = 5\sqrt{n}\cdot m\cdot\delta.$$

Here, the parameter δ is determined by the compatible algorithms corresponding to F. The following theorem addresses the security of the scheme.

Theorem 3. *If* $\mathsf{F} : \mathcal{K}\times\mathcal{X} \to \{0,1\}$ *is a partitioning function and* (Encode, $\mathsf{PubEval}$, $\mathsf{TrapEval}$) *are the corresponding* δ*-compatible algorithms, our scheme achieves adaptively-anonymous security assuming* $\mathsf{dLWE}_{n,m+1,q,\alpha}$.

5.3 Multi-bit Variant

Here, we explain how to extend our scheme to be a multi-bit variant without increasing much the size of the master public keys and ciphertexts following [PVW08, ABB10a, Yam16]. (However, it comes with longer private keys.) To modify the scheme so that it can deal with the message space of length ℓ_M, we replace $\mathbf{u} \in \mathbb{Z}_q^n$ in mpk with $\mathbf{U} \in \mathbb{Z}_q^{n\times\ell_M}$. The component c_0 in the ciphertext is replaced with $\mathbf{c}_0^\top = \mathbf{s}^\top\mathbf{U} + \mathbf{x}_0^\top + \mathsf{M}\lceil q/2\rceil$, where $\mathbf{x}_0 \stackrel{\$}{\leftarrow} D_{\mathbb{Z}^{\ell_M},\alpha q}$ and $\mathsf{M} \in \{0,1\}^{\ell_M}$ is the message to be encrypted. The private key is replaced to be $\mathbf{E} \in \mathbb{Z}^{m\times\ell_M}$, where $\mathbf{E}$ is chosen as $\mathbf{E} \stackrel{\$}{\leftarrow} [\mathbf{A}\|\mathbf{B}_0+\mathbf{B}_{\mathsf{ID}}]_\sigma^{-1}(\mathbf{U})$. We can prove security for the multi-bit variant from $\mathsf{dLWE}_{n,m+\ell_M,q,\alpha}$ by naturally extending the proof of Theorem 3. We note that the same parameters as in Sect. 5.2 will also work for the multi-bit variant. By this change, the sizes of the master public keys, ciphertexts, and private keys become $\tilde{O}(n^2u + n\ell_M)$, $\tilde{O}(n + \ell_M)$, and $\tilde{O}(n\ell_M)$ from $\tilde{O}(n^2u)$, $\tilde{O}(n)$, and $\tilde{O}(n)$, respectively. The sizes of the master public keys and ciphertexts will be asymptotically the same as long as $\ell_M = \tilde{O}(n)$. To deal with longer messages, we employ a KEM-DEM approach as suggested in [Yam16]. Namely, we encrypt a random ephemeral key of sufficient length and then encrypt the message by using the ephemeral key.

6 Our VRF Scheme Based on $\mathsf{F_{MAH}}$

6.1 Construction

Here, we construct a verifiable random function scheme based on the partitioning function $\mathsf{F_{MAH}}$. We let the input and output space of the scheme be $\mathcal{X} = \{0,1\}^k$ and $\mathcal{Y} = \mathbb{G}_T$, respectively. Let $\eta := \eta(\lambda)$, $\ell := \ell(\lambda)$, $C : \{0,1\}^k \to \{0,1\}^\ell$, and S be as in Sect. 4.3. We also introduce $\ell_1 := \ell_1(\lambda)$ and $\ell_2 = \ell_2(\lambda)$ such that $\ell = \ell_1\ell_2$. These parameters will control the trade-offs between sizes of proofs and verification keys. A typical choice would be $(\ell_1, \ell_2) = (O(\sqrt{\ell}), O(\sqrt{\ell}))$ or $(\ell_1, \ell_2) = (O(\ell), O(1))$.

$\mathsf{Gen}(1^\lambda)$: On input 1^λ, it chooses a group description $\Pi \xleftarrow{\$} \mathsf{GrpGen}(1^\lambda)$. It chooses random generators $g, h \xleftarrow{\$} \mathbb{G}^*$ and $w_1, \ldots, w_\eta \xleftarrow{\$} \mathbb{Z}_p$. It then outputs

$$\mathsf{vk} = \left(\Pi,\ g,\ h,\ \left\{W_{i,j_1} := g^{w_i^{j_1}}\right\}_{(i,j_1)\in[\eta]\times[\ell_1]}\right) \quad \text{and} \quad \mathsf{sk} = \left(\{w_i\}_{i\in[\eta]}\right).$$

$\mathsf{Eval}(\mathsf{sk}, X)$: Given $X \in \{0,1\}^k$, it first computes $\mathsf{S}(X) = \{s_1, \ldots, s_\ell\} \subset [2\ell]$,

$$\theta = \prod_{(i,j)\in[\eta]\times[\ell]} (w_i + s_j), \qquad \text{and} \qquad \theta_{i,j_2} = \prod_{(i',j')\in\Omega_{i,j_2}} (w_{i'} + s_{j'}) \tag{9}$$

for $(i, j_2) \in [\eta] \times [\ell_2]$, where

$$\Omega_{i,j_2} = \{(i',j') \in [\eta]\times[\ell] \ \mid \ (i' \in [i-1]) \vee (i' = i \wedge j' \in [j_2\ell_1])\}.$$

We note that $\theta = \theta_{\eta,\ell_2}$. If $\theta \equiv 0 \mod p$, it outputs $Y = 1_{\mathbb{G}_T}$ and $\pi = (\{\pi_{i,j_2} = 1_{\mathbb{G}}\}_{(i,j_2)\in[\eta]\times[\ell_2]})^4$. Otherwise, it outputs

$$Y = e(g,h)^{1/\theta} \qquad \text{and} \qquad \pi = \left(\left\{\pi_{i,j_2} = g^{1/\theta_{i,j_2}}\right\}_{(i,j_2)\in[\eta]\times[\ell_2]}\right).$$

$\mathsf{Verify}(\mathsf{vk}, X, Y, \pi)$: It first checks the validity of vk by the following steps. It outputs 0 if any of the following does not hold:

[4] The event occurs with only negligible probability. This choice of the output is arbitrary and can be replaced with any fixed group elements.

1. vk is of the form $(\Pi, g, h, \{W_{i,j_1}\}_{(i,j_1)\in[\eta]\times[\ell_1]})$.
2. $\mathsf{GrpVfy}(\Pi) \to 1$, $g, h \in \mathbb{G}^*$, and $W_{i,j_1} \in \mathbb{G}$ for all $(i, j_1) \in [\eta] \times [\ell_1]$.
3. $e(W_{i,1}, W_{i,j_1-1}) = e(g, W_{i,j_1})$ for all $(i, j_1) \in [\eta] \times [2, \ell_1]$.

It then checks the validity of Y and π. To do this, it computes $\Phi_{i,j_2} \in \mathbb{G}$ for $(i, j_2) \in [\eta] \times [\ell_2]$ as

$$\Phi_{i,j_2} := g^{\varphi_{j_2,0}} \cdot \prod_{j_1\in[\ell_1]} W_{i,j_1}^{\varphi_{j_2,j_1}}, \tag{10}$$

where $\{\varphi_{j_2,j_1} \in \mathbb{Z}_p\}_{(j_2,j_1)\in[\ell_2]\times[0,\ell_1]}$ are the coefficients of the following polynomial:

$$\prod_{j'\in[(j_2-1)\ell_1+1, j_2\ell_1]} (\mathsf{Z} + s_{j'}) = \varphi_{j_2,0} + \sum_{j_1\in[\ell_1]} \varphi_{j_2,j_1}\mathsf{Z}^{j_1} \in \mathbb{Z}_p[\mathsf{Z}].$$

It outputs 0 if any of the following does not hold:

4. $X \in \{0,1\}^k$, $Y \in \mathbb{G}_T$, π is of the form $\pi = (\{\pi_{i,j_2} \in \mathbb{G}\}_{(i,j_2)\in[\eta]\times[\ell_2]})$.
5. If there exists $(i, j_2) \in [\eta] \times [\ell_2]$ such that $\Phi_{i,j_2} = 1_{\mathbb{G}}$, we have $Y = 1_{\mathbb{G}_T}$ and $\pi_{i,j_2} = 1_{\mathbb{G}}$ for all $(i, j_2) \in [\eta] \times [\ell_2]$.
6. If $\Phi_{i,j_2} \neq 1_{\mathbb{G}}$ for all $(i, j_2) \in [\eta] \times [\ell_2]$, the following equation holds for all $(i, j_2) \in [\eta] \times [\ell_2]$:

$$e(\pi_{i,j_2}, \Phi_{i,j_2}) = e(\pi_{i,j_2-1}, g) \tag{11}$$

   where we define $\pi_{i,0} := \pi_{i-1,\ell_2}$ for $i \geq 2$ and $\pi_{1,0} := g$.
7. $e(\pi_{\eta,\ell_2}, h) = Y$ holds.

If all the above conditions hold, it outputs 1.

The correctness and unique provability of the scheme can be proven by a standard argument. The following theorem addresses the pseudorandomness of the scheme.

Theorem 4. *Our scheme satisfies pseudorandomness assuming* L-DDH *with* $L = (4\ell + 1)\eta + \ell_1$.

Proof. Let $\mathcal{A}$ be a PPT adversary that breaks pseudorandomness of the scheme. In addition, let $\epsilon = \epsilon(\lambda)$ and $Q = Q(\lambda)$ be its advantage and the upper bound on the number of evaluation queries, respectively. By assumption, $Q(\lambda)$ is polynomially bounded and there exists a noticeable function $\epsilon_0(\lambda)$ such that $\epsilon(\lambda) \geq \epsilon_0(\lambda)$ holds for infinitely many λ. By the property of the partitioning function (Definition 3, Item 1), we have that

$$|\mathsf{T}| < \eta \qquad \text{where} \qquad \mathsf{T} \overset{\$}{\leftarrow} \mathsf{PrtSmp}_{\mathsf{MAH}}(1^\lambda, Q, \epsilon_0)$$

holds with probability 1 for all sufficiently large λ. Therefore, in the following, we assume that this condition always holds. We show the security of the scheme via the following sequence of games. In each game, a value $\mathsf{coin}' \in \{0,1\}$ is defined. While it is set $\mathsf{coin}' = \widehat{\mathsf{coin}}$ in the first game, these values might be different in the later games. In the following, we define E_i be the event that $\mathsf{coin}' = \mathsf{coin}$.

Game_0 : This is the real security game. Recall that since the range of the function is $\mathcal{Y} = \mathbb{G}_T$, in the challenge phase, $Y_1^\star \overset{\$}{\leftarrow} \mathbb{G}_T$ is returned to $\mathcal{A}$ if $\mathsf{coin} = 1$. At the end of the game, $\mathcal{A}$ outputs a guess $\widehat{\mathsf{coin}}$ for coin. Finally, the challenger sets $\mathsf{coin}' = \widehat{\mathsf{coin}}$. By definition, we have

$$\left|\Pr[\mathsf{E}_0] - \frac{1}{2}\right| = \left|\Pr[\mathsf{coin}' = \mathsf{coin}] - \frac{1}{2}\right| = \left|\Pr[\widehat{\mathsf{coin}} = \mathsf{coin}] - \frac{1}{2}\right| = \epsilon.$$

Game_1 : In this game, we change Game_0 so that the challenger performs the following additional step at the end of the game. First, the challenger runs $\mathsf{PrtSmp}_{\mathsf{MAH}}(1^\lambda, Q, \epsilon_0) \to \mathsf{T} \subseteq [2\ell]$ and checks whether the following condition holds:

$$\mathsf{T} \not\subseteq \mathsf{S}(X^{(1)}) \ \wedge \ \cdots \ \wedge \ \mathsf{T} \not\subseteq \mathsf{S}(X^{(Q)}) \ \wedge \ \mathsf{T} \subseteq \mathsf{S}(X^\star) \tag{12}$$

where $X^\star$ is chosen by $\mathcal{A}$ at the challenge phase, and $X^{(1)}, \ldots, X^{(Q)}$ are inputs to the VRF for which $\mathcal{A}$ has queried the evaluation of the function. If it does not hold, the challenger ignores the output $\widehat{\mathsf{coin}}$ of $\mathcal{A}$, and sets $\mathsf{coin}' \overset{\$}{\leftarrow} \{0, 1\}$. In this case, we say that the challenger aborts. If condition (12) holds, the challenger sets $\mathsf{coin}' = \widehat{\mathsf{coin}}$. By Lemmas 1 and 3 (See also Definition 3, Item 2),

$$\left|\Pr[\mathsf{E}_1] - \frac{1}{2}\right| \geq \gamma_{\min}\epsilon - \frac{\gamma_{\max} - \gamma_{\min}}{2} \geq \gamma_{\min}\epsilon_0 - \frac{\gamma_{\max} - \gamma_{\min}}{2} = \tau$$

holds for infinitely many λ and a noticeable function $\tau = \tau(\lambda)$. Here, $\gamma_{\min}$, $\gamma_{\max}$, and τ are specified by ϵ_0, Q, and the underlying partitioning function $\mathsf{F}_{\mathsf{MAH}}$.

Game_2 : In this game, we change the way w_i are chosen. At the beginning of the game, the challenger picks $\mathsf{T} \overset{\$}{\leftarrow} \mathsf{PrtSmp}_{\mathsf{MAH}}(1^\lambda, Q, \epsilon_0)$ and parses it as $\mathsf{T} = \{t_1, \ldots, t_{\eta'}\} \subset [2\ell]$. Recall that by our assumption, we have $\eta' < \eta$. It then sets $t_i := 0$ for $i \in [\eta' + 1, \eta]$. It then samples $\alpha \overset{\$}{\leftarrow} \mathbb{Z}_p^*$, and $\tilde{w}_i \overset{\$}{\leftarrow} \mathbb{Z}_p^*$ for $i \in [\eta]$. Then, w_i are defined as

$$w_i = \tilde{w}_i \cdot \alpha - t_i \qquad \text{for } i \in [\eta].$$

The rest of the game is the same as in Game_1. The statistical distance of the distributions of $\{w_i\}_{i \in [\eta]}$ in Game_1 and Game_2 is at most η/p, which is negligible. Therefore, we have $|\Pr[\mathsf{E}_1] - \Pr[\mathsf{E}_2]| = \mathsf{negl}(\lambda)$.

Before describing the next game, for any $\Omega \subseteq [\eta] \times [\ell]$, $\mathsf{T} \subset [2\ell]$ with $|\mathsf{T}| = \eta' < \eta$, and $X \in \{0, 1\}^k$, we define polynomials $\mathsf{P}_{X,\Omega}(\mathsf{Z}), \mathsf{Q}(\mathsf{Z}) \in \mathbb{Z}_p[\mathsf{Z}]$ as

$$\mathsf{P}_{X,\Omega}(\mathsf{Z}) = \prod_{(i,j) \in \Omega} (\tilde{w}_i \mathsf{Z} - t_i + s_j)$$

$$\text{and} \qquad \mathsf{Q}(\mathsf{Z}) = \mathsf{Z}^{\eta' - 1} \cdot \prod_{(i,j) \in [\eta] \times [-2\ell, 2\ell] \setminus \{0\}} (\tilde{w}_i \mathsf{Z} + j),$$

where $\{s_j\}_{j\in[\ell]} = \mathsf{S}(X)$ and $\{t_i\}_{i\in[\eta]}$ are defined as in Game_2 (namely, $\mathsf{T} = \{t_i\}_{i\in[\eta']}$ and $t_i = 0$ for $i > \eta'$). In the special case of $\Omega = [\eta] \times [\ell]$, we denote $\mathsf{P}_X(\mathsf{Z}) := \mathsf{P}_{X,[\eta]\times[\ell]}(\mathsf{Z})$. We state the following lemma, which plays an important roll in our security proof.

Lemma 6. *There exist $\xi_X \in \mathbb{Z}_p^*$ and $\mathsf{R}_X(\mathsf{Z}) \in \mathbb{Z}_p[\mathsf{Z}]$ such that*

$$\frac{\mathsf{Q}(\mathsf{Z})}{\mathsf{P}_X(\mathsf{Z})} = \begin{cases} \frac{\xi_X}{\mathsf{Z}} + \mathsf{R}_X(\mathsf{Z}) & \text{if } \mathsf{T} \subseteq \mathsf{S}(X) \\ \mathsf{R}_X(\mathsf{Z}) & \text{if } \mathsf{T} \not\subseteq \mathsf{S}(X) \end{cases}.$$

From the above lemma, we can see that for any $\Omega \subseteq [\eta] \times [\ell]$, it holds that

$$\mathsf{P}_{X,\Omega}(\mathsf{Z}) \mid \mathsf{Q}(\mathsf{Z}) \qquad \text{if} \qquad \mathsf{T} \not\subseteq \mathsf{S}(X),$$

because $\mathsf{P}_{X,\Omega}(\mathsf{Z}) \mid \mathsf{P}_X(\mathsf{Z})$.

Game_3 Recall that in the previous game, the challenger aborts at the end of the game, if condition (12) is not satisfied. In this game, we change the game so that the challenger aborts as soon as the abort condition becomes true. Since this is only a conceptual change, we have $\Pr[\mathsf{E}_2] = \Pr[\mathsf{E}_3]$.

Game_4 In this game, we change the way g is sampled. Namely, Game_4 challenger first picks α and $\tilde{w}_i$ as specified in Game_2. It further picks $\hat{g} \xleftarrow{\$} \mathbb{G}^*$. Then, it computes (coefficients of) $\mathsf{Q}(\mathsf{Z})$ and sets

$$g := \hat{g}^{\mathsf{Q}(\alpha)}, \qquad W_{i,j_1} = g^{w_i^{j_1}} = \hat{g}^{\mathsf{Q}(\alpha)\cdot(\tilde{w}_i\alpha - t_i)^{j_1}} \qquad \text{for} \qquad (i, j_1) \in [\eta] \times [\ell_1].$$

It aborts and outputs a random bit if $g = 1_{\mathbb{G}} \Leftrightarrow \mathsf{Q}(\alpha) \equiv 0 \mod p$. It can be seen that the distribution of g and W_{i,j_1} is unchanged, unless $\mathsf{Q}(\alpha) \equiv 0 \mod p$. Since $\mathsf{Q}(\mathsf{Z})$ is a non-zero polynomial with degree $(4\eta\ell + \eta' - 1)$ and α is chosen uniformly at random from $\mathbb{Z}_p^*$, it follows from the Schwartz-Zippel lemma that this happens with probability at most $(4\eta\ell + \eta' - 1)/(p - 1) = \mathsf{negl}(\lambda)$. We therefore have $|\Pr[\mathsf{E}_3] - \Pr[\mathsf{E}_4]| = \mathsf{negl}(\lambda)$.

Game_5 In this game, we change the way the evaluation queries are answered. By the change introduced in Game_4, we assume $\mathsf{Q}(\alpha) \not\equiv 0 \mod p$ in the following. When $\mathcal{A}$ makes a query for an input X, the challenger first checks whether $\mathsf{T} \subseteq \mathsf{S}(X)$ and aborts if so (as specified in Game_3). Otherwise, it computes $\mathsf{R}_{X,\Omega_{i,j_2}}(\mathsf{Z}) \in \mathbb{Z}_p[\mathsf{Z}]$ such that $\mathsf{Q}(\mathsf{Z}) = \mathsf{P}_{X,\Omega_{i,j_2}}(\mathsf{Z}) \cdot \mathsf{R}_{X,\Omega_{i,j_2}}(\mathsf{Z})$ for $(i, j_2) \in [\eta] \times [\ell_2]$. Note that such polynomials exist by Lemma 6. Then, it returns

$$Y = e\left(\hat{g}^{\mathsf{R}_{X,\Omega_{\eta,\ell_2}}(\alpha)}, h\right), \qquad \pi = \left(\left\{\pi_{i,j_2} = \hat{g}^{\mathsf{R}_{X,\Omega_{i,j_2}}(\alpha)}\right\}_{(i,j_2)\in[\eta]\times[\ell_2]}\right)$$

to $\mathcal{A}$. We claim that this is only a conceptual change. To see this, we first observe that

$$\mathsf{P}_{X,\Omega_{i,j_2}}(\alpha) = \prod_{(i',j')\in\Omega_{i,j_2}} (\tilde{w}_{i'}\alpha - t_{i'} + s_{j'})$$

$$= \prod_{(i',j') \in \Omega_{i,j_2}} (w_{i'} + s_{j'}) = \theta_{i,j_2}. \quad (13)$$

We have $\theta_{i,j_2} \not\equiv 0 \mod p$, since otherwise we have $\mathsf{Q}(\alpha) \equiv \mathsf{P}_{X,\Omega_{i,j_2}}(\alpha) \cdot \mathsf{R}_{X,\Omega_{i,j_2}}(\alpha) \equiv \theta_{i,j_2} \cdot \mathsf{R}_{X,\Omega_{i,j_2}}(\alpha) \equiv 0 \mod p$, which is a contradiction. Thus, we have

$$\hat{g}^{\mathsf{R}_{X,\Omega_{i,j_2}}(\alpha)} = \hat{g}^{\mathsf{Q}(\alpha)/\mathsf{P}_{X,\Omega_{i,j_2}}(\alpha)} = g^{1/\mathsf{P}_{X,\Omega_{i,j_2}}(\alpha)} = g^{1/\theta_{i,j_2}}.$$

This indicates that the simulation by the challenger is perfect. Since the view of $\mathcal{A}$ is unchanged, we have $\Pr[\mathsf{E}_4] = \Pr[\mathsf{E}_5]$.

Game_6 : In this game, we change the way the challenge value $Y_0^\star = \mathsf{Eval}(\mathsf{sk}, X^\star)$ is created when $\mathsf{coin} = 0$. If $\mathsf{coin} = 0$, to generate $Y_0^\star$, it first computes $\xi_{X^\star} \in \mathbb{Z}_p^*$ and $\mathsf{R}_{X^\star}(\mathsf{Z}) \in \mathbb{Z}_p[\mathsf{Z}]$ such that $\mathsf{Q}(\mathsf{Z})/\mathsf{P}_{X^\star}(\mathsf{Z}) = \xi_{X^\star}/\mathsf{Z} + \mathsf{R}_{X^\star}(\mathsf{Z})$. Note that such $\xi_{X^\star}$ and $\mathsf{R}_{X^\star}(\mathsf{Z})$ exist by Lemma 6 whenever $\mathsf{T} \subseteq \mathsf{S}(X^\star)$. It then sets

$$Y_0^\star = \left(e\left(\hat{g}, h\right)^{1/\alpha}\right)^{\xi_{X^\star}} \cdot e\left(\hat{g}^{\mathsf{R}_{X^\star}(\alpha)}, h\right)$$

and returns it to $\mathcal{A}$. We claim that this is only a conceptual change. This can be seen by observing that

$$e\left(\hat{g}^{1/\alpha}, h\right)^{\xi_{X^\star}} \cdot e\left(\hat{g}^{\mathsf{R}_{X^\star}(\alpha)}, h\right) = e\left(\hat{g}^{\xi_{X^\star}/\alpha + \mathsf{R}_{X^\star}(\alpha)}, h\right)$$
$$= e\left(\hat{g}^{\mathsf{Q}(\alpha)/\mathsf{P}_{X^\star}(\alpha)}, h\right) = e\left(g, h\right)^{1/\mathsf{P}_{X^\star}(\alpha)}$$

and $\mathsf{P}_{X^\star}(\alpha) = \theta_{\eta,\ell_2}$, where the latter follows from Eq. (13). Since the view of $\mathcal{A}$ is unchanged, we therefore conclude that $\Pr[\mathsf{E}_5] = \Pr[\mathsf{E}_6]$.

Game_7 In this game, we change the challenge value to be a random element in $\mathbb{G}_T$ regardless of whether $\mathsf{coin} = 0$ or $\mathsf{coin} = 1$. Namely, Game_7 challenger sets $Y_0^\star \stackrel{\$}{\leftarrow} \mathbb{G}_T$. In this game, the value coin is independent from the view of $\mathcal{A}$. Therefore, $\Pr[\mathsf{E}_7] = 1/2$.

We claim that $|\Pr[\mathsf{E}_6] - \Pr[\mathsf{E}_7]|$ is negligible assuming L-DDH with $L = (4\ell+1)\eta + \ell_1$. To show this, we construct an adversary $\mathcal{B}$ against the problem using $\mathcal{A}$, which is described as follows.

$\mathcal{B}$ is given the problem instance $(\Pi, \hat{g}, h, \{\hat{g}^{\alpha^i}\}_{i\in[L]}, \Psi)$ of L-DDH where $\Psi = e(\hat{g}, h)^{1/\alpha}$ or $\Psi \stackrel{\$}{\leftarrow} \mathbb{G}_T$. At any point in the game, $\mathcal{B}$ aborts and sets $\mathsf{coin}' \stackrel{\$}{\leftarrow} \{0,1\}$ if condition (12) is not satisfied. It first sets g and W_{i,j_1} as in Game_4 and returns $\mathsf{vk} = (\Pi, g, h, \{W_{i,j_1}\}_{(i,j_1)\in[\eta]\times[\ell_1]})$ to $\mathcal{A}$. These terms can be efficiently computable from the problem instance because $\log_{\hat{g}} g$ and $\log_{\hat{g}} W_{i,j_1}$ can be written as polynomials in α with degree at most $\eta' - 1 + 4\eta\ell + \ell_1 < L$ and the coefficients of the polynomials can be efficiently computable. When $\mathcal{A}$ makes an evaluation query on input X, it computes (Y, π) as in Game_5 and returns it to $\mathcal{A}$. Again, these terms can be efficiently computable from the problem instance, because the degree of $\mathsf{R}_{X,\Omega_{i,j_2}}(\alpha)$ is at most L and coefficients of them can be efficiently computable. When $\mathcal{A}$ makes the challenge query on input $X^\star$, $\mathcal{B}$ first picks $\mathsf{coin} \overset{\$}{\leftarrow} \{0,1\}$ and returns $Y^\star \overset{\$}{\leftarrow} \mathbb{G}$ if $\mathsf{coin} = 1$. Otherwise, it returns

$$Y^\star = \Psi^{\xi_{X^\star}} \cdot e\left(\hat{g}^{\mathsf{R}_{X^\star}(\alpha)}, h\right)$$

to $\mathcal{A}$. Note that $\hat{g}^{\mathsf{R}_{X^\star}(\alpha)}$ can be efficiently computed from the problem instance because the degree of $\mathsf{R}_{X^\star}(\mathsf{Z})$ is at most L. At the end of the game, coin' is defined. Finally, $\mathcal{B}$ outputs 1 if $\mathsf{coin}' = \mathsf{coin}$ and 0 otherwise.
It can easily be seen that the view of $\mathcal{A}$ corresponds to that of Game_6 if $\Psi = e(\hat{g}, h)^{1/\alpha}$ and Game_7 if $\Psi \overset{\$}{\leftarrow} \mathbb{G}_T$. It is clear that the advantage of $\mathcal{B}$ is $|\Pr[\mathsf{E}_6] - \Pr[\mathsf{E}_7]|$. Assuming L-DDH, we have $|\Pr[\mathsf{E}_6] - \Pr[\mathsf{E}_7]| = \mathsf{negl}(\lambda)$.

Analysis. From the above, we have

$$\begin{aligned}\left|\Pr[\mathsf{E}_7] - \frac{1}{2}\right| &= \left|\Pr[\mathsf{E}_1] - \frac{1}{2} + \sum_{i=1}^{6} \Pr[\mathsf{E}_{i+1}] - \Pr[\mathsf{E}_i]\right| \\ &\geq \left|\Pr[\mathsf{E}_1] - \frac{1}{2}\right| - \sum_{i=1}^{6} |\Pr[\mathsf{E}_{i+1}] - \Pr[\mathsf{E}_i]| \geq \tau(\lambda) - \mathsf{negl}(\lambda).\end{aligned}$$

for infinitely many λ. Since $\Pr[\mathsf{E}_7] = 1/2$, this implies $\tau(\lambda) \leq \mathsf{negl}(\lambda)$ for infinitely many λ, which is a contradiction. This completes the proof of Theorem 4.

6.2 A Variant with Short Verification Keys

Here, we introduce a variant of our scheme in Sect. 6.1. In the variant, we remove $\{W_{i,j_1} = g^{w_i^{j_1}}\}_{(i,j_1)\in[\eta]\times[2,\ell_1]}$ from vk. Instead, we add these components to π. We do not change the verification algorithm and other parts of the scheme. It is straightforward to see that the correctness and pseudorandomness of the scheme can still be proven. To prove the unique provability, we observe that the only possible strategy to break is to include invalid $\{W_{i,j_1}\}_{(i,j_1)\in[\eta]\times[2,\ell_1]}$ in the proof. This is because if these values are correct, the unique provability of the original scheme immediately implies that of the modified scheme. However, this strategy does not work since the invalid values will be detected at Step 3 of the verification algorithm using $\{W_{i,1} = g^{w_i}\}_{i\in[\eta]}$ in vk. The advantage of the variant is that the size of vk is small. In particular, vk only consists of $\eta + 2$ group elements in this variant, whereas $\eta\ell_1 + 2$ group elements were required in the scheme in Sect. 6.1. Of course, this change increases the size of the proofs π. The number of group elements will become $\eta(\ell_1 + \ell_2 - 1)$ from $\eta\ell_2$ by this modification. To minimize the size of the proofs we choose $\ell_1 = \ell_2 = \sqrt{\ell}$.

7 Comparisons

Here, we compare our proposed schemes with previous schemes.

New Lattice IBE Schemes. In Sect. 5.2, we showed how to construct an IBE scheme from a partitioning function with associating compatible algorithms. We have two ways of instantiating the scheme.

- By using the partitioning function $\mathsf{F}_{\mathsf{MAH}}$ in Sect. 4.3 and the corresponding compatible algorithms, where the latter is given by Lemma 4, we obtain our first IBE scheme. The master public key of the scheme only consists of $\omega(\log^2 \lambda)$ matrices.
- By using the partitioning function $\mathsf{F}_{\mathsf{AFF}}$ in Sect. 4.4 and the corresponding compatible algorithms, where the latter is given by Lemma 5, we obtain our second IBE scheme. The master public key of the scheme is even shorter: It only consists of $\omega(\log \lambda)$ matrices.

Both our schemes achieve the best asymptotic space efficiency (namely, the sizes of the master public keys, ciphertexts, and private keys) among existing IBE schemes that are adaptively secure against *unbounded collusion without subexponential security assumptions.* In Table 1 in Sect. 1, we compare our schemes with previous schemes. Note that the scheme by Zhang et al. [ZCZ16] achieves shorter master public key size than ours, but only achieves Q-bounded security. This restriction cannot be removed by just making Q super-polynomial, since the encryption algorithm of the scheme runs in time proportional to Q.

Finally, we note that there are two drawbacks that are common in our schemes. The first drawback is that the encryption algorithm is heavy. Our first scheme requires $\tilde{O}(\lambda)$ times of matrix multiplications for the encryption algorithm. Our second scheme requires even heavier computation. It first computes the description of the "division in $\mathbf{NC}^1$ circuit" [BCH86] and then invokes Barrington's theorem [Bar89] to convert it into a branching program. The second drawback is that we have to rely on the LWE assumption with large (but polynomial) approximation factors to prove the security.

New VRF Schemes. Following [HJ16], we say that a VRF scheme has "all the desired properties" if it has exponential-sized input space and a proof of adaptive security under a non-interactive complexity assumption. Here, we compare our schemes proposed in this paper with previous schemes that satisfy all the desired properties.

- In Sect. 6.1, we proposed new VRF scheme based on $\mathsf{F}_{\mathsf{MAH}}$. The scheme is parametrized by the parameters ℓ_1 and ℓ_2. By setting $\ell_1 = \ell$ and $\ell_2 = 1$, we obtain a new VRF scheme with very short proofs. They only consist of $\omega(\log \lambda)$ group elements.
- In Sect. 6.2, we proposed a variant of the above scheme. The verification keys consist of $\omega(\log \lambda)$ group elements and proofs consist of $\omega(\sqrt{\lambda} \log \lambda)$ group elements.
- In the full version (Appendix C), we proposed a new VRF scheme based on $\mathsf{F}_{\mathsf{AFF}}$. The verification key of the scheme only consists of $\omega(\log \lambda)$ group elements. However, the proof size of the scheme is large.

We refer to Table 2 in Sect. 1 for the overview. From the table, it can be seen that all previous VRF schemes that satisfy all the desired properties [ACF14, BMR10, HW10, Jag15, HJ16] require $O(\lambda)$ group elements for *both* of verification keys and proofs. Our first scheme above significantly improves the size of proofs.

Our second scheme improves both of the sizes of the verification keys and proofs. Compared to our second scheme, only advantage of our third scheme is that the reduction cost is better. Still, we think that our third scheme is also of interest because the construction is quite different from previous schemes.

Acknowledgement. The author is grateful to the members of the study group "Shin-Akarui-Angou-Benkyokai" and anonymous reviewers of Eurocrypt 2017 and Crypto 2017 for insightful comments. In particular, the author would like to thank Shuichi Katsumata for precious comments on the presentation and for pointing out that our initial construction can be slightly simplified. The author also specially thanks Goichiro Hanaoka for helpful comments. This work was supported by JSPS KAKENHI Grant Number 16K16068 and JST CREST Grant No. JPMJCR1688.

References

[ACF09] Abdalla, M., Catalano, D., Fiore, D.: Verifiable random functions from identity-based key encapsulation. In: Joux, A. (ed.) EUROCRYPT 2009. LNCS, vol. 5479, pp. 554–571. Springer, Heidelberg (2009). doi:10.1007/978-3-642-01001-9_32

[ACF14] Abdalla, M., Catalano, D., Fiore, D.: Verifiable random functions: relations to identity-based key encapsulation and new constructions. J. Cryptology **27**(3), 544–593 (2014)

[ABB10a] Agrawal, S., Boneh, D., Boyen, X.: Efficient lattice (H)IBE in the standard model. In: Gilbert, H. (ed.) EUROCRYPT 2010. LNCS, vol. 6110, pp. 553–572. Springer, Heidelberg (2010). doi:10.1007/978-3-642-13190-5_28

[ABB10b] Agrawal, S., Boneh, D., Boyen, X.: Lattice basis delegation in fixed dimension and shorter-ciphertext hierarchical IBE. In: Rabin, T. (ed.) CRYPTO 2010. LNCS, vol. 6223, pp. 98–115. Springer, Heidelberg (2010). doi:10.1007/978-3-642-14623-7_6

[AFL16] Apon, D., Fan, X., Liu, F.: Compact identity based encryption from LWE. In: IACR Cryptology ePrint Archive, 2016:125 (2016)

[BGJS17] Badrinarayanan, S., Goyal, V., Jain, A., Sahai, A.: A note on VRFs from verifiable functional encryption. In: IACR Cryptology ePrint Archive, 2017:051 (2017)

[Bar89] Mix Barrington, D.A.: Bounded-width polynomial-size branching programs recognize exactly those languages in NC^1. J. Comput. Syst. Sci. **38**(1), 150–164 (1989)

[BCH86] Beame, P., Cook, S.A., Hoover, H.J.: Log depth circuits for division and related problems. SIAM J. Comput. **15**(4), 994–1003 (1986)

[BR09] Bellare, M., Ristenpart, T.: Simulation without the artificial abort: simplified proof and improved concrete security for Waters' IBE scheme. In: Joux, A. (ed.) EUROCRYPT 2009. LNCS, vol. 5479, pp. 407–424. Springer, Heidelberg (2009). doi:10.1007/978-3-642-01001-9_24

[Bit17] Bitansky, N.: Verifiable random functions from non-interactive witness-indistinguishable proofs. In: IACR Cryptology ePrint Archive, 2017: 18 (2017)

[BB04a] Boneh, D., Boyen, X.: Efficient selective-ID secure identity-based encryption without random oracles. In: Cachin, C., Camenisch, J.L. (eds.) EUROCRYPT 2004. LNCS, vol. 3027, pp. 223–238. Springer, Heidelberg (2004). doi:10.1007/978-3-540-24676-3_14

[BB04b] Boneh, D., Boyen, X.: Secure identity based encryption without random oracles. In: Franklin, M. (ed.) CRYPTO 2004. LNCS, vol. 3152, pp. 443–459. Springer, Heidelberg (2004). doi:10.1007/978-3-540-28628-8_27

[BF01] Boneh, D., Franklin, M.: Identity-based encryption from the weil pairing. In: Kilian, J. (ed.) CRYPTO 2001. LNCS, vol. 2139, pp. 213–229. Springer, Heidelberg (2001). doi:10.1007/3-540-44647-8_13

[BGG+14] Boneh, D., Gentry, C., Gorbunov, S., Halevi, S., Nikolaenko, V., Segev, G., Vaikuntanathan, V., Vinayagamurthy, D.: Fully key-homomorphic encryption, arithmetic circuit abe and compact garbled circuits. In: Nguyen, P.Q., Oswald, E. (eds.) EUROCRYPT 2014. LNCS, vol. 8441, pp. 533–556. Springer, Heidelberg (2014). doi:10.1007/978-3-642-55220-5_30

[BGH07] Boneh, D., Gentry, C., Hamburg, M.: Space-efficient identity based encryption without pairings. In: FOCS, pp. 647–657 (2007)

[BMR10] Boneh, D., Montgomery, H.W., Raghunathan, A.: Algebraic pseudorandom functions with improved efficiency from the augmented cascade. In: ACM-CCS, pp. 131–140 (2010)

[Boy10] Boyen, X.: Lattice mixing and vanishing trapdoors: a framework for fully secure short signatures and more. In: Nguyen, P.Q., Pointcheval, D. (eds.) PKC 2010. LNCS, vol. 6056, pp. 499–517. Springer, Heidelberg (2010). doi:10.1007/978-3-642-13013-7_29

[BL16] Boyen, X., Li, Q.: Towards tightly secure lattice short signature and Id-based encryption. In: Cheon, J.H., Takagi, T. (eds.) ASIACRYPT 2016. LNCS, vol. 10032, pp. 404–434. Springer, Heidelberg (2016). doi:10.1007/978-3-662-53890-6_14

[BLP+13] Brakerski, Z., Langlois, A., Peikert, C., Regev, O., Stehlé, D.: Classical hardness of learning with errors. In: STOC, pp. 575–584 (2013)

[BV16] Brakerski, Z., Vaikuntanathan, V.: Circuit-ABE from LWE: unbounded attributes and semi-adaptive security. In: Robshaw, M., Katz, J. (eds.) CRYPTO 2016. LNCS, vol. 9816, pp. 363–384. Springer, Heidelberg (2016). doi:10.1007/978-3-662-53015-3_13

[CHKP10] Cash, D., Hofheinz, D., Kiltz, E., Peikert, C.: Bonsai trees, or how to delegate a lattice basis. In: Gilbert, H. (ed.) EUROCRYPT 2010. LNCS, vol. 6110, pp. 523–552. Springer, Heidelberg (2010). doi:10.1007/978-3-642-13190-5_27

[CLL+12] Chen, J., Lim, H.W., Ling, S., Wang, H., Wee, H.: Shorter IBE and signatures via asymmetric pairings. In: Abdalla, M., Lange, T. (eds.) Pairing 2012. LNCS, vol. 7708, pp. 122–140. Springer, Heidelberg (2013). doi:10.1007/978-3-642-36334-4_8

[Coc01] Cocks, C.: An identity based encryption scheme based on quadratic residues. In: Honary, B. (ed.) Cryptography and Coding 2001. LNCS, vol. 2260, pp. 360–363. Springer, Heidelberg (2001). doi:10.1007/3-540-45325-3_32

[Dod03] Dodis, Y.: Efficient construction of (distributed) verifiable random functions. In: Desmedt, Y.G. (ed.) PKC 2003. LNCS, vol. 2567, pp. 1–17. Springer, Heidelberg (2003). doi:10.1007/3-540-36288-6_1

[DY05] Dodis, Y., Yampolskiy, A.: A verifiable random function with short proofs and keys. In: Vaudenay, S. (ed.) PKC 2005. LNCS, vol. 3386, pp. 416–431. Springer, Heidelberg (2005). doi:10.1007/978-3-540-30580-4_28

[FHPS13] Freire, E.S.V., Hofheinz, D., Paterson, K.G., Striecks, C.: Programmable hash functions in the multilinear setting. In: Canetti, R., Garay, J.A. (eds.) CRYPTO 2013. LNCS, vol. 8042, pp. 513–530. Springer, Heidelberg (2013). doi:10.1007/978-3-642-40041-4_28

[Gen06] Gentry, C.: Practical identity-based encryption without random oracles. In: Vaudenay, S. (ed.) EUROCRYPT 2006. LNCS, vol. 4004, pp. 445–464. Springer, Heidelberg (2006). doi:10.1007/11761679_27

[GPV08] Gentry, C., Peikert, C., Vaikuntanathan, V.: Trapdoors for hard lattices and new cryptographic constructions. In: STOC, pp. 197–206 (2008)

[Gol08] Goldreich, O.: Computational Complexity: A Conceptual Perspective, 1st edn. Cambridge University Press, New York (2008)

[GV15] Gorbunov, S., Vinayagamurthy, D.: Riding on asymmetry: efficient ABE for branching programs. In: Iwata, T., Cheon, J.H. (eds.) ASIACRYPT 2015. LNCS, vol. 9452, pp. 550–574. Springer, Heidelberg (2015). doi:10.1007/978-3-662-48797-6_23

[GKV10] Gordon, S.D., Katz, J., Vaikuntanathan, V.: A group signature scheme from lattice assumptions. In: Abe, M. (ed.) ASIACRYPT 2010. LNCS, vol. 6477, pp. 395–412. Springer, Heidelberg (2010). doi:10.1007/978-3-642-17373-8_23

[GHKW17] Goyal, R., Hohenberger, S., Koppula, V., Waters, B.: A generic approach to constructing and proving verifiable random functions. In: IACR Cryptology ePrint Archive, 2017:021 (2017)

[HJ16] Hofheinz, D., Jager, T.: Verifiable random functions from standard assumptions. In: Kushilevitz, E., Malkin, T. (eds.) TCC 2016. LNCS, vol. 9562, pp. 336–362. Springer, Heidelberg (2016). doi:10.1007/978-3-662-49096-9_14

[HK08] Hofheinz, D., Kiltz, E.: Programmable hash functions and their applications. In: Wagner, D. (ed.) CRYPTO 2008. LNCS, vol. 5157, pp. 21–38. Springer, Heidelberg (2008). doi:10.1007/978-3-540-85174-5_2

[HW10] Hohenberger, S., Waters, B.: Constructing verifiable random functions with large input spaces. In: Gilbert, H. (ed.) EUROCRYPT 2010. LNCS, vol. 6110, pp. 656–672. Springer, Heidelberg (2010). doi:10.1007/978-3-642-13190-5_33

[Jag15] Jager, T.: Verifiable random functions from weaker assumptions. In: Dodis, Y., Nielsen, J.B. (eds.) TCC 2015. LNCS, vol. 9015, pp. 121–143. Springer, Heidelberg (2015). doi:10.1007/978-3-662-46497-7_5

[JR13] Jutla, C.S., Roy, A.: Shorter quasi-adaptive NIZK proofs for linear subspaces. In: Sako, K., Sarkar, P. (eds.) ASIACRYPT 2013. LNCS, vol. 8269, pp. 1–20. Springer, Heidelberg (2013). doi:10.1007/978-3-642-42033-7_1

[KY16] Katsumata, S., Yamada, S.: Partitioning via non-linear polynomial functions: more compact IBEs from ideal lattices and bilinear maps. In: Cheon, J.H., Takagi, T. (eds.) ASIACRYPT 2016. LNCS, vol. 10032, pp. 682–712. Springer, Heidelberg (2016). doi:10.1007/978-3-662-53890-6_23

[LOS+10] Lewko, A., Okamoto, T., Sahai, A., Takashima, K., Waters, B.: Fully secure functional encryption: attribute-based encryption and (hierarchical) inner product encryption. In: Gilbert, H. (ed.) EUROCRYPT 2010. LNCS, vol. 6110, pp. 62–91. Springer, Heidelberg (2010). doi:10.1007/978-3-642-13190-5_4

[LW10] Lewko, A., Waters, B.: New techniques for dual system encryption and fully secure HIBE with short ciphertexts. In: Micciancio, D. (ed.) TCC 2010. LNCS, vol. 5978, pp. 455–479. Springer, Heidelberg (2010). doi:10.1007/978-3-642-11799-2_27

[Lys02] Lysyanskaya, A.: Unique signatures and verifiable random functions from the DH-DDH separation. In: Yung, M. (ed.) CRYPTO 2002. LNCS, vol. 2442, pp. 597–612. Springer, Heidelberg (2002). doi:10.1007/3-540-45708-9_38

[MRV99] Micali, S., Rabin, M.O., Vadhan, S.P.: Verifiable random functions. In: FOCS, pp. 191–201 (1999)

[MP12] Micciancio, D., Peikert, C.: Trapdoors for lattices: simpler, tighter, faster, smaller. In: Pointcheval, D., Johansson, T. (eds.) EUROCRYPT 2012. LNCS, vol. 7237, pp. 700–718. Springer, Heidelberg (2012). doi:10.1007/978-3-642-29011-4_41

[Pei09] Peikert, C.: Public-key cryptosystems from the worst-case shortest vector problem: extended abstract. In: STOC, pp. 333–342 (2009)

[PVW08] Peikert, C., Vaikuntanathan, V., Waters, B.: A framework for efficient and composable oblivious transfer. In: Wagner, D. (ed.) CRYPTO 2008. LNCS, vol. 5157, pp. 554–571. Springer, Heidelberg (2008). doi:10.1007/978-3-540-85174-5_31

[Reg05] Regev, O.: On lattices, learning with errors, random linear codes, and cryptography. In: STOC, pp. 84–93. ACM Press (2005)

[SOK00] Sakai, R., Ohgishi, K., Kasahara, M.: Cryptosystems based on pairings. In: SCIS (2000). (in Japanese)

[Sha85] Shamir, A.: Identity-based cryptosystems and signature schemes. In: Blakley, G.R., Chaum, D. (eds.) CRYPTO 1984. LNCS, vol. 196, pp. 47–53. Springer, Heidelberg (1985). doi:10.1007/3-540-39568-7_5

[SS96] Sipser, M., Spielman, D.A.: Expander codes. IEEE Trans. Inf. Theory **42**(6), 1710–1722 (1996)

[Wat05] Waters, B.: Efficient identity-based encryption without random oracles. In: Cramer, R. (ed.) EUROCRYPT 2005. LNCS, vol. 3494, pp. 114–127. Springer, Heidelberg (2005). doi:10.1007/11426639_7

[Wat09] Waters, B.: Dual system encryption: realizing fully secure IBE and HIBE under simple assumptions. In: Halevi, S. (ed.) CRYPTO 2009. LNCS, vol. 5677, pp. 619–636. Springer, Heidelberg (2009). doi:10.1007/978-3-642-03356-8_36

[Yam16] Yamada, S.: Adaptively secure identity-based encryption from lattices with asymptotically shorter public parameters. In: Fischlin, M., Coron, J.-S. (eds.) EUROCRYPT 2016. LNCS, vol. 9666, pp. 32–62. Springer, Heidelberg (2016). doi:10.1007/978-3-662-49896-5_2

[Yam17] Yamada, S.: Asymptotically compact adaptively secure lattice IBEs and verifiable random functions via generalized partitioning techniques. In: IACR Cryptology ePrint Archive, 2017: 096 (2017). (Full version of this paper)

[Zém01] Zémor, G.: On expander codes. IEEE Trans. Inf. Theory **47**(2), 835–837 (2001)

[ZCZ16] Zhang, J., Chen, Y., Zhang, Z.: Programmable hash functions from lattices: short signatures and IBEs with small key sizes. In: Robshaw, M., Katz, J. (eds.) CRYPTO 2016. LNCS, vol. 9816, pp. 303–332. Springer, Heidelberg (2016). doi:10.1007/978-3-662-53015-3_11

Identity-Based Encryption from Codes with Rank Metric

Philippe Gaborit[1(✉)], Adrien Hauteville[1,2], Duong Hieu Phan[1], and Jean-Pierre Tillich[2]

[1] Université de Limoges,
XLIM-DMI, 123, Av. Albert Thomas, 87060 Limoges Cedex, France
gaborit@unilim.fr

[2] Inria de Paris, 2 rue Simone Iff, CS 42112, 75589 Paris Cedex 12, France

Abstract. Code-based cryptography has a long history, almost as long as the history of public-key encryption (PKE). While we can construct almost all primitives from codes such as PKE, signature, group signature etc., it is a long standing open problem to construct an identity-based encryption from codes. We solve this problem by relying on codes with rank metric.

The concept of identity-based encryption (IBE), introduced by Shamir in 1984, allows the use of users' identifier information such as email as public key for encryption. There are two problems that makes the design of IBE extremely hard: the requirement that the public key can be an arbitrary string and the possibility to extract decryption keys from the public keys. In fact, it took nearly twenty years for the problem of designing an efficient method to implement an IBE to be solved. The known methods of designing IBE are based on different tools: from elliptic curve pairings by Sakai, Ohgishi and Kasahara and by Boneh and Franklin in 2000 and 2001 respectively; from the quadratic residue problem by Cocks in 2001; and finally from the Learning-with-Error problem by Gentry, Peikert, and Vaikuntanathan in 2008.

Among all candidates for post-quantum cryptography, there only exist thus lattice-based IBE. In this paper, we propose a new method, based on the hardness of learning problems with rank metric, to design the first code-based IBE scheme. In order to overcome the two above problems in designing an IBE scheme, we first construct a rank-based PKE, called RankPKE, where the public key space is dense and thus can be obtained from a hash of any identity. We then extract a decryption key from any public key by constructing an trapdoor function which relies on RankSign - a signature scheme from PQCrypto 2014.

In order to prove the security of our schemes, we introduced a new problem for rank metric: the Rank Support Learning problem (RSL). A high technical contribution of the paper is devoted to study in details the hardness of the RSL problem.

Keywords: Code-based cryptography · Rank metric · IBE · PKE

J. Katz and H. Shacham (Eds.): CRYPTO 2017, Part III, LNCS 10403, pp. 194–224, 2017.
DOI: 10.1007/978-3-319-63697-9_7

1 Introduction

1.1 Code-Based Cryptography

Code-based cryptography has a long history, which began by the McEliece cryptosystem in 1978, followed by the Niederreiter scheme in 1986 [39]. The difficult problem involved in these cryptosystems is the Syndrome Decoding problem, which consists in recovering from a random matrix $\boldsymbol{H}$ and from a syndrome $\boldsymbol{s} = \boldsymbol{H}\boldsymbol{e}^T$, the small (Hamming) weight error vector $\boldsymbol{e}$ associated to $\boldsymbol{s}$. The idea of these encryption schemes is to consider as public key a masking of a decodable code. Although this masking could be broken for some special families of codes like Reed-Solomon codes or Reed-Muller codes, the original family of binary Goppa codes proposed by McEliece in 1978 is still today considered as secure, and the indistinguishability of Goppa codes from random codes for standard encryption parameters remains unbroken. Few years later Alekhnovich proposed in 2003 [2] a cryptosystem relying on random instances of codes but with larger size of encrypted messages. Code-based cryptosystems had still very large public keys, but from the year 2005 [23], inspired by the NTRU approach, structured matrices, and in particular quasi-cyclic matrices, where also considered for public keys leading to cryptosystems with only a small hidden structure like for instance the MDPC cryptosystem of 2013 [38].

However, when signature schemes were already known for a long time in number theory based cryptography, finding a signature scheme (not based on the Fiat-Shamir heuristic) had been an open problem for quite some time, until the CFS scheme of Courtois, Finiasz and Sendrier in 2001 [16], the scheme is an hash-and-sign signature which computes a signature as a small (Hamming) weight vector associated to a random syndrome. Although this latter scheme has some advantages, like a short signature size, the small weight vector has a logarithmic weight in the length of the code, which implies a super polynomial complexity and very large public keys, which makes it difficult to use it for advanced encryption schemes like for instance identity-based encryption.

Beside systems based on the Hamming metric, cryptosystems relying on a different metric, the rank metric, were introduced in 1991 by Gabidulin *et al.* [22]. This system, which is an analogue of the McEliece cryptosystem but with a different metric was based on Gabidulin codes, which are analogue codes to Reed-Solomon codes for rank metric. These codes having a very strong structure, they were difficult to mask (as their Hamming counterpart the Reed-Solomon codes), and in practice all cryptosystems based on these codes were broken. Meanwhile the rank metric approach had a strong advantage over the Hamming approach, the fact that the generic decoding problems are inherently more difficult than for Hamming metric. In some sense the general decoding problems for rank metric are to Hamming metric, what is the discrete logarithm problem over the group of an elliptic curve rather than on the ring $\mathbb{Z}/p\mathbb{Z}$. Again, following the approach of NTRU and the (Hamming) MDPC cryptosystem, an analogue cryptosystem, was proposed in 2013 for rank metric: the Low Rank Parity Check (LRPC) cryptosystem [25], as its cousins the MDPC and the NTRU cryptosystems, this system benefits from a poor structure which also seems (as for MDPC and NTRU) to limit the attacks to general attacks on the rank syndrome decoding problem.

In 2014, a new signature scheme, the RankSign scheme, based on LRPC codes was introduced by Gaborit *et al.* at PQCrypto 2014, [28]. This signature scheme is also a hash-and-sign signature scheme which inverts a random syndrome, but at the difference of the CFS scheme, the weight of the returned signature is linear in the length of the code, which implies smaller size of public key. Moreover beside its poor structure, inherited from the LRPC structure, the system comes with a security proof on information leaking from signatures. Thus we are eventually able to use this hash-and-sign signature scheme as a brick for the first IBE scheme based on coding theory.

1.2 Identity Based Encryption

The notion of identity-based encryption (IBE) was introduced by Shamir [43]. This gives an alternative to the standard notion of public-key encryption. In an IBE scheme, the public key associated with a user can be an arbitrary identity string, such as his e-mail address, and others can send encrypted messages to a user using this arbitrary identity without having to rely on a public-key infrastructure.

The main technical difference between a public key encryption (PKE) and IBE is the way the public and private keys are bound and the way of verifying those keys. In a PKE scheme, verification is achieved through the use of a certificate which relies on a public-key infrastructure. In an IBE, there is no need of verification of the public key but the private key is managed by a Trusted Authority (TA).

Difficulty in designing an IBE. There are two main difficulties in designing an IBE in comparison with a PKE

1. In a PKE, one often generates a public key from a secret key and normally, well-formed public keys are exponentially sparse. In an IBE scheme, any identity should be mapped to a public key and there is no known technique to randomly generate a point in an exponentially sparse space. Regev's public key encryption is an example [41]. In order to circumvent this problem, Gentry et. al. proposed a "dual" of a public-key cryptosystem, in which public keys are first generated in a primal space such that they are *dense*: every point in the primal space corresponds to a public-key and thus via a random oracle, one can map any identity to a valid public key.
2. For some PKE, the public keys are dense and one can thus map any identity to a well-formed public key. However, the difficulty is to extract the corresponding secret key from the public key. ElGamal's public key encryption [18] is an example because from a public key y in a cyclic group generated by g, there is no trapdoor for the discrete log problem that allows to find the corresponding secret key x such that $g^x = y$. In order to circumvent this problem, bilinear maps have been used [10].

Beside the technical difficulties in the design, achieving security in IBE is much more complicated than in PKE. The main difference is that in IBE, except the challenge identity that the adversary aims to attack, any other identities can be corrupted. Therefore the simulator has to be able to generate secret keys for all identities but the challenge identity. Under the above difficulties in the design and in proving the security, it took nearly twenty years for finding efficient methods to implement IBE.

There are currently three classes of IBE schemes: from elliptic curve pairings introduced by Sakai, Ohgishi and Kasahara [42] and by Boneh and Franklin in [10]; from the quadratic residue problem by Cocks in 2001 [15]; and from hard problems on lattice by Gentry, Peikert, and Vaikuntanathan [31]. These pioneer works inspired then many other ideas to improve the efficiency or to strengthen the security, in particular to avoid the use of the random oracle. We can name some very interesting schemes in the standard model: pairing-based schemes [8,9,12,30,46,47] and lattice-based scheme [1,11,13]. It is still not known how to devise an IBE scheme from quadratic residue problem without random oracles. We explain below a new method to achieve the first IBE scheme in the coding theory, with the help of rank metric codes and in the random oracle model.

Achieving IBE in Euclidean Metric. Let us first recall the technique in lattice that helps to construct IBE schemes. One of the major breakthroughs in lattice cryptography was the work of Gentry, Peikert, and Vaikuntanathan [31], that showed how to use a short trapdoor basis to generate short lattice vectors without revealing the trapdoor. This was used to give the first lattice-based construction of a secure identity-based encryption scheme.

Let us start with Regev's scheme [41]. Associated to a matrix $\boldsymbol{A} \in \mathbb{Z}_q^{n\times m}$, one generates the public key as $\boldsymbol{p} = \boldsymbol{s}A + \boldsymbol{e}$ for $\boldsymbol{s} \in \mathbb{Z}_q^n$ and a short vector $\boldsymbol{e}$. The set of possible public keys are points near a lattice point and are thus exponentially sparse. Gentry, Peikert, and Vaikuntanathan introduced a dual version of the Regev's scheme in exchanging the role of public key and of secret key in defining the public key as $\boldsymbol{u} \stackrel{\text{def}}{=} A\boldsymbol{e}^T \mod q$ for short $\boldsymbol{e} \in \mathbb{Z}^m$. The public keys are now dense, any identity could be mapped via a random oracle to a point in $\mathbb{Z}_q^n$ which will then be used as the corresponding public key. The key property is, with a carefully designed trapdoor $\boldsymbol{T}$, from a random public key $\boldsymbol{u} \in \mathbb{Z}_q^n$, the preimage $\boldsymbol{e}$ of the function $f_{\boldsymbol{A}}(\boldsymbol{e}) := A\boldsymbol{e} \mod q$ can be sampled in a space of well-defined short vectors used as the secret keys.

Achieving IBE in Rank Metric: Our technique. It seems very hard to give a rank metric analogue version of the above lattice technique. The main reason is due to the difficulty of obtaining a robust analysis of such a presampling function. However, we can overcome this difficulty in another way which perfectly fits the rank metric. We still keep the public key as $\boldsymbol{p} = \boldsymbol{s}A + \boldsymbol{e}$ for $\boldsymbol{e}$ of low rank (say at most r) in $\mathbb{F}_{q^m}^n$, and for $\boldsymbol{A}$ and $\boldsymbol{s}$ drawn uniformly at random in $\mathbb{F}_{q^m}^{(n-k)\times n}$ and $\mathbb{F}_{q^m}^{n-k}$ respectively, where $\mathbb{F}_{q^m}$ is the finite field over q^m elements. The main feature of the rank metric which will be used in what follows is that we can choose the bound r to be above the Gilbert Varshamov (RGV) bound for rank codes and this gives us two ingredients to design an IBE:

- with r carefully chosen above the RGV bound, we can still invert the function $f(\boldsymbol{s}, \boldsymbol{e}) = \boldsymbol{s}A + \boldsymbol{e}$. This relies on the RankSign system with a trapdoor to compute the pre-image of the function f [28].
- with overwhelming probability, any point $\boldsymbol{p}$ has a preimage $(\boldsymbol{s}, \boldsymbol{e})$ such that $f(\boldsymbol{s}, \boldsymbol{e}) = \boldsymbol{p}$. We can thus map an arbitrary identity to a valid public key $\boldsymbol{p}$, by using a random oracle as in the case of the GPV scheme.

Rank Metric vs. Hamming and Euclidean Metric. Rank metric and Hamming metric are very different metrics. This difference reflects for instance in the size of balls: when the number of elements of a ball of radius r in the Hamming metric for $\{0,1\}^n$ is bounded above by 2^n, for rank metric the number of elements is exponential but with a quadratic exponent depending on r. In practice, it means that even if it is possible to construct a trapdoor function for the Hamming distance such as the CFS signature scheme [16], the dimension of the dual code used there has to be sublinear in its length, whereas for rank metric it is possible to obtain such a trapdoor function for constant rate codes. This latter property makes it very difficult to use such a trapdoor function for the Hamming distance in order to build an IBE scheme whereas it is tractable for the rank metric.

Moreover one strong advantage of rank metric is the potential size of public keys. If one considers the general syndrome decoding problem $\boldsymbol{H}\boldsymbol{x}^T = \boldsymbol{s}$ (for the hardest case), because of the complexity of the best known attacks for rank metric (see [27]), and for λ a security parameter, the size of $\boldsymbol{H}$ is in $\mathcal{O}(\lambda^{\frac{3}{2}})$ for rank metric when it is in $\mathcal{O}(\lambda^2)$ for Hamming and Euclidean metrics.

1.3 Hardness of Problems in Rank Metric

The computational complexity of decoding $\mathbb{F}_{q^m}$-linear codes for rank metric has been an open question for almost 25 years since the first paper on rank based cryptography in 1991 [22]. Recently a probabilistic reduction to decoding in Hamming distance was given in [29]. On a practical complexity point of view the complexity of practical attacks grows very fast with the size of parameters, and there is a structural reason for this: for Hamming distance a key notion in the attacks is counting the number of words of length n and support size t, which corresponds to the notion of Newton binomial coefficient $\binom{n}{t}$, whose value is exponential and upper bounded by 2^n. In the case of rank metric, counting the number of possible supports of size r for a rank code of length n over $\mathbb{F}_{q^m}$ corresponds to counting the number of subspaces of dimension r in $\mathbb{F}_{q^m}$: the Gaussian binomial coefficient of size roughly $q^{r(m-r)}$, whose value is also exponential but with a quadratic term in the exponent.

1.4 Our Contribution

The contributions of this paper are two-fold:

On the cryptographic aspect: we design new cryptographic primitives based on the rank metric. The final objective is to design an IBE scheme, but on the way, we also introduce a new PKE scheme which perfectly fits a transformation from PKE to IBE. This shows a potential versatility of the use of rank metric in cryptography: it gives a credible alternative to Euclidean metric in the perspective of post-quantum cryptography and it has some advantages compared to Hamming metric as it is still a open question to construct an IBE scheme based on the Hamming metric. We emphasize that the design of an IBE scheme often opens the way to reach more advanced primitives such as Broadcast Encryption, Attribute-based Encryption and Functional Encryption.

On the algorithmic aspect: the security of the new constructions that we introduce relies on the hardness of three algorithmic problems. Two of them are well known problems, namely the Rank Syndrome Decoding Problem and the Augmented Low Rank Parity Check Code problem. However the last one is new and we call it the Rank Support Learning problem. A large part of the paper is devoted to study the hardness of the Rank Support Learning problem and more specifically

- we prove the equivalence between the Rank Support Learning problem and Rank Decoding with parity-check matrices defined over a subfield;
- we show that this problem can also be tackled by finding low weight-codewords in a certain code;
- we show that this problem can be viewed as the rank metric analogue of a rather old problem in the Hamming metric for which the best known algorithms are exponential;
- based on this analogy we give an algorithm of exponential complexity to handle this problem over the rank metric.

2 Background on Rank Metric and Cryptography

2.1 Notation

In the whole article, q denotes a power of a prime p. The finite field with q elements is denoted by $\mathbb{F}_q$ and more generally for any positive integer m the finite field with q^m elements is denoted by $\mathbb{F}_{q^m}$. We will frequently view $\mathbb{F}_{q^m}$ as an m-dimensional vector space over $\mathbb{F}_q$.

We use bold lowercase and capital letters to denote vectors and matrices respectively. We will view vectors here either as column or row vectors. It will be clear from the context whether it is a column or a row vector. For two matrices $\boldsymbol{A}, \boldsymbol{B}$ of compatible dimensions, we let $(\boldsymbol{A}|\boldsymbol{B})$ and $\left(\frac{\boldsymbol{A}}{\boldsymbol{B}}\right)$ respectively denote the horizontal and vertical concatenations of $\boldsymbol{A}$ and $\boldsymbol{B}$.

If S is a finite set, $x \stackrel{\$}{\leftarrow} S$ denotes that x is chosen uniformly at random among S. If $\mathcal{D}$ is a distribution, $x \leftarrow \mathcal{D}$ denotes that x is chosen at random according to $\mathcal{D}$.

We also use the standard $\mathcal{O}()$, $\Omega()$ and $\Theta()$ notation and also the "soft-O" notation $\tilde{\mathcal{O}}(\,)$, where $f(x) = \tilde{\mathcal{O}}(g(x))$ means that $f(x) = \mathcal{O}(g(x)\log(g(x))^k)$ for some k.

2.2 Definitions

In the whole article, the space $\mathbb{F}_{q^m}^n$ will be endowed with the following metric

Definition 1 (Rank metric over $\mathbb{F}_{q^m}^n$). *Let $\boldsymbol{x} = (x_1, \ldots, x_n) \in \mathbb{F}_{q^m}^n$ and consider an arbitrary basis $(\beta_1, \ldots, \beta_m) \in \mathbb{F}_{q^m}^m$ of $\mathbb{F}_{q^m}$ viewed as an m-dimensional vector space over $\mathbb{F}_q$. We decompose each entry x_j in this basis $x_j = \sum_{i=1}^m m_{ij}\beta_i$. The $m \times n$ matrix associated to $\boldsymbol{x}$ is given by $\boldsymbol{M}(\boldsymbol{x}) = (m_{ij})_{\substack{1\leq i\leq m \\ 1\leq j\leq n}}$. The rank weight $\|\boldsymbol{x}\|$ of $\boldsymbol{x}$ is defined as*

$$\|\boldsymbol{x}\| \stackrel{def}{=} \operatorname{Rank} \boldsymbol{M}(\boldsymbol{x}).$$

The associated distance $\operatorname{rd}(\boldsymbol{x}, \boldsymbol{y})$ between elements $\boldsymbol{x}$ and $\boldsymbol{y}$ in $\mathbb{F}_{q^m}^n$ is defined by $\operatorname{rd}(\boldsymbol{x}, \boldsymbol{y}) = \|\boldsymbol{x} - \boldsymbol{y}\|$.

Remark 1. It is readily seen that this distance does not depend on the basis that is chosen. We refer to [37] for more details on the rank distance.

A rank code $\mathcal{C}$ of length n and dimension k over the field $\mathbb{F}_{q^m}$ is a subspace of dimension k of $\mathbb{F}_{q^m}^n$ embedded with the rank metric. The minimum rank distance of the code $\mathcal{C}$ is the minimum rank of non-zero vectors of the code. One also considers the usual inner product which allows to define the notion of dual code. An important notion which differs from the Hamming distance, is the notion of support. Let $\boldsymbol{x} = (x_1, x_2, \cdots, x_n) \in \mathbb{F}_{q^m}^n$ be a vector of rank weight r. We denote by $E \stackrel{\text{def}}{=} \langle x_1, x_2, \cdots, x_n\rangle_{\mathbb{F}_q}$ the $\mathbb{F}_q$-linear subspace of $\mathbb{F}_{q^m}$ generated by linear combinations over $\mathbb{F}_q$ of $x_1, x_2, \cdots, x_n$. The vector space E is called the **support** of $\boldsymbol{x}$ and is denoted by $\operatorname{Supp}(\boldsymbol{x})$. In the following, $\mathcal{C}$ is a rank metric code of length n and dimension k over $\mathbb{F}_{q^m}$. The matrix $\boldsymbol{G}$ denotes a $k \times n$ generator matrix of $\mathcal{C}$ and $\boldsymbol{H}$ is one of its parity check matrix.

Bounds for Rank Metric Codes. The classical bounds for the Hamming metric have straightforward rank metric analogues, since two of them are of interest for the paper we recall them below.

Definition 2 (Rank Gilbert-Varshamov bound (RGV)). *The number of elements $S(n, m, q, t)$ of a sphere of radius t in $\mathbb{F}_{q^m}^n$, is equal to the number of $m \times n$ q-ary matrices of rank t. For $t = 0$ $S_0 = 1$, for $t \geq 1$ we have (see [37]):*

$$S(n, m, q, t) = \prod_{j=0}^{t-1} \frac{(q^n - q^j)(q^m - q^j)}{q^t - q^j}.$$

From this we deduce the volume $B(n, m, q, t)$ of a ball of radius t in $\mathbb{F}_{q^m}^n$ to be:

$$B(n, m, q, t) = \sum_{i=0}^{t} S(n, m, q, i).$$

In the linear case the Rank Gilbert-Varshamov bound $RGV(n, k, m, q)$ for an $[n, k]$ linear code over $\mathbb{F}_{q^m}$ is then defined as the smallest integer t such that $B(n, m, q, t) \geq q^{m(n-k)}$.

The Gilbert-Varshamov bound for a rank code $\mathcal{C}$ with parity-check matrix $\boldsymbol{H}$, corresponds to the smallest rank weight r for which, for any syndrome $\boldsymbol{s}$, there exists on average a word $\boldsymbol{e}$ of rank weight r such that $\boldsymbol{H}\boldsymbol{e} = \boldsymbol{s}$. To give an idea of the behavior of this bound, it can be shown that, asymptotically in the case $m = n$ [37]: $\frac{RGV(n,k,m,q)}{n} \sim 1 - \sqrt{\frac{k}{n}}$.

Singleton Bound. The classical Singleton bound for a linear $[n, k]$ rank code of minimum rank r over $\mathbb{F}_{q^m}$ works in the same way as for linear codes (by finding an information set) and reads $r \leq n - k + 1$: in the case when $n > m$ this bound can be rewritten as $r \leq 1 + \lfloor \frac{(n-k)m}{n} \rfloor$ [37].

2.3 Decoding Rank Codes

We will be interested in codes for the rank metric which can be efficiently decoded. At the difference of Hamming metric, there do not exist many families which admit an efficient decoding for large rank weight error (ideally we would like to go up to the RGV bound).

Deterministic Decoding of Rank Codes. Essentially there is only one family of rank codes which can be decoded in a deterministic way: the Gabidulin codes [21]. These codes are an analogue of the Reed-Solomon codes where polynomials are replaced by q-polynomials and benefit from the same decoding properties (cf [21] for more properties on these codes). A Gabidulin code of length n and dimension k over $\mathbb{F}_{q^m}$ with $k \leq n \leq m$ can decode up to $\frac{n-k}{2}$ errors in a deterministic way.

Probabilistic Decoding of Rank Codes. Besides the deterministic decoding of Gabidulin codes, which does not reach the RGV bound and hence is not optimal, it is possible to decode up to the RGV bound a simple family of codes. In this subsection we present the construction which allows with a probabilistic decoding algorithm to attain the RGV bound. These codes are adapted from codes in the subspace metric (a metric very close from the rank metric) which can be found in [44].

Definition 3 (Simple codes). *A code $\mathcal{C}$ is said to be (n,k,t)-simple (or just simple when t, k n are clear from the context), when it has a parity-check matrix $\boldsymbol{H}$ of the form*

$$\boldsymbol{H} = \left(\begin{array}{c|c} \boldsymbol{I}_{n-k} & \begin{array}{c} \boldsymbol{0}_t \\ \hline \boldsymbol{R} \end{array} \end{array} \right)$$

where $\boldsymbol{I}_{n-k}$ the $(n-k)\times(n-k)$ identity matrix, $\boldsymbol{0}_t$ is the zero matrix of size $t \times k$ and $\boldsymbol{R}$ is a matrix over $\mathbb{F}_{q^m}$ of size $k \times (n-k-t)$. It is called a random simple code if $\boldsymbol{R}$ is chosen uniformly at random among matrices of this size.

Proposition 1. *Let $\mathcal{C}$ be a random (n,k,t)-simple code with $t < \frac{m+n-\sqrt{(m-n)^2+4\,\mathrm{km}}}{2}$ and w an integer. If $w \leqslant t$ then $\mathcal{C}$ can decode an error of weight w with probability of failure $p_f \sim \frac{1}{q^{t-w+1}}$ when $q \to \infty$.*

The proof of this proposition is given in the full version of this paper [26]. The success of decoding depends essentially on the probability $1-p_f$ to recover the space E from the t first coordinates of $\boldsymbol{s}$, this probability can be made as small as needed by decoding less than t errors or by increasing q.

In term of complexity of decoding, one has just a system to invert in $(n-t)w$ unknowns in $\mathbb{F}_q$. Notice that the bound $\frac{m+n-\sqrt{(m-n)^2+4\,\mathrm{km}}}{2}$ corresponds asymptotically to the Rank Gilbert-Varshamov bound. Thus a simple code can asymptotically decodes up to the Rank Gilbert-Varshamov bound with probability $1-\mathcal{O}(\frac{1}{q})$.

In the special case $m=n$ and $w=t \approx n\left(1-\sqrt{\frac{k}{n}}\right)$ (the Rank Gilbert-Varshamov bound), the system has $\mathcal{O}(n^2)$ unknowns, so the decoding complexity is bounded by $\mathcal{O}(n^6)$ operations in $\mathbb{F}_q$. This decoding algorithm is better than the Gabidulin code decoder in term of correction capability since it corrects up to $n\left(1-\sqrt{\frac{k}{n}}\right)$ errors when Gabidulin codes can not decode more than $\frac{n-k}{2}$ errors.

2.4 Difficult Problem for Rank-Based Cryptography

Rank-based cryptography generally relies on the hardness of syndrome decoding for the rank metric. It is defined as the well known syndrome decoding problem but here the Hamming metric is replaced by the rank metric.

Definition 4 (Rank (Metric) Syndrome Decoding Problem (RSD)). *Let $\boldsymbol{H}$ be a full-rank $(n-k)\times n$ matrix over $\mathbb{F}_{q^m}$ with $k \le n$, $\boldsymbol{s} \in \mathbb{F}_{q^m}^{n-k}$ and w an integer. The problem is to find $\boldsymbol{x} \in \mathbb{F}_{q^m}^n$ such that $\mathrm{rank}(\boldsymbol{x}) = w$ and $\boldsymbol{Hx} = \boldsymbol{s}$. We denote this problem as the $\mathsf{RSD}_{q,m,n,k,w}$ problem.*

The RSD problem has recently been proven hard in [29] on probabilistic reduction. This problem has an equivalent dual version. Let $\boldsymbol{H}$ be a parity-check matrix of a code $\mathcal{C}$ and $\boldsymbol{G}$ be a generator matrix. Then the RSD problem is equivalent to find $\boldsymbol{m} \in \mathbb{F}_{q^m}^k$ and $\boldsymbol{x} \in \mathbb{F}_{q^m}^n$ such that $\boldsymbol{m}\boldsymbol{G} + \boldsymbol{x} = \boldsymbol{y}$ with $\text{Rank}\, \boldsymbol{x} = r$ and $\boldsymbol{y}$ some preimage of $\boldsymbol{s}$ by $\boldsymbol{H}$. We can now give the decisional version of this problem:

Definition 5 (Decisional Rank Syndrome Decoding Problem (DRSD)**).** *Let $\boldsymbol{G}$ be a full-rank $k \times n$ matrix over $\mathbb{F}_{q^m}$, $\boldsymbol{m} \in \mathbb{F}_{q^m}^k$ and $\boldsymbol{x} \in \mathbb{F}_{q^m}^n$ of weight r. Can we distinguish the pair $(\boldsymbol{G}, \boldsymbol{m}\boldsymbol{G} + \boldsymbol{x})$ from $(\boldsymbol{G}, \boldsymbol{y})$ with $\boldsymbol{y} \xleftarrow{\$} \mathbb{F}_{q^m}^n$?*

The same problem in the Hamming metric Decisional Syndrome Decoding problem (DSD), viewed as an LPN problem with a fixed number of samples (which is equivalent to the syndrome decoding problem), is proven hard in [3] with a reduction to the syndrome decoding problem for the Hamming metric. We can use the same technique as in [24,29] to prove that DRSD is hard in the worst case. The general idea is that a distinguisher D_R with non negligible advantage for DRSD problem can be used to construct another distinguisher D for DSD with a non negligible advantage.

2.5 Complexity of the Rank Decoding Problem

As explained earlier in the introduction the complexity of practical attacks grows very fast with the size of parameters, there exist two types of generic attacks on the problem:

Combinatorial attacks: these attacks are usually the best ones for small values of q (typically $q = 2$) and when n and k are not too small; when q increases, the combinatorial aspect makes them less efficient. The best attacks generalize the basic information set decoding approach in a rank metric context. Interestingly enough, the more recent improvements based on birthday paradox do not seem to generalize in rank metric because of the different notion of support.

In practice, when $m \leqslant n$, the best combinatorial attacks have complexity $\mathcal{O}\big((n-k)^3 m^3 q^{(r-1)\lfloor \frac{(k+1)m}{n} \rfloor}\big)$ [27].

Algebraic attacks: the particular nature of rank metric makes it a natural field for algebraic attacks and solving by Groebner basis, since these attacks are largely independent of the value of q and in some cases may also be largely independent on m. These attacks are usually the most efficient ones when q increases. There exist different types of algebraic modeling which can then be solved with Groebner basis techniques [19,20,27,36]. Algebraic attacks usually consider algebraic systems on the base field $\mathbb{F}_q$, it implies that the number of unknowns is quadratic in the length of the code. Since the general complexity of Groebner basis attacks is exponential in the number of unknowns, it induces for cryptographic parameters, general attacks with a quadratic exponent in the length of the code, as for combinatorial attacks.

3 A New Public Key Encryption

3.1 Public-Key Encryption

Let us briefly remind that a public-key encryption scheme $\mathcal{S}$ is defined by three algorithms: the key generation algorithm KeyGen which, on input the security parameter, produces a pair of matching public and private keys (pk, sk); the encryption algorithm $\mathsf{Enc}_{pk}(m; r)$ which outputs a ciphertext c corresponding to the plaintext $m \in \mathcal{M}$, using random coins $r \in \mathcal{R}$; and the decryption algorithm $\mathsf{Dec}_{sk}(c)$ which outputs the plaintext m associated to the ciphertext c.

It is now well-admitted to require *semantic security* (*a.k.a. polynomial security* or *indistinguishability of encryptions* [32], denoted IND): if the attacker has some *a priori* information about the plaintext, it should not learn more with the view of the ciphertext. More formally, this security notion requires the computational indistinguishability between two messages, chosen by the adversary, one of which has been encrypted. The issue is to find which one has been actually encrypted with a probability significantly better than one half. More precisely, we define the advantage $\mathsf{Adv}^{\mathsf{ind}}_{\mathcal{S}}(\mathcal{A})$, where the adversary $\mathcal{A}$ is seen as a 2-stage Turing machine $(\mathcal{A}_1, \mathcal{A}_2)$ by

$$\mathsf{Adv}^{\mathsf{ind}}_{\mathcal{S}}(\mathcal{A}) \stackrel{\text{def}}{=} 2 \times \Pr\left[\begin{array}{l}(pk, sk) \leftarrow \mathsf{KeyGen}, (m_0, m_1, s) \leftarrow \mathcal{A}_1(pk), \\ b \stackrel{R}{\leftarrow} \{0,1\}, c = \mathsf{Enc}_{pk}(m_b) : \mathcal{A}_2(m_0, m_1, s, c) = b\end{array}\right] - 1.$$

This advantage should ideally be a negligible function of the security parameter.

3.2 Description of the Cryptosystem RankPKE

First, we need to define what we call a homogeneous matrix which will be used in encryption.

Definition 6 (Homogeneous Matrix). *A matrix* $\boldsymbol{M} = (m_{ij})_{\substack{1 \le i \le a \\ 1 \le j \le b}} \in \mathbb{F}_{q^m}^{a \times b}$ *is homogeneous of weight* d *if all its coefficients belong to the same* $\mathbb{F}_q$*-vector subspace of dimension* d*, that is to say*

$$\dim_{\mathbb{F}_q} \langle m_{ij} \rangle = d$$

We now introduce a public-key encryption, called RankPKE. Let $\boldsymbol{A}$ be drawn uniformly at random in $\mathbb{F}_{q^m}^{(n-k) \times n}$. We need it to be of full rank. This happens with overwhelming probability (i.e. $1 - \mathcal{O}(q^{-m(k+1)})$). Let W_r be the set of all the words of rank r and of length n, i.e. $W_r = \{\boldsymbol{x} \in \mathbb{F}_{q^m}^n : \|\boldsymbol{x}\| = r\}$. The system RankPKE works as follows:

- RankPKE.KeyGen:
  - generate $\boldsymbol{A} \stackrel{\$}{\leftarrow} \mathbb{F}_{q^m}^{(n-k) \times n}$
  - generate $\boldsymbol{s} \stackrel{\$}{\leftarrow} \mathbb{F}_{q^m}^{n-k}$ and $\boldsymbol{e} \stackrel{\$}{\leftarrow} W_r$
  - compute $\boldsymbol{p} = \boldsymbol{s}\boldsymbol{A} + \boldsymbol{e}$

 - define $G \in \mathbb{F}_{q^m}^{k' \times n'}$ a generator matrix of a public code $\mathcal{C}$ which can decode (efficiently) errors of weight up to wr, where w is defined just below.
 - define $sk = s$ and $pk = (A, p, G)$

– $\mathsf{RankPKE.Enc}((A, p, G), m)$:
Let $m \in \mathbb{F}_{q^m}^{k'}$ be the message we want to encrypt. We generate a random homogeneous matrix $U \in \mathbb{F}_{q^m}^{n \times n'}$ of weight w. Then we can compute the ciphertext (C, x) of m as :

$$\begin{pmatrix} A \\ \hline p \end{pmatrix} U + \begin{pmatrix} 0 \\ \hline mG \end{pmatrix} = \begin{pmatrix} C \\ \hline x \end{pmatrix}$$

– $\mathsf{RankPKE.Dec}(s, (C, x))$:
 - use the secret key s to compute:

$$\begin{aligned} \left(s \;\middle|\; -1 \right) \begin{pmatrix} C \\ \hline x \end{pmatrix} &= sC - x = sAU - pU - mG \\ &= sAU - (sA + e)U - mG = -eU - mG \end{aligned}$$

 - since U is homogeneous, we have $\|eU\| \leqslant wr$. Therefore, by using the decoding algorithm of $\mathcal{C}$, we recover m.

The expansion rate of this cryptosystem is $\frac{n-k+1}{R}$ where $R = \frac{k'}{n'}$ is the rate of $\mathcal{C}$.

3.3 Security

Definition 7 (Rank Support Learning (RSL)). *Let A be a random full-rank matrix of size $(n-k) \times n$ over $\mathbb{F}_{q^m}$ and V be a subspace of $\mathbb{F}_{q^m}$ of dimension w. Let $\mathcal{O}$ be an oracle which gives samples of the form (A, Au), where $u \overset{\$}{\leftarrow} V^n$. The $\mathsf{RSL}_{q,m,n,k,w}$ problem is to recover V given only access to the oracle.*

We say that the problem is (N, t, ε)-hard if for every probabilistic algorithm $\mathcal{A}$ running in time t, we have

$$\mathrm{Prob}[\mathcal{A}(A, AU) = V] \leqslant \varepsilon, \quad U \overset{\$}{\leftarrow} V^{n \times N}$$

When we want to stress the fact that we care about the problem where we are allowed to make exactly N calls to the oracle, we denote this the $\mathsf{RSL}_{q,m,n,k,w,N}$ problem. The pair (A, AU) is referred to as an instance of the $\mathsf{RSL}_{q,m,n,k,w,N}$ problem.

The corresponding decisional problem, namely DRSL, is to distinguish (A, AU) from (A, Y) where $Y \overset{\$}{\leftarrow} \mathbb{F}_{q^m}^{(n-k) \times N}$.

Proposition 2. *The* $\mathsf{RSL}_{q,m,n,k,w,N}$ *is as hard as the* $\mathsf{RSD}_{q,m,n,k,w}$ *problem.*

Proof. Let $\boldsymbol{A}$ be a full-rank $(n-k)\times n$ matrix over $\mathbb{F}_{q^m}$ and $\boldsymbol{x}\in\mathbb{F}_{q^m}^{n-k}$ of rank w. Let $\boldsymbol{s}=\boldsymbol{A}\boldsymbol{x}$. $(\boldsymbol{A},\boldsymbol{s})$ is an instance of the $\mathsf{RSD}_{q,m,n,k,w}$ problem.

Let $\boldsymbol{S}$ be a matrix obtained by the concatenation of N times the vector $\boldsymbol{s}$. $(\boldsymbol{A},\boldsymbol{S})$ is an instance of the $\mathsf{RSL}_{q,m,n,k,w,N}$ problem.

If we are able to solve any instances of the $\mathsf{RSL}_{q,m,n,k,w,N}$ problem, then we can recover the support of $\boldsymbol{x}$ and solve the instance $(\boldsymbol{A},\boldsymbol{s})$.

We can use this technique to solve any instances of the $\mathsf{RSD}_{q,m,n,k,w}$ problem, which proves that the $\mathsf{RSL}_{q,m,n,k,w,N}$ is as hard as the $\mathsf{RSD}_{q,m,n,k,w}$ problem in the worst case.

Security of the DRSL and DRSD Problems. We have already seen in the previous section that the DRSD problem is hard. As for other problems in cryptography (like DDH [7,17]), the best known attacks on the $\mathsf{DRSL}_{q,m,n,k,w,N}$ problem consist in solving the same instance of the $\mathsf{RSL}_{q,m,n,k,w,N}$ problem, so we make the assumption that the $\mathsf{DRSL}_{q,m,n,k,w,N}$ problem is difficult.

Theorem 1. *Under the assumption that* DRSL *is hard, the scheme* RankPKE *is semantically secure.*

Proof. We proceed by a sequence of games.

Game $\mathbf{G}_0$: This is the real IND-CPA attack game. The RankPKE.KeyGen is run and then, a 2-stage poly-time adversary $\mathcal{A}=(\mathcal{A}_1,\mathcal{A}_2)$ is fed with the public key $pk=(\boldsymbol{A},\boldsymbol{p},\boldsymbol{G}')$. Then, $\mathcal{A}_1$ outputs a pair of messages $(\boldsymbol{m}_0,\boldsymbol{m}_1)$. Next a challenge ciphertext is produced by flipping a coin b and producing a ciphertext $c^\star:=(C^\star,\boldsymbol{x}^\star)$ of $\boldsymbol{m}^\star=\boldsymbol{m}_b$.

This ciphertext $c^\star$ comes from a random homogeneous matrix $\boldsymbol{U}\in\mathbb{F}_{q^m}^{n\times n'}$ of weight w and then $c^\star=\mathsf{RankPKE.Enc}((\boldsymbol{A},\boldsymbol{p},\boldsymbol{G}'),\boldsymbol{m}_b)$. On input $c^\star$, $\mathcal{A}_2$ outputs bit b'. We denote by S_0 the event $b'=b$ and use the same notation S_n in any game $\mathbf{G}_n$ below.

$$\mathsf{Adv}^{\text{ind-cpa}}_{\mathsf{RankPKE}}(\mathcal{A})=\mid 2\Pr[\mathsf{S}_0]-1\mid$$

Game $\mathbf{G}_1$: In this game, we replace $\boldsymbol{p}=\boldsymbol{s}A+\boldsymbol{e}$ in RankPKE.KeyGen by $\boldsymbol{p}\xleftarrow{\$}\mathbb{F}_{q^m}^n$. Under the hardness of the DRSD problem, the two games $\mathbf{G}_1$ and $\mathbf{G}_0$ are indistinguishable:

$$\mid\Pr[\mathsf{S}_1]-\Pr[\mathsf{S}_0]\mid\leq\epsilon_{\mathsf{drsd}},$$

where ϵ_{drsd} is the bound on the successful probability of the attacks against the problem DRSD.

Game $\mathbf{G}_2$: In this game, we replace $(C^\star,\boldsymbol{x}^\star)$ in $\mathbf{G}_1$ by $(C^\star\xleftarrow{\$}\mathbb{F}_{q^m}^{(n-k)\times n'},\boldsymbol{x}^\star\xleftarrow{\$}\mathbb{F}_{q^m}^{n'})$.

As $\boldsymbol{x}^\star$ is perfectly random, $\boldsymbol{x}^\star-\boldsymbol{m}^\star\boldsymbol{G}$ is also perfectly random. In other words, this game replaces $\left(\frac{\boldsymbol{A}}{\boldsymbol{p}}\right)\boldsymbol{U}=\left(\frac{C^\star}{\boldsymbol{x}^\star-\boldsymbol{m}^\star\boldsymbol{G}}\right)$ by a perfectly random matrix. Therefore, the indistinguishability of the two games $\mathbf{G}_2$ and $\mathbf{G}_1$ follows from the hardness of the DRSL problem, applying it to the matrix $\boldsymbol{A}' = \begin{pmatrix} \boldsymbol{A} \\ \boldsymbol{p} \end{pmatrix}$ which is perfectly random because $\boldsymbol{A}$ and $\boldsymbol{p}$ are both perfectly random. Thus

$$|\Pr[\mathsf{S}_2] - \Pr[\mathsf{S}_1]| \leq \epsilon_{\mathsf{drsl}},$$

where ϵ_{drsl} is the bound on the successful probability of the attacks against the DRSL problem.

Advantage Zero. In this last game, as the ciphertext challenge $(C^\star, \boldsymbol{x}^\star)$ is perfectly random, b is perfectly hidden to any adversary $\mathcal{A}$.

$$|\Pr[\mathsf{S}_2]| = \frac{1}{2}$$

4 On the Difficulty of the Rank Support Learning Problem

The purpose of this section is to give some evidence towards the difficulty of the support learning problem $\mathsf{RSL}_{q,m,n,k,w,N}$ by

- explaining that it is the rank metric analogue of a problem in Hamming metric (the so called support learning problem) which has already been useful to devise signature schemes and for which after almost twenty years of existence only algorithms of exponential complexity are known;
- explaining that it is a problem which is provably hard for $N = 1$ and that it becomes easy only for very large values of N;
- giving an algorithm which is the analogue in the rank metric of the best known algorithm for the support learning problem which is of exponential complexity. This complexity is basically smaller by a multiplicative factor which is only of order $q^{-\beta N}$ (for some $\beta < 1$) than the complexity of solving the rank syndrome decoding problem $\mathsf{RSD}_{q,m,n,k,w}$;
- relating this problem to finding a codeword of rank weight w in a code where there are q^N codewords of this weight. It is reasonable to conjecture that the complexity of finding such a codeword gets reduced by a multiplicative factor which is at most q^N compared to the complexity of finding a codeword of rank weight w in a random code of the same length and dimension which has a single codeword of this weight;
- showing that this problem can also rephrased in terms of decoding a random code but defined over a larger alphabet ($\mathbb{F}_{q^{mN}}$ instead of $\mathbb{F}_{q^m}$).

4.1 A Related Problem: The Support Learning Problem

The rank support learning problem can be viewed as the rank metric analogue of the support learning problem which can be expressed as follows.

Problem 1 *(Support Learning)***.** Let $\boldsymbol{A}$ be a random full-rank matrix of size $(n-k)\times n$ over $\mathbb{F}_q$ and I be a subset of $\{1,\ldots,n\}$ of size w. Let V be the subspace of $\mathbb{F}_q^n$ of vectors with support I, that is the set of vectors $\boldsymbol{u} = (u_i)_{1\leq i\leq n} \in \mathbb{F}_q^n$ such that $u_i = 0$ when $i \notin I$. Let $\mathcal{O}$ be an oracle which gives samples of the form $(\boldsymbol{A}, \boldsymbol{A}\boldsymbol{u})$, where $\boldsymbol{u} \xleftarrow{\$} V$. The support learning problem is to recover I given only access to the oracle.

We say that the problem is (N, t, ε)-hard if for every probabilistic algorithm $\mathcal{A}$ running in time t, we have

$$\text{Prob}[\mathcal{A}(\boldsymbol{A}, \boldsymbol{A}\boldsymbol{U}) = V] \leqslant \varepsilon, \quad \boldsymbol{U} \xleftarrow{\$} V^N$$

When we want to stress the fact that we care about the problem where we are allowed to make exactly N calls to the oracle, we denote this the $\mathsf{SL}_{q,n,k,w,N}$ problem. The pair $(\boldsymbol{A}, \boldsymbol{A}\boldsymbol{U})$ is referred to as an instance of the $\mathsf{SL}_{q,n,k,w,N}$ problem.

When $N = 1$ this is just the usual decoding problem of a random linear code with parity check matrix $\boldsymbol{A}$. In this case, the problem is known to be NP-complete [5]. When N is greater than 1, this can be viewed as a decoding problem where we are given N syndromes of N errors which have a support included in the same set I. This support learning problem with $N > 1$ has already been considered before in [34]. Its presumed hardness for moderate values of N was used there to devise a signature scheme [34], the so called KKS-scheme. Mounting a key attack in this case (that is for the Hamming metric) without knowing any signature that has been computed for this key really amounts to solve this support learning problem even it was not stated exactly like this in the article. However, when we have signatures originating from this scheme, the problem is of a different nature. Indeed, it was found out in [14] that signatures leak information. The authors showed there that if we know M signatures, then we are given $\boldsymbol{A}$, $\boldsymbol{A}\boldsymbol{U}$ but also M vectors in $\mathbb{F}_q^n$, $\boldsymbol{v}_1, \ldots, \boldsymbol{v}_M$ whose support is included in I. The knowledge of those auxiliary $\boldsymbol{v}_i$'s help a great deal to recover I : it suffices to compute the union of their support which is very likely to reveal the whole set I. When the $\boldsymbol{v}_i$'s are random vectors in $\mathbb{F}_q^n$ of support included in I it is clearly enough to have a logarithmic number of them (in the size of the support I) to recover I. However this does not undermine the security of the support learning problem and just shows that the KKS-signature scheme is at best a one-time signature scheme.

Some progress on the support learning problem itself was achieved almost fifteen years later in [40]. Roughly speaking the idea there is to consider a code that has q^N codewords of weight at most w which correspond to all possible linear combinations of the $\boldsymbol{u}_i$'s and to use generic decoding algorithms of linear codes (which can also be used as low-weight codewords search algorithms) to recover one of those linear combinations. The process can then be iterated to reveal the whole support I. The fact that there are q^N codewords of weight $\leq w$ that are potential solutions for the low weight codeword search algorithm implies that we may expect to gain a factor of order q^N in the complexity of the algorithm when compared to finding a codeword of weight w in a random linear code which has a single codeword of weight w. Actually the gain is less than this in practice. This seems to be due to the fact that we have highly correlated codewords (their support is for instance included in I). However, still there is some exponential speedup when compared to the single codeword case. This allowed to break all the parameters proposed in [34,35] but also those of [4] which actually relied on the same problem. However, as has been acknowledged in [40], this does not give a polynomial time algorithm for the support learning problem, it just gives an exponential speedup when compared to solving a decoding problem with an error of weight w. The parameters of the KKS scheme can easily be chosen in order to thwart this attack.

4.2 Both Problems Reduce to Linear Algebra When N is Large Enough

As explained before when $N = 1$ the support learning problem is NP-complete. The rank support learning problem is also hard in this case since it is equivalent to decoding in the rank metric an $\mathbb{F}_{q^m}$-linear code for which there is a randomized reduction to the NP-complete decoding problem in the Hamming metric [29]. It is also clear that both problems become easy when N is large enough and for the same reason : they basically amount to compute a basis of a linear space.

In the Hamming metric, this corresponds to the case when $N = w$. Indeed in this case, notice that the dimension of the subspace V is w. When the $\boldsymbol{u}_i$'s are generated randomly with support included in I they have a constant probability $K(q)$ (which is increasing with q and bigger than 0.288 in the binary case) to generate the space $\boldsymbol{A}V$. Once we know this space, the problem becomes easy. Indeed let $\boldsymbol{e}_1, \dots, \boldsymbol{e}_n$ be the canonical generators of $\mathbb{F}_q^n$ (i.e. $\boldsymbol{e}_i$ has only one non-zero entry which is its i-th entry that is equal to 1). We recover I by checking for all positions i in $\{1, \dots, n\}$ whether $\boldsymbol{A}\boldsymbol{e}_i$ belongs to $\boldsymbol{A}V$ or not. If it is the case, then i belongs to I, if this is not the case, i does not belong to I.

There is a similar algorithm for the rank support learning problem. This should not come as a surprise since supports of code positions for the Hamming metric really correspond to subspaces of $\mathbb{F}_{q^m}$ for the rank metric metric as has been put forward in [27] (see also [33] for more details about this). The difference being however that we need much bigger values of N to mount a similar attack to the Hamming metric case. Indeed what really counts here is the space that can be generated by the $\boldsymbol{A}\boldsymbol{u}_i$'s where the $\boldsymbol{u}_i$'s are the columns of $\boldsymbol{U}$. It is nothing but the space $\boldsymbol{A}V^n$. Let us denote this space by W. This space is not $\mathbb{F}_{q^m}$-linear, however it is $\mathbb{F}_q$-linear and it is of dimension nw viewed as an $\mathbb{F}_q$-linear subspace of $\mathbb{F}_{q^m}^n$. When $N = nw$ we can mount a similar attack, namely we compute the space generated by linear combinations over $\mathbb{F}_q$ of $\boldsymbol{A}\boldsymbol{u}_1, \dots, \boldsymbol{A}\boldsymbol{u}_{nw}$. They generate W with constant probability $K(q)$. When we look all $\mathbb{F}_q$-linear subspaces V' of $\mathbb{F}_{q^m}$ of dimension 1 (there are less than q^m of them) and check whether the subspace W' of dimension n given by $\boldsymbol{A}V'^n$ is included in $W = \boldsymbol{A}V^n$ or not. By taking the sum of the spaces for which this is the case we recover V. Actually the complexity of this algorithm can be improved by using in a more clever way the knowledge of W, but this is beyond the scope of this article and this algorithm is just here to explain the deep similarities between both cases and to convey some intuition about when the rank support learning problem becomes easy.

This discussion raises the issue whether there is an algorithm "interpolating" standard decoding algorithms when $N = 1$ and linear algebra when $N = w$ in the Hamming metric case and $N = nw$ in the rank metric case. This is in essence what has been achieved in [40] for the Hamming metric and what we will do now here for the rank metric.

4.3 Solving the Subspace Problem with Information-Set Decoding

There are two ingredients in the algorithm for solving the support learning problem in [40]. The first one is to set up an equivalent problem which amounts to find a codeword of weight $\leq w$ in a code which has q^N codewords of this weight. The second one is to use standard information set decoding techniques to solve this task and to show that it behaves better than in the case where there is up to a multiplicative constant a single codeword of this weight in the code. We are going to follow the same route here for the rank metric.

We begin by introducing the following $\mathbb{F}_q$-linear code

$$\mathcal{C} \stackrel{\text{def}}{=} \{\boldsymbol{x} \in \mathbb{F}_{q^m}^n : \boldsymbol{A}\boldsymbol{x} \in W_U\}$$

where W_U is the $\mathbb{F}_q$-linear subspace of $\mathbb{F}_{q^m}^{n-k}$ generated by linear combinations of the form $\sum_i \alpha_i \boldsymbol{A}\boldsymbol{u}_i$ where α_i belongs to $\mathbb{F}_q$ and the $\boldsymbol{u}_i$'s are the N column vectors forming the matrix $\boldsymbol{U}$. This code has the following properties.

Lemma 1. *Let* $\mathcal{C}' \stackrel{def}{=} \{\sum_i \alpha_i \boldsymbol{u}_i : \alpha_i \in \mathbb{F}_q\}$. *We have*

1. $\dim_{\mathbb{F}_q} \mathcal{C} \leq km + N$
2. $\mathcal{C}' \subset \mathcal{C}$
3. *all the elements of* $\mathcal{C}'$ *are of rank weight* $\leq w$.

[27] gives several algorithms for decoding $\mathbb{F}_{q^m}$-linear codes for the rank metric. The first one can be generalized in a straightforward way to codes which are just $\mathbb{F}_q$-linear as explained in more detail in [33]. This article also explains how this algorithm can be used in a straightforward way to search for low rank codewords in such a code. Here our task is to look for codewords of rank $\leq w$ which are very likely to lie in $\mathcal{C}'$ which would reveal a linear combination $\boldsymbol{c} = \sum_i \alpha_i \boldsymbol{u}_i$. This reveals in general V when $\boldsymbol{c}$ is of rank weight w simply by computing the vector space over $\mathbb{F}_q$ generated by the entries of $\boldsymbol{c}$. When the rank of $\boldsymbol{c}$ is smaller this yields a subspace of V and we will discuss later on how we finish the attack.

Let us concentrate now on analyzing how the first decoding algorithm of [27] behaves when we use it to find codewords of $\mathcal{C}$ of rank $\leq w$. For this, we have to recall how the support attack of [27] works.

We assume that we want to find a codeword of weight w in an $\mathbb{F}_q$-linear code which is a $\mathbb{F}_q$-subspace of $\mathbb{F}_{q^m}$ of dimension K. For the purpose of this algorithm, a codeword $\boldsymbol{c} = (c_1, \ldots, c_n) \in \mathbb{F}_{q^m}^n$ is also viewed as a matrix $(c_{ij})_{\substack{1 \le i \le m \\ 1 \le j \le n}}$ over $\mathbb{F}_q$ by writing the c_i's in a arbitrary $\mathbb{F}_q$ basis $(\beta_1, \ldots, \beta_m) \in \mathbb{F}_{q^m}^m$ of $\mathbb{F}_{q^m}$ viewed as vector space over $\mathbb{F}_q$: $c_i = \sum_{j=1}^m c_{ij}\beta_j$. There are $nm - K$ linear equations which specify the code that are satisfied by the c_{ij}'s of the form

$$\sum_{1 \le i,j \le m} h_{ij}^s c_{ij} = 0 \tag{1}$$

for $s = 1, \ldots, mn - K$. Algorithm 1 explains how a codeword of weight $\le w$ is produced by the approach of [27]. The point of choosing r like this in this algorithm, i.e.

$$r \stackrel{\text{def}}{=} m - \left\lceil \frac{K}{n} \right\rceil \tag{2}$$

is that r is the smallest integer for which the linear system (3) has more equations than unknowns (and we therefore expect that it has generally only the all-zero solution).

Theorem 2. *Assume that* $w \le \min\left(\lfloor \frac{K}{n} \rfloor, \lfloor \frac{N}{n} \rfloor + 1\right)$ *and that* $\frac{w + \lfloor \frac{K}{n} \rfloor}{2} \ge \lfloor \frac{N}{n} \rfloor$. *Let*

$$e_- = \left(w - \left\lfloor \frac{N}{n} \right\rfloor\right)\left(\left\lfloor \frac{K}{n} \right\rfloor - \left\lfloor \frac{N}{n} \right\rfloor\right)$$

$$e_+ = \left(w - \left\lfloor \frac{N}{n} \right\rfloor - 1\right)\left(\left\lfloor \frac{K}{n} \right\rfloor - \left\lfloor \frac{N}{n} \right\rfloor - 1\right) + n\left(\left\lfloor \frac{N}{n} \right\rfloor + 1\right) - N$$

Algorithm 1 outputs an element of $\mathcal{C}'$ *with complexity* $\tilde{\mathcal{O}}\left(q^{\min(e_-, e_+)}\right)$. *We give the complete proof of this theorem in the the full version of this paper* [26].

Remark 2. 1. When N and $K = km + N$ are multiple of n, say $N = \delta n$ and $K = \alpha R n + \delta$ (with $\alpha \stackrel{\text{def}}{=} \frac{m}{n}$, $R = \frac{k}{n}$) the complexity above simplifies to $\tilde{\mathcal{O}}\left(q^{\alpha R n (w - \delta)}\right)$. In other words the complexity gets reduced by a factor $q^{\alpha R \delta n} = q^{\alpha R N}$ when compared to finding a codeword of weight w in a random $\mathbb{F}_q$-linear code of the same dimension and length.
2. This approach is really suited to the case $m \le n$. When $m > n$ we obtain better complexities by working on the transposed code (see [33] for more details about this approach).

Algorithm 1. algorithm that outputs a codeword of weight $\leq w$.

$r \leftarrow m - \lceil \frac{K}{n} \rceil$
loop
 $W \leftarrow$ random $\mathbb{F}_q$-subspace of dimension r of $\mathbb{F}_{q^m}$
 Compute a basis $\boldsymbol{f}^1 = (f_i^1)_{1 \leq i \leq m}, \ldots, \boldsymbol{f}^r = (f_i^r)_{1 \leq i \leq m}$ of W
 Make the assumption that the entries c_j of $\boldsymbol{c}$ can be written in the $\boldsymbol{f}^1, \ldots, \boldsymbol{f}^r$ basis as

$$c_j = \sum_{l=1}^{r} x_{lj} \boldsymbol{f}^l$$

 Rewrite the linear equations (1) by writing $c_{ij} = \sum_{l=1}^{r} x_{lj} f_i^l$ to obtain $mn - K$ equations of the form

$$\sum_{1 \leq i,j \leq m} h_{ij}^s \sum_{l=1}^{r} x_{lj} f_i^l = 0 \tag{3}$$

 Define $(x_{ij})_{\substack{1 \leq i \leq r \\ 1 \leq j \leq n}}$ by $c_{ij} = \sum_{l=1}^{r} x_{lj} f_i^l$
 Solve this system (in the x_{ij}'s)
 if this system has a non zero solution **then**
  if $(\sum_{l=1}^{r} x_{lj} \boldsymbol{f}^l)_{1 \leq j \leq n}$ has rank weight $\leq w$ **then**
   return $(\sum_{l=1}^{r} x_{lj} \boldsymbol{f}^l)_{1 \leq j \leq n}$
  end if
 end if
end loop

4.4 Link Between Rank Support Learning and Decoding over the Rank Metric

We have exploited here that for solving the rank support learning problem, it can be rephrased in terms of finding a codeword of low rank weight in a code that has many codewords of such low rank weight (namely the code $\mathcal{C}$ that has been introduced in this section). $\mathcal{C}$ is not a random code however, it is formed by a random subcode, namely the code $\mathcal{C}_0 = \{\boldsymbol{x} \in \mathbb{F}_{q^m}^n : \boldsymbol{A}\boldsymbol{x} = 0\}$ plus some non random part, namely $\mathcal{C}'$ which contains precisely the low rank codeword we are after. In other words $\mathcal{C}$ decomposes as

$$\mathcal{C} = \mathcal{C}_0 \oplus \mathcal{C}'$$

where $\mathcal{C}_0$ is a truly random code and $\mathcal{C}'$ is a subcode of $\mathcal{C}$ that contains the codewords of $\mathcal{C}$ of low-rank. $\mathcal{C}$ is therefore not really a random code.

There is a way however to rephrase the rank support learning problem as a problem of decoding a *random* code. The trick is to change the alphabet of the code. We define the code $\mathcal{C}_N$ as

$$\mathcal{C}_N = \{\boldsymbol{x} \in \mathbb{F}_{q^{mN}} : \boldsymbol{A}\boldsymbol{x} = 0\}.$$

In other words, $\mathcal{C}_N$ is a code defined over the extension field $\mathbb{F}_{q^{mN}}$ but with a random parity-check matrix with entries defined over $\mathbb{F}_{q^m}$.

There are several ways to equip $\mathbb{F}_{q^{mN}}^n$ with a rank metric. One of them consists in writing the entries c_i of a codeword $\boldsymbol{c} = (c_1, \dots, c_n) \in \mathbb{F}_{q^{mN}}^n$ of $\mathcal{C}_N$ as column vectors $(c_{ij})_{1 \le j \le mN} \in \mathbb{F}_q^{mN}$ by expressing the entry c_i in a $\mathbb{F}_q$ basis of $\mathbb{F}_{q^{mN}}$ $(\beta_1, \dots, \beta_{mN})$, i.e. $c_i = \sum_{1 \le j \le mN} c_{ij}\beta_j$ and replacing each entry by the corresponding vector to obtain an $mN \times n$ matrix. The rank of this matrix would then define the rank weight of a codeword. However, since $\mathbb{F}_{q^{mN}}$ is an extension field of $\mathbb{F}_{q^m}$ there are also other ways to define a rank metric. We will choose the following one here. First we decompose each entry c_i in an $\mathbb{F}_{q^m}$-basis $(\gamma_1, \dots, \gamma_N)$ of $\mathbb{F}_{q^{mN}}$:

$$c_i = \sum_{j=1}^{N} \alpha_{(i-1)N+j}\gamma_j$$

where the α_i's belong to $\mathbb{F}_{q^m}$. The rank weight of $(c_1, \dots, c_n)$ is then defined as the rank weight of the vector $(\alpha_i)_{1 \le i \le nN} \in \mathbb{F}_{q^m}^{nN}$ where the rank weight of the last vector is defined as we have done up to here, namely by replacing each entry α_i by a column vector $(\alpha_{ij})_{1 \le j \le m}$ obtained by taking the coordinates of α_i in some $\mathbb{F}_q$-basis of $\mathbb{F}_{q^m}$. In other words, the rank weight of $(c_1, \dots, c_n)$ is defined as the rank of the associated $m \times nN$ matrix.

Let us now introduce the rank decoding problem with random parity check matrices defined over a smaller field.

Definition 8 (Rank Decoding with parity-check matrices defined over a subfield (RDPCSF)). *Let $\boldsymbol{A}$ be a random full-rank matrix of size $(n - k) \times n$ over $\mathbb{F}_{q^m}$ and $\boldsymbol{e} \in \mathbb{F}_{q^{mN}}^n$ be a random word of rank weight w. The $\mathsf{RDPCSF}_{q,m,n,k,w,N}$ problem is to recover $\boldsymbol{e}$ from the knowledge of $\boldsymbol{A} \in \mathbb{F}_{q^m}^{(n-k)\times n}$ and $\boldsymbol{Ae} \in \mathbb{F}_{q^{mN}}^{n-k}$.*

It turns out that the support learning problem and the rank decoding problem with parity-check matrices defined over a smaller field are equivalent

Theorem 3. *The problems $\mathsf{RSL}_{q,m,n,w,N}$ and $\mathsf{RDPCSF}_{q,m,n,w,N}$ are equivalent : any randomized algorithm solving one of this problem with probability $\ge \epsilon$ in time t can be turned into an algorithm for the other problem solving it with probability $\ge \epsilon$ in time $t + P(q, m, n, w, N)$, where P is a polynomial function of its entries.*

Proof. Let us consider an instance $(\boldsymbol{A}, \boldsymbol{AU})$ of the $\mathsf{RSL}_{q,m,n,w,N}$ problem. Denote the j-th column of $\boldsymbol{U}$ by $\boldsymbol{u}_j$. Define now $\boldsymbol{e} \in \mathbb{F}_{q^{mN}}^n$ by $\boldsymbol{e} = \sum_{j=1}^N \gamma_j \boldsymbol{u}_j$, where $(\gamma_1, \dots, \gamma_N)$ is some $\mathbb{F}_{q^m}$-basis of $\mathbb{F}_{q^{mN}}$. From the definition of the rank weight we have chosen over $\mathbb{F}_{q^{mN}}^n$, it is clear that the rank weight of $\boldsymbol{e}$ is less than or equal to w. The pair $(A, \sum_{j=1}^N \gamma_j \boldsymbol{Au}_j)$ is then an instance of the $\mathsf{RDPCSF}_{q,m,n,w,N}$ problem. It is now straightforward to check that we transform in this way a uniformly distributed instance of the $\mathsf{RSL}_{q,m,n,w,N}$ problem into a uniformly distributed instance of the $\mathsf{RDPCSF}_{q,m,n,w,N}$ problem. The aforementioned claim on the equivalence of the two problems follows immediately from this and the fact that when we know the space generated by the entries of the $\boldsymbol{u}_j$'s, we just have to solve a linear system to recover a solution of the decoding problem (this accounts for the additive polynomial overhead in the complexity).

Note that this reduction of the rank support learning problem to the problem of decoding a linear code over an extension field $\mathbb{F}_{q^{mN}}$ defined from a random parity-check matrix defined over the base field $\mathbb{F}_{q^m}$ works also for the Hamming metric : the support learning problem $\mathsf{SL}_{q,n,w,N}$ also reduces to decoding a linear code over an extension field $\mathbb{F}_{q^{mN}}$ defined from a random parity-check matrix defined over the base field $\mathbb{F}_{q^m}$ but this time for the Hamming metric over $\mathbb{F}^n_{q^{mN}}$. All these considerations point towards the same direction, namely that when N is not too large, the rank support learning problem should be a hard problem. It is for instance tempting to conjecture that this problem can not be solved q^N faster than decoding errors of rank weight w for an $[n, k]$ random linear code over $\mathbb{F}_{q^m}$. A similar conjecture could be made for the support learning problem.

5 Identity Based Encryption

Identity-based encryption schemes. An identity-based encryption (IBE) scheme is a tuple of algorithms $\mathsf{IBE} = (\mathsf{Setup}, \mathsf{KeyDer}, \mathsf{Enc}, \mathsf{Dec})$ providing the following functionality. The trusted authority runs Setup to generate a master key pair (mpk, msk). It publishes the master public key mpk and keeps the master secret key msk private. When a user with identity ID wishes to become part of the system, the trusted authority generates a user decryption key $d_{ID} \stackrel{\$}{\leftarrow} \mathsf{KeyDer}(msk, ID)$, and sends this key over a secure and authenticated channel to the user. To send an encrypted message m to the user with identity ID, the sender computes the ciphertext $C \stackrel{\$}{\leftarrow} \mathsf{Enc}(mpk, ID, m)$, which can be decrypted by the user as $m \leftarrow \mathsf{Dec}(d_{ID}, C)$. We refer to [10] for details on the security definitions for IBE schemes.

Security. We define the security of IBE schemes through a game with an adversary. In the first phase, the adversary is run on input of the master public key of a freshly generated key pair $(mpk, msk) \stackrel{\$}{\leftarrow} \mathsf{Setup}$. In a chosen-plaintext attack ($\mathsf{IND-CPA}$), the adversary is given access to a key derivation oracle $\mathcal{O}$ that on input an identity $ID \in \{0, 1\}^*$ returns $d_{ID} \stackrel{\$}{\leftarrow} \mathsf{KeyDer}(msk, ID)$. At the end of the first phase, the adversary outputs two equal-length challenge messages $m_0, m_1 \in \{0, 1\}^*$ and a challenge identity $ID \in \{0, 1\}^\star$. The adversary is given a challenge ciphertext $C \stackrel{\$}{\leftarrow} \mathsf{Enc}(mpk, ID, m_b)$ for a randomly chosen bit b, and is given access to the same oracle $\mathcal{O}$ as during the first phase of the attack. The second phase ends when the adversary outputs a bit b'. The adversary is said to win the $\mathsf{IND-CPA}$ game if $b' = b$ and if it never queried the key derivation oracle for the keys of any identity that matches the target identity.

Definition 9. *An* IBE *scheme is* $\mathsf{IND-CPA}$*-secure if any poly-time adversary* $\mathcal{A} = (\mathcal{A}_1, \mathcal{A}_2)$ *making at most a polynomial number of queries to the key derivation oracle, only has a negligible advantage in the* $\mathsf{IND-CPA}$ *game described above,* i.e., *the following advantage is negligible:*

$$2 \times \Pr\left[\begin{matrix}(mpk, msk) \stackrel{\$}{\leftarrow} \mathsf{Setup}, (ID, m_0, m_1, s) \leftarrow \mathcal{A}_1^{\mathcal{O}}(mpk), \\ b \stackrel{\$}{\leftarrow} \{0, 1\}, c = \mathsf{Enc}(mpk, ID, (m_b)) : \mathcal{A}_2^{\mathcal{O}}(m_0, m_1, s, c) = b\end{matrix}\right] - 1.$$

5.1 Trapdoor Functions from RankSign

We now adapt the RankSign system to construct a trapdoor function, which is sufficient to convert our PKE to an IBE. Associated to a matrix $\boldsymbol{A} \in \mathbb{F}_{q^m}^{(n-k)\times n}$, we define the function $f_{\boldsymbol{A}}$ as follows:

$$f_{\boldsymbol{A}} : \mathbb{F}_{q^m}^{n-k} \times \mathbb{F}_{q^m}^{n} \to \mathbb{F}_{q^m}^{n}$$
$$(\boldsymbol{s}, \boldsymbol{e}) \mapsto \boldsymbol{s}\boldsymbol{A} + \boldsymbol{e}$$

The matrix $\boldsymbol{A}$ will be generated with a trapdoor $\boldsymbol{T}$ such that $f_{\boldsymbol{A}}$ is a trapdoor function: from a random $\boldsymbol{p} \in \mathbb{F}_{q^m}^{n}$, with the trapdoor $\boldsymbol{T}$, one can sample $(\boldsymbol{s}, \boldsymbol{e}) = f_{\boldsymbol{A}}^{-1}(\boldsymbol{p})$ such that $\boldsymbol{e}$ is indistinguishable from a random element in W_r, the set of all the words of rank r and of length n, as defined in RankPKE. These properties will be sufficient for us to construct an IBE and reduce its security to the security of RankPKE. We now describe how we can get such a trapdoor function by relying on the RankSign system [28].

RankSign. RankSign is a signature scheme based on the rank metric. Like other signature schemes based on coding theory [16], RankSign needs a family of codes with an efficient decoding algorithm. It takes on input a random word of the syndrome space (obtained from the hash of the file we want to sign) and outputs a word of small weight with the given syndrome. This is an instance of the RSD problem, with the difference that the matrix $\boldsymbol{H}$ has a trapdoor which makes the problem easy. The public key is a description of the code which hides its structure and the secret key, on the contrary, reveals the structure of the code, which allows the signer to solve the RSD problem. RankSign does not compute a codeword of weight below the Gilbert-Varshamov bound, but instead a codeword of weight r between the Gilbert-Varshamov bound and the Singleton bound. The idea is to use a family of the augmented Low Rank Parity Check codes (denoted $LRPC^{+}$), and an adapted decoding algorithm (called the General Errors/Erasures Decoding algorithm) to produce such a codeword from any syndrome. The decoding algorithm is probabilistic and the parameters of the code have to be chosen precisely in order to have a probability of success very close to 1. We refer to [28] for a complete description of the decoding algorithm and the signature algorithm.

Definition 10 (Augmented Low Rank Parity Check Codes). *Let $\boldsymbol{H}$ be an $\mathbb{F}_{q^m}^{(n-k)\times n}$ homogeneous matrix of full-rank and of weight d and $\boldsymbol{R} \in \mathbb{F}_{q^m}^{(n-k)\times t}$ be a random matrix. Let $\boldsymbol{P} \in GL_{n-k}(\mathbb{F}_{q^m})$ and $\boldsymbol{Q} \in GL_{n+t}(\mathbb{F}_q)$ be two invertible matrices (remark that the coefficients of $\boldsymbol{Q}$ belong to the base field). Let $\boldsymbol{H}' = \boldsymbol{P}(\boldsymbol{R}|\boldsymbol{H})\boldsymbol{Q}$ be the parity-check matrix of a code $\mathcal{C}$ of type $[n+t, t+k]$. By definition, such a code is an $LRPC^{+}$ code. If $t = 0$, $\mathcal{C}$ is an LRPC code.*

The public key of RankSign is the matrix $\boldsymbol{H}'$, the secret key is the structured matrix $(\boldsymbol{R}|\boldsymbol{H})$ and the trapdoor is the pair of matrices $(\boldsymbol{P}, \boldsymbol{Q})$.

We can now describe the trapdoor function $f_{\boldsymbol{A}}^{-1}$. Let $\boldsymbol{p} \in \mathbb{F}_{q^m}^{n+t}$ and $\boldsymbol{H}'$ the public key of an instance of RankSign. We choose $\boldsymbol{A}$ as a generator matrix of a code with parity-check matrix $\boldsymbol{H}'$, i.e. as a full-rank matrix over $\mathbb{F}_{q^m}$ of size $(k+t) \times (n+t)$ which is such that $\boldsymbol{H}'\boldsymbol{A}^T = 0$. First, we compute $\boldsymbol{H}'\boldsymbol{p}$ and then we apply RankSign with trapdoor T to this syndrome to obtain a vector $\boldsymbol{e}$ of weight r such that $\boldsymbol{H}'\boldsymbol{p}^T = \boldsymbol{H}'\boldsymbol{e}^T$. Finally, we solve the linear system $\boldsymbol{s}\boldsymbol{A} = \boldsymbol{p} - \boldsymbol{e}$ of unknown $\boldsymbol{s}$ and the secret key associated to $\boldsymbol{p}$ is set to be $\boldsymbol{s}$. The security of the RankSign system is based on the assumption that $\boldsymbol{H}'$ is computationally indistinguishable from a random matrix.

Definition 11 (LRPC$^+$ **problem** [28]). *Given an augmented LRPC code, distinguish it from a random code with the same parameters.*

The hardness of this problem is studied in [28]. Currently the best attacks consist in recovering the structure of the LRPC by looking for small-weight words in the code, and the best algorithms for that are generic algorithms whose complexity is exponential [33].

Proposition 3. *Let $\boldsymbol{H}'$ be a public RankSign matrix and $\boldsymbol{A}$ be a generator matrix of the associated code. The two following distributions are computationally indistinguishable:*

Let $\mathcal{D}_0$ the distribution $(\boldsymbol{p}, \boldsymbol{s}, \boldsymbol{e})$ where $\boldsymbol{p} \xleftarrow{\$} \mathbb{F}_{q^m}^{n+t}$, $\boldsymbol{e} \in W_r$ is sampled from RingSign Algorithm such that $\boldsymbol{H}'\boldsymbol{e}^T = \boldsymbol{H}'\boldsymbol{p}^T$ and $\boldsymbol{s}$ is the solution of the linear system $\boldsymbol{x}\boldsymbol{A} = \boldsymbol{p} - \boldsymbol{e}$ of unknown $\boldsymbol{x}$.

Let $\mathcal{D}_1$ be the distribution $(\boldsymbol{p}', \boldsymbol{s}', \boldsymbol{e}')$ with $\boldsymbol{s}' \xleftarrow{\$} \mathbb{F}_{q^m}^{k+t}$, $\boldsymbol{e}' \xleftarrow{\$} W_r$ and $\boldsymbol{p}' = \boldsymbol{s}'\boldsymbol{A} + \boldsymbol{e}'$.

Precisely, the maximum advantage ϵ of the adversaries to distinguish $\mathcal{D}_0$ et $\mathcal{D}_1$ is bounded by: $\epsilon \leq \frac{2}{q} + \epsilon_{\mathsf{drsd}}$

Proof. Let $\mathcal{D}_2$ be the distribution $(\boldsymbol{s}, \boldsymbol{e})$ where $\boldsymbol{s} \xleftarrow{\$} \mathbb{F}_{q^m}^{n-k}$ and $\boldsymbol{e}$ is a signature of $\boldsymbol{s}$ by RankSign with the public key $\boldsymbol{H}'$ (*i.e.*, $\|\boldsymbol{e}\| = r$ and $\boldsymbol{H}'\boldsymbol{e}^T = \boldsymbol{s}$). Let $\mathcal{D}_3$ be the distribution $(\boldsymbol{H}'\boldsymbol{e}'^T, \boldsymbol{e}'^T)$ with $\boldsymbol{e}' \xleftarrow{\$} W_r$.

According to the proof of Theorem 2 of [28], a sample $(\boldsymbol{H}'\boldsymbol{e}'^T, \boldsymbol{e}'^T) \leftarrow \mathcal{D}_3$ is distributed exactly as $\mathcal{D}_2$ except if $(\boldsymbol{H}'\boldsymbol{e}'^T, \boldsymbol{e}'^T)$ is not T-decodable and the probability that the latter occurs is less than $\frac{2}{q}$. Therefore an adversary can not distinguish $\mathcal{D}_2$ from $\mathcal{D}_3$ with an advantage larger than $\frac{2}{q}$.

Now, we can prove the proposition. First, let us examine the distribution $\mathcal{D}_0$. Since $\boldsymbol{H}'$ is a linear map and $\boldsymbol{p} \xleftarrow{\$} \mathbb{F}_{q^m}^{n+t}$, $\boldsymbol{s} = \boldsymbol{H}'\boldsymbol{p}^T$ is uniformly distributed among $\mathbb{F}_{q^m}^{n-k}$. This implies $(\boldsymbol{\sigma}, \boldsymbol{e}) \leftarrow \mathcal{D}_2$. Moreover, $\boldsymbol{p} - \boldsymbol{e}$ is uniformly distributed among the words of the code generated by $\boldsymbol{A}$, hence $\boldsymbol{s} \xleftarrow{\$} \mathbb{F}_{q^m}^{k+t}$.

According to the indistinguishability of $\mathcal{D}_2$ and $\mathcal{D}_3$, the distribution of $\boldsymbol{e}'$ and $\boldsymbol{e}$ are computationally indistinguishable. $\boldsymbol{s}'$ and $\boldsymbol{s}$ are both uniformly distributed. Finally, based on the assumption that the DRSD problem is hard, $\boldsymbol{p}'$ and $\boldsymbol{p}$ are indistinguishable.

Summing up these two steps, the advantage of an adversary to distinguish $\mathcal{D}_0$ from $\mathcal{D}_1$ is bounded by $\frac{2}{q} + \epsilon_{\mathsf{drsd}}$. □

5.2 Scheme

Our IBE system uses a random oracle H which maps the identity into the public keys space $\mathbb{F}_{q^m}^{n+t}$ of our encryption scheme.

- IBE.Setup
  - choose the parameters (n, m, k, d, t) of the scheme according to RankSign. The secret master key is the triplet of matrices $\boldsymbol{P}, (\boldsymbol{R}|\boldsymbol{H})$ and $\boldsymbol{Q}$ such that $\boldsymbol{H}$ is a parity-check matrix of an $[n, k]$ LRPC code of weight d over $\mathbb{F}_{q^m}$, $\boldsymbol{R} \xleftarrow{\$} \mathbb{F}_{q^m}^{(n-k)\times t}$, $\boldsymbol{P} \xleftarrow{\$} GL_{n-k}(\mathbb{F}_{q^m})$ and $\boldsymbol{Q} \xleftarrow{\$} GL_{n+t}(\mathbb{F}_q)$. Let $\boldsymbol{A}$ be a full rank $(k + t) \times (n + t)$ matrix over $\mathbb{F}_{q^m}$ such $\boldsymbol{H}'\boldsymbol{A}^T = 0$ with $\boldsymbol{H}' = \boldsymbol{P}(\boldsymbol{R}|\boldsymbol{H})\boldsymbol{Q}$ and the trapdoor $\boldsymbol{T}$ is $(\boldsymbol{P}, \boldsymbol{Q})$.
  - define $\boldsymbol{G} \in \mathbb{F}_{q^m}^{k'\times n'}$ to be a generator matrix of a public code $\mathcal{C}'$ which can decode (efficiently) errors of weight up to wr as in RankPKE.KeyGen.
  - return $mpk = (\boldsymbol{A}, \boldsymbol{G})$ and $msk = \boldsymbol{T}$
- IBE.KeyDer($\boldsymbol{A}, \boldsymbol{T}, id$) :
  - compute $\boldsymbol{p} = H(id)$
  - compute $(\boldsymbol{s}, \boldsymbol{e}) = f_{\boldsymbol{A}}^{-1}(\boldsymbol{p})$ by using the trapdoor $\boldsymbol{T}$
  - store $(id, \boldsymbol{s})$ and return $\boldsymbol{s}$
- IBE.Enc($id, \boldsymbol{m}$) :
  - compute $\boldsymbol{p} = H(id)$
  - return $\boldsymbol{c} =$ RankPKE.Enc($(\boldsymbol{A}, \boldsymbol{p}, \boldsymbol{G}), \boldsymbol{m}$)
- IBE.Dec($\boldsymbol{s}, \boldsymbol{c}$) : return RankPKE.Dec($\boldsymbol{s}, \boldsymbol{c}$).

5.3 Security

We now state the security of the IBE system.

Theorem 4. *Under the assumption that the* LRPC$^+$ *problem is hard and the* RankPKE *is secure, the* IBE *system described above is* IND − CPA*-secure in the random oracle model:*[1]

$$\epsilon_{\mathsf{ibe}} \leq \frac{2q_H}{q} + \epsilon_{\mathsf{lrpc^+}} + q_H(\epsilon_{\mathsf{drsd}} + \epsilon_{\mathsf{pke}})$$

where $\epsilon_{\mathsf{lrpc^+}}, \epsilon_{\mathsf{pke}}, \epsilon_{\mathsf{ibe}}$ *are respectively the bound on the advantage of the attacks against the* LRPC$^+$ *problem, the* RankPKE *system and the* IBE *system, and* q_H *is the maximum number of distinct hash queries to* H *that an adversary can make.*

[1] As in the lattice-based IBE scheme of Gentry, Peikert, and Vaikuntanathan [31], we lose a factor q_H in the reduction from PKE to IBE. Moreover, because of the lack of a statistical indistinguishability in the preimage sampling as in [31], we also lose an additional cost of $\frac{2q_H}{q} + q_H\epsilon_{\mathsf{drsd}}$ which require us to use a large q. Fortunately, the efficiency of our scheme is $\mathcal{O}(\log q)$.

Proof. We proceed by a sequence of games.

Game $\mathbf{G}_0$: This is the real IND-CPA attack game. The IBE.Setup is run and then, a 2-stage poly-time adversary $\mathcal{A} = (\mathcal{A}_1, \mathcal{A}_2)$ is fed with the public key $mpk = (\boldsymbol{A}, \boldsymbol{G})$. $\mathcal{A}_1$ can ask queries to H and key queries. Then, $\mathcal{A}_1$ outputs a challenge identity $id^\star$, which is different from the key queries $\mathcal{A}_1$ already asked, and a pair of messages $(\boldsymbol{m}_0, \boldsymbol{m}_1)$. Next a challenge ciphertext is produced by flipping a coin b and producing a ciphertext $c^\star = \mathsf{IBE.Enc}(id^\star, \boldsymbol{m}_b)$.

On input $c^\star$, $\mathcal{A}_2$ can continue to ask queries to H and key queries which are different from $id^\star$, and finally outputs bit b'. We denote by S_0 the event $b' = b$ and use the same notation S_n in any game $\mathbf{G}_n$ below.

$$\mathsf{Adv}^{\text{ind-cpa}}_{\mathsf{IBE}}(\mathcal{A}) =\mid 2\Pr[\mathsf{S}_0] - 1 \mid$$

We assume without loss of generality that, for any identity id that $\mathcal{A}$ wants to corrupt, $\mathcal{A}$ already queried H on id. In particular, we can assume that $\mathcal{A}$ will query the challenge identity $id^\star$ to H.

As this is the real attack game, for a key query on an identity id, the $\mathsf{IBE.KeyDer}(\boldsymbol{A}, \boldsymbol{T}, id)$ is run and the secret key is given to $\mathcal{A}$. We recall this algorithm:

- compute $\boldsymbol{p} = H(id)$
- compute $(\boldsymbol{s}, \boldsymbol{e}) = f_{\boldsymbol{A}}^{-1}(\boldsymbol{p})$ by using the trapdoor $\boldsymbol{T}$:
  - compute $\boldsymbol{H}'\boldsymbol{p}$ and then we apply RankSign with trapdoor $\boldsymbol{T}$ to this syndrome to obtain a vector $\boldsymbol{e}$ of weight r such that $\boldsymbol{H}'\boldsymbol{p} = \boldsymbol{H}'\boldsymbol{e}$.
  - solve the linear system $\boldsymbol{s}\boldsymbol{A} = \boldsymbol{p} - \boldsymbol{e}$ of unknown $\boldsymbol{s}$ and the secret key associated to $\boldsymbol{p}$ is set to be $\boldsymbol{s}$.
- store $(id, \boldsymbol{s})$ and return $\boldsymbol{s}$.

Game $\mathbf{G}_1$: In this game, we modify the answers to the key queries so that it does not require the trapdoor $\boldsymbol{T}$ anymore. In order to make the answers coherent, we also need to simulate the queries to the hash queries to H. We maintain a list List_H, initially set to empty, to store the tuples $(id, \boldsymbol{p}, \boldsymbol{s})$ where $\boldsymbol{p}$ is the value that we respond to the H query on id, and $\boldsymbol{s}$ is the secret key which corresponds to the public key $\boldsymbol{p}$ we generate. The simulation is given in the following way:

- Hash queries: on $\mathcal{A}$'s jth distinct query id_j to H:
  - randomly choose a vector $\boldsymbol{e}_j$ of weight r
  - randomly choose $\boldsymbol{s}_j$
  - define $\boldsymbol{p}_j = H(id) = \boldsymbol{s}_j\boldsymbol{A} + \boldsymbol{e}_j$
  - add the tuple $(id_j, \boldsymbol{p}_j, \boldsymbol{s}_j)$ to List_H and return $\boldsymbol{p}_j$ to $\mathcal{A}$.
- Secret key queries: when $\mathcal{A}$ asks for a secret key for the identity id, we retrieve the tuple $(id, \boldsymbol{p}, \boldsymbol{s})$ from the List_H and return $\boldsymbol{s}$ to $\mathcal{A}$.

Now, looking back at the Proposition 3, we remark that the set of q_H samples $(\boldsymbol{p}_j, \boldsymbol{s}_j, \boldsymbol{e}_j)$ in the previous game come from the distribution $\mathcal{D}_0^{q_H}$ and the set of q_H samples $(\boldsymbol{p}_j, \boldsymbol{s}_j, \boldsymbol{e}_j)$ in this game come from the distribution $\mathcal{D}_1^{q_H}$. We thus have:

$$|\Pr[\mathsf{S}_1] - \Pr[\mathsf{S}_0]| \leq \frac{2q_H}{q} + q_H\epsilon_{\mathsf{drsd}}$$

Game $\mathbf{G}_2$: As the objective is to reduce the security of the IBE to the security of RankPKE, in this game, we define the matrix $\boldsymbol{A}$ to be a random matrix as in the RankPKE. Because the simulation in the previous game does not use the trapdoor $\boldsymbol{T}$, we can keep the simulation for hash queries and key queries exactly unchanged. By the assumption that the LRPC$^+$ problem is hard, this game is indistinguishable from the previous game:

$$|\Pr[\mathsf{S}_2] - \Pr[\mathsf{S}_1]| \leq \epsilon_{\mathsf{lrpc}^+}$$

Game $\mathbf{G}_3$: We can now reduce the security of the IBE in the previous game to the security of RankPKE. We are given the public key $\boldsymbol{p}^\star$ of RankPKE and try to break the semantic security of RankPKE. Intuitively, we proceed as follows. We will try to embed the given public key $\boldsymbol{p}^\star$ of RankPKE to $H(id^\star)$. The IBE for $id^\star$ becomes thus a RankPKE with the same distribution of public keys. We can then use the given challenge ciphertext of RankPKE as the challenge ciphertext to $\mathcal{A}$ and whenever $\mathcal{A}$ can break IBE, we can break RankPKE. The difficulty in this strategy is that we should correctly guess the challenge identity $id^\star$. In a selective game where $\mathcal{A}$ has to announce $id^\star$ at the beginning of the game, we know this identity. However, in the adaptive game that we consider, we need make a guess on the challenge identity among all the identities queried to H. This explains why we lose a factor q_H in the advantage to attack RankPKE.

Now, formally, on input a random matrix $\boldsymbol{A}$ and a public key $\boldsymbol{p}^\star$ for the RankPKE, we choose an index i among $1, \ldots q_H$ uniformly at random and change the answer for the ith query to H and for the challenge as follows:

- Hash queries: on $\mathcal{A}$'s jth distinct query id_j to H: if $j = i$, then add the tuple $(id_j, \boldsymbol{p}^\star, \perp)$ to List_H and return $\boldsymbol{p}^\star$ to $\mathcal{A}$. Otherwise for $j \neq i$, do the same as in the previous game.
- Secret key queries: when $\mathcal{A}$ asks for a secret key for the identity id, retrieve the tuple $(id, \boldsymbol{p}, \boldsymbol{s})$ from the List_H. If $\boldsymbol{s} \neq \perp$, return $\boldsymbol{s}$ to $\mathcal{A}$, otherwise output a random bit and abort.
- Challenge ciphertext: when $\mathcal{A}$ submits a challenge identity $id^\star$, different from all its secret key queries, and two messages m_0, m_1, if $id^\star = id_i$, i.e., $(id^\star, \boldsymbol{p}^\star, \perp) \notin \mathsf{List}_H$, then output a random bit and abort. Otherwise, we also submits the messages m_0, m_1 to the challenger and receive a challenge ciphertext $c^\star$. We return then $c^\star$ to $\mathcal{A}$.

When $\mathcal{A}$ terminates and returns a bit b, we also outputs b. We now analyze the advantage to break RankPKE:

- We do not abort if we made a good guess, *i.e,* $id^\star = id_i$. As i is perfectly hidden from $\mathcal{A}$, the probability that we do not abort is $\frac{1}{q_H}$.

- Conditioned on not aborting, the view we provides to $\mathcal{A}$ is exactly the same as in the previous game. We get thus the same advantage in attacking RankPKE as $\mathcal{A}$'s advantage in attacking IBE

We finally have:

$$| 2\Pr[\mathsf{S}_3] - 1 | \leq q_H \epsilon_{\mathsf{pke}}$$

6 Parameters

In this section, we explain how to construct a set of parameters and give an analysis of the best known attacks against the IBE scheme.

6.1 General Parameters for RankSign and RankEnc

First, we have to carefully choose the parameters of the algorithm RankSign [28] used for the presampling phase. In the case where only RankPKE is used, the constraints are much weaker. Remember that RankSign is a probabilistic signature algorithm and the probability of returning a valid signature depends on the choice of the parameters. These parameters are:
- q, m : the cardinality of the base field and the degree of the extension field.
- n : the length of the hidden LRPC code used to sign.
- t : the number of random columns added to the LRPC to hide it.
- k, d : the dimension of the LRPC code and the weight of the LRPC code.
- r : the weight of the signature.

The conditions these parameters must verify are [28]

$$n = d(n-k), (r-t)(m-r) + (n-k)(rd-m) = 0, \; r = t + \frac{n-k}{d}$$

Let us explain the choice of our parameters. First we need to fix d for two reasons:

- if we look at the three conditions, they are homogeneous if d is constant. Thus, we can make other set of parameters from one set by multiply all the parameters (except for d) by a constant.
- d is the weight of the $LRPC^+$ code used for the public master key. It is very important to choose d not too small to ensure the security of the public master key.

Once d is fixed, we can easily test all the valid parameters and choose the most interesting ones, whether we need to optimize the security or the key size.

Then we need to choose the parameters of RankPKE. We need a code which can correct wr errors, where w is the weight of the matrix $\boldsymbol{U}$. We use (n', k', t')-simple codes because because they can asymptotically decode up to d_{GV} errors. In all cases, we have chosen $n' = m$ for simplicity, even if this is not a necessary condition.

Let us describe the size of the keys and of the messages, as well as the computation time of our cryptosystem:

- public master key $\boldsymbol{A}$ is a $(k+t) \times (n+t)$ matrix over $\mathbb{F}_{q^m}$: $(k+t)(n-k)m\lceil \log_2 q \rceil$ bits (under systematic form).
- public key $\boldsymbol{p}_{id}$ is an element of $\mathbb{F}_{q^m}^{n+t}$: $(n+t)m\lceil \log_2 q \rceil$ bits.
- secrete key $\boldsymbol{s}_{id}$ is an element of $\mathbb{F}_{q^m}^{n-k}$: $(n-k)m\lceil \log_2 q \rceil$ bits.
- plaintext $\boldsymbol{m}$ is an element of $\mathbb{F}_{q^m}^{k'}$: $k'm\lceil \log_2 q \rceil$ bits.
- ciphertext is a $(k+t+1) \times n'$ matrix over $\mathbb{F}_{q^m}$: $(k+t+1)n'm\lceil \log_2 q \rceil$ bits.
- to generate the secret key, we need to invert a syndrome with RankSign which takes $(n-k)(n+t)$ multiplications in $\mathbb{F}_{q^m}$ [28].
- encryption consists in a multiplication of two matrices of respective sizes $(k+t+1) \times (n+t)$ and $(n+t) \times n'$, which takes $(k+t+1)(n+t)n'$ multiplications in $\mathbb{F}_{q^m}$.
- decryption consists in a multiplication matrix-vector and the decoding of an error of weight wr with a (n', k', t')-simple code, which takes $(k+t+1)n'$ multiplications in $\mathbb{F}_{q^m}$ and $\mathcal{O}\big(((n'-t')wr)^3\big)$ operations in $\mathbb{F}_q$.

A multiplication in $\mathbb{F}_{q^m}$ costs $\tilde{\mathcal{O}}(m \log q)$ operations in $\mathbb{F}_2$ [45].

6.2 Practical Evaluation of the Security

In order to analyze the security of the IBE, we recall the result of the Theorem 4: $\epsilon_{\mathsf{ibe}} \leq \frac{2q_H}{q} + \epsilon_{\mathsf{lrpc^+}} + q_H(\epsilon_{\mathsf{drsd}} + \epsilon_{\mathsf{pke}})$. We want $\epsilon_{\mathsf{ibe}} \leqslant 2^{-\lambda}$, where λ is the security parameter. Since the first term only depends on q and on the number of queries, we need $q > q_H 2^{\lambda+1}$. We stress that the size of the data and the computation time are linear in the logarithm of q. In consequence, it is not a problem to have q exponential in the security parameter. Moreover, since all combinatorial attacks are polynomial in q, they are utterly inefficient to break the IBE.

The second type of attacks are the algebraic attacks. An adversary can either attack the public master key $\boldsymbol{A}$ by solving an instance of $\mathsf{LRPC^+}$ problem, a public key $\boldsymbol{p}$ of an user by solving an instance of DRSD or a ciphertext by solving an instance of RSL. By using the results in [6], we can estimate the complexity of the attacks and adapt the parameters in consequence.

We give an example of a set of parameters in the following table. We take the standard values $\lambda = 128$ for the security parameter and $q_H = 2^{60}$.

n	$n-k$	m	q	d	t	r	d_{GV}	d_{Sing}	Public master key Size (Bytes)	n'	k'	t'	w	Probability of failure
100	20	96	2^{192}	5	12	16	11	20	4,239,360	96	9	66	4	2^{-576}

The decoding algorithm for the simple codes is probabilistic, that is why there is a probability p_f that the decoding fails. However, $p_f \approx \frac{1}{q^{t'-wr+1}}$, since we have a very large q in this example, p_f is negligible. These parameters are large but still tractable, for a first code-based IBE scheme in post-quantum cryptography.

Acknowledgements. This work has been supported in part by the French ANR projects ALAMBIC (ANR-16-CE39-0006) and ID-FIX (ANR-16-CE39-0004). The work of Adrien Hauteville and Jean-Pierre Tillich was also supported in part by the European Commission through the ICT programme under contract H2020- ICT-2014-1 645622 PQCRYPTO. The authors would also like to thank warmly the reviewers for their insightful remarks (and especially the last reviewer for his remarks and his very detailed review that helped a lot to improve the editorial quality of this paper).

References

1. Agrawal, S., Boneh, D., Boyen, X.: Efficient lattice (H)IBE in the standard model. In: Gilbert, H. (ed.) EUROCRYPT 2010. LNCS, vol. 6110, pp. 553–572. Springer, Heidelberg (2010). doi:10.1007/978-3-642-13190-5_28
2. Alekhnovich, M.: More on average case vs approximation complexity. Comput. Complex. **20**(4), 755–786 (2011)
3. Applebaum, B.: Cryptography with constant input locality. Cryptography in Constant Parallel Time. ISC, pp. 147–185. Springer, Heidelberg (2014). doi:10.1007/978-3-642-17367-7_8
4. Barreto, P.S.L.M., Misoczki, R., Simplicio Jr., M.A.: One-time signature scheme from syndrome decoding over generic error-correcting codes. J. Syst. Softw. **84**(2), 198–204 (2011)
5. Berlekamp, E., McEliece, R., van Tilborg, H.: On the inherent intractability of certain coding problems. IEEE Trans. Inform. Theory **24**(3), 384–386 (1978)
6. Bettale, L.: Cryptanalyse algébrique : outils et applications. PhD thesis, Université Pierre et Marie Curie - Paris 6 (2012)
7. Boneh, D.: The decision Diffie-Hellman problem. In: Buhler, J.P. (ed.) ANTS 1998. LNCS, vol. 1423, pp. 48–63. Springer, Heidelberg (1998). doi:10.1007/BFb0054851
8. Boneh, D., Boyen, X.: Efficient selective-ID secure identity-based encryption without random oracles. In: Cachin, C., Camenisch, J.L. (eds.) EUROCRYPT 2004. LNCS, vol. 3027, pp. 223–238. Springer, Heidelberg (2004). doi:10.1007/978-3-540-24676-3_14
9. Boneh, D., Boyen, X.: Secure identity based encryption without random oracles. In: Franklin, M. (ed.) CRYPTO 2004. LNCS, vol. 3152, pp. 443–459. Springer, Heidelberg (2004). doi:10.1007/978-3-540-28628-8_27
10. Boneh, D., Franklin, M.: Identity-based encryption from the weil pairing. In: Kilian, J. (ed.) CRYPTO 2001. LNCS, vol. 2139, pp. 213–229. Springer, Heidelberg (2001). doi:10.1007/3-540-44647-8_13
11. Boyen, X.: Lattice mixing and vanishing trapdoors: a framework for fully secure short signatures and more. In: Nguyen, P.Q., Pointcheval, D. (eds.) PKC 2010. LNCS, vol. 6056, pp. 499–517. Springer, Heidelberg (2010). doi:10.1007/978-3-642-13013-7_29
12. Canetti, R., Halevi, S., Katz, J.: A forward-secure public-key encryption scheme. J. Cryptol. **20**(3), 265–294 (2007)
13. Cash, D., Hofheinz, D., Kiltz, E., Peikert, C.: Bonsai trees, or how to delegate a lattice basis. In: Gilbert, H. (ed.) EUROCRYPT 2010. LNCS, vol. 6110, pp. 523–552. Springer, Heidelberg (2010). doi:10.1007/978-3-642-13190-5_27
14. Cayrel, P.-L., Otmani, A., Vergnaud, D.: On kabatianskii-krouk-smeets signatures. In: Carlet, C., Sunar, B. (eds.) WAIFI 2007. LNCS, vol. 4547, pp. 237–251. Springer, Heidelberg (2007). doi:10.1007/978-3-540-73074-3_18

15. Cocks, C.: An identity based encryption scheme based on quadratic residues. In: Honary, B. (ed.) Cryptography and Coding 2001. LNCS, vol. 2260, pp. 360–363. Springer, Heidelberg (2001). doi:10.1007/3-540-45325-3_32
16. Courtois, N.T., Finiasz, M., Sendrier, N.: How to achieve a mceliece-based digital signature scheme. In: Boyd, C. (ed.) ASIACRYPT 2001. LNCS, vol. 2248, pp. 157–174. Springer, Heidelberg (2001). doi:10.1007/3-540-45682-1_10
17. Diffie, W., Hellman, M.: New directions in cryptography. IEEE Trans. Inf. Theory **22**(6), 644–654 (1976)
18. ElGamal, T.: A public key cryptosystem and a signature scheme based on discrete logarithms. In: Blakley, G.R., Chaum, D. (eds.) CRYPTO 1984. LNCS, vol. 196, pp. 10–18. Springer, Heidelberg (1985). doi:10.1007/3-540-39568-7_2
19. Faugère, J.-C., El Din, M.S., Spaenlehauer, P.-J.: Computing loci of rank defects of linear matrices using gröbner bases and applications to cryptology. In: Proceedings of the ISSAC 2010, pp. 257–264 (2010)
20. Faugère, J.-C., Levy-dit-Vehel, F., Perret, L.: Cryptanalysis of minrank. In: Wagner, D. (ed.) CRYPTO 2008. LNCS, vol. 5157, pp. 280–296. Springer, Heidelberg (2008). doi:10.1007/978-3-540-85174-5_16
21. Ernest Mukhamedovich Gabidulin: Theory of codes with maximum rank distance. Problemy Peredachi Informatsii **21**(1), 3–16 (1985)
22. Gabidulin, E.M., Paramonov, A.V., Tretjakov, O.V.: Ideals over a non-commutative ring and their application in cryptology. In: Davies, D.W. (ed.) EUROCRYPT 1991. LNCS, vol. 547, pp. 482–489. Springer, Heidelberg (1991). doi:10.1007/3-540-46416-6_41
23. Gaborit, P.: Shorter keys for code based cryptography. In: Proceedings of the 2005 International Workshop on Coding and Cryptography (WCC 2005), Bergen, Norway, pp. 81–91, March 2005
24. Gaborit, P., Hauteville, A., Tillich, J.-P.: RankSynd a PRNG based on rank metric. In: Takagi, T. (ed.) PQCrypto 2016. LNCS, vol. 9606, pp. 18–28. Springer, Cham (2016). doi:10.1007/978-3-319-29360-8_2
25. Gaborit, P., Murat, G., Ruatta, O., Zémor, G.: Low rank parity check codes and their application to cryptography. In: Proceedings of the Workshop on Coding and Cryptography WCC 2013, Bergen, Norway (2013). www.selmer.uib.no/WCC2013/pdfs/Gaborit.pdf
26. Gaborit, P., Phan, D.H., Hauteville, A., Tillich, J.-P.: Identity-based encryption from codes with rank metric, full version (2017). Available on ePrint. http://eprint.iacr.org/2017/623
27. Gaborit, P., Ruatta, O., Schrek, J.: On the complexity of the rank syndrome decoding problem. IEEE Trans. Inf. Theory **62**(2), 1006–1019 (2016)
28. Gaborit, P., Ruatta, O., Schrek, J., Zémor, G.: RankSign: an efficient signature algorithm based on the rank metric. In: Mosca, M. (ed.) PQCrypto 2014. LNCS, vol. 8772, pp. 88–107. Springer, Cham (2014). doi:10.1007/978-3-319-11659-4_6
29. Gaborit, P., Zémor, G.: On the hardness of the decoding and the minimum distance problems for rank codes. IEEE Trans. Inf. Theory **62**(12), 7245–7252 (2016)
30. Gentry, C.: Practical identity-based encryption without random oracles. In: Vaudenay, S. (ed.) EUROCRYPT 2006. LNCS, vol. 4004, pp. 445–464. Springer, Heidelberg (2006). doi:10.1007/11761679_27
31. Gentry, C., Peikert, C., Vaikuntanathan, V.: Trapdoors for hard lattices and new cryptographic constructions. In: Ladner, R.E., Dwork, C. (eds.) 40th ACM STOC, pp. 197–206. ACM Press, May 2008
32. Goldwasser, S., Micali, S.: Probabilistic encryption. J. Comput. Syst. Sci. **28**(2), 270–299 (1984)

33. Hauteville, A., Tillich, J.-P.: New algorithms for decoding in the rank metric and an attack on the LRPC cryptosystem (2015). arXiv:abs/1504.05431
34. Kabatianskii, G., Krouk, E., Smeets, B.: A digital signature scheme based on random error-correcting codes. In: Darnell, M. (ed.) Cryptography and Coding 1997. LNCS, vol. 1355, pp. 161–167. Springer, Heidelberg (1997). doi:10.1007/BFb0024461
35. Kabatianskii, G., Krouk, E., Smeets, B.J.M.: Error Correcting Coding and Security for Data Networks: Analysis of the Superchannel Concept. Wiley, Hoboken (2005)
36. Lévy-dit Vehel, F., Perret, L.: Algebraic decoding of codes in rank metric. In: Proceedings of YACC 2006, Porquerolles, France, June 2006. http://grim.univ-tln.fr/YACC06/abstracts-yacc06.pdf
37. Loidreau, P.: Properties of codes in rank metric (2006)
38. Misoczki, R., Tillich, J.-P., Sendrier, N., Barreto, P.S.L.M.: MDPC-McEliece: New McEliece variants from moderate density parity-check codes. IACR Cryptology ePrint Archive, Report 2012/409 (2012)
39. Niederreiter, H.: Knapsack-type cryptosystems and algebraic coding theory. Prob. Control Inf. Theory **15**(2), 159–166 (1986)
40. Otmani, A., Tillich, J.-P.: An efficient attack on all concrete KKS proposals. In: Yang, B.-Y. (ed.) PQCrypto 2011. LNCS, vol. 7071, pp. 98–116. Springer, Heidelberg (2011). doi:10.1007/978-3-642-25405-5_7
41. Regev, O.: On lattices, learning with errors, random linear codes, and cryptography. In: Gabow, H.N., Fagin, R. (eds.) 37th ACM STOC, pp. 84–93. ACM Press, May 2005
42. Sakai, R., Ohgishi, K., Kasahara, M.: Cryptosystems based on pairing. In: SCIS 2000, Okinawa, Japan, January 2000
43. Shamir, A.: Identity-based cryptosystems and signature schemes. In: Blakley, G.R., Chaum, D. (eds.) CRYPTO 1984. LNCS, vol. 196, pp. 47–53. Springer, Heidelberg (1985). doi:10.1007/3-540-39568-7_5
44. Silva, D., Kschischang, F.R., Kötter, R.: Communication over finite-field matrix channels. IEEE Trans. Inf. Theory **56**(3), 1296–1305 (2010)
45. von zur Gathen, J., Gerhard, J.: Modern Computer Algebra. Cambridge University Press, New York (2003)
46. Waters, B.: Dual system encryption: realizing fully secure IBE and HIBE under simple assumptions. In: Halevi, S. (ed.) CRYPTO 2009. LNCS, vol. 5677, pp. 619–636. Springer, Heidelberg (2009). doi:10.1007/978-3-642-03356-8_36
47. Waters, B.: Efficient identity-based encryption without random oracles. In: Cramer, R. (ed.) EUROCRYPT 2005. LNCS, vol. 3494, pp. 114–127. Springer, Heidelberg (2005). doi:10.1007/11426639_7

Stream Ciphers

Degree Evaluation of NFSR-Based Cryptosystems

Meicheng Liu(✉)

State Key Laboratory of Information Security, Institute of Information Engineering, Chinese Academy of Sciences, Beijing 100093, People's Republic of China
meicheng.liu@gmail.com

Abstract. In this paper, we study the security of NFSR-based cryptosystems from the algebraic degree point of view. We first present a general framework of iterative estimation of algebraic degree for NFSR-based cryptosystems, by exploiting a new technique, called *numeric mapping*. Then based on this general framework we propose a concrete and efficient algorithm to find an upper bound on the algebraic degree for Trivium-like ciphers. Our algorithm has linear time complexity and needs a negligible amount of memory. As illustrations, we apply it to Trivium, Kreyvium and TriviA-SC, and reveal various upper bounds on the algebraic degree of these ciphers by setting different input variables. By this algorithm, we can make use of a cube with any size in cube testers, which is generally believed to be infeasible for an NFSR-based cryptosystem before. Due to the high efficiency of our algorithm, we can exhaust a large set of the cubes with large size. As such, we obtain the best known distinguishing attacks on reduced Trivium and TriviA-SC as well as the first cryptanalysis of Kreyvium. Our experiments on Trivium show that our algorithm is not only efficient in computation but also accurate in estimation of attacked rounds. The best cubes we have found for Kreyvium and TriviA-SC are both of size larger than 60. To the best of our knowledge, our tool is the first formalized and systematic one for finding an upper bound on the algebraic degree of an NFSR-based cryptosystem, and this is the first time that a cube of size beyond practical computations can be used in cryptanalysis of an NFSR-based cryptosystem. It is also potentially useful in the future applications to key recovery attacks and more cryptographic primitives.

Keywords: Nonlinear feedback shift register · Stream cipher · Distinguishing attack · Cube tester · Trivium · Kreyvium · TriviA-SC

1 Introduction

A nonlinear feedback shift register (NFSR) is a common component in modern cryptographic primitives, especially in radio-frequency identification devices

This work was supported by the National Natural Science Foundation of China (Grant Nos. 61672516, 61303258 and 61379139) and the Strategic Priority Research Program of the Chinese Academy of Sciences under Grant XDA06010701.

J. Katz and H. Shacham (Eds.): CRYPTO 2017, Part III, LNCS 10403, pp. 227–249, 2017.
DOI: 10.1007/978-3-319-63697-9_8

(RFID) and wireless sensor networks applications. NFSRs are known to be more resistant to cryptanalytic attacks than linear feedback shift registers (LFSRs). Built on NFSRs are many well known lightweight cryptographic algorithms, including the stream ciphers Trivium [8,10] and Grain [1,27,28] that have been selected in the final eSTREAM portfolio of hardware-oriented stream ciphers, the authenticated cipher ACORN [44] that has been selected as one of the third-round candidates in the CAESAR competition, the block cipher family KATAN/KTANTAN [9], and the hash function Quark [4,5]. Among them, Trivium has attracted the most attention for its simplicity and performance, while it shows remarkable resistance to cryptanalysis. Inspired by the design of Trivium, a number of various cryptographic algorithms have been successively developed, for instance the block cipher family KATAN/KTANTAN, the authenticated cipher ACORN and the stream ciphers Kreyvium [11] and TriviA-SC [13].

Most cryptographic primitives, including NFSR-based cryptosystems, can be described by tweakable Boolean functions, which contain both secret variables (*e.g.*, key bits) and public variables (*e.g.*, plaintext bits or IV bits). The algebraic degree of these Boolean functions plays an important role in the security of the corresponding primitives. In fact, a cryptographic primitive with low algebraic degree is vulnerable to many known attacks, such as higher order differential attacks [30,32,35], algebraic attacks [15–18], cube attacks [19–22], and integral attacks [31].

For NFSR-based cryptosystems, cube attacks and higher order differential attacks are the most powerful cryptanalytic tools among the known attacks. The best known key recovery attacks faster than an exhaustive search on Trivium are cube attacks on its variant when the initialization is reduced to 799 rounds out of 1152 [21,26], and the best known distinguishing attacks on Trivium are reduced to 839 rounds derived by cube testers [3,33]. Note that here are not included the possible key recovery attacks with unknown probability, such as [41], or the attacks for a small percentage of weak keys, such as [29]. The weaknesses in the cipher Grain-128 against cube testers [2,39] partially leads to the design of Grain-128a [1]. Actually, the full Grain-128 was broken in theory by dynamic cube attacks [19,22]. All of these attacks exploit low-degree relations of the tweakable Boolean functions formed by the cryptosystems, that is, low-degree relations between the IV bits and keystream bits.

It is difficult to compute the exact value of the algebraic degree for modern cryptographic primitives. After the development of cryptanalysis in the past three decades, several theoretical tools have been developed to estimate the upper bound on the algebraic degree of iterated permutations, and concurrently exploited to attack iterated ciphers [6,7,12,40].

Yet for NFSR, there are few tools for estimating its algebraic degree, besides symbolic computation and statistical analysis. The known techniques highly depends on computational capabilities, and the cryptanalytic results are limited by existing computational resources. For instance, thus far the cubes with size larger than 54 have never been utilized in cryptanalysis of an NFSR-based cryptosystem, in either cube attacks or cube testers. To gain better attacks, the cryptanalysts have to utilize extremely the computational resources, *e.g.*, using dedicated reconfigurable hardware [19]. This usually requires high financial cost or high energy consumption. While dynamic cube attacks [19,22] can reach much higher attack complexity, they are still limited by the size of the cubes.

1.1 Our Contributions

In this paper, we devote our attention to evaluating the algebraic degree of NFSR-based cryptosystems. For the conquest of the existing limitation as mentioned above, we exploit a new technique, called *numeric mapping*, to iteratively estimate the upper bound on the algebraic degree of the internal states of an NFSR. Based on this new tool, we develop an algorithm for estimating the algebraic degree of NFSR-based cryptosystems.

As an illustration, we refine and apply our algorithm to Trivium-like ciphers, including Trivium, Kreyvium and TriviA-SC. Trivium uses an 80-bit key and an 80-bit IV, while Kreyvium and TriviA-SC both use a 128-bit key and a 128-bit IV. These three ciphers all have 1152 rounds of initialization. Our refined algorithm gives an upper bound on the algebraic degree of a Trivium-like cipher over a given set of input variables with any size, *e.g.*, all the key and IV bits, all or part of the IV bits. It has linear time complexity in the number of initialization rounds, and needs a negligible amount of memory. In other words, it is almost as fast as the cipher (up to at most a factor of some constant). Further, by this algorithm we perform several experiments on round-reduced Trivium, Kreyvium and TriviA-SC, and obtain various upper bounds on the algebraic degree by setting different input variables. As a result, we confirm that the maximum numbers of initialization rounds of Trivium, Kreyvium and TriviA-SC such that the generated keystream bit does not achieve maximum algebraic degree are at least 907, 982 and 1121 (out of the full 1152 rounds) respectively when taking all the key and IV bits as input variables; these numbers of rounds turn out to be 793, 862 and 987 while taking all the IV bits as input variables.

We further apply our algorithm to take advantage of the cubes with large size in cube testers, which is considered to be impossible for an NFSR-based cryptosystem in the literatures. In the experiments, we set the key bits as symbolic constants, *i.e.*, the algebraic degree of any key bit is considered to be 0 on the cube variables. This is consistent with a distinguisher in the setting of unknown key. Since our algorithm is very fast, we can exhaust all the cubes of size $37 \leq n \leq 40$ that contain no adjacent indexes for Trivium in a dozen minutes on a common PC. The total amount of such cubes is about 2^{25}. Before this paper, it needs around $c2^{62}$ cipher operations to test all those cubes, and the confidence of the test depends on c; while our algorithm is deterministic. We then find a cube of size 37 over which the algebraic degree of the keystream bit of 837-round Trivium is strictly less than 37. We also verify this result by performing experiments on 100 random keys. The minimum number of rounds that the sum over this cube, called superpoly in cube attacks and cube testers, is not zero-constant is detected to be 839 in our experiments, which implies that our algorithm is not only efficient in computation but also accurate in estimation of attacked rounds. Our experiments show that this cube can also be used to distinguish 842-round Trivium. All the cubes of size $61 \leq n \leq 64$ that contain no adjacent indexes for Kreyvium and TriviA-SC are exhausted in a few hours. The total amount of such cubes is about 2^{30}. By the conventional methods, it needs around $c2^{91}$ cipher operations. The best cube we have found for Kreyvium is of size 61, which can be used to distinguish 872-round Kreyvium. The best cubes we have found for TriviA-SC and its successor are respectively of size 63 and size 61, for distinguishing 1035 rounds and 1047 rounds respectively. To the best of our knowledge, this is the first time[1] that a cube of size larger than 60 can be used in the attack on an NFSR-based cryptosystem.

As such, we obtain the best distinguishing attacks for the stream ciphers Trivium and TriviA-SC so far and the first outside cryptanalysis of Kreyvium. Our results are summarized in Table 1 with the comparisons of the previous attacks. Note here that this table does not include the distinguishers worse than an exhaustive search or for a small percentage of weak keys. We detail the discussions of related work in the following.

Table 1. Distinguishing attacks on Trivium, Kreyvium and TriviA-SC

Cipher	#Rounds	Complexity	Ref.
Trivium	790	2^{30}	[3]
	798	2^{25}	[29]
	806	2^{44}	[39]
	829	2^{53}	[38]
	830	2^{39}	[43]
	839	2^{37}	[33]
	842	2^{39}	Sect. 4
Kreyvium	872	2^{61}	Sect. 4
TriviA-SC (v1)	930	2^{36}	[38]
	1035	2^{63}	Sect. 4
TriviA-SC (v2)	950	2^{36}	[38]
	1047	2^{61}	Sect. 5
Simplified TriviA-SC	1152	2^{120}	[45]
	1152	2^{63}	Sect. 4

[1] In parallel and independently with our work, large cubes have also been exploited by Todo *et al.* [41] in the attacks on NFSR-based cryptosystems, such as Trivium, Grain-128a and ACORN.

1.2 Related Work

Upper Bound on Algebraic Degree. At EUROCRYPT 2002, Canteaut and Videau [12] developed a theory to find an upper bound on the algebraic degree of a composite function using the Walsh spectrum, and applied it to higher order differential cryptanalysis on Feistel block ciphers and especially on a generalization of MISTY1. This theory was further improved by Boura *et al.* [6,7] in recent years with applications to cryptanalysis of several block ciphers and hash functions, including Rijndael-256 and KECCAK. These theories of estimating algebraic degree are suitable for iterated ciphers. Similarly, our work is started by an upper bound on the algebraic degree of a composite function, but without using the Walsh spectrum and based on a simple fact.

More recently, at EUROCRYPT 2015, Todo [40] discovered a new tool for searching upper bound on the algebraic degree of SPN and Feistel ciphers by introducing the division property with applications to integral cryptanalysis of various iterated cryptographic primitives. The bit-based division property proposed by Todo and Morii in [42] is more relevant to our work. In parallel with our work, this tool has been exploited by Todo *et al.* [41] for estimating the algebraic degree of NFSR-based cryptosystems, including TRIVIUM, Grain-128a and ACORN, and applied to cube attacks on these ciphers. Nevertheless, our idea is still essentially different with that of division property. In some ways, the tool based on division property is limited by the number of rounds and the size of input variables, due to its high time complexity. The bound found by division property is possibly more precise, while our tool is much faster and has no such limitations.

Attacks on Trivium-Like Ciphers. It is worth noticing that all but the attacks of [45] listed in Table 1 are cube tester, which is a variant of higher order differential attacks and was first introduced by Aumasson *et al.* in [3]. Cube testers are useful not only in distinguishing attacks but also in key recovery attacks, *e.g.*, dynamic cube attacks [19,22] and cube-attack-like cryptanalysis [20].

Before the work of Aumasson *et al.*, TRIVIUM (designed by Cannière and Preneel [8,10] in 2006) had already attracted a lot of similar cryptanalysis, especially for chosen IV statistical attacks, *e.g.*, [23,24,37]. After the effort of cryptanalysts in the past ten years, the cryptanalysis of TRIVIUM seems to be approaching a bottleneck, if not the summit. Several cube distinguishers under different statistical models reach around 830 rounds, *e.g.*, [33,38,43]. Though our distinguisher for TRIVIUM does not improve the previous ones much, our technique for finding cubes is novel and gives a new and global view on cube cryptanalysis of TRIVIUM.

In addition, Knellwolf *et al.* [29] showed distinguishers on 868-round and 961-round TRIVIUM respectively for 2^{31} and 2^{26} weak keys both with complexity of 2^{25}. The key recovery attacks are also well studied for TRIVIUM. In [21], Dinur and Shamir described a practical full key recovery on TRIVIUM reduced to 767 rounds, using cube attacks. Afterwards, Fouque and Vannet [26] improved the cube attacks on TRIVIUM, and provided a practical full key recovery after 784 rounds and a full key recovery after 799 rounds with complexity of 2^{62}. Recently, Todo *et al.* [41] proposed a possible key recovery after 832 rounds, in which one bit information of the key can be retrieved with unknown probability in around 2^{77}. Besides, Maximov and Biryukov [34] presented a state recovery attack on the full cipher with time complexity around $c2^{83.5}$, where c is the complexity of solving a system of linear equations with 192 variables.

TRIVIA-SC [13] is a stream cipher designed by Chakraborti *et al.* at CHES 2015 for using in the authenticated encryption scheme TriviA, which was selected as a second-round candidate in the CAESAR competition but was not retained for the third round. Its successor, TRIVIA-SC (v2) [14], retains the same design and only differs in flipping all but three bits of the constants loaded to the initial internal state. Sarkar *et al.* [38] showed cube distinguishers with complexity of 2^{36} on both versions of TRIVIA-SC reduced to 930 rounds and 950 rounds respectively. We improve these distinguishers to 1035 rounds and 1047 rounds respectively. The work of [45] by Xu *et al.* shows a linear distinguisher with complexity of 2^{120} for the full 1152 rounds of a simplified variant of TRIVIA-SC in which the unique nonlinear term of the output function is removed. As shown in Table 1, we cut down their complexity from 2^{120} to 2^{63} for this simplified TRIVIA-SC.

KREYVIUM is a variant of TRIVIUM with 128-bit security, designed by Canteaut *et al.* at FSE 2016 for efficient homomorphic-ciphertext compression [11]. As far as we know, this paper proposes the first cryptanalysis of KREYVIUM.

1.3 Organization

The rest of this paper is structured as follows. In Sect. 2, the basic definitions and notations are provided. Section 3 shows the general framework of our algorithm for estimating algebraic degree of NFSR-based cryptosystems. We propose in Sect. 4 a concrete algorithm for finding an upper bound on the algebraic degree of Trivium-like ciphers with applications to TRIVIUM, KREYVIUM and TRIVIA-SC, while Sect. 5 further presents an improved algorithm with applications to TRIVIA-SC. Section 6 concludes the paper.

2 Preliminaries

Boolean Functions and Algebraic Degree. Let $\mathbb{F}_2$ denote the binary field and $\mathbb{F}_2^n$ the n-dimensional vector space over $\mathbb{F}_2$. An n-variable Boolean function is a mapping from $\mathbb{F}_2^n$ into $\mathbb{F}_2$. Denote by $\mathbb{B}_n$ the set of all n-variable Boolean functions. An n-variable Boolean function f can be uniquely represented as a multivariate polynomial over $\mathbb{F}_2$,

$$f(x_1, x_2, \cdots, x_n) = \bigoplus_{c=(c_1,\cdots,c_n)\in\mathbb{F}_2^n} a_c \prod_{i=1}^{n} x_i^{c_i},\ a_c \in \mathbb{F}_2,$$

called the algebraic normal form (ANF). The algebraic degree of f, denoted by $\deg(f)$, is defined as $\max\{wt(c) \mid a_c \neq 0\}$, where $wt(c)$ is the Hamming weight of c. Let g_i $(1 \leq i \leq m)$ be Boolean functions on n variables. We denote $\deg(G) = (\deg(g_1), \deg(g_2), \cdots, \deg(g_m))$, for $G = (g_1, g_2, \cdots, g_m)$.

Cube Testers. Given a Boolean function f and a term t_I containing variables from an index subset I that are multiplied together, the function can be written as the sum of terms which are supersets of I and terms that miss at least one variable from I,

$$f(x_1, x_2, \cdots, x_n) = f_S(I) \cdot t_I \oplus q(x_1, x_2, \cdots, x_n),$$

where $f_S(I)$ is called the superpoly of I in f. The basic idea of cube testers is that the symbolic sum of all the derived polynomials obtained from the function f by assigning all the possible values to the subset of variables in the term t_I is exactly $f_S(I)$. Cube testers work by evaluating superpolys of carefully selected terms t_I which are products of public variables (*e.g.*, IV bits), and trying to distinguish them from a random function. Especially, the superpoly $f_S(I)$ is equal to a zero constant, if the algebraic degree of f in the variables from I is less than the size of I. In this paper, we mainly focus on this case. For more details of cube testers, we refer to [3].

Nonlinear Feedback Shift Registers. Nonlinear feedback shift registers (NFSRs) are the basic components of cryptographic primitives, especially of stream ciphers. Each time the system is clocked, the internal state is shifted right, and the new left bit is computed from the previous state by a nonlinear function f. The feedback bit is computed as

$$s_{t+1} = f(s_t, \cdots, s_{t-n+1}),$$

where f can be any function in n variables. According to implementation purposes, the most useful case is the binary case, in which each cell contains a bit, and f is a Boolean function. In this paper, we focus on this binary case. For more details of NFSRs, we refer to [25].

3 An Iterative Method for Estimating Algebraic Degree of NFSR-Based Cryptosystems

Compared with other types of cryptographic primitives, such as Feistel and SPN ciphers, an NFSR-Based Cryptosystem usually updates less bits each round and needs more rounds to ensure its security, and its algebraic degree is more irregular. Maybe due to this reason, besides experimental analysis there are few theoretical tools to estimate algebraic degree of NFSR-Based cryptosystems.

We will show in this section a general idea for iteratively estimating algebraic degree of NFSR-based cryptosystems. We first present a basic fact on the degree of a composite function, and then exploit it to estimate degrees of the internal states and outputs of NFSR-based cryptosystems.

Let $f(x_1, x_2, \cdots, x_m) = \bigoplus_{c=(c_1,\cdots,c_m)\in\mathbb{F}_2^m} a_c \prod_{i=1}^m x_i^{c_i}$ be a Boolean function on m variables. We define the following mapping, called *numeric mapping* and denoted by $\mathtt{DEG}$,

$$\mathtt{DEG}: \mathbb{B}_m \times \mathbb{Z}^m \to \mathbb{Z},$$
$$(f, D) \mapsto \max_{a_c \neq 0}\{\sum_{i=1}^m c_i d_i\},$$

where $D = (d_1, d_2, \cdots, d_m)$ and a_c's are coefficients of algebraic normal form of f as defined previously.

Let $g_1, g_2, \cdots, g_m$ be Boolean functions on n variables, $G = (g_1, g_2, \cdots, g_m)$ and $\deg(G) = (\deg(g_1), \deg(g_2), \cdots, \deg(g_m))$. The numeric degree of the composite function $h = f \circ G$ is defined as $\mathtt{DEG}(f, \deg(G))$, denoted by $\mathtt{DEG}(h)$ for short. We call $\mathtt{DEG}(f, D)$ a super numeric degree of h if $d_i \geq \deg(g_i)$ for all $1 \leq i \leq m$, where $D = (d_1, d_2, \cdots, d_m)$. We can check that the algebraic degree of h is always less than or equal to the numeric degree of h, *i.e.*,

$$\deg(h) = \deg(f(g_1, g_2, \cdots, g_m)) \leq \mathtt{DEG}(h) = \max_{a_c \neq 0}\{\sum_{i=1}^m c_i \deg(g_i)\}.$$

Proposition 1. *The algebraic degree of a composite function is less than or equal to its numeric degree.*

An NFSR-based cryptosystem usually consists of an update function g and an output function f. The internal state is updated by the update function g, while the output bit is generated by the output function f after an initialization of a sufficient number of rounds. To make the implementation efficient, the update function and output function usually have extremely sparse terms, *e.g.*, Trivium [8,10] and Grain [1,27,28]. Even though these functions are simple, there are few tools to exactly compute their algebraic degrees after updating the internal state by a sufficient number of rounds. A straightforward way to achieve this is to calculate the algebraic normal form, but it easily becomes out of memory as the number of rounds increases. A more efficient method is to test the coefficients of the algebraic normal form by statistical analysis, but it highly depends on the computational power and is limited by computational time. To overcome these limitations of computational resources, we exploit the numeric mapping to estimate the algebraic degree.

Corollary 2. *Denote by $s^{(t)}$ the internal state of an NFSR-based cryptosystem at t-th round, and let g and f be the update function and output function respectively. Then the algebraic degrees of the updated bit and output bit are respectively less than or equal to their numeric degrees, i.e.,* $\mathtt{DEG}(g, \deg(s^{(t)}))$ *and* $\mathtt{DEG}(f, \deg(s^{(t)}))$.

Example 1. Let $x_t = x_{t-2}x_{t-7} + x_{t-4}x_{t-5} + x_{t-8}$ be the update function of an NFSR with size 8. For $t = 16$, we have

$$x_{16} = x_{14}x_9 + x_{12}x_{11} + x_8.$$

We can iteratively compute

$$\begin{aligned} x_9 &= x_2x_7 + x_4x_5 + x_1, \\ x_{11} &= x_2x_4x_7 + x_1x_4 + x_4x_5 + x_6x_7 + x_3, \\ x_{12} &= x_3x_5x_8 + x_2x_5 + x_5x_6 + x_7x_8 + x_4, \\ x_{14} &= x_2x_3x_7x_8 + x_2x_5x_6x_7 + x_3x_4x_5x_8 + x_3x_5x_7x_8 \\ &\quad + x_1x_3x_8 + x_1x_5x_6 + x_2x_4x_5 + x_2x_5x_7 + x_4x_5x_6 \\ &\quad + x_5x_6x_7 + x_1x_2 + x_2x_7 + x_4x_7 + x_7x_8 + x_6. \end{aligned}$$

Then by numeric mapping, we have

$$\begin{aligned} \texttt{DEG}(x_{16}) &= \max\{\deg(x_{14}) + \deg(x_9), \deg(x_{12}) + \deg(x_{11}), \deg(x_8)\} \\ &= \max\{4 + 2, 3 + 3, 1\} \\ &= 6. \end{aligned}$$

We can verify that $\deg(x_{16}) = 6$ by calculating the algebraic normal form of x_{16}. As a matter of fact, we can also check that $\texttt{DEG}(x_t) = \deg(x_t)$ for all $t < 16$. This fact implies that we can get an accurate estimation of the algebraic degree of x_{16} by iteratively using numeric mapping starting at the beginning, without computations of the algebraic normal forms of internal bits.

The case that the numeric degree equals the algebraic degree usually happens when the intermediate variables appearing in the same nonlinear terms are independent. This scenario is reasonable for an ideal cryptosystem. For a concrete cipher, the numeric degree might be equal or close to the algebraic degree if we eliminate or reduce the dependent relationship between the intermediate variables.

Algorithm 1. Estimation of Degree of NFSR-Based Cryptosystems

Require: Given the ANFs of the internal state $s^{(0)}$, the ANFs of the update function G and output function f, and the set of variables X.

```
Set D^(0) and E^(0) to deg(s^(0), X);
For t from 1 to N do:
    Compute D^(t) = DegEst(G, E^(t-1));
    Set E^(t) to (D^(0), D^(1), ..., D^(t));
Return DegEst(f, E^(N)).
```

The algebraic degrees of output bits and the internal states can be estimated iteratively for NFSR-based cryptosystems. We describe this estimation in Algorithm 1. In the algorithm, $s^{(0)} = (s_1^{(0)}, s_2^{(0)}, \cdots, s_n^{(0)})$

denotes the internal state at time 0 with size n, and $\deg(s^{(0)}, X) = (\deg(s_1^{(0)}, X), \deg(s_2^{(0)}, X), \cdots, \deg(s_n^{(0)}, X))$, where the notation $\deg(s_i^{(0)}, X)$ denotes the algebraic degree of $s_i^{(0)}$ with X as variables. Especially, $\deg(0, X) = -\infty$, and $\deg(c, X) = 0$ for any nonzero c containing no variable in X. The update function G is written as vectorial Boolean functions from $\mathbb{F}_2^n$ to $\mathbb{F}_2^n$, where a few bits of input are updated and the rest of the bits are shifted. `DegEst` is a procedure for estimating algebraic degree. The output of this algorithm gives an upper bound on algebraic degree of the output of a given NFSR-based cryptosystem when setting $\texttt{DegEst}(\cdot, E^{(t)})$ to $\texttt{DEG}(\cdot, D^{(t)})$. This is based on the fact that $\deg(g(s^{(t)})) \le \texttt{DEG}(g, \deg(s^{(t)})) \le \texttt{DEG}(g, \texttt{DEG}(s^{(t)}))$ according to Corollary 2.

Now we have given a general framework of iterative estimation of algebraic degree of NFSR-Based Cryptosystems. To reach a sharper upper bound, we use a more delicate `DegEst` rather than `DEG` in Algorithm 1. We will show later the applications to Trivium-like ciphers, and the experimental results show that our estimated degree is very close to the real value of algebraic degree.

4 Applications to Trivium-Like Ciphers

In this section, we first briefly describe a generic view of a Trivium-like cipher to capture various cryptographic algorithms such as Trivium, TriviA-SC and Kreyvium. Then, based on our observations on the update functions of this kind of ciphers, we formalize and develop a linear-time algorithm for finding an upper bound on the algebraic degree of a Trivium-like cipher. Finally, we apply our algorithm to analyze the security of the ciphers Trivium, TriviA-SC and Kreyvium.

4.1 A Brief Description of Trivium-Like Ciphers

Let A, B and C be three registers with sizes of n_A, n_B and n_C, denoted by A_t, B_t and C_t their corresponding states at clock t,

$$A_t = (x_t, x_{t-1}, \cdots, x_{t-n_A+1}), \tag{1}$$
$$B_t = (y_t, y_{t-1}, \cdots, y_{t-n_B+1}), \tag{2}$$
$$C_t = (z_t, z_{t-1}, \cdots, z_{t-n_C+1}), \tag{3}$$

and respectively updated by the following three quadratic functions,

$$x_t = z_{t-r_C} \cdot z_{t-r_C+1} + \ell_A(s^{(t-1)}), \tag{4}$$
$$y_t = x_{t-r_A} \cdot x_{t-r_A+1} + \ell_B(s^{(t-1)}), \tag{5}$$
$$z_t = y_{t-r_B} \cdot y_{t-r_B+1} + \ell_C(s^{(t-1)}), \tag{6}$$

where $1 \le r_\lambda < n_\lambda$ for $\lambda \in \{A, B, C\}$ and ℓ_A, ℓ_B and ℓ_C are linear functions. We denote $A_t[i] = x_i$, $B_t[i] = y_i$ and $C_t[i] = z_i$, and define $g_A^{(t)} = z_{t-r_C} \cdot z_{t-r_C+1}$, $g_B^{(t)} = x_{t-r_A} \cdot x_{t-r_A+1}$ and $g_C^{(t)} = y_{t-r_B} \cdot y_{t-r_B+1}$. The internal state, denoted by

$s^{(t)}$ at clock t, consists of the three registers A, B, C, that is, $s^{(t)} = (A_t, B_t, C_t)$. Let f be the output function. After an initialization of N rounds, in which the internal state is updated for N times, the cipher generates a keystream bit by $f(s^{(t)})$ for each $t \geq N$.

TRIVIUM and TRIVIA-SC exactly fall into this kind of ciphers. As mentioned earlier, TRIVIA-SC and its successor TRIVIA-SC (v2) only differ in the constants loaded to the initial internal state. Hereinafter, TRIVIA-SC means its both versions, if not specified. KREYVIUM is a variant of TRIVIUM with 128-bit security. Compared with TRIVIUM, KREYVIUM uses two extra registers (K^*, V^*) without updating but shifting, *i.e.*, $s^{(t)} = (A_t, B_t, C_t, K^*, V^*)$, and add a single bit of (K^*, V^*) to each of ℓ_A and ℓ_B, where K^* and V^* only involve the key bits and IV bits respectively. We can easily adapt our techniques to KREYVIUM from TRIVIUM. TRIVIUM uses an 80-bit key and an 80-bit IV, while KREYVIUM and TRIVIA-SC both use a 128-bit key and a 128-bit IV. All these ciphers have 1152 rounds. For more details of the specifications of these ciphers, we refer to [10,11,13,14].

4.2 The Algorithm for Estimation of Degree of Trivium-Like Ciphers

We present here an algorithm for giving an upper bound on the algebraic degree of the output of f after N rounds for a Trivium-like cipher, as depicted in Algorithm 2. We first initialize the degree of the initial internal state, denoted by $D^{(0)}$, then iteratively compute $D^{(t)}$ for $t = 1, 2, \cdots, N$, and finally apply numeric mapping to calculate an estimated degree for the first bit of the keystream. In Algorithm 2, we also use three sequences, denoted by d_A, d_B and d_C, to record the estimated degrees of the three registers A, B, C. In each step of a Trivium-like cipher, three bits are updated as (4), (5) and (6). Accordingly, we compute estimated degrees for these three bits in each step t, denoted by $d_A^{(t)}, d_B^{(t)}$ and $d_C^{(t)}$. Then update $D^{(t)}$ from $D^{(t-1)}$. For estimating the algebraic degrees of x_t, y_t, z_t, we exploit two procedures `DegMul` and `DEG` for dealing with their "quadratic" and "linear" parts separately. An instance of `DegMul` is described in Algorithm 3. The other two cases are similar, and the full procedure of `DegMul` is given in Algorithm 5 in Appendix. Algorithm 3 is used to compute an upper bound on the algebraic degree of $g_A^{(t)} = z_{t-r_C} \cdot z_{t-r_C+1}$, and its correctness is shown in Lemma 4. We will demonstrate that for all t with $1 \leq t \leq N$ the estimated degrees $d_A^{(t)}, d_B^{(t)}, d_C^{(t)}$ for x_t, y_t, z_t are greater than or equal to their corresponding algebraic degrees, and therefore the output $\mathtt{DEG}(f, D^{(N)})$ of Algorithm 2 is a super numeric degree of the first bit of the keystream. In other words, Algorithm 2 gives an upper bound on algebraic degree of the N-round output bit of a Trivium-like cipher.

Theorem 3. *Algorithm 2 outputs a super numeric degree of the first keystream bit of an N-round Trivium-like cipher with X as variables.*

As mentioned previously, to prove Theorem 3, it is sufficient to show the following lemma.

Algorithm 2. Estimation of Degree of Trivium-Like Ciphers

Require: Given the ANFs of the initial internal state (A_0, B_0, C_0), and the set of variables X.

1: For λ in $\{A, B, C\}$ do:
2:     For t from $1 - n_\lambda$ to 0 do:
3:         $d_\lambda^{(t)} \leftarrow \deg(\lambda_0[t], X)$, where $A_0[t] = x_t$, $B_0[t] = y_t$, $C_0[t] = z_t$;
4: $D^{(0)} \leftarrow (d_A^{(1-n_A)}, \cdots, d_A^{(0)}, d_B^{(1-n_B)}, \cdots, d_B^{(0)}, d_C^{(1-n_C)}, \cdots, d_C^{(0)})$;
5: For t from 1 to N do:
6:     For λ in $\{A, B, C\}$ do:
7:         $d_\lambda^{(t)} \leftarrow \max\{\texttt{DegMul}(g_\lambda^{(t)}), \texttt{DEG}(\ell_\lambda, D^{(t-1)})\}$;
8:     $D^{(t)} \leftarrow (d_A^{(t-n_A+1)}, \cdots, d_A^{(t)}, d_B^{(t-n_B+1)}, \cdots, d_B^{(t)}, d_C^{(t-n_C+1)}, \cdots, d_C^{(t)})$;
9: Return $\texttt{DEG}(f, D^{(N)})$.

Algorithm 3. $\texttt{DegMul}(g_\lambda^{(t)})$ for $\lambda = A$

1: $t_1 \leftarrow t - r_C$;
2: If $t_1 \leq 0$ then:
    Return $d_C^{(t_1)} + d_C^{(t_1+1)}$.
3: $t_2 \leftarrow t_1 - r_B$;
4: $d_1 \leftarrow \min\{d_B^{(t_2)} + d_C^{(t_1+1)}, d_B^{(t_2+2)} + d_C^{(t_1)}, d_B^{(t_2)} + d_B^{(t_2+1)} + d_B^{(t_2+2)}\}$;
5: $d_2 \leftarrow \texttt{DEG}(\ell_C, D^{(t_1)}) + d_C^{(t_1)}$;
6: $d_3 \leftarrow \texttt{DEG}(\ell_C, D^{(t_1-1)}) + d_C^{(t_1+1)}$;
7: $d \leftarrow \max\{d_1, d_2, d_3\}$;
8: Return d.

Lemma 4. *In Algorithm 2, we have* $d_A^{(t)} \geq \deg(x_t, X)$, $d_B^{(t)} \geq \deg(y_t, X)$ *and* $d_C^{(t)} \geq \deg(z_t, X)$ *for* $t \leq N$.

Proof. It is trivial for $t \leq 0$. Next we simply write $\deg(\cdot, X)$ as $\deg(\cdot)$. By Eqs. (4), (5) and (6), it is sufficient to prove for $1 \leq t \leq N$ that

$$d_A^{(t)} \geq \max\{\deg(z_{t-r_C} \cdot z_{t-r_C+1}), \deg(\ell_A(s^{(t-1)}))\}, \tag{7}$$

$$d_B^{(t)} \geq \max\{\deg(x_{t-r_A} \cdot x_{t-r_A+1}), \deg(\ell_B(s^{(t-1)}))\}, \tag{8}$$

and

$$d_C^{(t)} \geq \max\{\deg(y_{t-r_B} \cdot y_{t-r_B+1}), \deg(\ell_C(s^{(t-1)}))\}. \tag{9}$$

We prove them by induction. Here we provide only the details of the proof for the first inequality due to the similarity. It is clear that (7) is true for $1 \leq t \leq r_C$. Assume that (7), (8) and (9) are true for all $i \leq t - 1$. Now we prove that (7) is true for t with $r_C < t \leq N$.

From Algorithm 2, we have $d_A^{(t)} \geq \texttt{DEG}(\ell_A, D^{(t-1)}) \geq \deg(\ell_A(s^{(t-1)}))$. Next we prove $d_A^{(t)} \geq \deg(z_{t-r_C} \cdot z_{t-r_C+1})$. By (6), we obtain that for $t - r_C \geq 1$,

$$z_{t-r_C} = y_{t-r_C-r_B} \cdot y_{t-r_C-r_B+1} + \ell_C(s^{(t-r_C-1)}),$$
$$z_{t-r_C+1} = y_{t-r_C-r_B+1} \cdot y_{t-r_C-r_B+2} + \ell_C(s^{(t-r_C)}),$$

and thus

$$\begin{aligned}
&z_{t-r_C} \cdot z_{t-r_C+1} \\
=&(y_{t-r_C-r_B} \cdot y_{t-r_C-r_B+1} + \ell_C(s^{(t-r_C-1)})) \cdot z_{t-r_C+1} \\
=&y_{t-r_C-r_B} \cdot y_{t-r_C-r_B+1} \cdot z_{t-r_C+1} + \ell_C(s^{(t-r_C-1)}) \cdot z_{t-r_C+1} \\
=&y_{t-r_C-r_B} \cdot y_{t-r_C-r_B+1} \cdot (y_{t-r_C-r_B+1} \cdot y_{t-r_C-r_B+2} + \ell_C(s^{(t-r_C)})) \\
&\quad + \ell_C(s^{(t-r_C-1)}) \cdot z_{t-r_C+1} \\
=&y_{t-r_C-r_B} \cdot y_{t-r_C-r_B+1} \cdot y_{t-r_C-r_B+2} + y_{t-r_C-r_B} \cdot y_{t-r_C-r_B+1} \cdot \ell_C(s^{(t-r_C)}) \\
&+ \ell_C(s^{(t-r_C-1)}) \cdot z_{t-r_C+1}.
\end{aligned}$$

Denote by Y_1, Y_2 and Y_3 respectively the three summands in the above equality. By the previous assumption, we have

$$\begin{aligned}
d_C^{(t-r_C)} &\geq \deg(y_{t-r_C-r_B} \cdot y_{t-r_C-r_B+1}), \\
d_C^{(t-r_C+1)} &\geq \deg(y_{t-r_C-r_B+1} \cdot y_{t-r_C-r_B+2}),
\end{aligned}$$

and thus

$$\begin{aligned}
\deg(Y_1) \leq &\min\{\deg(y_{t-r_C-r_B}) + \deg(y_{t-r_C-r_B+1} \cdot y_{t-r_C-r_B+2}), \\
&\quad \deg(y_{t-r_C-r_B+2}) + \deg(y_{t-r_C-r_B} \cdot y_{t-r_C-r_B+1}), \\
&\quad \deg(y_{t-r_C-r_B}) + \deg(y_{t-r_C-r_B+1}) + \deg(y_{t-r_C-r_B+2})\} \\
\leq &\min\{\deg(y_{t-r_C-r_B}) + d_C^{(t-r_C+1)}, \\
&\quad \deg(y_{t-r_C-r_B+2}) + d_C^{(t-r_C)}, \\
&\quad \deg(y_{t-r_C-r_B}) + \deg(y_{t-r_C-r_B+1}) + \deg(y_{t-r_C-r_B+2})\} \\
\leq &\min\{d_B^{(t-r_C-r_B)} + d_C^{(t-r_C+1)}, \\
&\quad d_B^{(t-r_C-r_B+2)} + d_C^{(t-r_C)}, \\
&\quad d_B^{(t-r_C-r_B)} + d_B^{(t-r_C-r_B+1)} + d_B^{(t-r_C-r_B+2)}\} = d_1.
\end{aligned}$$

From the assumption we also have

$$\begin{aligned}
\deg(Y_2) &\leq \mathtt{DEG}(\ell_C, D^{(t-r_C)}) + d_C^{(t-r_C)} = d_2, \\
\deg(Y_3) &\leq \mathtt{DEG}(\ell_C, D^{(t-r_C-1)}) + d_C^{(t-r_C+1)} = d_3.
\end{aligned}$$

Since $\deg(z_{t-r_C} \cdot z_{t-r_C+1}) \leq \max\{\deg(Y_1), \deg(Y_2), \deg(Y_3)\} \leq \max\{d_1, d_2, d_3\}$, by Algorithms 2 and 3 we know $\deg(z_{t-r_C} \cdot z_{t-r_C+1}) \leq d_A^{(t)}$. □

Complexity of the Algorithm. The size of the ANF of ℓ_λ is constant and thus $\mathtt{DEG}(\ell_\lambda)$ and $\mathtt{DegMul}(g_\lambda^{(t)})$ can be calculated in constant time, for $\lambda \in \{A, B, C\}$. Therefore Algorithm 2 has time complexity of $\mathcal{O}(N)$. It requires a memory of $\mathcal{O}(N)$.

4.3 Experimental Results

In this section, we implement the algorithm on TRIVIUM, KREYVIUM and TRIVIA-SC, and reveal various upper bounds on the algebraic degrees of these ciphers. For KREYVIUM, we use a modified $D^{(t)}$ in the algorithm which includes the degrees of the two extra registers (key and IV).

When Will the Key and IV Be Sufficiently Mixed? We take all the key and IV bits as input variables X, and do experiments on TRIVIUM, KREYVIUM and TRIVIA-SC using Algorithm 2. We list the results in Table 2. As shown in the table, TRIVIUM does not achieve the maximum degree 160 after an initialization of 907 rounds, while KREYVIUM and TRIVIA-SC do not achieve the maximum degree 256 after 982 rounds and 1108 rounds respectively. Though it is not an attack, this implies that TRIVIUM behaves best among the three ciphers while TRIVIA-SC has a small margin towards this test of maximum algebraic degree.

Table 2. Lower bound on the maximum number of rounds of not achieving maximum degree for TRIVIUM, KREYVIUM and TRIVIA-SC with all the key and IV bits as variables ($X = (key, IV)$)

Cipher	TRIVIUM	KREYVIUM	TRIVIA-SC
#Key+#IV	160	256	256
#Rounds	907	982	1108

When Will the IV Be Sufficiently Mixed? Taking a subset of the IV as input variables and the key as parameter, the algorithm gives a chosen IV distinguisher on the cipher. Such kind of distinguishers, including cube testers, have been widely investigated on stream ciphers, *e.g.*, [3,23,24,37].

We first apply the algorithm to TRIVIUM, KREYVIUM and TRIVIA-SC with all the IV bits as input variables, *i.e.*, $X = IV$. In our experiments, the key is taken as parameter, that is, $\deg(k_i, X) = 0$ for any bit k_i of the key. This is consistent with a distinguisher in the setting of unknown key. Our experiments show that TRIVIUM does not achieve the maximum degree 80 after an initialization of 793 rounds, while KREYVIUM and TRIVIA-SC do not achieve the maximum degree 128 after 862 rounds and 987 rounds respectively. We summarize our results in Table 3.

We next consider an exhaustive search on the sets of input variables X which have size of around half length of the IV and contain no adjacent indexes. This is not the first time to make use of a cube that contain no adjacent indexes. Actually, the results of Aumasson *et al.* [3] and Liu *et al.* [33] have shown that we can profit from such kind of cubes in cube testers due to the non-linear structure of the update functions of TRIVIUM. In our experiments, we set the key as parameter, and set the non-variable IV bits to be zeros. Using

Table 3. Lower bound on the maximum number of rounds of NOT achieving maximum degree for TRIVIUM, KREYVIUM and TRIVIA-SC with all the IV bits as variables ($X = IV$)

Cipher	TRIVIUM	KREYVIUM	TRIVIA-SC
#IV	80	128	128
#Rounds	793	862	987

Algorithm 2, we can exhaust all the cubes of size $37 \leq n \leq 40$ for TRIVIUM, which contain no adjacent indexes, in a dozen minutes on a common PC. The amount of such cubes is $\sum_{n=37}^{40} \binom{81-n}{n} \approx 2^{25}$. Before this paper, it needs $c\sum_{n=37}^{40} 2^n \binom{81-n}{n} \approx c2^{62}$ cipher operations to test all those cubes, and the confidence of the test depends on c. All the cubes containing no adjacent indexes of size $61 \leq n \leq 64$ for KREYVIUM and TRIVIA-SC are exhausted in a few hours. The amount of such cubes is $\sum_{n=61}^{64} \binom{129-n}{n} \approx 2^{30}$. By the existing methods, it needs $c\sum_{n=61}^{64} 2^n \binom{129-n}{n} \approx c2^{91}$ cipher operations to test all those cubes. The results are summarized in Table 4. The corresponding cubes are listed in Table 7 in Appendix.

As shown in Table 4, the output of 837-round TRIVIUM has degree strictly less than 37 over a subset of IV bits with size 37, and thus the outputs of 837-round TRIVIUM over this cube always sum to 0. Since 2^{37} is practical, we verify this by carrying out a test for random 100 keys. The minimum number of rounds such that the sum over this cube, *i.e.*, the superpoly of the cube, is not zero-constant is detected to be 839, which means the output of 839-round TRIVIUM achieves the maximum degree 37 over this subset of IV bits. This shows that our lower bound on the number of attacked rounds is very sharp, and our estimation of degree is, in some ways, very close to its real value. The test also implies a distinguisher for 842-round TRIVIUM with time complexity of around 2^{39}, since we detect a bias of 0.46 from the 842-round output bit. We summarize

Table 4. Cube testers on round-reduced TRIVIUM, KREYVIUM and TRIVIA-SC with around half of the IV bits as variables

Cipher	TRIVIUM	KREYVIUM	TRIVIA-SC (v1)	TRIVIA-SC (v2)	Simplified TRIVIA-SC
Size of cube	37	61	63	62	63
#Rounds	837	872	1035	1046	1152

Table 5. Superpoly of round-reduced TRIVIUM over a cube of size 37

#Rounds	837	838	839	840	841	842
rate(superpoly=1)	0	0	0.09	0.07	0.29	0.27

in Table 5 the results of the test, where the rate that the superpoly of this cube equals non-zero is given for starting from 837 rounds to 842 rounds.

As shown in Table 4, the output of 872-round Kreyvium has algebraic degree strictly less than 61 over a subset of IV bits with size 61, which implies a distinguisher on this reduced version of Kreyvium with complexity of 2^{61}.

Our experiments also show that the output of 1035-round TriviA-SC (v1) and 1046-round TriviA-SC (v2) do not achieve maximum algebraic degree on a subset of IV bits with size 63 and size 62 respectively, which implies that we can distinguish them from random functions in 2^{63} and 2^{62} respectively. In fact, these two cubes are found much earlier before the completion of our experiments. The former is found in a second, and the latter in three minutes. By using the cube of size 63, we can also obtain a distinguisher with complexity of 2^{63} on the full rounds of a simplified variant of TriviA-SC (for both versions), in which the unique nonlinear term of the output function is removed.

We have also tried to search for the cubes of large size under other strategies. We exhaust all the cubes with size close to the length of the IV. Besides, we use our algorithm together with the greedy algorithm, as done in [39], to search for the best cubes of any size. Nevertheless, no better results are found.

To further evaluate the accuracy of our algorithm, we perform more experiments specially on Trivium. We compute the exact value of the algebraic degree of the output bit of reduced Trivium from 66 rounds to 426 rounds, as well as estimate the degree by our algorithm. Our experiments show that

- our estimated bound is equal to its real value for most of cases (greater than 70%), and even for the other cases their gap is only one, when taking all the key and IV bits or all the IV bits as input variables.
- our estimated bound is always equal to its real value, when taking the best cube of size 37 as input variables.

They are strong evidence of high accuracy of our algorithm. We depict in Fig. 1 our full estimation of the upper bound on the algebraic degree of reduced Trivium for the mentioned three cases. From this figure, we can see that the algebraic degree on the IV bits is almost the same as that on all the key and IV bits, and it increases much faster than that of the best cube. The former is possible due to that the key and IV bits are loaded into different registers of Trivium, and the latter due to that two adjacent variable bits accelerate the growth of the algebraic degree.

Remarks. The algorithm is possibly improved by further refining the estimation of the degree of $y_i \cdot y_{i+1} \cdot y_{i+2}$. However, probably because in most of cases $y_i \cdot y_{i+1} \cdot y_{i+2}$ is not dominant on the algebraic degree of $z_{i+r_B} \cdot z_{i+r_B+1}$, no improvement is found by this way in our experiments. Another possible improvement is to store the estimated degree of $y_i \cdot y_{i+1}$ and replace some $d_C^{(i+r_B)}$ with it in the procedure `DegMul`. Again, it gives no better result, at least in our experiments, probably due to that the algebraic degree of z_{i+r_B} is usually equal to that of $y_i \cdot y_{i+1}$. Even though these methods show no advantages in our experiments,

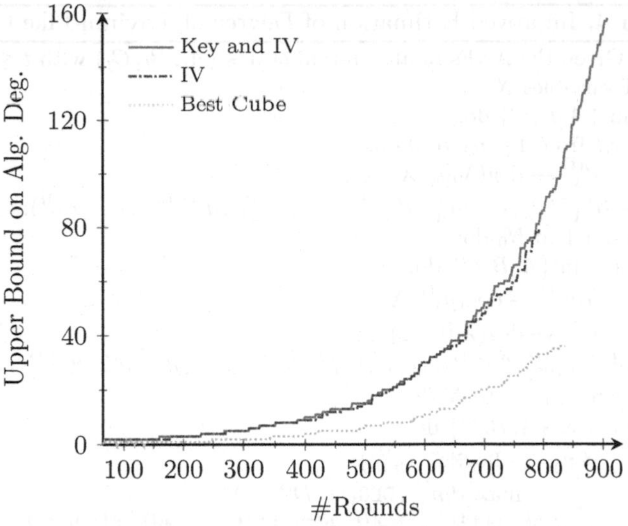

Fig. 1. Upper bound on the algebraic degree of reduced TRIVIUM

they may be useful in some cases. In the following, for an instance, we will show an improved algorithm by computing the exact degrees of the internal states of the first rounds, together with the second method.

5 Improved Estimation of Degree of Trivium-Like Ciphers

In this section, we present an improved algorithm for estimating algebraic degree of the output of f after N rounds for a Trivium-like cipher, as described in Algorithm 4.

It is similar to Algorithm 2. In the improved algorithm, we compute the exact algebraic degrees of the internal states for the first N_0 rounds, where the degrees of $g_A^{(t)}$, $g_B^{(t)}$ and $g_C^{(t)}$ are also recorded, and use a modified `DegMul*` to replace `DegMul`, as depicted in Algorithm 6 in Appendix. The rest of this algorithm is the same as Algorithm 2. The output of Algorithm 4 also gives an upper bound on algebraic degree of an N-round Trivium-like cipher with X as input variables. The replacing `DegMul` with `DegMul*` does not give the improvement but guarantees the validity of the algorithm. The proof is similar to that of Algorithm 2 and thus omitted in this paper.

It is hard to assess the complexity of Algorithm 4, which depends on N_0 and the complexities of the ANFs of the internal states (A_t, B_t, C_t) with $t \leq N_0$. It becomes much slower than Algorithm 2, as N_0 increases.

We apply the algorithm to TRIVIUM, KREYVIUM and TRIVIA-SC. It slightly improves the results in Sect. 4 for TRIVIA-SC, as shown in Table 6, while this is not the case for TRIVIUM and KREYVIUM. For both versions of TRIVIA-SC in

Algorithm 4. Improved Estimation of Degree of Trivium-Like Ciphers

Require: Given the ANFs of all internal states (A_t, B_t, C_t) with $t \leq N_0$, and the set of variables X.

For λ in $\{A, B, C\}$ do:
  For t from $1 - n_\lambda$ to 0 do:
    $d_\lambda^{(t)} \leftarrow \deg(\lambda_0[t], X)$;
$D^{(0)} \leftarrow (d_A^{(1-n_A)}, \cdots, d_A^{(0)}, d_B^{(1-n_B)}, \cdots, d_B^{(0)}, d_C^{(1-n_C)}, \cdots, d_C^{(0)})$;
For t from 1 to N_0 do:
  For λ in $\{A, B, C\}$ do:
    $dm_\lambda^{(t)} \leftarrow \deg(g_\lambda^{(t)}, X)$;
    $d_\lambda^{(t)} \leftarrow \deg(\lambda_t[t], X)$;
  $D^{(t)} \leftarrow (d_A^{(t-n_A+1)}, \cdots, d_A^{(t)}, d_B^{(t-n_B+1)}, \cdots, d_B^{(t)}, d_C^{(t-n_C+1)}, \cdots, d_C^{(t)})$;
For t from $N_0 + 1$ to N do:
  For λ in $\{A, B, C\}$ do:
    $dm_\lambda^{(t)} \leftarrow \texttt{DegMul}^*(g_\lambda^{(t)})$;
    $d_\lambda^{(t)} \leftarrow \max\{dm_\lambda^{(t)}, \texttt{DEG}(\ell_\lambda, D^{(t-1)})\}$;
  $D^{(t)} \leftarrow (d_A^{(t-n_A+1)}, \cdots, d_A^{(t)}, d_B^{(t-n_B+1)}, \cdots, d_B^{(t)}, d_C^{(t-n_C+1)}, \cdots, d_C^{(t)})$;
Return $\texttt{DEG}(f, D^{(N)})$.

the case $X = (key, IV)$, the number of rounds such that the output has degree less than 256 is improved from 1108 to 1121, by taking $N_0 = 340$. For TriviA-SC (v2) with X being a subset of IV with size of 61, the number of rounds is improved from 1032 to 1047, by taking $N_0 = 440$. This cube is listed in Table 7 in Appendix.

Table 6. Lower bounds on the number of rounds of NOT achieving maximum degree for TriviA-SC

Cipher	TriviA-SC	TriviA-SC (v2)
X	(key, IV)	Subset of IV
$\#X$	256	61
#Rounds (Algorithm 2)	1108	1032
#Rounds (Algorithm 4)	1121	1047

6 Conclusions

In this paper, we have shown a general framework of algebraic degree evaluation for NFSR-based cryptosystems. It is based on a new tool, named numeric mapping. We have also detailed the technique for efficiently finding an upper bound on the algebraic degree of Trivium-like ciphers. As illustrations, we applied it to Trivium, Kreyvium and TriviA-SC, and gained the best distinguishing attacks for all these ciphers, by an exhaustive search on a subset of the cubes that have size of around half length of the IV. To the best of our knowledge, our tool is the first theoretical one for finding an upper bound on the algebraic degree of an NFSR-based cryptosystem, and this is the first time that a cube of size beyond practical computations can be used in cryptanalysis of an NFSR-based cryptosystem. Note that cube testers are useful not only in distinguishing attacks but also in key recovery attacks. We believe that this tool is useful in both cryptanalysis and design of NFSR-based cryptosystems. In the future, it is worthy of working on its applications to key recovery attacks and to more cryptographic primitives. It is also worth a further generalization to other cryptosystems that are not built on NFSR.

Acknowledgement. We are grateful to Jian Guo, Wenhao Wang, and anonymous reviewers of CRYPTO 2017 for their fruitful discussions and helpful comments.

A The Full Procedures of DegMul and DegMul*

Algorithms 5 and 6 respectively describe the full procedures of $\texttt{DegMul}(g_\lambda^{(t)})$ and $\texttt{DegMul}^*(g_\lambda^{(t)})$ for $\lambda \in \{A, B, C\}$, where $\rho(A) = C, \rho(C) = B, \rho(B) = A$.

Algorithm 5. $\texttt{DegMul}(g_\lambda^{(t)})$ for $\lambda \in \{A, B, C\}$

1: $t_1 \leftarrow t - r_{\rho(\lambda)}$;
2: If $t_1 \leq 0$ then:
Return $d_{\rho(\lambda)}^{(t_1)} + d_{\rho(\lambda)}^{(t_1+1)}$.
3: $t_2 \leftarrow t_1 - r_{\rho^2(\lambda)}$;
4: $d_1 \leftarrow \min\{d_{\rho^2(\lambda)}^{(t_2)} + d_{\rho(\lambda)}^{(t_1+1)}, d_{\rho^2(\lambda)}^{(t_2+2)} + d_{\rho(\lambda)}^{(t_1)}, d_{\rho^2(\lambda)}^{(t_2)} + d_{\rho^2(\lambda)}^{(t_2+1)} + d_{\rho^2(\lambda)}^{(t_2+2)}\}$;
5: $d_2 \leftarrow \texttt{DEG}(\ell_{\rho(\lambda)}, D^{(t_1)}) + d_{\rho(\lambda)}^{(t_1)}$;
6: $d_3 \leftarrow \texttt{DEG}(\ell_{\rho(\lambda)}, D^{(t_1-1)}) + d_{\rho(\lambda)}^{(t_1+1)}$;
7: $d \leftarrow \max\{d_1, d_2, d_3\}$;
8: Return d.

Algorithm 6. $\texttt{DegMul}^*(g_\lambda^{(t)})$ for $\lambda \in \{A, B, C\}$

1: $t_1 \leftarrow t - r_{\rho(\lambda)}$;
2: If $t_1 \leq 0$ then:
Return $d_{\rho(\lambda)}^{(t_1)} + d_{\rho(\lambda)}^{(t_1+1)}$.
3: $t_2 \leftarrow t_1 - r_{\rho^2(\lambda)}$;
4: $d_1 \leftarrow \min\{d_{\rho^2(\lambda)}^{(t_2)} + dm_{\rho(\lambda)}^{(t_1+1)}, d_{\rho^2(\lambda)}^{(t_2+2)} + dm_{\rho(\lambda)}^{(t_1)}, d_{\rho^2(\lambda)}^{(t_2)} + d_{\rho^2(\lambda)}^{(t_2+1)} + d_{\rho^2(\lambda)}^{(t_2+2)}\}$;
5: $d_2 \leftarrow \texttt{DEG}(\ell_{\rho(\lambda)}, D^{(t_1)}) + dm_{\rho(\lambda)}^{(t_1)}$;
6: $d_3 \leftarrow \texttt{DEG}(\ell_{\rho(\lambda)}, D^{(t_1-1)}) + d_{\rho(\lambda)}^{(t_1+1)}$;
7: $d \leftarrow \max\{d_1, d_2, d_3\}$;
8: Return d.

B The Best Cube Testers

Table 7. The cubes in cube testers on round-reduced TRIVIUM, KREYVIUM and TRIVIA-SC with around half of the IV bits as variables

Cipher	Cube size	Cube
TRIVIUM	37	{0, 2, 4, 6, 8, 10, 12, 15, 17, 19, 21, 23, 25, 27, 30, 32, 34, 36, 38, 40, 42, 45, 47, 49, 51, 53, 55, 57, 60, 62, 64, 66, 68, 70, 72, 75, 79}
KREYVIUM	61	{0, 2, 4, 6, 8, 10, 12, 14, 16, 18, 20, 22, 24, 26, 29, 31, 33, 36, 38, 40, 42, 44, 46, 48, 50, 52, 54, 57, 59, 61, 63, 65, 67, 69, 72, 74, 76, 78, 80, 82, 84, 86, 88, 90, 92, 94, 96, 98, 100, 102, 104, 107, 109, 111, 113, 115, 117, 119, 122, 124, 126}
TRIVIA-SC	61	{0, 2, 4, 6, 8, 10, 12, 14, 16, 18, 20, 22, 24, 26, 28, 30, 32, 34, 36, 38, 40, 42, 44, 46, 48, 50, 52, 54, 56, 58, 60, 62, 64, 66, 68, 70, 75, 77, 79, 81, 83, 85, 87, 89, 91, 93, 95, 97, 99, 101, 103, 105, 107, 109, 111, 113, 115, 121, 123, 125, 127}
	62	{0, 2, 4, 6, 8, 10, 12, 14, 16, 18, 20, 22, 24, 26, 28, 30, 32, 34, 36, 38, 40, 42, 44, 46, 48, 50, 52, 54, 56, 58, 60, 62, 64, 66, 68, 70, 72, 77, 79, 81, 83, 85, 87, 89, 91, 93, 95, 97, 99, 101, 103, 105, 107, 109, 111, 113, 115, 117, 121, 123, 125, 127}
	63	{0, 2, 4, 6, 8, 10, 12, 14, 16, 18, 20, 22, 24, 26, 28, 30, 32, 34, 36, 38, 40, 42, 44, 46, 48, 50, 52, 54, 56, 58, 60, 62, 64, 66, 68, 70, 72, 74, 76, 78, 81, 83, 85, 87, 89, 91, 93, 95, 97, 99, 101, 103, 105, 107, 109, 111, 113, 115, 117, 121, 123, 125, 127}

References

1. Ågren, M., Hell, M., Johansson, T., Meier, W.: Grain-128a: a new version of Grain-128 with optional authentication. IJWMC **5**(1), 48–59 (2011)
2. Aumasson, J., Dinur, I., Henzen, L., Meier, W., Shamir, A.: Efficient FPGA implementations of high-dimensional cube testers on the stream cipher Grain-128. IACR Cryptology ePrint Archive **2009**, p. 218 (2009)
3. Aumasson, J.-P., Dinur, I., Meier, W., Shamir, A.: Cube testers and key recovery attacks on reduced-round MD6 and trivium. In: Dunkelman, O. (ed.) FSE 2009. LNCS, vol. 5665, pp. 1–22. Springer, Heidelberg (2009). doi:10.1007/978-3-642-03317-9_1
4. Aumasson, J.-P., Henzen, L., Meier, W., Naya-Plasencia, M.: QUARK: A lightweight hash. In: Mangard, S., Standaert, F.-X. (eds.) CHES 2010. LNCS, vol. 6225, pp. 1–15. Springer, Heidelberg (2010). doi:10.1007/978-3-642-15031-9_1
5. Aumasson, J., Henzen, L., Meier, W., Naya-Plasencia, M.: Quark: A lightweight hash. J. Cryptol. **26**(2), 313–339 (2013)

6. Boura, C., Canteaut, A.: On the influence of the algebraic degree of F^{-1} on the algebraic degree of $G \circ F$. IEEE Trans. Inf. Theor. **59**(1), 691–702 (2013)
7. Boura, C., Canteaut, A., Cannière, C.: Higher-order differential properties of KECCAK and *Luffa*. In: Joux, A. (ed.) FSE 2011. LNCS, vol. 6733, pp. 252–269. Springer, Heidelberg (2011). doi:10.1007/978-3-642-21702-9_15
8. Cannière, C.: TRIVIUM: A stream cipher construction inspired by block cipher design principles. In: Katsikas, S.K., López, J., Backes, M., Gritzalis, S., Preneel, B. (eds.) ISC 2006. LNCS, vol. 4176, pp. 171–186. Springer, Heidelberg (2006). doi:10.1007/11836810_13
9. Cannière, C., Dunkelman, O., Knežević, M.: KATAN and KTANTAN—A family of small and efficient hardware-oriented block ciphers. In: Clavier, C., Gaj, K. (eds.) CHES 2009. LNCS, vol. 5747, pp. 272–288. Springer, Heidelberg (2009). doi:10.1007/978-3-642-04138-9_20
10. Cannière, C., Preneel, B.: TRIVIUM. In: Robshaw, M., Billet, O. (eds.) New Stream Cipher Designs. LNCS, vol. 4986, pp. 244–266. Springer, Heidelberg (2008). doi:10.1007/978-3-540-68351-3_18
11. Canteaut, A., Carpov, S., Fontaine, C., Lepoint, T., Naya-Plasencia, M., Paillier, P., Sirdey, R.: Stream ciphers: A practical solution for efficient homomorphic-ciphertext compression. In: Peyrin, T. (ed.) FSE 2016. LNCS, vol. 9783, pp. 313–333. Springer, Heidelberg (2016). doi:10.1007/978-3-662-52993-5_16
12. Canteaut, A., Videau, M.: Degree of composition of highly nonlinear functions and applications to higher order differential cryptanalysis. In: Knudsen, L.R. (ed.) EUROCRYPT 2002. LNCS, vol. 2332, pp. 518–533. Springer, Heidelberg (2002). doi:10.1007/3-540-46035-7_34
13. Chakraborti, A., Chattopadhyay, A., Hassan, M., Nandi, M.: TriviA: A fast and secure authenticated encryption scheme. In: Güneysu, T., Handschuh, H. (eds.) CHES 2015. LNCS, vol. 9293, pp. 330–353. Springer, Heidelberg (2015). doi:10.1007/978-3-662-48324-4_17
14. Chakraborti, A., Nandi, M.: TriviA-ck-v2. CAESAR Submission (2015). http://competitions.cr.yp.to/round2/triviackv2.pdf
15. Courtois, N.T.: Fast algebraic attacks on stream ciphers with linear feedback. In: Boneh, D. (ed.) CRYPTO 2003. LNCS, vol. 2729, pp. 176–194. Springer, Heidelberg (2003). doi:10.1007/978-3-540-45146-4_11
16. Courtois, N., Klimov, A., Patarin, J., Shamir, A.: Efficient algorithms for solving overdefined systems of multivariate polynomial equations. In: Preneel, B. (ed.) EUROCRYPT 2000. LNCS, vol. 1807, pp. 392–407. Springer, Heidelberg (2000). doi:10.1007/3-540-45539-6_27
17. Courtois, N.T., Meier, W.: Algebraic attacks on stream ciphers with linear feedback. In: Biham, E. (ed.) EUROCRYPT 2003. LNCS, vol. 2656, pp. 345–359. Springer, Heidelberg (2003). doi:10.1007/3-540-39200-9_21
18. Courtois, N.T., Pieprzyk, J.: Cryptanalysis of block ciphers with overdefined systems of equations. In: Zheng, Y. (ed.) ASIACRYPT 2002. LNCS, vol. 2501, pp. 267–287. Springer, Heidelberg (2002). doi:10.1007/3-540-36178-2_17
19. Dinur, I., Güneysu, T., Paar, C., Shamir, A., Zimmermann, R.: An experimentally verified attack on full grain-128 using dedicated reconfigurable hardware. In: Lee, D.H., Wang, X. (eds.) ASIACRYPT 2011. LNCS, vol. 7073, pp. 327–343. Springer, Heidelberg (2011). doi:10.1007/978-3-642-25385-0_18
20. Dinur, I., Morawiecki, P., Pieprzyk, J., Srebrny, M., Straus, M.: Cube attacks and cube-attack-like cryptanalysis on the round-reduced keccak sponge function. In: Oswald, E., Fischlin, M. (eds.) EUROCRYPT 2015. LNCS, vol. 9056, pp. 733–761. Springer, Heidelberg (2015). doi:10.1007/978-3-662-46800-5_28

21. Dinur, I., Shamir, A.: Cube attacks on tweakable black box polynomials. In: Joux, A. (ed.) EUROCRYPT 2009. LNCS, vol. 5479, pp. 278–299. Springer, Heidelberg (2009). doi:10.1007/978-3-642-01001-9_16
22. Dinur, I., Shamir, A.: Breaking Grain-128 with dynamic cube attacks. In: Joux, A. (ed.) FSE 2011. LNCS, vol. 6733, pp. 167–187. Springer, Heidelberg (2011). doi:10.1007/978-3-642-21702-9_10
23. Englund, H., Johansson, T., Sönmez Turan, M.: A framework for chosen IV statistical analysis of stream ciphers. In: Srinathan, K., Rangan, C.P., Yung, M. (eds.) INDOCRYPT 2007. LNCS, vol. 4859, pp. 268–281. Springer, Heidelberg (2007). doi:10.1007/978-3-540-77026-8_20
24. Fischer, S., Khazaei, S., Meier, W.: Chosen IV statistical analysis for key recovery attacks on stream ciphers. In: Vaudenay, S. (ed.) AFRICACRYPT 2008. LNCS, vol. 5023, pp. 236–245. Springer, Heidelberg (2008). doi:10.1007/978-3-540-68164-9_16
25. Fontaine, C.: Nonlinear feedback shift register. In: van Tilborg, H.C.A., Jajodia, S. (eds.) Encyclopedia of Cryptography and Security, 2nd edn, pp. 846–848. Springer, US (2011)
26. Fouque, P.-A., Vannet, T.: Improving key recovery to 784 and 799 rounds of trivium using optimized cube attacks. In: Moriai, S. (ed.) FSE 2013. LNCS, vol. 8424, pp. 502–517. Springer, Heidelberg (2014). doi:10.1007/978-3-662-43933-3_26
27. Hell, M., Johansson, T., Maximov, A., Meier, W.: A stream cipher proposal: Grain-128. In: 2006 IEEE International Symposium on Information Theory, pp. 1614–1618. IEEE (2006)
28. Hell, M., Johansson, T., Maximov, A., Meier, W.: The grain family of stream ciphers. In: Robshaw, M., Billet, O. (eds.) New Stream Cipher Designs. LNCS, vol. 4986, pp. 179–190. Springer, Heidelberg (2008). doi:10.1007/978-3-540-68351-3_14
29. Knellwolf, S., Meier, W., Naya-Plasencia, M.: Conditional differential cryptanalysis of trivium and KATAN. In: Miri, A., Vaudenay, S. (eds.) SAC 2011. LNCS, vol. 7118, pp. 200–212. Springer, Heidelberg (2012). doi:10.1007/978-3-642-28496-0_12
30. Knudsen, L.R.: Truncated and higher order differentials. In: Preneel, B. (ed.) FSE 1994. LNCS, vol. 1008, pp. 196–211. Springer, Heidelberg (1995). doi:10.1007/3-540-60590-8_16
31. Knudsen, L., Wagner, D.: Integral cryptanalysis. In: Daemen, J., Rijmen, V. (eds.) FSE 2002. LNCS, vol. 2365, pp. 112–127. Springer, Heidelberg (2002). doi:10.1007/3-540-45661-9_9
32. Lai, X.: Higher order derivatives and differential cryptanalysis. In: Proceeding Symposium Communication and Coding Cryptography. Kluwer Academic Publishers, pp. 227–233 (1994)
33. Liu, M., Lin, D., Wang, W.: Searching cubes for testing Boolean functions and its application to Trivium. In: IEEE International Symposium on Information Theory (ISIT 2015), Hong Kong, China, 14–19 June 2015, pp. 496–500. IEEE (2015)
34. Maximov, A., Biryukov, A.: Two trivial attacks on TRIVIUM. In: Adams, C., Miri, A., Wiener, M. (eds.) SAC 2007. LNCS, vol. 4876, pp. 36–55. Springer, Heidelberg (2007). doi:10.1007/978-3-540-77360-3_3
35. Moriai, S., Shimoyama, T., Kaneko, T.: Higher order differential attak of CAST cipher. In: Vaudenay, S. (ed.) FSE 1998. LNCS, vol. 1372, pp. 17–31. Springer, Heidelberg (1998)
36. Oswald, E., Fischlin, M. (eds.): EUROCRYPT 2015. LNCS, vol. 9056. Springer, Heidelberg (2015)

37. Saarinen, M.O.: Chosen-IV statistical attacks on estream ciphers. In: Malek, M., Fernández-Medina, E., Hernando, J. (eds.): SECRYPT 2006, Proceedings of the International Conference on Security and Cryptography, Setúbal, Portugal, 7–10 August 2006, SECRYPT is part of ICETE - The International Joint Conference on e-Business and Telecommunications, pp. 260–266. INSTICC Press (2006)
38. Sarkar, S., Maitra, S., Baksi, A.: Observing biases in the state: case studies with Trivium and trivia-sc. Des. Codes Crypt. **82**(1–2), 351–375 (2017)
39. Stankovski, P.: Greedy distinguishers and nonrandomness detectors. In: Gong, G., Gupta, K.C. (eds.) INDOCRYPT 2010. LNCS, vol. 6498, pp. 210–226. Springer, Heidelberg (2010). doi:10.1007/978-3-642-17401-8_16
40. Todo, Y.: Structural evaluation by generalized integral property, pp. 287–314. [36]
41. Todo, Y., Isobe, T., Hao, Y., Meier, W.: Cube attacks on non-blackbox polynomials based on division property. In: Proceedings of 37th Annual International Cryptology Conference on Advances in Cryptology (CRYPTO 2017), Santa Barbara, CA, USA, 20–24 August 2017 (2017)
42. Todo, Y., Morii, M.: Bit-based division property and application to SIMON family. In: Peyrin, T. (ed.) FSE 2016. LNCS, vol. 9783, pp. 357–377. Springer, Heidelberg (2016). doi:10.1007/978-3-662-52993-5_18
43. Vardasbi, A., Salmasizadeh, M., Mohajeri, J.: Superpoly algebraic normal form monomial test on Trivium. IET Inform. Secur. **7**(3), 230–238 (2013)
44. Wu, H.: ACORN: a lightweight authenticated cipher (v3). CAESAR Submission, (2016). http://competitions.cr.yp.to/round3/acornv3.pdf
45. Xu, C., Zhang, B., Feng, D.: Linear cryptanalysis of FASER128/256 and TriviA-ck. In: Meier, W., Mukhopadhyay, D. (eds.) INDOCRYPT 2014. LNCS, vol. 8885, pp. 237–254. Springer, Cham (2014). doi:10.1007/978-3-319-13039-2_14

Cube Attacks on Non-Blackbox Polynomials Based on Division Property

Yosuke Todo[1(✉)], Takanori Isobe[2], Yonglin Hao[3], and Willi Meier[4]

[1] NTT Secure Platform Laboratories, Tokyo 180-8585, Japan
todo.yosuke@lab.ntt.co.jp
[2] University of Hyogo, Hyogo 650-0047, Japan
[3] Department of Computer Science and Technology, Tsinghua University, Beijing 100084, China
[4] FHNW, Windisch, Switzerland

Abstract. The cube attack is a powerful cryptanalytic technique and is especially powerful against stream ciphers. Since we need to analyze the complicated structure of a stream cipher in the cube attack, the cube attack basically analyzes it by regarding it as a blackbox. Therefore, the cube attack is an experimental attack, and we cannot evaluate the security when the size of cube exceeds an experimental range, e.g., 40. In this paper, we propose cube attacks on non-blackbox polynomials. Our attacks are developed by using the division property, which is recently applied to various block ciphers. The clear advantage is that we can exploit large cube sizes because it never regards the cipher as a blackbox. We apply the new cube attack to Trivium, Grain128a, and ACORN. As a result, the secret keys of 832-round Trivium, 183-round Grain128a, and 704-round ACORN are recovered. These attacks are the current best key-recovery attack against these ciphers.

Keywords: Cube attack · Stream cipher · Division property · Higher-order differential cryptanalysis · MILP · Trivium · Grain128a · ACORN

1 Introduction

Cube attack is one of general cryptanalytic techniques against symmetric-key cryptosystems proposed by Dinur and Shamir [11]. Especially, the cube attack has been successfully applied to various stream ciphers [4,10,12,14,25]. Let $\boldsymbol{x}$ and $\boldsymbol{v}$ be secret and public variables of stream ciphers, respectively, and let $f(\boldsymbol{x}, \boldsymbol{v})$ be the first bit of key stream. Some bits in $\boldsymbol{v}$ are active, where they take all possible combinations of values. The set of these values is denoted as a *cube*, and the sum of $f(\boldsymbol{x}, \boldsymbol{v})$ over all values of the cube is evaluated. Then, this sum is also represented as a polynomial whose inputs are $\boldsymbol{x}$ and $\boldsymbol{v}$, and the polynomial is denoted as a *superpoly* of the cube. The superpoly is more simplified than the original $f(\boldsymbol{x}, \boldsymbol{v})$, and secret variables $\boldsymbol{x}$ are recovered by analyzing this simplified polynomial. Unfortunately, it is really difficult to analyze the structure of the superpoly. Therefore, the target stream cipher $f(\boldsymbol{x}, \boldsymbol{v})$ is normally regarded as a

J. Katz and H. Shacham (Eds.): CRYPTO 2017, Part III, LNCS 10403, pp. 250–279, 2017.
DOI: 10.1007/978-3-319-63697-9_9

blackbox polynomial in the cube attack, and this blackbox polynomial is experimentally evaluated. In the original paper of the cube attack [11], the authors introduced a linearity test to reveal the structure of the superpoly. If the linearity test always passes, the Algebraic Normal Form (ANF) of the superpoly is recovered by assuming that the superpoly is linear. Moreover, a quadraticity test was introduced in [24], and the ANF of the superpoly is similarly recovered. The quadraticity test was also used in the current best key-recovery attack against Trivium [14]. Note that they are experimental cryptanalysis, and it is possible that cube attacks do not actually work. For example, if the superpoly is highly unbalanced function for specific variables, we cannot ignore the probability that the linearity and quadraticity tests fail.

The difference between the cube attack and higher-order differential attack has been often discussed. The higher-order differential attack was proposed by Lai [20]. Assuming the algebraic degree of f is at most d, Lai showed that the algebraic degree of the ith order difference is at most $d - i$. Then, Knudsen showed the effectiveness of the higher-order differential attack on toy block ciphers [18]. Nowadays, many advanced techniques similar to the higher-order differential attack have been developed to analyze block ciphers, e.g., integral attack [8,19,22].

The cube attack can in some way be seen as a type of higher-order differential attacks because it also evaluates the behavior of higher-order difference. However, the most major difference between the cube attack and common higher-order differential attack is whether or not secret variables are directly recovered from the characteristic, and understanding this difference is very important to consider key-recovery attacks against stream ciphers. When a block cipher is analyzed, attackers first evaluate the algebraic degree of the reduced-round block cipher and construct a higher-order differential characteristic, where the $(d+1)$th order difference is always 0 if the degree is at most d. Then, the key recovery is independently appended after the higher-order differential characteristic. Namely, attackers guess round keys used in last several rounds and compute the $(d+1)$th order difference of ciphertexts of the reduced-round block cipher. If the correct round key is guessed, the $(d + 1)$th order difference is always 0. In other words, if the $(d + 1)$th order difference is not 0, guessed round keys are incorrect.

Note that we cannot use this strategy for the key-recovery attack against many stream ciphers because the secret key is generally used during the initialization phase and is not involved when generating a keystream, i.e. even if there is a distinguisher in the keystream, it cannot be directly utilized for key recovery attacks by appending key recovery rounds in the key generation phase, unlike key recovery attacks of block ciphers. To execute the key-recovery attack of stream ciphers, we have to recover the secret key by using only key streams that attackers can observe. Therefore, more advanced and complicated analyses are required than the simple degree estimation of the common higher-order differential attack or square, saturation, and integral characteristics. In the context of the cube attack, we have to analyze the ANF of the superpoly. It is unlikely to well analyze because symmetric-key cryptosystems are complicated. Therefore, stream ciphers have been experimentally analyzed in the cube attack.

Another important related work to understand this paper is the division property, which is a new method to construct higher-order differential (integral) characteristics [31]. The division property is the generalization of the integral property [19] that can also exploit the algebraic degree at the same time, and it allows us to evaluate more accurate higher-order differential characteristics. Moreover, the bit-based division property was introduced in [32], and three propagation rules for basic operations, `and`, `xor`, and `copy` are shown. While arbitrary block ciphers are evaluated by using the bit-based division property, it requires much time and memory complexity [32]. Therefore, the application is first limited to block ciphers with small block length, like SIMON32 or Simeck32. In [34], Xiang et al. showed how to model the propagation of the bit-based division property by using the mixed integer linear programming (MILP). Moreover, they showed that MILP solvers can efficiently evaluate the propagation. To demonstrate the effectiveness, accurate propagations of the bit-based division property for six lightweight block ciphers including SIMON128 were shown.

Our Contribution. The most important step in a cube attack is the *superpoly recovery*. If the superpoly is more efficiently recovered than the brute-force search, it brings some vulnerability of symmetric-key ciphers. Superpolys are experimentally recovered in the conventional cube attack. The advantage of such approach is that we do not need to analyze the structure of f in detail. On the other hand, there are significant drawbacks in the experimental analysis.

- The size of a cube is limited to the experimental range because we have to compute the sum of f over a cube. It may be possible that we try a cube whose size is at most 40 in current computers, but it requires incredible effort in the aspect to both money and time. Therefore, it is practically infeasible to execute the cube attack when the cube size exceeds 40.
- The prediction of the true security of target stream ciphers is an important motivation of cryptanalyses. Since the evaluation is limited to the experimental range, it is difficult to predict the impact of the cube attack under future high-performance computers.
- Since the stream cipher is regarded as a blackbox, the feedback to designers is limited.

To overcome these drawbacks, we propose the cube attack on non-blackbox polynomials.

Our analysis is based on the propagation of the (bit-based) division property, and as far as we know, it is the first application of the division property to stream ciphers. Since the division property is a tool to find higher-order differential characteristics, the trivial application is only useful to find zero-sum integral distinguishers, where the sum of the first bit of the key stream over the cube is always 0 for any secret key. As mentioned earlier, it is nontrivial to recover the secret key of stream ciphers by using zero-sum integral distinguisher. Therefore, we propose a novel application of the division property to recover the secret key. Our technique uses the division property to analyze the ANF of $f(\boldsymbol{x}, \boldsymbol{v})$

by evaluating propagations from multiple input division property according to a cube. Finally, we can evaluate secret variables that are not involved to the superpoly of the cube. This allows us to compute the upper bound of the time complexity for the superpoly recovery. Note that the superpoly recovery directly brings some vulnerability of symmetric-key ciphers, and we discuss this issue in Sect. 4.

Let I be a set of cube indices. After the evaluation of the division property, we get a set of indices J, where x_j $(j \in J)$ is involved to the superpoly. Then, the variation of the sum over the cube is at most $2^{|J|}$ for each constant part of public variables, where $|J|$ denotes the size of J. All sums are evaluated by guessing $|J|$-bit secret variables, and the time complexity to recover the ANF of the superpoly is $2^{|I|+|J|}$ encryptions. Finally, we query the encryption oracle and get the sum over the cube. Then, we can get one polynomial about secret variables, and the secret variable is recovered from the polynomial.

Table 1. Summary of results. The time complexity in this table shows the time complexity to recover the superpoly of a cube.

Applications	# rounds	Cube size	Complexity	Key recovery	Reference
TRIVIUM	799	32[a]	Practical	✓	[14]
	832	72	2^{77}	✓	Sect. 5.1
Grain128a	177	33	Practical		[21]
	183	92	2^{108}	Speculative	Sect. 5.2
ACORN	503	5[b]	Practical[b]	✓	[25]
	704	64	2^{122}	✓	Sect. 5.3

[a]18 cubes whose size is from 32 to 37 are used, where the most efficient cube is shown to recover one bit of the secret key.
[b]The attack against 477 rounds is mainly described for the practical attack in [25]. However, when the goal is the superpoly recovery and to recover one bit of the secret key, 503 rounds are attacked.

Table 1 shows the summary of applications. We applied our new cube attack to TRIVIUM [6], Grain128a [3], and ACORN [33]. TRIVIUM is part of the eSTREAM portfolio [1], and it is one of the most analyzed stream ciphers. The initialization is 1152 rounds. The secret key of TRIVIUM with 767 initialization rounds was recovered in the proposal paper of the cube attack [11]. Then, an improved cube attack was proposed in [14], and the secret key of TRIVIUM with 799 initialization rounds is recovered. This is the current best key-recovery attack against TRIVIUM. Our new cube attack recovers the secret key of TRIVIUM with 832 initialization rounds. Grain128a is a member of Grain family of stream ciphers and is standardized by ISO/IEC 29167-13 [16]. The initialization is 256 rounds. The conditional differential cryptanalysis was applied to Grain128a, and a distinguishing attack against Grain128a with 177 initialization rounds was shown under the single-key setting [21]. On the other hand, the key-recovery attack is not known. Our new cube attack recovers the secret key of Grain128a with 183 initialization rounds. Unfortunately, when we applied our technique to practical cube attack, i.e., the cube size is small, we could not find balanced superpoly. In such case, the size of recovered bit of information is smaller than 1 bit. Since we cannot say that balanced superpoly is efficiently found in the large cube size, the feasibility of the key recovery is speculative. However, 183 rounds are at least vulnerable because the superpoly recovery is more efficient than the brute-force search. ACORN is an authenticated encryption and one of the 3rd round candidates in CAESAR competition [2]. The structure is based on non-linear feedback shift register (NLFSR) like Trivium and Grain. Before the output of key streams, the secret key and initialization vector (iv) are sequentially XORed with the NLFSR, and then associated data is sequentially XORed. In the nonce-respecting setting, we cannot select cube bits from the associated data. Therefore, the initialization is regarded as 2048 rounds when there is no associated data. The cube attack was applied in [25], and the secret key of ACORN with 503 initialization is recovered. Our new cube attack recovers the secret key of ACORN with 704 initialization rounds.

2 Preliminaries

2.1 Mixed Integer Linear Programming

The deployment of the mixed integer linear programming (MILP) to cryptanalysis was shown by Mouha et al. in [23]. Then, the MILP has been applied to search for differential [28,29], linear [28], impossible differential [7,26], zero-correlation linear [7], and integral characteristics with division property [34]. The use of MILP for the integral characteristic with division property is expanded in this paper.

The MILP problem is an optimization or feasibility program where variables are restricted to integers. We create an MILP model $\mathcal{M}$, which consists of variables $\mathcal{M}.var$, constraints $\mathcal{M}.con$, and an objective function $\mathcal{M}.obj$. As an example, let us consider the following optimization program.

Example 1.

$$\begin{aligned}
\mathcal{M}.var &\leftarrow x, y, z \text{ as binary.}\\
\mathcal{M}.con &\leftarrow x + 2y + 3z \leq 4\\
\mathcal{M}.con &\leftarrow x + y \geq 1\\
\mathcal{M}.obj &\leftarrow \text{maximize } x + y + 2z
\end{aligned}$$

The answer of the model $\mathcal{M}$ is 3, where $(x, y, z) = (1, 0, 1)$.

MILP solver can solve such optimization problem, and it returns *infeasible* if there is no feasible solution. Moreover, if there is no objective function, the MILP solver only evaluates whether this model is feasible or not.

We used Gurobi optimization as the solver in our experiments [15].

2.2 Cube Attack

The cube attack is a key-recovery attack proposed by Dinur and Shamir in 2009 [11] and is the extension of the higher-order differential cryptanalysis [20].

Let $\boldsymbol{x} = (x_1, x_2, \dots, x_n)$ and $\boldsymbol{v} = (v_1, v_2, \dots, v_m)$ be n secret variables and m public variables, respectively. Then, the symmetric-key cryptosystem is represented as $f(\boldsymbol{x}, \boldsymbol{v})$, where f denotes a polynomial and the size of input and output is $n + m$ bits and 1 bit, respectively. In the case of stream ciphers, $\boldsymbol{x}$ is the secret key, $\boldsymbol{v}$ is the initialization vector (iv), and $f(\boldsymbol{x}, \boldsymbol{v})$ is the first bit of the key stream. The core idea of the cube attack is to simplify the polynomial by computing the higher-order differential of $f(\boldsymbol{x}, \boldsymbol{v})$ and to recover secret variables from the simplified polynomial.

For a set of indices $I = \{i_1, i_2, \dots, i_{|I|}\} \subset \{1, 2, \dots, n\}$, which is referred as cube indices and denote by t_I the monomial as $t_I = v_{i_1} \cdots v_{i_{|I|}}$. Then, we can decompose $f(\boldsymbol{x}, \boldsymbol{v})$ as

$$f(\boldsymbol{x}, \boldsymbol{v}) = t_I \cdot p(\boldsymbol{x}, \boldsymbol{v}) + q(\boldsymbol{x}, \boldsymbol{v}),$$

where $p(\boldsymbol{x}, \boldsymbol{v})$ is independent of $\{v_{i_1}, v_{i_2}, \dots, v_{i_{|I|}}\}$ and the effective number of input variables of p is $n + m - |I|$ bits. Moreover, $q(\boldsymbol{x}, \boldsymbol{v})$ misses at least one variable from $\{v_{i_1}, v_{i_2}, \dots, v_{i_{|I|}}\}$.

Let C_I, which is referred as a cube (defined by I), be a set of $2^{|I|}$ values where variables in $\{v_{i_1}, v_{i_2}, \dots, v_{i_{|I|}}\}$ are taking all possible combinations of values, and all remaining variables are fixed to some arbitrary values. Then the sum of f over all values of the cube C_I is

$$\begin{aligned}\bigoplus_{C_I} f(\boldsymbol{x}, \boldsymbol{v}) &= \bigoplus_{C_I} t_I \cdot p(\boldsymbol{x}, \boldsymbol{v}) + \bigoplus_{C_I} q(\boldsymbol{x}, \boldsymbol{v}) \\ &= p(\boldsymbol{x}, \boldsymbol{v}).\end{aligned}$$

The first term is reduced to $p(\boldsymbol{x}, \boldsymbol{v})$ because t_I becomes 1 for only one case in C_I. The second term is always canceled out because $q(\boldsymbol{x}, \boldsymbol{v})$ misses at least one variable from $\{v_{i_1}, v_{i_2}, \dots, v_{i_{|I|}}\}$. Then, $p(\boldsymbol{x}, \boldsymbol{v})$ is called the *superpoly* of the cube C_I.

Blackbox Analysis. If the cube is appropriately chosen such that the superpoly is enough simplified to recover secret variables, the cube attack succeeds. However, $f(\boldsymbol{x}, \boldsymbol{v})$ in real symmetric-key cryptosystems is too complicated. Therefore, the cube attack regards f as a blackbox polynomial.

In the preprocessing phase, attackers first try out various cubes, change values of public and secret variables, and analyze the feature of the superpoly. The goal of this phase is to reveal the structure of $p(\boldsymbol{x}, \boldsymbol{v})$. Especially, the original cube attack searches for linear superpoly $p(\boldsymbol{x}, \boldsymbol{0})$ by the summation over the chosen cube. If the superpoly is linear,

$$p(\boldsymbol{x} \oplus \boldsymbol{x}', \boldsymbol{0}) = p(\boldsymbol{x}, \boldsymbol{0}) \oplus p(\boldsymbol{x}', \boldsymbol{0}) \oplus p(\boldsymbol{0}, \boldsymbol{0})$$

always holds for arbitrary $\boldsymbol{x}$ and $\boldsymbol{x}'$. By repeating this linearity test enough, attackers can know that the superpoly is linear with high probability, and the Algebraic Normal Form (ANF) of the superpoly is recovered by assuming its linearity.

In the online phase, attackers query to an encryption oracle by controlling only public variables and recover secret variables. Attackers evaluate the sum of $f(\boldsymbol{x}, \boldsymbol{v})$ over all values of the cube C_I. Since the sum is right hand side of the superpoly, the part of secret variables is recovered. Please refer to [4,11] to well understand the principle of the cube attack.

2.3 Higher-Order Differential Cryptanalysis and Division Property

Underlying mathematical background of the cube attack is the same as that of the higher-order differential attack. Unlike the cube attack, the common higher-order differential attack never regards the block cipher as a blackbox polynomial. Attackers analyze the structure of a block cipher and construct higher-order differential characteristics, where attackers prepare the set of chosen plaintexts such that the sum of corresponding ciphertexts of reduced-round block cipher is 0. After the proposal of the higher-order differential attack, many advanced techniques similar to the higher-order differential attack have been developed to analyze block ciphers, e.g., square attack [8], saturation attack [22], multi-set attack [5], and integral attack [19].

Division Property. At 2015, the division property, which is an improved technique to find higher-order differential (integral) characteristics for iterated ciphers, was proposed in [31]. Then, the bit-based variant was introduced in [32], and it is defined as follows[1].

Definition 1 ((Bit-Based) Division Property). *Let $\mathbb{X}$ be a multiset whose elements take a value of $\mathbb{F}_2^n$. Let $\mathbb{K}$ be a set whose elements take an n-dimensional bit vector. When the multiset $\mathbb{X}$ has the division property $\mathcal{D}_{\mathbb{K}}^{1^n}$, it fulfils the following conditions:*

$$\bigoplus_{\boldsymbol{x}\in\mathbb{X}} \boldsymbol{x}^{\boldsymbol{u}} = \begin{cases} \text{unknown} & \textit{if there exist } \boldsymbol{k}\in\mathbb{K} \textit{ s.t. } \boldsymbol{u}\succeq\boldsymbol{k}, \\ 0 & \textit{otherwise}, \end{cases}$$

where $\boldsymbol{u}\succeq\boldsymbol{k}$ if $u_i \geq k_i$ for all i, and $\boldsymbol{x}^{\boldsymbol{u}} = \prod_{i=1}^{n} x_i^{u_i}$.

We first evaluate the division property of the set of chosen plaintexts and then evaluate the division property of the set of corresponding ciphertexts by evaluating the propagation for every round function.

Some propagation rules for the division property are proven in [31,32]. Attackers determine indices $I = \{i_1, i_2, \ldots, i_{|I|}\} \subset \{1, 2, \ldots, n\}$ and prepare

[1] Two kinds of bit-based division property are proposed in [32]. In this paper, we only focus on the conventional bit-based division property.

$2^{|I|}$ chosen plaintexts where variables indexed by I are taking all possible combinations of values. The division property of such chosen plaintexts is $\mathcal{D}_{\boldsymbol{k}}^{1^n}$, where $k_i = 1$ if $i \in I$ and $k_i = 0$ otherwise. Then, the propagation of the division property from $\mathcal{D}_{\boldsymbol{k}}^{1^n}$ is evaluated as

$$\{\boldsymbol{k}\} \stackrel{\text{def}}{=} \mathbb{K}_0 \rightarrow \mathbb{K}_1 \rightarrow \mathbb{K}_2 \rightarrow \cdots \rightarrow \mathbb{K}_r,$$

where $\mathcal{D}_{\mathbb{K}_i}$ is the division property after i-round propagation. If the division property $\mathbb{K}_r$ does not have an unit vector $\boldsymbol{e}_i$ whose only ith element is 1, the ith bit of r-round ciphertexts is balanced.

Propagation of Division Property with MILP. Evaluating the propagation of the division property is not easy because the size of $\mathbb{K}_i$ extremely increases. At ASIACRYPT 2016, Xiang et al. showed that the propagation is efficiently evaluated by using MILP [34]. First, they introduced the *division trail* as follows.

Definition 2 (Division Trail). *Let us consider the propagation of the division property* $\{\boldsymbol{k}\} \stackrel{\text{def}}{=} \mathbb{K}_0 \rightarrow \mathbb{K}_1 \rightarrow \mathbb{K}_2 \rightarrow \cdots \rightarrow \mathbb{K}_r$. *Moreover, for any vector* $\boldsymbol{k}_{i+1}^* \in \mathbb{K}_{i+1}$, *there must exist a vector* $\boldsymbol{k}_i^* \in \mathbb{K}_i$ *such that* $\boldsymbol{k}_i^*$ *can propagate to* $\boldsymbol{k}_{i+1}^*$ *by the propagation rule of the division property. Furthermore, for* $(\boldsymbol{k}_0, \boldsymbol{k}_1, \ldots, \boldsymbol{k}_r) \in (\mathbb{K}_0 \times \mathbb{K}_1 \times \cdots \times \mathbb{K}_r)$ *if* $\boldsymbol{k}_i$ *can propagate to* $\boldsymbol{k}_{i+1}$ *for all* $i \in \{0, 1, \ldots, r-1\}$, *we call* $(\boldsymbol{k}_0 \rightarrow \boldsymbol{k}_1 \rightarrow \cdots \rightarrow \boldsymbol{k}_r)$ *an* r*-round division trail.*

Let E_k be the target r-round iterated cipher. Then, if there are division trails $\boldsymbol{k}_0 \xrightarrow{E_k} \boldsymbol{k}_r = \boldsymbol{e}_i$, attackers cannot know whether the ith bit of r-round ciphertexts is balanced or not. On the other hand, if we can prove that there is no division trail $\boldsymbol{k}_0 \xrightarrow{E_k} \boldsymbol{e}_i$, the ith bit of r-round ciphertexts is always balanced. Therefore, we have to evaluate all possible division trails to verify whether each bit of ciphertexts is balanced or not. In [30–32], all possible division trails are evaluated by using a breadth-first search. Unfortunately, such a search requires enormous memory and time complexity. Therefore, it is practically infeasible to apply this method to iterated ciphers whose block length is not small.

MILP can efficiently solve this problem. We generate an MILP model that covers all division trails, and the solver evaluates the feasibility whether there are division trails from the input division property to the output one or not. If the solver guarantees that there is no division trail, higher-order differential (integral) characteristics are found.

Let `copy`, `xor`, and `and` be three fundamental operations, where 1 bit is copied into m bits in `copy`, the xor of m bits is computed in `xor`, and the and of m bits is computed in `and`. Note that MILP models for `copy`, `xor`, and `and` are sufficient to represent any circuit.

Proposition 1 (MILP Model for COPY). *Let* $a \xrightarrow{COPY} (b_1, b_2, \ldots, b_m)$ *be a division trail of COPY. The following inequalities are sufficient to describe the propagation of the division property for* `copy`.

$$\begin{cases} \mathcal{M}.var \leftarrow a, b_1, b_2, \dots, b_m \; as \; binary. \\ \mathcal{M}.con \leftarrow a = b_1 + b_2 + \cdots + b_m \end{cases}$$

Proposition 2 (MILP Model for XOR). *Let $(a_1, a_2, \dots, a_m) \xrightarrow{XOR} b$ be a division trail of XOR. The following inequalities are sufficient to describe the propagation of the division property for* `xor`.

$$\begin{cases} \mathcal{M}.var \leftarrow a_1, a_2, \dots, a_m, b \; as \; binary. \\ \mathcal{M}.con \leftarrow a_1 + a_2 + \cdots + a_m = b \end{cases}$$

Proposition 3 (MILP Model for AND). *Let $(a_1, a_2, \dots, a_m) \xrightarrow{AND} b$ be a division trail of AND. The following inequalities are sufficient to describe the propagation of the division property for* `and`.

$$\begin{cases} \mathcal{M}.var \leftarrow a_1, a_2, \dots, a_m, b \; as \; binary. \\ \mathcal{M}.con \leftarrow b \geq a_i \; for \; all \; i \in \{1, 2, \dots, m\} \end{cases}$$

To accept multiple inputs and outputs, three propositions are generalized from the original ones shown in [34]. Moreover, Propositions 1 and 2 are also introduced in [27]. Note that Proposition 3 includes redundant propagations of the division property, but they do not affect obtained characteristics.

3 How to Analyze Non-Blackbox Polynomials

The cube attack basically regards $f(\boldsymbol{x}, \boldsymbol{v})$ as a blackbox polynomial and analyzes it experimentally because real $f(\boldsymbol{x}, \boldsymbol{v})$ are too complicated to analyze the structure in detail. Such experimental analysis is often advantageous but has significant drawbacks, e.g., the size of cube is limited to the experimental range.

In this section, we propose a new technique to analyze the polynomial, where our technique never regards the polynomial as a blackbox and can analyze the structure in detail. Accurately, we propose a new application of the division property that enables us to analyze the Algebraic Normal Form (ANF) coefficients of f. Secret variables that are not involved in the superpoly of a cube C_I are efficiently identified by using our new method. As a result, we can estimate the time complexity that the ANF of the superpoly of a cube C_I is recovered.

3.1 What Is Guaranteed by Division Property

We first revisit the definition of the division property and consider what the division property can do for stream ciphers.

Zero-Sum Integral Distinguisher. The trivial application is to find zero-sum integral distinguishers. Let us consider $f(\boldsymbol{x}, \boldsymbol{v})$ as a stream cipher, where $\boldsymbol{x}$ and $\boldsymbol{v}$ denote the secret and public variables, respectively, and f is designed by using iterative structure. For a cube C_I where the variables in $\{v_{i_1}, v_{i_2}, \ldots, v_{i_{|I|}}\}$ are taking all possible combinations of values, the propagation of the division property enables us to evaluate whether or not the sum of $f(\boldsymbol{x}, \boldsymbol{v})$ over all values of the cube C_I is balanced. Therefore, if the goal of attackers is to find zero-sum integral distinguishers, we can trivially use the division property.

Analysis of ANF Coefficients. Even if we can find a zero-sum integral distinguisher on stream ciphers, it is nontrivial to recover secret variables unlike block ciphers. Therefore, new techniques are required for the extension to the key-recovery attack.

We propose a novel application of the division property, where the division property is not used to find zero-sum integral distinguishers but used to analyze the ANF coefficients of f. Since our goal is to analyze the ANF coefficients, we do not need to distinguish public variables from secret ones. For the simplicity of notation, we consider $f(\boldsymbol{x})$ instead of $f(\boldsymbol{x}, \boldsymbol{v})$, and the ANF of $f(\boldsymbol{x})$ is represented as follows.

$$f(\boldsymbol{x}) = \bigoplus_{\boldsymbol{u} \in \mathbb{F}_2^n} a_{\boldsymbol{u}}^f \cdot \boldsymbol{x}^{\boldsymbol{u}},$$

where $a_{\boldsymbol{u}}^f \in \mathbb{F}_2$ denotes the ANF coefficients. Then, the following Lemma is derived.

Lemma 1. *Let $f(\boldsymbol{x})$ be a polynomial from $\mathbb{F}_2^n$ to $\mathbb{F}_2$ and $a_{\boldsymbol{u}}^f \in \mathbb{F}_2$ $(\boldsymbol{u} \in \mathbb{F}_2^n)$ be the ANF coefficients. Let $\boldsymbol{k}$ be an n-dimensional bit vector. Then, assuming there is no division trail such that $\boldsymbol{k} \xrightarrow{f} 1$, $a_{\boldsymbol{u}}^f$ is always 0 for $\boldsymbol{u} \succeq \boldsymbol{k}$.*

Proof. According to $\boldsymbol{k}$, we first decompose $f(\boldsymbol{x})$ into

$$\begin{aligned} f(\boldsymbol{x}) &= \bigoplus_{\boldsymbol{u} \in \mathbb{F}_2^n | \boldsymbol{u} \succeq \boldsymbol{k}} u_{\boldsymbol{u}}^f \cdot \boldsymbol{x}^{\boldsymbol{u}} \oplus \bigoplus_{\boldsymbol{u} \in \mathbb{F}_2^n | \boldsymbol{u} \not\succeq \boldsymbol{k}} a_{\boldsymbol{u}}^f \cdot \boldsymbol{x}^{\boldsymbol{u}}, \\ &= \boldsymbol{x}^{\boldsymbol{k}} \cdot \bigoplus_{\boldsymbol{u} \in \mathbb{F}_2^n | \boldsymbol{u} \succeq \boldsymbol{k}} a_{\boldsymbol{u}}^f \cdot \boldsymbol{x}^{\boldsymbol{u} \oplus \boldsymbol{k}} \oplus \bigoplus_{\boldsymbol{u} \in \mathbb{F}_2^n | \boldsymbol{u} \not\succeq \boldsymbol{k}} a_{\boldsymbol{u}}^f \cdot \boldsymbol{x}^{\boldsymbol{u}}. \end{aligned}$$

Assume that there is no division trail such that $\boldsymbol{k} \xrightarrow{f} 1$. Then, no division trail guarantees that the sum of $f(\boldsymbol{x})$ over all values of the cube C_I is always balanced independent of x_i $(i \in \{1, 2, \ldots, n\} - I)$. Namely,

$$\begin{aligned} \bigoplus_{C_I} f(\boldsymbol{x}) &= \bigoplus_{C_I} \left(\boldsymbol{x}^{\boldsymbol{k}} \cdot \bigoplus_{\boldsymbol{u} \in \mathbb{F}_2^n | \boldsymbol{u} \succeq \boldsymbol{k}} a_{\boldsymbol{u}}^f \cdot \boldsymbol{x}^{\boldsymbol{u} \oplus \boldsymbol{k}} \right) \\ &= \bigoplus_{\boldsymbol{u} \in \mathbb{F}_2^n | \boldsymbol{u} \succeq \boldsymbol{k}} a_{\boldsymbol{u}}^f \cdot \boldsymbol{x}^{\boldsymbol{u} \oplus \boldsymbol{k}} = 0 \end{aligned}$$

holds independent of x_i ($i \in \{1, 2, \dots, n\} - I$). It holds only if $a_{\boldsymbol{u}}^f$ is always 0 for all $\boldsymbol{u}$ such that $\boldsymbol{u} \succeq \boldsymbol{k}$. □

Lemma 1 is very important observation for our attack.

3.2 Superpoly Recovery

The most important part of a cube attack is to recover the superpoly, and we simply call it the *superpoly recovery* in this paper. Since public variables $\boldsymbol{v}$ are known and chosen for attackers, the ANF of $p_{\boldsymbol{v}}(\boldsymbol{x}) = p(\boldsymbol{v}, \boldsymbol{x})$ is evaluated, and the goal is to recover $p_{\boldsymbol{v}}(\boldsymbol{x})$ whose $\boldsymbol{v}$ is fixed. Once the superpoly $p_{\boldsymbol{v}}(\boldsymbol{x})$ is recovered, attackers query the cube to an encryption oracle and compute the sum of $f(\boldsymbol{x}, \boldsymbol{v})$ over the cube. Then, attackers can get one polynomial about secret variables, and the secret variables are recovered from the polynomial.

The size of secret variables recovered from one superpoly depends on the structure of the superpoly $p_{\boldsymbol{v}}(\boldsymbol{x})$. If a balanced superpoly is used, one bit of information in involved secret variables is always recovered. If an unbalanced superpoly is used, the size of recovered secret variables is less than 1 bit but some information of secret variables is leaked to attackers. Moreover, it is possible to recover more bits of information in secret variables by exploiting multiple cubes. As an extreme case, if the superpoly is constant function, no secret variable is recovered, but it trivially implies constant-sum integral distinguishers. Therefore, the superpoly recovery directly brings vulnerability of symmetric-key cryptosystems, and some information of secret variables is always recovered unless the superpoly is constant function.

Previous Method to Recover Superpoly. The previous cube attack experimentally recovered the superpoly of a cube whose size is feasible for current computer. Therefore, not every superpoly can be evaluated. Linearity and quadraticity tests are repeated, and the superpoly is regarded as the linear or quadratic polynomial if these tests are sufficiently passes. Then, assuming the superpoly is linear or quadratic, the superpoly is recovered.

Analyze ANF Coefficients of Superpoly by Division Property. Lemma 1 implies that the division property can be used as a tool to analyze ANF coefficients of the superpoly. The following proposition is shown from Lemma 1 and is useful to evaluate the upper bound of the complexity to recover the ANF of the superpoly.

Proposition 4. *Let $f(\boldsymbol{x}, \boldsymbol{v})$ be a polynomial, where $\boldsymbol{x}$ and $\boldsymbol{v}$ denote the secret and public variables, respectively. For a set of indices $I = \{i_1, i_2, \dots, i_{|I|}\} \subset \{1, 2, \dots, m\}$, let C_I be a set of $2^{|I|}$ values where the variables in $\{v_{i_1}, v_{i_2}, \dots, v_{i_{|I|}}\}$ are taking all possible combinations of values. Let $\boldsymbol{k}_I$ be an m-dimensional bit vector such that $\boldsymbol{v}^{\boldsymbol{k}_I} = t_I = v_{i_1} v_{i_2} \cdots v_{i_{|I|}}$, i.e. $k_i = 1$ if $i \in I$ and $k_i = 0$ otherwise. Assuming there is no division trail such that $(\boldsymbol{e}_j, \boldsymbol{k}_I) \xrightarrow{f} 1$, x_j is not involved in the superpoly of the cube C_I.*

Algorithm 1. Evaluate secret variables by MILP

```
procedure attackFramework(MILP model M, cube indices I)
    Let x be n MILP variables of M corresponding to secret variables.
    Let v be m MILP variables of M corresponding to public variables.
    M.con ← v_i = 1 for all i ∈ I
    M.con ← v_i = 0 for all i ∈ ({1, 2, ..., n} − I)
    M.con ← Σ_{i=1}^{m} x_i = 1
    do
        solve MILP model M
        if M is feasible then
            pick index j ∈ {1, 2, ..., n} s.t. x_j = 1
            J = J ∪ {j}
            M.con ← x_j = 0
        end if
    while M is feasible
    return J
end procedure
```

Proof. The ANF of $f(\boldsymbol{x}, \boldsymbol{v})$ is represented as follows.

$$f(\boldsymbol{x}, \boldsymbol{v}) = \bigoplus_{\boldsymbol{u} \in \mathbb{F}_2^{n+m}} a_{\boldsymbol{u}}^f \cdot (\boldsymbol{x} \| \boldsymbol{v})^{\boldsymbol{u}},$$

where $a_{\boldsymbol{u}}^f \in \mathbb{F}_2$ denotes the ANF coefficients. The polynomial $f(\boldsymbol{x}, \boldsymbol{v})$ is decomposed into

$$\begin{aligned} f(\boldsymbol{x}, \boldsymbol{v}) &= \bigoplus_{\boldsymbol{u} \in \mathbb{F}_2^{n+m} | \boldsymbol{u} \succeq (\boldsymbol{0} \| \boldsymbol{k}_I)} a_{\boldsymbol{u}}^f \cdot (\boldsymbol{x} \| \boldsymbol{v})^{\boldsymbol{u}} \oplus \bigoplus_{\boldsymbol{u} \in \mathbb{F}_2^{n+m} | \boldsymbol{u} \not\succeq (\boldsymbol{0} \| \boldsymbol{k}_I)} a_{\boldsymbol{u}}^f \cdot (\boldsymbol{x} \| \boldsymbol{v})^{\boldsymbol{u}} \\ &= t_I \cdot \bigoplus_{\boldsymbol{u} \in \mathbb{F}_2^{n+m} | \boldsymbol{u} \succeq (\boldsymbol{0} \| \boldsymbol{k}_I)} a_{\boldsymbol{u}}^f \cdot (\boldsymbol{x} \| \boldsymbol{v})^{\boldsymbol{u} \oplus (\boldsymbol{0} \| \boldsymbol{k}_I)} \oplus \bigoplus_{\boldsymbol{u} \in \mathbb{F}_2^{n+m} | \boldsymbol{u} \not\succeq (\boldsymbol{0} \| \boldsymbol{k}_I)} a_{\boldsymbol{u}}^f \cdot (\boldsymbol{x} \| \boldsymbol{v})^{(\boldsymbol{0} \| \boldsymbol{u})} \\ &= t_I \cdot p(\boldsymbol{x}, \boldsymbol{v}) \oplus q(\boldsymbol{x}, \boldsymbol{v}). \end{aligned}$$

Therefore, the superpoly $p(\boldsymbol{x}, \boldsymbol{v})$ is represented as

$$p(\boldsymbol{x}, \boldsymbol{v}) = \bigoplus_{\boldsymbol{u} \in \mathbb{F}_2^{n+m} | \boldsymbol{u} \succeq (\boldsymbol{0} \| \boldsymbol{k}_I)} a_{\boldsymbol{u}}^f \cdot (\boldsymbol{x} \| \boldsymbol{v})^{\boldsymbol{u} \oplus (\boldsymbol{0} \| \boldsymbol{k}_I)}.$$

If there is no division trail $(\boldsymbol{e}_j \| \boldsymbol{k}_I) \xrightarrow{f} 1$, $a_{\boldsymbol{u}}^f = 0$ for $\boldsymbol{u} \succeq (\boldsymbol{e}_j \| \boldsymbol{k}_I)$ because of Lemma 1. Therefore,

$$p(\boldsymbol{x}, \boldsymbol{v}) = \bigoplus_{\boldsymbol{u} \in \mathbb{F}_2^{n+m} | \boldsymbol{u} \succeq (\boldsymbol{0} \| \boldsymbol{k}_I), u_j = 0} a_{\boldsymbol{u}}^f \cdot (\boldsymbol{x} \| \boldsymbol{v})^{\boldsymbol{u} \oplus (\boldsymbol{0} \| \boldsymbol{k}_I)}.$$

This superpoly is independent of x_j because u_j is always 0 and $(x_j)^0 = 1$. □

We can evaluate which secret variables are involved to the superpoly of a given cube, and Algorithm 1 shows the algorithm supported by MILP. The input

$\mathcal{M}$ is an MILP model, where the target stream cipher is represented by the context of the division property. How to construct $\mathcal{M}$ for each specific stream cipher is shown in each application in Sect. 5. First, we pick MILP variables $\boldsymbol{x}$ and $\boldsymbol{v}$ from $\mathcal{M}$, where $\boldsymbol{x}$ and $\boldsymbol{v}$ correspond to MILP variables for secret and public variables, respectively. As an example, in Algorithm 2 for Trivium, let $\boldsymbol{x} = (s_1^0, s_2^0, \ldots, s_{80}^0)$ and $\boldsymbol{v} = (s_{93}^0, s_{94}^0, \ldots, s_{172}^0)$. Then, to represent the input division property, elements of $\boldsymbol{v}$ indexed by I are constrained by 1, and the others are constrained by 0. Since at least one element in secret variables is additionally constrained to 1 in our cube attack, the sum of $\boldsymbol{x}$ is constrained to 1. Next, we solve this MILP model by using the solver. If $\mathcal{M}$ is infeasible, there is no involved secret variables in superpoly and $\bigoplus_{C_I} f(\boldsymbol{x}, \boldsymbol{v}) = p(\boldsymbol{x}, \boldsymbol{v})$ is always constant. If $\mathcal{M}$ is feasible, we can get a satisfying division trail and pick an index $j \in \{1, 2, \ldots, n\}$ such that $x_j = 1$ in the division trail. Then, x_j is involved to the superpoly and the index j is stored to a set J. Once we detect that x_j is involved, we additionally constrain $x_j = 0$. By repeating this procedure, we can get the set J whose elements are an index of secret variables involved to the superpoly.

After the analysis of the superpoly by using Algorithm 1, we know that only x_j $(j \in J)$ are involved to the superpoly of the cube C_I. Attackers choose a value in constant part of iv and prepare the cube C_I by flipping bits in I. They then recover the superpoly by trying out all possible combinations of secret variables $\{x_{j_1}, x_{j_2}, \ldots, x_{j_{|J|}}\}$. The time complexity to recover the superpoly is $2^{|I|+|J|}$. Therefore, if $|I| + |J|$ is smaller than the security bit level, we can efficiently recover the superpoly.

4 Toward Key Recovery

The time complexity to recover the superpoly is estimated in Sect. 3. As described in Sect. 3, the superpoly recovery directly brings vulnerability of stream ciphers. On the other hand, if our goal is to recover secret variables, we have to find a preferable superpoly that is close to balancedness for secret variables. Under the condition that we already get the cube index I and index of involved secret variables J by using Algorithm 1, our attack strategy to recover secret variables consists of three phases: *offline phase*, *online phase*, and *brute-force search phase.*

1. **Offline phase.** The goal of this phase is to find a preferable superpoly. Attackers choose a value in the constant part of iv, and prepare a cube by flipping bits in I. They then compute $\bigoplus_{C_I} f(\boldsymbol{x}, \boldsymbol{v}) = p_{\boldsymbol{v}}(\boldsymbol{x})$ in local, where all possible combinations of secret variables $\{x_{j_1}, x_{j_2}, \ldots, x_{j_{|J|}}\}$ are tried out, and the superpoly is recovered. Finally, we search for the preferable superpoly by changing the constant part of iv.
2. **Online phase.** The goal of this phase is to recover the part of secret variables by using the preferable superpoly. After the balanced superpoly is given, attackers query the cube C_I to encryption oracle and get one bit $p_{\boldsymbol{v}}(\boldsymbol{x})$. Then, we get one polynomial about involved secret variables, and the half

of values in involved secret variables is discarded because the superpoly is balanced.

3. **Brute-force search phase.** Attackers guess the remaining secret variables to recover the entire value in secret variables.

We cannot know whether the superpoly is balanced or not unless it is actually recovered, and the actual superpoly recovery requires $2^{|I|+|J|}$ time complexity. Therefore, if $|I|+|J|$ exceeds the experimental range, it is practically infeasible to search for preferable superpolys. As a consequence, we introduce the following two assumptions about collecting preferable superpolys.

Assumption 1 (Strong Assumption). *For a cube C_I, there are many values in the constant part of iv whose corresponding superpoly is balanced.*

Assumption 2 (Weak Assumption). *For a cube C_I, there are many values in the constant part of iv whose corresponding superpoly is not a constant function.*

Assumption 2 is weaker than Assumption 1 because the superpoly satisfying Assumption 1 always holds Assumption 2. As long as Assumption 2 holds, the size of recovered secret variables is less than 1 bit but some secret information is at least leaked to attackers. If Assumption 1 holds and such superpoly is used in the online phase, values in involved secret variables are divided in exactly half, i.e., $p_{\boldsymbol{v}}(\boldsymbol{x})$ is 0 for $2^{|J|-1}$ values and is 1 for the others. Therefore, we can recover one bit of information in secret variables.

4.1 Evaluating Time Complexity

Assuming that Assumption 1 holds, we show the time complexity to recover the entire secret key. Then, the time complexity of the offline phase is estimated as $k \times 2^{|I|+|J|}$, where k denotes the required number of trials for finding a preferable superpoly. Note that we can expect that such superpoly can be reasonably found with high probability without trying out all possible values in involved secret variables. We evaluate a part of values in involved secret variables at random and check whether $p_{\boldsymbol{v}}(\boldsymbol{x})$ is almost balanced or not. If the output is highly biased for $\boldsymbol{x}$, the superpoly $p_{\boldsymbol{v}}$ is not preferable and changes to other values in the constant part of iv. The complexity of this method is $O(2^{|I|})$. Once we find an almost preferable superpoly, we entirely try out $2^{|J|}$ values in secret variables.

Even if the preferable superpoly is used, the size of recovered secret information is at most 1 bit. Therefore, when only one cube is used, the time complexity of the brute-force search phase is $2^{\kappa-1}$, where κ denotes the security bit level. Therefore, the total time complexity is

$$k \times 2^{|I|+|J|} + 2^{|I|} + 2^{\kappa-1}, \tag{1}$$

From Eq. (1), when $|I|+|J| = \kappa - 1$, the total time complexity is greater than 2^{κ} because k is at least 1. Therefore, such cube is not applied to the key-recovery attack. Moreover, when $|I|+|J| = \kappa - 2$, this attack is valid only if the best case ($k = 1$), where a preferable superpoly is found in the first trial.

If only one cube is exploited, the dominant time complexity is always that for the brute-force search phase. When ℓ cubes are found in the evaluation phase and all found cubes are exploited, the total time complexity is reduced to

$$\ell \times \left(k \times 2^{|I|+|J|} + 2^{|I|}\right) + 2^{\kappa-\ell}.$$

However, this paper only focuses on the case that only one cube is exploited for the simplicity. Note that the detection of one cube brings at least cryptographic vulnerability.

5 Applications

We apply our general attack method to three NLFSE-based ciphers. The first target is Trivium [6], which is one of eSTREAM portfolio [1] and one of the most analyzed stream ciphers. Another target is Grain128a [3], which is standardized by ISO/IEC 29167-13 [16]. The final application is ACORN [33], which is one of the 3rd round CAESAR candidates [2], and its design is based on stream ciphers.

5.1 Application to Trivium

Specification. Trivium is an NLFSR-based stream cipher, and the internal state is represented by 288-bit state $(s_1, s_2, \ldots, s_{288})$. Figure 1 shows the state update function of Trivium. The 80-bit key is loaded to the first register, and the 80-bit IV is loaded to the second register. The other state bits are set to 0

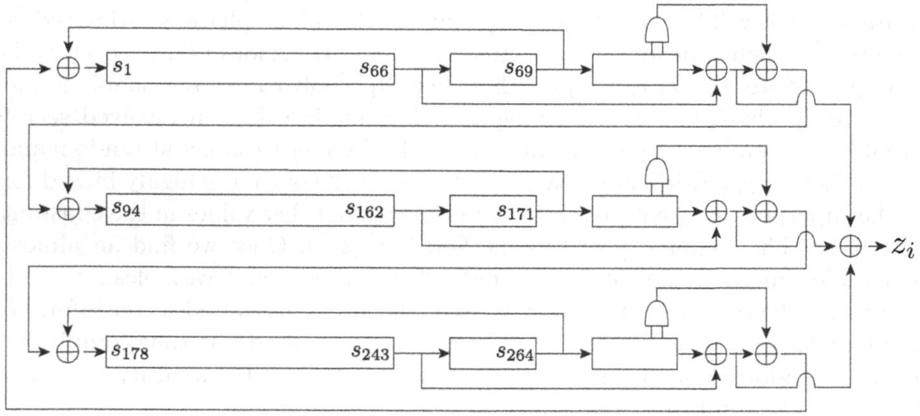

Fig. 1. Structure of Trivium

except the least three bits in the third register. Namely, the initial state bits are represented as

$$\begin{aligned}(s_1, s_2, \ldots, s_{93}) &= (K_1, K_2, \ldots, K_{80}, 0, \ldots, 0),\\ (s_{94}, s_{95}, \ldots, s_{177}) &= (IV_1, IV_2, \ldots, IV_{80}, 0, \ldots, 0),\\ (s_{178}, s_{279}, \ldots, s_{288}) &= (0, 0, \ldots, 0, 1, 1, 1).\end{aligned}$$

The pseudo code of the update function is given as follows.

$$\begin{aligned}&t_1 \leftarrow s_{66} \oplus s_{93}\\ &t_2 \leftarrow s_{162} \oplus s_{177}\\ &t_3 \leftarrow s_{243} \oplus s_{288}\\ &z \leftarrow t_1 \oplus t_2 \oplus t_3\\ &t_1 \leftarrow t_1 \oplus s_{91} \cdot s_{92} \oplus s_{171}\\ &t_2 \leftarrow t_2 \oplus s_{175} \cdot s_{176} \oplus s_{264}\\ &t_3 \leftarrow t_3 \oplus s_{286} \cdot s_{287} \oplus s_{69}\\ &(s_1, s_2, \ldots, s_{93}) \leftarrow (t_3, s_1, \ldots, s_{92})\\ &(s_{94}, s_{95}, \ldots, s_{177}) \leftarrow (t_1, s_{94}, \ldots, s_{176})\\ &(s_{178}, s_{279}, \ldots, s_{288}) \leftarrow (t_2, s_{178}, \ldots, s_{287})\end{aligned}$$

Here z denotes the 1-bit key stream. First, in the key initialization, the state is updated $4 \times 288 = 1152$ times without producing an output. After the key initialization, one bit key stream is produced by every update function.

MILP Model. `TriviumEval` in Algorithm 2 generates MILP model $\mathcal{M}$ as the input of Algorithm 1, and the model $\mathcal{M}$ can evaluate all division trails for Trivium whose initialization rounds are reduced to R. `TriviumCore` in Algorithm 2 generates MILP variables and constraints for each update function of register. Since one `TriviumCore` creates 10 MILP variables and 7 constraints, one update function creates 30 MILP variables and 21 constraints. Therefore, generated MILP model $\mathcal{M}$ consists of $288 + 30R$ MILP variables and $21R + 282 + 1$ MILP constraints. Note that constraints by the input division property are operated by Algorithm 1.

Experimental Verification. We implemented the MILP model $\mathcal{M}$ for the propagation of the division property on Trivium and evaluated involved secret variables by using Algorithm 1, where Gurobi optimizer [15] was used as the solver of MILP. Before the theoretical evaluation, we verify our attack and implementation by using small cube as $I = \{1, 11, 21, 31, 41, 51, 61, 71\}$. Table 2 summarizes involved secret variables from 576 to 594 rounds.

Example 2 (Verification of Our Attack against 590-round Trivium*).* We actually execute the offline phase against 590-round Trivium, and only K_{60} is

---

Algorithm 2. MILP model of division property for TRIVIUM

1: **procedure** TriviumCore($\mathcal{M}, x, i_1, i_2, i_3, i_4, i_5$)
2:     $\mathcal{M}.var \leftarrow y_{i_1}, y_{i_2}, y_{i_3}, y_{i_4}, y_{i_5}, z_1, z_2, z_3, z_4, a$ as binary
3:     $\mathcal{M}.con \leftarrow y_{i_j} = x_{i_j} - z_j$ for all $j \in \{1, 2, 3, 4\}$
4:     $\mathcal{M}.con \leftarrow a \geq z_3$
5:     $\mathcal{M}.con \leftarrow a \geq z_4$
6:     $\mathcal{M}.con \leftarrow y_{i_5} = x_{i_5} + a + z_1 + z_2$
7:     **for all** $i \in \{1, 2, \ldots, 288\}$ w/o i_1, i_2, i_3, i_4, i_5 **do**
8:         $y_i = x_i$
9:     **end for**
10:    **return** $(\mathcal{M}, y)$
11: **end procedure**
1: **procedure** TriviumEval(round R)
2:     Prepare empty MILP Model $\mathcal{M}$
3:     $\mathcal{M}.var \leftarrow s_i^0$ for $i \in \{1, 2, \ldots, 288\}$
4:     **for** $r = 1$ to R **do**
5:         $(\mathcal{M}, x) = $ TriviumCore$(\mathcal{M}, s^{r-1}, 66, 171, 91, 92, 93)$
6:         $(\mathcal{M}, y) = $ TriviumCore$(\mathcal{M}, x, 162, 264, 175, 176, 177)$
7:         $(\mathcal{M}, z) = $ TriviumCore$(\mathcal{M}, y, 243, 69, 286, 287, 288)$
8:         $s^r = z \ggg 1$
9:     **end for**
10:    **for all** $i \in \{1, 2, \ldots, 288\}$ w/o $66, 93, 162, 177, 243, 288$ **do**
11:        $\mathcal{M}.con \leftarrow s_i^r = 0$
12:    **end for**
13:    $\mathcal{M}.con \leftarrow (s_{66}^r + s_{93}^r + s_{162}^r + s_{177}^r + s_{243}^r + s_{288}^r) = 1$
14:    **return** $\mathcal{M}$
15: **end procedure**

---

involved to the superpoly. We randomly chose 100 superpolys by changing the constant part of iv and evaluated the sum of the cube. As a result, the sum is always 0 independent of K_{60} in 42 superpolys, where 0x00CA6124DE5F12043D62 is its example of the constant part of iv. Moreover, the sum corresponds to the value of K_{60} in 22 superpolys, where 0x2F0881B93B251C7079F2 is its example. Then, the ANF of the superpoly is represented as

$$p_v(x) = x_{60}.$$

Finally, the sum corresponds to the value of $K_{60} \oplus 1$ in 36 superpolys, where 0x5745A1944411D1374828 is its example. Then, the ANF of the superpoly is represented as

$$p_v(x) = x_{60} \oplus 1.$$

Balanced superpolys are preferable, and we found $22 + 36 = 58$ such superpolys. Therefore, the required number of trials for finding preferable superpolys is about $k = 2$.

Example 3 (Verification of Our Attack against 591-round TRIVIUM*).* We execute the offline phase against 591-round TRIVIUM, and $K_{23}, K_{24}, K_{25}, K_{66}, K_{67}$

Table 2. Involved secret variables in the superpoly of the cube $C_{\{1,11,21,31,41,51,61,71\}}$.

# rounds	Involved secret variables J	Size of J
576	48, 73, 74, 75	4
577	40, 65, 66, 67	4
583	48, 50, 62, 63, 66, 73, 74, 75, 76, 77	10
584	48, 50, 60, 61, 66, 67, 73, 74, 75, 76, 77	11
586	20, 30, 40, 45, 46, 47, 55, 56, 57, 58, 61, 65, 66, 67	14
587	30, 55, 56, 57, 58	5
590	60	1
591	23, 24, 25, 66, 67	5
592	...	25
593	...	57
594	...	47

are involved to the superpoly. Similarly to the attack against 590 rounds, we randomly chose 100 superpolys by changing the constant part of iv and evaluated the sum of the given cube. As a result, the sum is always 0 independent of 5 involved secret variables in 64 superpolys, where `0x39305FDD295BDACD2FBE` is its example of the constant part of iv. There are 11 superpolys such that the sum is 1 only when

$$K_{23}\|K_{24}\|K_{25}\|K_{66}\|K_{67} \in \{\mathtt{00, 05, 08, 0D, 10, 15, 19, 1C}\}$$

as the hexadecimal notation, where `0x03CC37748E34C601ADF5` is its example of the constant part of iv. Then, the ANF of the superpoly is represented as

$$p_v(\boldsymbol{x}) = (x_{66} \oplus 1)(x_{23}x_{24} \oplus x_{25} \oplus x_{67} \oplus 1).$$

There are 9 superpolys such that the sum is 1 when

$$K_{23}\|K_{24}\|K_{25}\|K_{66}\|K_{67} \in \{\mathtt{02, 07, 0A, 0F, 12, 17, 1B, 1E}\}$$

as the hexadecimal notation, where `0x78126459CB2384E6CCCE` is its example of the constant part of iv. Then, the ANF of the superpoly is represented as

$$p_v(\boldsymbol{x}) = x_{66}(x_{23}x_{24} \oplus x_{25} \oplus x_{67} \oplus 1).$$

Moreover, there are 16 superpolys such that the sum is 1 when the value of $K_{23}\|K_{24}\|K_{25}\|K_{66}\|K_{67}$ belongs to

$$\{\mathtt{00, 02, 05, 07, 08, 0A, 0D, 0F, 10, 12, 15, 17, 19, 1B, 1C, 1E}\}$$

as the hexadecimal notation, where `0x644BD671BE0C9241481A` is its example of the constant part of iv. Then, the ANF of the superpoly is represented as

$$p_v(\boldsymbol{x}) = x_{23}x_{24} \oplus x_{25} \oplus x_{67} \oplus 1,$$

Table 3. Summary of theoretical cube attacks on Trivium. The time complexity in this table shows the time complexity to recover the superpoly.

#rounds	$\|I\|$	Involved secret variables J	Time complexity
800	44	8, 33, 34, 35, 48, 59, 60, 61, 64, 73, 74, 75	$2^{44+12} = 2^{56}$
802	46	32, 34, 57, 58, 59, 60, 61, 62	$2^{46+8} = 2^{54}$
805	49	14, 39, 40, 41, 42, 44, 46, 58, 67,...,73	$2^{49+15} = 2^{64}$
806	51	42, 67, 68, 69	$2^{51+4} = 2^{55}$
808	52	26, 28, 40, 51, 52, 53, 54, 55, 58, 65, 66, 67	$2^{52+12} = 2^{64}$
809	53	24, 26, 36, 38, 40, 49,...,56, 58, 61,...,67, 77,...,80	$2^{53+25} = 2^{78}$
814	54	32, 34, 57, 58, 59, 60, 61	$2^{54+7} = 2^{61}$
816	55	6, 31, 32, 33, 48, 50, 52, 57,...,60, 62, 73,...,79	$2^{55+19} = 2^{74}$
818	58	34, 59, 60, 61	$2^{58+4} = 2^{62}$
819	61	15, 17, 40, 41, 42, 43, 44, 58	$2^{61+8} = 2^{69}$
820	62	15, 26, 40, 41, 42, 51, 52, 53	$2^{62+8} = 2^{70}$
822	64	42, 67, 68, 69	$2^{64+4} = 2^{68}$
825	65	52, 54, 66, 77, 78, 79, 80	$2^{65+7} = 2^{72}$
829	66	23, 25, 26, 27, 36, 42, 56, 67, 68, 69	$2^{66+10} = 2^{76}$
830	69	1, 37, 42, 56, 67, 68, 69	$2^{69+7} = 2^{76}$
831	71	49, 74, 75, 76	$2^{71+4} = 2^{75}$
832	72	34, 58, 59, 60, 61	$2^{72+5} = 2^{77}$

For any size of cube $|I|$, the odd index $1, 3, \ldots, 79$ and even index $2, 4, \ldots, 2(|I| - 40)$ is chosen as cube indices.

and this superpoly is balanced. Note that x_{66} is not involve to this superpoly. Balanced superpolys are preferable, and we found 16 such superpolys. Therefore, the required number of trials for finding preferable superpolys is about $k = 6$.

Theoretical Results. As experimental verification shows, Assumption 1 holds for Trivium in small example. Therefore, we can expect that theoretically recovered superpolys also fulfill Assumption 1.

Cube indices are chosen as the following in our experiments: the odd index $1, 3, \ldots, 2|I| - 1$ is chosen, and the even index $2, 4, \ldots, 2(|I| - 40)$ is additionally chosen. Then, we exhaustively evaluated involved secret variables, and Table 3 summarizes the result in our theoretical cube attack. Table 3 shows indices of involved secret variables and the time complexity for the superpoly recovery against Trivium with at least 800 initialization rounds. Since the previous best key-recovery attack is 799 rounds, all results at least improve the current best key-recovery attack. Under the condition that the time complexity for the superpoly recovery is less than 2^{79}, the largest number of initialization rounds that we can attack is 832 rounds. Compared with previous best key-recovery attack, it updates $832 - 799 = 33$ rounds.

We do not have plausible evidence that our choice of cube indices is appropriate, and the choice is still difficult because we need to try out $\binom{80}{|I|}$ cubes when we want to evaluate all cubes whose size is $|I|$. How to choose appropriate cubes is left as an open question.

5.2 Application to Grain128a

Specification. Grain128a is one of Grain family of NLFSR-based stream ciphers, and the internal state is represented by two 128-bit states, $(b_0, b_1, \ldots, b_{127})$ and $(s_0, s_1, \ldots, s_{127})$. The 128-bit key is loaded to the first register $\boldsymbol{b}$, and the 96-bit IV is loaded to the second register $\boldsymbol{s}$. The other state bits are set to 1 except the least one bit in the second register. Namely, the initial state bits are represented as

$$(b_0, b_1, \ldots, b_{127}) = (K_1, K_2, \ldots, K_{128}),$$
$$(s_0, s_1, \ldots, s_{127}) = (IV_1, IV_2, \ldots, IV_{96}, 1, \ldots, 1, 0).$$

The pseudo code of the update function in the initialization is given as follows.

$$\begin{aligned} g \leftarrow\ & b_0 + b_{26} + b_{56} + b_{91} + b_{96} \\ & + b_3 b_{67} + b_{11} b_{13} + b_{17} b_{18} + b_{27} b_{59} + b_{40} b_{48} + b_{61} b_{65} + b_{68} b_{84} \\ & + b_{88} b_{92} b_{93} b_{95} + b_{22} b_{24} b_{25} + b_{70} b_{78} b_{82}. \end{aligned} \quad (2)$$

$$f \leftarrow s_0 + s_7 + s_{38} + s_{70} + s_{81} + s_{96} \quad (3)$$
$$h \leftarrow b_{12} s_8 + s_{13} s_{20} + b_{95} s_{42} + s_{60} s_{79} + b_{12} b_{95} s_{94} \quad (4)$$
$$z \leftarrow h + s_{93} + \sum_{j \in A} b_j \quad (5)$$

$$(b_0, b_1, \ldots, b_{127}) \leftarrow (b_1, \ldots, b_{127}, g + s_0 + z)$$
$$(s_0, s_1, \ldots, s_{127}) \leftarrow (s_1, \ldots, s_{127}, f + z)$$

Here, $A = \{2, 15, 36, 45, 64, 73, 89\}$. First, in the key initialization, the state is updated 256 times without producing an output. After the key initialization, the update function is tweaked such that z is not fed to the state, and z is used as a key stream. Figure 2 shows the state update function of Grain128a.

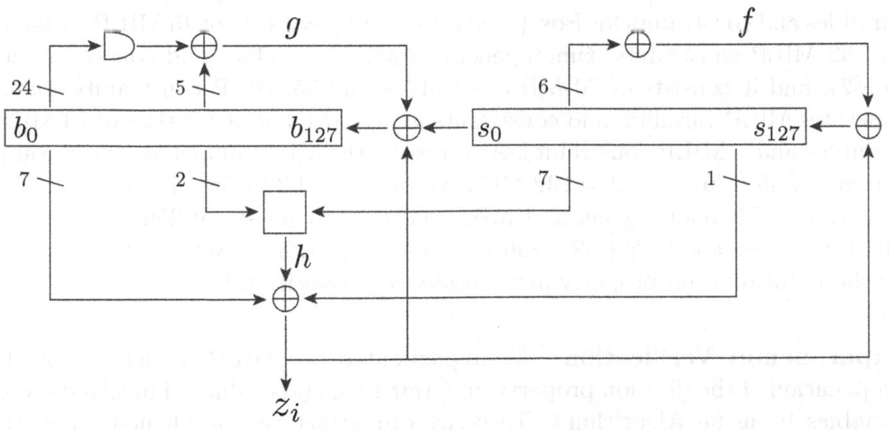

Fig. 2. Structure of Grain128a

Algorithm 3. MILP model for the initialization of Grain128a

procedure `Grain128aEval`(round R)
  Prepare empty MILP Model $\mathcal{M}$
  $\mathcal{M}.var \leftarrow b_i^0$ for $i \in \{0, 1, \dots, 127\}$ as binary
  $\mathcal{M}.var \leftarrow s_i^0$ for $i \in \{0, 1, \dots, 127\}$ as binary
  for $r = 1$ to R **do**
    $(\mathcal{M}, \boldsymbol{b}', \boldsymbol{s}', z) = \texttt{funcZ}(\mathcal{M}, \boldsymbol{b}^{r-1}, \boldsymbol{s}^{r-1})$
    $\mathcal{M}.var \leftarrow z_g, z_f$ as binary
    $\mathcal{M}.con \leftarrow z = z_g + z_f$
    $(\mathcal{M}, \boldsymbol{b}'', g) = \texttt{funcG}(\mathcal{M}, \boldsymbol{b}')$
    $(\mathcal{M}, \boldsymbol{s}'', f) = \texttt{funcF}(\mathcal{M}, \boldsymbol{s}')$
    for $i = 0$ to 126 **do**
      $b_i^r = b_{i+1}''$
      $s_i^r = s_{i+1}''$
    end for
    $\mathcal{M}.var \leftarrow b_{127}^r, s_{127}^r$ as binary
    $\mathcal{M}.con \leftarrow b_0'' = 0$
    $\mathcal{M}.con \leftarrow b_{127}^r = g + s_0'' + z_g$
    $\mathcal{M}.con \leftarrow s_{127}^r = f + z_f$
  end for
  $(\mathcal{M}, \boldsymbol{b}', \boldsymbol{s}', z) = \texttt{funcZ}(\mathcal{M}, \boldsymbol{b}^R, \boldsymbol{s}^R)$
  for all $i \in \{0, 1, \dots, 127\}$ **do**
    $\mathcal{M}.con \leftarrow b_i' = 0$
    $\mathcal{M}.con \leftarrow s_i' = 0$
  end for
  $\mathcal{M}.con \leftarrow z = 1$
  return $\mathcal{M}$
end procedure

MILP Model. `Grain128aEval` in Algorithm 3 generates MILP model $\mathcal{M}$ as the input of Algorithm 1, and the model $\mathcal{M}$ can evaluate all division trails for Grain128a whose initialization rounds are reduced to R. `funcZ` generates MILP variables and constraints for Eqs. (4) and (5), and it consists of 45 MILP variables and 32 MILP constraints. `funcG` generates MILP variables and constraints for Eq. (2), and it consists of 70 MILP variables and 55 MILP constraints. `funcF` generates MILP variables and constraints for Eq. (3), and it consists of 13 MILP variables and 7 MILP constraints. As a result, the MILP model for every round consists of $45 + 70 + 13 + 4 = 132$ MILP variables and $32 + 55 + 7 + 4 = 98$ MILP constraints. Therefore, generated MILP model $\mathcal{M}$ consists of $256 + 45 + 132R$ MILP variables and $98R + 32 + 256 + 1$ MILP constraints. Note that constraints by the input division property are operated by Algorithm 1.

Experimental Verification. We implemented the MILP model $\mathcal{M}$ for the propagation of the division property on Grain128a and evaluated involved secret variables by using Algorithm 1. To verify our attack and implementation, the offline phase is executed by using small cube as $I = \{1, 2, \dots, 9\}$.

Example 4 (Verification of Our Attack against 106-round Grain128a). The cube $C_{\{1,2,3,\ldots,9\}}$ brings the superpoly that involves only seven secret variables, (K_{46}, K_{53}, K_{85}, K_{119}, K_{122}, K_{126}, and K_{127}), and this result comes out of Algorithm 1. In our experiments, the Hamming weight of all superpolys $p_{\boldsymbol{v}}(\boldsymbol{x})$ is only 4. Specifically, in arbitrary iv satisfying $IV_{76} = 0$, $p_{\boldsymbol{v}}(\boldsymbol{x})$ is 1 only when the involved secret variables are represented as

$$\begin{aligned}(K_{46}, K_{53}, K_{85}, K_{119}, K_{122}, K_{126}, K_{127}) =& (*, 1, 0, 1, 1, 1, 1) \text{ or} \\ & (*, 0, 1, 1, 1, 1, 1),\end{aligned}$$

where $*$ is any bit. Moreover, in arbitrary iv satisfying $IV_{76} = 1$, $p_{\boldsymbol{v}}(\boldsymbol{x})$ is 1 only when the involved secret variables are represented as

$$\begin{aligned}(K_{46}, K_{53}, K_{85}, K_{119}, K_{122}, K_{126}, K_{127}) =& (*, 1, 0, 1, 0, 1, 1) \text{ or} \\ & (*, 0, 1, 1, 0, 1, 1).\end{aligned}$$

Namely, the superpoly is represented as

$$p_{\boldsymbol{v}}(\boldsymbol{x}) = (x_{53} \oplus x_{85}) \cdot x_{119} \cdot (x_{122} \oplus v_{76}) \cdot x_{126} \cdot x_{127}.$$

This superpoly is independent of x_{46}. Moreover, it is not balanced, and the Hamming weight of $p_{\boldsymbol{v}}(\boldsymbol{x})$ is 2 for six involved input bits. Therefore, the recovered bit of information in secret variables is represented as

$$\left| \log_2 \left(\frac{2 \times \frac{2}{2^6} + (62 \times \frac{62}{2^6})}{2^6} \right) \right| \approx 0.09.$$

Double bit of information can be recovered by flipping the bit IV_{76}, but the recovered information is still smaller than 1.

Theoretical Results. We cannot find superpolys satisfying Assumption 1 in our experiments using small cube. On the other hand, Assumption 2 holds. Therefore, we can expect that theoretically recovered superpolys also fulfill Assumption 2, and it leaks at least some information in secret variables which is smaller than 1 bit. Moreover, by collecting these superpolys, we can expect that multiple bits of information in secret variables are recovered.

Table 4 shows indices of involved secret variables and the time complexity for the superpoly recovery against Grain128a. Since the previous best attack is 177

Table 4. Summary of theoretical cube attacks on Grain128a. The time complexity in this table shows the time complexity to recover the superpoly.

#rounds	$\lvert I \rvert$	Involved secret variables J	Time complexity
182	88[a]	36, 40, 51, 52, 53, 54, 55, 56, 61, 62, 69, 79, 81, 82, 121, 122, 126, 127	$2^{88+18} = 2^{106}$
183	92[b]	48, 49, 50, 51, 52, 54, 55, 61, 63, 83, 84, 90, 93, 95, 120, 128	$2^{92+16} = 2^{108}$

[a] Following set of indices $I = \{1, \ldots, 40, 42, 44, \ldots, 51, 53, \ldots, 87, 89, 91, 93, 95\}$ is used as the cube.
[b] Following set of indices $I = \{1, \ldots, 51, 53, \ldots, 91, 93, 95\}$ is used as the cube.

rounds in the single-key setting, all results at least improve the current best key-recovery attack. Under the condition that the time complexity for the superpoly recovery is less than 2^{127}, the largest number of initialization rounds that we can attack is 183 rounds. Compared with previous best distinguishing attack, it updates $183 - 177 = 6$ rounds. Moreover it allows for some key recovery.

5.3 Application to ACORN

Specification. ACORN is an authenticated encryption and one of the 3rd round candidates in CAESAR competition. The structure is based on NLFSR, and the internal state is represented by 293-bit state $(S_0, S_1, \ldots, S_{292})$. There are two component functions, $ks = KSG128(S)$ and $f = FBK128(S)$, in the update function, and each is defined as

$$ks = S_{12} \oplus S_{154} \oplus maj(S_{235}, S_{61}, S_{193}) \oplus ch(S_{230}, S_{111}, S_{66}),$$
$$f = S_0 \oplus \tilde{S}_{107} \oplus maj(S_{244}, S_{23}, S_{160}) \oplus (ca \wedge S_{196}) \oplus (cb \wedge ks),$$

where ks is used as the key stream, and maj and ch are defined as

$$maj(x, y, z) = (x \wedge y) \oplus (x \wedge z) \oplus (y \wedge z),$$
$$ch(x, y, z) = (x \wedge y) \oplus ((x \oplus 1) \wedge z).$$

Then, the update function is given as follows.

$$\begin{aligned}
&S_{289} \leftarrow S_{289} \oplus S_{235} \oplus S_{230} \\
&S_{230} \leftarrow S_{230} \oplus S_{196} \oplus S_{193} \\
&S_{193} \leftarrow S_{193} \oplus S_{160} \oplus S_{154} \\
&S_{154} \leftarrow S_{154} \oplus S_{111} \oplus S_{107} \\
&S_{107} \leftarrow S_{107} \oplus S_{66} \oplus S_{61} \\
&S_{61} \leftarrow S_{61} \oplus S_{23} \oplus S_0 \\
&ks = KSG128(S) \\
&f = FBK128(S, ca, cb) \\
&(S_0, S_1, \ldots, S_{291}, S_{292}) \leftarrow (S_1, s_2, \ldots, S_{292}, f \oplus m)
\end{aligned}$$

The 293-bit state is first initialized to $\mathbf{0}$. Second, 128-bit secret key is sequentially loaded to the NLFSR via m. Third, 128-bit initialization vector is sequentially loaded to the NLFSR via m. Fourth, 128-bit secret key is sequentially loaded to the NLFSR via m twelve times. The constant bits ca and cb are always 1 in the initial 1792 rounds. The associated data is always loaded before the output of the key stream, but we do not care about this process in this paper because the number of rounds that we can attack is smaller than 1792 rounds. Figure 3 shows the structure of ACORN. Please refer to [33] in detail.

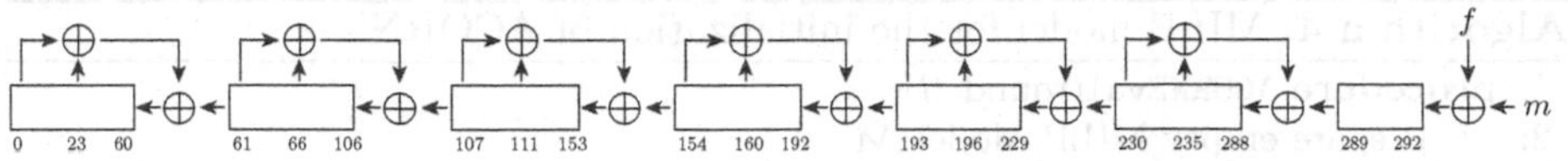

Fig. 3. Structure of ACORN

MILP Model. `ACORNEval` in Algorithm 4 generates MILP model $\mathcal{M}$ as the input of Algorithm 1, and the model $\mathcal{M}$ can evaluate all division trails for ACORN whose initialization rounds are reduced to R. `xorFB` generates MILP variables and constraints for feed-back function with XOR. `ksg128` and `fbk128` generates MILP variables and constraints for $KSG128$ and $FBK128$, respectively.

If there are zero constant bit in input of $KSG128$ and $FBK128$, the propagation of the division property for two functions `ksg128` and `fbk128` is limited. For example, when $maj(x, y, z)$ is computed under the condition $y = z = 0$, this function is represented as

$$maj(x, 0, 0) = 0,$$

and the division property of x never propagates to the output of maj. Such limitations of the propagation only happens in the first several rounds because the state $\boldsymbol{S}$ is initialized to $\mathbf{0}$. To control this behavior, there is the current number of rounds as the input of `ksg128` and `fbk128`. Note that constraints by the input division property are operated by Algorithm 1.

Experimental Verification. We implemented the MILP model $\mathcal{M}$ for the propagation of the division property on ACORN and evaluated involved secret variables by using Algorithm 1. We searched the small cube such that $|I| + |J|$ is practically feasible, and the following small cube

$$C_{\{1,2,3,4,5,8,20,125,126,127,128\}}$$

is used to verify our attack and implementation.

Example 5 (Verification of Our Attack against 517-round ACORN). The cube $C_{\{1,2,3,4,5,8,20,125,126,127,128\}}$ brings the superpoly that involves only nine secret variables, (K_6, K_8, K_{10}, K_{11}, K_{12}, K_{15}, K_{16}, K_{45}, and K_{49}), and this result comes out of Algorithm 1. We try out 100 randomly chosen constant part of iv. As a result, all superpolys $p_{\boldsymbol{v}}(\boldsymbol{x})$ are balanced independent of the value of the constant part of iv. Specifically, $p_{\boldsymbol{v}}(\boldsymbol{x})$ corresponds to the sum of involved secret variables. Namely, the superpoly is represented as

$$p_{\boldsymbol{v}}(\boldsymbol{x}) = x_6 \oplus x_8 \oplus x_{10} \oplus x_{11} \oplus x_{12} \oplus x_{15} \oplus x_{16} \oplus x_{45} \oplus x_{49}.$$

Algorithm 4. MILP model for the initialization of ACORN

1: **procedure** ACORNEval(round R)
2:    Prepare empty MILP Model $\mathcal{M}$
3:    $\mathcal{M}.var \leftarrow K_i$ for $i \in \{1, 2, \ldots, 128\}$ as binary
4:    $\mathcal{M}.var \leftarrow IV_i$ for $i \in \{1, 2, \ldots, 128\}$ as binary
5:    $\mathcal{M}.var \leftarrow S_i^0$ for $i \in \{0, 1, \ldots, 292\}$ as binary
6:    **for** $r = 1$ to R **do**
7:        $(\mathcal{M}, \boldsymbol{T}) = \texttt{xorFB}(\mathcal{M}, \boldsymbol{S}^{r-1}, 289, 235, 230)$
8:        $(\mathcal{M}, \boldsymbol{U}) = \texttt{xorFB}(\mathcal{M}, \boldsymbol{T}, 230, 196, 193)$
9:        $(\mathcal{M}, \boldsymbol{V}) = \texttt{xorFB}(\mathcal{M}, \boldsymbol{U}, 193, 160, 154)$
10:        $(\mathcal{M}, \boldsymbol{W}) = \texttt{xorFB}(\mathcal{M}, \boldsymbol{V}, 154, 111, 107)$
11:        $(\mathcal{M}, \boldsymbol{X}) = \texttt{xorFB}(\mathcal{M}, \boldsymbol{W}, 107, 66, 61)$
12:        $(\mathcal{M}, \boldsymbol{Y}) = \texttt{xorFB}(\mathcal{M}, \boldsymbol{X}, 61, 23, 0)$
13:        $(\mathcal{M}, \boldsymbol{Z}, ks) = \texttt{ksg128}(\mathcal{M}, \boldsymbol{Y}, r)$
14:        $(\mathcal{M}, \boldsymbol{A}, f) = \texttt{fbk128}(\mathcal{M}, \boldsymbol{Z}, r)$
15:        **for** $i = 0$ to 291 **do**
16:            $S_i^r = A_{i+1}$
17:        **end for**
18:        $\mathcal{M}.var \leftarrow S_{292}^r$ as binary
19:        **if** $128 < r \leq 256$ **then**
20:            $\mathcal{M}.con \leftarrow S_{292}^r = f \oplus IV_{r-128}$
21:        **else**
22:            $\mathcal{M}.var \leftarrow TK_r$ as binary
23:            $\mathcal{M}.con \leftarrow S_{292}^r = f \oplus TK_r$
24:        **end if**
25:    **end for**
26:    **for** $i = 0$ to 127 **do**
27:        $\mathcal{M}.con \leftarrow K_i = \sum_j TK_{i+128 \times j}$
28:    **end for**
29:    $(\mathcal{M}, \boldsymbol{T}) = \texttt{xorFB}(\mathcal{M}, \boldsymbol{S}^R, 289, 235, 230)$
30:    $(\mathcal{M}, \boldsymbol{U}) = \texttt{xorFB}(\mathcal{M}, \boldsymbol{T}, 230, 196, 193)$
31:    $(\mathcal{M}, \boldsymbol{V}) = \texttt{xorFB}(\mathcal{M}, \boldsymbol{U}, 193, 160, 154)$
32:    $(\mathcal{M}, \boldsymbol{W}) = \texttt{xorFB}(\mathcal{M}, \boldsymbol{V}, 154, 111, 107)$
33:    $(\mathcal{M}, \boldsymbol{X}) = \texttt{xorFB}(\mathcal{M}, \boldsymbol{W}, 107, 66, 61)$
34:    $(\mathcal{M}, \boldsymbol{Y}) = \texttt{xorFB}(\mathcal{M}, \boldsymbol{X}, 61, 23, 0)$
35:    $(\mathcal{M}, \boldsymbol{Z}, ks) = \texttt{ksg128}(\mathcal{M}, \boldsymbol{Y})$
36:    **for** $i = 0$ to 292 **do**
37:        $\mathcal{M}.con \leftarrow Z_i = 0$
38:    **end for**
39:    $\mathcal{M}.con \leftarrow ks = 1$
40:    **return** $\mathcal{M}$
41: **end procedure**

Theoretical Results. As experimental verification shows, Assumption 1 holds for ACORN in small example. Therefore, we can expect that theoretically recovered superpolys also fulfill Assumption 1.

Table 5 shows indices of involved secret variables and the time complexity for the superpoly recovery against ACORN. Since the previous best attack is

Table 5. Summary of theoretical cube attacks on ACORN. The time complexity in this table shows the time complexity to recover the superpoly.

#rounds	$\|I\|$	Involved secret variables J	Time complexity
647	35[a]	1, 2, 3, 5, 6, 7, 8, 9, 10, 11, 12, 13, 15, 16, 18, 19, 20, 21, 22, 23, 24, 25, 26, 27, 28, 29, 31, 32, 33, 35, 40, 45, 49, 52, 55, 57, 60, 61, 62, 65, 66, 94, 99	$2^{35+43} = 2^{78}$
649	35[a]	1, 2,...,39, 41,...,49, 52,...,69, 78, 86, 96, 97, 98, 100, 101, 102	$2^{35+74} = 2^{109}$
704	64[b]	1,...,12, 14,...21, 23,...,38, 40,...44, 48, 49, 50, 54, 58, 60, 63, 64, 65, 68, 69, 71, 74, 75, 97, 102, 108	$2^{64+58} = 2^{122}$

[a]Following set of indices $I = \{1, 2, \ldots, 16, 22, 29, 31, 113, 114, \ldots, 128\}$ is used as the cube.

[b]Following set of indices $I = \{1, 2, \ldots, 32, 97, 98, \ldots, 128\}$ is used as the cube.

503 rounds, all results at least improve the current best key-recovery attack. As far as we searched various cubes, the largest number of initialization rounds that we can attack is 704 rounds, where the cube size is 64 and the number of involved secret variables is 58. Compared with previous best key-recovery attack, it updates $704 - 503 = 201$ rounds.

6 Discussions

6.1 Validity of Assumptions 1 and 2

Whether the two assumptions hold depends on the structure of analyzed ciphers. In the three applications shown in this paper, we could easily find balanced superpoly for Trivium and ACORN by actually evaluating the offline phase using small cube. Therefore, we can expect that Assumption 1 holds in theoretical recovered superpolys for these two ciphers. On the other hand, we could not find balanced superpolys for Grain128a. This implies that Assumption 1 does not hold in theoretical recovered superpolys for Grain128a. However, since we could easily find non-constant superpolys, we can expect that Assumption 2 holds.

Note that Assumption 1 is introduced to estimate the time complexity to recover the entire secret key, and some information of secret variables is leaked to attackers even if only Assumption 2 holds. Moreover, even if both assumptions do not hold, the recovered superpoly is useful for distinguishing attacks. Therefore, if the superpoly recovery is more efficient than the brute-force attack, it immediately brings some vulnerability of symmetric-key cryptosystems. Therefore, the time complexity for the superpoly recovery discussed in this paper is very important.

Conventional cube attacks also have similar assumption because they experimentally verify whether the superpoly is linear, quadratic, or not. For example, in [11], the authors judged that the superpoly is linear if the superpoly passes at least 100 linearity tests. Moreover, Fouque and Vannet also introduced heuristic linearity and quadraticity tests in [14], where the superpoly is judged as linear and quadratic if it passes constant-order linearity and quadraticity tests, respectively. These constant-order tests may fail if there are terms of the superpoly that are highly biased. For example, assuming that the superpoly is represented as $K_1 + f(K_2, K_3, K_4, ..., K_{32})$ where f is unbalanced, the test used in previous cube attacks may judge the superpoly as K_1 in error. Namely, the conventional cube attack also assumes that the superpoly is balanced for each involved secret variables, and it fails to recover secret variables if this assumption is incorrect.

6.2 Multiple-Bits Recovery only from One Cube

There is a possibility that we can recover multiple bits from given cube by changing a value in constant part of iv. Indeed, Example 3 recovers more than one bit of information in secret variables by using an $\boldsymbol{v} =$ `0x03CC37748E34C601ADF5` or $\boldsymbol{v} =$ `0x78126459CB2384E6CCCE` together with $\boldsymbol{v} =$ `0x644BD671BE0C9241481A`. Moreover, two bits of information in secret variables are recovered if we find two independent balanced superpolys. On the other hand, the superpoly must be enough simplified for the key recovery. While we may be able to recover multiple bits only from one cube by changing values of the constant part of iv when the number of involved secret variables is high, we cannot claim that there are many independent balanced superpolys when the number of involved secret variables is small. Therefore, we do not claim that multiple bits are recovered from one cube by changing values of the constant part of iv.

6.3 Comparison with Previous Techniques

There is previous work that exploits non-randomness in high degree monomial structure in the ANF for the key recovery of stream ciphers: In [13], it is examined if every key bit in the parametrized expression of a coefficient of some high degree monomial in iv bits does occur, or more generally, how much influence each key bit does have on the value of the coefficient. If a coefficient depends on less than all key bits, this fact is exploited to filter those keys which do not satisfy the imposed value for the coefficient. As opposed to the present work, this method is mostly statistical in nature, whereas division property is fully algebraic.

Secondly, in [17], conditions are identified on the internal state to obtain a deterministic differential characteristic for some large number of rounds. Depending on whether these conditions involve public variables only, or also key variables, distinguishing and partial key-recovery attacks are derived. The technique is extended to (conditional) higher order differentials and enables to distinguish reduced round versions of some stream ciphers, and to recover parts of the key. Again, this method is quite different from the methods of this paper, and is not purely algebraic.

A third more recent approach is dynamic cube attack [12]. In contrast to standard cube attack that finds the key by solving a system of (linear) equations in the key bits, dynamic cube attack recovers the secret key by exploiting distinguishers obtained from cube testers. Dynamic cube attacks aim at creating lower degree representations of the given cipher. This method has been successfully applied to break the stream cipher Grain-128 [9]. All the previous methods share the restriction that they are experimental rather than theoretical, i.e., they are dependent on computing with cubes as large as practically feasible.

7 Conclusion

This paper revisited the cube attack proposed by Dinur and Shamir at Eurocrypt 2009. The conventional cube attack regards a target symmetric-key cryptosystem as a blackbox polynomial and analyzes the polynomial experimentally. Therefore, it is practically infeasible to evaluate the security when the size of cube exceeds the experimental size. In this paper, we proposed the cube attack on non-blackbox polynomials, and it leads the cube attack exploiting large number of cube size. Our method was developed by the division property, and as far as we know, this is the first application of the division property to stream ciphers. The trivial application brings only zero-sum integral distinguishers, and it is non-trivial to recover the secret key of stream ciphers by using the distinguisher. The novel application of the division property was proposed, where it is used to analyze the Algebraic Normal Form coefficients of polynomials. As a result, we can estimate the time complexity for the superpoly recovery. Then, the superpoly recovery immediately brings the vulnerability. We applied the new technique to Trivium, Grain128a, and ACORN, and the superpoly of 832-round Trivium, 183-round Grain128a, and 704-round ACORN are more efficiently recovered than the brute-force search. For Trivium and ACORN, we can expect that the recovered superpoly is useful for the key recovery attack, and they bring the current best key-recovery attacks. On the other hand, for Grain128a, we cannot expect that the recovered superpoly is balanced, and then the recovered bit of information may be significantly small. Therefore, the feasibility of the key recovery is speculative, but 183 rounds are at least vulnerable. We expect that our new tool becomes a new generic tool to measure the security of stream ciphers.

References

1. eSTREAM: the ECRYPT stream cipher project (2008). http://www.ecrypt.eu.org/stream/
2. CAESAR: Competition for authenticated encryption: Security, applicability, and robustness (2014). https://competitions.cr.yp.to/caesar.html
3. Ågren, M., Hell, M., Johansson, T., Meier, W.: Grain-128a: a new version of grain-128 with optional authentication. IJWMC **5**(1), 48–59 (2011)

4. Aumasson, J.-P., Dinur, I., Meier, W., Shamir, A.: Cube testers and key recovery attacks on reduced-round MD6 and Trivium. In: Dunkelman, O. (ed.) FSE 2009. LNCS, vol. 5665, pp. 1–22. Springer, Heidelberg (2009). doi:10.1007/978-3-642-03317-9_1
5. Biryukov, A., Shamir, A.: Structural cryptanalysis of SASAS. In: Pfitzmann, B. (ed.) EUROCRYPT 2001. LNCS, vol. 2045, pp. 395–405. Springer, Heidelberg (2001). doi:10.1007/3-540-44987-6_24
6. Cannière, C.D., Preneel, B.: Trivium specifications (2006). http://www.ecrypt.eu.org/stream/p.3ciphers/trivium/trivium_p.3.pdf. eSTREAM portfolio, Profile 2 (HW)
7. Cui, T., Jia, K., Fu, K., Chen, S., Wang, M.: New automatic search tool for impossible differentials and zero-correlation linear approximations (2016). http://eprint.iacr.org/2016/689
8. Daemen, J., Knudsen, L., Rijmen, V.: The block cipher Square. In: Biham, E. (ed.) FSE 1997. LNCS, vol. 1267, pp. 149–165. Springer, Heidelberg (1997). doi:10.1007/BFb0052343
9. Dinur, I., Güneysu, T., Paar, C., Shamir, A., Zimmermann, R.: An experimentally verified attack on full grain-128 using dedicated reconfigurable hardware. In: Lee, D.H., Wang, X. (eds.) ASIACRYPT 2011. LNCS, vol. 7073, pp. 327–343. Springer, Heidelberg (2011). doi:10.1007/978-3-642-25385-0_18
10. Dinur, I., Morawiecki, P., Pieprzyk, J., Srebrny, M., Straus, M.: Cube attacks and cube-attack-like cryptanalysis on the round-reduced Keccak sponge function. In: Oswald, E., Fischlin, M. (eds.) EUROCRYPT 2015. LNCS, vol. 9056, pp. 733–761. Springer, Heidelberg (2015). doi:10.1007/978-3-662-46800-5_28
11. Dinur, I., Shamir, A.: Cube attacks on tweakable black box polynomials. In: Joux, A. (ed.) EUROCRYPT 2009. LNCS, vol. 5479, pp. 278–299. Springer, Heidelberg (2009). doi:10.1007/978-3-642-01001-9_16
12. Dinur, I., Shamir, A.: Breaking Grain-128 with dynamic cube attacks. In: Joux, A. (ed.) FSE 2011. LNCS, vol. 6733, pp. 167–187. Springer, Heidelberg (2011). doi:10.1007/978-3-642-21702-9_10
13. Fischer, S., Khazaei, S., Meier, W.: Chosen IV statistical analysis for key recovery attacks on stream ciphers. In: Vaudenay, S. (ed.) AFRICACRYPT 2008. LNCS, vol. 5023, pp. 236–245. Springer, Heidelberg (2008). doi:10.1007/978-3-540-68164-9_16
14. Fouque, P.-A., Vannet, T.: Improving key recovery to 784 and 799 rounds of Trivium using optimized cube attacks. In: Moriai, S. (ed.) FSE 2013. LNCS, vol. 8424, pp. 502–517. Springer, Heidelberg (2014). doi:10.1007/978-3-662-43933-3_26
15. Gurobi Optimization Inc.: Gurobi optimizer 6.5. Official webpage (2015). http://www.gurobi.com/
16. ISO/IEC: JTC1: ISO/IEC 29167-13: Information technology - automatic identification and data capture techniques - part 13: Crypto suite Grain-128a security services for air interface communications (2015)
17. Knellwolf, S., Meier, W., Naya-Plasencia, M.: Conditional differential cryptanalysis of NLFSR-based cryptosystems. In: Abe, M. (ed.) ASIACRYPT 2010. LNCS, vol. 6477, pp. 130–145. Springer, Heidelberg (2010). doi:10.1007/978-3-642-17373-8_8
18. Knudsen, L.R.: Truncated and higher order differentials. In: Preneel, B. (ed.) FSE 1994. LNCS, vol. 1008, pp. 196–211. Springer, Heidelberg (1995). doi:10.1007/3-540-60590-8_16
19. Knudsen, L., Wagner, D.: Integral cryptanalysis. In: Daemen, J., Rijmen, V. (eds.) FSE 2002. LNCS, vol. 2365, pp. 112–127. Springer, Heidelberg (2002). doi:10.1007/3-540-45661-9_9

20. Lai, X.: Higher order derivatives and differential cryptanalysis. In: Blahut, R.E., Costello, D.J., Maurer, U., Mittelholzer, T. (eds.) Communications and Cryptography. The Springer International Series in Engineering and Computer Science, vol. 276, pp. 227–233. Springer, Boston (1994)
21. Lehmann, M., Meier, W.: Conditional differential cryptanalysis of Grain-128a. In: Pieprzyk, J., Sadeghi, A.-R., Manulis, M. (eds.) CANS 2012. LNCS, vol. 7712, pp. 1–11. Springer, Heidelberg (2012). doi:10.1007/978-3-642-35404-5_1
22. Lucks, S.: The saturation attack — a bait for Twofish. In: Matsui, M. (ed.) FSE 2001. LNCS, vol. 2355, pp. 1–15. Springer, Heidelberg (2002). doi:10.1007/3-540-45473-X_1
23. Mouha, N., Wang, Q., Gu, D., Preneel, B.: Differential and linear cryptanalysis using mixed-integer linear programming. In: Wu, C.-K., Yung, M., Lin, D. (eds.) Inscrypt 2011. LNCS, vol. 7537, pp. 57–76. Springer, Heidelberg (2012). doi:10.1007/978-3-642-34704-7_5
24. Mroczkowski, P., Szmidt, J.: The cube attack on stream cipher Trivium and quadraticity tests. Fundam. Inform. **114**(3–4), 309–318 (2012)
25. Salam, M.I., Bartlett, H., Dawson, E., Pieprzyk, J., Simpson, L., Wong, K.K.-H.: Investigating cube attacks on the authenticated encryption stream cipher ACORN. In: Batten, L., Li, G. (eds.) ATIS 2016. CCIS, vol. 651, pp. 15–26. Springer, Singapore (2016). doi:10.1007/978-981-10-2741-3_2
26. Sasaki, Y., Todo, Y.: New impossible differential search tool from design and cryptanalysis aspects - revealing structural properties of several ciphers. In: EUROCRYPT (3), pp. 185–215 (2017). doi:10.1007/978-3-319-56617-7_7
27. Sun, L., Wang, W., Wang, M.: MILP-aided bit-based division property for primitives with non-bit-permutation linear layers (2016). http://eprint.iacr.org/2016/811
28. Sun, S., Hu, L., Wang, M., Wang, P., Qiao, K., Ma, X., Shi, D., Song, L.: Towards finding the best characteristics of some bit-oriented block ciphers and automatic enumeration of (related-key) differential and linear characteristics with predefined properties (2014a). http://eprint.iacr.org/2014/747
29. Sun, S., Hu, L., Wang, P., Qiao, K., Ma, X., Song, L.: Automatic security evaluation and (related-key) differential characteristic search: application to SIMON, PRESENT, LBlock, DES(L) and other bit-oriented block ciphers. In: Sarkar, P., Iwata, T. (eds.) ASIACRYPT 2014. LNCS, vol. 8873, pp. 158–178. Springer, Heidelberg (2014). doi:10.1007/978-3-662-45611-8_9
30. Todo, Y.: Integral cryptanalysis on full MISTY1. In: Gennaro, R., Robshaw, M. (eds.) CRYPTO 2015. LNCS, vol. 9215, pp. 413–432. Springer, Heidelberg (2015). doi:10.1007/978-3-662-47989-6_20
31. Todo, Y.: Structural evaluation by generalized integral property. In: Oswald, E., Fischlin, M. (eds.) EUROCRYPT 2015. LNCS, vol. 9056, pp. 287–314. Springer, Heidelberg (2015). doi:10.1007/978-3-662-46800-5_12
32. Todo, Y., Morii, M.: Bit-based division property and application to SIMON family. In: Peyrin, T. (ed.) FSE 2016. LNCS, vol. 9783, pp. 357–377. Springer, Heidelberg (2016). doi:10.1007/978-3-662-52993-5_18
33. Wu, H.: Acorn v3 (2016). Submission to CAESAR competition
34. Xiang, Z., Zhang, W., Bao, Z., Lin, D.: Applying MILP method to searching integral distinguishers based on division property for 6 lightweight block ciphers. In: Cheon, J.H., Takagi, T. (eds.) ASIACRYPT 2016. LNCS, vol. 10031, pp. 648–678. Springer, Heidelberg (2016). doi:10.1007/978-3-662-53887-6_24

Lattice Crypto

Middle-Product Learning with Errors

Miruna Roşca[1,2](✉), Amin Sakzad[3], Damien Stehlé[1], and Ron Steinfeld[3]

[1] ENS de Lyon, Laboratoire LIP
(U. Lyon, CNRS, ENSL, INRIA, UCBL), Lyon, France
mirunarosca@gmail.com
[2] Bitdefender, Bucharest, Romania
[3] Faculty of Information Technology, Monash University, Melbourne, Australia

Abstract. We introduce a new variant MP-LWE of the Learning With Errors problem (LWE) making use of the Middle Product between polynomials modulo an integer q. We exhibit a reduction from the Polynomial-LWE problem (PLWE) parametrized by a polynomial f, to MP-LWE which is defined independently of any such f. The reduction only requires f to be monic with constant coefficient coprime with q. It incurs a noise growth proportional to the so-called expansion factor of f. We also describe a public-key encryption scheme with quasi-optimal asymptotic efficiency (the bit-sizes of the keys and the run-times of all involved algorithms are quasi-linear in the security parameter), which is secure against chosen plaintext attacks under the MP-LWE hardness assumption. The scheme is hence secure under the assumption that PLWE is hard for at least one polynomial f of degree n among a family of f's which is exponential in n.

Keywords: LWE · PLWE · Public-key encryption

1 Introduction

Lattice-based cryptography relies in great parts on the assumed hardness of two well-studied and closely related problems: the Small Integer Solution problem (SIS) introduced in [Ajt96] and the Learning With Errors problem (LWE) introduced in [Reg09]. They lead to numerous cryptographic constructions, are conjectured exponentially hard to solve even for quantum algorithms, and enjoy reductions from standard worst-case lattice problems such as finding a short non-zero vector in a lattice (ApproxSVP). However, the resulting cryptographic constructions suffer from large keys and/or rather inefficient algorithms. This is because the problems themselves involve large-dimensional random matrices over a ring $\mathbb{Z}_q$ (for some $q \geq 2$).

To obtain more efficient SIS-based primitives, Lyubashevsky and Micciancio [LM06], and Peikert and Rosen [PR06] introduced the Polynomial SIS

J. Katz and H. Shacham (Eds.): CRYPTO 2017, Part III, LNCS 10403, pp. 283–297, 2017.
DOI: 10.1007/978-3-319-63697-9_10

problem (PSIS), inspired from [Mic07,HPS98].[1] $\mathsf{PSIS}^{(f)}$ can be described in terms of elements of $\mathbb{Z}_q[x]/f$ for an integer $q \geq 2$ and a polynomial f that parametrizes the problem. Equivalently, it may be described as SIS where the uniform matrix is replaced by a structured matrix (the precise structure depends on f). PSIS allows the design of fast digital signatures, among other applications (see [Lyu09], for example).

This approach was extended to LWE by Stehlé *et al.* [SSTX09], who introduced and studied the (search version of) Polynomial-LWE problem (PLWE).[2] Lyubashevsky *et al.* [LPR13] introduced the Ring-LWE problem, which involves number fields rather than polynomials, and proposed a reduction from its search to decision versions, in the case of cyclotomic polynomials. Power-of-2 cyclotomic polynomials (for which PLWE and Ring-LWE match) have been exploited to design fast encryption schemes, among others (see [ADPS16], for example). Cryptographic schemes based on PLWE/Ring-LWE most often enjoy keys of $\widetilde{O}(\lambda)$ bit-sizes and algorithms with $\widetilde{O}(\lambda)$ runtime, where λ refers to the security parameter (i.e., all known attacks run in time $\geq 2^\lambda$) and the $\widetilde{O}(\cdot)$ notation hides poly-logarithmic factors.

Switching from unstructured SIS and LWE to their polynomial counterparts PSIS and PLWE has undeniable efficiency advantages. However, the security guarantees are severely degraded. PSIS and PLWE also enjoy reductions from worst-case lattice problems such as ApproxSVP, but these lattice problems, e.g., $\mathsf{ApproxSVP}^{(f)}$, are restricted to lattices that correspond to ideals of $\mathbb{Z}[x]/f$, where f is the polynomial that parametrizes PSIS and PLWE: under some conditions on f, there exists a reduction from $\mathsf{ApproxSVP}^{(f)}$ with small approximation factor, to $\mathsf{PSIS}^{(f)}$ and $\mathsf{PLWE}^{(f)}$ (see [LM06,PR06,SSTX09]). It is entirely possible that $\mathsf{PSIS}^{(f)}/\mathsf{PLWE}^{(f)}$ could be easy to solve for some polynomials f, and hard for others.[3] For instance, if f has a linear factor over the integers, then it is well-known that $\mathsf{PSIS}^{(f)}/\mathsf{PLWE}^{(f)}$ are computationally easy (we note that the reductions from $\mathsf{ApproxSVP}^{(f)}$ require f to be irreducible). Finding weak f's for PLWE has been investigated in a sequence of recent works [EHL14,ELOS15,CLS15,HCS16], although it was later established that the weaknesses of the studied instantiations lied in the choice of the noise distribution rather than in the choice of f [CIV16b,CIV16a,Pei16]. In another

[1] The problem was called Ideal-SIS in [LM06], Cyclotomic-SIS in [PR06], and is now commonly referred to as Ring-SIS. We prefer to call it PSIS as it is not defined in terms of number fields but polynomial rings (as opposed to Ring-LWE), similarly to the Polynomial-LWE problem (PLWE) we consider in this work. It is possible to define a SIS variant of Ring-LWE, i.e., involving number fields: in the common case of power-of-2 cyclotomics, PSIS and Ring-SIS match (as do PLWE and Ring-LWE). In this work, we are interested in larger classes of polynomials, making the distinction important.

[2] It was originally called Ideal-LWE, by analogy to Ideal-SIS.

[3] We note that the stability of the polynomial rings under multiplication by x can be exploited to accelerate some known lattice algorithms by small polynomial factors, but we are interested here in more drastic weaknesses.

sequence of works, Cramer *et al.* [CDPR16, CDW17] showed that $\mathsf{ApproxSVP}^{(f)}$ is easier for f a cyclotomic polynomial of prime-power conductor than for general lattices. More concretely, the authors of [CDW17] give a quantum polynomial-time algorithm for $\mathsf{ApproxSVP}^{(f)}$ with approximation factor $2^{\widetilde{O}(\sqrt{n})}$, where n is the degree of f. As a comparison, for such approximation factors and arbitrary lattices, the best known algorithms run in time $2^{\widetilde{O}(\sqrt{n})}$ (see [Sch87]). Finally, we note that the choice of non-cyclotomic polynomials in [BCLvV16] was motivated by such weaknesses. Even though the results in [CDPR16, CDW17] impact $\mathsf{ApproxSVP}^{(f)}$, it may be argued that it could have implications for $\mathsf{PLWE}^{(f)}$ as well, possibly even for lower approximation factors. On the other hand, it could be that similar weaknesses exist for $\mathsf{ApproxSVP}^{(f)}$ considered in [BCLvV16], although none is known at the moment. This lack of understanding of which f's correspond to hard $\mathsf{PLWE}^{(f)}$ problems motivates research into problems that are provably as hard as $\mathsf{PLWE}^{(f)}$ for the hardest f in a large class of polynomials, while preserving the computational efficiency advantages of PLWE. Our results are motivated by and make progress in this direction.

Recently, Lyubashevsky [Lyu16] introduced a variant $R^{<n}$-SIS of SIS that is not parametrized by a polynomial f and which enjoys the following desirable properties. First, an efficient algorithm for $R^{<n}$-SIS with degree bound n leads to an efficient algorithm for $\mathsf{PSIS}^{(f)}$ for all f's in a family of polynomials of size exponential in n. Second, there exists a signature scheme which is secure under the assumption that $R^{<n}$-SIS is hard, involves keys of bit-size $\widetilde{O}(\lambda) = \widetilde{O}(n)$ and whose algorithms run in time $\widetilde{O}(\lambda)$. In this sense, $R^{<n}$-SIS can serve as an alternative cryptographic foundation that hedges against the risk that $\mathsf{PSIS}^{(f)}$ is easy to solve for some f (as long as it stays hard for some f in the family).

Our contributions. Our main contribution is the introduction of an LWE counterpart to Lyubashevsky's $R^{<n}$-SIS problem. Let $n, q \geq 2$. We let $\mathbb{Z}_q^{<n}[x]$ denote the set of polynomials with coefficients in $\mathbb{Z}_q$ and degree $< n$. For $a \in \mathbb{Z}_q^{<n}[x]$ and $s \in \mathbb{Z}_q^{<2n-1}[x]$, we let $a \odot_n s = \lfloor (a \cdot s \bmod x^{2n})/x^n \rfloor \in \mathbb{Z}_q^{<n}[x]$ denote the polynomial obtained by multiplying a and s and keeping only the middle third of coefficients. Middle-Product LWE (MP-LWE), with parameters $n, q \geq 2$ and $\alpha \in (0,1)$, consists in distinguishing arbitrarily many samples (a_i, b_i) uniform in $\mathbb{Z}_q^{<n}[x] \times (\mathbb{R}/q\mathbb{Z})^{<n}[x]$, from the same number of samples (a_i, b_i) with a_i uniform in $\mathbb{Z}_q^{<n}[x]$ and $b_i = a_i \odot_n s + e_i$, where each coefficient of e_i is sampled from the Gaussian distribution of standard deviation $\alpha \cdot q$, and s is uniformly chosen in $\mathbb{Z}_q^{<2n-1}[x]$.

We give a reduction from (decision) $\mathsf{PLWE}^{(f)}$ to (decision) MP-LWE of parameter n, for every monic f of degree n whose constant coefficient is coprime with q. The noise parameter amplifies linearly with the so-called Expansion Factor of f, introduced in [LM06]. The noise parameter in MP-LWE can for example be set to handle all monic polynomials $f = x^n + g$ with constant coefficient coprime with q, $\deg g \leq n/2$ and $\|g\| \leq n^c$ for an arbitrary $c > 0$. For any c, this set of f's has exponential size in n. We note that similar restrictions involving the expansion factor appeared before in [LM06, SSTX09].

Finally, we describe a public-key encryption scheme that is IND-CPA secure under the MP-LWE hardness assumption, involves keys of bit-size $\widetilde{O}(\lambda)$ and whose algorithms run in time $\widetilde{O}(\lambda)$. The scheme is adapted from Regev's [Reg09]. Its correctness proof involves an associativity property of the middle product. To establish its security, we prove that a related hash function family involving middle products is universal, and apply a generalized version of the leftover hash lemma. The standard leftover hash lemma does not seem to suffice for our needs, as the first part of the ciphertext is not statistically close to uniform, contrarily to Regev's encryption scheme.

Open problems. Our reduction is from the decision version of $\mathsf{PLWE}^{(f)}$ to the decision version of MP-LWE. (It can be adapted to the search counterparts, but it is unclear how to use the hardness of search MP-LWE for cryptographic purposes). Unfortunately, the hardness of decision $\mathsf{PLWE}^{(f)}$ is currently supported by the presumed hardness of $\mathsf{ApproxSVP}^{(f)}$ for very few polynomials f. Such reductions for larger classes of polynomials f would strengthen our confidence in the hardness of MP-LWE. A first strategy towards this goal would be to design a reduction from search $\mathsf{PLWE}^{(f)}$ to decision $\mathsf{PLWE}^{(f)}$ for larger classes of f's than currently handled (the reduction from [LPR13] requires f to be cyclotomic). This reduction could then be combined with the one from $\mathsf{ApproxSVP}^{(f)}$ to $\mathsf{PLWE}^{(f)}$ from [SSTX09], which only requires f to be irreducible with bounded expansion factor. A second strategy would be to reduce decision $\mathsf{Ring}\text{-}\mathsf{LWE}^{(f)}$ to decision $\mathsf{PLWE}^{(f)}$ and rely on the new reduction from ApproxSVP restricted to ideals of the number field K_f to decision $\mathsf{Ring}\text{-}\mathsf{LWE}^{(f)}$ from [PRSD17]. Indeed, this new reduction is not restricted to cyclotomic polynomials.

We show the cryptographic relevance of MP-LWE by adapting Regev's encryption scheme to the middle-product algebraic setting. Adapting the dual-Regev scheme from [GPV08] does not seem straightforward. Indeed, it appears that we would need a leftover hash lemma for polynomials over $\mathbb{Z}_q[x]$ that are not folded modulo some polynomial f. The difficulty is that the constant coefficients of the polynomials are now "isolated", in the sense that the constant coefficient of a polynomial combination of polynomials only involves the constant coefficients of these polynomials. Hopefully, solving this difficulty would also enable the construction of a trapdoor for MP-LWE, similar to those that exist for LWE and SIS (see [MP12] and references therein). Independently, showing that the MP-LWE secret could be sampled from a small-norm distribution, as achieved for LWE in [ACPS09], may allow for a more efficient ElGamal-type encryption, similar to the one described in [LPR13].

Notations. We use the notation $U(X)$ for the uniform distribution over the set X. If D_1 and D_2 are two distributions over the same countable domain, we let $\Delta(D_1, D_2)$ denote their statistical distance. We let $\|\mathbf{b}\|$ and $\|\mathbf{b}\|_\infty$ denote the Euclidean and infinity norm of any vector $\mathbf{b}$ over the reals, respectively. Similarly, if b is a polynomial over the reals, we let $\|b\|$ denote the Euclidean norm of its coefficient vector. For a matrix $\mathbf{M}$ we let $\mathbf{M}_{i,j}$ denote its element in the i-th row and j-th column. We let $\|\mathbf{M}\|$ denote the largest singular value of $\mathbf{M}$.

2 Background

In this section, we provide the background definitions and results that are necessary to present our contributions.

2.1 Probabilities

We will use the following variant of the leftover hash lemma. We recall that a (finite) family $\mathcal{H}$ of hash functions $h : X \to Y$ is universal if $\Pr_{h \leftarrow U(\mathcal{H})}[h(x_1) = h(x_2)] = 1/|Y|$, for all $x_1 \neq x_2 \in X$.

Lemma 2.1. *Let X, Y, Z denote finite sets. Let $\mathcal{H}$ be a universal family of hash functions $h : X \to Y$. Let $f : X \to Z$ be arbitrary. Then for any random variable T taking values in X, we have:*

$$\Delta\big(\, (h, h(T), f(T)) \,,\, (h, U(Y), f(T)) \,\big) \;\leq\; \frac{1}{2} \cdot \sqrt{\gamma(T) \cdot |Y| \cdot |Z|},$$

where $\gamma(T) = \max_{t \in X} \Pr[T = t]$.

In the problems we will study, the so-called noise distributions will be Gaussian.

Definition 2.1. *We define the Gaussian function on $\mathbb{R}^n$ of covariance matrix $\mathbf{\Sigma}$ as $\rho_{\mathbf{\Sigma}}(\mathbf{x}) := \exp(-\pi \cdot \mathbf{x}^T \mathbf{\Sigma}^{-1} \mathbf{x})$ for every vector $\mathbf{x} \in \mathbb{R}^n$. The probability distribution whose density is proportional to $\rho_{\mathbf{\Sigma}}$ is called the Gaussian distribution and is denoted $D_{\mathbf{\Sigma}}$. When $\mathbf{\Sigma} = s^2 \cdot \mathsf{Id}_n$, we write ρ_s and D_s instead of $\rho_{\mathbf{\Sigma}}$ and $D_{\mathbf{\Sigma}}$, respectively.*

2.2 Polynomials and Structured Matrices

Let R be a ring. For $k > 0$, we let $R^{<k}[x]$ denote the set of polynomials in $R[x]$ of degree $< k$. Given a polynomial $a = a_0 + a_1 x + \cdots + a_{k-1} x^{k-1} \in R^{<k}[x]$ and some $j < k$, we use the following notations: $\mathbf{a} = (a_0, \ldots, a_{k-1})^T \in R^k$ and $\overline{\mathbf{a}} = (a_{k-1}, \ldots, a_0)^T \in R^k$. The latter notation is extended to the corresponding polynomial.

Definition 2.2. *Let f be a polynomial of degree m. For any $d > 0$ and any $a \in R[x]$, we let $\mathsf{Rot}_f^d(a)$ denote the matrix in $R^{d \times m}$ whose i-th row is given by the coefficients of the polynomial $(x^{i-1} \cdot a) \bmod f$, for any $i = 1, \ldots, d$. We will use the notation $\mathsf{Rot}_f(a)$ instead of $\mathsf{Rot}_f^m(a)$.*

Note that if $a' = a \bmod f$, then $\mathsf{Rot}_f^d(a) = \mathsf{Rot}_f^d(a')$ for any d. Note also that $\mathsf{Rot}_f(a \cdot b) = \mathsf{Rot}_f(a) \cdot \mathsf{Rot}_f(b)$ for any $a, b \in R[x]$.

Definition 2.3. *Let f be a polynomial of degree m. We define $\mathbf{M}_f$ as the (Hankel) matrix in $R^{m \times m}$ such that for any $1 \leq i, j \leq m$, the coefficient $(\mathbf{M}_f)_{i,j}$ is the constant coefficient of $x^{i+j-2} \bmod f$.*

Matrix $\mathbf{M}_f$ helps rewriting multiplication on the left by matrix $\mathsf{Rot}_f(a)$ as a multiplication on the right by $\mathbf{a}$.

Lemma 2.4. *For any $a \in R^{<m}[x]$, we have $\mathsf{Rot}_f(a) \cdot (1, 0, \ldots, 0)^T = \mathbf{M}_f \cdot \mathbf{a}$.*

Proof. First, the i-th coordinate of the left hand side is the constant coefficient of $x^{i-1} \cdot a \bmod f$. Second, the i-th entry of the right hand side is

$$((a_0 x^{i-1} \bmod f) \bmod x) + \cdots + ((a_{m-1} x^{m+i-2} \bmod f) \bmod x),$$

which can be re-written as $x^{i-1}(a_0 + \cdots + a_{m-1}x^{m-1} \bmod f) \bmod x = (x^{i-1} \cdot a \bmod f) \bmod x$. The latter is the constant coefficient of $x^{i-1} \cdot a \bmod f$. □

Definition 2.5. *For any $d, k > 0$ and $a \in R^{<k}[x]$, we let $\mathsf{Toep}^{d,k}(a)$ denote the matrix in $R^{d \times (k+d-1)}$ whose i-th row, for $i = 1, \ldots, d$, is given by the coefficients of $x^{i-1} \cdot a$.*

The following property will be useful in proving our main result.

Lemma 2.6. *For any $d, k > 0$ and any $a \in R^{<k}[x]$, we have $\mathsf{Rot}_f^d(a) = \mathsf{Toep}^{d,k}(a) \cdot \mathsf{Rot}_f^{k+d-1}(1)$.*

Proof. It is sufficient to prove that the rows of $\mathsf{Rot}_f^d(a)$ and $\mathsf{Toep}^{d,k}(a) \cdot \mathsf{Rot}_f^{k+d-1}(1)$ are equal. We just note that the i-th row of $\mathsf{Rot}_f^{k+d-1}(1)$ is $x^{i-1} \bmod f$, for $i = 1, \ldots, k+d$ and these will fill the gap in the definitions of $\mathsf{Rot}_f^d(a)$ and $\mathsf{Toep}^{d,k}(a)$. □

We now recall the definition of the expansion factor [LM06].

Definition 2.7. *Let $f \in \mathbb{Z}[x]$ of degree m. Then the expansion factor of f is defined as $\mathsf{EF}(f) = \max(\|g \bmod f\|_\infty / \|g\|_\infty : g \in \mathbb{Z}^{<2m-1}[x] \setminus \{0\})$.*

We remark that there are numerous polynomials with bounded expansion factor. One class of such polynomials [LM06] is the family of all $f = x^m + h$, for $h = \sum_{i \leq m/2} h_i x^i$ and $\|\mathbf{h}\|_\infty \in \text{poly}(m)$: we then have $\mathsf{EF}(f) \in \text{poly}(m)$.

Lemma 2.8. *For $f \in \mathbb{Z}[x]$, we have $\|\mathbf{M}_f\| \leq \deg(f) \cdot \mathsf{EF}(f)$.*

Proof. By definitions of $\mathbf{M}_f$ and $\mathsf{EF}(f)$, we have that $|(\mathbf{M}_f)_{i,j}| \leq \mathsf{EF}(f)$, for $1 \leq i, j \leq m$. Therefore, the largest singular value of $\mathbf{M}_f$ is bounded from above by $m \cdot \mathsf{EF}(f)$. □

2.3 The Polynomial Learning with Errors Problem (PLWE)

We first define the distribution the PLWE problem is based on. For the rest of this paper, we will use the notation $\mathbb{R}_q := \mathbb{R}/q\mathbb{Z}$.

Definition 2.9 (P **distribution**). *Let $q \geq 2$, $m > 0$, f a polynomial of degree m, χ a distribution over $\mathbb{R}[x]/f$. Given $s \in \mathbb{Z}_q[x]/f$, we define the distribution $\mathsf{P}_{q,\chi}^{(f)}(s)$ over $\mathbb{Z}_q[x]/f \times \mathbb{R}_q[x]/f$ obtained by sampling $a \hookleftarrow U(\mathbb{Z}_q[x]/f)$, $e \hookleftarrow \chi$ and returning $(a, b = a \cdot s + e)$.*

Definition 2.10 (PLWE). *Let $q \geq 2$, $m > 0$, f a polynomial of degree m, χ a distribution over $\mathbb{R}[x]/f$. The (decision) $\mathsf{PLWE}_{q,\chi}^{(f)}$ consists in distinguishing between arbitrarily many samples from $\mathsf{P}_{q,\chi}^{(f)}(s)$ and the same number of samples from $U(\mathbb{Z}_q[x]/f \times \mathbb{R}_q[x]/f)$, with non-negligible probability over the choices of $s \hookleftarrow U(\mathbb{Z}_q[x]/f)$.*

One can also define a search variant of $\mathsf{PLWE}_{q,\chi}^{(f)}$, which would consist in computing $s \in \mathbb{Z}_q[x]/f$ from arbitrarily many samples from $\mathsf{P}_{q,\chi}^{(f)}(s)$.

3 The Middle-Product Learning with Errors Problem

We first recall the definition of the middle product of two polynomials and some of its properties.

3.1 The Middle-Product

Let R be a ring. Assume we multiply two polynomials a and b of degrees $< d_a$ and $< d_b$, respectively. Assume that $d_a+d_b-1 = d+2k$ for some integers d and k. Then the middle-product of size d of a and b is obtained by multiplying a and b, deleting the (left) coefficients of $1, x, \ldots, x^{k-1}$, deleting the (right) coefficients of $x^{k+d}, x^{k+d+1}, \ldots, x^{d+2k-1}$, and dividing what remains (the middle) by x^k.

Definition 3.1. *Let d_a, d_b, d, k be integers such that $d_a + d_b - 1 = d + 2k$. The middle-product $\odot_d : R^{<d_a}[x] \times R^{<d_b}[x] \to R^{<d}[x]$ is the map:*

$$(a, b) \mapsto a \odot_d b = \left\lfloor \frac{(a \cdot b) \bmod x^{k+d}}{x^k} \right\rfloor .$$

We use the same notation $\odot_d$ for every d_a, d_b such that $d_a + d_b - 1 - d$ is non-negative and even.

The middle-product of polynomials is used in computer algebra to accelerate computations in polynomial rings (see, e.g., [Sho99,HQZ04]). As it is part of the output of polynomial multiplication, it can be computed with a number of ring additions and multiplications that is quasi-linear number in $d_a + d_b$. Faster algorithms exist [HQZ04].

The (reversed) coefficient vector of the middle-product of two polynomials is in fact equal to the product of the Toeplitz matrix associated to one polynomial by the (reversed) coefficient vector of the second polynomial.

Lemma 3.2. *Let $d, k > 0$. Let $r \in R^{<k+1}[x]$ and $a \in R^{<k+d}[x]$ and $b = r \odot_d a$. Then $\overline{\mathbf{b}} = \mathsf{Toep}^{d,k+1}(r) \cdot \overline{\mathbf{a}}$. In other words, we have $\mathbf{b} = \overline{\mathsf{Toep}^{d,k+1}(r) \cdot \overline{\mathbf{a}}}$.*

Proof. We first note that $\mathsf{Toep}^{d,2k+d}(r \cdot a) = \mathsf{Toep}^{d,k+1}(r) \cdot \mathsf{Toep}^{k+d,k+d}(a)$. Thus, by definition of the middle-product, we have that the coefficients of b appear in the first row of $\mathsf{Toep}(r \cdot a)$, namely $b_i = \mathsf{Toep}^{d,2k+d}(r \cdot a)_{1,k+i+1}$ for $i < d$. But since $\mathsf{Toep}(r \cdot a)$ is constant along its diagonals, we also have that b appear (in reversed order) in the $(k+d)$-th column of $\mathsf{Toep}^{d,2k+d}(r \cdot a)$, namely $b_i = \mathsf{Toep}^{d,2k+d}(r \cdot a)_{d-i,k+d}$ for $i < d$. Therefore, vector $\overline{\mathbf{b}}$ is the $(k+d)$-th column of $\mathsf{Toep}^{d,2k+d}(r \cdot a)$, which is equal to $\mathsf{Toep}^{d,k+1}(r) \cdot \mathbf{a}'$, where $\mathbf{a}'$ is the $(k+d)$-th column of $\mathsf{Toep}^{k+d,k+d}(a)$. Since $\mathsf{Toep}^{k+d,k+d}(a)$ is constant along its diagonals, its first row is equal to its reversed $(k+d)$-th column, so $\mathbf{a}' = \overline{\mathbf{a}}$, as required. □

The middle-product is an additive homomorphism when either of its inputs is fixed. As a consequence of the associativity of matrix multiplication and Lemma 3.2, the middle-product satisfies the following associativity property.

Lemma 3.3. *Let $d, k, n > 0$. For all $r \in R^{<k+1}[x]$, $a \in R^{<n}[x]$, $s \in R^{<n+d+k-1}[x]$, we have $r \odot_d (a \odot_{d+k} s) = (r \cdot a) \odot_d s$.*

Proof. Note first that the degree bounds match. Now, by Lemma 3.2, the vector associated to the reverse of $r \odot_d (a \odot_{d+k} s)$ is $\mathsf{Toep}^{d,k+1}(r) \cdot (\mathsf{Toep}^{d+k,n}(a) \cdot \overline{\mathbf{s}})$. Similarly, the vector associated to the reverse of $(r \cdot a) \odot_d s$ is $\mathsf{Toep}^{d,k+n}(r \cdot a) \cdot \overline{\mathbf{s}}$. The result follows from observing that $\mathsf{Toep}^{d,k+1}(r) \cdot \mathsf{Toep}^{d+k,n}(a) = \mathsf{Toep}^{d,k+n}(r \cdot a)$. □

3.2 Middle-Product Learning with Errors

Before stating MP-LWE, we first introduce a distribution its definition relies on.

Definition 3.4 (MP **distribution).** *Let $n, d > 0$, $q \geq 2$, and χ a distribution over $\mathbb{R}^{<d}[x]$. For $s \in \mathbb{Z}_q^{<n+d-1}[x]$, we define the distribution $\mathsf{MP}_{q,n,d,\chi}(s)$ over $\mathbb{Z}_q^{<n}[x] \times \mathbb{R}_q^{<d}[x]$ as the one obtained by: sampling $a \hookleftarrow U(\mathbb{Z}_q^{<n}[x])$, $e \hookleftarrow \chi$ and returning $(a, b = a \odot_d s + e)$.*

Definition 3.5 (MP-LWE). *Let $n, d > 0$, $q \geq 2$, and a distribution χ over $\mathbb{R}^{<d}[x]$. The (decision) $\mathsf{MP\text{-}LWE}_{n,d,q,\chi}$ consists in distinguishing between arbitrarily many samples from $\mathsf{MP}_{q,n,d,\chi}(s)$ and the same number of samples from $U(\mathbb{Z}_q^{<n}[x] \times \mathbb{R}_q^{<d}[x])$, with non-negligible probability over the choices of $s \hookleftarrow U(\mathbb{Z}_q^{<n+d-1}[x])$.*

It is possible to define a search variant of $\mathsf{MP\text{-}LWE}_{q,n,d,\chi}$, which would consist in computing $s \in \mathbb{Z}_q^{<n+d-1}[x]$ from arbitrarily many samples from $\mathsf{MP}_{q,n,d,\chi}(s)$.

Note that $\mathsf{MP\text{-}LWE}_{q,n,d,\chi}$ can also be viewed as a variant of LWE, in which the samples are correlated. Thanks to Lemma 3.2, it can indeed be restated as follows. Given many samples $(\mathsf{Toep}^{d,n}(a_i), \overline{\mathbf{b}}_i) \in \mathbb{Z}_q^{d\times(n+d-1)} \times \mathbb{R}_q^d$ for uniformly chosen $a_i \in \mathbb{Z}_q^{<n}[x]$, decide if the vectors $\overline{\mathbf{b}}_i$ are uniformly sampled in $\mathbb{R}_q^d$ or are of the form $\overline{\mathbf{b}}_i = \mathsf{Toep}^{d,n}(a_i) \cdot \overline{\mathbf{s}} + \overline{\mathbf{e}}_i$ for some common $s \hookleftarrow U(\mathbb{Z}_q^{<n+d-1}[x])$ and $e_i \hookleftarrow \chi$.

3.3 Hardness of MP-LWE

The following reduction from PLWE to MP-LWE is our main result.

Theorem 3.6. *Let $n, d > 0$, $q \geq 2$, and $\alpha \in (0,1)$. For $S > 0$, we let $\mathcal{F}(S,d,n)$ denote the set of polynomials $f \in \mathbb{Z}[x]$ that are monic, have constant coefficient coprime with q, have degree m in $[d,n]$ and that satisfy $\mathsf{EF}(f) < S$. Then there exists a* ppt *reduction from $\mathsf{PLWE}^{(f)}_{q,D_{\alpha\cdot q}}$ for any $f \in \mathcal{F}(S,d,n)$ to $\mathsf{MP\text{-}LWE}_{q,n,d,D_{\alpha'\cdot q}}$ with $\alpha' = \alpha d S$.*

Proof. We first reduce $\mathsf{PLWE}^{(f)}$ to a variant of MP-LWE whose only dependence on f lies in the noise distribution (see Lemma 3.7 below). Then we remove the latter dependence, by adding a compensating Gaussian distribution (see Lemma 3.8 below). The bound on the magnitude of matrix $\mathbf{M}_f$ from Lemma 2.8 for $\chi = D_{\alpha\cdot q}$ implies that

$$\|\mathbf{\Sigma}_0\| = \alpha q \|\mathbf{J}\cdot\mathbf{M}_f^d\| = \alpha q\|\mathbf{M}_f^d\| \leq \alpha q d \mathsf{EF}(f) < \alpha q d S.$$

Hence, taking $\alpha' q = \alpha q d S$ completes the proof. □

Lemma 3.7. *Let $n, d > 0$, $q \geq 2$, and χ a distribution over $\mathbb{R}^{<d}[x]$. Then there exists a* ppt *reduction from $\mathsf{PLWE}^{(f)}_{q,\chi}$ for any monic $f \in \mathbb{Z}[x]$ with constant coefficient coprime with q and degree $m \in [d,n]$, to $\mathsf{MP\text{-}LWE}_{q,n,d,\mathbf{J}\cdot\mathbf{M}_f^d\cdot\chi}$. Here, matrix $\mathbf{M}_f^d$ is the one obtained by keeping only the first d rows of $\mathbf{M}_f$, and $\mathbf{J} \in \mathbb{Z}^{d\times d}$ is the one with 1's on the anti-diagonal and 0's everywhere else.*

Proof. We describe below an efficient randomized mapping ϕ that takes as input a pair $(a_i, b_i) \in \mathbb{Z}_q[x]/f \times \mathbb{R}_q[x]/f$ and maps it to a pair $(a_i', b_i') \in \mathbb{Z}_q^{<n}[x] \times \mathbb{R}_q^{<d}[x]$, such that ϕ maps $U(\mathbb{Z}_q[x]/f \times \mathbb{R}_q[x]/f)$ to $U(\mathbb{Z}_q^{<n}[x] \times \mathbb{R}_q^{<d}[x])$ and $\mathsf{P}^{(f)}_{q,\chi}(s)$ to $\mathsf{MP}_{q,n,d,\chi'}(s')$, for some s' that depends on s and some χ' that depends on χ and f.

The reduction is then as follows:

- Sample $t \hookleftarrow U(\mathbb{Z}_q^{<n+d-1}[x])$.
- Each time the MP-LWE oracle requests a new sample, ask for a fresh PLWE sample (a_i, b_i), compute $(a_i', b_i') = \phi(a_i, b_i)$ and give $(a_i', b_i') + (0, a_i' \odot_d t)$ to the MP-LWE oracle.
- When MP-LWE terminates, return its output.

Assuming ϕ satisfies the specifications above, the reduction maps uniform samples to uniform samples, and $\mathsf{P}^{(f)}_{q,\chi}(s)$ samples for a uniform s that is common to all samples to $\mathsf{MP}_{q,n,d,\mathbf{J}\cdot\mathbf{M}_f^d\cdot\chi}(s'+t)$ samples for a uniform $s'+t$ that is common to all samples.

We now describe ϕ. Let $(a_i, b_i) \in \mathbb{Z}_q[x]/f \times \mathbb{R}_q[x]/f$ be an input pair. Let m denote the degree of f. We sample $r_i \hookleftarrow U(\mathbb{Z}_q^{<n-m}[x])$ and set $\phi(a_i, b_i) = (a_i', b_i')$ with:

$$a_i' = a_i + f\cdot r_i \in \mathbb{Z}_q^{<n}[x]\ ,\ \ \overline{\mathbf{b}_i'} = \mathbf{M}_f^d \cdot \mathbf{b}_i \in \mathbb{R}_q^{<d}[x].$$

As a_i and r_i are uniformly distributed in $\mathbb{Z}_q^{\leq m}[x]$ and $\mathbb{Z}_q^{<n-m}[x]$ respectively, the polynomial a_i' is uniformly distributed in $\mathbb{Z}_q^{<n}[x]$ (we refer to [Lyu16, Lemma 2.10] for a fully detailed proof). Here, we use the assumption that f is monic.

Further, if b_i is uniformly distributed, then so is its coefficient vector $\mathbf{b}_i$, and so is $\mathbf{M}_f^d \cdot \mathbf{b}_i$. Indeed, as the constant coefficient is coprime with q, matrix $\mathbf{M}_f$ is invertible modulo q (reordering its columns makes it triangular, with diagonal coefficients all equal to the constant coefficient of f).

Now, assume that $b_i = a_i \cdot s + e_i$, for some $s \in \mathbb{Z}_q[x]/f$ and $e_i \hookleftarrow \chi$. Thanks to Subsect. 2.2, we know that $\mathsf{Rot}_f(b_i) = \mathsf{Rot}_f(a_i) \cdot \mathsf{Rot}_f(s) + \mathsf{Rot}_f(e_i)$, and, by taking the first columns and d first rows, we have

$$\begin{aligned}\mathbf{M}_f^d \cdot \mathbf{b}_i &= \mathsf{Rot}_f^d(a_i) \cdot \mathbf{M}_f \cdot \mathbf{s} + \mathbf{M}_f^d \cdot \mathbf{e}_i \\ &= \mathsf{Rot}_f^d(a_i') \cdot \mathbf{M}_f \cdot \mathbf{s} + \mathbf{M}_f^d \cdot \mathbf{e}_i \\ &= \mathsf{Toep}^{d,n}(a_i') \cdot \mathsf{Rot}_f^{d+n-1}(1) \cdot \mathbf{M}_f \cdot \mathbf{s} + \mathbf{M}_f^d \cdot \mathbf{e}_i \\ &= \mathsf{Toep}^{d,n}(a_i') \cdot \overline{\mathbf{s}'} + \mathbf{M}_f^d \cdot \mathbf{e}_i,\end{aligned}$$

where $\mathbf{s}' = \overline{\mathsf{Rot}_f^{d+n-1}(1) \cdot \mathbf{M}_f \cdot \mathbf{s}}$. Since $\mathbf{b}_i' = \overline{\mathbf{M}_f^d \cdot \mathbf{b}_i} = \overline{\mathsf{Toep}(a_i') \cdot \overline{\mathbf{s}'}} + \overline{\mathbf{M}_f^d \cdot \mathbf{e}_i}$, we get that $\mathbf{e}_i' = \overline{\mathbf{M}_f^d \cdot \mathbf{e}_i}$, which makes the distribution in MP-LWE equals to the claimed $\mathbf{J} \cdot \mathbf{M}_f^d \cdot \chi$. This completes the proof. □

We now remove the dependence in f of the noise distribution.

Lemma 3.8. *Let $n, d > 0$, $q \geq 2$. Let $\sigma' > 0$. Let $\mathbf{\Sigma}_0 \in \mathbb{R}^{d \times d}$ be symmetric definite positive matrix with $\|\mathbf{\Sigma}_0\| < \sigma'$. Then there exists a* ppt *reduction from* $\mathsf{MP\text{-}LWE}_{q,n,d,D_{\mathbf{\Sigma}_0}}$ *to* $\mathsf{MP\text{-}LWE}_{q,n,d,D_{\sigma' \cdot \mathsf{Id}_d}}$, *where* Id_d *denotes the d-dimensional identity matrix.*

Proof. The reduction is as follows. We first note that, there exists a positive definite matrix $\mathbf{\Sigma}'$, such that $\mathbf{\Sigma}_0 + \mathbf{\Sigma}' = \sigma' \cdot \mathsf{Id}_d$. The positive definiteness is guaranteed by fact that $\|\mathbf{\Sigma}_0\| < \sigma'$. Then, for any $\mathsf{MP\text{-}LWE}_{q,n,d,D_{\mathbf{\Sigma}_0}}$ input sample (a_i, b_i), we sample $e_i' \hookleftarrow D_{\mathbf{\Sigma}'}$ and compute $(a_i', b_i') = (a_i, b_i + e_i')$.

Observe that the reduction maps uniform samples to uniform samples, and $\mathsf{MP}_{q,n,d,D_{\mathbf{\Sigma}_0}}(s)$ samples to $\mathsf{MP}_{q,n,d,D_{\sigma' \cdot \mathsf{Id}_d}}(s)$ samples. This completes the proof. □

4 Public-Key Encryption from MP-LWE

We now describe a public key encryption scheme that is IND-CPA secure, under the MP-LWE hardness assumption. The scheme is an adaptation of Regev's from [Reg09]. It relies on parameters $q, n, d, t \geq 2$, and a noise rate $\alpha \in (0, 1)$. We let $\chi = \lfloor D_{\alpha q} \rceil$ denote the distribution over $\mathbb{Z}^{<d+k}[x]$ where each coefficient is sampled from $D_{\alpha \cdot q}$ and then rounded to nearest integer. The plaintext space is $\{0,1\}^{<d}[x]$, while the ciphertext space is $\mathbb{Z}_q^{<k+n}[x] \times \mathbb{Z}_q^{<d}[x]$.

$\mathsf{KeyGen}(1^\lambda)$. Sample $s \hookleftarrow U(\mathbb{Z}_q^{<n+d+k-1}[x])$. For every $i \leq t$, sample $a_i \hookleftarrow U(\mathbb{Z}_q^{<n}[x])$, $e_i \hookleftarrow \chi$ and compute $b_i = a_i \odot_{d+k} s + 2 \cdot e_i \in \mathbb{Z}_q^{<d+k}[x]$. Return the secret key $\mathsf{sk} := s$ and the public key $pk := (a_i, b_i)_{i \leq t}$.

$\mathsf{Encrypt}(\mathsf{pk} = (a_i, b_i)_{i \leq t}, \mu)$. For $i \leq t$, sample $r_i \hookleftarrow U(\{0,1\}^{<k+1}[x])$, and return $c = (c_1, c_2)$ with:

$$c_1 = \sum_{i \leq t} r_i \cdot a_i \ , \quad c_2 = \mu + \sum_{i \leq t} r_i \odot_d b_i.$$

$\mathsf{Decrypt}(\mathsf{sk} = s, c)$. Return the plaintext $\mu' = (c_2 - c_1 \odot_d s \bmod q) \bmod 2$.

Example parameters are $n \geq \lambda$, $k = d = n/2$, $q = \Theta(n^{5/2+c}\sqrt{\log n})$, $t = \Theta(\log n)$ and $\alpha = \Theta(1/n\sqrt{\log n})$, for $c > 0$ arbitrary. For these parameters, the scheme is correct (by Lemma 4.1) and secure under $\mathsf{MP\text{-}LWE}_{q,n,n,D_{\alpha q}}$ (by Lemma 4.3). These parameters allow to rely on the assumed hardness of $\mathsf{PLWE}^{(f)}_{q,D_{\beta \cdot q}}$ via Theorem 3.6, for $\beta = \Omega(\sqrt{n}/q)$ (hence preventing attacks *à la* [AG11]) and for any f monic of degree n, with constant coefficient coprime with q and expansion factor $\leq n^c$. Finally, note that the scheme encrypts and decrypts n plain text bits in time $\widetilde{O}(n)$, and the key pair has bit-length $\widetilde{O}(n)$.

Correctness follows from Lemma 3.3 and the proof of correctness of Regev's encryption scheme.

Lemma 4.1 (Correctness). *Assume that* $\alpha < 1/(16\sqrt{\lambda t k})$ *and* $q \geq 16t(k+1)$. *With probability* $\geq 1 - d \cdot 2^{-\Omega(\lambda)}$ *over the randomness of* $(\mathsf{sk}, \mathsf{pk}) \hookleftarrow \mathsf{KeyGen}$, *for all plain text* μ *and with probability* 1 *over the randomness of* $\mathsf{Encrypt}$, *we have* $\mathsf{Decrypt}(\mathsf{sk}, \mathsf{Encrypt}(\mathsf{pk}, \mu)) = \mu$.

Proof. Assume that (c_1, c_2) is an encryption of μ under pk. Then we have, modulo q:

$$\begin{aligned} c_2 - c_1 \odot_d s &= \mu + \sum_{i \leq t} r_i \odot_d b_i - (\sum_{i \leq t} r_i \cdot a_i) \odot_d s \\ &= \mu + \sum_{i \leq t} \left(r_i \odot_d (a_i \odot_{d+k} s + 2 \cdot e_i) - (r_i \cdot a_i) \odot_d s\right) \\ &= \mu + 2 \sum_{i \leq t} r_i \odot_d e_i, \end{aligned}$$

where the last equality follows from Lemma 3.3. If $\|\mu + 2 \cdot \sum_{i \leq t} r_i \odot_d e_i\|_\infty < q/2$, then centered reduction modulo q of $c_2 - c_1 \odot_d s$ gives us $\mu + 2 \cdot \sum_{i \leq t} r_i \odot_d e_i$ (over the integers). Reducing modulo 2 then provides μ.

Now, each coefficient of $\sum_{i \leq t} r_i \odot_d e_i$ can be viewed as an inner product between a binary vector of dimension $t(k+1)$ and a vector sampled from $\lfloor D_{\alpha q} \rceil^{t(k+1)}$. Each coefficient individually has magnitude $\leq \alpha q \sqrt{\lambda t(k+1)} + t(k+1)$ with probability $\geq 1 - 2^{-\Omega(\lambda)}$, because of the Gaussian tail bound and the triangle inequality. By the union bound and triangular inequality, we obtain that $\|\mu + 2 \cdot \sum_{i \leq t} r_i \odot_d e_i\|_\infty < 2\alpha q \sqrt{t\lambda(k+1)} + 2t(k+1) + 1$ with probability $\geq 1 - d \cdot 2^{-\Omega(\lambda)}$. □

The security proof is adapted from that of Regev's encryption scheme from [Reg09], with a subtlety in the application of the leftover hash lemma. In Regev's scheme, if the public key is replaced by uniformly random elements, then the leftover hash lemma guarantees that the joint distribution of the public key and the encryption of an arbitrary plain text is within exponentially small statistical distance from uniform. This property does not hold in our case: indeed, if $a_1, \ldots, a_t$ all have constant coefficient equal to 0 (this event occurs with a probability $1/q^t$, which is not exponentially small for our parameters), then so does $\sum_i r_i a_i$. However, we can show that the second component c_2 of the ciphertext is statistically close to uniform, given the view of the first component c_1. This suffices, as the plain text is embedded in the second ciphertext component.

We first prove that the hash function family coming into play in the security proof is universal.

Lemma 4.2. *Let $q, k, d \geq 2$. For $(b_i)_i \in (\mathbb{Z}_q^{<d+k}[x])^t$, we let $h_{(b_i)_i}$ denote the map that sends $(r_i)_{i \leq t} \in (\{0,1\}^{<k+1}[x])^t$ to $\sum_{i \leq t} r_i \odot_d b_i \in \mathbb{Z}_q^{<d}[x]$. Then the hash function family $(h_{(b_i)_i})_{(b_i)_i}$ is universal.*

Proof. Our aim is to show that for $r_1, \ldots, r_t$ not all 0, we have

$$\Pr_{(b_i)_i, (b'_i)_i} \Big[\sum_{i \leq t} r_i \odot_d b_i = \sum_{i \leq t} r_i \odot_d b'_i\Big] = q^{-d}.$$

W.l.o.g. we may assume that $r_1 \neq 0$. By linearity, it suffices to prove that for all $y \in \mathbb{Z}_q^{<d}[x]$,

$$\Pr_{b_1}\big[r_1 \odot_d b_1 = y\big] = q^{-d}.$$

Let j be minimal such that the coefficient in x^j of r_1 is non-zero (i.e., equal to 1 as r_1 is binary). Then the equation $r_1 \odot_d b_1 = y$ restricted to entries $j+1$ to $j+d$ is a triangular linear system in the coefficients of b_1 with diagonal coefficients equal to 1. The map $b_1 \mapsto r_1 \odot_d b_1$ restricted to these coefficients of b_1 is hence a bijection. This gives the equality above. □

Lemma 4.3 (Security). *Assume that $t \geq (2 \cdot \lambda + (k+d+n) \cdot \log q)/(k+1)$. Then the scheme above is $\mathsf{IND\text{-}CPA}$ secure, under the $\mathsf{MP\text{-}LWE}_{q,n,d+k,D_{\alpha q}}$ hardness assumption.*

Proof. The $\mathsf{IND\text{-}CPA}$ security experiment is as follows. The challenger $\mathcal{C}$ samples a bit $b \hookleftarrow \{0,1\}$ and $(\mathsf{sk}, \mathsf{pk}) \hookleftarrow \mathsf{KeyGen}(1^\lambda)$; it gives pk to adversary $\mathcal{A}$ who sends back two plaintexts $\mu_0 \neq \mu_1$; the challenger computes $c \hookleftarrow \mathsf{Encrypt}(\mathsf{pk}, \mu_b)$ and sends it to $\mathcal{A}$, who outputs a bit b'. The scheme is secure if no ppt adversary $\mathcal{A}$ outputs $b' = b$ more probability that is non-negligibly away from $1/2$.

Now, consider the variant of the experiment above, in which $\mathcal{C}$ does not run $(\mathsf{sk}, \mathsf{pk}) \hookleftarrow \mathsf{KeyGen}(1^\lambda)$ but instead samples $\mathsf{pk} = (a_i, b_i)_i$ uniformly. Under the $\mathsf{MP\text{-}LWE}$ hardness assumption, the probabilities that $\mathcal{A}$ outputs $b' = b$ in both experiments are negligibly close. The reduction from $\mathsf{MP\text{-}LWE}$ to distinguishing the first and second experiments consists in rounding the real samples given by an MP-LWE oracle to the nearest integer modulo q, mapping MP-LWE with real noise to MP-LWE with rounded real noise (and uniform MP-LWE over the reals modulo q to a uniform MP-LWE over the integers modulo q).

We consider a third experiment, in which $\mathcal{C}$ also samples $\mathsf{pk} = (a_i, b_i)_i$, and additionally does not compute $c \hookleftarrow \mathsf{Encrypt}(\mathsf{pk}, \mu_b)$ before sending it to $\mathcal{A}$, but instead computes $c = (c_1, c_2)$ as follows. For $i \leq t$, it samples $r_i \hookleftarrow U(\{0,1\}^{<k+1}[x])$, $u \hookleftarrow U(\mathbb{Z}_q^{<d}[x])$, and sets:

$$c_1 = \sum_{i \leq t} r_i \cdot a_i \ , \quad c_2 = u.$$

Note that in this game, the view of $\mathcal{A}$ is independent of b, and hence the probability that it outputs $b' = b$ is exactly 1/2. We argue below that the distributions of $((a_i, b_i)_i, c_1, c_2)$ in this new experiment and the latter one are within exponentially small statistical distance. The combination of these two facts provides the result.

It remains to prove that

$$\Delta\Big(((a_i, b_i)_i, \sum_{i \leq t} r_i \cdot a_i, \sum_{i \leq t} r_i \odot_d b_i) \ , \ \ ((a_i, b_i)_i, \sum_{i \leq t} r_i \cdot a_i, u) \Big) \leq 2^{-\lambda},$$

where the a_i's, b_i's, r_i's and u are uniformly sampled in $\mathbb{Z}_q^{<n}[x]$, $\mathbb{Z}_q^{<d+k}[x]$, $U(\{0,1\}^{<k+1}[x])$ and $\mathbb{Z}_q^{<d}[x]$, respectively. By Lemma 4.2, the hash function family $h_{(b_i)_i}$ is universal. Further, the quantity $\sum_{i \leq t} r_i \cdot a_i$ belongs to $\mathbb{Z}_q^{<k+n}$, of cardinality q^{k+n}. Hence, by the Generalized Leftover Hash Lemma (see Lemma 2.1), the statistical distance above is bounded from above by $(2^{-(k+1)\cdot t} \cdot q^{k+d+n})^{1/2}/2$. □

Acknowledgments. We thank Guillaume Hanrot for helpful discussions. This work has been supported in part by ERC Starting Grant ERC-2013-StG-335086-LATTAC, and the Australian Research Council Discovery Grant DP150100285.

References

[ACPS09] Applebaum, B., Cash, D., Peikert, C., Sahai, A.: Fast cryptographic primitives and circular-secure encryption based on hard learning problems. In: Halevi, S. (ed.) CRYPTO 2009. LNCS, vol. 5677, pp. 595–618. Springer, Heidelberg (2009). doi:10.1007/978-3-642-03356-8_35

[ADPS16] Alkim, E., Ducas, L., Pöppelmann, T., Schwabe, P.: Post-quantum key exchange - A new hope. In: Proceeding of USENIX, pp. 327–343 (2016)

[AG11] Arora, S., Ge, R.: New algorithms for learning in presence of errors. In: Aceto, L., Henzinger, M., Sgall, J. (eds.) ICALP 2011. LNCS, vol. 6755, pp. 403–415. Springer, Heidelberg (2011). doi:10.1007/978-3-642-22006-7_34

[Ajt96] Ajtai, M.: Generating hard instances of lattice problems (extended abstract). In: Proceeding of STOC, pp. 99–108. ACM (1996)

[BCLvV16] Bernstein, D.J., Chuengsatiansup, C., Lange, T., van Vredendaal, C.: NTRU Prime. Cryptology ePrint Archive (2016). http://eprint.iacr.org/2016/461

[CDPR16] Cramer, R., Ducas, L., Peikert, C., Regev, O.: Recovering short generators of principal ideals in cyclotomic rings. In: Fischlin, M., Coron, J.-S. (eds.) EUROCRYPT 2016. LNCS, vol. 9666, pp. 559–585. Springer, Heidelberg (2016). doi:10.1007/978-3-662-49896-5_20

[CDW17] Cramer, R., Ducas, L., Wesolowski, B.: Short stickelberger class relations and application to ideal-SVP. In: Coron, J.-S., Nielsen, J.B. (eds.) EUROCRYPT 2017. LNCS, vol. 10210, pp. 324–348. Springer, Cham (2017). doi:10.1007/978-3-319-56620-7_12

[CIV16a] Castryck, W., Iliashenko, I., Vercauteren, F.: On the tightness of the error bound in Ring-LWE. LMS J. Comput. Math. (2016)

[CIV16b] Castryck, W., Iliashenko, I., Vercauteren, F.: Provably weak instances of ring-LWE revisited. In: Fischlin, M., Coron, J.-S. (eds.) EUROCRYPT 2016. LNCS, vol. 9665, pp. 147–167. Springer, Heidelberg (2016). doi:10.1007/978-3-662-49890-3_6

[CLS15] Chen, H., Lauter, K., Stange, K.E.: Attacks on search RLWE. Cryptology ePrint Archive (2015). http://eprint.iacr.org/2015/971

[EHL14] Eisenträger, K., Hallgren, S., Lauter, K.: Weak instances of PLWE. In: Joux, A., Youssef, A. (eds.) SAC 2014. LNCS, vol. 8781, pp. 183–194. Springer, Cham (2014). doi:10.1007/978-3-319-13051-4_11

[ELOS15] Elias, Y., Lauter, K.E., Ozman, E., Stange, K.E.: Provably weak instances of ring-LWE. In: Gennaro, R., Robshaw, M. (eds.) CRYPTO 2015. LNCS, vol. 9215, pp. 63–92. Springer, Heidelberg (2015). doi:10.1007/978-3-662-47989-6_4

[GPV08] Gentry, C., Peikert, C., Vaikuntanathan, V.: Trapdoors for hard lattices and new cryptographic constructions. In: Proceeding of STOC, pp. 197–206. ACM (2008)

[HCS16] Lauter, K., Chen, H., Stange, K.E.: Vulnerable Galois RLWE families and improved attacks. Cryptology ePrint Archive (2016). http://eprint.iacr.org/2016/193

[HPS98] Hoffstein, J., Pipher, J., Silverman, J.H.: NTRU: A ring-based public key cryptosystem. In: Buhler, J.P. (ed.) ANTS 1998. LNCS, vol. 1423, pp. 267–288. Springer, Heidelberg (1998). doi:10.1007/BFb0054868

[HQZ04] Hanrot, G., Quercia, M., Zimmermann, P.: The middle product algorithm I. Appl. Algebra Engrg. Comm. Comput. **14**(6), 415–438 (2004)

[LM06] Lyubashevsky, V., Micciancio, D.: Generalized compact knapsacks are collision resistant. In: Bugliesi, M., Preneel, B., Sassone, V., Wegener, I. (eds.) ICALP 2006. LNCS, vol. 4052, pp. 144–155. Springer, Heidelberg (2006). doi:10.1007/11787006_13

[LPR13] Lyubashevsky, V., Peikert, C., Regev, O.: On ideal lattices and learning with errors over rings. J. ACM **60**(6), 43 (2013)

[Lyu09] Lyubashevsky, V.: Fiat-shamir with aborts: applications to lattice and factoring-based signatures. In: Matsui, M. (ed.) ASIACRYPT 2009. LNCS, vol. 5912, pp. 598–616. Springer, Heidelberg (2009). doi:10.1007/978-3-642-10366-7_35

[Lyu16] Lyubashevsky, V.: Digital signatures based on the hardness of ideal lattice problems in all rings. In: Cheon, J.H., Takagi, T. (eds.) ASIACRYPT 2016. LNCS, vol. 10032, pp. 196–214. Springer, Heidelberg (2016). doi:10.1007/978-3-662-53890-6_7

[Mic07] Micciancio, D.: Generalized compact knapsacks, cyclic lattices, and efficient one-way functions. Comput. Complex. **16**(4), 365–411 (2007)

[MP12] Micciancio, D., Peikert, C.: Trapdoors for lattices: simpler, tighter, faster, smaller. In: Pointcheval, D., Johansson, T. (eds.) EUROCRYPT 2012. LNCS, vol. 7237, pp. 700–718. Springer, Heidelberg (2012). doi:10.1007/978-3-642-29011-4_41

[Pei16] Peikert, C.: How (Not) to instantiate ring-LWE. In: Zikas, V., Prisco, R. (eds.) SCN 2016. LNCS, vol. 9841, pp. 411–430. Springer, Cham (2016). doi:10.1007/978-3-319-44618-9_22

[PR06] Peikert, C., Rosen, A.: Efficient collision-resistant hashing from worst-case assumptions on cyclic lattices. In: Halevi, S., Rabin, T. (eds.) TCC 2006. LNCS, vol. 3876, pp. 145–166. Springer, Heidelberg (2006). doi:10.1007/11681878_8

[PRSD17] Peikert, C., Regev, O., Stephens-Davidowitz, N.: Pseudorandomness of Ring-LWE for any ring and modulus. In: Proceeding of STOC. ACM (2017)

[Reg09] Regev, O.: On lattices, learning with errors, random linear codes, and cryptography. J. ACM **56**(6), 34 (2009)

[Sch87] Schnorr, C.P.: A hierarchy of polynomial time lattice basis reduction algorithms. Theor. Comput. Sci. **53**(2–3), 201–224 (1987)

[Sho99] Shoup, V.: Efficient computation of minimal polynomials in algebraic extensions of finite fields. In: Proceeding of ISSAC, pp. 53–58. ACM (1999)

[SSTX09] Stehlé, D., Steinfeld, R., Tanaka, K., Xagawa, K.: Efficient public key encryption based on ideal lattices. In: Matsui, M. (ed.) ASIACRYPT 2009. LNCS, vol. 5912, pp. 617–635. Springer, Heidelberg (2009). doi:10.1007/978-3-642-10366-7_36

All-But-Many Lossy Trapdoor Functions from Lattices and Applications

Xavier Boyen* and Qinyi Li(✉)

Queensland University of Technology, Brisbane, Australia

Abstract. "All-but-many lossy trapdoor functions" (ABM-LTF) are a powerful cryptographic primitive studied by Hofheinz (Eurocrypt 2012). ABM-LTFs are parametrised with tags: a lossy tag makes the function lossy; an injective tag makes the function injective, and invertible with a trapdoor. Existing ABM-LTFs rely on non-standard assumptions.

Our first result is an ABM-LTF construction from lattices, based on the learning-with-errors (LWE) problem. Unlike the previous schemes which behaved as "encrypted signatures", the core of our construction is an "encrypted, homomorphic-evaluation-friendly, weak pseudorandom function". The weak pseudorandom function outputs matrices, where the lossy tags are preimages of the zero matrix, and the injective tags are preimages of random full-rank matrices.

Our second result is a public-key system tightly secure against "selective opening" attacks, where an attacker gets many challenges and can ask to see the random bits of any of them. Following the steps of Hemenway et al. (Asiacrypt 2011) and Hofheinz (Eurocrypt 2012), our ABM-LTF gives the first lattice-based, compact public-key encryption (PKE) scheme that has indistinguishability against adaptive chosen-ciphertext and selective opening attacks (IND-SO-CCA2), with tight security, and whose public-key size and security reduction are independent of the number of decryption queries and ciphertext challenges.

Meanwhile, this result provides an alternative solution to the problem of building pairing-free IND-CCA2 PKE schemes with tight security in the multi-challenge setting, which was firstly answered by Gay et al. (Eurocrypt 2016). Additionally, our ABM-LTF answers the open question of constructing (non-necessarily lossy) all-but-many trapdoor functions from lattices, first asked by Alperin-Sheriff and Peikert (PKC 2012).

1 Introduction

All-but-many lossy trapdoor functions (ABM-LTF) are a useful cryptographic primitive formalised by Hofheinz [29]. ABM-LTFs generalise lossy trapdoor functions (LTFs) [39], all-but-one lossy trapdoor functions (ABO-LTFs) [39], and all-but-N lossy trapdoor functions (ABN-LTFs) [27]. ABM-LTF have shown their

*Research supported in part by ARC Discovery Project grant number DP140103885 and ARC Future Fellowship FT140101145 from the Australian Research Council.

J. Katz and H. Shacham (Eds.): CRYPTO 2017, Part III, LNCS 10403, pp. 298–331, 2017.
DOI: 10.1007/978-3-319-63697-9_11

usefulness in constructing public-key encryption schemes with strong security properties including selective opening security, e.g., [29], key-dependent message security, e.g., [30] and key leakage resilience, e.g., [40].

An ABM-LTF is a function described by public evaluation parameters and parametrised by a tag from some set. The tag set consists of two disjoint super-polynomially large subsets: the set of injective tags and the set of lossy tags. An injective tag makes the function injective and, hence, invertible with trapdoors. A lossy tag makes the function lossy meaning that the function looses information of its inputs and, therefore, can not be inverted in the information-theoretical sense (except negligible probability). Note that there *could* exist a spurious set of invalid tags, that make the function injective yet disable its trapdoor invertibility: in our construction we need to avoid this possibility. An ABM-LTF is equipped with two trapdoors: one is the inversion trapdoor which allows one to correctly invert the function in case of the tag is injective; the other is a lossy tags generation trapdoor which allows security reduction to generate lossy tags.

ABM-LTFs have two main security properties. The first one, "lossy-tag indistinguishability", guarantees that a lossy tag is computationally indistinguishable from a random tag, even given access to the lossy tag generation oracle. The second one, "evasiveness", prevents efficient adversaries from generating lossy tags (notice that this implies that a random tag is an injective tag w.h.p.). Theses two security properties make ABM-LTFs particularly useful for handling adaptive attacks in the multi-challenge setting, in which adversaries are able to obtain multiple challenge targets (e.g., challenge ciphertext). For instance, evasiveness forces that all adaptive queries be made with injective tags, enabling inversion trapdoors in security reductions. Indistinguishability allows security reductions to use multiple lossy tags for creating multiple challenges embedding the same computational problem, without tipping off adversaries.

Constructions of ABM-LTFs. Not very surprisingly, with such powerful properties, ABM-LTFs have more complicated constructions than its simpler counterparts, say plain LTFs. So far, essentially two types of constructions of ABM-LTFs exist. The first type is based on Paillier/Damgard-Jurik encryption [19, 37] together with some non-standard assumptions, and first instantiated by Hofheinz [29] and latter improved by Fujisaki [23]. The second type, based on subgroup indistinguishable problems over composite-order bilinear groups, was design by Hofheinz [29]. Though relying on different assumptions and algebraic structures, the two types of constructions share the same flavour at a conceptual level. Both of them can be seen as "encrypted signature" schemes in which a lossy tag corresponds to a valid (but disguised) signature. Existential unforgeability of signatures guarantees the evasiveness. Tag indistinguishability is provided by the semantic security of Paillier/Damgard-Jurik encryption or hardness of subgroup decisional problems. Roughly, the two types of construction utilise either additive homomorphism of Paillier/Damgard-Jurik ciphertexts, or group exponentiation operations, to conduct the lossy trapdoor function evaluations. Apart from the elegance of existing constructions, one of their disadvantages is their need for non-standard assumptions. Thus, a first motivation for our present work is to solve the open problem of finding different constructions of ABM-LTFs under reasonable assumptions, first posed by Hofheinz [29].

All-but-Many Trapdoor Function. Without regard to lossines, a notion similar to ABM-LTF is that of all-but-many trapdoor function (ABM-TF). An ABM-TF's inversion trapdoor can be concealed among super-polynomially many tags. Candidate constructions from assumptions related to factoring or discrete logarithm have already been proposed [23,29]. On the other hand, while there exist many constructions and applications of lattice-based all-but-one trapdoor functions [1,4,35] and all-but-N trapdoor functions for N bounded a priori [5], lattice-based ABM-TFs appears to be harder to construct. Therefore, a second motivation for this work is to solve the open problem stated in [5], namely to construct lattice-based ABM-TFs (and, a fortiori, ABM-LTFs).

IND-SO-CCA2 Public-Key Encryption. A direct application of ABM-LTFs, shown in [29], is to construct compact public-key encryption schemes that have ciphertext indistinguishability against adaptively chosen-ciphertext attacks and selective opening attacks (IND-SO-CCA2).[1]

In selective opening attacks (SOA), an adversary gets a collection of some arbitrary N challenge ciphertexts $(\mathsf{ct}_i = \mathsf{Encrypt}(\mathsf{pk}, \mathsf{m}_i; r_i))_{i \in [N]}$ that encrypt m_i with randomness r_i under public key pk, where $\{\mathsf{m}_i\}_{i \in [N]}$ satisfy some joint distribution dist chosen by the adversary. The adversary may choose some subset $\mathcal{I} \subset [N]$ and ask that the corresponding ciphertexts ct_i be "opened" to get (m_i, r_i). The adversary must try to extract information on the messages in the unopened ciphertexts $(\mathsf{ct}_i)_{i \in [N] \setminus \mathcal{I}}$. IND-SO-CCA2 security ensures that no adversary can distinguish the unopened messages from new messages which are freshly and *efficiently* sampled according to dist conditioned on the opened messages. One drawback of this definition of IND-SO-CCA2 is that it requires that the joint message distributions be efficiently re-sampleable conditionally on opened messages. Unfortunately, it is not difficult to come up with examples of efficiently sampleable joint distributions whose conditionals as above would *not* be efficiently sampleable.

A stronger version of indistinguishability-based security definition (sometimes called Full IND-SO-CCA2, see Definition 2 of [31]) does not have the requirement of efficient conditional resampling. This *appears* preferable, but problems remain. First, such stronger definition neither has any known instantiation nor is implied by any known realisable definition, suggesting that it could be too strong to achieve. Second, the existence of efficiently sampleable joint distributions with inefficient conditionals could be exploited by an adversary to use the challenger as a hard-problem oracle, rather than the other way around. Nevertheless, it has been shown by Hofheinz and Rupp [31] that even the first version of IND-SO-CCA2 is stronger than traditional IND-CCA2 security. Therefore it is well motivated to find efficient constructions that are IND-SO-CCA2 secure.

[1] "Compact" here means that the size of public keys is independent of the number of challenge ciphertexts adversary asks for. ABN-LTFs results in IND-SO-CCA2 PKE schemes but the size of public keys is at least linear in N.

For completeness, we mention that stronger and/or more natural definitions than IND-SO-CCA2 are possible, especially in a simulation-based real/ideal framework. We mention the SIM-SO-CCA2 definition (see [8,11] for details) and several PKE schemes that meet it (see, e.g., [22,23,27,29,32]). Nevertheless, SIM-SO-CCA2 secure PKE schemes from lattice assumptions remain unknown.

1.1 Our Contribution

In this paper, we address Hofheinz's [29] open problem of building tightly secure ABM-LTFs under reasonable assumptions. We propose a new ABM-LTF from widely accepted lattice assumptions: specifically, all the security properties of our ABM-LTF can be tightly and ultimately reduced to the computational hardness of Learning with Errors (LWE). Our ABM-LTF also provides a solution to Alperin-Sheriff and Peikert's [5] open problem of constructing ABM-TFs from lattices.

Moreover, by following the pathway given in [27,29,42], our ABM-LTF further leads to the first IND-SO-CCA2 public-key cryptosystem from lattices with a tight security reduction. In turn, such a scheme provides an alternative solution to the question of building tightly secure PKE (without bilinear maps) in the multi-challenge setting, recently and very differently answered by Gay et al. [24]. Being high-dimensional-lattice-based, all of our constructions are conjectured to be quantum-safe.

Our Approach. At a high level, instead of building ABM-LTFs as "encrypted signatures" which is the approach of [29], our ABM-LTF builds an "encrypted homomorphic-evaluation-friendly pseudorandom function" whose outputs are (encrypted) matrices whose rank controls the function's lossiness.

Our starting point is the lattice-based (and lossy) trapdoor function from [10], given by $g(\mathbf{s}, \mathbf{e}) = \mathbf{s}^t \cdot [\mathbf{A}|\mathbf{AR} + \mathbf{HG}] + \mathbf{e}^t \bmod q$, where the matrix $\mathbf{R}$ has low-norm, and $\mathbf{G}$ is the now famous "gadget" matrix (a public matrix with a public trapdoor $\mathbf{T_G}$ such that $\mathbf{G} \cdot \mathbf{T_G} = \mathbf{0}$ with very low norm).

The trapdoor function $g()$ traces back to the two-sided lattice trapdoor framework from [1,13] and the efficient strong lattice trapdoor generators from [35]. It was showed by Bellare et al. [10] that if $\mathbf{A}$ is built from LWE samples (to consist of a truly random matrix on its top and a pseudorandom matrix on its bottom), then for certain parameters, the function is injective and invertible if $\mathbf{H}$ has full column-rank, and is lossy if $\mathbf{H} = \mathbf{0}$. The indistinguishability property of all-but-many trapdoors requires that there must be unbounded many tags that can be mapped to $\mathbf{H} = \mathbf{0}$ and this mapping should be oblivious to "outside" evaluators. Boyen and Li [14] recently showed such a way in another context by embedding a pseudorandom function (PRF) into the above trapdoor function to compute $\mathbf{H}$, i.e., $\mathbf{H} = \mathsf{PRF}(K, \mathsf{tag}) \cdot \mathbf{I}$, where $\mathsf{PRF}(K, \mathsf{tag}) \in \{0, 1\}$ and $\mathbf{I}$ is the identity matrix (in this case $\mathbf{H}$ is square). However, their method only allows two values for $\mathbf{H}$.[2] This makes a random tag lossy with probability half, for hitting $\mathbf{H} = \mathbf{0}$, thereby violating the evasiveness property (i.e., lossy tags should be hard to find without trapdoor).

Our first idea is to parallelly apply multiple PRFs and expand their pseudorandom outputs from bit strings to matrices, through universal hash functions. Particularly, we set tags with form $\mathsf{tag} = (\mathbf{D}, \mu)$. $\mathbf{D}$ is a matrix, which allows us to add additional control on generating $\mathbf{H}$. μ is the input for PRFs. Then we set $\mathbf{H} = \mathbf{ZD} + \sum \mathsf{PRF}(K_i, \mu) \cdot \mathbf{H}_i \bmod q$ for randomly sampled, encrypted matrices $\mathbf{H}_i$, and full-rank matrix $\mathbf{Z}$. Firstly, the subset-sum operation $\sum \mathsf{PRF}(K_i, \mu) \cdot \mathbf{H}_i$ and $\mathbf{ZD}$ can be easily performed by existing evaluation techniques with small adjustments on the dimensions of gadget matrices as we will show. Secondly, for any "outside" evaluator, as the outputs of PRFs are unpredictable, the output of the subset-sum formula, and, hence, $\mathbf{H}$ will be pseudorandom. For one who knows the keys of PRFs and the matrix $\mathbf{Z}$, a lossy tag can be generated by randomly selecting μ and solving $\mathbf{D}$ for the equation $\mathbf{0} = \mathbf{ZD} + \sum \mathsf{PRF}(K_i, \mu) \cdot \mathbf{H}_i \pmod q$. Now the problem we have is that the adversary can reuse μ from a prior lossy tag $(\mathbf{D}, \mu)$ it was given, to create a new tag $(\bar{\mathbf{D}}, \mu)$ where $\bar{\mathbf{D}} = \mathbf{D} + \mathbf{D}'$ for non-full-rank $\mathbf{D}'$. This special tag — we call it an "invalid tag" — could disable the gadget trapdoors while still making the function injective. To solve this problem, we use a chameleon hash function to tie $\mathbf{D}$ and μ together (say μ is the output of the chameleon hash on input $\mathbf{D}$ and some fresh randomness) to enforce the one-time use of μ. For generating lossy tags in the simulation, we can pick random μ, solve for $\mathbf{D}$ and use the trapdoor of the chameleon hash function to find randomness under which μ chameleon-hashes to $\mathbf{D}$.

As a consequence of using a chameleon hash function, the inputs to the PRFs (i.e., μ) will be random for all randomly generated tags in the real schemes and all responses from the lossy tag generation oracle to queries in the security reductions. Moreover, the collision-resistant property of the chameleon hash function essentially forces all adversarially generated PRF inputs (i.e., μ) to be different. This fact drives us towards relaxing the PRFs into so-called "weak PRFs" [3], which only guarantee pseudorandomness for *random* inputs. The advantages of using weak PRFs is that weak PRFs admit potentially much simpler, more efficient constructions from weaker assumptions, with shallower circuit implementations than normal PRFs. The remaining problem of using a weak PRF (WPRF for short) instead of a usual PRF is that, in the evasiveness security game, the adversary is allowed adaptively to come up with lossy tag guesses in which μ may not be random, and receive binary answers of "lossy/invalid" or "injective". Such answers may leak damaging information to the adversary,

[2] The binary restriction on $\mathbf{H}$ in [14] comes from the fact that the fully homomorphic evaluation techniques from [12,16,26] usually supports operations on two bits or two small scalars. It would be very useful to find a way to do such evaluation over two vectors or matrices. We note that Hiromasa et al. [28] showed how to do homomorphic evaluation on matrices for GSW-FHE scheme [26]. But it is not clear how to apply such technique to the gadget-based trapdoors.

since the WPRF indistinguishability from random may not apply on non-random inputs μ.

We resolve this last problem by pre-processing μ with a (very basic) universal hash, essentially XOR-ing μ with a secret constant. This keeps the WPRF input random for all the challenger-generated μ_i, and further randomises one of the adversarially generated μ to make it jointly random with the random μ_i. This restores WPRF indistinguishability for one adversarial queries, which in turns all but guarantees (with probability overwhelmingly close to 1) that the response to the adversary's guess will be "injective". Because the response was a foregone conclusion, it is devoid of information, and could have been answered without looking at μ. This allows us to consider the *second* adversarial query without regard for the first one (which we answered without even looking at it). Repeating the previous argument, this *second* adversarial query μ together with the random μ_i induce a set of jointly random WPRF inputs after universal hashing, and thus the adversary will also expect an "injective" answer with all but negligible probability on this second query, as for the first query. The conclusion carries inductively for any polynomially bounded number of queries.

For our purpose of constructing ABM-LTF and PKE schemes without relying on any of the "pre-quantum" assumptions of existing schemes, WPRFs can be instantiated directly from the Learning-With-Rounding assumption [7]. Such WPRFs can be implemented as Boolean NAND circuits in the $\mathbf{NC}^1$ circuit class, which allows us to use smaller modulus in our construction (or nearly equivalently, larger relative LWE noise). The addition of a universal hash (or a simple XOR) at the input of the WPRF barely makes the circuit more complex.

Finally, we also mention that we need that random tags (and even adversarially chosen tags) make the column-rank of $\mathbf{H}$ full, with overwhelming probability, as required for evasiveness of ABM-LTFs. Since we are able to use a polynomial rather than sub-exponential modulus (in the security parameter), a randomly sampled square matrix $\mathbf{H}$ will not overwhelmingly likely be full-rank. We resolve this by adding extra columns to $\mathbf{H}$, making it "wider", and to such end we also adjust the dimension of the gadget matrices. (We note that if the WPRF, which we can view as a black-box, is instantiated from LWR problem, it would use another modulus which unfortunately is slightly super-polynomial [7].)

A Parallel and Independent Work. In concurrent and independent work, Libert et al. [34] propose an ABM-LTF and a SIM-SO-CCA2 secure PKE scheme using rather similar techniques. Both papers give ABM-LTF constructions based on embedding key-homomorphic PRF evaluation into the lattice-based LTF of Bellare et al. [9], and give applications to PKE with selective-opening security.

The first notabale difference is that our ABM-LTF uses the weaker notion of weak PRF in the homomorphic evaluation. Unlike the stronger usual PRFs, weak PRFs need not to be pseudo-random on all inputs; only on random ones. They have more efficient constructions from weaker assumptions, along with tighter reductions. Using weak PRFs gives us shallower circuit implementations, which cause milder noise growth in the key-homomorphic evaluations. In turn, this lessens our LWE assumptions for the construction of ABM-LTF.

The second important difference is that the PKE scheme in [34] does achieve SIM-SO-CCA2 security, compared to ours which has IND-SO-CCA2 security. It is the first lattice-based PKE scheme that enjoys such strong notion of selective-opening security. At a high level, they first build an IND-SO-CCA2-secure PKE scheme from their ABM-LTF, then give an efficient mechanism to "explain" any lossy ciphertext as an encryption of an arbitrary message to get SIM-SO-CCA2.

A natural question, given the complementary strengths of our respective papers, would be to combine them and achieve the best of both worlds.

1.2 Other Related Works

Lossy trapdoor functions (LTFs) were proposed by Peikert and Waters [39]. They admit instantiations from standard assumptions, e.g., DDH, DCR and LWE. They also have enormous applications, e.g., in the construction of IND-CCA2 public-key schemes, the first lattice trapdoor function, lossy encryption [8]. All-but-N LTFs (ABN-LTFs) were firstly proposed by Hemenway et al. [27] as a means to construct PKE secure against chosen-ciphertext and selective opening attacks. In contrast to ABM-LTFs in which unbounded many lossy tags are provided, an ABN-LTF contains exact N lossy tags. ABN-LTFs suffer from a drawback that N has to be fixed when generating the public parameters, making the size of public parameters grow at least linearly in N. Last, we mention that lossiness arguments have been used in a LWE context for establishing the hardness of the LWE problem with uniform rather than Gaussian noise [21,36].

2 Preliminaries

Notation. 'PPT' abbreviates "probabilistic polynomial-time". If S is a set, we denote by $a \xleftarrow{\$} S$ the uniform sampling of a random element of S. For a positive integer n, we denote by $[n]$ the set of positive integers no greater than n. We use bold lowercase letters (e.g. $\mathbf{a}$) to denote vectors and bold capital letters (e.g. $\mathbf{A}$) to denote matrices. For a positive integer $q \geq 2$, let $\mathbb{Z}_q$ be the ring of integers modulo q. We denote the group of $n \times m$ matrices in $\mathbb{Z}_q$ by $\mathbb{Z}_q^{n \times m}$. Vectors are treated as column vectors. The transpose of a vector $\mathbf{a}$ (resp. a matrix $\mathbf{A}$) is denoted by $\mathbf{a}^t$ (resp. $\mathbf{A}^t$). For $\mathbf{A} \in \mathbb{Z}_q^{n \times m}$ and $\mathbf{B} \in \mathbb{Z}_q^{n \times m'}$, let $[\mathbf{A}|\mathbf{B}] \in \mathbb{Z}_q^{n \times (m+m')}$ be the concatenation of $\mathbf{A}$ and $\mathbf{B}$. We write $\|\mathbf{x}\|$ for the Euclidean norm of a vector $\mathbf{x}$. The Euclidean norm of a matrix $\mathbf{R} = \{\mathbf{r}_1, \ldots, \mathbf{r}_m\}$ is denoted by $\|\mathbf{R}\| = \max_i \|\mathbf{r}_i\|$. The spectral norm of $\mathbf{R}$ is denoted by $s_1(\mathbf{R}) = \sup_{\mathbf{x} \in \mathbb{R}^{m+1}} \|\mathbf{R} \cdot \mathbf{x}\|$. The inner product of two vectors $\mathbf{x}$ and $\mathbf{y}$ is written $\langle \mathbf{x}, \mathbf{y} \rangle$. For a security parameter λ, a function $\mathsf{negl}(\lambda)$ is negligible in λ if it is smaller than all polynomial fractions for a sufficiently large λ. The logarithm function $\log_2(\cdot)$ is abbreviated as $\log(\cdot)$.

We will be using the following lemma which is directly implied by the Theorem 1.1 of [17]

Lemma 1. *Let an integer $n \geq 2$, and a prime $q \geq 2$. A randomly sampled $\mathbb{Z}_q^{n \times 2n}$-matrx $\mathbf{H}$ will have n linearly independent columns, i.e., rank n, with all but negligible probability in n.*

Proof. By the Theorem 1.1 of [17] the probability that $\mathbf{H}$ has rank n is

$$\prod_{i=1}^{n}(1-\frac{1}{q^{n+i}}) \geq (1-\frac{1}{q^{n+1}})^n \geq 1-n\cdot q^{-(n+1)} \geq 1-\mathsf{negl}(n)$$

as required. □

2.1 Randomness Extractor

Let X and Y be two random variables over some finite set S. The statistical distance between X and Y, denoted as $\Delta(X,Y)$, is defined as

$$\Delta(X,Y)=\frac{1}{2}\sum_{s\in S}\left|\Pr[X=s]-\Pr[Y=s]\right|.$$

Let X_λ and Y_λ be ensembles of random variables indexed by the security parameter λ. X and Y are statistically close if $\Delta(X_\lambda,Y_\lambda)=\mathsf{negl}(\lambda)$.

The min-entropy of a random variable X over a set S is defined as

$$H_\infty(X)=-\log(\max_{s\in S}\Pr[X=s]).$$

The average min-entropy of a random variable X given Y is defined as

$$\tilde{H}_\infty(X|Y)=-\log\left(\mathbb{E}_{y\leftarrow Y}\left[2^{-H_\infty(X|Y=y)}\right]\right)$$

Lemma 2 ([38], Lemma 2.1). *If Y takes at most 2^r possible values and X is any random variable, then*

$$\tilde{H}_\infty(X|Y)\geq H_\infty(X)-r.$$

Definition 1 (Universal Hash Functions). *A family of functions $\mathcal{UH}=\{\mathsf{UH}_\mathbf{k}:\mathcal{X}\to\mathcal{Y}\}$ is called a family of universal hash functions with index (key) $\mathbf{k}$, if for all $x,x'\in\mathcal{X}$, with $x\neq x'$, we have $\Pr[\mathsf{UH}_\mathbf{k}(x)=\mathsf{UH}_\mathbf{k}(x')]\leq\frac{1}{|\mathcal{X}|}$ over the random choice of $\mathsf{UH}_\mathbf{k}$.*

Lemma 3 ([38], Lemma 2.2). *Let X, Y be random variables such that $X\in\{0,1\}^n$ and $\tilde{H}_\infty(X|Y)\geq k$. Let $\mathcal{UH}$ be a family of universal hash functions from $\{0,1\}^n$ to $\{0,1\}^\ell$ where $\ell\leq k-2\log(1/\epsilon)$. It holds that for $\mathsf{UH}_\mathbf{k}\xleftarrow{\$}\mathcal{UH}$ and $r\xleftarrow{\$}\{0,1\}^\ell$, $\Delta\left((\mathsf{UH}_\mathbf{k},\mathsf{UH}_\mathbf{k}(X),Y),(\mathsf{UH}_\mathbf{k},r,Y)\right)\leq\epsilon$.*

Corollary 1. *Let $q>2$, $\epsilon>0$. Let $\mathcal{UH}=\{\mathsf{UH}_\mathbf{h}:\{0,1\}^\ell\to\mathbb{Z}_q\}$ be a family of hash functions where $\ell\geq\log(q/(\epsilon^2))$, $y=\mathsf{UH}_\mathbf{h}(x)=\sum_{i=1}^{\ell}h_ix_i \bmod q$ for $x=x_1\dots x_\ell\in\{0,1\}^\ell$, $\mathbf{h}=h_1\dots h_\ell\xleftarrow{\$}\mathbb{Z}_q^\ell$. Let $r\xleftarrow{\$}\mathbb{Z}_q$, we have $\Delta((\mathsf{UH}_\mathbf{h},\mathsf{UH}_\mathbf{h}(x)),(\mathsf{UH}_\mathbf{h},r))\leq\epsilon$.*

Proof. It is easy to see that for different inputs x and x', and $\mathbf{h}\xleftarrow{\$}\mathbb{Z}_q^\ell$, $\mathsf{UH}_\mathbf{h}(x)=\mathsf{UH}_\mathbf{h}(x')$ happens with probability $1/q$. So $\mathcal{UH}$ is a family of universal hash function. Applying Lemma 3 concludes the proof. □

2.2 Discrete Gaussians

Let $m \in \mathbb{Z}_{>0}$ be a positive integer. Let an integer lattice $\Lambda \subset \mathbb{Z}^m$. For any real vector $\mathbf{c} \in \mathbb{R}^m$ and positive parameter $\sigma \in \mathbb{R}_{>0}$, let the Gaussian function $\rho_{\sigma,\mathbf{c}}(\mathbf{x}) = \exp\left(-\pi\|\mathbf{x}-\mathbf{c}\|^2/\sigma^2\right)$ on $\mathbb{R}^m$ with centre $\mathbf{c}$ and parameter σ. Define the discrete Gaussian distribution over Λ with centre $\mathbf{c}$ and parameter σ as $D_{\Lambda,\sigma} = \rho_{\sigma,\mathbf{c}}(\mathbf{y})/\rho_\sigma(\Lambda)$ for $\forall \mathbf{y} \in \Lambda$, where $\rho_\sigma(\Lambda) = \sum_{\mathbf{x}\in\Lambda} \rho_{\sigma,\mathbf{c}}(\mathbf{x})$. For notational convenience, $\rho_{\sigma,\mathbf{0}}$ and $D_{\Lambda,\sigma,\mathbf{0}}$ are abbreviated as ρ_σ and $D_{\Lambda,\sigma}$.

Lemma 4 (**[9], Lemma 5.1**)**.** *Let $h > 0$, $w > 0$ be integers and $\sigma > 0$ be Gaussian parameter. For $\mathbf{R} \leftarrow D_{\mathbb{Z},\sigma}^{h\times w}$, we have $s_1(\mathbf{R}) \leq \sigma \cdot O(\sqrt{h}+\sqrt{w})$ with all but probability $2^{-\Omega(h+w)}$.*

Lemma 5 (**[9], Lemma 5.2**)**.** *For prime q and integer $b \geq 2$, let $\bar{m} \geq n\log_b q + \omega(\log n)$. With overwhelming probability over the uniformly random choice of $\mathbf{A} \in \mathbb{Z}_q^{n\times\bar{m}}$, the following holds: for $\mathbf{r} \leftarrow D^{\bar{m}}_{\mathbb{Z},b\cdot\omega(\sqrt{\log n})}$, the distribution of $\mathbf{Ar}$ is statistically close to the uniform distribution over $\mathbb{Z}_q^n$.*

2.3 Gadget Matrices

We define two gadget matrices with different dimensions than the canonical gadget matrix given by Micciancio and Peikert [35]. Let an integer $n \geq 2$, a primt $q \geq 2$, a radix $b \geq 2$, and let $w = \log_b q$. Let $\mathbf{G}^*$ be the primitive matrix defined as $\mathbf{G}^* = \mathbf{I}_n \otimes [1, b, b^2, \ldots, b^{w-1}] \in \mathbb{Z}_q^{n\times nw}$. We define the gadget matrices

$$\mathbf{G} = \left[\mathbf{G}^* |\ \mathbf{0}\right] \in \mathbb{Z}_q^{n\times 2nw}$$

and

$$\hat{\mathbf{G}} = \mathbf{I}_{2n} \otimes [1, b, b^2, \ldots, b^{w-1}] = \begin{bmatrix}\mathbf{G} & \mathbf{0}\\ \mathbf{0} & \mathbf{G}\end{bmatrix} \in \mathbb{Z}_q^{2n\times 2nw}.$$

Those gadget matrices have useful properties as stated below.

Lemma 6 (**[12], Lemma 2.1**)**.** *There is a deterministic algorithm, denoted $\mathbf{G}^{-1}(\cdot) : \mathbb{Z}_q^{n\times m} \to \mathbb{Z}^{m\times m}$, that takes any matrix $\mathbf{A} \in \mathbb{Z}_q^{n\times m}$ as input, and outputs the preimage $\mathbf{G}^{-1}(\mathbf{A})$ of $\mathbf{A}$ such that $\mathbf{G}\cdot\mathbf{G}^{-1}(\mathbf{A}) = \mathbf{A} \pmod q$ and $s_1\left(\mathbf{G}^{-1}(\mathbf{A})\right) \leq (b-1)m$.*

There is a deterministic algorithm, denoted $\hat{\mathbf{G}}^{-1}(\cdot) : \mathbb{Z}_q^{2n\times m} \to \mathbb{Z}^{m\times m}$, that takes any matrix $\mathbf{A} \in \mathbb{Z}_q^{2n\times m}$ as input, and outputs the preimage $\hat{\mathbf{G}}^{-1}(\mathbf{A})$ of $\mathbf{A}$ such that $\hat{\mathbf{G}}\cdot\hat{\mathbf{G}}^{-1}(\mathbf{A}) = \mathbf{A} \pmod q$ and $s_1(\hat{\mathbf{G}}^{-1}(\mathbf{A})) \leq (b-1)m$.

Lemma 7 (**[35], Theorem 3**)**.** *Let $\mathbf{A} \in \mathbb{Z}_q^{n\times\bar{m}}$, $\mathbf{R} \in \mathbb{Z}^{\bar{m}\times 2nw}$. Let $\mathbf{H} \in \mathbb{Z}_q^{n\times 2nw}$ with rank n. Let $\hat{\mathbf{G}} \in \mathbb{Z}_q^{2n\times 2nw}$ be the gadget matrix. For $\mathbf{y}^t = g_{\mathbf{F}}(\mathbf{x}) = \mathbf{x}^t\begin{bmatrix}\mathbf{I}_m\\ \mathbf{F}\end{bmatrix} = \mathbf{x}_1^t + \mathbf{x}_2^t \cdot \mathbf{F} \bmod q$ where $\mathbf{F} = [\mathbf{A}|\mathbf{AR} + \mathbf{H}\hat{\mathbf{G}}]$, there is a PPT algorithm $\mathsf{Invert}(\mathbf{F}, \mathbf{R}, \mathbf{H}, \mathbf{y})$ that outputs $\mathbf{x}$ with overwhelming probability if $\|\mathbf{x}_1\| \leq q/\Theta(b\cdot s_1(\mathbf{R}))$.*

2.4 Homomorphic Evaluation Algorithms

In our construction we use the homomorphic evaluation algorithms developed in [12,16,26]. The next lemma follows directly from Claim 3.4.2, the Lemma 3.6, and Theorem 3.5 of [16]. It has been used in [14].

Lemma 8. *Let* $C : \{0,1\}^\ell \to \{0,1\}$ *be a NAND Boolean circuit in class* $\boldsymbol{NC}^1$*, i.e. C has depth* $d = \eta \log \ell$ *for some constant* η*. Let* $\{\mathbf{A}_i = \mathbf{A}\mathbf{R}_i + x_i\mathbf{G} \in \mathbb{Z}_q^{n\times 2nw}\}_{i\in[\ell]}$ *be* ℓ *matrices correspond to the* ℓ *input wires of C where* $\mathbf{A} \xleftarrow{\$} \mathbb{Z}_q^{n\times \bar{m}}$, $\mathbf{R}_i \leftarrow D^{\bar{m}\times 2nw}_{\mathbb{Z},b\cdot\omega(\sqrt{\log n})}$, $x_i \in \{0,1\}$ *and* $\mathbf{G} \in \mathbb{Z}_q^{n\times 2nw}$ *is the gadget matrix. There is an efficient deterministic algorithm* $\mathsf{Eval}_{\mathsf{BV}}$ *that takes as input C and* $\{\mathbf{A}_i\}_{i\in[\ell]}$ *and outputs a matrix* $\mathbf{A}_C = \mathbf{A}\mathbf{R}_C + C(x_1, \ldots, x_\ell)\mathbf{G} = \mathsf{Eval}_{\mathsf{BV}}(C, \mathbf{A}_1, \ldots, \mathbf{A}_\ell)$ *where* $\mathbf{R}_C \in \mathbb{Z}^{\bar{m}\times 2nw}$ *can be computed deterministically from* $\{\mathbf{R}_i\}_{i\in[\ell]}$ *and* $\{x_1\}_{i\in[\ell]}$*, and* $C(x_1, \ldots, x_\ell)$ *is the output of C on the arguments* $x_1, \ldots, x_\ell$*.* $\mathsf{Eval}_{\mathsf{BV}}$ *runs in time poly*$(4^d, \ell, n, \log q)$*.*

Let $2nw \le \bar{m}$*. So* $s_1(\mathbf{R}_{max}) = max\{s_1(\mathbf{R}_i)\}_{i\in[\ell]} \le b\cdot O(\sqrt{\bar{m}})$ *by Lemma 4. the spectral norm of* $\mathbf{R}_C$ *can be bounded, with overwhelming probability, by* $s_1(\mathbf{R}_C) \le O(4^d \cdot \bar{m}^{3/2}) = O(\ell^{2\eta}\cdot \bar{m}^{3/2})$*.*

We also explicitly use the following two evaluation formulas. Let $\mathbf{C} = \mathbf{A}\mathbf{R} + x\mathbf{G}$ and $\hat{\mathbf{C}} = \mathbf{A}\hat{\mathbf{R}} + \mathbf{H}\hat{\mathbf{G}}$ where $\mathbf{A} \in \mathbb{Z}_q^{n\times\bar{m}}$, $\mathbf{R}, \hat{\mathbf{R}} \in \mathbb{Z}^{\bar{m}\times 2nw}$ has low norm, $x \in \{0,1\}$, $\mathbf{H} \in \mathbb{Z}^{n\times 2n}$, and $\mathbf{G} \in \mathbb{Z}_q^{n\times 2nw}$, $\hat{\mathbf{G}} \in \mathbb{Z}_q^{2n\times 2nw}$ be gadget matrices. We can multiplicatively evaluate $\mathbf{C}$ and $\hat{\mathbf{C}}$ with respect to the "message" product $x\mathbf{H}$ by computing

$$\begin{aligned} \hat{\mathbf{C}}' &= \mathbf{C}\cdot\mathbf{G}^{-1}(\hat{\mathbf{C}}) \pmod q \\ &= \mathbf{A}\mathbf{R}\cdot\mathbf{G}^{-1}(\hat{\mathbf{C}}) + x(\mathbf{A}\hat{\mathbf{R}}) + x\mathbf{H}\hat{\mathbf{G}} \pmod q \\ &= \mathbf{A}\hat{\mathbf{R}}' + x\mathbf{H}\hat{\mathbf{G}} \pmod q \end{aligned}$$

Let $\hat{\mathbf{C}}_1 = \mathbf{A}\hat{\mathbf{R}}_1 + \mathbf{Z}\hat{\mathbf{G}}$ and $\hat{\mathbf{C}}_2 = \mathbf{M}\hat{\mathbf{G}}$[3] where $\mathbf{A} \in \mathbb{Z}_q^{n\times\bar{m}}$, $\hat{\mathbf{R}}_1, \hat{\mathbf{R}}_2 \in \mathbb{Z}^{\bar{m}\times 2nw}$ have low norm, $\mathbf{Z} \in \mathbb{Z}_q^{n\times 2n}$, $\mathbf{M} \in \mathbb{Z}_q^{2n\times 2n}$, and $\hat{\mathbf{G}}$ is the gadget matrix. We compute the "encryption" of $\mathbf{Z}\mathbf{M} \in \mathbb{Z}_q^{n\times 2n}$ by computing:

$$\begin{aligned} \hat{\mathbf{C}} &= \hat{\mathbf{C}}_1\cdot\hat{\mathbf{G}}^{-1}(\hat{\mathbf{C}}_2) \pmod q \\ &= \mathbf{A}\left(\hat{\mathbf{R}}_1\cdot\hat{\mathbf{G}}^{-1}(\hat{\mathbf{C}}_2)\right) + (\mathbf{Z}\mathbf{M})\hat{\mathbf{G}} \pmod q \\ &= \mathbf{A}\hat{\mathbf{R}} + (\mathbf{Z}\mathbf{M})\hat{\mathbf{G}} \pmod q \end{aligned}$$

2.5 Computational Assumptions

We use the classic variant of learning-with-errors (LWE) problem where the secret components have the same distribution as the noise components. Such variant is known as the normal-form LWE problem and is no easier than the

[3] In our construction, $\mathbf{Z}$ will be hidden and $\mathbf{M}$ will be publicly samplable.

LWE problem with uniform secret, up to a small difference in the number of available samples (see e.g., [6]). Additionally, we consider the LWE problem in which the secret is a matrix in $\mathbb{Z}^{n\times h}$ rather than single vector in $\mathbb{Z}^n$. By a standard hybrid argument, such problem, as shown in Lemma 6.2 of [39], can be reduced to the LWE problem with a single vector secret, while loosing a factor h of security. We point out that in our constructions h is independent of the number of adversarial queries.

Definition 2. *Let n, q, h be positive integers. Let χ be be a distribution over $\mathbb{Z}_q$. Let $\mathbf{S} \leftarrow \chi^{n\times h}$ be a secret matrix. Define two oracles:*

- $\mathcal{O}_{\mathbf{S}}$: *samples* $\mathbf{a} \xleftarrow{\$} \mathbb{Z}_q^n$, $\mathbf{e} \leftarrow \chi^h$; *returns* $(\mathbf{a}, \mathbf{S}^t\mathbf{a} + \mathbf{e}^t \bmod q)$.
- $\mathcal{O}_{\$}$: *samples* $\mathbf{a} \xleftarrow{\$} \mathbb{Z}_q^n$, $\mathbf{b} \xleftarrow{\$} \mathbb{Z}_q^h$; *returns* $(\mathbf{a}, \mathbf{b})$.

The normal form of the $\mathsf{LWE}_{n,h,q,\chi}$ problem with matrix secret asks for distinguishing between $\mathcal{O}_{\mathbf{S}}$ and $\mathcal{O}_{\$}$. The advantage of a distinguishing algorithm $\mathcal{A}$ in the security parameter λ is defined as

$$\mathsf{Adv}_{\mathsf{NF},\mathcal{A}}^{\mathsf{LWE}_{n,h,q,\chi}}(\lambda) = \left|\Pr[\mathcal{A}^{\mathcal{O}_{\mathbf{S}}}(1^\lambda) = 1] - \Pr[\mathcal{A}^{\mathcal{O}_{\$}}(1^\lambda) = 1]\right|$$

We also implicity make the short integer solution (SIS) assumption [2,25] for invoking the lattice-based chameleon hash function by Cash et al. [18], which is viewed as a black box in our constructions. Since the SIS assumption is quantitatively much weaker than the LWE assumption we use, and is implied by it, our constructions are ultimately based on LWE assumption.

3 Definitions

3.1 Weak Pseudorandom Functions

Weak pseudorandom functions (weak PRFs) [3] are keyed functions that have pseudorandom outputs on *random* inputs. They hav many applications in protocol design, e.g., [20,33], improving efficiency when a full PRF is not needed.

Let λ be a security parameter, $t = t(\lambda)$, and $\ell = \ell(\lambda)$. An efficiently computable, deterministic (one-bit-output) function family $F : \{0,1\}^t \times \{0,1\}^\ell \to \{0,1\}$ is called weak PRF if it satisfies the following: For every $Q = \mathsf{poly}(\lambda)$, the ensemble $\mathcal{X} = \{(x_i, F_K(x_i)\}_{i\in[Q]}$ is computationally indistinguishable from the ensemble $\mathcal{Y} = \{(x_i, R(x_i))\}_{i\in[Q]}$, where K is random in $\{0,1\}^t$, x_i is random in $\{0,1\}^\ell$, and $R : \{0,1\}^\ell \to \{0,1\}$ is a random function.

Weak PRFs, which turn out to be much weaker that normal PRFs, admit simple and efficient constructions from various assumptions. To base our ABM-LTF purely on lattice assumptions, we can use a weak PRF from [7]

$$F_K(\cdot) = \lfloor \frac{p}{q}\langle \mathbf{s}, \cdot\rangle \rceil \bmod p \qquad \text{where } 2 \le p \ll q$$

For binary output, $p = 2$. The key $K = \mathbf{s}$ is a randomly chosen vector in $\mathbb{Z}_q^n$. $F_K(\cdot)$ has input space $\mathbb{Z}_q^n$. The security of $F_K(\cdot)$ is based on the hardness of learning with rounding (LWR), a deterministic variation on LWE, defined in [7].

Let $q > p \geq 2$. For a vector $\mathbf{s} \in \mathbb{Z}_q^n$, the LWR distribution $L_{\mathbf{s}}$ over $\mathbb{Z}_q^n \times \mathbb{Z}_p$ is obtained by randomly choosing $\mathbf{a}$ form $\mathbb{Z}_q^n$, and outputting $(\mathbf{a}, \lfloor \frac{p}{q} \langle \mathbf{s}, \mathbf{a} \rangle \rceil \bmod p)$. The $\mathsf{LWR}_{n,p,q}$ problem asks for distinguishing between any desired number of independent samples from $L_{\mathbf{s}}$, and the same number of samples from uniform distribution over $\mathbb{Z}_q^n \times \mathbb{Z}_p$. It has been shown that the hardness of the decision LWR problem can be based on the decision LWE problem for certain parameters.

Notice that $F_K(\cdot)$ with $p = 2$ is exactly an instance of the decision-$\mathsf{LWR}_{n,2,q}$ problem, and it is a weak pseudorandom function if the $\mathsf{LWR}_{n,2,q}$ problem is hard. It has been shown that for $q/2 \geq (\alpha q) \cdot n^{\omega(1)}$, the $\mathsf{LWR}_{n,2,q}$ problem is no easier than the $\mathsf{LWE}_{n,q,D_{\mathbb{Z}},\alpha q}$ problem where $\alpha \leq n^{-\omega(1)}$.[4] We note that F_K here is essentially the same decryption circuit as in many lattice-based encryption schemes (e.g., [15,16,26]) and belongs to a very shallow $\mathbf{NC}^1$ circuit class.

3.2 Chameleon Hash Functions

A chameleon hash function $\mathsf{CH} = (\mathsf{CH.Gen}, \mathsf{CH.Eval}, \mathsf{CH.Equiv})$ has three PPT algorithms. The key generation algorithm $\mathsf{CH.Gen}$ takes as input a security parameter λ, outputs a hash key and trapdoor pair $(\mathsf{Hk}, \mathsf{Td})$. The randomised hashing algorithm takes as input a message X, random coins $r \in \mathcal{R}_{\mathsf{CH}}$, and outputs $Y = \mathsf{CH.Eval}(\mathsf{Hk}, X; R)$. The equivocation algorithm takes as input a trapdoor Td, an arbitrary valid hash value y and an arbitrary message x, and outputs a valid randomness $R \in \mathcal{R}_{\mathsf{CH}}$ such that $Y = \mathsf{CH.Eval}(\mathsf{Hk}, X; R)$.

A chameleon hash function has output uniformity which guarantees the distribution of hashes is independent of the messages. Particularly, for all Hk, two messages X, X', the distributions $\{R \xleftarrow{\$} \mathcal{R}_{\mathsf{CH}} : \mathsf{CH.Eval}(\mathsf{Hk}, X; R)\}$ and $\{R \xleftarrow{\$} \mathcal{R}_{\mathsf{CH}} : \mathsf{CH.Eval}(\mathsf{Hk}, X'; R)\}$ are identical. A chameleon hash function is collision-resistant. That is, for all PPT adversary $\mathcal{A}$, for random $(\mathsf{Hk}, \mathsf{Td}) \leftarrow \mathsf{CH.Gen}(1^\lambda)$, the advantage

$$\mathsf{Adv}^{\mathsf{coll}}_{\mathsf{CH},\mathcal{A}}(\lambda) = \left[\begin{array}{c} ((X, R), (X', R')) \leftarrow \mathcal{A}(1^\lambda, \mathsf{Hk}) \\ (X, R) \neq (X', R'), \\ \mathsf{CH.Eval}(\mathsf{Hk}, X; R) = \mathsf{CH.Eval}(\mathsf{Hk}, X'; R') \end{array} \right]$$

must be negligible in λ.

As in the definition of chameleon hash function from [29], the message space is assumed to be $\{0,1\}^*$. This is not a big issue since we can always apply a collision-resistant hash function on the input to get a chameleon-hash input with fixed size. We additionally require the chameleon hash function used in

[4] Unfortunately, this proof indicates that if such LWR-based weak PRFs are used in our construction, we need to make a slightly stronger LWE assumption with super-polynomial modulus q. However, such LWE assumption remains weaker than widely used LWE assumptions with sub-exponential moduli q, e.g., [12].

our ABM-LTF construction to have the following property in order to achieve selective opening security:

Definition 3. *Let* $CH = (CH.Gen, CH.Eval, CH.Equiv)$ *be a secure chameleon hash function. We say* CH *has* ***equivocation indistinguishability*** *if, for random* $(Hk, Td) \leftarrow CH.Gen(1^\lambda)$*, given a fixed message* $X \in \mathcal{X}_{CH}$*, the following two distributions of tuple* (X, R, Y) *are statistically indistinguishable:*

$$\{X \in \mathcal{X}_{CH}, R \xleftarrow{\$} \mathcal{R}_{CH}, Y \leftarrow CH.Eval(Hk, X; R)) \in \mathcal{Y}_{CH}\}$$

and

$$\{X \in \mathcal{X}_{CH}, Y \xleftarrow{\$} \mathcal{Y}_{CH}, R \leftarrow CH.Equiv(Td, Y, X) \in \mathcal{R}_{CH}\}$$

Cash et al. [18] constructed a chameleon hash function from the short integer solutions (SIS) assumption [2]. Such construction has equivocation indistinguishability and output uniformity which follow directly from the properties of preimage-sampleable functions given by Gentry et al. [25].

3.3 Lossy Trapdoor Functions

A lossy trapdoor function with domain D consists of three PPT algorithms:

- $\mathsf{LTF.Gen}(1^\lambda, \mathsf{mode})$: a key generation algorithm that takes as input a security parameter and a mode parameter $\mathsf{mode} = \{\mathsf{inj}, \mathsf{loss}\}$, then behaves as follows:
  - $\mathsf{LTF.Gen}(1^\lambda, \mathsf{inj})$ outputs $(\mathsf{LTF.ek}, \mathsf{LTF.ik})$ where $\mathsf{LTF.ek}$ is a injective evaluation key and $\mathsf{LTF.ik}$ is an inversion trapdoor.
  - $\mathsf{LTF.Gen}(1^\lambda, \mathsf{loss})$ outputs $(\mathsf{LTF.ek}, \perp)$ where $\mathsf{LTF.ek}$ is a lossy evaluation key.
- $\mathsf{LTF.Eval}(\mathsf{LTF.ek}, X)$: an evaluation function that evaluates the function on input $X \in \mathsf{D}$ using evaluation key $\mathsf{LTF.ek}$.
- $\mathsf{LTF.Inv}(\mathsf{LTF.ik}, Y)$: an inversion function that takes as input a value Y, and uses the inversion key $\mathsf{LTF.ik}$ to find a value X.

A lossy trapdoor function has the following properties.

Invertibility. For all $(\mathsf{LTF.ek}, \mathsf{LTF.ik}) \leftarrow \mathsf{LTF.Gen}(1^\lambda, \mathsf{inj})$, $X \in \mathsf{D}$, and $Y = \mathsf{LTF.Eval}(\mathsf{LTF.ek}, X)$, we have

$$\Pr[X = \mathsf{LTF.Inv}(\mathsf{LTF.ik}, Y)] = 1 - \mathsf{negl}(\lambda)$$

Lossiness. We say that the lossy trapdoor function is ℓ-lossy if for all $\mathsf{LTF.ek} = \mathsf{LTF.Gen}(1^\lambda, \mathsf{loss})$, the image set of $\mathsf{LTF.Eval}(\mathsf{LTF.ek}, \mathsf{D})$ has size at most $|\mathsf{D}|/2^\ell$.

Indistinguishability. The first outputs of $\mathsf{LTF.Gen}(1^\lambda, \mathsf{inj})$ and $\mathsf{LTF.Gen}(1^\lambda, \mathsf{loss})$ are computationally indistinguishable. That is, for all PPT adversary $\mathcal{A}$, the advantage $\mathsf{Adv}^{\mathsf{ind}}_{\mathsf{LTF},\mathcal{A}}(\lambda)$, given by

$$\left|\Pr\left[\mathcal{A}(1^\lambda, \mathsf{LTF.ek}) = 1\right] - \Pr\left[\mathcal{A}(1^\lambda, \mathsf{LTF.ek}') = 1\right]\right|$$

is negligible in λ, where $(\mathsf{LTF.ek}, \mathsf{LTF.ik}) \leftarrow \mathsf{LTF.Gen}(1^\lambda, \mathsf{inj})$ and $(\mathsf{LTF.ek}', \perp) \leftarrow \mathsf{LTF.Gen}(1^\lambda, \mathsf{loss})$.

3.4 All-But-Many Lossy Trapdoor Functions

Our definition mainly follows the original definition given by Hofheinz [29], and maintains the same tagging mechanism. That is, a tag tag is divided into two parts: the primary part $\mathbf{t}_\mathsf{p}$ and the auxiliary part $\mathbf{t}_\mathsf{a}$. The auxiliary part is usually just a random string. For any $\mathbf{t}_\mathsf{a}$, given a lossy tag generation trapdoor, one can compute $\mathbf{t}_\mathsf{p}$ to make $\mathsf{tag} = (\mathbf{t}_\mathsf{p}, \mathbf{t}_\mathsf{a})$ a lossy tag. As in [29], the auxiliary part helps us to embed auxiliary information (e.g., a one-time signature verification key).

One difference between our definition (and construction) and that of Hofheinz, is that we divide a tag set into *three* disjoint subsets: (1) a lossy tag set, (2) an injective tag set and (3) an invalid tag set. This is because in our lattice-based construction, some tags can simultaneously make the function injective and disable the inversion trapdoor. We will need to make sure that those tags are generally hard to find (except when knowing a trapdoor).

We now define ABM-LTFs. An all-but-many lossy trapdoor function with domain D consists of four PPT algorithms:

- $\mathsf{ABM.Gen}(1^\lambda)$: a key generation algorithm. It takes as input a security parameter, and outputs an evaluation key $\mathsf{ABM.ek}$, an inversion key $\mathsf{ABM.ik}$, and a lossy tag generation key $\mathsf{ABM.tk}$. The evaluation key $\mathsf{ABM.ek}$ defines the tag space $\mathcal{T} = \mathbf{t}_\mathsf{p} \times \{0,1\}^*$ consisting of three disjoint sets: injective tags $\mathcal{T}_{\mathsf{inj}}$, lossy tags $\mathcal{T}_{\mathsf{loss}}$, and invalid tags $\mathcal{T}_{\mathsf{invalid}}$. All tags have form $\mathsf{tag} = (\mathbf{t}_\mathsf{p}, \mathbf{t}_\mathsf{a})$ where $\mathbf{t}_\mathsf{p}$ is the primary part of the tag, and $\mathbf{t}_\mathsf{a} \in \{0,1\}^*$ is the auxiliary part of the tag.
- $\mathsf{ABM.Eval}(\mathsf{ABM.ek}, \mathsf{tag}, X)$: an evaluation algorithm. It takes as input $\mathsf{ABM.ek}$, a tag $\mathsf{tag} \in \mathcal{T}$, and $X \in \mathsf{D}$. It produces $Y = \mathsf{ABM.Eval}(\mathsf{ABM.ek}, \mathsf{tag}, X)$.
- $\mathsf{ABM.Inv}(\mathsf{ABM.ik}, \mathsf{tag}, Y)$: an inversion algorithm. It takes as input $\mathsf{ABM.ik}$, a injective tag $\mathsf{tag} \in \mathcal{T}_{\mathsf{inj}}$ and Y, where $Y = \mathsf{ABM.Eval}(\mathsf{ABM.ek}, \mathsf{tag}, X)$. It outputs $X = \mathsf{ABM.Inv}(\mathsf{ABM.ik}, \mathsf{tag}, Y)$.
- $\mathsf{ABM.LTag}(\mathsf{ABM.tk})$: a lossy tag generation algorithm. It uses $\mathsf{ABM.tk}$ to generate a lossy tag $\mathsf{tag} \in \mathcal{T}_{\mathsf{loss}}$.

We require the following properties of ABM-LTFs.

Invertibility. The invertibility property consists of two sub-properties. Firstly, it requires that randomly sampled tags be injective tags with all but negligible probability, i.e.,

$$\Pr\left[\mathsf{tag} \in \mathcal{T}_{\mathsf{inj}} \mid \mathsf{tag} \xleftarrow{\$} \mathcal{T}\right] \geq 1 - \mathsf{negl}(\lambda)$$

for some negligible function $\mathsf{negl}(\lambda)$ in the security parameter λ. Secondly, it requires that for all injective tags, the ABM-LTF be invertible with all bat negligible probability. That is, for all $(\mathsf{ABM.ek}, \mathsf{ABM.ik}, \mathsf{ABM.tk}) \leftarrow \mathsf{ABM.Gen}(1^\lambda)$, $\mathsf{tag} \in \mathcal{T}_{\mathsf{inj}}$, $X \in \mathsf{D}$, and $Y = \mathsf{ABM.Eval}(\mathsf{ABM.ek}, \mathsf{tag}, X)$ we have

$$\Pr\left[\mathsf{ABM.Inv}(\mathsf{ABM.ik}, \mathsf{tag}, Y) = X\right] = 1 - \mathsf{negl}(\lambda)$$

Lossiness. An ABM-LTF is ℓ-lossy if for all $(\mathsf{ABM.ek}, \mathsf{ABM.ik}, \mathsf{ABM.tk}) \leftarrow \mathsf{ABM.Gen}(1^\lambda)$, and all $\mathsf{tag} \in \mathcal{T}_{\mathsf{loss}}$, the image set $\mathsf{ABM.Eval}(\mathsf{ABM.ek}, \mathsf{tag}, \mathsf{D})$ has size $\leq |\mathsf{D}|/2^\ell$.

Indistinguishability. The indistinguishability property requires that even multiple lossy tags be indistinguishable from random tags. That is, for all PPT adversary $\mathcal{A}$'s, the advantage $\mathsf{Adv}^{\mathsf{ind}}_{\mathsf{ABM\text{-}LTF},\mathcal{A}}(\lambda)$ given by

$$\left| \Pr\left[\mathcal{A}^{\mathsf{ABM.LTag}(\mathsf{ABM.tk},\cdot)}(1^\lambda, \mathsf{ABM.ek}) = 1 \right] - \Pr\left[\mathcal{A}^{\mathcal{O}_{\mathcal{T}}(\cdot)}(1^\lambda, \mathsf{ABM.ek}) = 1 \right] \right|$$

is negligible in λ, where $(\mathsf{ABM.ek}, \mathsf{ABM.ik}, \mathsf{ABM.tk}) \leftarrow \mathsf{ABM.Gen}(1^\lambda)$, the call $\mathsf{ABM.LTag}(\mathsf{ABM.tk}, \cdot)$ returns a lossy tag, and $\mathcal{O}_{\mathcal{T}}(\cdot)$ returns a random tag in $\mathcal{T}$.

Evasiveness. Evasiveness asks that lossy and invalid tags be computationally hard to find, even given multiple lossy tags. That is, for all PPT adversary $\mathcal{A}$, for $(\mathsf{ABM.ek}, \mathsf{ABM.ik}, \mathsf{ABM.tk}) \leftarrow \mathsf{ABM.Gen}(1^\lambda)$, $\mathcal{A}$ has negligible advantage

$$\mathsf{Adv}^{\mathsf{eva}}_{\mathsf{ABM\text{-}LTF},\mathcal{A}}(\lambda) = \Pr\left[\mathcal{A}^{\mathsf{ABM.LTag}(\mathsf{ABM.tk},\cdot),\mathcal{O}(\cdot)}(1^\lambda, \mathsf{ABM.ek}) = \mathsf{tag} \in \mathcal{T}_{\mathsf{loss}} \cup \mathcal{T}_{\mathsf{invalid}} \right]$$

where the oracle $\mathcal{O}(\cdot)$ takes as input a tag tag output from $\mathcal{A}$ and returns answers "lossy/invalid" and "injective" indicating the type of tag.

4 All-But-Many Lossy Trapdoor Function from LWE

We now present our main construction, which borrows and combines various ideas from many different sources, primarily [7,10,14,29]; we also credit an anonymous source for suggesting the marriage of weak PRFs with chameleon hashing.

4.1 Basic LTF from [10]

We recall the lattice-based LTF proposed by Bellare et al. [10], which is the basis of our ABM-LTF construction.

Let $c > 1$ and $b \geq 2$ be two constants. Let $n_1 \geq 2$ be an integer, $q \geq 2$ be a large enough prime. Let $n = cn_1$ and $w = \log_b q$. Let $\bar{m}$ be any integer such that $\bar{m} > n \log_b q + \omega(\log n)$, and $m = \bar{m} + 2nw = \Theta(n \log_b q)$. Let β and γ be integers such that $1 < \gamma < \beta < q$. Define $I_\beta = \{0, 1, \cdots, \beta - 1\}$ and $I_\gamma = \{0, 1, \cdots, \gamma - 1\}$. Let $\hat{\mathbf{G}} \in \mathbb{Z}_q^{2n \times 2nw}$ be the gadget matrix.

- $\mathsf{LTF.Gen}(1^\lambda, \mathsf{loss})$ The lossy function generation algorithm dose the following:
  1. Sample $\mathbf{A}' \in \mathbb{Z}_q^{n_1 \times \bar{m}}$, $\mathbf{E}_1 \leftarrow \chi^{\bar{m} \times (n - n_1)}$, $\mathbf{E}_2 \leftarrow \chi^{n_1 \times (n - n_1)}$.
  2. Compute $\mathbf{A} = \begin{bmatrix} \mathbf{A}' \\ \mathbf{E}_1^t + \mathbf{E}_2^t \mathbf{A}' \end{bmatrix} \in \mathbb{Z}_q^{n \times \bar{m}}$.
  3. Sample $\mathbf{R} \leftarrow D^{\bar{m} \times 2nw}_{\mathbb{Z}, b \cdot \omega(\sqrt{\log n})}$.
  4. Set $\mathsf{LTF.ek}$: $\mathbf{F} = [\mathbf{A} | \mathbf{AR}] \in \mathbb{Z}_q^{n \times (\bar{m} + 2nw)}$.

- $\mathsf{LTF.Gen}(1^\lambda, \mathsf{inj})$ The injective trapdoor function generation algorithm does the following:
  1. Sample $\mathbf{A}' \in \mathbb{Z}_q^{n_1 \times \bar{m}}$, $\mathbf{E}_1 \leftarrow \chi^{\bar{m}\times(n-n_1)}$, $\mathbf{E}_2 \leftarrow \chi^{n_1\times(n-n_1)}$.
  2. Compute $\mathbf{A} = \begin{bmatrix} \mathbf{A}' \\ \mathbf{E}_1^t + \mathbf{E}_2^t\mathbf{A}' \end{bmatrix} \in \mathbb{Z}_q^{n\times\bar{m}}$.
  3. Sample $\mathbf{R} \leftarrow D^{\bar{m}\times 2nw}_{\mathbb{Z},b\cdot\omega(\sqrt{\log n})}$ and $\mathbf{H} \in \mathbb{Z}_q^{n\times 2n}$ with rank n.
  4. Set $\mathsf{LTF.ek} = \mathbf{F} = [\mathbf{A}|\mathbf{AR} + \mathbf{H}\hat{\mathbf{G}}] \in \mathbb{Z}_q^{n\times(\bar{m}+2nw)}$ and $\mathsf{LTF.ik} = (\mathbf{R}, \mathbf{H}, \hat{\mathbf{G}})$
- $\mathsf{LTF.Eval}(\mathsf{LTF.ek}, \mathbf{x})$ For $\mathbf{x} \in I_\beta^{m+n_1} \times I_\gamma^{n-n_1}$, the evaluation algorithm returns

$$\mathbf{y}^t = g_{\mathbf{F}}(\mathbf{x}) = \mathbf{x}^t \begin{bmatrix} \mathbf{I}_m \\ \mathbf{F} \end{bmatrix} \bmod q$$

- $\mathsf{LTF.Inv}(\mathsf{LTF.ik}, \mathbf{y})$ Given $\mathbf{y}$, the inversion algorithm outputs $\mathbf{x} = \mathsf{Invert}(\mathbf{F}, \mathbf{R}, \mathbf{H}, \mathbf{y})$.

The invertibility of the basic lossy trapdoor function directly relies on Lemma 7. The lossiness and the indistinguishability of the function $g_{\mathbf{F}}(\cdot)$ relies on the following two lemmas.

Lemma 9 (Lemma 5.4, [9]). *Let $\mathbf{F} = [\mathbf{A}|\mathbf{AR}] \in \mathbb{Z}_q^{n\times m}$ be as generated by $\mathsf{LTF.Gen}(1^\lambda, \mathsf{loss})$ under the conditions $\gamma^{c-1} \geq 2^{\Omega(m/n_1)}$ and $\beta \geq \gamma \cdot s_1(\tilde{\mathbf{E}})$ where $\tilde{\mathbf{E}}^t = [\mathbf{E}_1^t|\mathbf{E}_1^t \cdot \mathbf{R}|\mathbf{E}_2^t]$. The function $g_{\mathbf{F}}(\mathbf{x}) = \mathbf{x}^t \begin{bmatrix} \mathbf{I}_m \\ \mathbf{F} \end{bmatrix} \bmod q$, where $\mathbf{x} \in I_\beta^{m+n_1} \times I_\gamma^{n-n_1}$, is an $\Omega(m)$-lossy function.*

Lemma 10 (Lemma 5.7, [9]). *For any PPT adversary $\mathcal{A}$ against the indistinguishability of above LTF with advantage $\mathsf{Adv}^{ind}_{\mathsf{LTF},\mathcal{A}}(\lambda)$, there exists an adversary $\mathcal{B}$ against $\mathsf{LWE}_{n_1,q,\chi}$ such that*

$$\mathsf{Adv}^{ind}_{\mathsf{LTF},\mathcal{A}}(\lambda) \leq 2 \cdot \mathsf{Adv}^{\mathsf{LWE}_{n_1,n-n_1,q,\chi}}_{\mathsf{NF},\mathcal{B}} + \mathsf{negl}(\lambda)$$

for some negligible probability $\mathsf{negl}(\lambda)$.

4.2 Our Construction of ABM-LTF

Let $n_1 \geq 2$, $\bar{m} \geq 2$ be integers, $q \geq 2$ be a prime. Let $n = cn_1$, $w = \log_b q$ for constants c and b. Set $m = \bar{m} + 2nw$. Let β and γ be integers such that $1 < \gamma < \beta < q$. Define $I_\beta = \{0, 1, \cdots, \beta - 1\}$ and $I_\gamma = \{0, 1, \cdots, \gamma - 1\}$. Let $\mathsf{CH} = (\mathsf{CH.Gen}, \mathsf{CH.Eval}, \mathsf{CH.Equiv})$ be a secure chameleon hash function with equivocation indistinguishability. Let $\mathcal{UH} = \{\mathsf{UH}_\mathbf{s} : \{0,1\}^{\ell'} \to \{0,1\}^{\ell}\}$ for $\mathbf{s} \in \{0,1\}^{t'}$.

- $\mathsf{ABM.Gen}(1^\lambda, d)$ The key generation algorithm does the following steps:
  1. Choose $\mathbf{A}' \xleftarrow{\$} \mathbb{Z}_q^{n_1\times\bar{m}}$, $\mathbf{E}_2 \xleftarrow{\$} \chi^{n_1\times(n-n_1)}$, $\mathbf{E}_1 \leftarrow \chi^{\bar{m}\times(n-n_1)}$ and set

$$\mathbf{A} = \begin{bmatrix} \mathbf{A}' \\ \mathbf{E}_2^t\mathbf{A}' + \mathbf{E}_1^t \end{bmatrix} \in \mathbb{Z}_q^{n\times\bar{m}}$$

2. Select a weak PRF WPRF : $\{0,1\}^t \times \{0,1\}^\ell \to \{0,1\}$. Select $\mathbf{K} \xleftarrow{\$} \{0,1\}^{h\times t}$. We denote by $\mathbf{k}_i \in \{0,1\}^t$ the i-th row of $\mathbf{K}$, to serve as an independent key for WPRF. We denote by $k_{i,j} \in \{0,1\}$ the j-th bit of $\mathbf{k}_i$. Select a universal hash function $\mathsf{UH}_\mathbf{s} \xleftarrow{\$} \mathcal{UH}$ with hidden key $\mathbf{s} = s_1 \dots s_{t'} \in \{0,1\}^{t'}$. Express the function $\mathsf{WPRF}(\cdot, \mathsf{UH}.(\cdot))$ as a Boolean circuit C_{WPRF} with gate fan-in 2 and depth d.
3. Sample a set of low-norm matrices $\{\mathbf{R}_{k_{i,j}}\}_{i\in[h],j\in[t]}$, $\{\mathbf{R}_{s_i}\}_{i\in[t']}$ from the distribution $D^{\bar{m}\times 2nw}_{\mathbb{Z},b\cdot\omega(\sqrt{\log n})}$. Compute $\mathbf{C}_{k_{i,j}} = \mathbf{A}\mathbf{R}_{k_{i,j}} + k_{i,j}\mathbf{G}$ and $\mathbf{C}_{s_i} = \mathbf{A}\mathbf{R}_{s_i} + s_i\mathbf{G}$.[5]
4. Sample a set of low-norm matrices $\{\mathbf{R}_{\mathbf{H}_i}\}_{i\in[h]}$ for $\mathbf{R}_{\mathbf{H}_i} \leftarrow D^{\bar{m}\times 2nw}_{\mathbb{Z},b\cdot\omega(\sqrt{\log n})}$. Sample a set of random rank-n matrices $\{\mathbf{H}_i\}_{i\in[h]}$ for $\mathbf{H}_i \xleftarrow{\$} \mathbb{Z}_q^{n\times 2n}$. Compute $\hat{\mathbf{C}}_{\mathbf{H}_i} = \mathbf{A}\mathbf{R}_{\mathbf{H}_i} + \mathbf{H}_i\hat{\mathbf{G}} \in \mathbb{Z}_q^{n\times 2nw}$ for $i \in [h]$.[6]
5. Select $\mathbf{Z} \leftarrow D^{\bar{m}\times 2nw}_{\mathbb{Z},b\cdot\omega(\sqrt{\log n})}$, and compute $\hat{\mathbf{C}}_\mathbf{Z} = \mathbf{A}\mathbf{R}_\mathbf{Z} + \mathbf{Z}\hat{\mathbf{G}}$.
6. Run $\mathsf{CH.Gen}(1^\lambda)$ to generate a chameleon hash key Hk and a trapdoor Td. Assume this chameleon hash function has message space $\mathcal{X}_{\mathsf{CH}} = \{0,1\}^*$, randomness space $\mathcal{R}_{\mathsf{CH}}$ and output space $\{0,1\}^{\ell'}$.
7. Set the public evaluation key

$$\mathsf{ABM.ek} = \begin{pmatrix} \mathsf{WPRF}, C_{\mathsf{WPRF}}, \mathbf{A}, \{\mathbf{C}_{k_{i,j}}\}_{i\in[h],j\in[t]}, \\ \{\mathbf{C}_{s_i}\}_{i\in[t']}, \{\hat{\mathbf{C}}_{\mathbf{H}_i}\}_{i\in[h]}, \hat{\mathbf{C}}_\mathbf{Z}, \mathsf{Hk} \end{pmatrix}$$

the private inversion key

$$\mathsf{ABM.ik} = \begin{pmatrix} \mathsf{WPRF}, C_{\mathsf{WPRF}}, \mathbf{K}, \mathbf{s}, \{\mathbf{R}_{k_{i,j}}\}_{i\in[h],j\in[t]}, \\ \{\mathbf{R}_{s_i}\}_{i\in[t']}, \{\mathbf{H}_i\}_{i\in[h]}, \{\mathbf{R}_{\mathbf{H}_i}\}_{i\in[h]}, \mathbf{Z}, \mathbf{R}_\mathbf{Z} \end{pmatrix}$$

and the lossy tag generation key

$$\mathsf{ABM.tk} = \left(\mathsf{WPRF}, C_{\mathsf{WPRF}}, \mathbf{K}, \mathbf{s}, \{\mathbf{H}_i\}_{i\in[h]}, \mathbf{Z}, \mathsf{Td}\right)$$

– **Tags.** A tag has form $\mathsf{tag} = (\mathbf{t}_\mathsf{p}, \mathbf{t}_\mathsf{a})$. The primary tag part $\mathbf{t}_\mathsf{p} = (\mathbf{D}, R) \in \mathbb{Z}_q^{2n\times 2n} \times \mathcal{R}_{\mathsf{CH}}$ and the auxiliary tag part $\mathbf{t}_\mathsf{a} \in \{0,1\}^*$. Set the tag space as $\mathcal{T} = \mathbb{Z}_q^{2n\times 2n} \times \mathcal{R}_{\mathsf{CH}} \times \{0,1\}^*$. With a tag $\mathsf{tag} = ((\mathbf{D}, R), \mathbf{t}_\mathsf{a})$, we can compute $\mu = \mathsf{CH.Eval}(\mathsf{Hk}, (\mathbf{D}, \mathbf{t}_\mathsf{a}); R) \in \{0,1\}^{\ell'}$. Let

$$\mathbf{H} = \mathbf{Z}\mathbf{D} - \sum_{i=1}^{h} \mathsf{WPRF}(\mathbf{k}_i, \mathsf{UH}_\mathbf{s}(\mu)) \cdot \mathbf{H}_i \pmod q$$

We define

$$\mathsf{tag} \in \begin{cases} \mathcal{T}_{\mathsf{inj}} & \text{if } \mathbf{H} \text{ has rank } n; \\ \mathcal{T}_{\mathsf{loss}} & \text{if } \mathbf{H} = \mathbf{0}; \\ \mathcal{T}_{\mathsf{invalid}} & \text{if } \mathbf{H} \text{ has rank} \neq 0 \text{ and} \neq n. \end{cases}$$

[5] $\mathbf{G}$ is the gadget matrix with dimensions n-by-$2nw$.

[6] $\hat{\mathbf{G}}$ is the gadget matrix with dimensions $2n$-by-$2nw$.

– $\mathsf{ABM.Eval}(\mathsf{ABM.ek}, \mathsf{tag}, \mathbf{x})$ For input $\mathbf{x} \in I_{\beta}^{m+n_1} \times I_{\gamma}^{n-n_1}$, the algorithm does:
  1. Let $\mathsf{tag} = (\mathbf{t}_\mathsf{p}, \mathbf{t}_\mathsf{a}) = ((\mathbf{D}, R), \mathbf{t}_\mathsf{a}) \in \mathcal{T}$, compute $\mu = \mathsf{CH.Eval}((\mathbf{D}, \mathbf{t}_\mathsf{a}); R) \in \{0,1\}^{\ell'}$.
  2. Let $\mu_i \in \{0,1\}$ be the i-th bit of μ. Compute

$$\begin{aligned}\tilde{\mathbf{C}}_i &= \mathsf{Eval}_{\mathsf{BV}}(C_{\mathsf{WPRF}}, \mathbf{C}_{k_{i,1}}, \ldots, \mathbf{C}_{k_{i,t}}, \mathbf{C}_{s_1}, \ldots, \mathbf{C}_{s_{t'}}, \mu_1 \mathbf{G}, \ldots, \mu_{\ell'} \mathbf{G}) \\ &= \mathbf{A}\tilde{\mathbf{R}}_i + \mathsf{WPRF}(\mathbf{k}_i, \mathsf{UH}_\mathbf{s}(\mu))\mathbf{G} \pmod q\end{aligned}$$

  for some low-norm $\tilde{\mathbf{R}}_i \in \mathbb{Z}^{\bar{m} \times 2nw}$ and $i \in [h]$.
  3. Compute $\bar{\mathbf{C}} = \hat{\mathbf{C}}_\mathbf{Z} \hat{\mathbf{G}}^{-1}(\mathbf{D}\hat{\mathbf{G}}) = \mathbf{A}(\mathbf{R}_\mathbf{Z}\hat{\mathbf{G}}^{-1}(\mathbf{D}\hat{\mathbf{G}})) + (\mathbf{Z}\mathbf{D})\hat{\mathbf{G}} = \mathbf{A}\bar{\mathbf{R}} + (\mathbf{Z}\mathbf{D})\mathbf{G}$, where $\bar{\mathbf{R}} \in \mathbb{Z}^{\bar{m} \times 2nw}$ is of low norm.
  4. Set

$$\begin{aligned}\mathbf{F} &= [\mathbf{A}|\bar{\mathbf{C}}] - [\mathbf{0}|\sum\nolimits_{i=1}^{h} \tilde{\mathbf{C}}_i \cdot \mathbf{G}^{-1}(\hat{\mathbf{C}}_{\mathbf{H}_i})] \bmod q \\ &= [\mathbf{A}|\mathbf{A}\mathbf{R} + (\mathbf{Z}\mathbf{D} - \sum\nolimits_{i=1}^{h} (\mathsf{WPRF}(\mathbf{k}_i, \mathsf{UH}_\mathbf{s}(\mu)) \cdot \mathbf{H}_i)\hat{\mathbf{G}}] \bmod q \\ &= [\mathbf{A}|\mathbf{A}\mathbf{R} + \mathbf{H}\hat{\mathbf{G}}] \bmod q\end{aligned}$$

  for the unknown low-norm $\mathbb{Z}^{\bar{m} \times 2nw}$-matrix

$$\mathbf{R} = \bar{\mathbf{R}} - \sum\nolimits_{i=1}^{h} \left(\tilde{\mathbf{R}}_i \cdot \mathbf{G}^{-1}(\hat{\mathbf{C}}_{\mathbf{H}_i}) + \mathsf{WPRF}(\mathbf{k}_i, \mathsf{UH}_\mathbf{s}(\mu)) \cdot \mathbf{R}_{\mathbf{H}_i} \right) \quad (1)$$

  Notice that here $\mathbf{R}$ is unknown to the the function evaluator, and, however, is known to the inversion algorithm $\mathsf{ABM.Inv}$ which has the knowledge of $\mathsf{ABM.ik}$.
  5. Compute the output of the function $\mathbf{y}^t = g_\mathbf{F}(\mathbf{x}) = \mathbf{x}^t \begin{bmatrix} \mathbf{I}_{\bar{m}+2nw} \\ \mathbf{F} \end{bmatrix} \bmod q$.

– $\mathsf{ABM.Inv}(\mathsf{ABM.ik}, \mathsf{tag}, \mathbf{y})$ The inversion algorithm takes as input an inversion key $\mathsf{ABM.ik}$, an injective tag $\mathsf{tag} \in \mathcal{T}_\mathsf{inj}$ and an image $\mathbf{y}$. It does the following:
  1. Let $\mathsf{tag} = ((\mathbf{D}, R), \mathbf{t}_\mathsf{a})$, compute $\mu = \mathsf{CH.Eval}(\mathsf{Hk}, (\mathbf{D}, \mathbf{t}_\mathsf{a}); R) \in \{0,1\}^{\ell'}$.
  2. Compute $\mathbf{F} = [\mathbf{A}|\mathbf{A}\mathbf{R} + \mathbf{H}\hat{\mathbf{G}}]$ as the algorithm $\mathsf{ABM.Eval}$.
  3. Use the knowledge of $\mathsf{ABM.ik}$ to compute the low-norm $\mathbf{R}$ by the formula 1 and compute $\mathbf{H} = \mathbf{Z}\mathbf{D} - \sum_{i=1}^{h} \mathsf{WPRF}(\mathbf{k}_i, \mathsf{UH}_\mathbf{s}(\mu)) \cdot \mathbf{H}_i \pmod q$. Notice $\mathbf{H}$ has rank n.
  4. Call the algorithm $\mathsf{Invert}(\mathbf{F}, \mathbf{R}, \mathbf{H}, \mathbf{y})$ to get $\mathbf{x}$.

– $\mathsf{ABM.LTag}(\mathsf{ABM.tk})$ The lossy tag generation algorithm takes as input the lossy tag generation key $\mathsf{ABM.tk}$. It does the following:
  1. Randomly select a tag $\mathsf{tag}' = ((\mathbf{D}', R'), \mathbf{t}'_\mathsf{a}) \in \mathcal{T}$ and compute $\mu = \mathsf{CH.Eval}(\mathsf{Hk}, (\mathbf{D}', \mathbf{t}'_\mathsf{a}); R')$.
  2. Solve for $\mathbf{D} \in \mathbb{Z}_q^{2n \times 2n}$ such that $\mathbf{Z}\mathbf{D} = \sum_{i=1}^{h} (\mathsf{WPRF}(\mathbf{k}_i, \mathsf{UH}_\mathbf{s}(\mu)) \cdot \mathbf{H}_i) \pmod q$.
  3. Randomly select $\mathbf{t}_\mathsf{a} \in \{0,1\}^*$.
  4. Compute $R = \mathsf{CH.Equiv}(\mathsf{Td}, ((\mathbf{D}', \mathbf{t}'_\mathsf{a}), R'), \mathbf{D})$ and output $\mathsf{tag} = ((\mathbf{D}, R), \mathbf{t}_\mathsf{a})$.

It is easy to check that the algorithm indeed outputs a lossy tag.

4.3 Correctness

We show in the following theorems that our ABM-LTFs are invertible with injective tags and lossy with lossy tags.

Theorem 1. *For our construction, randomly sampled tags are injective tags with all but negligible probability. In addition, for any injective tag* $\mathsf{tag} \in \mathcal{T}_{\mathsf{inj}}$*, the function* $g_{\mathbf{F}}(\cdot)$ *is invertible with overwhelming probability, where* $\mathbf{F} = [\mathbf{A}|\mathbf{AR} + \mathbf{H}\hat{\mathbf{G}}] \in \mathbb{Z}_q^{n \times m}$ *was computed via* $\mathsf{ABM.Eval}$ *with* tag.

Proof. Let $\mathsf{tag} = ((\mathbf{D}, R), \mathbf{t_p})$ be a randomly sampled tag; that is, $\mathbf{D} \xleftarrow{\$} \mathbb{Z}_q^{2n \times 2n}$, $R \xleftarrow{\$} \mathcal{R}_{\mathsf{CH}}$ and $\mathbf{t_p} \xleftarrow{\$} \{0,1\}^*$. We have $\mathbf{ZD} \bmod q$ is uniformly random over $\mathbb{Z}_q^{n \times 2n}$, thus, so is $\mathbf{H}$. By Lemma 1, $\mathbf{H}$ has rank n except negligible probability. Hence, $\mathsf{tag} = ((\mathbf{D}, R), \mathbf{t_p})$ is an injective tag.

Since $\|\mathbf{x}\| \le \beta \cdot \sqrt{m}$, we can bound β (with large enough q) to ensure that $\|\mathbf{x}\| \le q/\Theta(b \cdot s_1(\mathbf{R}))$. We then apply Lemma 7 to conclude the proof. □

Theorem 2. *With our parameter restrictions (see also parameter selection in Sect. 4.4), for any lossy tag* $\mathsf{tag} \in \mathcal{T}_{\mathsf{loss}}$*, the function* $g_{\mathbf{F}}(\cdot)$ *is* $\Omega(m)$*-lossy, where* $\mathbf{F} = [\mathbf{A}|\mathbf{AR}] \in \mathbb{Z}_q^{n \times m}$ *computed via* $\mathsf{ABM.Eval}$ *using* tag*, and* $m = \Theta(n \log_b q)$.

Proof. This proof borrows from the proof of Lemma 9 which follows directly from the proof of Lemma 5.4 of [9].

By the construction of $\mathbf{F} \in \mathbb{Z}_q^{n \times m}$ we have

$$g_{\mathbf{F}}(\mathbf{x}) = \mathbf{x}^t \begin{bmatrix} \mathbf{I}_m \\ \mathbf{F} \end{bmatrix} \bmod q = (\mathbf{x}^t \begin{bmatrix} \mathbf{I}_{\bar{m}} & & \\ & \mathbf{I}_{2nw} & \\ & & \mathbf{I}_{n_1} \\ \mathbf{E}_1^t & \mathbf{E}_1^t \cdot \mathbf{R} & \mathbf{E}_2^t \end{bmatrix}) \begin{bmatrix} \mathbf{I}_{\bar{m}} & \\ & \mathbf{I}_{2nw} \\ \mathbf{A}' & \mathbf{A}'\mathbf{R} \end{bmatrix} \bmod q$$

$$= (\mathbf{x}^t \begin{bmatrix} \mathbf{I}_{m+n_1} \\ \tilde{\mathbf{E}}^t \end{bmatrix}) \begin{bmatrix} \mathbf{I}_m \\ \mathbf{F}' \end{bmatrix} \bmod q$$

It suffices to bound the number of possible values of $\mathbf{x}^t \begin{bmatrix} \mathbf{I}_{m+n_1} \\ \tilde{\mathbf{E}}^t \end{bmatrix} \in \mathbb{Z}^{n_1+m}$.

By the triangle inequality, we have

$$\left\| \mathbf{x}^t \begin{bmatrix} \mathbf{I}_{m+n_1} \\ \tilde{\mathbf{E}}^t \end{bmatrix} \right\| \le \beta\sqrt{n_1 + m} + s_1(\tilde{\mathbf{E}}) \cdot \gamma\sqrt{n - n_1} \le \sqrt{n_1 + m} \cdot (\beta + \gamma \cdot s_1(\tilde{\mathbf{E}}))$$

Define $N_d(r)$ to be the number of integer points in a d-dimensional Euclidean ball of radius r. For $r \ge \sqrt{d}$, from the volume of the ball and Stirling's approximation, we have $N_d(r) = O(r/\sqrt{d})^d$. So the number of possible values of $\mathbf{x}^t \begin{bmatrix} \mathbf{I}_{m+n_1} \\ \tilde{\mathbf{E}}^t \end{bmatrix}$ is $O(\beta + \gamma \cdot s_1(\tilde{\mathbf{E}}))^{n_1+m}$.

By the structure of $\mathbf{F}$, $\gamma \ge 2^{\Omega(m/n_1)}$ and $\gamma \le q^{1/C}$, the base-2 logarithm of the domain of the function $g_{\mathbf{F}}(\cdot)$ is

$$(n_1 + m) \log \beta + n_1 \log \gamma^{c-1} \ge (n_1 + m) \log \beta + \Omega(m)$$

Since $\beta \geq \gamma \cdot s_1(\tilde{\mathbf{E}})$, the base-2 logarithm of the range of the function $g_{\mathbf{F}}(\cdot)$ is at most

$$(n_1 + m) \log O(\beta + \gamma \cdot s_1(\tilde{\mathbf{E}})) = (n_1 + m) \log \beta + O(m)$$

By choosing a sufficiently large constant in the Ω notation, we have $\log |\mathsf{D}| - \log |\mathsf{R}| = \Omega(m)$. We conclude that the function $g_{\mathbf{F}}(\cdot)$ is $\Omega(m)$-lossy. □

Setting β and γ. The restrictions on β and γ originate from two lemmas.

Firstly, for invertibility (Lemma 7), we need $\|\mathbf{x}\| \leq \beta\sqrt{m} < q/\Theta(b \cdot s_1(\mathbf{R}))$.

Secondly, for lossiness (Lemma 9), we need $\gamma^{c-1} \geq 2^{\Omega(m/n_1)}$ where $m = \Theta(n \log_b q) = \Theta(cn_1 \log_b q)$, and $\gamma \cdot s_1(\tilde{\mathbf{E}}) \leq \beta$; hence $\gamma \geq q^{\Theta(1/\log b)\cdot c/(c-1)}$.

For any desired constant $C > 1$, we can set up constants $c > 1$ and $b \geq 2$ so that $\gamma \leq q^{1/C}$. This gives

$$q^{1/C} \cdot s_1(\tilde{\mathbf{E}}) \leq \beta \leq q/\Theta(b \cdot s_1(\mathbf{R}) \cdot \sqrt{m}) \tag{2}$$

Therefore, it is sufficient to take q large enough such that

$$q^{1-1/C} \geq \Omega\left(s_1(\mathbf{R}) \cdot s_1(\tilde{\mathbf{E}}) \cdot \sqrt{m}\right) \tag{3}$$

4.4 Parameter Selections

An instance of parameter selection that meets all requirements of correctness and security properties is given here.

Firstly, to enable the statistical argument for security, i.e., Lemma 5 and 3, we set $\bar{m} > n \log_b q + \omega(\log n)$, and for any $\epsilon > 0$, set $h = \mathsf{poly}(\lambda)$ such that $\log(q/(\epsilon^2)) \leq h$.

We set the constant $C = 6$ for Eq. (2), which we can do by picking a suitable constant c and logarithm radix b.

Instantiating WPRF by the weak PRF from [7], which has fan-in-2 Boolean circuit implementation in class NC^1, and a universal hash function from Corollary 1, we can get the fan-in-2 Boolean circuit C_{WPRF} in class NC^1, i.e., C_{WPRF} has input length $\ell' + t' + t = \mathsf{poly}(\lambda)$, and depth $\eta \log(\ell' + t' + t) = \eta \log(\mathsf{poly}(\lambda))$, for some constant $\eta > 0$.

We now bound the norm of $\mathbf{R} \in \mathbb{Z}^{\bar{m} \times 2nw}$ per the formula 1. Firstly we have

$$\begin{aligned} & s_1\left(\textstyle\sum_{i=1}^{h} \tilde{\mathbf{R}}_i \cdot \mathbf{G}^{-1}(\hat{\mathbf{C}}_{\mathbf{H}_i}) + \mathsf{WPRF}(\mathbf{k}_i, \mathsf{UH}_{\mathbf{s}}(\mu)) \cdot \mathbf{R}_{\mathbf{H}_i}\right) \\ \leq\ & O\left(h \cdot 4^d \cdot \bar{m}^{3/2}\right) \cdot ((b-1) \cdot 2nw) \quad \text{(Lemma 8 and 6)} \\ \leq\ & O\left(h \cdot 4^d \cdot \bar{m}^{3/2} \cdot \bar{m}\right) \qquad ((b-1) \cdot 2nw \leq O(\bar{m})) \\ \leq\ & O\left(h \cdot 4^d \cdot \bar{m}^2\right) \end{aligned}$$

and

$$\begin{aligned} s_1(\bar{\mathbf{R}}) &\leq 3 \cdot b \cdot \omega(\sqrt{\log n}) \cdot O(\sqrt{\bar{m}}) \cdot (b-1) \cdot 2nw \\ &\leq \tilde{O}(\bar{m}^{3/2}) \end{aligned}$$

So we have

$$\begin{aligned} s_1(\mathbf{R}) &\leq s_1\left(\sum_{i=1}^{h} \tilde{\mathbf{R}}_i \cdot \mathbf{G}^{-1}(\hat{\mathbf{C}}_{\mathbf{H}_i}) + \mathsf{WPRF}(\mathbf{k}_i, \mathsf{UH}_{\mathbf{s}}(\mu))) \cdot \mathbf{R}_{\mathbf{H}_i}\right) + s_1(\bar{\mathbf{R}}) \\ &\leq O\left(h \cdot 4^d \cdot \bar{m}^2\right) + \tilde{O}(\bar{m}^{3/2}) \\ &= \tilde{O}(h \cdot 4^d \cdot n_1^2) \end{aligned} \tag{4}$$

We now choose the LWE noise distribution $\chi = D_{\mathbb{Z},2\sqrt{n_1}}$ for accommodating the average-case to worst-case hardness reduction from classical lattice problems, e.g. SIVP, given by [41]. We bound $s_1(\tilde{\mathbf{E}})$ where $\tilde{\mathbf{E}}^t = [\mathbf{E}_1^t | \mathbf{E}_1^t \cdot \mathbf{R} | \mathbf{E}_2^t]$ according to Lemma 9.

$$\begin{aligned} s_1(\tilde{\mathbf{E}}) &\leq s_1(\mathbf{E})(1 + s_1(\mathbf{R})) \\ &\leq 2\sqrt{n_1} \cdot (\sqrt{\bar{m} + n_1} + \sqrt{n - n_1})(1 + s_1(\mathbf{R})) \qquad \text{(by Lemma 4)} \\ &= \tilde{O}(h \cdot 4^d \cdot n_1^3) \end{aligned}$$

We now set q through Eq. (3) as

$$\begin{aligned} q &= \Theta\left((s_1(\mathbf{R}) \cdot s_1(\tilde{\mathbf{E}}) \cdot \sqrt{m})^{C/(C-1)}\right) \\ &= \tilde{\Theta}\left((h \cdot 4^d \cdot n_1^3 \cdot h \cdot 4^d \cdot n_1^2 \cdot n_1^{0.5})^{C/(C-1)}\right) \\ &= \tilde{\Theta}\left(h^{2.4} \cdot 2^{4.8d} \cdot n_1^{6.6}\right) \end{aligned}$$

Lastly we fix $\gamma = \tilde{O}\left((h^2 \cdot 2^{4d} \cdot n_1^{5.5})^{1/(C-1)}\right) = \tilde{O}\left(h^{0.4} \cdot 2^{0.8d} \cdot n_1^{1.1}\right) \leq q^{1/C}$. To fix β we have $\gamma \cdot s_1(\tilde{\mathbf{E}}) = \tilde{O}\left(h^{1.4} \cdot 2^{2.8} \cdot n_1^{4.1}\right)$ and $q/\Theta(b \cdot s_1(\mathbf{R})\sqrt{m}) = \tilde{O}\left(h^{2.4} \cdot 2^{2.8d} \cdot n_1^{4.1}\right)$, so to satisfy Eq. (2), we set

$$\gamma \cdot s_1(\tilde{\mathbf{E}}) \leq \beta = \tilde{\Theta}\left(h^{2.4} \cdot 2^{4.8d} \cdot n_1^{6.6}\right) \leq q/\Theta(b \cdot s_1(\mathbf{R})\sqrt{m})$$

Summing up, an example of parameter selection per the foregoing, is:

$$d = O\left(\log(\mathsf{poly}(\lambda))\right) \quad ; \quad q = \tilde{\Theta}\left(h^{2.4} \cdot 2^{4.8d} \cdot n_1^{6.6}\right) \quad ; \quad m = \Theta(n_1 \log_b q)$$

$$\beta = \tilde{\Theta}\left(h^{2.4} \cdot 2^{4.8d} \cdot n_1^{6.6}\right) \quad ; \quad \gamma = \tilde{O}\left(h^{0.4} \cdot 2^{0.8d} \cdot n_1^{1.1}\right)$$

4.5 Security Proofs

Theorem 3 (Indistinguishability). *For any PPT adversary $\mathcal{A}$ against indistinguishablity of the above ABM-LTF with advantage $\mathsf{Adv}^{\mathsf{ind}}_{\mathsf{ABM},\mathcal{A}}(\lambda)$, there exist two adversaries $\mathcal{A}_1$, $\mathcal{A}_2$ and a negligibly small error $\mathsf{negl}(\lambda)$ such that*

$$\mathsf{Adv}^{\mathsf{ind}}_{\mathsf{ABM},\mathcal{A}}(\lambda) \leq \mathsf{Adv}^{\mathsf{LWE}_{n_1,n-n_1,q,\chi}}_{\mathsf{NF},\mathcal{A}_1}(\lambda) + h \cdot \mathsf{Adv}^{\mathsf{WPRF}}_{\mathcal{A}_2}(\lambda) + \mathsf{negl}(\lambda) + \epsilon$$

Proof. We proceed with the proof using a game sequence. Let S_i be the event that $\mathcal{A}$ outputs 1 in the game **Game** i. In **Game** 1, all algorithms work exactly the same as the real scheme. $\mathcal{A}$ interacts with $\mathsf{ABM.LTag}(\mathsf{ABM.tk}, \cdot)$ which outputs lossy tags. So we have

$$\Pr[S_1] = \Pr\left[\mathcal{A}^{\mathsf{ABM.LTag}(\mathsf{ABM.tk},\cdot)}(1^\lambda, \mathsf{ABM.ek}) = 1\right]$$

In **Game** 2, we change the way of generating public matrix $\mathbf{A}$. Particularly, we sample $\mathbf{A}$ from $\mathbb{Z}_q^{n\times\bar{m}}$ uniformly at random. Because $\mathbf{A}$ does not affect the output distribution of $\mathsf{ABM.LTag}$, by the LWE assumption, this change is not noticeable to $\mathcal{A}$, lest it give an LWE distinguisher. So we have

$$|\Pr[S_2] - \Pr[S_1]| \le \mathsf{Adv}_{\mathsf{NF},\mathcal{A}_1}^{\mathsf{LWE}_{n_1,n-n_1,q,\chi}}(\lambda)$$

for a suitable $\mathsf{LWE}_{n_1,q,\chi}$ adversary $\mathcal{A}_1$.

In **Game** 3, the public evaluation key of the ABM-LTF is set as

$$\mathsf{ABM.ek} = \left(\mathsf{WPRF}, C_{\mathsf{WPRF}}, \mathbf{A}, \{\mathbf{C}_{k_{i,j}}\}_{i\in[h],j\in[t]}, \{\mathbf{C}_{s_i}\}_{i\in[t']}, \{\hat{\mathbf{C}}_{\mathbf{H}_i}\}_{i\in[h]}, \hat{\mathbf{C}}_{\mathbf{Z}}, \mathsf{Hk}\right)$$

where $\{\mathbf{C}_{k_{i,j}}\}_{i\in[h],j\in[t]}$, $\{\mathbf{C}_{s_i}\}_{i\in[t']}$, $\{\hat{\mathbf{C}}_{\mathbf{H}_i}\}_{i\in[h]}$, and $\hat{\mathbf{C}}_{\mathbf{Z}}$ are chosen uniformly random from $\mathbb{Z}_q^{n\times 2nw}$. Accordingly, the low-norm secret matrices in $\mathsf{ABM.ik}$, which include $\{\mathbf{R}_{k_{i,j}}\}_{i\in[h],j\in[t]}$, $\{\mathbf{R}_{s_i}\}_{i\in[t']}$, $\{\mathbf{R}_{\mathbf{H}_i}\}_{i\in[h]}$, and $\mathbf{R}_{\mathbf{Z}}$ are no longer needed. It is easy to see that this change does not affect the (output distribution of) algorithm $\mathsf{ABM.LTag}$. Moreover, by Lemma 5, $\mathsf{ABM.ek}$ in **Game** 3 has a distribution that is statistically close to the distribution of $\mathsf{ABM.ek}$ in **Game** 2. So for some negligibly small statistical error $\mathsf{negl}(\lambda)$, we have

$$|\Pr[S_3] - \Pr[S_2]| \le \mathsf{negl}(\lambda)$$

In **Game** 4, we change the algorithm $\mathsf{ABM.LTag}$. Specifically, in step 2 of $\mathsf{ABM.LTag}$, we compute $\mathsf{r}_i(\mathsf{UH}_{\mathbf{s}}(\mu))$ with random functions $\mathsf{r}_i : \{0,1\}^\ell \to \{0,1\}$ instead of $\mathsf{WPRF}(\mathbf{k}_i, \mathsf{UH}_{\mathbf{s}}(\mu))$ for $i \in [h]$. (Note this does not affect $\mathsf{ABM.Eval}$ which still uses C_{WPRF}.) As μ is uniformly random, for a PPT adversary $\mathcal{A}_2$ against WPRF, a straightforward hybrid argument shows that

$$|\Pr[S_4] - \Pr[S_3]| \le h \cdot \mathsf{Adv}_{\mathcal{A}_2}^{\mathsf{WPRF}}(\lambda)$$

In **Game** 5, we randomly sample a matrix $\mathbf{S} \xleftarrow{\$} \mathbb{Z}_q^{n\times 2n}$ instead of computing $\mathbf{S} = \sum_{i=1}^{h} \mathsf{r}_i(\mathsf{UH}_{\mathbf{s}}(\mu))\, \mathbf{H}_i \bmod q$ as in **Game** 4. By Corollary 1 with $h \ge \log(q/(\epsilon^2))$, the statistical distance between the distribution of the random variable $\sum_{i=1}^{h} \mathsf{r}_i(\mathsf{UH}_{\mathbf{s}}(\mu)) \cdot \mathbf{H}_i \bmod q$ and the uniform distribution over $\mathbb{Z}_q^{n\times 2n}$ is less than ϵ. Hence, we have

$$|\Pr[S_5] - \Pr[S_4]| \le \epsilon$$

On the other hand, in **Game** 5, $\mathbf{H} = \mathbf{ZD} - \mathbf{S} \bmod q$ with random $\mathbf{S}$. Thus the pair $(\mathbf{D}, R)$ is independent of $\mathbf{H}$. Therefore all tags generated in **Game** 5 are random tags. So we have

$$\Pr[S_5] = \Pr\left[\mathcal{A}^{\mathcal{O}_{\mathcal{T}}(\cdot)}(1^\lambda, \mathsf{ABM.ek}) = 1\right]$$

Summing up, we find that adversary $\mathcal{A}$'s advantage $\mathsf{Adv}^{\mathsf{ind}}_{\mathsf{ABM\text{-}LTF},\mathcal{A}}(\lambda)$ is

$$\left|\Pr\left[\mathcal{A}^{\mathsf{ABM.LTag(ABM.tk,\cdot)}}(1^\lambda, \mathsf{ABM.ek}) = 1\right] - \Pr\left[\mathcal{A}^{\mathcal{O}_{\mathcal{T}}(\cdot)}(1^\lambda, \mathsf{ABM.ek}) = 1\right]\right|$$
$$\leq \mathsf{Adv}^{\mathsf{LWE}_{n_1,n-n_1,q,\chi}}_{\mathsf{NF},\mathcal{A}_1}(\lambda) + h \cdot \mathsf{Adv}^{\mathsf{WPRF}}_{\mathcal{A}_2}(\lambda) + \mathsf{negl}(\lambda) + \epsilon \quad (5)$$

which completes the proof. □

Theorem 4 (Evasiveness). *For any PPT adversary $\mathcal{A}$ against the evasiveness of the above ABM-LTF with advantage $Adv^{eva}_{ABM\text{-}LTF,\mathcal{A}}(\lambda)$, there exist $\mathcal{A}_1$, $\mathcal{A}_2$, $\mathcal{A}_3$ and a negligible function $negl(\lambda)$ such that*

$$Adv^{eva}_{ABM\text{-}LTF,\mathcal{A}}(\lambda) \leq Adv^{LWE_{n_1,n-n_1,q,\chi}}_{NF,\mathcal{A}_1}(\lambda) + h \cdot Adv^{WPRF}_{\mathcal{A}_2}(\lambda) + Adv^{coll}_{CH,\mathcal{A}_3}(\lambda) + \epsilon + negl(\lambda)$$

Proof. We prove the theorem using a game sequence. Let S_i be the event that $\mathcal{A}$ outputs a lossy or invalid tag in **Game** i. We further consider two types of (lossy or invalid) tag output by $\mathcal{A}$. We say that a tag $\mathsf{tag} = ((\mathbf{D}^*, R^*), \mathbf{t}^*_{\mathsf{a}})$ has Type I if μ^*, which is equal to $\mathsf{CH.Eval}(\mathsf{Hk}, (\mathbf{D}^*, \mathbf{t}^*_{\mathsf{a}}); R^*)$, is also the chameleon hash output of some previously generated tag. A tag $\mathsf{tag} = ((\mathbf{D}^*, R^*), \mathbf{t}^*_{\mathsf{a}})$ has Type II if $\mu^* = \mathsf{CH.Eval}(\mathsf{Hk}, (\mathbf{D}^*, \mathbf{t}^*_{\mathsf{a}}); R^*)$ is not the chameleon hash output of any previously generated tag. W.l.o.g., we assume that the adversary gets $N = \mathsf{poly}(\lambda)$ lossy tags $\{\mathsf{tag}_i\}_{i\in[N]} = \{(\mathbf{D}_i, R_i), \mathbf{t}_{\mathsf{a}i}\}_{i\in[N]}$ generated by the lossy tag generation oracle. Then the adversary adaptively comes up with $N' = \mathsf{poly}(\lambda)$ tags $\{\mathsf{tag}^*_i\}_{i\in[N']} = \{(\mathbf{D}^*_i, R^*_i), \mathbf{t}_{\mathsf{a}i}{}^*\}_{i\in[N']}$ and gets answers "lossy/invalid" or "injective" from the oracle $\mathcal{O}$ indicating whether theses tags are lossy/invalid or injective.

In **Game** 1, $\mathcal{A}$ interacts with $\mathsf{ABM.LTag(ABM.tk,\cdot)}$ which works exactly as in the real system. By hypothesis, we have

$$\mathsf{Adv}^{\mathsf{eva}}_{\mathsf{ABM\text{-}LTF},\mathcal{A}}(\lambda) = \Pr[S_1]$$

In **Game** 2, we sample the public matrix $\mathbf{A}$ randomly from $\mathbb{Z}_q^{n\times\bar{m}}$. This does not affect the output distribution of $\mathsf{ABM.LTag}$. By the LWE assumption, the change is not noticeable to $\mathcal{A}$; if it is, there is an LWE distinguisher. So we have

$$|\Pr[S_2] - \Pr[S_1]| \leq \mathsf{Adv}^{\mathsf{LWE}_{n_1,n-n_1,q,\chi}}_{\mathsf{NF},\mathcal{A}_1}(\lambda)$$

for a suitable LWE adversary $\mathcal{A}_1$.

In **Game** 3, the public evaluation ABM-LTFs is set as

$$\mathsf{ABM.ek} = \left(\mathsf{WPRF}, C_{\mathsf{WPRF}}, \mathbf{A}, \{\mathbf{C}_{k_{i,j}}\}_{i\in[h],j\in[t]}, \{\mathbf{C}_{s_i}\}_{i\in[t']}, \{\hat{\mathbf{C}}_{\mathbf{H}_i}\}_{i\in[h]}, \hat{\mathbf{C}}_{\mathbf{Z}}, \mathsf{Hk}\right)$$

where $\{\mathbf{C}_{k_{i,j}}\}_{i\in[h],j\in[t]}$, $\{\mathbf{C}_{s_i}\}_{i\in[t']}$, $\{\hat{\mathbf{C}}_{\mathbf{H}_i}\}_{i\in[h]}$, and $\hat{\mathbf{C}}_{\mathbf{Z}}$ are chosen uniformly random from $\mathbb{Z}_q^{n\times 2nw}$. Accordingly, the low-norm secret matrices in $\mathsf{ABM.ik}$, including $\{\mathbf{R}_{k_{i,j}}\}_{i\in[h],j\in[t]}$, $\{\mathbf{R}_{s_i}\}_{i\in[t']}$, $\{\mathbf{R}_{\mathbf{H}_i}\}_{i\in[h]}$, $\mathbf{R}_{\mathbf{Z}}$, are not needed anymore. It is easy to see that this change does not affect the (output distribution of) algorithm $\mathsf{ABM.LTag}$. Moreover, by Lemma 5, $\mathsf{ABM.ek}$ in **Game** 3 has a distribution that is statistically close to the distribution of $\mathsf{ABM.ek}$ in **Game** 2. So for some negligibly small statistical error $\mathsf{negl}_1(\lambda)$, we have

$$|\Pr[S_3] - \Pr[S_2]| \leq \mathsf{negl}_1(\lambda)$$

In **Game** 4, we make the following changes. In step 2 of $\mathsf{ABM.LTag}$, for any μ, instead of computing $\mathbf{S} = \sum_{i=1}^{h} \mathsf{WPRF}(\mathbf{k}_i, \mathsf{UH}_\mathbf{s}(\mu))\mathbf{H}_i \bmod q$, we sample $\mathbf{S} \xleftarrow{\$} \mathbb{Z}_q^{n\times 2n}$. For all queries $\{\mathsf{tag}_i^*\}_{i\in[N']}$ to $\mathcal{O}$, we return the answer "injective".

We prove by induction that distinguishing between this game and the previous one implies a distinguisher for the WPRF. Notice that since the μ_i for all the issued lossy tags are random according to $\mathsf{ABM.LTag}$, their images $\mathsf{UH}_\mathbf{s}(\mu_i)$ are also random.

For the base step, suppose $N' = 1$ (the case $N' = 0$ is vacuous). In **Game** 3, $\mathcal{O}$ answers honestly by computing $\mathbf{H} = \mathbf{ZD} - \sum_{i=1}^{h} \mathsf{WPRF}(\mathbf{k}_i, \mathsf{UH}_\mathbf{s}(\mu_1^*))\,\mathbf{H}_i \bmod q$. Since $\mathsf{UH}_\mathbf{s}(\mu_1^*)$ is random and jointly random with all independently sampled $\mathsf{UH}_\mathbf{s}(\mu_i)$, by Corollary 1 and the security of WPRF, the **Game**-3 distribution $\{\sum_{j=1}^{h} \mathsf{WPRF}(\mathbf{K}_j, \mathsf{UH}_\mathbf{s}(\mu_i))\mathbf{H}_{i}j\}_{i\in[N]} \cup \{\sum_{j=1}^{h} \mathsf{WPRF}(\mathbf{K}_j, \mathsf{UH}_\mathbf{s}(\mu_1^*))\mathbf{H}_j\}$ and the **Game**-4 distribution $\{\mathbf{S}_i \xleftarrow{\$} \mathbb{Z}_q^{n\times 2n}\}_{i\in[N]} \cup \{\mathbf{S} \xleftarrow{\$} \mathbb{Z}_q^{n\times 2n}\}$ are computationally distinguishable with probability at most $h\cdot \mathsf{Adv}_{\mathcal{A}_2}^{\mathsf{WPRF}}(\lambda) + \epsilon$ for a suitable WPRF adversary $\mathcal{A}_2$. Moreover, since for μ_1^* from tag_1^* in **Game** 4 the matrix $\mathbf{S}$ is random, so is $\mathbf{H}$, the adversary always gets the answer "injective" except with negligible probability ε. This shows that $|\Pr[S_4] - \Pr[S_3]| \leq h\cdot \mathsf{Adv}_{\mathcal{A}_2}^{\mathsf{WPRF}}(\lambda) + \epsilon + N'\cdot\varepsilon$ when $N' = 1$.

For the inductive step, assume that the above holds for $k = N' - 1 \geq 1$. Accordingly, in **Game** 4, for tags $\{\mathsf{tag}_i^*\}_{i\in[k]}$, we simply answer "injective" without even looking at the query μ_i^*; we look at the N'-th query tag tag_{k+1}^*. In **Game** 3, we honestly derived the same "injective" answers for the first k guesses, and the last answer is computed as $\mathbf{H} = \mathbf{ZD} - \sum_{i=1}^{h} \mathsf{WPRF}(\mathbf{k}_i, \mathsf{UH}_\mathbf{s}(\mu_{k+1}^*))\,\mathbf{H}_i \bmod q$. Since WPRF in **Game** 4 is only evaluated on $\{\mathsf{UH}_\mathbf{s}(\mu_i)\}_{i\in[N]} \cup \{\mathsf{UH}_\mathbf{s}(\mu_{k+1}^*)\}$ which by construction is jointly uniformly random, and since in **Game** 3 by inductive hypothesis the answers were all "injective", the inductive hypothesis continues to hold, and we have $|\Pr[S_4] - \Pr[S_3]| \leq h\cdot\mathsf{Adv}_{\mathcal{A}_2}^{\mathsf{WPRF}}(\lambda) + \epsilon + k\cdot\varepsilon + \varepsilon$. Therefore we have for all $N' = \mathsf{poly}(\lambda)$, and taking $N'\cdot\varepsilon = \mathsf{negl}_2(\lambda)$,

$$|\Pr[S_4] - \Pr[S_3]| \leq h\cdot \mathsf{Adv}_{\mathcal{A}_2}^{\mathsf{WPRF}}(\lambda) + \epsilon + \mathsf{negl}_2(\lambda)$$

Notice that $\{\mathsf{tag}_i\}_{i\in[N]}$ generated in **Game** 4 are distributed as random tags.

In **Game** 5, the trapdoor Td of the chameleon hash function is not available. All primary tags are generated randomly, i.e., $(\mathbf{D}, R) \xleftarrow{\$} \mathbb{Z}_q^{2n\times 2n} \times \mathcal{R}_{\mathsf{CH}}$. Hence,

$$\Pr[S_5] = \Pr[S_4]$$

Moreover, for any fresh μ that was not derived from previous queries, $\mathbf{S} \in \mathbb{Z}_q^{n\times 2n}$ will be chosen randomly and independently. In other words, there does not exist an adversary that outputs Type II tags with more than some negligible probability $\mathsf{negl}_2(\lambda)$. So we have $\Pr[S_{5,\mathsf{II}}] \leq \mathsf{negl}_3(\lambda)$. Any Type I output breaches the collision-resistance of the chameleon hash function, therefore $\Pr[S_{5,\mathsf{I}}] \leq \mathsf{Adv}^{\mathsf{coll}}_{\mathsf{CH},\mathcal{A}_3}(\lambda)$ for some adversary $\mathcal{A}_3$. Since $\Pr[S_5] \leq \Pr[S_{5,\mathsf{I}}] + \Pr[S_{5,\mathsf{II}}]$, we obtain

$$\Pr[S_5] \leq \mathsf{negl}_3(\lambda) + \mathsf{Adv}^{\mathsf{coll}}_{\mathsf{CH},\mathcal{A}_3}(\lambda)$$

To sum up, letting $\mathsf{negl}(\lambda) = \mathsf{negl}_1(\lambda) + \mathsf{negl}_2(\lambda) + \mathsf{negl}_3(\lambda) + \epsilon$, we have

$$\begin{aligned}\mathsf{Adv}^{\mathsf{eva}}_{\mathsf{ABM\text{-}LTF},\mathcal{A}}(\lambda) \leq \mathsf{Adv}^{\mathsf{LWE}_{n_1,n-n_1,q,\chi}}_{\mathsf{NF},\mathcal{A}_1}(\lambda) + h \cdot \mathsf{Adv}^{\mathsf{WPRF}}_{\mathcal{A}_2}(\lambda) \\ + \mathsf{Adv}^{\mathsf{coll}}_{\mathsf{CH},\mathcal{A}_3}(\lambda) + \mathsf{negl}(\lambda)\end{aligned} \tag{6}$$

This concludes the proof. □

5 IND-SO-CCA2 Secure PKE from Lattices

Using the constructions from [27,29] as a guide, we build the first LWE-based IND-SO-CCA2-secure public-key encryption scheme with our LWE-based ABM-LTF. In our construction, we take the advantage of the chameleon hash function embedded in our ABM-LTF. Our apprach also draws the idea from [42] in which transformations from tag-based PKE schemes to IND-CCA2 PKE schemes are proposed with the help of chameleon hashing.

5.1 Definition of IND-SO-CCA2 Security

A public-key encryption scheme Π consists of three PPT algorithms: KeyGen, Encrypt and Decrypt. $\mathsf{KeyGen}(1^\lambda)$ takes as input a security parameter λ, outputs a public key pk and a private key sk. We define the message space $\mathcal{M}_\lambda$, randomness space $\mathcal{R}_\lambda$ and the ciphertext space $\mathcal{C}_\lambda$ in the obvious way. $\mathsf{Encrypt}(\mathsf{pk}, \mathsf{m}; r)$ encrypts a message $\mathsf{m} \in \mathcal{M}_\lambda$ using pk and randomness $r \xleftarrow{\$} \mathcal{R}_\lambda$, and outputs a ciphertext ct. $\mathsf{Decrypt}(\mathsf{sk}, \mathsf{ct})$ recovers the message m from ct using sk. The correctness of a PKE scheme requires that for all $\mathsf{m} \in \mathcal{M}_\lambda$, valid randomness $r \in \mathcal{R}_\lambda$, and $(\mathsf{pk}, \mathsf{sk}) \leftarrow \mathsf{KeyGen}(1^\lambda)$,

$$\Pr\left[\mathsf{m} = \mathsf{Decrypt}\left(\mathsf{sk}, \mathsf{Encrypt}(\mathsf{pk}, \mathsf{m}; r)\right)\right] \geq 1 - \mathsf{negl}(\lambda)$$

for some negligible function $\mathsf{negl}(\lambda)$.

Selective Opening Security. Suppose that a vector of messages, coming from some joint distribution dist, has been encrypted into a vector of ciphertexts, and sent out. A “selective opening” attack allows an adversary to choose a subset of these ciphertexts and have them “opened”, revealing their messages and the random coins used during encryption.

The opened messages, random coins, and distribution dist might help the adversary to learn information about the remaining messages, in the unopend ciphertexts. Selective opening security means that the content of the unopend ciphertexts remains secure in that scenario.

There are a few different ways of formalising selective opening security. As in [29], we are considering the indistinguishability-based definition of security against chosen-ciphertext attacks (referred to as IND-SO-CCA2) with respect to joint message distributions that are efficiently re-sampleable.

Definition 4. (Efficient Resampling). *Let $N = N(\lambda) > 0$, let $\mathcal{M}_\lambda$ be the message space, and let dist be a joint distribution over $\mathcal{M}_\lambda^N$. We say that dist is efficiently re-samplable if there is a PPT algorithm $\mathsf{ResSamp}$ such that for any $\mathcal{I} \subset [N]$ and any partial vector $(\mathsf{m}'^{(i)})_{i \in \mathcal{I}} \in \mathcal{M}_\lambda^{|\mathcal{I}|}$, ReSamp samples from the distribution dist, conditioned on $\mathsf{m}^{(i)} = \mathsf{m}'^{(i)}$ for all $i \in \mathcal{I}$.*

The IND-SO-CCA2 security essentially requires that no efficient adversary can distinguish the unopened messages from fresh messages drawn from the same joint distribution conditioned on the opened messages.

Definition 5. (IND-SO-CCA2 Security). *A public-key encryption scheme $\Pi = (\mathsf{KeyGen}, \mathsf{Encrypt}, \mathsf{Decrypt})$ has IND-SO-CCA2 security iff for every polynomial $N = N(\lambda)$, and every PPT adversary $\mathcal{A}$, we have that*

$$\mathsf{Adv}_{\Pi,\mathcal{A}}^{\text{ind-so-cca}}(\lambda) = \left| \Pr\left[\mathsf{Exp}_{\Pi,\mathcal{A}}^{\text{ind-so-cca-b}}(\lambda) = 1 \right] - 1/2 \right|$$

is negligible, where the experiment $\mathsf{Exp}_{\Pi,\mathcal{A}}^{\text{ind-so-cca-b}}(\lambda)$ is defined in Fig. 1.

The adversary $\mathcal{A}$ is required to output the resampling algorithm ReSamp as per Fig. 1, and never to submit any challenge ciphertext $\mathsf{ct}^{(i)}$ to the decryption oracle $\mathsf{Decrypt}(\mathsf{sk}, \cdot)$.

Experiment $\mathsf{Exp}_{\Pi,\mathcal{A}}^{\text{ind-so-cca-b}}(\lambda)$

1. $b \xleftarrow{\$} \{0,1\}$
2. $(\mathsf{pk}, \mathsf{sk}) \leftarrow \mathsf{KeyGen}(1^\lambda)$
3. $(\mathsf{dist}, \mathsf{ReSamp}) \leftarrow \mathcal{A}^{\mathsf{Decrypt}(\mathsf{sk},\cdot)}(\mathsf{pk})$
4. $\mathbf{m}_0 = (\mathsf{m}^{(i)})_{i \in [N]} \leftarrow \mathsf{dist}$
5. $\mathbf{r} = (r^{(i)})_{i \in [N]} \leftarrow (\mathcal{M}_\lambda)^N$
6. $\mathbf{c} = \left(\mathsf{ct}^{(i)}\right)_{i \in [N]} = \left(\mathsf{Encrypt}(\mathsf{pk}, \mathsf{m}^{(i)}; r^{(i)})\right)_{i \in [N]}$
7. $\mathcal{I} \leftarrow \mathcal{A}^{\mathsf{Decrypt}(\mathsf{sk},\cdot)}(\mathsf{pk}, \mathbf{c})$
8. $\mathbf{m}_1 = \mathsf{ReSamp}(\mathsf{dist}, \mathbf{m}_\mathcal{I})$
9. $b' \leftarrow \mathcal{A}^{\mathsf{Decrypt}(\mathsf{sk},\cdot)}\left(\mathbf{m}_b, \{\mathsf{m}^{(i)}, r^{(i)}\}_{i \in \mathcal{I}}\right)$
10. Return 1 if $b' = b$, and 0 otherwise

Fig. 1. Security experiment of IND-SO-CCA2 security

5.2 Construction of IND-SO-CCA2 PKE

Let λ be the security parameter and $\kappa = \omega(\log \lambda)$. Let $\mathsf{ABM\text{-}LTF} = (\mathsf{ABM.Gen}, \mathsf{ABM.Eval}, \mathsf{ABM.Inv})$ be an l-lossy ABM-LTF with domain $\mathsf{D} = I_\beta^{m+n_1} \times I_\gamma^{n-n_1}$ as constructed before. Assume $\mathsf{X} = I_\beta^{n_1} \times I_\gamma^{n-n_1}$. Let $\mathsf{LTF} = (\mathsf{LTF.Gen}, \mathsf{LTF.Eval}, \mathsf{LTF.Inv})$ be an l'-lossy LTF with domain D. Without loss of generality, we assume $l \geq l'$. Let $\mathcal{UH}$ be a family of universal hash functions from $\mathsf{D} \times I_\beta^m \rightarrow \{0,1\}^\tau$ with $\tau \leq (l + l' - \log|\mathsf{X}| - 2\lambda) - 2\log(1/\epsilon)$ for some negligible $\epsilon = \mathsf{negl}(\lambda)$[7]. Let $B = \Theta(b \cdot s_1(\mathbf{R}))$ as in Lemma 7. The message space is $\{0,1\}^\tau$. The PKE scheme $\Pi = (\mathsf{KeyGen}, \mathsf{Encrypt}, \mathsf{Decrypt})$ is as follows.

- $\mathsf{KeyGen}(1^\lambda)$ The key generation algorithm does:
  1. Run $(\mathsf{ABM.ek}, \mathsf{ABM.ik}, \mathsf{ABM.tk}) \leftarrow \mathsf{ABM.Gen}(1^\lambda)$.
  2. Run $(\mathsf{LTF.ek}, \mathsf{LTF.ik}) \leftarrow \mathsf{LTF.Gen}(1^\lambda, \mathsf{inj})$.
  3. Set the public key $\mathsf{pk} = (\mathsf{LTF.ek}, \mathsf{ABM.ek})$ and private key $\mathsf{sk} = (\mathsf{LTF.ik}, \mathsf{ABM.ik})$.
- $\mathsf{Encrypt}(\mathsf{pk}, \mathsf{m}; r)$ To encrypt $\mathsf{m} \in \{0,1\}^\tau$, the encryption algorithm does:
  1. Randomly select $\mathbf{e}_1, \mathbf{e}_2 \xleftarrow{\$} I_\beta^m$, $\mathbf{x} \xleftarrow{\$} I_\beta^{n_1} \times I_\gamma^{n-n_1}$; Set $\mathbf{x}_1^t = [\mathbf{e}_1^t|\mathbf{x}^t]$, $\mathbf{x}_2^t = [\mathbf{e}_2^t|\mathbf{x}^t] \in \mathsf{D}$.
  2. Randomly select a universal hash function $\mathsf{UH}_\mathbf{k} \xleftarrow{\$} \mathcal{UH}$.[8]
  3. Compute $\mathbf{y}_1 = \mathsf{LTF.Eval}(\mathsf{LTF.ek}, \mathbf{x}_1)$ and $\rho = \mathsf{UH}_\mathbf{k}(\mathbf{x}, \mathbf{e}_1, \mathbf{e}_2) \oplus \mathsf{m}$.
  4. Set $\mathsf{tag} = (\mathbf{t}_\mathsf{p}, \mathbf{t}_\mathsf{a})$ for randomly sampled $\mathbf{t}_\mathsf{p} = (\mathbf{D}, R)$ and $\mathbf{t}_\mathsf{a} = (\mathsf{UH}_\mathbf{k}, \rho, \mathbf{x}_2)$, then compute $\mu = \mathsf{CH.Eval}(\mathsf{Hk}, (\mathbf{D}, \mathbf{t}_\mathsf{a}, \mathbf{y}_1); R)$.
  5. Use μ as the input of the step 2 of the algorithm $\mathsf{ABM.Eval}$, and compute the output of ABM-LTF: $\mathbf{y}_2 = \mathsf{ABM.Eval}(\mathsf{ABM.ek}, \mathsf{tag}, \mathbf{x}_2)$.
  6. Set the ciphertext $\mathsf{ct} = (\mathbf{y}_1, \mathbf{y}_2, \mathbf{t}_\mathsf{p}, \mathsf{UH}_\mathbf{k}, \rho, \mu)$.

  Note the randomness of this encryption $r = \mathsf{tag}$ where all elements in tag are public except $\mathbf{x}_2$.
- $\mathsf{Decrypt}(\mathsf{sk}, \mathsf{ct})$ The decryption algorithm does:
  1. Parse the ciphertext as $\mathsf{ct} = (\mathbf{y}_1, \mathbf{y}_2, \mathbf{t}_\mathsf{p}, \mathsf{UH}_\mathbf{k}, \rho, \mu)$.
  2. Run $\mathsf{LTF.Inv}(\mathsf{LTF.ik}, \mathbf{y}_1)$ to get $\mathbf{x}_1^t = [\mathbf{e}_1^t|\mathbf{x}^t]$; Reject if $\|\mathbf{e}_1\| > B$.
  3. Let $\mathbf{F}$ be the matrix derived at the step 2 of $\mathsf{ABM.Inv}$. Compute $\mathbf{e}_2^t = \mathbf{y}_2^t - \mathbf{x}^t\mathbf{F}$; Reject if $\|\mathbf{e}_2\| > B$; Otherwise, go to the next step.
  4. Compute $\mu' = \mathsf{CH.Eval}(\mathsf{Hk}, (\mathbf{D}, \mathbf{t}_\mathsf{a}, \mathbf{y}_1); R)$ where $\mathbf{t}_\mathsf{a} = (\mathsf{UH}_\mathbf{k}, \rho, \mathbf{x}_2)$; if $\mu' \neq \mu$, reject; Otherwise go to the next step.
  5. Output the message $\mathsf{m} = \rho \oplus \mathsf{UH}_\mathbf{k}(\mathbf{x}, \mathbf{e}_1, \mathbf{e}_2)$.

The correctness of decryption algorithm can be easily checked.

[7] We can satisfy this condition with large enough l, l' from the LTF and our ABM-LTF.

[8] Note the family of universal hash functions is used for masking the message and not the one used in the construction of ABM-LTF.

5.3 Security Proof

Theorem 5. *Suppose that the ABM-LTF specified above is secure. Then the PKE scheme $\Pi = (\mathsf{KeyGen}, \mathsf{Encrypt}, \mathsf{Decrypt})$ is IND-SO-CCA2 secure. In particular, for every PPT adversary $\mathcal{A}$ against Π with advantage $\mathsf{Adv}^{\text{ind-so-cca}}_{\Pi,\mathcal{A}}(\lambda)$, there exist PPT adversaries $\mathcal{B}_1$, $\mathcal{B}_2$ and $\mathcal{B}_3$ such that $\mathsf{Adv}^{\text{ind-so-cca}}_{\Pi,\mathcal{A}}(\lambda)$*

$$\leq \mathsf{Adv}^{coll}_{CH,\mathcal{B}_1}(\lambda) + \mathsf{Adv}^{ind}_{ABM\text{-}LTF,\mathcal{B}_2}(\lambda) + \mathsf{Adv}^{eva}_{ABM\text{-}LTF,\mathcal{B}_3}(\lambda) + \mathsf{Adv}^{ind}_{LTF,\mathcal{B}_4}(\lambda) + negl(\lambda)$$

for the same chameleon hash function CH used in the construction of ABM-LTF, where $\mathsf{Adv}^{coll}_{CH,\mathcal{B}_1}(\lambda)$ is the advantage of $\mathcal{B}_1$ against CH that is used in ABM-LTF.

Proof. Recall that in the IND-SO-CCA2 security game (Fig. 1), we have N challenge ciphertexts. We denote the i-th challenge ciphertext by

$$\mathsf{ct}^{(i)} = (\mathbf{y}_1^{(i)}, \mathbf{y}_2^{(i)}, \mathbf{t}_\mathsf{p}^{(i)}, \mathsf{UH}_{\mathbf{k}^{(i)}}, \rho^{(i)}, \mu^{(i)})$$

where $\mathbf{t}_\mathsf{p}^{(i)} = (\mathbf{D}^{(i)}, R^{(i)})$. Also recall $\mathbf{t}_\mathsf{a} = (\mathsf{UH}_\mathbf{k}, \rho, \mathbf{x}_2)$ for some $\mathbf{x}_2^t = [\mathbf{e}_2^t|\mathbf{x}^t]$. And $\mathbf{x}_2$ is applied to $\mathsf{ABM.Eval}$ with tag $= (\mathbf{t}_\mathsf{p}, \mathbf{t}_\mathsf{a}, \mu)$ to generate $\mathbf{y}_2$.

We prove the theorem through a game sequence. Let S_i be the event that $\mathcal{A}$ outputs 1 in **Game** i. The first game **Game** 1 is the same as the experiment $\mathsf{Exp}^{\text{ind-so-cca-b}}_{\Pi,\mathcal{A}}(\lambda)$. By definition we have

$$|\Pr[S_1] - 1/2| = \mathsf{Adv}^{\text{ind-so-cca}}_{\Pi,\mathcal{A}}(\lambda).$$

In **Game** 2, we reject all the decryption queries in which the component μ has already appeared in one of the challenge ciphertexts. If the adversary makes a decryption query on ciphertext $\mathsf{ct} = (\mathbf{y}_1, \mathbf{y}_2, \mathbf{t}_\mathsf{p} = (\mathbf{D}, R), \mathsf{UH}_\mathbf{k}, \rho, \mu^{(i)})$ where $\mu^{(i)}$ is from some $\mathsf{ct}^{(i)} = (\mathbf{y}_1{}^{(i)}, \mathbf{y}_2^{(i)}, \mathbf{t}_\mathsf{p}^{(i)}, \mathsf{UH}_{\mathbf{k}^{(i)}}, \rho^{(i)}, \mu^{(i)})$, we argue that such query will be rejected unless the collision resistant property of the chameleon hash function is broken. Notice that R is the randomness, $\mathbf{y}_2$ is the only ciphertext component that is *not* a part of the message of the chameleon hash function. Let $\mathbf{t}_\mathsf{a} = (\mathsf{UH}_\mathbf{k}, \rho, \mathbf{x}_2)$ and $\mathbf{t}_\mathsf{a}^{(i)} = (\mathsf{UH}_{\mathbf{k}^{(i)}}, \rho^{(i)}, \mathbf{x}_2^{(i)})$. There are three cases:

- If $\mathbf{y}_2 = \mathbf{y}_2^{(i)}$ and$(\mathbf{t}_\mathsf{p}, \mathsf{UH}, \rho) = (\mathbf{t}_\mathsf{p}^{(i)}, \mathsf{UH}_{\mathbf{k}^{(i)}}, \rho^{(i)})$: In this case the query is exactly the i-th challenge ciphertext which is invalid.
- If $\mathbf{y}_2 = \mathbf{y}_2^{(i)}$ and $(\mathbf{t}_\mathsf{p}, \mathsf{UH}, \rho) \neq (\mathbf{t}_\mathsf{p}^{(i)}, \mathsf{UH}_{\mathbf{k}^{(i)}}, \rho^{(i)})$: The decryption algorithm will output $\mathbf{x}_2$ in the step 3 (when the ciphertext passes through all test up to step 3) and recompute μ'. We would have $\mu \neq \mu$, thus reject the query, unless $\mathsf{CH.Eval}(\mathsf{Hk}, (\mathbf{D}, \mathbf{t}_\mathsf{a}, \mathbf{y}_1); R) = \mathsf{CH.Eval}(\mathsf{Hk}, (\mathbf{D}^{(i)}, \mathbf{t}_\mathsf{a}^{(i)}, \mathbf{y}_1^{(i)}); R^{(i)})$, which corresponds to a collision to the chameleon hash function.
- If $\mathbf{y}_2 \neq \mathbf{y}_2^{(i)}$: Recall that $\mu = \mu^{(i)}$ is derived from an injective tag. If the query makes decryption algorithm output $\mathbf{x}_2$ at step 3, we must have $\mathbf{x}_2 \neq \mathbf{x}_2^{(i)}$ and, thus, $\mathbf{t}_\mathsf{a} \neq \mathbf{t}_\mathsf{a}^{(i)}$. Then the query will be reject at step 4 unless an explicit collision, $((\mathbf{D}, \mathbf{t}_\mathsf{a}, \mathbf{y}_1); R)$ and $(\mathbf{D}^{(i)}, \mathbf{t}_\mathsf{a}^{(i)}, \mathbf{y}_1^{(i)}); R^{(i)})$, happens to the chameleon hash function.

So **Game** 2 and **Game** 1 behave the same unless the collision resistancy of the chameleon hashing is broken. Thus we have

$$|\Pr[S_2] - \Pr[S_1]| \leq \mathsf{Adv}^{\mathsf{coll}}_{\mathsf{CH},\mathcal{B}_1}(\lambda)$$

for some suitable adversary $\mathcal{B}_1$.

In **Game** 3, lossy tags are generated using $\mathsf{ABM.LTag}$ for all challenge ciphertexts, i.e., $\mathsf{ct}^{(i)}$ for $i \in [N]$. Notice that here we allow the decryption queries made with lossy tags in which $\mu \neq \mu^{(i)}$. (Of course it is computationally hard to come up with such queries by the evasiveness of ABM-LTF, which we have not used yet.) This is because the decryption algorithm in **Game** 3 does not use ABM-LTF to invert to get $\mathbf{x}$. Instead, $\mathbf{x}$ is recovered by LTF from $\mathbf{y}_1$ and then $\mathbf{e}_2$ can be uniquely recovered from $\mathbf{x}$ and $\mathbf{y}_2$. By tag indistinguishability of the ABM-LTF,

$$|\Pr[S_3] - \Pr[S_2]| \leq \mathsf{Adv}^{\mathsf{ind}}_{\mathsf{ABM\text{-}LTF},\mathcal{B}_2}(\lambda)$$

for some suitable adversary $\mathcal{B}_2$.

Recall that in **Game** 3, we use LTF to invert $\mathbf{y}_1$ to get $\mathbf{x}_1^t = [\mathbf{e}_1^t|\mathbf{x}^t]$ and use $\mathbf{y}_2$ and $\mathbf{x}$ to recover $\mathbf{e}_2$ and, thus $\mathbf{x}_2$. In **Game** 4, we directly use $\mathsf{ABM.ik}$ to invert $\mathbf{y}_2$ and get $\mathbf{x}_2$. By our correctness of LTF and ABM-LTF, this gives the same result unless μ in the decryption query is from one of the challenge ciphertexts, or the queries are made with lossy or invalid tags. The first case is already excluded in **Game** 3. The latter case would not happen under the evasiveness of ABM-LTF. So we have

$$|\Pr[S_4] - \Pr[S_3]| \leq \mathsf{Adv}^{\mathsf{eva}}_{\mathsf{ABM\text{-}LTF},\mathcal{B}_3}(\lambda)$$

for some suitable adversary $\mathcal{B}_3$.

In **Game** 5, we generate a lossy evaluation key for LTF. We have

$$|\Pr[S_5] - \Pr[S_4]| \leq \mathsf{Adv}^{\mathsf{ind}}_{\mathsf{LTF},\mathcal{B}_4}(\lambda)$$

for some suitable adversary $\mathcal{B}_4$.

In **Game** 6, we produce the ρ component in each challenge ciphertext by randomly sampling a string $\mathbf{r} \xleftarrow{\$} \{0,1\}^\tau$ and setting $\rho = \mathbf{r} \oplus \mathsf{m}$. As in **Game** 5, the $\mathbf{y}_2$ components are computed from ABM-LTF with lossy tags on $\mathbf{x}_2 \in \mathsf{D}$ for all challenge ciphertexts. Let $|\mathsf{E}_2|$ and $|\mathsf{X}|$ be the number of possible values of $\mathbf{e}_2$ and $\mathbf{x}$ respectively[9]. Recall $\mathbf{x}_1^t = [\mathbf{e}_1^t|\mathbf{x}^t]$ and $\mathbf{x}_2^t = [\mathbf{e}_2^t|\mathbf{x}^t]$. By the parameter selection and Lemma 2, we have

$$\begin{aligned}
\tilde{H}_\infty(\mathbf{x}_1, \mathbf{x}_2|\mathbf{y}_1, \mathbf{y}_2, \mu) &= \tilde{H}_\infty(\mathbf{x}, \mathbf{e}_1, \mathbf{e}_2|\mathbf{y}_1, \mathbf{y}_2, \mu) \\
&\geq H_\infty(\mathbf{x}, \mathbf{e}_1, \mathbf{e}_2) - (\log|\mathsf{D}| - l) - (\log|\mathsf{D}| - l') - 2\lambda \\
&\geq \log|\mathsf{D}| + \log|\mathsf{E}_2| - (\log|\mathsf{D}| - l) - (\log|\mathsf{X}| + \log|\mathsf{E}_2| - l') - 2\lambda \\
&= l + l' - \log|\mathsf{X}| - 2\lambda
\end{aligned}$$

[9] Recall that $\mathbf{x}$, $\mathbf{e}_1$, $\mathbf{e}_2$ are chosen uniformly at random from certain intervals.

Consequently, by the hypothesis that $\tau \leq (l - 2\lambda) - 2\log(1/\epsilon)$ and Lemma 3,

$$\Delta\left((\mathbf{y}_1, \mathbf{y}_2, \mu, \mathsf{UH}_{\mathbf{k}}, \mathsf{UH}_{\mathbf{k}}(\mathbf{x})), (\mathbf{y}_1, \mathbf{y}_2, \mu, \mathsf{UH}_{\mathbf{k}}, \mathcal{U}_\tau)\right) \leq \epsilon = \mathsf{negl}(\lambda)$$

where $\mathcal{U}_\tau$ stands for the uniform distribution over $\{0,1\}^\tau$. So we get

$$|\Pr[S_6] - \Pr[S_5]| \leq \mathsf{negl}(\lambda)$$

In **Game** 6, as all challenge messages are masked by an one-time pad, $\mathcal{A}$ gets no information about them. The original message vector $\mathbf{m}_0$ and the conditionally resampled message vector $\mathbf{m}_1$ come from the same distribution, thus

$$\Pr[S_6] = 1/2$$

Summing up, we obtain that $\mathsf{Adv}_{\Pi,\mathcal{A}}^{\mathsf{ind\text{-}so\text{-}cca}}(\lambda)$

$$\leq \mathsf{Adv}_{\mathsf{CH},\mathcal{B}_1}^{\mathsf{coll}}(\lambda) + \mathsf{Adv}_{\mathsf{ABM\text{-}LTF},\mathcal{B}_2}^{\mathsf{ind}}(\lambda) + \mathsf{Adv}_{\mathsf{ABM\text{-}LTF},\mathcal{B}_3}^{\mathsf{eva}}(\lambda) + \mathsf{Adv}_{\mathsf{LTF},\mathcal{B}_4}^{\mathsf{ind}}(\lambda) + \mathsf{negl}(\lambda)$$

which completes the proof. □

5.4 Tightly Secure IND-CCA2 PKE

The above PKE scheme is also a tightly secure PKE scheme with respect to the multi-ciphertext IND-CCA2 definition adopted by Gay et al. [24] (Definition 6). One can easily modify the IND-SO-CCA2 security proofs into a tight security proof with respect to the IND-CCA2 definition, where the security loss is independent of the number of decryption queries and the number of encryption queries.

Particularly, such a reduction is able to answer all the decryption queries and construct all challenge ciphertexts with lossy tags simultaneously, making the challenge ciphertexts information-theoretically unrecoverable. This IND-CCA2 secure PKE scheme we just outlined is thus the first tightly secure PKE scheme in the multi-ciphertext IND-CCA2 security model based on the LWE assumptions (or more generally without using quantumly broken assumptions).

Definition 6 (Multi-ciphertext IND-CCA2 security). *A PKE scheme $\Pi = (\mathsf{KeyGen}, \mathsf{Encrypt}, dec)$ is IND-CCA2 secure in the multi-ciphertext setting if for every PPT adversary $\mathcal{A}$, we have $\mathcal{A}$'s advantage*

$$\mathsf{Adv}_{\Pi,\mathcal{A}}^{\mathsf{ind\text{-}cc2a}}(\lambda) = \left|\Pr\left[\mathsf{Exp}_{\Pi,\mathcal{A}}^{\mathsf{ind\text{-}cca2}}(\lambda) = 1\right] - 1/2\right|$$

is negligible in λ where the experiment $\mathsf{Exp}_{\Pi,\mathcal{A}}^{\mathsf{ind\text{-}cca2}}(\lambda)$ is defined in Fig. 2.

Experiment $\mathsf{Exp}^{\text{ind-cca2}}_{\Pi,\mathcal{A}}(\lambda)$	$\mathcal{O}_{\mathsf{enc}}(\mathsf{m}_0, \mathsf{m}_1)$	$\mathcal{O}_{\mathsf{dec}}(\mathsf{ct})$
1. $\mathcal{L} \leftarrow \emptyset$	1. If $\lvert\mathsf{m}_0\rvert \neq \lvert\mathsf{m}_1\rvert$ return $\perp$	1. If $\mathsf{ct} \in \mathcal{L}$, return $\perp$
2. $(\mathsf{pk}, \mathsf{sk}) \leftarrow \mathsf{KeyGen}((1^\lambda)$	2. $r \xleftarrow{\$} \mathcal{R}_\Pi$	2. return $\mathsf{Decrypt}(\mathsf{sk}, \mathsf{ct})$
3. $b \xleftarrow{\$} \{0, 1\}$	3. $\mathsf{ct} \leftarrow \mathsf{Encrypt}(\mathsf{pk}, \mathsf{m}_b; r)$	
4. $b' \leftarrow \mathcal{A}^{\mathcal{O}_{\mathsf{enc}}(\cdot,\cdot), \mathcal{O}_{\mathsf{dec}}(\cdot)}(\mathsf{pk})$	4. $\mathcal{L} \leftarrow \mathcal{L} \cup \mathsf{ct}$	
5. return 1 if $b' = b$, 0 otherwise		

Fig. 2. Security experiment of IND-CCA2 security

6 Conclusion

In this paper, we have proposed the first All-But-Many Lossy Trapdoor Function based on lattice assumptions. ABM-LTFs are a very powerful primitive with potentially many applications in the construction of multi-challenge or multi-user cryptosystems. Our result answers the two open questions of constructing, from lattices, ABM-TF (originally posed by Alperin-Sheriff and Peikert [5]) and ABM-LTF (posed by Hofheinz [29]).

In addition, we have constructed an IND-SO-CCA2-secure PKE scheme from lattices by taking our ABM-LTF along the path of [27,29]. Our PKE scheme enjoys a tight security reduction, in the sense that the reduction is independent of all adversarial queries, including decryption, opening, and challenge ciphertexts. This gives the first tightly IND-CCA2 secure PKE scheme from LWE, and an alternative solution, lattice-based, to the problem of constructing tightly secure CCA PKE without bilinear or multilinear parings [24].

Acknowledgement. We thank Benoît Libert and Damien Stehlé and the anonymous reviewers for useful comments.

References

1. Agrawal, S., Boneh, D., Boyen, X.: Efficient lattice (H)IBE in the standard model. In: Gilbert, H. (ed.) EUROCRYPT 2010. LNCS, vol. 6110, pp. 553–572. Springer, Heidelberg (2010). doi:10.1007/978-3-642-13190-5_28
2. Ajtai, M.: Generating hard instances of lattice problems (extended abstract). In: STOC 1996. ACM (1996)
3. Akavia, A., Bogdanov, A., Guo, S., Kamath, A., Rosen, A.: Candidate weak pseudorandom functions in AC0∘MOD2. In: ITCS 2014. ACM (2014)
4. Alperin-Sheriff, J.: Short signatures with short public keys from homomorphic trapdoor functions. In: Katz, J. (ed.) PKC 2015. LNCS, vol. 9020, pp. 236–255. Springer, Heidelberg (2015). doi:10.1007/978-3-662-46447-2_11
5. Alperin-Sheriff, J., Peikert, C.: Circular and KDM security for identity-based encryption. In: Fischlin, M., Buchmann, J., Manulis, M. (eds.) PKC 2012. LNCS, vol. 7293, pp. 334–352. Springer, Heidelberg (2012). doi:10.1007/978-3-642-30057-8_20

6. Applebaum, B., Cash, D., Peikert, C., Sahai, A.: Fast cryptographic primitives and circular-secure encryption based on hard learning problems. In: Halevi, S. (ed.) CRYPTO 2009. LNCS, vol. 5677, pp. 595–618. Springer, Heidelberg (2009). doi:10.1007/978-3-642-03356-8_35
7. Banerjee, A., Peikert, C., Rosen, A.: Pseudorandom functions and lattices. In: Pointcheval, D., Johansson, T. (eds.) EUROCRYPT 2012. LNCS, vol. 7237, pp. 719–737. Springer, Heidelberg (2012). doi:10.1007/978-3-642-29011-4_42
8. Bellare, M., Hofheinz, D., Yilek, S.: Possibility and impossibility results for encryption and commitment secure under selective opening. In: Joux, A. (ed.) EUROCRYPT 2009. LNCS, vol. 5479, pp. 1–35. Springer, Heidelberg (2009). doi:10.1007/978-3-642-01001-9_1
9. Bellare, M., Kiltz, E., Peikert, C., Waters, B.: Identity-based (lossy) trapdoor functions and applications. Cryptology ePrint Archive, Report 2011/479 (2011)
10. Bellare, M., Kiltz, E., Peikert, C., Waters, B.: Identity-based (Lossy) trapdoor functions and applications. In: Pointcheval, D., Johansson, T. (eds.) EUROCRYPT 2012. LNCS, vol. 7237, pp. 228–245. Springer, Heidelberg (2012). doi:10.1007/978-3-642-29011-4_15
11. Böhl, F., Hofheinz, D., Kraschewski, D.: On definitions of selective opening security. In: Fischlin, M., Buchmann, J., Manulis, M. (eds.) PKC 2012. LNCS, vol. 7293, pp. 522–539. Springer, Heidelberg (2012). doi:10.1007/978-3-642-30057-8_31
12. Boneh, D., Gentry, C., Gorbunov, S., Halevi, S., Nikolaenko, V., Segev, G., Vaikuntanathan, V., Vinayagamurthy, D.: Fully key-homomorphic encryption, arithmetic circuit ABE and compact garbled circuits. In: Nguyen, P.Q., Oswald, E. (eds.) EUROCRYPT 2014. LNCS, vol. 8441, pp. 533–556. Springer, Heidelberg (2014). doi:10.1007/978-3-642-55220-5_30
13. Boyen, X.: Lattice mixing and vanishing trapdoors: a framework for fully secure short signatures and more. In: Nguyen, P.Q., Pointcheval, D. (eds.) PKC 2010. LNCS, vol. 6056, pp. 499–517. Springer, Heidelberg (2010). doi:10.1007/978-3-642-13013-7_29
14. Boyen, X., Li, Q.: Towards tightly secure lattice short signature and id-based encryption. In: Cheon, J.H., Takagi, T. (eds.) ASIACRYPT 2016. LNCS, vol. 10032, pp. 404–434. Springer, Heidelberg (2016). doi:10.1007/978-3-662-53890-6_14
15. Brakerski, Z., Vaikuntanathan, V.: Efficient fully homomorphic encryption from (standard) LWE. In: IEEE FOCS 2011 (2011)
16. Brakerski, Z., Vaikuntanathan, V.: Lattice-based FHE as secure as PKE. In: ITCS 2014. ACM (2014)
17. Brent, R.P., McKay, B.D.: Determinants and ranks of random matrices over zm. Discret. Math. **66**(1), 35–49 (1987)
18. Cash, D., Hofheinz, D., Kiltz, E., Peikert, C.: Bonsai trees, or how to delegate a lattice basis. J. Cryptol. **25**(4), 601–639 (2012)
19. Damgård, I., Jurik, M.: A generalisation, a simpli.cation and some applications of paillier's probabilistic public-key system. In: Kim, K. (ed.) PKC 2001. LNCS, vol. 1992, pp. 119–136. Springer, Heidelberg (2001). doi:10.1007/3-540-44586-2_9
20. Dodis, Y., Kiltz, E., Pietrzak, K., Wichs, D.: Message authentication, revisited. In: Pointcheval, D., Johansson, T. (eds.) EUROCRYPT 2012. LNCS, vol. 7237, pp. 355–374. Springer, Heidelberg (2012). doi:10.1007/978-3-642-29011-4_22
21. Döttling, N., Müller-Quade, J.: Lossy codes and a new variant of the learning-with-errors problem. In: Johansson, T., Nguyen, P.Q. (eds.) EUROCRYPT 2013. LNCS, vol. 7881, pp. 18–34. Springer, Heidelberg (2013). doi:10.1007/978-3-642-38348-9_2

22. Fehr, S., Hofheinz, D., Kiltz, E., Wee, H.: Encryption schemes secure against chosen-ciphertext selective opening attacks. In: Gilbert, H. (ed.) EUROCRYPT 2010. LNCS, vol. 6110, pp. 381–402. Springer, Heidelberg (2010). doi:10.1007/978-3-642-13190-5_20
23. Fujisaki, E.: All-but-many encryption. In: Sarkar, P., Iwata, T. (eds.) ASIACRYPT 2014. LNCS, vol. 8874, pp. 426–447. Springer, Heidelberg (2014). doi:10.1007/978-3-662-45608-8_23
24. Gay, R., Hofheinz, D., Kiltz, E., Wee, H.: Tightly CCA-secure encryption without pairings. In: Fischlin, M., Coron, J.-S. (eds.) EUROCRYPT 2016. LNCS, vol. 9665, pp. 1–27. Springer, Heidelberg (2016). doi:10.1007/978-3-662-49890-3_1
25. Gentry, C., Peikert, C., Vaikuntanathan, V.: Trapdoors for hard lattices and new cryptographic constructions. In: STOC 2008. ACM (2008)
26. Gentry, C., Sahai, A., Waters, B.: Homomorphic encryption from learning with errors: conceptually-simpler, asymptotically-faster, attribute-based. In: Canetti, R., Garay, J.A. (eds.) CRYPTO 2013. LNCS, vol. 8042, pp. 75–92. Springer, Heidelberg (2013). doi:10.1007/978-3-642-40041-4_5
27. Hemenway, B., Libert, B., Ostrovsky, R., Vergnaud, D.: Lossy encryption: constructions from general assumptions and efficient selective opening chosen ciphertext security. In: Lee, D.H., Wang, X. (eds.) ASIACRYPT 2011. LNCS, vol. 7073, pp. 70–88. Springer, Heidelberg (2011). doi:10.1007/978-3-642-25385-0_4
28. Hiromasa, R., Abe, M., Okamoto, T.: Packing messages and optimizing bootstrapping in GSW-FHE. In: Katz, J. (ed.) PKC 2015. LNCS, vol. 9020, pp. 699–715. Springer, Heidelberg (2015). doi:10.1007/978-3-662-46447-2_31
29. Hofheinz, D.: All-but-many lossy trapdoor functions. In: Pointcheval, D., Johansson, T. (eds.) EUROCRYPT 2012. LNCS, vol. 7237, pp. 209–227. Springer, Heidelberg (2012). doi:10.1007/978-3-642-29011-4_14
30. Hofheinz, D.: Circular chosen-ciphertext security with compact ciphertexts. In: Johansson, T., Nguyen, P.Q. (eds.) EUROCRYPT 2013. LNCS, vol. 7881, pp. 520–536. Springer, Heidelberg (2013). doi:10.1007/978-3-642-38348-9_31
31. Hofheinz, D., Rupp, A.: Standard versus selective opening security: separation and equivalence results. In: Lindell, Y. (ed.) TCC 2014. LNCS, vol. 8349, pp. 591–615. Springer, Heidelberg (2014). doi:10.1007/978-3-642-54242-8_25
32. Huang, Z., Liu, S., Qin, B.: Sender-equivocable encryption schemes secure against chosen-ciphertext attacks revisited. In: Kurosawa, K., Hanaoka, G. (eds.) PKC 2013. LNCS, vol. 7778, pp. 369–385. Springer, Heidelberg (2013). doi:10.1007/978-3-642-36362-7_23
33. Lyubashevsky, V., Masny, D.: Man-in-the-middle secure authentication schemes from LPN and weak PRFs. In: Canetti, R., Garay, J.A. (eds.) CRYPTO 2013. LNCS, vol. 8043, pp. 308–325. Springer, Heidelberg (2013). doi:10.1007/978-3-642-40084-1_18
34. Libert, B., Sakzad, A., Stehlé, D., Steinfeld, R.: All-But-Many Lossy Trapdoor Functions and Selective Opening Chosen-Ciphertext Security from LWE. In: Jonathan, K., Hovav, S. (eds.) CRYPTO 2017. LNCS, vol. 10403, pp. 332–364. Springer, Cham (2017)
35. Micciancio, D., Peikert, C.: Trapdoors for lattices: simpler, tighter, faster, smaller. In: Pointcheval, D., Johansson, T. (eds.) EUROCRYPT 2012. LNCS, vol. 7237, pp. 700–718. Springer, Heidelberg (2012). doi:10.1007/978-3-642-29011-4_41
36. Micciancio, D., Peikert, C.: Hardness of SIS and LWE with small parameters. In: Canetti, R., Garay, J.A. (eds.) CRYPTO 2013. LNCS, vol. 8042, pp. 21–39. Springer, Heidelberg (2013). doi:10.1007/978-3-642-40041-4_2

37. Paillier, P.: Public-key cryptosystems based on composite degree residuosity classes. In: Stern, J. (ed.) EUROCRYPT 1999. LNCS, vol. 1592, pp. 223–238. Springer, Heidelberg (1999). doi:10.1007/3-540-48910-X_16
38. Peikert, C., Vaikuntanathan, V., Waters, B.: A framework for efficient and composable oblivious transfer. In: Wagner, D. (ed.) CRYPTO 2008. LNCS, vol. 5157, pp. 554–571. Springer, Heidelberg (2008). doi:10.1007/978-3-540-85174-5_31
39. Peikert, C., Waters, B.: Lossy trapdoor functions and their applications. SIAM J. Comput. **40**(6), 1803–1844 (2011)
40. Qin, B., Liu, S.: Leakage-resilient chosen-ciphertext secure public-key encryption from hash proof system and one-time lossy filter. In: Sako, K., Sarkar, P. (eds.) ASIACRYPT 2013. LNCS, vol. 8270, pp. 381–400. Springer, Heidelberg (2013). doi:10.1007/978-3-642-42045-0_20
41. Regev, O.: On lattices, learning with errors, random linear codes, and cryptography. In: STOC 2005. ACM (2005)
42. Zhang, R.: Tweaking TBE/IBE to PKE transforms with chameleon hash functions. In: Katz, J., Yung, M. (eds.) ACNS 2007. LNCS, vol. 4521, pp. 323–339. Springer, Heidelberg (2007). doi:10.1007/978-3-540-72738-5_21

All-But-Many Lossy Trapdoor Functions and Selective Opening Chosen-Ciphertext Security from LWE

Benoît Libert[1,2(✉)], Amin Sakzad[3], Damien Stehlé[2], and Ron Steinfeld[3]

[1] CNRS, Laboratoire LIP, Lyon, France
[2] ENS de Lyon, Laboratoire LIP (U. Lyon, CNRS, ENSL, INRIA, UCBL), Lyon, France
benoit.libert@ens-lyon.fr, damien.stehle@gmail.com
[3] Faculty of Information Technology, Monash University, Clayton, Australia
{amin.sakzad,ron.steinfeld}@monash.edu

Abstract. Selective opening (SO) security refers to adversaries that receive a number of ciphertexts and, after having corrupted a subset of the senders (thus obtaining the plaintexts and the senders' random coins), aim at breaking the security of remaining ciphertexts. So far, very few public-key encryption schemes are known to provide simulation-based selective opening (SIM-SO-CCA2) security under chosen-ciphertext attacks and most of them encrypt messages bit-wise. The only exceptions to date rely on *all-but-many* lossy trapdoor functions (as introduced by Hofheinz; Eurocrypt'12) and the Composite Residuosity assumption. In this paper, we describe the first all-but-many lossy trapdoor function with security relying on the presumed hardness of the Learning-With-Errors problem (LWE) with standard parameters. Our construction exploits homomorphic computations on lattice trapdoors for lossy LWE matrices. By carefully embedding a lattice trapdoor in lossy public keys, we are able to prove SIM-SO-CCA2 security under the LWE assumption. As a result of independent interest, we describe a variant of our scheme whose multi-challenge CCA2 security tightly relates to the hardness of LWE and the security of a pseudo-random function.

Keywords: LWE · Lossy trapdoor functions · Chosen-ciphertext security · Selective-opening security · Tight security reductions

1 Introduction

Lossy Trapdoor Functions. As introduced by Peikert and Waters [66], lossy tradpoor functions (LTFs) are function families where injective functions – which can be inverted using a trapdoor – are indistinguishable from lossy functions, where the image is much smaller than the domain. The last decade, they received continuous attention (see, e.g., [3,37,46,49,71,72]) and found many amazing applications in cryptography. These include black-box realizations of cryptosystems with chosen-ciphertext (IND-CCA2) security [66], deterministic public-key

J. Katz and H. Shacham (Eds.): CRYPTO 2017, Part III, LNCS 10403, pp. 332–364, 2017.
DOI: 10.1007/978-3-319-63697-9_12

encryption in the standard model [19,26,68] and encryption schemes retaining some security in the absence of reliable randomness [8,10]. As another prominent application, they enabled the design [11,16] of encryption schemes secure against selective-opening (SO) adversaries, thereby providing an elegant solution to a 10 year-old problem raised by Dwork *et al.* [35].

When it comes to constructing CCA2-secure [67] encryption schemes, LTFs are often combined with *all-but-one* trapdoor functions (ABO-LTFs) [66], which enable a variant of the two-key simulation paradigm [63] in the security proof. In ABO-LTF families, each function takes as arguments an input x and a tag t in such a way that the function $f_{\mathsf{abo}}(t, \cdot)$ is injective for any t, except a special tag t^* for which $f_{\mathsf{abo}}(t^*, \cdot)$ behaves as a lossy function. In the security proof of [66], the lossy tag t^* is used to compute the challenge ciphertext, whereas decryption queries are handled by inverting $f_{\mathsf{abo}}(t, \cdot)$ for all injective tags $t \neq t^\star$. One limitation of ABO-LTFs is the uniqueness of the lossy tag t^* which must be determined at key generation time. As such, ABO-LTFs are in fact insufficient to prove security in attack models that inherently involve multiple challenge ciphertexts: examples include the key-dependent message [17] and selective opening [11] settings, where multi-challenge security does *not* reduce to single-challenge security via the usual hybrid argument [7].

To overcome the aforementioned shortcoming, Hofheinz [49] introduced *all-but-many* lossy trapdoor functions (ABM-LTFs) which extend ABO-LTFs by allowing the security proof to dynamically create arbitrarily many lossy tags using a trapdoor. Each tag $t = (t_{\mathsf{c}}, t_{\mathsf{a}})$ is comprised of an auxiliary component t_{a} and a core component t_{c} so that, by generating t_{c} as a suitable function of t_{a}, the reduction is able to assign a lossy (but random-looking) tag to each challenge ciphertext while making sure that the adversary will be unable to create lossy tags by itself in decryption queries. Using carefully designed ABM-LTFs and variants thereof [50], Hofheinz gave several constructions [49,50] of public-key encryption schemes in scenarios involving multiple challenge ciphertexts.

Selective Opening Security. In the context of public-key encryption, selective opening (SO) attacks take place in a scenario involving a receiver and N senders. Those encrypt possibly correlated messages $(\mathsf{Msg}_1, \ldots, \mathsf{Msg}_N)$ under the receiver's public key PK and, upon receiving the ciphertexts $(\mathbf{C}_1, \ldots, \mathbf{C}_N)$, the adversary decides to corrupt a subset of the senders. Namely, by choosing $I \subset [N]$, it obtains the messages $\{\mathsf{Msg}_i\}_{i \in I}$ as well as the random coins $\{r_i\}_{i \in I}$ for which $\mathbf{C}_i = \mathsf{Encrypt}(PK, \mathsf{Msg}_i, r_i)$. Then, the adversary aims at breaking the security of unopened ciphertexts $\{\mathbf{C}_i\}_{i \in [N] \setminus I}$. It is tempting to believe that standard notions like semantic security carry over to such adversaries due to the independence of random coins $\{r_i\}_{i \in [N]}$. However, this is not true in general [29] as even the strong standard notion of IND-CCA security [67] was shown [9,55] not to guarantee anything under selective openings. Proving SO security turns out to be a challenging task for two main reasons. The first one is that the adversary must also obtain the random coins $\{r_i\}_{i \in I}$ of opened ciphertexts (and not only the underlying plaintexts) as reliably erasing them can be very difficult in practice. Note that having the reduction guess the set I of corrupted senders beforehand is not an option since it is only possible with negligible probability $1/\binom{N}{N/2}$. The second difficulty arises from the potential correlation between $\{\mathsf{Msg}_i\}_{i\in I}$ and $\{\mathsf{Msg}_i\}_{i\in[N]\setminus I}$, which hinders the use of standard proof techniques and already makes selective opening security non-trivial to formalize.

Towards properly defining SO security, the indistinguishability-based (IND-SO) approach [11,16] demands that unopened plaintexts $\{\mathsf{Msg}_i\}_{i\in[N]\setminus I}$ be indistinguishable from independently resampled ones $\{\mathsf{Msg}'_i\}_{i\in[N]\setminus I}$ conditionally on the adversary's view. However, such definitions are not fully satisfactory. Indeed, since $\{\mathsf{Msg}_i\}_{i\in[N]}$ may be correlated, the resampling of $\{\mathsf{Msg}'_i\}_{i\in[N]\setminus I}$ must be conditioned on $\{\mathsf{Msg}_i\}_{i\in I}$ to make the adversary's task non-trivial. This implies that, in the security game, the challenger can only be efficient for message distributions that admit efficient conditional resampling, which is a much stronger restriction than efficient samplability. Indeed, many natural message distributions (e.g., where some messages are hard-to-invert functions of other messages) do not support efficient conditional resampling.

Bellare *et al.* [11,16] defined a stronger, simulation-based (SIM-SO) flavor of selective opening security. This notion mandates that, whatever the adversary outputs after having seen $\{\mathbf{C}_i\}_{i\in[N]}$ and $\{(\mathsf{Msg}_i, r_i)\}_{i\in I}$ can be efficiently simulated from $\{\mathsf{Msg}_i\}_{i\in I}$, without seeing the ciphertexts nor the public key. Unlike its indistinguishability-based counterpart, SIM-SO security does not imply any restriction on the message distributions. While clearly preferable, it turns out to be significantly harder to achieve. Indeed, Böhl *et al.* [18] gave an example of IND-SO-secure scheme that fails to achieve SIM-SO security.

On the positive side, simulation-based chosen-plaintext (SIM-SO-CPA) security was proved attainable under standard number theoretic assumptions like Quadratic Residuosity [16], Composite Residuosity [45] or the Decision Diffie-Hellman assumption [16,54]. In the chosen-ciphertext (SIM-SO-CCA) scenario, additionally handling decryption queries makes the problem considerably harder: indeed, very few constructions achieve this security property and most of them [36,56,57,59] proceed by encrypting messages in a bit-by-bit manner. The only exceptions [38,49] to date rely on all-but-many lossy trapdoor functions and Paillier's Composite Residuosity assumption [64].

In this paper, we provide SIM-SO-CCA-secure realizations that encrypt many bits at once under lattice assumptions. Our constructions proceed by homomorphically evaluating a low-depth pseudorandom function (PRF) using the fully homomorphic encryption (FHE) scheme of Gentry, Sahai and Waters [41].

1.1 Our Results

Our contribution is three-fold. We first provide an all-but-many lossy trapdoor function based on the Learning-With-Errors (LWE) assumption [69]. We tightly relate the security of our ABM-LTF to that of the underlying PRF and the hardness of the LWE problem.

As a second result, we use our ABM-LTF to pave the way towards public-key encryption schemes with *tight* (or, more precisely, *almost tight* in the terminology of [31]) chosen-ciphertext security in the multi-challenge setting [7].

By "tight CCA security", as in [39,51–53,58], we mean that the multiplicative gap between the adversary's advantage and the hardness assumption only depends on the security parameter and not on the number of challenge ciphertexts. The strength of the underlying LWE assumption depends on the specific PRF used to instantiate our scheme. So far, known tightly secure lattice-based PRFs rely on rather strong LWE assumptions with exponential modulus and inverse error rate [5], or only handle polynomially-bounded adversaries [34] (and hence do not fully exploit the conjectured exponential hardness of LWE). However, any future realization of low-depth PRF with tight security under standard LWE assumptions (i.e., with polynomial approximation factor) could be plugged into our scheme so as to obtain tight CCA security under the same assumption. Especially, if we had such a tightly secure PRF with an evaluation circuit in NC^1, our scheme would be instantiable with a polynomial-size modulus by translating the evaluation circuit into a branching program via Barrington's theorem [6] and exploiting the asymmetric noise growth of the GSW FHE as in [27,44].

As a third and main result, we modify our construction so as to prove it secure against selective opening chosen-ciphertext attacks in the indistinguishability-based (i.e., IND-SO-CCA2) sense. By instantiating our system with a carefully chosen universal hash function, we finally upgrade it from IND-SO-CCA2 to SIM-SO-CCA2 security. For this purpose, we prove that the upgraded scheme is a *lossy encryption* scheme with *efficient opening*. As defined by Bellare *et al.* [11,16], a lossy encryption scheme is one where normal public keys are indistinguishable from *lossy keys*, for which ciphertexts statistically hide the plaintext. It was shown in [11,16] that any lossy cryptosystem is in fact IND-SO-CPA-secure. Moreover, if a lossy ciphertext $\mathbf{C}$ can be efficiently opened to any desired plaintext Msg (i.e., by finding plausible random coins r that explain $\mathbf{C}$ as an encryption of Msg) using the secret key, the scheme also provides SIM-SO-CPA security. We show that our IND-SO-CCA-secure construction satisfies this property when we embed a lattice trapdoor [40,60] in lossy secret keys.

This provides us with the first multi-bit LWE-based public-key cryptosystem with SIM-SO-CCA security. So far, the only known method [59] to attain the same security notion under quantum-resistant assumptions was to apply a generic construction where each bit of plaintext requires a full key encapsulation (KEM) using a CCA2-secure KEM. In terms of ciphertext size, our system avoids this overhead and can be instantiated with a polynomial-size modulus as long as the underlying PRF can be evaluated in NC^1. For example, the Banerjee-Peikert PRF [4] – which relies on a much weaker LWE assumption than [5] as it only requires on a slightly superpolynomial modulus – satisfies this condition when the input of the PRF is hardwired into the circuit.

As a result of independent interest, we show in the full version of the paper that lattice trapdoors can also be used to reach SIM-SO-CPA security in lossy encryption schemes built upon lossy trapdoor functions based on DDH-like assumptions. This shows that techniques from lattice-based cryptography can also come in handy to obtain simulation-based security from conventional number theoretic assumptions.

1.2 Our Techniques

Our ABM-LTF construction relies on the observation – previously used in [3, 12] – that the LWE function $f_{\mathsf{LWE}} : \mathbb{Z}_q^n \times \mathbb{Z}^m \to \mathbb{Z}_q^m : (\mathbf{x}, \mathbf{e}) \to \mathbf{A} \cdot \mathbf{x} + \mathbf{e}$ is lossy. Indeed, under the LWE assumption, the random matrix $\mathbf{A} \in \mathbb{Z}_q^{m \times n}$ can be replaced by a matrix of the form $\mathbf{A} = \mathbf{B} \cdot \mathbf{C} + \mathbf{F}$, for a random $\mathbf{B} \in \mathbb{Z}_q^{m \times \ell}$ such that $\ell < n$ and a small-norm $\mathbf{F} \in \mathbb{Z}^{m \times n}$, without the adversary noticing. However, we depart from [3,12] in several ways.

First, in lossy mode, we sample $\mathbf{C}$ uniformly in $\mathbb{Z}_q^{\ell \times n}$ (rather than as a small-norm matrix as in [12]) because, in order to achieve SIM-SO security, we need to generate $\mathbf{C}$ with a trapdoor. Our application to SIM-SO security also requires to sample $(\mathbf{x}, \mathbf{e})$ from discrete Gaussian distributions, rather than uniformly over an interval as in [12]. Second, we assume that the noise $\mathbf{e} \in \mathbb{Z}^m$ is part of the input instead of using the Rounding technique[1] [5] as in the lossy function of Alwen *et al.* [3]. The reason is that, in our ABM-LTF, we apply the LWE-based function $(\mathbf{x}, \mathbf{e}) \to \mathbf{A}_t \cdot \mathbf{x} + \mathbf{e}$ for tag-dependent matrices $\mathbf{A}_t$ and, if we were to use the rounding technique, the lower parts of matrices $\mathbf{A}_t$ would have to be statistically independent for different tags. Since we cannot guarantee this independence, we consider the noise term $\mathbf{e}$ to be part of the input. In this case, we can prove that, for any lossy tag, the vector $\mathbf{x}$ retains at least $\Omega(n \log n)$ bits of min-entropy conditionally on $\mathbf{A}_t \cdot \mathbf{x} + \mathbf{e}$ and this holds even if $\{\mathbf{A}_t\}_t$ are not statistically independent for distinct lossy tags t.

One difficulty is that our ABM-LTF only loses less than half of its input bits for lossy tags, which prevents it from being correlation-secure in the sense of [70]. For this reason, our encryption schemes *cannot* proceed exactly as in [49,66] by simultaneously outputting an ABM-LTF evaluation $f_{\mathsf{ABM}}(\mathbf{x}, \mathbf{e}) = \mathbf{A}_t \cdot \mathbf{x} + \mathbf{e}$ and a lossy function evaluation $f_{\mathsf{LTF}}(\mathbf{x}, \mathbf{e}) = \mathbf{A} \cdot \mathbf{x} + \mathbf{e}$ as this would leak $(\mathbf{x}, \mathbf{e})$. Fortunately, we can still build CCA2-secure systems by evaluating $f_{\mathsf{LTF}}(\cdot)$ and $f_{\mathsf{ABM}}(\cdot)$ for the same $\mathbf{x}$ and distinct noise vectors $\mathbf{e}_0, \mathbf{e}$. In this case, we can prove that the two functions are jointly lossy: conditionally on $(f_{\mathsf{LTF}}(\mathbf{x}, \mathbf{e}_0), f_{\mathsf{ABM}}(\mathbf{x}, \mathbf{e}))$, the input $\mathbf{x}$ retains $\Omega(n \log n)$ bits of entropy, which allows us to blind the message as $\mathsf{Msg} + h(\mathbf{x})$ using a universal hash function h.

Our ABM-LTF extends the all-but-one trapdoor function of Alwen *et al.* [3] by homomorphically evaluating a pseudorandom function. Letting $\bar{\mathbf{A}} \in \mathbb{Z}_q^{m \times n}$ be a lossy matrix and $\mathbf{G} \in \mathbb{Z}_q^{m \times n}$ denote the gadget matrix of Micciancio and Peikert [60], the evaluation key of our ABM-LTF contains Gentry-Sahai-Waters (GSW) encryptions $\mathbf{B}_i = \mathbf{R}_i \cdot \bar{\mathbf{A}} + K[i] \cdot \mathbf{G} \in \mathbb{Z}_q^{m \times n}$ of the bits $K[i]$ of a PRF seed $K \in \{0,1\}^\lambda$, where $\mathbf{R}_i \in \{-1,1\}^{m \times m}$. Given a tag $t = (t_{\mathsf{c}}, t_{\mathsf{a}})$, the evaluation algorithm computes a GSW encryption $\mathbf{B}_t = \mathbf{R}_t \cdot \bar{\mathbf{A}} + h_t \cdot \mathbf{G} \in \mathbb{Z}_q^{m \times n}$ of the Hamming distance h_t between t_{c} and $\mathsf{PRF}(K, t_{\mathsf{a}})$ before using $\mathbf{A}_t = [\bar{\mathbf{A}}^\top \mid \mathbf{B}_t^\top]^\top$ to evaluate $f_{\mathsf{ABM}}(\mathbf{x}, \mathbf{e}) = \mathbf{A}_t \cdot \mathbf{x} + \mathbf{e}$. In a lossy tag $t = (\mathsf{PRF}(K, t_{\mathsf{a}}), t_{\mathsf{a}})$, we have $h_t = 0$, so that the matrix $\mathbf{A}_t = [\bar{\mathbf{A}}^\top \mid (\mathbf{R}_t \cdot \bar{\mathbf{A}})^\top]^\top$ induces a lossy function $f_{\mathsf{ABM}}(t, \cdot)$. At the same time, any injective tag $t = (t_{\mathsf{c}}, t_{\mathsf{a}})$ satisfies $t_{\mathsf{c}} \neq \mathsf{PRF}(K, t_{\mathsf{a}})$

[1] The function of [3] maps $\mathbf{x}$ to $f_{\mathsf{LWR}}(\mathbf{x}) = \lfloor (p/q) \cdot \mathbf{A} \cdot \mathbf{x} \rfloor$, for some prime moduli $p < q$.

and thus $h_t \neq 0$, which allows inverting $f_{\mathsf{ABM}}(\mathbf{x}, \mathbf{e}) = \mathbf{A}_t \cdot \mathbf{x} + \mathbf{e}$ using the public trapdoor [60] of the matrix $\mathbf{G}$.

The pseudorandomness of the PRF ensures that: (i) Lossy tags are indistinguishable from random tags; (ii) They are computationally hard to find without the seed K. In order to prove both statements, we resort to the LWE assumption as the matrix $\bar{\mathbf{A}}$ is not statistically uniform over $\mathbb{Z}_q^{m \times n}$.

Our tightly CCA2-secure public-key cryptosystem uses ciphertexts of the form $(f_{\mathsf{LTF}}(\mathbf{x}, \mathbf{e}_0), f_{\mathsf{ABM}}(\mathbf{x}, \mathbf{e}), \mathsf{Msg} + h(\mathbf{x}))$, where t_{a} is the verification key of the one-time signature. Instantiating this scheme with a polynomial-size modulus requires a tightly secure PRF which is computable in NC^1 when the input of the circuit is the *key* (rather than the input of the PRF).[2] To overcome this problem and as a result of independent interest, we provide a tighter proof for the key-homomorphic PRF of Boneh *et al.* [21] (where the concrete security loss is made independent of the number of evaluation queries), which gives us tight CCA2-security under a strong LWE assumption.

In our IND-SO-CCA2 system, an additional difficulty arises since we cannot use one-time signatures to bind ciphertext components altogether. One alternative is to rely on the hybrid encryption paradigm as in [24] by setting $t_{\mathsf{a}} = f_{\mathsf{LTF}}(\mathbf{x}, \mathbf{e}_0)$ and encrypting Msg using a CCA-secure secret-key encryption scheme keyed by $h(\mathbf{x})$. In a direct adaptation of this technique, the chosen-ciphertext adversary can modify $f_{\mathsf{ABM}}(\mathbf{x}, \mathbf{e})$ by re-randomizing the underlying $\mathbf{e}$. Our solution to this problem is to apply the encrypt-then-MAC approach and incorporate $f_{\mathsf{ABM}}(\mathbf{x}, \mathbf{e})$ into the inputs of the MAC so as to prevent the adversary from randomizing $\mathbf{e}$. Using the lossiness of $f_{\mathsf{ABM}}(\cdot)$ and $f_{\mathsf{LTF}}(\cdot)$, we can indeed prove that the hybrid construction provides IND-SO-CCA2 security.

In order to obtain SIM-SO-CCA2 security, we have to show that lossy ciphertexts can be equivocated in the same way as a chameleon hash function. Indeed, the result of [11,16] implies that any lossy encryption scheme with this property is simulation-secure and the result carries over to the chosen-ciphertext setting. We show that ciphertexts can be trapdoor-opened if we instantiate the scheme using a particular universal hash function $h : \mathbb{Z}^n \to \mathbb{Z}_q^L$ which maps $\mathbf{x} \in \mathbb{Z}^n$ to $h(\mathbf{x}) = \mathbf{H}_{\mathcal{UH}} \cdot \mathbf{x} \in \mathbb{Z}_q^L$, for a random matrix $\mathbf{H}_{\mathcal{UH}} \in \mathbb{Z}_q^{L \times n}$. In order to generate the evaluation keys ek' and ek of f_{LTF} and f_{ABM}, we use random matrices $\mathbf{B}_{\mathsf{LTF}} \in \mathbb{Z}_q^{2m \times \ell}$, $\mathbf{C}_{\mathsf{LTF}} \in \mathbb{Z}_q^{\ell \times n}$, $\mathbf{B}_{\mathsf{ABM}} \in \mathbb{Z}_q^{m \times \ell}$, $\mathbf{C}_{\mathsf{ABM}} \in \mathbb{Z}_q^{\ell \times n}$ as well as small-norm $\mathbf{F}_{\mathsf{LTF}} \in \mathbb{Z}^{2m \times n}$, $\mathbf{F}_{\mathsf{ABM}} \in \mathbb{Z}^{m \times n}$ so as to set up lossy matrices $\mathbf{A}_{\mathsf{LTF}} = \mathbf{B}_{\mathsf{LTF}} \cdot \mathbf{C}_{\mathsf{LTF}} + \mathbf{F}_{\mathsf{LTF}}$ and $\mathbf{A}_{\mathsf{ABM}} = \mathbf{B}_{\mathsf{ABM}} \cdot C_{\mathsf{ABM}} + \mathbf{F}_{\mathsf{ABM}}$. The key idea is to run the trapdoor generation algorithm of [60] to generate a statistically uniform $\mathbf{C} = [\mathbf{C}_{\mathsf{LTF}}^\top \mid \mathbf{C}_{\mathsf{ABM}}^\top \mid \mathbf{H}_{\mathcal{UH}}^\top]^\top \in \mathbb{Z}_q^{(2\ell+L) \times n}$ together with a trapdoor allowing to sample short integer vectors in any coset of the lattice $\Lambda^\perp(\mathbf{C})$. By choosing the target vector $\mathbf{t} \in \mathbb{Z}_q^{2\ell+L}$ as a function of the desired message Msg_1, the initial message Msg_0 and the initial random coins $(\mathbf{x}, \mathbf{e}_0, \mathbf{e})$, we can find a short $\mathbf{x}' \in \mathbb{Z}^n$ such that $\mathbf{C} \cdot \mathbf{x}' = \mathbf{t} \mod q$ and subsequently define $(\mathbf{e}_0', \mathbf{e}') \in \mathbb{Z}^{2m} \times \mathbb{Z}^m$

[2] Note that the same holds for the construction of [22], in which the PRF from [5] should be replaced by another one which is in NC^1 as a function the key (e.g., the one from [21]).

so that they explain the lossy ciphertext as an encryption of Msg_1 using the coins $(\mathbf{x}', \mathbf{e}_0', \mathbf{e}')$. Moreover, we prove that these have the suitable distribution conditionally on the lossy ciphertext and the target message Msg_1.

1.3 Related Work

While selective opening security was first considered by Dwork *et al.* [35], the feasibility of SOA-secure public-key encryption remained open until the work of Bellare, Hofheinz and Yilek [11,16]. They showed that IND-SO security can be generically achieved from any lossy trapdoor function and, more efficiently, under the DDH assumption. They also achieved SIM-SO-CPA security under the Quadratic Residuosity and DDH assumptions, but at the expense of encrypting messages bitwise. In particular, they proved the SIM-SO security of the Goldwasser-Micali system [42] and their result was extended to Paillier [45]. Hofheinz, Jager and Rupp recently described space-efficient schemes under DDH-like assumption. Meanwhile, the notion of SIM-SO-CPA security was realized in the identity-based setting by Bellare, Waters and Yilek [15]. Recently, Hoang *et al.* [48] investigated the feasibility of SO security using imperfect randomness.

Selective opening security was considered for chosen-ciphertext adversaries in several works [36,49,56,57,59]. Except constructions [38,49] based on (variants of) the Composite Residuosity assumption, all of them process messages in a bitwise fashion, incurring an expansion factor $\Omega(\lambda)$. In the random oracle model [13], much more efficient solutions are possible. In particular, Heuer *et al.* [47] gave evidence that several practical schemes like RSA-OAEP [14] are actually secure in the SIM-SO-CCA sense.

The exact security of public-key encryption in the multi-challenge, multi-user setting was first taken into account by Bellare, Boldyreva and Micali [7] who proved that Cramer-Shoup [32] was tightly secure in the number of users, but not w.r.t. the number Q of challenge ciphertexts. Using ABM-LTFs, Hofheinz managed to obtain tight multi-challenge security [49] (i.e., without a security loss $\Omega(Q)$ between the advantages of the adversary and the reduction) at the expense of non-standard, variable-size assumptions. Under simple DDH-like assumptions, Hofheinz and Jager [53] gave the first feasibility results in groups with a bilinear map. More efficient tight multi-challenge realizations were given in [39,51,52,58] but, for the time being, the only solutions that do not rely on bilinear maps are those of [39,52]. In particular, constructions from lattice assumptions have remained lacking so far. By instantiating our scheme with a suitable PRF [5], we take the first step in this direction (albeit under a strong LWE assumption with an exponential approximation factor). Paradoxically, while we can tightly reduce the security of the underlying PRF to the multi-challenge security of our scheme, we do not know how to prove tight multi-user security.

A common feature between our security proofs and those of [39,51,52,58] is that they (implicitly) rely on the technique of the Naor-Reingold PRF [62]. However, while they gradually introduce random values in semi-functional spaces (which do not appear in our setting), we exploit a different degree of freedom enabled by lattices, which is the homomorphic evaluation of low-depth PRFs.

The GSW FHE scheme [41] inspired homomorphic manipulations [20] of Micciancio-Peikert trapdoors [60], which proved useful in the design of attribute-based encryption (ABE) for circuits [20,28] and fully homomorphic signatures [43]. In particular, the homomorphic evaluation of PRF circuits was considered by Brakerski and Vaikuntanathan [28] to construct an unbounded ABE system. Boyen and Li [22] used similar ideas to build tightly secure IBE and signatures from lattice assumptions. Our constructions depart from [22] in that PRFs are also used in the schemes, and not only in the security proofs. Another difference is that [22,28] only need PRFs with binary outputs, whereas our ABM-LTFs require a PRF with an exponentially-large range in order to prevent the adversary from predicting its output with noticeable probability.

We finally remark that merely applying the Canetti-Halevi-Katz paradigm [30] to the Boyen-Li IBE [22] does not imply tight CCA2 security in the multi-challenge setting since the proof of [22] is only tight for one identity: in a game with Q challenge ciphertexts, the best known reduction would still lose a factor Q via the standard hybrid argument.

Concurrent Work. In a concurrent and independent paper, Boyen and Li [23] proposed an LWE-based all-but-many lossy trapdoor function. While their construction relies on a similar idea of homomorphically evaluating a PRF over GSW ciphertexts, it differs from our ABM-LTF in several aspects. First, their evaluation keys contain GSW-encrypted matrices while our scheme encrypts scalars. As a result, their security proofs have to deal with invalid tags (which are neither lossy nor efficiently invertible with a trapdoor) that do not appear in our construction. Secondly, while their ABM-LTF loses more information on its input than ours, it does not seem to enable simulation-based security. The reason is that their use of small-norm LWE secrets (which allows for a greater lossiness) makes it hard to embed a lattice trapdoor in lossy keys. As a result, their IND-SO-CCA2 system does not readily extend to provide SIM-SO-CCA2 security. An advantage of their scheme is that it requires only a weak PRF rather than a strong PRF. This is a real benefit as weak PRFs are much easier to design with a low-depth evaluation circuit.

2 Background

For any $q \geq 2$, we let $\mathbb{Z}_q$ denote the ring of integers with addition and multiplication modulo q. We always set q as a prime integer. If $\mathbf{x}$ is a vector over $\mathbb{R}$, then $\|\mathbf{x}\|$ denotes its Euclidean norm. If $\mathbf{M}$ is a matrix over $\mathbb{R}$, then $\|\mathbf{M}\|$ denotes its induced norm. We let $\sigma_n(\mathbf{M})$ denote the least singular value of $\mathbf{M}$, where n is the rank of $\mathbf{M}$. For a finite set S, we let $U(S)$ denote the uniform distribution over S. If X is a random variable over a countable domain, the min-entropy of X is defined as $H_\infty(X) = \min_x(-\log_2 \Pr[X = x])$. If X and Y are distributions over the same domain, then $\Delta(X, Y)$ denotes their statistical distance.

2.1 Randomness Extraction

We first recall the Leftover Hash Lemma, as it was stated in [1].

Lemma 1 ([1]). *Let $\mathcal{H} = \{h : X \to Y\}_{h \in \mathcal{H}}$ be a family of universal hash functions, for countable sets X, Y. For any random variable T taking values in X, we have $\Delta\big((h, h(T)), (h, U(Y))\big) \leq \frac{1}{2} \cdot \sqrt{2^{-H_\infty(T)} \cdot |Y|}$. More generally, let $(T_i)_{i \leq k}$ be independent random variables with values in X, for some $k > 0$. We have $\Delta\big((h, (h(T_i))_{i \leq k}), (h, (U(Y))^{(i)})_{i \leq k})\big) \leq \frac{k}{2} \cdot \sqrt{2^{-H_\infty(T)} \cdot |Y|}$.*

A consequence of Lemma 1 was used by Agrawal *et al.* [1] to re-randomize matrices over $\mathbb{Z}_q$ by multiplying them with small-norm matrices.

Lemma 2 ([1]). *Let us assume that $m > 2n \cdot \log q$, for some prime $q > 2$. For any $k \in \mathsf{poly}(n)$, if $\mathbf{A} \hookleftarrow U(\mathbb{Z}_q^{m \times n})$, $\mathbf{B} \hookleftarrow U(\mathbb{Z}_q^{k \times n})$, $\mathbf{R} \hookleftarrow U(\{-1, 1\}^{k \times m})$, the distributions $(\mathbf{A}, \mathbf{R} \cdot \mathbf{A})$ and $(\mathbf{A}, \mathbf{B})$ are within $2^{-\Omega(n)}$ statistical distance.*

2.2 Reminders on Lattices

Let $\mathbf{\Sigma} \in \mathbb{R}^{n \times n}$ be a symmetric definite positive matrix, and $\mathbf{c} \in \mathbb{R}^n$. We define the Gaussian function on $\mathbb{R}^n$ by $\rho_{\mathbf{\Sigma},\mathbf{c}}(\mathbf{x}) = \exp(-\pi(\mathbf{x} - \mathbf{c})^\top \mathbf{\Sigma}^{-1}(\mathbf{x} - \mathbf{c}))$ and if $\mathbf{\Sigma} = \sigma^2 \cdot \mathbf{I}_n$ and $\mathbf{c} = \mathbf{0}$ we denote it by ρ_σ. For an n-dimensional lattice Λ, we define $\eta_\varepsilon(\Lambda)$ as the smallest $r > 0$ such that $\rho_{1/r}(\widehat{\Lambda} \setminus \mathbf{0}) \leq \varepsilon$ with $\widehat{\Lambda}$ denoting the dual of Λ, for any $\varepsilon \in (0, 1)$. In particular, we have $\eta_{2^{-n}}(\mathbb{Z}^n) \leq O(\sqrt{n})$. We denote by $\lambda_1^\infty(\Lambda)$ the infinity norm of the shortest non-zero vector of Λ.

For a matrix $\mathbf{A} \in \mathbb{Z}_q^{m \times n}$, we define $\Lambda^\perp(\mathbf{A}) = \{\mathbf{x} \in \mathbb{Z}^m : \mathbf{x}^\top \cdot \mathbf{A} = \mathbf{0} \bmod q\}$ and $\Lambda(\mathbf{A}) = \mathbf{A} \cdot \mathbb{Z}^n + q\mathbb{Z}^m$.

Lemma 3 (Adapted from [40, Lemma 5.3]**).** *Let $m \geq 2n$ and $q \geq 2$ prime. With probability $\geq 1 - 2^{-\Omega(n)}$, we have $\eta_{2^{-n}}(\Lambda^\perp(\mathbf{A})) \leq \eta_{2^{-m}}(\Lambda^\perp(\mathbf{A})) \leq O(\sqrt{m}) \cdot q^{n/m}$ and $\lambda_1^\infty(\Lambda(\mathbf{A})) \geq q^{1-n/m}/4$.*

Let Λ be a full-rank n-dimensional lattice, $\mathbf{\Sigma} \in \mathbb{R}^{n \times n}$ be a symmetric definite positive matrix, and $\mathbf{x}', \mathbf{c} \in \mathbb{R}^n$. We define the discrete Gaussian distribution of support $\Lambda + \mathbf{x}'$ and parameters $\mathbf{\Sigma}$ and $\mathbf{c}$ by $D_{\Lambda+\mathbf{x}',\mathbf{\Sigma},\mathbf{c}}(\mathbf{x}) \sim \rho_{\mathbf{\Sigma},\mathbf{c}}(\mathbf{x})$, for every $\mathbf{x} \in \Lambda + \mathbf{x}'$. For a subset $S \subseteq \Lambda + \mathbf{x}'$, we denote by $D^S_{\Lambda+\mathbf{x}',\mathbf{\Sigma},\mathbf{c}}$ the distribution obtained by restricting the distribution $D_{\Lambda+\mathbf{x}',\mathbf{\Sigma},\mathbf{c}}$ to the support S. For $\mathbf{x} \in S$, we have $D^S_{\Lambda+\mathbf{x}',\mathbf{\Sigma},\mathbf{c}}(\mathbf{x}) = D_{\Lambda+\mathbf{x}',\mathbf{\Sigma},\mathbf{c}}(\mathbf{x})/p_a$, where $p_a(S) = D_{\Lambda+\mathbf{x}',\mathbf{\Sigma},\mathbf{c}}(S)$. Assuming that $1/p_a(S) = n^{O(1)}$, membership in S is efficiently testable and $D_{\Lambda+\mathbf{x}',\mathbf{\Sigma},\mathbf{c}}$ is efficiently samplable, the distribution $D^S_{\Lambda+\mathbf{x}',\mathbf{\Sigma},\mathbf{c}}$ can be efficiently sampled from using rejection sampling.

We will use the following standard results on lattice Gaussians.

Lemma 4 (Adapted from [25, Lemma 2.3]**).** *There exists a* ppt *algorithm that, given a basis $(\mathbf{b}_i)_{i \leq n}$ of a full-rank lattice Λ, $\mathbf{x}', \mathbf{c} \in \mathbb{R}^n$ and $\mathbf{\Sigma} \in \mathbb{R}^{n \times n}$ symmetric definite positive such that $\Omega(\sqrt{\log n}) \cdot \max_i \|\mathbf{\Sigma}^{-1/2} \cdot \mathbf{b}_i\| \leq 1$, returns a sample from $D_{\Lambda+\mathbf{x}',\mathbf{\Sigma},\mathbf{c}}$.*

Lemma 5 (Adapted from [61, Lemma 4.4]**).** *For any n-dimensional lattice Λ, $\mathbf{x}', \mathbf{c} \in \mathbb{R}^n$ and symmetric positive definite $\mathbf{\Sigma} \in \mathbb{R}^{n \times n}$ satisfying $\sigma_n(\sqrt{\mathbf{\Sigma}}) \geq \eta_{2^{-n}}(\Lambda)$, we have $\Pr_{\mathbf{x} \hookleftarrow D_{\Lambda+\mathbf{x}',\mathbf{\Sigma},\mathbf{c}}}[\|\mathbf{x} - \mathbf{c}\| \geq \sqrt{n} \cdot \|\sqrt{\mathbf{\Sigma}}\|] \leq 2^{-n+2}$.*

Lemma 6 (Adapted from [61, Lemma 4.4]**).** *For any n-dimensional lattice* Λ, $\mathbf{x}', \mathbf{c} \in \mathbb{R}^n$ *and symmetric positive definite* $\mathbf{\Sigma} \in \mathbb{R}^{n \times n}$ *satisfying* $\sigma_n(\sqrt{\mathbf{\Sigma}}) \geq \eta_{2^{-n}}(\Lambda)$, *we have* $\rho_{\mathbf{\Sigma},\mathbf{c}}(\Lambda + \mathbf{x}') \in [1 - 2^{-n}, 1 + 2^{-n}] \cdot \det(\Lambda)/\det(\mathbf{\Sigma})^{1/2}$.

We will also use the following result on the singular values of discrete Gaussian random matrices.

Lemma 7 ([2, Lemma 8])**.** *Assume that* $m \geq 2n$. *Let* $\mathbf{F} \in \mathbb{Z}^{m \times n}$ *with each entry sampled from* $D_{\mathbb{Z},\sigma}$, *for some* $\sigma \geq \Omega(\sqrt{n})$. *Then with probability* $\geq 1 - 2^{-\Omega(n)}$, *we have* $\|\mathbf{F}\| \leq O(\sqrt{m}\sigma)$ *and* $\sigma_n(\mathbf{F}) \geq \Omega(\sqrt{m}\sigma)$.

2.3 The Learning with Errors Problem

We recall the Learning With Errors problem [69]. Note that we make the number of samples m explicit in our definition.

Definition 1. *Let* $\lambda \in \mathbb{N}$ *be a security parameter and let integers* $n = n(\lambda)$, $m = m(\lambda)$, $q = q(\lambda)$. *Let* $\chi = \chi(\lambda)$ *be an efficiently samplable distribution over* $\mathbb{Z}_q$. *The* $\mathsf{LWE}_{n,m,q,\chi}$ *assumption posits that the following distance is a negligible function for any* ppt *algorithm* $\mathcal{A}$:

$$\begin{aligned}\mathbf{Adv}^{\mathcal{A},\mathsf{LWE}}_{\ell,m,q,\chi}(\lambda) := \big| &\Pr[\mathcal{A}(1^\lambda, \mathbf{A}, \mathbf{u}) = 1 \mid \mathbf{A} \hookleftarrow U(\mathbb{Z}_q^{n \times m}), \mathbf{u} \hookleftarrow U(\mathbb{Z}_q^m)] \\ &- \Pr[\mathcal{A}(1^\lambda, \mathbf{A}, \mathbf{A} \cdot \mathbf{s} + \mathbf{e}) = 1 \mid \mathbf{A} \hookleftarrow U(\mathbb{Z}_q^{m \times n}), \mathbf{s} \hookleftarrow U(\mathbb{Z}_q^n), \mathbf{e} \hookleftarrow \chi^m]\big|.\end{aligned}$$

A typical choice for χ is the integer Gaussian distribution $D_{\mathbb{Z},\alpha \cdot q}$ for some parameter $\alpha \in (\sqrt{n}/q, 1)$. In particular, in this case, there exist reductions from standard lattice problems to LWE (see [25,69]).

In [60], Micciancio and Peikert described a trapdoor mechanism for LWE. Their technique uses a "gadget" matrix $\mathbf{G} \in \mathbb{Z}_q^{m \times n}$ for which anyone can publicly sample short vectors $\mathbf{x} \in \mathbb{Z}^m$ such that $\mathbf{x}^\top \mathbf{G} = \mathbf{0}$. As in [60], we call $\mathbf{R} \in \mathbb{Z}^{m \times m}$ a $\mathbf{G}$-trapdoor for a matrix $\mathbf{A} \in \mathbb{Z}_q^{2m \times n}$ if $[\mathbf{R} \mid \mathbf{I}_m] \cdot \mathbf{A} = \mathbf{G} \cdot \mathbf{H}$ for some invertible matrix $\mathbf{H} \in \mathbb{Z}_q^{n \times n}$ which is referred to as the trapdoor tag. If $\mathbf{H} = \mathbf{0}$, then $\mathbf{R}$ is called a "punctured" trapdoor for $\mathbf{A}$.

Lemma 8 ([60, Sect. 5])**.** *Assume that* $m \geq 2n \log q$. *There exists a* ppt *algorithm* $\mathsf{GenTrap}$ *that takes as inputs matrices* $\bar{\mathbf{A}} \in \mathbb{Z}_q^{m \times n}$, $\mathbf{H} \in \mathbb{Z}_q^{n \times n}$ *and outputs matrices* $\mathbf{R} \in \{-1, 1\}^{m \times m}$ *and*

$$\mathbf{A} = \begin{bmatrix} \bar{\mathbf{A}} \\ -\mathbf{R}\bar{\mathbf{A}} + \mathbf{G}\mathbf{H} \end{bmatrix} \in \mathbb{Z}_q^{2m \times n}$$

such that if $\mathbf{H} \in \mathbb{Z}_q^{n \times n}$ *is invertible, then* $\mathbf{R}$ *is a* $\mathbf{G}$*-trapdoor for* $\mathbf{A}$ *with tag* $\mathbf{H}$; *and if* $\mathbf{H} = \mathbf{0}$, *then* $\mathbf{R}$ *is a punctured trapdoor.*

Further, in case of a $\mathbf{G}$*-trapdoor, one can efficiently compute from* $\mathbf{A}, \mathbf{R}$ *and* $\mathbf{H}$ *a basis* $(\mathbf{b}_i)_{i \leq 2m}$ *of* $\Lambda^\perp(\mathbf{A})$ *such that* $\max_i \|\mathbf{b}_i\| \leq O(m^{3/2})$.

Micciancio and Peikert also showed that a $\mathbf{G}$-trapdoor for $\mathbf{A} \in \mathbb{Z}_q^{2m \times n}$ can be used to invert the LWE function $(\boldsymbol{s}, \boldsymbol{e}) \mapsto \mathbf{A} \cdot \boldsymbol{s} + \boldsymbol{e}$, for any $\boldsymbol{s} \in \mathbb{Z}_q^n$ and any sufficiently short $\boldsymbol{e} \in \mathbb{Z}^{2m}$.

Lemma 9 ([60, Theorem 5.4]). *There exists a deterministic polynomial time algorithm* Invert *that takes as inputs matrices* $\mathbf{R} \in \mathbb{Z}^{m \times m}$, $\mathbf{A} \in \mathbb{Z}_q^{2m \times n}$, $\mathbf{H} \in \mathbb{Z}_q^{n \times n}$ *such that* $\mathbf{R}$ *is a* $\mathbf{G}$*-trapdoor for* $\mathbf{A}$ *with invertible tag* $\mathbf{H}$*, and a vector* $\mathbf{A} \cdot \mathbf{s} + \mathbf{e}$ *with* $\mathbf{s} \in \mathbb{Z}_q^n$ *and* $\|\mathbf{e}\| \leq q/(10 \cdot \|\mathbf{R}\|)$*, and outputs* $\mathbf{s}$ *and* $\mathbf{e}$.

As showed in [20,41], homomorphic computations can be performed on $\mathbf{G}$-trapdoors with respect to trapdoor tags $\mathbf{H}_i$ corresponding to scalars. As observed in [27], when the circuit belongs to NC^1, it is advantageous to convert the circuit into a branching program, using Barrington's theorem. This is interesting to allow for a polynomial modulus q but imposes a circuit depth restriction (so that the evaluation algorithms are guaranteed to run in polynomial-time).

Lemma 10 (Adapted from [20,41]). *Let* $C : \{0,1\}^\kappa \rightarrow \{0,1\}$ *be a NAND Boolean circuit of depth* d*. Let* $\mathbf{B}_i = \mathbf{R}_i \cdot \bar{\mathbf{A}} + x_i \cdot \mathbf{G} \in \mathbb{Z}_q^{m \times n}$ *with* $\bar{\mathbf{A}} \in \mathbb{Z}_q^{m \times n}$, $\mathbf{R}_i \in \{-1,1\}^{m \times m}$ *and* $x_i \in \{0,1\}$*, for* $i \leq \kappa$.

- *There exist deterministic algorithms* $\mathsf{Eval}^{\mathsf{pub}}_{\mathsf{CCT}}$ *and* $\mathsf{Eval}^{\mathsf{priv}}_{\mathsf{CCT}}$ *with running times* $\mathsf{poly}(|C|, \kappa, m, n, \log q)$*, that satisfy:*
$$\mathsf{Eval}^{\mathsf{pub}}_{\mathsf{CCT}}(C, (\mathbf{B}_i)_i) = \mathsf{Eval}^{\mathsf{priv}}_{\mathsf{CCT}}(C, (\mathbf{R}_i)_i) \cdot \bar{\mathbf{A}} + C(x_1, \ldots, x_\kappa) \cdot \mathbf{G},$$
and $\|\mathsf{Eval}^{\mathsf{priv}}_{\mathsf{CCT}}(C, (\mathbf{R}_i)_i)\| \leq m^{O(d)}$.
- *There exist deterministic algorithms* $\mathsf{Eval}^{\mathsf{pub}}_{\mathsf{BP}}$ *and* $\mathsf{Eval}^{\mathsf{priv}}_{\mathsf{BP}}$ *with running times* $\mathsf{poly}(4^d, \kappa, m, n, \log q)$*, that satisfy:*
$$\mathsf{Eval}^{\mathsf{pub}}_{\mathsf{BP}}(C, (\mathbf{B}_i)_i) = \mathsf{Eval}^{\mathsf{priv}}_{\mathsf{BP}}(C, (\mathbf{R}_i)_i) \cdot \bar{\mathbf{A}} + C(x_1, \ldots, x_\kappa) \cdot \mathbf{G},$$
and $\|\mathsf{Eval}^{\mathsf{priv}}_{\mathsf{BP}}(C, (\mathbf{R}_i)_i)\| \leq 4^d \cdot O(m^{3/2})$.

Note that we impose that the $\mathsf{Eval}^{\mathsf{pub}}$ and $\mathsf{Eval}^{\mathsf{priv}}$ algorithms are deterministic, although probabilistic variants are considered in the literature. This is important in our case, as it will be used in the function evaluation algorithm of our all-but-many lossy trapdoor function family LTF function evaluation.

2.4 Lossy Trapdoor Functions

We consider a variant of the notion of Lossy Trapdoor Functions (LTF) introduced by [66], for which the function input may be sampled from a distribution that differs from the uniform distribution. In our constructions, for lossiness security, we actually allow the function evaluation algorithm to sample from a larger domain Dom^E_λ than the domain Dom^D_λ on which the inversion algorithm guaranteed to succeed. A sample over Dom^E_λ has an overwhelming probability to land in Dom^D_λ with respect to the sampling distribution.

Definition 2. *For an integer* $l(\lambda) > 0$*, a family of* l*-lossy trapdoor functions* LTF *with security parameter* λ*, evaluation sampling domain* Dom^E_λ*, efficiently samplable distribution* $D_{\mathsf{Dom}^E_\lambda}$ *on* Dom^E_λ*, inversion domain* $\mathsf{Dom}^D_\lambda \subseteq \mathsf{Dom}^E_\lambda$ *and range* Rng_λ *is a tuple* (IGen, LGen, Eval, Invert) *of* ppt *algorithms with the following functionalities:*

Injective key generation. $\mathsf{LTF.IGen}(1^\lambda)$ *outputs an evaluation key ek for an injective function together with an inversion key ik.*

Lossy key generation. $\mathsf{LTF.LGen}(1^\lambda)$ *outputs an evaluation key ek for a lossy function. In this case, there is no inversion key and we define* $ik = \perp$.

Evaluation. $\mathsf{LTF.Eval}(ek, X)$ *takes as inputs the evaluation key ek and a function input* $X \in \mathsf{Dom}_\lambda^E$. *It outputs an image* $Y = f_{ek}(X)$.

Inversion. $\mathsf{LTF.Invert}(ik, Y)$ *inputs the inversion key* $ik \neq \perp$ *and a* $Y \in \mathsf{Rng}_\lambda$. *It outputs the unique* $X = f_{ik}^{-1}(Y)$ *such that* $Y = f_{ek}(X)$ *(if it exists).*

In addition, LTF *has to meet the following requirements:*

Inversion Correctness. *For an injective key pair* $(ek, ik) \leftarrow \mathsf{LTF.IGen}(1^\lambda)$, *we have, except with negligible probability over* (ek, ik), *that for all inputs* $X \in \mathsf{Dom}_\lambda^D$, $X = f_{ik}^{-1}(f_{ek}(X))$.

Eval Sampling Correctness. *For* X *sampled from* $D_{\mathsf{Dom}_\lambda^E}$, *we have* $X \in \mathsf{Dom}_\lambda^D$ *except with negligible probability.*

l-Lossiness. *For* $(ek, \perp) \hookleftarrow \mathsf{LTF.LGen}(1^\lambda)$ *and* $X \hookleftarrow D_{\mathsf{Dom}_\lambda^E}$, *we have that* $H_\infty(X \mid ek = \overline{ek}, f_{ek}(X) = \overline{y}) \geq l$, *for all* $(\overline{ek}, \overline{y})$ *except a set of negligible probability.*

Indistinguishability. *The distribution of lossy functions is computationally indistinguishable from that of injective functions, namely:*

$$\mathbf{Adv}^{\mathcal{A},\mathsf{LTF}}(\lambda) := \big| \Pr[\mathcal{A}(1^\lambda, ek) = 1 \mid (ek, ik) \hookleftarrow \mathsf{LTF.IGen}(1^\lambda)] - \Pr[\mathcal{A}(1^\lambda, ek) = 1 \mid (ek, \perp) \hookleftarrow \mathsf{LTF.LGen}(1^\lambda)] \big|$$

is a negligible function for any ppt *algorithm* $\mathcal{A}$.

2.5 All-But-Many Lossy Trapdoor Functions

We consider a variant of the definition of All-But-Many Lossy Trapdoor Functions (ABM-LTF) from [49], in which the distribution over the function domain may not be the uniform one.

Definition 3. *For an integer* $l(\lambda) > 0$, *a family of all-but-many* l*- lossy trapdoor functions* ABM *with security parameter* λ, *evaluation sampling domain* Dom_λ^E, *efficiently samplable distribution* $D_{\mathsf{Dom}_\lambda^E}$ *on* Dom_λ^E, *inversion domain* $\mathsf{Dom}_\lambda^D \subseteq \mathsf{Dom}_\lambda^E$, *and range* Rng_λ *consists of the following* ppt *algorithms:*

Keygeneration. $\mathsf{ABM.Gen}(1^\lambda)$ *outputs an evaluation key ek, an inversion key ik and a tag key tk. The evaluation key ek defines a set* $\mathcal{T} = \mathcal{T}_\mathsf{c} \times \mathcal{T}_\mathsf{a}$ *containing the disjoint sets of lossy tags* $\mathcal{T}_{\mathsf{loss}}$ *and injective tags* $\mathcal{T}_{\mathsf{inj}}$. *Each tag* $t = (t_\mathsf{c}, t_\mathsf{a})$ *is described by a core part* $t_\mathsf{c} \in \mathcal{T}_\mathsf{c}$ *and an auxiliary part* $t_\mathsf{a} \in \mathcal{T}_\mathsf{a}$.

Evaluation. $\mathsf{ABM.Eval}(ek, t, X)$ *takes as inputs an evaluation key ek, a tag* $t \in \mathcal{T}$ *and a function input* $X \in \mathsf{Dom}_\lambda^E$. *It outputs an image* $Y = f_{ek,t}(X)$.

Inversion. $\mathsf{ABM.Invert}(ik, t, Y)$ *takes as inputs an inversion key ik, a tag* $t \in \mathcal{T}$ *and a* $Y \in \mathsf{Rng}_\lambda$. *It outputs the unique* $X = f_{ik,t}^{-1}(Y)$ *such that* $Y = f_{ek,t}(X)$.

Lossy tag generation. $\mathsf{ABM.LTag}(tk, t_a)$ *takes as input an auxiliary part* $t_a \in \mathcal{T}_a$ *and outputs a core part* t_c *such that* $t = (t_c, t_a)$ *forms a lossy tag.*

In addition, ABM *has to meet the following requirements:*

Inversion Correctness. *For* (ek, ik, tk) *produced by* $\mathsf{ABM.Gen}(1^\lambda)$*, we have, except with negligible probability over* (ek, ik, tk)*, that for all injective tags* $t \in \mathcal{T}_{\mathsf{inj}}$ *and all inputs* $X \in \mathsf{Dom}^D_\lambda$*, that* $X = f^{-1}_{ik,t}(f_{ek,t}(X))$*.*

Eval Sampling Correctness. *For* X *sampled from* $D_{\mathsf{Dom}^E_\lambda}$*, we have* $X \in \mathsf{Dom}^D_\lambda$ *except with negligible probability.*

Lossiness. *For* $(ek, ik, tk) \hookleftarrow \mathsf{ABM.Gen}(1^\lambda)$*, any* $t_a \in \mathcal{T}_a$*,* $t_c \hookleftarrow \mathsf{ABM.LTag}(tk, t_a)$ *and* $X \hookleftarrow D_{\mathsf{Dom}^E_\lambda}$*, we have that* $H_\infty(X \mid ek = \overline{ek}, f_{ek,(t_c,t_a)}(X) = \overline{y}) \geq l$*, for all* $(\overline{ek}, \overline{y})$ *except a set of negligible probability.*

Indistinguishability. *Multiple lossy tags are computationally indistinguishable from random tags, namely:*

$$\mathbf{Adv}^{\mathcal{A},\mathsf{ind}}_Q(\lambda) := \left| \Pr[\mathcal{A}(1^\lambda, ek)^{\mathsf{ABM.LTag}(tk,\cdot)} = 1] - \Pr[\mathcal{A}(1^\lambda, ek)^{\mathcal{O}_{\mathcal{T}_c}(\cdot)} = 1] \right|$$

is negligible for any ppt *algorithm* $\mathcal{A}$*, where* $(ek, ik, tk) \hookleftarrow \mathsf{ABM.Gen}(1^\lambda)$ *and* $\mathcal{O}_{\mathcal{T}_c}(\cdot)$ *is an oracle that assigns a random core tag* $t_c \hookleftarrow U(\mathcal{T}_c)$ *to each auxiliary tag* $t_a \in \mathcal{T}_a$ *(rather than a core tag that makes* $t = (t_c, t_a)$ *lossy). Here* Q *denotes the number of oracle queries made by* $\mathcal{A}$*.*

Evasiveness. *Non-injective tags are computationally hard to find, even with access to an oracle outputting multiple lossy tags, namely:*

$$\mathbf{Adv}^{\mathcal{A},\mathsf{eva}}_{Q_1,Q_2}(\lambda) := \Pr[\mathcal{A}(1^\lambda, ek)^{\mathsf{ABM.LTag}(tk,\cdot),\mathsf{ABM.IsLossy}(tk,\cdot)} \in \mathcal{T} \backslash \mathcal{T}_{\mathsf{inj}}]$$

is negligible for legitimate adversary $\mathcal{A}$*, where* $(ek, ik, tk) \hookleftarrow \mathsf{ABM.Gen}(1^\lambda)$ *and* $\mathcal{A}$ *is given access to the following oracles:*

- $\mathsf{ABM.LTag}(tk, \cdot)$ *which acts exactly as the lossy tag generation algorithm.*
- $\mathsf{ABM.IsLossy}(tk, \cdot)$ *that takes as input a tag* $t = (t_c, t_a)$ *and outputs* 1 *if* $t \in \mathcal{T} \backslash \mathcal{T}_{\mathsf{inj}}$ *and otherwise outputs* 0*.*

We denote by Q_1 *and* Q_2 *the number of queries to these two oracles. By "legitimate adversary", we mean that* $\mathcal{A}$ *is* ppt *and never outputs a tag* $t = (t_c, t_a)$ *such that* t_c *was obtained by invoking the* ABM.LTag *oracle on* t_a*.*

As pointed out in [49], the evasiveness property mirrors the notion of strong unforgeability for signature schemes. Indeed, the adversary is considered successful even if it outputs a (t_c, t_a) such that t_a was submitted to $\mathsf{ABM.LTag}(tk, \cdot)$ as long as the response t'_a of the latter was such that $t'_a \neq t_a$.

In order to simplify the tight proof of our public-key encryption scheme, we slightly modified the original definition of evasiveness in [49] by introducing a lossiness-testing oracle $\mathsf{ABM.IsLossy}(tk, \cdot)$. When it comes to proving tight CCA security, it will save the reduction from having to guess which decryption query contradicts the evasiveness property of the underlying ABM-LTF.

2.6 Selective-Opening Chosen-Ciphertext Security

A public-key encryption scheme consists of a tuple of ppt algorithms (Par-Gen, Keygen, Encrypt,Decrypt), where Par-Gen takes as input a security parameter 1^λ and generates common public parameters Γ, Keygen takes in Γ and outputs a key pair (SK, PK), while Encrypt and Decrypt proceed in the usual way.

As a first step, we will consider encryption schemes that provide SO security in the sense of an indistinguishability-based definition (or IND-SOA security). This notion is captured by a game where the adversary obtains $N(\lambda)$ ciphertexts, opens an arbitrary subset of these (meaning that it obtains both the plaintexts and the encryption coins) and asks that remaining ciphertexts be indistinguishable from messages that are independently re-sampled conditionally on opened ones. In the IND-SO-CCA2 scenario, this should remain true even if the adversary has a decryption oracle. A formal definition is recalled in the full paper.

A stronger notion is that of simulation-based security, which demands that an efficient simulator be able to perform about as well as the adversary without seeing neither the ciphertexts nor the public key. Formally, two experiments are required to have indistinguishable output distributions.

In the real experiment, the challenger samples $\mathbf{Msg} = (\mathsf{Msg}_1, \ldots, \mathsf{Msg}_N) \leftarrow \mathcal{M}$ from the joint message distribution and picks random coins $r_1, \ldots, r_N \leftarrow \mathcal{R}$ to compute ciphertexts $\{\mathbf{C}_i \leftarrow \mathsf{Encrypt}(PK, \mathsf{Msg}_i, r_i)\}_{i\in[N]}$ which are given to the adversary $\mathcal{A}$. The latter responds by choosing a subset $I \subset [N]$ and gets back $\{(\mathsf{Msg}_i, r_i)\}_{i\in I}$. The adversary $\mathcal{A}$ outputs a string $out_\mathcal{A}$ and the output of the experiment is a predicate $\mathfrak{R}(\mathcal{M}, \mathbf{Msg}, out_\mathcal{A})$.

In the ideal experiment, the challenger samples $\mathbf{Msg} = (\mathsf{Msg}_1, \ldots, \mathsf{Msg}_N) \leftarrow \mathcal{M}$ from the joint message distribution. Without seeing any encryptions, the simulator chooses a subset I and some state information st. After having seen the messages $\{\mathsf{Msg}_i\}_{i\in I}$ and the state information but without seeing any randomness, the simulator outputs a string out_S. The outcome of the ideal experiment is the predicate $\mathfrak{R}(\mathcal{M}, \mathbf{Msg}, out_S)$. As in [36,54], we allow the adversary to choose the message distribution $\mathcal{M}$. While this distribution should be efficiently samplable, it is *not* required to support efficient conditional re-sampling.

Definition 4 ([36,54]). *A PKE scheme* (Par-Gen, Keygen, Encrypt, Decrypt) *provides* **simulation-based selective opening** *(SIM-SO-CPA) security if, for any* ppt *function* $\mathfrak{R}$ *and any* ppt *adversary* $\mathcal{A} = (\mathcal{A}_0, \mathcal{A}_1, \mathcal{A}_2)$ *in the real experiment* $\mathbf{Exp}^{\mathsf{cpa\text{-}so\text{-}real}}(\lambda)$*, there is an efficient simulator* $S = (S_0, S_1, S_2)$ *in the ideal experiment* $\mathbf{Exp}^{\mathsf{so\text{-}ideal}}(\lambda)$ *s.t.* $|\Pr[\mathbf{Exp}^{\mathsf{cpa\text{-}so\text{-}real}}(\lambda) = 1] - \Pr[\mathbf{Exp}^{\mathsf{so\text{-}ideal}}(\lambda) = 1]|$ *is negligible, where the two experiments are defined as follows:*

$\mathbf{Exp}^{\mathsf{cpa\text{-}so\text{-}real}}(\lambda)$:	$\mathbf{Exp}^{\mathsf{so\text{-}ideal}}(\lambda)$:
$\Gamma \leftarrow \mathsf{Par\text{-}Gen}(1^\lambda)$;	$\Gamma \leftarrow \mathsf{Par\text{-}Gen}(1^\lambda)$;
$(PK, SK) \leftarrow \mathsf{Keygen}(\Gamma)$	$(\mathcal{M}, st_0) \leftarrow S_0(\Gamma)$
$(\mathcal{M}, st_0) \leftarrow \mathcal{A}_0(PK, \Gamma)$	$\mathbf{Msg} = (\mathsf{Msg}_1, \ldots, \mathsf{Msg}_N) \leftarrow \mathcal{M}$
$\mathbf{Msg} = (\mathsf{Msg}_1, \ldots, \mathsf{Msg}_N) \leftarrow \mathcal{M}$	$(I, st_1) \leftarrow S_1(st_0, 1^{\lvert\mathsf{Msg}_i\rvert})$
$r_1, \ldots, r_n \leftarrow \mathcal{R}$	$out_S \leftarrow S_2(st_1, \{\mathsf{Msg}_i\}_{i\in I})$
$\mathbf{C}_i \leftarrow \mathsf{Encrypt}(PK, \mathsf{Msg}_i, r_i) \quad \forall i \in [N]$,	*Output* $\mathfrak{R}(\mathcal{M}, \mathbf{Msg}, out_S)$
$(I, st_1) \leftarrow \mathcal{A}_1(st_0, \mathbf{C}_1, \ldots, \mathbf{C}_N)$	
$out_\mathcal{A} \leftarrow \mathcal{A}_2(st_1, (\mathsf{Msg}_i, r_i)_{i\in I})$	
Output $\mathfrak{R}(\mathcal{M}, \mathbf{Msg}, out_\mathcal{A})$	

As usual, the adversarially-chosen message distribution $\mathcal{M}$ is efficiently samplable and encoded as a polynomial-size circuit.

The notion of simulation-based chosen-ciphertext (SIM-SO-CCA) security is defined analogously. The only difference is in the real experiment $\mathbf{Exp}^{\mathsf{cca\text{-}so\text{-}real}}$, which is obtained from $\mathbf{Exp}^{\mathsf{cpa\text{-}so\text{-}real}}$ by granting the adversary access to a decryption oracle at all stages. Of course, the adversary is disallowed to query the decryption of any ciphertext in the set $\{\mathbf{C}_i\}_{i\in[N]}$ of challenge ciphertexts.

It is known [11] that SIM-SO-CPA security can be achieved from lossy encryption schemes [16] when there exists an efficient Opener algorithm which, using the lossy secret key, can explain a lossy ciphertext $\mathbf{C}$ as an encryption of any given plaintext. As observed in [16,54], this Opener algorithm can use the initial coins used in the generation of $\mathbf{C}$ for this purpose. This property (for which a formal definition is recalled in the full version of the paper) is called efficient weak opening.

3 An All-But-Many Lossy Trapdoor Function from LWE

As a warm-up, we first describe a variant of the lossy trapdoor function suggested by Bellare *et al.* [12, Sect. 5.2] that is better suited to our needs. We then extend this LWE-based LTF into an ABM-LTF in Sect. 3.2.

3.1 An LWE-Based Lossy Trapdoor Function

All algorithms use a prime modulus $q > 2$, integers $n \in \mathsf{poly}(\lambda)$, $m \geq 2n\log q$ and $\ell > 0$, an LWE noise distribution χ, and parameters $\sigma_x, \sigma_e, \gamma_x, \gamma_e > 0$. The function evaluation sampling domain $\mathsf{Dom}^E_\lambda = \mathsf{Dom}^E_x \times \mathsf{Dom}^E_e$ where Dom^E_x (resp. Dom^E_e) is the set of $\mathbf{x}$ (resp. $\mathbf{e}$) in $\mathbb{Z}^n$ (resp. $\mathbb{Z}^{2m}$) with $\|\boldsymbol{x}\| \leq \gamma_x \cdot \sqrt{n} \cdot \sigma_x$ (resp. $\|\boldsymbol{e}\| \leq \gamma_e\sqrt{2m}\cdot\sigma_e$). Its inversion domain is $\mathsf{Dom}^D_\lambda = \mathsf{Dom}^D_x \times \mathsf{Dom}^D_e$, where Dom^D_x (resp. Dom^D_e) is the set of $\mathbf{x}$ (resp. $\mathbf{e}$) in $\mathbb{Z}^n$ (resp. $\mathbb{Z}^{2m}$) with $\|\boldsymbol{x}\| \leq \sqrt{n}\cdot\sigma_x$ (resp. $\|\boldsymbol{e}\| \leq \sqrt{2m}\cdot\sigma_e$) and its range is $\mathsf{Rng}_\lambda = \mathbb{Z}_q^{2m}$. The function inputs are sampled from the distribution $D_{\mathsf{Dom}^E_\lambda} = D^{\mathsf{Dom}^E_x}_{\mathbb{Z}^n,\sigma_x} \times D^{\mathsf{Dom}^E_e}_{\mathbb{Z}^{2m},\sigma_e}$.

Injective key generation. $\mathsf{LTF.IGen}(1^\lambda)$ samples $\bar{\mathbf{A}} \hookleftarrow U(\mathbb{Z}_q^{m\times n})$ and runs $(\mathbf{A}, \mathbf{R}) \hookleftarrow \mathsf{GenTrap}(\bar{\mathbf{A}}, \mathbf{I}_n)$ to obtain $\mathbf{A} \in \mathbb{Z}_q^{2m\times n}$ together with a $\mathbf{G}$-trapdoor $\mathbf{R} \in \{-1, 1\}^{m\times m}$. It outputs $ek := \mathbf{A}$ and $ik := \mathbf{R}$.

Lossy key generation. $\mathsf{LTF.LGen}(1^\lambda)$ generates $\mathbf{A} \in \mathbb{Z}_q^{2m\times n}$ as a matrix of the form $\mathbf{A} = \mathbf{B} \cdot \mathbf{C} + \mathbf{F}$ with $\mathbf{B} \hookleftarrow U(\mathbb{Z}_q^{2m\times \ell})$, $\mathbf{C} \hookleftarrow U(\mathbb{Z}_q^{\ell\times n})$ and $\mathbf{F} \hookleftarrow \chi^{2m\times n}$. It outputs $ek := \mathbf{A}$ and $ik := \perp$.

Evaluation. $\mathsf{LTF.Eval}(ek, (\mathbf{x}, \mathbf{e}))$ takes as input a domain element $(\mathbf{x}, \mathbf{e}) \in \mathsf{Dom}_\lambda^E$ and maps it to $\mathbf{y} = \mathbf{A} \cdot \mathbf{x} + \mathbf{e} \in \mathbb{Z}_q^{2m}$.

Inversion. $\mathsf{LTF.Invert}(ik, \mathbf{y})$ inputs a vector $\mathbf{y} \in \mathbb{Z}_q^{2m}$, uses the $\mathbf{G}$-trapdoor $ik = \mathbf{R}$ of $\mathbf{A}$ to find the unique $(\mathbf{x}, \mathbf{e}) \in \mathsf{Dom}_\lambda^D$ such that $\mathbf{y} = \mathbf{A} \cdot \mathbf{x} + \mathbf{e}$. This is done by applying the LWE inversion algorithm from Lemma 9.

Note that the construction differs from the lossy function of [12] in two ways. First, in [12], the considered distribution over the function domain is uniform over a parallelepiped. We instead consider a discrete Gaussian distribution. Second, in [12], the matrix $\mathbf{C}$ is chosen as a small-norm integer matrix sampled from the LWE noise distribution. We instead sample it uniformly. Both modifications are motivated by our application to SO-CCA security. Indeed, in the security proof, we will generate $\mathbf{C}$ along with a lattice trapdoor (using $\mathsf{GenTrap}$), which we will use to simulate the function domain distribution conditioned on an image value.

We first study the conditional distribution of the pair $(\mathbf{x}, \mathbf{e})$ given its image under a lossy function. This will be used to quantify the lossiness of the LTF.

Lemma 11. *Let* $\mathbf{C} \in \mathbb{Z}_q^{\ell\times n}$ *and* $\mathbf{F} \in \mathbb{Z}^{2m\times n}$. *Sample* $(\mathbf{x}, \mathbf{e}) \hookleftarrow D_{\mathbb{Z}^n,\sigma_x}^{\mathsf{Dom}_x} \times D_{\mathbb{Z}^{2m},\sigma_e}^{\mathsf{Dom}_e}$ *and define* $(\mathbf{u}, \mathbf{f}) = (\mathbf{C} \cdot \mathbf{x}, \mathbf{F} \cdot \mathbf{x} + \mathbf{e}) \in \mathbb{Z}_q^n \times \mathbb{Z}^{2m}$. *Note that* $\mathbf{e}$ *is fully determined by* $\mathbf{x}, \mathbf{u}$ *and* $\mathbf{f}$. *Further, the conditional distribution of* $\mathbf{x}$ *given* $(\mathbf{u}, \mathbf{f})$ *is* $D_{\Lambda^\perp(\mathbf{C}^\top)+\mathbf{x}',\sqrt{\mathbf{\Sigma}},\mathbf{c}}^{S_{\mathbf{F},\mathbf{u},\mathbf{f}}}$, *with support*

$$S_{\mathbf{F},\mathbf{u},\mathbf{f}} = \left\{\bar{\mathbf{x}} \in \Lambda^\perp(\mathbf{C}^\top) + \mathbf{x}' : \bar{\mathbf{x}} \in \mathsf{Dom}_x,\ \mathbf{f} - \mathbf{F} \cdot \bar{\mathbf{x}} \in \mathsf{Dom}_e\right\},$$

where $\mathbf{x}'$ *is any solution to* $\mathbf{C} \cdot \mathbf{x}' = \mathbf{u}$ *and:*

$$\mathbf{\Sigma} = \sigma_x^2 \cdot \sigma_e^2 \cdot (\sigma_x^2 \cdot \mathbf{F}^\top \cdot \mathbf{F} + \sigma_e^2 \cdot \mathbf{I}_n)^{-1}, \quad \mathbf{c} = \sigma_x^2 \cdot (\sigma_x^2 \mathbf{F}^\top \cdot \mathbf{F} + \sigma_e^2 \cdot \mathbf{I}_n)^{-1} \cdot \mathbf{F}^\top \cdot \mathbf{f}.$$

Proof. We first remark that the support of $\mathbf{x}|(\mathbf{u}, \mathbf{f})$ is $S_{\mathbf{F},\mathbf{u},\mathbf{f}}$, since the set of solutions $\bar{\mathbf{x}} \in \mathbb{Z}^n$ to $\mathbf{u} = \mathbf{C} \cdot \mathbf{x} \in \mathbb{Z}_q^\ell$ is $\Lambda^\perp(\mathbf{C}^\top) + \mathbf{x}'$ and each such $\bar{\mathbf{x}}$ has a non-zero conditional probability if and only if the corresponding $\bar{\mathbf{e}} = \mathbf{f} - \mathbf{F} \cdot \mathbf{x}$ is in Dom_e. Now, for $\bar{\mathbf{x}} \in \mathbb{Z}^n$ in the support $S_{\mathbf{F},\mathbf{u},\mathbf{f}}$, we have

$$\begin{aligned}\Pr[\mathbf{x} = \bar{\mathbf{x}}|(\mathbf{u}, \mathbf{f})] &\sim D_{\mathbb{Z}^n,\sigma_x}(\bar{\mathbf{x}}) \cdot D_{\mathbb{Z}^{2m},\sigma_e}(\mathbf{f} - \mathbf{F} \cdot \bar{\mathbf{x}}) \\ &\sim \exp\left(-\pi\left(\frac{\|\bar{\mathbf{x}}\|^2}{\sigma_x^2} + \frac{\|\mathbf{f} - \mathbf{F} \cdot \bar{\mathbf{x}}\|^2}{\sigma_e^2}\right)\right) \\ &\sim \exp\left(-\pi\left((\bar{\mathbf{x}} - \mathbf{c})^\top \cdot \mathbf{\Sigma}^{-1} \cdot (\bar{\mathbf{x}} - \mathbf{c})\right)\right).\end{aligned}$$

The last equality follows from expanding the norms and collecting terms. □

We now formally state for which parameters we can prove that the scheme above is an LTF. The second part of the theorem will be useful for our SO-CCA encryption application.

Theorem 1. *Let $\chi = D_{\mathbb{Z},\beta/(2\sqrt{\lambda})}$ for some $\beta > 0$. Let us assume that $\ell \geq \lambda$, $n = \Omega(\ell \log q)$ and $m \geq 2n \log q$, $\gamma_x \geq 3\sqrt{m/n}$ and $\gamma_e \geq 3$. Assume further that $\sigma_x \geq \Omega(n)$, $\sigma_e \geq \Omega(\sqrt{mn} \cdot \beta \cdot \sigma_x)$ and $\sigma_e \leq O(q/m^{3/2})$. Then, under the $\mathsf{LWE}_{\ell,2m,q,\chi}$ hardness assumption, the above construction is an l-lossy LTF with $l \geq n \log \sigma_x - 2 - \ell \log q > \Omega(n \log n)$. Further, any* ppt *indistinguishability adversary $\mathcal{A}$ implies an* LWE *distinguisher $\mathcal{D}$ with comparable running time such that*

$$\mathbf{Adv}^{\mathcal{A},\mathsf{LTF}}(\lambda) \leq n \cdot \mathbf{Adv}^{\mathcal{D},\mathsf{LWE}}_{\ell,2m,q,\chi}(\lambda).$$

Moreover, there exists a ppt *sampling algorithm, that given $(\mathbf{B}, \mathbf{C}, \mathbf{F})$ generated by* $\mathsf{LTF.LGen}(1^\lambda)$, *a trapdoor basis $(\boldsymbol{b}_i)_{i \leq n}$ for $\Lambda^\perp(\mathbf{C}^\top)$ such that $\max_i \|\boldsymbol{b}_i\| \leq \sigma_x \sigma_e / (\Omega(\log n) \cdot \sqrt{2mn\beta^2\sigma_x^2 + \sigma_e^2})$ and a function output $\boldsymbol{y} = \mathsf{LTF.Eval}(ek, (\mathbf{x}, \mathbf{e}))$ for an input $(\mathbf{x}, \mathbf{e}) \hookleftarrow D^{\mathsf{Dom}^E_x}_{\mathbb{Z}^n,\sigma_x} \times D^{\mathsf{Dom}^E_e}_{\mathbb{Z}^{2m},\sigma_e}$, outputs, with probability $\geq 1 - 2^{-\Omega(\lambda)}$ over ek and $(\mathbf{x}, \mathbf{e})$, an independent sample $(\bar{\mathbf{x}}, \bar{\mathbf{e}})$ from the conditional distribution of $(\mathbf{x}, \mathbf{e})$ conditioned on $\boldsymbol{y} = \mathsf{LTF.Eval}(ek, (\mathbf{x}, \mathbf{e}))$.*

Proof. First, the construction is correct. Indeed, by Lemmas 4 and 5, if $\sigma_x \geq \Omega(\sqrt{m})$ and $\sigma_e \geq \Omega(\sqrt{m})$, the distribution $D_{\mathbb{Z}^n,\sigma_x} \times D_{\mathbb{Z}^{2m},\sigma_e}$ is efficiently samplable, and a sample from it belongs to Dom^E_λ with probability $\geq 1 - 2^{-\Omega(\lambda)}$, so $D_{\mathsf{Dom}^E_\lambda}$ is efficiently samplable. For inversion correctness, we consider $(\mathbf{x}, \mathbf{e}) \in \mathsf{Dom}^D_\lambda$, and set $\mathbf{y} = \mathbf{A} \cdot \mathbf{x} + \mathbf{e}$. By Lemma 9, we can recover $(\mathbf{x}, \mathbf{e})$ from $\mathbf{y}$ using the $\mathbf{G}$-trapdoor $\mathbf{R}$ of $\mathbf{A}$ if $\|\mathbf{e}\| \leq q/(10 \cdot \|\mathbf{R}\|)$. The fact that $\|\mathbf{R}\| \leq m$ and the parameter choices guarantee this.

The lossy and injective modes are computationally indistinguishable under the $\mathsf{LWE}_{\ell,2m,q,\chi}$ assumption. A standard hybrid argument over the columns of $\mathbf{A} \in \mathbb{Z}_q^{2m \times n}$ provides the inequality between the respective success advantages.

We now focus on the lossiness property. Note that Lemma 11 describes the conditional distribution of $(\mathbf{x}, \mathbf{e})$ conditioned on $(\mathbf{C} \cdot \mathbf{x}, \mathbf{F} \cdot \mathbf{x} + \mathbf{e})$. We claim that, except with probability $\leq 2^{-\Omega(\lambda)}$ over ek generated by $\mathsf{LTF.LGen}(1^\lambda)$, this is also the distribution of $(\mathbf{x}, \mathbf{e})$ conditioned on $\mathsf{LTF.Eval}(ek, (\mathbf{x}, \mathbf{e}))$. Indeed, $\mathsf{LTF.Eval}(ek, (\mathbf{x}, \mathbf{e})) = \mathbf{B} \cdot \mathbf{C} \cdot \mathbf{x} + \mathbf{F} \cdot \mathbf{x} + \mathbf{e} \in \mathbb{Z}_q^{2m}$ uniquely determines $\mathbf{u} = \mathbf{C} \cdot \mathbf{x} \in \mathbb{Z}_q^\ell$ and $\mathbf{f} = \mathbf{F} \cdot \mathbf{x} + \mathbf{e} \in \mathsf{Dom}_e$ if $\|\mathbf{f}\|_\infty < \lambda_1^\infty(\Lambda(\mathbf{B}))/2$ for all $(\mathbf{x}, \mathbf{e}) \in \mathsf{Dom}^E$. The latter condition is satisfied except with probability $\leq 2^{-\Omega(\lambda)}$ over the choice of ek. This is because $\|\mathbf{f}\|_\infty \leq \sqrt{2m} \cdot \beta\sqrt{n}\sigma_x + \sqrt{2m}\sigma_x \leq 2\sqrt{2m} \cdot \sigma_e < q/8$ except with probability $2^{-\Omega(\lambda)}$ over the choice of $\mathbf{F}$, and $\lambda_1^\infty(\Lambda(\mathbf{B}))/2 \geq q/4$ with probability $\leq 2^{-\Omega(\lambda)}$ over the choice of $\mathbf{B}$, by Lemma 3.

We now show that the conditional distribution $D^{S_{\mathbf{F},\mathbf{u},\mathbf{f}}}_{\Lambda^\perp(\mathbf{C}^\top)+\mathbf{x}',\sqrt{\mathbf{\Sigma}},\mathbf{c}}$ given by Lemma 11 for $\mathbf{x}$ conditioned on $\mathsf{LTF.Eval}(ek, (\mathbf{x}, \mathbf{e}))$ has min-entropy at least l and is efficiently samplable. For every $\bar{\mathbf{x}} \in S_{\mathbf{F},\mathbf{u},\mathbf{f}}$, we have

$$D^{S_{\mathbf{F},\mathbf{u},\mathbf{f}}}_{\Lambda^\perp(\mathbf{C}^\top)+\mathbf{x}',\sqrt{\mathbf{\Sigma}},\mathbf{c}}(\bar{\mathbf{x}}) = \frac{1}{p_a} D_{\Lambda^\perp(\mathbf{C}^\top)+\mathbf{x}',\sqrt{\mathbf{\Sigma}},\mathbf{c}}(\bar{\mathbf{x}}), \quad p_a = D_{\Lambda^\perp(\mathbf{C}^\top)+\mathbf{x}',\sqrt{\mathbf{\Sigma}},\mathbf{c}}(S_{\mathbf{F},\mathbf{u},\mathbf{f}}).$$

For min-entropy, we observe that, by Lemma 6, the point with highest probability in $D_{\Lambda^\perp(\mathbf{C}^\top)+\mathbf{x}',\sqrt{\mathbf{\Sigma}},\mathbf{c}}$ has probability $\leq 2\det(\Lambda^\perp(\mathbf{C}^\top)/\sqrt{\det(\mathbf{\Sigma})}$. We can apply Lemma 6 because $\sigma_n(\sqrt{\mathbf{\Sigma}}) \geq \eta_{2^{-n}}(\Lambda^{\perp}(\mathbf{C}^{\top}))$ with overwhelming probability. Indeed, thanks to assumption on χ, we have $\|\mathbf{F}^{\top} \cdot \mathbf{F}\| \leq 2mn\beta^2$ with probability $\geq 1 - 2^{-\Omega(\lambda)}$. When this inequality holds, we have

$$\sigma_n(\sqrt{\mathbf{\Sigma}}) \geq \sigma_x \sigma_e / \sqrt{2mn\beta^2\sigma_x^2 + \sigma_e^2}.$$

Further, by Lemma 3, we have $\eta_{2^{-n}}(\Lambda^{\perp}(\mathbf{C}^{\top})) \leq O(\sqrt{n}q^{\ell/n})$ with probability $\geq 1 - 2^{-\Omega(\ell)}$. Hence the assumption of Lemma 6 holds, thanks to our parameter choices. Overall, we obtain that the scheme is l-lossy for

$$l \geq \log\sqrt{\det(\mathbf{\Sigma})} - \log\det(\Lambda^{\perp}(\mathbf{C}^{\top})) - 1 - \log(1/p_a).$$

By calculations similar to those above, we have that $\sqrt{\det \mathbf{\Sigma}} \leq \sigma_x^n$. Further, matrix $\mathbf{C}$ has rank ℓ with probability $\geq 1 - 2^{-\Omega(\ell)}$, and, when this is the case, we have $\det(\Lambda^{\perp}(\mathbf{C}^{\top})) = q^{\ell}$. We obtain $l \geq n\log\sigma_x - 1 - \ell\log q - \log(1/p_a)$.

To complete the lossiness proof, we show that $p_a \geq 1 - 2^{-\Omega(\lambda)}$ so that $\log(1/p_a) \leq 1$, except with probability $\leq 2^{-\Omega(\lambda)}$ over $(\mathbf{F}, \mathbf{C}, \mathbf{x}, \mathbf{e})$. For this, we have by a union bound that $p_a \geq 1 - (p_x + p_e)$, where p_x is the probability that a sample $\bar{\mathbf{x}}$ from $D_{\Lambda^{\perp}(\mathbf{C}^{\top})+\mathbf{x}',\sqrt{\mathbf{\Sigma}},\mathbf{c}}$ lands outside Dom_x^E (i.e., $\|\bar{\mathbf{x}}\| > \gamma_x \cdot \sqrt{n} \cdot \sigma_x$), and p_e is the probability that a sample $\bar{\mathbf{x}}$ from $D_{\Lambda^{\perp}(\mathbf{C}^{\top})+\mathbf{x}',\sqrt{\mathbf{\Sigma}},\mathbf{c}}$ is such that $\mathbf{f} - \mathbf{F} \cdot \bar{\mathbf{x}}$ lands outside Dom_e^E (i.e., $\|\mathbf{f} - \mathbf{F} \cdot \bar{\mathbf{x}}\| > \gamma_e \cdot \sqrt{2m} \cdot \sigma_e$).

In order to bound p_x, we observe that it is at most

$$p'_x = \Pr_{\bar{\mathbf{x}} \hookleftarrow D_{\Lambda^{\perp}(\mathbf{C}^{\top})+\mathbf{x}',\sqrt{\mathbf{\Sigma}},\mathbf{c}}}[\|\bar{\mathbf{x}} - \mathbf{c}\| > \|\sqrt{\mathbf{\Sigma}}\| \cdot \sqrt{n}]$$

if $\gamma_x \cdot \sqrt{n} \cdot \sigma_x \geq \|\mathbf{c}\| + \|\sqrt{\mathbf{\Sigma}}\| \cdot \sqrt{n}$. Now, using that $\|\mathbf{F}\| \leq \sqrt{2mn} \cdot \beta$, $\|\mathbf{x}\| \leq \sqrt{n} \cdot \sigma_x$ and $\|\mathbf{e}\| \leq \sqrt{2m} \cdot \sigma_e$ except with probability $2^{-\Omega(\lambda)}$, by Lemma 5, we get with the same probability that $\|\mathbf{c}\| \leq (\sigma_x/\sigma_e)^2 \cdot \sqrt{2mn}\beta \cdot (\sqrt{2mn} \cdot \beta \cdot \sigma_x \cdot \sqrt{n} + \sigma_e \cdot \sqrt{2m})$. Furthermore, using $\|\sqrt{\mathbf{\Sigma}}\| \leq \sigma_x/\sigma_e$, we have that the condition $\gamma_x \cdot \sqrt{n} \cdot \sigma_x \geq \|\mathbf{c}\| + \|\sqrt{\mathbf{\Sigma}}\| \cdot \sqrt{n}$ is satisfied by our choice of parameters. Also, as shown above, we have $\sigma_n(\sqrt{\mathbf{\Sigma}}) \geq \eta_{2^{-n}}(\Lambda^{\perp}(\mathbf{C}^{\top}))$ with overwhelming probability, so that we can apply Lemma 5 to conclude that $p_x \leq p'_x \leq 2^{-n+2}$ with probability $\geq 1 - 2^{-\Omega(\lambda)}$.

To bound p_e, we follow a similar computation as for p_x. Namely, we first observe that, if $\bar{\mathbf{x}}$ is sampled from $D_{\Lambda^{\perp}(\mathbf{C}^{\top})+\mathbf{x}',\sqrt{\mathbf{\Sigma}},\mathbf{c}}$, then $\bar{\mathbf{e}} = \mathbf{f} - \mathbf{F} \cdot \bar{\mathbf{x}}$ is distributed as $D_{\mathbf{F}\cdot\Lambda^{\perp}(\mathbf{C}^{\top})+\mathbf{f}-\mathbf{F}\cdot\mathbf{x}',\sqrt{\mathbf{F}\mathbf{\Sigma}\mathbf{F}^{\top}},\mathbf{f}-\mathbf{F}\cdot\mathbf{c}}$. Therefore, the probability p_e is at most the probability p'_e that a sample $\bar{\mathbf{e}}$ from $D_{\mathbf{F}\cdot\Lambda^{\perp}(\mathbf{C}^{\top})+\mathbf{f}-\mathbf{F}\cdot\mathbf{x}',\sqrt{\mathbf{F}\mathbf{\Sigma}\mathbf{F}^{\top}},\mathbf{f}-\mathbf{F}\cdot\mathbf{c}}$ satisfies $\|\bar{\mathbf{e}} - (\mathbf{f} - \mathbf{F} \cdot \mathbf{c})\| > \|\sqrt{\mathbf{F}\mathbf{\Sigma}\mathbf{F}^{\top}}\| \cdot \sqrt{2m}$, assuming that the condition

$$\gamma_e \cdot \sqrt{2m} \cdot \sigma_e \geq \|\mathbf{f} - \mathbf{F} \cdot \mathbf{c}\| + \|\sqrt{\mathbf{F}\mathbf{\Sigma}\mathbf{F}^{\top}}\| \cdot \sqrt{2m}, \tag{1}$$

is satisfied. Now, using $\|\mathbf{f} - \mathbf{F} \cdot \mathbf{c}\| \leq \|\mathbf{f}\| + \|\mathbf{F}\| \cdot \|\mathbf{c}\|$ and the above bounds on $\|\mathbf{F}\|$, $\|\mathbf{f}\|$ and $\|\mathbf{c}\|$ and our choice of parameters, we have that condition (1) is satisfied with overwhelming probability. To apply Lemma 5 to bound p'_e, we also need to show that $\sigma_n(\sqrt{\mathbf{F}\mathbf{\Sigma}\mathbf{F}^{\top}}) \geq \eta_{2^{-n}}(\mathbf{F} \cdot \Lambda^{\perp}(\mathbf{C}^{\top}))$. Now, note that

$$\sigma_n(\sqrt{\mathbf{F}\mathbf{\Sigma}\mathbf{F}^{\top}}) = \sigma_x \cdot \sigma_e / \sqrt{\sigma_x^2 + \sigma_e^2/\sigma_n(\mathbf{F})^2}.$$

By Lemma 7, we have $\sigma_n(\mathbf{F}) \geq \Omega(\sqrt{m} \cdot \beta)$ with overwhelming probability. We conclude that $\sigma_n(\sqrt{\mathbf{F}\boldsymbol{\Sigma}\mathbf{F}^\top}) \geq \Omega(\sigma_x \cdot \sqrt{m} \cdot \beta)$. On the other hand, we have $\eta_{2^{-n}}(\mathbf{F} \cdot \Lambda^\perp(\mathbf{C}^\top)) \leq \|\mathbf{F}\| \cdot \eta_{2^{-n}}(\Lambda^\perp(\mathbf{C}^\top)) = O(\|\mathbf{F}\| \cdot \sqrt{n}) \leq O(\beta \cdot \sqrt{m} \cdot n)$ with overwhelming probability, also by Lemma 7. For this reason, the condition $\sigma_n(\sqrt{\mathbf{F}\boldsymbol{\Sigma}\mathbf{F}^\top}) \geq \eta_{2^{-n}}(\mathbf{F} \cdot \Lambda^\perp(\mathbf{C}^\top))$ holds with with the same probability thanks to our choice of parameters. We can thus apply Lemma 5 to conclude that $p_e \leq p'_e \leq 2^{-n+2}$ with overwhelming probability.

Overall, we have that $p_a \geq 1 - (p_x + p_e) \geq 1 - 2^{-\Omega(\lambda)}$ which completes the proof of lossiness. This also immediately implies that the conditional distribution $D^{S_{\mathbf{F},\mathbf{u},\mathbf{f}}}_{\Lambda^\perp(\mathbf{C}^\top)+\mathbf{x}',\sqrt{\boldsymbol{\Sigma}},\mathbf{c}}$ is efficiently samplable by rejection sampling, given an efficient sampler for $D_{\Lambda^\perp(\mathbf{C}^\top)+\mathbf{x}',\sqrt{\boldsymbol{\Sigma}},\mathbf{c}}$. The latter sampler can be implemented with a ppt algorithm by Lemma 4 and the fact that $\max_i \|\boldsymbol{b}_i\| < \sigma_n(\boldsymbol{\Sigma})$ with overwhelming probability by the bound on $\sigma_n(\sqrt{\boldsymbol{\Sigma}})$. □

3.2 An All-But-Many Lossy Trapdoor Function from LWE

Parameters and domains are defined as in Sect. 3.1.

Key generation. $\mathsf{ABM.Gen}(1^\lambda)$ conducts the following steps.

1. For parameters n, ℓ, m, γ, χ, generate $\bar{\mathbf{A}} \in \mathbb{Z}_q^{m\times n}$ as $\bar{\mathbf{A}} = \mathbf{B} \cdot \mathbf{C} + \mathbf{F}$ with $\mathbf{B} \hookleftarrow U(\mathbb{Z}_q^{m\times\ell})$, $\mathbf{C} \hookleftarrow U(\mathbb{Z}_q^{\ell\times n})$ and $\mathbf{F} \hookleftarrow \chi^{m\times n}$.
2. Choose a PRF family $\mathsf{PRF} : \{0,1\}^\lambda \times \{0,1\}^k \to \{0,1\}^\lambda$ with input length $k = k(\lambda)$ and key length λ. Choose a seed $K \hookleftarrow U(\{0,1\}^\lambda)$ for PRF.
3. Sample matrices $\mathbf{R}_1, \ldots, \mathbf{R}_\lambda \hookleftarrow U(\{-1,1\}^{m\times m})$ and compute
$$\mathbf{B}_i = \mathbf{R}_i \cdot \bar{\mathbf{A}} + K[i] \cdot \mathbf{G} \in \mathbb{Z}_q^{m\times n} \qquad \forall i \leq \lambda.$$
4. Output the evaluation key ek, the inversion key ik and the lossy tag generation key tk, which consist of
$$ek := \Big(\bar{\mathbf{A}}, (\mathbf{B}_i)_{i\leq\lambda}\Big), \qquad ik := \big((\mathbf{R}_i)_{i\leq\lambda}, K\big), \qquad tk := K. \tag{2}$$

A tag $t = (t_{\mathsf{c}}, t_{\mathsf{a}}) \in \{0,1\}^\lambda \times \{0,1\}^k$ will be injective whenever $t_{\mathsf{c}} \neq \mathsf{PRF}(K, t_{\mathsf{a}})$.

Lossy tag generation. $\mathsf{ABM.LTag}(tk, t_{\mathsf{a}})$ takes as input an auxiliary tag component $t_{\mathsf{a}} \in \{0,1\}^k$ and uses $tk = K$ to compute and output$t_{\mathsf{c}} = \mathsf{PRF}(K, t_{\mathsf{a}})$.

Evaluation. $\mathsf{ABM.Eval}(ek, t, (\mathbf{x}, \mathbf{e}))$ takes in the function input $(\mathbf{x}, \mathbf{e}) \in \mathsf{Dom}^E_\lambda$, the tag $t = (t_{\mathsf{c}}, t_{\mathsf{a}}) \in \{0,1\}^\lambda \times \{0,1\}^k$ and proceeds as follows.

1. For each $j \leq \lambda$, let $C_{\mathsf{PRF},j}(t_{\mathsf{a}}) : \{0,1\}^\lambda \to \{0,1\}$ be the NAND Boolean circuit, where $t_{\mathsf{a}} \in \{0,1\}^k$ is hard-wired, which evaluates the j-th bit of $\mathsf{PRF}(\widetilde{K}, t_{\mathsf{a}}) \in \{0,1\}^\lambda$ for any $\widetilde{K} \in \{0,1\}^\lambda$. Run the public evaluation algorithm of Lemma 10 to obtain[3] $\mathbf{B}_{\mathsf{PRF},j} \leftarrow \mathsf{Eval}^{\mathsf{pub}}(C_{\mathsf{PRF},j}(t_{\mathsf{a}}), (\mathbf{B}_i)_{i\leq\lambda})$.

[3] One may use either $\mathsf{Eval}^{\mathsf{pub}}_{\mathsf{CCT}}$ or $\mathsf{Eval}^{\mathsf{pub}}_{\mathsf{BP}}$, but the choice must be consistent with the $\mathsf{Eval}^{\mathsf{priv}}$ variant used in function inversion.

2. Define the matrix

$$\mathbf{A}_t = \left[\frac{\bar{\mathbf{A}}}{\sum_{j\leq\lambda}\left((-1)^{t_c[j]}\cdot\mathbf{B}_{\mathsf{PRF},j} + t_c[j]\cdot\mathbf{G}\right)}\right] \in \mathbb{Z}_q^{2m\times n},$$

and compute the output $\mathbf{y} = \mathbf{A}_t\cdot\mathbf{x} + \mathbf{e} \in \mathbb{Z}_q^{2m}$.

Inversion. $\mathsf{ABM.Invert}(ik, t, \mathbf{y})$ inputs the inversion key $ik := \left((\mathbf{R}_i)_{i\leq\lambda}, K\right)$, the tag $t = (t_c, t_a) \in \{0,1\}^\lambda \times \{0,1\}^k$ and $\mathbf{y} \in \mathsf{Rng}_\lambda$, and proceeds as follows.

1. Return $\perp$ if $t_c = \mathsf{PRF}(K, t_a)$.
2. Otherwise, for each $j \leq \lambda$, run the private evaluation algorithm from Lemma 10 to obtain $\mathbf{R}_{\mathsf{PRF},j} \leftarrow \mathsf{Eval}^{\mathsf{priv}}(C_{\mathsf{PRF},j}(t_a), (\mathbf{R}_i)_{i\leq\lambda})$ and compute the (small-norm) matrix $\mathbf{R}_t = \sum_{j\leq\lambda}(-1)^{t_c[j]}\cdot\mathbf{R}_{\mathsf{PRF},j} \in \mathbb{Z}^{m\times m}$.
3. Let h_t denote the Hamming distance between t_c and $\mathsf{PRF}(K, t_a)$. Use the $\mathbf{G}$-trapdoor $\mathbf{R}_t$ of $\mathbf{A}_t$ with tag h_t to find the unique $(\mathbf{x}, \mathbf{e}) \in \mathsf{Dom}_\lambda^D$ such that $\mathbf{y} = \mathbf{A}_t\cdot\mathbf{x} + \mathbf{e}$. This is done by applying the LWE inversion algorithm of Lemma 9.

All algorithms involved run in polynomial-time, if one uses $\mathsf{Eval}^{\mathsf{pub}}_{\mathsf{CCT}}$ and $\mathsf{Eval}^{\mathsf{priv}}_{\mathsf{CCT}}$ from Lemma 10. If the circuits $C_{\mathsf{PRF},j}(t_a)$ (having the PRF key as input, and the PRF input hardwired) have logarithmic depth $d \leq O(\log\lambda)$, then it is preferable to use $\mathsf{Eval}^{\mathsf{pub}}_{\mathsf{BP}}$ and $\mathsf{Eval}^{\mathsf{priv}}_{\mathsf{BP}}$ instead. Indeed, under this small-depth assumption, these algorithms still run in polynomial-time, and have the advantage of leading to smaller $\mathbf{R}_t$'s. This eventually allows one to set q as a polynomial function of λ. In the rest of this section, we choose these variants of $\mathsf{Eval}^{\mathsf{pub}}$ and $\mathsf{Eval}^{\mathsf{priv}}$. The results can be readily adapted to the other option.

Theorem 2. *Let $\chi = D_{\mathbb{Z},\beta/(2\sqrt{\lambda})}$ for some $\beta > 0$. Assume that* PRF *has depth $d = O(\log\lambda)$ when the circuit input is the key and the PRF input is hard-coded in the circuit. Assume that $\ell \geq \lambda$, $n = \Omega(\ell\log q)$ and $m \geq 2n\log q$, $\gamma_x \geq 3\sqrt{m/n}$ and $\gamma_e \geq 3$. Assume also that $\sigma_x \geq \Omega(n)$, $\sigma_e \geq \Omega(4^d\cdot m^2\cdot\beta\cdot\sqrt{n}\cdot\sigma_x)$ and $\sigma_e \leq O(q/(\lambda\cdot 4^d\cdot m^2))$. Then, under the PRF security and $\mathsf{LWE}_{\ell,2m,q,\chi}$ hardness assumptions, the above function is an l-lossy ABM LTF with $l = \Omega(n\log n)$.*

The theorem follows from the lemmas below.

Lemma 12 (Correctness). *Let us assume that and $q/\sigma_e \geq \lambda\cdot 4^d\cdot O(m^2)$. Assume that* PRF *has logarithmic depth $O(\log\lambda)$ when the circuit input is the key and the PRF input is hard-coded in the circuit. Then, for any triple (ek, ik, tk) produced by $\mathsf{ABM.Gen}(1^\lambda)$, for any tag $t = (t_c, t_a) \in \{0,1\}^\lambda \times \{0,1\}^k$ satisfying $t_c \neq \mathsf{PRF}(K, t_a)$ and for any input $(\mathbf{x}, \mathbf{e}) \in \mathsf{Dom}_\lambda^D$, the inversion correctness condition $(\mathbf{x}, \mathbf{e}) = \mathsf{ABM.Invert}(ik, t, \mathsf{ABM.Eval}(ek, t, (\mathbf{x}, \mathbf{e})))$ is satisfied.*

Proof. By Lemma 10, we have $\|\mathbf{R}_t\| \leq \lambda\cdot 4^d\cdot O(m^{3/2})$ and

$$\mathbf{A}_t = \left[\frac{\bar{\mathbf{A}}}{\mathbf{R}_t\cdot\bar{\mathbf{A}} + h_t\cdot\mathbf{G}}\right] \bmod q,$$

where h_t is the Hamming distance between t_c and $\mathsf{PRF}(K, t_a) \in \{0,1\}^\lambda$. As $q > \lambda$ is prime, integer h_t is invertible modulo q, and $\mathbf{R}_t$ is a $\mathbf{G}$-trapdoor with tag h_t for $\mathbf{A}_t$. Thanks to our parameters, we have $\|\mathbf{e}\| \leq q/(10 \cdot \|\mathbf{R}_t\|)$ and hence algorithm Invert from Lemma 9 recovers $(\mathbf{x}, \mathbf{e})$. □

Our ABM-LTF provides evasiveness unless the PRF family is not unpredictable, which would contradict its pseudorandomness. In order to meaningfully rely on the pseudorandomness of PRF, the proof of Lemma 13 also appeals to the LWE assumption so as to first move to a game where the lossy matrix $\bar{\mathbf{A}} \in \mathbb{Z}_q^{m \times n}$ is traded for a random matrix. Since the matrices $\mathbf{B}_i = \mathbf{R}_i \cdot \bar{\mathbf{A}} + K[i] \cdot \mathbf{G}$ depend the bits of the seed K, moving to a uniform matrix $\bar{\mathbf{A}}$ is necessary to make sure that the evaluation key ek is statistically independent of K.

Lemma 13 (Evasiveness). *Assume that $m \geq 2n \log q$. Any* ppt *evasiveness adversary $\mathcal{A}$ making Q_1 and Q_2 queries to* ABM.LTag *and* ABM.IsLossy*, respectively, implies an* LWE *distinguisher $\mathcal{D}_1$ and a PRF distinguisher $\mathcal{D}_2$ such that*

$$\mathbf{Adv}_{Q_1,Q_2}^{\mathcal{A},\mathsf{eva}}(\lambda) \leq n \cdot \mathbf{Adv}_{\ell,m,q,\chi}^{\mathcal{D}_1,\mathsf{LWE}}(\lambda) + \mathbf{Adv}_{Q_1+Q_2}^{\mathcal{D}_2,\mathsf{PRF}}(\lambda) + \frac{Q_2+1}{2^\lambda}.$$

(The proof is deferred to the full version of the paper.)

The pseudo-randomness of core tag components also guarantees that lossy tags are computationally indistinguishable from uniformly random tags. The proof of Lemma 14 also relies on the LWE assumption since the evaluation key ek only hides the PRF seed K in the computational sense. It follows the same strategy as the proof of Lemma 13 and given in the full version of the paper.

Lemma 14 (Indistinguishability). *Assume that $m > 2n \log q$. Then* ppt *indistinguishability adversary $\mathcal{A}$ implies either either an* LWE *distinguisher $\mathcal{D}_1$ or a PRF distinguisher $\mathcal{D}_2$ such that:*

$$\mathbf{Adv}_{Q}^{\mathcal{A},\mathsf{ind}}(\lambda) \leq 2n \cdot \mathbf{Adv}_{\ell,m,q,\chi}^{\mathcal{D}_1,\mathsf{LWE}}(\lambda) + \mathbf{Adv}_{Q}^{\mathcal{D}_2,\mathsf{PRF}}(\lambda) + \frac{1}{2^{\lambda-1}},$$

where Q denotes the number of (genuine or uniform) lossy tag generation queries.

The proof of lossiness is essentially identical to that of the LTF (Theorem 1).

Lemma 15 (Lossiness). *Let $\chi = D_{\mathbb{Z},\beta/(2\sqrt{\lambda})}$ for some $\beta > 0$. Assume that the depth d of* PRF *is in $O(\log \lambda)$, when the circuit input is the key and the PRF input is hardwired in the circuit. Let us assume that $\ell \geq \lambda$ and $n = \Omega(\ell \log q)$. Assume also that $\sigma_e \geq \Omega(4^d \cdot m^2 \cdot \beta \cdot \sigma_x \cdot \sqrt{n})$. Then, for any lossy tag $t = (t_c, t_a)$, the above ABM-LTF is l-lossy with $l = \Omega(n \log n)$.*

Proof. We rely on the fact that, for any lossy tag $t = (t_c, t_a)$ (i.e., for which $t_c = \mathsf{PRF}(K, t_a)$), we have

$$\mathbf{A}_t = \left[\frac{\bar{\mathbf{A}}}{\mathbf{R}_t \cdot \bar{\mathbf{A}}}\right] = \left[\frac{\mathbf{B}}{\mathbf{R}_t \cdot \mathbf{B}}\right] \cdot \mathbf{C} + \left[\frac{\mathbf{F}}{\mathbf{R}_t \cdot \mathbf{F}}\right], \quad (3)$$

where $\mathbf{B} \hookleftarrow U(\mathbb{Z}_q^{m\times\ell})$, $\mathbf{C} \hookleftarrow U(\mathbb{Z}_q^{\ell\times n})$, $\mathbf{F} \hookleftarrow \chi^{m\times n}$ and $\mathbf{R}_t$ is as in the ABM.Invert description.

As a consequence, by the same argument as in the proof of Theorem 1, the distribution of the input $(\mathbf{x}, \mathbf{e})$ conditioned on $\mathsf{ABM.Eval}(ek, t, (\mathbf{x}, \mathbf{e}))$ is the same as the distribution of $(\mathbf{x}, \mathbf{e})$ conditioned on $(\mathbf{C}\cdot\mathbf{x}, \mathbf{F}\cdot\mathbf{x}+\mathbf{e})$. From this point, the proof is identical to that of Theorem 1, with $\mathbf{F}_{new} = [\mathbf{F}^\top \mid (\mathbf{R}_t \cdot \mathbf{F})^\top]^\top$ playing the role of $\mathbf{F}$ in the original proof. The two properties of $\mathbf{F}_{new}$ used in the proof are $\|\mathbf{F}_{new}\| \leq (1+\|\mathbf{R}_t\|)\cdot\|\mathbf{F}\| \leq O(4^d \cdot m^{3/2})\cdot\|\mathbf{F}\|$, using Lemma 10, which leads to a larger σ_e by the factor $O(4^d \cdot m^{3/2})$. The other property is a lower bound on $\sigma_n(\mathbf{F}_{new})$ and since the latter is $\geq \sigma_n(\mathbf{F})$, no parameters are affected. □

In [3, Sect. 7], Alwen *et al.* used the a rounding technique [5] to build an all-but-one trapdoor function. While our construction bears resemblance with theirs, our proof of lossiness is very different. In [3, Theorem 7.3], they consider a matrix of the form (3) and crucially rely on the statistical independence of the rows of $[\mathbf{B}^\top \mid (\mathbf{R}_0 \cdot \mathbf{B})^\top]^\top$, for some $\mathbf{R}_0 \in \{-1, 1\}^{m\times m}$, conditionally on $\mathbf{R}_0 \cdot \mathbf{F}$. Here, we cannot guarantee that matrices $\mathbf{R}_t \cdot \mathbf{B}$ be statistically independent for different tags t, and hence it does not seem possible to directly use the rounding technique from [3]. Fortunately, the proof of Lemma 15 does not require the rows of the matrix $[\mathbf{B}^\top \mid (\mathbf{R}_t \cdot \mathbf{B})^\top]^\top$ to be statistically independent and neither does it rely on the independence of $\mathbf{R}_t \cdot \mathbf{B}$ for different tags t.

3.3 Joint Use of Lossy and All-But-Many Functions

We remark that our LTF and ABM-LTF are not lossy enough to be correlation-secure in the sense of Rosen and Segev [70]: indeed, the result of [70, Theorem 3.3] requires lossy functions that lose at least half of their input. In particular, we cannot reveal $\mathbf{y}_0 = \mathbf{A}\cdot\mathbf{x} + \mathbf{e}$ and $\mathbf{y} = \mathbf{A}_t \cdot \mathbf{x} + \mathbf{e}$ for the same input $(\mathbf{x}, \mathbf{e})$ as this would expose $\mathbf{y} - \mathbf{y}_0 = (\mathbf{A} - \mathbf{A}_t)\cdot\mathbf{x}$, which would leak $(\mathbf{x}, \mathbf{e})$. However, we can safely reveal $\mathbf{y}_0 = \mathsf{LTF.Eval}(ek', (\mathbf{x}, \mathbf{e}_0)) = \mathbf{A}\cdot\mathbf{x} + \mathbf{e}_0$ and $\mathbf{y} = \mathsf{ABM.Eval}(ek, t, (\mathbf{x}, \mathbf{e})) = \mathbf{A}_t \cdot \mathbf{x} + \mathbf{e}$ for distinct Gaussian terms $\mathbf{e}_0, \mathbf{e} \in \mathbb{Z}^{2m}$.

Indeed, conditionally on $\mathsf{LTF.Eval}(ek', (\mathbf{x}, \mathbf{e}_0))$ and $\mathsf{ABM.Eval}(ek, t, (\mathbf{x}, \mathbf{e}))$, the distribution of $\mathbf{x}$ retains l bits of min-entropy, where $l = \Omega(n \cdot \log n)$. As in the proof of Theorem 1, this follows by observing that the residual distribution on $\mathbf{x}$ is a discrete Gaussian (by Lemma 15) whose covariance matrix is above the smoothing parameter of the support.

Lemma 16. *The LTF of Sect. 3.1 and the above ABM-LTF are jointly lossy when they share the first part* $\mathbf{x}$ *of their inputs.*

Let $\chi = D_{\mathbb{Z},\beta/(2\sqrt{\lambda})}$ *for some* $\beta > 0$. *Assume that the depth* d *of* PRF *is in* $O(\log\lambda)$, *when the circuit input is the key and the PRF input is hardwired in the circuit. Let us assume that* $\ell \geq \lambda$ *and* $n = \Omega(\ell \log q)$. *Assume also that* $\sigma_e \geq \Omega(4^d \cdot m^2 \cdot \beta \cdot \sqrt{n} \cdot \sigma_x)$. *Then, except with probability* $\leq 2^{-\Omega(\lambda)}$ *over the choice of* $ek' \hookleftarrow \mathsf{LTF.LGen}(1^\lambda)$, $ek \hookleftarrow \mathsf{ABM.Gen}(1^\lambda)$, $\mathbf{x} \hookleftarrow \mathsf{Dom}_x$, *and* $\mathbf{e}_0, \mathbf{e} \hookleftarrow \mathsf{Dom}_e$, *we have, for any lossy tag* t:

$$H_\infty(\mathbf{x} \mid \mathsf{LTF.Eval}(ek', (\mathbf{x}, \mathbf{e}_0)),\ \mathsf{ABM.Eval}(ek, t, (\mathbf{x}, \mathbf{e}))) \geq n \cdot \log \sigma_x - 2 - \ell \log q > \Omega(n \cdot \log n).$$

Proof. The result follows by generalizing the proofs of Theorem 1 and Lemma 15 in a straightforward manner. Indeed, if $\mathbf{A}_{\mathsf{LTF}} = \mathbf{B}_{\mathsf{LTF}} \cdot \mathbf{C}_{\mathsf{LTF}} + \mathbf{F}_{\mathsf{LTF}} \in \mathbb{Z}_q^{2m \times n}$ and $\bar{\mathbf{A}} = \mathbf{B}_{\mathsf{ABM}} \cdot \mathbf{C}_{\mathsf{ABM}} + \mathbf{F}_{\mathsf{ABM}} \in \mathbb{Z}_q^{m \times n}$ are the lossy matrices of both functions, the information revealed by $\mathsf{LTF.Eval}(ek', (\mathbf{x}, \mathbf{e}_0))$ and $\mathsf{ABM.Eval}(ek, t, (\mathbf{x}, \mathbf{e}))$ is

$$\left[\begin{array}{c|c} \mathbf{B}_{\mathsf{LTF}} & \mathbf{0}^{2m \times \ell} \\ \hline \mathbf{0}^{m \times \ell} & \mathbf{B}_{\mathsf{ABM}} \\ \mathbf{0}^{m \times \ell} & \mathbf{R}_t \cdot \mathbf{B}_{\mathsf{ABM}} \end{array}\right] \cdot \left[\begin{array}{c} \mathbf{C}_{\mathsf{LTF}} \\ \hline \mathbf{C}_{\mathsf{ABM}} \end{array}\right] \cdot \mathbf{x} + \left[\begin{array}{c} \mathbf{F}_{\mathsf{LTF}} \\ \hline \mathbf{F}_{\mathsf{ABM}} \\ \mathbf{R}_t \cdot \mathbf{F}_{\mathsf{ABM}} \end{array}\right] \cdot \mathbf{x} + \left[\begin{array}{c} \mathbf{e}_0 \\ \hline \mathbf{e} \end{array}\right].$$

It is thus entirely determined by the vectors $[\mathbf{C}_{\mathsf{LTF}}^\top \mid \mathbf{C}_{\mathsf{ABM}}^\top]^\top \cdot \mathbf{x} \in \mathbb{Z}_q^{2\ell}$ and $[\mathbf{F}_{\mathsf{LTF}}^\top \mid \mathbf{F}_{\mathsf{ABM}}^\top \mid (\mathbf{R}_t \cdot \mathbf{F}_{\mathsf{ABM}})^\top]^\top \cdot \mathbf{x} + [\mathbf{e}_0^\top \mid \mathbf{e}_1^\top]^\top \in \mathbb{Z}^{4m}$ and we obtain the result by repeating the arguments in the proof of Theorem 1 and Lemma 15. □

4 Selective Opening Chosen-Ciphertext Security

We now combine our ABM-LTF and the LWE-based LTF of Sect. 3 to build an IND-SO-CCA2-secure public-key encryption scheme from the LWE assumption. The scheme can be seen as instantiating a variant of the Peikert-Waters methodology [66], as generalized by Hofheinz [49, Sect. 6.3] to the case of multiple lossy tags. In [49], ciphertexts consists of $(f_{\mathsf{lossy}}(x), f_{\mathsf{ABM}}(t, x), \mathsf{Msg} \oplus h(x))$, where $f_{\mathsf{lossy}}(x)$ (resp. $f_{\mathsf{ABM}}(t, x)$) is a lossy (resp. all-but-many) function of the input x; t is the tag of the ciphertext; and $h(x)$ is a universal hash of x.

Nevertheless, our scheme is *not* a generic instantiation of this paradigm as we cannot use exactly the same input x in the two functions $f_{\mathsf{lossy}}(\cdot)$ and $f_{\mathsf{ABM}}(t, \cdot)$. As we mentioned earlier, we cannot give out function outputs $\mathbf{y}_0 = \mathbf{A} \cdot \mathbf{x} + \mathbf{e}$ and $\mathbf{y} = \mathbf{A}_t \cdot \mathbf{x} + \mathbf{e}$ for the same input $(\mathbf{x}, \mathbf{e})$. For this reason, our lossy and ABM functions have to use distinct noise terms $(\mathbf{e}_0, \mathbf{e})$ in the two evaluations $\mathbf{y}_0 = \mathbf{A} \cdot \mathbf{x} + \mathbf{e}_0$ and $\mathbf{y} = \mathbf{A}_t \cdot \mathbf{x} + \mathbf{e}$. The decryption algorithm can proceed by inverting $(\mathbf{x}, \mathbf{e}_0) \leftarrow f_{\mathsf{lossy}}^{-1}(\mathbf{y}_0)$ as before. However, instead of simply testing if $\mathbf{y} = f_{\mathsf{ABM}}(t, (\mathbf{x}, \mathbf{e}_0))$ by evaluating $f_{\mathsf{ABM}}(t, .)$ in the forward direction as in [49,66], the receiver has to test whether $\mathbf{y} - \mathbf{A}_t \cdot \mathbf{x}$ is a small-norm vector, analogously to [65, Sect. 4.4]. For this reason, the message Msg is hidden by the universal hash of $\mathbf{x}$ only, which is sufficient in our security proof. Moreover, our extension to SIM-SO-CCA2 security requires $h(\cdot)$ to operate on $\mathbf{x}$ alone.

Unlike [66], we cannot use one-time signatures to bind ciphertext components in a non-malleable manner. Indeed, at each corruption query, the challenger would have to reveal the one-time secret keys of the challenge ciphertexts, which would allow the adversary to make decryption queries for lossy tags.

Instead, we can proceed analogously to Boyen *et al.* [24] and define the auxiliary tags to be the output $\mathbf{y}_0 = \Pi^{\mathsf{LTF}}.\mathsf{Eval}(ek', (\mathbf{x}, \mathbf{e}_0))$ of the lossy function while resorting to the hybrid encryption paradigm and authenticate the message-carrying part $\mathbf{c}_0 = \mathsf{Msg} + h(\mathbf{x})$ of the ciphertext via the encrypt-then-MAC approach. One difficulty is that, since $\mathbf{y}_0 = \Pi^{\mathsf{LTF}}.\mathsf{Eval}(ek', (\mathbf{x}, \mathbf{e}_0))$ and

$\mathbf{y} = \Pi^{\mathsf{ABM}}.\mathsf{Eval}(ek, t, (\mathbf{x}, \mathbf{e}))$ involve distinct small-norm vectors $\mathbf{e}_0$, $\mathbf{e}$, we must find a different way to prevent the adversary from tampering with $\mathbf{e}$ in one of the challenge ciphertexts (indeed, $\mathbf{y}$ is no longer authenticated by a one-time signature). Our solution to this problem is to include $\mathbf{y} = \Pi^{\mathsf{ABM}}.\mathsf{Eval}(ek, t, (\mathbf{x}, \mathbf{e}))$ in the input of the MAC, which simultaneously authenticates $\mathbf{y}$ and $\mathbf{c}_0$. For simplicity, we assume MACs with the uniqueness property but the proof can be adapted to rely on any strongly unforgeable MAC.

As mentioned in [49, Sect. 6], the application to IND-SO-CCA2 security requires the core tag space $\mathcal{T}_{\mathsf{c}}$ of ABM-LTFs to be efficiently samplable and explainable. As defined in [49, Definition 6.2], "explainability" (a.k.a. "invertible samplability" [33]) means that any core tag t_{c} can be explained by the challenger as having been uniformly chosen "without ulterior motive" when the adversary opens a given ciphertext. Our ABM-LTF clearly satisfies this property since core tags t_{c} are just random λ-bit strings.

4.1 Description

Par-Gen(1^λ): Selects public parameters consisting of:
- A modulus $q > 2$, integers $\ell, \ell_0, \ell_1, n \in \mathsf{poly}(\lambda)$, $m = \lceil cn \cdot \log q \rceil$, for some constant $c > 0$, and parameters $\beta, \sigma_x, \sigma_e > 0$.
- The specification $\mathsf{MAC} = (\mathsf{KG}, \mathsf{Sig}, \mathsf{Ver})$ of a unique MAC with message space $\mathsf{MsgSp}^{mac} := \mathbb{Z}_q^{2m} \times \mathbb{Z}_q^{\ell_0}$ and key space $\mathcal{K}^{mac} := \mathbb{Z}_q^{\ell_1}$.
- A family $\mathcal{UH}$ of universal hash functions $h : [-\sigma_x\sqrt{n}, \sigma_x\sqrt{n}]^n \rightarrow \mathbb{Z}_q^{\ell_0+\ell_1}$ that range over $\mathsf{MsgSp} := \mathbb{Z}_q^{\ell_0}$.

The public parameters $\Gamma = \{\ell, \ell_0, \ell_1, n, m, q, \beta, \sigma_x, \sigma_e, \mathsf{MAC}\}$ define the plaintext space $\mathsf{MsgSp} := \mathbb{Z}_q^{\ell_0}$ and will be shared by the LWE-based LTF of Sect. 3.1 and our ABM-LTF of Sect. 3.2.

Keygen(Γ): Let $\Pi^{\mathsf{LTF}} = (\mathsf{IGen}, \mathsf{LGen}, \mathsf{Eval}, \mathsf{Invert})$ be an instance of the LTF of Sect. 3.1 and let $\Pi^{\mathsf{ABM}} = (\mathsf{Gen}, \mathsf{Eval}, \mathsf{Invert}, \mathsf{LTag})$ be an instance of the ABM-LTF of Sect. 3.2. We assume Π^{LTF} and Π^{ABM} both operate over the domain $\mathsf{Dom}_\lambda^D := \{(\mathbf{x}, \mathbf{e}) \in \mathbb{Z}^n \times \mathbb{Z}^{2m} \mid \|\mathbf{x}\| \leq \sigma_x\sqrt{n},\ \|\mathbf{e}\| \leq \sigma_e\sqrt{2m}\}$. The public key is generated via the following steps.

1. Generate a pair $(ek', ik') \leftarrow \Pi^{\mathsf{LTF}}.\mathsf{IGen}(1^\lambda)$ for an injective function of the lossy trapdoor function family Π^{LTF}.
2. Generate $(ek, ik, tk) \leftarrow \Pi^{\mathsf{ABM}}.\mathsf{Gen}(1^\lambda)$ as an ABM-LTF key pair. We assume that the space of auxiliary tags is $\mathcal{T}_{\mathsf{a}} = \mathbb{Z}_q^m$
3. Choose a random member $h \leftarrow \mathcal{UH}$ of the universal hash family.

Output (PK, SK) where $PK = \big(ek', ek, h\big)$ and $SK = ik'$.

Encrypt(PK, Msg): To encrypt $\mathsf{Msg} \in \mathbb{Z}_q^{\ell_0}$, choose $\mathbf{x} \hookleftarrow D_{\mathbb{Z}^n, \sigma_x}$, $\mathbf{e}_0 \hookleftarrow D_{\mathbb{Z}^{2m}, \sigma_e}$, $\mathbf{e} \hookleftarrow D_{\mathbb{Z}^{2m}, \sigma_e}$ and do the following.

1. Compute $\mathbf{y}_0 = \Pi^{\mathsf{LTF}}.\mathsf{Eval}(ek', (\mathbf{x}, \mathbf{e}_0)) = \mathbf{A} \cdot \mathbf{x} + \mathbf{e}_0 \ \in \mathbb{Z}_q^{2m}$.
2. Define $t_{\mathsf{a}} = \mathbf{y}_0$ and choose a random $t_{\mathsf{c}} \hookleftarrow U(\mathcal{T}_{\mathsf{c}})$. Then, let $t = (t_{\mathsf{c}}, t_{\mathsf{a}})$ and compute $\mathbf{y} = \Pi^{\mathsf{ABM}}.\mathsf{Eval}(ek, t, (\mathbf{x}, \mathbf{e})) = \mathbf{A}_t \cdot \mathbf{x} + \mathbf{e} \ \in \mathbb{Z}_q^{2m}$.
3. Compute $(\mathbf{k}^{sym}, \mathbf{k}^{mac}) = h(\mathbf{x}) \in \mathbb{Z}_q^{\ell_0} \times \mathbb{Z}_q^{\ell_1}$.

4. Set $\mathbf{c}_0 = \mathsf{Msg} + \mathbf{k}^{sym} \in \mathbb{Z}_q^{\ell_0}$ and $\mathbf{c}_1 = \mathsf{MAC.Sig}(\mathbf{k}^{mac}, (\mathbf{y}, \mathbf{c}_0))$.

Output the ciphertext $\mathbf{C} = (t_{\mathsf{c}}, \mathbf{c}_0, \mathbf{c}_1, \mathbf{y}_0, \mathbf{y})$.

Decrypt(SK, C): To decrypt $\mathbf{C} = (t_{\mathsf{c}}, \mathbf{c}_0, \mathbf{c}_1, \mathbf{y}_0, \mathbf{y})$ using $SK = ik'$,

1. Compute $(\mathbf{x}, \mathbf{e}_0) \leftarrow \Pi^{\mathsf{LTF}}.\mathsf{Invert}(ik', \mathbf{y}_0)$. Return $\perp$ if $\mathbf{y}_0$ is not in the range[4] of $\Pi^{\mathsf{LTF}}.\mathsf{Eval}(ek', \cdot)$ or if $(\mathbf{x}, \mathbf{e}_0) \notin \mathsf{Dom}_\lambda^D$.
2. Define the tag $t = (t_{\mathsf{c}}, \mathbf{y}_0)$. If $\|\mathbf{y} - \mathbf{A}_t \cdot \mathbf{x}\| > \sigma_e \sqrt{2m}$, return $\perp$.
3. Compute $(\mathbf{k}^{sym}, \mathbf{k}^{mac}) = h(\mathbf{x}) \in \mathbb{Z}_q^{\ell_0} \times \mathbb{Z}_q^{\ell_1}$.
4. If $\mathsf{MAC.Ver}(\mathbf{k}^{mac}, (\mathbf{y}, \mathbf{c}_0), \mathbf{c}_1) = 0$, return $\perp$. Otherwise, return the plaintext $\mathsf{Msg} = \mathbf{c}_0 - \mathbf{k}^{sym} \in \mathbb{Z}_q^{\ell_0}$.

In order to instantiate the scheme with a polynomial-size modulus q, we need a PRF with an evaluation circuit in NC^1, which translates into a polynomial-length branching program. By applying Lemma 10 and exploiting the asymmetric noise growth of the GSW FHE as in [27], we can indeed keep q small.

For this purpose, the Banerjee-Peikert PRF [4] is a suitable candidate. While its evaluation circuit is in NC^2 in general, we can still homomorphically evaluate input-dependent circuits $C_{\mathsf{PRF},j}(\cdot)$ over the encrypted key K using an NC^1 circuit. For public moduli p, q and matrices $\mathbf{A}_0, \mathbf{A}_1 \in \mathbb{Z}_q^{n \times n\lceil \log q \rceil}$, their PRF maps an input $x \in \{0,1\}^k$ to $\lfloor (p/q) \cdot (\mathbf{k}^\top \cdot \mathbf{A}_x \bmod q) \rfloor$, where $\mathbf{k} \in \mathbb{Z}_q^n$ is the secret key and the input-dependent matrix $\mathbf{A}_x$ is publicly computable from $\mathbf{A}_0, \mathbf{A}_1$. This allows hard-coding $\mathbf{A}_x$ into an NC^1 circuit to be evaluated over the "encrypted" bits of $\mathbf{k}$ in order to obtain "encryptions" of the bits of $\lfloor (p/q) \cdot \mathbf{k}^\top \cdot \mathbf{A}_x \rfloor$. Indeed, matrix-vector products and rounding can both be computed in $\mathsf{TC}^0 \subseteq \mathsf{NC}^1$, which allows using a polynomial-size q by applying Lemma 10. The resulting instantiation relies on the same LWE assumption as the Banerjee-Peikert PRF [4], where the modulus-to-noise ratio is only slightly super-polynomial.

4.2 Indistinguishability-Based (IND-SO-CCA2) Security

We first prove that the scheme provides IND-SO-CCA2 security. While we can tightly relate the IND-SO-CCA security of the scheme to the pseudorandomness of the underlying PRF, the reduction from the unforgeability of the MAC loses a factor proportional to the number of challenges.

Theorem 3. *The scheme provides IND-SO-CCA2 security assuming that: (i)* Π^{LTF} *is a LTF; (ii)* Π^{ABM} *is an ABM-LTF; (iii)* PRF *is a pseudorandom function family; (iv)* MAC *provides sUF-OT-CMA security. In our instantiation, for any adversary* $\mathcal{A}$*, there exists an* $\mathsf{LWE}_{\ell,m,q,\chi}$ *distinguisher* $\mathcal{D}_1$*, a PRF adversary* $\mathcal{D}_2$ *and a MAC forger* $\mathcal{B}$ *with comparable running time and such that*

$$\mathbf{Adv}_{\mathcal{A}}^{\text{IND-SO-CCA2}}(\lambda) \leq 4n \cdot \mathbf{Adv}_{\ell,m,q,\chi}^{\mathcal{D}_1,\mathsf{lwe}}(\lambda) + 2 \cdot \mathbf{Adv}_{N+Q_D}^{\mathcal{D}_2,\mathrm{prf}}(\lambda) + \frac{Q_D + 2 + N \cdot (Q_D + 1)}{2^{\lambda - 2}} + N \cdot \mathbf{Adv}_{\mathcal{B}}^{\mathrm{mac},Q_D}(\lambda),$$

[4] Note that $\mathbf{y}_0$ may be far from the image of $\mathbf{A}$ in an invalid ciphertext but the inversion algorithm can detect this using ik'.

where N is the number of challenge ciphertexts and Q_D is the number of decryption queries made by the adversary. (The proof is given in the full paper.)

In the full version of this paper, we describe a variant of the scheme which, while not secure under selective openings, can be proved tightly CCA2-secure in the multi-challenge setting as long as the PRF is itself tightly secure. In order to enable instantiations with a polynomial-size modulus q, we give a tighter security proof for the PRF of [21] in the full version of the paper.

4.3 Achieving Simulation-Based (SIM-SO-CCA2) Security

We show that our scheme can be instantiated so as to achieve the stronger notion of SIM-SO-CCA2 security. To this end, we show that it is in fact a lossy encryption scheme with weak efficient opening. We first detail the lossy key generation algorithm (which can be used in the final game in the proof of IND-SO-CCA2 security) and the Opener algorithm.

In order for Opener to run efficiently, we instantiate our scheme with a universal hash family $\mathcal{UH}$, where each function $h : [-\sigma_x\sqrt{n}, \sigma_x\sqrt{n}]^n \rightarrow \mathbb{Z}_q^{\ell_0+\ell_1}$ is keyed by a public matrix $\mathbf{H}_{\mathcal{UH}} \in \mathbb{Z}_q^{(\ell_0+\ell_1)\times n}$, which is included in the public key PK_{loss} and allows evaluating

$$h_{\mathbf{H}_{\mathcal{UH}}}(\mathbf{x}) = \begin{bmatrix} \mathbf{k}^{sym} \\ \mathbf{k}^{mac} \end{bmatrix} = \mathbf{H}_{\mathcal{UH}} \cdot \mathbf{x} \mod q$$

before computing $\mathbf{c}_0 = \mathsf{Msg} + \mathbf{k}^{sym} \in \mathbb{Z}_q^{\ell_0}$ and $\mathbf{c}_1 = \mathsf{MAC.Sig}(\mathbf{k}^{sym}, (\mathbf{y}, \mathbf{c}_0))$.

We also require Par-Gen to output public parameters ℓ, ℓ_0, n satisfying the constraint $n > 2\cdot(2\ell+\ell_0+\ell_1)\cdot\log q$, where ℓ_0 is the message length, ℓ_1 is the key length of the MAC and ℓ is the dimension of the underlying LWE assumption.

Keygen(Γ, loss): Given public parameters $\Gamma = \{\ell, \ell_0, \ell_1, n, m, q, \beta, \sigma_x, \sigma_e\}$ containing integers ℓ, ℓ_0, n, m such that $n > 2 \cdot (2\ell + \ell_0 + \ell_1) \cdot \lceil \log q \rceil$ and $m > 2(n + \ell) \cdot \log q$, conduct the following steps.

1. Choose a random matrix $\mathbf{C}_0 \hookleftarrow U(\mathbb{Z}_q^{\bar{n}\times\bar{\ell}})$, where $\bar{\ell} = (2\ell + \ell_0 + \ell_1)$ and $\bar{n} = n - \bar{\ell}\cdot\lceil\log q\rceil$ which is used to run the $(\mathbf{C}, \mathbf{R}_{sim}) \leftarrow \mathsf{GenTrap}(\mathbf{C}_0, \mathbf{I}_{\bar{\ell}}, \sigma_x)$ algorithm of Lemma 8 to produce a statistically uniform $\mathbf{C} \in \mathbb{Z}_q^{\bar{\ell}\times n}$ with a a small-norm $\mathbf{R}_{sim} \in \mathbb{Z}^{\bar{\ell}\cdot\lceil\log q\rceil\times\bar{n}}$ forming a $\mathbf{G}_{sim}$-trapdoor, where $\mathbf{G}_{sim} \in \mathbb{Z}_q^{\bar{\ell}\cdot\lceil\log q\rceil\times\bar{\ell}}$ is the gadget matrix of [60]. Parse $\mathbf{C} \in \mathbb{Z}_q^{\bar{\ell}\times n}$ as

$$\mathbf{C} = \begin{bmatrix} \mathbf{C}_{\mathsf{LTF}} \\ \hline \mathbf{C}_{\mathsf{ABM}} \\ \hline \mathbf{H}_{\mathcal{UH}} \end{bmatrix} \in \mathbb{Z}_q^{\bar{\ell}\times n}, \tag{4}$$

   where $\mathbf{C}_{\mathsf{LTF}}, \mathbf{C}_{\mathsf{ABM}} \in \mathbb{Z}_q^{\ell\times n}$ and $\mathbf{H}_{\mathcal{UH}} \in \mathbb{Z}_q^{(\ell_0+\ell_1)\times n}$.

2. Sample matrices $\mathbf{B}_{\mathsf{LTF}} \hookleftarrow U(\mathbb{Z}_q^{2m\times\ell})$, $\mathbf{B}_{\mathsf{ABM}} \hookleftarrow U(\mathbb{Z}_q^{m\times\ell})$, $\mathbf{F}_{\mathsf{LTF}} \hookleftarrow \chi^{2m\times n}$, $\mathbf{F}_{\mathsf{ABM}} \hookleftarrow \chi^{m\times n}$ in order to define $\mathbf{A}_{\mathsf{LTF}} = \mathbf{B}_{\mathsf{LTF}} \cdot \mathbf{C}_{\mathsf{LTF}} + \mathbf{F}_{\mathsf{LTF}} \in \mathbb{Z}_q^{2m\times n}$ and $\mathbf{A}_{\mathsf{ABM}} = \mathbf{B}_{\mathsf{ABM}} \cdot \mathbf{C}_{\mathsf{ABM}} + \mathbf{F}_{\mathsf{ABM}} \in \mathbb{Z}_q^{m\times n}$, which are statistically close to outputs of $\mathsf{Lossy}(1^n, 1^m, 1^\ell, q, \chi)$ as $\mathbf{C}_{\mathsf{LTF}}$ and $\mathbf{C}_{\mathsf{ABM}}$ are statistically uniform over $\mathbb{Z}_q^{\ell\times n}$.
3. Define $ek' = \mathbf{A}_{\mathsf{LTF}} \in \mathbb{Z}_q^{2m\times n}$ to be the evaluation key of Π^{LTF}. Then, run Steps 2-4 of the key generation algorithm of Π^{ABM} while setting $\bar{\mathbf{A}} = \mathbf{A}_{\mathsf{ABM}} \in \mathbb{Z}_q^{m\times n}$ at Step 1. The resulting keys (ek, ik, tk) consist of

$$ek := \Big(\mathbf{A}_{\mathsf{ABM}}, \{\mathbf{B}_i\}_{i=1}^{\lambda}\Big), \qquad ik := \big(\{\mathbf{R}_i\}_{i=1}^{\lambda}, K\big), \qquad tk := K$$

and are statistically close to the output distribution (2) of $\Pi^{\mathsf{ABM}}.\mathsf{Gen}$.

Return $PK_{\mathsf{loss}} = (ek', ek, \mathbf{H}_{\mathcal{UH}})$ and

$$SK_{\mathsf{loss}} = \big(\mathbf{R}_{sim}, \mathbf{C}_0, \mathbf{B}_{\mathsf{LTF}}, \mathbf{B}_{\mathsf{ABM}}, \mathbf{F}_{\mathsf{LTF}}, \mathbf{F}_{\mathsf{ABM}}, ik\big). \tag{5}$$

Opener$(\Gamma, PK_{\mathsf{loss}}, SK_{\mathsf{loss}}, \mathsf{Msg}_0, (\mathbf{x}, \mathbf{e}_0, \mathbf{e}_1), \mathsf{Msg}_1)$**:** Parse SK_{loss} as in (5) and conduct the following steps.

1. Compute $\mathbf{t}_{\mathsf{LTF},\mathbf{x}} = \mathbf{C}_{\mathsf{LTF}} \cdot \mathbf{x} \in \mathbb{Z}_q^{\ell}$, $\mathbf{t}_{\mathsf{ABM},\mathbf{x}} = \mathbf{C}_{\mathsf{ABM}} \cdot \mathbf{x} \in \mathbb{Z}_q^{\ell}$ and

$$\begin{bmatrix}\mathbf{k}^{sym,\mathbf{x}} \\ \mathbf{k}^{mac,\mathbf{x}}\end{bmatrix} = \mathbf{H}_{\mathcal{UH}} \cdot \mathbf{x} \ \in \mathbb{Z}_q^{\ell_0+\ell_1}.$$

Then, set $\mathbf{t}_{\mathsf{Msg},\mathbf{x}} = (\mathsf{Msg}_0 - \mathsf{Msg}_1) + \mathbf{k}^{sym,\mathbf{x}} \in \mathbb{Z}_q^{\ell_0}$ and define

$$\mathbf{t}_{\mathbf{x}} = \Big[\ \mathbf{t}_{\mathsf{LTF},\mathbf{x}}^\top \mid \mathbf{t}_{\mathsf{ABM},\mathbf{x}}^\top \mid \mathbf{t}_{\mathsf{Msg},\mathbf{x}}^\top \mid \mathbf{k}^{mac,\mathbf{x}\top}\ \Big]^\top \in \mathbb{Z}_q^{\bar{\ell}}.$$

2. Using the trapdoor $\mathbf{R}_{sim} \in \mathbb{Z}^{\bar{\ell}\cdot\lceil\log q\rceil\times\bar{n}}$, sample a small-norm vector $\mathbf{x}' \hookleftarrow D^{S_{\underline{\mathbf{F}},\mathbf{t}_{\mathbf{x}},\mathbf{f}}}_{\Lambda^\perp(\mathbf{C})+\mathbf{z},\sqrt{\mathbf{\Sigma}},\mathbf{c}}$ so as to have a short integer vector $\mathbf{x}' \in \mathbb{Z}^n$ satisfying $\mathbf{C}\cdot\mathbf{x}' = \mathbf{t}_{\mathbf{x}} \bmod q$, using an arbitrary solution $\mathbf{z} \in \mathbb{Z}^n$ of $\mathbf{C}\cdot\mathbf{z} = \mathbf{t}_{\mathbf{x}} \in \mathbb{Z}_q^{\bar{\ell}}$, where $\mathbf{\Sigma}$ and $\mathbf{c}$ are defined based on Lemma 11, for

$$\underline{\mathbf{F}} := \begin{bmatrix}\mathbf{F}_{\mathsf{LTF}} \\ \hline \mathbf{F}_{\mathsf{ABM}} \\ \hline \mathbf{R}_t\cdot\mathbf{F}_{\mathsf{ABM}}\end{bmatrix} \in \mathbb{Z}^{4m\times n}, \underline{\mathbf{e}} := \begin{bmatrix}\mathbf{e}_0 \\ \hline \mathbf{e}\end{bmatrix} \in \mathbb{Z}^{4m}, \ \mathbf{f} := \underline{\mathbf{F}}\cdot\mathbf{x} + \underline{\mathbf{e}} \in \mathbb{Z}^{4m}. \tag{6}$$

3. Output $(\mathbf{x}', \mathbf{e}_0', \mathbf{e}')$ where

$$\begin{cases}\mathbf{e}_0' = \mathbf{F}_{\mathsf{LTF}}\cdot(\mathbf{x}-\mathbf{x}') + \mathbf{e}_0 \ \in \mathbb{Z}^{2m} \\ \mathbf{e}' \ = \begin{bmatrix}\mathbf{F}_{\mathsf{ABM}} \\ \hline \mathbf{R}_t\cdot\mathbf{F}_{\mathsf{ABM}}\end{bmatrix}\cdot(\mathbf{x}-\mathbf{x}') + \mathbf{e} \ \in \mathbb{Z}^{2m}\end{cases} \tag{7}$$

We observe that algorithm Opener is efficient. In particular, at Step 2, it can compute the matrix $\mathbf{\Sigma}$ and the vector $\mathbf{c}$ of Lemma 11 by first reconstructing the matrix $\underline{\mathbf{F}} \in \mathbb{Z}^{4m\times n}$ of (6) and the vector $\mathbf{f} = \underline{\mathbf{F}}\cdot\mathbf{x} + \underline{\mathbf{e}} \in \mathbb{Z}^{4m}$, which requires to deterministically re-compute the integer matrix $\mathbf{R}_t$ obtained at Step 2 of $\mathsf{ABM.Invert}(ik, t, .)$ using $ik = ((\mathbf{R}_i)_{i\leq\lambda}, K)$.

We easily check that, for any vector $\mathbf{x}'$ sampled at Step 2, the corresponding

$$\begin{bmatrix} \mathbf{k}^{sym,\mathbf{x}'} \\ \mathbf{k}^{mac,\mathbf{x}'} \end{bmatrix} = \mathbf{H}_{\mathcal{UH}} \cdot \mathbf{x}' \in \mathbb{Z}_q^{\ell_0+\ell_1}$$

satisfy $\mathbf{k}^{mac,\mathbf{x}'} = \mathbf{k}^{mac,\mathbf{x}_0}$ and $\mathbf{k}^{sym,\mathbf{x}'} = (\mathsf{Msg}_0 - \mathsf{Msg}_1) + \mathbf{k}^{sym,\mathbf{x}} \mod q$.

As a consequence, if $C = (t_{\mathsf{c}}, \mathbf{c}_0, \mathbf{c}_1, \mathbf{y}_0, \mathbf{y})$ is the ciphertext obtained by running $\mathsf{Encrypt}(PK_{\mathsf{loss}}, \mathsf{Msg}_0, (\mathbf{x}, \mathbf{e}_0, \mathbf{e}))$, this ciphertext contains

$$\mathbf{c}_0 = \mathsf{Msg}_0 + \mathbf{k}^{sym,\mathbf{x}} \mod q, \qquad \mathbf{c}_1 = \mathsf{MAC.Sig}(\mathbf{k}^{mac,\mathbf{x}}, (\mathbf{y}, \mathbf{c}_0)),$$

which coincide with $\mathbf{c}_0 = \mathsf{Msg}_1 + \mathbf{k}^{sym,\mathbf{x}'}$ and $\mathbf{c}_1 = \mathsf{MAC.Sig}(\mathbf{k}^{mac,\mathbf{x}'}, (\mathbf{y}, \mathbf{c}_0))$. Moreover, we also have $\mathbf{C}_{\mathsf{LTF}} \cdot \mathbf{x} = \mathbf{C}_{\mathsf{LTF}} \cdot \mathbf{x}'$ and $\mathbf{C}_{\mathsf{ABM}} \cdot \mathbf{x} = \mathbf{C}_{\mathsf{ABM}} \cdot \mathbf{x}'$.

The following theorem formally states the correctness of the Opener algorithm.

Theorem 4. *For any key pair* $(PK_{\mathsf{loss}}, SK_{\mathsf{loss}})$ *in the support of* $\mathsf{Keygen}(\Gamma, \mathsf{loss})$, *algorithm* Opener *outputs* $(\mathbf{x}', \mathbf{e}_0', \mathbf{e}')$ *with the correct distribution conditionally on* $\mathsf{Encrypt}(PK_{\mathsf{loss},}, \mathsf{Msg}_0, (\mathbf{x}, \mathbf{e}_0, \mathbf{e})) = \mathsf{Encrypt}(PK_{\mathsf{loss},}, \mathsf{Msg}_1, (\mathbf{x}', \mathbf{e}_0', \mathbf{e}'))$.

Proof. For any lossy tag $t = (t_{\mathsf{c}}, t_{\mathsf{a}})$, the matrix $\mathbf{A}_t$ used by $\Pi^{\mathsf{ABM}}.\mathsf{Eval}(ek, t, .)$ is of the form

$$\mathbf{A}_t = \left[\frac{\mathbf{A}_{\mathsf{ABM}}}{\mathbf{R}_t \cdot \mathbf{A}_{\mathsf{ABM}}}\right] = \left[\frac{\mathbf{B}_{\mathsf{ABM}}}{\mathbf{R}_t \cdot \mathbf{B}_{\mathsf{ABM}}}\right] \cdot \mathbf{C}_{\mathsf{ABM}} + \left[\frac{\mathbf{F}_{\mathsf{ABM}}}{\mathbf{R}_t \cdot \mathbf{F}_{\mathsf{ABM}}}\right], \tag{8}$$

where $\mathbf{R}_t \in \mathbb{Z}^{m \times m}$ is the integer matrix obtained in $\mathsf{ABM.Invert}(ik, t, .)$. At the same time, ek' consists of a matrix of the form $\mathbf{A}_{\mathsf{LTF}} = \mathbf{B}_{\mathsf{LTF}} \cdot \mathbf{C}_{\mathsf{LTF}} + \mathbf{F}_{\mathsf{LTF}}$.

We now claim that, due to the way to sample $\mathbf{x}'$ and $\mathbf{e}_0'$ and $\mathbf{e}'$ at Steps 2 and 3 of Opener, the distribution of $\mathbf{y}_0'$ and $\mathbf{y}'$, with

$$\begin{cases} \mathbf{y}_0' = \mathbf{A}_{\mathsf{LTF}} \cdot \mathbf{x}' + \mathbf{e}_0' \in \mathbb{Z}^{2m} \\ \mathbf{y}' = \mathbf{A}_t \cdot \mathbf{x}' + \mathbf{e}' \in \mathbb{Z}^{2m} \end{cases} \tag{9}$$

is the same as that of the real encryptions explained in the beginning of this Section. By replacing $\mathbf{A}_{\mathsf{LTF}}, \mathbf{A}_t$ and $\mathbf{e}_0'$ and $\mathbf{e}'$ we get:

$$\begin{aligned} \mathbf{y}_0' &= (\mathbf{B}_{\mathsf{LTF}} \cdot \mathbf{C}_{\mathsf{LTF}} + \mathbf{F}_{\mathsf{LTF}}) \cdot \mathbf{x}' + (\mathbf{F}_{\mathsf{LTF}} \cdot (\mathbf{x} - \mathbf{x}') + \mathbf{e}_0) \\ &= \mathbf{B}_{\mathsf{LTF}} \cdot \mathbf{C}_{\mathsf{LTF}} \cdot \mathbf{x}' + \mathbf{F}_{\mathsf{LTF}} \cdot \mathbf{x} + \mathbf{e}_0 \\ &= \mathbf{B}_{\mathsf{LTF}} \cdot \mathbf{C}_{\mathsf{LTF}} \cdot \mathbf{x} + \mathbf{F}_{\mathsf{LTF}} \cdot \mathbf{x} + \mathbf{e}_0 \\ &= \mathbf{A}_{\mathsf{LTF}} \cdot \mathbf{x} + \mathbf{e}_0 \in \mathbb{Z}^m \end{aligned}$$

and

$$\begin{aligned}\mathbf{y}' &= \left(\left[\frac{\mathbf{B}_{\mathsf{ABM}}}{\mathbf{R}_t \cdot \mathbf{B}_{\mathsf{ABM}}}\right] \cdot \mathbf{C}_{\mathsf{ABM}} + \left[\frac{\mathbf{F}_{\mathsf{ABM}}}{\mathbf{R}_t \cdot \mathbf{F}_{\mathsf{ABM}}}\right]\right) \cdot \mathbf{x}' \\ &\quad + \left(\left[\frac{\mathbf{F}_{\mathsf{ABM}}}{\mathbf{R}_t \cdot \mathbf{F}_{\mathsf{ABM}}}\right] \cdot (\mathbf{x} - \mathbf{x}') + \mathbf{e}\right) \\ &= \left[\frac{\mathbf{B}_{\mathsf{ABM}}}{\mathbf{R}_t \cdot \mathbf{B}_{\mathsf{ABM}}}\right] \cdot \mathbf{C}_{\mathsf{ABM}} \cdot \mathbf{x}' + \left[\frac{\mathbf{F}_{\mathsf{ABM}}}{\mathbf{R}_t \cdot \mathbf{F}_{\mathsf{ABM}}}\right] \cdot \mathbf{x} + \mathbf{e} \\ &= \left[\frac{\mathbf{B}_{\mathsf{ABM}}}{\mathbf{R}_t \cdot \mathbf{B}_{\mathsf{ABM}}}\right] \cdot \mathbf{C}_{\mathsf{ABM}} \cdot \mathbf{x} + \left[\frac{\mathbf{F}_{\mathsf{ABM}}}{\mathbf{R}_t \cdot \mathbf{F}_{\mathsf{ABM}}}\right] \cdot \mathbf{x} + \mathbf{e} \\ &= \mathbf{A}_t \cdot \mathbf{x} + \mathbf{e} \in \mathbb{Z}^{2m}\end{aligned} \tag{10}$$

It remains to show that $(\mathbf{x}', \mathbf{e}'_0, \mathbf{e}')$ have the correct distribution. By applying Lemma 11 to the matrix $\mathbf{C}$ of (4) with $\mathbf{u} = \mathbf{t_x}$, the conditional distribution of $\mathbf{x}'$ given $(\mathbf{t_x}, \underline{\mathbf{F}} \cdot \mathbf{x} + \underline{\mathbf{e}})$ is statistically close to $D^{S_{\mathbf{\Sigma},\mathbf{t_x},\mathbf{f}}}_{\Lambda^{\perp}(\mathbf{C})+\mathbf{z},\sqrt{\mathbf{\Sigma}},\mathbf{c}}$, where $\mathbf{z}$ is an arbitrary solution of $\mathbf{C} \cdot \mathbf{z} = \mathbf{t_x}$. It is also efficiently samplable, by Theorem 1. This provides the claimed result. □

In the full version of the paper, we show that lattice trapdoors can also be used to obtain SIM-SO-CPA security from LTFs based on DDH-like assumptions.

Acknowledgements. We thank Fabrice Benhamouda for useful discussions. Part of this research was funded by the French ANR ALAMBIC project (ANR-16-CE39-0006) and by the BPI-funded project RISQ. The third author was supported by ERC Starting Grant ERC-2013-StG-335086-LATTAC. The second and fourth authors were supported by Australian Research Council Discovery Grant DP150100285.

References

1. Agrawal, S., Boneh, D., Boyen, X.: Efficient lattice (H)IBE in the standard model. In: Gilbert, H. (ed.) EUROCRYPT 2010. LNCS, vol. 6110, pp. 553–572. Springer, Heidelberg (2010). doi:10.1007/978-3-642-13190-5_28
2. Agrawal, S., Gentry, C., Halevi, S., Sahai, A.: Discrete gaussian leftover hash lemma over infinite domains. In: Sako, K., Sarkar, P. (eds.) ASIACRYPT 2013. LNCS, vol. 8269, pp. 97–116. Springer, Heidelberg (2013). doi:10.1007/978-3-642-42033-7_6
3. Alwen, J., Krenn, S., Pietrzak, K., Wichs, D.: Learning with rounding, revisited. In: Canetti, R., Garay, J.A. (eds.) CRYPTO 2013. LNCS, vol. 8042, pp. 57–74. Springer, Heidelberg (2013). doi:10.1007/978-3-642-40041-4_4
4. Banerjee, A., Peikert, C.: New and improved key-homomorphic pseudorandom functions. In: Garay, J.A., Gennaro, R. (eds.) CRYPTO 2014. LNCS, vol. 8616, pp. 353–370. Springer, Heidelberg (2014). doi:10.1007/978-3-662-44371-2_20
5. Banerjee, A., Peikert, C., Rosen, A.: Pseudorandom functions and lattices. In: Pointcheval, D., Johansson, T. (eds.) EUROCRYPT 2012. LNCS, vol. 7237, pp. 719–737. Springer, Heidelberg (2012). doi:10.1007/978-3-642-29011-4_42
6. Barrington, D.: Bounded-width polynomial-size branching programs recognize exactly those languages in nc1. In: STOC (1986)

7. Bellare, M., Boldyreva, A., Micali, S.: Public-key encryption in a multi-user setting: security proofs and improvements. In: Preneel, B. (ed.) EUROCRYPT 2000. LNCS, vol. 1807, pp. 259–274. Springer, Heidelberg (2000). doi:10.1007/3-540-45539-6_18
8. Bellare, M., Brakerski, Z., Naor, M., Ristenpart, T., Segev, G., Shacham, H., Yilek, S.: Hedged public-key encryption: how to protect against bad randomness. In: Matsui, M. (ed.) ASIACRYPT 2009. LNCS, vol. 5912, pp. 232–249. Springer, Heidelberg (2009). doi:10.1007/978-3-642-10366-7_14
9. Bellare, M., Dowsley, R., Waters, B., Yilek, S.: Standard security does not imply security against selective-opening. In: Pointcheval, D., Johansson, T. (eds.) EUROCRYPT 2012. LNCS, vol. 7237, pp. 645–662. Springer, Heidelberg (2012). doi:10.1007/978-3-642-29011-4_38
10. Bellare, M., Hoang, V.T.: Resisting randomness subversion: fast deterministic and hedged public-key encryption in the standard model. In: Oswald, E., Fischlin, M. (eds.) EUROCRYPT 2015. LNCS, vol. 9057, pp. 627–656. Springer, Heidelberg (2015). doi:10.1007/978-3-662-46803-6_21
11. Bellare, M., Hofheinz, D., Yilek, S.: Possibility and impossibility results for encryption and commitment secure under selective opening. In: Joux, A. (ed.) EUROCRYPT 2009. LNCS, vol. 5479, pp. 1–35. Springer, Heidelberg (2009). doi:10.1007/978-3-642-01001-9_1
12. Bellare, M., Kiltz, E., Peikert, C., Waters, B.: Identity-based (lossy) trapdoor functions and applications. In: Pointcheval, D., Johansson, T. (eds.) EUROCRYPT 2012. LNCS, vol. 7237, pp. 228–245. Springer, Heidelberg (2012). doi:10.1007/978-3-642-29011-4_15
13. Bellare, M., Rogaway, P.: Random oracles are practical: a paradigm for designing efficient protocols. In: ACM-CCS (1993)
14. Bellare, M., Rogaway, P.: Optimal asymmetric encryption. In: Santis, A. (ed.) EUROCRYPT 1994. LNCS, vol. 950, pp. 92–111. Springer, Heidelberg (1995). doi:10.1007/BFb0053428
15. Bellare, M., Waters, B., Yilek, S.: Identity-based encryption secure against selective opening attack. In: Ishai, Y. (ed.) TCC 2011. LNCS, vol. 6597, pp. 235–252. Springer, Heidelberg (2011). doi:10.1007/978-3-642-19571-6_15
16. Bellare, M., Yilek, S.: Encryption schemes secure under selective opening attack. Cryptology ePrint Archive: Report 2009/101 (2009)
17. Black, J., Rogaway, P., Shrimpton, T.: Encryption-scheme security in the presence of key-dependent messages. In: Nyberg, K., Heys, H. (eds.) SAC 2002. LNCS, vol. 2595, pp. 62–75. Springer, Heidelberg (2003). doi:10.1007/3-540-36492-7_6
18. Böhl, F., Hofheinz, D., Kraschewski, D.: On definitions of selective opening security. In: Fischlin, M., Buchmann, J., Manulis, M. (eds.) PKC 2012. LNCS, vol. 7293, pp. 522–539. Springer, Heidelberg (2012). doi:10.1007/978-3-642-30057-8_31
19. Boldyreva, A., Fehr, S., O'Neill, A.: On notions of security for deterministic encryption, and efficient constructions without random oracles. In: Wagner, D. (ed.) CRYPTO 2008. LNCS, vol. 5157, pp. 335–359. Springer, Heidelberg (2008). doi:10.1007/978-3-540-85174-5_19
20. Boneh, D., Gentry, C., Gorbunov, S., Halevi, S., Nikolaenko, V., Segev, G., Vaikuntanathan, V., Vinayagamurthy, D.: Fully key-homomorphic encryption, arithmetic circuit ABE and compact garbled circuits. In: Nguyen, P.Q., Oswald, E. (eds.) EUROCRYPT 2014. LNCS, vol. 8441, pp. 533–556. Springer, Heidelberg (2014). doi:10.1007/978-3-642-55220-5_30
21. Boneh, D., Lewi, K., Montgomery, H., Raghunathan, A.: Key homomorphic PRFs and their applications. In: Canetti, R., Garay, J.A. (eds.) CRYPTO

2013. LNCS, vol. 8042, pp. 410–428. Springer, Heidelberg (2013). doi:10.1007/978-3-642-40041-4_23
22. Boyen, X., Li, Q.: Towards tightly secure lattice short signature and ID-based encryption. In: Cheon, J.H., Takagi, T. (eds.) ASIACRYPT 2016. LNCS, vol. 10032, pp. 404–434. Springer, Heidelberg (2016). doi:10.1007/978-3-662-53890-6_14
23. Boyen, X., Li, Q.: All-but-many lossy trapdoor functions from lattices and applications. In: Katz, J., Shacham, H. (eds.) CRYPTO 2017, Part III. LNCS, vol. 10403, pp. 298–331. Springer, Cham (2017)
24. Boyen, X., Mei, Q., Waters, B.: Direct chosen ciphertext security from identity-based technique. In: ACM-CCS (2005)
25. Brakerski, Z., Langlois, A., Peikert, C., Regev, O., Stehlé, D.: On the classical hardness of learning with errors. In: STOC (2013)
26. Brakerski, Z., Segev, G.: Better security for deterministic public-key encryption: the auxiliary-input setting. In: Rogaway, P. (ed.) CRYPTO 2011. LNCS, vol. 6841, pp. 543–560. Springer, Heidelberg (2011). doi:10.1007/978-3-642-22792-9_31
27. Brakerski, Z., Vaikuntanathan, V.: Lattice-based FHE as secure as PKE. In: ITCS (2014)
28. Brakerski, Z., Vaikuntanathan, V.: Circuit-ABE from LWE: unbounded attributes and semi-adaptive security. In: Robshaw, M., Katz, J. (eds.) CRYPTO 2016. LNCS, vol. 9816, pp. 363–384. Springer, Heidelberg (2016). doi:10.1007/978-3-662-53015-3_13
29. Canetti, R., Feige, U., Goldreich, O., Naor, M.: Adaptively secure multi-party computation. In: STOC (1996)
30. Canetti, R., Halevi, S., Katz, J.: Chosen-ciphertext security from identity-based encryption. In: Cachin, C., Camenisch, J.L. (eds.) EUROCRYPT 2004. LNCS, vol. 3027, pp. 207–222. Springer, Heidelberg (2004). doi:10.1007/978-3-540-24676-3_13
31. Chen, J., Wee, H.: Fully, (almost) tightly secure IBE and dual system groups. In: Canetti, R., Garay, J.A. (eds.) CRYPTO 2013. LNCS, vol. 8043, pp. 435–460. Springer, Heidelberg (2013). doi:10.1007/978-3-642-40084-1_25
32. Cramer, R., Shoup, V.: A practical public key cryptosystem provably secure against adaptive chosen ciphertext attack. In: Krawczyk, H. (ed.) CRYPTO 1998. LNCS, vol. 1462, pp. 13–25. Springer, Heidelberg (1998). doi:10.1007/BFb0055717
33. Damgård, I., Nielsen, J.B.: Improved non-committing encryption schemes based on a general complexity assumption. In: Bellare, M. (ed.) CRYPTO 2000. LNCS, vol. 1880, pp. 432–450. Springer, Heidelberg (2000). doi:10.1007/3-540-44598-6_27
34. Döttling, N., Schröder, D.: Efficient pseudorandom functions via on-the-fly adaptation. In: Gennaro, R., Robshaw, M. (eds.) CRYPTO 2015. LNCS, vol. 9215, pp. 329–350. Springer, Heidelberg (2015). doi:10.1007/978-3-662-47989-6_16
35. Dwork, C., Naor, M., Reingold, O., Stockmeyer, L.: Magic functions. J. ACM **50**(6) (2003)
36. Fehr, S., Hofheinz, D., Kiltz, E., Wee, H.: Encryption schemes secure against chosen-ciphertext selective opening attacks. In: Gilbert, H. (ed.) EUROCRYPT 2010. LNCS, vol. 6110, pp. 381–402. Springer, Heidelberg (2010). doi:10.1007/978-3-642-13190-5_20
37. Freeman, D., Goldreich, O., Kiltz, E., Rosen, A., Segev, G.: More constructions of lossy and correlation-secure trapdoor functions. J. Cryptology **26**(1), 39–74 (2013)
38. Fujisaki, E.: All-but-many encryption - a new framework for fully-equipped UC commitments. In: Sarkar, P., Iwata, T. (eds.) ASIACRYPT 2014. LNCS, vol. 8874, pp. 426–447. Springer, Heidelberg (2014). doi:10.1007/978-3-662-45608-8_23

39. Gay, R., Hofheinz, D., Kiltz, E., Wee, H.: Tightly CCA-secure encryption without pairings. In: Fischlin, M., Coron, J.-S. (eds.) EUROCRYPT 2016. LNCS, vol. 9665, pp. 1–27. Springer, Heidelberg (2016). doi:10.1007/978-3-662-49890-3_1
40. Gentry, C., Peikert, C., Vaikuntanathan, V.: Trapdoors for hard lattices and new cryptographic constructions. In: STOC (2008)
41. Gentry, C., Sahai, A., Waters, B.: Homomorphic encryption from learning with errors: conceptually-simpler, asymptotically-faster, attribute-based. In: Canetti, R., Garay, J.A. (eds.) CRYPTO 2013. LNCS, vol. 8042, pp. 75–92. Springer, Heidelberg (2013). doi:10.1007/978-3-642-40041-4_5
42. Goldwasser, S., Micali, S.: Probabilistic encryption. J. Comput. Syst. Sci. **28**, 270–299 (1984)
43. Gorbunov, S., Vaikuntanathan, V., Wichs, D.: Leveled fully homomorphic signatures from standard lattices. In: STOC (2015)
44. Gorbunov, S., Vinayagamurthy, D.: Riding on asymmetry: efficient ABE for branching programs. In: Iwata, T., Cheon, J.H. (eds.) ASIACRYPT 2015. LNCS, vol. 9452, pp. 550–574. Springer, Heidelberg (2015). doi:10.1007/978-3-662-48797-6_23
45. Hemenway, B., Libert, B., Ostrovsky, R., Vergnaud, D.: Lossy encryption: constructions from general assumptions and efficient selective opening chosen ciphertext security. In: Lee, D.H., Wang, X. (eds.) ASIACRYPT 2011. LNCS, vol. 7073, pp. 70–88. Springer, Heidelberg (2011). doi:10.1007/978-3-642-25385-0_4
46. Hemenway, B., Ostrovsky, R.: Extended-DDH and lossy trapdoor functions. In: Fischlin, M., Buchmann, J., Manulis, M. (eds.) PKC 2012. LNCS, vol. 7293, pp. 627–643. Springer, Heidelberg (2012). doi:10.1007/978-3-642-30057-8_37
47. Heuer, F., Jager, T., Kiltz, E., Schäge, S.: On the selective opening security of practical public-key encryption schemes. In: Katz, J. (ed.) PKC 2015. LNCS, vol. 9020, pp. 27–51. Springer, Heidelberg (2015). doi:10.1007/978-3-662-46447-2_2
48. Hoang, V.T., Katz, J., O'Neill, A., Zaheri, M.: Selective-opening security in the presence of randomness failures. In: Cheon, J.H., Takagi, T. (eds.) ASIACRYPT 2016. LNCS, vol. 10032, pp. 278–306. Springer, Heidelberg (2016). doi:10.1007/978-3-662-53890-6_10
49. Hofheinz, D.: All-but-many lossy trapdoor functions. In: Pointcheval, D., Johansson, T. (eds.) EUROCRYPT 2012. LNCS, vol. 7237, pp. 209–227. Springer, Heidelberg (2012). doi:10.1007/978-3-642-29011-4_14
50. Hofheinz, D.: Circular chosen-ciphertext security with compact ciphertexts. In: Johansson, T., Nguyen, P.Q. (eds.) EUROCRYPT 2013. LNCS, vol. 7881, pp. 520–536. Springer, Heidelberg (2013). doi:10.1007/978-3-642-38348-9_31
51. Hofheinz, D.: Algebraic partitioning: fully compact and (almost) tightly secure cryptography. In: Kushilevitz, E., Malkin, T. (eds.) TCC 2016. LNCS, vol. 9562, pp. 251–281. Springer, Heidelberg (2016). doi:10.1007/978-3-662-49096-9_11
52. Hofheinz, D.: Adaptive partitioning. In: Coron, J.-S., Nielsen, J.B. (eds.) EUROCRYPT 2017. LNCS, vol. 10212, pp. 489–518. Springer, Cham (2017). doi:10.1007/978-3-319-56617-7_17
53. Hofheinz, D., Jager, T.: Tightly secure signatures and public-key encryption. In: Safavi-Naini, R., Canetti, R. (eds.) CRYPTO 2012. LNCS, vol. 7417, pp. 590–607. Springer, Heidelberg (2012). doi:10.1007/978-3-642-32009-5_35
54. Hofheinz, D., Jager, T., Rupp, A.: Public-key encryption with simulation-based selective-opening security and compact ciphertexts. In: Hirt, M., Smith, A. (eds.) TCC 2016. LNCS, vol. 9986, pp. 146–168. Springer, Heidelberg (2016). doi:10.1007/978-3-662-53644-5_6

55. Hofheinz, D., Rao, V., Wichs, D.: Standard security does not imply indistinguishability under selective opening. In: Hirt, M., Smith, A. (eds.) TCC 2016. LNCS, vol. 9986, pp. 121–145. Springer, Heidelberg (2016). doi:10.1007/978-3-662-53644-5_5
56. Huang, Z., Liu, S., Qin, B.: Sender-equivocable encryption schemes secure against chosen-ciphertext attacks revisited. In: Kurosawa, K., Hanaoka, G. (eds.) PKC 2013. LNCS, vol. 7778, pp. 369–385. Springer, Heidelberg (2013). doi:10.1007/978-3-642-36362-7_23
57. Lai, J., Deng, R.H., Liu, S., Weng, J., Zhao, Y.: Identity-based encryption secure against selective opening chosen-ciphertext attack. In: Nguyen, P.Q., Oswald, E. (eds.) EUROCRYPT 2014. LNCS, vol. 8441, pp. 77–92. Springer, Heidelberg (2014). doi:10.1007/978-3-642-55220-5_5
58. Libert, B., Peters, T., Joye, M., Yung, M.: Compactly hiding linear spans. In: Iwata, T., Cheon, J.H. (eds.) ASIACRYPT 2015. LNCS, vol. 9452, pp. 681–707. Springer, Heidelberg (2015). doi:10.1007/978-3-662-48797-6_28
59. Liu, S., Paterson, K.G.: Simulation-based selective opening CCA security for PKE from key encapsulation mechanisms. In: Katz, J. (ed.) PKC 2015. LNCS, vol. 9020, pp. 3–26. Springer, Heidelberg (2015). doi:10.1007/978-3-662-46447-2_1
60. Micciancio, D., Peikert, C.: Trapdoors for lattices: simpler, tighter, faster, smaller. In: Pointcheval, D., Johansson, T. (eds.) EUROCRYPT 2012. LNCS, vol. 7237, pp. 700–718. Springer, Heidelberg (2012). doi:10.1007/978-3-642-29011-4_41
61. Micciancio, D., Regev, O.: Worst-case to average-case reductions based on gaussian measures. SIAM J. Comput. **37**(1), 267–302 (2007)
62. Naor, M., Reingold, O.: Number-theoretic constructions of efficient pseudo-random functions. In: FOCS (1997)
63. Naor, M., Yung, M.: Public-key cryptosystems provably secure against chosen ciphertext attacks. In: STOC (1990)
64. Paillier, P.: Public-key cryptosystems based on composite degree residuosity classes. In: Stern, J. (ed.) EUROCRYPT 1999. LNCS, vol. 1592, pp. 223–238. Springer, Heidelberg (1999). doi:10.1007/3-540-48910-X_16
65. Peikert, C.: Public-key cryptosystems from the worst-case shortest vector problem. In: STOC (2009)
66. Peikert, C., Waters, B.: Lossy trapdoor functions and their applications. In: STOC (2008)
67. Rackoff, C., Simon, D.R.: Non-interactive zero-knowledge proof of knowledge and chosen ciphertext attack. In: Feigenbaum, J. (ed.) CRYPTO 1991. LNCS, vol. 576, pp. 433–444. Springer, Heidelberg (1992). doi:10.1007/3-540-46766-1_35
68. Raghunathan, A., Segev, G., Vadhan, S.: Deterministic public-key encryption for adaptively chosen plaintext distributions. In: Johansson, T., Nguyen, P.Q. (eds.) EUROCRYPT 2013. LNCS, vol. 7881, pp. 93–110. Springer, Heidelberg (2013). doi:10.1007/978-3-642-38348-9_6
69. Regev, O.: On lattices, learning with errors, random linear codes, and cryptography. In: STOC (2005)
70. Rosen, A., Segev, G.: Chosen-ciphertext security via correlated products. In: Reingold, O. (ed.) TCC 2009. LNCS, vol. 5444, pp. 419–436. Springer, Heidelberg (2009). doi:10.1007/978-3-642-00457-5_25
71. Wee, H.: Dual projective hashing and its applications - lossy trapdoor functions and more. In Eurocrypt, 2012
72. Zhandry, M.: The magic of ELFs. In Crypto, 2016

Amortization with Fewer Equations for Proving Knowledge of Small Secrets

Rafael del Pino[1,2,3,4(✉)] and Vadim Lyubashevsky[4]

[1] INRIA, Paris, France
afe@zurich.ibm.com
[2] École Normale Supérieure, Paris, France
[3] CNRS, Paris, France
[4] IBM Research Zurich, Zurich, Switzerland

Abstract. For a linear function f, a vector $\mathbf{x}$ with small coefficients, and a vector $y = f(\mathbf{x})$, we would like to be able to give a zero-knowledge proof for the knowledge of an $\mathbf{x}'$ with small coefficients that satisfies $f(\mathbf{x}') = y$. This is a common scenario in lattice-based cryptography, and there is currently no satisfactory solution for this problem. All known protocols are built via the repetition of a basic protocol that only has constant (1/2 or 2/3) soundness error. This implies that the communication complexity of the final protocol will be at least a factor of k larger than that of the basic one, where k is the security parameter.

One can do better if one considers simultaneously proving the knowledge of many instances of the above linear equation. The protocol that has the smallest amortized communication complexity while achieving close-to-optimal slack (i.e. the ratio between the coefficients in the secret and those that can be extracted from the proof) is due to Cramer et al. (Eurocrypt '17) which builds on an earlier work of Baum et al. (Crypto '16). The main downside of this protocol is that the amortization only kicks in when the number of equations is rather large – $4k^2$. This means that for $k = 128$, it is only truly optimal when one has more than 2^{16} equations to prove. The aforementioned work of Cramer et al. also shows how to achieve a protocol requiring $o(k^2)$ samples, but it is only applicable for much larger values of k and the number of required samples ends up being larger than 2^{16}.

The main result of our work is reducing the concrete minimal number of equations required for the amortization, while keeping the communication complexity almost unchanged. The cost of this is an increase in the running time of the zero-knowledge proof. More specifically, we show that one can decrease the required number of equations by a factor of $\Omega(\log^2 \alpha)$ at the cost of increasing the running time by a factor of $\Omega(\alpha)$. For example, increasing the running time by a factor of 8 allows us to decrease the required number of samples from 69000 to 4500 – a factor of 15. As a side benefit, the slack of our protocol decreases by a factor of $\log \alpha$ as well.

We also show that in the case that f is a function over the polynomial ring $\mathbb{Z}[X]/(X^d + 1)$ and we would like to give a proof of knowledge of an $\mathbf{x}'$ with small coefficients such that $f(\mathbf{x}') = 2y$, then the number of samples needed for amortization is even lower. Without any trade-offs

J. Katz and H. Shacham (Eds.): CRYPTO 2017, Part III, LNCS 10403, pp. 365–394, 2017.
DOI: 10.1007/978-3-319-63697-9_13

in the running time, our algorithm requires around 2000 samples, and for the same factor 8 increase in the running time, the requirement goes down to 850.

1 Introduction

Every lattice-based cryptographic construction relies on the fact that when given a matrix $\mathbf{A}$ and a vector y over some ring R (such as $\mathbb{Z}_q$ or $\mathbb{Z}_q[X]/(X^d+1)$ with the usual addition and multiplication operations), it is hard to recover a vector $\mathbf{x}$ with small coefficients such that

$$\mathbf{A}\mathbf{x} = y. \tag{1}$$

In many instances, one would also like to construct a zero-knowledge protocol where the prover, who knows $\mathbf{x}$, is able to convince a verifier (who only has $\mathbf{A}$ and y) that he possesses this knowledge.

There are several known approaches for constructing such protocols. The first method is to adapt the classic Stern protocol [Ste93], which was used for a similar code-based problem, to working over larger rings [KTX08,LNSW13]. The main issue with this protocol is that each round has soundness error 2/3 and therefore needs to be repeated 192 times (to achieve 128 bits of security). For most practical applications, this technique is therefore unsuitable.

A second approach is to use the "Fiat-Shamir with Aborts" idea of Lyubashevsky [Lyu08,Lyu09,Lyu12] whose original application was to digital signatures. If one uses a ring R that contains a lot of elements with small coefficients (e.g. $R = \mathbb{Z}_q[X]/(X^d + 1)$), then one can prove the knowledge of a short $\mathbf{x}'$ and $c \in R$ such that $\mathbf{A}\mathbf{x}' = cy$. This is not exactly equivalent to proving (1), but it suffices for the purposes of digital signatures, commitments [BKLP15], and to some applications of verifiable encryption [LN17].

The most natural and useful scenario, however, is proving the knowledge of some $\mathbf{s}'$ that exactly satisfies (1). One could directly apply the "Fiat-Shamir with Aborts" technique with 0/1 challenges, but this leads to protocols with soundness error 1/2, which is essentially as inefficient as those using the Stern technique. When working over the ring $R = \mathbb{Z}_q[X]/(X^d + 1)$, it was shown that one can decrease the soundness error to $1/(2d + 1)$ [BCK+14] and prove the knowledge of an $\mathbf{x}'$ such that $\mathbf{A}\mathbf{x}' = 2y$. The main observation in that paper was that rather than using challenges from the set 0/1, one could use them from the set $\{0, X^i\}$ for $0 \le i < 2d$. Even though this latter proof does not exactly prove (1), the fact that one can prove the knowledge for a constant multiple of y (rather than some arbitrary, unknown c) makes this type of proof suitable for a variety of applications. But still, the soundness error of $1/(2d+1)$ would require the proof to be repeated around a dozen times for typical values of $d = 1024$.

Amortized Proofs. A very interesting line of work, which built upon ideas from [CD09], considered the *amortized* complexity of the [Lyu08,Lyu09] protocol. In [DPSZ12], it was shown that one could prove the knowledge of a linear (in the security parameter) number of equations with essentially optimal communication per equation. The main downside was that, for a security parameter k, while the prover may have known $\mathbf{x}_i$ with small coefficients that satisfied $\mathbf{A}\mathbf{x}_i = y_i$, he would only be able to prove knowledge of $\mathbf{x}'_i$ whose coefficients were on the order of $2^{\Omega(k)}$ larger. In practice, this *slack* is quite bad as it would require setting all the parameters to be very large so as to make the proofs non-vacuous (i.e. so that there isn't an efficient algorithm that can simply compute such $\mathbf{x}'$ from $\mathbf{A}$ and y).

More recently, using different and novel ideas, Baum et al. [BDLN16] showed how to reduce the slack to super-polynomial in the security parameter, and the most recent work of Cramer et al. [CDXY17] reduced this slack to being only a factor k larger than what one would get by running the basic protocol from [Lyu08,Lyu09] with 0/1 challenges. The main downside of this latter algorithm is that it requires doing at least $4k^2$ proofs at the same time. So for $k = 128$, this implies that one needs to have at least 2^{16} equations that one wishes to prove simultaneously. When wanting to prove fewer than that, one could include some "dummy" values, but this will have the effect of increasing the per-proof communication complexity and running time. The main open direction in this line of work is therefore to reduce the necessary number of equations while keeping the slack and communication to be as low as in [CDXY17]. This is the main result of the current paper.

1.1 Prior Work

High-level overview of [BDLN16, CDXY17]. We will use the notation from [CDXY17]. The setup is that the prover has a linear function f and ordered pairs $(y_1, \mathbf{x}_1), \ldots, (y_n, \mathbf{x}_n)$ such that $f(\mathbf{x}_i) = y_i$ (in (1), the function f is defined by the matrix $\mathbf{A}$). He wishes to prove the knowledge of $\mathbf{x}'_i$ with small coefficients such that $f(\mathbf{x}'_i) = y_i$. The algorithm from [CDXY17] works in two stages. In the first stage, it runs the "imperfect prover" from [BDLN16] which proves the knowledge of all-but-k $\mathbf{x}'_i$. The main issue is that after the first stage, we do not know which k secrets the extractor cannot extract.

In the second stage, the prover creates $4k^2$ additive combinations of y_i, for which the pre-image is the corresponding additive combination of the $\mathbf{x}_i$ due to the linearity of the function f.[1] The main result of the paper is showing a strategy for producing these combinations such that for any set S of $\mathbf{x}_i$ of size k, each $\mathbf{x}_i$ from S appears in at least $k+1$ combinations without any other $\mathbf{x}_i$ from S. One can then run the imperfect proof on the $4k^2$ linear combinations and again get the guarantee that all but k secrets can be extracted. Each element in S therefore appears in some extracted combination in which all other elements were already extracted in the first stage. And due to the linearity of f, we can now extract the sole element from the set S appearing in the combination.

[1] To be more precise, the number of combinations is p^2, with p the first prime greater than $2k + 1$.

An asymptotically more efficient construction is also given in [CDXY17]. This construction uses two different additive combinations of the y_i, the first one is a relaxed version in which for any set S of $\mathbf{x}_i$ of size k, all but $k - 5k^{0.75}$ of the $\mathbf{x}_i$ from S appears in at least $k + 1$ combinations without any other $\mathbf{x}_i$ from S. By running the imperfect proof on these sums all but $5k^{0.75}$ secrets can now be extracted. The second additive combination is identical to the one of the previous proof but is now used on sets of size $5k^{0.75}$, ensuring that after another execution of the imperfect proof all secrets can be extracted. This improved version requires at least $4(5k^{0.75})^2 = 100k^{1.5} = O(k^{1.5})$ secrets. However it is clear that this construction only makes sense if $k > 5k^{0.75}$, i.e. $k > 625$. So while this construction is more efficient asymptotically we only consider the previous one which is better for all reasonable security parameters.

More concrete description of the "imperfect proof" from [BDLN16]. The original protocol from [BDLN16] is a Σ-protocol that can be seen as a very particular type of parallel composition of the protocol from [Lyu08]. The basic protocol from [Lyu08] for proving the knowledge of $\mathbf{x}'$ such that $f(\mathbf{x}') = y$ is as follows: The prover starts by choosing a mask $\mathbf{g}$ from some distribution and sends $h = f(\mathbf{g})$. The verifier then chooses a random bit $c \in \{0,1\}$ as a challenge and sends it to the prover. The prover computes $c\mathbf{x}+\mathbf{g}$ and performs a rejection sampling step, i.e. he aborts with a probability that depends on the value of $c\mathbf{x}+\mathbf{g}$ (this is necessary for zero-knowledge). If it passes, then the prover sends $c\mathbf{x}+\mathbf{g}$ to the verifier. The verifier checks that $f(c\mathbf{x}+\mathbf{g}) = cy + h$.

The idea in [BDLN16] for giving "imperfect proofs" for n equations was to choose $T = 2\kappa n$ masking parameters $\mathbf{g}_j$ (for some small constant κ) and send $h_j = f(\mathbf{g}_j)$ to the verifier. The verifier then sends a T-bit challenge string $c_1, \ldots, c_T$, and the prover sends the $\mathbf{g}_j$ for which $c_j = 0$. For every $1 \le i \le n$, the prover also tries to send $\mathbf{x}_i + \mathbf{g}_j$ for the first non-used $\mathbf{g}_j$ (a $\mathbf{g}_j$ is considered used if it was revealed in the clear or was previously tried to be used for masking another $\mathbf{x}_{i'}$ with $i' < i$ – there should initially be approximately κn unused $\mathbf{g}_j$). If the rejection sampling step passes, then the prover indeed sends the $\mathbf{x}_i + \mathbf{g}_j$. Otherwise, he tries to send $\mathbf{x}_i + \mathbf{g}_{j'}$ where $\mathbf{g}_{j'}$ is the next unused $\mathbf{g}$. The verifier checks that all the revealed $\mathbf{g}_j$ satisfy $f(\mathbf{g}_j) = h_j$, and then checks that $y_i + h_j = f(\mathbf{x}_i + \mathbf{g}_j)$ for all i. It is then shown that if a prover succeeds with probability 2^{-k+1}, then an extractor can extract $n - k$ vectors $\mathbf{x}'_i$ that satisfy $f(\mathbf{x}'_i) = y_i$. Thus the protocol is a proof of knowledge of all-but-k pre-images.

1.2 Our Results

Our main result builds upon the works of [BDLN16,CDXY17] and allows us to reduce the required minimum number of proofs at the expense of a higher running time. Most importantly, the communication complexity per equation does not increase too much. As an example, if we increase the running-time by a factor of 8, we can decrease the required number of equations from 69000 to around 4500 (see Table 1). We also construct a protocol for proving knowledge of $\mathbf{s}_i$ with small coefficients over the ring $R = \mathbb{Z}_q[X]/(X^d + 1)$ such that

$\mathbf{A}\mathbf{s}_i = 2\mathbf{t}_i$. This protocol gets an even better trade-off between running time and the minimum number of samples. For the same factor of 8 increase in running time, we only now need to have 841 equations.

The importance of these trade-offs becomes even more substantial in the quantum setting. If we model a hash function with k bits of output as a random oracle, it is commonly assumed that while finding a preimage takes classical time 2^k, by using Grover's algorithm one only needs time $2^{k/2}$ on a quantum computer. In most practical uses the Fiat-Shamir transform [FS86] is used to make the zero-knowledge protocol non interactive by replacing the verifier by a random oracle. This entails that to achieve 128 bits of security one would use a security parameter $\mathrm{k} = 256$, in turn forcing amortization to be done on at least $4k^2 = 2^{18}$ equations. When using our construction we obtain the same factor 4 between the number of equations needed to achieve 128 bits of classical and quantum security (see Table 1).

Table 1. Trade-offs between the running time and the minimum number of samples for either 128 bits of classical or quantum security. We are considering proofs for (Ring)-LWE instances of dimension 1024 where the secrets and errors have coefficients drawn from $\{-1, 0, 1\}$.

	[CDXY17]	0/1 challenges			$\mathbf{x}^i$ challenges			
variable parameter α	2	16	64	256	2	16	64	256
Minimum equations n (128 bit classical security)	69169	4489	2209	1369	2209	841	529	361
Communication/equation (kB) (128 bit classical security)	8.8	9.2	9.7	10.3	8.2	8.9	9.5	10.1
Minimum equations n (128 bit quantum security)	249001	16129	7921	4489	7921	2209	1681	1369
Communication/equation (kB) (128 bit quantum security)	9.1	9.5	10.0	10.6	8.4	9.1	9.7	10.3
Time/equation (OWF evaluation)	16	128	512	2048	16	128	512	2048

Figure 1 shows a graph that illustrates how increasing the running time by a factor α reduces the minimum number of required equations. The implication is that for larger values of α, the added reduction in the minimum number of equations is not worth the increase in the running time. For practical purposes, the best trade-offs are achieved for small α's. Figure 2 illustrates the small effect that increasing α has on the communication complexity of the protocol. Even increasing α by 2^{20}, which is not advisable as we just mentioned, would result in the communication complexity growing by less than a factor of 2.

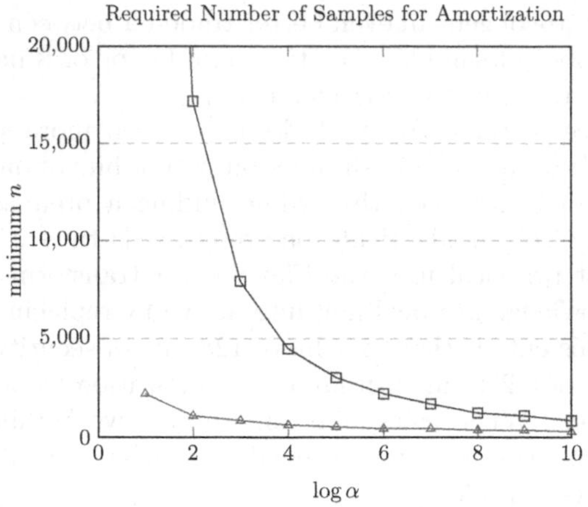

Fig. 1. The minimum number of samples required for amortization as a function of $\log \alpha$. The squares represent our first protocol (with 0/1 challenges) and the triangles represent the second (with challenges of the form X^i) when working over the ring $\mathbb{Z}[X]/(X^d + 1)$ for $d = 1024$.

Techniques. We achieve this improvement by modifying the first stage of the protocol – that is, the "imperfect proof" from [BDLN16]. Improving this protocol to make it a proof of knowledge of all-but-τ pre-images for some $\tau < k$, allows us to only do the amortized second stage of [CDXY17] with only $4\tau^2 < 4k^2$ equations. A way to reduce τ is for the prover to produce a larger number of h_j in the first step of the Σ-protocol and then for the verifier to demand that the prover reveal the pre-images of a larger fraction of the h_j. The protocol of [BDLN16] can be thought of as a cut-and-choose protocol, thus more reveals intuitively implies a higher probability of the correctness of the non-revealed parts. If we introduce a parameter α, then the prover produces $T = \alpha\kappa n$ elements h_j in the first part, sends them to the verifier, and receives a challenge $c_1, \ldots, c_T$ where a $1 - 1/\alpha$ fraction of the c_j are 0. The prover reveals the pre-images of the corresponding h_j and then uses the non-revealed $\mathbf{g}_j$ (of which there are κn) to send $\mathbf{x}_i + \mathbf{g}_j$ in the same manner as in [BDLN16] described in Sect. 1.1. We prove that this results in a protocol that proves the knowledge of all-but-τ pre-images for $\tau = k/\log \alpha$. Therefore, now only $4(k/\log \alpha)^2$ equations are needed for amortization to kick in.

One issue that still needs to be resolved is the communication complexity. Naively, it seems that one would need to send $T = \alpha\kappa n$ elements h_j which would increase the communication complexity by a factor α. We instead give an approach in which the communication is only logarithmically dependent on α – furthermore it will only be small additive factors that have a dependence on $\log \alpha$. Rather than sending $h_1, \ldots, h_T$, the prover can instead send a hash $h = H(h_1, \ldots, h_T)$ where H is a collision-resistant hash function. This does not completely solve the problem because at some point the prover will need to send

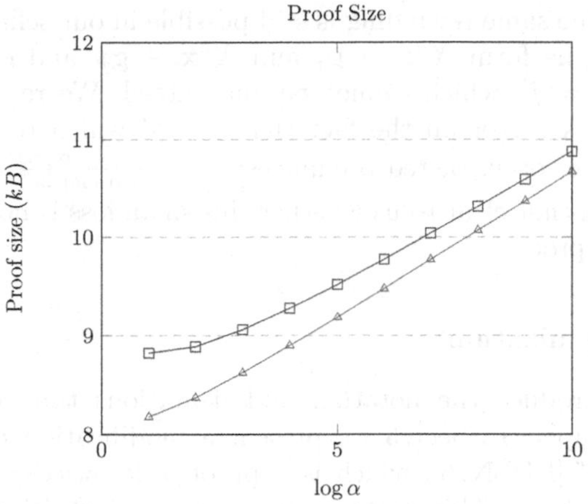

Fig. 2. Proof sizes as a function of $\log \alpha$. We are considering proofs for the same types of instances as in Table 1. The squares represent our first protocol (with 0/1 challenges) and the triangles represent the second (with X^i challenges) when working over the ring $\mathbb{Z}[X]/(X^d+1)$ for $d = 1024$.

the h_j so that the verifier can check the validity of h. But here we use the fact that all except κn of the h_j will have their pre-images simply revealed. Our strategy is therefore as follows: we create the $\mathbf{g}_j$ from 256-bit seeds s_j which are leaves on a tree generated by a pseudorandom function. That is, from the root of the tree, one can generate the entire tree. When required to reveal pre-images of a set of h_j, the prover does not need to send the $\mathbf{g}_j$ (or their seeds) individually. He can instead send roots of sub-trees which only include the seeds that will be revealed. We prove that with this strategy, rather than sending $\alpha\kappa n$ seeds, one only needs to send a maximum of $\kappa n \log \alpha$ many elements from the tree (which are themselves 256 bits each).

Putting everything together, we show that at the expense of increasing the running time by a factor of α, one can reduce the minimum number of samples required for amortization by a factor of $\log^2 \alpha$. Our second contribution is showing that when working over the ring $\mathbb{Z}[X]/(X^d+1)$, proving the knowledge of $\mathbf{x}_i$ such that $f(\mathbf{x}_i) = 2y_i$ has an even better trade-off between running-time and the minimum number of samples. In particular, we show that at the expense of an α-fold increase in running time, one can reduce the minimum number of vectors by a factor of $\left(\frac{\log \alpha + \log 2d}{1 + 1/\log \alpha}\right)^2$.

To obtain such an improvement we adapt the proof of [BCK+14] to the framework of [BDLN16]. Though merging the two protocols is rather straightforward, the knowledge extractors of both of these schemes don't combine as nicely. The knowledge extractor of [BDLN16] first recovers a set of all but k of the masking parameters $\mathbf{g}_j$ and then simply extracts $\mathbf{x}_i$ from $\mathbf{x}_i + \mathbf{g}_j$. This method falls apart when used with the protocol of [BCK+14] as the latter scheme uses rewinding to obtain two equations $X^a\mathbf{x} + \mathbf{g}$ and $X^b\mathbf{x} + \mathbf{g}$ and recovers a pre-image from their difference. The same rewinding is still possible in our scheme but will yield two equations of the form $X^a\mathbf{x}_i + \mathbf{g}_j$ and $X^b\mathbf{x}_i + \mathbf{g}_{j'}$ and extraction will be only possible if $j = j'$, which cannot be guaranteed. We resolve this issue by conditioning our extractor on the fact that $j = j'$ which results in a slightly sub-optimal number of extracted preimages: $n - \frac{k\cdot(1+1/\log\alpha)}{\log\alpha+\log 2d}$ instead of simply $n - \frac{k}{\log\alpha+\log 2d}$. It is not clear to us whether this small loss is necessary or simply an artifact of our proof.

1.3 Paper Organization

In Sect. 2, we introduce the notation and definitions that we will be using throughout the paper. In Sect. 3 we present a modification of the "imperfect proof" protocol of [BDLN16], which is a proof of knowledge of all-but-τ preimages for $\tau = k/\log\alpha$. This protocol only serves as intuition, and we do not formally prove its correctness or security because the communication complexity (i.e. the proof size) grows linearly in α. In Sect. 4, we show how to reduce the communication complexity of the interactive protocol from Sect. 3 and prove its correctness, zero-knowledge, and soundness. We only show honest-verifier zero-knowledge because this is enough to convert the protocol to a non-interactive one using the Fiat-Shamir transform, which is the manner in which one would use these schemes in practice. Analyzing the size of the communication is delayed until in Sect. 6 because this analysis also applies to the protocol in Sect. 5. In Sect. 5, we show that if the proof is done over the ring $\mathbb{Z}[X]/(X^d+1)$, then the number of required equations can be made even smaller if one wants to prove $f(\mathbf{x}') = 2y$.

2 Preliminaries

2.1 Notation

We will write vectors such as $\mathbf{b}$ or $\mathbf{B}$ in bold face. We refer to the ith position of a vector $\mathbf{b}$ as $\mathbf{b}[i]$. Define $[r] = \{1,\ldots,r\}$. The Euclidean norm of a vector, $\mathbf{b} \in \mathbb{Z}^r$ is $\|\mathbf{b}\| = \sqrt{\sum_{i\in[r]} \mathbf{b}[i]^2}$. For a set $\mathcal{S}$, we write $s \xleftarrow{\$} \mathcal{S}$ to denote that s was drawn uniformly at random from $\mathcal{S}$. For a distribution D, we write $s \leftarrow D$ to denote that s is drawn from D.

2.2 Homomorphic OWF

In this section we follow the framework of [BDLN16] in defining homomorphic one-way functions over integer vectors (which includes polynomial rings) as well as amortized zero-knowledge proofs of preimage for these functions. Let $\lambda \in \mathbb{N}$ be a security parameter, G be an Abelian group, $\beta, r \in \mathbb{N}$, $f : \mathbb{Z}^r \to G$ be a function and $\mathcal{A}$ be any algorithm. Consider the following game:

Invert$_{\mathcal{A},f,\beta}(\lambda)$:

1. Choose $\mathbf{x} \in \mathbb{Z}^r$, $\|\mathbf{x}\| \leq \beta$ and compute $y = f(\mathbf{x})$.
2. On input $(1^\lambda, y)$ the algorithm $\mathcal{A}$ computes an $\mathbf{x}'$.
3. Output 1 iff $f(\mathbf{x}') = y$, $\|\mathbf{x}'\| \leq \beta$, and 0 otherwise.

Definition 2.1 (Homomorphic OWF over Integer Vectors (ivOWF)). *A function $f : \mathbb{Z}^r \to G$ is called a homomorphic one-way function over the integers if the following conditions hold:*

- *There exist a polynomial time algorithm $eval_f$ such that $eval_f(\mathbf{x}) = f(\mathbf{x})$ for all $\mathbf{x} \in \mathbb{Z}^r$.*
- *for all $\mathbf{x}, \mathbf{x}' \in \mathbb{Z}^r$ it holds that $f(\mathbf{x}) + f(\mathbf{x}') = f(\mathbf{x} + \mathbf{x}')$.*
- *for every PPT algorithm $\mathcal{A}$ there exists a negligible function* $\text{negl}(\lambda)$ *such that:*

$$\Pr\left[\mathbf{Invert}_{\mathcal{A},f,\beta}(\lambda) = 1\right] \leq \text{negl}(\lambda).$$

2.3 Rejection Sampling and the Normal Distribution

For a protocol to be zero-knowledge, the output of the prover needs to be independent of his secret. In certain situations achieving this independence requires rejection sampling. While [BDLN16] used rejection sampling in the infinity norm (as in [Lyu08,Lyu09]) we use the euclidean norm and thus rejection sampling over the ℓ_2 norm using normal distributions (as in [Lyu12]), which allows for tighter parameters. But all our techniques easily work for the ℓ_∞ norm as well.

Definition 2.2 (Continuous Normal Distribution). *The continuous Normal distribution over $\mathbb{R}^r$ centered at $\mathbf{v}$ with standard deviation σ is defined by the probability density function $\rho^r_{\mathbf{v},\sigma}(\mathbf{x}) = \left(\frac{1}{\sqrt{2\pi\sigma^2}}\right)^r e^{-\frac{\|\mathbf{x}-\mathbf{v}\|^2}{2\sigma^2}}$.*

Definition 2.3 (Discrete Normal Distribution). *The discrete Normal distribution over $\mathbb{Z}^r$ centered at $\mathbf{v}$ with standard deviation σ is defined by the probability mass function $\mathcal{D}^r_{\mathbf{v},\sigma}(\mathbf{x}) = \rho^r_{\mathbf{v},\sigma}(\mathbf{x}) / \rho^r_{\mathbf{v},\sigma}(\mathbb{Z}^r)$.*

Lemma 2.4 (Tail-Cut Bound [Ban93]). $\Pr\left[\|\mathbf{z}\| \geq 2\sigma\sqrt{r}; \mathbf{z} \leftarrow \mathcal{D}^r_\sigma\right] < 2^{-r}$.

Theorem 2.5 (Rejection sampling [Lyu12] Theorem 4.6). *Let V be a subset of $\mathbb{Z}^r$ with elements of norm less than T, let h be a distribution over V. Let $\sigma = 11T$, for $\mathbf{v}, \mathbf{z} \in \mathbb{Z}^r$ let* $\mathbf{Rej}(\mathbf{v}, \mathbf{z})$ *be the algorithm that outputs 1 with probability* $\min\left(\mathcal{D}^r_\sigma(\mathbf{z})/(3\mathcal{D}^r_{\mathbf{v},\sigma}(\mathbf{z})), 1\right)$ *and 0 otherwise. Then we have:*

$$(\mathbf{v}, \mathbf{z} \mid \mathbf{Rej}(\mathbf{v}, \mathbf{z}) = 1) \sim_s (\mathbf{v}, \mathbf{z}')$$

where $\mathbf{v} \leftarrow h$, $\mathbf{z} \leftarrow \mathcal{D}^r_{\mathbf{v},\sigma}$, and $\mathbf{z}' \leftarrow \mathcal{D}^r_\sigma$, i.e. the distribution of $\mathbf{z}$ conditioned on $\mathbf{Rej}(\mathbf{v}, \mathbf{z}) = 1$ *is exactly a discrete Normal distribution centered on 0. Moreover the probability, taken over the choice of $\mathbf{v} \leftarrow h$ and $\mathbf{z} \leftarrow \mathcal{D}^r_{\mathbf{v},\sigma}$ that* $\mathbf{Rej}$ *outputs 1 is exponentially close to 1/3:*

$$\left| \Pr_{\mathbf{v} \leftarrow h, \mathbf{z} \leftarrow \mathcal{D}^r_{\mathbf{v},\sigma}} \left[\mathbf{Rej}(\mathbf{v}, \mathbf{z}) = 1\right] - \frac{1}{3} \right| \leq 2^{-100}$$

2.4 Zero-Knowledge Proofs of Knowledge

We will consider amortized proofs of knowledge for preimages of an ivOWF. Formally, given an ivOWF f the relation we want to give a zero-knowledge proof of knowledge for is:

$$\mathcal{R}_{\mathrm{KSP}}(n, f, \beta) = \left\{ (Y, \mathbf{X}) \in (G \times \mathbb{Z}^r)^n \,\middle|\, Y = (y_1, \ldots, y_n) \wedge \mathbf{X} = (\mathbf{x}_1, \ldots, \mathbf{x}_n) \right.$$
$$\left. \wedge \left[y_i = f(\mathbf{x}_i) \wedge \|\mathbf{x}_i\| \leq \beta \right]_{i \in [n]} \right\}$$

We define a second binary relation $\mathcal{R}'$, such that $\mathcal{R} \subset \mathcal{R}'$, which characterizes the soundness slack of the protocol, i.e. while the input to the protocol is a pair $(Y, \mathbf{X}) \in \mathcal{R}$ the knowledge extractor can only extract values in $\mathcal{R}'$. Typically the relation $\mathcal{R}'$ is identical to $\mathcal{R}$ except for the fact that the components of $\mathbf{X}$ are bounded in norm by a constant $\beta' > \beta$. We will however see in Sect. 5 a ZKPOK for a different relation $\mathcal{R}'$.

Definition 2.6 (Zero-Knowledge Proof of Knowledge). *Let $\mathcal{P}_{ZK}$ be a two-party protocol, let $\mathcal{R}, \mathcal{R}'$ be binary relations such that $\mathcal{R} \subseteq \mathcal{R}'$, let k be a statistical security parameter. $\mathcal{P}_{ZK}$ is a zero-knowledge proof of knowledge if the following properties hold:*

Correctness: *If $\mathcal{P}, \mathcal{V}$ are honest and run $\mathcal{P}_{ZK}$ on an instance of $\mathcal{R}$, then the protocol terminates with probability greater than $1 - 2^{O(k)}$.*

Computational Honest-Verifier Zero-Knowledge: *There exists an expected PPT simulator $\mathcal{S}$ such that for any $(a, b) \in \mathcal{R}$, and for any PPT algorithm $\mathcal{A}$. $\mathcal{A}$ has advantage* negl(k) *in distinguishing between the two following distributions:*

- *$View_{\mathcal{V}}[\mathcal{P}(a, b) \leftrightarrow \mathcal{V}(a)]$ the view of $\mathcal{V}$ consisting in the transcript of the protocol as well as the random coins of $\mathcal{V}$.*
- *$\mathcal{S}(a)$.*

Soundness: *For any pair $(a, b) \in \mathcal{R}$, for any deterministic prover $\hat{\mathcal{P}}$ that succeeds with probability $p > 2^{-k}$ one can extract b' such that $(a, b') \in \mathcal{R}'$ in expected time $poly(s, k) \cdot 1/p$, where s is the size of the input to the protocol.*

2.5 Imperfect Proof of Knowledge and a Compiler

In [BDLN16], the authors introduce the concept of an imperfect proof of knowledge. An imperfect proof of knowledge is a protocol that proves knowledge of pre-images in the relation $\mathcal{R}_{\mathrm{KSP}}$, however the knowledge extractor is not required to be able to extract all the pre-images.

Definition 2.7 (Imperfect Proof of knowledge). *Let $\mathcal{P}_{IProof}$ be a two-party protocol, let f be an ivOWF, let $\mathcal{R}_{KSP}(n, f, \beta)$ and $\mathcal{R}_{KSP}(n, f, \beta')$ be two binary relations on f, k be the security parameter. The protocol $\mathcal{P}_{IProof}$ is an imperfect proof of knowledge with imperfection $\tau(k)$ if the following properties hold:*

Correctness: *$\mathcal{P}_{IProof}$ is correct as in Definition 2.6.*

Computational Honest-Verifier Zero-Knowledge: *$\mathcal{P}_{IProof}$ is honest verifier zero-knowledge as in Definition 2.6.*

Impefect Soundness: *For any pair $(Y = (y_1, \ldots, y_n), \mathbf{X} = (\mathbf{x}_1, \ldots, \mathbf{x}_n)) \in \mathcal{R}_{KSP}(n, f, \beta)$, for any deterministic prover $\hat{\mathcal{P}}$ that succeeds with probability $p > 2^{-k}$ one can extract at least $n - \tau(k)$ values $\mathbf{x}'_i$ such that $f(\mathbf{x}'_i) = y_i$ and $\|\mathbf{x}'_i\| \leq \beta'$ in expected time $poly(s, k) \cdot 1/p$, where s is the size of the input to the protocol.*

[BDLN16] introduced a ZKPOK that uses an imperfect proof as a building block. The construction was later improved in [CDXY17] allowing for very efficient proofs that only require two executions of the imperfect proof system, while only introducing an additional soundness slack of k. The protocol, however, requires the amortization to be done on at least $4k^2$ secrets, which can be impractical. We give a somewhat refined statement of this construction as the proof of [CDXY17] can be straightforwardly adapted to using the imperfection $\tau(k)$ instead of k.

Theorem 2.8 (Compiler [CDXY17] Theorem 2). *Let f be an ivOWF, let k be a statistical security parameter, let $\mathcal{R}_{KSP}(n, f, \beta)$ and $\mathcal{R}_{KSP}(n, f, \beta')$ be two binary relations on f. Let $\mathcal{P}_{IProof}$ be an imperfect proof with imperfection $\tau(k)$. If $n \geq 4\tau(k)^2 + O(\log k)$ then there exists an efficient construction for a zero-knowledge proof of knowledge $\mathcal{P}_{CProof}$ with soundness slack $\tau(k)\beta'$.*

In this paper, we give constructions that can reduce the imperfection $\tau(k)$ of the imperfect proof to values less than k, thus allowing for more efficient zero-knowledge protocols in cases where the number of available equations is less than $\tau(k)$.

3 Warmup Construction

We present a first construction that achieves imperfection $\tau(k) = k/log(\alpha) + 1$ for any parameter α, but has proof size that grows linearly in α. This first construction is similar to the one of [BDLN16]. Their protocol works in two phases: first the prover samples masking parameters $\mathbf{g}_j, j \in [T]$ and a cut-and-choose protocol reveals each one with probability one half. After this step, the verifier is convinced that with probability $1 - 2^{-k}$ all but k of them are well formed. In the second phase the masking parameters that were not revealed are used to hide the secrets of the prover. We modify the first phase of this protocol so that the prover reveals each masking parameter with probability $1 - 1/\alpha$. For $\alpha \geq 2$, this reduces the percentage of $\mathbf{g}_j$ on which the prover can cheat and, in turn, reduces the imperfection of the proof. However, the number of masking parameters necessary for the second phase is on the order of n, meaning that, since the prover will reveal a fraction $1 - 1/\alpha$ of them, the protocol then requires $T = \Theta(\alpha n)$ masking parameters.

We describe this protocol in Fig. 3. We do not give a formal proof that it is an imperfect proof of knowledge with imperfection $k/\log \alpha + 1$ as the protocol

$\mathcal{P}$		$\mathcal{V}$
$\mathbf{X} := (\mathbf{x}_1, \ldots, \mathbf{x}_n)$		$\mathbf{Y}$
$\mathbf{Y} := (y_1 := f(\mathbf{x}_1), \ldots, y_n := f(\mathbf{x}_n))$		
$\mathbf{g}_1, \ldots, \mathbf{g}_T \leftarrow \mathcal{D}_\sigma^r$		
$a_1, \ldots, a_T := f(\mathbf{g}_1), \ldots, f(\mathbf{g}_t)$		
$h_1, \ldots, h_T := H(a_1), \ldots, H(a_T)$	$\xrightarrow{h_1, \ldots, h_T}$	
	$\xleftarrow{\mathbf{c}}$	$\mathbf{c} \leftarrow \chi^T \in \{0,1\}^T$
$\mathcal{O} := \{j, \mathbf{c}[j] = 0\}, \mathcal{C} := [T] \setminus \mathcal{O}$	$\xrightarrow{(\mathbf{g}_j)_{j \in \mathcal{O}}}$	
		$\forall j \in \mathcal{O}$, Check : $\begin{cases} H(f(\mathbf{g}_j)) = h_j \\ \Vert\mathbf{g}_j\Vert \leq B \end{cases}$
$\Phi := \emptyset$ $\forall i \in [n]$: find the first $j \in \mathcal{C}, j > max(\Phi)$ s.t. $\mathbf{Rej}(\mathbf{x}_i, \mathbf{x}_i + \mathbf{g}_j) = 1$ $\mathbf{z}_i := \mathbf{x}_i + \mathbf{g}_j$ $\Phi := \Phi \cup \{j\}$		
If $\vert\Phi\vert < n$ abort	$\xrightarrow{\Phi, (\mathbf{z}_i)_{i \in [n]}}$	
		$\forall i \in [n]$: Check $\begin{cases} H(f(\mathbf{z}_i) - y_i) = h_{\Phi_i} \\ \Vert\mathbf{z}_i\Vert \leq B \end{cases}$

Fig. 3. Warm-up construction. For $\alpha \geq 2$, we fix $T = 5\alpha n$ and χ the bernouilli distribution of parameter $1/\alpha$. Resulting in an imperfect proof of knowledge with imperfection $k/\log \alpha + 1$ and communication that grows linearly with α

presented in the next section is a strict improvement upon this one. While this first protocol achieves better imperfection than the one of [BDLN16], it has a major downside in that the communication cost grows linearly with α, since we need $T \geq \alpha n$. This voids any improvement over the previous protocol. To remedy this problem we will modify this protocol as follows:

- Rather than sending the hash of every a_i in the first round the prover will only send $h = H(h_1, \ldots, h_T)$, thus making the first flow of the protocol constant size.
- In his second move, the prover sends $\mathbf{g}_j, j \in \mathcal{O}$. This is an issue because $|\mathcal{O}| \simeq (\alpha - 1)4n$, but also because the $\mathbf{g}_i$ can be rather large. We solve these problems by sending a set of seeds from which a PRG will be used to derive the $\mathbf{g}_i$. This way only 256 bits need to be sent for each seed. Most crucially, by using a tree data-structure, we show that the prover only needs to send $4n \log \alpha$ seeds in his second move.

4 Amortized Proof for $f(\mathbf{x}_i) = y_i$ with Fewer Equations

In this section we describe our first concrete imperfect proof of knowledge and prove that it has imperfection $\tau(k) = k/\log\alpha + 1$. We show that the proof is only slightly dependent on α in Sect. 6.

We will need the following two functions, which can both be efficiently implemented using an extendable output function (e.g. SHAKE128 [BDPA16]):

- **PRF:** $\{0,1\}^{256} \to \{0,1\}^{512}$ a size doubling pseudo-random function
- **PRG:** $\{0,1\}^{256} \to \{0,1\}^{*}$ a pseudo-random generator

For a randomized algorithm h and a seed $s \in \{0,1\}^{256}$ we will write $h\,[\mathbf{PRG}(s)]$ to denote an execution of h using as randomness the bits output by $\mathbf{PRG}(s)$.

We first describe the tree structure that we will use. From now on we will only consider $T = 2^t$ a power of two, which simplifies the description of the protocols and does not affect efficiency – all the results we obtain can be adapted to general T. A tree Γ is a binary tree with nodes labeled in $\{0,1\}^*$ (the root will have the label $\emptyset$, its left child will have label 0, its right child will have label 1, etc.). We consider complete binary trees of depth t, which implies that the leaves will be labeled in $\{0,1\}^t$. We map the range $[T]$ to the labels of the leaves through the mapping where the image of $t \in [T]$ is the leaf labeled by the binary decomposition of $t-1$. Each node will have two extra attributes, one will be the seed associated to the node (which can be bottom for the verifier since he will not know all the seeds), the other will be a bit indicating whether the associated seed must be sent to the verifier in the first flow.

The purpose of this seed tree is twofold. We will use the leaves as seeds for the **PRG** when generating the $\mathbf{g}_j, j \in [T]$. This way sending the seeds to the verifier in the first flow will be sufficient as he can then reconstruct the $\mathbf{g}_j, j \in \mathcal{O}$ using the **PRG**. More importantly, rather than directly sending the leaves of the seed tree, it will be more efficient to send the smallest set of nodes needed to recover the leaves for indices that lie in $\mathcal{O}$. We define the tree structure as follows:

Tree T:

- Label $\subset \{0,1\}^*$
- Left $\in$ **Tree** $\cup \perp$
- Right $\in$ **Tree** $\cup \perp$
- Leaf $\in \{0,1\}$
- Sel $\in \{0,1\}$
- Seed $\in \{0,1\}^{256} \cup \perp$

For $j \in \{0,1\}^*$ we denote by $\Gamma[j]$ the node with label j. We will describe four algorithms: the first to initialize the tree will be performed by both parties, the second to initialize the seeds will only be used by the prover, the third to compute the indexes of the seeds that will be sent in the first flow of the protocol will be used by both parties, and the fourth to recover the seeds needed to compute the $\mathbf{g}_j, j \in \mathcal{O}$ will only be used by the verifier.

$\underline{\mathcal{P}}$		$\underline{\mathcal{V}}$
$\mathbf{X} := (\mathbf{x}_1, \ldots, \mathbf{x}_n)$		$\mathbf{Y}$
$\mathbf{Y} := (y_1 := f(\mathbf{x}_1), \ldots, y_n := f(\mathbf{x}_n))$		
Tree $\Gamma_{\mathcal{P}}$:= **new Tree**		**Tree** $\Gamma_{\mathcal{V}}$:= **new Tree**
Initialize$(\Gamma_{\mathcal{P}}, \emptyset, t)$		**Initialize**$(\Gamma_{\mathcal{V}}, \emptyset, t)$
$s \xleftarrow{\$} \{0,1\}^{256}$		
SeedTree$(\Gamma_{\mathcal{P}}, s)$		
$\forall i \in [T] : \mathbf{g}_i \leftarrow \mathcal{D}_\sigma^r\left[\mathbf{PRG}(s_i)\right]$		
$a_1, \ldots, a_T := f(\mathbf{g}_1), \ldots, f(\mathbf{g}_t)$		
$h_1, \ldots, h_T := H(a_1), \ldots, H(a_T)$		
$h := H(h_1, \ldots, h_T)$	$\xrightarrow{h}$	
	$\xleftarrow{\mathbf{c}}$	$\mathbf{c} \leftarrow \chi^T \in \{0,1\}^T$
$\mathcal{O} := \{j, \mathbf{c}[j] = 0\}, \mathcal{C} := [T] \setminus \mathcal{O}$		
Prefix$(\Gamma_{\mathcal{P}}, \mathcal{O})$		
$\mathcal{S} := \left\{j \subset \{0,1\}^t,\ \Gamma_{\mathcal{P}}[j].Sel = 1\right\}$	$\xrightarrow[(h_j)_{j\in\mathcal{C}}]{(s_j)_{j\in\mathcal{S}}}$	
		$\mathcal{O} := \{j, \mathbf{c}[j] = 0\}, \mathcal{C} := [T] \setminus \mathcal{O}$
		Prefix$(\Gamma_{\mathcal{V}}, \mathcal{O})$
		Reconstruct$(\Gamma_{\mathcal{V}}, (s_j)_{j\in\mathcal{S}}, \mathcal{O})$
		$(s_j)_{j\in\mathcal{O}} := \left(\Gamma_{\mathcal{V}}[j].Seed\right)_{j\in\mathcal{O}}$
		$\forall j \in \mathcal{O} \begin{cases} \mathbf{g}_j := f(\mathcal{D}_\sigma^r\left[\mathbf{PRG}(s_j)\right]) \\ h_j := H(\mathbf{g}_j) \\ \text{Check: } \lVert\mathbf{g}_j\rVert \le B \end{cases}$
		$Check : H(h_1, \ldots, h_T) = h$
$\Phi := \emptyset$		
$\forall i \in [n]:$		
find the first $j \in \mathcal{C}, j > max(\Phi)$		
s.t. $\mathbf{Rej}(\mathbf{x}_i, \mathbf{x}_i + \mathbf{g}_j) = 1$		
$\mathbf{z}_i := \mathbf{x}_i + \mathbf{g}_j$		
$\Phi := \Phi \cup \{j\}$		
If $\lvert\Phi\rvert < n$ abort	$\xrightarrow{\Phi, (\mathbf{z}_i)_{i\in[n]}}$	
		$\forall i \in [n]:$
		$\text{Check} \begin{cases} H(f(\mathbf{z}_i) - y_i) = h_{\Phi_i} \\ \lVert\mathbf{z}_i\rVert \le B \end{cases}$

Fig. 4. Our first construction: For $\alpha \ge 2$, we fix $T = 5\alpha n$ and χ the bernouilli distribution of parameter $1/\alpha$. We obtain an imperfect proof of knowledge with imperfection $\frac{k}{\log \alpha} + 1$. The communication complexity only has a small dependence on $\log \alpha$.

Algorithm 1. Initialize(Γ, l, d)

Require: A tree Γ, a label $l \subset \{0,1\}^t$, a depth d
$\Gamma.Label := l$
$\Gamma.Sel := 0$
$\Gamma.Seed := \perp$
if $d = 0$ **then**
  $Self.Leaf := 1$
  $Self.Left := \perp$
  $Self.Right := \perp$
else
  $Self.Leaf := 0$
  Initialise$(\Gamma.Left, (l, 0), d-1)$
  Initialise$(\Gamma.Right, (l, 1), d-1)$
end if

The second algorithm **Initialize** will use a seed fixed by the prover and compute the seed associated with the children of each node as the first and second half of **PRF** applied on the seed of the parent node.

Algorithm 2. SeedTree(Γ, v)

Require: A tree Γ, $v \in \{0,1\}^{256}$
$\Gamma.Seed := v$
if $\Gamma.Leaf = 0$ **then**
  $(v_1, v_2) :=$ **PRF**(v)
  SeedTree$(\Gamma.left, v_1)$
  SeedTree$(\Gamma.right, v_2)$
end if

The **Prefix** algorithm will compute the prefix of a set of nodes and set their attribute *Sel* to 1. A node n will be in the prefix of a set $\mathcal{O}$ if all the leaves that descend from n are in $\mathcal{O}$ and none of the ancestors of n are in the prefix of $\mathcal{O}$. The algorithm ensues directly from this definition.

The **Reconstruct** algorithm will use a tree in which the prefix $\mathcal{S}$ of $\mathcal{O}$ has been computed as well as a set of seeds $s_j, j \in \mathcal{S}$ and will reconstruct the seeds $s_j, j \in \mathcal{O}$ by using **SeedTree** for each node in $\mathcal{S}$.

We give in Fig. 5 an example of a seed tree as well as a set $\mathcal{O}$ and its prefix. We describe our improved protocol in Fig. 4.

Theorem 4.1. *Let f be an ivOWF, k be a statistical security parameter, H a collision resistant hash function, $r \geq 128$ be an integer, χ the bernouilli distribution of parameter $1/\alpha$ (i.e. $P[\chi = 0] = 1 - P[\chi = 1] = 1 - 1/\alpha$). Let $T = 5\alpha n$, $\sigma = 11\beta$, $B = 2\sigma\sqrt{r}$. The protocol $\mathcal{P}_{IProof}$ given in Fig. 4 is an imperfect proof of knowledge for inputs in $\mathcal{R}_{KSP}(n, f, \beta)$, with soundness extractor in $\mathcal{R}_{KSP}(n, f, 2B)$ and imperfection $\frac{k}{\log \alpha} + 1$.*

Algorithm 3. Prefix($\Gamma, \mathcal{O}$)

Require: A tree Γ, a set of indices $\mathcal{O} \subset [T]$
if $\Gamma.Leaf = 1 \wedge \Gamma.label \in \mathcal{O}$ **then**
  $\Gamma.Sel := 1$
  return 1
else if $\Gamma.Leaf = 0 \wedge$ **Prefix**$(\Gamma.Left, \mathcal{O}) = 1 \wedge$ **Prefix**$(\Gamma.Right, \mathcal{O}) = 1$ **then**
  $\Gamma.Sel := 1$
  $\Gamma.Left.Sel := 0$
  $\Gamma.Right.Sel := 0$
  return 1
end if
return 0

Algorithm 4. Reconstruct($\Gamma, S, \mathcal{O}$)

Require: A tree Γ, a list of seeds $S = [s_j]$, a set $\mathcal{O} \subset [T]$. We assume that **Prefix**$(\Gamma, \mathcal{O})$ was applied.
if $\Gamma.Sel = 1$ **then**
  SeedTree$(\Gamma, S[0])$
  $S := S[1:]$
else
  Reconstruct$(\Gamma.Left, S)$
  Reconstruct$(\Gamma.Right, S)$
end if

Proof. We prove correctness in Lemma 4.2, honest-verifier zero-knowledge in Lemma 4.3, and soundness in Lemma 4.4.

We first prove correctness.

Lemma 4.2 (Correctness). *With parameters set as in Theorem 4.1, the protocol $\mathcal{P}_{IProof}$ described in Fig. 4 completes with probability greater than $1-2^{-100}$.*

Proof. By the homomorphic property of f and by construction of **Initialize**, **SeedTree**, **Prefix**, and **Reconstruct** all the checked equalities hold. We fist consider the probability that $\mathcal{P}$ aborts. $\mathcal{P}$ will abort if he runs out of samples during the rejection sampling. For each $\mathbf{g}_j, j \in [T]$ the probability that $\mathbf{g}_j$ will not be revealed is $1/\alpha$, and by Theorem 2.5 the probability that the rejection sampling will succeed is $1/3$, in which case the vector obtained will be of norm less than B with overwhelming probability (2.4). We can model the probability that each g_j will not be revealed and will pass both checks of the rejection step by a Bernoulli variable X_j s.t $\Pr[X_j = 1] = 1/(3\alpha) - 2^{-O(n)}$. $\mathcal{P}$ will abort if $\sum_{j \in [T]} X_j < n$. Using the Chernoff bound we obtain:

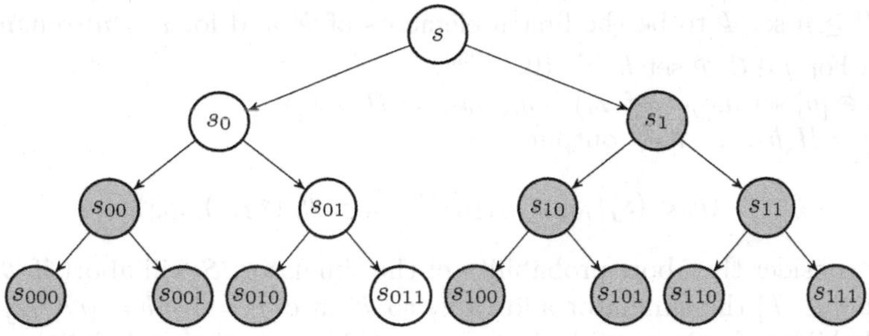

Fig. 5. Seed tree for $t = 3$, and $\mathcal{O} = \{1, 2, 3, 5, 6, 7, 8\}$, the nodes needed to reconstruct $(s_j)_{j \in \mathcal{O}}$ are those in $prefix(\mathcal{O}) = \{00, 010, 1\}$.

$$\Pr\left[\sum_{j\in[T]} X_j < n\right] \leq \exp\left(-\frac{(T - 3\alpha n)^2}{3\alpha T} + 2^{-O(n)}\right)$$
$$= \exp\left(-\frac{4n}{15} + 2^{-O(n)}\right),$$

which is negligible asymptotically (and in practice less than 2^{-100} whenever we amortize over $n \geq 260$ secrets.)

We now consider the probability that $\mathcal{V}$ aborts. $\mathcal{V}$ will abort if there exists either $j \in \mathcal{O}$ such that $\|\mathbf{g}_j\| > B$ or $i \in [n]$ such that $\|\mathbf{z}_i\| > B$. Since the $\mathbf{g}_j$ and the $\mathbf{z}_i$ are drawn independently from the distribution $\mathcal{D}_\sigma^r$ by using a union bound we have that the probability that the norm of one of them exceeds B is less than $(T + n)2^{-r}$. □

We now show that this protocol is honest-verifier zero-knowledge.

Lemma 4.3 (HVZK). *With parameters set as in Theorem 4.1, the protocol $\mathcal{P}_{IProof}$ described in Fig. 4 is computationally honest-verifier zero-knowledge.*

Proof. The honest-verifier zero-knowledge proof is very close to that of [BDLN16], but we still include it here for completeness as there are slight differences. Consider the following algorithm $\mathcal{S}_{IProof}$:

- On input $(\mathbf{Y} = (y_1, \ldots, y_n), \beta)$ sample $s \xleftarrow{\$} \{0,1\}^{256}$ and $(s_j)_{j \subset \{0,1\}^t}$ using **SeedTree**.
- Sample $\mathbf{c} \leftarrow \chi^T$, compute the sets $\mathcal{O}$ and $\mathcal{C}$.
- Set $\Phi' = \emptyset$, for $j \in \mathcal{C}$ sample $\mathbf{z}_j \leftarrow \mathcal{D}_\sigma^r$ and do the following:
  - Sample $b \xleftarrow{\$} \{0, 1, 2\}$
  - If $b = 0 \wedge \|\mathbf{z}_j\| \leq B$ then $\Phi' = \Phi' \cup j$
- For $j \in \mathcal{O}$ set $h_j = H(f(\mathcal{D}_\sigma^r[\mathbf{PRG}(s_j)]))$.
- If $|\Phi'| < n$ then for $j \in \mathcal{C}$ set $h_j \xleftarrow{\$} \{0,1\}^{256}$, $h = H(h_1, \ldots, h_T)$, output $(h, \mathbf{c}, (s_j)_{j \in prefix(\mathcal{O})}, (h_j)_{j \in \mathcal{C}})$ and abort.

- If $|\Phi'| \geq n$ set Φ to be the first n elements of Φ' and for $i \in [n]$ rename $\mathbf{z}_{\Phi[i]}$ as $\mathbf{z}_i$. For $j \in \mathcal{C}\backslash\Phi$ set $h_j \xleftarrow{\$} \{0,1\}^{256}$.
- For $i \in [n]$ set $a_{\Phi[i]} = f(\mathbf{z}_i) - y_i$, $h_{\Phi[i]} = H(a_{\Phi[i]})$.
- Set $h = H(h_1, \ldots, h_T)$, output

$$(h, \mathbf{c}, (s_j)_{j \in prefix(\mathcal{O})}, (h_j)_{j \in \mathcal{C}}, \Phi, (\mathbf{z}_{\Phi[i]})_{i \in [n]}).$$

We first consider the abort probability of the simulator: $\mathcal{S}$ will abort if $|\Phi'| < n$. For each $j \in [T]$ the simulator adds a $\mathbf{z}_j$ to Φ' iff $\mathbf{c}[j] = 1 \wedge b = 0 \wedge \|\mathbf{z}_j\| \leq B$, the probability of this event is $1/(3\alpha) - 2^{-O(n)}$, thus the probability of abort will be exponentially close to the one of $\mathcal{P}_{IProof}$. Regardless of whether the simulator aborts or not, all the checks performed by the verifier will accept: h is set to be $h = H(h_1, \ldots, h_T)$, and when $\mathcal{S}$ does not abort he sets $h_{\Phi[i]}$ so that $H(f(\mathbf{z}_i) - y_i) = h_{\Phi[i]}$. The sets $\mathcal{O}$ and $\mathcal{C}$ are defined in the same way as in $\mathcal{P}_{IProof}$ and the $s_j, j \in prefix(\mathcal{O})$ are also sampled according to the protocol. Note that in $\mathcal{P}_{IProof}$ for $j \in \mathcal{C}\backslash\Phi$ the h_j are distributed uniformly since H is modeled as a random oracle and no preimages of the h_j are given (note that for some leaves of the tree the verifier knows half of the output of **PRF** on the parent node, even conditioning on this knowledge the second half of the output is uniform as **PRF** is modeled as a random oracle). It remains to analyze the distribution of $\mathbf{z}_i$ for $i \in [n]$. We have by Theorem 2.5 that the distribution of $\mathbf{z}_i, i \in [n]$ in $\mathcal{P}_{IProof}$ is that of a discrete gaussian centered in 0 with standard deviation σ and thus identical to the distribution of $\mathbf{z}_i$ in $\mathcal{S}$. □

We finally show the soundness of the protocol, i.e. that one can extract all but $\tau(k) = k/\log\alpha + 1$ preimages from a prover that succeeds with probability greater than 2^{-k}.

Lemma 4.4 (Soundness). *With parameters set as per Theorem 4.1, the protocol $\mathcal{P}_{IProof}$ has imperfection $\tau(k) = k/\log\alpha + 1$ and slack $2B$.*

Proof. The soundness proof is similar to the one of [BDLN16] as the use of the hashes and seed trees does not affect it significantly. We will however give a detailed proof, first to address the differences with the proof of [BDLN16], and second because the soundness proof of the protocol described in Sect. 5 will build upon this first proof.

Let $k' = k/\log\alpha + 1$, let $\hat{\mathcal{P}}$ be a deterministic prover that makes an honest verifier accept with probability $p > 2^{-k}$. We will construct an extractor $\mathcal{E}$ that extracts $n - k'$ values $\mathbf{x}'_i, i \in I \subset [n]$ such that $f(\mathbf{x}'_i) = y_i$ and $\|\mathbf{x}'_i\| \leq 2B$. $\mathcal{E}$ will run in expected time $poly(s,k) \cdot 1/p$ where s is the size of the input to $\mathcal{P}_{IProof}$.

We first give a high-level overview of the proof. Remark that by collision resistance of H we can consider $\mathbf{g}_1, \ldots, \mathbf{g}_T$ as being fixed by the value of h. $\mathcal{E}$ will begin by running $\hat{\mathcal{P}}$ on random challenges, and thus random sets $\mathcal{O} \subset [T]$. Each time $\hat{\mathcal{P}}$ is successful $\mathcal{E}$ will be able to extract $\mathbf{g}_j$ for j in $\mathcal{O}$ (since the prover is effectively revealing $\mathbf{g}_j, j \in \mathcal{O}$ in his first message after the challenge). $\mathcal{E}$ will repeat this step until he has extracted all but k' vectors $\mathbf{g}_j$, we will prove that this takes expected time $O(1/p)$. Once this is done $\mathcal{E}$ can run $\hat{\mathcal{P}}$ until he succeeds and obtain vectors $\mathbf{z}_i, i \in [n]$ such that, by collision resistance of H, $f(\mathbf{z}_i) = y_i + f(\mathbf{g}_{\Phi[i]})$. If $\mathcal{E}$ has previously extracted $\mathbf{g}_{\Phi[i]}$ he can compute $\mathbf{z}_i - \mathbf{g}_{\Phi[i]}$ which is a preimage of y_i. Since $\mathcal{E}$ knows all but k' vectors $\mathbf{g}_j$, $\mathcal{E}$ will be able to obtain preimages for all but k' secrets y_i.

Formally: $\mathcal{E}$ starts $\hat{\mathcal{P}}$ who outputs h and runs the protocol on random challenges until he outputs $(s_j)_{j \in prefix(\mathcal{O})}$ and $(h_j)_{j \in \mathcal{C}}$, from this $\mathcal{E}$ can recover hashes $(h_j)_{j\in[T]}$ such that $H(h_1, \ldots, h_T) = h$, fix $\overline{h} := h$ and $\overline{h}_j := h_j$. Set $A := \emptyset$ and run T instances of $\hat{\mathcal{P}}$ in parallel, which we denote $\hat{\mathcal{P}}_1, \ldots, \hat{\mathcal{P}}_T$. Do the following until $|A| \geq T - k'$:

- For each $\hat{\mathcal{P}}_j$ sample a random challenge $\mathbf{c}_j \leftarrow \chi^T$ subject to $\mathbf{c}_j[j] = 0$ and run $\hat{\mathcal{P}}_j$ on challenge $\mathbf{c}_j$.
- For each instance $\hat{\mathcal{P}}_j$ that does not abort, reconstruct s_j from the prover's response and set $\mathbf{g}_j = \mathcal{D}^r_\sigma[\mathbf{PRG}(s_j)]$. Verify the proof output by $\hat{\mathcal{P}}_j$ and set $A = A \cup \mathbf{g}_j$. Note that if the proof is valid then the verifier can reconstruct $h_1, \ldots, h_T$ s.t
$$H(h_1, \ldots, h_T) = \overline{h} = H(\overline{h}_1, \ldots, \overline{h}_T)$$
since H is collision resistant we have in particular that $h_j = \overline{h}_j$ which implies $H(f(\mathbf{g}_j)) = \overline{h}_j$. We also have $\|\mathbf{g}_j\| \leq B$.

Observe that if this algorithm terminates we obtain a set A of at least $T - k'$ preimages of the $\overline{h}_j$ by the function $H \circ f$. We will now show that this extractor finishes in expected polynomial time. This proof is very similar to the one of [BDLN16] but we choose to present it anyway as it will be reused in the next section.

Let p_j be the probability that $\hat{\mathcal{P}}_j$ outputs a good $\mathbf{g}_j$ (i.e. such that $H(f(\mathbf{g}_j)) = \overline{h}_j \wedge \|\mathbf{g}_j\| \leq B$). We say that p_j is bad if $p_j < p/k'$ and good otherwise. Let X_j be the event that $\hat{\mathcal{P}}_j$ eventually outputs a good $\mathbf{g}_j$, where $X_j = 1$ if the event happens and $X_j = 0$ otherwise. If p_j is good then after l iterations:
$$\Pr[X_j = 0] \leq (1 - p/k')^l \leq e^{-lp/k'}$$
so after at most $l = k \cdot k'/p$ iterations we can expect that $\mathbf{g}_j$ was extracted except with probability negligible in k. This can be generalized to the success of all $\hat{\mathcal{P}}_j$ (where p_j is good) by a union bound, and the probability of failing is still negligible because T is polynomial in k. The resulting extractor thus runs in time $O(Tk^2/p \log \alpha)$ provided there are less than k' bad p_j.

Assume there are k' bad p_j which, for simplicity, are $p_1, \ldots, p_{k'}$. In the protocol the challenge is taken according to the distribution χ^T. The success probability of $\hat{\mathcal{P}}$ can be conditioned on the value of $\mathbf{c}[1]$ as
$$\begin{aligned} p &= \Pr\left[\hat{\mathcal{P}} \text{ succeeds} \middle| \mathbf{c}[1] = 0\right] \cdot \Pr[\mathbf{c}[1] = 0] \\ &\quad + \Pr\left[\hat{\mathcal{P}} \text{ succeeds} \middle| \mathbf{c}[1] = 1\right] \cdot \Pr[\mathbf{c}[1] = 1] \\ &= p_1\left(1 - \frac{1}{\alpha}\right) + \frac{1}{\alpha}\Pr\left[\hat{\mathcal{P}} \text{ succeeds} \middle| \mathbf{c}[1] = 1\right] \end{aligned}$$

Conditioning additionally on $\mathbf{c}[2]$ yields

$$p \le p_1\left(1-\frac{1}{\alpha}\right)+\frac{1}{\alpha}\left(\left(1-\frac{1}{\alpha}\right)\alpha p_2+\frac{1}{\alpha}\Pr\left[\hat{\mathcal{P}}\text{ succeeds}\middle|\mathbf{c}[1]=1\wedge\mathbf{c}[2]=1\right]\right)$$
$$=\left(1-\frac{1}{\alpha}\right)(p_1+p_2)+\frac{1}{\alpha^2}\Pr\left[\hat{\mathcal{P}}\text{ succeeds}\middle|\mathbf{c}[1]=1\wedge\mathbf{c}[2]=1\right]$$

The reason the inequality holds is as follows: the probability that a random challenge s.t $\mathbf{c}[2]$ will yield a preimage of $\overline{h}_2$ is p_2. Now conditioning on $\mathbf{c}[1]=1$, which occurs with probability $1/\alpha$, will increase that probability from p_2 to at most αp_2.

Repeating the above argument generalizes to

$$\begin{aligned} p \le &\left(1-\frac{1}{\alpha}\right)(p_1+p_2+\ldots+p_{k'}) \\ &+\frac{1}{\alpha^{k'}}\Pr\left[\hat{\mathcal{P}}\text{ succeeds}\middle|\mathbf{c}[1]=1\wedge\ldots\wedge\mathbf{c}[k']=1\right] \\ <&\left(1-\frac{1}{\alpha}\right)p+\frac{1}{\alpha^{k'}} \end{aligned}$$

This entails that

$$p<\frac{1}{\alpha^{k'-1}}=\alpha^{-k/log\alpha}=2^{-k}$$

From this we conclude that there are less than k' bad p_j, and thus that $\mathcal{E}$ has extracted a set A of size at least $T-k'$ of elements $\mathbf{g}_j$ s.t

$$H(f(\mathbf{g}_j))=\overline{h}_j\wedge\|\mathbf{g_j}\|\le B.$$

We will now show how to use this set A to extract $n-k'$ secrets $\mathbf{x}'_i$.

$\mathcal{E}$ runs $\hat{\mathcal{P}}$ on random challenges until it succeeds. Call this successful instance $\widetilde{\mathcal{P}}$, this takes expected time $1/p$. From the output of $\widetilde{\mathcal{P}}$, $\mathcal{E}$ obtains a set $\widetilde{\Phi}$ as well as $(\widetilde{\mathbf{z}}_i)_{i\in[n]}$ s.t $H(f(\widetilde{\mathbf{z}}_i)-y_i)=\overline{h}_{\widetilde{\Phi}[i]}$ (by collision resistance of H and by the fact that $H(\widetilde{h}_1,\ldots,\widetilde{h}_T)=\overline{h}$) and $\|\widetilde{\mathbf{z}}_i\|\le B$. For each $i\in[n]$ if there exists $\mathbf{g}_{\widetilde{\Phi}[i]}\in A$, then we have $H(f(\widetilde{\mathbf{z}}_i)-y_i)=H(f(\mathbf{g}_{\widetilde{\Phi}[i]}))$, setting $\mathbf{x}'_i=\widetilde{\mathbf{z}}_i-\mathbf{g}_{\widetilde{\Phi}[i]}$ gives $f(\mathbf{x}'_i)=y_i$ and $\|\mathbf{x}'_i\|\le 2B$. Since $|A|\ge T-k'$ there are at most k' of the $\widetilde{\Phi}[i]$ that are not in this set and $\mathcal{E}$ can extract $n-k'$ preimages $\mathbf{x}'_i$. □

Using this imperfect proof with the compiler of Theorem 2.8 results in a proof of knowledge with soundness slack $4k\sqrt{r}\beta/\log\alpha$, communication overhead $O(1)$ (we will discuss this in further details in Sect. 6) and amortization over $4\left(\frac{k}{\log\alpha}+1\right)^2$ secrets. e.g. for $\alpha=2^{10}$ one can create amortized proofs for as few as 853 secrets with a security parameter $k=128$, while the construction of [CDXY17] needs to amortize over at least 67103 secrets for the same security. However this protocol is not strictly better in the sense that the computation cost, which is essentially the number of evaluations of the function f, increases multiplicatively in α for both the prover and the verifier, making this protocol impractical for very large α. In the next section we describe a new variant of the scheme inspired by the work of [BCK+14] that reduces the soundness errror $\tau(k)$ without necessarily increasing the computational cost of the protocol.

5 Proving $f(\mathbf{x}_i) = 2y_i$ with Even Fewer Equations

In this section we use an idea from the zero-knowledge proof of [BCK+14] to improve the imperfection of our previous scheme. In [BCK+14] the authors prove knowledge of preimages for an ivOWF over a polynomial ring of dimension d, they take advantage of this structure by replacing the binary challenge of the classic 3-round ZKPOK with a challenge in $\{0, \pm 1, \pm X, \dots, \pm X^{d-1}\}$ this improves the soundness error of the protocol from $1/2$ to $1/(2d+1)$. We adapt this technique to further improve the imperfection of our imperfect proof. The knowledge extractor becomes however substantially more complicated.

Let $\mathcal{R}$ be the polynomial ring $\mathbb{Z}[X]/\langle X^d + 1\rangle$. For $(a_1, \dots, a_l) \in \mathcal{R}^l$ and for $b \in \mathcal{R}$ let $\star$ be the following product $\star : \mathcal{R} \times \mathcal{R}^l \rightarrow \mathcal{R}^l$ such that $b \star (a_1, \dots, a_l) = (ba_1, \dots, ba_l)$.

In this section we will consider ivOWFs $f : \mathbb{Z}^r \simeq \mathcal{R}^l \rightarrow \mathcal{R}$ such that for $b \in \mathcal{R}$ and $a \in \mathcal{R}^l$ we have $f(b \star a) = bf(a)$. This type of one-way function is often used in ideal-lattice constructions.

Lemma 5.1 ([BCK+14] Lemma 3.2). *Let d be a power of 2, let $a, b \in \{\pm 1, \dots, \pm X^{d-1}\}$. Then $2(a-b)^{-1} \bmod X^d + 1$ only has coefficients in $\{-1, 0, 1\}$. In particular $\|2(a-b)^{-1}\| \leq \sqrt{d}$.*

We now prove that the construction of Fig. 6 is an imperfect proof of knowledge.

Theorem 5.2. *Let $f : \mathcal{R}^l \rightarrow \mathcal{R}$ be an ivOWF, $r = ld \geq 128$ be an integer, let $f' = 2f$, let k be a statistical security parameter, H a collision resistant hash function, χ a distribution over $\{0, \pm 1, \pm X, \dots, \pm X^{d-1}\}$ with $\Pr[\chi = 0] = 1 - 1/\alpha$ and $\forall c \in \{\pm 1, \dots, \pm X^{d-1}\}$, $\Pr[\chi = c] = 1/(2d\alpha)$. Let $T = 5\alpha n$, $\sigma = 11\beta$, $B = 2\sqrt{r}\sigma$. The protocol $\mathcal{P}_{IProof}$ given in Fig. 6 is an imperfect proof of knowledge for inputs in $\mathcal{R}_{KSP}(f, n, \beta)$, with soundness extractor in $\mathcal{R}_{KSP}(f', n, \sqrt{d}B)$ and imperfection $\frac{k(1+1/\log\alpha)}{\log\alpha + \log 2d} + 1$.*

Proof. The proofs for the correctness and zero-knowledge of the protocol are identical to the proofs in the previous section. On the other hand the soundness proof is more involved.

Soundness: Let $k' = \frac{k(1+1/\log\alpha)}{\log\alpha + \log 2d} + 1$, let $\hat{\mathcal{P}}$ be a deterministic prover that makes an honest verifier accept with probability $p > 2^{-k}$. We will construct an extractor $\mathcal{E}$ that extracts $n - k'$ values $\mathbf{x}'_i, i \in I \subset [n]$ such that $f(\mathbf{x}'_i) = 2y_i$ and $\|\mathbf{x}'_i\| \leq \sqrt{d}B$. $\mathcal{E}$ will run in time $poly(s, k) \cdot 1/p^{1+2/\log\alpha}$ where s is the size of the input to $\mathcal{P}_{IProof}$.

$\underline{\mathcal{P}}$		$\underline{\mathcal{V}}$
$\mathbf{X} := (\mathbf{x}_1, \ldots, \mathbf{x}_n)$ $\mathbf{Y} := (y_1 := f(\mathbf{x}_1), \ldots, y_n := f(\mathbf{x}_n))$		$\mathbf{Y}$
Tree $\Gamma_{\mathcal{P}}$:= **new Tree** **Initialize**$(\Gamma_{\mathcal{P}}, \emptyset, t)$ $s \xleftarrow{\$} \{0,1\}^{256}$ **SeedTree**$(\Gamma_{\mathcal{P}}, s)$ $\forall i \in [T]: \; \mathbf{g}_i \leftarrow \mathcal{D}_\sigma^r\,[\mathbf{PRG}(s_i)]$ $a_1, \ldots, a_T := f(\mathbf{g}_1), \ldots, f(\mathbf{g}_t)$ $h_1, \ldots, h_T := H(a_1), \ldots, H(a_T)$ $h := H(h_1, \ldots, h_T)$	$\xrightarrow{h}$	**Tree** $\Gamma_{\mathcal{V}}$:= **new Tree** **Initialize**$(\Gamma_{\mathcal{V}}, \emptyset, t)$
	$\xleftarrow{\mathbf{c}}$	$\mathbf{c} \leftarrow \chi^T \in \{0, \pm 1, \ldots, \pm X^{d-1}\}^T$
$\mathcal{O} := \{j, \mathbf{c}[j] = 0\}, \mathcal{C} := [T] \setminus \mathcal{O}$ **Prefix**$(\Gamma_{\mathcal{P}}, \mathcal{O})$ $\mathcal{S} := \{j \subset \{0,1\}^t, \; \Gamma_{\mathcal{P}}[j].Sel = 1\}$	$\xrightarrow[(h_j)_{j \in \mathcal{C}}]{(s_j)_{j \in \mathcal{S}}}$	
		$\mathcal{O} := \{j, \mathbf{c}_j = 0\}, \mathcal{C} := [T] \setminus \mathcal{O}$ **Prefix**$(\Gamma_{\mathcal{V}}, \mathcal{O})$ **Reconstruct**$(\Gamma_{\mathcal{V}}, (s_j)_{j \in \mathcal{S}}, \mathcal{O})$ $(s_j)_{j \in \mathcal{O}} := (\Gamma_{\mathcal{V}}[j].Seed)_{j \in \mathcal{O}}$ $\forall j \in \mathcal{O} \begin{cases} \mathbf{g}_j := f(\mathcal{D}_\sigma^r\,[\mathbf{PRG}(s_j)]) \\ h_j := H(\mathbf{g}_j) \\ \text{Check: } \Vert\mathbf{g}_j\Vert \leq B \end{cases}$ $Check: H(h_1, \ldots, h_T) = h$
$\Phi := \emptyset$ $\forall i \in [n]:$ find the first $j \in \mathcal{C}, j > max(\Phi)$ s.t.**Rej**$(\mathbf{c}[j] \cdot \mathbf{x}_i, \mathbf{c}[j] \cdot \mathbf{x}_i + \mathbf{g}_j) = 1$ $\mathbf{z}_i := \mathbf{c}[j] \cdot \mathbf{x}_i + \mathbf{g}_j$ $\Phi := \Phi \cup \{j\}$ If $\lvert\Phi\rvert < n$ abort	$\xrightarrow{\Phi, (\mathbf{z}_i)_{i \in [n]}}$	
		$\forall i < i' \in [n]$, Check : $\Phi_i < \Phi_{i'}$ $\forall i \in [n]:$ Check : $\begin{cases} H(f(\mathbf{z}_i) - \mathbf{c}[\Phi_i]\, y_i) = h_{\Phi_i} \\ \Vert\mathbf{z}_i\Vert \leq B \end{cases}$

Fig. 6. Our second construction: an imperfect proof of knowledge for $f(\mathbf{x}_i) = 2y_i$ with imperfection $\frac{k(1+1/\log\alpha)}{\log\alpha + \log 2d} + 1$

We first give a high level overview of the soundness proof. $\mathcal{E}$ starts by running the extractor from Lemma 4.4 to obtain all but $k/\log\alpha+1$ vectors $\mathbf{g}_j$ as well as all but $k/\log\alpha+1$ preimages $\mathbf{x}_i$. Next we would like to have $\mathcal{E}$ run $\hat{\mathcal{P}}$ until he is successful twice and obtain two outputs:

- $\mathbf{z}_1,\ldots,\mathbf{z}_n$ such that $f(\mathbf{z}_i)=\mathbf{c}[\Phi[i]]\cdot y_i+\mathbf{g}_{\Phi[i]}$
- $\mathbf{z}'_1,\ldots,\mathbf{z}'_n$ such that $f(\mathbf{z}'_i)=\mathbf{c}'[\Phi'[i]]\cdot y_i+\mathbf{g}_{\Phi'[i]}$

Now if for a given $i\in[n]$ we have both:

$$\Phi[i]=\Phi'[i] \tag{2}$$

$$\mathbf{c}[\Phi[i]]\neq\mathbf{c}'[\Phi[i]] \tag{3}$$

Then $\mathcal{E}$ can extract $(\mathbf{z}_i-\mathbf{z}'_i)\cdot 2\left(\mathbf{c}[\Phi[i]]-\mathbf{c}[\Phi'[i]]\right)^{-1}$ which is a preimage of $2y_i$. We would thus like to show that there are at least $n-k'$ indices $i\in[n]$ for which both of these equations are true with non negligible probability. However proving such a thing is difficult as the probabilities that (2) is true for each $i\in[n]$ are not independent. We instead show a somewhat stronger statement: we prove that there exists a function g, going from the set of indices i for which $\mathbf{x}_i$ was not extracted to the set of indices j for which $\mathbf{g}_j$ was not extracted, such that if $\hat{\mathcal{P}}$ succeeds on a random challenge then with good probability $\Phi[i]=g(i)$ for all indices i for which $\mathbf{x}_i$ was not extracted. Intuitively we simply show that one mapping Φ from the unextracted $\mathbf{x}_i$ to the unextracted $\mathbf{g}_j$ has to occur more often than the others, which we call g. Since there are not too many such mappings (less than $2^{k/\log\alpha}$) we can restrict our extractor to only consider the outputs of $\hat{\mathcal{P}}$ where he uses $\Phi=g$. Now $\mathcal{E}$ can run $\hat{\mathcal{P}}$ until he outputs two valid proofs, for which we are guaranteed that for all relevant $i\in[n]$, $\Phi[i]=\Phi'[i]=g(i)$. To conclude we show that there exist at least $n-k'$ indices i for which the success probability of $\hat{\mathcal{P}}$ is still high even when conditioned on $\mathbf{c}[\Phi[i]]\neq\mathbf{c}'[\Phi[i]]$. Doing so we obtain $n-k'$ indices $i\in[n]$ for which both (2) and (3) are true, and $\mathcal{E}$ can extract all but $n-k'$ preimages.

Formally: We first use the same extractor as in the proof of Lemma 4.4. Though this scheme is different, the same extractor applies with the only difference being that the equation verified by the extracted $\mathbf{x}'_i$ will be of the form $f(\mathbf{x}'_i)=bX^a y_i$ for some $b\in\{-1,1\}, a\in[d]$. Which directly gives $f(-bX^{d-a}\mathbf{x}'_i)=y_i$, since this new pre-image has the same norm we can rename it and obtain the same result. We thus obtain the following:

- $\overline{h}$ the hash sent by $\hat{\mathcal{P}}$ on his first flow.
- $\overline{h}_1,\ldots,\overline{h}_T$ such that $H(\overline{h}_1,\ldots,\overline{h}_T)=\overline{h}$.
- A set A of at least $T-k/\log\alpha-1$ vectors $\mathbf{g}'_j$ such that $H(f(\mathbf{g}'_j))=\overline{h}_j$. We define $\Psi\subset[T]$ to be the indices of the $\overline{h}_j$ for which a preimage was not extracted.
- A set S of at least $n-k/\log\alpha-1$ vectors $\mathbf{x}'_i$ such that $f(\mathbf{x}'_i)=y_i$. We define $\Upsilon\subset[n]$ to be the indices of the y_i for which a preimage was not extracted.

By construction of this extractor we have $|\Upsilon|\leq|\Psi|\leq k/\log\alpha+1$.

Observe that, on a successful run of $\hat{\mathcal{P}}$, the set Φ is a strictly increasing mapping from $[n]$ to $[T]$ (this is explicitly checked by the verifier). In the previous protocol this was used to show zero-knowledge, as reusing randomness could leak information, but this is now crucial for soundness. We also note that since Φ is a function from $[n]$ to $[T]$ we have either:

(A) $\Phi(\Upsilon) \subset \Psi$
(B) Or $\exists i \in \Upsilon$ s.t. $\Phi[i] \notin \Psi$

If on a run $\hat{\mathcal{P}}$ is successful and (B) occurs then there exist $i, j \in [n] \times [T]$ such that $H(f(\mathbf{z}_i) - \mathbf{c}[j]\, y_i) = h_j$ and $j = \Phi[i] \notin \Psi$. As we have already extracted $\mathbf{g}'_j$ with $H(f(\mathbf{g}'_j)) = \overline{h}_j = h_j$ we obtain that $\mathbf{x}'_i = \mathbf{c}[j]^{-1}(\mathbf{z}_i - \mathbf{g}'_j)$ is a preimage of y_i. We can thus redefine the set Υ to be $\Upsilon := \Upsilon \backslash i$. Suppose that on a successful run of $\hat{\mathcal{P}}$, (B) occurs with probability greater than $1/2$. The extractor can then run $\hat{\mathcal{P}}$ $O(2/p)$ times, successfully extract a new preimage of the y_i and reduce the size of Υ by 1. After repeating this procedure $O(k)$ times we have either that $|\Upsilon| < k'$, in which case the extractor is done, or that (B) occurs with probability strictly lower than $1/2$ on a successful run. For the rest of the proof we assume the latter. Since either (A) or (B) occurs on a successful run this implies that (A) happens with probability strictly greater than $1/2$.

On any run where (A) occurs, Φ induces a strictly increasing mapping from Υ to Ψ, let $\mathcal{G}$ be the set of all such mappings, we have

$$|\mathcal{G}| = \binom{|\Psi|}{|\Upsilon|} \leq 2^{|\Psi|} \leq 2^{k/\log\alpha+1}.$$

The extractor runs $|\mathcal{G}|$ parallel instances of $\hat{\mathcal{P}}$ denoted as $\hat{\mathcal{P}}^g, g \in \mathcal{G}$, and does the following until $|S| \geq n - k'$.

- Run instance $\hat{\mathcal{P}}^g$ with fresh randomness until it succeeds, (A) occurs and $\Phi(\Psi) = g(\Psi)$. Denote the challenge used as $\widetilde{\mathbf{c}}^g$ and the output of the prover as $\widetilde{\mathbf{z}}^g_i, i \in [n]$.
- Run $|\Upsilon|$ parallel instances of $\hat{\mathcal{P}}^g$ denoted as $\hat{\mathcal{P}}^g_i, i \in \Upsilon$, do the following:
  - For each $\hat{\mathcal{P}}^g_i$ sample a random challenge $\mathbf{c}^g_i \leftarrow \chi^T$ subject to $\mathbf{c}^g_i[i] \neq \widetilde{\mathbf{c}}^g[i]$ and run $\hat{\mathcal{P}}^g_i$ on challenge $\mathbf{c}^g_i$.
  - For each instance $\hat{\mathcal{P}}^g_i$ that does not abort. If (A) occurs and $\Phi(\Psi) = g(\Psi)$, then the vector $\mathbf{z}_i$ output by the prover verifies:

    $$H(f(\mathbf{z}_i) - \mathbf{c}^g_i[g(i)]\, y_i) = \overline{h}_i.$$

    From the previous step we had $\widetilde{\mathbf{z}}^g_i$ such that

    $$H(f(\widetilde{\mathbf{z}}^g_i) - \widetilde{\mathbf{c}}^g[g(i)]\, y_i) = \overline{h}_i.$$

    The extractor sets

    $$\mathbf{x}'_i = (\mathbf{z}^g_i - \widetilde{\mathbf{z}}^g_i) \cdot 2\left(\mathbf{c}^g_i[g(i)] - \widetilde{\mathbf{c}}^g[g(i)]\right)^{-1}$$

    Note that $f(\mathbf{x}'_i) = 2y_i$ and by Lemma 5.1 $\|\mathbf{x}'_i\| \leq \sqrt{d}B$.

We now prove that this extractor terminates in expected time $\frac{\text{poly}(s,k)}{p^{1+2/\log\alpha}}$. Since $|\mathcal{G}| \leq 2/p^{1/\log\alpha}$ it is sufficient to show that there exists g in $\mathcal{G}$ such that $\hat{\mathcal{P}}^g$ runs in time $\text{poly}(s,k) \cdot 1/p^{1+1/\log\alpha}$. On any run where (A) occurs, $\Phi(\Upsilon)$ is a function in $\mathcal{G}$, this implies that

$$\Pr\left[\hat{\mathcal{P}}\ \textit{succeeds} \wedge (A)\right] = \sum_{g\in\mathcal{G}} \Pr\left[\hat{\mathcal{P}}\ \textit{succeeds} \wedge (A) \wedge \Phi(\Upsilon) = g\right]$$

and thus

$$\begin{aligned}\exists\gamma \in \mathcal{G} \text{ s.t. } \Pr\left[\hat{\mathcal{P}}\ \textit{succeeds} \wedge (A) \wedge \Phi(\Upsilon) = \gamma\right] &\geq \frac{\Pr\left[\hat{\mathcal{P}}\ \textit{succeeds} \wedge (A)\right]}{|\mathcal{G}|} \\ &\geq \frac{p^{1+1/\log\alpha}}{2}\end{aligned}$$

We will use the shorthand $\hat{\mathcal{P}} \wedge \gamma$ for the event $\hat{\mathcal{P}}$ *succeeds* $\wedge (A) \wedge \Phi(\Upsilon) = \gamma$. Let p_i be the probability that $\hat{\mathcal{P}}_i^\gamma$ succeeds, i.e.

$$p_i = \Pr\left[\hat{\mathcal{P}} \wedge \gamma \middle| \mathbf{c}\left[\gamma(i)\right] \neq \tilde{\mathbf{c}}^\gamma\left[\gamma(i)\right]\right],$$

we say that p_i is bad if $p_i < \frac{\Pr[\hat{\mathcal{P}}\wedge\gamma]}{k'}$ and good otherwise. If there are less than k' bad p_i then the extractor terminates in expected time

$$\text{poly}(s,k) \cdot \frac{|\mathcal{G}|}{\Pr\left[\hat{\mathcal{P}} \wedge \gamma\right]} = \text{poly}(s,k) \cdot 2^{k(1+2/\log\alpha)}$$

(c.f. the proof of Lemma 4.4). Assume that there are k' bad p_i which, for simplicity, are $p_1, \ldots, p_{k'}$. Then the event $\hat{\mathcal{P}} \wedge \gamma$ can be conditioned on the value of $\mathbf{c}[\gamma(1)]$ as

$$\begin{aligned}\Pr\left[\hat{\mathcal{P}} \wedge \gamma\right] &= \Pr\left[\hat{\mathcal{P}} \wedge \gamma \middle| \mathbf{c}\left[\gamma(1)\right] \neq \tilde{\mathbf{c}}^\gamma\left[\gamma(1)\right]\right] \cdot \Pr\left[\mathbf{c}\left[\gamma(1)\right] \neq \tilde{\mathbf{c}}^\gamma\left[\gamma(1)\right]\right] \\ &\quad + \Pr\left[\hat{\mathcal{P}} \wedge \gamma \middle| \mathbf{c}\left[\gamma(1)\right] = \tilde{\mathbf{c}}^\gamma\left[\gamma(1)\right]\right] \cdot \Pr\left[\mathbf{c}\left[\gamma(1)\right] = \tilde{\mathbf{c}}^\gamma\left[\gamma(1)\right]\right] \\ &= \frac{2d\alpha - 1}{2d\alpha} p_1 + \frac{1}{2d\alpha} \Pr\left[\hat{\mathcal{P}} \wedge \gamma \middle| \mathbf{c}\left[\gamma(1)\right] = \tilde{\mathbf{c}}^\gamma\left[\gamma(1)\right]\right]\end{aligned}$$

Conditioning on $\mathbf{c}\left[\gamma(2)\right], \ldots, \mathbf{c}\left[\gamma(k')\right]$ we have

$$\begin{aligned}\Pr\left[\hat{\mathcal{P}} \wedge \gamma\right] &\leq \frac{2d\alpha - 1}{2d\alpha}(p_1 + \ldots + p_{k'}) \\ &\quad + \frac{1}{(2d\alpha)^{k'}} \Pr\left[\hat{\mathcal{P}} \wedge \gamma \middle| \mathbf{c}\left[\gamma(1)\right] = \tilde{\mathbf{c}}^\gamma\left[\gamma(1)\right], \ldots, \mathbf{c}\left[\gamma(k')\right] = \tilde{\mathbf{c}}^\gamma\left[\gamma(k')\right]\right] \\ &< \frac{2d\alpha - 1}{2d\alpha} \Pr\left[\hat{\mathcal{P}} \wedge \gamma\right] + \frac{1}{(2d\alpha)^{k'}} \\ &\leq \frac{1}{(2d\alpha)^{k'-1}} \\ &< 2^{-k(1+1/\log\alpha)-1}\end{aligned}$$

which contradicts the fact that $\Pr\left[\hat{\mathcal{P}} \wedge \gamma\right] \geq \frac{p^{1+1/\log\alpha}}{2}$.

From this we conclude that there are less than k' bad p_i, and thus that the extractor has extracted a set S of $n - k'$ vectors $\mathbf{x}'_i$ such that $\|\mathbf{x}'_i\| \leq \sqrt{d}B$ and $f(\mathbf{x}'_i) = 2y_i$ in time $\text{poly}(s, k) \cdot 2^{k(1+2/\log\alpha)}$. □

6 Proof Size

In this section we will go more in-depth in the trade-offs offered by the schemes described in Sects. 4 and 5. We first give the expected value as well as an upper bound on the size of the prefix $\mathcal{S}$ of the set $\mathcal{O}$ as the second flow of the prover will consist in sending $|\mathcal{S}|$ seeds (and $|\mathcal{C}|$ hashes).

Lemma 6.1. *Let $T = 2^t$, let $\mathbf{c} \leftarrow \chi^T \in C^T$ (the set C from which the values of $\mathbf{c}$ are taken does not matter, all that matters is the probability with which 0 is sampled) with χ such that $\Pr[\chi = 0] = 1 - 1/\alpha$, let $\mathcal{O} = \{j \in [T], \mathbf{c}[j] = 0\}$, and let $\mathcal{S}(\mathbf{c}) = prefix(\mathcal{O})$ be as defined in Sect. 4. Then:*

- *With overwhelming probability we can bound the size of $\mathcal{S}(\mathbf{c})$ by*

$$|\mathcal{S}(\mathbf{c})| \leq \left\lfloor \frac{1.4T}{\alpha} \log \frac{\alpha}{1.4} \right\rfloor$$

Proof. Consider the binary tree Γ which leaves are numbered according to $[T]$, we will say that a leaf $j \in [T]$ is selected if $\mathbf{c}[j] = 0$. First observe that we can split Γ into two trees Γ_L and Γ_R of size $T/2$, Γ_L being the binary tree associated to the first $T/2$ values $\mathbf{c}_L$ of $\mathbf{c}$ and Γ_R the tree associated to the last $T/2$ vales $\mathbf{c}_R$ of $\mathbf{c}$. The prefix $\mathcal{S}(\mathbf{c})$ of Γ will be the union of the prefixes $\mathcal{S}(\mathbf{c}_L)$ and $\mathcal{S}(\mathbf{c}_R)$, except if all the leaves of Γ are selected, in which case its prefix will be its root. i.e. $\forall \mathbf{c} \neq (0, \ldots, 0)$, $\mathcal{S} = \mathcal{S}(\mathbf{c}_L) \cup \mathcal{S}(\mathbf{c}_R)$, which implies $|\mathcal{S}(\mathbf{c})| = |\mathcal{S}(\mathbf{c}_L)| + |\mathcal{S}(\mathbf{c}_R)|$.

We first use the Chernoff bound to obtain a lower bound on the size of $\mathcal{O}$. Let $\mathcal{C} = [T] \setminus \mathcal{O}$, we have:

$$\Pr[|\mathcal{C}| > 1.4T/\alpha] \leq e^{-\frac{T}{15\alpha}} = e^{-\frac{n}{3}}$$

since for all practical parameters we will have $n \geq 250$, we can assume that $|\mathcal{C}| \leq 1.4T/\alpha$. We consider the worst case for the size of $\mathcal{S}$ for a given $|\mathcal{C}| = a$, i.e. we define

$$W(T, a) = \max_{\#_0(\mathbf{c}) = T - a} (|\mathcal{S}(\mathbf{c})|).$$

We will prove that $\forall a \in [T], W(T, a) \leq a \log(T/a)$. Remark that for all T, $W(T, 0) = 1$. Since for all $\mathbf{c} \in C^T$ we have

$$|\mathcal{S}(\mathbf{c})| \leq |\mathcal{S}(\mathbf{c}_L)| + |\mathcal{S}(\mathbf{c}_R)|,$$

we get

$$W(T, a) \leq \max_b (W(T/2, b) + W(T/2, a - b))$$

where $\max(0, a - T/2) \leq b \leq \min(a, T/2)$. We prove that

$$\forall a \in [T], W(T, a) \leq a \log (T/a)$$

by induction over $T = 2^t$:

- For $T = 1$, $W(1, 1) = 1$
- For $2T$: Assume that for all $1 \leq b \leq T$, $W(T, b) \leq b \log (T/b)$ (and $W(T, 0) = 1$). Fix $a \in [2T]$. Let $f(b) = W(T, b) + W(T, a - b)$, then

$$W(2T, a) \leq \max_b (f(b))$$

for $\max(0, a - T/2) \leq b \leq \min(a, T/2)$.
  - For $b = a$ or $b = 0$,

$$f(b) = W(T, a) + W(T, 0) \leq a \log(T/a) + 1 \leq a \log(2T/a)$$

  - For $b \neq a$ and $b \neq 0$,

$$f(b) \leq a \log(T/a) + (a - b) \log(T/(a - b)).$$

    Simple analysis shows that this function reaches its maximum for $b = a/2$, and thus $f(b) \leq a \log(2T/a)$

We conclude by using the fact that $W(T, a)$ is an integer. Finally, with high probability

$$|\mathcal{S}(\mathbf{c})| \leq W(T, 1.4T/\alpha) \leq \left\lfloor \frac{1.4T}{\alpha} \log \frac{\alpha}{1.4} \right\rfloor$$

□

We will show that the size of the protocol given in Fig. 4 can be made nearly independent of the parameter α by cleverly encoding each flow. We will consider the four flows of the protocol each on its own (though it is clear that the proof really is a three-move protocol since the last two flows can be sent simultaneously).

First Flow: The prover sends $h \in \{0, 1\}^{256}$ to the verifier, this is clearly independent of α.

$$\text{Flow size} = 256 \text{ bits}$$

Second Flow: The verifier sends $\mathbf{c} \in \{0, 1\}^T$ to the prover, this takes $5\alpha n$ bits since $T = 5\alpha n$. However the verifier can compute the sets $\mathcal{O}$ and $\mathcal{C} = [T] \backslash \mathcal{O}$ before sending $\mathbf{c}$ (rather than doing it afterwards) and equivalently send the set $\mathcal{C}$. We have $|\mathcal{C}| \leq 7n$ and since the indices of $\mathcal{C}$ are in $[T]$ they can be encoded in $\log(5\alpha n)$ bits. The second flow only depends on α logarithmically.

$$\text{Flow size} \leq 7n \log(5\alpha n) \text{ bits}$$

Third Flow: The prover sends $(s_j)_{j \in \mathcal{S}}$ and $(h_j)_{j \in \mathcal{C}}$ to the verifier. From Lemma 6.1 we have that $|\mathcal{S}| \leq 7n \log(\alpha/1.4)$ and similarly $|\mathcal{C}| \leq 7n$, since the seeds and hash all are in $\{0, 1\}^{256}$ this flow depends logarithmically on α.

$$\text{Flow size} \leq 7n \log \left(\frac{2\alpha}{1.4}\right) \cdot 256 \text{ bits}$$

Fourth Flow (i.e. second part of the Third Flow): The prover sends Φ and $(\mathbf{z}_i)_{i\in[n]}$ to the verifier. Since $\Phi \in [T]^n$ sending it naively would require $n\log(5\alpha n)$ bits, however all the elements of Φ correspond to non-zero indices of $\mathbf{c}$, i.e. they are in $\mathcal{C}$. Φ can thus be encoded using $n\log(|\mathcal{C}|) \leq n\log(7n)$ bits. The coefficients of the $\mathbf{z}_i$ come form $\mathcal{D}_\sigma$ by a tail cutting argument they can be represented in $\log(11\sigma) = \log(11^2\beta)$ bits each and there are nr of them. The fourth flow is independent of α.

$$\text{Flow size} \leq n\log(7n) + nr\log(11^2\beta) \text{ bits}$$

The proof in Fig. 6 only differs in size from this proof on the second flow, where the challenge $\mathbf{c}$ is in $\{0, \pm 1, \pm X, \ldots, \pm X^{d-1}\}^T$. But similarly to the encoding we use for the first protocol, the verifier can simply send the set $\mathcal{C}$ as well as a vector of dimension $|\mathcal{C}|$ containing the challenges in $\{\pm 1, \pm X, \ldots, \pm X^{d-1}\}$. The size of the second flow now becomes $7n\log(5\alpha n) + 7n\log(2d)$. The total size of the proof is finally upper bounded by:

$$256 + n\left(7\log(5\alpha n) + 1792\log\left(\frac{2\alpha}{1.4}\right) + \log(7n) + \boxed{7\log(2d)} + r\log(11^2\beta)\right) \text{ bits}$$

where the boxed term only exists in the protocol from Fig. 6. Note that this size only has a very slight dependence on α. In fact the largest summand will be the one corresponding to the $\mathbf{z}_i$ up to $\alpha \sim 2^{30}$, for which the computation requirements of the proof will already be the bottleneck. The complete proof consists in two iterations of the imperfect proof, one with parameter β and the second with parameter $\tau(k)\beta$, the size of the complete proof is thus:

$$512 + n\Bigg(14\log(5\alpha n) + 3584\log\left(\frac{2\alpha}{1.4}\right) + 2\log(7n) + \boxed{14\log(2d)} + r\log(\tau(k)11^4\beta^2)\Bigg) \text{ bits}$$

And if we consider the average case rather than the worst case we can assume that $|\mathcal{S}| \leq 5n\log\alpha$ and $|\mathcal{C}| = 5n$. Which gives the expected proof size:

$$512 + n\Bigg(10\log(5\alpha n) + 2560\log(2\alpha) + 2\log(5n) + \boxed{10\log(2d)} + r\log(\tau(k)11^4\beta^2)\Bigg) \text{ bits}$$

We compare in Table 2 our scheme with the one of [CDXY17] for the (Ring)-LWE one-way function with dimension $d = 1024$ (so $r = 2048$), and binary secrets (so $\beta = \sqrt{r}$). For a fair comparison we consider the protocol of [CDXY17] in the euclidean norm and with our improvements (only one hash in the first flow and seeds instead of $\mathbf{g}_j$ in the third flow). The communication cost per secret and the slack are rather similar in all three protocols. The main difference being that our protocols allows for amortization over very few secrets but at

Table 2. Comparison between [CDXY17] and our protocols for the R-LWE ivOWF with binary secrets. Masking parameters are revealed with probability $1-1/\alpha$, k is the security parameter, $\tau(k)$ the imperfection of the protocol, and n the number of secrets. The communication is per secret and the run-time is in number of evaluations of the ivOWF per secret per player.

	[CDXY17]	Protocol I			Protocol II			
α	2	16	64	256	2	16	64	256
k	128	128	128	128	128	128	128	128
$\tau(k)$	129	33	23	17	23	12	10	9
n	69169	4489	2209	1369	2209	841	529	361
T	$6.9 \cdot 10^6$	$3.6 \cdot 10^5$	$7.1 \cdot 10^5$	$1.8 \cdot 10^6$	$2.2 \cdot 10^4$	$6.7 \cdot 10^4$	$1.7 \cdot 10^5$	$4.6 \cdot 10^5$
Slack	$2.6 \cdot 10^5$	$6.7 \cdot 10^4$	$4.7 \cdot 10^4$	$3.7 \cdot 10^4$	$1.5 \cdot 10^6$	$9.2 \cdot 10^5$	$7.2 \cdot 10^5$	$6.1 \cdot 10^5$
Proof size	8.8 kB	9.2 kB	9.7 kB	10.3 kB	8.2 kB	8.9 kB	9.5 kB	10.1 kB
Run-time	16	128	512	2048	16	128	512	2048

a larger computation cost. In Fig. 1 we plot the number n of secrets we can amortize over as a function of $\log \alpha$. It is apparent that increasing $\log \alpha$ past a certain threshold yields very little advantage while drastically increasing the computation cost (which grows linearly in α). It is also clear that our second protocol gives better amortization than the first one, though this only proves the knowledge of short pre-images of $2y$.

References

[Ban93] Banaszczyk, W.: New bounds in some transference theorems in the geometry of numbers. Mathematische Annalen **296**, 625–635 (1993)

[BCK+14] Benhamouda, F., Camenisch, J., Krenn, S., Lyubashevsky, V., Neven, G.: Better zero-knowledge proofs for lattice encryption and their application to group signatures. In: Sarkar, P., Iwata, T. (eds.) ASIACRYPT 2014. LNCS, vol. 8873, pp. 551–572. Springer, Heidelberg (2014). doi:10.1007/978-3-662-45611-8_29

[BDLN16] Baum, C., Damgård, I., Larsen, K.G., Nielsen, M.: How to prove knowledge of small secrets. In: Robshaw, M., Katz, J. (eds.) CRYPTO 2016. LNCS, vol. 9816, pp. 478–498. Springer, Heidelberg (2016). doi:10.1007/978-3-662-53015-3_17

[BDPA16] Bertoni, G., Daemen, J., Peeters, M., Van Assche, G.: The keccak sponge function family (2016)

[BKLP15] Benhamouda, F., Krenn, S., Lyubashevsky, V., Pietrzak, K.: Efficient zero-knowledge proofs for commitments from learning with errors over rings. In: Pernul, G., Ryan, P.Y.A., Weippl, E. (eds.) ESORICS 2015. LNCS, vol. 9326, pp. 305–325. Springer, Cham (2015). doi:10.1007/978-3-319-24174-6_16

[CD09] Cramer, R., Damgård, I.: On the amortized complexity of zero-knowledge protocols. In: Halevi, S. (ed.) CRYPTO 2009. LNCS, vol. 5677, pp. 177–191. Springer, Heidelberg (2009). doi:10.1007/978-3-642-03356-8_11

[CDXY17] Cramer, R., Damgård, I., Xing, C., Yuan, C.: Amortized complexity of zero-knowledge proofs revisited: achieving linear soundness slack. In: Coron, J.-S., Nielsen, J.B. (eds.) EUROCRYPT 2017. LNCS, vol. 10210, pp. 479–500. Springer, Cham (2017). doi:10.1007/978-3-319-56620-7_17

[DPSZ12] Damgård, I., Pastro, V., Smart, N., Zakarias, S.: Multiparty computation from somewhat homomorphic encryption. In: Safavi-Naini, R., Canetti, R. (eds.) CRYPTO 2012. LNCS, vol. 7417, pp. 643–662. Springer, Heidelberg (2012). doi:10.1007/978-3-642-32009-5_38

[FS86] Fiat, A., Shamir, A.: How to prove yourself: practical solutions to identification and signature problems. In: Odlyzko, A.M. (ed.) CRYPTO 1986. LNCS, vol. 263, pp. 186–194. Springer, Heidelberg (1987). doi:10.1007/3-540-47721-7_12

[KTX08] Kawachi, A., Tanaka, K., Xagawa, K.: Concurrently secure identification schemes based on the worst-case hardness of lattice problems. In: Pieprzyk, J. (ed.) ASIACRYPT 2008. LNCS, vol. 5350, pp. 372–389. Springer, Heidelberg (2008). doi:10.1007/978-3-540-89255-7_23

[LN17] Lyubashevsky, V., Neven, G.: One-shot verifiable encryption from lattices. In: Coron, J.-S., Nielsen, J.B. (eds.) EUROCRYPT 2017. LNCS, vol. 10210, pp. 293–323. Springer, Cham (2017). doi:10.1007/978-3-319-56620-7_11

[LNSW13] Ling, S., Nguyen, K., Stehlé, D., Wang, H.: Improved zero-knowledge proofs of knowledge for the ISIS problem, and applications. In: Kurosawa, K., Hanaoka, G. (eds.) PKC 2013. LNCS, vol. 7778, pp. 107–124. Springer, Heidelberg (2013). doi:10.1007/978-3-642-36362-7_8

[Lyu08] Lyubashevsky, V.: Lattice-based identification schemes secure under active attacks. In: Cramer, R. (ed.) PKC 2008. LNCS, vol. 4939, pp. 162–179. Springer, Heidelberg (2008). doi:10.1007/978-3-540-78440-1_10

[Lyu09] Lyubashevsky, V.: Fiat-Shamir with aborts: applications to lattice and factoring-based signatures. In: Matsui, M. (ed.) ASIACRYPT 2009. LNCS, vol. 5912, pp. 598–616. Springer, Heidelberg (2009). doi:10.1007/978-3-642-10366-7_35

[Lyu12] Lyubashevsky, V.: Lattice signatures without trapdoors. In: Pointcheval, D., Johansson, T. (eds.) EUROCRYPT 2012. LNCS, vol. 7237, pp. 738–755. Springer, Heidelberg (2012). doi:10.1007/978-3-642-29011-4_43

[Ste93] Stern, J.: A new identification scheme based on syndrome decoding. In: Stinson, D.R. (ed.) CRYPTO 1993. LNCS, vol. 773, pp. 13–21. Springer, Heidelberg (1994). doi:10.1007/3-540-48329-2_2

Leakage and Subversion

Private Multiplication over Finite Fields

Sonia Belaïd[1(✉)], Fabrice Benhamouda[2], Alain Passelègue[3], Emmanuel Prouff[4,5], Adrian Thillard[6], and Damien Vergnaud[7,8]

[1] Thales Communications & Security, Gennevilliers, France
sonia.belaid@live.fr
[2] IBM Research, Yorktown Heights, USA
[3] UCLA, Los Angeles, USA
[4] Safran Identity and Security, Paris, France
[5] Sorbonne Universitès, UPMC Univ Paris 06, CNRS, INRIA, Laboratoire d'Informatique de Paris 6 (LIP6), Équipe PolSys, 4 Place Jussieu, 75252 Paris, France
[6] ANSSI, Paris, France
[7] Département d'informatique de L'ENS, École normale supérieure, CNRS, PSL Research University, 75005 Paris, France
[8] INRIA, Paris, France

Abstract. The notion of privacy in the probing model, introduced by Ishai, Sahai, and Wagner in 2003, is nowadays frequently involved to assess the security of circuits manipulating sensitive information. However, provable security in this model still comes at the cost of a significant overhead both in terms of arithmetic complexity and randomness complexity. In this paper, we deal with this issue for circuits processing multiplication over finite fields. Our contributions are manifold. Extending the work of Belaïd, Benhamouda, Passelègue, Prouff, Thillard, and Vergnaud at Eurocrypt 2016, we introduce an algebraic characterization of the privacy for multiplication in any finite field and we propose a novel algebraic characterization for *non-interference* (a stronger security notion in this setting). Then, we present two generic constructions of multiplication circuits in finite fields that achieve non-interference in the probing model. Denoting by d the number of probes used by the adversary, the first proposal reduces the number of *bilinear* multiplications (i.e., of general multiplications of two non-constant values in the finite field) to only $2d+1$ whereas the state-of-the-art was $O(d^2)$. The second proposal reduces the randomness complexity to d random elements in the underlying finite field, hence improving the $O(d \log d)$ randomness complexity achieved by Belaïd et al. in their paper. This construction is almost optimal since we also prove that $d/2$ is a lower bound. Eventually, we show that both algebraic constructions can always be instantiated in large enough finite fields. Furthermore, for the important cases $d \in \{2, 3\}$, we illustrate that they perform well in practice by presenting explicit realizations for finite fields of practical interest.

Keywords: Side-channel analysis · Probing model · Bilinear complexity · Randomness complexity · Constructions · Lower bounds · Probabilistic method

J. Katz and H. Shacham (Eds.): CRYPTO 2017, Part III, LNCS 10403, pp. 397–426, 2017.
DOI: 10.1007/978-3-319-63697-9_14

1 Introduction

While most symmetric cryptographic algorithms are now assumed to be secure against classical black-box attacks (e.g., when the attacker gets the knowledge of some inputs and/or outputs), their implementation can still be vulnerable to *side-channel attacks*. These attacks, revealed by Kocher in the 1990s [19], make additional use of the physical leakage of the underlying device (e.g., temperature, power consumption, execution time, ...) during the algorithm execution to recover the secret key.

These side-channel attacks are actually very powerful both against hardware and software implementations. In practice, keys from a classical block cipher can be recovered in a few minutes on many devices. Therefore, there is a huge need in efficient and secure countermeasures. Among the many ones proposed by the community, *masking* (a.k.a. *splitting* or *sharing*) [9,16] is probably the most widely deployed. The main idea is to split each sensitive data, which depends both on the secret key and on known variables (e.g., inputs or outputs) into $d+1$ shares. The first d shares are generated uniformly at random and the last one is computed so that the combination of the $d+1$ shares with some group law $*$ is equal to the initial value. With this technique, the attacker actually needs the whole set of $d+1$ shares to learn any information on the initial value. Since each share's observation comes with noise, the higher the order d is, the more complex the attack is [9,21].

In order to evaluate the security of masking schemes, the cryptographic community has made important efforts to define leakage models which properly reflect the reality of embedded devices. In 2003 [18], Ishai, Sahai, and Wagner introduced the *d-probing model* in which the attacker can get access to the exact values of at most d intermediate variables of its choice in the targeted implementation. While in practice, the attacker has access to the noisy values of all the manipulated variables, this model may still make sense, since recovering the exact value of d variables from their noisy observations is exponentially hard in the order d. Furthermore, it is widely used for its convenience to realize security proofs. Ten years later [21], Prouff, and Rivain extended a model initially introduced by Chari et al. [9], referred to as the *noisy leakage model*. This time, the model fits the reality of embedded devices since the attacker is assumed to get the noisy observations of all the intermediate variables of the implementation. However, because it requires the manipulation of noisy data (i.e., real values), this model is not convenient to make security proofs. Fortunately, Duc, Dziembowski, and Faust [13] exhibited a reduction from the noisy leakage model to the d-probing model, later improved in practice by Duc, Faust, and Standaert [14]. In other words, they proved that if an implementation is secure in the d-probing model, then it is also secure in the realistic noisy leakage model for specific number of shares, level of noise and circuit sizes. This sequence of works makes the d-probing model both realistic and convenient to make security proofs of masking schemes. An implementation secure in the d-probing model is said to satisfy the *d-privacy property* or equivalently to be *d-private* [18].

1.1 Our Problem

For the large majority of symmetric cryptographic algorithms which manipulate Boolean values, we naturally protect their implementation using Boolean masking for which $* = \oplus$. Each sensitive data is thus split into $d+1$ shares whose Boolean addition returns the initial value.[1]

In this context, the protection of linear functions is trivial since they just need to be applied independently to each share. However, the protection of non-linear functions is more complicated since the shares cannot be manipulated independently from each other. Concretely, additional randomness is required to randomize the computations which manipulate several shares of the same data. In particular, it is not trivial to evaluate the best way to build such counter-measures while minimizing the quantity of additional randomness as well as the number of operations.

The first proposal to perform a d-private multiplication over the finite field $\mathbb{F}_2$ was made by Ishai, Sahai, and Wagner in their seminal paper [18] (further referred to as ISW multiplication). They achieved d-privacy with $d(d+1)/2$ additional random bits and $(d+1)^2$ products over $\mathbb{F}_2$. Their multiplication then became the cornerstone of a sequence of works to build more complex d-private implementations [3,10,13,14,24]. Their proposal was described to securely compute a d-private multiplication over $\mathbb{F}_2$, but it can actually be transposed to secure a multiplication over any finite field $\mathbb{F}_q$ (e.g. [15,24]) (in which case it requires $d(d+1)/2$ random field elements and $(d+1)^2$ products over $\mathbb{F}_q$). Secure implementation of multiplications over larger finite fields $\mathbb{F}_q$ (in particular for finite fields of characteristic 2), is of utmost practical interest to evaluate an S-box expressed as a polynomial over a such a finite field. For instance, it has been shown in [24] and [12] respectively that the implementation of the AES S-box (resp. the DES S-boxes) may be done with 4 (resp. 3) multiplications over $\mathbb{F}_{2^8}$ (resp. $\mathbb{F}_{2^6}$), instead of several dozens of multiplications over $\mathbb{F}_2$. However, with the order d growing up in practice for security reasons, this multiplication remains quite expensive. In particular, it consumes a large amount of randomness, which is generated by a physical source followed by a deterministic random bit generator, and it also requires a large number of multiplications, which are more expensive than linear operations.

That is why the community started to investigate more efficient d-private multiplications. Belaïd et al. [4] proposed a new d-private multiplication over the finite field $\mathbb{F}_2$ with twice as less randomness while preserving the number of multiplications. They also proved that any d-private multiplication over $\mathbb{F}_2$ requires at least d random bits and they proved a $O(d \log d)$ quasi-linear (non-constructive) upper bound for this randomness complexity. Most of their results can be readily generalized to d-private multiplication over any finite field $\mathbb{F}_{2^n}$

[1] An alternative is to apply so-called *threshold implementations* [20]. In [23], Reparaz et al. have shown that the latter implementations can be built from circuits that are made secure in the probing model. Thus, any improvement of the complexity of arithmetic circuits secure in the probing model may lead to complexity improvement for higher-order threshold implementations.

of characteristic 2 (except for the lower bound which holds only in $\mathbb{F}_2$). While their multiplication is d-private, it offers less security than the ISW one since it does not compose necessarily securely with other private circuits (see below for formal security definitions). It still can be used in symmetric algorithms to improve their performances: for instance, in the S-box of the block cipher AES defined over $\mathbb{F}_{2^8}$, three of the four multiplications can be replaced by theirs. Nevertheless, the proposal remains expensive and there is still a huge need in more efficient d-private multiplications.

1.2 Related Work

Other methods of encoding have been proposed in the literature. The *inner product masking*, proposed by Balasch et al. [2] encodes, over any finite field $\mathbb{F}_q$, the secret as a pair of vectors (L, R) such that the secret equals the inner product of L and R. In [1], this construction was enhanced by fixing a public value for L, hence allowing to achieve d-privacy using $d+1$ shares. The subsequent randomness and computation complexities for the multiplication are however still quadratic in d. Another approach, proposed by Prouff, and Roche [22] uses *polynomial masking*. Based on Shamir's secret sharing scheme, the secret is viewed as the constant coefficient of a certain polynomial, whose values when evaluated at some public points $(\alpha_i)_{i \leq d}$ constitute the shares.[2]. Though the complexity for the multiplication of the original proposal is cubic in d, Coron, Prouff, and Roche [11] achieved a complexity in $O(d^2 \log^4 d)$ for fields of characteristic 2. The recent work [17], which aims at achieving higher-order security in the presence of so-called *glitches*, is based on ISW multiplication and therefore requires $O(d^2)$ random values and field multiplications. It may moreover be noticed that this work directly benefits from the improvement proposed in [4] and in this paper.

1.3 Our Contributions

In this work, we aim to go further in the research of efficient d-private multiplications over finite fields $\mathbb{F}_q$ (where q is some prime power). Given two sharings $\boldsymbol{a} = (a_0, \ldots, a_d) \in \mathbb{F}_q^{d+1}$ and $\boldsymbol{b} = (b_0, \ldots, b_d) \in \mathbb{F}_q^{d+1}$, we aim to exhibit an output sharing $\boldsymbol{c} = (c_0, \ldots, c_d) \in \mathbb{F}_q^{d+1}$ such that

$$\sum_{i=0}^{d} c_i = \left(\sum_{i=0}^{d} a_i \right) \cdot \left(\sum_{i=0}^{d} b_i \right)$$

where the sum and product denote $\mathbb{F}_q$ operations. The computation of this sharing $\boldsymbol{c}$ should achieve the d-privacy (and actually will achieve a stronger security

[2] It may be remarked that the inner product masking with fixed public values for L is very close to polynomial masking, where R plays a similar role as the tuple of polynomial evaluations and where L plays a similar role as the reconstruction vector (deduced from the public values $(\alpha_i)_{i \leq d}$).

notion) with the use of a minimal number of random $\mathbb{F}_q$ elements and a minimal number of products in $\mathbb{F}_q$.

Extending the work of Belaïd et al. [4], we first present an algebraic characterization for privacy in the d-probing model for multiplication in any finite field. Contrary to the work done in [4] in which the authors limited themselves to multiplications based on the sum of shares' products, in this paper, we extend the possibilities by authorizing products of sums of shares.

As mentioned above, the scheme proposed by Belaïd et al. offers less security than the original ISW proposal since it does not compose necessarily securely with other private circuits. It is thus necessary to consider new security properties which strengthen the d-privacy. The introduction of such properties was made by Barthe, Belaïd, Dupressoir, Fouque, Grégoire, Strub, and Zucchini in [3], under the name of *non-interference*, *tight non-interference*, and *strong non-interference* (see Sect. 2 for formal definitions and for a comparison of these notions).

We then propose a novel algebraic characterization for *non-interference* in the d-probing model for multiplication in any finite field (and actually for any bivariate function over a finite field, as long as intermediate values are linear in the randomness and linear or bilinear in the inputs).

Theorem 3.5 ***(informal).*** A multiplication algorithm is non-interfering in the d-probing model if and only if there does not exist a set of $\ell \leq d$ intermediate results $\{p_1, \ldots, p_\ell\}$ and a $\mathbb{F}_q$-linear combination of $\{p_1, \ldots, p_\ell\}$ that can be written as

$$\boldsymbol{a}^\intercal \cdot \boldsymbol{M} \cdot \boldsymbol{b} + \boldsymbol{a}^\intercal \cdot \boldsymbol{\mu} + \boldsymbol{\nu}^\intercal \cdot \boldsymbol{b} + \tau,$$

where $\boldsymbol{M} \in \mathbb{F}_q^{(d+1)\times(d+1)}$, $\boldsymbol{\mu}, \boldsymbol{\nu} \in \mathbb{F}_q^{d+1}$, and $\tau \in \mathbb{F}_q$, and all the rows of the matrix $(\boldsymbol{M}|\boldsymbol{\mu}) \in \mathbb{F}_q^{(d+1)\times(d+2)}$ or the matrix $(\boldsymbol{M}^\intercal|\boldsymbol{\nu}) \in \mathbb{F}_q^{(d+1)\times(d+2)}$ are non-zero.

We then present two generic algebraic constructions of multiplication circuits in finite fields (based on this characterization) that achieve non-interference in the d-probing model. Both constructions are explicit and improve the complexity of previous proposals and their security is ensured as soon as some matrices satisfy some precise linear algebraic condition.

The first proposal (Algorithm 4) aims at reducing the number of *bilinear* multiplications (i.e., of general multiplications of two non-constant values in the finite field). The scheme requires only $2d+1$ bilinear multiplications whereas all previous proposals need $O(d^2)$ such multiplications (at the cost of increasing the number of linear multiplications, i.e. multiplications by some constant). This leads to an important efficiency improvement in practice since bilinear multiplications over $\mathbb{F}_q$ cannot be tabulated for $q \geqslant 2^6$ (such a tabulation indeed requires $\log_2(q)q^2$ bits of ROM memory which is quickly too high for constrained devices), while multiplications by a constant can often be tabulated as long as $q \leqslant 2^{10}$ (such a tabulation indeed requires $\log_2(q)q$ bits of ROM memory). When the processing cannot be tabulated, it must be computed on-the-fly, which implies a non-negligible timing penalty: for instance a multiplication over $\mathbb{F}_{2^8}$ based on *log-alog* tables[3] would take around 40 CPU cycles on a classical AVR 8-bit architecture, while a direct lookup table access only takes 2 cycles (see [6] for more details about the different time/memory trade-offs for the multiplication processing). Additionally, our new scheme (Algorithm 4) achieves the strong non-interference security notion (Theorem 4.3) and composes therefore securely with other private circuits.

The goal of the second construction (Algorithm 5) is to reduce the randomness complexity; it needs only d random elements in the underlying finite field (improving the non-constructive upper bound $O(d \log d)$ proven in [4]). This constitutes an important improvement both from a theoretical and practical point of views since the generation of random values on a constrained device may be very time-consuming. Our second proposal achieves the non-interference security notion (which is stronger than the privacy notion achieved in [4]).

We show (using the probabilistic method) that both algebraic constructions can always be instantiated in large enough finite fields (Theorems 4.5 and 5.4). The second construction is almost optimal (for randomness complexity) since from our algebraic characterization, we can deduce the following lower bound on the randomness complexity:

Proposition 5.6 ***(informal).*** A non-interfering multiplication algorithm in the d-probing model uses more than $\lfloor (d-1)/2 \rfloor$ random elements in $\mathbb{F}_q$.

With our upper-bound, this proposition shows that the randomness complexity is therefore in $\Theta(d)$. These asymptotic results provide strong theoretical insights on the complexity of private multiplication. However, we also show that our constructions perform well in practice. In particular, for the important cases $d \in \{2, 3\}$, that are used in real-world implementations, we present explicit realizations of our constructions for finite fields of practical interest (and in particular for $\mathbb{F}_{2^8}$ used by the AES).

In terms of performance, we also compared the efficiency of our proposed constructions with the state of the art [4], for the practical masking orders $d \in \{2, 3\}$ and the finite field $\mathbb{F}_{2^8}$. The simulations have been done on a classical AVR 8-bit architecture; for different timing complexities of randomness generation[4] and of field multiplication, we measured the number of CPU cycles necessary to run the algorithms.

For $d = 2$ and a field multiplication taking 45 CPU cycles,[5] the proposal of [4] is more efficient, as soon as the generation of a random byte takes more than 7 cycles. In the event where this generation is shorter, our Algorithm 4 (Sect. 4.1)

---

[3] More precisely, the non-zero field elements to multiplied are first represented as powers of a primitive element α such that $z = x \times y$ becomes $\alpha^c = \alpha^{a+b}$ with $(x, y, z) = (\alpha^a, \alpha^b, \alpha^c)$. The mappings $x \to \alpha^a$, $y \to \alpha^b$ and $\alpha^c \to z$ have been tabulated for efficiency reasons. The particular case $x = 0$ or $y = 0$ has been treated with care to not introduce timing dependency.

[4] For comparison/testing purpose, we did not call the device random generator but, instead, simulated the generation by a software code.

[5] This timing corresponds to a code written in assembly and involving log-alog look-up tables.

is better. Algorithm 5 (Sect. 5.1) is, in this case, always worse than the state of the art proposal, but it still outperforms Algorithm 4 as soon as the generation of random takes more than 12 cycles.

When the masking order is $d = 3$, Algorithm 4 is better when the random generation takes less than 16 cycles. Then, the algorithm of [4] is better when this number is lower than 60. Finally, Algorithm 5 outperforms both other constructions when the generation takes more than 60 cycles.

Similarly, we ran several simulations studying the impact of the complexity of the multiplication on our constructions. By fixing at 20 the number of cycles for the random generation, we observed that Algorithm 4 outperforms state of the art algorithms when the multiplication takes more than 6 cycles (resp. 93 cycles) for $d = 2$ (resp. $d = 3$). A comparison of the complexities of state of the art algorithms and our new proposals can be found in Table 1.

Table 1. Complexities of ISW, EC16, our new d-private compression gadget for multiplication and our specific gadgets at several orders

Complexities	ISW	EC16 [4]/small cases	Algorithm 4	Algorithm 5
Second-order masking ($d = 2$)				
Sums	12	12 / 10	38	12
Linear products	0	0 / 0	8	6
Products	9	9 / 9	5	9
Random scalars	3	3 / 2	9	2
Third-order masking ($d = 3$)				
Sums	24	22 / 20	84	24
Linear products	0	0 / 0	18	12
Products	16	16 / 16	7	16
Random scalars	6	5 / 4	21	3
Fourth-order masking ($d = 4$)				
Sums	40	38 / 30	148	40
Linear products	0	0 / 0	32	20
Products	25	25 / 25	9	25
Random scalars	10	8 / 5	38	4
d^{th}-order masking				
Sums	$2d(d+1)$	$\begin{cases} d(7d+10)/4 & (d \text{ even}) \\ (7d+1)(d+1)/4 & (d \text{ odd}) \end{cases}$	$9d^2 + d$	$2d(d+1)$
Linear products	0	0	$2d^2$	$d(d+1)$
Products	$(d+1)^2$	$(d+1)^2$	$2d+1$	$(d+1)^2$
Random scalars	$d(d+1)/2$	$\begin{cases} d^2/4 + d & (d \text{ even}) \\ (d^2-1)/4 + d & (d \text{ odd}) \end{cases}$	$2d^2 + \frac{d(d-1)}{2}$	d

2 Preliminaries

This section defines notation and basic notions that we use in this paper.

2.1 Notation

For a finite set S, we denote by $|S|$ its cardinality, and by $s \xleftarrow{\$} S$ the operation of picking up an element s of S uniformly at random. We denote by $\mathbb{F}_q$ the finite field with q elements. Vectors are denoted by lower case bold font letters, and matrices are denoted by bold font letters. All vectors are column vectors unless otherwise specified. The *image* of the linear map associated to a matrix $\boldsymbol{M}$ is denoted by $\mathrm{im}(\boldsymbol{M})$. For a vector $\boldsymbol{x}$, we denote by x_i its i-th coordinate and by $\mathsf{hw}(\boldsymbol{x})$ its Hamming weight (i.e., the number of its coordinates that are different from 0). When double indexing will be needed, we shall denote by $x_{i,j}$ the j-th coordinate of the vector $\boldsymbol{x}_i$. For vectors $\boldsymbol{x}_1, \ldots, \boldsymbol{x}_t$ in $\mathbb{F}_q^n$, we denote $\langle \boldsymbol{x}_1, \ldots, \boldsymbol{x}_t \rangle$ the vector space generated by the set $\{\boldsymbol{x}_1, \ldots, \boldsymbol{x}_t\}$.

The *probability density function* associated to a discrete random variable X defined over S (e.g., $\mathbb{F}_q$) is the function which maps $x \in S$ to $\Pr[X = x]$. It is denoted by $\{X\}$ or by $\{X\}_r$ if there is a need to specify the randomness source r over which the *distribution* is considered.

Throughout the rest of this paper, when not specified, we consider the elements to belong to the finite field $\mathbb{F}_q$ for some prime power q. Some of our results require q to be larger than some lower bound that is then specified in the corresponding statements. We denote by $r \leftarrow \$$ the fact of sampling a fresh uniform element from $\mathbb{F}_q$ and assigning it to r.

2.2 Arithmetic Circuits and Privacy

An arithmetic circuit C is a directed acyclic graph whose vertices are input gates, output gates, addition gates, multiplication gates, or constant-scalar gates (over $\mathbb{F}_q$) and whose edges are wires carrying the inputs/outputs of the operations performed by the vertices. A constant-scalar gate is parameterized by a scalar $\gamma \in \mathbb{F}_q$, has fan-in 0, and outputs γ. A *randomized circuit* is a circuit augmented with random-scalar gates. A random-scalar gate is a gate with fan-in 0 that produces a random scalar in $\mathbb{F}_q$ and sends it along its output wire; the scalar is selected uniformly and independently of everything else afresh for each invocation of the circuit.

For a circuit C, we denote by $(y_1, y_2, \ldots) \leftarrow C(x_1, x_2, \ldots)$ the operation of running C on inputs $(x_1, x_2, \ldots)$ and letting $(y_1, y_2, \ldots)$ denote the outputs. Moreover, if C is *randomized*, we denote by $(y_1, y_2, \ldots) \xleftarrow{\$} C(x_1, x_2, \ldots)$ the operation of running C on inputs $(x_1, x_2, \ldots)$ and with uniform fresh randomness. When we will need to specify this randomness we shall use the notation $(y_1, y_2, \ldots) \leftarrow C(x_1, x_2, \ldots; r)$. Eventually, for any subset P of wires in C, we denote by $C_P(x_1, x_2, \ldots; r)$ (or $C_P(x_1, x_2, \ldots)$ if the randomness is not specified) the list of values on the wires in P.

We hereafter give a formal definition of the notion of *gadget* used in prior works (e.g., [15]).

Definition 2.1 (gadget). *Let n, m be two positive integers and f be a function from $\mathbb{F}_q^n$ to $\mathbb{F}_q^m$. Let u, v be two positive integers. A (u,v)-*gadget for f *is an arithmetic (randomized) circuit C such that for every tuple $(\boldsymbol{x}_1, \boldsymbol{x}_2, \ldots, \boldsymbol{x}_n)^\mathsf{T} \in (\mathbb{F}_q^u)^n$ and every randomness r, $(\boldsymbol{y}_1, \boldsymbol{y}_2, \ldots, \boldsymbol{y}_m)^\mathsf{T} \leftarrow C(\boldsymbol{x}_1, \boldsymbol{x}_2, \ldots, \boldsymbol{x}_n; r)$ satisfies*

$$\left(\sum_{j=1}^{v} y_{1,j}, \sum_{j=1}^{v} y_{2,j}, \ldots, \sum_{j=1}^{v} y_{m,j}\right)^\mathsf{T} = f\left(\sum_{j=1}^{u} x_{1,j}, \sum_{j=1}^{u} x_{2,j}, \ldots, \sum_{j=1}^{u} x_{n,j}\right).$$

We usually define $x_i = \sum_{j=1}^{u} x_{i,j}$ and $y_i = \sum_{j=i}^{v} y_{i,j}$. The element $x_{i,j}$ (resp. $y_{i,j}$) is called the j-th *share* of x_i (resp. y_i).

Let us now define the notion of privacy for a gadget.

Definition 2.2 (d-private gadget). *Let n be a positive integer and let f be a function defined over $\mathbb{F}_q^n$. Let u and v be two positive integers. A (u,v)-gadget C for f is* d-private *if and only if for any set P of d wires in C, the distribution $\{C_P(\boldsymbol{x}_1, \boldsymbol{x}_2, \ldots, \boldsymbol{x}_n; r) \mid \forall i \in \{1, \ldots, n\},\ \sum_{j=1}^{u} x_{i,j} = x_i\}_{\boldsymbol{x}_1, \boldsymbol{x}_2, \cdots, \boldsymbol{x}_n, r}$ is the same for every $(x_1, x_2, \ldots, x_n)^\mathsf{T} \in \mathbb{F}_q^n$.*

Remark 2.3. In Definition 2.2, we recall that x_i denotes the i-th input of f, while $\boldsymbol{x}_i$ represents a sharing of x_i.

Remark 2.4. When there is no ambiguity, and for simplicity, the mention of the privacy order d will sometimes be omitted.

From now on, and to clarify the link with the *probing attack model* introduced in [18], the wires in a set P used to attack an implementation are referred as the *probes* and the corresponding values in $C_P(\ldots; r)$ as the *intermediate results.* To simplify the descriptions, a probe p is sometimes used to directly denote the corresponding intermediate result. When the inputs w and the circuit C are clear from the context, the distribution $\{C_P(\boldsymbol{x}_1, \ldots, \boldsymbol{x}_n; r)\}_r$ is simplified to $\{(p)_{p \in P}\}$.

2.3 Compositional Security Notions

A (u,w)-gadget for the function $f \circ f'$ can be obviously built by composing a (v,w)-gadget of f and a (u,v)-gadget of f'. However, the composition $C \circ C'$ of two d-private gadgets C and C' is not necessarily itself d-private. For the latter to hold, gadget C' must satisfy a property which strengthens the privacy. The introduction of such a property has been made by Barthe et al. in [3]. Before recalling their definitions, we first need to introduce the notion of *t-simulatability.*

Definition 2.5 (t-simulatability). *Let u and v be two positive integers. Let C be a (u,v)-gadget for a function defined over $\mathbb{F}_q^n$. For some positive integers ℓ and t, a set $P = \{p_1, \ldots, p_\ell\}$ of ℓ probes on C is* t-simulatable, *if* *there exist n sets I_1, I_2, ..., I_n of at most t indices in $\{1, \dots, u\}$ and a randomized function* sim *defined from $(\mathbb{F}_q^t)^n$ to $\mathbb{F}_q^\ell$ such that for any fixed tuple $(\boldsymbol{x}_1, \boldsymbol{x}_2, \dots, \boldsymbol{x}_n) \in (\mathbb{F}_q^u)^n$, the distributions $\{p_1, \dots, p_\ell\}$ (which implicitly depends on $(\boldsymbol{x}_1, \boldsymbol{x}_2, \dots, \boldsymbol{x}_n)$, and the random values used by the gadget) and $\{\mathsf{sim}((x_{1,i})_{i \in I_1}, (x_{2,i})_{i \in I_2}, \dots, (x_{n,i})_{i \in I_n})\}$ are identical.*

Remark 2.6. The notation $\mathsf{sim}((x_{1,i})_{i \in I_1}, (x_{2,i})_{i \in I_2}, \dots, (x_{n,i})_{i \in I_n})$ will be simplified to $\mathsf{sim}(\boldsymbol{x}_{I_1}, \boldsymbol{x}_{I_2}, \dots, \boldsymbol{x}_{I_n})$. Moreover, depending on the context, we will sometimes call a t-simulatable set of probes, a set of probes which can be simulated with at most t shares of each of the n inputs of the gadget (which is an equivalent definition).

We now provide the notions of security that we will be using throughout the rest of the paper.

Definition 2.7 (d-non-interference). *A (u, v)-gadget C for a function f defined over $\mathbb{F}_q^n$ is* d-non-interfering (or d-NI) *if and only if every set of at most d probes can be simulated with at most d shares of each of its n inputs.*

Definition 2.8 (d-tight non-interference) *[3]. A gadget C is* d-tight non-interfering (or d-TNI) *if and only if every set of $t \leq d$ probes can be simulated with at most t shares of each input.*

Definition 2.9 (d-strong non-interference). *A (u, v)-gadget C for a function f defined over $\mathbb{F}_q^n$ is* d-strong non-interfering (or d-SNI) *if and only if for every set P_1 of d_1 probes on internal wires (i.e., no output wires nor output shares) and every set P_2 of d_2 probes on output shares such that $d_1 + d_2 \leq d$, the set $P_1 \cup P_2$ of probes can be simulated by only d_1 shares of each of its n inputs.*

The d-SNI property is stronger than the d-NI property, which is itself stronger than the d-privacy property. The relations between all these notions are discussed in more details below.

2.4 Relations Between Compositional Security Notions

We recall that, from [3], if C is d-SNI (see Definition 2.9), then it is d-NI (see Definition 2.7); and if it is d-NI, then it is d-private. But a d-private gadget is not necessarily d-NI (see the counterexample given in [4, Appendix B]), and a d-NI gadget is not necessarily d-SNI (see for instance gadgets implementing SecMult in [24] or Algorithm 3 in [4]). Furthermore, in [4, Proposition 7.4], it is proven that d-NI and d-TNI are equivalent. These relations are depicted in Fig. 1.

From [3], the composition of a d-TNI (or d-NI) gadget with a d-SNI[6] is d-SNI, while the composition of d-TNI gadgets is not necessarily d-NI. This implies that d-SNI gadgets can be directly composed while maintaining the d-privacy property, whereas a d-SNI *refreshing* gadget (which randomizes the shares of its inputs using fresh random values) must sometimes be involved before the composition of d-NI gadgets.

[6] The inputs of the final gadget correspond to the inputs of the d-TNI one, while the outputs of the final gadget correspond to the outputs of the d-SNI one.

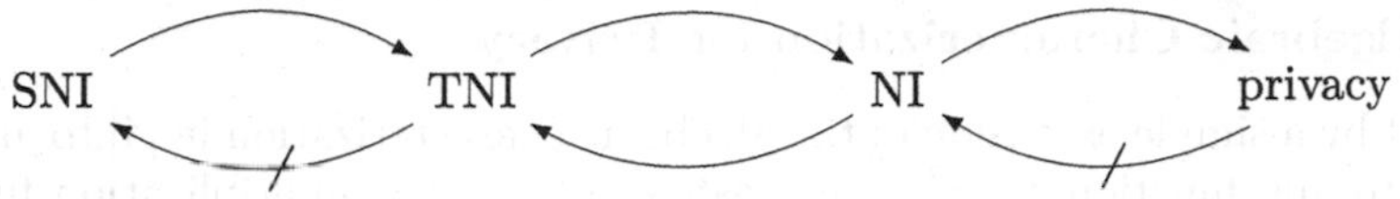

Fig. 1. Relations between privacy, NI, TNI, and SNI (normal arrows are implications, strike out arrows are separations)

2.5 Case of Study

In this paper, we focus on the construction of efficient d-NI or d-SNI multiplication gadgets over $\mathbb{F}_q$ for any order d.

Definition 2.10 (multiplication gadget). *A* multiplication (u, v)-gadget *is a (u, v)-gadget C for the function $f : (a, b) \in \mathbb{F}_q^2 \mapsto a \cdot b \in \mathbb{F}_q$.*

Remark 2.11. When the sharing orders u and v will be clear from the context, the term (u, v) will be omitted.

In the sequel, the two inputs of a multiplication (u, v)-gadget C are denoted by a and b. Their respective sharings are thus denoted by $\boldsymbol{a} = (a_0, \ldots, a_{u-1})^\intercal \in \mathbb{F}_q^u$ and $\boldsymbol{b} = (b_0, \ldots, b_{u-1})^\intercal \in \mathbb{F}_q^u$. The output is denoted by c and its sharing is denoted by $\boldsymbol{c} = (c_0, \ldots, c_{v-1})^\intercal \in \mathbb{F}_q^v$. We also denote by $\boldsymbol{r} = (r_1, \ldots, r_R)^\intercal \in \mathbb{F}_q^R$ the vector of the random scalars that are involved in the gadget C. Thus, any intermediate result, a.k.a. probe, in the evaluation of C is a function of $a_0, \ldots, a_{u-1}, b_0, \ldots, b_{u-1}, r_1, \ldots, r_R$.

3 Algebraic Characterizations

This section aims at introducing algebraic characterizations for the privacy and the non-interference properties of a multiplication $(d + 1, v)$-gadget (for some positive integers d and v) over $\mathbb{F}_q$.

3.1 Bilinear Probes and Matrix Notation

For our algebraic characterizations, we focus on specific probes we call *bilinear probes*.

Definition 3.1. *Let C be a $(d + 1, v)$-gadget for a function f: $\mathbb{F}_q^2 \to \mathbb{F}_q$. A bilinear probe p is a probe on C (and thus an expression of $a_0, \ldots, a_d, b_0, \ldots, b_d$, $r_1, \ldots, r_R$), which is an affine functions of a_ib_j, a_i, b_j and r_k (for $0 \leq i, j \leq d$ and $1 \leq k \leq R$). In other words, a bilinear probe p can be written as:*

$$\boldsymbol{a}^\intercal \cdot \boldsymbol{M_p} \cdot \boldsymbol{b} + \boldsymbol{a}^\intercal \cdot \boldsymbol{\mu}_p + \boldsymbol{\nu}_p^\intercal \cdot \boldsymbol{b} + \boldsymbol{\sigma}_p^\intercal \cdot \boldsymbol{r} + \tau_p,$$

where $M_p \in \mathbb{F}_q^{(d+1)\times(d+1)}$, $\boldsymbol{\mu}_p \in \mathbb{F}_q^{d+1}$, $\boldsymbol{\nu}_p \in \mathbb{F}_q^{d+1}$, $\boldsymbol{\sigma}_p \in \mathbb{F}_q^R$, and $\tau_p \in \mathbb{F}_q$.

In the following sections we shall say that an expression $f(x_1, \ldots, x_n, r)$ functionally depends on the variable r if there exists $a_1, \ldots, a_n$ such that the function $r \mapsto f(a_1, \ldots, a_n, r)$ is not constant.

3.2 Algebraic Characterization for Privacy

We start by a simple extension of the algebraic characterization in [4] to any field $\mathbb{F}_q$ and to any function $f\colon \mathbb{F}_q^2 \to \mathbb{F}_q$ instead of just the multiplication function $f(a,b) = a \cdot b$ (however, please note that our characterization consider only bilinear probes). We consider the following condition:

Condition 3.1. *Let C be a $(d+1, v)$-gadget for a two-input function $f\colon \mathbb{F}_q^2 \to \mathbb{F}_q$. A set of bilinear probes $P = \{p_1, \ldots, p_\ell\}$ on C satisfies Condition 3.1 if and only if there exists a vector $\boldsymbol{\lambda} \in \mathbb{F}_q^\ell$ such that the expression $\sum_{i=1}^{\ell} \lambda_i p_i$ can be written as*

$$\sum_{i=1}^{\ell} \lambda_i p_i = \boldsymbol{a}^\intercal \cdot \boldsymbol{M} \cdot \boldsymbol{b} \,+\, \boldsymbol{a}^\intercal \cdot \boldsymbol{\mu} \,+\, \boldsymbol{\nu}^\intercal \cdot \boldsymbol{b} \,+\, \tau\,,$$

where $M \in \mathbb{F}_q^{(d+1)\times(d+1)}$, $\boldsymbol{\mu} \in \mathbb{F}_q^{d+1}$, $\boldsymbol{\nu} \in \mathbb{F}_q^{d+1}$, and $\tau \in \mathbb{F}_q$, and such that the all-one vector $\boldsymbol{u}_{d+1} = (1, \ldots, 1)^\intercal \in \mathbb{F}_q^{d+1}$ is in the affine space $\boldsymbol{\mu} + \operatorname{im}(\boldsymbol{M})$ or $\boldsymbol{\nu} + \operatorname{im}(\boldsymbol{M}^\intercal)$, where $\operatorname{im}(\boldsymbol{M})$ is the column space of $\boldsymbol{M}$.

We point out that, using notation of the above condition, for any set of bilinear probes $P = \{p_1, \ldots, p_\ell\}$ on C and any $\boldsymbol{\lambda} \in \mathbb{F}_q^\ell$, the expression $\sum_{i=1}^{\ell} \lambda_i p_i$ can be written as

$$\sum_{i=1}^{\ell} \lambda_i p_i = \boldsymbol{a}^\intercal \cdot \boldsymbol{M}_{\boldsymbol{\lambda}} \cdot \boldsymbol{b} \,+\, \boldsymbol{a}^\intercal \cdot \boldsymbol{\mu}_{\boldsymbol{\lambda}} \,+\, \boldsymbol{\nu}_{\boldsymbol{\lambda}}^\intercal \cdot \boldsymbol{b} \,+\, \boldsymbol{\sigma}_{\boldsymbol{\lambda}}^\intercal \cdot \boldsymbol{r} \,+\, \tau_{\boldsymbol{\lambda}}\,, \tag{1}$$

where $M_{\boldsymbol{\lambda}} \in \mathbb{F}_q^{(d+1)\times(d+1)}$, $\boldsymbol{\mu}_{\boldsymbol{\lambda}} \in \mathbb{F}_q^{d+1}$, $\boldsymbol{\nu}_{\boldsymbol{\lambda}} \in \mathbb{F}_q^{d+1}$, $\boldsymbol{\sigma}_{\boldsymbol{\lambda}} \in \mathbb{F}_q^{R}$, and $\tau_{\boldsymbol{\lambda}} \in \mathbb{F}_q$. Condition 3.1 is therefore equivalent to asking that there exists $\boldsymbol{\lambda} \in \mathbb{F}_q^\ell$ such that:

$$\boldsymbol{\sigma}_{\boldsymbol{\lambda}} = \boldsymbol{0} \quad \text{and} \quad \boldsymbol{u}_{d+1} \in (\boldsymbol{\mu}_{\boldsymbol{\lambda}} + \operatorname{im}(\boldsymbol{M}_{\boldsymbol{\lambda}})) \cup (\boldsymbol{\nu}_{\boldsymbol{\lambda}} + \operatorname{im}(\boldsymbol{M}_{\boldsymbol{\lambda}}^\intercal)).$$

Theorem 3.2. *Let C be a $(d+1, v)$-gadget for a two-input function $f\colon \mathbb{F}_q^2 \to \mathbb{F}_q$. Let P be a set of bilinear probes on C. Then P satisfies Condition 3.1 if and only if there exist $a^{(0)}, b^{(0)}, a^{(1)}, b^{(1)} \in \mathbb{F}_q$, such that:*

$$\{(p)_{p\in P} \mid (a,b) = (a^{(0)}, b^{(0)})\} \neq \{(p)_{p\in P} \mid (a,b) = (a^{(1)}, b^{(1)})\}.$$

That is, the distribution $\{(p)_{p\in P}\}$ does depend on the value of (a,b).

The proof essentially uses the same ideas as the proof of Theorem A.1 of [4] and is detailed in the full version.

Remark 3.3. We do not restrict the size of the set P. Furthermore, the proof does not rely on the correctness property of C.

Corollary 3.4. *Let C be a $(d+1, v)$-gadget for a two-input function $f\colon \mathbb{F}_q^2 \to \mathbb{F}_q$. We suppose that any possible probe on C is bilinear. Then, C is d-private if and only if there does not exist any set P of d probes on C satisfying Condition 3.1.*

Proof. The proof is straightforward from Theorem 3.2. □

When $q = 2$ and when $f(a, b) = a \cdot b$, this corollary is actually equivalent to Theorem A.1 of [5]. Contrary to this former theorem, we only need to consider set of exactly d probes, as Condition 3.1 allows for discarding some probes (by choosing $\lambda_i = 0$). Furthermore, the gadget C has at least $2d + 2 \geq d$ possible probes: $a_0, \ldots, a_d, b_0, \ldots, b_d$. Thus, any set $\ell < d$ probes can be completed into a set of d probes.

3.3 Algebraic Characterization for Non-Interference

In this subsection, we introduce a novel algebraic characterization for Non-Interference (NI). We consider the following condition:

Condition 3.2. *Let C be a $(d + 1, v)$-gadget for a two-input function $f\colon \mathbb{F}_q^2 \to \mathbb{F}_q$. A set of bilinear probes $P = \{p_1, \ldots, p_\ell\}$ on C satisfies Condition 3.2 if and only if there exists $\boldsymbol{\lambda} \in \mathbb{F}_q^\ell$ such that the expression $\sum_{i=1}^{\ell} \lambda_i p_i$ can be written as*

$$\sum_{i=1}^{\ell} \lambda_i p_i = \boldsymbol{a}^\mathsf{T} \cdot \boldsymbol{M} \cdot \boldsymbol{b} \; + \; \boldsymbol{a}^\mathsf{T} \cdot \boldsymbol{\mu} \; + \; \boldsymbol{\nu}^\mathsf{T} \cdot \boldsymbol{b} \; + \; \tau,$$

where $\boldsymbol{M} \in \mathbb{F}_q^{(d+1)\times(d+1)}$, $\boldsymbol{\mu} \in \mathbb{F}_q^{d+1}$, $\boldsymbol{\nu} \in \mathbb{F}_q^{d+1}$, and $\tau \in \mathbb{F}_q$, and such that all the rows of the matrix $\begin{pmatrix}\boldsymbol{M} & \boldsymbol{\mu}\end{pmatrix} \in \mathbb{F}_q^{(d+1)\times(d+2)}$ (which is the concatenation of the matrix $\boldsymbol{M}$ and the column vector μ) are non-zero or all the columns of the matrix $\begin{pmatrix}\boldsymbol{M} \\ \boldsymbol{\nu}^\mathsf{T}\end{pmatrix} \in \mathbb{F}_q^{(d+2)\times(d+1)}$ are non-zero.

We recall that, using notation of the above condition, for any set of bilinear probes $P = \{p_1, \ldots, p_\ell\}$ on C and any $\boldsymbol{\lambda} \in \mathbb{F}_q^\ell$, the expression $\sum_{i=1}^{\ell} \lambda_i p_i$ can be written as in Eq. 1. Therefore, Condition 3.2 is equivalent to asking that there exists $\boldsymbol{\lambda} \in \mathbb{F}_q^\ell$ such that $\sum_{i=1}^{\ell} \lambda_i p_i$ is functionally independent from any r_k $(0 \leq k \leq R)$ and functionally depends on every a_i $(0 \leq i \leq d)$ or on every b_j $(0 \leq j \leq d)$. This condition is therefore quite natural.

Theorem 3.5. *Let C be a $(d{+}1, v)$-gadget for a two-input function $f\colon \mathbb{F}_q^2 \to \mathbb{F}_q$. Let P be a set of bilinear probes on C. Then if P satisfies Condition 3.2, P is not d-simulatable. Furthermore, if P is not d-simulatable and $q > d + 1$, then P satisfies Condition 3.2.*

We point out that the first part of the theorem does not require $q > d + 1$. As the second part is used for constructions while the first part is used for lower bounds, the restriction $q > d + 1$ is never an issue in our paper.

Proof. Let us start by proving the first direction, the second being more complex.

Direction 1: Left to right. By contrapositive, let us assume that there exists a set $P = \{p_1, \ldots, p_\ell\}$ of probes that satisfies Condition 3.2: that is, there exists $\lambda \in \mathbb{F}_q^\ell$ such that the sum $\sum_{i=1}^{\ell} \lambda_i p_i$ can be written as:

$$s = \sum_{i=1}^{\ell} \lambda_i p_i = \boldsymbol{a}^\intercal \cdot \boldsymbol{M} \cdot \boldsymbol{b} + \boldsymbol{a}^\intercal \cdot \boldsymbol{\mu} + \boldsymbol{\nu}^\intercal \cdot \boldsymbol{b},$$

and, without loss of generality, such that all the rows of the matrix $M' = (\boldsymbol{M}\ \boldsymbol{\mu}) \in \mathbb{F}_q^{(d+1)\times(d+2)}$ are non-zero, meaning that s *does* functionally depend on every a_i but *does not* functionally depend on any r_i.

Then, assume that the set P can be simulated with at most d values of the a_i's, e.g., using only $a_1, \ldots, a_d$, and let us further assume that the simulator has access to all the b_i's. That is, there exists a randomized function sim that takes as inputs $(a_1, \ldots, a_d)$ and $(b_0, \ldots, b_d)$ such that the distribution $\mathsf{sim}(a_1, \ldots, a_d, b_0, \ldots, b_d)$ is exactly the same as the distribution P.

Since s functionally depends on a_0, there exist specific values $a_1, \ldots, a_d$, $b_0, \ldots, b_d$ such that the function:

$$f_{(a_1,\ldots,a_d,b_1,\ldots,b_d)} : a_0 \mapsto \boldsymbol{a}^\intercal \cdot \boldsymbol{M} \cdot \boldsymbol{b} + \boldsymbol{a}^\intercal \cdot \boldsymbol{\mu} + \boldsymbol{\nu}^\intercal \cdot \boldsymbol{b},$$

is not constant, by definition of s functionally depending on a_0.

Therefore, since $\mathsf{sim}(a_1, \ldots, a_d, b_0, \ldots, b_d)$ does not depend on a_0, it is impossible that it perfectly simulates the distribution P. This implies that one cannot simulate such a set of probes with at most d shares of each input and concludes the proof of this first direction.

Direction 2: Right to left. Let us now consider a set $P = \{p_1, \ldots, p_\ell\}$ of bilinear probes that cannot be simulated with at most d shares of each input. Probes in P being bilinear, any linear combination of these probes can be written as

$$s_\lambda = \sum_{i=1}^{\ell} \lambda_i p_i = \boldsymbol{a}^\intercal \cdot \boldsymbol{M}_\lambda \cdot \boldsymbol{b} + \boldsymbol{a}^\intercal \cdot \boldsymbol{\mu}_\lambda + \boldsymbol{\nu}_\lambda^\intercal \cdot \boldsymbol{b} + \boldsymbol{\sigma}_\lambda^\intercal \cdot \boldsymbol{r},$$

by definition. We want to show that, since P cannot be simulated with at most d shares of each input, there exists a particular λ such that $\boldsymbol{\sigma}_\lambda = \boldsymbol{0}$ and all the rows of $(\boldsymbol{M}_\lambda\ \boldsymbol{\mu}_\lambda)$ are non-zero or all the columns of $\begin{pmatrix} \boldsymbol{M}_\lambda \\ \boldsymbol{\nu}_\lambda^\intercal \end{pmatrix}$ are non-zero.

Let us once again consider the matrix $\boldsymbol{S} \in \mathbb{F}_q^{\ell \times R}$ whose coefficients $s_{i,j}$ are defined as $s_{i,j} = \alpha$ if and only if p_i can be written as $\alpha r_j + z_i$ where z_i does not functionally depend on r_j. That is, if we write $p_i = \boldsymbol{a}^\intercal \cdot \boldsymbol{M}_{p_i} \cdot \boldsymbol{b} + \boldsymbol{a}^\intercal \cdot \boldsymbol{\mu}_i + \boldsymbol{\nu}_i^\intercal \cdot \boldsymbol{b} + \boldsymbol{s}_{p_i}^\intercal \cdot \boldsymbol{r}$, the i-th row of $\boldsymbol{S}$ is $\boldsymbol{s}_{p_i}^\intercal$. We can permute the columns of $\boldsymbol{S}$ and the rows of $\boldsymbol{r}$ such that a row reduction on the matrix $\boldsymbol{S}$ yields a matrix of the form:

$$\boldsymbol{S}' = \begin{pmatrix} \boldsymbol{0}_{t,t} & \boldsymbol{0}_{t,\ell-t} \\ \boldsymbol{I}_t & \boldsymbol{S}'' \end{pmatrix}.$$

Again, it is clear that since the distribution $\{p_1, \ldots, p_\ell\}$ cannot be simulated with at most d shares of each input, we have $t > 0$. Indeed, otherwise we can simply simulate all probes by uniformly random values (and thus do not even need shares of the input). Let $\boldsymbol{N}$ be the invertible matrix in $\mathbb{F}_q^{\ell\times\ell}$ such that $\boldsymbol{N}\cdot\boldsymbol{S}=\boldsymbol{S}'$. We write $(p'_1,\dots,p'_\ell)^\intercal=\boldsymbol{N}\cdot\boldsymbol{p}$. Then, the distribution $\{p'_1,\dots,p'_\ell\}$ also cannot be simulated with at most d shares of each input. In addition, for $t<i\leq\ell$, p'_i does functionally depend on r_i and no other p'_j does functionally depend on r_j (due to the shape of $\boldsymbol{S}'$). Therefore, it is immediate that these probes can be simulated by setting them to uniformly random values, and thus the distribution $\{p'_1,\dots,p'_t\}$ also cannot be simulated with at most d shares of each input.

We remark that $(p'_1,\dots,p'_t)$ does not functionally depend on any random bit, due to the shape of $\boldsymbol{S}'$. Therefore, for each $1\leq i\leq t$, we can write:

$$p'_i=\boldsymbol{a}^\intercal\cdot\boldsymbol{M}'_i\cdot\boldsymbol{b}+\boldsymbol{a}^\intercal\cdot\boldsymbol{\mu}'_i+\boldsymbol{\nu}'^\intercal_i\cdot\boldsymbol{b},$$

for some matrices $\boldsymbol{M}'_i\in\mathbb{F}_q^{(d+1)\times(d+1)}$ and vectors $\boldsymbol{\mu}'_i,\boldsymbol{\nu}'_i\in\mathbb{F}_q^{d+1}$. Clearly, up to switching to roles of a and b, this implies that for any a_i, $i\in\{0,\dots,d\}$, there exists $j\in\{1,\dots,t\}$ such that p'_j functionally depends on a_i, otherwise one can simulate all the p'_i's with at most d shares of a, and then one can simulate $P=\{p_1,\dots,p_\ell\}$ as well.

We then just need to show that there exist $\boldsymbol{\lambda}\in\mathbb{F}_q^t$ such that $\sum_{i=1}^t\lambda_i\cdot p'_i$ satisfies Condition 3.2. This is actually immediate as soon as $q>d+1$: for $i=0,\dots,d$ the set $\mathcal{H}_i=\{\boldsymbol{\lambda}\in\mathbb{F}_q^t\mid\sum_{i=1}^t\lambda_i p'_i$ *does not functionally depends on* $a_i\}$ is a hyperplane, and thus we just need to prove that there exists $\boldsymbol{\lambda}\in\mathbb{F}_q^t\setminus\cup_{i=0}^d\mathcal{H}_i$, which is true as soon as $q>d+1$. This concludes the proof of Theorem 3.5. □

Remark 3.6. As for Theorem 3.2, we do not restrict the size of the set P in Theorem 3.5. Furthermore, the proof does not rely on the correctness property of C.

Corollary 3.7. *Let C be a $(d+1,v)$-gadget for a two-input function f: $\mathbb{F}_q^2\to\mathbb{F}_q$. We suppose that any possible probe on C is bilinear. If $q>d+1$ and there does not exist any set P of d probes on C satisfying Condition 3.2, then C is d-NI. Furthermore, if C is d-NI, then there does not exist any set P of d probes on C satisfying Condition 3.2.*

Proof. The proof is straightforward from Theorem 3.5. □

4 Construction with a Linear Number of Bilinear Multiplications

Let us now show our generic d-SNI construction with a linear number of bilinear multiplications (i.e., multiplications by a value which is not constant), in the order d. The construction is in two steps. We first construct a d-NI multiplication $(d+1,2d+1)$-gadget. In other words, our first construction outputs $2d+1$ shares instead of $d+1$. We then show how to compress these $2d+1$ shares into $d+1$ shares to get a d-SNI multiplication $(d+1,d+1)$-gadget, using the gadget

SharingCompress from the Appendix C.1 of [8], that we recall and prove to be d-SNI (while it was only implicitly proved d-NI in [8]).

We start by presenting the generic construction and its security proof. The first part of our construction uses a matrix $\gamma \in \mathbb{F}_q^{d\times d}$ satisfying some conditions. That is why we then show that such a matrix exists for any d when q is large enough (but we only prove that q being exponential in $d \log d$ is sufficient) using the probabilistic method. We conclude by explicitly constructing matrices γ for small values of d.

4.1 Construction

Construction with $2d+1$ output shares. Let $\gamma = (\gamma_{i,j})_{1\le i,j\le d} \in \mathbb{F}_q^{d\times d}$ be a constant matrix and let $\boldsymbol{\delta} \in \mathbb{F}_q^{d\times d}$ be the matrix defined by $\delta_{i,j} = 1 - \gamma_{j,i}$.

The main idea of our construction with $2d+1$ output shares is to remark that:

$$
\begin{aligned}
a \cdot b = &\left(a_0 + \sum_{i=1}^{d}(r_i + a_i)\right) \cdot \left(b_0 + \sum_{i=1}^{d}(s_i + b_i)\right) \\
&- \sum_{i=1}^{d} r_i \cdot \left(b_0 + \sum_{j=1}^{d}(\delta_{i,j}s_j + b_j)\right) - \sum_{i=1}^{d} s_i \cdot \left(a_0 + \sum_{j=1}^{d}(\gamma_{i,j}r_j + a_j)\right)
\end{aligned}
$$

if $a = \sum_{i=0}^{d} a_i$ and $b = \sum_{j=0}^{d} b_j$. On the right-hand side of the above equation there are only $2d+1$ bilinear multiplications.

We can then construct a multiplication $(d+1, 2d+1)$-gadget which outputs the following $2d+1$ shares (the computation is performed with the usual priorities: parenthesis first, then products, then from left to right):

- $c_0 = \left(a_0 + \sum_{i=1}^{d}(r_i + a_i)\right) \cdot \left(b_0 + \sum_{i=1}^{d}(s_i + b_i)\right)$;
- $c_i = -r_i \cdot \left(b_0 + \sum_{j=1}^{d}(\delta_{i,j}s_j + b_j)\right)$, for $i = 1, \dots, d$;
- $c_{i+d} = -s_i \cdot \left(a_0 + \sum_{j=1}^{d}(\gamma_{i,j}r_j + a_j)\right)$, for $i = 1, \dots, d$.

The corresponding gadget is given in Algorithm 1 and is clearly correct.

However, the latter gadget has two issues. First, it outputs $2d+1$ shares instead of $d+1$. Second, it is obviously not secure for every matrix γ. For example, if γ is a matrix of zeros or the identity matrix, the gadget is clearly not d-private, let alone d-NI or d-SNI. Actually, it is not even clear that there exists a matrix γ for which the gadget is private. Let us now deal with these two issues.

From $2d+1$ output shares to $d+1$. For the first issue, we use the gadget SharingCompress from the Appendix C.1 of [8] to compress the shares $c_0, \dots, c_{2d}$ into $d+1$ shares. We recall this gadget in Algorithm 2.

Algorithm 1. ExtendedMult

Require: $\boldsymbol{a} = (a_0, \ldots, a_d), \boldsymbol{b} = (b_0, \ldots, b_d)$
Ensure: $\mathbf{c} = (c_0, \ldots, c_{2d})$ such that $\sum_{i=0}^{2d} c_i = (\sum_{i=0}^{d} a_i) \cdot (\sum_{i=0}^{d} b_i)$

```
x ← a_0;  y ← b_0
for i = 1 to d do
    c_i ← b_0
    c_{i+d} ← a_0
    for j = 1 to d do
        s_j ← $
        r_j ← $
        t ← δ_{i,j} s_j + b_j
        c_i ← c_i + t
        y ← y + (s_j + b_j)
        t ← γ_{i,j} r_j + a_j
        c_{i+d} ← c_{i+d} + t
        x ← x + (r_j + a_j)
    c_i ← −r_i · c_i
    c_{i+d} ← −s_i · c_{i+d}
c_0 ← x · y
return (c_0, c_1, ... c_{2d})
```

Proposition 4.1. *The gadget SharingCompress*$[k : \ell]$ *depicted in Algorithm 2 is* $(\ell - 1)$*-SNI.*

This proof is given in the full version. From this proposition, we deduce that the instance SharingCompress$[2d + 1 : d + 1]$ that we need is d-SNI.

Finally, the full gadget with a linear number of bilinear multiplications is depicted in Algorithm 4. It essentially calls Algorithm 3 which handles the special case where the number of input shares is twice the number of output shares.

As we are composing the gadget SharingCompress with our multiplication gadget above, we need to prove that the former gadget satisfies a security property which behaves well with composition. In [8], only privacy is proven which does not behave well with composition. That is why we prove instead the following proposition in the full version.

Conditions on γ and δ. As mentioned before, the construction is completely insecure for some matrices γ, such as the matrix of zeros. Let us now exhibit necessary conditions for the scheme to be d-NI.

The probes involving only the a_i's and the r_i's[7] are of the following forms:

- a_i, r_i, $r_i + a_i$, $\gamma_{j,i} r_i$, $\gamma_{j,i} r_i + a_i$, (for $0 \le i \le d$ and $1 \le j \le d$)
- $a_0 + \sum_{i=1}^{k} (r_i + a_i)$ (for $1 \le k \le d$),
- $a_0 + \sum_{i=1}^{k} (\gamma_{j,i} r_i + a_i)$ (for $1 \le j \le d$ and $1 \le k \le d$).

[7] By probes involving only the a_i's and the r_i's, we mean probes that do not functionally depend on any b_i nor any s_i.

Algorithm 2. SharingCompress$[k : \ell]$ from [8, Appendix C.1]

Require: k-sharing $(x_i)_{1 \leq i \leq k}$
Ensure: ℓ-sharing $(y_i)_{1 \leq i \leq \ell}$ such that $\sum_{i=1}^{\ell} y_i = \sum_{i=1}^{k} x_i$

```
K ← ℓ⌈k/ℓ⌉
for j = k + 1 to K do
    x_j ← 0
for j = 1 to ℓ do
    y_j ← x_j
for j = 1 to (K−ℓ)/ℓ do
    (y_1, ..., y_ℓ) ← SharingCompress[2ℓ : ℓ](y_1, ... y_ℓ, x_{jℓ+1}, ..., x_{jℓ+ℓ})
return (y_1, ..., y_ℓ)
```

Algorithm 3. SharingCompress$[2d : d]$ from [8, Appendix C.1]

Require: $2d$-sharing $(x_i)_{1 \leq i \leq 2d}$
Ensure: d-sharing $(y_i)_{1 \leq i \leq d}$ such that $\sum_{i=1}^{d} y_i = \sum_{i=1}^{2d} x_i$

```
for i = 1 to d do
    for j = i + 1 to d do
        r_{i,j} ← $
for i = 1 to d do
    v_i ← 0
for i = 1 to d do
    for j = 1 to i − 1 do
        v_i ← v_i − r_{j,i}
    for j = i + 1 to d do
        v_i ← v_i + r_{i,j}
for i = 1 to d do
    y_i ← x_i + v_i
    y_i ← y_i + x_{i+d}
return (y_1, ... y_d)
```

Algorithm 4. Construction with a Linear Number of Bilinear Multiplications

Require: $\boldsymbol{a} = (a_0, \ldots, a_d), \boldsymbol{b} = (b_0, \ldots, b_d)$
Ensure: $\boldsymbol{c'} = (c'_0, \ldots, c'_d)$ such that $\sum_{i=0}^{d} c'_i = (\sum_{i=0}^{d} a_i) \cdot (\sum_{i=0}^{d} b_i)$

```
(c_0, ... c_{2d}) ← ExtendedMult(a, b)
(c'_0, ... c'_d) ← SharingCompress[2d + 1 : d + 1](c_0, ... c_{2d})
return (c'_0, c'_1, ... c'_d)
```

Thanks to Theorem 3.5, a necessary condition for d-NI is that there is no linear combination of at most d of these expressions, which do not functionally depend on any r_i but which does depend on all the a_i's.

The probes involving only the b_i's and the s_i's are similar except that a_i, r_i, and $\gamma_{j,i}$ are replaced by b_i, s_i, $\delta_{j,i}$ respectively. A similar necessary condition can be deduced from Theorem 3.5.

Formally, let us introduce a first necessary condition on the matrix γ.

Condition 4.1. *Let $\ell = (2d+4) \cdot d + 1$. Let $\boldsymbol{I}_d \in \mathbb{F}_q^{d \times d}$ be the identity matrix, $\mathbf{0}_{m \times n} \in \mathbb{F}_q^{m \times n}$ be a matrix of zeros (when $n = 1$, $\mathbf{0}_{m \times n}$ is also written $\mathbf{0}_m$), $\mathbf{1}_{m \times n} \in \mathbb{F}_q^{m \times n}$ be a matrix of ones, $\boldsymbol{D}_{\gamma,j} \in \mathbb{F}_q^{d \times d}$ be the diagonal matrix such that $D_{\gamma,j,i,i} = \gamma_{j,i}$, $\boldsymbol{T}_d \in \mathbb{F}_q^{d \times d}$ be the upper-triangular matrix with just ones, and $\boldsymbol{T}_{\gamma,j} \in \mathbb{F}_q^{d \times d}$ be the upper-triangular matrix for which $T_{\gamma,j,i,k} = \gamma_{j,i}$ for $i \leq k$. In other words, we have:*

$$\boldsymbol{I}_d = \begin{pmatrix} 1 & 0 & \cdots & 0 \\ 0 & 1 & & 0 \\ \vdots & & \ddots & \vdots \\ 0 & \cdots & 0 & 1 \end{pmatrix} \qquad \boldsymbol{D}_{\gamma,j} = \begin{pmatrix} \gamma_{j,1} & 0 & \cdots & 0 \\ 0 & \gamma_{j,2} & & 0 \\ \vdots & & \ddots & \vdots \\ 0 & \cdots & 0 & \gamma_{j,d} \end{pmatrix}$$

$$\boldsymbol{T}_d = \begin{pmatrix} 1 & 1 & \cdots & 1 \\ 0 & 1 & & 1 \\ \vdots & & \ddots & \vdots \\ 0 & \cdots & 0 & 1 \end{pmatrix} \qquad \boldsymbol{T}_{\gamma,j} = \begin{pmatrix} \gamma_{j,1} & \gamma_{j,1} & \cdots & \gamma_{j,1} \\ 0 & \gamma_{j,2} & & \gamma_{j,2} \\ \vdots & & \ddots & \vdots \\ 0 & \cdots & 0 & \gamma_{j,d} \end{pmatrix}$$

We define the following matrices:

$$\boldsymbol{L} = \left(\begin{array}{c|c|c|c|c|c|c|c|c|c|c} 1 & \mathbf{0}_{1\times d} & \mathbf{0}_{1\times d} & \mathbf{0}_{1\times d} & \mathbf{0}_{1\times d} & \cdots & \mathbf{0}_{1\times d} & \mathbf{1}_{1\times d} & \mathbf{1}_{1\times d} & \cdots & \mathbf{1}_{1\times d} \\ \mathbf{0}_d & \boldsymbol{I}_d & \mathbf{0}_{d\times d} & \boldsymbol{I}_d & \boldsymbol{I}_d & \cdots & \boldsymbol{I}_d & \boldsymbol{T}_d & \boldsymbol{T}_d & \cdots & \boldsymbol{T}_d \end{array} \right)$$

$$\boldsymbol{M} = \left(\begin{array}{c|c|c|c|c|c|c|c|c|c|c} \mathbf{0}_d & \mathbf{0}_{d\times d} & \boldsymbol{I}_d & \boldsymbol{I}_d & \boldsymbol{D}_{\gamma,1} & \cdots & \boldsymbol{D}_{\gamma,d} & \boldsymbol{T}_d & \boldsymbol{T}_{\gamma,1} & \cdots & \boldsymbol{T}_{\gamma,d} \end{array} \right)$$

Condition *4.1* is satisfied for a matrix γ *if for any vector $\boldsymbol{v} \in \mathbb{F}_q^\ell$ of Hamming weight $\mathsf{hw}(\boldsymbol{v}) \leq d$ such that $\boldsymbol{L} \cdot \boldsymbol{v}$ contains no coefficient equal to* 0 *then $\boldsymbol{M} \cdot \boldsymbol{v} \neq \mathbf{0}_d$.*

Let us explain how this condition was constructed. The rows of $\boldsymbol{L}$ correspond to $a_0, \ldots, a_d$. The rows of $\boldsymbol{M}$ correspond to $r_1, \ldots, r_d$. Any linear combination of the probes involving only the a_i's and the r_i's can be written as

$$(a_0, \ldots, a_d) \cdot \boldsymbol{L} \cdot \boldsymbol{v} + (r_1, \ldots, r_d) \cdot \boldsymbol{M} \cdot \boldsymbol{v}.$$

Hence the above condition.

Remark 4.2. If all the vectors $\boldsymbol{v} \in \mathbb{F}_q^\ell$ of Hamming weight $\mathsf{hw}(\boldsymbol{v}) \leq d$ were considered, this condition would be equivalent to saying that the linear code of parity-check matrix $\boldsymbol{M}$ has minimum distance at least d. However, as we only consider vectors $\boldsymbol{v}$ such that additionally $\boldsymbol{L} \cdot \boldsymbol{v}$ contains no coefficient equal to 0, this simple relation to codes is not true. We remark however that if the linear code of parity-check matrix $\boldsymbol{M}$ has minimum distance at least d, then the condition would be satisfied. Unfortunately for us, this code clearly has minimum distance 1, as it contains the vector $(1, 0, \ldots, 0)^\intercal \in \mathbb{F}_q^\ell$. That is why we cannot naively use classical coding theory results to prove the existence of a matrix γ satisfying Condition 4.1.

We remark that the same necessary condition should hold for the matrix $\boldsymbol{\delta}$ by symmetry between a_i, r_i, γ and $b_i, s_i, \boldsymbol{\delta}$. Therefore, the formal condition we are considering is the following.

Condition 4.2. Condition *4.2* holds (for a matrix $\gamma \in \mathbb{F}_q^{d\times d}$) *if Condition 4.1 is satisfied for both* $\boldsymbol{\gamma}$ *and* $\boldsymbol{\delta}$*, where* $\boldsymbol{\delta} \in \mathbb{F}_q^{d\times d}$ *is the matrix defined by* $\delta_{i,j} = 1 - \gamma_{j,i}$.

4.2 Security Analysis

We have shown that Condition 4.2 is necessary for our gadget (Algorithm 4) to be d-NI. The next theorem shows it is also sufficient for it to be d-SNI.

Theorem 4.3. *If* $\gamma \in \mathbb{F}_q^{d\times d}$ *satisfies Condition 4.2 and if* $q > d+1$*, then Algorithm 4 is d-SNI.*

To prove this theorem, we use the following lemma.

Lemma 4.4. *Let* P *be a set of* t *probes in Algorithm 1 such that* $t \leq d$*. Then, there exists a set* Q_1 *of at most* t *probes involving only the* a_i*'s and the* r_i*'s and a set* Q_2 *of at most* t *probes involving only the* b_i*'s and the* s_i*'s, such that the set* P *can be simulated by the probes in* $Q_1 \cup Q_2$.

Proof (Lemma 4.4*).* We list hereafter all the possible probes in Algorithm 1. We gather them by sets for the needs of the proof.

Set 1: a_i, r_i, $r_i + a_i$, $\gamma_{j,i} r_i$, $\gamma_{j,i} r_i + a_i$, (for $0 \leq i \leq d$ and $1 \leq j \leq d$);
Set 2: $a_0 + \sum_{i=1}^{k}(r_i + a_i)$ (for $1 \leq k \leq d$);
Set 3: $a_0 + \sum_{i=1}^{k}(\gamma_{j,i} r_i + a_i)$ (for $1 \leq j \leq d$ and $1 \leq k \leq d$);
Set 4: b_i, s_i, $s_i + b_i$, $\delta_{j,i} s_i$, $\delta_{j,i} s_i + b_i$, (for $0 \leq i \leq d$ and $1 \leq j \leq d$);
Set 5: $b_0 + \sum_{i=1}^{k}(s_i + b_i)$ (for $1 \leq k \leq d$);
Set 6: $b_0 + \sum_{i=1}^{k}(\delta_{j,i} s_i + b_i)$ (for $1 \leq j \leq d$ and $1 \leq k \leq d$);
Set 7: $-r_i \cdot \left(b_0 + \sum_{j=1}^{d}(\delta_{i,j} s_j + b_j)\right)$ (for $1 \leq i \leq d$);
Set 8: $-s_i \cdot \left(a_0 + \sum_{j=1}^{d}(\gamma_{i,j} r_j + a_j)\right)$ (for $1 \leq i \leq d$);
Set 9: $(a_0 + \sum_{i=1}^{d}(r_i + a_i)) \cdot (b_0 + \sum_{i=1}^{d}(s_i + b_i))$.

Let us now consider a set P of t probes among the listed ones. We initialize two sets Q_1 and Q_2 to the empty set and show how to fill them with at most t probes involving only the a_i's and the r_i's for Q_1 and at most t probes involving only the b_i's and the s_i's for Q_2 in such a way that P can be perfectly simulated by probes of $Q_1 \cup Q_2$.

For all the probes of P which belong to Sets 1 to 3, then we add them directly to Q_1 since they only depend on a_i's, r_i's and constants. Similarly, for all the probes of P which belong to Sets 4 to 6, then we add them directly to Q_2 since they only depend on b_i's, s_i's and constants. For P's probes belonging to Set 7, we add probe $-r_i$ to Q_1 and $b_0 + \sum_{j=1}^{d}(\delta_{i,j} s_i + b_j)$ to Q_2. For P's probes belonging to Set 8, we add probe $-s_i$ to Q_2 and $a_0 + \sum_{j=1}^{d}(\gamma_{i,j} r_i + a_j)$ to Q_1. Finally, for probes of P from Set 9, we add $a_0 + \sum_{i=1}^{d}(r_i + a_i)$ to Q_1 and $b_0 + \sum_{i=1}^{d}(s_i + b_i)$ to Q_2. Since for each probe of P, at most one probe was added to Q_1 and at most one probe was added to Q_2, it is clear that after all the t probes of P are processed, Q_1 and Q_2 contain at most t probes each.

Let us now prove that all the probes of P can be perfectly simulated by the probes of $Q_1 \cup Q_2$. For probes of P belonging to six first sets, the exact same values were added to Q_1 (for the three first sets) or Q_2 (for Set 4 to 6) thus the simulation is trivial. For probes of P in Set 7, $-r_i$ was added to Q_1 and $b_0 + \sum_{j=1}^{d}(\delta_{i,j}s_i + b_j)$ to Q_2. The multiplication of these two probes perfectly simulate the initial probe of P. The same conclusions can be made for probes of P in Sets 8 and 9 since each time probes were added to Q_1 and Q_2 so that their product corresponds to the initial probe of P. □

Proof (Theorem 4.3). From Lemma 4.4, any set P of $t \leq d$ probes in Algorithm 1 can be perfectly simulated by probes of two sets Q_1 and Q_2 of cardinal at most t and containing probes involving only the a_i's and the r_i's for Q_1 and probes involving only the b_i's and the s_i's for Q_2.

From Condition 4.2, any combination of the t probes of Q_1 either depend on strictly less than t a_i's or it is functionally dependent on at least one r_i. Thanks to Theorem 3.5 and the fact that $q > d+1$, the t probes of Q_1 can be perfectly simulated using at most t shares a_i. The same statement can be made for the probes of Q_2. Therefore, from Lemma 4.4, any set of $t \leq d$ probes on Algorithm 1 can be perfectly simulated by at most t shares a_i and t shares b_i, which proves that Algorithm 1 is d-TNI.

Since from Proposition 4.1, SharingCompress$[2d+1 : d+1]$ is d-SNI, from the composition theorems established in [3], Algorithm 4 is d-SNI. □

4.3 Probabilistic Construction

In order to prove the existence of a matrix γ which satisfies Condition 4.1 for q large enough (but only exponential in $d \log d$), we state Theorem 4.5 that makes use of the non-constructive "probabilistic method." More precisely, we prove that if one chooses γ uniformly at random in $\mathbb{F}_q^{d\times d}$, the probability that the matrix γ satisfies Condition 4.2 is more than zero, when q is large enough. The proof of Theorem 4.5 uses probability but the existence of a matrix γ which satisfies Condition 4.2 (for q large enough) is guaranteed without any possible error.

Theorem 4.5. *For any $d \geq 1$, for any prime power q, if γ is chosen uniformly in $\mathbb{F}_q^{d\times d}$, then*

$$\Pr[\gamma \textit{ satisfies Condition 4.2}] \geq 1 - 2 \cdot (12d)^d \cdot d \cdot q^{-1}.$$

In particular, for any $d \geq 1$, there exists an integer $Q = O(d)^{d+1}$, such that for any prime power $q \geq Q$, there exists a matrix $\gamma \in \mathbb{F}_q^{d\times d}$ satisfying Condition 4.2.

As when γ is uniformly random, so is $\boldsymbol{\delta}$, Theorem 4.5 immediately follows from the following proposition and the union bound.

Proposition 4.6. *For any $d \geq 1$, for any prime power q, if γ is chosen uniformly in $\mathbb{F}_q^{d \times d}$, then*

$$\Pr[\gamma \text{ satisfies Condition 4.1}] \geq 1 - (12d)^d \cdot d \cdot q^{-1}.$$

In particular, for any $d \geq 1$, there exists an integer $Q = O(d)^{d+1}$, such that for any prime power $q \geq Q$, there exists a matrix $\gamma \in \mathbb{F}_q^{d \times d}$ satisfying Condition 4.1.

The proof of this proposition is very technical and is provided in the full version.

Remark 4.7. Note that the constants in the previous proof are not the best possible and can be improved. In the following, we present explicit constructions for small values of d.

4.4 Small Cases

We show here the instantiation for $d = 2$. The case for $d = 3$ is similar and is provided in details in the full version.

Let $d = 2$. Let us now explicitly instantiate our construction for any non-prime field $\mathbb{F}_q$ where $q = p^k$, $k \geq 2$. Let ξ be any element in $\mathbb{F}_q \setminus \mathbb{F}_p$. A possible instantiation is:

$$\gamma = \begin{pmatrix} \xi & \xi+1 \\ \xi+1 & \xi \end{pmatrix}, \quad \delta = \begin{pmatrix} -\xi+1 & -\xi \\ -\xi & -\xi+1 \end{pmatrix}.$$

The computed shares are hence:

- $c_0 = (a_0 + (r_1 + a_1) + (r_2 + a_2)) \cdot (b_0 + (s_1 + b_1) + (s_2 + b_2))$
- $c_1 = -r_1 \cdot (b_0 + ((-\xi + 1)s_1 + b_1) + (-\xi s_2 + b_2))$
- $c_2 = -r_2 \cdot (b_0 + (-\xi s_1 + b_1) + ((-\xi + 1)s_2 + b_2))$
- $c_3 = -s_1 \cdot (a_0 + (\xi r_1 + a_1) + ((\xi + 1)r_2 + a_2))$
- $c_4 = -s_2 \cdot (a_0 + ((\xi + 1)r_1 + a_1) + (\xi r_2 + a_2))$

Let us now prove that this scheme satisfies Condition 4.2. Let us consider the matrices $\boldsymbol{L}$ and $\boldsymbol{M}$ as defined in Condition 4.1:

$$\boldsymbol{L} = \left(\begin{array}{c|cc|cc|cc|cc|cc|cc|cc|cc} 1 & 0 & 0 & 0 & 0 & 0 & 0 & 0 & 0 & 0 & 0 & 1 & 1 & 1 & 1 & 1 & 1 \\ 0 & 1 & 0 & 0 & 0 & 1 & 0 & 1 & 0 & 1 & 0 & 1 & 1 & 1 & 1 & 1 & 1 \\ 0 & 0 & 1 & 0 & 0 & 0 & 1 & 0 & 1 & 0 & 1 & 0 & 1 & 0 & 1 & 0 & 1 \end{array}\right)$$

$$\boldsymbol{M} = \left(\begin{array}{c|cc|cc|cc|cc|cc|cc|cc|cc} 0 & 0 & 0 & 1 & 0 & 1 & 0 & \xi & 0 & \xi+1 & 0 & 1 & 1 & \xi & \xi & \xi+1 & \xi+1 \\ 0 & 0 & 0 & 0 & 1 & 0 & 1 & 0 & \xi+1 & 0 & \xi & 0 & 1 & 0 & \xi+1 & 0 & \xi \end{array}\right)$$

We will prove that, for any vector $\boldsymbol{v}$ such that $\mathsf{hw}(\boldsymbol{v}) \leq 2$, it holds that if $\boldsymbol{M} \cdot \boldsymbol{v} = \boldsymbol{0}_2$, then $\boldsymbol{L} \cdot \boldsymbol{v}$ has a 0 coefficient.

Let us start by the case $\mathsf{hw}(\boldsymbol{v}) = 1$. If $\boldsymbol{M} \cdot \boldsymbol{v} = \boldsymbol{0}_2$, the only non-zero coefficient of $\boldsymbol{v}$ clearly must be in one of the first $1 + d = 3$ coordinates. Denote by i the index of this coefficient. Since $i \leq 3$, from the definition of $\boldsymbol{L}$, we have

$\boldsymbol{L} \cdot \boldsymbol{v} = \boldsymbol{I}_3 \cdot (v_1, v_2, v_3)^\mathsf{T}$, and thus its i-th coefficient is equal to the non-zero coefficient of $\boldsymbol{v}$ but the two other coefficients of $\boldsymbol{L} \cdot \boldsymbol{v}$ are equal to 0. This concludes this case.

Let us tackle the case $\mathsf{hw}(\boldsymbol{v}) = 2$. Note that $\boldsymbol{L} \cdot \boldsymbol{v}$ hence corresponds to a linear combination of exactly two columns of $\boldsymbol{L}$. By construction of $\boldsymbol{L}$, all first columns (until the occurrence of $\boldsymbol{T}_d$) are of Hamming weight 1. Consequently, for $\boldsymbol{L} \cdot \boldsymbol{v}$ to have only non-zero coefficients, at least one of the $3 \cdot d = 6$ last coordinates of $\boldsymbol{v}$ must be non-zero. The corresponding columns of $\boldsymbol{L}$ have two possible values : $(1,1,0)^\top$ or $(1,1,1)^\top$. Let us consider the cases where one coordinate of $\boldsymbol{v}$ corresponding to a column $(1,1,0)^\top$ is set. The corresponding column in $\boldsymbol{M}$ is of the form $(\alpha, 0)^\top$, where α can be $1, \xi, \xi+1$. In order for $\boldsymbol{L} \cdot \boldsymbol{v}$ to have only non-zero coefficients, the other non-zero coordinate of $\boldsymbol{v}$ must correspond to a column of $\boldsymbol{L}$ where the last coefficient is non-zero. However, for all of these columns, the corresponding column of $\boldsymbol{M}$ is always of the form (λ, β), with $\beta \neq 0$, in which case $\boldsymbol{M} \cdot \boldsymbol{v} \neq \boldsymbol{0}_2$. It just remains to consider the case where one non-zero coordinate of $\boldsymbol{v}$ corresponds to a column $(1,1,1)^\top$ of $\boldsymbol{L}$. The corresponding columns in $\boldsymbol{M}$ can be $(1,1)^\top$, $(\xi, \xi+1)^\top$, or $(\xi+1, \xi)^\top$. Note that for no other column in $\boldsymbol{L}$ one can retrieve a corresponding column in $\boldsymbol{M}$ whose coefficients are both non-zero. Consequently, both non-zero coordinates of $\boldsymbol{v}$ must correspond to columns $(1,1,1)^\top$ of $\boldsymbol{L}$. Since no two vectors among $(1,1)$, $(\xi, \xi+1)$, and $(\xi+1, \xi)$ are proportional, then we always have $\boldsymbol{M} \cdot \boldsymbol{v} \neq \boldsymbol{0}_2$.

The exact same reasoning can be held for $\boldsymbol{\delta}$, since no two vectors among $(1,1)$, $(-\xi+1, -\xi)$, $(-\xi, -\xi+1)$ are proportional.

5 Construction with Linear Randomness Complexity

In this section, we describe a construction that only requires a linear randomness complexity. That is, our $(d+1, d+1)$-gadget only uses d random scalars. In particular, our construction breaks the linear bound of $d+1$ random scalars (for order $d > 3$) proven in [4]. There is no contradiction since this lower bound is proven only in $\mathbb{F}_2$. Our construction is described below and once again makes use of a matrix of scalars that needs to satisfy certain properties, as explained later in this section.

5.1 Construction

Construction. Let $\boldsymbol{\gamma} = (\gamma_{i,j})_{\substack{0 \le i \le d \\ 1 \le j \le d}} \in \mathbb{F}_q^{(d+1) \times d}$ be a constant matrix (with $d+1$ rows instead of d for the previous construction).

Following the previous gadget with the objective of minimizing the randomness complexity, we can construct a multiplication $(d+1, d+1)$-gadget which outputs the shares $(c_0, \dots, c_d)$ defined as follows:

$$c_i = a_0 b_i + \sum_{j=1}^{d} (\gamma_{i,j} r_j + a_j b_i) \,,$$

Algorithm 5. New Construction with Linear Randomness

Require: $\boldsymbol{a} = (a_0, \ldots, a_d), \boldsymbol{b} = (b_0, \ldots, b_d)$
Ensure: $\boldsymbol{c} = (c_0, \ldots, c_d)$ such that $\sum_{i=0}^{d} c_i = (\sum_{i=0}^{d} a_i) \cdot (\sum_{i=0}^{d} b_i)$
  for $i = 1$ to d **do**
    $c_i \leftarrow a_0 b_i$
  for $j = 1$ to d **do**
    $r_j \leftarrow \$$
    for $i = 0$ to d **do**
      $c_i \leftarrow c_i + (\gamma_{i,j} r_j + a_j b_i)$
  return $(c_0, \ldots, c_d)$

for $0 \leq i \leq d$. The gadget is formally depicted in Algorithm 5 and is correct under the condition that for any $0 \leq j \leq d$,

$$\sum_{i=0}^{d} \gamma_{i,j} = 0.$$

We remark that if this construction is secure, it breaks the randomness complexity lower bound of $d+1$ random bits proven in [4] when $q = 2$. Furthermore, it is the first construction with a linear number of random scalars (in d). Previously, the construction with the best randomness complexity used a quasi-linear number of random scalars [4].

However, as for our construction in Sect. 4.1, the construction is clearly not secure for every matrix γ. For example, if γ is a matrix of zeros, the gadget is clearly not private, let alone NI or SNI. Actually, it is not even clear that there exists a matrix γ for which the gadget is private. We prove in the following that this is indeed the case if the finite field is large enough and we provide explicit choices of the matrix γ for small orders $d \in \{2, 3\}$ over small finite fields.

Condition on γ. Similarly to Sect. 4.1, the following condition is necessary for the above construction to be d-NI.

Condition 5.1. *Let $\ell = (2d+4) \cdot d + 1$. Let $\boldsymbol{I}_d \in \mathbb{F}_q^{d \times d}$ be the identity matrix, $\boldsymbol{0}_{m \times n} \in \mathbb{F}_q^{m \times n}$ be a matrix of zeros (when $n = 1$, $\boldsymbol{0}_{m \times n}$ is also written $\boldsymbol{0}_m$), $\boldsymbol{1}_{m \times n} \in \mathbb{F}_q^{m \times n}$ be a matrix of ones, $\boldsymbol{D}_{\gamma,j} \in \mathbb{F}_q^{d \times d}$ be the diagonal matrix such that $D_{\gamma,j,i,i} = \gamma_{j,i}$, $\boldsymbol{T}_d \in \mathbb{F}_q^{d \times d}$ be the upper-triangular matrix with just ones, $\boldsymbol{T}_{\gamma,j} \in \mathbb{F}_q^{d \times d}$ be the upper-triangular matrix for which $T_{\gamma,j,i,k} = \gamma_{j,i}$ for $i \leq k$. Let $\omega_0, \ldots, \omega_d$ be $(d+1)$ indeterminates and we consider the field of rational fractions $\mathbb{F}_q(\omega_0, \ldots, \omega_d)$. In other words, we have:*

$$I_d = \begin{pmatrix} 1 & 0 & \cdots & 0 \\ 0 & 1 & & 0 \\ \vdots & & \ddots & \vdots \\ 0 & \cdots & 0 & 1 \end{pmatrix} \qquad D_{\gamma,j} = \begin{pmatrix} \gamma_{j,1} & 0 & \cdots & 0 \\ 0 & \gamma_{j,2} & & 0 \\ \vdots & & \ddots & \vdots \\ 0 & \cdots & 0 & \gamma_{j,d} \end{pmatrix}$$

$$T_d = \begin{pmatrix} 1 & 1 & \cdots & 1 \\ 0 & 1 & & 1 \\ \vdots & & \ddots & \vdots \\ 0 & \cdots & 0 & 1 \end{pmatrix} \qquad T_{\gamma,j} = \begin{pmatrix} \gamma_{j,1} & \gamma_{j,1} & \cdots & \gamma_{j,1} \\ 0 & \gamma_{j,2} & & \gamma_{j,2} \\ \vdots & & \ddots & \vdots \\ 0 & \cdots & 0 & \gamma_{j,d} \end{pmatrix}$$

We define the following matrices:

$$L' = \left(\begin{array}{c|c|c|c|c|c|c|c|c|c|c} 1 & \mathbf{0}_{1\times d} & \mathbf{0}_{1\times d} & \mathbf{0}_{1\times d} & \mathbf{0}_{1\times d} & \cdots & \mathbf{0}_{1\times d} & \omega_0 \mathbf{1}_{1\times d} & \omega_1 \mathbf{1}_{1\times d} & \cdots & \omega_d \mathbf{1}_{1\times d} \\ \mathbf{0}_d & I_d & \mathbf{0}_{d\times d} & \omega_0 I_d & \omega_1 I_d & \cdots & \omega_d I_d & \omega_0 T_d & \omega_1 T_d & \cdots & \omega_d T_d \end{array} \right)$$

$$M' = \left(\begin{array}{c|c|c|c|c|c|c|c|c|c|c} \mathbf{0}_d & \mathbf{0}_{d\times d} & I_d & D_{\gamma,0} & D_{\gamma,1} & \cdots & D_{\gamma,d} & T_{\gamma,0} & T_{\gamma,1} & \cdots & T_{\gamma,d} \end{array} \right)$$

where $L' \in \mathbb{F}_q(\omega_0, \ldots, \omega_d)^{(d+1)\times \ell}$ *and* $M' \in \mathbb{F}_q^{d\times \ell}$.
Condition *5.1* is satisfied for a matrix γ *if for any vector* $v \in \mathbb{F}_q^{\ell}$ *of Hamming weight* $\mathsf{hw}(v) \le d$ *such that* $L' \cdot v$ *contains no coefficient equal to* 0 *then* $M' \cdot v \neq \mathbf{0}_d$.

5.2 Security Analysis

Lemma 5.1. *Each probe contains at most one share* b_i *of* b.

Proof. A probe can only target the partial expression of an output or an entire output. In this construction, each output c_i is built with a single share b_i of b. Therefore, a probe can contain at most one such share. □

Corollary 5.2. *Any set of at most* d *probes contains at most* d *shares of* b.

Proposition 5.3. *The above construction with* d *random scalars is* d*-NI, if* γ *satisfies Condition 5.1.*

Proof. From Condition 5.1, any combination of at most d probes in our construction is either functionally dependent on at most d shares a_i or on at least one random scalar. Furthermore, using in addition Corollary 5.2, any combination of at most d probes is functionally dependent on at most d shares b_i. Therefore, thanks to Theorem 3.5 and the fact that $q > d + 1$, the construction is d-NI. □

5.3 Probabilistic Construction

As in the previous section, in order to prove the existence of a matrix γ which satisfies Condition 4.2 for q large enough (but only exponential in $d \log d$), we state Theorem 5.4 that makes also use of the non-constructive "probabilistic method." Its proof is detailed in the full version.

Theorem 5.4. *For any $d \geq 1$, for any prime power q, if γ is chosen uniformly in $\gamma \in \mathbb{F}_q^{(d+1)\times d}$ under the condition that $\sum_{i=0}^{d} \gamma_{i,j} = 0$ for $0 \leq i \leq d$, then*

$$\Pr[\gamma \text{ satisfies Condition 4.2}] \geq 1 - d(d+1) \cdot (12d)^d \cdot q^{-1}$$

In particular, for any $d \geq 1$, there exists an integer $Q = O(d)^{d+2}$, such that for any prime power $q \geq Q$, there exists a matrix $\gamma \in \mathbb{F}_q^{d\times d}$ satisfying Condition 5.1.

5.4 Small Cases

We show here the instantiation for $d \in \{2, 3\}$.

$d = 2$. Let d equal 2. Let us now explicitly instantiate our construction for any non-prime field $\mathbb{F}_q$ where $q = p^k$, $k \geq 2$. Let ξ be any element in $\mathbb{F}_q \setminus \mathbb{F}_p$. A possible instantiation is:

$$\gamma = \begin{pmatrix} 1 & \xi \\ \xi & 1 \\ -\xi - 1 & -\xi - 1 \end{pmatrix}.$$

The computed shares are hence:

- $c_0 = a_0 b_0 + (1 \cdot r_1 + a_1 b_0) + (\xi \cdot r_2 + a_2 b_0)$
- $c_1 = a_0 b_1 + (\xi \cdot r_1 + a_1 b_1) + (1 \cdot r_2 + a_2 b_1)$
- $c_2 = a_0 b_2 + ((-\xi - 1) \cdot r_1 + a_1 b_2) + (-\xi - 1) \cdot r_2 + a_2 b_2)$

Let us now prove that this scheme satisfies Condition 5.1. The reasoning is similar to the proof in Sect. 4.4.

In order for $\boldsymbol{M'} \cdot \boldsymbol{v}$ to be null, and for $\boldsymbol{L'} \cdot \boldsymbol{v}$ to be of full Hamming weight, we observe that the two non-zero coefficients of $\boldsymbol{v}$ must correspond to two columns of full Hamming weight of $\boldsymbol{M'}$. However, no two vectors in $(1, \xi), (\xi, 1), (-\xi - 1, -\xi - 1)$ are proportional. This ensures that Condition 5.1 is satisfied for γ.

$d = 3$. Let d equal 3. Let us now explicitly instantiate our construction for any non-prime field $\mathbb{F}_q$ where $q = 2^k$, $k \geq 4$. Let ξ be any element in $\mathbb{F}_q \setminus \mathbb{F}_p$. A possible instantiation is:

$$\gamma = \begin{pmatrix} 1 & \xi & \xi + 1 \\ 1 & \xi^2 + 1 & \xi \\ 1 & \xi + 1 & \xi^2 + \xi + 1 \\ 1 & \xi^2 + \xi + 1 & \xi + 1 \end{pmatrix}.$$

The computed shares are hence:

- $c_0 = a_0 b_0 + (1 \cdot r_1 + a_1 b_0) + (\xi \cdot r_2 + a_2 b_0) + ((\xi + 1) \cdot r_3 + a_3 b_0)$
- $c_1 = a_0 b_1 + (1 \cdot r_1 + a_1 b_1) + ((\xi^2 + 1) \cdot r_2 + a_2 b_1) + (\xi \cdot r_3 + a_3 b_1)$
- $c_2 = a_0 b_2 + (1 \cdot r_1 + a_1 b_2) + ((\xi + 1) \cdot r_2 + a_2 b_2) + ((\xi^2 + \xi + 1\xi) \cdot r_3 + a_3 b_2)$
- $c_3 = a_0 b_3 + (1 \cdot r_1 + a_1 b_3) + ((\xi^2 + \xi + 1) \cdot r_2 + a_2 b_3) + ((\xi + 1) \cdot r_3 + a_3 b_3)$

Let us now prove that this scheme satisfies Condition 5.1. The reasoning is similar to the proof in Sect. 4.4. We check the non-proportionality of the relevant vectors $(1, \xi, \xi + 1), (1, \xi^2 + 1, \xi), (1, \xi + 1, \xi^2 + \xi + 1), (1, \xi^2 + \xi + 1, \xi + 1)$, and finish by computing all left determinants using a computer algebra system. It follows that this construction satisfies Condition 5.1.

5.5 Lower Bound

Let us now show a lower bound on the randomness complexity of d-NI multiplication gadgets satisfying the following condition.

Condition 5.2. *A multiplication gadget satisfies Condition 5.2 if the output shares are affine functions (over $\mathbb{F}_q$) of the products $a_i b_j$ and of the input shares a_i and b_j (coefficients of the affine functions may depend on the random scalars). In other words, each output share c_i can be written as (possibly after expansion and simplification):*

$$c_i = \boldsymbol{a}^\intercal \cdot \boldsymbol{M_i}(\boldsymbol{r}) \cdot \boldsymbol{b} \; + \; \boldsymbol{a}^\intercal \cdot \boldsymbol{\mu_i}(\boldsymbol{r}) \; + \; \boldsymbol{\nu}_i^\intercal(\boldsymbol{r}) \cdot \boldsymbol{b} \; + \; \tau_i(\boldsymbol{r}) \,,$$

where $\boldsymbol{M_i}(\boldsymbol{r}) \in \mathbb{F}_q^{(d+1)\times(d+1)}$, $\boldsymbol{\mu}_i(\boldsymbol{r}) \in \mathbb{F}_q^{d+1}$, $\boldsymbol{\nu}_i(\boldsymbol{r}) \in \mathbb{F}_q^{d+1}$, and $\tau_i(\boldsymbol{r}) \in \mathbb{F}_q$ are arbitrary functions of the vector $\boldsymbol{r} \in \mathbb{F}_q^R$ of random scalars.

This condition is very weak. In particular, it does not restrict output shares to be bilinear and do not restrict internal values of the circuit at all. All the d-NI multiplication gadgets we know [4,10,18,24] including the ours in Sects. 4.1 and 5.1 satisfy this condition. We first need the following lemma.

Lemma 5.5. *Let $\boldsymbol{U} \in \mathbb{F}_q^{(d+1)\times(d+1)}$ be the matrix of ones. Let $\boldsymbol{M}, \boldsymbol{M}'$ be two matrices in $\mathbb{F}_q^{(d+1)\times(d+1)}$ such that $\boldsymbol{M} + \boldsymbol{M}' = \boldsymbol{U}$. Then all the columns or all the rows of $\boldsymbol{M}$, or all the columns or all the rows of $\boldsymbol{M}'$ are non-zero.*

Proof. Let us prove the lemma by contraposition. We suppose that both $\boldsymbol{M}$ and $\boldsymbol{M}'$ have a column of zeros and a row of zeros. Let us suppose that the i-th row of $\boldsymbol{M}$ is a zero row and the j-th column of $\boldsymbol{M}'$ is a zero column. Then $M_{i,j} = M'_{i,j} = 0 \neq 1 = U_{i,j}$ and $\boldsymbol{M} + \boldsymbol{M}' \neq \boldsymbol{U}$. □

We can now state our lower bound.

Proposition 5.6. *Let C be a d-NI multiplication gadget satisfying Condition 5.2. Then C uses more than $\lfloor (d-1)/2 \rfloor$ random scalars (i.e., $R \geq d/2$).*

A d-NI multiplication gadget satisfying Condition 5.2 thus requires a linear number of random scalars in d. We recall our construction in Sect. 5.1 uses d random scalars, which is linear in d.

Proof. Let us suppose that C uses only $R \leq \lfloor (d-1)/2 \rfloor$ random scalars. Let $k = \lfloor d/2 \rfloor$. Let us construct a set of probes which cannot be simulated by at most d shares of each input a and b. As C satisfies Condition 5.2, we can write:

$$\begin{aligned} c_0 + \cdots + c_k &= \boldsymbol{a}^\intercal \cdot \boldsymbol{M}(\boldsymbol{r}) \cdot \boldsymbol{b} \; + \; \boldsymbol{a}^\intercal \cdot \boldsymbol{\mu}(\boldsymbol{r}) \; + \; \boldsymbol{\nu}^\intercal(\boldsymbol{r}) \cdot \boldsymbol{b} \; + \; \tau(\boldsymbol{r}) \,, \\ c_{k+1} + \cdots + c_d &= \boldsymbol{a}^\intercal \cdot \boldsymbol{M}'(\boldsymbol{r}) \cdot \boldsymbol{b} \; + \; \boldsymbol{a}^\intercal \cdot \boldsymbol{\mu}'(\boldsymbol{r}) \; + \; \boldsymbol{\nu}'^\intercal(\boldsymbol{r}) \cdot \boldsymbol{b} \; + \; \tau'(\boldsymbol{r}) \,, \end{aligned}$$

where $\boldsymbol{M}(\boldsymbol{r}), \boldsymbol{M}'(\boldsymbol{r}) \in \mathbb{F}_q^{(d+1)\times(d+1)}$, $\boldsymbol{\mu}(\boldsymbol{r}), \boldsymbol{\mu}(\boldsymbol{r}) \in \mathbb{F}_q^{d+1}$, $\boldsymbol{\nu}(\boldsymbol{r}), \boldsymbol{\nu}(\boldsymbol{r}) \in \mathbb{F}_q^{d+1}$, and $\tau(\boldsymbol{r}), \tau'(\boldsymbol{r}) \in \mathbb{F}_q$ are arbitrary functions of the vector $\boldsymbol{r} \in \mathbb{F}_q^R$ of random scalars.

Let $\boldsymbol{U} \in \mathbb{F}_q^{(d+1)\times(d+1)}$ be the matrix of ones. As $\sum_{i=0}^{d} c_i = ab = \boldsymbol{a}^\intercal \cdot \boldsymbol{U} \cdot \boldsymbol{b}$ by correctnesss of C, we have $\boldsymbol{M}(\boldsymbol{r}) + \boldsymbol{M'}(\boldsymbol{r}) = \boldsymbol{U}$. In particular, when $\boldsymbol{r} = \boldsymbol{0}$ (for example), Lemma 5.5 ensures that $c_0 + \cdots + c_k$ or $c_{k+1} + \cdots + c_d$ functionally depends on every a_i $(0 \le i \le d)$ or on every b_j $(0 \le j \le d)$. Therefore, one of the following set of probes cannot be simulated by at most d shares of each input a and b:

$$\{r_1, \ldots, r_R, c_0, \ldots, c_k\} \quad \text{and} \quad \{r_1, \ldots, r_R, c_{k+1}, \ldots, c_d\}.$$

We conclude by remarking that $R + (k+1) \le \lfloor (d-1)/2 \rfloor + \lfloor d/2 \rfloor + 1 \le d$, as either $d-1$ or d is odd and so either $\lfloor (d-1)/2 \rfloor \le (d-1)/2 - 1$ or $\lfloor d/2 \rfloor \le d/2 - 1$. □

Acknowledgements. The second author was supported by the Defense Advanced Research Projects Agency (DARPA) and Army Research Office (ARO) under Contract No. W911NF-15-C-0236. The third author was supported in part from a DARPA/ARL SAFEWARE award, NSF Frontier Award 1413955, NSF grants 1619348, 1228984, 1136174, and 1065276, BSF grant 2012378, a Xerox Faculty Research Award, a Google Faculty Research Award, an equipment grant from Intel, and an Okawa Foundation Research Grant. This material is based upon work supported by the Defense Advanced Research Projects Agency through the ARL under Contract W911NF-15-C-0205. The views expressed are those of the authors and do not reflect the official policy or position of the Department of Defense, the National Science Foundation, or the U.S. Government. The fourth and fifth authors were supported in part by the European Union's H2020 Programme under grant agreement number ICT-731591 (REASSURE). The fifth author was supported in part by the French ANR project BRUTUS, ANR-14-CE28-0015.

References

1. Balasch, J., Faust, S., Gierlichs, B.: Inner product masking revisited. In: Oswald, E., Fischlin, M. (eds.) EUROCRYPT 2015. LNCS, vol. 9056, pp. 486–510. Springer, Heidelberg (2015). doi:10.1007/978-3-662-46800-5_19
2. Balasch, J., Faust, S., Gierlichs, B., Verbauwhede, I.: Theory and practice of a leakage resilient masking scheme. In: Wang, X., Sako, K. (eds.) ASIACRYPT 2012. LNCS, vol. 7658, pp. 758–775. Springer, Heidelberg (2012). doi:10.1007/978-3-642-34961-4_45
3. Barthe, G., Belaïd, S., Dupressoir, F., Fouque, P.A., Grégoire, B., Strub, P.Y., Zucchini, R.: Strong non-interference and type-directed higher-order masking. In: Weippl, E.R., Katzenbeisser, S., Kruegel, C., Myers, A.C., Halevi, S. (eds.) ACM CCS 16, pp. 116-129. ACM Press, October 2016
4. Belaïd, S., Benhamouda, F., Passelègue, A., Prouff, E., Thillard, A., Vergnaud, D.: Randomness complexity of private circuits for multiplication. In: Fischlin, M., Coron, J.-S. (eds.) EUROCRYPT 2016. LNCS, vol. 9666, pp. 616–648. Springer, Heidelberg (2016). doi:10.1007/978-3-662-49896-5_22
5. Belaïd, S., Benhamouda, F., Passelègue, A., Prouff, E., Thillard, A., Vergnaud, D.: Randomness complexity of private circuits for multiplication. Cryptology ePrint Archive, Report 2016/211 (2016). full version of [4]. http://eprint.iacr.org/2016/211

6. Carlet, C., Prouff, E.: Polynomial evaluation and side channel analysis. In: Ryan, P.Y.A., Naccache, D., Quisquater, J.-J. (eds.) The New Codebreakers. LNCS, vol. 9100, pp. 315–341. Springer, Heidelberg (2016). doi:10.1007/978-3-662-49301-4_20. http://dx.doi.org/10.1007/978-3-662-49301-4_20
7. Carlet, C., Prouff, E., Rivain, M., Roche, T.: Algebraic decomposition for probing security. In: Gennaro, R., Robshaw, M. (eds.) CRYPTO 2015. LNCS, vol. 9215, pp. 742–763. Springer, Heidelberg (2015). doi:10.1007/978-3-662-47989-6_36
8. Carlet, C., Prouff, E., Rivain, M., Roche, T.: Algebraic decomposition for probing security. Cryptology ePrint Archive, Report 2016/321 (2016). full version of [7]. http://eprint.iacr.org/2016/321
9. Chari, S., Jutla, C.S., Rao, J.R., Rohatgi, P.: Towards sound approaches to counteract power-analysis attacks. In: Wiener, M. (ed.) CRYPTO 1999. LNCS, vol. 1666, pp. 398–412. Springer, Heidelberg (1999). doi:10.1007/3-540-48405-1_26
10. Coron, J.-S., Prouff, E., Rivain, M., Roche, T.: Higher-order side channel security and mask refreshing. In: Moriai, S. (ed.) FSE 2013. LNCS, vol. 8424, pp. 410–424. Springer, Heidelberg (2014). doi:10.1007/978-3-662-43933-3_21
11. Coron, J.-S., Prouff, E., Roche, T.: On the use of Shamir's secret sharing against side-channel analysis. In: Mangard, S. (ed.) CARDIS 2012. LNCS, vol. 7771, pp. 77–90. Springer, Heidelberg (2013). doi:10.1007/978-3-642-37288-9_6
12. Coron, J.-S., Roy, A., Vivek, S.: Fast evaluation of polynomials over binary finite fields and application to side-channel countermeasures. In: Batina, L., Robshaw, M. (eds.) CHES 2014. LNCS, vol. 8731, pp. 170–187. Springer, Heidelberg (2014). doi:10.1007/978-3-662-44709-3_10
13. Duc, A., Dziembowski, S., Faust, S.: Unifying leakage models: from probing attacks to noisy leakage. In: Nguyen, P.Q., Oswald, E. (eds.) EUROCRYPT 2014. LNCS, vol. 8441, pp. 423–440. Springer, Heidelberg (2014). doi:10.1007/978-3-642-55220-5_24
14. Duc, A., Faust, S., Standaert, F.-X.: Making masking security proofs concrete. In: Oswald, E., Fischlin, M. (eds.) EUROCRYPT 2015. LNCS, vol. 9056, pp. 401–429. Springer, Heidelberg (2015). doi:10.1007/978-3-662-46800-5_16
15. Faust, S., Rabin, T., Reyzin, L., Tromer, E., Vaikuntanathan, V.: Protecting circuits from leakage: the computationally-bounded and noisy cases. In: Gilbert, H. (ed.) EUROCRYPT 2010. LNCS, vol. 6110, pp. 135–156. Springer, Heidelberg (2010). doi:10.1007/978-3-642-13190-5_7
16. Goubin, L., Patarin, J.: DES and differential power analysis the "duplication" method. In: Koç, Ç.K., Paar, C. (eds.) CHES 1999. LNCS, vol. 1717, pp. 158–172. Springer, Heidelberg (1999). doi:10.1007/3-540-48059-5_15
17. Gross, H., Mangard, S., Korak, T.: Domain-oriented masking: compact masked hardware implementations with arbitrary protection order. IACR Cryptology ePrint Archive 2016, p. 486 (2016). http://eprint.iacr.org/2016/486. To appear in the proceedings of CARDIS 2016
18. Ishai, Y., Sahai, A., Wagner, D.: Private circuits: securing hardware against probing attacks. In: Boneh, D. (ed.) CRYPTO 2003. LNCS, vol. 2729, pp. 463–481. Springer, Heidelberg (2003). doi:10.1007/978-3-540-45146-4_27
19. Kocher, P.C.: Timing attacks on implementations of Diffie-Hellman, RSA, DSS, and other systems. In: Koblitz, N. (ed.) CRYPTO 1996. LNCS, vol. 1109, pp. 104–113. Springer, Heidelberg (1996). doi:10.1007/3-540-68697-5_9
20. Nikova, S., Rijmen, V., Schläffer, M.: Secure hardware implementation of non-linear functions in the presence of glitches. J Cryptol. **24**(2), 292–321 (2011). http://dx.doi.org/10.1007/s00145-010-9085-7

21. Prouff, E., Rivain, M.: Masking against side-channel attacks: a formal security proof. In: Johansson, T., Nguyen, P.Q. (eds.) EUROCRYPT 2013. LNCS, vol. 7881, pp. 142–159. Springer, Heidelberg (2013). doi:10.1007/978-3-642-38348-9_9
22. Prouff, E., Roche, T.: Higher-order glitches free implementation of the AES using secure multi-party computation protocols. In: Preneel, B., Takagi, T. (eds.) CHES 2011. LNCS, vol. 6917, pp. 63–78. Springer, Heidelberg (2011). doi:10.1007/978-3-642-23951-9_5
23. Reparaz, O., Bilgin, B., Nikova, S., Gierlichs, B., Verbauwhede, I.: Consolidating masking schemes. In: Gennaro, R., Robshaw, M. (eds.) CRYPTO 2015. LNCS, vol. 9215, pp. 764–783. Springer, Heidelberg (2015). doi:10.1007/978-3-662-47989-6_37
24. Rivain, M., Prouff, E.: Provably secure higher-order masking of AES. In: Mangard, S., Standaert, F.-X. (eds.) CHES 2010. LNCS, vol. 6225, pp. 413–427. Springer, Heidelberg (2010). doi:10.1007/978-3-642-15031-9_28

Anonymous Attestation with Subverted TPMs

Jan Camenisch[1(✉)], Manu Drijvers[1,2], and Anja Lehmann[1]

[1] IBM Research – Zurich, Säumerstrasse 4, 8803 Rüschlikon, Switzerland
{jca,mdr,anj}@zurich.ibm.com

[2] Department of Computer Science, ETH Zurich, 8092 Zürich, Switzerland

Abstract. Various sources have revealed that cryptographic standards and components have been subverted to undermine the security of users, reigniting research on means to achieve security in presence of such subverted components. In this paper we consider direct anonymous attestation (DAA) in this respect. This standardized protocol allows a computer with the help of an embedded TPM chip to remotely attest that it is in a healthy state. Guaranteeing that different attestations by the same computer cannot be linked was an explicit and important design goal of the standard in order to protect the privacy of the user of the computer. Surprisingly, none of the standardized or otherwise proposed DAA protocols achieves privacy when the TPM is subverted, but they all rely on the honesty of the TPM. As the TPM is a piece of hardware, it is hardly possible to tell whether or not a given TPM follows the specified protocol. In this paper we study this setting and provide a new protocol that achieves privacy also in presence of subverted TPMs.

1 Introduction

Direct anonymous attestation (DAA) is a cryptographic protocol for a platform consisting of a host and a TPM chip (Trusted Platform Module). The TPM serves as a trust anchor of the platform and anonymously attests either to the host's current state or some other message chosen by the host. Thus, DAA can be used to convince a communication partner that the platform has not been compromised, i.e., modified by malware. The main design goal of DAA is that such attestations are anonymous, i.e., while a verifier can check that the signature stems from a legitimate platform, it does not learn the identity of the platform, or even recognize that multiple attestations stem from the same platform.

DAA was introduced by Brickell, Camenisch, and Chen [15] for the Trusted Computing Group and was standardized in the TPM 1.2 specification in 2004 [59]. Their paper inspired a large body of work on DAA schemes [9,16–18,23,25,36–38,40], including more efficient schemes using bilinear pairings as well as different security definitions and proofs. One result of these works is the recent TPM 2.0 specification [50,60] that includes support for multiple pairing-based DAA schemes, two of which are standardized by ISO [49]. Over 500 million TPMs have been sold, making DAA probably the most complex

This work has been supported by the ERC under Grant PERCY #321310.

J. Katz and H. Shacham (Eds.): CRYPTO 2017, Part III, LNCS 10403, pp. 427–461, 2017.
DOI: 10.1007/978-3-319-63697-9_15

cryptographic scheme that is widely implemented. Recently, the protocol has gotten renewed attention for authentication: An extension of DAA called EPID is used in Intel SGX [41], the most recent development in the area of trusted computing. Further, the FIDO alliance, an industry consortium designing standards for strong user authentication, is in the process of standardizing a specification using DAA to attest that authentication keys are securely stored [21].

The first version of the TPM specification and attestation protocol had received strong criticism from privacy groups and data protection authorities as it imposed linkability and full identification of all attestations. As a consequence, guaranteeing the privacy of the platform, i.e., ensuring that an attestation does not carry any identifier, became an important design criteria for such hardware-based attestation. Indeed, various privacy groups and data protection authorities had been consulted in the design process of DAA.

Trusting Hardware for Privacy? Surprisingly, despite the strong concerns of having to trust a piece of hardware when TPMs and hardware-based attestation were introduced, the problem of privacy-preserving attestation in the presence of fraudulent hardware has not been fully solved yet. The issue is that the original DAA protocol as well as all other DAA protocols crucially rely on the honesty of the entire platform, i.e., host and TPM, for guaranteeing privacy. Clearly, assuming that the host is honest is unavoidable for privacy, as it communicates directly with the outside world and can output any identifying information it wants. However, further requiring that the TPM behaves fully honest and aims to preserve the host's privacy is an unnecessarily strong assumption and contradicts the initial design goal of not having to trust the TPM.

Even worse, it is impossible to verify this strong assumption as the TPM is a chip that comes with pre-installed software, to which the user only has black-box access. While black-box access might allow one to partly verify the TPM's functional correctness, it is impossible to validate its *privacy* guarantees. A compromised TPM manufacturer can ship TPMs that provide seemingly correct outputs, but that are formed in a way that allows dedicated entities (knowing some trapdoor) to trace the user, for instance by encoding an identifier in a nonce that is hashed as part of the attestation signature. It could further encode its secret key in attestations, allowing a fraudulent manufacturer to *frame* an honest host by signing a statement on behalf of the platform. We stress that such attacks are possible on all current DAA schemes, meaning that, by compromising a TPM manufacturer, all TPMs it produces can be used as mass surveillance devices. The revelations of subverted cryptographic standards [5,56] and tampered hardware [46] indicate that such attack scenarios are very realistic.

In contrast to the TPM, the host software can be verified by the user, e.g., being compiled from open source, and will likely run on hardware that is not under the control of the TPM manufacturer. Thus, while the honesty of the host is vital for the platform's privacy and there are means to verify or enforce such honesty, requiring the TPM to be honest is neither necessary nor verifiable.

1.1 Our Contribution

In this paper we address this problem of anonymous attestation without having to trust a piece of hardware, a problem which has been open for more than a decade. We further exhibit a new DAA protocol that provides privacy even if the TPM is subverted. More precisely, our contributions are twofold: we first show how to model subverted parties within the Universal Composability (UC) model and then propose a protocol that is secure against subverted TPMs.

Modeling Subversion Attacks in UC. We modify the UC-functionality of DAA recently proposed by Camenisch, Drijvers, and Lehmann [25] to model the preserved privacy guarantees in the case where the TPM is corrupt and the host remains honest. Modeling corruption in the sense of subverted parties is not straightforward: if the TPM was simply controlled by the adversary, then, using the standard UC corruption model, only very limited privacy can be achieved. The TPM has to see and approve every message it signs but, when corrupted, all these messages are given to the adversary as well. In fact, the adversary will learn which particular TPM is asked to sign which message. That is, the adversary can later recognize a certain TPM attestation via its message, even if the signatures are anonymous.

Modeling corruption of TPMs like this gives the adversary much more power than in reality: even if a TPM is subverted and runs malicious algorithms, it is still embedded into a host who controls all communication with the outside world. Thus, the adversary cannot communicate directly with the TPM, but only via the (honest) host. To model such subversions more accurately, we introduce *isolated* corruptions in UC. When a TPM is corrupted like this, we allow the ideal-world adversary (simulator) to specify a piece of code that the isolated, yet subverted TPM will run. Other than that, the adversary has no control over the isolated corrupted party, i.e., it cannot directly interact with the isolated TPM and cannot see its state. Thus, the adversary will also not automatically learn anymore which TPM signed which message.

A New DAA Protocol with Optimal Privacy. We further discuss why the existing DAA protocols do not offer privacy when the TPM is corrupt and propose a new DAA protocol which we prove to achieve our strong security definition. In contrast to most existing schemes, we construct our protocol from generic building blocks which yields a more modular design. A core building block are *split signatures* which allow two entities – in our case the TPM and host – each holding a secret key share to jointly generate signatures. Using such split keys and signatures is a crucial difference compared with all existing schemes, where only the TPM contributed to the attestation key which inherently limits the possible privacy guarantees. We also redesign the overall protocol such that the main part of the attestation, namely proving knowledge of a membership credential on the attestation key, can be done by the host instead of the TPM.

By shifting more responsibility and computations to the host, we do not only increase privacy, but also achieve stronger notions of non-frameability and unforgeability than all previous DAA schemes. Interestingly, this design change also improves the efficiency of the TPM, which is usually the bottleneck in a DAA scheme. In fact, we propose a pairing-based instantiation of our generic protocol which, compared to prior DAA schemes, has the most efficient TPM signing operation. This comes for the price of higher computational costs for the host and verifier. However, we estimate signing and verification times of under 40 ms, which is sufficiently fast for most practical applications.

1.2 Related Work

The idea of combining a piece of tamper-resistant hardware with a user-controlled device was first suggested by Chaum [33] and applied to the context of e-cash by Chaum and Pedersen [34], which got later refined by Cramer and Pedersen [42] and Brands [14]. A user-controlled wallet is required to work with a piece of hardware, the observer, to be able to withdraw and spend e-cash. The wallet ensures the user's privacy while the observer prevents a user from double-spending his e-cash. Later, Brands in 2000 [13] considered the more general case of user-bound credentials where the user's secret key is protected by a smart card. Brands proposes to let the user's host add randomness to the smart card contribution as a protection against subliminal channels. All these works use a blind signature scheme to issue credentials to the observers and hence such credentials can only be used a single time.

Young and Yung further study the protection against subverted cryptographic algorithms with their work on kleptography [62,63] in the late 1990s. Recently, caused by the revelations of subverted cryptographic standards [5,56] and tampered hardware [46] as a form of mass-surveillance, this problem has again gained substantial attention.

Subversion-Resilient Cryptography. Bellare et al. [7] provided a formalization of algorithm-substitution attacks and considered the challenge of securely encrypting a message with an encryption algorithm that might be compromised. Here, the corruption is limited to attacks where the subverted party's behavior is indistinguishable from that of a correct implementation, which models the goal of the adversary to remain undetected. This notion of algorithm-substitution attacks was later applied to signature schemes, with the goal of preserving unforgeability in the presence of a subverted signing algorithm [4].

However, these works on subversion-resilient cryptography crucially rely on honestly generated keys and aim to prevent key or information leakage when the algorithms using these keys get compromised.

Recently, Russell et al. [57,58] extended this line of work by studying how security can be preserved when *all* algorithms, including the key generation can be subverted. The authors also propose immunization strategies for a number of primitives such as one-way permutations and signature schemes. The approach of replacing a correct implementation with an indistinguishable yet corrupt one is similar to the approach in our work, and like Russell et al. we allow the subversion of all algorithms, and aim for security (or rather privacy) when the TPM behaves maliciously already when generating the keys.

The DAA protocol studied in this work is more challenging to protect against subversion attacks though, as the signatures produced by the TPM must not only be unforgeable and free of a subliminal channel which could leak the signing key, but also be anonymous and unlinkable, i.e., signatures must not leak any information about the signer even when the key is generated by the adversary. Clearly, allowing the TPM to run subverted keys requires another trusted entity on the user's side in order to hope for any privacy-protecting operations. The DAA setting naturally satisfies this requirement as it considers a platform to consist of two individual entities: the TPM and the host, where all of TPM's communication with the outside world is run via the host.

Reverse Firewalls. This two-party setting is similar to the concept of reverse firewalls recently introduced by Mironov and Stephens-Davidowitz [53]. A reverse firewall sits in between a user's machine and the outside world and guarantees security of a joint cryptographic operation even if the user's machine has been compromised. Moreover, the firewall-enhanced scheme should maintain the original functionality and security, meaning the part run on the user's computer must be fully functional and secure on its own without the firewall. Thus, the presence of a reverse firewall can enhance security if the machine is corrupt but is not the source of security itself. This concept has been proven very powerful and manages to circumvent the negative results of resilience against subversion-attacks [39,43].

The DAA setting we consider in this paper is not as symmetric as a reverse firewall though. While both parties contribute to the unforgeability of attestations, the privacy properties are only achievable if the host is honest. In fact, there is no privacy towards the host, as the host is fully aware of the identity of the embedded TPM. The requirement of privacy-protecting and unlinkable attestation only applies to the final output produced by the host.

Divertible Protocols and Local Adversaries. A long series of related work explores divertible and mediated protocols [3,11,20,54], where a special party called the mediator controls the communication and removes hidden information in messages by rerandomizing them. The host in our protocol resembles the mediator, as it adds randomness to every contribution to the signature from the TPM. However, in our case the host is a normal protocol participant, whereas the mediator's sole purpose is to control the communication.

Alwen et al. [2] and Canetti and Vald [32] consider local adversaries to model isolated corruptions in the context of multi-party protocols. These works thoroughly formalize the setting of multi-party computations where several parties can be corrupted, but are controlled by different and non-colluding adversaries. In contrast, the focus of this work is to limit the communication channel that the adversary has to the corrupted party itself. We leverage the flexibility of the UC model to define such isolated corruptions.

Generic MPC. Multi-party computation (MPC) was introduced by Yao [61] and allows a set of parties to securely compute any function on private inputs. Although MPC between the host and TPM could solve our problem, a negative result by Katz and Ostrovsky [52] shows that this would require at least five rounds of communication, whereas our tailored solution is much more efficient. Further, none of the existing MPC models considers the type of subverted corruptions that is crucial to our work, i.e., one first would have to extend the existing models and schemes to capture such isolated TPM corruption. This holds in particular for the works that model tamper-proof hardware [48,51], as therein the hardware is assumed to be "perfect" and unsubvertable.

TPM2.0 Interfaces and Subliminal Channels. Camenisch et al. [22] recently studied the DAA-related interfaces that are provided by hardware modules following the current TPM2.0 specification, and propose a revision to obtain better security and privacy guarantees from such hardware. The current APIs do not allow to prove the unforgeability of the TPM's parts in the DAA protocols, and provide a static Diffie-Hellman oracle. Fixes to these problems have been proposed, but they create new issues: they enable a fraudulent TPM to encode information into an attestation signature, which could be used to break anonymity or to leak the secret key. This creates a subliminal channel already on the hardware level, which would annihilate any privacy guarantees against malicious TPMs that are achieved on the protocol level. Camenisch et al. address this problem and present a revised set of interfaces that allow for provable security and do not introduce a subliminal channel. Further, two new DAA protocols are presented that can be build from these revised APIs and guarantee privacy even when the hardware is subverted, which is termed *strong* privacy and builds upon our isolated corruption model. In contrast to our work, the protocols in [22] do not provide privacy against malicious TPMs in the standard corruption model, and the privacy guarantees in the isolated model are slightly weaker than in our optimal privacy definition. We give a brief comparison of strong and optimal privacy in Sect. 2.3 and refer to [22] for a detailed discussion. The protocols proposed in [22] are realizable with only minor modifications to the TPM specification, though, whereas our protocol with optimal privacy would require more significant changes.

2 A Security Model for DAA with Optimal Privacy

This section presents our security definition for anonymous attestation with optimal privacy. First, we informally describe how DAA works and what the desired security and (optimal) privacy properties are. Then we present our formal definition in Sect. 2.1, and describe how it improves upon existing work in Sect. 2.2. Finally, in Sect. 2.3, we elaborate on the inherent limitations the UC framework imposes on privacy in the presence of fully corrupted parties and introduce the concept of *isolated corruptions*, which allow one to overcome this limitations yet capture the power of subverted TPMs.

High-Level Functional and Security Properties. In a DAA scheme, we have four kinds of entities: a number of TPMs, a number of hosts, an issuer, and a number of verifiers. A TPM and a host together form a platform which performs the *join protocol* with the issuer who decides if the platform is allowed to become a member. Once being a member, the TPM and host together can *sign* messages with respect to basenames *bsn*, where the basename steers the platform's anonymity. If a platform signs with a fresh basename, the signature must be anonymous and unlinkable to any previous signatures. That is, any verifier can check that the signature stems from a legitimate platform via a deterministic *verify* algorithm, but the signature does not leak any information about the identity of the signer. However, signatures the platform makes with the *same* basename can be linked to each other via a (deterministic) *link* algorithm.

For security, one requires **unforgeability**: when the issuer is honest, the adversary can only sign in the name of corrupt platforms. More precisely, if n platforms are corrupt, the adversary can forge at most n unlinkable signatures for one basename. By corrupt platform we mean that both the host and TPM are corrupt, and thus a platform is called honest if at least one of the TPM or host is honest. This is in fact stronger than the unforgeability notion covered in all previous definitions which only rely on the honesty of the TPM.

Non-frameability captures the property that no adversary can create signatures on a message m w.r.t. basename *bsn* that links to a signature created by a platform with an honest host, when this platform never signed m w.r.t. *bsn*.

Finally, we require **anonymity** for attestations. An adversary that is given two signatures, w.r.t. two *different* basenames cannot determine whether both signatures stem from the same platform. All previous works considered anonymity only for fully honest platforms, i.e., consisting of an honest TPM and honest host, whereas our goal is to guarantee anonymity even if the TPM is corrupt. Note that anonymity can only hold if the host is honest, though, as it has full control over its output and can, e.g., always choose to append its identity to a signature. Thus, the best one can hope for is preserved anonymity when the TPM is corrupt but the host is honest, which is the setting that this work addresses.

Universal Composability. Our security definition has the form of an ideal functionality $\mathcal{F}_{\mathsf{pdaa}}$ in the Universal Composability (UC) framework [31]. Informally, a protocol Π securely realizes an ideal functionality $\mathcal{F}$ if the real world is as secure as the ideal world. As $\mathcal{F}$ performs the task at hand in an ideal fashion, i.e., $\mathcal{F}$ is secure by construction, there are no meaningful attacks on the ideal world, so there are no meaningful attacks on the real world. More precisely, Π securely realizes $\mathcal{F}$ if for every adversary $\mathcal{A}$, there exists a simulator $\mathcal{S}$ such that no environment $\mathcal{E}$ can distinguish the real world (with Π and $\mathcal{A}$) from the ideal world (with $\mathcal{F}$ and $\mathcal{S}$).

2.1 Ideal Functionality $\mathcal{F}_{\mathsf{pdaa}}$

We now formally define our ideal DAA-with-optimal-privacy functionality $\mathcal{F}_{\mathsf{pdaa}}$, which is based on $\mathcal{F}^{l}_{\mathsf{daa}}$ by Camenisch et al. [25]. The crucial difference between the two functionalities is the resilience against corrupt TPMs: $\mathcal{F}^{l}_{\mathsf{daa}}$ guarantees anonymity, non-frameability and unforgeability only when both the TPM and the host are honest. Our modified version $\mathcal{F}_{\mathsf{pdaa}}$ guarantees all properties as long as the host is honest, i.e., even when the TPM is corrupt. We explain these differences in detail in Sect. 2.2. We start by describing the interfaces and guaranteed security properties in an informal manner, and present the detailed definition of $\mathcal{F}_{\mathsf{pdaa}}$ in Fig. 1.

Setup. The SETUP interface on input $sid = (\mathcal{I}, sid')$ initiates a new session for the issuer $\mathcal{I}$ and expects the adversary to provide algorithms (ukgen, sig, ver, link, identify) that will be used inside the functionality. ukgen creates a new key gsk and a tracing trapdoor τ that allows $\mathcal{F}_{\mathsf{pdaa}}$ to trace signatures generated with gsk. sig, ver, and link are used by $\mathcal{F}_{\mathsf{pdaa}}$ to create, verify, and link signatures, respectively. Finally, identify allows to verify whether a signature belongs to a certain tracing trapdoor. This allows $\mathcal{F}_{\mathsf{pdaa}}$ to perform multiple consistency checks and enforce the desired non-frameability and unforgeability properties.

Note that the ver and link algorithms assist the functionality only for signatures that are not generated by $\mathcal{F}_{\mathsf{pdaa}}$ itself. For signatures generated by the functionality, $\mathcal{F}_{\mathsf{pdaa}}$ will enforce correct verification and linkage using its internal records. While ukgen and sig are probabilistic algorithms, the other ones are required to be deterministic. The link algorithm also has to be symmetric, i.e., for all inputs it must hold that $\mathsf{link}(\sigma, m, \sigma', m', bsn) \leftrightarrow \mathsf{link}(\sigma', m', \sigma, m, bsn)$.

Join. A host $\mathcal{H}_j$ can request to join with a TPM $\mathcal{M}_i$ using the JOIN interface. If both the TPM and the issuer approve the join request, the functionality stores an internal membership record for $\mathcal{M}_i, \mathcal{H}_j$ in `Members` indicating that from now on that platform is allowed to create attestations.

If the host is corrupt, the adversary must provide $\mathcal{F}_{\mathsf{pdaa}}$ with a tracing trapdoor τ. This value is stored along in the membership record and allows the functionality to check via the identify function whether signatures were created by this platform. $\mathcal{F}_{\mathsf{pdaa}}$ uses these checks to ensure non-frameability and unforgeability whenever it creates or verifies signatures. To ensure that the adversary cannot provide bad trapdoors that would break the completeness or non-frameability properties, $\mathcal{F}_{\mathsf{pdaa}}$ checks the legitimacy of τ via the "macro" function CheckTtdCorrupt. This function checks that for all previously generated or verified signatures for which $\mathcal{F}_{\mathsf{pdaa}}$ has already seen another matching tracing trapdoor $\tau' \neq \tau$, the new trapdoor τ is not identified as a matching key as well. The detailed definition is given in the full version of this paper [24].

Sign. After joining, a host $\mathcal{H}_j$ can request a signature on a message m with respect to basename bsn using the SIGN interface. The signature will only be

1. `Issuer Setup`. On input (SETUP, sid) from issuer $\mathcal{I}$.
   - Verify that $sid = (\mathcal{I}, sid')$.
   - Output (SETUP, sid) to $\mathcal{A}$ and wait for input (ALG, sid, sig, ver, link, identify, ukgen) from $\mathcal{A}$.
   - Check that ver, link and identify are deterministic.
   - Store (sid, sig, ver, link, identify, ukgen) and output (SETUPDONE, sid) to $\mathcal{I}$.

Join

2. `Join Request`. On input (JOIN, $sid, jsid, \mathcal{M}_i$) from host $\mathcal{H}_j$.
   - Create a join session record $\langle jsid, \mathcal{M}_i, \mathcal{H}_j, status\rangle$ with $status \leftarrow request$.
   - Output (JOIN, $sid, jsid, \mathcal{H}_j$) to $\mathcal{M}_i$.
3. `M Join Proceed`. On input (JOIN, $sid, jsid$) from TPM $\mathcal{M}_i$.
   - Update the session record $\langle jsid, \mathcal{M}_i, \mathcal{H}_j, status\rangle$ with $status = request$ to $delivered$.
   - Output (JOINPROCEED, $sid, jsid, \mathcal{M}_i, \mathcal{H}_j$) to $\mathcal{A}$, wait for input (JOINPROCEED, $sid, jsid$) from $\mathcal{A}$.
   - Abort if $\mathcal{I}$ or $\mathcal{M}_i$ is honest and a record $\langle \mathcal{M}_i, *, *\rangle \in$ `Members` already exists.
   - Output (JOINPROCEED, $sid, jsid, \mathcal{M}_i$) to $\mathcal{I}$.
4. `I Join Proceed`. On input (JOINPROCEED, $sid, jsid$) from $\mathcal{I}$.
   - Update the session record $\langle jsid, \mathcal{M}_i, \mathcal{H}_j, status\rangle$ with $status = delivered$ to $complete$.
   - Output (JOINCOMPLETE, $sid, jsid$) to $\mathcal{A}$ and wait for input (JOINCOMPLETE, $sid, jsid, \tau$) from $\mathcal{A}$.
   - If $\mathcal{H}_j$ is honest, set $\tau \leftarrow \perp$. *(strong non-frameability)*
   - Else, verify that the provided tracing trapdoor τ is eligible by checking CheckTtdCorrupt(τ) = 1.
   - Insert $\langle \mathcal{M}_i, \mathcal{H}_j, \tau\rangle$ into `Members` and output (JOINED, $sid, jsid$) to $\mathcal{H}_j$.

Sign

5. `Sign Request`. On input (SIGN, $sid, ssid, \mathcal{M}_i, m, bsn$) from $\mathcal{H}_j$.
   - If $\mathcal{H}_j$ is honest and no entry $\langle \mathcal{M}_i, \mathcal{H}_j, *\rangle$ exists in `Members`, abort.
   - Create a sign session record $\langle ssid, \mathcal{M}_i, \mathcal{H}_j, m, bsn, status\rangle$ with $status \leftarrow request$.
   - Output (SIGNPROCEED, $sid, ssid, m, bsn$) to $\mathcal{M}_i$.
6. `Sign Proceed`. On input (SIGNPROCEED, $sid, ssid$) from $\mathcal{M}_i$.
   - Look up record $\langle ssid, \mathcal{M}_i, \mathcal{H}_j, m, bsn, status\rangle$ with $status = request$ and update it to $status \leftarrow complete$.
   - If $\mathcal{I}$ is honest, check that $\langle \mathcal{M}_i, \mathcal{H}_j, *\rangle$ exists in `Members`.
   - Generate the signature for a fresh or established key: *(strong privacy)*
     - Retrieve (gsk, τ) from $\langle \mathcal{M}_i, \mathcal{H}_j, bsn, gsk, \tau\rangle \in$ `DomainKeys`. If no such entry exists, set $(gsk, \tau) \leftarrow$ ukgen(), check CheckTtdHonest(τ) = 1, and store $\langle \mathcal{M}_i, \mathcal{H}_j, bsn, gsk, \tau\rangle$ in `DomainKeys`.
     - Compute signature $\sigma \leftarrow$ sig(gsk, m, bsn), check ver(σ, m, bsn) = 1.
     - Check identify(σ, m, bsn, τ) = 1 and that there is no $(\mathcal{M}', \mathcal{H}') \neq (\mathcal{M}_i, \mathcal{H}_j)$ with tracing trapdoor τ' registered in `Members` or `DomainKeys` with identify(σ, m, bsn, τ') = 1.
   - Store $\langle \sigma, m, bsn, \mathcal{M}_i, \mathcal{H}_j\rangle$ in `Signed` and output (SIGNATURE, $sid, ssid, \sigma$) to $\mathcal{H}_j$.

Verify & Link

7. `Verify`. On input (VERIFY, sid, m, bsn, σ, RL) from some party $\mathcal{V}$.
   - Retrieve all tuples $(\tau_i, \mathcal{M}_i, \mathcal{H}_j)$ from $\langle \mathcal{M}_i, \mathcal{H}_j, \tau_i\rangle \in$ `Members` and $\langle \mathcal{M}_i, \mathcal{H}_j, *, *, \tau_i\rangle \in$ `DomainKeys` where identify(σ, m, bsn, τ_i) = 1. Set $f \leftarrow 0$ if at least one of the following conditions hold:
     - More than one τ_i was found.
     - $\mathcal{I}$ is honest and no pair $(\tau_i, \mathcal{M}_i, \mathcal{H}_j)$ was found.
     - $\mathcal{M}_i$ or $\mathcal{H}_j$ is honest but no entry $\langle *, m, bsn, \mathcal{M}_i, \mathcal{H}_j\rangle \in$ `Signed` exists. *(strong unforgeability)*
     - There is a $\tau' \in$ RL where identify(σ, m, bsn, τ') = 1 and no pair $(\tau_i, \mathcal{M}_i, \mathcal{H}_j)$ for an honest $\mathcal{H}_j$ was found.
   - If $f \neq 0$, set $f \leftarrow$ ver(σ, m, bsn).
   - Add $\langle \sigma, m, bsn, \mathrm{RL}, f\rangle$ to `VerResults` and output (VERIFIED, sid, f) to $\mathcal{V}$.
8. `Link`. On input (LINK, $sid, \sigma, m, \sigma', m', bsn$) from a party $\mathcal{V}$.
   - Output $\perp$ to $\mathcal{V}$ if at least one signature (σ, m, bsn) or (σ', m', bsn) is not valid (verified via the `verify` interface with RL = $\emptyset$).
   - For each τ_i in `Members` and `DomainKeys` compute $b_i \leftarrow$ identify(σ, m, bsn, τ_i) and $b'_i \leftarrow$ identify(σ', m', bsn, τ_i) and do the following:
     - Set $f \leftarrow 0$ if $b_i \neq b'_i$ for some i.
     - Set $f \leftarrow 1$ if $b_i = b'_i = 1$ for some i.
   - If f is not defined yet, set $f \leftarrow$ link($\sigma, m, \sigma', m', bsn$).
   - Output (LINK, sid, f) to $\mathcal{V}$.

Fig. 1. Our ideal functionality $\mathcal{F}_{\mathsf{pdaa}}$ for DAA with optimal privacy.

created when the TPM $\mathcal{M}_i$ explicitly agrees to signing m w.r.t. bsn and a join record for $\mathcal{M}_i, \mathcal{H}_j$ in `Members` exists (if the issuer is honest).

When a platform wants to sign message m w.r.t. a fresh basename bsn, $\mathcal{F}_{\mathsf{pdaa}}$ generates a new key gsk (and tracing trapdoor τ) via ukgen and then signs m with that key. The functionality also stores the fresh key (gsk, τ) together with bsn in `DomainKeys`, and reuses the same key when the platform wishes to sign repeatedly under the same basename. Using fresh keys for every signature naturally enforces the desired privacy guarantees: the signature algorithm does not receive any identifying information as input, and thus the created signatures are guaranteed to be anonymous (or pseudonymous in case bsn is reused).

Our functionality enforces this privacy property whenever the host is honest. Note, however, that $\mathcal{F}_{\mathsf{pdaa}}$ does not behave differently when the host is corrupt, as in this case its output does not matter due to way corruptions are handled in UC. That is, $\mathcal{F}_{\mathsf{pdaa}}$ always outputs anonymous signatures to the host, but if the host is corrupt, the signature is given to the adversary, who can choose to discard it and output anything else instead.

To guarantee non-frameability and completeness, our functionality further checks that every freshly generated key, tracing trapdoor and signature does not falsely match with any existing signature or key. More precisely, $\mathcal{F}_{\mathsf{pdaa}}$ first uses the CheckTtdHonest macro to verify whether the new key does not match to any existing signature. (The detailed definition of CheckTtdHonest is given in the full version of this paper [24].) Likewise, before outputting σ, the functionality checks that no one else already has a key which would match this newly generated signature.

Finally, for ensuring unforgeability, the signed message, basename, and platform are stored in `Signed` which will be used when verifying signatures.

Verify. Signatures can be verified by any party using the VERIFY interface. $\mathcal{F}_{\mathsf{pdaa}}$ uses its internal `Signed`, `Members`, and `DomainKeys` records to enforce unforgeability and non-frameability. It uses the tracing trapdoors τ stored in `Members` and `DomainKeys` to find out which platform created this signature. If no match is found and the issuer is honest, the signature is a forgery and rejected by $\mathcal{F}_{\mathsf{pdaa}}$. If the signature to be verified matches the tracing trapdoor of some platform with an honest TPM or host, but the signing records do not show that they signed this message w.r.t. the basename, $\mathcal{F}_{\mathsf{pdaa}}$ again considers this to be a forgery and rejects. If the records do not reveal any issues with the signature, $\mathcal{F}_{\mathsf{pdaa}}$ uses the ver algorithm to obtain the final result.

The verify interface also supports verifier-local revocation. The verifier can input a revocation list `RL` containing tracing trapdoors, and signatures matching any of those trapdoors are no longer accepted.

Link. Using the LINK interface, any party can check whether two signatures (σ, σ') on messages (m, m') respectively, generated with the same basename bsn originate from the same platform or not. $\mathcal{F}_{\mathsf{pdaa}}$ again uses the tracing trapdoors τ stored in `Members` and `DomainKeys` to check which platforms created the two signatures. If they are the same, $\mathcal{F}_{\mathsf{pdaa}}$ outputs that they are linked. If it finds a platform that signed one, but not the other, it outputs that they are unlinked, which prevents framing of platforms with an honest host.

The full definition of $\mathcal{F}_{\mathsf{pdaa}}$ is given in Fig. 1. Note that when $\mathcal{F}_{\mathsf{pdaa}}$ runs one of the algorithms sig, ver, identify, link, and ukgen, it does so without maintaining state. This means all user keys have the same distribution, signatures are equally distributed for the same input, and ver, identify, and link invocations only depend on the current input, not on previous inputs.

2.2 Comparison with $\mathcal{F}^l_{\mathsf{daa}}$

Our functionality $\mathcal{F}_{\mathsf{pdaa}}$ is a strengthened version of $\mathcal{F}^l_{\mathsf{daa}}$ [25], as it requires fewer trust assumptions on the TPM for anonymity, non-frameability and unforgeability. It also includes a syntactical change which allows for more efficient constructions, as we discuss at the end of this section.

Optimal Privacy. The most important difference is that $\mathcal{F}^l_{\mathsf{daa}}$ guarantees anonymity only when both the TPM and the host are honest, whereas our modified version $\mathcal{F}_{\mathsf{pdaa}}$ guarantees anonymity as long as the host is honest, i.e., even when the TPM is corrupt. As discussed, the honesty of the host is strictly necessary, as privacy is impossible to guarantee otherwise.

In the ideal functionality $\mathcal{F}^l_{\mathsf{daa}}$ proposed by Camenisch et al. [25] the signatures are created in the SIGNPROCEED step in two different ways, depending on whether the TPM is honest or not. For the case of a corrupt TPM, the signature is provided by the adversary, which reflects that the adversary can recognize and link the signatures and $\mathcal{F}^l_{\mathsf{daa}}$ does not guarantee any privacy. If the TPM (and the host) is honest, $\mathcal{F}^l_{\mathsf{daa}}$ creates anonymous signatures inside the functionality using the signing algorithm sig and ukgen. As signatures are generated with fresh keys for every new basename, the functionality enforces the desired unlinkability and anonymity.

In our functionality $\mathcal{F}_{\mathsf{pdaa}}$, we also apply that approach of internally and anonymously creating signatures to the case where the TPM is corrupt, instead of relying on a signature input by the adversary. Thus, $\mathcal{F}_{\mathsf{pdaa}}$ guarantees the same strong privacy for both settings of a corrupt and honest TPM. In fact, for the sake of simplicity we let $\mathcal{F}_{\mathsf{pdaa}}$ even generate the signatures for corrupt hosts within the functionality now (whereas $\mathcal{F}^l_{\mathsf{daa}}$ used adversarially provided ones). However, as $\mathcal{F}_{\mathsf{pdaa}}$ outputs that signature to the host $\mathcal{H}_i$, who will be the adversary if $\mathcal{H}_i$ is corrupt, the behaviour of $\mathcal{F}_{\mathsf{pdaa}}$ with respect to privacy does not matter in that case: the adversary can simply ignore the output. We present a summary of the privacy properties guaranteed by $\mathcal{F}^l_{\mathsf{daa}}$ and $\mathcal{F}_{\mathsf{pdaa}}$ in Table 1.

Another difference between both functionalities is that in $\mathcal{F}_{\mathsf{pdaa}}$ we assume a direct communication channel between the host and TPM, which is necessary to achieve the desired privacy properties (see Sect. 2.3). Note that in the real-world, such a direct channel is naturally enforced by the physical proximity of the host and TPM forming the platform, i.e., if both are honest, an adversary can neither alter nor read their internal communication, or even notice that communication

Table 1. Overview of privacy guarantees by $\mathcal{F}^{l}_{\mathsf{daa}}$ [25], $\mathcal{F}_{\mathsf{pdaa+}}$ [22] and $\mathcal{F}_{\mathsf{pdaa}}$ (this work).

Corruption setting	$\mathcal{F}^{l}_{\mathsf{daa}}$	$\mathcal{F}_{\mathsf{pdaa+}}$	$\mathcal{F}_{\mathsf{pdaa}}$	
Honest host, honest TPM	+	+	+	
Honest host, isolated corrupt TPM	-	(+)	+	*Optimal privacy*
Honest host, fully corrupt TPM	-	-	(+)	*Conditional privacy*
Corrupt host	-	-	-	*Impossible*

is happening. Consequently, our functionality gets a bit simpler compared to $\mathcal{F}^{l}_{\mathsf{daa}}$ as we omit in JOIN and SIGN all dedicated interfaces and outputs that informed the simulator about communication between $\mathcal{H}_j$ and $\mathcal{M}_i$ and waited for a proceed input by the simulator to complete their communication.

Stronger Non-frameability and Unforgeability. While the focus of this work is strengthening the privacy properties in the presence of a subverted TPM, we also lift the trust assumption for non-frameability and unforgeability. Whereas $\mathcal{F}^{l}_{\mathsf{daa}}$ and all other prior security models [15, 17] guarantee non-frameability only if the entire platform is honest, our modified definition $\mathcal{F}_{\mathsf{pdaa}}$ enforces that property as long as the host is honest. Our stronger version of non-frameability is enforced by modifying the JOINPROCEED interface such that it allows the adversary to provide a tracing trapdoor τ (which steers the non-frameability checks by $\mathcal{F}_{\mathsf{pdaa}}$) only when the host is corrupt, as it set $\tau \leftarrow \bot$ whenever the host is honest. This replaces the original condition of discarding the adversarial τ when both, the host and TPM are honest. Note that similar to anonymity, requiring an honest host is strictly necessary for non-frameability too, as we can never control the signatures that a corrupt host outputs. In particular, a corrupt host with an honest TPM could additionally run a corrupt TPM and "frame itself" by outputting signatures from the corrupt TPM.

In terms of unforgeability, all previous definitions including $\mathcal{F}^{l}_{\mathsf{daa}}$ solely rely on the honesty of the TPM (and issuer of course). In $\mathcal{F}_{\mathsf{pdaa}}$ we provide a stronger version and guarantee that attestations cannot be forged unless the entire platform is corrupted, i.e., here we ensure unforgeability if at least one of two entities, TPM or host, is honest. This change is reflected in our functionality $\mathcal{F}_{\mathsf{pdaa}}$ as follows: In the SIGNPROCEED interface we store the host identity as part of the signature record $\langle \sigma, m, bsn, \mathcal{M}_i, \mathcal{H}_j \rangle \in \texttt{Signed}$ when signatures are created. Further, the VERIFY interface now requires the existence of such record whenever the signature to be verified belongs to an honest host or honest TPM. In $\mathcal{F}^{l}_{\mathsf{daa}}$ only $\langle \sigma, m, bsn, \mathcal{M}_i \rangle$ was stored and required when the TPM was honest. For unforgeability, relaxing the condition on the honesty of the TPM is not as crucial as for privacy and non-frameability. Thus, if only the standard unforgeability notion is sufficient, one can easily derive a functionality with optimal privacy but standard unforgeability by reverting the changes we just described.

Dedicated Tracing Key. Our functionality also includes some syntactical changes. $\mathcal{F}_{\mathsf{daa}}^{l}$ uses keys gsk for two purposes: to create signatures for honest platforms (via sig), and to trace signatures (via identify) when enforcing non-frameability and unforgeability. A key gsk can be provided by the adversary when a JOIN request is completed for a corrupt host, or is generated internally via ukgen whenever an anonymous signature is created. In $\mathcal{F}_{\mathsf{pdaa}}$ we split this into two dedicated values: gsk which is used to sign, and τ to trace signatures. Consequently, the identify algorithm now takes τ instead of gsk as input. The adversary has to provide τ in the JOIN interface, as its input is only used to ensure that a corrupt host cannot impersonate or frame another honest platform. The internally created keys are used for both, signing and tracing, and hence we modify ukgen to output a tuple (gsk, τ) instead of gsk only.

The idea behind that change is to allow for more efficient schemes, as the tracing key τ is usually a value that needs to be extracted by the simulator in the security proof. In the scheme we propose, it is sufficient that τ is the public key of the platform whereas gsk is its secret key. Using only a single gsk would have required the join protocol to include an extractable encryption of the platform's secret key, which would not only be less efficient but also a questionable protocol design. Clearly, our approach is more general than in $\mathcal{F}_{\mathsf{daa}}^{l}$, one can simply set $\tau = gsk$ to derive the same definition as $\mathcal{F}_{\mathsf{daa}}^{l}$.

2.3 Modeling Subverted Parties in the UC Framework

As just discussed, our functionality $\mathcal{F}_{\mathsf{pdaa}}$ guarantees that signatures created with an honest host are unlinkable and do not leak any information about the signing platform, even if the TPM is corrupt. However, the adversary still learns the message and basename when the TPM is corrupt, due to the way UC models corruptions. We discuss how this standard corruption model inherently limits the achievable privacy level, and then present our approach of isolated corruptions which allow one to overcome this limitation yet capture the power of subverted TPMs. While we discuss the modeling of isolated corruptions in the context of our DAA functionality, we consider the general concept to be of independent interest as it is applicable to any other scenario where such subversion attacks can occur.

Conditional Privacy Under Full TPM Corruption. According to the UC corruption model, the adversary gains full control over a corrupted party, i.e., it receives all inputs to that party and can choose its responses. For the case of a corrupt TPM this means that the adversary sees the message m and basename bsn whenever the honest host wants to create a signature. In fact, the adversary will learn which particular TPM $\mathcal{M}_i$ is asked to sign m w.r.t. bsn. Thus, even though the signature σ on m w.r.t. bsn is then created by $\mathcal{F}_{\mathsf{pdaa}}$ and does not leak any information about the identity of the signing platform, the adversary might still be able to recognize the platform's identity via the signed values. That is, if a message m or basename bsn is unique, i.e., only a single (and corrupt) TPM has ever signed m w.r.t. bsn, then, when later seeing a signature on m w.r.t. bsn, the adversary can derive which platform had created the signature.

A tempting idea for better privacy would be to change the functionality such that the TPM does not receive the message and basename when asked to approve an attestation via the SIGNPROCEED message. As a result, this information will not be passed to the adversary if the TPM is corrupt. However, that would completely undermine the purpose of the TPM that is supposed to serve as a trust anchor: verifiers accept a DAA attestation because they know a trusted TPM has approved them. Therefore, it is essential that the TPM sees and acknowledges the messages it signs.

Thus, in the presence of a fully corrupt TPM, the amount of privacy that can be achieved depends which messages and basenames are being signed – the more unique they are, the less privacy $\mathcal{F}_{\mathsf{pdaa}}$ guarantees.

Optimal Privacy Under *Isolated* TPM Corruption. The aforementioned leakage of all messages and basenames that are signed by a corrupt TPM is enforced by the UC corruption model. Modeling corruption of TPMs like this gives the adversary much more power than in reality: even if a TPM is subverted and runs malicious algorithms, it is still embedded into a host who controls all communication with the outside world. Thus, the adversary cannot communicate directly with the TPM, but only via the (honest) host.

To model such subversions more accurately and study the privacy achievable in the presence of subverted TPMs, we define a relaxed level of corruption that we call *isolated corruption*. When the adversary corrupts a TPM in this manner, it can specify code for the TPM but cannot directly communicate with the TPM.

We formally define such isolated corruptions via the body-shell paradigm used to model UC corruptions [31]. Recall that the body of a party defines its behavior, whereas the shell models the communication with that party. Thus, for our isolated corruptions, the adversary gets control over the body but not the shell. Interestingly, this is exactly the inverse of honest-but-curious corruptions in UC, where the adversary controls the shell and thus sees all inputs and outputs, but cannot change the body, i.e., the parties behavior remains honest.

In our case, an adversary performing an isolated corruption can provide a body, which models the tampered algorithms that an isolated corrupt TPM may use. The shell remains honest though and handles inputs, and subroutine outputs, and only forwards the ones that are allowed to the body. In the real world, the shell would only allow communication with the host in which the TPM is embedded. In the ideal world, the shell allows inputs to and outputs from the functionality, and blocks anything else.

Figures 2 and 3 depict the different levels of corruption in the real world and ideal world, respectively. In the ideal word, an isolated corruption of a TPM replaces the dummy TPM that forwards inputs and outputs between the environment and the ideal functionality with an *isolated simulator* comprising of the adversarial body and honest shell.

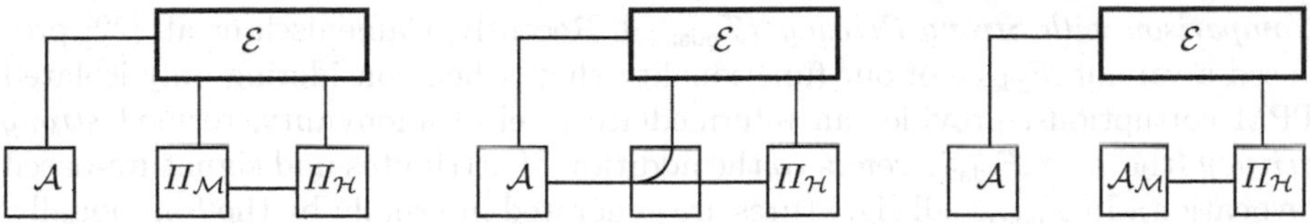

Fig. 2. Modeling of corruption in the real world. Left: an honest TPM applies the protocol $\Pi_{\mathcal{M}}$, and communicates with the host running $\Pi_{\mathcal{H}}$. Middle: a corrupt TPM sends any input the adversary instructs it to, and forwards any messages received to the adversary. Right: an isolated corrupt TPM is controlled by an isolated adversary $\mathcal{A}_{\mathcal{M}}$, who can communicate with the host, but not with any other entities.

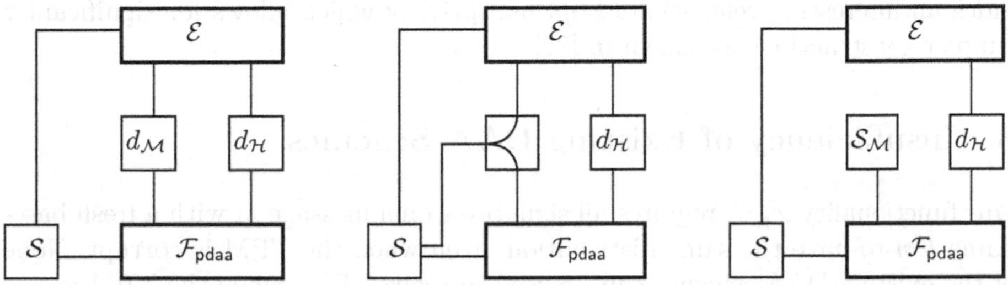

Fig. 3. Modeling of corruption in the ideal world. Left: an honest TPM is a dummy party $d_{\mathcal{M}}$ that forwards inputs and outputs between the environment $\mathcal{E}$ and the functionality $\mathcal{F}_{\mathsf{pdaa}}$. Middle: a corrupt TPM sends any input the adversary instructs it to, and forwards any subroutine output to the adversary. Right: an isolated corrupt TPM is controlled by an isolated simulator $\mathcal{S}_{\mathcal{M}}$, who may send inputs and receive outputs from $\mathcal{F}_{\mathsf{pdaa}}$, but not communicate with any other entities.

When designing a UC functionality, then all communication between a host and the "embedded" party that can get corrupted in such isolated manner must be modeled as direct channel (see e.g., the SIGN related interfaces in $\mathcal{F}_{\mathsf{pdaa}}$). Otherwise the simulator/adversary will be aware of the communication between both parties and can delay or block messages, which would contradict the concept of an isolated corruption where the adversary has no direct channel to the embedded party. Note that the perfect channel of course only holds if the host entity is honest, if it is corrupt (in the standard sense), the adversary can see and control all communication via the host anyway.

With such isolated adversaries we specify much stronger privacy. The adversary no longer automatically learns which isolated corrupt TPM signed which combination of messages and basenames, and the signatures created by $\mathcal{F}_{\mathsf{pdaa}}$ are guaranteed to be unlinkable. Of course the message m and basename bsn must not leak information about the identity of the platform. In certain applications, the platform would sign data generated or partially controlled by other functions contained in a TPM. This is out of scope of the attestation scheme, but the higher level scheme using $\mathcal{F}_{\mathsf{pdaa}}$ should ensure that this does not happen, by, e.g., letting the host randomize or sanitize the message.

Comparison with Strong Privacy ($\mathcal{F}_{\mathsf{pdaa+}}$). Recently, Camenisch et al. [22] proposed a variant $\mathcal{F}_{\mathsf{pdaa+}}$ of our functionality that, when considering only isolated TPM corruptions, provides an intermediate level of anonymity, termed *strong privacy* (the + in $\mathcal{F}_{\mathsf{pdaa+}}$ refers to the addition of attributes and signature-based revocation). In $\mathcal{F}_{\mathsf{pdaa+}}$ all signatures are generated internally by the functionally, just as in optimal privacy. The difference is that in strong privacy these signatures are revealed to the TPM which can then base its behavior on the signature value. Thus, while the actual signature shown to the TPM is still guaranteed to be anonymous, the TPM can influence the final distribution of the signatures by blocking certain values. In the isolated corruption model, where the corrupt TPM cannot communicate the learned signatures to the adversary, $\mathcal{F}_{\mathsf{pdaa+}}$ provides an interesting relaxation of optimal privacy which allows for significantly simpler constructions as shown in [22].

3 Insufficiency of Existing DAA Schemes

Our functionality $\mathcal{F}_{\mathsf{pdaa}}$ requires all signatures on a message m with a fresh basename bsn to have the same distribution, even when the TPM is corrupt. None of the existing DAA schemes can be used to realize $\mathcal{F}_{\mathsf{pdaa}}$ when the TPM is corrupted (either fully or isolated). The reason is inherent to the common protocol design that underlies all DAA schemes so far, i.e., there is no simple patch that would allow upgrading the existing solutions to achieve optimal privacy.

In a nutshell, in all existing DAA schemes, the TPM chooses a secret key gsk for which it blindly receives a membership credential of a trusted issuer. To create a signature on message m with basename bsn, the platform creates a signature proof of knowledge signing message m and proving knowledge of gsk and the membership credential.

In the original RSA-based DAA scheme [15], and the more recent qSDH-based schemes [18, 19, 23, 40], the proof of knowledge of the membership credential is created jointly by the TPM and host. After jointly computing the commitment values of the proof, the host computes the hash over these values and sends the hash c to the TPM. To prevent leaking information about its key, the TPM must ensure that the challenge is a hash of fresh values. In all the aforementioned schemes this is done by letting the TPM choose a fresh nonce n and computing the final hash as $c' \leftarrow \mathsf{H}(n, c)$. An adversarial TPM can embed information in n instead of taking it uniformly at random, clearly altering the distribution of the proof and thus violating the desired privacy guarantees.

At a first glance, deriving the hash for the proof in a more robust manner might seem a viable solution to prevent such leakage. For instance, setting the nonce as $n \leftarrow n_t \oplus n_h$, with n_t being the TPM's and n_h the host's contribution, and letting the TPM commit to n_t before receiving n_h. While this indeed removes the leakage via the nonce, it still reveals the hash value $c' \leftarrow \mathsf{H}(n, c)$ to the TPM with the hash becoming part of the completed signature. Thus, the TPM can base its behavior on the hash value and, e.g., only sign messages for hashes that start with a 0-bit. When considering only isolated corruptions for the TPM, the impact of such leakage is limited though as argued by Camenisch et al. [22] and formalized in their notion of strong privacy. In fact, Camenisch et al. show that by using such jointly generated nonces, and also letting the host contribute to the platform's secret key, the existing DAA schemes can be modified to achieve strong privacy in the isolated corruption model. However, it clearly does not result in signatures that are equally distributed as required by our functionality, and thus the approach is not sufficient to obtain *optimal* privacy.

The same argument applies to the LRSW-based DAA schemes [9,25,38], where the proof of a membership credential is done solely by the TPM, and thus can leak information via the Fiat-Shamir hash output again. The general problem is that the signature proofs of knowledge are not randomizable. If the TPM would create a randomizable proof of knowledge, e.g., a Groth-Sahai proof [47], the host could randomize the proof to remove any hidden information, but this would yield a highly inefficient signing protocol for the TPM.

4 Building Blocks

In this section we introduce the building blocks for our DAA scheme. In addition to standard components such as additively homomorphic encryption and zero-knowledge proofs, we introduce two non-standard types of signature schemes. One signature scheme we require is for the issuer to blindly sign the public key of the TPM and host. The second signature scheme is needed for the TPM and host to jointly create signed attestations, which we term *split signatures*.

The approach of constructing a DAA scheme from modular building blocks rather than basing it on a concrete instantiation was also used by Bernhard et al. [9,10]. As they considered a simplified setting, called pre-DAA, where the host and platform have a joint corruption state, and we aim for much stronger privacy, their "linkable indistinguishable tag" is not sufficient for our construction. We replace this with our split signatures.

As our protocol requires "compatible" building blocks, i.e., the different schemes have to work in the same group, we assume the availability of public system parameters $spar \xleftarrow{\$} \mathsf{SParGen}(\tau)$ generated for security parameter τ. We give *spar* as dedicated input to the individual key generation algorithms instead of the security parameter τ. For the sake of simplicity, we omit the system parameters as dedicated input to all other algorithms and assume that they are given as implicit input.

4.1 Proof Protocols

Let $\mathit{NIZK}\{(w) : s(w)\}(\mathit{ctxt})$ denote a generic non-interactive zero-knowledge proof that is bound to a certain context *ctxt* and proves knowledge of a witness w such that statement $s(w)$ is true. Sometimes we need witnesses to be online-extractable, which we denote by underlining them: $\mathit{NIZK}\{(\underline{w_1}, w_2) : s(w_1, w_2)\}$ allows for online extraction of w_1.

All the *NIZK* we give have efficient concrete instantiations for the instantiations we propose for our other building blocks. We will follow the notation introduced by Camenisch and Stadler [29] and formally defined by Camenisch, Kiayias, and Yung [26] for these protocols. For instance, $PK\{(a) : y = g^a\}$ denotes a "*zero-knowledge Proof of Knowledge of integer* a *such that* $y = g^a$ *holds.*" $SPK\{\ldots\}(m)$ denotes a signature proof of knowledge on m, that is a non-interactive transformation of a proof with the Fiat-Shamir heuristic [45].

4.2 Homomorphic Encryption Schemes

We require an encryption scheme (EncKGen, Enc, Dec) that is semantically secure and that has a cyclic group $\mathbb{G} = \langle g \rangle$ of order q as message space. It consists of a key generation algorithm $(epk, esk) \xleftarrow{\$} \mathsf{EncKGen}(spar)$, where $spar$ defines the group $\mathbb{G}$, an encryption algorithm $C \xleftarrow{\$} \mathsf{Enc}(epk, m)$, with $m \in \mathbb{G}$, and a decryption algorithm $m \leftarrow \mathsf{Dec}(esk, C)$.

We further require that the encryption scheme has an appropriate *homomorphic property*, namely that there is an efficient operation $\odot$ on ciphertexts such that, if $C_1 \in \mathsf{Enc}(epk, m_1)$ and $C_2 \in \mathsf{Enc}(epk, m_2)$, then $C_1 \odot C_2 \in \mathsf{Enc}(epk, m_1 \cdot m_2)$. We will also use exponents to denote the repeated application of $\odot$, e.g., C^2 to denote $C \odot C$.

ElGamal Encryption. We use the ElGamal encryption scheme [44], which is homomorphic and chosen plaintext secure. The semantic security is sufficient for our construction, as the parties always prove to each other that they formed the ciphertexts correctly. Let $spar$ define a group $\mathbb{G} = \langle g \rangle$ of order q such that the DDH problem is hard w.r.t. τ, i.e., q is a τ-bit prime.

$\mathsf{EncKGen}(spar)$: Pick $x \xleftarrow{\$} \mathbb{Z}_q$, compute $y \leftarrow g^x$, and output $esk \leftarrow x$, $epk \leftarrow y$.
$\mathsf{Enc}(epk, m)$: To encrypt a message $m \in \mathbb{G}$ under $epk = y$, pick $r \xleftarrow{\$} \mathbb{Z}_q$ and output the ciphertext $(C_1, C_2) \leftarrow (y^r, g^r m)$.
$\mathsf{Dec}(esk, C)$: On input the secret key $esk = x$ and a ciphertext $C = (C_1, C_2) \in \mathbb{G}^2$, output $m' \leftarrow C_2 \cdot C_1^{-1/x}$.

4.3 Signature Schemes for Encrypted Messages

We need a signature scheme that supports the signing of encrypted messages and must allow for (efficient) proofs proving that an encrypted value is correctly signed and proving knowledge of a signature that signs an encrypted value. Dual-mode signatures [27] satisfy these properties, as therein signatures on plaintext as well as on encrypted messages can be obtained. As we do not require signatures on plaintexts, though, we can use a simplified version.

A signature scheme for encrypted messages consists of the algorithms (SigKGen, EncSign, DecSign, Vf) and also uses an encryption scheme (EncKGen, Enc, Dec) that is compatible with the message space of the signature scheme. In particular, the algorithms working with encrypted messages or signatures also get the keys $(epk, esk) \xleftarrow{\$} \mathsf{EncKGen}(spar)$ of the encryption scheme as input.

$\mathsf{SigKGen}(spar)$: On input the system parameters, this algorithm outputs a public verification key spk and secret signing key ssk.

$\mathsf{EncSign}(ssk, epk, C)$: On input signing key ssk, a public encryption key epk, and ciphertext $C = \mathsf{Enc}(epk, m)$, outputs an "encrypted" signature $\overline{\sigma}$ of C.

$\mathsf{DecSign}(esk, spk, \overline{\sigma})$: On input an "encrypted" signature $\overline{\sigma}$, secret decryption key esk and public verification key spk, outputs a standard signature σ.

$\mathsf{Vf}(spk, \sigma, m)$: On input a public verification key spk, signature σ and message m, outputs 1 if the signature is valid and 0 otherwise.

In terms of security, we require completeness and unforgeability as defined in [27], but omit the oracle for signatures on plaintext messages in the unforgeability experiment. Clearly, any secure dual-mode signature is also unforgeable according to our notion. The simplified security model is given in the full version of this paper [24].

AGOT+ Signature Scheme. To instantiate the building block of signatures for encrypted messages we will use the AGOT+ scheme of [27], which was shown to be a secure instantiation of a dual-mode signature, hence is also secure in our simplified setting. Again, as we do not require signatures on plaintext messages we omit the standard signing algorithm. The AGOT+ scheme is based on the structure-preserving signature scheme by Abe et al. [1], which is proven to be unforgeable in the generic group model.

The AGOT+ scheme assumes the availability of system parameters $(q, \mathbb{G}_1, \mathbb{G}_2, \mathbb{G}_T, e, g_1, g_2, x)$, where $\mathbb{G}_1, \mathbb{G}_2, \mathbb{G}_T$ are groups of prime order q generated by g_1, g_2, and $e(g_1, g_2)$ respectively, e is a non-degenerate bilinear map $e : \mathbb{G}_1 \times \mathbb{G}_2 \rightarrow \mathbb{G}_T$, and x is an additional random group element in $\mathbb{G}_1$.

$\mathsf{SigKGen}(spar)$: Draw $v \xleftarrow{\$} \mathbb{Z}_q$, compute $y \leftarrow g_2^v$, and return $spk = y$, $ssk = v$.

$\mathsf{EncSign}(ssk, epk, M)$: On input a proper encryption $M = \mathsf{Enc}(epk, m)$ of a message $m \in \mathbb{G}_1$ under epk, and secret key $ssk = v$, choose a random $u \xleftarrow{\$} \mathbb{Z}_q^*$, and output the (partially) encrypted signature $\bar{\sigma} = (r, S, T, w)$:

$$r \leftarrow g_2^u, \quad S \leftarrow (M^v \odot \mathsf{Enc}(epk, x))^{1/u}, \quad T \leftarrow (S^v \odot \mathsf{Enc}(epk, g_1))^{1/u}, \quad w \leftarrow g_1^{1/u}.$$

$\mathsf{DecSign}(esk, spk, \overline{\sigma})$: Parse $\overline{\sigma} = (r, S, T, w)$, compute $s \leftarrow \mathsf{Dec}(esk, S)$, $t \leftarrow \mathsf{Dec}(esk, T)$ and output $\sigma = (r, s, t, w)$.

$\mathsf{Vf}(spk, \sigma, m)$: Parse $\sigma = (r, s, t, w')$ and $spk = y$ and output 1 iff $m, s, t \in \mathbb{G}_1$, $r \in \mathbb{G}_2$, $e(s, r) = e(m, y) \cdot e(x, g_2)$, and $e(t, r) = e(s, y) \cdot e(g_1, g_2)$.

Note that for notational simplicity, we consider w part of the signature, i.e., $\sigma = (r, s, t, w)$, altough signature verification will ignore w. As pointed out by Abe et al., a signature $\sigma = (r, s, t)$ can be randomized using the randomization token w to obtain a signature $\sigma' = (r', s', t')$ by picking a random $u' \xleftarrow{\$} \mathbb{Z}_q^*$ and computing $r' \leftarrow r^{u'}$, $s' \leftarrow s^{1/u'}$, $t' \leftarrow (tw^{(u'-1)})^{1/u'^2}$.

For our construction, we also require the host to prove that it knows an encrypted signature on an encrypted message. In Sect. 6 we describe how such a proof can be done.

4.4 Split Signatures

The second signature scheme we require must allow two different parties, each holding a share of the secret key, to jointly create signatures. Our DAA protocol performs the joined public key generation and the signing operation in a strict sequential order. That is, the first party creates his part of the key, and the second party receiving the 'pre-public key' generates a second key share and completes the joined public key. Similarly, to sign a message the first signer creates a 'pre-signature' and the second signer completes the signature. We model the new signature scheme for that particular sequential setting rather than aiming for a more generic building block in the spirit of threshold or multi-signatures, as the existence of a strict two-party order allows for substantially more efficient constructions.

We term this new building block *split signatures* partially following the notation by Bellare and Sandhu [8] who formalized different two-party settings for RSA-based signatures where the signing key is split between a client and server. Therein, the case "MSC" where the first signature contribution is produced by an external server and then completed by the client comes closest to out setting.

Formally, we define a split signature scheme as a tuple of the algorithms $\mathsf{SSIG} = (\mathsf{PreKeyGen}, \mathsf{CompleteKeyGen}, \mathsf{VerKey}, \mathsf{PreSign}, \mathsf{CompleteSign}, \mathsf{Vf})$:

$\mathsf{PreKeyGen}(spar)$: On input the system parameters, this algorithm outputs the pre-public key ppk and the first share of the secret signing key ssk_1.

$\mathsf{CompleteKeyGen}(ppk)$: On input the pre-public key, this algorithm outputs a public verification key spk and the second secret signing key ssk_2.

$\mathsf{VerKey}(ppk, spk, ssk_2)$: On input the pre-public key ppk, the full public key spk, and a secret key share ssk_2, this algorithm outputs 1 iff the pre-public key combined with secret key part ssk_2 leads to full public key spk.

$\mathsf{PreSign}(ssk_1, m)$: On input a secret signing key share ssk_1, and message m, this algorithm outputs a pre-signature σ'.

$\mathsf{CompleteSign}(ppk, ssk_2, m, \sigma')$: On input the pre-public key ppk, the second signing key share ssk_2, message m, and pre-signature σ', this algorithm outputs the completed signature σ.

$\mathsf{Vf}(spk, \sigma, m)$: On input the public key spk, signature σ, and message m, this algorithm outputs a bit b indicating whether the signature is valid or not.

We require a number of security properties from our split signatures. The first one is unforgeability which must hold if at least one of the two signers is honest. This is captured in two security experiments: type-1 unforgeability allows the first signer to be corrupt, and type-2 unforgeability considers a corrupt second signer. Our definitions are similar to the ones by Bellare and Sandhu, with the difference that we do not assume a trusted dealer creating *both* secret key shares. Instead, we let the adversary output the key share of the party he controls. For type-2 unforgeability we must ensure, though, that the adversary indeed integrates the honestly generated pre-key ppk when producing the completed public key spk, which we verify via VerKey. Formally, unforgeability for split signatures is defined as follows.

Experiment $\mathsf{Exp}_{\mathcal{A}}^{\mathsf{Unforgeability\text{-}1}}(\tau)$:
$spar \xleftarrow{\$} \mathsf{SParGen}(1^\tau)$
$(ppk, state) \leftarrow \mathcal{A}(spar)$
$(spk, ssk_2) \leftarrow \mathsf{CompleteKeyGen}(ppk)$
$\mathbf{L} \leftarrow \emptyset$
$(m^*, \sigma^*) \leftarrow \mathcal{A}^{\mathcal{O}^{\mathsf{CompleteSign}(ppk, ssk_2, \cdot, \cdot)}}(state, spk)$
where $\mathcal{O}^{\mathsf{CompleteSign}}$ on input (m_i, σ_i'):
set $\mathbf{L} \leftarrow \mathbf{L} \cup m_i$
return $\sigma_i \leftarrow \mathsf{CompleteSign}(ppk, ssk_2, m_i, \sigma_i')$
return 1 if $\mathsf{Vf}(spk, \sigma^*, m^*) = 1$ and $m^* \notin \mathbf{L}$

Experiment $\mathsf{Exp}_{\mathcal{A}}^{\mathsf{Unforgeability\text{-}2}}(\tau)$:
$spar \xleftarrow{\$} \mathsf{SParGen}(1^\tau)$
$(ppk, ssk_1) \leftarrow \mathsf{PreKeyGen}(spar)$
$\mathbf{L} \leftarrow \emptyset$
$(m^*, \sigma^*, spk, ssk_2) \leftarrow \mathcal{A}^{\mathcal{O}^{\mathsf{PreSign}(ssk_1, \cdot)}}(spar, ppk)$
where $\mathcal{O}^{\mathsf{PreSign}}$ on input m_i:
set $\mathbf{L} \leftarrow \mathbf{L} \cup m_i$
return $\sigma_i' \leftarrow \mathsf{PreSign}(ssk_1, m_i)$
return 1 if $\mathsf{Vf}(spk, \sigma^*, m^*) = 1$, and $m^* \notin \mathbf{L}$
and $\mathsf{VerKey}(ppk, spk, ssk_2) = 1$

Fig. 4. Unforgeability-1 (1st signer is corrupt) and unforgeability-2 (2nd signer is corrupt) experiments.

Definition 1 (Type-1/2 Unforgeability of SSIG). *A split signature scheme is* type-1/2 unforgeable *if for any efficient algorithm $\mathcal{A}$ the probability that the experiments given in Fig. 4 return 1 is negligible (as a function of τ).*

Further, we need a property that we call *key-hiding*, which ensures that signatures do not leak any information about the public key for which they are generated. This is needed in the DAA scheme to get unlinkability even in the presence of a corrupt TPM that contributes to the signatures and knows part of the secret key, yet should not be able to recognize "his" signatures afterwards. Our key-hiding notion is somewhat similar in spirit to key-privacy for encryption schemes as defined by Bellare et al. [6], which requires that a ciphertext should not leak anything about the public key under which it is encrypted.

Formally, this is captured by giving the adversary a challenge signature for a chosen message either under the real or a random public key. Clearly, the property can only hold as long as the real public key *spk* is not known to the adversary, as otherwise he can simply verify the challenge signature. As we want the property to hold even when the first party is corrupt, the adversary can choose the first part of the secret key and also contribute to the challenge signature. The adversary is also given oracle access to $\mathcal{O}^{\mathsf{CompleteSign}}$ again, but is not allowed to query the message used in the challenge query, as he could win trivially otherwise (by the requirement of signature-uniqueness defined below and the determinism of CompleteSign). The formal experiment for our key-hiding property is given below. The oracle $\mathcal{O}^{\mathsf{CompleteSign}}$ is defined analogously as in type-1 unforgeability.

Definition 2 (Key-hiding property of SSIG). *We say a split signature scheme is* key-hiding *if for any efficient algorithm $\mathcal{A}$ the probability that the experiment given in Fig. 5 returns 1 is negligible (as a function of τ).*

Finally, we need correctness, i.e., honestly generated signatures verify correctly, and two uniqueness properties for our split signatures. The first is *key-uniqueness*, which states that every signature is only valid under one public key.

Experiment $\mathsf{Exp}_{\mathcal{A}}^{\mathsf{Key\text{-}Hiding}}(\tau)$:
$spar \xleftarrow{\$} \mathsf{SParGen}(1^\tau)$
$(ppk, state) \xleftarrow{\$} \mathcal{A}(spar)$
$(spk, ssk_2) \xleftarrow{\$} \mathsf{CompleteKeyGen}(ppk)$
$\mathbf{L} \leftarrow \emptyset$
$(m, \sigma', state') \xleftarrow{\$} \mathcal{A}^{\mathcal{O}^{\mathsf{CompleteSign}(ppk, ssk_2, \cdot, \cdot)}}(state)$
$b \xleftarrow{\$} \{0,1\}$
if $b = 0$ *(signature under spk):*
  $\sigma \leftarrow \mathsf{CompleteSign}(ppk, ssk_2, m, \sigma')$
if $b = 1$ *(signature under random key)*:
  $(ppk^*, ssk_1^*) \xleftarrow{\$} \mathsf{PreKeyGen}(spar)$
  $(spk^*, ssk_2^*) \xleftarrow{\$} \mathsf{CompleteKeyGen}(ppk^*)$
  $\sigma' \xleftarrow{\$} \mathsf{PreSign}(ssk_1^*, m)$
  $\sigma \leftarrow \mathsf{CompleteSign}(ppk^*, ssk_2^*, m, \sigma')$
$b' \leftarrow \mathcal{A}^{\mathcal{O}^{\mathsf{CompleteSign}(ppk, ssk_2, \cdot, \cdot)}}(state', \sigma)$
return 1 if $b = b'$, $m \notin \mathbf{L}$, and $\mathsf{Vf}(spk, \sigma, m) = 1$

Fig. 5. Key-hiding experiment for split signatures.

Second, we require *signature-uniqueness*, which guarantees that one can compute only a single valid signature on a certain message under a certain public key. These properties are formally defined in the full version of this paper [24].

Instantiation of split signatures (split-BLS). To instantiate split signatures, we use a modified BLS signature [12]. Let H be a hash function $\{0,1\} \to \mathbb{G}_1^*$ and the public system parameters be the description of a bilinear map, i.e., $spar = (\mathbb{G}_1, \mathbb{G}_2, \mathbb{G}_T, g_1, g_2, e, q)$.

$\mathsf{PreKeyGen}(spar)$: Take $ssk_1 \xleftarrow{\$} \mathbb{Z}_q^*$, set $ppk \leftarrow g_2^{ssk_1}$, and output (ppk, ssk_1).
$\mathsf{CompleteKeyGen}(spar, ppk)$: Check $ppk \in \mathbb{G}_2$ and $ppk \neq 1_{\mathbb{G}_2}$. Take $ssk_2 \xleftarrow{\$} \mathbb{Z}_q^*$ and compute $spk \leftarrow ppk^{ssk_2}$. Output (spk, ssk_2).
$\mathsf{VerKey}(spar, ppk, spk, ssk_2)$: Output 1 iff $ppk \neq 1_{\mathbb{G}_2}$ and $spk = ppk^{ssk_2}$.
$\mathsf{PreSign}(spar, ssk_1, m)$: Output $\sigma' \leftarrow \mathsf{H}(m)^{ssk_1}$.
$\mathsf{CompleteSign}(spar, ppk, ssk_2, m, \sigma')$: If $e(\sigma', g_2) = e(\mathsf{H}(m), ppk)$, output $\sigma \leftarrow \sigma'^{ssk_2}$, otherwise $\perp$.
$\mathsf{Vf}(spar, spk, \sigma, m)$: Output 1 iff $\sigma \neq 1_{\mathbb{G}_1}$ and $e(\sigma, g_2) = e(\mathsf{H}(m), spk)$.

The proof of the following theorem is given in the full version of this paper [24].

Theorem 1. *The split-BLS signature scheme is a secure split signature scheme, satisfying correctness, unforgeability-1, unforgeability-2, key-hiding, key-uniqueness, and signature-uniqueness, under the computational co-Diffie-Hellman assumption and the DDH assumption in* $\mathbb{G}_1$*, in the random oracle model.*

5 Construction

This section describes our DAA protocol achieving optimal privacy. On a very high level, the protocol follows the core idea of existing DAA protocols: The platform, consisting of the TPM and a host, first generates a secret key *gsk* that gets blindly certified by a trusted issuer. Subsequently, the platform can use the key *gsk* to sign attestations and basenames and then prove that it has a valid credential on the signing key, certifying the trusted origin of the attestation.

This high-level procedure is the main similarity to existing schemes though, as we significantly change the role of the host to satisfy our notion of optimal privacy. First, we no longer rely on a single secret key *gsk* that is fully controlled by the TPM. Instead, both the TPM and host generate secret shares, *tsk* and *hsk* respectively, that lead to a joint public key *gpk*. For privacy reasons, we cannot reveal this public key to the issuer in the join protocol, as any exposure of the joint public key would allow to trace any subsequent signed attestations of the platform. Thus, we let the issuer sign only an encryption of the public key, using the signature scheme for encrypted messages. When creating this membership credential *cred* the issuer is assured that the blindly signed key is formed correctly and the credential is strictly bound to that unknown key.

After having completed the JOIN protocol, the host and TPM can together sign a message m with respect to a basename *bsn*. Both parties use their individual key shares and create a split signature on the message and basename (denoted as *tag*), which shows that the platform intended to sign this message and basename, and a split signature on only the basename (denoted as *nym*), which is used as a pseudonym. Recall that attestations from one platform with the same basename should be linkable. By the uniqueness of split signatures, *nym* will be constant for one platform and basename and allow for such linkability. Because split signatures are key-hiding, we can reveal *tag* and *nym* while preserving the unlinkability of signatures with different basenames.

When signing, the host proves knowledge of a credential that signs *gpk*. Note that the host can create the full proof of knowledge because the membership credential signs a joint public key. In existing DAA schemes, the membership credential signs a TPM secret, and therefore the TPM must always be involved to prove knowledge of the credential, which prevents optimal privacy as we argued in Sect. 3.

5.1 Our DAA Protocol with Optimal Privacy Π_{pdaa}

We now present our generic DAA protocol with optimal privacy Π_{pdaa} in detail. Let $\mathsf{SSIG} = (\mathsf{PreKeyGen}, \mathsf{CompleteKeyGen}, \mathsf{VerKey}, \mathsf{PreSign}, \mathsf{CompleteSign}, \mathsf{Vf})$ denote a secure split signature scheme, as defined in Sect. 4.4, and let $\mathsf{ESIG} = (\mathsf{SigKGen}, \mathsf{EncSign}, \mathsf{DecSign}, \mathsf{Vf})$ denote a secure signature scheme for encrypted messages, as defined in Sect. 4.3. In addition, we use a CPA secure encryption scheme $\mathsf{ENC} = (\mathsf{EncKGen}, \mathsf{Enc}, \mathsf{Dec})$. We require all these algorithms to be compatible, meaning they work with the same system parameters.

We further assume that functionalities ($\mathcal{F}_{\mathsf{crs}}, \mathcal{F}_{\mathsf{ca}}, \mathcal{F}_{\mathsf{auth*}}$) are available to all parties. The certificate authority functionality $\mathcal{F}_{\mathsf{ca}}$ allows the issuer to register his public key, and we assume that parties call $\mathcal{F}_{\mathsf{ca}}$ to retrieve the public key whenever needed. As the issuer key (ipk, π_{ipk}) also contains a proof of well-formedness, we also assume that each party retrieving the key will verify π_{ipk}.

The common reference string functionality $\mathcal{F}_{\mathsf{crs}}$ provides all parties with the system parameters *spar* generated via $\mathsf{SParGen}(1^\tau)$. All the algorithms of the building blocks take *spar* as an input, which we omit – except for the key generation algorithms – for ease of presentation.

For the communication between the TPM and issuer (via the host) in the join protocol, we use the semi-authenticated channel $\mathcal{F}_{\mathsf{auth*}}$ introduced by Camenisch et al. [25]. This functionality abstracts the different options on how to realize the authenticated channel between the TPM and issuer that is established via an unauthenticated host. We assume the host and TPM can communicate directly, meaning that they have an authenticated and perfectly secure channel. This models the physical proximity of the host and TPM forming the platform: if the host is honest an adversary can neither alter nor read their internal communication, or even notice that communication is happening.

To make the protocol more readable, we omit the explicit calls to the sub-functionalities with sub-session IDs and simply say e.g., issuer $\mathcal{I}$ registers its public key with $\mathcal{F}_{\mathsf{ca}}$. For definitions of the standard functionalities $\mathcal{F}_{\mathsf{crs}}$ and $\mathcal{F}_{\mathsf{ca}}$ we refer to [30,31].

`1. Issuer Setup.` In the setup phase, the issuer $\mathcal{I}$ creates a key pair of the signature scheme for encrypted messages and registers the public key with $\mathcal{F}_{\mathsf{ca}}$.

(a) $\mathcal{I}$ upon input (SETUP, sid) generates his key pair:
  - Check that $sid = (\mathcal{I}, sid')$ for some sid'.
  - Get $(ipk, isk) \xleftarrow{\$} \mathsf{ESIG.SigKGen}(spar)$ and prove knowledge of the secret key via $\pi_{ipk} \leftarrow \mathsf{NIZK}\{(\underline{isk}) : (ipk, isk) \in \mathsf{ESIG.SigKGen}(spar)\}(sid)$.
  - Initiate $\mathcal{L}_{\mathsf{JOINED}} \leftarrow \emptyset$.
  - Register the public key (ipk, π_{ipk}) at $\mathcal{F}_{\mathsf{ca}}$, and store $(isk, \mathcal{L}_{\mathsf{JOINED}})$.
  - Output $(\mathsf{SETUPDONE}, sid)$.

Join Protocol. The join protocol runs between the issuer $\mathcal{I}$ and a platform, consisting of a TPM $\mathcal{M}_i$ and a host $\mathcal{H}_j$. The platform authenticates to the issuer and, if the issuer allows the platform to join, obtains a credential *cred* that subsequently enables the platform to create signatures. The credential is a signature on the encrypted joint public key *gpk* to which the host and TPM each hold a secret key share. To show the issuer that a TPM has contributed to the joint key, the TPM reveals an authenticated version of his (public) key contribution to the issuer and the host proves that it correctly incorporated that share in *gpk*. A unique sub-session identifier *jsid* distinguishes several join sessions that might run in parallel.

2. **Join Request.** The join request is initiated by the host.

(a) Host $\mathcal{H}_j$, on input $(\mathsf{JOIN}, sid, jsid, \mathcal{M}_i)$ parses $sid = (\mathcal{I}, sid')$ and sends $(sid, jsid)$ to $\mathcal{M}_i$. [1]

(b) TPM $\mathcal{M}_i$, upon receiving $(sid, jsid)$ from a party $\mathcal{H}_j$, outputs $(\mathsf{JOIN}, sid, jsid)$.

3. **$\mathcal{M}$-Join Proceed.** The join session proceeds when the TPM receives an explicit input telling him to proceed with the join session *jsid*.

(a) TPM $\mathcal{M}_i$, on input $(\mathsf{JOIN}, sid, jsid)$ creates a key share for the split signature and sends it authenticated to the issuer (via the host):
   - Run $(tpk, tsk) \xleftarrow{\$} \mathsf{SSIG.PreKeyGen}(spar)$.
   - Send tpk over $\mathcal{F}_{\mathsf{auth}*}$ to $\mathcal{I}$ via $\mathcal{H}_j$, and store the key $(sid, \mathcal{H}_j, tsk)$.

(b) When $\mathcal{H}_j$ notices $\mathcal{M}_i$ sending tpk over $\mathcal{F}_{\mathsf{auth}*}$ to the issuer, it generates its key share for the split signature and appends an encryption of the jointly produced gpk to the message sent towards the issuer.
   - Complete the split signature key as $(gpk, hsk) \xleftarrow{\$} \mathsf{SSIG.CompleteKeyGen}(tpk)$.
   - Create an ephemeral encryption key pair $(epk, esk) \xleftarrow{\$} \mathsf{EncKGen}(spar)$.
   - Encrypt gpk under epk as $C \xleftarrow{\$} \mathsf{Enc}(epk, gpk)$.
   - Prove that C is an encryption of a public key gpk that is correctly derived from the TPM public key share tpk:

$$\pi_{\mathsf{JOIN},\mathcal{H}} \leftarrow \mathsf{NIZK}\{(\underline{gpk}, hsk) : C \in \mathsf{Enc}(epk, gpk) \\ \wedge\ \mathsf{SSIG.VerKey}(tpk, gpk, hsk) = 1\}(sid, jsid).$$

   - Append $(\mathcal{H}_j, epk, C, \pi_{\mathsf{JOIN},\mathcal{H}})$ to the message $\mathcal{M}_i$ is sending to $\mathcal{I}$ over $\mathcal{F}_{\mathsf{auth}*}$ and store $(sid, jsid, \mathcal{M}_i, esk, hsk, gpk)$.

(c) $\mathcal{I}$, upon receiving tpk authenticated by $\mathcal{M}_i$ and $(\mathcal{H}_j, epk, C, \pi_{\mathsf{JOIN},\mathcal{H}})$ in the unauthenticated part, verifies that the request is legitimate:
   - Verify $\pi_{\mathsf{JOIN},\mathcal{H}}$ w.r.t. the authenticated tpk and check that $\mathcal{M}_i \notin \mathcal{L}_{\mathsf{JOINED}}$.
   - Store $(sid, jsid, \mathcal{H}_j, \mathcal{M}_i, epk, C)$ and output $(\mathsf{JOINPROCEED}, sid, jsid, \mathcal{M}_i)$.

4. **$\mathcal{I}$-Join Proceed.** The join session is completed when the issuer receives an explicit input telling him to proceed with join session *jsid*.

(a) $\mathcal{I}$ upon input $(\mathsf{JOINPROCEED}, sid, jsid)$ signs the encrypted public key C using the signature scheme for encrypted messages:
   - Retrieve $(sid, jsid, \mathcal{H}_j, \mathcal{M}_i, epk, C)$ and set $\mathcal{L}_{\mathsf{JOINED}} \leftarrow \mathcal{L}_{\mathsf{JOINED}} \cup \mathcal{M}_i$.
   - Sign C as $cred' \xleftarrow{\$} \mathsf{ESIG.EncSign}(isk, epk, C)$ and prove that it did so correctly. (This proof is required to allow verification in the security proof: ENC is only CPA-secure and thus we cannot decrypt $cred'$.)

$$\pi_{\mathsf{JOIN},\mathcal{I}} \leftarrow \mathsf{NIZK}\{isk : cred' \in \mathsf{ESIG.EncSign}(isk, epk, C) \\ \wedge\ (ipk, isk) \in \mathsf{ESIG.SigKGen}(spar)\}(sid, jsid).$$

[1] Recall that we use direct communication between a TPM and host, i.e., this message is authenticated and unnoticed by the adversary.

- Send $(sid, jsid, cred', \pi_{\mathsf{JOIN},\mathcal{I}})$ to $\mathcal{H}_j$ (via the network).

(b) Host $\mathcal{H}_j$, upon receiving $(sid, jsid, cred', \pi_{\mathsf{JOIN},\mathcal{I}})$ decrypts and stores the membership credential:
   - Retrieve the session record $(sid, jsid, \mathcal{M}_i, esk, hsk, gpk)$.
   - Verify proof $\pi_{\mathsf{JOIN},\mathcal{I}}$ w.r.t. $ipk, cred', C$ and decrypt the credential as $cred \leftarrow \mathsf{ESIG.DecSign}(esk, cred')$.
   - Store the completed key record $(sid, hsk, tpk, gpk, cred, \mathcal{M}_i)$ and output $(\mathsf{JOINED}, sid, jsid)$.

Sign Protocol. The sign protocol runs between a TPM $\mathcal{M}_i$ and a host $\mathcal{H}_j$. After joining, together they can sign a message m w.r.t. a basename bsn using the split signature. Sub-session identifier $ssid$ distinguishes multiple sign sessions.

5. `Sign Request`. The signature request is initiated by the host.

(a) $\mathcal{H}_j$ upon input $(\mathsf{SIGN}, sid, ssid, \mathcal{M}_i, m, bsn)$ prepares the signature process:
   - Check that it joined with $\mathcal{M}_i$ (i.e., a completed key record for $\mathcal{M}_i$ exists).
   - Create signature record $(sid, ssid, \mathcal{M}_i, m, bsn)$.
   - Send $(sid, ssid, m, bsn)$ to $\mathcal{M}_i$.

(b) $\mathcal{M}_i$, upon receiving $(sid, ssid, m, bsn)$ from $\mathcal{H}_j$, stores $(sid, ssid, \mathcal{H}_j, m, bsn)$ and outputs $(\mathsf{SIGNPROCEED}, sid, ssid, m, bsn)$.

6. `Sign Proceed`. The signature is completed when $\mathcal{M}_i$ gets permission to proceed for $ssid$.

(a) $\mathcal{M}_i$ on input $(\mathsf{SIGNPROCEED}, sid, ssid)$ creates the first part of the split signature on m w.r.t. bsn:
   - Retrieve the signature request $(sid, ssid, \mathcal{H}_j, m, bsn)$ and key $(sid, \mathcal{H}_j, tsk)$.
   - Set $tag' \xleftarrow{\$} \mathsf{SSIG.PreSign}(tsk, (0, m, bsn))$ and $nym' \xleftarrow{\$} \mathsf{SSIG.PreSign}(tsk, (1, bsn))$.
   - Send $(sid, ssid, tag', nym')$ to $\mathcal{H}_j$.

(b) $\mathcal{H}_j$ upon receiving $(sid, ssid, tag', nym')$ from $\mathcal{M}_i$ completes the signature:
   - Retrieve the signature request $(sid, ssid, \mathcal{M}_i, m, bsn)$ and key $(sid, hsk, tpk, gpk, cred, \mathcal{M}_i)$.
   - Compute $tag \leftarrow \mathsf{SSIG.CompleteSign}(hsk, tpk, (0, m, bsn), tag')$.
   - Compute $nym \leftarrow \mathsf{SSIG.CompleteSign}(hsk, tpk, (1, bsn), nym')$.
   - Prove that tag and nym are valid split signatures under public key gpk and that it owns a valid issuer credential $cred$ on gpk, without revealing gpk or $cred$.

$$\pi_{\mathsf{SIGN}} \leftarrow \mathsf{NIZK}\{(gpk, cred) : \mathsf{ESIG.Vf}(ipk, cred, gpk) = 1 \\ \wedge\ \mathsf{SSIG.Vf}(gpk, tag, (0, m, bsn)) = 1 \wedge \mathsf{SSIG.Vf}(gpk, nym, (1, bsn)) = 1\}$$

   - Set $\sigma \leftarrow (tag, nym, \pi_{\mathsf{SIGN}})$ and output $(\mathsf{SIGNATURE}, sid, ssid, \sigma)$.

Verify and Link. Any party can use the following verify and link algorithms to determine the validity of a signature and whether two signatures for the same basename were created by the same platform.

7. `Verify`. The verify algorithm allows one to check whether a signature σ on message m w.r.t. basename bsn and private key revocation list $\texttt{RL}$ is valid.

(a) $\mathcal{V}$ upon input $(\mathsf{VERIFY}, sid, m, bsn, \sigma, \texttt{RL})$ verifies the signature:
- Parse σ as $(tag, nym, \pi_{\mathsf{SIGN}})$.
- Verify π_{SIGN} with respect to m, bsn, tag, and nym.
- For every $gpk_i \in \texttt{RL}$, check that $\mathsf{SSIG.Vf}(gpk_i, nym, (1, bsn)) \neq 1$.
- If all tests pass, set $f \leftarrow 1$, otherwise $f \leftarrow 0$.
- Output $(\mathsf{VERIFIED}, sid, f)$.

8. `Link`. The link algorithm allows one to check whether two signatures σ and σ', on messages m and m' respectively, that were generated for the same basename bsn were created by the same platform.

(a) $\mathcal{V}$ upon input $(\mathsf{LINK}, sid, \sigma, m, \sigma', m', bsn)$ verifies the signatures and compares the pseudonyms contained in σ, σ':
- Check that both signatures σ and σ' are valid with respect to (m, bsn) and (m', bsn) respectively, using the `Verify` algorithm with $\texttt{RL} \leftarrow \emptyset$. Output $\perp$ if they are not both valid.
- Parse the signatures as $(tag, nym, \pi_{\mathsf{SIGN}})$ and $(tag', nym', \pi'_{\mathsf{SIGN}})$.
- If $nym = nym'$, set $f \leftarrow 1$, otherwise $f \leftarrow 0$.
- Output (LINK, sid, f).

5.2 Security

We now prove that that our generic protocol is a secure DAA scheme with optimal privacy under isolated TPM corruptions (and also achieves conditional privacy under full TPM corruption) as defined in Sect. 2.

Theorem 2. *Our protocol Π_{pdaa} described in Sect. 5, securely realizes $\mathcal{F}_{\mathsf{pdaa}}$ defined in Sect. 2, in the $(\mathcal{F}_{\mathsf{auth*}}, \mathcal{F}_{\mathsf{ca}}, \mathcal{F}_{\mathsf{crs}})$-hybrid model, provided that*

- SSIG *is a secure split signature scheme (as defined in Sect. 4.4),*
- ESIG *is a secure signature scheme for encrypted messages,*
- ENC *is a CPA-secure encryption scheme, and*
- NIZK *is a zero-knowledge, simulation-sound and online-extractable (for the underlined values) proof system.*

To prove Theorem 2, we have to show that there exists a simulator $\mathcal{S}$ as a function of $\mathcal{A}$ such that no environment can distinguish Π_{pdaa} and $\mathcal{A}$ from $\mathcal{F}_{\mathsf{pdaa}}$ and $\mathcal{S}$. We let the adversary perform both isolated corruptions and full corruptions on TPMs, showing that this proof both gives optimal privacy with respect to adversaries that only perform isolated corruptions on TPMs, and conditional privacy otherwise. The full proof is given in the full version of this paper [24], we present a proof sketch below.

Proof Sketch

Setup. For the setup, the simulator has to provide the functionality the required algorithms $(\mathsf{sig}, \mathsf{ver}, \mathsf{link}, \mathsf{identify}, \mathsf{ukgen})$, where $\mathsf{sig}, \mathsf{ver}, \mathsf{link}$, and ukgen simply reflect the corresponding real-world algorithms. Thereby the signing algorithm also includes the issuer's secret key. When the issuer is corrupt, $\mathcal{S}$ can learn the issuer secret key by extracting from the proof π_{ipk}. When the issuer is honest, it is simulated by $\mathcal{S}$ in the real-world and thus $\mathcal{S}$ knows the secret key.

The algorithm $\mathsf{identify}(\sigma, m, bsn, \tau)$ that is used by $\mathcal{F}_{\mathsf{pdaa}}$ to internally ensure consistency and non-frameability is defined as follows: parse σ as $(tag, nym, \pi_{\mathsf{SIGN}})$ and output $\mathsf{SSIG.Vf}(\tau, nym, (1, bsn))$. Recall that τ is a tracing trapdoor that is either provided by the simulator (when the host is corrupt) or generated internally by $\mathcal{F}_{\mathsf{pdaa}}$ whenever a new gpk is generated.

Join. The join-related interfaces of $\mathcal{F}_{\mathsf{pdaa}}$ notify $\mathcal{S}$ about any triggered join request by a platform consisting of host $\mathcal{H}_j$ and TPM $\mathcal{M}_i$ such that $\mathcal{S}$ can simulate the real-world protocol accordingly. If the host is corrupt, the simulator also has to provide the functionality with the tracing trapdoor τ. For our scheme the joint key gpk of the split signature serves that purpose. For privacy reasons the key is never revealed, but the host proves knowledge and correctness of the key in $\pi_{\mathsf{JOIN},\mathcal{H}}$. Thus, if the host is corrupt, the simulator extracts gpk from this proof and gives it $\mathcal{F}_{\mathsf{pdaa}}$.

Sign. For platforms with an honest host, $\mathcal{F}_{\mathsf{pdaa}}$ creates anonymous signatures using the sig algorithm $\mathcal{S}$ defined in the setup phase. Thereby, $\mathcal{F}_{\mathsf{pdaa}}$ enforces unlinkability by generating and using fresh platform keys via ukgen whenever a platform requests a signature for a new basename. For signature requests where a platform repeatedly uses the same basename, $\mathcal{F}_{\mathsf{pdaa}}$ re-uses the corresponding key accordingly. We now briefly argue that no environment can notice this difference. Recall that signatures consist of signatures tag and nym, and a proof π_{SIGN}, with the latter proving knowledge of the platform's key gpk and credential $cred$, such that tag and nym are valid under gpk which is in turn certified by $cred$. Thus, for every new basename, the credential $cred$ is now based on different keys gpk. However, as we never reveal these values but only prove knowledge of them in π_{SIGN}, this change is indistinguishable to the environment.

The signature tag and pseudonym nym, that are split signatures on the message and basename, are revealed in plain though. For repeated attestations under the same basename, $\mathcal{F}_{\mathsf{pdaa}}$ consistently re-uses the same key, whereas the use of a fresh basename will now lead to the disclosure of split signatures under different keys. The key-hiding property of split signatures guarantees that this change is unnoticeable, even when the TPM is corrupt and controls part of the key. Note that the key-hiding property requires that the adversary does not know the joint public key gpk, which we satisfy as gpk is never revealed in our scheme; the host only proves knowledge of the key in $\pi_{\mathsf{JOIN},\mathcal{H}}$ and π_{SIGN}.

Verify. For the verification of DAA signatures $\mathcal{F}_{\mathsf{pdaa}}$ uses the provided ver algorithm but also performs additional checks that enforce the desired non-frameability and unforgeability properties. We show that these additional checks will fail with negligible probability only, and therefore do not noticeably change the verification outcome.

First, $\mathcal{F}_{\mathsf{pdaa}}$ uses the identify algorithm and the tracing trapdoors τ_i to check that there is only a unique signer that matches to the signature that is to be verified. Recall that we instantiated the identify algorithm with the verification algorithm of the split signature scheme SSIG and $\tau = gpk$ are the (hidden) joint platform keys. By the key-uniqueness property of SSIG the check will fail with negligible probability only.

Second, $\mathcal{F}_{\mathsf{pdaa}}$ rejects the signature when no matching tracing trapdoor was found and the issuer is honest. For platforms with an honest hosts, theses trapdoors are created internally by the functionality whenever a signature is generated, and $\mathcal{F}_{\mathsf{pdaa}}$ immediately checks that the signature matches to the trapdoor (via the identify algorithm). For platforms where the host is corrupt, our simulator $\mathcal{S}$ ensures that a tracing trapdoor is stored in $\mathcal{F}_{\mathsf{pdaa}}$ as soon as the platform has joined (and received a credential). If a signature does not match any of the existing tracing trapdoors, it must be under a $gpk = \tau$ that was neither created by $\mathcal{F}_{\mathsf{pdaa}}$ nor signed by the honest issuer in the real-world. The proof π_{SIGN} that is part of every signature σ proves knowledge of a valid issuer credential on gpk. Thus, by the unforgeability of the signature scheme for encrypted messages ESIG, such invalid signatures can occur only with negligible probability.

Third, if $\mathcal{F}_{\mathsf{pdaa}}$ recognizes a signature on message m w.r.t. basename bsn that matches the tracing trapdoor of a platform with an honest TPM or honest host, but that platform has never signed m w.r.t. bsn, it rejects the signature. This can be reduced to unforgeability-1 (if the host is honest) or unforgeability-2 (if the TPM is honest) of the split signature scheme SSIG.

The fourth check that $\mathcal{F}_{\mathsf{pdaa}}$ makes corresponds to the revocation check in the real-world verify algorithm, i.e., it does not impose any additional check.

Link. Similar as for verification, $\mathcal{F}_{\mathsf{pdaa}}$ is not relying solely on the provided link algorithm but performs some extra checks when testing for the linkage between two signatures σ and σ'. It again uses identify and the internally stored tracing trapdoor to derive the final linking output. If there is one tracing trapdoor matching one signature but not the other, it outputs that they are not linked. If there is one tracing trapdoor matching both signatures, it enforces the output that they are linked. Only if no matching tracing trapdoor is found, $\mathcal{F}_{\mathsf{pdaa}}$ derives the output via link algorithm.

We now show that the two checks and decisions imposed by $\mathcal{F}_{\mathsf{pdaa}}$ are consistent with the real-world linking algorithm. In the real world, signatures $\sigma = (tag, nym, \pi_{\mathsf{SIGN}})$ and $\sigma' = (tag', nym', \pi'_{\mathsf{SIGN}})$ w.r.t basename bsn are linked iff $nym = nym'$. Tracing trapdoors are instantiated by the split signature scheme public keys gpk, and identify verifies nym under the key gpk. If one key matches one signature but not the other, then by the fact that the verification algorithm of the split signatures is deterministic, we must have $nym \neq nym'$, showing that the real world algorithm also outputs unlinked. If one key matches both signatures, we have $nym = nym'$ by the signature-uniqueness of split signatures, so the real-world algorithm also outputs linked. □

6 Concrete Instantiation and Efficiency

In this section we describe on a high level how to efficiently instantiate the generic building blocks to instantiate our generic DAA scheme presented in Sect. 5. The details are presented in the full version of this paper [24].

The split signature scheme is instantiated with the split-BLS signatures (as described in Sect. 4.4), the signatures for encrypted messages with the AGOT+ signature scheme (as described in Sect. 4.3) and the encryption scheme with ElGamal, both working in $\mathbb{G}_2$. All the zero-knowledge proofs are instantiated with non-interactive Schnorr-type proofs about discrete logarithms, and witnesses that have to be online extractable are encrypted using ElGamal for group elements and Camenisch-Shoup encryption [28] for exponents. Note that the latter is only used by the issuer to prove that its key is correctly formed, i.e., every participant will only work with Camenisch-Shoup ciphertexts once.

Security. When using the concrete instantiations as presented above we can derive the following corollary from Theorem 2 and the required security assumptions of the deployed building blocks. We have opted for a highly efficient instantiation of our scheme, which comes for the price of stronger assumptions such as the generic group (for AGOT+ signatures) and random oracle model (for split-BLS signatures and Fiat-Shamir NIZKs). We would like to stress that our generic scheme based on abstract building blocks, presented in Sect. 5, does not require either of the models, and one can use less efficient instantiations to avoid these assumptions.

Corollary 1. *Our protocol Π_{pdaa} described in Sect. 5 and instantiated as described above, securely realizes $\mathcal{F}_{\mathsf{pdaa}}$ in the $(\mathcal{F}_{\mathsf{auth*}}, \mathcal{F}_{\mathsf{ca}}, \mathcal{F}_{\mathsf{crs}})$-hybrid model under the following assumptions:*

	Instantiation	Assumption
SSIG	split-BLS	co-DHP* [35] and DDH in $\mathbb{G}_1$, RO model
ESIG	AGOT+	generic group model (security of AGOT)
ENC	ElGamal	DDH in $\mathbb{G}_2$
NIZK	Fiat-Shamir, ElGamal, Camenisch-Shoup	DDH in $\mathbb{G}_2$, DCR [55], RO model

Efficiency. We now give an overview of the efficiency of our protocol when instantiated as described above. Our analysis focuses on signing and verification, which will be used the most and thus have the biggest impact on the performance of the scheme. The detailed efficiency analysis is presented in the full version of this paper [24].

When signing, the TPM only performs 2 exponentiations in $\mathbb{G}_1$, making it the DAA scheme with the most efficient TPM signing operation to date, according to the efficiency overview by Camenisch et al. [23]. The host performs 3 exponentiations in $\mathbb{G}_1$, 6 exponentiations in $\mathbb{G}_2$, and 10 pairings. Verification requires 4 exponentiations in $\mathbb{G}_T$ and 8 pairings.

We measured the speed of the Apache Milagro Cryptographic Library (AMCL)[2] and found that exponentiations in $\mathbb{G}_1$, $\mathbb{G}_2$, and $\mathbb{G}_T$ require 0.6 ms, 1.0 ms, and 1.4 ms respectively. A pairing costs 1.6 ms. Using these numbers, we estimate a signing time of 23.8 ms for the host, and a verification time of 18.4 ms, showing that also for the host our protocol is efficient enough to be used in practice. Table 2 gives an overview of the efficiency of our concrete instantiation.

Table 2. Efficiency of our concrete DAA scheme.

	$\mathcal{M}$ sign	$\mathcal{H}$ sign	Verify
Operations	$2\mathbb{G}_1$	$3\mathbb{G}_1$, $6\mathbb{G}_2$, $10P$	$4\mathbb{G}_T$, $8P$
Est. time		23.8 ms	18.4 ms

References

1. Abe, M., Groth, J., Ohkubo, M., Tibouchi, M.: Unified, minimal and selectively randomizable structure-preserving signatures. In: Lindell, Y. (ed.) TCC 2014. LNCS, vol. 8349, pp. 688–712. Springer, Heidelberg (2014). doi:10.1007/978-3-642-54242-8_29
2. Alwen, J., Katz, J., Maurer, U., Zikas, V.: Collusion-preserving computation. In: Safavi-Naini, R., Canetti, R. (eds.) CRYPTO 2012. LNCS, vol. 7417, pp. 124–143. Springer, Heidelberg (2012). doi:10.1007/978-3-642-32009-5_9
3. Alwen, J., Shelat, A., Visconti, I.: Collusion-free protocols in the mediated model. In: Wagner, D. (ed.) CRYPTO 2008. LNCS, vol. 5157, pp. 497–514. Springer, Heidelberg (2008). doi:10.1007/978-3-540-85174-5_28
4. Ateniese, G., Magri, B., Venturi, D.: Subversion-resilient signature schemes. In: CCS 2015 (2015)
5. Ball, J., Borger, J., Greenwald, G.: Revealed: how US and UK spy agencies defeat internet privacy and security. Guardian Weekly, September 2013
6. Bellare, M., Boldyreva, A., Desai, A., Pointcheval, D.: Key-privacy in public-key encryption. In: Boyd, C. (ed.) ASIACRYPT 2001. LNCS, vol. 2248, pp. 566–582. Springer, Heidelberg (2001). doi:10.1007/3-540-45682-1_33

[2] See https://github.com/miracl/amcl. We used the C-version of the library, configured to use the BN254 curve. The program `benchtest_pair.c` has been used to retrieve the timings, executed on an Intel i5-4300U CPU.

7. Bellare, M., Paterson, K.G., Rogaway, P.: Security of symmetric encryption against mass surveillance. In: Garay, J.A., Gennaro, R. (eds.) CRYPTO 2014. LNCS, vol. 8616, pp. 1–19. Springer, Heidelberg (2014). doi:10.1007/978-3-662-44371-2_1
8. Bellare, M., Sandhu, R.: The security of practical two-party RSA signature schemes. Cryptology ePrint Archive, Report 2001/060 (2001)
9. Bernhard, D., Fuchsbauer, G., Ghadafi, E., Smart, N., Warinschi, B.: Anonymous attestation with user-controlled linkability. Int. J. Inf. Secur. **12**(3), 219–249 (2013)
10. Bernhard, D., Fuchsbauer, G., Ghadafi, E.: Efficient signatures of knowledge and DAA in the standard model. In: Jacobson, M., Locasto, M., Mohassel, P., Safavi-Naini, R. (eds.) ACNS 2013. LNCS, vol. 7954, pp. 518–533. Springer, Heidelberg (2013). doi:10.1007/978-3-642-38980-1_33
11. Blaze, M., Bleumer, G., Strauss, M.: Divertible protocols and atomic proxy cryptography. In: Nyberg, K. (ed.) EUROCRYPT 1998. LNCS, vol. 1403, pp. 127–144. Springer, Heidelberg (1998). doi:10.1007/BFb0054122
12. Boneh, D., Lynn, B., Shacham, H.: Short signatures from the weil pairing. J. Crypt. **17**(4), 297–319 (2004)
13. Brands, S.: Rethinking Public Key Infrastructures and Digital Certificates: Building in Privacy. MIT Press, Cambridge (2000)
14. Brands, S.: Untraceable off-line cash in wallet with observers. In: Stinson, D.R. (ed.) CRYPTO 1993. LNCS, vol. 773, pp. 302–318. Springer, Heidelberg (1994). doi:10.1007/3-540-48329-2_26
15. Brickell, E., Camenisch, J., Chen, L.: Direct anonymous attestation. In: CCS 2004 (2004)
16. Brickell, E., Chen, L., Li, J.: A new direct anonymous attestation scheme from bilinear maps. In: Lipp, P., Sadeghi, A.-R., Koch, K.-M. (eds.) Trust 2008. LNCS, vol. 4968, pp. 166–178. Springer, Heidelberg (2008). doi:10.1007/978-3-540-68979-9_13
17. Brickell, E., Chen, L., Li, J.: Simplified security notions of direct anonymous attestation and a concrete scheme from pairings. Int. J. Inf. Secur. **8**(5), 315–330 (2009)
18. Brickell, E., Li, J.: A pairing-based DAA scheme further reducing TPM resources. Cryptology ePrint Archive, Report 2010/067 (2010)
19. Brickell, E., Li, J.: Enhanced privacy ID from bilinear pairing for hardware authentication and attestation. Int. J. Inf. Priv. Secur. Integr. **1**(1), 3–33 (2011)
20. Burmester, M.V.D., Desmedt, Y.: All languages in NP have divertible zero-knowledge proofs and arguments under cryptographic assumptions. In: Damgård, I.B. (ed.) EUROCRYPT 1990. LNCS, vol. 473, pp. 1–10. Springer, Heidelberg (1991). doi:10.1007/3-540-46877-3_1
21. Camenisch, J., Drijvers, M., Edgington, A., Lehmann, A., Lindemann, R., Urian, R.: FIDO ECDAA algorithm, implementation draft. https://fidoalliance.org/specs/fido-uaf-v1.1-id-20170202/fido-ecdaa-algorithm-v1.1-id-20170202.html
22. Camenisch, J., Chen, L., Drijvers, M., Lehmann, A., Novick, D., Urian, R.: One TPM to bind them all: fixing TPM 2.0 for provably secure anonymous attestation. In: IEEE S&P 2017 (2017)
23. Camenisch, J., Drijvers, M., Lehmann, A.: Anonymous attestation using the strong Diffie Hellman assumption revisited. In: Franz, M., Papadimitratos, P. (eds.) Trust 2016. LNCS, vol. 9824, pp. 1–20. Springer, Cham (2016). doi:10.1007/978-3-319-45572-3_1
24. Camenisch, J., Drijvers, M., Lehmann, A.: Anonymous attestation with subverted TPMs. Cryptology ePrint Archive, Report 2017/200 (2017)

25. Camenisch, J., Drijvers, M., Lehmann, A.: Universally composable direct anonymous attestation. In: Cheng, C.-M., Chung, K.-M., Persiano, G., Yang, B.-Y. (eds.) PKC 2016. LNCS, vol. 9615, pp. 234–264. Springer, Heidelberg (2016). doi:10.1007/978-3-662-49387-8_10
26. Camenisch, J., Kiayias, A., Yung, M.: On the portability of generalized schnorr proofs. In: Joux, A. (ed.) EUROCRYPT 2009. LNCS, vol. 5479, pp. 425–442. Springer, Heidelberg (2009). doi:10.1007/978-3-642-01001-9_25
27. Camenisch, J., Lehmann, A.: (Un)linkable pseudonyms for governmental databases. In: CCS 2015 (2015)
28. Camenisch, J., Shoup, V.: Practical verifiable encryption and decryption of discrete logarithms. In: Boneh, D. (ed.) CRYPTO 2003. LNCS, vol. 2729, pp. 126–144. Springer, Heidelberg (2003). doi:10.1007/978-3-540-45146-4_8
29. Camenisch, J., Stadler, M.: Efficient group signature schemes for large groups. In: Kaliski, B.S. (ed.) CRYPTO 1997. LNCS, vol. 1294, pp. 410–424. Springer, Heidelberg (1997). doi:10.1007/BFb0052252
30. Canetti, R.: Universally composable signature, certification, and authentication. In: CSFW 2004 (2004)
31. Canetti, R.: Universally composable security: a new paradigm for cryptographic protocols. Cryptology ePrint Archive, Report 2000/067 (2000)
32. Canetti, R., Vald, M.: Universally composable security with local adversaries. In: Visconti, I., Prisco, R. (eds.) SCN 2012. LNCS, vol. 7485, pp. 281–301. Springer, Heidelberg (2012). doi:10.1007/978-3-642-32928-9_16
33. Chaum, D.: Achieving electronic privacy. Sci. Am. **267**(2), 96–101 (1992)
34. Chaum, D., Pedersen, T.P.: Wallet databases with observers. In: Brickell, E.F. (ed.) CRYPTO 1992. LNCS, vol. 740, pp. 89–105. Springer, Heidelberg (1993). doi:10.1007/3-540-48071-4_7
35. Chatterjee, S., Hankerson, D., Knapp, E., Menezes, A.: Comparing two pairing-based aggregate signature schemes. Des. Codes Crypt. **55**(2), 141–167 (2010)
36. Chen, L.: A DAA scheme requiring less TPM resources. In: Bao, F., Yung, M., Lin, D., Jing, J. (eds.) Inscrypt 2009. LNCS, vol. 6151, pp. 350–365. Springer, Heidelberg (2010). doi:10.1007/978-3-642-16342-5_26
37. Chen, L., Morrissey, P., Smart, N.P.: Pairings in trusted computing. In: Galbraith, S.D., Paterson, K.G. (eds.) Pairing 2008. LNCS, vol. 5209, pp. 1–17. Springer, Heidelberg (2008). doi:10.1007/978-3-540-85538-5_1
38. Chen, L., Page, D., Smart, N.P.: On the design and implementation of an efficient DAA scheme. In: Gollmann, D., Lanet, J.-L., Iguchi-Cartigny, J. (eds.) CARDIS 2010. LNCS, vol. 6035, pp. 223–237. Springer, Heidelberg (2010). doi:10.1007/978-3-642-12510-2_16
39. Chen, R., Mu, Y., Yang, G., Susilo, W., Guo, F., Zhang, M.: Cryptographic reverse firewall via malleable smooth projective hash functions. In: Cheon, J.H., Takagi, T. (eds.) ASIACRYPT 2016. LNCS, vol. 10031, pp. 844–876. Springer, Heidelberg (2016). doi:10.1007/978-3-662-53887-6_31
40. Chen, X., Feng, D.: Direct anonymous attestation for next generation TPM. J. Comput. **3**(12), 43–50 (2008)
41. Costan, V., Devadas, S.: Intel SGX explained. Cryptology ePrint Archive, Report 2016/086 (2016)
42. Cramer, R.J.F., Pedersen, T.P.: Improved privacy in wallets with observers. In: Helleseth, T. (ed.) EUROCRYPT 1993. LNCS, vol. 765, pp. 329–343. Springer, Heidelberg (1994). doi:10.1007/3-540-48285-7_29

43. Dodis, Y., Mironov, I., Stephens-Davidowitz, N.: Message transmission with reverse firewalls—secure communication on corrupted machines. In: Robshaw, M., Katz, J. (eds.) CRYPTO 2016. LNCS, vol. 9814, pp. 341–372. Springer, Heidelberg (2016). doi:10.1007/978-3-662-53018-4_13
44. ElGamal, T.: A public key cryptosystem and a signature scheme based on discrete logarithms. In: Blakley, G.R., Chaum, D. (eds.) CRYPTO 1984. LNCS, vol. 196, pp. 10–18. Springer, Heidelberg (1985). doi:10.1007/3-540-39568-7_2
45. Fiat, A., Shamir, A.: How to prove yourself: practical solutions to identification and signature problems. In: Odlyzko, A.M. (ed.) CRYPTO 1986. LNCS, vol. 263, pp. 186–194. Springer, Heidelberg (1987). doi:10.1007/3-540-47721-7_12
46. Greenwald, G.: No Place to Hide: Edward Snowden, the NSA, and the U.S. Surveillance State. Metropolitan Books, New York (2014)
47. Groth, J., Sahai, A.: Efficient non-interactive proof systems for bilinear groups. In: Smart, N. (ed.) EUROCRYPT 2008. LNCS, vol. 4965, pp. 415–432. Springer, Heidelberg (2008). doi:10.1007/978-3-540-78967-3_24
48. Hazay, C., Polychroniadou, A., Venkitasubramaniam, M.: Composable security in the tamper-proof hardware model under minimal complexity. In: Hirt, M., Smith, A. (eds.) TCC 2016. LNCS, vol. 9985, pp. 367–399. Springer, Heidelberg (2016). doi:10.1007/978-3-662-53641-4_15
49. International Organization for Standardization: ISO/IEC 20008–2: Information Technology - Security Techniques - Anonymous Digital Signatures - Part 2: Mechanisms Using a Group Public Key (2013)
50. International Organization for Standardization: ISO/IEC 11889: Information Technology - Trusted Platform Module Library (2015)
51. Katz, J.: Universally composable multi-party computation using tamper-proof hardware. In: Naor, M. (ed.) EUROCRYPT 2007. LNCS, vol. 4515, pp. 115–128. Springer, Heidelberg (2007). doi:10.1007/978-3-540-72540-4_7
52. Katz, J., Ostrovsky, R.: Round-optimal secure two-party computation. In: Franklin, M. (ed.) CRYPTO 2004. LNCS, vol. 3152, pp. 335–354. Springer, Heidelberg (2004). doi:10.1007/978-3-540-28628-8_21
53. Mironov, I., Stephens-Davidowitz, N.: Cryptographic reverse firewalls. In: Oswald, E., Fischlin, M. (eds.) EUROCRYPT 2015. LNCS, vol. 9057, pp. 657–686. Springer, Heidelberg (2015). doi:10.1007/978-3-662-46803-6_22
54. Okamoto, T., Ohta, K.: Divertible zero knowledge interactive proofs and commutative random self-reducibility. In: Quisquater, J.-J., Vandewalle, J. (eds.) EUROCRYPT 1989. LNCS, vol. 434, pp. 134–149. Springer, Heidelberg (1990). doi:10.1007/3-540-46885-4_16
55. Paillier, P.: Public-key cryptosystems based on composite degree residuosity classes. In: Stern, J. (ed.) EUROCRYPT 1999. LNCS, vol. 1592, pp. 223–238. Springer, Heidelberg (1999). doi:10.1007/3-540-48910-X_16
56. Perlroth, N., Larson, J., Shane, S.: N.S.A. able to foil basic safeguards of privacy on web. The New York Times, September 2013
57. Russell, A., Tang, Q., Yung, M., Zhou, H.-S.: Cliptography: clipping the power of kleptographic attacks. In: Cheon, J.H., Takagi, T. (eds.) ASIACRYPT 2016. LNCS, vol. 10032, pp. 34–64. Springer, Heidelberg (2016). doi:10.1007/978-3-662-53890-6_2
58. Russell, A., Tang, Q., Yung, M., Zhou, H.: Destroying steganography via amalgamation: kleptographically CPA secure public key encryption. Cryptology ePrint Archive, Report 2016/530 (2016)
59. Trusted Computing Group: TPM main specification version 1.2 (2004)

60. Trusted Computing Group: Trusted platform module library specification, family "2.0" (2014)
61. Yao, A.C.C.: Protocols for secure computations (extended abstract). In: FOCS 1982 (1982)
62. Young, A., Yung, M.: Kleptography: using cryptography against cryptography. In: Fumy, W. (ed.) EUROCRYPT 1997. LNCS, vol. 1233, pp. 62–74. Springer, Heidelberg (1997). doi:10.1007/3-540-69053-0_6
63. Young, A., Yung, M.: The prevalence of kleptographic attacks on discrete-log based cryptosystems. In: Kaliski, B.S. (ed.) CRYPTO 1997. LNCS, vol. 1294, pp. 264–276. Springer, Heidelberg (1997). doi:10.1007/BFb0052241

Hedging Public-Key Encryption in the Real World

Alexandra Boldyreva[1(✉)], Christopher Patton[2], and Thomas Shrimpton[2]

[1] Georgia Institute of Technology, Atlanta, GA, USA
sasha@gatech.edu
[2] University of Florida, Gainesville, FL, USA

Abstract. Hedged PKE schemes are designed to provide useful security when the per-message randomness fails to be uniform, say, due to faulty implementations or adversarial actions. A simple and elegant theoretical approach to building such schemes works like this: Synthesize fresh random bits by hashing all of the encryption inputs, and use the resulting hash output as randomness for an underlying PKE scheme.

In practice, implementing this simple construction is surprisingly difficult, as the high- and mid-level APIs presented by the most commonly used crypto libraries (e.g. OpenSSL and forks thereof) *do not* permit one to specify the per-encryption randomness. Thus application developers are forced to piece together low-level functionalities and attend to any associated, security-critical algorithmic choices. Other approaches to hedged PKE present similar problems in practice.

We reconsider the matter of building hedged PKE schemes, and the security notions they aim to achieve. We lift the current best-possible security notion for hedged PKE (IND-CDA) from the CPA setting to the CCA setting, and then show how to achieve it using primitives that are readily available from high-level APIs. We also propose a new security notion, MM-CCA, which generalizes traditional IND-CCA to admit imperfect randomness. Like IND-CCA, and unlike IND-CDA, our notion gives the adversary the public key. We show that MM-CCA is achieved by RSA-OAEP in the random-oracle model; this is significant in practice because RSA-OAEP is directly available from high-level APIs across all libraries we surveyed. We sort out relationships among the various notions, and also develop new results for existing hedged PKE constructions.

Keywords: Hedged public-key encryption · Cryptographic APIs

1 Introduction

The security of many cryptographic primitives relies on access to reliable, high-quality randomness. However, generating good randomness is a complex process that often fails, due to use of ill-designed random number generators (RNGs), software bugs, or malicious subversion [18,20,21,26,30,31]. Such failures have

J. Katz and H. Shacham (Eds.): CRYPTO 2017, Part III, LNCS 10403, pp. 462–494, 2017.
DOI: 10.1007/978-3-319-63697-9_16

led to serious breaches of security in deployed cryptographic schemes [12,18,27, 35]. Recent high-profile examples include security vulnerabilities in a significant fraction of TLS and SSH servers caused by problems with RNGs as exposed by Heninger et al. [27] and the vulnerabilities with Juniper NetScreen-branded firewalls that use Dual EC RNG designed by NSA to have a backdoor, as studied by Checkoway et al. in [18].

Theorists have begun to address the practical issue of weak randomness. Of particular interest has been the case of public-key encryption (PKE), since there are no shared secrets upon which to bootstrap security. In their seminal work [5], Bellare et al. introduce the notion of hedged public-key encryption. Informally, hedged encryption guarantees traditional semantic security when the per-message randomness is perfect, and retains best-possible security guarantees when not, assuming there is sufficient min-entropy in the joint distribution over the plaintext messages and the per-message randomness. Such security is called hedged security.

A particularly simple and elegant approach to building hedged PKE is what Bellare et al. refer to as Encrypt-with-Hash (EwH)[1]. Loosely, to encrypt a message M (and potentially some auxiliary input I) using public key pk and randomness r, one computes a string $\tilde{r}$ by hashing (pk, M, I, r), and then returns a ciphertext $\mathcal{E}(pk, M; \tilde{r})$. In the random oracle model (ROM) [8], any entropy contained among the hash inputs is harvested to synthesize new randomness $\tilde{r}$ that can be treated as uniform. Intuitively, unless the attacker manages to guess (pk, M, I, r), or $\tilde{r}$ directly, this EwH scheme remains hedged-secure if the underlying scheme $\mathcal{E}$ is IND-CPA.

Other works on hedged PKE and related efforts to deal with imperfect per-message randomness have followed this approach [11,32,34,38]. It has also been used to construct deterministic encryption [4,13,34]. In fact, this trick of synthesizing randomness for encryption dates back (at least) to Fujisaki and Okamoto [24], who used this as part of a transform to turn CPA-secure encryption into CCA-secure encryption.

EwH in Practice. Say that a developer is aware of the security breaches caused by bad randomness, and wants to implement EwH using the best-known and most widely-deployed cryptographic library, OpenSSL. To protect application developers from having to understand and properly handle lower-level algorithmic details, OpenSSL encourages the use of high-level "envelope" API calls. For public-key encryption, the interface is

```
int EVP_PKEY_encrypt(EVP_PKEY_CTX *ctx, unsigned char *out,
    size_t *outlen, const unsigned char *in, size_t inlen)
```

where `ctx` points to the so-called encryption context, which acts as state across calls. Among other things, it contains the public key and a descriptor of the particular PKE scheme to be used: Textbook RSA, PKCS #1 v1.5 RSA encryption (RFC 2313), and a variant of RSA-OAEP [9] specified in PKCS #1 v2.2

[1] To be precise, [5] refers to their constructions as REwH, and those are extensions of the EwH scheme from [4]. We use the name EwH for simplicity.

(RFC 8017). The plaintext input is pointed to by `in`, and `out` points to where the ciphertext output should be written. Notice: *Nowhere is one able to specify the randomness to be used.* The mid-level function calls that are wrapped by `EVP_PKEY_encrypt` also do not expose the randomness to the caller. One could try to manipulate the source of randomness, `RAND_bytes`, used by the higher-level calls. Indeed, OpenSSL provides an interface for adding entropy into the state of the underlying (P)RNG; doing so, however, presents several technical challenges, which we discuss at length in Sect. 2. Hence, to implement EwH in OpenSSL, the developer is forced to cobble together low-level functionalities, which implies needing to attend to security-critical details, such as parameters, padding schemes, or how the randomness is generated. The same is true for the two most popular forks of OpenSSL (BoringSSL and LibreSSL) and several other common libraries. We give a survey of crypto libraries in Sect. 2.

Encrypt-with-Hash is not the only approach to building hedged PKE (or deterministic PKE, etc.), and we will discuss some others shortly. But the punchline there will be the same: Developers face similar hurdles when they attempt to instantiate those constructions with modern crypto libraries.

To summarize, while hedged PKE has received significant theoretical study, the gap between theory and practice remains large. Existing theoretical constructions offer little to developers who respect the guidance of widely deployed crypto libraries to use high-level APIs.

Reconsidering hedged PKE. We reconsider the matter of constructing PKE schemes that maintain useful security guarantees when forced to use imperfect randomness. There are two important questions that guide us:

- What simple and efficient schemes can we implement via high-level APIs exported by standard crypto libraries?
- What security notions can we hope to achieve with these schemes?

To the latter question, we take as our starting point the IND-CDA notion of [5], which we rename as MMR-CPA. In the MMR-CPA experiment, the adversary may query an encryption oracle with sources $\mathcal{M}$, each of these outputting a triple $(\boldsymbol{M}_0, \boldsymbol{M}_1, \boldsymbol{r})$, consisting of a pair of vectors of messages and a vector of randomness to be used for encryption (hence MMR). The oracle, which contains the public key pk and a secret challenge bit b, returns a vector of component-wise encryption of $\boldsymbol{M}_b$, each under the corresponding component randomness from $\boldsymbol{r}$. The adversary's goal is to guess the value of b. Crucially, the adversary is not provided with the public key pk until after all encryption queries are made; otherwise, pk-dependent $\mathcal{M}$ can be crafted that would make MMR-CPA unachievable, even when $\mathcal{M}$ is a high min-entropy source [5]. Also implicit is that the public key was generated using uniform coins, and that only the per-message randomness is under suspicion.

Achieving MMR-CCA. As a small definitional contribution, we extend MMR to the CCA setting, and both the CPA and CCA notions are formalized for PKE with associated data (AD). Associated data was originally called "labels" in the

PKE literature [1,17,19,37]. But AD seems to be more often used among practitioners, so we adopt it. (This also aligns better with the language of symmetric encryption.)

The MMR attack effectively assumes the adversary can arbitrarily and adaptively re-corrupt the randomness source used by the libraries when producing ciphertexts. In many settings, where the per-message randomness source is provided by the operating system (or even hardware), this equates to re-corrupting the OS (or hardware) at will with each encryption. The strength of this attack model makes RSA-OAEP, for example, unable to achieve MMR-CPA (let alone -CCA) security.[2] This is unfortunate, as RSA-OAEP is the only provably-secure scheme implemented by `EVP_PKEY_encrypt`, and it is available across virtually all libraries. In fact, there are currently *no* positive results for RSA-OAEP in the presence of imperfect randomness.

That said, we give the first MMR-CCA secure PKE scheme. It is a hybrid-encryption construction that uses a trapdoor function, a hash function (modeled as a random oracle), and a symmetric-key authenticated encryption scheme. Each of these components can be called with most crypto libraries, including OpenSSL, via high-level APIs. We prove that the scheme is MMR-CCA in the ROM assuming the standard assumptions on security of the base schemes. Despite the simplicity of the scheme, the security proof is quite involved. See Sect. 6.2 for details.

THE MM NOTIONS. The MMR notions define security in the hedged PKE setting with imperfect randomness, yet no common crypto library explicitly exposes a single primitive that achieves it. We define a new pair of notions, MM-{CPA,CCA}, which are identical to their MMR counterparts but with two important exceptions. First, the adversary is provided the public key as initial input. Second, the per-message randomness source $\mathcal{R}$ may be corrupted *once*, prior to any encryptions. This models scenarios in which the OS code base, a standards document, or a hardware RNG may have been modified (maliciously or otherwise) to produce faulty randomness prior to widespread distribution. And, while it is good practice to be cautious, we are unaware of any practical scenarios or documented attacks in which the randomness source may be continuously re-corrupted to depend on previously observed ciphertexts and the messages about to be encrypted, as is allowed in the MMR attack setting.

We show that RSA-OAEP is MM-CCA secure (in the ROM) whenever $\mathcal{R}$ has min-entropy sufficient to stop attacks that would break *any* PKE scheme in the MM setting. Not only does this give the first positive result for RSA-OAEP in the presence of imperfect randomness, but it also gives developers an immediate option across virtually all libraries.

Because MM adversaries are given the public key, MM security against adaptive attackers follows "for free" (via a standard hybrid argument) from MM security against non-adaptive attackers. On the other hand, in general one converts

[2] Consider the plaintext-recovery attack by Brown [15] on RSA-OAEP with public exponent $e = 3$. The attack exploits low entropy coins and is effective even if messages have high min-entropy.

Construction	Assumptions	Achieves
F-EME-OAEP	F is POWF	MM+IND-CCA
HE[F, AEAD]	F is OWF, AEAD is IND-CPA+AUTH	MMR+IND-CCA
PtD[F-DOAEP]	F is OWF	MM+IND-CCA
RtD[Π_r, F-DOAEP]	Π_r is IND-CPA, F is OWF	MM+IND-CPA

Fig. 1. A summary of our constructions and the security they achieve.

non-adaptive MMR security into adaptive MMR security only with the addition of an extra key-anonymity property (ANON); Bellare et al. [5] show this in the CPA setting, and we give an analogous result in the CCA setting (Theorem 1).

RELATING THE NOTIONS. We view MM-{CPA,CCA} as a direct generalization of IND-{CPA,CCA}. In the latter, the randomness source is perfect, and the adversary queries (effectively) a source whose support contains exactly one pair (M_0, M_1), i.e., a source with zero min-entropy. We work out relationships among the MM, MMR and IND notions. Among them, we show that IND-CCA $\not\Rightarrow$ MM-CCA in general, which makes our positive result for RSA-OAEP non-trivial.

Perhaps unintuitively, we show that the MMR notions are *not* stronger security notions than the MM notions. They are incomparable: in the MMR setting, the adversary is allowed to re-corrupt the randomness source but does not have the public key; in the MM setting, the adversary has the public key, but may only use it to produce message sources, and may not re-corrupt the randomness source.

HEDGING BEYOND EwH. Not all previous proposals for hedged encryption require direct manipulation of the randomness used by some underlying PKE scheme. For example, Bellare et al. [5] propose doing $\mathcal{E}_d(pk_d, \mathcal{E}_r(pk_r, M; r))$, which first encrypts the message M using a randomized PKE scheme $\mathcal{E}_r$, and then re-encrypts the resulting ciphertext using a deterministic scheme. They call this the Randomized-then-Deterministic (RtD) composition. (Note that this means two public-keys are needed, potentially requiring the issuing of new certificates, among other deployment issues.) They also propose a construction called Pad-then-Deterministic (PtD), where $\mathcal{E}(pk_d, M)$ is defined by sampling randomness r and then returning $\mathcal{E}_d(pk_d, M \parallel r)$. In both cases, to provide security against weak randomness, it is necessary (although not sufficient) that the deterministic scheme is PRIV-secure in the sense of [4].

Here, too, we run into problems in practice. Standard crypto libraries do not offer function calls that directly implement any PRIV-secure deterministic PKE schemes. Several such schemes are known in the literature [4,5,13,34], but implementing these would require piecing together calls to low-level functionalities, precisely what modern APIs attempt to avoid.

One potential exception is RSA-DOAEP [4], a three-round Feistel construction followed by a single call to RSA. This is the most amenable scheme to being implemented from high-level calls—OpenSSL exposes EVP calls for hashing, and the EVP_PKEY_encrypt function admits raw RSA as one of its options.

We show that RtD, where the deterministic scheme is DOAEP, is both MM-CPA and IND-CPA secure. Better yet, we are able to show, under appropriate conditions, that PtD with DOAEP is MM+IND-CCA secure.

OPEN QUESTIONS. Our work leaves open some interesting questions. For one, is MM-CCA achievable in the standard model? In particular, from reasonable assumptions and via primitives that are available in crypto libraries (without making very low-level calls)? Asking a bit less, is MM-CPA achievable with the same restrictions? By composing two of the theorems we give, any scheme that is (non-adaptive) MMR-CCA and ANON-CCA in the standard model would be MM-CCA, too. But this only shifts the focus to the question of how to build schemes that achieve these two properties, and within the constraints we mentioned.

In an analogous result, we show that a scheme that is (non-adaptive) MMR-CPA and ANON-CPA in the standard model is MM-CPA. Prior work does give schemes that are non-adaptive MMR-CPA and ANON-CPA (e.g., the RtD and PtD schemes from [5]), but none that can be realized from typical high-level APIs. So from our perspective, achieving MM-CPA in the standard model remains open in practice.

A CALL TO ACTION. A theoretician's viewpoint on this work might be to suggest that libraries should be modified to keep up with the nice primitives that our community provides. In practice, this viewpoint is unhelpful. The design of good APIs, like the design of good cryptography, is hard work. A recent study by Acar et al. [2] reveals that modern APIs make even simple tasks difficult to implement, which has been shown time and time again to result in security vulnerabilities in real systems. Yet, the question of what is the "right" level of exposure to the user is a complex trade-off between usability and flexibility. APIs have very long lifetimes because, once adopted, changing them potentially implies altering all of the applications upon which they are built. Our thesis is that raising awareness of real APIs in our research community will better serve cryptographic practice, and will uncover interesting new theory challenges (like those we explore) as well.

RELATED WORK. Raghunathan et al. [34] extend the security notion for deterministic encryption to the setting where the adversary is given the public key. They also consider chosen-ciphertext attacks and argue that their extension can be applied to hedged encryption. So that their notion is achievable, the adversary is restricted to choosing sources for its queries from a finite set (whose size is bounded by a parameter of the experiment) of sources that do not depend on the public key. We note a similar restriction in the MM-CCA setting; the randomness source may not depend on the public key, since otherwise the source could be crafted to leak information about the plaintext. Their definition is incomparable to our MM-CCA notion, and it is not clear what practical threat model it captures. Moreover, their definition deems RSA-OAEP insecure, while our

MM-CCA definition permits for useful security analysis of the most deployed PKE scheme, in case of imperfect randomness.

Paterson et al. [32] give notions of security under related-randomness attacks (RRA). Here, too, the adversary is provided with the public key. The RRA notions generalize the reset attack (RA) notions due to Yilek [38] by allowing the adversary to specify certain functions to be applied to fresh uniform randomness, or to previously sampled uniform randomness, and have the result used to encrypt chosen plaintexts. These functions must be output-unpredictable, loosely meaning that they cannot allow the attacker to guess the randomness that will be used for encryption, and collision-resistant, meaning that the queried functions, if applied to the same uniform random string, should not produce the same output. If either of these conditions is violated, there is an attack that makes RRA security impossible for any scheme. This is similar to our requirement in the MM notions that the encryption randomness have min-entropy that is $\omega(\log k)$, where k is the security parameter. Again, their definition is incomparable to our MM-CCA notion, and unlike our definition, does not allow to consider randomness sources with arbitrary high-min-entropy distributions. We note that again, RRA security is not achievable by randomness-recovering PKE schemes, such as RSA-OAEP.

Bellare and Tackmann [11] give notions of hedged security in the presence of nonces. They consider a setting where a sender uses a uniform seed and a nonce, and security is guaranteed if either the seed is secret and the nonces are non-repeating, or the seed is compromised and the nonces are unpredictable. Brzuska et al. and Bellare and Hoang [7,16] show that assuming the existence of indistinguishability obfuscation (iO), the random oracle in the EwH construction is uninstantiable. Finally, Hoang et al. [28] study public-key encryption security against selective-opening attacks in the presence of randomness failures.

2 Crypto Libraries

In this section we provide a brief survey of real-world libraries: In particular, the extent to which their APIs for PKE expose the per-message encryption randomness.

We begin with OpenSSL, the most widely-used library for encryption on the Web. As discussed in the introduction, OpenSSL encourages the use of "envelopes", which are designed to abstract the details of the algorithm used. We have noted that the high-level call `EVP_PKEY_encrypt` does not allow the programmer to specify the source of entropy. This call is a wrapper for RSA-based encryption, internally invoked by calling `RSA_public_encrypt`. This function has the interface

```
int RSA_public_encrypt(int flen, unsigned char *from,
    unsigned char *to, RSA *pk, int padding)
```

It allows one to specify one of three padding schemes (via `padding`), which is passed down from the `ctx` input of `EVP_PKEY_encrypt`. So we see that here, too, there is no explicit place to insert external randomness.

This design pattern is maintained by BoringSSL and LibreSSL, the two most popular forks of the OpenSSL codebase. It is also adopted by a number of other libraries, including the popular open source libraries libgcrypt and PyCrypto, as well as the commercial library cryptlib.

The *SSL API style reflects the opinion that APIs should not allow application developers to touch the coins, as doing so invites errors that can fatally impact security. Indeed, at Real World Cryptography 2017, Google security-team developers said interfaces should "Never ask users to provide critical input (e.g., randomness, etc.)" [22].

HEDGING VIA PROVIDING THE COINS SOURCE. Of course, there are APIs that surface access to the coins directly. For example, in Go's native crypto library the function call for RSA-OAEP has the signature

```
func EncryptOAEP(hash hash.Hash, random io.Reader,
    pub *PublicKey, msg []byte, label []byte)
```

The randomness source is the second parameter of this routine. One can hedge RSA-OAEP by implementing the `io.Reader` interface. Other examples of APIs that expose the coins are Botan, Crypto++, wolfSSL, and SCAPI.

Falling (somewhat confusingly) in the middle is the popular Java library known as Bouncy Castle. Java provides a built-in interface for various security-related functionalities. The programmer can control which library implements these functionalities by specifying a *security provider*, e.g., Bouncy Castle. Bouncy Castle's own API does *not* surface coins. On the other hand, the native Java API does. For instance, one initializes a structure for ElGamal encryption [23] as follows. Let `pubKey` be an ElGamal public key:

```
Cipher cipher = Cipher.getInstance("ElGamal/None/NoPadding", "BC");
cipher.init(Cipher.ENCRYPT_MODE, pubKey, new SecureRandom());
```

The string `"BC"` means the security provider is Bouncy Castle. So one could instantiate EwH (over ElGamal) here by providing their own implementation of `SecureRandom`.

HEDGING VIA RESEEDING THE COINS SOURCE. Although OpenSSL does not explicitly surface the coins, it exposes an interface for manipulating the coins used to provide randomness for higher-level calls. Coins are sampled in OpenSSL via the interface `RAND_bytes(unsigned char *buf, int num)`, which writes the next `num` bytes output by the source to `buf`. By default, the output is a stream of bytes generated by a PRNG seeded with entropy gathered by the system, e.g., by reading from `/dev/urandom`. When the PRNG is called, it generates the requested bytes and updates its internal state by applying a cryptographic hash function. (The hash function may be specified by the programmer.) Alternatively, a hardware-based RNG can be used. For our purposes, there are two relevant ways to manipulate the state:

- `RAND_seed(const void *buf, int num)`: Resets the state using the first `num` bytes of `buf` as a seed.

- `RAND_add(const void *buf, int num, double entropy)`: "Mixes" the first `num` bytes of `buf` into the state. `entropy` is an estimate of the number of full bytes of entropy of the input.

A search of the source code[3] reveals that the implementation of the padding scheme calls `RAND_bytes`. To hedge RSA-OAEP using this interface, one might do as follows:

```
RAND_add((const void *)in, in_len, in_entropy);
ctxt_len = RSA_public_encrypt(msg_len, msg, ctxt, pk,
                              RSA_PKCS1_OAEP_PADDING);
```

where `in_entropy` is an estimate of the bytes of entropy of the string `in`, which encodes `pk`, and `msg`. There are a number of technical details to attend to here. First, estimating the entropy of `in` is non-trivial. (The OpenSSL documentation refers the reader to RFC 1750 for estimation methodologies.[4]) Second, the documentation does not specify how the state is updated, except that if `entropy` is equal to `num`, then this call is equivalent to resetting the state via `RAND_seed`, effectively evicting the initial entropy provided by the system. Third, if a hardware RNG is used to instantiate `RAND_bytes`, then calling `RAND_add` fails silently, meaning *the call has no effect on the randomness.* Alternatively, one might first call `RAND_bytes(rand, rand_len)`, then reset the state via `RAND_seed` on input of a buffer containing `pk`, `msg`, and `rand`. Again, if a hardware RNG is used, then calling `RAND_seed` has no effect.

Apart from these practical considerations, we note a subtle theoretical issue with hedging OpenSSL in this manner. At first glance, it would appear that if one is careful with the technical details, then these interfaces could be used to implement EwH. However, since the PRNG is stateful, the coins used to encrypt a message necessarily depend on the inputs of all prior encryptions. It is not clear that the proof security for EwH holds for this instantiation, since the message-coins source is assumed to be stateless [5, Theorem 6.1].

To summarize, if a developer chooses to (or must) use a library whose APIs do not expose the encryption randomness, e.g., any of the widely-deployed *SSL libraries, they are forced to work with low-level functionalities and attend to security-critical details about parameters, padding, the implementation of the (P)RNG, etc. If they are free to work with, say, the Go native library, then they can implement EwH by extending the functionality of the exposed randomness source.

3 Preliminaries

NOTATION. If n is an integer we write $[n]$ for the set $\{1, 2, \ldots, n\}$. If i and j are integers such that $i \leq j$, we let $[i..j]$ denote the set $\{i, i+1, \ldots, j\}$. (If $i > j$, then let $[i..j] = \emptyset$.) The implicit, unambiguous encoding of one or more objects

[3] See https://github.com/openssl/openssl/blob/OpenSSL_1_0_2-stable/crypto.

[4] See https://wiki.openssl.org/index.php/Manual:RAND_add(3).

as a bit string is written as $\langle X, Y, \ldots \rangle$. We write vectors in boldface, e.g., $\boldsymbol{X}$. We let $\boldsymbol{X}_i$ and $\boldsymbol{X}[i]$ denote the i-th element of $\boldsymbol{X}$. We say that $\boldsymbol{X}, \boldsymbol{Y}$ are *length-equivalent* if $|\boldsymbol{X}| = |\boldsymbol{Y}| = m$ and, for all $i \in [m]$, $|\boldsymbol{X}_i| = |\boldsymbol{Y}_i|$. We let Λ denote the empty vector. All algorithms, unless noted otherwise, are randomized. An *adversary* is a randomized algorithm. The runtime of adversary $\mathcal{A}$ (at security parameter k) is denoted $\mathsf{time}_{\mathcal{A}}(k)$.

GAMES. We adopt the game-playing framework of Bellare and Rogaway [10]. The notation $\mathbf{Exp}(\mathcal{A}, k)$ denotes the execution of game $\mathbf{Exp}$ with adversary $\mathcal{A}$ at security parameter k. Let $\mathbf{Exp}(\mathcal{A}, k) \Rightarrow x$ be the random variable denoting the event that game $\mathbf{Exp}$ outputs x when played by $\mathcal{A}$ at security parameter k. If the outcome of the game is either true or false, then we write $\mathbf{Exp}(\mathcal{A}, k)$ as short hand for $\mathbf{Exp}(\mathcal{A}, k) \Rightarrow \mathsf{true}$.

3.1 Public-Key Encryption with Associated Data

A public-key encryption scheme with associated data PKEAD is a triple of algorithms $(\mathsf{Kgen}, \mathsf{Enc}, \mathsf{Dec})$ with associated data space $\mathsf{AD} \subseteq \{0,1\}^*$ and randomness length $\rho(\cdot)$. The *key-generation algorithm* Kgen takes 1^k as input, and outputs a pair of strings (pk, sk), the public key and secret key respectively. The *encryption algorithm* takes as input the public key pk, associated data $H \in \mathsf{AD}$, message $M \in \{0,1\}^*$, and coins $r \in \{0,1\}^{\rho(k)}$ and outputs a ciphertext $C \in \{0,1\}^*$ or the distinguished symbol $\perp$, indicating that encryption failed. When the value of the coins used is not important, we write $\mathsf{Enc}(pk, H, M)$ or $\mathsf{Enc}_{pk}^{H}(M)$ as short hand for $r \leftarrow\!\!\$\ \{0,1\}^{\rho(k)}; \mathsf{Enc}(pk, H, M; r)$. Otherwise, we write $\mathsf{Enc}(pk, H, M; r)$ or $\mathsf{Enc}_{pk}^{H}(M; r)$. The *decryption algorithm* takes the secret key sk, associated data $H \in \mathsf{AD}$, and a ciphertext $C \in \{0,1\}^*$ and outputs a message $M \in \{0,1\}^*$ or $\perp$, indicating failure to decrypt. Just as for encryption, we write $M \leftarrow \mathsf{Dec}(sk, H, C)$ or $M \leftarrow \mathsf{Dec}_{sk}^{H}(C)$.

It will be convenient to define vector-valued encryption. To that end, let $v \in \mathbb{N}$, $\boldsymbol{M} \in (\{0,1\}^*)^v$, and $\boldsymbol{H} \in \mathsf{AD}^v$. Then the notation $\boldsymbol{C} \leftarrow\!\!\$\ \mathsf{Enc}(pk, \boldsymbol{H}, \boldsymbol{M})$ means to compute $\boldsymbol{C}_i \leftarrow\!\!\$\ \mathsf{Enc}(pk, \boldsymbol{H}_i, \boldsymbol{M}_i)$ for every $i \in [v]$, and to assemble $\boldsymbol{C} = (\boldsymbol{C}_1, \ldots, \boldsymbol{C}_v)$ as the return value.

In this work, we consider schemes for which the following holds: If for every $k \in \mathbb{N}$, $(pk, sk) \in [\mathsf{Kgen}(1^k)]$, $H \in \mathsf{AD}$, and $M \in \{0,1\}^*$, there exists an $r' \in \{0,1\}^{\rho(k)}$ such that $\mathsf{Enc}_{pk}^{H}(M; r') \neq \perp$, then for every $r \in \{0,1\}^{\rho(k)}$, it holds that $\mathsf{Enc}_{pk}^{H}(M; r) \neq \perp$. Such a scheme is *correct* if for every $k \in \mathbb{N}$, $(pk, sk) \in [\mathsf{Kgen}(1^k)]$, $H \in \mathsf{AD}$, $M \in \{0,1\}^*$ and $r \in \{0,1\}^{\rho(k)}$, we have $C \neq \perp \implies \mathsf{Dec}_{sk}^{H}(C) = M$, where $C = \mathsf{Enc}_{pk}^{H}(M; r)$. As this condition makes clear, proper operation is demanded when both encryption and decryption are in possession of H. We note H may be the empty string, recovering more traditional public-key encryption.

3.2 Sources

In our security definitions, we will rely on the notion of a *source*, so we start with generalizing this notion as described in [5]. Let β and γ be non-negative integers, k be a positive integer, and $\mu, v, \rho_0, \ldots, \rho_{\gamma-1} : \mathbb{N} \to \mathbb{N}$ be functions. We define a $(\mu, v, \rho_0, \rho_1, \ldots, \rho_{\gamma-1})$-$\mathrm{m}^\beta\mathrm{r}^\gamma$-*source* $\mathcal{M}$ as an algorithm that on input 1^k returns a tuple $(\boldsymbol{M}_0, \boldsymbol{M}_1, \ldots, \boldsymbol{M}_{\beta-1}, \boldsymbol{r})$ with the following properties: one, for every $b \in [0..\beta-1]$, vector $\boldsymbol{M}_b$ is over strings; two, vector $\boldsymbol{r}$ is over γ-tuples of strings; three, each of the vectors has $v(k)$ elements; four, for every $i \in [v(k)]$ and $c \in [0..\gamma-1]$, string r_c has length $\rho_c(k)$ where $(r_0, \ldots, r_{\gamma-1}) = \boldsymbol{r}[i]$; five, for every $b, b' \in [0..\beta-1]$, vectors $\boldsymbol{M}_b$ and $\boldsymbol{M}_{b'}$ are length-equivalent; and six, for every $k \in \mathbb{N}$, $b \in [0..\beta-1]$, $i \in [v(k)]$, and $(M, r) \in \{0,1\}^{|\boldsymbol{M}_b[i]|} \times (\{0,1\}^{\rho_0(k)} \times \cdots \times \{0,1\}^{\rho_{\gamma-1}(k)})$ it holds that

$$\Pr\left[\, (\boldsymbol{M}_0, \ldots, \boldsymbol{M}_{\beta-1}, \boldsymbol{r}) \leftarrow\!\!\$\; \mathcal{M}(1^k) : (\boldsymbol{M}_b[i], \boldsymbol{r}[i]) = (M, r) \,\right] \leq 2^{-\mu(k)}.$$

We say that such a source has output length $v(\cdot)$ and min-entropy $\mu(\cdot)$. When stating the parameters is not important, we refer to the source as an $\mathrm{m}^\beta\mathrm{r}^\gamma$-source. In this paper we will consider mr-, mmr-, mm-, and r-sources.

We define the *equality pattern* of $v(k)$-vectors $\boldsymbol{M}$ and $\boldsymbol{r}$ as the bit-valued matrix $\mathrm{E}^{\boldsymbol{M},\boldsymbol{r}}$ defined by $\mathrm{E}^{\boldsymbol{M},\boldsymbol{r}}[i,j] = 1 \iff (\boldsymbol{M}[i], \boldsymbol{r}[i]) = (\boldsymbol{M}[j], \boldsymbol{r}[j])$ for every $i, j \in [v(k)]$. A $(\mu, v, \rho_0, \ldots, \rho_{\gamma-1})$-$\mathrm{m}^\beta\mathrm{r}^\gamma$-source is *distinct* if for every $k \in \mathbb{N}$ and $b \in [0..\beta-1]$, it holds that $\Pr[(\boldsymbol{M}_0, \ldots, \boldsymbol{M}_{\beta-1}, \boldsymbol{r}) \leftarrow\!\!\$\; \mathcal{M}(1^k) : \mathrm{E}^{\boldsymbol{M}_b,\boldsymbol{r}} = \mathrm{I}_{v(k)}] = 1$, where $\mathrm{I}_{v(k)}$ denotes the $v(k) \times v(k)$ identity matrix. Security against chosen distribution attacks will be defined with respect to adversaries that specify distinct sources. We remark that it is possible to relax this requirement somewhat [5, Sect. 4.3], but we will not belabor this point.

4 Security Notions

Let $\mathsf{PKEAD} = (\mathsf{Kgen}, \mathsf{Enc}, \mathsf{Dec})$ be a PKEAD scheme with associated data space AD and randomness length $\rho(\cdot)$. (We will refer to PKEAD throughout this section.) In this section we define three notions of privacy. The first, IND-CCA, is standard (IND-CCA2 in the taxonomy of [6]), except that it considers associated data. In this notion, the source of coins for encryption is fixed and uniform. The second, MMR-CCA is a lifting of the MMR-CPA notion from [5] (where it is called IND-CDA) to the CCA setting with associated data. In this notion, the adversary is free to re-corrupt the source of coins on each encryption. The third, MM-CCA, is entirely new. In this notion, the coins source is corrupted once prior to the keys being chosen and any encryption are made. We now discuss the notions (presented in Fig. 2) in more detail. For each attack and setting $(\mathrm{ATK}, \mathrm{STG}) \in \{\mathrm{IND}, \mathrm{MMR}, \mathrm{MM}\} \times \{\mathrm{CPA}, \mathrm{CCA}\}$ we define $\mathbf{Adv}^{\text{atk-stg}}_{\mathsf{PKEAD}}(\mathcal{A}, k) = 2 \cdot \Pr\left[\mathbf{Exp}^{\text{atk-stg}}_{\mathsf{PKEAD}}(\mathcal{A}, k)\right] - 1$.

4.1 IND Security

The standard notion of indistinguishability under chosen-ciphertext attacks is generalized to incorporate associated data in Fig. 2. We say that PKEAD is IND-CCA secure if for every PT ("polynomial-time") adversary $\mathcal{A}$, the function

$\mathbf{Exp}^{\text{ind-cca}}_{\mathsf{PKEAD}}(\mathcal{A},k)$: $Q \leftarrow \emptyset$ $(pk, sk) \leftarrow_{\$} \mathsf{Kgen}(1^k)$ $b \leftarrow_{\$} \{0,1\}$ $b' \leftarrow_{\$} \mathcal{A}^{\mathbf{LR},\mathbf{Dec}}(1^k, pk)$ return $b = b'$	$\mathbf{Exp}^{\text{mmr-cca}}_{\mathsf{PKEAD}}(\mathcal{A},k)$: $Q \leftarrow \emptyset$; $\mathsf{pkout} \leftarrow \mathsf{false}$ $(pk, sk) \leftarrow_{\$} \mathsf{Kgen}(1^k)$ $b \leftarrow_{\$} \{0,1\}$ $b' \leftarrow_{\$} \mathcal{A}^{\mathbf{LR},\mathbf{Dec},\mathbf{PKout}}(1^k)$ return $b = b'$	$\mathbf{Exp}^{\text{mm-cca}}_{\mathsf{PKEAD},\mathcal{R}}(\mathcal{A},k)$: $Q \leftarrow \emptyset$ $(pk, sk) \leftarrow_{\$} \mathsf{Kgen}(1^k)$ $b \leftarrow_{\$} \{0,1\}$ $b' \leftarrow_{\$} \mathcal{A}^{\mathbf{LR},\mathbf{Dec}}(1^k, pk)$ return $b = b'$

Oracle LR(H, M_0, M_1):
if $\|M_0\| \neq \|M_1\|$ then
  return $\lightning$
$C \leftarrow_{\$} \mathsf{Enc}^{H}_{pk}(M_b)$
$Q \leftarrow Q \cup \{(H, C)\}$
return C
	Oracle LR$(\boldsymbol{H}, \mathcal{M})$:
	if $\mathsf{pkout} = \mathsf{true}$ then return $\lightning$
	$(\boldsymbol{M}_0, \boldsymbol{M}_1, \boldsymbol{r}) \leftarrow_{\$} \mathcal{M}(1^k)$
	$\boldsymbol{C} \leftarrow \mathsf{Enc}^{\boldsymbol{H}}_{pk}(\boldsymbol{M}_b\,; \boldsymbol{r})$
	for $i \leftarrow 1$ to $\|\boldsymbol{H}\|$ do
	  $Q \leftarrow Q \cup \{(\boldsymbol{H}_i, \boldsymbol{C}_i)\}$
	return $\boldsymbol{C}$
		Oracle LR$(\boldsymbol{H}, \mathcal{M})$:
		$\boldsymbol{r} \leftarrow_{\$} \mathcal{R}(1^k)$
		$(\boldsymbol{M}_0, \boldsymbol{M}_1) \leftarrow_{\$} \mathcal{M}(1^k)$
		$\boldsymbol{C} \leftarrow \mathsf{Enc}^{\boldsymbol{H}}_{pk}(\boldsymbol{M}_b\,; \boldsymbol{r})$
		for $i \leftarrow 1$ to $\|\boldsymbol{H}\|$ do
		  $Q \leftarrow Q \cup \{(\boldsymbol{H}_i, \boldsymbol{C}_i)\}$
		return $\boldsymbol{C}$

Oracle Dec(H, C):
if $(H, C) \in Q$ then
  return $\lightning$
return $\mathsf{Dec}^{H}_{sk}(C)$
	Oracle Dec(H, C):
	if $(H, C) \in Q$ then
	  return $\lightning$
	return $\mathsf{Dec}^{H}_{sk}(C)$
	Oracle PKout():
	$\mathsf{pkout} \leftarrow \mathsf{true}$; return pk
		Oracle Dec(H, C):
		if $(H, C) \in Q$ then
		  return $\lightning$
		return $\mathsf{Dec}^{H}_{sk}(C)$

Fig. 2. Security notions for public-key encryption with associated data.

$\mathbf{Adv}^{\text{ind-cca}}_{\mathsf{PKEAD}}(\mathcal{A}, \cdot)$ is negligible. The corresponding notion in the chosen-plaintext attack setting is obtained by denying the adversary access to the decryption oracle. Let $\mathbf{Exp}^{\text{ind-cpa}}_{\mathsf{PKEAD}}(\mathcal{A}, k)$ denote this experiment. We say that PKEAD is IND-CPA secure if for every PT adversary $\mathcal{A}$, the function $\mathbf{Adv}^{\text{ind-cpa}}_{\mathsf{PKEAD}}(\mathcal{A}, \cdot)$ is negligible.

4.2 MMR Security

We adapt the definition of security against chosen-distribution attacks (IND-CDA) from [5] to deal with associated data and chosen-ciphertext attacks.

Consider the MMR-CCA experiment defined in Fig. 2 associated to PKEAD, adversary $\mathcal{A}$, and security parameter k. The output of the **LR** oracle is well-defined if for every $k \in \mathbb{N}$ and some $\mu, v : \mathbb{N} \to \mathbb{N}$, it holds that $\mathcal{M}$ is a (μ, v, ρ)-mmr-source, and $\boldsymbol{H} \in \mathsf{AD}^{v(k)}$. Fix functions $\mu, v : \mathbb{N} \to \mathbb{N}$ where $\mu(k) \in \omega(\log k)$. We call $\mathcal{A}$ a (μ, v, ρ)-mmr-adversary if its queries are well-defined and its **LR** queries consist of distinct (μ, v, ρ)-mmr-sources. We say that PKEAD is MMR-CCA secure with respect to distinct (μ, v, ρ)-mmr-sources if for every polynomial-time (μ, v, ρ)-mmr-adversary $\mathcal{A}$, the function $\mathbf{Adv}^{\text{mmr-cca}}_{\mathsf{PKEAD}}(\mathcal{A}, \cdot)$ is negligible.

The corresponding notion in the chosen-plaintext attack setting is obtained by denying $\mathcal{A}$ access to **Dec**. Let $\mathbf{Exp}^{\text{mmr-cpa}}_{\mathsf{PKEAD}}(\mathcal{A}, k)$ denote this experiment and let MMR-CPA security be defined analogously to MMR-CCA.

REMARKS ABOUT MMR. Notice that the adversary is not given the public key until after it is done seeing the challenge ciphertexts. It has previously been observed (in [5], building on [4]) that otherwise, the adversary may craft an mmr-source, which depends on the public key, and completely leaks the challenge bit with one query. Therefore, giving the adversary the public key would render the notion unachievable.

MIN-ENTROPY REQUIREMENTS. Just as in prior work [4,5], we require that the joint message-coins distribution have high min-entropy. In the MMR setting, this means the sources queried by the adversary have min-entropy $\mu = \mu(k) \in \omega(\log k)$. This is sufficient to thwart trial-encryption attacks by which the adversary, given the public key, exhaustively encrypts message-coins pairs until a ciphertext matches the output of its **LR** oracle.

4.3 ANON Security

Bellare et al. [5] studied how key anonymity is important for achieving adaptivity against MMR attacks. Unlike with the standard IND-CPA or -CCA notions, non-adaptive MMR (MMR1) security does not imply adaptive security. This is due to the fact that the adversary is not given the public key when it makes the queries to see the challenge ciphertexts. They observed that in the CPA setting, a property called key anonymity suffices to gain adaptivity. We extend their notion to the CCA setting; refer to the game defined in Fig. 3.

$\mathbf{Exp}^{\text{anon-cca}}_{\mathsf{PKEAD}}(\mathcal{D}, k)$	**Oracle LR**$(\boldsymbol{H}, \mathcal{M})$:	**Oracle Enc**$(\boldsymbol{H}, \mathcal{M})$:
$Q \leftarrow \emptyset$	if $\mathsf{pkout} = \mathsf{true}$ then return $\lightning$	if $\mathsf{pkout} = \mathsf{true}$ then return $\lightning$
$d \leftarrow\!\!\$\ \{0, 1\}$	$\mathsf{pkout} \leftarrow \mathsf{true}$	$(\boldsymbol{M}, \boldsymbol{r}) \leftarrow\!\!\$\ \mathcal{M}(1^k)$
$(pk_0, sk_0) \leftarrow\!\!\$\ \mathsf{Kgen}(1^k)$	if $(\boldsymbol{H}, \mathcal{M}) = (\bot, \bot)$ then	$\boldsymbol{C} \leftarrow \mathsf{Enc}(pk_0, \boldsymbol{H}, \boldsymbol{M}; \boldsymbol{r})$
$(pk_1, sk_1) \leftarrow\!\!\$\ \mathsf{Kgen}(1^k)$	return (pk_0, pk_1, Λ)	return $\boldsymbol{C}$
$d' \leftarrow\!\!\$\ \mathcal{D}^{\mathbf{LR},\mathbf{Enc},\mathbf{Dec}}(1^k)$	$(\boldsymbol{M}, \boldsymbol{r}) \leftarrow\!\!\$\ \mathcal{M}(1^k)$	
return $d = d'$	$\boldsymbol{C} \leftarrow \mathsf{Enc}(pk_d, \boldsymbol{H}, \boldsymbol{M}; \boldsymbol{r})$	
	for $i \leftarrow 1$ to $\lvert \boldsymbol{H} \rvert$ do	**Oracle Dec**$_b(H, C)$:
	$Q \leftarrow Q \cup \{(\boldsymbol{H}_i, \boldsymbol{C}_i)\}$	if $(H, C) \in Q$ then return $\lightning$
	return $(pk_0, pk_1, \boldsymbol{C})$	return $\mathsf{Dec}(sk_b, H, C)$

Fig. 3. Key anonymity of public-key encryption as formalized by [5], lifted to the CCA setting.

The game begins by choosing two key pairs (pk_0, sk_0) and (pk_1, sk_1) and a challenge bit d. The adversary is executed with the security parameter as input and with access to three oracles as defined in the figure. The outcome of the game is true if and only if the adversary's output is equal to d. The output of the **LR** and **Enc** oracles is well-defined when $\boldsymbol{H} \in \mathsf{AD}^{v(k)}$ and $\mathcal{M}$ is an (μ, v, ρ)-mr-source for some $\mu, v : \mathbb{N} \to \mathbb{N}$. Following the lead of [3], we provide a decryption oracle for both the primary and alternate secret key. On input (b, H, C) where

$b \in \{0,1\}$, $H \in \mathsf{AD}$, and $C \in \{0,1\}^*$, oracle **Dec** decrypts (H, C) under sk_b and returns the result as long as (H, C) was never output by **LR**.

Fix functions $\mu, v : \mathbb{N} \to \mathbb{N}$ such that $\mu(k) \in \omega(\log k)$. We define a (μ, v, ρ)-mr-adversary as one whose oracle queries consist of well-defined inputs and distinct (μ, v, ρ)-mr-sources. We say that PKEAD is ANON-CCA secure with respect to distinct (μ, v, ρ)-mr-sources if the function $\mathbf{Adv}^{\text{anon-cca}}_{\mathsf{PKEAD}}(\mathcal{A}, \cdot)$ is negligible for every PT (μ, v, ρ)-mr-adversary $\mathcal{A}$. As usual, we capture ANON-CPA security by denying the adversary access to the **Dec** oracle. This is equivalent to the ANON notion of [5], which in turn lifts [3] to the hedged setting.

NON-ADAPTIVE TO ADAPTIVE MMR VIA ANON. Intuitively, key anonymity captures the adversary's ability to discern information about the public key given adaptively-chosen encryptions under the public key and, in our setting, decryptions under the corresponding secret key. This property suffices for the following result, lifting [5, Theorem 5.2] to the CCA setting.

Theorem 1 (MMR1+ANON-CCA $\implies$ MMR-CCA). *Let $\mu, v, \rho : \mathbb{N} \to \mathbb{N}$ be functions where $\mu(k) \in \omega(\log k)$. Let $\mathcal{A}$ be a (μ, v, ρ)-mmr-adversary who makes q queries to its* **LR** *oracle. There exists a (μ, v, ρ)-mmr-adversary $\mathcal{B}$, who makes one query to its* **LR** *oracle, and a (μ, v, ρ)-mr-adversary $\mathcal{D}$ such that*

$$\mathbf{Adv}^{mmr\text{-}cca}_{\mathsf{PKEAD}}(\mathcal{A}, k) \leq q \cdot \mathbf{Adv}^{mmr\text{-}cca}_{\mathsf{PKEAD}}(\mathcal{B}, k) + 2q \cdot \mathbf{Adv}^{anon\text{-}cca}_{\mathsf{PKEAD}}(\mathcal{D}, k) .$$

where $\mathcal{D}$ and $\mathcal{B}$ have the same runtime as $\mathcal{A}$. Moreover, adversary $\mathcal{D}$ makes as many decryption queries as $\mathcal{A}$, $q - 1$ encryption queries, and one query to **LR***, and adversary $\mathcal{B}$ makes as many decryption queries as $\mathcal{A}$ and one query to* **LR***.*

The proof is a simple extension of [5, Theorem 5.2] that takes the decryption oracle into account; we refer the reader to the full version of this paper for the details [14]. The intuition is that leakage of the public key in the ciphertext is tolerable in the non-adaptive setting since the adversary may obtain the public key after making its **LR** query. In the adaptive setting, this leakage could lead to attacks based on key-dependent message-coins distributions in subsequent **LR** queries.

REMARK. We note that the converse is not true: MMR-CPA does *not* imply ANON-CPA. Suppose we modify an MMR-CPA secure PKEAD scheme by appending the hash of the public key to the end of the ciphertext. Modeling the hash function as a random oracle, this construction remains MMR-CPA secure. However, it is clearly not ANON-CPA. Since the adversary is given the primary and alternate key in response to its **LR** query, it can easily check (with one random oracle query) which key was used to encrypt.

4.4 MM Security

Next, we consider the practical setting in which the coins are non-adaptively corrupted. Consider the MM-CCA experiment defined in Fig. 2 associated to PKEAD, adversary $\mathcal{A}$, *randomness source* $\mathcal{R}$, and security parameter k.

The output of the **LR** oracle is well-defined if for every $k \in \mathbb{N}$ and some $\mu_1, \mu_2, v : \mathbb{N} \to \mathbb{N}$, it holds that $\mathcal{M}$ is a (μ_1, v)-mm-source, $\boldsymbol{H} \in \mathsf{AD}^{v(k)}$, and $\mathcal{R}$ is a (μ_2, v, ρ)-r-source. Fix functions $\mu_1, \mu_2, v : \mathbb{N} \to \mathbb{N}$ where $\mu_2(k) \in \omega(\log k)$. We call $\mathcal{A}$ a (μ_1, v)-mm-adversary if its queries are well-defined and its **LR** queries consist of distinct (μ_1, v)-mm-sources. We say that PKEAD is MM-CCA secure with respect to distinct (μ_1, v)-mm-sources and (μ_2, v, ρ)-r-sources if for every PT (μ_1, v)-mm-adversary $\mathcal{A}$ and for every PT (μ_2, v, ρ)-r-source $\mathcal{R}$, the function $\mathbf{Adv}^{\text{mm-cca}}_{\mathsf{PKEAD},\mathcal{R}}(\mathcal{A}, \cdot)$ is negligible. Again, we let $\mathbf{Exp}^{\text{mm-cpa}}_{\mathsf{PKEAD},\mathcal{R}}(\mathcal{A}, k)$ be the experiment associated to PKEAD, $\mathcal{A}$, k, and randomness source $\mathcal{R}$, which is identical to $\mathbf{Exp}^{\text{mm-cca}}_{\mathsf{PKEAD},\mathcal{R}}(\mathcal{A}, k)$, but the adversary has no **Dec** oracle. MM-CPA security is defined analogously to MM-CCA security.

NON-ADAPTIVE TO ADAPTIVE MM "FOR FREE". Unlike in the MMR attack setting, in the MM-CCA game, the adversary is given the public key. This is achievable because the coin source may not be adaptively corrupted to depend upon it. It follows that one does get adaptivity "for free" in this setting, via a standard hybrid argument.

Theorem 2 (MM1-CCA $\implies$ MM-CCA). *Let $\mu_1, \mu_2, v : \mathbb{N} \to \mathbb{N}$ be functions where $\mu_2(k) \in \omega(\log k)$. Let $\mathcal{R}$ be a (μ_2, v, ρ)-r-source and $\mathcal{A}$ be a (μ_1, v)-mm-adversary who makes q queries to its* **LR** *oracle. There exists a (μ_1, v)-mm-adversary $\mathcal{B}$ who makes one query to its* **LR** *oracle such that*

$$\mathbf{Adv}^{\text{mm-cca}}_{\mathsf{PKEAD},\mathcal{R}}(\mathcal{A}, k) \leq q \cdot \mathbf{Adv}^{\text{mm-cca}}_{\mathsf{PKEAD},\mathcal{R}}(\mathcal{B}, k)\,,$$

and $\mathcal{B}$ has the same runtime as $\mathcal{A}$, making as many decryption queries.

MIN-ENTROPY REQUIREMENTS. As in the MMR setting, achieving MM security demands restrictions upon the sources. Minimally, we will need to require that $\mu_1(k) + \mu_2(k) \in \omega(\log k)$, where $\mu_1(\cdot)$ is the min-entropy of the mm-sources specified by the adversary and $\mu_2(\cdot)$ is the min-entropy of the r-source parameterizing the experiment. In fact, we need a bit more. As an illustration, suppose that $\mu_1(k) \in \omega(\log k)$ and $\mu_2(k) = 0$. This means that the randomness source always outputs the same sequence of coins. This allows the adversary to mount the key-dependent distribution attack identified by [5] when the adversary is given the public key. (Indeed, this kind of attack is effective whenever the randomness source has low min-entropy. Therefore, it is crucial in the MM setting that the entropy of the randomness source μ_2 be of order $\omega(\log k)$.

5 Relations Among the Notions

We summarize the min-entropy requirements of each notion as follows: IND requires uniform random coins, MMR requires that the joint distribution on messages and coins have high min-entropy, and MM requires that the coins have high min-entropy. MMR tolerates bad randomness, but only if the message has high entropy. On the other hand, MM fails if the randomness is low

Result	Shown By
MMR-CPA (resp. MM-CPA) $\not\Rightarrow$ ANON-CPA:	CE1
ANON-CPA $\not\Rightarrow$ MMR-CPA (resp. MM-CPA):	CE2
MM-CPA $\not\Rightarrow$ MMR-CPA:	CE3
IND-CPA $\not\Rightarrow$ MM-CPA (resp. MMR-CPA):	CE4
MMR1+ANON-CCA $\Longrightarrow$ MMR-CCA	Theorem 1
MM1-CCA $\Longrightarrow$ MM-CCA	Theorem 2
MMR1+ANON-CCA $\Longrightarrow$ MM1-CCA	Theorem 3
MM-CCA $\Longrightarrow$ IND-CCA where $\mu_1(k) \in O(\log k)$	Theorem 4

Fig. 4. Summary of relations. **Top:** separations using **CE1:** $\mathsf{Enc}^H_{pk}(M; r) = \mathcal{E}^H_{pk}(M; r) \,\|\, \mathsf{H}(pk)$, where $\mathcal{E}$ is {MM,MMR}-CPA and H a random oracle; **CE2:** $\mathsf{Enc}^H_{pk}(M; r) = M$; **CE3:** EME-OAEP (see Sect. 6.1); **CE4:** $\mathsf{Enc}^H_{pk}(M; r \,\|\, b) = \mathcal{E}^H_{pk}(M; r) \,\|\, (b \oplus M[1])$, where $\mathcal{E}$ is IND-CPA. We note that the corresponding CCA separations are implied by the CPA separations. **Bottom:** implications, where we note that the corresponding CPA implications are implied by the CCA implications.

min-entropy. Thus, the MM setting captures systems that are pretty good at gathering entropy, but not perfect. This is a realistic scenario, as evidenced by the analysis of the entropy-gathering mechanisms in the Linux kernel in [27]. Catastrophic failures, on the other hand, such as the infamous OpenSSL bug in the Debian distribution, which resulted in the PRNG seed having only 15 bits of entropy on many systems [31], or the "boot-time entropy hole" described in [27], are out of scope. With these distinctions in mind, we study the relationships between IND, MMR, and MM attack settings. Our results are summarized in Fig. 4.

Relationship between MMR and MM attacks. Intuitively, the MMR attack captures a stronger setting, since the adversary can adaptively corrupt the coins. The notions are incomparable, however, since the adversary has the public key in the MM attack setting. Nevertheless, we are able to show that a scheme that is both MMR- and ANON-CCA secure is MM-CCA secure.

Theorem 3 (MMR1+ANON-CCA $\Longrightarrow$ MM1-CCA). *Let* PKEAD *be an encryption scheme with randomness length $\rho(\cdot)$. Let $\mu_1, \mu_2, v : \mathbb{N} \to \mathbb{N}$ be functions, where $\mu_2(k) \in \omega(\log k)$. Let $\mathcal{R}$ be a (μ_2, v, ρ)-r-source and $\mathcal{A}$ be a (μ_1, v)-mm-adversary who makes one query to its* **LR** *oracle. There exist a $(\mu_1 + \mu_2, v, \rho)$-mmr-adversary $\mathcal{B}$ who makes one query to its* **LR** *oracle and a $(\mu_1 + \mu_2, v, \rho)$-mr adversary $\mathcal{D}$ such that*

$$\mathbf{Adv}^{\text{mm-cca}}_{\mathsf{PKEAD},\mathcal{R}}(\mathcal{A}, k) \le \mathbf{Adv}^{\text{mm-cca}}_{\mathsf{PKEAD}}(\mathcal{B}, k) + 4 \cdot \mathbf{Adv}^{\text{anon-cca}}_{\mathsf{PKEAD}}(\mathcal{D}, k),$$

where and $\mathcal{B}$ and $\mathcal{D}$ have the same runtime as $\mathcal{A}$. Each makes as many decryption queries as $\mathcal{A}$ and one query to its **LR** *oracle.*

Roughly speaking, our argument is that if the scheme is key anonymous, then the public key provides the adversary with negligible advantage in the MM-CCA setting. Therefore, we can give the adversary a public key different from the one used to answer its queries with it being none the wiser. The full proof can be found in the full version of this paper [14].

Finally, we exhibit a scheme that is MM-CPA, but *not* MMR-CPA in Sect. 6.1, thus concluding that MMR+ANON-CCA is a properly stronger notion than MM-CCA.

Relationship between MM and IND attacks. Let $\Pi = (\mathcal{K}, \mathcal{E}, \mathcal{D})$ be an encryption scheme. Define PKEAD as $(\mathcal{K}, \mathsf{Enc}, \mathsf{Dec})$ where $\mathsf{Enc}^H_{pk}(M\,; r \,\|\, b) = \mathcal{E}^H_{pk}(M\,; r) \,\|\, (b \oplus M[1])$ and $\mathsf{Dec}^H_{sk}(C \,\|\, z) = \mathcal{D}^H_{sk}(C)$. (Note that if Π has randomness length $\rho(\cdot)$, then PKEAD has randomness length $\rho(k) + 1$ for all k.) Then PKEAD is IND-CPA secure as long as Π is. But PKEAD is not MM-CPA secure, since bit b might be fixed by the randomness source. It follows that IND-CPA security does not imply MM-CPA security in general. (A similar argument holds for MMR-CPA.) But what about the converse?

Recall that our notions are parameterized by the min-entropy and output length of the source(s). We may also consider finer-grained notions of security. Let $\Pi^{\text{mmr-cca}}_{\mu,v}$ denote the set of PKE schemes MMR-CCA secure with respect to distinct (μ, v, ρ)-mmr-sources, where $\rho(\cdot)$ is the randomness length of the scheme. Similarly, let $\Pi^{\text{mm-cca}}_{\mu_1,\mu_2,v}$ denote the set of PKE schemes MM-CCA secure with respect to distinct (μ_1, v)-mm-sources and (μ_2, v, ρ)-r-sources. Finally, let $\Pi^{\text{ind-cca}}$ denote the set of IND-CCA secure schemes. First, we observe that if $\varphi, \psi, v : \mathbb{N} \to \mathbb{N}$ are functions and $\varphi(k) \in O(\psi(k))$, then $\Pi^{\text{mmr-cca}}_{\varphi,v} \subseteq \Pi^{\text{mmr-cca}}_{\psi,v}$. This means that if a scheme is secure with respect to the lowest min-entropy requirement (of order $\omega(\log k)$), then it is also secure with respect to sources with more entropy. Analogously, we have that $\Pi^{\text{mm-cca}}_{\varphi_1,\varphi_2,v} \subseteq \Pi^{\text{mm-cca}}_{\psi_1,\psi_2,v}$ where $\varphi_1, \varphi_2, \psi_1, \psi_2, v : \mathbb{N} \to \mathbb{N}$ are functions such that $\varphi_1(k) \in O(\psi_1(k))$ and $\varphi_2(k) \in O(\psi_2(k))$.

As a special case, we have that $\Pi^{\text{mm-cca}}_{0,\varphi,1} \subseteq$ ind-cca for every $\varphi(k) \in \omega(\log k)$. More generally, we can show that for certain classes of functions $\mu_1, \mu_2, v : \mathbb{N} \to \mathbb{N}$, it holds that $\Pi^{\text{mm-cca}}_{\mu_1,\mu_2,v} \subseteq \Pi^{\text{ind-cca}}$. First, we observe the following:

Lemma 1. *Let* PKEAD *be an encryption scheme with randomness length* $\rho(\cdot)$. *Let* $\mu_1, v : \mathbb{N} \to \mathbb{N}$ *be functions. Let* $\mathcal{A}$ *be an adversary who makes one query to its* **LR** *oracle, and* $\mathcal{U}$ *be the* (ρ, v, ρ)*-r-source defined by:* $\boldsymbol{r} \leftarrow\!\!\$\, (\{0,1\}^{\rho(k)})^{v(k)}$*; return* $\boldsymbol{r}$. *There exists a* (μ_1, v)*-mm-adversary* $\mathcal{B}$ *who makes one query to its* **LR** *oracle such that* $\mathbf{Adv}^{\text{ind-cca}}_{\mathsf{PKEAD}}(\mathcal{A}, k) \le v(k)2^{\mu_1(k)} \cdot \mathbf{Adv}^{\text{mm-cca}}_{\mathsf{PKEAD},\mathcal{U}}(\mathcal{B}, k)$*, where* $\mathsf{time}_{\mathcal{B}}(k) = \mathsf{time}_{\mathcal{A}}(k) + O(v(k)2^{\mu_1(k)})$.

Proof. Fix $k \in \mathbb{N}$ and let $\mu_1 = \mu_1(k)$, $\rho = \rho(k)$, and $v = v(k)$. Assume that $\mathcal{A}$'s query to its **LR** oracle is (H, M_0, M_1) where $H \in \mathsf{AD}$ and M_0 and M_1 are distinct, equal-length strings. This is without loss of generality, since otherwise **LR** would reject. Let $n = |M_0| = |M_1|$. We construct adversary $\mathcal{B}$ from $\mathcal{A}$. On input $(1^k, pk)$ and with oracles **LR** and **Dec**, adversary $\mathcal{B}$ executes $b' \leftarrow\!\!\$\, \mathcal{A}^{\mathbf{LR}',\mathbf{Dec}}(1^k, pk)$ and returns b', where $\mathbf{LR}'$ is defined below.

Let $\mathcal{M}$ be the following mm-source: on input 1^k, first construct a set $S \subseteq (\{0,1\}^n)^2$ such that: (1) $|S| = v2^{\mu_1}$; (2) $(M_0, M_1) \in S$; and (3) for every distinct (X_0, X_1) and (Y_0, Y_1) in S, it holds that $X_0 \ne Y_0$ and $X_1 \ne Y_1$. Next, for each $i \in [v]$, sample a pair (X, Y) uniformly and *without replacement* from S, and let $\boldsymbol{M}_0[i] = X$ and $\boldsymbol{M}_1[i] = Y$. Finally, output $(\boldsymbol{M}_0, \boldsymbol{M}_1)$. Sampling each $(\boldsymbol{M}_0[i], \boldsymbol{M}_1[i])$ without replacement means $\mathcal{M}$ is distinct. Since $|S| = v2^{\mu_1}$, for each $X \in \{0,1\}^n$, $b \in \{0,1\}$, and $i \in [v]$, it holds that

$$\Pr\left[\, (\boldsymbol{M}_0, \boldsymbol{M}_1) \leftarrow\!\!\$\; \mathcal{M}(1^k) : \boldsymbol{M}_b[i] = X \,\right] \le 1 - \frac{v2^{\mu_1} - 1}{v2^{\mu_1}} \cdot \frac{v2^{\mu_1} - 2}{v2^{\mu_1} - 1} \cdots$$
$$= \frac{v}{v2^{\mu_1}} = \frac{1}{2^{\mu_1}} .$$

It follows that $\mathcal{M}$ is a distinct (μ_1, v)-mm-source. Returning now to answering $\mathcal{A}$'s **LR** queries: on input (H, M_0, M_1), oracle $\mathbf{LR}'$ first lets $\boldsymbol{H}[i] = H$ for each $i \in [v]$. It then executes $\boldsymbol{C} \leftarrow\!\!\$\; \mathbf{LR}(\boldsymbol{H}, \mathcal{M})$, samples $j \leftarrow\!\!\$\; [v]$, and returns $\boldsymbol{C}[j]$ to $\mathcal{A}$.

Adversary $\mathcal{B}$'s simulation of $\mathcal{A}$'s **LR** query (and subsequent **Dec** queries) is perfect as long as $\boldsymbol{M}_0[j] = M_0$ and $\boldsymbol{M}_1[j] = M_1$. Let good denote this event. This occurs with probability $1/v2^{\mu_1}$. Then

$$\begin{aligned}\Pr\left[\, \mathbf{Exp}^{\text{mm-cca}}_{\mathsf{PKEAD},\mathcal{U}}(\mathcal{B}, k) \,\right] &= \Pr\left[\, \mathbf{Exp}^{\text{mm-cca}}_{\mathsf{PKEAD},\mathcal{U}}(\mathcal{B}, k) \mid \mathsf{good} \,\right] \Pr\left[\, \mathsf{good} \,\right] \\ &\quad + \Pr\left[\, \mathbf{Exp}^{\text{mm-cca}}_{\mathsf{PKEAD},\mathcal{U}}(\mathcal{B}, k) \mid \overline{\mathsf{good}} \,\right] \Pr\left[\, \overline{\mathsf{good}} \,\right] \\ &\ge \frac{1}{v2^{\mu_1}} \cdot \Pr\left[\, \mathbf{Exp}^{\text{ind-cca}}_{\mathsf{PKEAD}}(\mathcal{A}, k) \,\right] ,\end{aligned}$$

which yields the bound. To complete the proof, we need only to comment on the runtime of $\mathcal{B}$. Constructing the set S requires time $O(v2^{\mu_1})$. Since this dominates the time to simulate $\mathcal{A}$'s **LR** query, it follows that the runtime $\mathcal{B}$ is $\mathsf{time}_{\mathcal{A}}(k) + O(v2^{\mu_1})$. □

This yields, almost immediately, the following corollary:

Theorem 4. *Let $\mu_1, \mu_2, v : \mathbb{N} \to \mathbb{N}$ be functions such that $\mu_1(k) \in O(\log k)$, $\mu_2(k) \in \omega(\log k)$, and $v(k)$ is polynomial in k. Then $\Pi^{\text{mm-cca}}_{\mu_1,\mu_2,v} \subseteq \Pi^{\text{ind-cca}}$.*

Proof. Let $\mathsf{PKEAD} \in \Pi^{\text{mm-cca}}_{\mu_1,\mu_2,v}$ have randomness length $\rho(\cdot)$. By definition, we have that $\mathsf{PKEAD} \in \Pi^{\text{mm-cca}}_{\mu_1,\rho,v}$. By Lemma 1, for every PT adversary $\mathcal{A}$, there is a PT (μ_1, v)-mm-adversary $\mathcal{B}$ such that

$$\mathbf{Adv}^{\text{ind-cca}}_{\mathsf{PKEAD}}(\mathcal{A}, k) \le v(k) 2^{\mu_1(k)} \cdot \mathbf{Adv}^{\text{mm-cca}}_{\mathsf{PKEAD},\mathcal{U}}(\mathcal{B}, k).$$

Hence, $\mathsf{PKEAD} \in \Pi^{\text{ind-cca}}$. □

6 Constructions

In this section we present several constructions of hedged PKEAD schemes. To begin, we give a result showing that EME-OAEP (the version of RSA-OAEP that is implemented in OpenSSL) is not MMR-CPA, but is provably MM-CCA in the ROM, under a standard assumption on RSA. This gives the first positive result for RSA-OAEP in the presence of imperfect randomness, and is callable via the high-level APIs exposed by all major libraries.

To achieve MMR+IND-CCA, we give a hybrid-encryption PKEAD scheme. This, too, can be realized by high-level API calls in modern libraries, using RSA as the trapdoor function, and available hash function and symmetric authenticated encryption functionalities.

We then revisit the generic compositions RtD and PtD from Bellare et al. [5]. We show that if the deterministic scheme is instantiated specifically by RSA-DOAEP [4], which can be done via high-level API calls to hash functions and RSA, then PtD achieves MM+IND-CCA, and RtD achieves MM+IND-CPA. We also suggest specific conditions under which RtD would be MMR+IND-CCA, extending prior work [5].

TRAPDOOR PERMUTATIONS. Some of our constructions make use of trapdoor permutations, so we recall this primitive and its security here. Let $k \in \mathbb{N}$. A *trapdoor permutation generator* is a probabilistic algorithm F with associated input length[5] $n(\cdot)$ that on input 1^k outputs the encoding of a pair of functions $f, f^{-1} : \{0,1\}^* \to \{0,1\}^*$ such that for every $x \in \{0,1\}^{n(k)}$, it holds that $f^{-1}(f(x)) = x$. We say that F is OWF secure if for every PT adversary $\mathcal{A}$, the quantity

$$\mathbf{Adv}^{\mathrm{owf}}_{F}(\mathcal{A}, k) = \Pr\Big[(f, f^{-1}) \leftarrow_{\$} F(1^k); x \leftarrow_{\$} \{0,1\}^{n(k)} : \mathcal{A}(1^k, f, f(x)) \Rightarrow x \Big]$$

is a negligible function of k.

We will also use the stronger security notion of *partial-domain one-wayness* formalized by Fujisaki et al. [25], which asserts that it is difficult to partially invert a value in the range of the trapdoor permutation. Let F be a trapdoor permutation generator with input length $n(\cdot)$ and let $m(\cdot)$ be a function such that $m(k) \leq n(k)$ for every $k \in \mathbb{N}$. We say that F is m-POWF secure if for every PT adversary $\mathcal{A}$, the following function is negligible in k:

$$\mathbf{Adv}^{\mathrm{powf}}_{F,m}(\mathcal{A}, k) = \Pr\Big[(f, f^{-1}) \leftarrow_{\$} F(1^k); x \leftarrow_{\$} \{0,1\}^{n(k)} : \mathcal{A}(1^k, f, f(x)) \Rightarrow x[1..m(k)] \Big].$$

6.1 EME-OAEP

We first look at RSA-OAEP [9], the only provably-secure PKE scheme available in OpenSSL, and indeed most libraries.[6] It is known to be IND-CCA secure assuming that the underlying trapdoor permutation is POWF secure, or under the RSA assumption [25,36].

[5] For example, the input length might be the number of modulus bits in RSA.

[6] Some implement ElGamal or hybrid encryption schemes as well.

$\mathsf{Kgen}(1^k)$	$\mathsf{Enc}^H_{pk}(M)$	$\mathsf{Dec}^H_{sk}(C)$
$(f, f^{-1}) \leftarrow_\$ F(1^k)$	$\langle f \rangle \leftarrow pk$; $PM \leftarrow \mathsf{pad}(M)$	$\langle f^{-1} \rangle \leftarrow sk$; $P \leftarrow f^{-1}(C)$
return $(\langle f \rangle, \langle f^{-1} \rangle)$	if $PM = \bot$ then return $\bot$	if $\lvert P \rvert \neq n$ then return $\bot$
	$X_0 \leftarrow PM \,\Vert\, \mathsf{H}_1(H)$	$X_1 \,\Vert\, Y_1 \,\Vert\, [z] \leftarrow P$ $\# \lvert Y_1 \rvert = \rho$
	$Y_0 \leftarrow_\$ \{0,1\}^\rho$	$Y_0 \leftarrow Y_1 \oplus \mathsf{H}_2(X_1)$
	$X_1 \leftarrow X_0 \oplus \mathsf{G}(Y_0)$	$X_0 \leftarrow X_1 \oplus \mathsf{G}(Y_0)$
	$Y_1 \leftarrow Y_0 \oplus \mathsf{H}_2(X_1)$	$PM \,\Vert\, T \leftarrow X_0$ $\# \lvert T \rvert = \tau$
	$P \leftarrow X_1 \,\Vert\, Y_1 \,\Vert\, [0]$	if $\mathsf{H}_1(H) \neq T$ then return $\bot$
	return $f(P)$	return $\mathsf{unpad}(PM)$

Fig. 5. Specification of F-$\mathsf{EME\text{-}OAEP}$ encryption (RFC 8017) where F is a trapdoor permutation generator with input length $n(\cdot)$. Let $\tau(\cdot)$ and $\rho(\cdot)$ be functions where for every $k \in \mathbb{N}$, it holds that $\rho(k) + \tau(k) + 16 \leq n(k)$. Fix $k \in \mathbb{N}$ and let $n = n(k)$, $\tau = \tau(k)$, $\rho = \rho(k)$, and $m = n - \rho - 8$. The syntax $[i]$ denotes integer i, where $0 \leq i \leq 255$, encoded as a byte. Let $\mathsf{H}_1 : \{0,1\}^* \to \{0,1\}^\tau$, $\mathsf{G} : \{0,1\}^* \to \{0,1\}^m$, and $\mathsf{H}_2 : \{0,1\}^* \to \{0,1\}^\rho$ be functions. Define $\mathsf{pad} : \{0,1\}^* \to \{0,1\}^{m-\tau} \cup \{\bot\}$ by $\mathsf{pad}(M) = M \,\Vert\, [1] \,\Vert\, [0] \cdots [0]$ if $\lvert M \rvert$ is less than or equal to $m - \tau - 8$ and is a multiple of 8, and $\mathsf{pad}(M) = \bot$ otherwise. Define its inverse $\mathsf{unpad} : \{0,1\}^{m-\tau} \to \{0,1\}^* \cup \{\bot\}$ in the natural way.

We specify the EME-OAEP variant standardized in PKCS #1 version 2.2 (RFC 8017). Let F be a trapdoor permutation generator. Refer to the encryption scheme F-$\mathsf{EME\text{-}OAEP}$ specified in Fig. 5. This scheme resembles standard OAEP except that a hash of the associated data (called a *label* in RFC 8017) is appended to the message.[7] Instead of checking for a string of zero-bytes, the decrypting party checks that the hash of the associated data matches. In addition, a zero-byte is appended to the pad before applying the trapdoor.[8]

F-$\mathsf{EME\text{-}OAEP}$ IS NOT MMR-CPA. This scheme is not MMR-CPA secure, due to an attack by Brown [15] on $\mathsf{RSA\text{-}OAEP}$ with exponent $e = 3$. The attack exploits low entropy coins. An adversary who knows (or is able to guess) the coins can recover the entire plaintext, meaning the attack is effective even if the message has high min-entropy. Since this attack does not exploit the tag used to check if the ciphertext is valid during decryption, it is equally effective in breaking $\mathsf{RSA\text{-}EME\text{-}OAEP}$.

F-EME-OAEP IS MM-CCA. We prove the scheme does achieve our new notion. The standard cites the result of [25] to establish the IND-CCA security of this scheme, but this result makes no formal claim for the security of the associated data. Moreover, no security guarantee is known in case randomness is not perfect. We extend their analysis to account for associated data and imperfect randomness and prove, in the random oracle model, that F-$\mathsf{EME\text{-}OAEP}$ is MM-CCA secure with respect to high min-entropy coins sources, assuming that F is POWF

[7] Interestingly, no API we surveyed exposes AD as a parameter, although the standard supports AD.

[8] The zero-byte is intended to ensure that the message is in $\mathbb{Z}_N^*$ in the case of RSA.

secure. By [25, Lemma 4.2], instantiating the trapdoor with RSA is secure assuming only that RSA is OWF secure.

Theorem 5 (F-EME-OAEP is MM-CCA). *Let F be a length $n(\cdot)$ trapdoor permutation generator. Let $\mu_1, \mu_2, v, \tau, \rho : \mathbb{N} \to \mathbb{N}$ be functions where $\mu_2(k) \in \omega(\log k)$ and $\rho(k)+\tau(k)+16 \leq n(k)$ for every $k \in \mathbb{N}$. Let $m(k) = n(k) - \rho(k) - 8$. Let PKEAD $= F$-EME-OAEP as defined in Fig. 5, where H_1, H_2, and G are modeled as random oracles. Let $\mathcal{A}$ be a (μ_1, v)-mm-adversary who makes q_e queries to* **LR**, *q_d queries to* **Dec**, *and q_1, q_2, and q_G queries to H_1, H_2, and G respectively. Let $\mathcal{R}$ be a (μ_2, v, ρ)-r-source. There exists an adversary $\mathcal{B}$ such that*

$$\mathbf{Adv}^{\text{mm-cca}}_{\mathsf{PKEAD},\mathcal{R}}(\mathcal{A}, k) \leq 512 q_e q_2 v(k) \cdot \mathbf{Adv}^{\text{powf}}_{F,m}(\mathcal{B}, k) + \frac{q_e(q_1 + q_d)^2}{2^{\tau(k)-1}} + \frac{q_e(q_G + q_d)^2}{2^{\rho(k)-1}} + \frac{q_e v(k)(q_G + q_d)}{2^{\mu_2(k)-1}},$$

where $\mathsf{time}_{\mathcal{B}}(k) = \mathsf{time}_{\mathcal{A}}(k) + O(q_d q_1 q_G q_2)$.

The proof appears in the full version [14]. Note that the security bound does not depend on the min-entropy of the message source, but only on the min-entropy of the randomness source. This is undesirable from a concrete security standpoint, since any entropy in the messages is thrown away. In Sect. 6.3, we show that adding an additional Feistel round is sufficient to establish a concrete security bound that depends on the message entropy. Note that the loss of 2^8 in the bound is the result of fixing the most significant byte as $[0]$.

In real-world terms, this result suggests that it is safe to use RSA-EME-OAEP barring catastrophic failure of the (P)RNG. If the adversary is able to guess the coins used, then there is an attack [15], and so the Dual EC DRBG attack [18], for example, completely breaks the security of RSA-EME-OAEP. Even cases where the coins still have *some* entropy [31] we consider insecure in an asymptotic sense, since an adversary can guess the coins with non-negligible probability.

MMR DOES NOT IMPLY MM SECURITY. Since F-EME-OAEP is not MMR-CPA, we conclude that MMR-CPA does not imply MM-CPA in general.

6.2 Hybrid Encryption Construction

Next, we present a novel scheme that is MMR-CCA in the random oracle model, and at the same time can be implemented using most high-level APIs, including OpenSSL. The scheme is a hybrid construction combining a trapdoor permutation, an authenticated encryption scheme with authenticated data (AEAD, now a standard notion in crypto libraries), and hash functions modeled as random oracles. We recall the notion of AEAD and then proceed to define the PKEAD scheme.

AUTHENTICATED ENCRYPTION WITH ASSOCIATED DATA (AEAD). An AEAD scheme consists of three algorithms AEAD = (Kgen, Enc, Dec). The randomized *key generation* algorithm Kgen samples a key K from a finite, non-empty set $\mathcal{K}$

$\underline{\mathsf{Kgen}(1^k)}$:	$\underline{\mathsf{Enc}_{pk}(M, H)}$	$\underline{\mathsf{Dec}_{sk}(H, C_1 \parallel C_2)}$
$(f, f^{-1}) \leftarrow_{\$} F(1^k)$	$X \leftarrow_{\$} \{0,1\}^{\rho(k)}$	$K_P \leftarrow f^{-1}(C_1)$
$R \leftarrow_{\$} \{0,1\}^r$	$K_P \leftarrow \mathsf{H}_1(\langle f \parallel R, H, M, X\rangle)$	$K \leftarrow \mathsf{H}_2(\langle f \parallel R, H, K_P\rangle)$
return $(f \parallel R, f^{-1})$	$C_1 \leftarrow f(K_P)$	$\tilde{H} \leftarrow \langle H, C_1\rangle$
	$K \leftarrow \mathsf{H}_2(\langle f \parallel R, H, K_P\rangle)$	$N \leftarrow \mathsf{extract}(\tilde{H})$
	$\tilde{H} \leftarrow \langle H, C_1\rangle$	$M \leftarrow \mathsf{AEAD.Dec}(K, N, \tilde{H}, C_2)$
	$N \leftarrow \mathsf{extract}(\tilde{H})$	return M
	$C_2 \leftarrow \mathsf{AEAD.Enc}(K, N, \tilde{H}, M)$	
	return $C_1 \parallel C_2$	

Fig. 6. Hybrid encryption construction $\mathsf{HE}[F, \mathsf{AEAD}]$ with randomness length $\rho(\cdot)$ and additional parameters $n, \lambda, k_P \in \mathbb{N}$. Let F be a length $n(\cdot)$ trapdoor permutation generator, such that $n(k) \geq k_P$ for sufficiently large k, and let AEAD be an AEAD scheme with key space $\{0,1\}^\lambda$, nonce space $\{0,1\}^n$, and associated-data space $\{0,1\}^*$. Let $\mathsf{H}_1 : \{0,1\}^* \to \{0,1\}^{k_P}$ and $\mathsf{H}_2 : \{0,1\}^* \to \{0,1\}^\lambda$ be functions. Let $\mathsf{extract}\colon \{0,1\}^* \to \{0,1\}^n$ be a function that on input $\tilde{H}$ returns the n-bit nonce.

called the *key space*. The deterministic *encryption algorithm* $\mathsf{Enc}\colon \mathcal{K} \times \mathcal{N} \times \mathsf{AD} \times \{0,1\}^* \to \{0,1\}^* \cup \{\perp\}$ takes as input a key K, a nonce $N \in \mathcal{N}$, associated data $H \in \mathsf{AD}$, and a message $M \in \{0,1\}^*$, and it returns a ciphertext $C \in \{0,1\}^*$ or the distinguished symbol $\perp$. We sometimes write $C \leftarrow \mathsf{Enc}_K^{H,N}(M)$ as a shorthand for $C \leftarrow \mathsf{Enc}(K, N, H, M)$. The deterministic *decryption algorithm* $\mathsf{Dec}\colon \mathcal{K} \times \mathcal{N} \times \mathsf{AD} \times \{0,1\}^* \to \{0,1\}^* \cup \{\perp\}$ takes as input a key K, a nonce $N \in \mathcal{N}$, associated data $H \in \mathsf{AD}$, and ciphertext $C \in \{0,1\}^*$, and outputs either the plaintext M or $\perp$. We sometimes write $M \leftarrow \mathsf{Dec}_K^{H,N}(C)$ as shorthand for $M \leftarrow \mathsf{Dec}(K, N, H, C)$. For correctness, it is required that for all $K \in \mathcal{K}$, $H \in \mathsf{AD}$, $N \in \mathcal{N}$ and $M \in \{0,1\}^*$, we have $\mathsf{Enc}_K^{H,N}(M) \neq \perp \implies \mathsf{Dec}_K^{H,N}(\mathsf{Enc}_K^{H,N}(M)) = M$.

Message privacy. To define message privacy, let $\mathcal{A}$ be an adversary and consider the experiment $\mathbf{Exp}_{\mathsf{AEAD}}^{\text{ind-cpa}}(\mathcal{A})$. The experiment first generates the key $K \leftarrow_{\$} \mathsf{Kgen}$ and samples a bit $b \leftarrow_{\$} \{0,1\}$. The adversary has access to the encryption oracle $\mathsf{Enc}(K, \cdot, \cdot, LR(\cdot, \cdot, b))$, where $LR(\cdot, \cdot, b)$ on inputs $M_0, M_1 \in \{0,1\}^*$ with $|M_0| = |M_1|$ returns M_b. We say that $\mathcal{A}$ is *nonce-respecting* if it never repeats N in its oracle queries. (Hereafter, we assume the IND-CPA attacker is nonce-respecting.) Finally, adversary $\mathcal{A}$ outputs a bit b'. The outcome of the game is the predicate $(b = b')$. We define $\mathcal{A}$'s advantage as $\mathbf{Adv}_{\mathsf{AEAD}}^{\text{ind-cpa}}(\mathcal{A}) = 2 \cdot \Pr[\mathbf{Exp}_{\mathsf{AEAD}}^{\text{ind-cpa}}(\mathcal{A})] - 1$.

Authenticity. To define message authenticity, let $\mathcal{A}$ be an adversary and consider the experiment $\mathbf{Exp}_{\mathsf{AEAD}}^{\text{auth}}(\mathcal{A})$. It first generates a key $K \leftarrow_{\$} \mathsf{Kgen}$, then provides $\mathcal{A}$ access to oracle $\mathsf{Enc}(K, \cdot, \cdot, \cdot)$. (Note that the AUTH adversary need not be nonce-respecting.) The adversary can also query a special decryption oracle on triples (N, H, C). This oracle returns 1 if $\mathsf{Dec}_K^{H,IV}(C) \neq \perp$, and 0 otherwise. The game outputs true if and only if the special decryption oracle returns 1 on some query (N, H, C) and $\mathcal{A}$ never queried (N, H, M) for some $M \in \{0,1\}^*$ and got C in response. Let $\mathbf{Adv}^{\text{auth}}_{\mathsf{AEAD}}(\mathcal{A}) = \Pr[\mathbf{Exp}^{\text{auth}}_{\mathsf{AEAD}}(\mathcal{A})]$.

HYBRID PKEAD FROM A TDP AND AEAD. We propose a PKEAD scheme that uses a trapdoor permutation and an AEAD symmetric encryption scheme. Its algorithms can be implemented using the library calls to RSA function with no padding and to any AEAD scheme such as AES-GCM. The scheme is defined in Fig. 6. The functions H_1 and H_2 are realized using cryptographic hash functions, but are modeled as random oracles in the analysis. We assume that there is an efficient function $\mathsf{extract}$ that on input associated data $\tilde{H}$ returns the n-bit nonce for AEAD scheme. The goal of $\mathsf{extract}$ is to make sure that the outputs do not repeat. If H contains a counter, or some other non-repeating string, then that could be used as an extracted nonce. Alternatively, C_1 or its part could be used as a nonce. (In the analysis we take into account that the asymmetric parts of ciphertexts do not repeat with overwhelming probability.) We leave the particular instantiation of $\mathsf{extract}$ to the applications.

$\mathsf{HE}[F, \mathsf{AEAD}]$ IS MMR+IND-CCA. The following theorem establishes MMR- and IND-CCA security of our hybrid construction.

Theorem 6. *Let F be a trapdoor permutation generator,* AEAD *be an AEAD scheme, and* $\mathsf{PKEAD} = \mathsf{HE}[\mathrm{F}, \mathsf{AEAD}]$ *as defined in Fig. 6, where H_1 and H_2 are modeled as random oracles.*

– *(MMR-CCA) Let $\mu, v : \mathbb{N} \to \mathbb{N}$ be functions such that $\mu(k) \in \omega(\log k)$. Let $\mathcal{A}$ be a (μ, v, ρ)-mmr-adversary attacking* PKEAD *and making q queries to its* **LR** *oracle, q_d queries to its* **Dec** *oracle, and q_{H_1} and q_{H_2} queries to H_1 and H_2 respectively. Then there exist adversary $\mathcal{B}$ attacking F and adversaries $\mathcal{C}$ and $\mathcal{D}$ attacking* AEAD*, such that*

$$\mathbf{Adv}^{\text{mmr-cca}}_{\mathsf{PKEAD}}(\mathcal{A}, k) \leq \frac{q_{\mathsf{H}_1} + q_d}{2^{r-1}} + \frac{(q_{\mathsf{H}_1} + q^2 v(k))}{2^{\mu(k)-1}} + \frac{q_d + q^2 v^2(k)}{2^{k_P - 1}}$$
$$+ 2v(k)q \cdot \left(\mathbf{Adv}^{\text{owf}}_{F}(\mathcal{B}, k) + \mathbf{Adv}^{\text{ind-cpa}}_{\mathsf{AEAD}}(\mathcal{C}, k) + \mathbf{Adv}^{\text{auth}}_{\mathsf{AEAD}}(\mathcal{D}, k)\right).$$

– *(IND-CCA) Let $\mathcal{A}$ be an adversary attacking* PKEAD *and making q queries to its* **LR** *oracle, q_d queries to its* **Dec** *oracle, and q_{H_1} and q_{H_2} queries to H_1 and H_2. Then there exist an adversary $\mathcal{B}$ attacking F and adversaries $\mathcal{C}$ and $\mathcal{D}$ attacking* AEAD*, such that*

$$\mathbf{Adv}^{\text{ind-cca}}_{\mathsf{PKEAD}}(\mathcal{A}, k) \leq \frac{q_{\mathsf{H}_1}}{2^{\rho(k)-1}} + \frac{q_d}{2^{k_P - 1}}$$
$$+ 2v(k)q \cdot \left(\mathbf{Adv}^{\text{owf}}_{F}(\mathcal{B}, k) + \mathbf{Adv}^{\text{ind-cpa}}_{\mathsf{AEAD}}(\mathcal{C}, k) + \mathbf{Adv}^{\text{auth}}_{\mathsf{AEAD}}(\mathcal{D}, k)\right).$$

In both cases, we have that $\mathsf{time}_{\mathcal{B}}(k), \mathsf{time}_{\mathcal{C}}(k), \mathsf{time}_{\mathcal{D}}(k) \approx \mathsf{time}_{\mathcal{A}}(k)$, $\mathcal{C}$ makes at most $v(k)q$ queries to its encryption oracle, and $\mathcal{D}$ makes $v(k)q$ queries to its encryption oracle, and q_d queries to its decryption oracle.

The proof is in the full version of this paper [14]. Here we sketch the more challenging proof of MMR-CCA security. We consider a sequence of games that starts with the MMR-CCA experiment and ends with the one where random messages are encrypted with the AEAD.Enc under random keys, which are independent from the asymmetric ciphertexts. The view of the adversary in the last game is independent of the challenge bit. As we move between games, we consider a series of "bad" events. The first bad event happens if the H_1 oracle is queried on the values colliding with those output by the mmr-source during encryption computation. We can bound such an event by relying on the entropy of the mmr-source, if the collision occurs after the public key is revealed, or using the fact that the adversary does not know the public key and cannot guess its randomizer value if the collision happens before the public key is revealed. If this "bad" event never happens, then K_p values used to compute the asymmetric parts of the challenge ciphertexts can be chosen at random. Another bad event is set when a H_2 oracle query is made so it contains the K_p that was used as input to f during encryption. If this does not happen, we can use random symmetric keys for AEAD.Enc. If this bad event does happen, we can construct the OWF adversary for trapdoor permutation generator F. Once we are in a game where random symmetric keys are used, we can use the IND-CPA security of AEAD. Here we have to make sure that the IND-CPA adversary is nonce-respecting. This follows from the fact that the asymmetric parts of the challenge ciphertexts, from which nonces are derived, do not repeat with overwhelming probability.

Care is needed to ensure that the adversary does not get information about the public key from the decryption queries and that the adversaries we construct can answer the decryption oracle queries. If the adversary makes a valid decryption oracle query, so that the asymmetric part is the same as that of some challenge ciphertext, then we can construct an adversary breaking authenticity of the AEAD scheme. If the asymmetric part of the ciphertext in the decryption oracle query is new, i.e., it is different from those of all challenge ciphertexts, and no corresponding H_2 query was made, the ciphertext can be rejected, as it can be valid only with negligible probability. Before the public key is revealed, such a hash query can only be made by the adversary with negligible probability. If the public key has been revealed, than such a ciphertext can be decrypted without the knowledge of the secret key.

6.3 Generic Constructions

We describe two black-box constructions of [5], which compose generic randomized and *deterministic* encryption schemes. Appealing to the security properties of their constituents, these constructions are shown to be MMR+IND-CPA secure in the standard model. We consider lifting these results to the CCA setting, and consider security against MM attacks. First, we specify deterministic encryption and briefly describe its associated security notions. It will be convenient formulate the syntax without associated data.

DETERMINISTIC ENCRYPTION. A deterministic PKE scheme Π is a triple of algorithms $(\mathcal{K}, \mathcal{E}, \mathcal{D})$. On input 1^k, algorithm $\mathcal{K}$ probabilistically outputs a key pair (pk, sk). Encryption deterministically maps the public key pk and a string M to an element of $\{0,1\}^* \cup \{\perp\}$. Decryption deterministically maps the secret key sk and a string C to an element of $\{0,1\}^* \cup \{\perp\}$. The scheme is correct if for every $k \in \mathbb{N}$, $(pk, sk) \in [\mathcal{K}(1^k)]$, and $M \in \{0,1\}^*$, it holds that $\mathcal{E}_{pk}(M) \neq \perp$ implies $\mathcal{D}_{sk}(\mathcal{E}_{pk}(M)) = M$. It will be helpful to assume that deterministic schemes are defined on all strings of a particular length. We say Π has input length $n(\cdot)$ if encryption is defined for all strings of length $n(k)$ and all k.

We consider both MMR-CPA and -CCA security of deterministic schemes against $(\mu, v, 0)$-mmr adversaries for functions $\mu, v : \mathbb{N} \to \mathbb{N}$, where $\mu(k) \in \omega(\log k)$. In order to instantiate a deterministic scheme in the game, we allow encryption to take coins as input, but these are simply ignored. Similarly, we allow encryption and decryption to take associated data as input, but this is ignored. Note that it does not make sense to consider MM-CPA or -CCA security of deterministic schemes, since we cannot defend against key-dependent distribution attacks in this setting. Security of deterministic encryption was first formalized by [4]. Their CPA notion, PRIV, is equivalent to MMR1-CPA security. However, their CCA notion, PRIV-CCA, is *not* equivalent to MMR1-CCA. In our notion, the message source specified by the adversary is allowed to depend on prior decryption queries, whereas in the PRIV-CCA game, the adversary makes decryption queries only after it gets its challenge.

BLOCK-SOURCES. Recall the notion of an $\mathrm{m}^\beta\mathrm{r}^\gamma$-source given in Sect. 4. In the standard model, we consider security with respect to $\mathrm{m}^\beta\mathrm{r}^\gamma$*-block-sources*, where the outputs have high *conditional* min-entropy. Intuitively, this means that, from the adversary's perspective, each output of a block-source has high min-entropy even having seen the prior elements of the vector. (See [5] for a precise definition.)

LOSSY AND ALL-BUT-ONE TRAPDOOR FUNCTIONS. LTDFs were first described by Peikert and Waters [33]. Informally, an *LTDF generator* F is a probabilistic algorithm that on input 1^k and $b \in \{0,1\}$ outputs a pair of strings (s,t) such that s encodes a function f. If $b = 1$, then function f is injective, and t encodes a function f^{-1} giving its inverse; otherwise, the image of f is significantly smaller than the injective mode (i.e., $b = 1$). The generator is secure if no reasonable adversary, given s, can distinguish injective mode from the lossy mode (i.e., $b = 0$). We call F *universal-inducing* if the lossy mode is a universal hash function. Motivated by the goal of instantiating IND-CCA secure probabilistic encryption, [33] introduce ABO ("all-but-one") TDFs as a richer abstraction. Instead of having an injective and lossy mode, an ABO TDF has a *set of modes*, one of which is lossy. Here, security demands that every pair of modes are computationally indistinguishable. Both primitives have been constructed from a number of hardness assumptions: For example, the Φ-hiding assumption for RSA [29] and LWE ("learning with errors") for lattices [33]. A universal LTDF is given by Boldyreva, Fehr, and O'Neill [13] based on the DDH assumption.

Pad-then-Deterministic. The transformation of a deterministic encryption scheme into a probabilistic one via a randomized padding scheme is defined in the

$\mathsf{PtD}[\Pi_d].\mathsf{Kgen}(1^k)$	$\mathsf{PtD}[\Pi_d].\mathsf{Enc}^H_{pk}(M)$	$\mathsf{PtD}[\Pi_d].\mathsf{Dec}^H_{sk}(C)$
$(pk, sk) \leftarrow_{\$} \mathcal{K}_d(1^k)$ return (pk, sk)	if $\lvert H \rvert \neq k_0$ then return $\perp$ $r \leftarrow_{\$} \{0,1\}^{\rho}$ $PM \leftarrow \mathsf{pad}_{n-k_0}(\langle M, r \rangle)$ return $\mathcal{E}_d(pk, H \parallel PM)$	$H' \parallel PM \leftarrow \mathcal{D}_d(sk, C)$ # $\lvert H' \rvert = k_0$ if $H' \neq H$ then return $\perp$ $\langle M, r \rangle \leftarrow \mathsf{unpad}_{n-k_0}(PM)$ return M

$\mathsf{RtD}[\Pi_r, \Pi_d].\mathsf{Kgen}(1^k)$	$\mathsf{RtD}[\Pi_r, \Pi_d].\mathsf{Enc}^H_{pk}(M)$	$\mathsf{RtD}[\Pi_r, \Pi_d].\mathsf{Dec}^H_{sk}(C)$
$(pk_r, sk_r) \leftarrow_{\$} \mathcal{K}_r(1^k)$ $(pk_d, sk_d) \leftarrow_{\$} \mathcal{K}_d(1^k)$ return $(\langle pk_r, pk_d \rangle, \langle sk_r, sk_d \rangle)$	$\langle pk_r, pk_d \rangle \leftarrow pk$ $C' \leftarrow_{\$} \mathcal{E}_r(pk_r, H, M)$ return $\mathcal{E}_d(pk_d, \mathsf{pad}_n(C'))$	$\langle sk_r, sk_d \rangle \leftarrow sk$ $X \leftarrow \mathcal{D}_d(sk_d, C)$ $C' \leftarrow \mathsf{unpad}_n(X)$ return $\mathcal{D}_r(sk_r, H, C')$

$F\text{-}\mathsf{DOAEP}.\mathcal{K}(1^k)$	$F\text{-}\mathsf{DOAEP}.\mathcal{E}_{pk}(X)$	$F\text{-}\mathsf{DOAEP}.\mathcal{D}_{sk}(Y)$
$(f, f^{-1}) \leftarrow_{\$} F(1^k)$ return $(\langle f \rangle, \langle f^{-1} \rangle)$	if $\lvert X \rvert \neq n$ then return $\perp$ $\langle f \rangle \leftarrow pk$ $X_\ell \leftarrow X[1..k_0]$ $X_r \leftarrow X[k_0+1..\lvert X \rvert]$ $S_0 \leftarrow \mathsf{H}_1(pk \parallel X_r) \oplus X_\ell$ $T_0 \leftarrow \mathsf{G}(pk \parallel S_0) \oplus X_r$ $S_1 \leftarrow \mathsf{H}_2(pk \parallel T_0) \oplus S_0$ $Y_\ell \parallel Y_r \leftarrow S_1 \parallel T_0$ # $\lvert Y_r \rvert = k_1$ return $Y_\ell \parallel f(Y_r)$	if $\lvert Y \rvert < n - k_1$ then return $\perp$ $\langle f^{-1} \rangle \leftarrow sk$ $Y_\ell \leftarrow Y[1..a]$ $Y_r \leftarrow f^{-1}(Y[a+1..\lvert Y \rvert])$ $S_1 \parallel T_0 \leftarrow Y_\ell \parallel Y_r i$ # $\lvert S_1 \rvert = k_0$ $S_0 \leftarrow \mathsf{H}_2(pk \parallel T_0) \oplus S_1$ $X_r \leftarrow \mathsf{G}(pk \parallel S_0) \oplus T_0$ $X_\ell \leftarrow \mathsf{H}_1(pk \parallel X_r) \oplus S_0$ return $X_\ell \parallel X_r$

Fig. 7. Generic constructions. Let $k_0, k_1, n, \rho : \mathbb{N} \to \mathbb{N}$ be such that $k_0(k) + \rho(k) \leq n(k)$ for all k. Let $\Pi_d = (\mathcal{K}_d, \mathcal{E}_d, \mathcal{D}_d)$ be a deterministic scheme with input length $n(\cdot)$ and let $\Pi_r = (\mathcal{K}_r, \mathcal{E}_r, \mathcal{D}_r)$ be a randomized encryption scheme. Let F be a trapdoor permutation generator with input length $k_1(\cdot)$. Let $\mathsf{pad}_\ell : \{0,1\}^* \to \{0,1\}^\ell \cup \{\perp\}$ be an invertible encoding scheme with $\mathsf{unpad}_\ell : \{0,1\}^* \to \{0,1\}^* \cup \{\perp\}$ as its inverse. Fix $k \in \mathbb{N}$ and let $k_0 = k_0(k)$, $k_1 = k_1(k)$, $n = n(k)$, $\rho = \rho(k)$, and $a = \max\{0, n - k_1\}$. If Y is a string and $a \leq 0$, then let $Y[1..a] = \varepsilon$. Let $\mathsf{H}_1, \mathsf{H}_2 : \{0,1\}^* \to \{0,1\}^{k_0}$ and $\mathsf{G} : \{0,1\}^* \to \{0,1\}^{n-k_0}$ be functions.

top panel of Fig. 7. This is the same as the construction proposed by [5], except we account for associated data. the message space of $\mathsf{PtD}[\Pi]$ is determined by Π. The associated data is restricted to bit strings of the length $k_0(\cdot)$. We first review the results known for PtD in the standard model, then consider its extension to the MMR- and MM-CCA settings.

Let Π be a deterministic scheme and $\mathsf{PtD}[\Pi]$ be as defined in Fig. 7. Bellare et al. [5, Theorem 6.3] prove this construction is MMR-CPA if Π is MMR-CPA, and IND-CPA if Π is a u-LTDF. [9] By Theorem 1, any scheme that is both MMR1- and ANON-CPA secure is also MMR-CPA secure. If Π is a u-LTDF, then it is MMR1-CPA secure for block-sources [13, Theorem 5.1], and ANON-CPA secure for block-sources [5, Theorem 5.3]. Thus, the scheme $\mathsf{PtD}[\Pi]$ is MMR-hedged secure (for block-sources) against chosen-distribution attacks as long

[9] Note that a family of trapdoor permutations is syntactically the same as a deterministic encryption scheme.

as Π is a u-LTDF. Note that universal-inducing property is not essential; see [5, Sect. 6.2] for details.

Unfortunately, this property of the base scheme does not suffice for security in the CCA setting. Nevertheless, a similar construction gets us a step in the right direction. Peikert and Waters [33] suggest the composition of an LTDF generator, an ABO TDF generator, and a strongly unforgeable one-time signature scheme to achieve IND-CCA. Boldyreva, Fehr, and O'Neill [13] give a similar construction (with the signature scheme replaced by a target-collision resistant hash function) that achieves PRIV-CCA for block-sources.

As pointed out above, this result does not lift generically to MMR1-CCA. Of course, it is possible that one or both of these constructions satisfy our stronger notion, but this requires a fresh proof.[10] It remains open to instantiate MMR-CCA in the standard model, but prior work suggests that LTDFs and ABO LTDFs are a promising approach.

PtD[F-DOAEP] IS MM+IND-CCA. Security against MM attacks is achievable with a scheme that is both MMR1- and ANON-CCA via Theorem 3. Here we show that, under certain restrictions, instantiating the base scheme with F-DOAEP is MM-CCA assuming only that F is OWF secure.

Theorem 7 (PtD[F-DOAEP] *is MM+*IND-*CCA*). *Let* PKEAD *be defined by* PtD[F-DOAEP] *with parameters* $n, k_0, k_1, \rho : \mathbb{N} \to \mathbb{N}$ *in Fig. 7, where functions* H_1, H_2, *and* G *are modeled as random oracles. Suppose that* $n(k) \geq k_0(k) + k_1(k)$ *for all* k. *There exists an adversary* $\mathcal{B}$ *such that the following conditions hold:*

- *(MM-CCA) Let* $\mu_1, \mu_2, v : \mathbb{N} \to \mathbb{N}$ *be functions where* $\mu_2(k) \in \omega(\log k)$. *Let* $\mathcal{A}$ *be a* (μ_1, v)*-mm-adversary and* $\mathcal{R}$ *be a* (μ_2, v, ρ)*-r-source. Suppose that* $\mathcal{A}$ *makes exactly* q_e *queries to its* **LR** *oracle,* q_d *queries to its* **Dec** *oracle, and* q_1, q_2, *and* q_G *to oracles* H_1, H_2, *and* G *respectively. Then*

$$\mathbf{Adv}^{\text{mm-cca}}_{\mathsf{PKEAD},\mathcal{R}}(\mathcal{A}, k) \leq 2q_e v(k) \cdot \mathbf{Adv}^{\text{owf}}_{F}(\mathcal{B}, k) + \frac{5q_e v(k)(q_1 + q_d)}{2^{\mu_1(k)+\mu_2(k)-1}} + \frac{3q_e v(k)(q_G + q_d) + v(k)(q_2 + q_d) + 2q_d}{2^{k_0(k)-1}} + \frac{q_e(q_1 + q_d)^2}{2^{\rho(k)-1}} .$$

- *(IND-CCA) Let* $\mathcal{A}$ *be an adversary, which makes* q_e *queries to its* **LR** *oracle,* q_d *queries to its* **Dec** *oracle, and* q_1, q_2, *and* q_G *to oracles* H_1, H_2, *and* G *respectively. Then*

$$\mathbf{Adv}^{\text{ind-cca}}_{\mathsf{PKEAD},\mathcal{R}}(\mathcal{A}, k) \leq 2q_e \cdot \mathbf{Adv}^{\text{owf}}_{F}(\mathcal{B}, k) + \frac{6q_e q_d + 3q_e q_G + q_e q_2}{2^{k_0(k)-1}} + \frac{6q_e(q_1 + q_d)^2}{2^{\rho(k)-1}} .$$

In each case, we have $\mathsf{time}_{\mathcal{B}}(k) = \mathsf{time}_{\mathcal{A}}(k) + O(q_d q_1 q_G q_2)$.

[10] In another direction, [34] consider novel notions of LTDFs for their adaptive CCA setting.

Let us explain this claim a bit. (The proof is in the full version [14].) First, we only consider the case where $n \geq k_0 + k_1$. The designers of F-DOAEP give two bounds for its PRIV security [4, Theorem 5.2]: one for inputs of length less than $k_0 + k_1$ and another for inputs of length greater than $k_0 + k_1$. The distinction arises from the fact that, in the former case, $\mathcal{A}$'s random oracle queries consist of strings less than k_1 bits in length. The problem is that $\mathcal{B}$ is looking for the preimage under f of its input y, which is a k_1-bit string. The solution is a lemma that relates the OWF advantage of $\mathcal{B}$ to the advantage of another inverter adversary whose task is to return a substring of the preimage rather than the whole string [4, Lemma A.1]. (This is closely related to the POWF notion of [25].) We focus on the $n \geq k_0 + k_1$ case for simplicity.

Second, restricting the associated data space to strings of length k_0 ensures that the entropy contained in the message and the random padding is encoded by the right side of the input. This restriction is not strictly necessary to achieve security, but it allows us to appeal directly to the OWF security of the trapdoor permutation in the analysis. It is worth noting that the associated data is encrypted along with the message and randomizer, and that this is undesirable if the associated data is a long string. In practice, the associated data might actually be a hash of the associated data, but we emphasize that security is achieved only for the hash and *not* the associated data itself.

Remark. In Sect. 6.1, we showed that F-EME-OAEP, a variant of F-OAEP, is secure against MM attacks, but that its concrete security depends only on the entropy in the coins. Here we see that adding an additional Feistel round yields improved concrete security against MM attacks, since we are able to prove a bound for F-DOAEP that does take the message entropy into account. This would be the case even without restricting the messages and associated data as we have.

Randomized-then-Deterministic. The composition of a randomized and a deterministic encryption scheme suggested by Bellare et al. is defined in Fig. 7. The idea is to first encrypt the message and associated data using a randomized scheme, then encrypt the result using a deterministic scheme. Security appeals to the randomized scheme when the coins are uniform and appeals to the deterministic scheme when the message-coins are only high min-entropy. The $\mathsf{RtD}[\Pi_r, \Pi_d]$ composition has message space determined by both Π_r and Π_d; the associated data is the same as for Π_r.

$\mathsf{RtD}[\Pi_r, \Pi_d]$ is MMR+IND-CCA. Let $\mathsf{PKEAD} = \mathsf{RtD}[\Pi_r, \Pi_d]$. It is clearly IND-CPA if Π_r is IND-CPA. Bellare et al. show that PKEAD, under certain conditions, is MMR-CPA if Π_d is MMR-CPA [5, theorem 6.2]. Their argument easily extends to the CCA setting, as shown below. In order to prove this composition works, it is necessary that the output of the randomized scheme Π_r has as much entropy as its inputs. The following property, formalized by [5], suffices for entropy-preserving encryption.

Injective encryption. A PKEAD scheme PKEAD with associated data space AD and randomness length $\rho(\cdot)$ is said to be *injective* if for every $k \in \mathbb{N}$, $(pk, sk) \in [\mathsf{PKEAD.Kgen}(1^k)]$, $H \in \mathsf{AD}$, and $(M, r), (M', r') \in \{0,1\}^* \times \{0,1\}^{\rho(k)}$, if $(M, r) \neq (M', r')$, then $\mathsf{PKEAD.Enc}_{pk}^{H}(M\,; r) \neq \mathsf{PKEAD.Enc}_{pk}^{H}(M'\,; r')$. This gives us two useful properties: one, if the equality pattern of $\boldsymbol{M}$ and $\boldsymbol{r}$ is distinct, then so is the equality pattern of $\mathsf{Enc}_{pk}^{H}(\boldsymbol{M}\,; \boldsymbol{r})$; two, if $\langle M, r \rangle$ has min-entropy $\mu(\cdot)$, then $C = \mathsf{Enc}_{pk}^{H}(M\,; r)$ has min-entropy $\mu(\cdot)$. Many schemes possess this property, including ElGamal [23] and OAEP [9].

Theorem 8 ($\mathsf{RtD}[\Pi_r, \Pi_d]$ *is* **MMR+IND-CCA**). *Let Π_r be an injective and randomized PKEAD scheme with associated data space* AD *and randomness length $\rho(\cdot)$, let Π_d be a deterministic PKE scheme, and let* $\mathsf{PKEAD} = \mathsf{RtD}[\Pi_r, \Pi_d]$ *as defined in Fig. 7.*

- *(MMR-CCA) Let $\mu, v : \mathbb{N} \to \mathbb{N}$ be functions where $\mu(k) \in \omega(\log k)$. Let $\mathcal{A}$ be a (μ, v, ρ)-mmr adversary. There exists a $(\mu, v, 0)$-mmr adversary $\mathcal{B}$ such that for every k, it holds that $\mathbf{Adv}_{\mathsf{PKEAD}}^{\text{mmr-cca}}(\mathcal{A}, k) = \mathbf{Adv}_{\Pi_d}^{\text{mmr-cca}}(\mathcal{B}, k)$, where $\mathcal{B}$ has the same runtime as $\mathcal{A}$.*
- *(IND-CCA) Let $\mathcal{A}$ be an adversary. There exists an adversary $\mathcal{B}$ such that for every k, it holds that $\mathbf{Adv}_{\mathsf{PKEAD}}^{\text{ind-cca}}(\mathcal{A}, k) = \mathbf{Adv}_{\Pi_r}^{\text{ind-cca}}(\mathcal{B}, k)$, where $\mathcal{B}$ has the same runtime as $\mathcal{A}$.*

The proof is by a simple extension of [5, Theorem 6.2]; The details appear in the full version of this paper [14]. This result gives us a simple way to securely realize MMR+IND-CCA encryption, but we need to show how to instantiate the deterministic scheme Π_d. The same result we have for PtD applies here; if Π_d is a u-LTDF, then $\mathsf{RtD}[\Pi_r, \Pi_{d,}]$ is MMR-CPA for block-sources. Again, securely instantiating MMR-CCA in the standard model remains open.

$\mathsf{RtD}[\Pi_r, F\text{-}\mathsf{DOAEP}]$ is MM+IND-CPA. As before, we consider security against MM attacks when the deterministic scheme is F-DOAEP. MMR-CCA security is out of reach for this particular composition, as evidenced by an attack against the PRIV-CCA-security of RSA-DOAEP pointed out by [4]. (Their attack can be carried out in the MM-CCA game.) Nonetheless, we show the following:

Theorem 9 ($\mathsf{RtD}[\Pi_r, F\text{-}\mathsf{DOAEP}]$ *is* **MMR+IND-CPA**). *Let F be a trapdoor permutation generator with randomness length $k_1(\cdot)$. Let F-DOAEP be the deterministic scheme defined in Fig. 7 with parameters $k_0, k_1, n : \mathbb{N} \to \mathbb{N}$. Let Π be an injective PKEAD scheme with associated data space* AD *and randomness length $\rho(\cdot)$. Let* $\mathsf{PKEAD} = \mathsf{RtD}[\Pi, F\text{-}\mathsf{DOAEP}]$ *as defined in Fig. 7, where* H_1, H_2, *and* G *are random oracles.*

- *(MM-CPA) Let $\mu_1, \mu_2, v : \mathbb{N} \to \mathbb{N}$ be functions where $\mu_2(k) \in \omega(\log k)$. Let $\mathcal{A}$ be a (μ_1, v)-mm-adversary and $\mathcal{R}$ be a (μ_2, v, ρ)-r-source. Suppose that $\mathcal{A}$ makes q_e queries to its* **LR** *oracle and q_1, q_2, and q_G to oracles* H_1, H_2, *and* G *respectively. Suppose that $n(k) < k_0(k) + k_1(k)$ for all k. Then there exists an adversary $\mathcal{B}$ such that*

$$\mathbf{Adv}^{\text{mm-cpa}}_{\mathsf{PKEAD},\mathcal{R}}(\mathcal{A},k) \le q_e v(k) q_G \cdot \sqrt{\delta_2(k) + \mathbf{Adv}^{\text{owf}}_F(\mathcal{B},k)} + q_e\delta_1(k) + \frac{4q_e v(k)\cdot q_1 q_G}{2^{\mu_1(k)+\mu_2(k)}} + \frac{4q_e v(k)(q_G+q_2)}{2^{k_0(k)}},$$

where $\delta_c(k) = 2^{ck_1(k)-2c(n(k)-k_0(k))+5}$ *and* $\mathsf{time}_{\mathcal{B}}(k) = \mathsf{time}_{\mathcal{A}}(k) + O(\log v(k) + q_2 \log q_2 + k_1(k)^3)$. *Suppose that* $n(k) \ge k_0(k) + k_1(k)$ *for all* k. *Then there exists an adversary* $\mathcal{B}$ *such that*

$$\mathbf{Adv}^{\text{mm-cpa}}_{\mathsf{PKEAD},\mathcal{R}}(\mathcal{A},k) \le q_e v(k) \cdot \mathbf{Adv}^{\text{owf}}_F(\mathcal{B},k) + \frac{4q_e v(k)\cdot q_1 q_G}{2^{\mu_1(k)+\mu_2(k)}} + \frac{4q_e v(k)(q_G+q_2)}{2^{k_0(k)}}$$

and $\mathsf{time}_{\mathcal{B}}(k) = \mathsf{time}_{\mathcal{A}}(k) + O(\log v(k) + q_2 \log q_2)$.

- *(IND-CPA) Let* $\mathcal{A}$ *be an IND-CPA adversary. There exists an IND-CPA adversary* $\mathcal{B}$ *such that* $\mathbf{Adv}^{\text{ind-cpa}}_{\mathsf{PKEAD}}(\mathcal{A},k) = \mathbf{Adv}^{\text{ind-cpa}}_{\Pi}(\mathcal{B},k)$ *and* $\mathcal{B}$ *has the same run time as* $\mathcal{A}$.

The first part of the claim follows from an argument built upon the proof that RSA-DOAEP is PRIV secure [4, Theorem 5.2]. Our results differ from theirs in the following way. In the PRIV experiment, the adversary is given the public key only *after* it submits its **LR** query. This means that the public key has entropy from the perspective of the adversary at this point in the game. This fact is used to bound the advantage $\mathcal{A}$ gets from its random oracle queries *before* it queries **LR**. This is why the inputs to the RO in the DOAEP construction are prepended with the public key (See Fig. 7). Because the adversary is given the public key in our setting, we must find another way to bound this advantage. Once we have done this, however, we can use their argument directly to obtain the claim. We refer the reader to the full version of this paper for the proof [14].

Acknowledgments. Christopher Patton and Thomas Shrimpton are supported by NSF grant CNS-1564446. Alexandra Boldyreva is supported in part by NSF grants CNS-1318511 and CNS-1422794. We thank Cihan Eryonucu for providing an initial survey of APIs during his visit to Georgia Tech. We also thank Mihir Bellare and the anonymous reviewers for valuable feedback, as well as Joseph Choi and Animesh Chhotaray for bug fixes.

References

1. Abdalla, M., Benhamouda, F., Pointcheval, D.: Public-key encryption indistinguishable under plaintext-checkable attacks. IET Inf. Secur. **10**(6), 288–303 (2016)
2. Acar, Y., Backes, M., Fahl, S., Garfinkel, S., Kim, D., Mazurek, M.L., Stransky, C.: Comparing the usability of cryptographic apis. In: Proceedings of the 38th IEEE Symposium on Security and Privacy (2017)
3. Bellare, M., Boldyreva, A., Desai, A., Pointcheval, D.: Key-privacy in public-key encryption. In: Boyd, C. (ed.) ASIACRYPT 2001. LNCS, vol. 2248, pp. 566–582. Springer, Heidelberg (2001). doi:10.1007/3-540-45682-1_33

4. Bellare, M., Boldyreva, A., O'Neill, A.: Deterministic and efficiently searchable encryption. In: Menezes, A. (ed.) CRYPTO 2007. LNCS, vol. 4622, pp. 535–552. Springer, Heidelberg (2007). doi:10.1007/978-3-540-74143-5_30
5. Bellare, M., Brakerski, Z., Naor, M., Ristenpart, T., Segev, G., Shacham, H., Yilek, S.: Hedged public-key encryption: how to protect against bad randomness. In: Matsui, M. (ed.) ASIACRYPT 2009. LNCS, vol. 5912, pp. 232–249. Springer, Heidelberg (2009). doi:10.1007/978-3-642-10366-7_14
6. Bellare, M., Desai, A., Pointcheval, D., Rogaway, P.: Relations among notions of security for public-key encryption schemes. In: Krawczyk, H. (ed.) CRYPTO 1998. LNCS, vol. 1462, pp. 26–45. Springer, Heidelberg (1998). doi:10.1007/BFb0055718
7. Bellare, M., Hoang, V.T.: Resisting randomness subversion: fast deterministic and hedged public-key encryption in the standard model. In: Oswald, E., Fischlin, M. (eds.) EUROCRYPT 2015. LNCS, vol. 9057, pp. 627–656. Springer, Heidelberg (2015). doi:10.1007/978-3-662-46803-6_21
8. Bellare, M., Rogaway, P.: Random oracles are practical: a paradigm for designing efficient protocols. In: CCS 1993 Proceedings of the 1st ACM Conference on Computer and Communications Security (1993)
9. Bellare, M., Rogaway, P.: Optimal asymmetric encryption. In: Santis, A. (ed.) EUROCRYPT 1994. LNCS, vol. 950, pp. 92–111. Springer, Heidelberg (1995). doi:10.1007/BFb0053428
10. Bellare, M., Rogaway, P.: The security of triple encryption and a framework for code-based game-playing proofs. In: Vaudenay, S. (ed.) EUROCRYPT 2006. LNCS, vol. 4004, pp. 409–426. Springer, Heidelberg (2006). doi:10.1007/11761679_25
11. Bellare, M., Tackmann, B.: Nonce-based cryptography: retaining security when randomness fails. In: Fischlin, M., Coron, J.-S. (eds.) EUROCRYPT 2016. LNCS, vol. 9665, pp. 729–757. Springer, Heidelberg (2016). doi:10.1007/978-3-662-49890-3_28
12. Bernstein, D.J., Chang, Y.-A., Cheng, C.-M., Chou, L.-P., Heninger, N., Lange, T., Someren, N.: Factoring RSA keys from certified smart cards: Coppersmith in the wild. In: Sako, K., Sarkar, P. (eds.) ASIACRYPT 2013. LNCS, vol. 8270, pp. 341–360. Springer, Heidelberg (2013). doi:10.1007/978-3-642-42045-0_18
13. Boldyreva, A., Fehr, S., O'Neill, A.: On notions of security for deterministic encryption, and efficient constructions without random oracles. In: Wagner, D. (ed.) CRYPTO 2008. LNCS, vol. 5157, pp. 335–359. Springer, Heidelberg (2008). doi:10.1007/978-3-540-85174-5_19
14. Boldyreva, A., Patton, C., Shrimpton, T.: Hedging public-key encryption in the real world. Cryptology ePrint Archive, Report 2017/510 (2017). http://eprint.iacr.org/2017/510
15. Brown, D.R.L.: A weak-randomizer attack on RSA-OAEP with $e = 3$. Cryptology ePrint Archive, Report 2005/189 (2005). http://eprint.iacr.org/2005/189
16. Brzuska, C., Farshim, P., Mittelbach, A.: Random-oracle uninstantiability from indistinguishability obfuscation. In: Dodis, Y., Nielsen, J.B. (eds.) TCC 2015. LNCS, vol. 9015, pp. 428–455. Springer, Heidelberg (2015). doi:10.1007/978-3-662-46497-7_17
17. Camenisch, J., Chandran, N., Shoup, V.: A public key encryption scheme secure against key dependent chosen plaintext and adaptive chosen ciphertext attacks. In: Joux, A. (ed.) EUROCRYPT 2009. LNCS, vol. 5479, pp. 351–368. Springer, Heidelberg (2009). doi:10.1007/978-3-642-01001-9_20

18. Checkoway, S., Maskiewicz, J., Garman, C., Fried, J., Cohney, S., Green, M., Heninger, N., Weinmann, R.P., Rescorla, E., Shacham, H.: A systematic analysis of the Juniper Dual EC incident. In: CCS 2016 Proceedings of the 23rd ACM Conference on Computer and Communications Security (2016)
19. Dodis, Y., Katz, J.: Chosen-ciphertext security of multiple encryption. In: Kilian, J. (ed.) TCC 2005. LNCS, vol. 3378, pp. 188–209. Springer, Heidelberg (2005). doi:10.1007/978-3-540-30576-7_11
20. Dodis, Y., Pointcheval, D., Ruhault, S., Vergniaud, D., Wichs, D.: Security analysis of pseudo-random number generators with input: /dev/random is not robust. In: CCS 2013 Proceedings of the 20th ACM Conference on Computer and Communications Security (2013)
21. Dorrendorf, L., Gutterman, Z., Pinkas, B.: Cryptanalysis of the random number generator of the windows operating system. ACM Trans. Inf. Syst. Secur. **13**(1), 10 (2009)
22. Duong, T., Kasper, E., Nguyen, Q.: Scaling Crypto Testing with Project Wycheproof. https://www.cs.bris.ac.uk/Research/CryptographySecurity/RWC/2017/thai.duong.pdf
23. ElGamal, T.: A public key cryptosystem and a signature scheme based on discrete logarithms. In: Blakley, G.R., Chaum, D. (eds.) CRYPTO 1984. LNCS, vol. 196, pp. 10–18. Springer, Heidelberg (1985). doi:10.1007/3-540-39568-7_2
24. Fujisaki, E., Okamoto, T.: Secure integration of asymmetric and symmetric encryption schemes. In: Wiener, M. (ed.) CRYPTO 1999. LNCS, vol. 1666, pp. 537–554. Springer, Heidelberg (1999). doi:10.1007/3-540-48405-1_34
25. Fujisaki, E., Okamoto, T., Pointcheval, D., Stern, J.: RSA-OAEP is secure under the RSA assumption. J. Cryptol. **17**(2), 81–104 (2004)
26. Gutterman, Z., Malkhi, D.: Hold your sessions: an attack on java session-id generation. In: Menezes, A. (ed.) CT-RSA 2005. LNCS, vol. 3376, pp. 44–57. Springer, Heidelberg (2005). doi:10.1007/978-3-540-30574-3_5
27. Heninger, N., Durumeric, Z., Wustrow, E., Halderman, J.A.: Mining your Ps and Qs: detection of widespread weak keys in network devices. In: USENIX 2012 Proceedings of the 21st USENIX Conference on Security Symposium (2012)
28. Hoang, V.T., Katz, J., O'Neill, A., Zaheri, M.: Selective-opening security in the presence of randomness failures. In: Cheon, J.H., Takagi, T. (eds.) ASIACRYPT 2016. LNCS, vol. 10032, pp. 278–306. Springer, Heidelberg (2016). doi:10.1007/978-3-662-53890-6_10
29. Kiltz, E., O'Neill, A., Smith, A.: Instantiability of RSA-OAEP under chosen-plaintext attack. In: Rabin, T. (ed.) CRYPTO 2010. LNCS, vol. 6223, pp. 295–313. Springer, Heidelberg (2010). doi:10.1007/978-3-642-14623-7_16
30. Michaelis, K., Meyer, C., Schwenk, J.: Randomly failed! the state of randomness in current java implementations. In: Dawson, E. (ed.) CT-RSA 2013. LNCS, vol. 7779, pp. 129–144. Springer, Heidelberg (2013). doi:10.1007/978-3-642-36095-4_9
31. Mueller, M.: Debian OpenSSL predictable PRNG (2008). https://www.exploit-db.com/exploits/5622/
32. Paterson, K.G., Schuldt, J.C.N., Sibborn, D.L.: Related randomness attacks for public key encryption. In: Krawczyk, H. (ed.) PKC 2014. LNCS, vol. 8383, pp. 465–482. Springer, Heidelberg (2014). doi:10.1007/978-3-642-54631-0_27
33. Peikert, C., Waters, B.: Lossy trapdoor functions and their applications. In: STOC 2008 Proceedings of the 40th Annual ACM Symposium on Theory of Computing (2008)

34. Raghunathan, A., Segev, G., Vadhan, S.: Deterministic public-key encryption for adaptively chosen plaintext distributions. In: Johansson, T., Nguyen, P.Q. (eds.) EUROCRYPT 2013. LNCS, vol. 7881, pp. 93–110. Springer, Heidelberg (2013). doi:10.1007/978-3-642-38348-9_6
35. Ristenpart, T., Yilek, S.: When good randomness goes bad: virtual machine reset vulnerabilities and hedging deployed cryptography. In: NDSS 2010 Proceedings of the 17th Annual Network and Distributed System Security Symposium (2010)
36. Shoup, V.: OAEP reconsidered. J. Cryptol. **15**(4), 223–249 (2002)
37. Shoup, V.: ISO18033-2: An emerging standard for public-key encryption (final committee draft) (2004). http://shoup.net/iso
38. Yilek, S.: Resettable public-key encryption: how to encrypt on a virtual machine. In: Pieprzyk, J. (ed.) CT-RSA 2010. LNCS, vol. 5985, pp. 41–56. Springer, Heidelberg (2010). doi:10.1007/978-3-642-11925-5_4

Symmetric-Key Crypto

Information-Theoretic Indistinguishability via the Chi-Squared Method

Wei Dai[1], Viet Tung Hoang[2(✉)], and Stefano Tessaro[3(✉)]

[1] Department of Computer Science and Engineering, University of California San Diego, San Diego, USA
weidai@eng.ucsd.edu

[2] Department of Computer Science, Florida State University, Tallahassee, USA
tvhoang@cs.fsu.edu

[3] Department of Computer Science, University of California Santa Barbara, Santa Barbara, USA
tessaro@cs.ucsb.edu

Abstract. Proving tight bounds on information-theoretic indistinguishability is a central problem in symmetric cryptography. This paper introduces a new method for information-theoretic indistinguishability proofs, called "the chi-squared method". At its core, the method requires upper-bounds on the so-called χ^2 divergence (due to Neyman and Pearson) between the output distributions of two systems being queries. The method morally resembles, yet also considerably simplifies, a previous approach proposed by Bellare and Impagliazzo (ePrint, 1999), while at the same time increasing its expressiveness and delivering tighter bounds.

We showcase the chi-squared method on some examples. In particular: (1) We prove an optimal bound of $q/2^n$ for the XOR of two permutations, and our proof considerably simplifies previous approaches using the H-coefficient method, (2) we provide improved bounds for the recently proposed encrypted Davies-Meyer PRF construction by Cogliati and Seurin (CRYPTO '16), and (3) we give a tighter bound for the Swap-or-not cipher by Hoang, Morris, and Rogaway (CRYPTO '12).

Keywords: Symmetric cryptography · Information-theoretic indistinguishability · Provable security

1 Introduction

Information-theoretic indistinguishability proofs are fundamental tools in cryptography, and take a particularly prominent role in symmetric cryptography. In this context, it is imperative to derive bounds which are as precise as possible – a tighter bound yields a better understanding of the actual security of the system at hand, and avoids potential inefficiency provoked by the choice of unnecessarily large parameters, such as the key- and block-lengths, and the number of rounds.

This paper falls within a line of works investigating generic techniques to obtain best-possible information-theoretic bounds. We investigate a new approach to indistinguishability proofs – which we refer to as the *chi-squared method*

J. Katz and H. Shacham (Eds.): CRYPTO 2017, Part III, LNCS 10403, pp. 497–523, 2017.
DOI: 10.1007/978-3-319-63697-9_17

– which will help us tighten (and simplify) proofs for certain examples where proofs so-far have evaded more classical methods, such as the H-coefficient method.

Specifically, we apply our methodology to the analyses of three, a priori seemingly unrelated, constructions – the XOR of permutations (initially studied by Hall, Wagner, Kelsey, and Schneier [12]), the Encrypted Davies-Meyer construction by Cogliati and Seurin [10], and the Swap-or-not construction by Hoang, Morris, and Rogaway [13]. Previously, no connections between these problems have been observed, but we give significantly improved bounds as an application of our framework.

Information-theoretic indistinguishability. Many cryptographic security proofs require showing, for a *distinguisher* A with access to one of two systems, $\mathbf{S}_0$ and $\mathbf{S}_1$,[1] an upper bound on

$$\mathsf{Adv}^{\mathsf{dist}}_{\mathbf{S}_0,\mathbf{S}_1}(A) = \Pr[A(\mathbf{S}_0) = 1] - \Pr[A(\mathbf{S}_1) = 1] ,$$

where $A(\mathbf{S}_b)$ denotes the probability that A outputs 1 when interacting with $\mathbf{S}_b$.

While it is customary to only target the case where A is computationally bounded, in many cases, the actual proofs themselves are concerned with the information-theoretic case where the advantage is maximized over *all* distinguishers, only bounded by their number q of *queries*, but with no further restrictions on their time complexities. A first example in this domain is the analysis of Feistel networks in the seminal work of Luby and Rackoff [16], whose main step is a proof that the Feistel construction with truly random round functions is information-theoretically indistinguishable from a random permutation. (This was first pointed out explicitly by Maurer [18].) Another class of inherently information-theoretic analyses – dating back to the analysis of the Even-Mansour [11] block cipher – studies constructions in ideal models (such as the ideal-cipher or random-permutation models), where adversaries are also only bounded in their query-complexity.

In this context, the perhaps most widely-used proof technique is that of bounding the probability of a certain failing condition, where $\mathbf{S}_0$ and $\mathbf{S}_1$ behave *identically*, in some well-defined sense, as long as the condition is not violated. This approach was abstracted e.g. in Maurer's random systems [19] and Bellare-Rogaway game playing [4] frameworks. Unfortunately, such methods are fairly crude, and often fall short of providing tight bounds, especially for so-called beyond-birthday security.[2]

More sophisticated approaches [5,23,25] directly bound the *statistical distance* $\|\mathsf{p}_{\mathbf{S}_1,A}(\cdot) - \mathsf{p}_{\mathbf{S}_0,A}(\cdot)\|$, where $\mathsf{p}_{\mathbf{S}_1,A}$ and $\mathsf{p}_{\mathbf{S}_0,A}$ are the respective probability distributions of the answers obtained by A, which is assumed to be deterministic. This is an upper bound on $\mathsf{Adv}^{\mathsf{dist}}_{\mathbf{S}_0,\mathbf{S}_1}(A)$. In particular, Patarin's H-coefficient

[1] For now, it suffices to understand such systems informally as interactive objects, or "oracles.".

[2] A not-so-widely known fact is that Maurer, Renner, and Pietrzak [20] show that this method *is* actually optimal, the caveat being however that describing the suitable tight condition may be infeasible, and the result is merely existential.

method [25] has recently re-gained substantial popularity, mostly thanks to Chen and Steinberger's exposition [6]. The technique was further refined by Hoang and Tessaro [14], who provided a "smoothed" version of the H-coefficient method, called the "expectation method."

A DIFFERENT AVENUE. Techniques such as the H-coefficient method heavily exploit computing the probabilities $\mathsf{ps}_{1,A}(\boldsymbol{Z})$ and $\mathsf{ps}_{0,A}(\boldsymbol{Z})$ that a *full* sequence of q outputs $\boldsymbol{Z} = (Z_1, \ldots, Z_q)$ occur. Often, these probabilities are easy to compute and compare under the condition that the sequence of outputs belongs to a set of good transcripts. One case where such methods however do not yield a good bound is where we are only given local information, e.g., the distance between $\mathsf{ps}_{1,A}(\cdot \mid \boldsymbol{Z}_{i-1})$ and $\mathsf{ps}_{0,A}(\cdot \mid \boldsymbol{Z}_{i-1})$ for all sequences $\boldsymbol{Z}_{i-1}$ and all $i \geq 1$, where $\boldsymbol{Z}_{i-1}$ is the sequence of the first $i-1$ outputs. Here, the naïve approach is to use a so-called hybrid argument, and bound the distance as

$$\|\mathsf{ps}_{1,A}(\cdot) - \mathsf{ps}_{0,A}(\cdot)\| \leq \sum_{i=1}^{q} \mathbf{E}\Big[\|\mathsf{ps}_{0,A}(\cdot \mid \boldsymbol{X}_{i-1}) - \mathsf{ps}_{1,A}(\cdot \mid \boldsymbol{X}_{i-1})\|\Big], \quad (1)$$

where $\boldsymbol{X}_{i-1}$ is the vector of answers to A's first $i-1$ queries, according to $\mathsf{ps}_{0,A}(\cdot)$. (Symmetrically, they can be all sampled according to $\mathsf{ps}_{1,A}(\cdot)$.) If all summands are upper bounded by ϵ, we obtain a bound of $q\epsilon$. This is rarely tight, and often sub-optimal. A different avenue was explored by Bellare and Impagliazzo (BI) [2], in an unpublished note. They consider the sequence of random variables $U_1, \ldots, U_q$, where

$$U_i = \frac{\mathsf{ps}_{1,A}(X_i|\boldsymbol{X}_{i-1})}{\mathsf{ps}_{0,A}(X_i|\boldsymbol{X}_{i-1})},$$

and $\boldsymbol{X}_{i-1}$ and X_i are sampled from A's interaction with $\mathbf{S}_0$. Roughly, they show that if $|U_i - 1|$ is sufficiently concentrated, say $|U_i - 1| \leq \epsilon$ for all i, except with probability δ, then the bound becomes

$$\|\mathsf{ps}_{1,A}(\cdot) - \mathsf{ps}_{0,A}(\cdot)\| \leq O(\sqrt{q} \cdot \epsilon\lambda) + e^{-\lambda^2/2} + \delta.$$

Unfortunately, the BI method is rather complex to use – it requires a careful balancing act in order to assess the trade-off between ϵ and δ, and the additional slackness due to the λ term is also problematic and appear to be an artifact of the proof technique.[3] To the best of our knowledge, the BI method was never used elsewhere.

OUR METHOD: THE CHI-SQUARED METHOD. In this work, we consider a different version of the above method. In particular, we revisit the setting of (1), and change our metric to measure distance between $\mu(\cdot) = \mathsf{ps}_{0,A}(\cdot \mid \boldsymbol{Z}_{i-1})$ and

[3] Indeed, it is known [29] that in many cases, if X and Y have statistical distance ϵ, then if one takes vectors $(X_1, \ldots, X_q)$ and $(Y_1, \ldots, Y_q)$ of q independent copies of X and Y, respectively, the statistical distance increases as $\sqrt{q}\epsilon$, this seemingly showing that the BI bound is far from tight.

$\nu(\cdot) = \mathsf{ps}_{1,A}(\cdot \mid \boldsymbol{Z}_{i-1})$. Instead of statistical distance, we will use the so-called χ^2-divergence, as proposed by Neyman and Pearson,[4]

$$\chi^2(\mu, \nu) = \sum_x \frac{(\mu(x) - \nu(x))^2}{\nu(x)} \ .$$

where the sum is over all x such that $\nu(x) > 0$, and we assume that if $\mu(x) > 0$, then $\nu(x) > 0$, too. In particular, let $\chi^2(\boldsymbol{Z}_{i-1}) = \chi^2(\mu; \nu)$ as above, then, we show that

$$\|\mathsf{ps}_{1,A}(\cdot) - \mathsf{ps}_{0,A}(\cdot)\| \leq \sqrt{\frac{1}{2}\sum_{i=1}^{q} \mathbf{E}\left[\chi^2(\boldsymbol{X}_{i-1}))\right]} \ ,$$

where for all $i = 1, \ldots, q$, $\boldsymbol{X}_{i-1}$ is sampled according to $\mathsf{ps}_{1,A}(\cdot)$. We refer to the method of obtaining a bound by upper bounding the q expectations $\mathbf{E}\left[\chi^2(\boldsymbol{X}_{i-1}))\right]$ as the *chi-squared method.* A crucial property that will make calculations manageable and elegant is that the distribution of $\boldsymbol{X}_{i-1}$ and the distribution in the denominator of the χ^2-divergence are with respect to different systems. In many case, we will be able to show that $\mathbf{E}\left[\chi^2(\boldsymbol{X}_{i-1}))\right]$ is much smaller than the statistical distance ϵ – even *quadratically*, i.e., $O(\epsilon^2)$ – and thus the method gives a very good bound of the order $O(\sqrt{q}\epsilon)$.

In contrast to the proof behind BI's method, which relies on somewhat heavy machinery, such as Azuma's inequality, the proof behind the chi-squared method is fairly simple, and relies on Pinsker's and Jensen's inequalities. In fact, we are *not* claiming that relations between the statistical distance and χ^2-divergence are novel, but we believe this methodology to be new in the context of cryptography indistinguishability proofs for interactive systems. Our method, as we discuss below in the body of the paper, can also be seen as a generalization of a technique by Chung and Vadhan [8], used in a different context.

We will apply our method to three different problems, improving (or simplifying) existing bounds.

APPLICATION: XOR OF RANDOM PERMUTATIONS. A potential drawback of block ciphers is that their permutation structure makes them unsuitable to be used as good pseudorandom *functions*, as they become distinguishable from a truly random function when reaching $q \approx 2^{n/2}$ queries, where n is the block length. For this reason, Hall, Wagner, Kelsey, and Schneier [12] initiated the study of constructions of good pseudorandom functions from block ciphers with security beyond the so-called Birthday barrier, i.e., above $2^{n/2}$. A particularly simple construction they proposed – which we refer to as the *XOR construction* – transforms a permutation $\pi : \{0,1\}^n \rightarrow \{0,1\}^n$ into a function $f : \{0,1\}^{n-1} \rightarrow \{0,1\}^n$ by computing $f(x) = \pi(0\|x) \oplus \pi(1\|x)$, where π is meant to be instantiated by a block cipher which is a good pseudorandom permutation, but is treated as a random permutation in the core argument of the proof, which we focus on.

[4] This is in fact Neyman's version—the divergence is not symmetric, and Pearson's version swaps the order of μ and ν.

Lucks [17] proved this construction be secure up to roughly $q = 2^{2n/3}$, whereas Bellare and Impagliazzo [2] gave a better bound of $O(n)q/2^n$, but also only provided a proof sketch. Patarin [24] gave an improved bound of $O(q/2^n)$, but the proof was quite complex. This bound was further improved to $q/2^n$ in an unpublished manuscript [26]. Patarin's tight proof is very involved, using an approach he refers to as "mirror theory",[5] with some claims remaining open or unproved. (Also, as a related problem, Cogliati, Lampe, and Patarin [9] gave weaker bounds for the case of the sum of at least three permutations.) The XOR construction is particularly helpful as a tool for beyond-birthday security, and has been used for example within Iwata's CENC mode of operation [15].

Here, as an application of the chi-squared method, we give a fairly simple proof giving us a bound of $(1.5q + 3\sqrt{q})/2^n$. One can argue that the improvement is small (and in fact, if the bound in [26] is indeed correct, ours is slightly worse). However, we believe the analysis of the XOR construction to be fundamental, and it has evaded simple proofs for nearly two decades. While Patarin's proof deals with precise bounds on number of permutations satisfying a given input-output relationship, our approach is simpler in that it does not require a fine-grained understanding of the underlying distribution, but only requires computing certain expectations.

A related version of the construction is the one computing $f'(x) = \pi_1(x) \oplus \pi_2(x)$ for two independent permutations π_1, π_2. We also analyze this variant in Appendix A, giving a bound of $q^{1.5}/2^{1.5n}$, and in the body focus on the "single-key" variant which is somewhat harder to analyze and more efficient.

Application: The EDM construction. As another application of the chi-squared method, we study the *encrypted Davies-Meyer* (EDM) construction recently introduced by Cogliati and Seurin [10]. The construction depends on two random permutations π and π', and on input x outputs the value $\pi'(\pi(x) \oplus x)$. Again, the goal is to show that this is a good PRF, with security beyond the birthday barrier. In [10], a security bound showing security up to $q = 2^{2n/3}$ queries was shown. Using the chi-squared method, we show that security up to $q = 2^{3n/4}$ is achieved. We note that in concurrent work to ours, Mennink and Neves [21] prove that EDM security approaches 2^n. Their bound uses Patarin's mirror theory, and has a different purpose than ours – we aim for a simpler-to-use framework, and the question of whether our approach yields better bounds remains open for future work.

The EDM construction is the underlying structure of a nonce-based misuse-resistant MAC that CS proposed. CS proved that the MAC construction also achieves $2n/3$-bit of security and conjecture that it actually has n-bit security. While our chi-squared technique seems to be able to handle the MAC construction as well, the combinatorics (also in CS's work) will be very complex, and thus we leave this analysis for future work.

[5] In essence, what mirror theory accounts to is reducing the problem of applying the H-coefficient method to a combinatorial problem counting solutions of a system of linear equations with contraints on their (discrete) solutions.

Application: Swap-or not. As our final application, we consider the swap-or-not block cipher, introduce by Hoang, Morris, and Rogaway [13]. Swap-or-not is a block cipher that supports an arbitrary abelian group $\mathbb{G}$ with size N as its domain, and, for sufficiently many rounds $r = \Omega(\log(N))$, is meant to with stand up to $q < N/c$ queries, for a small constant $c \geq 2$. This makes it particularly suitable as cipher for format-preserving encryption (FPE) [3], both because of its flexibility to support multiple domain formats, as well as for its high security making it suitable to smaller domains. Subsequent work [22,30] focused on boosting its security to $q = N$, at the cost of higher (worst-case) round complexity. The Swap-or-not example is particularly interesting object to analyze, as it uses a very different structure than more usual Feistel-like designs. The original proof in [13] uses a fairly ad-hoc analysis, which however as an intermediate step ends up upper bounding exactly the quantity $\mathbf{E}\left[\chi^2(\boldsymbol{X}_{i-1})\right]$. As a result of this, we end up saving a factor $\sqrt{N}$ on final advantage bound.

For example, for $N = 2^{64}$, $q = 2^{60}$, and r rounds, the original analysis gives a CCA-security advantage $2^{90-0.415r}$ vs one of approximately $2^{62-0.415r}$ for our new analysis. Thus, if we are interested in achieving security 2^{-64}, we would need $r \geq 371$ rounds according to the old analysis, whereas our analysis shows that 293 rounds are sufficient.

A perspective and further related works. We conclude by stressing that with respect to our current state of knowledge, there does not seem to be a universal method to obtain tight bounds on information-theoretic indistinguishability, and ultimately the best method depends on the problem at hand. This situation is not different than what encountered in statistics, where proving bounds on the variational distance require different tools depending on the context.

We are certainly not the first to observe the importance of using different metrics as a tool in cryptographic security proofs and reductions. For example, in symmetric cryptography, Steinberger [31] used the Hellinger distance to sharpen bounds on key-alternating ciphers. The H-coefficient technique itself can be seen as bounding a different distance metric between distributions. Further, cryptographic applications have often relied on using the KL-divergence, e.g., in parallel repetition theorems [7,28], and Renyi divergences, e.g., in lattice-based cryptography [1].

2 Preliminaries

Notation. Let n be a positive integer. We use $[n]$ to denote the set $\{1, \ldots, n\}$. For a finite set S, we let $x \leftarrow\$ S$ denote the uniform sampling from S and assigning the value to x. Let $|x|$ denote the length of the string x, and for $1 \leq i < j \leq |x|$, let $x[i, j]$ denote the substring from the ith bit to the jth bit (inclusive) of x. If A is an algorithm, we let $y \leftarrow A(x_1, \ldots; r)$ denote running A with randomness r on inputs $x_1, \ldots$ and assigning the output to y. We let $y \leftarrow\$ A(x_1, \ldots)$ be the resulting of picking r at random and letting $y \leftarrow A(x_1, \ldots; r)$.

PRF SECURITY. Let $F : \mathcal{K} \times \{0,1\}^m \to \{0,1\}^n$ be a family of functions. Let $\mathrm{Func}(m,n)$ be the set of all functions $g : \{0,1\}^m \to \{0,1\}^n$. For an adversary A, define

$$\mathsf{Adv}_F^{\mathrm{prf}}(A) = \Pr[K \leftarrow_{\$} \mathcal{K}; A^{F_K(\cdot)} \Rightarrow 1] - \Pr[f \leftarrow_{\$} \mathrm{Func}(m,n); A^{f(\cdot)} \Rightarrow 1]$$

as the PRF advantage of A attacking F.

DISTANCE MEASURES. Let μ and ν be two distributions on a finite event space Ω. The *statistical distance* between μ and ν is defined as

$$\|\mu - \nu\| = \sum_{x \in \Omega} \max\{0, \mu(x) - \nu(x)\}.$$

The *Kullback-Leibler (KL) divergence* between μ and ν is defined as

$$\Delta_{\mathrm{KL}}(\mu, \nu) = \sum_{x \in \Omega} \mu(x) \ln\Big(\frac{\mu(x)}{\nu(x)}\Big).$$

Note that for Δ_{KL} to be well-defined, we need ν to have full support, i.e. Ω. The well-known Pinsker's inequality relates the previous two notions.

Lemma 1 (Pinsker's inequality). Let μ and ν be two distributions on a finite event space Ω such that ν has full support. Then

$$(\|\mu - \nu\|)^2 \leq \frac{1}{2}\Delta_{\mathrm{KL}}(\mu, \nu).$$

Another well-known fact for KL-divergence is that it decomposes nicely for product distributions. The *chi-squared divergence* between μ and ν is defined as

$$\chi^2(\mu, \nu) = \sum_{x \in \Omega} \frac{(\mu(x) - \nu(x))^2}{\nu(x)}.$$

Note that for $\chi^2(\mu, \nu)$ to be well-defined, again ν needs to have full support. We remark that $\chi^2(\mu, \nu)$ is related to the notion of collision probability. To justify this remark, let Ω be some finite set and let $M = |\Omega|$. Let ν be the uniform distribution over Ω and μ be any distribution over Ω. Let X_1, X_2 be two i.i.d. samples from μ. Then

$$\begin{aligned}\chi^2(\mu, \nu) &= \sum_{x \in \Omega} M \cdot (\mu(x) - 1/M)^2 \\ &= M \cdot \Pr[X_1 = X_2] - 1.\end{aligned}$$

The following lemma relates the chi-squared divergence and the KL-divergence.

Lemma 2. Let Ω be a finite set, and let μ and ν be two distribution on Ω such that ν has full support. Then

$$\Delta_{\mathrm{KL}}(\mu, \nu) \leq \chi^2(\mu, \nu).$$

Proof. Since function $\ln(x)$ is concave, by using Jensen's inequality,

$$\sum_{x\in\Omega} \mu(x) \ln\Big(\frac{\mu(x)}{\nu(x)}\Big) \le \ln\Big(\sum_{x\in\Omega} \frac{(\mu(x))^2}{\nu(x)}\Big). \tag{2}$$

Next,

$$\sum_{x\in\Omega} \frac{(\mu(x)-\nu(x))^2}{\nu(x)} = \sum_{x\in\Omega} \frac{(\mu(x))^2}{\nu(x)} - \sum_{x\in\Omega}(2\mu(x)-\nu(x)) = \sum_{x\in\Omega} \frac{(\mu(x))^2}{\nu(x)} - 1. \tag{3}$$

Finally, using the inequality that $e^t - 1 \ge t$ for any real number t, we have

$$\sum_{x\in\Omega} \frac{(\mu(x))^2}{\nu(x)} - 1 \ge \ln\Big(\sum_{x\in\Omega} \frac{(\mu(x))^2}{\nu(x)}\Big). \tag{4}$$

From Eqs. (2)–(4), we obtain the claimed result.

3 The Chi-Squared Method

In this section, we describe the chi-squared method, which simplifies previous results by Bellare and Impagliazzo (BI), and Chung and Vadhan (CV) [2,8].

NOTATIONAL SETUP. Let A be an adversary that tries to distinguish two stateless systems $\mathbf{S}_1$ and $\mathbf{S}_0$. Since we allow A to be computationally unbounded, without loss of generality, assume that A is deterministic. Assume further that the adversary always makes exactly q queries. Since the adversary is deterministic, for any $i \le q-1$, the answers for the first i queries completely determine the first $i+1$ queries. For a system $\mathbf{S} \in \{\mathbf{S}_1, \mathbf{S}_0\}$ and strings $z_1, \dots, z_i$, let $\mathsf{p}_{\mathbf{S},A}(z_1, \dots, z_i)$ denote the probability that when the adversary A interacts with system $\mathbf{S}$, the answers for the first i queries that it receives is $z_1, \dots, z_i$. If $\mathsf{p}_{\mathbf{S},A}(z_1, \dots, z_i) > 0$, let $\mathsf{p}_{\mathbf{S},A}(z_{i+1} \mid z_1, \dots, z_i)$ denote the conditional probability that the answer for the $(i+1)$-th query when the adversary interacts with system $\mathbf{S}$ is z_{i+1}, given that the answers for the first i queries are $z_1, \dots, z_i$ respectively. For each $\boldsymbol{Z} = (z_1, \dots, z_q)$, let $\boldsymbol{Z}_i = (z_1, \dots, z_i)$, and for $\mathbf{S} \in \{\mathbf{S}_1, \mathbf{S}_0\}$, let $\mathsf{p}_{\mathbf{S},A}(\cdot \mid \boldsymbol{Z}_i)$ denote $\mathsf{p}_{\mathbf{S},A}(\cdot \mid z_1, \dots, z_i)$. We let $\boldsymbol{Z}_0$ be the empty vector, and $\mathsf{p}_{\mathbf{S},A}(\cdot \mid \boldsymbol{Z}_0)$ is understood as $\mathsf{p}_{\mathbf{S},A}(\cdot)$.

THE TECHNIQUE. We first give a brief intuition regarding our technique. On the high level, the chi-squared method relates the statistical distance of a product distribution to the expected chi-squared divergence of the components, via Kullback-Leibler divergence. The advantage of this approach is that the term that depends on the number of components, say q, is "under the square-root", because of Pinsker's inequality. The details follow.

For each $i \le q$ and each vector $\boldsymbol{Z}_{i-1} = (z_1, \ldots, z_{i-1})$, define (with sligh abuse of notation)

$$\begin{aligned}\chi^2(\boldsymbol{Z}_{i-1}) &= \chi^2(\mathsf{p}_{\mathbf{S}_1,A}(\cdot \mid \boldsymbol{Z}_{i-1}), \mathsf{p}_{\mathbf{S}_0,A}(\cdot \mid \boldsymbol{Z}_{i-1})) \\ &= \sum_{z_i} \frac{\left(\mathsf{p}_{\mathbf{S}_1,A}(z_i \mid \boldsymbol{Z}_{i-1}) - \mathsf{p}_{\mathbf{S}_0,A}(z_i \mid \boldsymbol{Z}_{i-1})\right)^2}{\mathsf{p}_{\mathbf{S}_0,A}(z_i \mid \boldsymbol{Z}_{i-1})},\end{aligned}$$

where the sum is taken over all z_i in the support of the distribution $\mathsf{p}_{\mathbf{S}_0,A}(\cdot \mid \boldsymbol{Z}_{i-1})$. We require that if $\mathsf{p}_{\mathbf{S}_1,A}(\boldsymbol{Z}_i) > 0$, then so is $\mathsf{p}_{\mathbf{S}_0,A}(\boldsymbol{Z}_i)$. Thus, $\chi^2(\boldsymbol{Z}_{i-1})$ is well-defined. Typically, in applications, $\mathbf{S}_0$ is the "ideal" system, and this technical constraint is always met.

The following lemma bounds the distinguishing advantage of A.

Lemma 3. Suppose whenever $\mathsf{p}_{\mathbf{S}_1,A}(\boldsymbol{Z}_i) > 0$ then $\mathsf{p}_{\mathbf{S}_0,A}(\boldsymbol{Z}_i) > 0$. Then,

$$\|\mathsf{p}_{\mathbf{S}_1,A}(\cdot) - \mathsf{p}_{\mathbf{S}_0,A}(\cdot)\| \le \Big(\frac{1}{2}\sum_{i=1}^{q} \mathbf{E}[\chi^2(\boldsymbol{X}_{i-1})]\Big)^{1/2},$$

where the expectation is taken over vectors $\boldsymbol{X}_{i-1}$ of the $i-1$ first answers sampled according to the interaction with $\mathbf{S}_1$.

Discussion. To illustrate the power of the chi-squared method, suppose that

$$\left|\frac{\mathsf{p}_{\mathbf{S}_1,A}(z_i \mid \boldsymbol{Z}_{i-1})}{\mathsf{p}_{\mathbf{S}_0,A}(z_i \mid \boldsymbol{Z}_{i-1})} - 1\right| \le \varepsilon$$

for every i and every $\boldsymbol{Z}_i$. If one uses the H-coefficient technique, the first step is to give a lower bound for the ratio $\mathsf{p}_{\mathbf{S}_1,A}(\boldsymbol{Z})/\mathsf{p}_{\mathbf{S}_0,A}(\boldsymbol{Z})$, which is

$$\prod_{i=1}^{q} \frac{\mathsf{p}_{\mathbf{S}_1,A}(z_i \mid \boldsymbol{Z}_{i-1})}{\mathsf{p}_{\mathbf{S}_0,A}(z_i \mid \boldsymbol{Z}_{i-1})} \ge (1-\varepsilon)^q \ge 1 - \varepsilon q.$$

Thus the distinguishing advantage is at most the statistical distance between $\mathsf{p}_{\mathbf{S}_0,A}(\cdot)$ and $\mathsf{p}_{\mathbf{S}_1,A}(\cdot)$, which is

$$\sum_{\boldsymbol{Z}} \max\{0, \mathsf{p}_{\mathbf{S}_0,A}(\boldsymbol{Z}) - \mathsf{p}_{\mathbf{S}_1,A}(\boldsymbol{Z})\} \le \sum_{\boldsymbol{Z}} \varepsilon q \cdot \mathsf{p}_{\mathbf{S}_0,A}(\boldsymbol{Z}) \le \varepsilon q.$$

In contrast, from Lemma 3, the distinguishing advantage is at most $\varepsilon\sqrt{q/2}$, because

$$\begin{aligned}\chi^2(\boldsymbol{Z}_{i-1}) &= \sum_{z_i} \mathsf{p}_{\mathbf{S}_0,A}(z_i \mid \boldsymbol{Z}_{i-1})\Big(\frac{\mathsf{p}_{\mathbf{S}_1,A}(z_i \mid \boldsymbol{Z}_{i-1})}{\mathsf{p}_{\mathbf{S}_0,A}(z_i \mid \boldsymbol{Z}_{i-1})} - 1\Big)^2 \\ &\le \sum_{z_i} \mathsf{p}_{\mathbf{S}_0,A}(z_i \mid \boldsymbol{Z}_{i-1}) \cdot \varepsilon^2 = \varepsilon^2.\end{aligned}$$

This is why the chi-square method can substantially improve the security bound in many settings, as we'll demonstrate in subsequent sections.

Proof (of Lemma 3). Recall that the adversary's distinguishing advantage is at most the statistical distance between $\mathsf{p}_{\mathbf{S}_0,A}(\cdot)$ and $\mathsf{p}_{\mathbf{S}_1,A}(\cdot)$. On the other hand, from Pinsker's inequality,

$$2\Big(\| \mathsf{p}_{\mathbf{S}_1,A}(\cdot) - \mathsf{p}_{\mathbf{S}_0,A}(\cdot)\|\Big)^2 \le \sum_{\boldsymbol{Z}} \mathsf{p}_{\mathbf{S}_1,A}(\boldsymbol{Z}) \ln\Big(\frac{\mathsf{p}_{\mathbf{S}_1,A}(\boldsymbol{Z})}{\mathsf{p}_{\mathbf{S}_0,A}(\boldsymbol{Z})}\Big)$$

$$= \sum_{\boldsymbol{Z}=(z_1,\ldots,z_q)} \mathsf{p}_{\mathbf{S}_1,A}(\boldsymbol{Z}) \ln\Big(\prod_{i=1}^{q} \frac{\mathsf{p}_{\mathbf{S}_1,A}(z_i \mid \boldsymbol{Z}_{i-1})}{\mathsf{p}_{\mathbf{S}_0,A}(z_i \mid \boldsymbol{Z}_{i-1})}\Big)$$

$$= \sum_{\boldsymbol{Z}=(z_1,\ldots,z_q)} \sum_{i=1}^{q} \mathsf{p}_{\mathbf{S}_1,A}(\boldsymbol{Z}) \ln\Big(\frac{\mathsf{p}_{\mathbf{S}_1,A}(z_i \mid \boldsymbol{Z}_{i-1})}{\mathsf{p}_{\mathbf{S}_0,A}(z_i \mid \boldsymbol{Z}_{i-1})}\Big)$$

$$= \sum_{i=1}^{q} \sum_{\boldsymbol{Z}_i=(z_1,\ldots,z_i)} \mathsf{p}_{\mathbf{S}_1,A}(\boldsymbol{Z}_{i-1}) \cdot \mathsf{p}_{\mathbf{S}_1,A}(z_i \mid \boldsymbol{Z}_{i-1}) \cdot \ln\Big(\frac{\mathsf{p}_{\mathbf{S}_1,A}(z_i \mid \boldsymbol{Z}_{i-1})}{\mathsf{p}_{\mathbf{S}_0,A}(z_i \mid \boldsymbol{Z}_{i-1})}\Big) \quad (5)$$

Fix $i \le q$ and $\boldsymbol{Z}_{i-1}$. Let μ and ν be the distributions $\mathsf{p}_{\mathbf{S}_1,A}(\cdot \mid \boldsymbol{Z}_{i-1})$ and $\mathsf{p}_{\mathbf{S}_0,A}(\cdot \mid \boldsymbol{Z}_{i-1})$ respectively. Let S be the support of ν, and recall that the support of μ is a subset of S. Notice that from Lemma 2, we have

$$\sum_{x\in S} \mu(x) \ln\Big(\frac{\mu(x)}{\nu(x)}\Big) \le \sum_{x\in S} \frac{(\mu(x)-\nu(x))^2}{\nu(x)}. \quad (6)$$

From Eqs. (5) and (6),

$$2\Big(\|\mathsf{p}_{\mathbf{S}_0,A}(\cdot) - \mathsf{p}_{\mathbf{S}_1,A}(\cdot)\|\Big)^2$$

$$\le \sum_{i=1}^{q} \sum_{\boldsymbol{Z}_i=(z_1,\ldots,z_i)} \mathsf{p}_{\mathbf{S}_1,A}(\boldsymbol{Z}_{i-1}) \frac{\Big(\mathsf{p}_{\mathbf{S}_1,A}(z_i \mid \boldsymbol{Z}_{i-1}) - \mathsf{p}_{\mathbf{S}_0,A}(z_i \mid \boldsymbol{Z}_{i-1})\Big)^2}{\mathsf{p}_{\mathbf{S}_0,A}(z_i \mid \boldsymbol{Z}_{i-1})}$$

$$= \sum_{i=1}^{q} \sum_{\boldsymbol{Z}_i=(z_1,\ldots,z_i)} \mathsf{p}_{\mathbf{S}_1,A}(\boldsymbol{Z}_{i-1}) \cdot \chi^2(\boldsymbol{Z}_{i-1}) = \sum_{i=1}^{q} \mathbf{E}[\chi^2(\boldsymbol{X}_{i-1})].$$

This concludes the proof. □

Comparison with CV's framework. Underneath CV's work is, in essence, a specialized treatment of our framework for the case that the ideal system $\mathbf{S}_0$ implements an ideal random function. Thus their method can be used to justify the security of the xor of two permutations (Sect. 4) and Encrypted Davies-Meyer PRF (Sect. 5), but it does not work for the Swap-or-Not shuffle (Sect. 6). CV however do not realize these potential applications, and focus only on the Generalized Leftover Hash Lemma (GLHL) of block sources. To the best of our knowledge, CV's method is never used for any other application, perhaps because it is written in a specific language for the context of GLHL.

Comparison with BI's framework. Compared to BI's framework, ours is better in both usability and tightness.

- In BI's method, the bound is a formula of two user-provided parameters. Consequently, to use BI's method, one has to fine-tune the parameters to optimize the bound. Moreover, since BI's method requires strong concentration bounds, in applications such as the xor of two permutations, one has to make non-trivial use of martingales and Azuma's inequality.[6] In contrast, under the chi-squared method, in Sect. 4, when we handle the xor of two permutations, we only compute an expectation and there's no need to use advanced probabilistic tools.
- Due to BI's requirement of strong concentration bounds, in some settings the results that BI's method obtains can be sub-optimal. The looseness in BI's method varies greatly among different settings. For example, in the xor of two permutations, BI's bound is about $nq/2^n$, whereas ours is just $q/2^n$. For Encrypted Davies-Meyer PRF, BI's method only gives $\frac{2n}{3}$-bit security, which is on par with the result of Cogliati and Seurin via the H-Coefficient technique, but our method yields $\frac{3n}{4}$-bit security. Finally, for the Swap-or-Not shuffle, BI's framework doesn't mesh with the analysis in [13], whereas our method can easily make use of the analysis in [13] to improve their result.

4 The XOR Construction

In this section, we consider the so called xor-construction, which was initially proposed in [12], and which is used to obtain, efficiently, a good pseudorandom function from a block cipher. Here, in particular, we consider a version which only involved *one* permutation (at the price of a slightly smaller domain). We analyze a two-permutation version in Appendix A.

SETUP AND MAIN THEOREM. Let Perm(n) be the set of permutations $\pi : \{0,1\}^n \to \{0,1\}^n$. Define $\mathsf{XOR}[n] : \mathrm{Perm}(n) \times \{0,1\}^{n-1} \to \{0,1\}^n$ to be the construction that takes a permutation $\pi \in \mathrm{Perm}(n)$ as a key, and on input x it returns $\pi(x \,\|\, 0) \oplus \pi(x \,\|\, 1)$. Theorem 1 below gives the PRF security of $\mathsf{XOR}[n]$.

Theorem 1. Fix an integer $n \geq 8$. For any adversary A that makes $q \leq 2^{n-5}$ queries we have

$$\mathsf{Adv}^{\mathrm{prf}}_{\mathsf{XOR}[n]}(A) \leq \frac{1.5q + 3\sqrt{q}}{2^n}.$$

DISCUSSION. Before we proceed into the proof, we have a few remarks. First, the bound in Theorem 1 is tight, since in the real system (the one implementing $\mathsf{XOR}[n]$), no answer can be 0^n. Hence if one simply looks for a 0^n-answer among q queries, one can distinguish the two systems with advantage

[6] This fact was not explicit. Indeed, BI provided only a proof sketch, claiming a bound $O(n)q^{1.5}/2^{1.5n}$ for the xor of two permutations, and their proof relies on the Chernoff bound. However, in their application, the resulting Bernoulli random variables are dependent, and thus a correct proof would need to use Azuma's inequality. We made non-trivial attempts to fix their proof using Azuma inequality, but could only recover a bound around $20nq/2^n$.

$1-(1-1/2^n)^q \approx q/2^n$. Next, if we blindly use the chi-squared method, with $\mathbf{S}_1$ being the real system, and $\mathbf{S}_0$ the ideal one (the one implementing a uniformly random function), then the bound is weak, around $\sqrt{q/2^n}$. The reason is that, for each $i \le q$ and $\boldsymbol{Z}_{i-1} = (z_1, \ldots, z_{i-1})$ that the real system can produce for its first $i-1$ answers,

$$\chi^2(\boldsymbol{Z}_{i-1}) \ge \frac{\left(\mathsf{ps}_{\mathbf{S}_1}(0^n \mid \boldsymbol{Z}_{i-1}) - \mathsf{ps}_{\mathbf{S}_0}(0^n \mid \boldsymbol{Z}_{i-1})\right)^2}{\mathsf{ps}_{\mathbf{S}_0}(0^n \mid \boldsymbol{Z}_{i-1})} = \frac{1}{2^n}.$$

Hence when we sample $\boldsymbol{X}_{i-1}$ according to the interaction with $\mathbf{S}_1$, it holds that $\mathbf{E}[\chi^2(\boldsymbol{X}_{i-1})] \ge 1/2^n$, and consequently we end up with an inferior bound $\sqrt{q/2^n}$. To avoid this issue, the system $\mathbf{S}_0$ in our proof is instead a "normalized" version of the ideal system. It only outputs uniformly random answers in $\{0,1\}^n \backslash \{0^n\}$. This normalization introduces a term $q/2^n$ in the bound, but the important point is that this term won't be under the square-root. We will use the chi-squared method with $\mathbf{S}_1$ being the real system, and $\mathbf{S}_0$ being the normalized ideal system.

*Proof (*Theorem 1*).* Let $\mathbf{S}_1$ be the real system, and let $\mathbf{S}_2$ be the ideal system. To obtain a good advantage, as explained above, we'll first "normalize" $\mathbf{S}_2$ to obtain another system $\mathbf{S}_0$. Let $\mathbf{S}_0$ be the system that implements an ideal random function mapping $\{0,1\}^{n-1}$ to $\{0,1\}^n \backslash \{0^n\}$. Let $\Gamma_{\text{good}} = (\{0,1\}^n \backslash \{0^n\})^q$, and $\Gamma_{\text{bad}} = (\{0,1\}^n)^q \backslash \Gamma_{\text{good}}$. Recall that $\mathsf{Adv}^{\text{xor}}(A, n)$ is at most the statistical distance between $\mathsf{ps}_{\mathbf{S}_1,A}$ and $\mathsf{ps}_{\mathbf{S}_2,A}$. From triangle inequality,

$$\|\mathsf{ps}_{\mathbf{S}_1,A}(\cdot) - \mathsf{ps}_{\mathbf{S}_2,A}(\cdot)\| \le \|\mathsf{ps}_{\mathbf{S}_1,A}(\cdot) - \mathsf{ps}_{\mathbf{S}_0,A}(\cdot)\| + \|\mathsf{ps}_{\mathbf{S}_0,A}(\cdot) - \mathsf{ps}_{\mathbf{S}_2,A}(\cdot)\|.$$

Let T be the random variable for the q answers in $\mathbf{S}_2$. Then

$$\begin{aligned} \|\mathsf{ps}_{\mathbf{S}_0,A}(\cdot) - \mathsf{ps}_{\mathbf{S}_2,A}(\cdot)\| &= \sum_{\boldsymbol{Z}} \max\{0, \mathsf{ps}_{\mathbf{S}_2,A}(\boldsymbol{Z}) - \mathsf{ps}_{\mathbf{S}_0,A}(\boldsymbol{Z})\} \\ &= \sum_{\boldsymbol{Z} \in \Gamma_{\text{bad}}} \mathsf{ps}_{\mathbf{S}_2,A}(\boldsymbol{Z}) = \Pr[T \in \Gamma_{\text{bad}}] \end{aligned}$$

where the second equality is due to the fact that $\mathsf{ps}_{\mathbf{S}_2,A}(\boldsymbol{Z}) > \mathsf{ps}_{\mathbf{S}_0,A}(\boldsymbol{Z})$ if and only if $\boldsymbol{Z} \in \Gamma_{\text{bad}}$, and $\mathsf{ps}_{\mathbf{S}_0,A}(\boldsymbol{Z}) = 0$ for every $\boldsymbol{Z} \in \Gamma_{\text{bad}}$. Note that $\Pr[T \in \Gamma_{\text{bad}}]$ is the probability that among q answers in $\mathbf{S}_2$ (the system implementing a uniformly random function), there is at least a 0^n-answer, which happens with probability at most $q/2^n$.

What is left is to bound $\|\mathsf{ps}_{\mathbf{S}_0,A}(\cdot) - \mathsf{ps}_{\mathbf{S}_1,A}(\cdot)\|$. We shall use the chi-squared method. Let $\boldsymbol{X} = (X_1, \ldots, X_q)$ be the random variable for the q answers in $\mathbf{S}_1$, and let $\boldsymbol{X}_i = (X_1, \ldots, X_i)$ for every $i \le q$. Fix $i \le q$ and fix $x \in \{0,1\}^n \backslash \{0^n\}$. Let $Y_{i,x}$ be the following random variable. If $\boldsymbol{X}_{i-1}$ takes values $(z_1, \ldots, z_{i-1})$ then $Y_{i,x}$ takes the value $\mathsf{ps}_{\mathbf{S}_1,A}(x \mid z_1, \ldots, z_{i-1})$. Recall that

$$\begin{aligned} \chi^2(\boldsymbol{X}_{i-1}) &= \sum_{x \in \{0,1\}^n \backslash \{0^n\}} \frac{(Y_{i,x} - 1/(2^n-1))^2}{1/(2^n-1)} \\ &\le \sum_{x \in \{0,1\}^n \backslash \{0^n\}} 2^n \cdot (Y_{i,x} - 1/(2^n-1))^2. \end{aligned} \tag{7}$$

We now expand $Y_{i,x}$ into a more expressive and convenient formula to work with. Let $\pi \in \mathrm{Perm}(n)$ be the secret key of $\mathsf{XOR}[n]$. Let $m_1, \ldots, m_i$ be the first i queries of the adversary. Let $V_1 = \pi(m_1 \parallel 0), V_2 = \pi(m_1 \parallel 1), \ldots, V_{2i-3} = \pi(m_{i-1} \parallel 0)$, and $V_{2i-2} = \pi(m_{i-1} \parallel 1)$. Regardless of how the adversary chooses its queries, marginally, these $V_1, \ldots, V_{2i-2}$ are simply random variables sampled uniformly without replacement from $\{0,1\}^n$. Let $S = \{V_1, \ldots, V_{2i-2}\}$. Let $D_{i,x}$ be the number of pairs $(u, u \oplus x)$ such that both u and $u \oplus x$ belongs to S. Note that S and $D_{i,x}$ are both random variables, and in fact functions of the random variables $V_1, \ldots, V_{2i-2}$. If $\pi(m_i \parallel 0) \oplus \pi(m_i \parallel 1) = x$, there are exactly $2^n - 4(i-1) + D_{i,x}$ choices for the pair $(\pi(m_i \parallel 0), \pi(m_i \parallel 1))$:

- First, $\pi(m_i \| 0)$ must take value in $\{0,1\}^n \backslash (S \cup S^*)$, where $S^* = \{u \oplus x \mid u \in S\}$. There are exactly $2^n - |S \cup S^*| = 2^n - |S| - |S^*| + |S \cap S^*| = 2^n - 4(i-1) + D_{i,x}$ choices for $\pi(m_i \parallel 0)$.
- Once $\pi(m_i \parallel 0)$ is fixed, the value of $\pi(m_i \parallel 1)$ is determined.

Hence

$$Y_{i,x} = \frac{2^n - 4(i-1) + D_{i,x}}{(2^n - 2i + 1)(2^n - 2i)},$$

and thus

$$|Y_{i,x} - 1/(2^n - 1)| = \frac{|(2^n - 1)D_{i,x} - 4(i-1)^2 + 2(2^n - i)|}{(2^n - 2i + 1)(2^n - 2i)(2^n - 1)}.$$

Note that

$$\begin{aligned}
&\frac{|(2^n - 1)D_{i,x} - 4(i-1)^2 + 2(2^n - i)|}{2^n - 1} \\
&= \left| D_{i,x} - \frac{4(i-1)^2}{2^n - 1} + 2 - \frac{2(i-1)}{2^n - 1} \right| \\
&= \left| D_{i,x} - \frac{4(i-1)^2}{2^n} + 2 - \frac{2(i-1)}{2^n - 1} - \frac{4(i-1)^2}{2^n(2^n - 1)} \right| \\
&\leq \left| D_{i,x} - \frac{4(i-1)^2}{2^n} \right| + 2 - \frac{2(i-1)}{2^n - 1} - \frac{4(i-1)^2}{2^n(2^n - 1)} \\
&\leq \left| D_{i,x} - \frac{4(i-1)^2}{2^n} \right| + 2,
\end{aligned}$$

where the first inequality is due to the facts that (i) $|a + b| \leq |a| + |b|$ for any numbers a and b, and (ii) $2 - \frac{2(i-1)}{2^n-1} - \frac{4(i-1)^2}{2^n(2^n-1)} > 0$, which is in turn due to the hypothesis that $i \leq q \leq 2^{n-5}$, and $n \geq 8$. Dividing both sides by $(2^n - 2i + 1)(2^n - 2i)$ we have

$$\begin{aligned}|Y_{i,x} - 1/(2^n - 1)| &\le \frac{|D_{i,x} - 4(i-1)^2/2^n| + 2}{(2^n - 2i + 1)(2^n - 2i)} \\ &\le \frac{|D_{i,x} - 4(i-1)^2/2^n| + 2}{\frac{7}{8} \cdot 2^{2n}} \\ &= \frac{\frac{8}{7} \cdot |D_{i,x} - 4(i-1)^2/2^n| + \frac{16}{7}}{2^{2n}} \\ &\le \frac{\frac{8}{7} \cdot |D_{i,x} - 4(i-1)^2/2^n| + 3}{2^{2n}},\end{aligned}$$

where the second inequality is also due to the hypothesis that $i \le q \le 2^{n-5}$, and $n \ge 8$. Using the fact that $(a+b)^2 \le 2(a^2+b^2)$ for every real numbers a and b,

$$\begin{aligned}(Y_{i,x} - 1/(2^n - 1))^2 &\le \frac{\frac{128}{49}(D_{i,x} - 4(i-1)^2/2^n)^2 + 18}{2^{4n}} \\ &\le \frac{3(D_{i,x} - 4(i-1)^2/2^n)^2 + 18}{2^{4n}}.\end{aligned}$$

From Eq. (7),

$$\begin{aligned}\mathbf{E}[\chi^2(\boldsymbol{X}_{i-1})] &\le \sum_{x \in \{0,1\}^n \backslash \{0^n\}} 2^n \cdot \mathbf{E}\Big[(Y_{i,x} - 1/(2^n - 1))^2\Big] \\ &\le \sum_{x \in \{0,1\}^n \backslash \{0^n\}} \frac{18}{2^{3n}} + \frac{3}{2^{3n}}\ \mathbf{E}\Big[\Big(D_{i,x} - \frac{4(i-1)^2}{2^n}\Big)^2\Big].\end{aligned}$$

In the last formula, it is helpful to think of each $D_{i,x}$ as a function of $V_1, \ldots, V_{2n-2}$, and the expectation is taken over the choices of $V_1, \ldots, V_{2n-2}$ sampled uniformly without replacement from $\{0,1\}^n$. We will show that for any $x \in \{0,1\}^n \backslash \{0^n\}$,

$$\mathbf{E}\Big[\Big(D_{i,x} - \frac{4(i-1)^2}{2^n}\Big)^2\Big] \le \frac{4(i-1)^2}{2^n}, \tag{8}$$

and thus

$$\mathbf{E}[\chi^2(\boldsymbol{X}_{i-1})] \le \sum_{x \in \{0,1\}^n \backslash \{0^n\}} \Big(\frac{18}{2^{3n}} + \frac{12(i-1)^2}{2^{4n}}\Big) \le \frac{18}{2^{2n}} + \frac{12(i-1)^2}{2^{3n}}.$$

Summing up, from Lemma 3,

$$\begin{aligned}(\|\mathsf{ps}_{0,A}(\cdot) - \mathsf{ps}_{1,A}(\cdot)\|)^2 &\le \frac{1}{2}\sum_{i=1}^{q} \mathbf{E}[\chi^2(X_{i-1})] \\ &\le \frac{1}{2}\sum_{i=1}^{q} \frac{18}{2^{2n}} + \frac{12(i-1)^2}{2^{3n}} \\ &\le \frac{1}{2}\Big(\frac{18q}{2^{2n}} + \frac{4q^3}{2^{3n}}\Big) \le \frac{9q + 0.25q^2}{2^{2n}},\end{aligned}$$

where the last inequality is due to the hypothesis that $q \le 2^{n-5}$.

We now justify Eq. (8). Fix $x \in \{0,1\}^n \backslash \{0^n\}$. For each $1 \le j \le 2i-2$, let B_j be the Bernoulli random variable such that $B_j = 1$ if and only if $V_j \in \{V_1 \oplus x, \ldots, V_{j-1} \oplus x\}$. Then $D_{i,x} = 2(B_1 + \cdots B_{2i-2})$: if $V_j = V_k \oplus x$ for some $k < j$, then these account for two pairs (u, v) such that $v = u \oplus x$, whereas $B_k = 0$ and $B_j = 1$. Let $S_k = B_1 + \cdots + B_k$, and $L_k = S_k - k^2/2^{n+1}$. We will prove by induction that for any $k \le 2i-2$,

$$\mathbf{E}\Big[(L_k)^2\Big] \le \frac{2k^2}{2^{n+1}}, \text{ and}$$
$$\mathbf{E}\Big[L_k\Big] \ge \frac{-k}{2^{n+1}}.$$

This subsumes Eq. (8) as the special case for $k = 2i - 2$. The base case $k = 1$ is vacuous, since $B_1 = 0$. Suppose this holds for $k - 1$; we'll prove that it holds for k as well. Given $B_1, \ldots, B_{k-1}$, the conditional probability that $B_k = 1$ is exactly

$$p = \frac{k - 1 - 2S_{k-1}}{2^n - (k-1)}$$

because it is equally likely for V_k to take any value in $\{0,1\}^n \backslash P$, where $P = \{V_1, \ldots, V_{k-1}\}$ and $2S_{k-1}$ is the number of elements $u \in P$ such that $u \oplus x$ is also in P. Moreover,

$$\frac{k-1-2S_{k-1}}{2^n-(k-1)} = \frac{k-1-2(L_{k-1}+(k-1)^2/2^{n+1})}{2^n-(k-1)} = \frac{k-1}{2^n} - \frac{2L_{k-1}}{2^n-(k-1)}.$$

Hence $p = \frac{k-1}{2^n} - \frac{2L_{k-1}}{2^n-(k-1)}$, and thus

$$\begin{aligned}
\mathbf{E}[L_k] &= \mathbf{E}[L_{k-1} + B_k - (2k-1)/2^{n+1}] = \mathbf{E}[L_{k-1} + p - (2k-1)/2^{n+1}] \\
&= \mathbf{E}\Big[\Big(1 - \frac{2}{2^n-(k-1)}\Big)L_{k-1} - \frac{1}{2^{n+1}}\Big] \\
&= \Big(1 - \frac{2}{2^n-(k-1)}\Big)\mathbf{E}[L_{k-1}] - \frac{1}{2^{n+1}} \\
&\ge \Big(1 - \frac{2}{2^n-(k-1)}\Big)\frac{(1-k)}{2^{n+1}} - \frac{1}{2^{n+1}} \ge \frac{-k}{2^{n+1}},
\end{aligned}$$

where the second last inequality is due to the induction hypothesis. On the other hand,

$$\begin{aligned}
&\mathbf{E}[(L_k)^2] = \mathbf{E}\Big[\Big(L_{k-1} + B_k - (2k-1)/2^{n+1}\Big)^2\Big] \\
&= \mathbf{E}\Big[p\Big(L_{k-1} + 1 - (2k-1)/2^{n+1}\Big)^2 + (1-p)\Big(L_{k-1} - (2k-1)/2^{n+1}\Big)^2\Big]. \quad (9)
\end{aligned}$$

By substituting $p = \frac{k-1}{2^n} - \frac{2L_{k-1}}{2^n-(k-1)}$ and using some simple algebraic manipulations,

$$\begin{aligned}
&p\Big(L_{k-1} + 1 - (2k-1)/2^{n+1}\Big)^2 + (1-p)\Big(L_{k-1} - (2k-1)/2^{n+1}\Big)^2 \\
&= \Big(1 - \frac{4}{2n-k-1}\Big)(L_{k-1})^2 - \Big(\frac{1}{2^n} + \frac{2}{2^n-(k-1)}\Big)L_{k-1} + \frac{(2k-1)^2}{2^{2n+2}} + \frac{(2k-1)}{2^{n+1}} \\
&\le (L_{k-1})^2 - \Big(\frac{1}{2^n} + \frac{2}{2^n-(k-1)}\Big)L_{k-1} + \frac{3(2k-1)}{2^{n+2}}, \qquad (10)
\end{aligned}$$

where the last inequality is due to the fact that $k \le 2q \le 2^{n-4}$. Taking expectation of both sides of Eq. (10), and using the induction hypothesis yield

$$\mathbf{E}\Big[\Big(L_k\Big)^2\Big] \le \frac{2(k-1)^2}{2^{n+1}} + \Big(\frac{1}{2^n} + \frac{2}{2^n-(k-1)}\Big)\frac{k-1}{2^{n+1}} + \frac{3(2k-1)}{2^{n+2}} \le \frac{2k^2}{2^{n+1}},$$

where the last inequality is again due to the fact that $k \le 2q \le 2^{n-4}$. This concludes the proof. □

5 The Encrypted Davies-Meyer Construction

In this section we consider the PRF construction EDM that Cogliati and Seurin (CS) recently propose [10]. They show that EDM achieves $\frac{2n}{3}$-bit security and conjecture that it actually achieves n-bit security. Here we'll give a $\frac{3n}{4}$-bit security proof for EDM. We begin by describing the EDM construction.

SETUP AND RESULTS. The construction $\mathrm{EDM}[n] : (\mathrm{Perm}(n))^2 \times \{0,1\}^n \to \{0,1\}^n$ takes two secret permutations $\pi, \pi' \in \mathrm{Perm}(n)$ as its key, and outputs $\pi'(\pi(x) \oplus x)$ on input x. Theorem 2 below shows that $\mathsf{Adv}^{\mathrm{prf}}_{\mathrm{EDM}[n]}(A) \le \frac{7q^2}{2^{3n/2}}$, namely $\frac{3n}{4}$-bit security, whereas CS's result shows that $\mathsf{Adv}^{\mathrm{prf}}_{\mathrm{EDM}[n]}(A) \le \frac{5q^{3/2}}{2^n}$.

We note that a concurrent work by Mennink and Neves (MN) [21] shows that $\mathsf{Adv}^{\mathrm{prf}}_{\mathrm{EDM}[n]}(A) \le \frac{q}{2^n} + \frac{\binom{q}{t+1}}{2^{nt}}$ for any integer $t \ge 1$ and any $q \le 2^n/67t$. While MN's bound is quite better than ours, their work relies on Patarin's "mirror theory" [26]. Here, our goal is to give a much simpler proof and we leave it as an open question of whether our bound can be tightened without resorting to mirror theory. A graphical comparison of the three bounds is shown in Fig. 1.

Theorem 2. *Let $n \ge 16$ be an integer. Then for any adversary A that makes at most q queries,*

$$\mathsf{Adv}^{\mathrm{prf}}_{\mathrm{EDM}[n]}(A) \le \frac{7q^2}{2^{1.5n}}.$$

Proof. Without loss of generality, assume that $q \le 2^{n-4}$; otherwise the claimed bound is moot. Assume that the adversary is deterministic and never repeats a

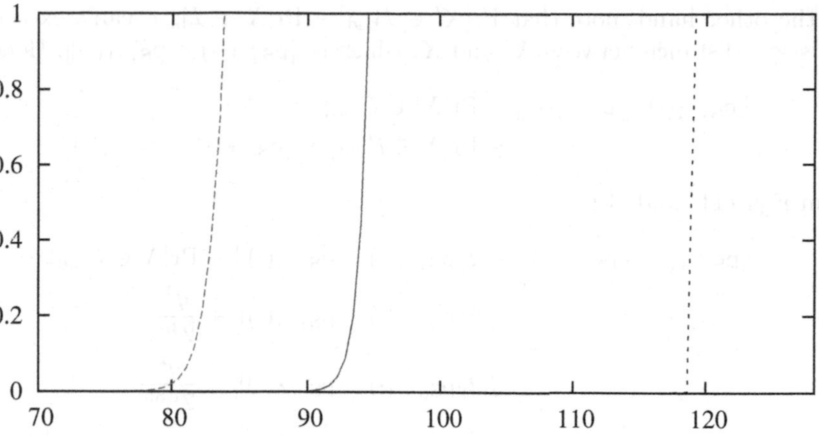

Fig. 1. Comparison among CS's bound (left), ours (middle), and MN's (right) for $n = 128$. The x-axis gives the log (base 2) of q, and the y-axis gives the security bounds. For MN's bound, we use $t = 9$ as suggested by MN.

past query. For convenience of analysis, instead of working directly with the real system (the one implementing EDM), we will "normalize" it to ensure that it has nice behaviors even if the past answers are bad.

Specifically, let $\mathbf{S}_0$ be the ideal system (the one implementing a uniform random function), and $\mathbf{S}_2$ be the real system. We will construct a system $\mathbf{S}_1$ that is the "normalized" version of $\mathbf{S}_2$ as follows. The system $\mathbf{S}_1$ keeps a secret boolean bad that is initially set to false. Initially, it implements $\mathbf{S}_2$, but if among the past queries, there are 4 answers that are the same, then it sets bad to true. Once bad is set, $\mathbf{S}_1$ instead implements $\mathbf{S}_0$. We now show that the advantage $\mathsf{Adv}^{\mathrm{prf}}_{\mathrm{EDM}}(A)$ can be bounded via the statistical distance between $\mathsf{p}_{\mathbf{S}_0,A}(\cdot)$ and $\mathsf{p}_{\mathbf{S}_1,A}(\cdot)$, and then bound the latter via the chi-squared method. First, recall that $\mathsf{Adv}^{\mathrm{prf}}_{\mathrm{EDM}}(A)$ is at most

$$\|\mathsf{p}_{\mathbf{S}_0,A}(\cdot) - \mathsf{p}_{\mathbf{S}_2,A}(\cdot)\| \le \|\mathsf{p}_{\mathbf{S}_0,A}(\cdot) - \mathsf{p}_{\mathbf{S}_1,A}(\cdot)\| + \|\mathsf{p}_{\mathbf{S}_1,A}(\cdot) - \mathsf{p}_{\mathbf{S}_2,A}(\cdot)\|. \quad (11)$$

Let X and X' be the random variables for the q-answers on $\mathbf{S}_0$ and $\mathbf{S}_1$ respectively. Let Γ_{bad} be the subset of $(\{0,1\}^n)^q$ such that for any $\boldsymbol{Z} \in \Gamma_{\mathrm{bad}}$, there are 4 components of $\boldsymbol{Z}$ that are the same. Then $\mathsf{p}_{\mathbf{S}_1,A}(\boldsymbol{Z}) = \mathsf{p}_{\mathbf{S}_2,A}(\boldsymbol{Z})$ for every $\boldsymbol{Z} \in (\{0,1\}^n)^q \backslash \Gamma_{\mathrm{bad}}$, and thus

$$\begin{aligned}
\|\mathsf{p}_{\mathbf{S}_1,A}(\cdot) - \mathsf{p}_{\mathbf{S}_2,A}(\cdot)\| &= \sum_{\boldsymbol{Z} \in (\{0,1\}^n)^q} \max\{0, \mathsf{p}_{\mathbf{S}_1,A}(\boldsymbol{Z}) - \mathsf{p}_{\mathbf{S}_2,A}(\boldsymbol{Z})\} \\
&= \sum_{\boldsymbol{Z} \in \Gamma_{\mathrm{bad}}} \max\{0, \mathsf{p}_{\mathbf{S}_1,A}(\boldsymbol{Z}) - \mathsf{p}_{\mathbf{S}_2,A}(\boldsymbol{Z})\} \\
&\le \sum_{\boldsymbol{Z} \in \Gamma_{\mathrm{bad}}} \mathsf{p}_{\mathbf{S}_1,A}(\boldsymbol{Z}) = \Pr[X' \in \Gamma_{\mathrm{bad}}].
\end{aligned}$$

On the other hand, note that $\Pr[X' \in \Gamma_{\text{bad}}] - \Pr[X \in \Gamma_{\text{bad}}]$ can't exceed the statistical distance between X' and X, which is $\|\mathsf{ps}_{0,A}(\cdot) - \mathsf{ps}_{1,A}(\cdot)\|$. Hence

$$\begin{aligned}\|\mathsf{ps}_{1,A}(\cdot) - \mathsf{ps}_{2,A}(\cdot)\| &\le \Pr[X' \in \Gamma_{\text{bad}}] \\ &\le \Pr[X \in \Gamma_{\text{bad}}] + \|\mathsf{ps}_{0,A}(\cdot) - \mathsf{ps}_{1,A}(\cdot)\|. \end{aligned} \tag{12}$$

From Eqs. (11) and (12),

$$\begin{aligned}\|\mathsf{ps}_{0,A}(\cdot) - \mathsf{ps}_{2,A}(\cdot)\| &\le 2\|\mathsf{ps}_{0,A}(\cdot) - \mathsf{ps}_{1,A}(\cdot)\| + \Pr[X \in \Gamma_{\text{bad}}] \\ &\le 2\|\mathsf{ps}_{0,A}(\cdot) - \mathsf{ps}_{1,A}(\cdot)\| + \frac{q^4}{2^{3n}} \\ &\le 2\|\mathsf{ps}_{0,A}(\cdot) - \mathsf{ps}_{1,A}(\cdot)\| + \frac{q^2}{2^{1.5n}}.\end{aligned}$$

Hence what's left is to bound $\|\mathsf{ps}_{0,A}(\cdot) - \mathsf{ps}_{1,A}(\cdot)\|$. Fix $i \le q$ and $\boldsymbol{Z}_{i-1} = (z_1, \ldots, z_{i-1}) \in (\{0,1\}^n)^{i-1}$. Recall that

$$\chi^2(\boldsymbol{Z}_{i-1}) = \sum_{z_i \in \{0,1\}^n} \frac{(\mathsf{ps}_{1,A}(z_i \mid \boldsymbol{Z}_{i-1}) - 1/2^n)^2}{1/2^n}.$$

We claim that if $z_i \in \{z_1, \ldots, z_{i-1}\}$ then

$$\frac{1}{2^n} - \frac{4i}{2^{2n}} \le \mathsf{ps}_{1,A}(z_i \mid \boldsymbol{Z}_{i-1}) \le \frac{1}{2^n} + \frac{2i}{2^{2n}}, \tag{13}$$

and if $z_i \notin \{z_1, \ldots, z_{i-1}\}$

$$\frac{1}{2^n} - \frac{2i^2}{2^{3n}} \le \mathsf{ps}_{1,A}(z_i \mid \boldsymbol{Z}_{i-1}) \le \frac{1}{2^n} + \frac{5i^2}{2^{3n}}. \tag{14}$$

Consequently,

$$\chi^2(\boldsymbol{Z}_{i-1}) \le (i-1)\frac{16i^2}{2^{3n}} + (2^n - i + 1)\frac{25i^4}{2^{5n}} \le \frac{18i^3}{2^{3n}}.$$

Hence from Lemma 3, if one samples vectors $\boldsymbol{X}_{i-1}$ according to interaction with system $\mathbf{S}_1$,

$$(\|\mathsf{ps}_{0,A}(\cdot) - \mathsf{ps}_{1,A}(\cdot)\|)^2 \le \frac{1}{2}\sum_{i=1}^{q} \mathbf{E}[\chi^2(\boldsymbol{X}_{i-1})] \le \frac{1}{2}\sum_{i=1}^{q} \frac{18i^3}{2^{3n}} \le \frac{9q^4}{2^{3n}}.$$

We now justify the two claims above, namely Eqs. (13) and (14). Note that if there are 4 components of $\boldsymbol{Z}_{i-1}$ that are the same, then the claims are obviously true, as $\mathsf{ps}_{1,A}(z_i \mid \boldsymbol{Z}_{i-1}) = 1/2^n$. Suppose that there are no 4 components of $\boldsymbol{Z}_{i-1}$ that are the same. Let $(m_1, \ldots, m_i)$ be the queries that are uniquely determined from $\boldsymbol{Z}_{i-1}$. Let $v_j = \pi(m_j) \oplus m_j$ for every $j \le i$.

We first justify Eq. (13), namely $z_i \in \{z_1, \ldots, z_{i-1}\}$. First consider the upper bound. Let S be the subset of $\{1, \ldots, i-1\}$ such that $z_i = z_j$, for every $j \in S$. Then $0 < |S| \le 3$. Let ℓ be an arbitrary element of S. Note that $\mathbf{S}_1$ outputs z_i

on query m_i if and only if $\pi(m_i) = v_\ell \oplus m_i$. For each fixed choice of $v_1, \ldots, v_{i-1}$, the conditional probability that $\pi(m_i) = v_\ell \oplus m_i$, given $\pi(m_j) = v_j \oplus m_j$ for every $j \le i-1$, is either 0 or $1/(2^n - i)$. Hence

$$\mathsf{ps}_{1,A}(z_i \mid \boldsymbol{Z}_{i-1}) \le \frac{1}{2^n - i} \le \frac{1}{2^n} + \frac{2i}{2^{2n}},$$

where the last inequality is due to the hypothesis that $i \le q \le 2^{n-4}$. Next, consider the lower bound in Eq. (13). For each fixed choice of v_j, with $j \in \{1, \ldots, i-1\} \backslash S$, there are at least $2^n - 4i$ choices for v_ℓ, out of at most 2^n possible choices, such that $v_\ell \oplus m_k \ne v_j \oplus m_j$, for every $j \in \{1, \ldots, i-1\} \backslash S$ and every $k \in S \cup \{i\}$. For each such tuple $(v_1, \ldots, v_{i-1})$, the conditional probability that $\pi(m_i) = v_\ell \oplus m_i$, given $\pi(m_j) = v_j \oplus m_j$ for every $j \le i-1$, is exactly $1/(2^n - i)$. Hence

$$\mathsf{ps}_{1,A}(z_i \mid \boldsymbol{Z}_{i-1}) \ge \frac{2^n - 4i}{2^n(2^n - i)} \ge \frac{1}{2^n} - \frac{4i}{2^{2n}},$$

where the last inequality is due to the hypothesis that $i \le q \le 2^{n-4}$.

We now justify Eq. (14), namely $z_i \notin \{z_1, \ldots, z_{i-1}\}$. First consider the lower bound. Let r be the number of elements in $\{z_1, \ldots, z_{i-1}\}$, and thus $r \le i-1$. The system $\mathbf{S}_1$ will give an answer not in $\{z_1, \ldots, z_{i-1}\}$ if and only if $v_i \notin \{v_1, \ldots, v_{i-1}\}$. Note that for each $x, x' \in \{0,1\}^n \backslash \{z_1, \ldots, z_{i-1}\}$, we have $\mathsf{ps}_{1,A}(x \mid \boldsymbol{Z}_{i-1}) = \mathsf{ps}_{1,A}(x' \mid \boldsymbol{Z}_{i-1})$, since as long as $v_i \notin \{v_1, \ldots, v_{i-1}\}$, $\pi'(v_i)$ is equally likely to take any value in $\{0,1\}^n \backslash \{z_1, \ldots, z_{i-1}\}$. Hence

$$\begin{aligned}
\mathsf{ps}_{1,A}(z_i \mid \boldsymbol{Z}_{i-1}) &= \frac{1}{2^n - r}\Big(1 - \sum_{x \in \{z_1, \ldots, z_{i-1}\}} \mathsf{ps}_{1,A}(x \mid \boldsymbol{Z}_{i-1})\Big)\\
&\ge \frac{1}{2^n - r}\Big(1 - \sum_{x \in \{z_1, \ldots, z_{i-1}\}} \frac{1}{2^n}(1 + 2i/2^n)\Big)\\
&\ge \frac{1}{2^n - r}\Big(1 - \frac{r}{2^n}(1 + 2i/2^n)\Big)\\
&\ge \frac{1}{2^n} - \frac{2ri}{2^{2n}(2^n - r)} \ge \frac{1}{2^n} - \frac{2i^2}{2^{3n}}.
\end{aligned}$$

For the upper bound of Eq. (14),

$$\begin{aligned}
\mathsf{ps}_{1,A}(z_i \mid \boldsymbol{Z}_{i-1}) &= \frac{1}{2^n - r}\Big(1 - \sum_{x \in \{z_1, \ldots, z_{i-1}\}} \mathsf{ps}_{1,A}(x \mid \boldsymbol{Z}_{i-1})\Big)\\
&\le \frac{1}{2^n - r}\Big(1 - \sum_{x \in \{z_1, \ldots, z_{i-1}\}} \frac{1}{2^n}(1 - 4i/2^n)\Big)\\
&\le \frac{1}{2^n - r}\Big(1 - \frac{r}{2^n}(1 - 4i/2^n)\Big)\\
&\le \frac{1}{2^n} + \frac{4ri}{2^{2n}(2^n - r)} \le \frac{1}{2^n} + \frac{5i^2}{2^{3n}}\ .
\end{aligned}$$

This concluses the proof. □

6 The Swap-or-Not Construction

As a final application of our framework, we prove a tighter bound on the security of the swap-or-not construction by Hoang, Morris, and Rogaway [13] using the chi-squared method. We start by reviewing the construction, before turning to its analysis.

THE SWAP-OR-NOT CONSTRUCTION. Let $r \geq 1$ be a round parameter. Let $\mathbb{G}$ be a finite abelian group, for which we use additive notation to denote the associated operation. Then, the *swap-or-not construction* SN_r uses r functions $f_1, \ldots, f_r : \mathbb{G} \to \{0,1\}$ (to be chosen independently and uniformly at random in the proof), and additionally uses r rounds keys $K = (K_1, \ldots, K_r) \in \mathbb{G}$. Then, on input $X \in \mathbb{G}$, it computes states $X_0, X_1, \ldots, X_r \in \mathbb{G}$, where $X_0 = X$, and for $i \in \{1, \ldots, r\}$, let $V_i = \max\{X_{i-1}, K_i - X_{i-1}\}$,[7]

$$X_i = \begin{cases} X_{i-1} & \text{if } f_i(V_i) = 0 \ , \\ K_i - X_{i-1} & \text{else.} \end{cases} \quad . \tag{15}$$

Finally, it outputs X_r. The corresponding inversion operation occurs by taking these steps backwards. We denote the resulting construction as $\mathrm{SN}_r[\mathbb{G}]$.

SECURITY NOTIONS. For a block cipher $E : \mathcal{K} \times \mathcal{M} \to \mathcal{M}$ and an adversary A, the CCA advantage $\mathsf{Adv}^{\mathrm{cca}}_{E}(A)$ of A against E is defined as

$$\Pr[K \leftarrow\!\!\$\ \mathcal{K}; A^{E_K(\cdot), E_K^{-1}(\cdot)} \Rightarrow 1] - \Pr[\pi \leftarrow\!\!\$\ \mathrm{Perm}(\mathcal{M}); A^{\pi(\cdot), \pi^{-1}(\cdot)} \Rightarrow 1],$$

where $\mathrm{Perm}(\mathcal{M})$ is the set of all permutations on $\mathcal{M}$. We emphasize that here $\mathcal{M}$ is an arbitrary set. If the adversary only queries its first oracle, and makes only *non-adaptive* queries, then we write $\mathsf{Adv}^{\mathrm{ncpa}}_{E}(A)$ instead. We write $\mathsf{Adv}^{\mathrm{cca}}_{E}(q)$ and $\mathsf{Adv}^{\mathrm{ncpa}}_{E}(q)$ to denote the CCA and NCPA advantage of the best adversaries of q queries against E, respectively.

If we have two block ciphers F and G on the same message space that are just NCPA-secure, one can have a CCA-secure block cipher E by composing $E = F \circ G^{-1}$, meaning that $E_{K,K'}(x) = G^{-1}_{K'}(F_K(x))$. The following well-known theorem by Maurer, Pietrzak, and Renner [20] bounds the CCA security of E based on the NCPA security of F and G.

Lemma 4 ([20]). Let F and G be block ciphers on the same message space, and let $E = F \circ G^{-1}$. Then for any q,

$$\mathsf{Adv}^{\mathrm{cca}}_{E}(q) \leq \mathsf{Adv}^{\mathrm{ncpa}}_{F}(q) + \mathsf{Adv}^{\mathrm{ncpa}}_{G}(q). \qquad \square$$

[7] Here, max is with respect to some encoding. The key point is that $K_i - (K_i - X) = X$, so this will reach a unique representative for this pair of elements of $\mathbb{G}$.

We note that Lemma 4 only holds in the information-theoretic setting where one consider the best possible, computationally unbounded adversaries. Pietrzak shows that this lemma does not hold in the computational setting [27].

NCPA SECURITY OF SWAP-OR-NOT. Following the route in the analysis of [13], we'll first consider the NCPA security of Swap-or-Not, and then use Lemma 4 to amplify it to CCA security.

Lemma 5. For any adversary A that makes at most q queries and an abelian group $\mathbb{G}$ of N elements,

$$\mathsf{Adv}^{\text{ncpa}}_{\text{SN}_r[\mathbb{G}]}(A) \le \frac{N}{\sqrt{r+1}}\left(\frac{N+q}{2N}\right)^{(r+1)/2} .$$

Proof. We assume without loss of generality that A is deterministic, and doesn't make redundant queries. The adversary A interacts with the construction $\text{SN}_r[\mathbb{G}]$ with r secret and randomly chosen functions $f_1, \ldots, f_r : \mathbb{G} \to \{0, 1\}$, and r keys $K = (K_1, \ldots, K_r)$. We denote by $\mathbf{S}_1$ the system resulting from $\text{SN}_r[\mathbb{G}]$ and by $\mathbf{S}_0$ the system resulting from interacting with the random permutation π. We will bound

$$\mathsf{Adv}^{\text{ncpa}}_{\text{SN}_r[\mathbb{G}]}(A) \le \|\mathsf{p}_{\mathbf{S}_1,A}(\cdot) - \mathsf{p}_{\mathbf{S}_0,A}(\cdot)\|.$$

For each $i \in \{0, 1, \ldots, q\}$, we define $\boldsymbol{X}_i$ to be the vector of outputs from the first i queries of A to $\mathbf{S}_1$. Let $m_i = N - i + 1$. We will use the following lemma from [13] to bound $\mathbf{E}[\chi^2(\boldsymbol{X}_{i-1})]$.

Lemma 6 ([13])**.** For any NCPA adversary A making q queries and for any $i \le q$,

$$\mathbf{E}\Big(\sum_{x \in \mathbb{G}\backslash\{x_1,\ldots,x_{i-1}\}} (\mathsf{p}_{\mathbf{S}_1,A}(x \mid \boldsymbol{X}_{i-1}) - 1/m_i)^2\Big) \le \left(\frac{N+i}{2N}\right)^r ,$$

where the expectation is taken over a vector $\boldsymbol{X}_{i-1} = (x_1, \ldots, x_{i-1})$ sampled according to interaction with $\mathbf{S}_1$. □

Fix some $\boldsymbol{Z}_{i-1} = (z_1, \ldots, z_{i-1})$ such that $\mathsf{p}_{\mathbf{S}_0}(\boldsymbol{Z}_{i-1}) > 0$. Notice that the i-th output of $\mathbf{S}_0$, given that the first $i-1$ outputs are $\boldsymbol{Z}_{i-1}$, is uniformly distributed over $\mathbb{G}\backslash\{z_1, \ldots, z_{i-1}\}$. In other words, for any $x \in \mathbb{G}\backslash\{z_1, \ldots, z_{i-1}\}$.

$$\mathsf{p}_{\mathbf{S}_0,A}(x \mid \boldsymbol{Z}_{i-1}) = 1/m_i.$$

Hence, from Lemma 6,

$$\begin{aligned}\mathbf{E}[\chi^2(\boldsymbol{X}_{i-1})] &= \mathbf{E}\Big(\sum_{x \in \mathbb{G}\backslash\{x_1,\ldots,x_{i-1}\}} m_i \cdot (\mathsf{p}_{\mathbf{S}_1,A}(x \mid \boldsymbol{X}_{i-1}) - 1/m_i)^2\Big) \\ &\le m_i \left(\frac{N+i}{2N}\right)^r \le N\left(\frac{N+i}{2N}\right)^r . \qquad (16)\end{aligned}$$

Using Lemma 3, we obtain,

$$
\begin{aligned}
(\|\mathsf{ps}_{0,A}(\cdot) - \mathsf{ps}_{1,A}(\cdot)\|)^2 &\leq \frac{1}{2} \cdot \sum_{i=1}^{q} \mathbf{E}[\chi^2(\boldsymbol{X}_{i-1})] \\
&\leq \frac{1}{2} \sum_{i=1}^{q} N \left(\frac{N+i}{2N}\right)^r \\
&\leq N^2 \int_0^{q/2N} \left(\frac{1}{2} + x\right)^r dx \leq \frac{N^2}{r+1} \left(\frac{N+q}{2N}\right)^{r+1} .
\end{aligned}
$$

CCA SECURITY OF SWAP-OR-NOT. Note that the inverse of $\mathrm{SN}_r[G]$ is also another $\mathrm{SN}_r[\mathbb{G}]$ (but the round functions and round-keys are bottom up). Hence from Lemmas 4 and 5, we conclude that

Theorem 3. For any $q, r \in \mathbb{N}$ and any abelian group $\mathbb{G}$ of N elements,

$$
\mathsf{Adv}^{\mathrm{cca}}_{\mathrm{SN}_{2r}[\mathbb{G}]}(q) \leq \frac{2N}{\sqrt{r+1}} \Big(\frac{N+q}{2N}\Big)^{(r+1)/2} .
$$

□

Note that in Theorem 3, the number of rounds in the Swap-or-Not shuffle is $2r$. The original bound in [13] is

$$
\mathsf{Adv}^{\mathrm{cca}}_{\mathrm{SN}_{2r}[\mathbb{G}]}(q) \leq \frac{4N^{3/2}}{r+2} \left(\frac{N+q}{2N}\right)^{r/2+1} .
$$

Typically one uses $r = \Theta(\log(N))$, and thus our result improves the original analysis by a factor of $\Theta(\sqrt{N/\log(N)})$. We note that our result is probably not tight, meaning that it might be possible to improve the security of Swap-or-Not further.

Acknowledgments. We thank the anonymous reviewers for insightful comments. Wei Dai's work was done in part while at UCSB and he was supported in part by NSF grant CNS-1526801. Viet Tung Hoang was supported in part by the First Year Assistant Professor Award of Florida State University. Stefano Tessaro was supported in part by NSF grants CNS-1423566, CNS-1528178, CNS-1553758 (CAREER), and IIS-152804, and by the Glen and Susanne Culler Chair.

A Another Variant of the Xor of Two Permutations

Let $\mathrm{Perm}(n)$ be the set of permutations $\pi : \{0,1\}^n \to \{0,1\}^n$. In Sect. 4 we show that $\mathsf{XOR}[n]$ is a goof PRF. In this section, we consider the related construction $\mathsf{XOR2}[n] : (\mathrm{Perm}(n))^2 \times \{0,1\}^n \to \{0,1\}^n$ that takes $\pi, \pi' \in \mathrm{Perm}(n)$ as its key, and outputs $\pi(x) \oplus \pi'(x)$ on input x. Theorem 4 below gives a bound on the PRF security of $\mathsf{XOR2}[n]$.

Theorem 4. Fix an integer $n \geq 4$. For any adversary A that makes $q \leq 2^{n-4}$ queries we have

$$\mathsf{Adv}^{\mathrm{prf}}_{\mathsf{XOR2}[n]}(A) \leq \frac{q^{1.5}}{2^{1.5n}}.$$

Proof. Let $\mathbf{S}_1$ be the real system, and let $\mathbf{S}_0$ be the ideal system. We shall use the chi-squared method. Let $\boldsymbol{X} = (X_1, \dots, X_q)$ be the random variable for the q answers in $\mathbf{S}_1$, and let $\boldsymbol{X}_i = (X_1, \dots, X_i)$ for every $i \leq q$. Fix $i \leq q$ and fix $x \in \{0,1\}^n$. Let $Y_{i,x}$ be the following random variable. If $\boldsymbol{X}_{i-1}$ takes values $(z_1, \dots, z_{i-1})$ then $Y_{i,x}$ takes the value $\mathsf{p}_{\mathbf{S}_1,A}(x \mid z_1, \dots, z_{i-1})$. Recall that

$$\begin{aligned}\chi^2(\boldsymbol{X}_{i-1}) &= \sum_{x \in \{0,1\}^n} \frac{(Y_{i,x} - 1/2^n)^2}{1/2^n} \\ &= \sum_{x \in \{0,1\}^n} 2^n \cdot (Y_{i,x} - 1/2^n)^2. \end{aligned} \tag{17}$$

We now expand $Y_{i,x}$ into a more expressive and convenient formula to work with. Let π and π' be the secret permutations of $\mathsf{XOR2}[n]$. Let $m_1, \dots, m_i$ be the first i queries of the adversary. Let $V_k = \pi(m_k)$ and $U_k = \pi'(m_k)$ for every $k \leq i$. Regardless of how the adversary chooses its queries, $V_1, V_2, \dots$ are simply random variables sampled uniformly without replacement from $\{0,1\}^n$. Likewise, $U_1, U_2, \dots$ are sampled uniformly without replacement from $\{0,1\}^n$ independent of $V_1, V_2, \dots$. Let $S = \{V_1, \dots, V_{i-1}\}$ and $S' = \{U_1, \dots, U_{i-1}\}$. Let $D_{i,x}$ be the number of strings u such that $u \in S$ and $u \oplus x \in S'$. If $\pi(m_i) \oplus \pi'(m_i) = x$, there are exactly $2^n - 2(i-1) + D_{i,x}$ choices for the pair $(\pi(m_i), \pi'(m_i))$:

- First, $\pi(m_i)$ must take value in $\{0,1\}^n \backslash (S \cup S^*)$, where $S^* = \{u \oplus x \mid u \in S'\}$. There are exactly $2^n - |S \cup S^*| = 2^n - |S| - |S^*| + |S \cap S^*| = 2^n - 2(i-1) + D_{i,x}$ choices for $\pi(m_i)$.
- Once $\pi(m_i)$ is fixed, the value of $\pi'(m_i)$ is determined.

Hence

$$Y_{i,x} = \frac{2^n - 2(i-1) + D_{i,x}}{(2^n - i + 1)^2},$$

and thus

$$(Y_{i,x} - 1/2^n)^2 = \frac{(D_{i,x} - (i-1)^2/2^n)^2}{(2^n - 2i + 1)^4} \leq \frac{2(D_{i,x} - (i-1)^2/2^n)^2}{2^{4n}},$$

where the last inequality is due to the fact that $i \leq q \leq 2^{n-4}$. From Eq. (17),

$$\begin{aligned}\mathbf{E}[\chi^2(\boldsymbol{X}_{i-1})] &\leq \sum_{x \in \{0,1\}^n} 2^n \cdot \mathbf{E}\Big[(Y_{i,x} - 1/2^n)^2\Big] \\ &\leq \frac{2}{2^{3n}} \sum_{x \in \{0,1\}^n} \mathbf{E}\Big[\Big(D_{i,x} - \frac{(i-1)^2}{2^n}\Big)^2\Big].\end{aligned}$$

We will show that for any $x \in \{0,1\}^n$,

$$\mathbf{E}\Big[\Big(D_{i,x} - \frac{(i-1)^2}{2^n}\Big)^2\Big] \le \frac{(i-1)^2}{2^n}, \tag{18}$$

and thus

$$\mathbf{E}[\chi^2(\boldsymbol{X}_{i-1})] \le \frac{2(i-1)^2}{2^{3n}} .$$

Summing up, from Lemma 3,

$$\begin{aligned}(\|\mathsf{ps}_{0,A}(\cdot) - \mathsf{ps}_{1,A}(\cdot)\|)^2 &\le \frac{1}{2}\sum_{i=1}^{q} \mathbf{E}[\chi^2(X_{i-1})] \\ &\le \sum_{i=1}^{q} \frac{(i-1)^2}{2^{3n}} \le \frac{q^3}{2^{3n}}.\end{aligned}$$

We now justify (18). Fix $x \in \{0,1\}^n$. For each $j \le i-1$, let B_j be the Bernoulli random variable such that $B_j = 1$ if and only if $V_j \oplus x \in S'$. Then $D_{i,x} = B_1 + \cdots + B_{i-1}$. Moreover, for each $j \le i-1$, we have $\mathbf{E}[B_j] = (i-1)/2^n$, because marginally, V_j is uniformly distributed in $\{0,1\}^n$ independent of $U_1, \ldots, U_{i-1}$. Then

$$\mathbf{E}[D_{i,x}] = \sum_{j=1}^{i-1} \mathbf{E}[B_j] = \frac{(i-1)^2}{2^n}.$$

Note that

$$\begin{aligned}\mathbf{E}\Big[\Big(D_{i,x} - \frac{(i-1)^2}{2^n}\Big)^2\Big] &= \mathbf{Var}(D_{i,x}) = \mathbf{E}[(D_{i,x})^2] - (\mathbf{E}[D_{i,x}])^2 \\ &= \mathbf{E}[(D_{i,x})^2] - \frac{(i-1)^4}{2^{2n}}.\end{aligned} \tag{19}$$

On the other hand,

$$\begin{aligned}(D_{i,x})^2 &= \Big(\sum_{j=1}^{i-1} B_j\Big)^2 \\ &= (B_1^2 + \cdots + B_{i-1}^2) + 2 \sum_{1 \le j < k \le i-1} B_j B_k \\ &= (B_1 + \cdots + B_{i-1}) + 2 \sum_{1 \le j < k \le i-1} B_j B_k,\end{aligned}$$

where the last equality is due to the fact that $R^2 = R$ for any Bernoulli random variable R. Taking expectation of both sides gives us

$$\mathbf{E}[(D_{i,x})^2] = \frac{(i-1)^2}{2^n} + 2 \sum_{1 \le j < k \le i-1} \mathbf{E}[B_j B_k].$$

We claim that for any $1 \le j < k \le i$, we have

$$\mathbf{E}[B_j B_k] = \frac{(i-1)(i-2)}{2^n(2^n-1)} \tag{20}$$

and thus

$$\mathbf{E}[(D_{i,x})^2] = \frac{(i-1)^2}{2^n} + \frac{(i-1)^2(i-2)^2}{2^n(2^n-1)}.$$

Combing this with (19) we have

$$\begin{aligned}\mathbf{E}\Big[\Big(D_{i,x} - \frac{(i-1)^2}{2^n}\Big)^2\Big] &= \frac{(i-1)^2}{2^n} + \frac{(i-1)^2(i-2)^2}{2^n(2^n-1)} - \frac{(i-1)^4}{2^{2n}}\\ &\le \frac{(i-1)^2}{2^n}.\end{aligned}$$

What remains is to justify (20). Note that given S' and V_j, we have $V_k \oplus x \in S'$ with condition probability $(i-2)/(2^n-1)$ if $V_j \oplus x \in S'$, and with conditional probability $(i-1)/(2^n-1)$ otherwise. That is, given B_j, the random variable B_k takes value 1 with conditional probability $(i-1-B_j)/(2^n-1)$. Hence

$$\begin{aligned}\mathbf{E}[B_j B_k] = \mathbf{E}\Big[B_j \frac{(i-1-B_j)}{2^n-1}\Big] &= \frac{(i-1)\cdot\mathbf{E}[B_j]}{2^n-1} - \frac{\mathbf{E}[B_j^2]}{2^n-1}\\ &= \frac{(i-1)\cdot\mathbf{E}[B_j]}{2^n-1} - \frac{\mathbf{E}[B_j]}{2^n-1} = \frac{(i-2)(i-1)}{2^n(2^n-1)}.\end{aligned}$$

This completes the proof. □

References

1. Bai, S., Langlois, A., Lepoint, T., Stehlé, D., Steinfeld, R.: Improved security proofs in lattice-based cryptography: using the Rényi divergence rather than the statistical distance. In: Iwata, T., Cheon, J.H. (eds.) ASIACRYPT 2015. LNCS, vol. 9452, pp. 3–24. Springer, Heidelberg (2015). doi:10.1007/978-3-662-48797-6_1
2. Bellare, M., Impagliazzo, R.: A tool for obtaining tighter security analyses of pseudorandom function based constructions, with applications to PRP to PRF conversion. Cryptology ePrint Archive, Report 1999/024 (1999). http://eprint.iacr.org/1999/024
3. Bellare, M., Ristenpart, T., Rogaway, P., Stegers, T.: Format-preserving encryption. In: Jacobson, M.J., Rijmen, V., Safavi-Naini, R. (eds.) SAC 2009. LNCS, vol. 5867, pp. 295–312. Springer, Heidelberg (2009). doi:10.1007/978-3-642-05445-7_19
4. Bellare, M., Rogaway, P.: The security of triple encryption and a framework for code-based game-playing proofs. In: Vaudenay, S. (ed.) EUROCRYPT 2006. LNCS, vol. 4004, pp. 409–426. Springer, Heidelberg (2006). doi:10.1007/11761679_25
5. Bernstein, D.J.: How to stretch random functions: the security of protected counter sums. J. Cryptol. **12**(3), 185–192 (1999)
6. Chen, S., Steinberger, J.: Tight security bounds for key-alternating ciphers. In: Nguyen, P.Q., Oswald, E. (eds.) EUROCRYPT 2014. LNCS, vol. 8441, pp. 327–350. Springer, Heidelberg (2014). doi:10.1007/978-3-642-55220-5_19

7. Chung, K.-M., Pass, R.: Tight parallel repetition theorems for public-coin arguments using KL-divergence. In: Dodis, Y., Nielsen, J.B. (eds.) TCC 2015. LNCS, vol. 9015, pp. 229–246. Springer, Heidelberg (2015). doi:10.1007/978-3-662-46497-7_9
8. Chung, K.-M., Vadhan, S.: Tight bounds for hashing block sources. In: Goel, A., Jansen, K., Rolim, J.D.P., Rubinfeld, R. (eds.) APPROX/RANDOM - 2008. LNCS, vol. 5171, pp. 357–370. Springer, Heidelberg (2008). doi:10.1007/978-3-540-85363-3_29
9. Cogliati, B., Lampe, R., Patarin, J.: The indistinguishability of the XOR of k permutations. In: Cid, C., Rechberger, C. (eds.) FSE 2014. LNCS, vol. 8540, pp. 285–302. Springer, Heidelberg (2015). doi:10.1007/978-3-662-46706-0_15
10. Cogliati, B., Seurin, Y.: EWCDM: an efficient, beyond-birthday secure, nonce-misuse resistant MAC. In: Robshaw, M., Katz, J. (eds.) CRYPTO 2016. LNCS, vol. 9814, pp. 121–149. Springer, Heidelberg (2016). doi:10.1007/978-3-662-53018-4_5
11. Even, S., Mansour, Y.: A construction of a cipher from a single pseudorandom permutation. J. Cryptol. **10**(3), 151–162 (1997)
12. Hall, C., Wagner, D., Kelsey, J., Schneier, B.: Building PRFs from PRPs. In: Krawczyk, H. (ed.) CRYPTO 1998. LNCS, vol. 1462, pp. 370–389. Springer, Heidelberg (1998). doi:10.1007/BFb0055742
13. Hoang, V.T., Morris, B., Rogaway, P.: An enciphering scheme based on a card shuffle. In: Safavi-Naini, R., Canetti, R. (eds.) CRYPTO 2012. LNCS, vol. 7417, pp. 1–13. Springer, Heidelberg (2012). doi:10.1007/978-3-642-32009-5_1
14. Hoang, V.T., Tessaro, S.: Key-alternating ciphers and key-length extension: exact bounds and multi-user security. In: Robshaw, M., Katz, J. (eds.) CRYPTO 2016. LNCS, vol. 9814, pp. 3–32. Springer, Heidelberg (2016). doi:10.1007/978-3-662-53018-4_1
15. Iwata, T.: New blockcipher modes of operation with beyond the birthday bound security. In: Robshaw, M. (ed.) FSE 2006. LNCS, vol. 4047, pp. 310–327. Springer, Heidelberg (2006). doi:10.1007/11799313_20
16. Luby, M., Rackoff, C.: How to construct pseudorandom permutations from pseudorandom functions. SIAM J. Comput. **17**(2), 373–386 (1988)
17. Lucks, S.: The sum of PRPs is a secure PRF. In: Preneel, B. (ed.) EUROCRYPT 2000. LNCS, vol. 1807, pp. 470–484. Springer, Heidelberg (2000). doi:10.1007/3-540-45539-6_34
18. Maurer, U.M.: A simplified and generalized treatment of luby-rackoff pseudorandom permutation generators. In: Rueppel, R.A. (ed.) EUROCRYPT 1992. LNCS, vol. 658, pp. 239–255. Springer, Heidelberg (1993). doi:10.1007/3-540-47555-9_21
19. Maurer, U.: Indistinguishability of random systems. In: Knudsen, L.R. (ed.) EUROCRYPT 2002. LNCS, vol. 2332, pp. 110–132. Springer, Heidelberg (2002). doi:10.1007/3-540-46035-7_8
20. Maurer, U., Pietrzak, K., Renner, R.: Indistinguishability amplification. In: Menezes, A. (ed.) CRYPTO 2007. LNCS, vol. 4622, pp. 130–149. Springer, Heidelberg (2007). doi:10.1007/978-3-540-74143-5_8
21. Mennink, B., Neves, S.: Encrypted Davies-Meyer and its dual: towards optimal security using mirror theory. In: Katz, J., Shacham, H. (eds.) CRYPTO 2017, Part III. LNCS, pp. 556–583. Springer, Cham (2017)
22. Morris, B., Rogaway, P.: Sometimes-recurse shuffle. In: Nguyen, P.Q., Oswald, E. (eds.) EUROCRYPT 2014. LNCS, vol. 8441, pp. 311–326. Springer, Heidelberg (2014). doi:10.1007/978-3-642-55220-5_18

23. Nandi, M.: A simple and unified method of proving indistinguishability. In: Barua, R., Lange, T. (eds.) INDOCRYPT 2006. LNCS, vol. 4329, pp. 317–334. Springer, Heidelberg (2006). doi:10.1007/11941378_23
24. Patarin, J.: A proof of security in $O(2^n)$ for the Xor of two random permutations. In: Safavi-Naini, R. (ed.) ICITS 2008. LNCS, vol. 5155, pp. 232–248. Springer, Heidelberg (2008). doi:10.1007/978-3-540-85093-9_22
25. Patarin, J.: The "Coefficients H" technique. In: Avanzi, R.M., Keliher, L., Sica, F. (eds.) SAC 2008. LNCS, vol. 5381, pp. 328–345. Springer, Heidelberg (2009). doi:10.1007/978-3-642-04159-4_21
26. Patarin, J.: Introduction to mirror theory: analysis of systems of linear equalities and linear non equalities for cryptography. Cryptology ePrint Archive, Report 2010/287 (2010). http://eprint.iacr.org/2010/287
27. Pietrzak, K.: Composition does not imply adaptive security. In: Shoup, V. (ed.) CRYPTO 2005. LNCS, vol. 3621, pp. 55–65. Springer, Heidelberg (2005). doi:10.1007/11535218_4
28. Raz, R.: A parallel repetition theorem. SIAM J. Comput. **27**(3), 763–803 (1998)
29. Renner, R.: On the variational distance of independently repeated experiments. CoRR, abs/cs/0509013 (2005)
30. Ristenpart, T., Yilek, S.: The mix-and-cut shuffle: small-domain encryption secure against N queries. In: Canetti, R., Garay, J.A. (eds.) CRYPTO 2013. LNCS, vol. 8042, pp. 392–409. Springer, Heidelberg (2013). doi:10.1007/978-3-642-40041-4_22
31. Steinberger, J.: Improved security bounds for key-alternating ciphers via hellinger distance. Cryptology ePrint Archive, Report 2012/481 (2012). http://eprint.iacr.org/2012/481

Indifferentiability of Iterated Even-Mansour Ciphers with Non-idealized Key-Schedules: Five Rounds Are Necessary and Sufficient

Yuanxi Dai[1](✉), Yannick Seurin[2], John Steinberger[1], and Aishwarya Thiruvengadam[3]

[1] Tsinghua University, Beijing, People's Republic of China
dyx13@mails.tsinghua.edu.cn, jpsteinb@gmail.com
[2] ANSSI, Paris, France
yannick.seurin@m4x.org
[3] University of Maryland, College Park, USA
aish@cs.umd.edu

Abstract. We prove that the 5-round iterated Even-Mansour (IEM) construction with a non-idealized key-schedule (such as the trivial key-schedule, where all round keys are equal) is indifferentiable from an ideal cipher. In a separate result, we also prove that five rounds are necessary by describing an attack against the corresponding 4-round construction. This closes the gap regarding the exact number of rounds for which the IEM construction with a non-idealized key-schedule is indifferentiable from an ideal cipher, which was previously only known to lie between four and twelve. Moreover, the security bound we achieve is comparable to (in fact, slightly better than) the previously established 12-round bound.

Keywords: Key-alternating cipher · Iterated Even-Mansour construction · Indifferentiability

1 Introduction

BACKGROUND. A large number of block ciphers are so-called *key-alternating ciphers*. Such block ciphers alternatively apply two types of transformations to the current state: the addition (usually bitwise) of a secret key and the application of a public permutation. In more detail, an r-round key-alternating cipher with message space $\{0,1\}^n$ is a transformation of the form

$$y = k_r \oplus P_r(k_{r-1} \oplus P_{r-1}(\cdots P_2(k_1 \oplus P_1(k_0 \oplus x))\cdots)), \qquad (1)$$

where $(k_0, \ldots, k_r)$ are n-bit round keys (usually derived from a master key k of size close to n), where $P_1, \ldots, P_r$ are fixed, key-independent permutations and

J. Katz and H. Shacham (Eds.): CRYPTO 2017, Part III, LNCS 10403, pp. 524–555, 2017.
DOI: 10.1007/978-3-319-63697-9_18

where x and y are the plaintext and ciphertext, respectively. In particular, virtually all[1] SPNs (*Substitution-Permutation Networks*) have this form, including, e.g., the AES family.

A recent trend has been to analyze this class of block ciphers in the so-called Random Permutation Model (RPM), which models the permutations $P_1, \ldots, P_r$ as oracles that the adversary can only query (from both sides) in a black-box way, each behaving as a perfectly random permutation. This approach allows to assert the nonexistence of *generic attacks*, i.e., attacks not exploiting the particular structure of "concrete" permutations endowed with short descriptions. This approach dates back to Even and Mansour [25] who studied the case $r = 1$. For this reason, construction (1), once seen as a way to define a block cipher from an arbitrary tuple of permutations $\mathbf{P} = (P_1, \ldots, P_r)$, is often called the *iterated Even-Mansour (IEM) construction*. The general case of $r \geq 2$ rounds was only considered more than 20 years later in a series of papers [11–13,31,37,45], primarily focusing on the standard security notion for block ciphers, namely pseudorandomness, which requires that no computationally bounded adversary with (usually two-sided) black-box access to a permutation can distinguish whether it is interacting with the block cipher under a random key or a perfectly random permutation. Pseudorandomness of the IEM construction with independent round keys is by now well understood, the security bound increasing beyond the "birthday bound" (the original bound proved for the 1-round Even-Mansour construction [24,25]) as the number of rounds increases [13,31].

THE IDEAL CIPHER MODEL. Although pseudorandomness has been the primary security requirement for a block cipher, in some cases this property is not enough to establish the security of higher-level cryptosystems using the block cipher. For example, the security of some real-world authenticated encryption protocols such as 3GPP confidentiality and integrity protocols f8 and f9 [33] rely on the stronger block cipher security notion of *indistinguishability under related-key attacks* [3,7]. Problems also arise in the context of block-cipher based hash functions [36,42] where the adversary can control both the message and the key of the block cipher, and hence can exploit "known-key" or "chosen-key" attacks [8,35] in order to break the collision- or preimage-resistance of the hash function.

Hence, cryptographers have come to view a good block cipher as something close to an *ideal cipher (IC)*, i.e., a family of 2^κ uniformly random and independent permutations, where κ is the key-length of the block cipher. Perhaps not surprisingly, this view turned out to be very fruitful for proving the security of constructions based on a block cipher when the PRP assumption is not enough [4,6,10,22,28,34,41,46], an approach often called the *ideal cipher model (ICM)*. This ultimately remains a heuristic approach, as one can construct (artificial) schemes that are secure in the ICM but insecure for any concrete instantiation of the block cipher, similarly to the random oracle model [5,9,27]. On

[1] Some SPNs do not adhere to the key-alternating abstraction because they introduce the key at the permutation stage as well—e.g., by using keyed S-boxes.

the other hand, a proof in the ideal cipher model is typically considered a good indication of security from the point of view of practice.

INDIFFERENTIABILITY. While an IC remains unachievable in the standard model for reasons stated above (and which boil down to basic considerations on the amount of entropy in the system), it remains an interesting problem to "build" ICs (secure in some provable sense) from *other* ideal primitives. This is precisely the approach taken by the indifferentiability framework, introduced by Maurer et al. [40] and popularized by Coron et al. [17]. Indifferentiability is a simulation-based framework that helps assess whether a construction of a target primitive A (e.g., a block cipher) from a lower-level ideal primitive B (e.g., for the IEM construction, a small number of random permutations $P_1, \ldots, P_r$) is "structurally close" to the ideal version of A (e.g., an IC). Indifferentiability comes equipped with a composition theorem [40] which implies that a large class of protocols (see [21,43] for restrictions) are provably secure in the ideal-B model if and only if they are provably secure in the ideal-A model.

We note that indifferentiability does not presuppose the presence of a private key; indeed, a number of indifferentiability proofs concern the construction of a keyless primitive (such as a hash function, compression function or permutation) from a lower-level primitive [1,17,32]. In the case of a block cipher, thus, the key is "just another input" to the construction.

PREVIOUS RESULTS. Two papers have previously explored the indifferentiability of the IEM construction from an ideal cipher, modeling the underlying permutations as random permutations. Andreeva et al. [1] showed that the 5-round IEM construction with an idealized key-schedule (i.e., the function(s) mapping the master key onto the round key(s) are modeled as random oracles) is indifferentiable from an IC. Lampe and Seurin [38] showed that the 12-round IEM construction with the trivial key-schedule, i.e., in which all round keys are equal, is also indifferentiable from an IC. Moreover, both papers included impossibility results for the indifferentiability of the 3-round IEM construction with a trivial key-schedule, showing that at least four rounds must be necessary in that context. In both settings, the question of the exact number of rounds needed to make the IEM construction indifferentiable from an ideal cipher remained open.

OUR RESULTS. We improve both the positive and negative results for the indifferentiability of the IEM construction with the trivial (and more generally, non-idealized) key-schedule. Specifically, we show an attack on the 4-round IEM construction, and prove that the 5-round IEM construction is indifferentiable from an IC, in both cases for the trivial key-schedule.[2] Hence, our work resolves the question of the exact number of rounds needed for the IEM construction with a non-idealized key-schedule to achieve indifferentiability from an IC.

[2] Actually we consider a slight variant of the trivial key-schedule where the first and last round keys are omitted, but both our negative and positive results are straightforward to extend to the "standard" trivial key-schedule. See Sect. 2 for a discussion.

Our 4-round impossibility result improves on the afore-mentioned 3-round impossibility results [1,38]. It can be seen as an extension of the attack against the 3-round IEM with the trivial key-schedule [38]. However, unlike this 3-round attack, our 4-round attack does not merely consist in finding a tuple of key/plaintext/ciphertext triples for the construction satisfying a so-called "evasive" relation (i.e., a relation which is hard to find with only black-box access to an ideal cipher, e.g., a triple (k, x, y) such that $x \oplus y = 0$). Instead, it relies on relations on the "internal" variables of the construction (which makes the attack harder to analyze rigorously). We note that a simple "evasive-relation-finding" attack against four rounds had previously been excluded by Cogliati and Seurin [14] (in technical terms, they proved that the 4-round IEM construction is *sequentially*-indifferentiable from an IC, see the remark after Theorem 1 in Sect. 3) so the extra complexity of our 4-round attack is in a sense inevitable.

Our 5-round feasibility result can be seen as improving both the 5-round result for the IEM construction with idealized key-schedules [1] (albeit see the fine-grained metrics below) and on the 12-round feasibility result for the IEM construction with the trivial key-schedule [38]. Our simulator runs in time $O(q^5)$, makes $O(q^5)$ IC queries, and achieves security $2^{41} \cdot q^{12}/2^n$, where q is the number of distinguisher queries. By comparison, these metrics are respectively

$$O(q^3),\ O(q^2),\ 2^{34} \cdot q^{10}/2^n$$

for the 5-round simulator of Andreeva et al. [1] with idealized key-schedule, and

$$O(q^4),\ O(q^4),\ 2^{91} \cdot q^{12}/2^n$$

for the 12-round simulator of Lampe and Seurin [38]. Hence, as far as the security bound is concerned at least, we achieve a slight improvement over the previous (most directly comparable) work.

A Glimpse at the Simulator. Our 5-round simulator follows the traditional "chain detection/completion" paradigm, pioneered by Coron et al. [16,18,32] for proving indifferentiability of the Feistel construction, which has since been used for the IEM construction as well [1,38]. However, it is, in a sense, conceptually simpler and more "systematic" than previous simulators for the IEM construction (something we pay for by a more complex "termination" proof). In a nutshell, our new 5-round simulator detects and completes *any* path of length 3, where a path is a sequence of adjacent permutation queries "chained" by the same key (and which might "wrap around" the ideal cipher). In contrast, the 12-round simulator of [38] used a much more parsimonious chain detection strategy (inherited from [16,18,32,44]) which allowed a much simpler termination argument.

Once a tentative simulator has been determined, the indifferentiability proof usually entails two technical challenges: on the one hand, proving that the simulator works hard enough to ensure that it will never be trapped in an inconsistency, and on the other hand, proving that it does not work in more than polynomial time. Finding the right balance between these two requirements is at the heart of the design of a suitable simulator.

The proof that our new 5-round simulator remains consistent with the IC roughly follows the same ideas as in previous indifferentiability proofs. In short, since the simulator completes all paths of length 3, at the moment the distinguisher makes a permutation query, only incomplete paths of length at most two can exist. Hence any incomplete path has three "free" adjacent positions, two of which (the ones on the edge) will be sampled at random, while the middle one will be adapted to match the IC. The most delicate part consists in proving that no path of length 3 can appear "unexpectedly" and remain unnoticed by the simulator (which will therefore not complete it), except with negligible probability.

The more innovative part of our proof lies in the "termination argument", i.e., in proving that the simulator is efficient and that the recursive chain detection/completion process does not "chain react" beyond a fixed polynomial bound. As in many previous termination arguments [16,18,23,32,44], we first observe that certain types of paths (namely those that wrap around the IC) are only ever detected and completed if the distinguisher made the corresponding IC query. Hence, assuming the distinguisher makes at most q queries, at most q such paths will be triggered and completed. In virtually all previous indifferentiability proofs, this fact easily allows to upper bound the size of permutation histories for all other "detect zones" used by the simulator, and hence to upper bound the total number of paths that will ever be detected and completed. (Indeed, all of the indifferentiability results in the afore-mentioned list actually have quite simple termination arguments!) But in the case of our 5-round simulator, this observation only allows us to upper bound the size of the middle permutation P_3, which by itself is not sufficient to upper bound the number of other detected paths. To push the argument further, we make some additional observations—essentially, that every triggered path that is not a "wraparound" path associated to some distinguisher query is uniquely (i.e., injectively) associated to one of: (i) a pair of P_3 and P_1 entries, where the P_1 entry was directly queried by the distinguisher, or (ii) symmetrically, a pair of P_3 and P_5 entries, where the P_5 entry was directly queried by the distinguisher, or (iii) a *pair* of P_3 entries. (In some sense, the crucial "trick" that allows to fall back on (iii) in all other cases is the observation that every query that is left over from a previous query cycle and that is not the direct result of a distinguisher query is in a completed path, and this completed path contains a query at P_3.) This suffices, because the distinguisher makes only q queries and because of the afore-mentioned bound on the size of P_3. In order to show that the association described above is truly injective, a structural property of P_2 and P_4 is needed, namely that the table maintaining answers of the simulator for P_2 (resp. P_4) never contains 4 distinct input/output pairs $(x^{(i)}, y^{(i)})$, such that $\bigoplus_{1 \le i \le 4}(x^{(i)} \oplus y^{(i)}) = 0$. Since some queries are "adapted" to fit the IC, proving this part ends up being a source of some tedium as well.

Related Work. Several papers have studied security properties of the IEM construction that are stronger than pseudorandomness yet weaker than indifferentiability, such as resistance to related-key [14,26], known-key [2,15], or chosen-key attacks [14,29]. A recent preprint shows that the 3-round IEM construction with a (non-invertible) idealized key-schedule is indifferentiable from an IC [30]. This complements our work by settling the problem analogous to ours in the case of idealized key-schedules. In both cases, the main open question is whether the concrete indifferentiability bounds (which are typically poor) can be improved.

ORGANIZATION. Preliminary definitions are given in Sect. 2. The attack against the 4-round IEM construction is given in Sect. 3. Our 5-round simulator is described in Sect. 4, while the indifferentiability proof is in Sect. 5.

2 Preliminaries

Throughout the paper, n will denote the block length of permutations $P_1, \ldots, P_r$ of the IEM construction and will play the role of security parameter for asymptotic statements. Given a finite non-empty set S, we write $s \leftarrow_{\$} S$ to mean that an element is drawn uniformly at random from S and assigned to s.

A *distinguisher* is an oracle algorithm $\mathcal{D}$ with oracle access to a finite list of oracles $(\mathcal{O}_1, \mathcal{O}_2, \ldots)$ and that outputs a single bit b, which we denote $\mathcal{D}^{\mathcal{O}_1, \mathcal{O}_2, \ldots} = b$ or $\mathcal{D}[\mathcal{O}_1, \mathcal{O}_2, \ldots] = b$.

A block cipher with key space $\{0,1\}^\kappa$ and message space $\{0,1\}^n$ is a mapping $E : \{0,1\}^\kappa \times \{0,1\}^n \to \{0,1\}^n$ such that for any key $k \in \{0,1\}^\kappa$, $x \mapsto E(k,x)$ is a permutation. An ideal cipher with block length n and key length κ is a block cipher drawn uniformly at random from the set of all block ciphers with block length n and key length κ.

THE IEM CONSTRUCTION. Fix integers $n, r \geq 1$. Let $\mathbf{f} = (f_0, \ldots, f_r)$ be a $(r+1)$-tuple of functions from $\{0,1\}^n$ to $\{0,1\}^n$. The r-round iterated Even-Mansour construction $\mathrm{EM}[n, r, \mathbf{f}]$ specifies, from any r-tuple $\mathbf{P} = (P_1, \ldots, P_r)$ of permutations of $\{0,1\}^n$, a block cipher with n-bit keys and n-bit messages, simply denoted $\mathrm{EM}^{\mathbf{P}}$ in all the following (parameters $[n, r, \mathbf{f}]$ will always be clear from the context), which maps a plaintext $x \in \{0,1\}^n$ and a key $k \in \{0,1\}^n$ to the ciphertext defined by

$$\mathrm{EM}^{\mathbf{P}}(k,x) = f_r(k) \oplus P_r(f_{r-1}(k) \oplus P_{r-1}(\cdots P_2(f_1(k) \oplus P_1(f_0(k) \oplus x)) \cdots)).$$

We say that the key-schedule is *trivial* when all f_i's are the identity.

Note that the first and last key additions do not play any role for indifferentiability where the key is just a "public" input to the construction, much like the plaintext/ciphertext. What provides security are the random permutations, that remain secret for inputs that have not been queried by the attacker. So, we will focus on a slight variant of the trivial key-schedule where $f_0 = f_r = 0$ (see Fig. 1), but our results carry over to the trivial key-schedule (and more generally to any non-idealized key-schedule where the f_i's are permutations on $\{0,1\}^n$).

INDIFFERENTIABILITY. We recall the standard definition of indifferentiability for the IEM construction.

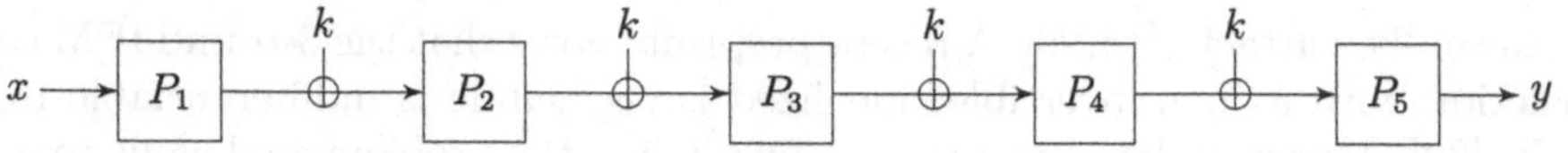

Fig. 1. The 5-round iterated Even-Mansour construction with independent permutations and identical round keys. The first and last round key additions are omitted since they do not play any role for the indifferentiability property.

Definition 1. The construction $\mathrm{EM}^{\mathbf{P}}$ with access to an r-tuple $\mathbf{P} = (P_1, \ldots, P_r)$ of random permutations is $(t_{\mathcal{S}}, q_{\mathcal{S}}, \varepsilon)$-*indifferentiable* from an ideal cipher IC if there exists a simulator $\mathcal{S} = \mathcal{S}(q)$ such that $\mathcal{S}$ runs in total time $t_{\mathcal{S}}$ and makes at most $q_{\mathcal{S}}$ queries to IC, and such that

$$\left| \Pr[D^{\mathrm{EM}^{\mathbf{P}},\mathbf{P}} = 1] - \Pr[D^{\mathrm{IC},\mathcal{S}^{\mathrm{IC}}} = 1] \right| \leq \varepsilon$$

for every (information-theoretic) distinguisher D making at most q queries in total.

We say that the r-round IEM construction is indifferentiable from an ideal cipher if for any q polynomial in n, it is $(t_{\mathcal{S}}, q_{\mathcal{S}}, \varepsilon)$-indifferentiable from an ideal cipher with $t_{\mathcal{S}}, q_{\mathcal{S}}$ polynomial in n and ε negligible in n.

Remark 1. Definition 1 allows the simulator $\mathcal{S}$ to depend on the number of queries q. In fact, our simulator (cf. Figs. 4 and 5) does not depend on q, but is efficient only with high probability. In the full version of the paper [19], we discuss an optimized implementation of our simulator that, among others, uses knowledge of q to abort whenever its runtime exceeds the limit of a "good" execution, thus ensuring that it is efficient with probability 1.

3 Attack Against 4-Round Simulators

We describe an attack against the 4-round IEM construction, improving previous attacks against 3 rounds [1,38]. Consider the distinguisher $\mathcal{D}$ whose pseudocode is given in Fig. 2 (see also Fig. 3 for an illustration of the attack). This distinguisher can query the permutations/simulator through the interface $\mathrm{Query}(i, \delta, z)$, and the EM construction/ideal cipher through interfaces $\mathrm{Enc}(k, x)$ and $\mathrm{Dec}(k, y)$.

We prove that $\mathcal{D}$ has advantage close to 1/2 against any simulator making a polynomial number of queries to the IC. More formally, we have the following result, whose proof can be found in the full version of the paper [19]:

Theorem 1. *Let $\mathcal{S}$ be any simulator making at most σ IC queries when interacting with $\mathcal{D}$. Then the advantage of $\mathcal{D}$ in distinguishing* $(\mathrm{EM}^{\mathbf{P}}, \mathbf{P})$ *and* $(\mathrm{IC}, \mathcal{S}^{\mathrm{IC}})$ *is at least*

$$\frac{1}{2} - \frac{4\sigma}{2^n} - \frac{7}{2^n}.$$

1   $y_3 \leftarrow_\$ \{0,1\}^n$

2   $x_4 \leftarrow_\$ \{0,1\}^n$

3   $x_4' \leftarrow_\$ \{0,1\}^n \setminus \{x_4\}$

4   $k := y_3 \oplus x_4$

5   $k' := y_3 \oplus x_4'$

6   $y_4 := \text{Query}(4, +, x_4)$

7   $y_4' := \text{Query}(4, +, x_4')$

8   $x_1 := \text{Dec}(k, y_4)$

9   $x_1' := \text{Dec}(k', y_4')$

10 if $x_1 = x_1'$ then

11   return 0

12 $y_1 := \text{Query}(1, +, x_1)$

13 $y_1' := \text{Query}(1, +, x_1')$

14 $x_2 := y_1 \oplus k$

15 $x_2' := y_1' \oplus k'$

16 $k'' := y_1 \oplus x_2'$

17 $k''' := k'' \oplus k \oplus k'$

18 $y_4'' := \text{Enc}(k'', x_1)$

19 $y_4''' := \text{Enc}(k''', x_1')$

20 if y_4, y_4', y_4'', y_4''' are not distinct then

21   return 0

22 draw $b \leftarrow_\$ \{0,1\}$

23 if $b = 1$ then

24      $y_4'' \leftarrow_\$ \{0,1\}^n \setminus \{y_4, y_4'\}$

25      $y_4''' \leftarrow_\$ \{0,1\}^n \setminus \{y_4, y_4', y_4''\}$

26 $x_4'' := \text{Query}(4, -, y_4'')$

27 $x_4''' := \text{Query}(4, -, y_4''')$

28 if $b = 0$ then

29   return $x_4'' \oplus x_4''' = x_4 \oplus x_4'$

30 else $(b = 1)$

31   return $x_4'' \oplus x_4''' \neq x_4 \oplus x_4'$

Fig. 2. Pseudocode of the attack against the 4-round IEM construction.

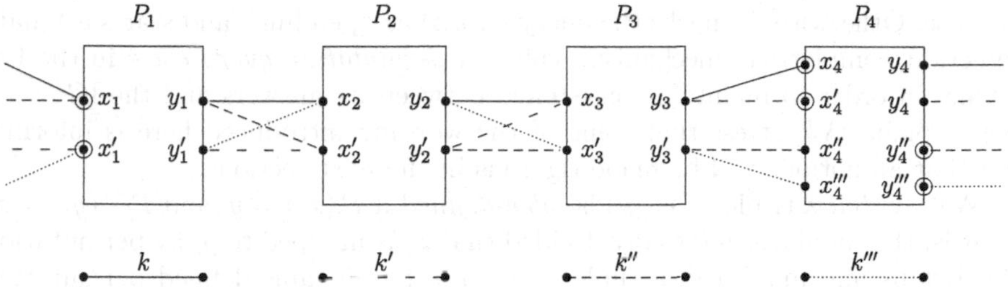

Fig. 3. Illustration of the attack against the 4-round IEM construction. The circled dots correspond to queries made by the distinguisher to the permutations/simulator.

As an additional remark, say that a distinguisher is *sequential* [14,39] if it first queries only its right interface (random permutations/simulator), and then only its left interface (IEM construction/ideal cipher), but not its right interface anymore. Many "natural" attacks against indifferentiability are sequential (in particular, the attack against 5-round Feistel of [18] and the attack against 3-round IEM of [38]), running in two phases: first, the distinguisher looks for input/output pairs satisfying some relation which is hard to satisfy for an ideal cipher (a so-called "evasive" relation) by querying the right interface; then, it checks consistency of these input/output pairs by querying the left interface (since the relation is hard to satisfy for an ideal cipher, any polynomially-bounded simulator will fail to consistently simulate the inner permutations in the ideal world). We note that the attack described in this section is *not* sequential. This does not come as a surprise since Cogliati and Seurin [14] showed that the 4-round IEM construction is *sequentially* indifferentiable from an IC, i.e., indifferentiable from an IC by any sequential distinguisher. Hence, our new attack yields a natural separation between (full) indifferentiability and sequential indifferentiability.

4 The 5-Round Simulator

We start with a high-level overview of how the simulator $\mathcal{S}$ works, deferring the formal description in pseudocode to Sect. 4.1. For each $i \in \{1, \ldots, 5\}$, the simulator maintains a pair of tables P_i and P_i^{-1} with 2^n entries containing either an n-bit value or a special symbol $\perp$, allowing the simulator to keep track of values that have already been assigned internally for the i-th permutation. Initially, these tables are empty, meaning that $P_i(x) = P_i^{-1}(y) = \perp$ for all $x, y \in \{0,1\}^n$. The simulator sets $P_i(x) \leftarrow y$, $P_i^{-1}(y) \leftarrow x$ to indicate that the i-th permutation maps x to y. The simulator never overwrites entries in P_i or P_i^{-1}, and always keeps these two tables consistent, so that P_i always encodes a "partial permutation" of $\{0,1\}^n$. We sometimes write $x \in P_i$ (resp. $y \in P_i^{-1}$) to mean that $P_i(x) \neq \perp$ (resp. $P_i^{-1}(y) \neq \perp$).

The simulator offers a single public interface $\text{Query}(i, \delta, z)$ allowing the distinguisher to request the value $P_i(z)$ when $\delta = +$ or $P_i^{-1}(z)$ when $\delta = -$ for $z \in \{0,1\}^n$. Upon reception of a query (i, δ, z), the simulator checks whether $P_i^\delta(z)$ has already been defined, and returns the corresponding value if this is the case. Otherwise, it marks the query (i, δ, z) as "pending" and starts a "chain detection/completion" mechanism, called a *permutation query cycle* in the following, in order to maintain consistency between its answers and the IC as we now explain. (We stress that some of the wording introduced here is informal and that all notions will be made rigorous in the next sections.)

We say that a triple (i, x_i, y_i) is *table-defined* if $P_i(x_i) = y_i$ and $P_i^{-1}(y_i) = x_i$ (that is, the simulator internally decided that x_i is mapped to y_i by permutation P_i). Let us informally call a tuple of $j - i + 1 \geq 2$ table-defined permutation queries at adjacent positions $((i, x_i, y_i), \ldots, (j, x_j, y_j))$ (indices taken mod 5) such that $x_{i+1} = y_i \oplus k$ if $i \neq 5$ and $x_{i+1} = \text{IC}^{-1}(k, y_i)$ if $i = 5$ a "k-path of length $j + i - 1$" (hence, paths might "wrap around" the IC).

The very simple idea at the heart of the simulator is that, before answering any query of the distinguisher to some simulated permutation, it ensures that any path of length three (or more) has been preemptively extended to a "complete" path of length five $((1, x_1, y_1), \ldots, (5, x_5, y_5))$ compatible with the ideal cipher (i.e., such that $\text{IC}(k, x_1) = y_5$). For this, assume that at the moment the distinguisher makes a permutation query (i, δ, z) which is not table-defined yet (otherwise the simulator just returns the existing answer), any path of length three is complete. This means that any existing incomplete path has length at most two. These length-2 paths will be called (table-defined[3]) *2chains* in the main body of the proof, and will play a central role. For ease of the discussion to come, let us call the pair of adjacent positions $(i, i+1)$ of the table-defined queries constituting a 2chain the *type* of the 2chain. (Note that as any path, a 2chain can "wrap around", i.e., consists of two table-defined queries $(5, x_5, y_5)$ and $(1, x_1, y_1)$ such that $\text{IC}(k, x_1) = y_5$, so that possible types are $(1,2)$, $(2,3)$, $(3,4)$, $(4,5)$, and $(5,1)$.) Let us also call the direct input to permutation P_{i+2}

[3] While the difference between a table-defined and table-undefined 2chain will be important in the formal proof, we ignore this subtlety for the moment.

and the inverse input to permutation P_{i-1} when extending the 2chain in the natural way the *right endpoint* and *left endpoint* of the 2chain, respectively.[4]

The "pending" permutation query (i, δ, z) asked by the distinguisher might create new incomplete paths of length 3 (once answered by the simulator) when combined with adjacent 2chains, that is, 2chains at position $(i-2, i-1)$ for a direct query $(i, +, x_i)$ or 2chains at position $(i+1, i+2)$ for an inverse query $(i, -, y_i)$. Hence, just after having marked the initial query of the distinguisher as "pending", the simulator immediately detects all 2chains that will form a length-3 path with this pending query, and marks these 2chains as "triggered". Following the high-level principle of completing any length-3 path, any triggered 2chain should (by the end of the query cycle) be extended to a complete path.

To ease the discussion, let us slightly change the notation and assume that the query that initiates the query cycle is either a forward query $(i+2, +, x_{i+2})$ or an inverse query $(i-1, -, y_{i-1})$. In both cases, adjacent 2chains that might be triggered are of type $(i, i+1)$. For each such 2chain, the simulator computes the endpoint *opposite* the initial query, and marks it "pending" as well. Thus if the initiating query was $(i+2, +, x_{i+2})$, new pending queries of the form $(i-1, -, \cdot)$ are (possibly) created, while if the initiating query was $(i-1, -, y_{i-1})$, new pending queries of the form $(i+2, +, \cdot)$ are (possibly) created. For each of these new pending queries, the simulator recursively detects whether they form a length-3 path with other $(i, i+1)$-2chains, marks these 2chains as "triggered", and so on. Hence, if the initiating query of the distinguisher was of the form $(i+2, +, \cdot)$ or $(i-1, -, \cdot)$, all "pending" queries will be of the form $(i+2, +, \cdot)$ or $(i-1, -, \cdot)$, and all triggered 2chains will be of type $(i, i+1)$. For this reason, we say that such a query cycle is of "type $(i, i+1)$". Note that while this recursive process is taking place, the simulator does *not* assign any new values to the partial permutations $P_1, \ldots, P_5$—indeed, each pending query remains defined only "at one end" during this phase.

Once all 2chains that must eventually be completed have been detected as described above, the simulator starts the completion process. First, it randomly samples the missing endpoints of all "pending" queries. (Thus, a pending query of the form $(i+2, +, x_{i+2})$ will see a value of y_{i+2} sampled; a pending query of the form $(i-1, -, y_{i-1})$ will see a value of x_{i-1} sampled. The fact that each pending query really *does* have a missing endpoint to be sampled is argued in the proof.) Secondly, for each triggered 2chain, the simulator adapts the corresponding path by computing the corresponding input x_{i+3} and output y_{i+3} at position $i+3$ and "forcing" $P_{i+3}(x_{i+3}) = y_{i+3}$. If an overwrite attempt occurs when trying to assign a value for some permutation, the simulator aborts. This completes the high-level description of the simulator's behavior. The important characteristics of an $(i, i+1)$-query cycle are summarized in Table 1.

[4] Again, there is a slight subtlety for the left endpoint of a $(1, 2)$-2chain and the right endpoint of a $(4, 5)$-2chain since this involves the ideal cipher, but we ignore it here.

Table 1. The five types of $(i, i+1)$-query cycles of the simulator.

Type $(i, i+1)$	Initiating query type $(i-1, -)$ and $(i+2, +)$	Adapt at $i+3$
(1,2)	$(5, -)$ and $(3, +)$	4
(2,3)	$(1, -)$ and $(4, +)$	5
(3,4)	$(2, -)$ and $(5, +)$	1
(4,5)	$(3, -)$ and $(1, +)$	2
(5,1)	$(4, -)$ and $(2, +)$	3

4.1 Pseudocode of the Simulator and Game Transitions

We now give the full pseudocode for the simulator, and by the same occasion describe the intermediate worlds that will be used in the indifferentiability proof. The distinguisher $\mathcal{D}$ has access to the public interface $\text{Query}(i, \delta, z)$, which in the ideal world is answered by the simulator, and to the ideal cipher/IEM construction interface, that we formally capture with two interfaces $\text{Enc}(k, x)$ and $\text{Dec}(k, y)$ for encryption and decryption respectively. We will refer to queries to any of these two interfaces as *cipher queries*, by opposition to *permutation queries* made to interface $\text{Query}(\cdot, \cdot, \cdot)$. In the ideal world, cipher queries are answered by an ideal cipher IC. We make the randomness of IC explicit through two random tapes $\mathsf{ic}, \mathsf{ic}^{-1} : \{0,1\}^n \times \{0,1\}^n \to \{0,1\}^n$ such that for any $k \in \{0,1\}^n$, $\mathsf{ic}(k, \cdot)$ is a uniformly random permutation and $\mathsf{ic}^{-1}(k, \cdot)$ is its inverse. Hence, in the ideal world, a query $\text{Enc}(k, x)$, resp. $\text{Dec}(k, y)$, is simply answered with $\mathsf{ic}(k, x)$, resp. $\mathsf{ic}^{-1}(k, y)$. The randomness used by the simulator for lazily sampling permutations $P_1, \ldots, P_5$ when needed is also made explicit in the pseudocode through uniformly random permutations tapes $\mathbf{p} = (p_1, p_1^{-1}, \ldots, p_5, p_5^{-1})$ where $p_i : \{0,1\}^n \to \{0,1\}^n$ is a uniformly random permutation and p_i^{-1} is its inverse. Hence, randomness in game G_1 is fully captured by ic and $\mathbf{p}$.

Since we will use two intermediate games, the real world will be denoted G_4. In this world, queries to $\text{Query}(\cdot, \cdot, \cdot)$ are simply answered with the corresponding value stored in the random permutation tapes $\mathbf{p}$, while queries to Enc or Dec are answered by the IEM construction based on random permutations $\mathbf{p}$. Randomness in G_4 is fully captured by $\mathbf{p}$.

Intermediate Games. The indifferentiability proof relies on two intermediate games G_2 and G_3. In game G_2, following an approach of [32], the Check procedure used by the simulator (see Line 30 of Fig. 4) to detect new external chains is modified such that it does not make explicit queries to the ideal cipher; instead, it first checks to see if the entry exists in table T recording cipher queries and if not, returns false. In game G_3, the ideal cipher is replaced with the 5-round IEM construction that uses the same random permutation tapes $\mathbf{p}$ as the simulator (and hence both the distinguisher *and* the simulator interact with the 5-round IEM construction instead of the IC).

Summing up, randomness is fully captured by ic and **p** in games G_1 and G_2, and by **p** in games G_3 and G_4 (since the ideal cipher is replaced by the IEM construction $\mathrm{EM}^{\mathbf{P}}$ when transitioning from G_2 to G_3).

NOTES ABOUT THE PSEUDOCODE. The pseudocode for the public (i.e., accessible by the distinguisher) procedures Query, Enc, and Dec is given in Fig. 4, together with helper procedures that capture the changes from games G_1 to G_4. The pseudocode for procedures that are internal to the simulator is given in Fig. 5. Lines commented with "\\G_i" apply only to game G_i. In the pseudocode and more generally throughout this paper, the result of arithmetic on indices in $\{1, 2, 3, 4, 5\}$ is automatically wrapped into that range (e.g., $i + 1 = 1$ if $i = 5$). For any table or tape $\mathcal{T}$ and $\delta \in \{+, -\}$, we let $\mathcal{T}^\delta$ be $\mathcal{T}$ if $\delta = +$ and be $\mathcal{T}^{-1}$ if $\delta = -$. Given a list L, $L \hookleftarrow x$ means that x is appended to L. If the simulator aborts (Line 86), we assume it returns a special symbol $\perp$ to the distinguisher.

Tables T and T^{-1} are used to record the cipher queries that have been issued (by the distinguisher *or* the simulator). Note that tables P_i and P_i^{-1} are modified only by procedure Assign. The table entries are never overwritten, due to the check at Line 86.

5 Proof of Indifferentiability

5.1 Main Result and Proof Overview

Our main result is the following theorem which uses the simulator described in Sect. 4. We present an overview of the proof following the theorem statement.

Theorem 2. *The 5-round iterated Even-Mansour construction* $\mathrm{EM}^{\mathbf{P}}$ *with random permutations* $\mathbf{P} = (P_1, \ldots, P_5)$ *is* (t_S, q_S, ε)*-indifferentiable from an ideal cipher with* $t_S = O(q^5)$, $q_S = O(q^5)$ *and* $\varepsilon = 2 \times 10^{12} q^{12}/2^n$.

Moreover, the bounds hold even if the distinguisher is allowed to make q permutation queries in each position (i.e., it can call Query$(i, *, *)$ *q times for each $i \in \{1, 2, 3, 4, 5\}$) and make q cipher queries (i.e.,* Enc *and* Dec *can be called q times in total).*

PROOF STRUCTURE. Our proof uses a sequence of games G_1, G_2, G_3 and G_4 as described in Sect. 4.1, with G_1 being the simulated world and G_4 being the real world.

Throughout the proof we will fix an arbitrary information-theoretic distinguisher $\mathcal{D}$ that can make a total of $6q$ queries: at most q cipher queries and at most q queries to Query$(i, \cdot, \cdot)$ for each $i \in \{1, \ldots, 5\}$, as stipulated in Theorem 2. (Giving the distinguisher q queries at *each* position gives it more power while not significantly affecting the proof or the bounds, and the distinguisher's extra power actually leads to *better* bounds at the final stages of the proof [20].[5]) We can assume without loss of generality that $\mathcal{D}$ is *deterministic*,

[5] In the randomness mapping, we will need to convert an arbitrary distinguisher to one that "completes all paths". If the distinguisher is only allowed q arbitrary queries in total, the number of queries will balloon up to $6q$; but if D is given extra power as described here, the reduction only increases q to $2q$.

```
Game G_i(ic, p), i = 1, 2 / G_i(p), i = 3, 4

Variables:
  Tables of cipher queries T, T^{-1}
  Tables of defined permutation queries P_i, P_i^{-1}, i ∈ {1, ..., 5}
  Ordered list of pending queries Pending
  Ordered list of triggered paths Triggered

public procedure Query(i, δ, z):
  return SimQuery(i, δ, z) \\ G1, G2, G3
  return p_i^δ(z) \\ G4

public procedure Enc(k, x_1):
  if T(k, x_1) = ⊥ then
    y_5 ← ic(k, x_1) \\ G1, G2
    y_5 ← EM(k, x_1) \\ G3, G4
    T(k, x_1) ← y_5, T^{-1}(k, y_5) ← x_1
  return T(k, x_1)

public procedure Dec(k, y_5):
  if T^{-1}(k, y_5) = ⊥ then
    x_1 ← ic^{-1}(k, y_5) \\ G1, G2
    x_1 ← EM^{-1}(k, y_5) \\ G3, G4
    T(k, x_1) ← y_5, T^{-1}(k, y_5) ← x_1
  return T^{-1}(k, y_5)

private procedure EM(k, x_1):
  for i = 1 to 4 do
    x_{i+1} = p_i(x_i) ⊕ k
  return p_5(x_5)

private procedure EM^{-1}(k, y_5):
  for i = 5 to 2 do
    y_{i-1} = p_i^{-1}(y_i) ⊕ k
  return p_1^{-1}(y_1)

private procedure Check(k, x_1, y_5):
  return Enc(k, x_1) = y_5 \\ G1
  return T(k, x_1) = y_5 \\ G2, G3, G4
```

Fig. 4. Public procedures Query, Enc, and Dec for games G_1-G_4, and helper procedures EM, EM^{-1}, and Check. This set of procedures captures all changes from game G_1 to G_4, namely: from game G_1 to G_2 only procedure Check is modified; from game G_2 to G_3, the only change is in procedures Enc and Dec where the ideal cipher is replaced by the IEM construction; and from game G_3 to G_4, only procedure Query is modified to return directly the value read in random permutation tables $\mathbf{p}$.

as any distinguisher can be derandomized using the "optimal" random tape and achieve at least the same advantage.

Without loss of generality, we assume that $\mathcal{D}$ outputs 1 with higher probability in the simulated world G_1 than in the real world G_4. We define the *advantage* of $\mathcal{D}$ in distinguishing between G_i and G_j by

$$\Delta_{\mathcal{D}}(\mathsf{G}_i, \mathsf{G}_j) := \Pr_{\mathsf{G}_i}[\mathcal{D}^{\text{Query,Enc,Dec}} = 1] - \Pr_{\mathsf{G}_j}[\mathcal{D}^{\text{Query,Enc,Dec}} = 1].$$

Our primary goal is to upper bound $\Delta_{\mathcal{D}}(\mathsf{G}_1, \mathsf{G}_4)$ (in Theorem 20), while the secondary goals of upper bounding the simulator's query complexity and running time will be obtained as corollaries along the way.

```
private procedure SimQuery(i, δ, z):
  if P_i^δ(z) = ⊥ then
    Pending ← ((i, δ, z)), Triggered ← ∅
    forall (i, δ, z) in Pending do FindNewPaths(i, δ, z)
    forall (i, δ, z) in Pending do ReadTape(i, δ, z)
    forall (i, i+1, y_i, x_{i+1}, k) in Triggered do AdaptPath(i, i+1, y_i, x_{i+1}, k)
  return P_i^δ(z)

private procedure FindNewPaths(i, δ, z):
case (δ = +):
x_i ← z
forall (x_{i−2}, x_{i−1}) in (P_{i−2}, P_{i−1}) do
  y_{i−2} ← P_{i−2}(x_{i−2}), y_{i−1} ← P_{i−1}(x_{i−1})
  if i = 2 then k ← y_{i−1} ⊕ x_i
  else k ← y_{i−2} ⊕ x_{i−1}
  C ← (i−2, i−1, y_{i−2}, x_{i−1}, k)
  if C ∈ Triggered then continue
  case i ∈ {1, 2}:
    if ¬Check(k, x_1, y_5) then
      continue
  case i ∈ {3, 4, 5}:
    if Next(i−1, y_{i−1}, k) ≠ x_i then
      continue
  Triggered ←↩ C
  y_{i−3} ← Prev(i−2, x_{i−2}, k)
  if (i−3, −, y_{i−3}) ∉ Pending then
    Pending ←↩ (i−3, −, y_{i−3})

case (δ = −):
y_i ← z
forall (x_{i+1}, x_{i+2}) in (P_{i+1}, P_{i+2}) do
  y_{i+1} ← P_{i+1}(x_{i+1}), y_{i+2} ← P_{i+2}(x_{i+2})
  if i = 4 then k ← y_i ⊕ x_{i+1}
  else k ← y_{i+1} ⊕ x_{i+2}
  C ← (i+1, i+2, y_{i+1}, x_{i+2}, k)
  if C ∈ Triggered then continue
  case i ∈ {4, 5}:
    if ¬Check(k, x_1, y_5) then
      continue
  case i ∈ {1, 2, 3}:
    if Prev(i+1, x_{i+1}, k) ≠ y_i then
      continue
  Triggered ←↩ C
  x_{i+3} ← Next(i+2, y_{i+2}, k)
  if (i+3, +, x_{i+3}) ∉ Pending then
    Pending ←↩ (i+3, +, x_{i+3})

private procedure ReadTape(i, δ, z):
  if δ = + then Assign(i, z, p_i(z)) else Assign(i, p_i^{−1}(z), z)

private procedure AdaptPath(i, i+1, y_i, x_{i+1}, k):
  y_{i+1} ← P_{i+1}(x_{i+1}), x_{i+2} ← Next(i+1, y_{i+1}, k), y_{i+2} ← P_{i+2}(x_{i+2})
  x_{i+3} ← Next(i+2, y_{i+2}, k)
  x_i ← P_i^{−1}(y_i), y_{i−1} ← Prev(i, x_i, k), x_{i−1} ← P_{i−1}^{−1}(y_{i−1})
  y_{i−2} ← Prev(i−1, x_{i−1}, k)
  Assign(i+3, x_{i+3}, y_{i−2}) \\ subscripts are equal because of the wrapping

private procedure Assign(i, x_i, y_i):
  if P_i(x_i) ≠ ⊥ or P_i^{−1}(y_i) ≠ ⊥ then abort
  P_i(x_i) ← y_i, P_i^{−1}(y_i) ← x_i

private procedure Next(i, y_i, k):
  if i = 5 then return Dec(k, y_i)
  else return y_i ⊕ k

private procedure Prev(i, x_i, k):
  if i = 1 then return Enc(k, x_i)
  else return x_i ⊕ k
```

Fig. 5. Private procedures used by the simulator.

Our proof starts with discussions about the game G_2, which is in some sense the "anchor point" of the first two game transitions. As usual, there are *bad events* that might cause the simulator to fail. We will prove that bad events are unlikely, and show properties of *good executions* in which bad events do not occur. The proof of efficiency of the simulator (in good executions of G_2) is the most interesting part of this paper; the technical content is in Sect. 5.4, and a separate high-level overview of the argument is also included immediately below (see "Termination Argument"). During the proof of efficiency we also obtain upper bounds on the sizes of the tables and on the number of calls to each procedure, which will be a crucial component for the transition to G_4 (see below).

For the G_1-G_2 transition (found in the full version [19]), note that the only difference between the two games is in Check. If the simulator is efficient, the probability that the two executions diverge in a call to Check is negligible. Therefore, if an execution of G_2 is good, it is identical to the G_1-execution with the same random tapes except with negligible probability. In particular, this implies that an execution of G_1 is efficient with high probability.

For the G_2-G_3 transition, we use a standard randomness mapping argument. We will map the randomness of good executions of G_2 to the randomness of non-aborting executions of G_3, so that the G_3-executions with the mapped randomness are identical to the G_2-executions with the preimage randomness. We will show that if the randomness of a G_3-execution has a preimage, then the answers of the permutation queries output by the simulator must be compatible with the random permutation tapes. Thus the G_3-execution is identical to the G_4-execution with the same random tapes, where the permutation queries are answered by the corresponding entries of the random tapes. This enables a transition directly from G_2 to G_4 using the randomness mapping, which is a small novelty of our proof. The details of this transition can be found in the full version [19].

TERMINATION ARGUMENT. Since the termination argument—i.e., the fact that our simulator does not run amok with excessive path completions, except with negligible probability—is one of the more novel aspects of our proof, we provide a separate high-level overview of this argument here.

To start with, observe that at the moment when an $(i, i+1)$-path is triggered, 3 queries on the path are either already in existence or already scheduled for future existence regardless of this event: the queries at position i and $i+1$ are already defined, while the pending query that triggers the path was already scheduled to become defined even before the path was triggered; hence, each triggered path only "accounts" for 2 new queries, positioned either at $i+2$, $i+3$ or at $i-1$, $i-2$ $(= i+3)$, depending on the position of the pending query.

A second observation is that...

- $(1, 2)$-2chains triggered by pending queries of the form $(5, -, \cdot)$, and
- $(4, 5)$-2chains triggered by pending queries of the form $(1, +, \cdot)$, and
- $(5, 1)$-2chains triggered by either pending queries of the form $(2, +, \cdot)$ or $(4, -, \cdot)$

...all involve a cipher query (equivalently, a call to Check, in G_2) to check the trigger condition, and one can argue that this query must have been made by the distinguisher itself. (Because when the simulator makes a query to Enc/Dec that is not for the purpose of detecting paths, it is for the purpose of completing a path.) Hence, because the distinguisher only has q cipher queries, only q such path completions should occur in total. Moreover, these three types of path completions are exactly those that "account" for a new (previously unscheduled) query to be created at P_3. Hence, and because the only source of new queries are path completions and queries coming directly from the distinguisher, the size of P_3 never grows more than $q + q = 2q$, with high probability.

Of the remaining types of 2chain completions (i.e., those that do not involve the presence of a previously made "wraparound" cipher query), those that contribute a new entry to P_2 are the following:

- $(3, 4)$-2chains triggered by pending queries of the form $(5, +, \cdot)$
- $(4, 5)$-2chains triggered by pending queries of the form $(3, -, \cdot)$

We can observe that either type of chain completion involves values y_3, x_4, y_4, x_5 that are well-defined at the time the chain is detected. We will analyze both types of path completion simultaneously, but dividing into two cases according to whether (a) the distinguisher ever made the query Query$(5, +, x_5)$, or else received the value x_5 as an answer to a query of the form Query$(5, -, y_5)$, or (b) the query $P_5(x_5)$ is being defined/is already defined as the result of a path completion. (Crucially, (a) and (b) are the *only* two options for x_5.)

For (a), at most q such values of x_5 can ever exist, since the distinguisher makes at most q queries to Query$(5, \cdot, \cdot)$; moreover, there are at most $2q$ possibilities for y_3, as already noted; and we have the relation

$$y_3 \oplus x_5 = x_4 \oplus y_4 \tag{2}$$

from the fact that y_3, x_4, y_4 and x_5 lie on a common path. One can show that, with high probability,

$$x_4 \oplus y_4 \neq x'_4 \oplus y'_4$$

for all x_4, y_4, x'_4, y'_4 such that $P_4(x_4) = y_4$, $P_4(x'_4) = y'_4$ and such that $x_4 \neq x'_4$.[6] Hence, with high probability (2) has at most a unique solution x_4, y_4 for each y_3, x_5, and scenario (a) accounts for at most $2q^2$ path completions (one for each possible left-hand side of (2)) of either type above.

For (b), there must exist a separate (table-defined) 2chain $(3, x'_3, y'_3)$, $(4, x'_4, y'_4)$ whose right endpoint is x_5. (This is the case if x_5 is part of a previously completed path, and is also the case if $(5, +, x_5)$ became a pending query during the current query cycle without being the initiating query.) The relation

$$y'_3 \oplus x'_4 \oplus y'_4 = y_3 \oplus x_4 \oplus y_4$$

[6] Probabilistically speaking, this trivially holds if P_4 is a random partial permutation defined at only polynomially many points, though our proof is made more complicated by the fact that P_4 also contains "adapted" queries.

(both sides are equal to x_5) implies

$$y_3 \oplus y_3' = x_4 \oplus y_4 \oplus x_4' \oplus y_4' \tag{3}$$

and, similarly to (a), one can show that (with high probability)

$$x_4 \oplus y_4 \oplus x_4' \oplus y_4' \neq X_4 \oplus Y_4 \oplus X_4' \oplus Y_4'$$

for all table-defined queries $(4, x_4, y_4), \ldots, (4, X_4', Y_4')$ with $\{(x_4, y_4), (x_4', y_4')\} \neq \{(X_4, Y_4), (X_4', Y_4')\}$. Thus, we have (modulo the ordering of (x_4, y_4) and (x_4', y_4')[7]) at most one solution to the RHS of (3) for each LHS; hence, scenario (b) accounts for at most $4q^2$ path completions[8] of either type above, with high probability.

Combining these bounds, we find that P_2 never grows to size more than $2q + 2q^2 + 4q^2 = 6q^2 + 2q$ with high probability, where the term of $2q$ accounts for (the sum of) direct distinguisher queries to Query$(2, \cdot, \cdot)$ and "wraparound" path completions involving a distinguisher cipher query. Symmetrically, one can show that P_4 also has size at most $6q^2 + 2q$, with high probability.

One can now easily conclude the termination argument; e.g., the number of $(2,3)$- or $(3,4)$-2chains that trigger path completions is each at most $2q \cdot (6q^2 + 2q)$ (the product of the maximum size of P_3 with the maximum size of P_2/P_4); or, e.g., the number of $(1,2)$-2chains triggered by a pending query $(3, +, \cdot)$ is at most $2q \cdot (6q^2 + 2q)$ (the product of the maximum size of P_3 with the maximum size of P_2), and so forth.

5.2 Executions of G_2: Definitions and Basic Properties

We start by introducing some notation and establishing properties of executions of G_2. Then, we define a set of bad events that may occur in G_2. An execution of G_2 is *good* if none of these bad events occur. We will prove that in good executions of G_2, the simulator does not abort and runs in polynomial time.

QUERIES AND 2CHAINS. The central notion for reasoning about the simulator is the notion of 2chain, that we develop below.

Definition 2. A *permutation query* is a triple (i, δ, z) where $1 \leq i \leq 5$, $\delta \in \{+, -\}$ and $z \in \{0,1\}^n$. We call i the *position* of the query, δ the *direction* of the query, and the pair (i, δ) the *type* of the query.

Definition 3. A *cipher query* is a triple (δ, k, z) where $\delta \in \{+, -\}$ and $k, z \in \{0,1\}^n$. We call δ the *direction* and k the *key* of the cipher query.

[7] As argued within the proof, this ordering issue does not actually introduce an extra factor of two into the bounds.

[8] Or more exactly, to at most $2q(2q-1)$ path completions, which leads to slightly better bounds used in the proof.

Definition 4. A permutation query (i, δ, z) is *table-defined* if $P_i^\delta(z) \neq \bot$, and *table-undefined* otherwise. Similarly, a cipher query (δ, k, z) is *table-defined* if $T^\delta(k, z) \neq \bot$, and *table-undefined* otherwise.

For permutation queries, we may omit i and δ when clear from the context and simply say that x_i, resp. y_i, is table-(un)defined to mean that $(i, +, x_i)$, resp. $(i, -, y_i)$, is table-(un)defined.

Note that if $(i, +, x_i)$ is table-defined and $P_i(x_i) = y_i$, then necessarily $(i, -, y_i)$ is also table-defined and $P_i^{-1}(y_i) = x_i$. Indeed, tables P_i and P_i^{-1} are only modified in procedure Assign, where existing entries are never overwritten due to the check at Line 86. Thus the two tables always encode a partial permutation and its inverse, i.e., $P_i(x_i) = y_i$ if and only if $P_i^{-1}(y_i) = x_i$. In fact, we will often say that a triple (i, x_i, y_i) is *table-defined* as a shorthand to mean that both $(i, +, x_i)$ and $(i, -, y_i)$ are table-defined with $P_i(x_i) = y_i$, $P_i^{-1}(y_i) = x_i$.

Similarly, if a cipher query $(+, k, x)$ is table-defined and $T(k, x) = y$, then necessarily $(-, k, y)$ is table-defined and $T^{-1}(k, y) = x$. Indeed, these tables are only modified by calls to Enc/Dec, and always according to the IC tape ic, hence these two tables always encode a partial cipher and its inverse, i.e., $T(k, x) = y$ if and only if $T^{-1}(k, y) = x$. Similarly, we will say that a triple (k, x, y) is *table-defined* as a shorthand to mean that both $(+, k, x)$ and $(-, k, y)$ are table-defined with $T(k, x) = y$, $T^{-1}(k, y) = x$.

Definition 5 (2chain)**.** An *inner 2chain* is a tuple $(i, i+1, y_i, x_{i+1}, k)$ such that $i \in \{1, 2, 3, 4\}$, $y_i, x_{i+1} \in \{0,1\}^n$, and $k = y_i \oplus x_{i+1}$. A *(5,1)-2chain* is a tuple $(5, 1, y_5, x_1, k)$ such that $y_5, x_1, k \in \{0,1\}^n$. An $(i, i+1)$-2chain refers either to an inner or a $(5,1)$-2chain, and is generically denoted $(i, i+1, y_i, x_{i+1}, k)$. We call $(i, i+1)$ the *type* of the 2chain.

Remark 2. Note that for a 2chain of type $(i, i+1)$ with $i \in \{1, 2, 3, 4\}$, given y_i and x_{i+1}, there is a unique key k such that $(i, i+1, y_i, x_{i+1}, k)$ is a 2chain (hence k is "redundant" in the notation), while for a 2chain of type $(5, 1)$, the key might be arbitrary. This convention allows to have a unified notation independently of the type of the 2chain. See also Remark 3 below.

Definition 6. An inner 2chain $(i, i+1, y_i, x_{i+1}, k)$ is *table-defined* if both $(i, -, y_i)$ and $(i+1, +, x_{i+1})$ are table-defined permutation queries, and *table-undefined* otherwise. A (5,1)-2chain $(5, 1, y_5, x_1, k)$ is *table-defined* if both $(5, -, y_5)$ and $(1, +, x_1)$ are table-defined permutation queries and if $T(k, x_1) = y_5$, and *table-undefined* otherwise.

Remark 3. Our definitions above ensure that whether a tuple $(i, i+1, y_i, x_{i+1}, k)$ is a 2chain or not is independent of the state of tables P_i/P_i^{-1} and T/T^{-1}. Only the fact that a 2chain is table-defined or not depends on these tables.

Definition 7 (endpoints)**.** Let $C = (i, i+1, y_i, x_{i+1}, k)$ be a table-defined 2chain. The *right endpoint* of C, denoted $r(C)$ is defined as

$$\begin{aligned} r(C) &= P_{i+1}(x_{i+1}) \oplus k && \text{if } i \in \{1,2,3,5\} \\ &= T^{-1}(k, P_5(x_5)) && \text{if } i = 4 \text{ and } (-, k, P_5(x_5)) \text{ is table-defined} \\ &= \bot && \text{if } i = 4 \text{ and } (-, k, P_5(x_5)) \text{ is table-undefined.} \end{aligned}$$

The *left endpoint* of C, denoted $\ell(C)$ is defined as

$$\begin{aligned}\ell(C) &= P_i^{-1}(y_i) \oplus k && \text{if } i \in \{2,3,4,5\}\\ &= T(k, P_1^{-1}(y_1)) && \text{if } i = 1 \text{ and } (+, k, P_1^{-1}(y_1)) \text{ is table-defined}\\ &= \perp && \text{if } i = 1 \text{ and } (+, k, P_1^{-1}(y_1)) \text{ is table-undefined.}\end{aligned}$$

We say that an endpoint is *dummy* when it is equal to $\perp$, and *non-dummy* otherwise. Hence, only the right endpoint of a 2chain of type $(4,5)$ or the left endpoint of a 2chain of type $(1,2)$ can be dummy.

We sometimes identify the right and left (non-dummy) endpoints $r(C)$, $\ell(C)$ of an $(i, i+1)$-2chain C with the corresponding permutation queries $(i+2, +, r(C))$ and $(i-1, -, \ell(C))$. In particular, if we say that $r(C)$ or $\ell(C)$ is "table-defined" this implicitly means that the endpoint in question is non-dummy and that the corresponding permutation query is table-defined. More importantly—and more subtly!—when we say that one of the endpoints of C is "table-undefined" we also implicitly mean that it is non-dummy. (Hence, an endpoint is in exactly one of these three possible states: dummy, table-undefined, table-defined.)

Definition 8. A *complete path* (with key k) is a 5-tuple of table-defined permutation queries $((1, x_1, y_1), \ldots, (5, x_5, y_5))$ such that

$$y_i \oplus x_{i+1} = k \text{ for } i = 1,2,3,4 \text{ and } T(k, x_1) = y_5. \tag{4}$$

The five table-defined queries (i, x_i, y_i) and the five table-defined 2chains $(i, i+1, y_i, x_{i+1}, k)$, $i \in \{1, \ldots, 5\}$, are said to *belong* to the (complete) path.

A 2chain C is also said to be *complete* if it belongs to some complete path. Note that such a 2chain is table-defined; also, its endpoints $r(C)$, $\ell(C)$ are (non-dummy and) table-defined.

Lemma 3. *In any execution of* G_2, *any 2chain belongs to at most one complete path.*

Proof. This follows from the fact that, by definition, a 2chain stipulates a value of k, and from the fact that the tables P_i/P_i^{-1} as well as $T(k,\cdot)/T^{-1}(k,\cdot)$ encode partial permutations. □

Query Cycles. When the distinguisher makes a permutations query (i, δ, z) that is already table-defined, the simulator returns the answer immediately. The definition below introduces some vocabulary related to the simulator's behavior when the distinguisher makes a permutation query that is table-undefined.

Definition 9 (query cycle)**.** A *query cycle* is the period of execution between when the distinguisher issues a permutation query (i_0, δ_0, z_0) which is table-undefined and when the answer to this query is returned by the simulator. We call (i_0, δ_0, z_0) the *initiating query* of the query cycle.

A query cycle is called an $(i, i+1)$-*query cycle* if the initiating query is of type $(i-1, -)$ or $(i+2, +)$ (see Lemma 4(a) and Table 1).

The portion of the query cycle consisting of calls to FindNewPaths at Line 36 is called the *detection phase* of the query cycle; the portion of the query cycle consisting of calls to ReadTape at Line 37 and to AdaptPath at Line 38 is called the *completion phase* of the query cycle.

Definition 10 (cipher query cycle). A *cipher query cycle* is the period of execution between when the distinguisher issues a table-undefined cipher query (δ, k, z) and when the answer to this query is returned. We call (δ, k, z) the *initiating query* of the cipher query cycle.

Remark 4. Note that a "query cycle" as defined above is a "permutation query cycle" in the informal description in Sect. 4, and cipher query cycles are not a special case of query cycles. Both query cycles and cipher query cycles require the initiating query to be table-undefined, since otherwise the answer already exists in the tables and is directly returned.

Definition 11 (pending queries, triggered 2chains). During a query cycle, we say that a permutation query (i, δ, z) is *pending* (or that z is pending when i and δ are clear from the context) if it is appended to list Pending at Line 35, 58, or 76. We say that a 2chain $C = (i, i+1, y_i, x_{i+1}, k)$ is *triggered* if the simulator appends C to the list Triggered at Line 55 or 73.

We present a few lemmas below that give some basic properties of query cycles and will help understand the simulator's behavior.

Lemma 4. *During an $(i, i+1)$-query cycle whose initiating query was (i_0, δ_0, z_0), the following properties always hold:*

(a) Only 2chains of type $(i, i+1)$ are triggered.
(b) Only permutations queries of type $(i-1, -)$, $(i+2, +)$ become pending.
(c) Any 2chain that is triggered was table-defined at the beginning of the query cycle.
(d) At the end of the detection phase, any pending query is either the initiating query, or the endpoint of a triggered 2chain.
(e) If a 2chain C is triggered during the query cycle, and the simulator does not abort, then C is complete at the end of the query cycle.

Proof. The proof of (a) and (b) proceeds by inspection of the pseudocode: note that calls to FindNewPaths$(i-1, -, \cdot)$ can only add 2chains of type $(i, i+1)$ to Triggered and permutations queries of type $(i+2, +)$ to Pending, whereas calls to FindNewPaths$(i+2, +, \cdot)$ can only add 2chains of type $(i, i+1)$ to Triggered and permutations queries of type $(i-1, -)$ to Pending. Hence, if the initiating query is of type $(i-1, -)$ or $(i+2, +)$, only 2chains of type $(i, i+1)$ will ever be added to Triggered, and only permutation queries of type $(i-1, -)$ or $(i+2, +)$ will ever be added to Pending. The proof of (c) also follows easily from inspection of the pseudocode. The sole subtlety is to note that for a $(5, 1)$-query cycle (where calls to FindNewPaths are of the form $(2, +, \cdot)$ and $(4, -, \cdot)$), for a $(5, 1)$-2chain to be triggered one must obviously have $x_1 \in P_1$ and $y_5 \in P_5^{-1}$, but also $T(k, x_1) = y_5$ since otherwise the call to Check(k, x_1, y_5) would return false. The proof of (d) is also immediate, since for a permutation query to be added to Pending, it must be either the initiating query, or computed at Line 56 or Line 74 as the endpoint of a triggered 2chain. Finally, the proof of (e) follows from the fact that, assuming the simulator does not abort, all values computed during the call to AdaptPath(C) form a complete path to which C belongs.

Lemma 5. *In any execution of* G_2*, the following properties hold:*

(a) During a $(1, 2)$*-query cycle, tables* T/T^{-1} *are only modified during the detection phase by calls to* Enc$(\cdot, \cdot)$ *resulting from calls to* Prev$(1, \cdot, \cdot)$ *at Line 56.*
(b) During a $(2, 3)$*-query cycle, tables* T/T^{-1} *are only modified during the completion phase by calls to* Enc$(\cdot, \cdot)$ *resulting from calls to* Prev$(1, \cdot, \cdot)$ *at Line 83.*
(c) During a $(3, 4)$*-query cycle, tables* T/T^{-1} *are only modified during the completion phase by calls to* Dec$(\cdot, \cdot)$ *resulting from calls to* Next$(5, \cdot, \cdot)$ *at Line 81.*
(d) During a $(4, 5)$*-query cycle, tables* T/T^{-1} *are only modified during the detection phase by calls to* Dec$(\cdot, \cdot)$ *resulting from calls to* Next$(5, \cdot, \cdot)$ *at Line 74.*
(e) During a $(5, 1)$*-query cycle, tables* T/T^{-1} *are not modified.*

Proof. This follows by inspection of the pseudocode. The only non-trivial point concerns $(1, 2)$-, resp. $(4, 5)$-query cycles, since Prev$(1, \cdot, \cdot)$, resp. Next$(5, \cdot, \cdot)$ are also called during the completion phase, but they are always called with arguments (x_1, k), resp. (y_5, k) that were previously used during the detection phase, so that this cannot modify the tables T/T^{-1}. □

5.3 Bad Events

In order to define certain bad events that may happen during an execution of G_2, we introduce the following definitions.

Definition 12 ($\mathcal{H}$, $\mathcal{K}$ and $\mathcal{E}$)**.** Consider a permutation query (i_0, δ_0, z_0) or a cipher query (δ_0, k_0, z_0) made by the distinguisher. The following sets are defined with respect to the state of tables when the query occurs. We define the "history" $\mathcal{H}$ as the multiset consisting of the following elements (each n-bit string may appear and be counted multiple times):

- for each table-defined permutation query (i, x_i, y_i), $\mathcal{H}$ contains corresponding elements x_i, y_i and $x_i \oplus y_i$.
- for each table-defined cipher query (k, x_1, y_5), $\mathcal{H}$ contains corresponding elements k, x_1 and y_5.

We define $\mathcal{K}$ as the multiset of all keys of 2chains *triggered in the current query cycle*, and $\mathcal{E}$ as the multiset of non-dummy endpoints of *all* table-defined 2chain plus the value z_0 (the query issued by the distinguisher).

Remark 5. When referring to sets $\mathcal{H}$, $\mathcal{K}$ and $\mathcal{E}$ with respect to a query cycle, we mean with respect to its initiating permutation query (and the state of tables at the beginning of the query cycle). These sets are time-dependent, but they don't change during a query cycle (in particular, the set of triggered 2chains do not depend on the queries that become table-defined during the query cycle). Also note that $\mathcal{K}$ only concerns 2chains triggered in the query cycle, while $\mathcal{E}$ concerns all 2chains that are table-defined at the beginning of the query cycle.

Definition 13 ($\mathcal{P}$, $\mathcal{P}^*$, $\mathcal{A}$ and $\mathcal{C}$)**.** Given a query cycle, let $\mathcal{P}$ be the multiset of random values read by ReadTape on tapes $(p_1, p_1^{-1}, \ldots, p_5, p_5^{-1})$ in the current query cycle, and $\mathcal{P}^*$ be the multiset of $x_i \oplus p_i(x_i)$ and $y_i \oplus p_i^{-1}(y_i)$ for each random value $p_i(x_i)$ or $p_i^{-1}(y_i)$ read from the tapes in the current query cycle.

Let $\mathcal{A}$ be the multiset of the values of $x_i \oplus y_i$ for each adapted query (i, x_i, y_i) with $i \in \{2, 4\}$. Note that $\mathcal{A}$ is non-empty only for $(4, 5)$- and $(1, 2)$-query cycles.

Given a query cycle or a cipher query cycle, we denote $\mathcal{C}$ the multiset of random values read by Enc and Dec on tapes ic or ic^{-1}.[9]

We define the operations $\cap$, $\cup$ and $\oplus$ of two multisets $\mathcal{S}_1, \mathcal{S}_2$ in the natural way: For each element e that appears s_1 and s_2 times $(s_1, s_2 \geq 0)$ in $\mathcal{S}_1$ and $\mathcal{S}_2$ respectively, $\mathcal{S}_1 \cap \mathcal{S}_2$ contains $\min\{s_1, s_2\}$ copies of e and $\mathcal{S}_1 \cup \mathcal{S}_2$ contains $s_1 + s_2$ copies of e. To define $\mathcal{S}_1 \oplus \mathcal{S}_2$, we start from an empty multiset; for each pair of $e_1 \in \mathcal{S}_1$ and $e_2 \in \mathcal{S}_2$ that appear s_1 and s_2 times respectively $(s_1, s_2 \geq 1)$, add $s_1 \cdot s_2$ copies of $e_1 \oplus e_2$ to the multiset.

Definition 14. Let $\mathcal{H}^{\oplus i}$ be the multiset of values equal to the exclusive-or of exactly i *distinct* elements in $\mathcal{H}$, and let $\mathcal{H}^{\oplus 0} := \{0\}$. The multisets $\mathcal{K}^{\oplus i}$, $\mathcal{E}^{\oplus i}$, $\mathcal{P}^{\oplus i}$, $\mathcal{P}^{*\oplus i}$, $\mathcal{A}^{\oplus i}$ and $\mathcal{C}^{\oplus i}$ are defined similarly.[10]

We are now ready to define the afore-mentioned "bad events" on executions of G_2.

Definition 15. $\mathsf{BadPerm}$ is the event that at least one of the following occurs in a query cycle:

- $\mathcal{P}^{\oplus i} \cap \mathcal{H}^{\oplus j} \neq \emptyset$ for $i \geq 1$ and $i + j \leq 4$;
- $\mathcal{P}^{*\oplus i} \cap \mathcal{H}^{\oplus j} \neq \emptyset$ for $i \geq 1$ and $i + j \leq 4$;
- $\mathcal{P} \cap \mathcal{E} \neq \emptyset$, $\mathcal{P} \cap (\mathcal{E} \oplus \mathcal{K}) \neq \emptyset$, $\mathcal{P} \cap (\mathcal{K} \oplus \mathcal{H}) \neq \emptyset$, $\mathcal{P} \cap (\mathcal{K} \oplus \mathcal{H}^{\oplus 2}) \neq \emptyset$;
- $\mathcal{P}^{\oplus 2} \cap \mathcal{K}^{\oplus 2} \neq \emptyset$ or $\mathcal{P}^{\oplus 2} \cap (\mathcal{H} \oplus \mathcal{K}) \neq \emptyset$;
- $\mathcal{P}^* \cap (\mathcal{H} \oplus \mathcal{E}) \neq \emptyset$.

Definition 16. $\mathsf{BadAdapt}$ is the event that in a $(1, 2)$- or $(4, 5)$-query cycle, $\mathcal{A}^{\oplus i} \cap \mathcal{H}^{\oplus j} \neq \emptyset$ for $i \geq 1$ and $i + j \leq 4$.

Definition 17. BadIC is the event that in a query cycle or in a cipher query cycle, either $\mathcal{C} \cap (\mathcal{H} \cup \mathcal{E}) \neq \emptyset$ or $\mathcal{C}$ contains two equal entries.

[9] For a query cycle, these Enc/Dec queries are made by the simulator, while for a cipher query cycle, a single call to Enc or Dec is made by the distinguisher.

[10] Since $\mathcal{H}$, $\mathcal{K}$, $\mathcal{E}$, $\mathcal{P}$, $\mathcal{P}^*$, $\mathcal{A}$ and $\mathcal{C}$ are multisets, two distinct elements may be equal. Because of the distinctness requirement, we have $\mathcal{H}^{\oplus 2} \neq \mathcal{H} \oplus \mathcal{H}$, etc.

Note that $\mathcal{P}^{\oplus i}$, $\mathcal{P}^{*\oplus i}$, $\mathcal{A}^{\oplus i}$ and $\mathcal{C}^{\oplus i}$ are random sets built from values read from tapes $(p_1, p_1^{-1}, \ldots, p_5, p_5^{-1})$ and $\mathsf{ic}/\mathsf{ic}^{-1}$ during the query cycle, while $\mathcal{H}^{\oplus i}$, $\mathcal{K}^{\oplus i}$ and $\mathcal{E}^{\oplus i}$ are fixed and determined by the states of the tables at the beginning of the query cycle.

Definition 18 (Good Executions). An execution of G_2 is said to be *good* if none of BadPerm, BadAdapt and BadIC occurs in the execution.

The main result of this section is to prove that the simulator does not abort in good executions of G_2. Due to space constraints, however, the proof of the following lemma is relegated to the full version [19].

Lemma 6. *The simulator does not abort in a good execution of* G_2.

5.4 Efficiency of the Simulator

We analyze the running time of the simulator in a good execution of G_2. A large part of this analysis consists of upper bounding the size of tables T, T^{-1}, P_i, P_i^{-1}. Since $|T| = |T^{-1}|$ and $|P_i| = |P_i^{-1}|$ we state the results only for T and P_i.

Note that during a query cycle, any triggered 2chain C can be associated with the query that became pending just before C was triggered and, reciprocally, any pending query (i, δ, z), except the initiating query, can be associated with the 2chain C that was triggered just before (i, δ, z) became pending. We make these observations formal through the following definitions.

Definition 19. During a query cycle, we say that a 2chain C is *triggered by query* (i, δ, z) if it is added to Triggered during a call to FindNewPaths(i, δ, z). We say C is an (i, δ)-triggered 2chain if it is triggered by a query of type (i, δ).

By Lemma 4(b), a triggered $(i, i+1)$-2chain is either $(i-1, -)$- or $(i+2, +)$-triggered. For brevity, we group 4 special types of triggered 2chains under a common name.

Definition 20. A (triggered) *wrapping* 2chain is either

- a $(4, 5)$-2chain that was $(1, +)$-triggered,
- a $(1, 2)$-2chain that was $(5, -)$-triggered,
- a $(5, 1)$-2chain that was either $(2, +)$- or $(4, -)$-triggered.

Note that wrapping 2chains are exactly those for which the simulator makes a call to procedure Check to decide whether to trigger the 2chain or not.

Definition 21. Consider a query cycle with initiating query (i_0, δ_0, z_0) and a permutation query $(i, \delta, z) \neq (i_0, \delta_0, z_0)$ which becomes pending. We call the (unique) 2chain that was triggered just before (i, δ, z) became pending the *2chain associated with* (i, δ, z).

Note that uniqueness of the 2chain associated with a non-initiating pending query follows easily from the checks at Lines 57 and 75.

The proof of the following lemma can be found in the full version [19]. The proof relies on the fact that, in a good execution, an $(i, i+1)$-2chain that is complete at the beginning of a query cycle cannot be triggered again in that cycle.

Lemma 7. *Consider a good execution of* G_2*, and assume that a complete path exists at the end of the execution. Then at most one of the five 2chains belonging to the complete path has been triggered during the execution.*

Lemma 8. *For* $i \in \{1, \ldots, 5\}$*, the number of table-defined permutation queries* (i, x_i, y_i) *during an execution of* G_2 *can never exceed the sum of the number of*

- *distinguisher's calls to* Query$(i, \cdot, \cdot)$*,*
- $(i+1, i+2)$*-2chains that were* $(i+3, +)$*-triggered,*
- $(i-2, i-1)$*-2chains that were* $(i-3, -)$*-triggered,*
- $(i+2, i+3)$*-2chains that were either* $(i+1, -)$*- or* $(i+4, +)$*-triggered.*

Proof. Entries are added to P_i/P_i^{-1} either by a call to ReadTape during an $(i+1, i+2)$- or an $(i-2, i-1)$-query cycle or by a call to AdaptPath during an $(i+2, i+3)$-query cycle (see Table 1).

We first consider entries that were added by a call to ReadTape during an $(i+1, i+2)$- or an $(i-2, i-1)$-query cycle. The number of such table-defined queries cannot exceed the sum of the total number $N_{i,+}$ of queries of type $(i, +)$ that became pending during an $(i-2, i-1)$-query cycle and the total number $N_{i,-}$ of queries of type $(i, -)$ that became pending during an $(i+1, i+2)$-query cycle. $N_{i,+}$ cannot exceed the sum of the total number of initiating and non-initiating pending queries of type $(i, +)$ over all $(i-2, i-1)$-query cycles. The total number of initiating queries of type $(i, +)$ is at most the number of distinguisher's calls to Query$(i, +, \cdot)$, while the total number of non-initiating pending queries of type $(i, +)$ over all $(i-2, i-1)$-query cycles cannot exceed the total number of $(i-3, -)$-triggered 2chains (as a non-initiating pending query of type $(i, +)$ cannot be associated with an $(i, +)$ triggered $(i-2, i-1)$-2chain). Similarly, $N_{i,-}$ cannot exceed the sum of the total number of distinguisher's call to Query$(i, -, \cdot)$ and the total number of $(i-3, -)$-triggered $(i+1, i+2)$-2chains. All in all, we see that the total number of triples (i, x_i, y_i) that became table-defined because of a call to ReadTape cannot exceed the sum of

- the number of distinguisher's calls to Query$(i, \cdot, \cdot)$,
- the number of $(i+1, i+2)$-2chains that were $(i+3, +)$-triggered,
- the number of $(i-2, i-1)$-2chains that were $(i-3, -)$-triggered.

Consider now a triple (i, x_i, y_i) which became table-defined during a call to AdaptPath in an $(i+2, i+3)$-query cycle. The total number of such triples cannot exceed the total number of $(i+2, i+3)$-2chains that are triggered over all $(i+2, i+3)$-query cycles (irrespective of whether they are $(i+1, -)$- or $(i+4, +)$-triggered). The result follows. □

The following lemma contains the standard "bootstrapping" argument introduced in [18]. The proof of the lemma can be found in the full version [19].

Lemma 9. *In a good execution of* G_2*, at most* q *wrapping 2chains are triggered in total.*

Lemma 10. *In a good execution of* G_2*, one always has* $|P_3| \le 2q$.

Proof. By Lemma 8, the number of table-defined permutation queries $(3, x_3, y_3)$ (and hence the size of P_3) cannot exceed the sum of

- the number of distinguisher's calls to Query$(3, \cdot, \cdot)$,
- the number of $(4, 5)$-2chains that were $(1, +)$-triggered,
- the number of $(1, 2)$-2chains that were $(5, -)$-triggered,
- the number of $(5, 1)$-2chains that were either $(2, +)$- or $(4, -)$-triggered.

The number of entries of the first type is at most q by the assumption that the distinguisher makes at most q oracle queries to each permutation. Further note that any 2chain mentioned for the 3 other types are wrapping 2chains. Hence, by Lemma 9, there are at most q such entries in total, so that $|P_3| \le 2q$. □

Before proceeding further, we state the following properties of good executions which will be used in the proof of Lemma 13. These properties are proven in the full version [19].

Lemma 11. *In a good execution of* G_2*, for* $i \in \{2, 4\}$*, there do not exist two distinct table-defined queries* (i, x_i, y_i) *and* (i, x_i', y_i') *such that* $x_i \oplus y_i = x_i' \oplus y_i'$.

Lemma 12. *In a good execution of* G_2*, for* $i \in \{2, 4\}$ *there never exist four distinct table-defined queries* $(i, x_i^{(j)}, y_i^{(j)})$ *with* $j = 1, 2, 3, 4$ *such that* $\sum_{j=1}^{4}(x_i^{(j)} \oplus y_i^{(j)}) = 0$.

Lemma 13. *In a good execution of* G_2*, the sum of the total numbers of* $(3, -)$*- and* $(5, +)$*-triggered 2chains, resp. of* $(1, -)$*- and* $(3, +)$*-triggered 2chains, is at most* $6q^2 - 2q$.

Proof. Let C be a 2chain which is either $(3, -)$- or $(5, +)$-triggered during the execution. (The case of $(1, -)$- or $(3, +)$-triggered 2chains is similar by symmetry.) By Lemma 4(e), C belongs to a complete path $((1, x_1, y_1), \ldots, (5, x_5, y_5))$ at the end of the execution (since the simulator does not abort), and $C = (3, 4, y_3, x_4, k)$ if it was $(5, +)$-triggered, whereas $C = (4, 5, y_4, x_5, k)$ if it was $(3, -)$-triggered.

Note that when C was triggered, $(5, +, x_5)$ was necessarily table-defined or pending. If $C = (4, 5, y_4, x_5, k)$ was $(3, -)$-triggered, $(5, +, x_5)$ must be table-defined. If $C = (3, 4, y_3, x_4, k)$ was $(5, +)$-triggered, then it was necessarily during the call to FindNewPaths$(5, +, x_5)$ which implies that x_5 was pending.

We now distinguish two cases depending on how $(5, +, x_5)$ became table-defined or pending. Assume first that this was because of a distinguisher's call to Query$(5, \cdot, \cdot)$. There are at most q such calls, hence there are at most q possibilities for x_5. There are at most $2q$ possibilities for y_3 by Lemma 10. Moreover, for each possible pair (y_3, x_5), there is at most one possibility for the table-defined query $(4, x_4, y_4)$ since otherwise this would contradict Lemma 11 (note that one must have $x_4 \oplus y_4 = y_3 \oplus x_5$). Hence there are at most $2q^2$ possibilities in that case.

Assume now that $(5, +, x_5)$ was a non-initiating pending query in the same query cycle in which C was triggered, or became table-defined during a previous query cycle than the one where C was triggered and for which $(5, +, x_5)$ was neither the initiating query nor became table-defined during the ReadTape call for the initiating query. In all cases there exists a table-defined (3, 4)-2chain $C' = (3, 4, y_3', x_4', k')$ distinct from $(3, 4, y_3, x_4, k)$ such that $x_5 = r(C') = y_4' \oplus x_4' \oplus y_3'$. Since we also have $x_5 = y_4 \oplus x_4 \oplus y_3$, we obtain $x_4 \oplus y_4 \oplus x_4' \oplus y_4' = y_3 \oplus y_3'$. If $y_3 = y_3'$, by Lemma 11 we have $x_4 = x_4'$ and $C' = (3, 4, y_3, x_4, k) = C$, contradicting our assumption. On the other hand, for a fixed (orderless) pair of $y_3 \neq y_3'$, the (orderless) pair of $(4, x_4, y_4)$ and $(4, x_4', y_4')$ is unique by Lemmas 11 and 12 (otherwise, one of the lemmas must be violated by the two pairs). There are at most $\binom{2q}{2} = q(2q - 1)$ choices of y_3 and y_3'; for each pair there is at most one (orderless) pair of $(4, x_4, y_4)$ and $(4, x_4', y_4')$, so there are 2 ways to combine the queries to form two 2chains. Moreover, C' must either have been completed during a previous query cycle than the one where C is triggered, or must have been triggered *before* C in the same query cycle and have made x_5 pending (in which case C was triggered by $(5, +, x_5)$). Thus each way to combine y_3, y_3', $(4, x_4, y_4)$ and $(4, x_4', y_4')$ to form two 2chains corresponds to at most one $(3, +)$- or $(5, -)$-triggered 2chain, so at most $4q^2 - 2q$ such 2chains are triggered. Combining both cases, the number of $(3, -)$- or $(5, +)$-triggered 2chains is at most $6q^2 - 2q$.

Lemma 14. *In a good execution of* G_2, $|P_2| \leq 6q^2$ *and* $|P_4| \leq 6q^2$.

Proof. By Lemma 8, the number of table-defined queries $(2, x_2, y_2)$ (and hence the size of P_2) cannot exceed the sum of

- the number of distinguisher's calls to Query$(2, \cdot, \cdot)$,
- the number of (3, 4)-2chains that were $(5, +)$-triggered,
- the number of (5, 1)-2chains that were $(4, -)$-triggered,
- the number of (4, 5)-2chains that were either $(3, -)$- or $(1, +)$-triggered.

There are at most q entries of the first type by the assumption that the distinguisher makes at most q oracle queries. Any 2chain mentioned for the other cases are either wrapping, $(3, -)$-triggered, or $(5, +)$-triggered 2chains. By Lemmas 9 and 13, there are at most $q + 6q^2 - 2q$ entries of the three other types in total. Thus, we have $|P_2| \leq q + q + 6q^2 - 2q = 6q^2$. Symmetrically, $|P_4| \leq 6q^2$. □

Lemma 15. *In a good execution of* G_2, *at most* $12q^3$ *2chains are triggered in total.*

Proof. Since the simulator doesn't abort in good executions by Lemma 6, any triggered 2chain belongs to a complete path at the end of the execution. By Lemma 7, at most one of the five 2chains belonging to a complete path is triggered in a good execution. Hence, there is a bijective mapping from the set of triggered 2chains to the set of complete paths existing at the end of the execution. Consider all $(3,4)$-2chains which are table-defined at the end of the execution. Each such 2chain belongs to at most one complete path by Lemma 3. Hence, the number of complete paths at the end of the execution cannot exceed the number of table-defined $(3,4)$-2chains, which by Lemmas 10 and 14 is at most $2q \cdot 6q^2 = 12q^3$. □

Lemma 16. *In a good execution of* G_2, *we have* $|T| \leq 12q^3 + q$.

Proof. Recall that the table T is used to maintain the cipher queries that have been issued. In G_2, no new cipher query is issued in Check called in procedure Trigger. So the simulator issues a table-undefined cipher query only if the path containing the cipher query has been triggered. The number of triggered paths is at most $12q^3$, while the distinguisher issues at most q cipher queries. Thus the number of table-defined cipher queries is at most $12q^3 + q$. □

Lemma 17. *In a good execution of* G_2, $|P_1| \leq 12q^3 + q$ *and* $|P_5| \leq 12q^3 + q$.

Proof. By Lemma 8, the number of table-defined queries $(1, x_1, y_1)$ (and hence the size of P_1) cannot exceed the sum of the number of distinguisher's call to Query$(1, \cdot, \cdot)$, which is at most q, and the total number of triggered 2chains, which is at most $12q^3$ by Lemma 15. Therefore, the size of $|P_1|$ is at most $12q^3 + q$. The same reasoning applies to $|P_5|$. □

The proof of the following lemma can be found in the full version. It follows in a straightforward manner from the previous lemmas and by inspection of the pseudocode.

Lemma 18. *In good executions of* G_2, *the simulator runs in time* $O(q^8)$ *and uses* $O(q^3)$ *space.*

Due to space limitations, we present the proofs of the remaining theorems in the full version [19].

5.5 Probability of Good Executions

Theorem 19. *An execution of* G_2 *is good with probability at least*

$$1 - 4.2 \times 10^8 q^{12}/2^n.$$

5.6 Indistinguishability of $\mathbf{G}_1$ and $\mathbf{G}_4$

Theorem 20. *Any distinguisher with* q *queries cannot distinguish* G_1 *from* G_4 *with advantage more than* $2 \times 10^{12} q^{12}/2^n$.

6 Final Thoughts: 4 and 6 Rounds

We conclude the paper with some more remarks on 4- and 6-round simulators, as a means of providing some extra intuition on our work. The 6-round simulator outlined below is also interesting for reasons of its own, as it achieves significantly better security and efficiency than what we achieve in this paper at 5 rounds.

A FAILED 4-ROUND SIMULATOR. Naturally, any simulator for 4-round iterated Even-Mansour with a non-idealized key schedule can only fail (at least, as long as the distinguisher is allowed to be non-sequential) given the attack presented in Sect. 3. Nonetheless, it can be interesting to review where the indifferentiability proof breaks down if we attempt a straightforward "collapsation" of our 5-round simulator to 4 rounds.

Recall that our 5-round simulator completes chains of length 3. E.g., a forward query $P_3(x_3)$ will cause a chain to be completed for each previously established pair of queries $P_1(x_1) = y_1$, $P_2(x_2) = y_2$ such that $y_1 \oplus x_2 = y_2 \oplus x_3$, and in the course of completing such a chain a new query $P_5^{-1}(y_5)$ will be made and the chain will be adapted at P_4. As the P_5^{-1}-query may trigger several fresh chain completions of its own, the process recurses, "bouncing back" between chains triggered by $P_3(\cdot)$- and $P_5^{-1}(\cdot)$-queries. Finally, as described, the 5-round simulator actually waits for the recursive process of chain detections to stop before adapting all detected chains at P_4, with each detected chain ultimately being adapted at "its own" P_4-query.

Similarly, one can imagine a 4-round simulator that attempts to complete all paths of length 3 in the same recursive fashion, but that adapts paths slightly differently: because of the missing round, a path is not adapted by "plugging values in at both ends" of a table P_i, but rather by sampling two adjacent values y_i, x_{i+1} non-independently such that $y_i \oplus x_{i+1} = k$ where k is the key for the path in question. In a nutshell, the problem with this approach is that because endpoints are shared between paths, *simultaneous* systems of equations can arise that have no solutions. (In turn, the existence of such unsolvable systems can be traced back to configurations in which "cycles of paths" arise. Such a counterexample can be reconstructed, e.g., from the attack of Sect. 3.)

A 6-ROUND SIMULATOR. At the opposite, our 5-round simulator enjoys a rather straightforward adaption to 6 rounds. The 6-round version holds some interest because it has a (theoretically) simpler analysis as well as improved efficiency and security.

The basic idea for the 6-round simulator is to detect paths of length 3 as well, but due to the extra round some leeway is afforded, and not all paths need be detected.[11] Specifically, the 6-round simulator detects paths at positions 2–3–4, 3–4–5, 6–1–2 and 5–6–1. We shall refer to these position groups as *detect zones*. For example, a forward query $P_5(x_5)$ for which there exist two previous queries

[11] Indeed, detecting all paths of length 3 would also be problematic for the termination argument, given the larger number of rounds.

$P_3(x_3) = y_3$ and $P_4(x_4) = y_4$ such that $y_3 \oplus x_4 = y_4 \oplus x_5$ would trigger a path by virtue of the 3–4–5 detect zone. We refer to 2–3–4 and 3–4–5 as the *middle detect zones* and to 6–1–2 and 5–6–1 as the *outer detect zones*. One can observe that four distinct detect zones exist, each of which has two "trigger points". (E.g., the 2–3–4 detect zone is triggered by queries $P_4(\cdot)$ and $P_2^{-1}(\cdot)$.) Structurally this makes the 6-round simulator very similar to the 8-round Feistel simulator of [20] (which was indeed an early source of inspiration for this work).

One can then observe that path completions triggered by either of the middle detect zones do not add queries to positions 3 and 4, while each path triggered by an outer detect zone will require a separate distinguisher query to set up. By a standard termination argument due to Seurin [44], this caps the number of paths completed by the simulator to $O(q^2)$ (the product of the size of P_3 and P_4), an improvement over the $O(q^3)$ bound from our 5-round simulator. Further, a refined analysis of bad events (some of which can be omitted for the 6-round simulator) pushes security all the way to $O(q^6/2^n)$, a substantial improvement over previous indifferentiability bounds. However, further details are deferred to the full version of this paper.

Acknowledgments. We thank Dana Dachman-Soled and Jonathan Katz for discussions that led to the termination argument used in this work. The first author was supported by the National Basic Research Program of China Grant 2011CBA00300, 2011CBA00301, the National Natural Science Foundation of China Grant 61033001, 61361136003. The second author was partially supported by the French Agence Nationale de la Recherche through the BRUTUS project under Contract ANR-14-CE28-0015. The third author was supported by National Natural Science Foundation of China Grant 20131351464. Work of the fourth author was performed under financial assistance award 70NANB15H328 from the U.S. Department of Commerce, National Institute of Standards and Technology.

References

1. Andreeva, E., Bogdanov, A., Dodis, Y., Mennink, B., Steinberger, J.P.: On the indifferentiability of key-alternating ciphers. In: Canetti, R., Garay, J.A. (eds.) CRYPTO 2013. LNCS, vol. 8042, pp. 531–550. Springer, Heidelberg (2013). doi:10.1007/978-3-642-40041-4_29
2. Andreeva, E., Bogdanov, A., Mennink, B.: Towards understanding the known-key security of block ciphers. In: Moriai, S. (ed.) FSE 2013. LNCS, vol. 8424, pp. 348–366. Springer, Heidelberg (2014). doi:10.1007/978-3-662-43933-3_18
3. Bellare, M., Kohno, T.: A theoretical treatment of related-key attacks: RKA-PRPs, RKA-PRFs, and applications. In: Biham, E. (ed.) EUROCRYPT 2003. LNCS, vol. 2656, pp. 491–506. Springer, Heidelberg (2003). doi:10.1007/3-540-39200-9_31
4. Bellare, M., Pointcheval, D., Rogaway, P.: Authenticated key exchange secure against dictionary attacks. In: Preneel, B. (ed.) EUROCRYPT 2000. LNCS, vol. 1807, pp. 139–155. Springer, Heidelberg (2000). doi:10.1007/3-540-45539-6_11
5. Bellare, M., Rogaway, P.: Random oracles are practical: a paradigm for designing efficient protocols. In: ACM Conference on Computer and Communications Security, pp. 62–73 (1993)

6. Bellare, M., Rogaway, P.: The security of triple encryption and a framework for code-based game-playing proofs. In: Vaudenay, S. (ed.) EUROCRYPT 2006. LNCS, vol. 4004, pp. 409–426. Springer, Heidelberg (2006). doi:10.1007/11761679_25. Full version: http://eprint.iacr.org/2004/331
7. Biham, E.: New types of cryptanalytic attacks using related keys. J. Cryptol. **7**(4), 229–246 (1994)
8. Biryukov, A., Khovratovich, D., Nikolić, I.: Distinguisher and related-key attack on the full AES-256. In: Halevi, S. (ed.) CRYPTO 2009. LNCS, vol. 5677, pp. 231–249. Springer, Heidelberg (2009). doi:10.1007/978-3-642-03356-8_14
9. Black, J.: The ideal-cipher model, revisited: an uninstantiable blockcipher-based hash function. In: Robshaw, M. (ed.) FSE 2006. LNCS, vol. 4047, pp. 328–340. Springer, Heidelberg (2006). doi:10.1007/11799313_21
10. Black, J., Rogaway, P., Shrimpton, T.: Black-box analysis of the block-cipher-based hash-function constructions from PGV. In: Yung, M. (ed.) CRYPTO 2002. LNCS, vol. 2442, pp. 320–335. Springer, Heidelberg (2002). doi:10.1007/3-540-45708-9_21
11. Bogdanov, A., Knudsen, L.R., Leander, G., Standaert, F.-X., Steinberger, J., Tischhauser, E.: Key-alternating ciphers in a provable setting: encryption using a small number of public permutations - (Extended abstract). In: Pointcheval, D., Johansson, T. (eds.) EUROCRYPT 2012. LNCS, vol. 7237, pp. 45–62. Springer, Heidelberg (2012). doi:10.1007/978-3-642-29011-4_5
12. Chen, S., Lampe, R., Lee, J., Seurin, Y., Steinberger, J.: Minimizing the two-round Even-Mansour cipher. In: Garay, J.A., Gennaro, R. (eds.) CRYPTO 2014. LNCS, vol. 8616, pp. 39–56. Springer, Heidelberg (2014). doi:10.1007/978-3-662-44371-2_3. Full version: http://eprint.iacr.org/2014/443
13. Chen, S., Steinberger, J.: Tight security bounds for key-alternating ciphers. In: Nguyen, P.Q., Oswald, E. (eds.) EUROCRYPT 2014. LNCS, vol. 8441, pp. 327–350. Springer, Heidelberg (2014). doi:10.1007/978-3-642-55220-5_19. Full version: http://eprint.iacr.org/2013/222
14. Cogliati, B., Seurin, Y.: On the provable security of the iterated Even-Mansour cipher against related-key and chosen-key attacks. In: Oswald, E., Fischlin, M. (eds.) EUROCRYPT 2015. LNCS, vol. 9056, pp. 584–613. Springer, Heidelberg (2015). doi:10.1007/978-3-662-46800-5_23. Full version: http://eprint.iacr.org/2015/069
15. Cogliati, B., Seurin, Y.: Strengthening the known-key security notion for block ciphers. In: Peyrin, T. (ed.) FSE 2016. LNCS, vol. 9783, pp. 494–513. Springer, Heidelberg (2016). doi:10.1007/978-3-662-52993-5_25
16. Coron, J., Holenstein, T., Künzler, R., Patarin, J., Seurin, Y., Tessaro, S.: How to build an ideal cipher: the indifferentiability of the Feistel construction. J. Cryptol. **29**(1), 61–114 (2016)
17. Coron, J.-S., Dodis, Y., Malinaud, C., Puniya, P.: Merkle-Damgård revisited: how to construct a hash function. In: Shoup, V. (ed.) CRYPTO 2005. LNCS, vol. 3621, pp. 430–448. Springer, Heidelberg (2005). doi:10.1007/11535218_26
18. Coron, J.-S., Patarin, J., Seurin, Y.: The random oracle model and the ideal cipher model are equivalent. In: Wagner, D. (ed.) CRYPTO 2008. LNCS, vol. 5157, pp. 1–20. Springer, Heidelberg (2008). doi:10.1007/978-3-540-85174-5_1
19. Dai, Y., Seurin, Y., Steinberger, J.P., Thiruvengadam, A.: Five rounds are sufficient and necessary for the indifferentiability of iterated Even-Mansour. IACR Cryptology ePrint Archive, Report 2017/042 (2017). http://eprint.iacr.org/2017/042

20. Dai, Y., Steinberger, J.: Indifferentiability of 8-round Feistel networks. In: Robshaw, M., Katz, J. (eds.) CRYPTO 2016. LNCS, vol. 9814, pp. 95–120. Springer, Heidelberg (2016). doi:10.1007/978-3-662-53018-4_4. Full version: http://eprint.iacr.org/2015/1069
21. Demay, G., Gaži, P., Hirt, M., Maurer, U.: Resource-restricted indifferentiability. In: Johansson, T., Nguyen, P.Q. (eds.) EUROCRYPT 2013. LNCS, vol. 7881, pp. 664–683. Springer, Heidelberg (2013). doi:10.1007/978-3-642-38348-9_39. Full version: http://eprint.iacr.org/2012/613
22. Desai, A.: The security of all-or-nothing encryption: protecting against exhaustive key search. In: Bellare, M. (ed.) CRYPTO 2000. LNCS, vol. 1880, pp. 359–375. Springer, Heidelberg (2000). doi:10.1007/3-540-44598-6_23
23. Dodis, Y., Stam, M., Steinberger, J., Liu, T.: Indifferentiability of confusion-diffusion networks. In: Fischlin, M., Coron, J.-S. (eds.) EUROCRYPT 2016. LNCS, vol. 9666, pp. 679–704. Springer, Heidelberg (2016). doi:10.1007/978-3-662-49896-5_24
24. Dunkelman, O., Keller, N., Shamir, A.: Minimalism in cryptography: the Even-Mansour scheme revisited. In: Pointcheval, D., Johansson, T. (eds.) EUROCRYPT 2012. LNCS, vol. 7237, pp. 336–354. Springer, Heidelberg (2012). doi:10.1007/978-3-642-29011-4_21
25. Even, S., Mansour, Y.: A construction of a cipher from a single pseudorandom permutation. J. Cryptol. **10**(3), 151–162 (1997)
26. Farshim, P., Procter, G.: The related-key security of iterated Even–Mansour ciphers. In: Leander, G. (ed.) FSE 2015. LNCS, vol. 9054, pp. 342–363. Springer, Heidelberg (2015). doi:10.1007/978-3-662-48116-5_17. Full version: http://eprint.iacr.org/2014/953
27. Fiat, A., Shamir, A.: How To prove yourself: practical solutions to identification and signature problems. In: Odlyzko, A.M. (ed.) CRYPTO 1986. LNCS, vol. 263, pp. 186–194. Springer, Heidelberg (1987). doi:10.1007/3-540-47721-7_12
28. Granboulan, L.: Short signatures in the random oracle model. In: Zheng, Y. (ed.) ASIACRYPT 2002. LNCS, vol. 2501, pp. 364–378. Springer, Heidelberg (2002). doi:10.1007/3-540-36178-2_23
29. Guo, C., Lin, D.: Separating invertible key derivations from non-invertible ones: sequential indifferentiability of 3-round Even-Mansour. Designs Codes Cryptogr. **81**, 109–129 (2015). http://dx.doi.org/10.1007/s10623-015-0132-0
30. Guo, C., Lin, D.: Indifferentiability of 3-round Even-Mansour with random oracle key derivation. IACR Cryptology ePrint Archive, Report 2016/894 (2016). http://eprint.iacr.org/2016/894
31. Hoang, V.T., Tessaro, S.: Key-alternating ciphers and key-length extension: exact bounds and multi-user security. In: Robshaw, M., Katz, J. (eds.) CRYPTO 2016. LNCS, vol. 9814, pp. 3–32. Springer, Heidelberg (2016). doi:10.1007/978-3-662-53018-4_1
32. Holenstein, T., Künzler, R., Tessaro, S.: The equivalence of the random oracle model and the ideal cipher model, revisited. In: Fortnow, L., Vadhan, S.P. (eds.) Symposium on Theory of Computing - STOC 2011, pp. 89–98. ACM (2011). Full version http://arxiv.org/abs/1011.1264
33. Iwata, T., Kohno, T.: New security proofs for the 3GPP confidentiality and integrity algorithms. In: Roy, B., Meier, W. (eds.) FSE 2004. LNCS, vol. 3017, pp. 427–445. Springer, Heidelberg (2004). doi:10.1007/978-3-540-25937-4_27
34. Kilian, J., Rogaway, P.: How to protect DES against exhaustive key search. In: Koblitz, N. (ed.) CRYPTO 1996. LNCS, vol. 1109, pp. 252–267. Springer, Heidelberg (1996). doi:10.1007/3-540-68697-5_20

35. Knudsen, L.R., Rijmen, V.: Known-key distinguishers for some block ciphers. In: Kurosawa, K. (ed.) ASIACRYPT 2007. LNCS, vol. 4833, pp. 315–324. Springer, Heidelberg (2007). doi:10.1007/978-3-540-76900-2_19
36. Lai, X., Massey, J.L.: Hash functions based on block ciphers. In: Rueppel, R.A. (ed.) EUROCRYPT 1992. LNCS, vol. 658, pp. 55–70. Springer, Heidelberg (1993). doi:10.1007/3-540-47555-9_5
37. Lampe, R., Patarin, J., Seurin, Y.: An asymptotically tight security analysis of the iterated Even-Mansour cipher. In: Wang, X., Sako, K. (eds.) ASIACRYPT 2012. LNCS, vol. 7658, pp. 278–295. Springer, Heidelberg (2012). doi:10.1007/978-3-642-34961-4_18
38. Lampe, R., Seurin, Y.: How to construct an ideal cipher from a small set of public permutations. In: Sako, K., Sarkar, P. (eds.) ASIACRYPT 2013. LNCS, vol. 8269, pp. 444–463. Springer, Heidelberg (2013). doi:10.1007/978-3-642-42033-7_23
39. Mandal, A., Patarin, J., Seurin, Y.: On the public indifferentiability and correlation intractability of the 6-round Feistel construction. In: Cramer, R. (ed.) TCC 2012. LNCS, vol. 7194, pp. 285–302. Springer, Heidelberg (2012). doi:10.1007/978-3-642-28914-9_16. Full version: http://eprint.iacr.org/2011/496
40. Maurer, U., Renner, R., Holenstein, C.: Indifferentiability, impossibility results on reductions, and applications to the random oracle methodology. In: Naor, M. (ed.) TCC 2004. LNCS, vol. 2951, pp. 21–39. Springer, Heidelberg (2004). doi:10.1007/978-3-540-24638-1_2
41. Merkle, R.C.: One way hash functions and DES. In: Brassard, G. (ed.) CRYPTO 1989. LNCS, vol. 435, pp. 428–446. Springer, New York (1990). doi:10.1007/0-387-34805-0_40
42. Preneel, B., Govaerts, R., Vandewalle, J.: Hash functions based on block ciphers: a synthetic approach. In: Stinson, D.R. (ed.) CRYPTO 1993. LNCS, vol. 773, pp. 368–378. Springer, Heidelberg (1994). doi:10.1007/3-540-48329-2_31
43. Ristenpart, T., Shacham, H., Shrimpton, T.: Careful with composition: limitations of the indifferentiability framework. In: Paterson, K.G. (ed.) EUROCRYPT 2011. LNCS, vol. 6632, pp. 487–506. Springer, Heidelberg (2011). doi:10.1007/978-3-642-20465-4_27
44. Seurin, Y.: Primitives et protocoles cryptographiques à sécurité prouvée. Ph.D. thesis, Université de Versailles Saint-Quentin-en-Yvelines, France (2009)
45. Steinberger, J.: Improved security bounds for key-alternating ciphers via Hellinger distance. IACR Cryptology ePrint Archive, Report 2012/481 (2012). http://eprint.iacr.org/2012/481
46. Winternitz, R.S.: A secure one-way hash function built from DES. In: IEEE Symposium on Security and Privacy, pp. 88–90 (1984)

Encrypted Davies-Meyer and Its Dual: Towards Optimal Security Using Mirror Theory

Bart Mennink[1,2(✉)] and Samuel Neves[3]

[1] Digital Security Group, Radboud University, Nijmegen, The Netherlands
b.mennink@cs.ru.nl
[2] CWI, Amsterdam, The Netherlands
[3] CISUC, Department of Informatics Engineering, University of Coimbra, Coimbra, Portugal
sneves@dei.uc.pt

Abstract. At CRYPTO 2016, Cogliati and Seurin introduced the Encrypted Davies-Meyer construction, $p_2(p_1(x) \oplus x)$ for two n-bit permutations p_1, p_2, and proved security up to $2^{2n/3}$. We present an improved security analysis up to $2^n/(67n)$. Additionally, we introduce the dual of the Encrypted Davies-Meyer construction, $p_2(p_1(x)) \oplus p_1(x)$, and prove even tighter security for this construction: $2^n/67$. We finally demonstrate that the analysis neatly generalizes to prove almost optimal security of the Encrypted Wegman-Carter with Davies-Meyer MAC construction. Central to our analysis is a modernization of Patarin's mirror theorem and an exposition of how it relates to fundamental cryptographic problems.

Keywords: PRP-to-PRF · Encrypted Davies-Meyer · Encrypted Davies-Meyer dual · EWCDM · Optimal security

1 Introduction

Many cryptographic primitives rest on the assumption that their building blocks behave as perfectly random functions. This is the case for, among many others, encryption modes [4], authenticators [5,9], or random permutations [28]. Yet, for all their utility, very few pseudorandom functions are actually available to practitioners. Instead, the leading cryptographic building block is the pseudorandom permutation, also known as the block cipher. It is therefore common practice to employ block ciphers as stand-ins for pseudorandom functions.

To a first approximation, this solves the problem. The PRP-PRF switch [6, 8,13,21,24] tells us that a PRF can be safely replaced by a PRP up to approximately $2^{n/2}$ queries. With large blocks this is often acceptable, but for lightweight block ciphers, whose number has grown tremendously in recent years (e.g., [1,2,11,12,18,20,22,27,46,51]), this $2^{n/2}$ birthday bound severely limits the application range. For example, Bhargavan and Leurent [10] recently presented practical collision attacks on TLS if a 64-bit cipher is used.

J. Katz and H. Shacham (Eds.): CRYPTO 2017, Part III, LNCS 10403, pp. 556–583, 2017.
DOI: 10.1007/978-3-319-63697-9_19

In order to save these ciphers from obsolescence, various PRP-to-PRF constructions have been presented that achieve security beyond the $2^{n/2}$ security bound. We can categorize these into truncation-based solutions and xor-based solutions.[1] Here and throughout, we simply talk about permutations to refer to block ciphers instantiated with a secret key, unless explicitly stated otherwise.

Truncation. Hall et al. [21] suggested simple truncation. Bellare and Impagliazzo [3] and Gilboa and Gueron [19] proved that truncating an n-bit permutation by $m < n$ bits has security up to approximately $2^{\frac{m+n}{2}}$ queries. This result was, as a matter of fact, already derived around 20 years earlier by Stam [47], be it in a non-cryptographic context.

Xor of Permutations. The xor (or more generally, sum) of two permutations,

$$\mathrm{XoP}^{p_1,p_2}(x) = p_1(x) \oplus p_2(x)\,, \tag{1}$$

where p_1, p_2 are two permutations, was initially mentioned by Bellare et al. [7] as a "natural" PRP-to-PRF method, and was later analyzed by Lucks [29] and Bellare and Impagliazzo [3]. Patarin achieved $2^n/67$ security [39,40,42]. The results are natively inherited by the construction that consists of the xor of three or more independent permutations [16,30].

The xor of permutations evidently requires independence between p_1 and p_2. If only a single permutation is to be used, one can simulate this independence through domain separation, as suggested by Lucks [29] and Bellare and Impagliazzo [3]:

$$\mathrm{XoP'}^{p}(x) = p(0\|x) \oplus p(1\|x)\,. \tag{2}$$

Patarin [40] proved that this single permutation construction achieves a similar level of security as XoP.

A New Contender. At CRYPTO 2016, Cogliati and Seurin [17] introduced the Encrypted Davies-Meyer (EDM) construction (see Fig. 1a):

$$\mathrm{EDM}^{p_1,p_2}(x) = p_2(p_1(x) \oplus x)\,, \tag{3}$$

where p_1, p_2 are two permutations. Cogliati and Seurin proved that EDM^{p_1,p_2} behaves like a random function up to complexity $2^{2n/3}$, and actually conjectured that 2^n is possible.

EDM^{p_1,p_2} shows structural differences with the xor of permutations, and these differences allowed Cogliati and Seurin to devise the misuse-resistant MAC

[1] Another notable approach is data-dependent rekeying by Bellare et al. [7]: given a block cipher E_k, data-dependent rekeying computes $E_{E_k(x)}(x)$. However, this approach only achieves approximately $2^{n/2}$ security, and it inherently requires rekeying of the block cipher which could be a costly operation in practice.

function Encrypted Wegman-Carter with Davies-Meyer (EWCDM), defined as follows:

$$\mathrm{EWCDM}^{h,p_1,p_2}(\nu, m) = p_2(p_1(\nu) \oplus \nu \oplus h(m)), \tag{4}$$

where h is an almost xor universal hash function, p_1, p_2 are two permutations, and where ν denotes the nonce and m the message, which may be arbitrarily large. Cogliati and Seurin proved that $\mathrm{EWCDM}^{h,p_1,p_2}$ achieves security up to $2^{2n/3}$ in the nonce-respecting setting, and $2^{n/2}$ security in the nonce-misusing setting. They likewise conjectured optimal 2^n security in the nonce-respecting setting.

1.1 Our Contribution

We improve the security of EDM^{p_1,p_2} as well as $\mathrm{EWCDM}^{h,p_1,p_2}$ from $2^{2n/3}$, as derived by Cogliati and Seurin [17], to $2^n/(67n)$. Furthermore, we introduce the dual of EDM, the Encrypted Davies-Meyer Dual (EDMD) construction:

$$\mathrm{EDMD}^{p_1,p_2}(x) = p_2(p_1(x)) \oplus p_1(x). \tag{5}$$

The dual is depicted in Fig. 1b, and as can be seen from a simple comparison with EDM^{p_1,p_2} of Fig. 1a, the constructions are very much related, and equally expensive. We show that the EDMD construction achieves security up to $2^n/67$ queries.

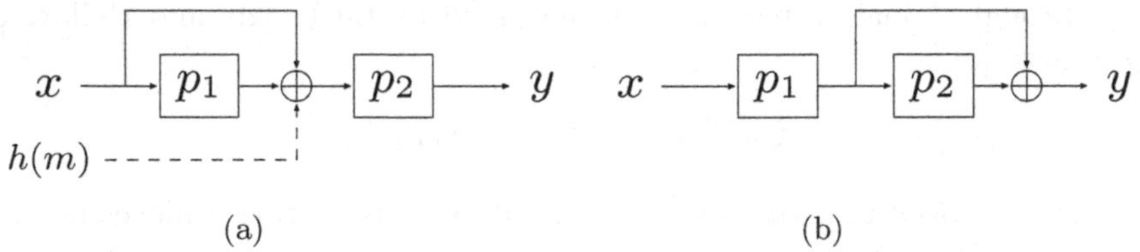

Fig. 1. Encrypted Davies-Meyer (a) and its dual (b). The dashed line represents the necessary addition to yield EWCDM.

Mirror Theory. The backbone of our security analysis is Patarin's mirror theory [31,36,40,43], a very powerful but rather unknown technique. We refurbish and modernize it in Sect. 3 in order to be able to neatly apply it in our analyses.

At a basic level, the idea of Patarin's mirror theory is to consider $q \geq 1$ equations in $r \geq q$ unknowns, and to determine a lower bound on the number of possible solutions to the unknowns. Some conditions naturally apply: the q equations are of the form $P_a \oplus P_b = \lambda$,[2] where P_a and P_b are two unknowns, and the solution to the unknowns should not contain collisions.

[2] Generalizations to multiple unknowns are possible [40,43], but are irrelevant for our work.

Consider the following example system of equations:

$$P_a \oplus P_b = \lambda_1 \,,\; P_b \oplus P_c = \lambda_2 \,,\; P_d \oplus P_e = \lambda_3 \,. \tag{6}$$

We have 2^n choices for P_a, after which P_b is determined by λ_1 and P_c by λ_2. Next, we have $2^n - 3$ options for P_d (as P_d should not collide with P_a, P_b, and P_c), after which P_e is determined by λ_3. This naive counting gives $2^n(2^n - 3)$ solutions to the system of equations, but it disregards two potential problems: (i) the choice may result in a collision in the unknowns and (ii) the system of equations may be inconsistent in the first place. Problem (i) may occur in a straightforward way if, for instance, $\lambda_1 = 0$, as in this case the first equation states that $P_a = P_b$. It could also happen in a more delicate setting, for example if $P_b = P_e$ (even though P_d does not collide with P_a). To understand problem (ii), consider the system of equations of (6) *appended with* equation $P_a \oplus P_c = \lambda_4$. From the first two equations of (6) and the appended equation we can conclude that the system is inconsistent if $\lambda_1 \oplus \lambda_2 \oplus \lambda_4 \neq 0$.

If problem (i) or (ii) occurs, the system of equations naturally has no solution. Disregarding these two problems, the fundamental mirror theorem states that if the number of q equations is "small enough," then the number of solutions to the r unknowns is at least $\frac{(2^n)_r}{2^{nq}}$, where $(2^n)_r$ is the falling factorial. What it means for q to be "small enough" depends on the system of equations under investigation. We refer to Theorem 2 for the details. We will in fact use a generalization of this theorem, where the solution to the unknowns may contain some collisions (see Theorem 3).

The bound itself is merely a combinatorial lower bound whose relevance is not that clear at first sight. Its strength lies in the fact that it can be nicely employed within the H-coefficient technique by Patarin [15,33,37], and in particular, it forms a crucial part in proving the (almost) optimal security of EDM, EWCDM, and EDMD.

Patarin's mirror theorem (or variants thereof) has been used already to analyze the security of Feistel constructions and the xor of permutations by Patarin [34–36,38–42,45], Cogliati et al. [16], and Volte et al. [48,49]. Iwata et al. [26] recently pointed out that a result from Patarin's mirror theorem implies almost optimal security of CENC [25].

Security of EDM. By looking at EDM^{p_1,p_2} from a different angle, we can prove $2^n/(67n)$ security for the case of independent permutations p_1, p_2 (Sect. 4). In more detail, we regard EDM^{p_1,p_2} as a sum of permutations *in the middle*, where an evaluation $y = \mathrm{EDM}^{p_1,p_2}(x)$ corresponds to a xor of permutations as $p_1(x) \oplus p_2^{-1}(y) = x$. After this we only need to overcome a few technicalities in order to apply the mirror theorem.

Security of EWCDM. Our analysis of EDM^{p_1,p_2}, namely the restructuring of the data flows, generalizes to $\mathrm{EWCDM}^{h,p_1,p_2}$ *almost verbatim*. In more detail, we prove in Sect. 5 that, in the nonce-respecting setting, $\mathrm{EWCDM}^{h,p_1,p_2}$ achieves close to optimal $2^n/(67n)$ PRF security. The analysis straightforwardly generalizes to MAC security. Security in the nonce-misusing setting cannot exceed the birthday bound as derived in [17].

Security of EDMD. Similar techniques allow us to prove optimal security of EDMD based on independent permutations. However, in Sect. 6 we observe that its security reduces quite elegantly to the xor of two independent permutations, XoP^{p_1,p_2} of (1). Therefore, EDMD based on independent permutations achieves $2^n/67$ security.

Towards a Single Permutation. Our results on EDM^{p_1,p_2} and $\mathrm{EWCDM}^{h,p_1,p_2}$ satisfactorily resolve the conjecture put forward by Cogliati and Seurin [17] up to a logarithmic factor, and our construction EDMD^{p_1,p_2} even achieves better security than EDM^{p_1,p_2}. Cogliati and Seurin furthermore conjectured that optimal security is already achieved *in the identical permutation case*, i.e., where $p_1 = p_2$. We support this conjecture, and think that it also holds for the dual, but it appears unlikely that the techniques used in this work can be employed to prove optimal security of EDM^p or EDMD^p, let alone $\mathrm{EWCDM}^{h,p}$. In Sect. 7 we give informal justification for this claim, and discuss further possibilities to investigate EDM^p and EDMD^p.

A Dual of EWCDM? An earlier version of this article suggested, as a side result, the dual construction

$$\mathrm{EWCDMD}^{h,p_1,p_2}(\nu, m) = p_2(p_1(\nu) \oplus h(m)) \oplus p_1(\nu) \oplus h(m)\,, \qquad (7)$$

with a claimed security of $2^n/(67n)$. However, Nandi [32] pointed out that $\mathrm{EWCDMD}^{h,p_1,p_2}$ can be seen as a cascade of two non-injective functions, therewith having twice as many collisions as expected, and can be distinguished from random in about $2^{n/2}$ queries. Closer inspection of the security proof revealed a very subtle issue in the application of the mirror theory, namely that it cannot readily handle systems of equations with a *conditional* existence of (in-)equalities, e.g., where two unknowns must be equal if two other unknowns satisfy a certain condition.[3] Broadly speaking, the problem is similar to (but more subtle than) issues encountered when analyzing a single permutation variant EDM^p, EDMD^p, or $\mathrm{EWCDM}^{h,p}$ (cf. Sect. 7). As such, we consider it to be a non-trivial exercise to derive a dual of $\mathrm{EWCDM}^{h,p}$ that provably achieves security beyond the birthday bound. We remark that $\mathrm{EWCDMD}^{h,p_1,p_2}$ may still achieve MAC security beyond the birthday bound, however, we have not considered MAC security in this work as it is beyond the scope of the article.

[3] The issue does not appear for EDM^{p_1,p_2} or $\mathrm{EWCDM}^{h,p_1,p_2}$. It even does not appear for EDMD^{p_1,p_2} as the inputs to the second permutation are always distinct.

2 Preliminaries

For a natural number n, $\{0,1\}^n$ denotes the set of all n-bit strings, and we denote by $\{0,1\}^*$ the set of bit strings of arbitrary length. $\mathsf{func}(n)$ denotes the set of all functions on $\{0,1\}^n$, and $\mathsf{perm}(n)$ the set of all permutations. We denote by $\mathsf{func}(n+*,n)$ the set of all functions with domain $\{0,1\}^n \times \{0,1\}^*$ and range $\{0,1\}^n$. For a natural number $m \geq n$, we write $(m)_n = m(m-1)\cdots(m-n+1)$ as the falling factorial. For a set $\mathcal{X}$, $x \xleftarrow{\$} \mathcal{X}$ denotes uniformly random sampling of x from $\mathcal{X}$.

2.1 Universal Hash Functions

For two non-empty sets $\mathcal{X}, \mathcal{Y}$, a family of hash functions $H = \{h : \mathcal{X} \to \mathcal{Y}\}$ is said to be ϵ-AXU (almost xor universal) if for any distinct $x, x' \in \mathcal{X}$ and $y \in \mathcal{Y}$, we have

$$\mathbf{Pr}\left[h \xleftarrow{\$} H \;:\; h(x) \oplus h(x') = y\right] \leq \epsilon\,.$$

2.2 Distinguishers

A distinguisher $\mathcal{D}$ is a computationally unbounded adversary that is given adaptive access to an oracle $\mathcal{O}$ and outputs a bit 0/1. For two oracles $\mathcal{O}$ and $\mathcal{P}$ with identical interface, we denote the distinguishing advantage of $\mathcal{D}$ by

$$\Delta_{\mathcal{D}}(\mathcal{O}\,;\,\mathcal{P}) = \mathbf{Pr}\left[\mathcal{D}^{\mathcal{O}} \Rightarrow 1\right] - \mathbf{Pr}\left[\mathcal{D}^{\mathcal{P}} \Rightarrow 1\right]. \tag{8}$$

Throughout this work, we only consider computationally unbounded distinguishers whose complexities are solely measured by the number of queries to the oracle. Without loss of generality, it suffices to only focus on deterministic distinguishers, as for any probabilistic distinguisher there exists a deterministic one with at least the same success probability, and we will assume so henceforth.

2.3 H-Coefficient Technique

Central to our analysis will be the H-coefficient technique by Patarin [33,37], and as a matter of fact, the mirror theory of Sect. 3 will be a useful tool *within* this technique. We will follow the renewed description of Chen and Steinberger [15].

Consider two oracles $\mathcal{O}$ and $\mathcal{P}$, and an information-theoretic deterministic distinguisher $\mathcal{D}$ with query complexity q that tries to distinguish both oracles: $\Delta_{\mathcal{D}}(\mathcal{O}\,;\,\mathcal{P})$ of (8). The communication that $\mathcal{D}$ has with its oracle is recorded in a transcript τ. Denote by $X_{\mathcal{O}}$ the probability distribution of transcripts when $\mathcal{D}$ is interacting with $\mathcal{O}$, and similarly by $X_{\mathcal{P}}$ the distribution of transcripts for interaction with $\mathcal{P}$. Say that a transcript is "attainable" if $\mathbf{Pr}\left[X_{\mathcal{P}} = \tau\right] > 0$ and denote by $\mathcal{T}$ the set of all attainable transcripts.

The H-coefficient technique states the following:

Theorem 1 (H-coefficient technique). *Let $\delta, \varepsilon \in [0,1]$. Consider a partition $\mathcal{T} = \mathcal{T}_{\text{bad}} \cup \mathcal{T}_{\text{good}}$ of the set of attainable transcripts such that*

1. $\mathbf{Pr}[X_{\mathcal{P}} \in \mathcal{T}_{\text{bad}}] \leq \delta$,
2. *for all* $\tau \in \mathcal{T}_{\text{good}}$, $\dfrac{\mathbf{Pr}[X_{\mathcal{O}} = \tau]}{\mathbf{Pr}[X_{\mathcal{P}} = \tau]} \geq 1 - \varepsilon$.

Then, the distinguishing advantage satisfies $\Delta_{\mathcal{D}}(\mathcal{O}\,;\,\mathcal{P}) \leq \delta + \varepsilon$.

Proof. A proof of the technique is given among others in [14,15], and we repeat it briefly. As we consider a deterministic distinguisher $\mathcal{D}$, its advantage is equal to the statistical distance between the distributions of views $X_{\mathcal{O}}$ and $X_{\mathcal{P}}$:

$$\begin{aligned}\Delta_{\mathcal{D}}(\mathcal{O}\,;\,\mathcal{P}) &= \frac{1}{2}\sum_{\tau\in\mathcal{T}} \left|\mathbf{Pr}[X_{\mathcal{O}} = \tau] - \mathbf{Pr}[X_{\mathcal{P}} = \tau]\right| \\ &= \sum_{\tau\in\mathcal{T}:\mathbf{Pr}[X_{\mathcal{P}}=\tau]>\mathbf{Pr}[X_{\mathcal{O}}=\tau]} \left(\mathbf{Pr}[X_{\mathcal{P}} = \tau] - \mathbf{Pr}[X_{\mathcal{O}} = \tau]\right) \\ &= \sum_{\tau\in\mathcal{T}:\mathbf{Pr}[X_{\mathcal{P}}=\tau]>\mathbf{Pr}[X_{\mathcal{O}}=\tau]} \mathbf{Pr}[X_{\mathcal{P}} = \tau]\left(1 - \frac{\mathbf{Pr}[X_{\mathcal{O}} = \tau]}{\mathbf{Pr}[X_{\mathcal{P}} = \tau]}\right).\end{aligned}$$

Making a distinction between bad and good views, we find:

$$\Delta_{\mathcal{D}}(\mathcal{O}\,;\,\mathcal{P}) \leq \sum_{\tau\in\mathcal{T}_{\text{bad}}} \mathbf{Pr}[X_{\mathcal{P}} = \tau] + \sum_{\tau\in\mathcal{T}_{\text{good}}} \mathbf{Pr}[X_{\mathcal{P}} = \tau]\,\varepsilon \leq \delta + \varepsilon\,,$$

which completes the proof. □

The basic idea of the technique is that a large number of transcripts are almost equally likely in both worlds, and the odd ones appear only with negligible probability δ. Note that the partitioning of $\mathcal{T}$ into bad and good transcripts is directly reflected in the terms δ and ε in the bound: if $\mathcal{T}_{\text{good}}$ is too large, ε will become large, whereas if $\mathcal{T}_{\text{bad}}$ is too large, δ will become large.

For a given transcript $\tau = \{(x_1, y_1), \ldots, (x_q, y_q)\}$ consisting of q input/output tuples, we say that an oracle $\mathcal{O}$ *extends* τ, denoted $\mathcal{O} \vdash \tau$, if

$$\mathcal{O}(x_i) = y_i$$

for $i = 1, \ldots, q$.

2.4 Pseudorandom Function Security

Let $F^{p_1,p_2} \in \mathsf{func}(n)$ be a fixed-input-length function that internally uses two permutations $p_1, p_2 \in \mathsf{perm}(n)$. We denote the PRF security of F as a random function by

$$\mathbf{Adv}^{\text{prf}}_{F^{p_1,p_2}}(\mathcal{D}) = \Delta_{\mathcal{D}}(F^{p_1,p_2}\,;\,f) \tag{9}$$

where the probabilities are taken over the drawing of $p_1, p_2 \xleftarrow{\$} \mathsf{perm}(n)$ and $f \xleftarrow{\$} \mathsf{func}(n)$.

The model generalizes to the security of variable-input-length functions as follows. Let $F^{h,p_1,p_2} \in \mathsf{func}(n + *, n)$ be a variable-input-length function that internally uses two permutations $p_1, p_2 \in \mathsf{perm}(n)$ and a universal hash function h from some hash function family H. We denote the PRF security of F as a random function by

$$\mathbf{Adv}^{\mathrm{prf}}_{F^{h,p_1,p_2}}(\mathcal{D}) = \Delta_{\mathcal{D}}(F^{h,p_1,p_2}\,;\, f) \tag{10}$$

where the probabilities are taken over the drawing of $h \xleftarrow{\$} H$, $p_1, p_2 \xleftarrow{\$} \mathsf{perm}(n)$, and $f \xleftarrow{\$} \mathsf{func}(n + *, n)$. For variable-input-length functions, we will impose that $\mathcal{D}$ is nonce-respecting, i.e., it never makes two queries to its oracle with the same first component.

Remark 1. We focus on PRF security in the information-theoretic setting, where the underlying primitives are secret permutations uniformly randomly drawn from $\mathsf{perm}(n)$. Our results straightforwardly generalize to the complexity-theoretic setting, where the permutations are instantiated as E_{k_1}, E_{k_2} for secret keys k_1, k_2. The bounds of this work carry over with an additional loss of $2\mathbf{Adv}^{\mathrm{prp}}_E(q)$, where $\mathbf{Adv}^{\mathrm{prp}}_E(q)$ denotes the maximum advantage of distinguishing E_k for secret k from a uniformly random permutation in q queries. Note that in our analyses, the distinguisher can *only* induce forward evaluations of the underlying primitive. Therefore, the block cipher only needs to be prp secure, and not necessarily sprp secure.

3 Mirror Theory

We revisit an important result from Patarin's mirror theory [36,40] in our context of pseudorandom function security. For the sake of presentation and interoperability with the results in the remainder of this paper, we use different parametrization and naming of definitions.

3.1 System of Equations

Let $q \geq 1$ and $r \geq 1$. Let $\mathcal{P} = \{P_1, \ldots, P_r\}$ be r unknowns, and consider a system of q equations

$$\mathcal{E} = \{P_{a_1} \oplus P_{b_1} = \lambda_1, \cdots, P_{a_q} \oplus P_{b_q} = \lambda_q\} \tag{11}$$

where a_i, b_i for $i = 1, \ldots, q$ are mapped to $\{1, \ldots, r\}$ using some surjective index mapping

$$\varphi : \{a_1, b_1, \ldots, a_q, b_q\} \to \{1, \ldots, r\}\,.$$

Note that for a given system of equations, the index mapping is unique up to a reordering of the unknowns. There is a one-to-one correspondence between $\mathcal{E}$ on the one hand and $(\varphi, \lambda_1, \ldots, \lambda_q)$ on the other hand, and below definitions are mostly formalized based on the latter description (but it is convenient to think about them with respect to $\mathcal{E}$). For a subset $I \subseteq \{1, \ldots, q\}$ we define by $\mathcal{M}_I$ the multiset

$$\mathcal{M}_I = \bigcup_{i \in I} \{\varphi(a_i), \varphi(b_i)\}\,.$$

We give three definitions with respect to the system of equations $\mathcal{E}$.

Definition 1 (circle-freeness). *The system of equations $\mathcal{E}$ is* circle-free *if there is no $I \subseteq \{1, \ldots, q\}$ such that the multiset $\mathcal{M}_I$ has even multiplicity elements only.*

Definition 2 (block-maximality). *Let $\{1, \ldots, r\} = \mathcal{R}_1 \cup \cdots \cup \mathcal{R}_s$ be a partition of the r indices into s minimal "blocks" such that for all $i \in \{1, \ldots, q\}$ there exists an $\ell \in \{1, \ldots, s\}$ such that $\{\varphi(a_i), \varphi(b_i)\} \subseteq \mathcal{R}_\ell$. The system of equations $\mathcal{E}$ is* ξ-block-maximal *for $\xi \geq 2$ if there is no $\ell \in \{1, \ldots, s\}$ such that $|\mathcal{R}_\ell| > \xi$.*

Definition 3 (non-degeneracy). *The system of equations $\mathcal{E}$ is* non-degenerate *if there is no $I \subseteq \{1, \ldots, q\}$ such that the multiset $\mathcal{M}_I$ has exactly two odd multiplicity elements and such that $\bigoplus_{i \in I} \lambda_i = 0$.*

Informally, circle-freeness means that there is no linear combination of one or more equations in $\mathcal{E}$ that is independent of the unknowns, block-maximality means that the unknowns can be partitioned into blocks of a certain maximum size such that there is no linear combination of two or more equations in $\mathcal{E}$ that relates two unknowns P_a, P_b from different blocks $\mathcal{R}_i, \mathcal{R}_j$, and non-degeneracy means that there is no linear combination of one or more equations that implies $P_a = P_b$ for some $P_a, P_b \in \mathcal{P}$.

3.2 Main Result

The main theorem of Patarin's mirror theory, simply dubbed "mirror theorem", is the following. It corresponds to "Theorem $P_i \oplus P_j$ for any ξ_{max}" of Patarin [40, Theorem 6].

Theorem 2 (mirror theorem). *Let $\xi \geq 2$. Let $\mathcal{E}$ be a system of equations over the unknowns $\mathcal{P}$ that is (i) circle-free, (ii) ξ-block-maximal, and (iii) non-degenerate. Then, as long as $(\xi - 1)^2 \cdot r \leq 2^n/67$, the number of solutions for $\mathcal{P}$ such that $P_a \neq P_b$ for all distinct $a, b \in \{1, \ldots, r\}$ is at least*

$$\frac{(2^n)_r}{2^{nq}}\,.$$

The quantity measured in above theorem (the number of solutions...) is called h_r in [40]. H_r is subsequently defined as $2^{nq} h_r$. The parameter H has slightly different meanings in [39,41,42], namely the number of oracles whose outputs could solve the system of equations. In the end, these definitions yielded the naming of the H-coefficient technique of Theorem 1. For the mirror theorem, we have opted to stick to the convention of [40] as its definition is pure in the sense that it is independent of the actual oracles in use.

In Appendix A, we give a proof sketch of Theorem 2, referring to [40] for the details. In the proof sketch, it becomes apparent that the side condition $(\xi - 1)^2 \cdot r \le 2^n/67$ can be improved (even up to $2^n/16$) quite easily. Patarin first derived the side condition symbolically and only then derived the specific constants. Knowing the constants in advance, we reverted the reasoning. However, to remain consistent with the theorem statement of [40], we deliberately opted to leave the 67 in; the improvement is nevertheless only constant. The term $(\xi - 1)^2$ is present to cover worst-case systems of equations; it can be improved to $(\xi - 1)$ in certain cases [44]. Fortunately, in most cases ξ is a small number and the loss is relatively insignificant.

3.3 Extension to Relaxed Inequality Conditions

We consider a generalization to the case where the condition that $P_a \neq P_b$ whenever $a \neq b$ is released to some degree. More detailed, let $\{1, \ldots, r\} = \mathcal{R}_1 \cup \cdots \cup \mathcal{R}_t$ be any partition of the r indices. We will require that $P_a \neq P_b$ whenever $a, b \in \mathcal{R}_j$ for some $j \in \{1, \ldots, t\}$. Definition 3 generalizes the obvious way in order to comply with this condition:

Definition 4 (relaxed non-degeneracy). *The system of equations $\mathcal{E}$ is* relaxed non-degenerate *with respect to partition $\{1, \ldots, r\} = \mathcal{R}_1 \cup \cdots \cup \mathcal{R}_t$ if there is no $I \subseteq \{1, \ldots, q\}$ such that the multiset $\mathcal{M}_I$ has exactly two odd multiplicity elements from a single set $\mathcal{R}_j$ ($j \in \{1, \ldots, t\}$) and such that $\bigoplus_{i \in I} \lambda_i = 0$.*

Note that a relaxed non-degenerate system of equations may induce equations of the form $P_a = P_b$ where a, b are from distinct index sets; such an equation does not make the system degenerate. The extension of Theorem 2 to relaxed inequality conditions is the following, which corresponds to [40, Theorem 7].

Theorem 3 (relaxed mirror theorem). *Let $\xi \ge 2$. Let $\{1, \ldots, r\} = \mathcal{R}_1 \cup \cdots \cup \mathcal{R}_t$ be any partition of the r indices. Let $\mathcal{E}$ be a system of equations over the unknowns $\mathcal{P}$ that is (i) circle-free, (ii) ξ-block-maximal, and (iii) relaxed non-degenerate with respect to partition $\{1, \ldots, r\} = \mathcal{R}_1 \cup \cdots \cup \mathcal{R}_t$. Then, as long as $(\xi - 1)^2 \cdot \max_j |\mathcal{R}_j| \le 2^n/67$, the number of solutions for $\mathcal{P}$ such that $P_a \neq P_b$ for all distinct $a, b \in \{1, \ldots, r\}$ is at least*

$$\frac{\mathrm{NonEq}(\mathcal{R}_1, \ldots, \mathcal{R}_t; \mathcal{E})}{2^{nq}},$$

where $\mathrm{NonEq}(\mathcal{R}_1, \ldots, \mathcal{R}_t; \mathcal{E})$ denotes the number of solutions to $\mathcal{P}$ that satisfy $P_a \neq P_b$ for all $a, b \in \mathcal{R}_j$ ($j = 1, \ldots, t$) as well as the inequalities imposed by $\mathcal{E}$ (but the equalities themselves released).

The quantity $\text{NonEq}(\mathcal{R}_1, \ldots, \mathcal{R}_t; \mathcal{E})$ sounds rather technical, but for most systems it is fairly obvious to determine. If $P_a \oplus P_b = \lambda \neq 0$ is an equation in $\mathcal{E}$, then this equation imposes $P_a \neq P_b$; if in addition a, b are in distinct index sets, then this inequality $P_a \neq P_b$ imposes an *extra* inequality over the ones suggested by $\mathcal{R}_1, \ldots, \mathcal{R}_t$. An obvious lower bound is

$$\text{NonEq}(\mathcal{R}_1, \ldots, \mathcal{R}_t; \mathcal{E}) \geq (2^n)_{|\mathcal{R}_1|}(2^n - (\xi - 1))_{|\mathcal{R}_2|} \cdots (2^n - (\xi - 1))_{|\mathcal{R}_t|},$$

as every unknown is in exactly one block, and this block imposes at most $\xi - 1$ additional inequalities on the unknowns. Better lower bounds can be derived for specific systems of equations. The relaxed theorem is equivalent to the original Theorem 2 if $t = 1$ and $\mathcal{R}_1 = \{1, \ldots, r\}$.

3.4 Example

The strength of the mirror theorem becomes visible by considering the sum of permutations, XoP^{p_1,p_2} of (1) and XoP'^{p} of (2). As a stepping stone to the analyses of EDM, EWCDM, and EDMD in the remainder of the paper, we prove that XoP^{p_1,p_2} is a secure PRF as long as $q \leq 2^n/67$. The proof is almost directly taken from [40] and is an immediate application of Theorem 3. Its single-key variant XoP'^{p} can be proved similarly from Theorem 2, provided $2q \leq 2^n/67$.

Proposition 1. *For any distinguisher $\mathcal{D}$ with query complexity at most $q \leq 2^n/67$, we have*

$$\mathbf{Adv}^{\text{prf}}_{\text{XoP}^{p_1,p_2}}(\mathcal{D}) \leq q/2^n. \tag{12}$$

Proof. Let $p_1, p_2 \xleftarrow{\$} \mathsf{perm}(n)$ and $f \xleftarrow{\$} \mathsf{func}(n)$. Consider any fixed deterministic distinguisher $\mathcal{D}$ that has access to either $\mathcal{O} = \text{XoP}^{p_1,p_2}$ (real world) or $\mathcal{P} = f$ (ideal world). It makes q construction queries recorded in a transcript $\tau = \{(x_1, y_1), \ldots, (x_q, y_q)\}$. Without loss of generality, we assume that $x_i \neq x_j$ whenever $i \neq j$.

In the real world, each tuple $(x_i, y_i) \in \tau$ corresponds to an evaluation of the function XoP^{p_1,p_2} and thus to evaluations $x_i \mapsto p_1(x_i)$ and $x_i \mapsto p_2(x_i)$, such that $p_1(x_i) \oplus p_2(x_i) = y_i$. Writing $P_{2i-1} := p_1(x_i)$ and $P_{2i} := p_2(x_i)$, the transcript τ defines q equations on the unknowns:

$$\begin{aligned} P_1 \oplus P_2 &= y_1, \\ P_3 \oplus P_4 &= y_2, \\ &\vdots \\ P_{2q-1} \oplus P_{2q} &= y_q. \end{aligned} \tag{13}$$

As $x_i \neq x_j$ whenever $i \neq j$, and additionally we use two independent permutations, all unknowns are formally distinct. In line with Sect. 3.1, denote the system of q equations of (13) by $\mathcal{E}$, and let $\mathcal{P} = \{P_1, \ldots, P_{2q}\}$ be the $2q$ unknowns. We can divide the indices $\{1,\ldots,2q\}$ into two index sets: $\mathcal{R}_1 = \{1,3,\ldots,2q-1\}$ are the indices corresponding to oracle p_1 and $\mathcal{R}_2 = \{2,4,\ldots,2q\}$ the indices corresponding to oracle p_2.

Patarin's H-coefficient technique of Theorem 1 states that $\mathbf{Adv}^{\mathrm{prf}}_{\mathrm{XoP}^{p_1,p_2}}(\mathcal{D}) \leq \varepsilon$, where ε is such that for any transcript τ (we do not consider bad transcripts),

$$\frac{\mathbf{Pr}\left[X_{\mathrm{XoP}^{p_1,p_2}} = \tau\right]}{\mathbf{Pr}\left[X_f = \tau\right]} \geq 1 - \varepsilon\,. \tag{14}$$

For the computation of $\mathbf{Pr}\left[X_{\mathrm{XoP}^{p_1,p_2}} = \tau\right]$ and $\mathbf{Pr}\left[X_f = \tau\right]$, it suffices to compute the probability, over the drawing of the oracles, that a good transcript is obtained. For the real world XoP^{p_1,p_2}, the transcript τ defines a system of equations $\mathcal{E}$ which is circle-free, has q blocks of size 2 (so it is 2-block-maximal), and it is relaxed non-degenerate with respect to partition $\{1,\ldots,r\} = \mathcal{R}_1 \cup \mathcal{R}_2$. We can subsequently apply Theorem 3 for $\xi = 2$, and obtain that, provided $q \leq 2^n/67$, the number of solutions for the output values $\mathcal{P}$ is at least $\frac{\mathrm{NonEq}(\mathcal{R}_1,\mathcal{R}_2;\mathcal{E})}{2^{nq}}$. To lower bound $\mathrm{NonEq}(\mathcal{R}_1,\mathcal{R}_2;\mathcal{E})$, note that we have $(2^n)_q$ possible choices for $P_1, P_3, \ldots, P_{2q-1}$, at least $2^n - 1$ choices for P_2 (if $y_1 \neq 0$ then P_2 should be unequal to P_1), at least $2^n - 2$ choices for P_4 (it should be unequal to P_2, and if $y_2 \neq 0$, it should moreover be unequal to P_3), etc., and we obtain

$$\mathrm{NonEq}(\mathcal{R}_1,\mathcal{R}_2;\mathcal{E}) \geq (2^n)_q (2^n-1)_q\,.$$

We have $(2^n - q)!$ possible choices for the remaining output values of p_1, and similarly of p_2. Thus,

$$\begin{aligned}\mathbf{Pr}\left[X_{\mathrm{XoP}^{p_1,p_2}} = \tau\right] &= \frac{|\{p_1,p_2 \in \mathsf{perm}(n) \mid \mathrm{XoP}^{p_1,p_2} \vdash \tau\}|}{|\mathsf{perm}(n)|^2} \\ &\geq \frac{\frac{(2^n)_q(2^n-1)_q}{2^{nq}} \cdot ((2^n-q)!)^2}{(2^n!)^2} = \frac{1}{2^{nq}}\left(1 - \frac{q}{2^n}\right)\,.\end{aligned} \tag{15}$$

For the ideal world f, we similarly obtain

$$\mathbf{Pr}\left[X_f = \tau\right] = \frac{|\{f \in \mathsf{func}(n) \mid f \vdash \tau\}|}{|\mathsf{func}(n)|} = \frac{1}{2^{nq}}\,. \tag{16}$$

We thus obtain for the ratio of (14):

$$\frac{\mathbf{Pr}\left[X_{\mathrm{XoP}^{p_1,p_2}} = \tau\right]}{\mathbf{Pr}\left[X_f = \tau\right]} \geq 1 - \frac{q}{2^n}\,.$$

We have obtained $\varepsilon = \frac{q}{2^n}$, provided $q \leq 2^n/67$. □

4 Security of EDM^{p_1,p_2}

Consider EDM of (3) for the case of independent permutations p_1, p_2. We will prove that this construction achieves close to optimal security.

Theorem 4. *Let $\xi \geq 1$ be any threshold. For any distinguisher $\mathcal{D}$ with query complexity at most $q \leq 2^n/(67\xi^2)$, we have*

$$\mathbf{Adv}^{\mathrm{prf}}_{\mathrm{EDM}^{p_1,p_2}}(\mathcal{D}) \leq \frac{q}{2^n} + \frac{\binom{q}{\xi+1}}{2^{n\xi}}. \tag{17}$$

The proof will be given in the remainder of this section. It relies on the mirror theorem, although this application is not straightforward. Most importantly, rather than considering EDM^{p_1,p_2}, we consider $\mathrm{EDM}^{p_1,p_2^{-1}}$. As p_1, p_2 are mutually independent, these two constructions are provably equally secure, but it is more convenient to reason about the latter one: we can view an evaluation $y = \mathrm{EDM}^{p_1,p_2^{-1}}(x)$ as the xor of two permutations in the middle of the function, $p_1(x) \oplus p_2(y) = x$. Therefore, q evaluations of $\mathrm{EDM}^{p_1,p_2^{-1}}$ can be translated to a system of q equations on the outputs of p_1, p_2 of the form (11). Some technicalities persist, such as the fact that y may be identical for different evaluations of the construction, and make it impossible to apply the mirror theorem directly.

The ξ functions as a threshold: as long as the largest block is of size at most $\xi+1$, this means that the result of Patarin applies provided that $q \leq 2^n/(67\xi^2)$. The probability that there is a block of size $> \xi+1$ is at most $\binom{q}{\xi+1}/2^{n\xi}$. Taking $\xi = 1$ gives condition $q \leq 2^n/67$ but the bound is capped by $q^2/2^n$. The optimal choice of ξ is when $q = 2^n/(67\xi^2)$ still yields a reasonable bound, i.e., when $(67\xi^2)^{\xi+1}(\xi+1)! \geq 2^n$. For $n = 128$ this is the case for $\xi \geq 9$. For $n = 256$ this is the case for $\xi \geq 15$.

For general n, we can observe that the above definitely holds if $(67\xi^2)^\xi = 2^n$ (a better but more complicated bound can be obtained using Stirling's approximation). Solving this for ξ results in

$$\begin{aligned}
\left(67\xi^2\right)^\xi &= 2^n \\
\left(\sqrt{67}\xi\right)^\xi &= 2^{n/2} \\
\left(\sqrt{67}\xi\right)^{\sqrt{67}\xi} &= 2^{\sqrt{67}n/2} \\
\sqrt{67}\xi &= e^{W\left(\ln\left(2^{\sqrt{67}n/2}\right)\right)} \\
\frac{\ln\left(2^{\sqrt{67}n/2}\right)}{\ln\ln\left(2^{\sqrt{67}n/2}\right)} \leq \sqrt{67}\xi &\leq \frac{\ln\left(2^{\sqrt{67}n/2}\right)}{\sqrt{\ln\ln\left(2^{\sqrt{67}n/2}\right)}},
\end{aligned}$$

where the last inequality comes from the approximation $\ln x - \ln\ln x \leq W(x) \leq \ln x - \frac{1}{2}\ln\ln x$ on the Lambert W function [23]. Coupled with Theorem 4, this guarantees security as long as $q \leq \frac{2^n}{(67n/\sqrt{\ln 67n})}$.

As suggested by Patarin [40, Generalization 2], it may be possible to eschew the condition $\xi^2 \cdot q \leq 2^n/67$ in favor of $\xi^2_{\mathrm{average}} \cdot q \leq 2^n/67$, where ξ_{average} denotes the average block size. For EDM^{p_1,p_2}, the probability of a given block being of size $\xi+1$ is significantly lower than of it being of size ξ; thus, the number of blocks with 2 variables is expected to dominate, and contribute the largest amount of solutions of the mirror system.

The proof of Theorem 4 consists of five steps: in Sect. 4.1 we describe how transcripts are generated, in Sect. 4.2 we discuss attainable index mappings, in Sect. 4.3 we give a definition of bad transcripts, in Sect. 4.4 we derive an upper bound on the probability of a bad transcript in the ideal world, and in Sect. 4.5 a lower bound on the ratio for good transcripts. Theorem 4 immediately follows from the H-coefficient technique of Theorem 1.

4.1 General Setting and Transcripts

Let $p_1, p_2 \xleftarrow{\$} \mathsf{perm}(n)$ and $f \xleftarrow{\$} \mathsf{func}(n)$. Consider any fixed deterministic distinguisher $\mathcal{D}$ that has access to either $\mathcal{O} = \text{EDM}^{p_1,p_2^{-1}}$ (real world) or $\mathcal{P} = f$ (ideal world). It makes q construction queries recorded in a transcript $\tau = \{(x_1, y_1), \ldots, (x_q, y_q)\}$. Without loss of generality, we assume that $x_i \neq x_j$ whenever $i \neq j$.

4.2 Attainable Index Mappings

In the real world, each tuple $(x_i, y_i) \in \tau$ corresponds to an evaluation of the function $\text{EDM}^{p_1,p_2^{-1}}$ and thus to a one call to p_1 and one to p_2: $x_i \mapsto p_1(x_i)$ and $y_i \mapsto p_2(y_i)$, such that $p_1(x_i) \oplus p_2(y_i) = x_i$. Indeed, p_1 and p_2 xor to x_i in the middle of the function $\text{EDM}^{p_1,p_2^{-1}}$. Writing $P_{a_i} := p_1(x_i)$ and $P_{b_i} := p_2(y_i)$, the transcript τ defines q equations on the unknowns:

$$\begin{aligned} P_{a_1} \oplus P_{b_1} &= x_1 \,, \\ P_{a_2} \oplus P_{b_2} &= x_2 \,, \\ &\vdots \\ P_{a_q} \oplus P_{b_q} &= x_q \,. \end{aligned} \tag{18}$$

In line with Sect. 3.1, denote the system of q equations of (18) by $\mathcal{E}$, let $\mathcal{P} = \{P_1, \ldots, P_r\}$ be the r unknowns, for $r \in \{q, \ldots, 2q\}$, and let

$$\varphi : \{a_1, b_1, \ldots, a_q, b_q\} \to \{1, \ldots, r\}$$

be the unique index mapping corresponding to the system of Eq. (18). Denote $\mathcal{R}_1 = \{\varphi(a_1), \ldots, \varphi(a_q)\}$ and $\mathcal{R}_2 = \{\varphi(b_1), \ldots, \varphi(b_q)\}$.

There is a relation between the index mapping and the permutations p_1, p_2, and different permutations could entail a different index mapping. Nevertheless, as $x_i \neq x_j$ whenever $i \neq j$, and additionally we consider independent permutations, any possible index mapping in the real world satisfies the following property.

Claim. $\varphi(a_i) \neq \varphi(a_j)$ if and only if $i \neq j$, and $\varphi(b_i) \neq \varphi(b_j)$ if and only if $y_i \neq y_j$. Furthermore, $\varphi(a_i) \neq \varphi(b_j)$ for any i, j.

Stated differently, φ should satisfy the input-output pattern induced by τ, and for any φ that does not satisfy this constraint, $\mathbf{Pr}[\varphi \mid \tau] = 0$. This particularly means that, if τ is given, there is a unique index mapping φ^τ (up to a reordering of the unknowns) that could have yielded the transcript. This index mapping has a range of size $q + q'$, where $q' = |\{y_1, \ldots, y_q\}| \leq q$ denotes the number of distinct range values in τ.

4.3 Bad Transcripts

In the real world, φ only exposes collisions of the form $\varphi(b_i) = \varphi(b_j)$, or equivalently $y_i = y_j$, for some i, j. As a matter of fact, multi-collisions in the range values in τ correspond to blocks in the mirror theory. Therefore, we say that a transcript τ is *bad* if there exist $\xi+1$ distinct equation indices $i_1, \ldots, i_{\xi+1} \in \{1, \ldots, q\}$ such that $y_{i_1} = \cdots = y_{i_{\xi+1}}$, where ξ is the threshold given in the theory statement.

4.4 Probability of Bad Transcripts (δ)

In accordance with Theorem 1, it suffices to analyze the probability of a bad transcript in the ideal world. We have:

$$\mathbf{Pr}\left[X_f \in \mathcal{T}_{\text{bad}}\right] = \mathbf{Pr}\left[\exists i_1, \ldots, i_{\xi+1} \in \{1, \ldots, q\} \;:\; y_{i_1} = \cdots = y_{i_{\xi+1}}\right] \leq \frac{\binom{q}{\xi+1}}{2^{n\xi}},$$

where we recall that in the ideal world the randomness in the transcript τ is in the values $y_1, \ldots, y_q \xleftarrow{\$} \{0,1\}^n$. We have obtained $\delta = \frac{\binom{q}{\xi+1}}{2^{n\xi}}$.

4.5 Ratio for Good Transcripts (ε)

Recall from Sect. 4.2 that for a given transcript τ, there is a unique index mapping φ^τ that could have resulted in the transcript. Pivotal to our proof is the following lemma.

Lemma 1. *Consider good transcript τ, and denote by $\mathcal{E}$ the system of q equations corresponding to $(\varphi^\tau, x_1, \ldots, x_q)$. This system of equations is (i) circle-free, (ii) $(\xi+1)$-block-maximal, and (iii) relaxed non-degenerate with respect to partition $\{1, \ldots, r\} = \mathcal{R}_1 \cup \mathcal{R}_2$.*

Proof. The proof relies on the fact that $\varphi^\tau(a_i) \neq \varphi^\tau(a_j)$ whenever $i \neq j$, and additionally that $\varphi^\tau(a_i) \neq \varphi^\tau(b_j)$ for any i, j. Particularly, for any $I \subseteq \{1, \ldots, q\}$ the corresponding multiset $\mathcal{M}_I$ has at least $|I|$ odd multiplicity elements, and there exists (i) no circle (Definition 1).

(ii) Suppose that $\mathcal{E}$ is not $(\xi+1)$-block-maximal (Definition 2). Then, there exists a minimal subset $\mathcal{R} \subseteq \{1, \ldots, r\}$ of size $\geq \xi + 2$ such that for any $i \in \{1, \ldots, q\}$ we either have $\{\varphi^\tau(a_i), \varphi^\tau(b_i)\} \subseteq \mathcal{R}$ or $\{\varphi^\tau(a_i), \varphi^\tau(b_i)\} \cap \mathcal{R} = \emptyset$. Let $I \subseteq \{1, \ldots, q\}$ be the subset such that $\{\varphi^\tau(a_i), \varphi^\tau(b_i)\} \subseteq \mathcal{R}$ for all $i \in I$.

Due to our definition of φ^τ, there must be an ordering $I = \{i_1, \ldots, i_{\xi+1}\}$ such that $\varphi^\tau(b_{i_1}) = \cdots = \varphi^\tau(b_{i_{\xi+1}})$, or equivalently, $y_{i_1} = \cdots = y_{i_{\xi+1}}$, therewith contradicting that τ is good and does not contain a $(\xi+1)$-fold collision.

(iii) Suppose that the system of equations is relaxed degenerate (Definition 4). Then, there exists a minimal subset $I \subseteq \{1, \ldots, q\}$ such that the multiset $\mathcal{M}_I$ has exactly two odd multiplicity elements corresponding to the same oracle and such that $\bigoplus_{i \in I} x_i = 0$. If $|I| = 1$, then $\mathcal{M}_I$ has two elements from different oracles. If $|I| = 2$, then $\bigoplus_{i \in I} x_i \neq 0$ as the x_i are all distinct. Finally, if $|I| \geq 3$ then $\mathcal{M}_I$ has at least 3 odd multiplicity elements. □

For the computation of $\mathbf{Pr}\left[X_{\mathrm{EDM}^{p_1,p_2^{-1}}} = \tau\right]$ and $\mathbf{Pr}\left[X_f = \tau\right]$, it suffices to compute the probability, over the drawing of the oracles, that a good transcript is obtained. Starting with the real world $\mathrm{EDM}^{p_1,p_2^{-1}}$, for the transcript τ, there is a unique index mapping φ^τ. It concerns q input-output tuples of p_1 and q' input-output tuples of p_2, where $|\mathrm{rng}(\varphi^\tau)| = q + q'$. Due to Lemma 1, we can apply Theorem 3 and obtain that, provided $\xi^2 \cdot q \leq 2^n/67$, the number of solutions to these $q + q'$ unknowns is at least $\frac{\mathrm{NonEq}(\mathcal{R}_1,\mathcal{R}_2;\mathcal{E})}{2^{nq}}$. We have $(2^n - q)!$ possible choices for the remaining output values of p_1, and $(2^n - q')!$ for p_2. Thus,

$$\mathbf{Pr}\left[X_{\mathrm{EDM}^{p_1,p_2^{-1}}} = \tau\right] = \mathbf{Pr}\left[p_1, p_2 \xleftarrow{\$} \mathsf{perm}(n) \;:\; \mathrm{EDM}^{p_1,p_2^{-1}} \vdash \tau\right]$$
$$\geq \frac{\frac{\mathrm{NonEq}(\mathcal{R}_1,\mathcal{R}_2;\mathcal{E})}{2^{nq}} \cdot (2^n - q)!(2^n - q')!}{(2^n!)^2} = \frac{\mathrm{NonEq}(\mathcal{R}_1,\mathcal{R}_2;\mathcal{E})}{2^{nq}(2^n)_q(2^n)_{q'}}.$$

To lower bound $\mathrm{NonEq}(\mathcal{R}_1,\mathcal{R}_2;\mathcal{E})$, note that we have $(2^n)_{q'}$ possible choices for $\{P_j \mid j \in \mathcal{R}_2\}$, and subsequently at least $(2^n - 1)_q$ possible choices for $\{P_j \mid j \in \mathcal{R}_1\}$, as every index in $\mathcal{R}_1$ is in a block with exactly one unknown from $\mathcal{R}_2$. Thus,

$$\mathbf{Pr}\left[X_{\mathrm{EDM}^{p_1,p_2^{-1}}} = \tau\right] \geq \frac{(2^n - 1)_q (2^n)_{q'}}{2^{nq}(2^n)_q(2^n)_{q'}} = \frac{1}{2^{nq}}\left(1 - \frac{q}{2^n}\right). \tag{19}$$

For the ideal world, we obtain

$$\mathbf{Pr}\left[X_f = \tau\right] = \mathbf{Pr}\left[f \xleftarrow{\$} \mathsf{func}(n) \;:\; f \vdash \tau\right] = \frac{1}{2^{nq}}. \tag{20}$$

We obtain for the ratio:

$$\frac{\mathbf{Pr}\left[X_{\mathrm{EDM}^{p_1,p_2^{-1}}} = \tau\right]}{\mathbf{Pr}\left[X_f = \tau\right]} \geq \frac{\frac{1}{2^{nq}}\left(1 - \frac{q}{2^n}\right)}{\frac{1}{2^{nq}}} = 1 - \frac{q}{2^n}.$$

We have obtained $\varepsilon = \frac{q}{2^n}$, provided $\xi^2 \cdot q \leq 2^n/67$.

5 Security of $\mathrm{EWCDM}^{h,p_1,p_2}$

We prove that EWCDM of (4) for the case independent permutations p_1, p_2 achieves close to optimal PRF security in the nonce-respecting setting. We remark that Cogliati and Seurin proved PRF security of $\mathrm{EWCDM}^{h,p_1,p_2}$ up to about $2^{2n/3}$ queries (cf., [17, Theorem 3] for $q_v = 0$). In a similar vein as the analysis of Cogliati and Seurin [17] on $\mathrm{EWCDM}^{h,p_1,p_2}$, our analysis straightforwardly generalizes to the analysis for unforgeability or for the nonce-misusing setting.

Theorem 5. *Let $\xi \geq 1$ be any threshold. For any distinguisher $\mathcal{D}$ with query complexity at most $q \leq 2^n/(67\xi^2)$, we have*

$$\mathbf{Adv}^{\mathrm{prf}}_{\mathrm{EWCDM}^{h,p_1,p_2}}(\mathcal{D}) \leq \frac{q}{2^n} + \frac{\binom{q}{2}\epsilon}{2^n} + \frac{\binom{q}{\xi+1}}{2^{n\xi}}, \tag{21}$$

where h is an ϵ-AXU hash function.

The proof follows the same strategy as the one of EDM^{p_1,p_2}, i.e., replacing p_2 by p_2^{-1} for readability and noting that $t = \mathrm{EWCDM}^{h,p_1,p_2^{-1}}(\nu, m)$ corresponds to the xor of two permutations as $p_1(\nu) \oplus p_2(t) = \nu \oplus h(m)$. An additional hurdle has to be overcome, namely cases where $\nu \oplus h(m) = \nu' \oplus h(m')$: if this happens, and additionally we have $t = t'$, the system of equations cannot be solved. (In retrospect, one can view the proof of EDM^{p_1,p_2} as a special case of the new proof by keeping m constant.) As before, ξ functions as a threshold and the computations of Sect. 4 likewise apply.

5.1 General Setting and Transcripts

Let $h \xleftarrow{\$} H$ be an ϵ-AXU hash function, $p_1, p_2 \xleftarrow{\$} \mathsf{perm}(n)$, and $f \xleftarrow{\$} \mathsf{func}(n{+}*, n)$. Consider any fixed deterministic distinguisher $\mathcal{D}$ that has access to either $\mathcal{O} = \mathrm{EWCDM}^{h,p_1,p_2^{-1}}$ (real world) or $\mathcal{P} = f$ (ideal world). It makes q construction queries recorded in a transcript $\tau_{\mathrm{cq}} = \{(\nu_1, m_1, t_1), \ldots, (\nu_q, m_q, t_q)\}$, where the q nonces ν_i are mutually different.

We will reveal after $\mathcal{D}$'s interaction with its oracle, but before its final decision, a universal hash function h. In the real world, h is the hash function that is actually used. In the ideal world, h will be drawn uniformly at random from the ϵ-AXU universal hash function family H. The extended transcript is denoted

$$\tau = (\tau_{\mathrm{cq}}, h).$$

5.2 Attainable Index Mappings

In the real world, each tuple $(\nu_i, m_i, t_i) \in \tau_{\mathrm{cq}}$ corresponds to an evaluation of the function $\mathrm{EWCDM}^{h,p_1,p_2^{-1}}$ and thus evaluations $\nu_i \mapsto p_1(\nu_i)$ and $t_i \mapsto p_2(t_i)$, such that $p_1(\nu_i) \oplus p_2(t_i) = \nu_i \oplus h(m_i)$ (note the fundamental difference with respect to the analysis of $\mathrm{EDM}^{p_1,p_2^{-1}}$ of Sect. 4, namely the addition of $h(m_i)$). Writing $P_{a_i} := p_1(\nu_i)$ and $P_{b_i} := p_2(t_i)$, the transcript τ_{cq} defines q equations on the unknowns:

$$\begin{aligned} P_{a_1} \oplus P_{b_1} &= \nu_1 \oplus h(m_1)\,, \\ P_{a_2} \oplus P_{b_2} &= \nu_2 \oplus h(m_2)\,, \\ &\vdots \\ P_{a_q} \oplus P_{b_q} &= \nu_q \oplus h(m_q)\,. \end{aligned} \tag{22}$$

(The system of equations differs from that of (18) as the unknowns should now sum to $\nu_i \oplus h(m_i)$.) In line with Sect. 3.1, denote the system of q equations of (22) by $\mathcal{E}$, let $\mathcal{P} = \{P_1, \ldots, P_r\}$ be the r unknowns, for $r \in \{q, \ldots, 2q\}$, and let

$$\varphi : \{a_1, b_1, \ldots, a_q, b_q\} \to \{1, \ldots, r\}$$

be the unique index mapping corresponding to the system of Eq. (22). Denote $\mathcal{R}_1 = \{\varphi(a_1), \ldots, \varphi(a_q)\}$ and $\mathcal{R}_2 = \{\varphi(b_1), \ldots, \varphi(b_q)\}$.

From the fact that $\nu_i \neq \nu_j$ whenever $i \neq j$, and additionally that we consider two independent permutations, we can derive the exact same property of φ as in Sect. 4.2, with ν replacing x and t replacing y.

Claim. $\varphi(a_i) \neq \varphi(a_j)$ if and only if $i \neq j$, and $\varphi(b_i) \neq \varphi(b_j)$ if and only if $t_i \neq t_j$. Furthermore, $\varphi(a_i) \neq \varphi(b_j)$ for any i, j.

As before, for a given transcript τ_{cq}, there is a unique index mapping φ^τ that could have yielded the transcript. It has a range of size $q + q'$, where $q' = |\{t_1, \ldots, t_q\}| \leq q$ denotes the number of distinct range values in τ_{cq}.

5.3 Bad Transcripts

Unlike for the analysis of $\text{EDM}^{p_1,p_2^{-1}}$, it is insufficient to just require that there is no $(\xi+1)$-fold collision, we must also take degeneracy of the system of equations into account. Indeed, if for two queries $(\nu_i, m_i, t_i), (\nu_j, m_j, t_j)$, we have that $t_i = t_j$ (or, equivalently, $\varphi(b_i) = \varphi(b_j)$) and $\nu_i \oplus h(m_i) = \nu_j \oplus h(m_j)$, the system of equations would imply that we need $\varphi(a_i) = \varphi(a_j)$, which is impossible by design.

Formally, we say that a transcript $\tau = (\tau_{\text{cq}}, h)$ is *bad* if

- there exist $\xi + 1$ distinct equation indices $i_1, \ldots, i_{\xi+1} \in \{1, \ldots, q\}$ such that $t_{i_1} = \cdots = t_{i_{\xi+1}}$, where ξ is the threshold given in the theory statement, or
- there exist two distinct equation indices $i, j \in \{1, \ldots, q\}$ such that $t_i = t_j$ and $\nu_i \oplus h(m_i) = \nu_j \oplus h(m_j)$.

5.4 Probability of Bad Transcripts (δ)

As in Sect. 4.4, it suffices to analyze the probability of a bad transcript in the ideal world, and we have:

$$\begin{aligned} \mathbf{Pr}\left[X_f \in \mathcal{T}_{\text{bad}}\right] \leq\ & \mathbf{Pr}\left[\exists i_1, \ldots, i_{\xi+1} \in \{1, \ldots, q\}\ :\ t_{i_1} = \cdots = t_{i_{\xi+1}}\right] \\ &+ \mathbf{Pr}\left[\exists i, j \in \{1, \ldots, q\}\ :\ t_i = t_j \wedge \nu_i \oplus h(m_i) = \nu_j \oplus h(m_j)\right], \end{aligned} \tag{23}$$

where we recall that in the ideal world the randomness in the transcript τ is in the values $t_1, \ldots, t_q \xleftarrow{\$} \{0,1\}^n$ and in the uniform drawing $h \xleftarrow{\$} H$. The first probability of (23) is identical to the one analyzed in Sect. 4.4 and upper bounded by $\binom{q}{\xi+1}/2^{n\xi}$. For the second probability of (23), there are $\binom{q}{2}$ possible indices, the first equation is satisfied with probability $1/2^n$ (due to the drawing of the t_i), and the second equation is satisfied with probability ϵ (as h is an ϵ-AXU hash function). Thus, the second probability is upper bounded by $\binom{q}{2}\epsilon/2^n$.

We thus obtain from (23):

$$\mathbf{Pr}\left[X_f \in \mathcal{T}_{\text{bad}}\right] \leq \frac{\binom{q}{2}\epsilon}{2^n} + \frac{\binom{q}{\xi+1}}{2^{n\xi}} =: \delta\,.$$

5.5 Ratio for Good Transcripts (ε)

Recall from Sect. 5.2 that for a given transcript τ_{cq}, there is a unique index mapping φ^τ that could have resulted in the transcript. We can derive the following result.

Lemma 2. *Consider good transcript $\tau = (\tau_{cq}, h)$ and denote by $\mathcal{E}$ the system of q equations corresponding to $(\varphi^\tau, \nu_1 \oplus h(m_1), \ldots, \nu_q \oplus h(m_q))$. This system of equations is (i) circle-free, (ii) $(\xi+1)$-block-maximal, and (iii) relaxed non-degenerate with respect to partition $\{1, \ldots, r\} = \mathcal{R}_1 \cup \mathcal{R}_2$.*

Proof. The proof is a generalization of the one of Lemma 1. Nothing changes for circle-freeness and $(\xi+1)$-block-maximality.

Suppose that the system of equations is relaxed degenerate (Definition 4). Then, there exists a minimal subset $I \subseteq \{1, \ldots, q\}$ such that the multiset $\mathcal{M}_I$ has exactly two odd multiplicity elements corresponding to the same oracle and such that $\bigoplus_{i \in I} \nu_i \oplus h(m_i) = 0$. As in Lemma 1, this implies that $|I| = 2$, say $I = \{i, j\}$, for which $\varphi^\tau(b_i) = \varphi^\tau(b_j)$ and $\nu_i \oplus h(m_i) = \nu_j \oplus h(m_j)$, therewith contradicting that τ is good. □

The remaining analysis is almost identical to the one for $\text{EDM}^{p_1, p_2^{-1}}$ in Sect. 4.5, the sole exception being that both probabilities have an additional factor $1/|H|$, and henceforth omitted.

6 Security of EDMD^{p_1,p_2}

Consider EDMD^{p_1,p_2} of (5) for the case of independent permutations p_1, p_2. We will prove that this construction achieves optimal PRF security without a logarithmic loss.

Theorem 6. *For any distinguisher $\mathcal{D}$ with query complexity at most $q \leq 2^n/67$, we have*

$$\mathbf{Adv}^{\text{prf}}_{\text{EDMD}^{p_1,p_2}}(\mathcal{D}) \leq q/2^n\,. \tag{24}$$

The proof can be performed along the same lines of that of EDM^{p_1,p_2}, with the difference that for EDMD^{p_1,p_2} no collisions among the evaluations of the permutations occur. However, the exact same security bound can be derived fairly elegantly from Proposition 1.

Proof. Let $p_1, p_2, p_3 \xleftarrow{\$} \mathsf{perm}(n)$ and $f \xleftarrow{\$} \mathsf{func}(n)$. Write $\mathrm{EDMD}^{p_1,p_2} = p_2 \circ p_1 \oplus p_1$. By a simple hybrid argument we obtain:

$$\Delta(p_2 \circ p_1 \oplus p_1\, ;\, f) \leq \Delta(p_2 \circ p_1 \oplus p_1\, ;\, p_3 \oplus p_1) + \Delta(p_3 \oplus p_1\, ;\, f)\,.$$

The former distance equals 0 (reveal p_1 to the distinguisher prior to the experiment, and it effectively has to distinguish p_2 from p_3). The latter distance is bounded by $q/2^n$ provided that $q \leq 2^n/67$, cf., Proposition 1. □

7 Towards a Single Permutation

Given our results on EDM^{p_1,p_2} of Theorem 4 and EDMD^{p_1,p_2} of Theorem 6, one may expect that similar techniques apply to the case where $p_1 = p_2$. However, it seems unlikely, if not impossible, to apply the mirror theory to these constructions. The reason is that the mirror theory works particularly well if only the input values of the functions are determined, and not the output values.

For example, for EDM^{p_1,p_2}, an evaluation $y = \mathrm{EDM}^{p_1,p_2}(x)$ corresponds to evaluations $p_1(x)$ and $p_2(p_1(x) \oplus x)$, where $y = p_2(p_1(x) \oplus x)$. Thus, the query-response tuple (x, y) reveals one input value to p_1 and one output value of p_2. By, without loss of generality, replacing p_2 by its inverse we nicely obtained a system where only input values of the permutations are fixed. Now, consider EDM^p: a single evaluation $y = \mathrm{EDM}^p(x)$ reveals an input value x to p as well as an output value y of p, and there seems to be no way to properly employ the mirror theorem in this case. The trick to view $\mathrm{EDM}^{p,p^{-1}}$ does not work as the construction is not equally secure as $\mathrm{EDM}^p = \mathrm{EDM}^{p,p}$. (In fact, $\mathrm{EDM}^{p,p^{-1}}$ is trivially insecure as it maps 0 to 0.)

For the single permutation variant of EDMD, the problem appears at a different surface: the chaining. In more detail, an evaluation $y = \mathrm{EDMD}^p(x)$ corresponds to two evaluations of p: $p(x)$ and $p(p(x))$, where $y = p(x) \oplus p(p(x))$. Suppose we have a different evaluation $y' = \mathrm{EDMD}^p(x')$ such that, accidentally, $p(p(x)) = p(x')$. This implies that the permutation p necessarily satisfies the following constraints:

$$p(x) = x'\ ,\ p(p(x)) = p(x') = y \oplus x'\ ,\ p(p(x')) = y' \oplus y \oplus x'\,.$$

In other words, a collision between two evaluations of p imposes conditions on the input-output pattern of p, and the mirror theorem does not allow to handle this case nicely. (Technically, the collision in this example forms a block of size 3 in the terminology of Definition 2, but the amount of freedom we have in fixing the unknowns in the block is not 2^n (as for normal systems of equations of Sect. 3), but at most 1).

We are not aware of any potential attack on EDM^p or EDMD^p that may exploit these properties. In fact, we believe that the conjecture posed by Cogliati and Seurin [17] holds for EDM^p, and that also EDMD^p achieves optimal security. It is interesting to note that

$$\mathrm{EDM}^p \circ p = p \circ \mathrm{EDMD}^p ,$$

and any attack on EDM^p performed by, for instance, chaining multiple evaluations of EDM^p would have its equivalent attack for EDMD^p.

Acknowledgments. Bart Mennink is supported by a postdoctoral fellowship from the Netherlands Organisation for Scientific Research (NWO) under Veni grant 016.Veni.173.017. The authors would like to thank Jacques Patarin for helpful discussions, the anonymous reviewers of CRYPTO 2017 for their useful technical comments, and Mridul Nandi for identifying an oversight in the analysis of the earlier EWCDMD construction [32].

A Proof Sketch of Theorem 2

Proof (sketch). Patarin's proof of Theorem 2 is very technical, and we only sketch its idea here. We refer to [36,40,41] for the technical details.

First consider the case of $\xi = 2$, i.e., $r = 2q$ and every unknown appears in exactly one equation. Without loss of generality (by reshuffling the unknowns), the system of equations reads

$$\mathcal{E} = \{P_1 \oplus P_2 = \lambda_1, \cdots, P_{2q-1} \oplus P_{2q} = \lambda_q\} . \tag{25}$$

For $u \in \{1, \ldots, q\}$, denote by $\mathcal{E}_u$ the first u equations of $\mathcal{E}$ and by h_{2u} the number of solutions to $\mathcal{E}_u$. Our target is to prove that $h_{2q} \geq \frac{(2^n)_{2q}}{2^{nq}}$, and we will prove this by induction on u. Clearly, for $u = 1$, $h_2 = 2^n$.

Suppose we have h_{2u} solutions for the first u equations. Then, h_{2u+2} counts the number of solutions to $\{P_1, \ldots, P_{2u+2}\}$ such that

- $\{P_1, \ldots, P_{2u}\}$ is a valid solution to the first u equations $\mathcal{E}_u$;
- $P_{2u+1} \oplus P_{2u+2} = \lambda_{u+1}$;
- $P_{2u+1} \notin \{P_1, \ldots, P_{2u}\} =: V_1$;
- $P_{2u+1} \notin \{P_1 \oplus \lambda_{u+1}, \ldots, P_{2u} \oplus \lambda_{u+1}\} =: V_2$.

Thus, for a given set of solutions to $\mathcal{E}_u$, we have $2^n - |V_1 \cup V_2|$ solutions for $\{P_{2u+1}, P_{2u+2}\}$. As $|V_1 \cup V_2| = |V_1| + |V_2| - |V_1 \cap V_2| = 4u - |V_1 \cap V_2|$, we obtain

$$\begin{aligned} h_{2u+2} &= \sum_{\{P_1,\ldots,P_{2u}\} \text{ solving } \mathcal{E}_u} 2^n - |V_1 \cup V_2| \\ &= \sum_{\{P_1,\ldots,P_{2u}\} \text{ solving } \mathcal{E}_u} 2^n - 4u + |V_1 \cap V_2| \\ &= (2^n - 4u)h_{2u} + \sum_{\{P_1,\ldots,P_{2u}\} \text{ solving } \mathcal{E}_u} |V_1 \cap V_2| . \end{aligned} \tag{26}$$

Obviously, $|V_1 \cap V_2| \geq 0$, but this gives only a poor estimation of h_{2q}, namely

$$h_{2q} \geq (2^n - 4(q-1))h_{2q-2} \geq \cdots \geq \left(\prod_{u=1}^{q-1} 2^n - 4u\right) h_2 \geq \prod_{u=0}^{q-1} 2^n - 4u\,,$$

for which

$$\begin{aligned}\frac{h_{2q}2^{nq}}{(2^n)_{2q}} &\geq \prod_{u=0}^{q-1} \frac{(2^n-4u)2^n}{(2^n-2u)(2^n-2u-1)} \\ &= \prod_{u=0}^{q-1} 1 - \frac{-2^n+4u^2+2u}{(2^n-2u)(2^n-2u-1)} \\ &\geq \prod_{u=0}^{q-1} 1 - \frac{4u^2}{(2^n-2q)^2} = 1 - O\left(\frac{q^3}{2^{2n}}\right).\end{aligned}$$

Instead, we would prefer to have a lower bound on $|V_1 \cap V_2|$ that can be used to undo the $4u^2$-term. If we could, hypothetically, prove that $|V_1 \cap V_2| \geq 4u^2/2^n$, the derivation would depart from (26) as

$$\begin{aligned}\frac{h_{2q}2^{nq}}{(2^n)_{2q}} &\geq \prod_{u=0}^{q-1} \frac{(2^n-4u+\frac{4u^2}{2^n})2^n}{(2^n-2u)(2^n-2u-1)} \\ &= \prod_{u=0}^{q-1} 1 - \frac{-2^n+2u}{(2^n-2u)(2^n-2u-1)} \geq 1\,.\end{aligned}$$

Unfortunately, for some solutions $\{P_1, \ldots, P_{2u}\}$ satisfying $\mathcal{E}_u$, the number $|V_1 \cap V_2|$ may be well below this bound, while for others it may be much higher. Patarin proved that, in fact, a slightly worse bounding already does the job.

Rewrite the crucial quantity of (26) as

$$\sum_{\{P_1,\ldots,P_{2u}\}\text{ solving }\mathcal{E}_u} |V_1 \cap V_2| = \sum_{1\leq i,j\leq 2u} \underbrace{\left|\left\{\text{solutions to } \mathcal{E}_u \cup \{P_i \oplus P_j = \lambda_{u+1}\}\right\}\right|}_{=:h'_{2u}(i,j)}. \tag{27}$$

Denote by I_{u+1} the set of indices whose value λ_l equals λ_{u+1}, and by J_{u+1} the set of pairs of indices whose value $\lambda_l \oplus \lambda_{l'}$ equals λ_{u+1}:

$$\begin{aligned}I_{u+1} &= \{l \in \{1, \ldots, u\} \mid \lambda_l = \lambda_{u+1}\}\,, \\ J_{u+1} &= \{(l, l') \in \{1, \ldots, u\}^2 \mid \lambda_l \oplus \lambda_{l'} = \lambda_{u+1}\}\,.\end{aligned}$$

The value $h'_{2u}(i,j)$ may attain different values depending on (i,j):

- If $i, j \in \{2l-1, 2l\}$ for some $l \in \{1, \ldots, u\}$, the two unknowns come from the same equation in $\mathcal{E}_u$:

- If $i = j$, then $h'_{2u}(i,j) = 0$, as the appended equation forms a contradiction on its own;
- If $i \neq j$ and $l \in I_{u+1}$, then $h'_{2u}(i,j) = h_{2u}$, as the appended equation is identical to the l-th equation in $\mathcal{E}_u$, and is redundant;
- If $i \neq j$ and $l \notin I_{u+1}$, then $h'_{2u}(i,j) = 0$, as the appended equation forms a contradiction with the l-th equation: $\lambda_l = P_i \oplus P_j = \lambda_{u+1}$;

- If $i \in \{2l-1, 2l\}$ and $j \notin \{2l-1, 2l\}$ for some $l \in I_{u+1}$, then $h'_{2u}(i,j) = 0$, as the appended equation forms a contradiction with the l-th equation. For example, if $i = 2l-1$, then the two equations imply that $P_{2l} \oplus P_j = 0$;
- If $j \in \{2l-1, 2l\}$ and $i \notin \{2l-1, 2l\}$ for some $l \in I_{u+1}$, we have $h'_{2u}(i,j) = 0$ by symmetry;
- If $i \in \{2l-1, 2l\}$ and $j \in \{2l'-1, 2l'\}$ for some $(l, l') \in J_{u+1}$, then $h'_{2u}(i,j) = 0$, as the l-th, l'-th, and appended equation form a contradiction. For example, if $i = 2l-1$ and $j = 2l'-1$, then the three equations imply that $P_{2l} = P_{2l'}$;
- If neither of the above applies, we are in the hard case. Denote by M_{u+1} the set of indices covered by this case:

$$\begin{aligned} M_{u+1} = \Big\{(i,j) \in \{1,\ldots,2u\}^2\Big\} \Big\backslash \\ &\Big\{(2l-1, 2l-1), (2l-1, 2l), (2l, 2l-1), (2l, 2l) \;\Big|\; l \in \{1,\ldots,u\}\Big\} \cup \\ &\Big\{(2l-1, *), (2l, *), (*, 2l-1), (*, 2l) \;\Big|\; l \in I_{u+1}\Big\} \cup \\ &\Big\{(2l-1, 2l'-1), (2l-1, 2l'), (2l, 2l'-1), (2l, 2l') \;\Big|\; (l, l') \in J_{u+1}\Big\}. \end{aligned}$$

Effectively, we have obtained from (26) and (27) that

$$\begin{aligned} h_{2u+2} &= (2^n - 4u)h_{2u} + \sum_{1 \le i,j \le 2u} h'_{2u}(i,j) \\ &= (2^n - 4u)h_{2u} + 2|I_{u+1}|h_{2u} + \sum_{(i,j) \in M_{u+1}} h'_{2u}(i,j)\,. \end{aligned} \tag{28}$$

Patarin proves the following two claims.

Claim (Patarin [40, Theorem 10]). $|M_{u+1}| \ge 4u^2 - 8u - 12|I_{u+1}|u$.
Claim (Patarin [40, Theorem 18]). For any $(i,j) \in M_{u+1}$, provided $2u \le 2^n/32$,[4]

$$h'_{2u}(i,j) \ge \frac{h_{2u}}{2^n}\left(1 - \frac{124u}{2^{2n}} - \frac{104|I_{u+2}|u}{2^{2n}}\right).$$

The former claim relies on the observation that, without loss of generality, the equations are ordered in such a way that λ_{u+1} is the most-frequent value so far. The second claim captures the technical heart of the result. From (28) and above two claims, we derive

$$\begin{aligned} \frac{h_{2u+2}}{h_{2u}} &\ge 2^n - 4u + 2|I_{u+1}| + \frac{4u^2 - 8u - 12|I_{u+1}|u}{2^n}\left(1 - \frac{124u}{2^{2n}} - \frac{104|I_{u+2}|u}{2^{2n}}\right) \\ &\ge 2^n - 4u + 2|I_{u+1}| + \frac{4u^2 - 8u - 12|I_{u+1}|u}{2^n} - \frac{4u^2}{2^n}\left(\frac{124u}{2^{2n}} + \frac{104|I_{u+2}|u}{2^{2n}}\right), \end{aligned}$$

[4] Closer inspection of the proof reveals that $2u \le 2^n/16$ suffices.

and subsequently,

$$\begin{aligned}
&\frac{h_{2u+2}}{h_{2u}} \cdot \frac{2^n}{(2^n-2u)(2^n-2u-1)} \\
&\geq \frac{2^{2n} - 4u2^n + 2|I_{u+1}|2^n + 4u^2 - 8u - 12|I_{u+1}|u - 4u^2\left(\frac{124u}{2^{2n}} + \frac{104|I_{u+2}|u}{2^{2n}}\right)}{(2^n-2u)(2^n-2u-1)} \\
&= 1 + \frac{\left(2^n - 10u - \frac{496u^3}{2^{2n}}\right) + |I_{u+1}|\left(2\cdot 2^n - 12u - \frac{416u^3}{2^{2n}}\right)}{(2^n-2u)(2^n-2u-1)} \\
&\overset{\star}{\geq} 1 + \frac{2^n - 10u - \frac{496u^3}{2^{2n}}}{(2^n-2u)(2^n-2u-1)} \overset{\star\star}{\geq} 1\,,
\end{aligned}$$

where $\overset{\star}{\geq}$ holds for $2u \leq 2^n/5$ and $\overset{\star\star}{\geq}$ under the condition that $2u \leq 2^n/7$.[5] Note that the bounding is done on $2u$ rather than u: we are currently still looking at the case of $\xi = 2$, and every block has 2 unknowns. The condition states an upper bound on the number of unknowns.

The bound $h_{2u+2}/h_{2u} \geq 1$ holds for any $u = 2, \ldots, q-1$. As, in addition, $h_2 = 2^n$, we derive

$$h_{2q} \geq \frac{(2^n-2q+1)(2^n-2q+2)}{2^n} h_{2q-2} \geq \cdots \geq \frac{(2^n-2)_{2q-2}}{2^{n(q-1)}} h_2 \geq \frac{(2^n)_{2q}}{2^{nq}}\,,$$

as long as $2(q-1) \leq 2^n/32$. This completes the proof.

The induction step in the proof is performed over the number of equations, and every step implicitly goes per two: two new unknowns are fixed and they should not hit any of the previously fixed unknowns. If we generalize this to systems of equations with larger values of ξ and where the blocks may be of different sizes, the induction would go over the number of blocks, and the size of every step corresponds to the number of unknowns in that block. This also results in more constraints *per induction step.*

For example, consider a system of equations $\mathcal{E}$, consisting of q' *blocks.* For $u \in \{1, \ldots, q'\}$ denote by $\mathcal{E}_u$ all equations that correspond to the first u blocks. If the first u blocks in total cover $v(u)$ unknowns, the value $h_{v(u)}$ is similarly defined as the number of solutions to $\mathcal{E}_u$. Suppose we have fixed the first $v(u)$ unknowns over the first u blocks, and consider a new block of ξ unknowns: the target is to determine $h_{v(u+1)} = h_{v(u)+\xi}$ from $h_{v(u)}$. Denote $v := v(u)$ for brevity. As $P_{v+1}, \ldots, P_{v+\xi}$ are in the same block, all values are fixed through the $\mathcal{E}_{u+1}$ once P_{v+1} is fixed: say that the system fixes $P_{v+i} = P_{v+1} \oplus \lambda'_i$ for some λ'_i, for $i = 2, \ldots, \xi$. (In the specific case of $\xi = 2$ treated before, $v = 2u$ and $\lambda'_2 = \lambda_{u+1}$.)

[5] We remark that Patarin derived upper bound $2^n/67$: he stated the claim on $h'_{2u}(i,j)$ for unknown constants, subsequently derived the side condition, and only then derived the constants (and hence the 67). Knowing the constants in retrospect allows us to obtain a better bounding. In the end, the side condition in the theorem statement is the most dominant one (the one of the second claim).

The value $h_{v+\xi}$ counts the number of solutions $\{P_1, \ldots, P_v, P_{v+1}, \ldots, P_{v+\xi}\}$ such that

- $\{P_1, \ldots, P_v\}$ is a valid solution to the first u *blocks* $\mathcal{E}_u$;
- $\{P_{v+1}, \ldots, P_{v+\xi}\}$ satisfy the $(u+1)$-th block $\mathcal{E}_{u+1} \backslash \mathcal{E}_u$;
- $P_{v+1} \notin \{P_1, \ldots, P_v\} =: V_1$;
- $P_{v+1} \notin \{P_1 \oplus \lambda'_2, \ldots, P_v \oplus \lambda'_2\} =: V_2$;
- $\ldots$;
- $P_{v+1} \notin \{P_1 \oplus \lambda'_\xi, \ldots, P_v \oplus \lambda'_\xi\} =: V_\xi$.

Note that the values $\{P_{v+1}, \ldots, P_{v+\xi}\}$ are distinct by hypothesis on the system of equations, or stated differently, $\lambda'_i \neq \lambda'_j \neq 0$ for any $i \neq j$. Now, in this generalized case, for a given set of solutions to $\mathcal{E}_u$, we have $2^n - |V_1 \cup \cdots \cup V_\xi|$ solutions for $\{P_{v+1}, \ldots, P_{v+\xi}\}$. By the inclusion-exclusion principle,

$$\begin{aligned} |V_1 \cup \cdots \cup V_\xi| &= \sum_{i=1}^{\xi} |V_i| - \sum_{j=2}^{\xi} (-1)^j \sum_{i_1 < \cdots < i_j} |V_{i_1} \cap \cdots \cap V_{i_j}| \\ &= \xi \cdot v - \sum_{j=2}^{\xi} (-1)^j \sum_{i_1 < \cdots < i_j} |V_{i_1} \cap \cdots \cap V_{i_j}|, \end{aligned}$$

from which

$$\begin{aligned} h_{v+\xi} &= \sum_{\{P_1,\ldots,P_v\} \text{ solving } \mathcal{E}_u} 2^n - |V_1 \cup \cdots \cup V_\xi| \\ &= \sum_{\{P_1,\ldots,P_v\} \text{ solving } \mathcal{E}_u} 2^n - \xi \cdot v + \sum_{j=2}^{\xi} (-1)^j \sum_{i_1 < \cdots < i_j} |V_{i_1} \cap \cdots \cap V_{i_j}| \\ &= (2^n - \xi \cdot v) h_v + \sum_{\{P_1,\ldots,P_v\} \text{ solving } \mathcal{E}_u} \sum_{j=2}^{\xi} (-1)^j \sum_{i_1 < \cdots < i_j} |V_{i_1} \cap \cdots \cap V_{i_j}|. \end{aligned} \tag{29}$$

Instead of the quantity of (27), it now requires to lower bound

$$\sum_{\{P_1,\ldots,P_v\} \text{ solving } \mathcal{E}_u} \sum_{j=2}^{\xi} (-1)^j \sum_{i_1 < \cdots < i_j} |V_{i_1} \cap \cdots \cap V_{i_j}|,$$

which is beyond the scope of the sketch of the proof. What is important to note is the term $\xi \cdot v$ in (29), which demonstrates an additional loss compared to the $4u$ in (26) for the case where all blocks are of size $\xi = 2$ unknowns. This loss, among others, eventually constitutes a stronger side condition. □

References

1. Beaulieu, R., Shors, D., Smith, J., Treatman-Clark, S., Weeks, B., Wingers, L.: The SIMON and SPECK families of lightweight block ciphers. Cryptology ePrint Archive, Report 2013/404 (2013)
2. Beierle, C., Jean, J., Kölbl, S., Leander, G., Moradi, A., Peyrin, T., Sasaki, Y., Sasdrich, P., Sim, S.M.: The SKINNY family of block ciphers and its low-latency variant MANTIS. In: Robshaw, M., Katz, J. (eds.) CRYPTO 2016. LNCS, vol. 9815, pp. 123–153. Springer, Heidelberg (2016). doi:10.1007/978-3-662-53008-5_5
3. Bellare, M., Impagliazzo, R.: A tool for obtaining tighter security analyses of pseudorandom function based constructions, with applications to PRP to PRF conversion. Cryptology ePrint Archive, Report 1999/024 (1999)
4. Bellare, M., Desai, A., Jokipii, E., Rogaway, P.: A concrete security treatment of symmetric encryption. In: FOCS 1997, pp. 394–403. IEEE Computer Society (1997)
5. Bellare, M., Guérin, R., Rogaway, P.: XOR MACs: new methods for message authentication using finite pseudorandom functions. In: Coppersmith, D. (ed.) CRYPTO 1995. LNCS, vol. 963, pp. 15–28. Springer, Heidelberg (1995). doi:10.1007/3-540-44750-4_2
6. Bellare, M., Kilian, J., Rogaway, P.: The security of cipher block chaining. In: Desmedt, Y.G. (ed.) CRYPTO 1994. LNCS, vol. 839, pp. 341–358. Springer, Heidelberg (1994). doi:10.1007/3-540-48658-5_32
7. Bellare, M., Krovetz, T., Rogaway, P.: Luby-Rackoff backwards: increasing security by making block ciphers non-invertible. In: Nyberg, K. (ed.) EUROCRYPT 1998. LNCS, vol. 1403, pp. 266–280. Springer, Heidelberg (1998). doi:10.1007/BFb0054132
8. Bellare, M., Rogaway, P.: The security of triple encryption and a framework for code-based game-playing proofs. In: Vaudenay, S. (ed.) EUROCRYPT 2006. LNCS, vol. 4004, pp. 409–426. Springer, Heidelberg (2006). doi:10.1007/11761679_25
9. Bernstein, D.J.: How to stretch random functions: the security of protected counter sums. J. Cryptology **12**(3), 185–192 (1999)
10. Bhargavan, K., Leurent, G.: On the practical (in-)security of 64-bit block ciphers: Collision attacks on HTTP over TLS and OpenVPN. In: Weippl, E.R., Katzenbeisser, S., Kruegel, C., Myers, A.C., Halevi, S. (eds.) ACM SIGSAC. pp. 456–467. ACM (2016)
11. Bogdanov, A., Knudsen, L.R., Leander, G., Paar, C., Poschmann, A., Robshaw, M.J.B., Seurin, Y., Vikkelsoe, C.: PRESENT: an ultra-lightweight block cipher. In: Paillier, P., Verbauwhede, I. (eds.) CHES 2007. LNCS, vol. 4727, pp. 450–466. Springer, Heidelberg (2007). doi:10.1007/978-3-540-74735-2_31
12. Borghoff, J., Canteaut, A., Güneysu, T., Kavun, E.B., Knezevic, M., Knudsen, L.R., Leander, G., Nikov, V., Paar, C., Rechberger, C., Rombouts, P., Thomsen, S.S., Yalçın, T.: PRINCE – a low-latency block cipher for pervasive computing applications. In: Wang, X., Sako, K. (eds.) ASIACRYPT 2012. LNCS, vol. 7658, pp. 208–225. Springer, Heidelberg (2012). doi:10.1007/978-3-642-34961-4_14
13. Chang, D., Nandi, M.: A short proof of the PRP/PRF switching lemma. Cryptology ePrint Archive, Report 2008/078 (2008)
14. Chen, S., Lampe, R., Lee, J., Seurin, Y., Steinberger, J.: Minimizing the two-round even-mansour cipher. In: Garay, J.A., Gennaro, R. (eds.) CRYPTO 2014. LNCS, vol. 8616, pp. 39–56. Springer, Heidelberg (2014). doi:10.1007/978-3-662-44371-2_3

15. Chen, S., Steinberger, J.: Tight security bounds for key-alternating ciphers. In: Nguyen, P.Q., Oswald, E. (eds.) EUROCRYPT 2014. LNCS, vol. 8441, pp. 327–350. Springer, Heidelberg (2014). doi:10.1007/978-3-642-55220-5_19
16. Cogliati, B., Lampe, R., Patarin, J.: The indistinguishability of the XOR of k permutations. In: Cid, C., Rechberger, C. (eds.) FSE 2014. LNCS, vol. 8540, pp. 285–302. Springer, Heidelberg (2015). doi:10.1007/978-3-662-46706-0_15
17. Cogliati, B., Seurin, Y.: EWCDM: an efficient, beyond-birthday secure, nonce-misuse resistant MAC. In: Robshaw, M., Katz, J. (eds.) CRYPTO 2016. LNCS, vol. 9814, pp. 121–149. Springer, Heidelberg (2016). doi:10.1007/978-3-662-53018-4_5
18. Cannière, C., Dunkelman, O., Knežević, M.: KATAN and KTANTAN—a family of small and efficient hardware-oriented block ciphers. In: Clavier, C., Gaj, K. (eds.) CHES 2009. LNCS, vol. 5747, pp. 272–288. Springer, Heidelberg (2009). doi:10.1007/978-3-642-04138-9_20
19. Gilboa, S., Gueron, S.: The advantage of truncated permutations. CoRR abs/1610.02518 (2016)
20. Gong, Z., Nikova, S., Law, Y.W.: KLEIN: a new family of lightweight block ciphers. In: Juels, A., Paar, C. (eds.) RFIDSec 2011. LNCS, vol. 7055, pp. 1–18. Springer, Heidelberg (2012). doi:10.1007/978-3-642-25286-0_1
21. Hall, C., Wagner, D., Kelsey, J., Schneier, B.: Building PRFs from PRPs. In: Krawczyk, H. (ed.) CRYPTO 1998. LNCS, vol. 1462, pp. 370–389. Springer, Heidelberg (1998). doi:10.1007/BFb0055742
22. Hong, D., Sung, J., Hong, S., Lim, J., Lee, S., Koo, B.-S., Lee, C., Chang, D., Lee, J., Jeong, K., Kim, H., Kim, J., Chee, S.: HIGHT: a new block cipher suitable for low-resource device. In: Goubin, L., Matsui, M. (eds.) CHES 2006. LNCS, vol. 4249, pp. 46–59. Springer, Heidelberg (2006). doi:10.1007/11894063_4
23. Hoorfar, A., Hassani, M.: Inequalities on the Lambert W function and hyperpower function. J. Inequalities Pure Appl. Math. **9**(2), 5–9 (2008)
24. Impagliazzo, R., Rudich, S.: Limits on the provable consequences of one-way permutations. In: Goldwasser, S. (ed.) CRYPTO 1988. LNCS, vol. 403, pp. 8–26. Springer, New York (1990). doi:10.1007/0-387-34799-2_2
25. Iwata, T.: New blockcipher modes of operation with beyond the birthday bound security. In: Robshaw, M. (ed.) FSE 2006. LNCS, vol. 4047, pp. 310–327. Springer, Heidelberg (2006). doi:10.1007/11799313_20
26. Iwata, T., Mennink, B., Vizár, D.: CENC is optimally secure. Cryptology ePrint Archive, Report 2016/1087 (2016)
27. Lim, C.H., Korkishko, T.: mCrypton – a lightweight block cipher for security of low-cost RFID tags and sensors. In: Song, J.-S., Kwon, T., Yung, M. (eds.) WISA 2005. LNCS, vol. 3786, pp. 243–258. Springer, Heidelberg (2006). doi:10.1007/11604938_19
28. Luby, M., Rackoff, C.: How to construct pseudorandom permutations from pseudorandom functions. SIAM J. Comput. **17**(2), 373–386 (1988)
29. Lucks, S.: The sum of PRPs is a secure PRF. In: Preneel, B. (ed.) EUROCRYPT 2000. LNCS, vol. 1807, pp. 470–484. Springer, Heidelberg (2000). doi:10.1007/3-540-45539-6_34
30. Mennink, B., Preneel, B.: On the XOR of multiple random permutations. In: Malkin, T., Kolesnikov, V., Lewko, A.B., Polychronakis, M. (eds.) ACNS 2015. LNCS, vol. 9092, pp. 619–634. Springer, Cham (2015). doi:10.1007/978-3-319-28166-7_30
31. Nachef, V., Patarin, J., Volte, E.: Feistel Ciphers - Security Proofs and Cryptanalysis. Springer, Cham (2017). doi:10.1007/978-3-319-49530-9

32. Nandi, M.: Birthday attack on dual EWCDM. Cryptology ePrint Archive, Report 2017/579 (2017)
33. Patarin, J.: Étude des Générateurs de Permutations Basés sur le Schéma du D.E.S. Ph.D. thesis, Université Paris 6, Paris, France, November 1991
34. Patarin, J.: Luby-Rackoff: 7 rounds are enough for $2^{n(1-\epsilon)}$ security. In: Boneh, D. (ed.) CRYPTO 2003. LNCS, vol. 2729, pp. 513–529. Springer, Heidelberg (2003). doi:10.1007/978-3-540-45146-4_30
35. Patarin, J.: Security of random feistel schemes with 5 or more rounds. In: Franklin, M. (ed.) CRYPTO 2004. LNCS, vol. 3152, pp. 106–122. Springer, Heidelberg (2004). doi:10.1007/978-3-540-28628-8_7
36. Patarin, J.: On linear systems of equations with distinct variables and small block size. In: Won and Kim [49], pp. 299–321 (2006)
37. Patarin, J.: The "Coefficients H" Technique. In: Avanzi, R.M., Keliher, L., Sica, F. (eds.) SAC 2008. LNCS, vol. 5381, pp. 328–345. Springer, Heidelberg (2009). doi:10.1007/978-3-642-04159-4_21
38. Patarin, J.: A proof of security in $O(2^n)$ for the benes scheme. In: Vaudenay, S. (ed.) AFRICACRYPT 2008. LNCS, vol. 5023, pp. 209–220. Springer, Heidelberg (2008). doi:10.1007/978-3-540-68164-9_14
39. Patarin, J.: A proof of security in $O(2^n)$ for the XOR of two random permutations. In: Safavi-Naini, R. (ed.) ICITS 2008. LNCS, vol. 5155, pp. 232–248. Springer, Heidelberg (2008). doi:10.1007/978-3-540-85093-9_22
40. Patarin, J.: Introduction to mirror theory: analysis of systems of linear equalities and linear non equalities for cryptography. Cryptology ePrint Archive, Report 2010/287 (2010)
41. Patarin, J.: Security of balanced and unbalanced Feistel schemes with linear non equalities. Cryptology ePrint Archive, Report 2010/293 (2010)
42. Patarin, J.: Security in $O(2^n)$ for the xor of two random permutations. Proof with the standard H technique. Cryptology ePrint Archive, Report 2013/368 (2013)
43. Patarin, J.: Mirror theory and cryptography. Cryptology ePrint Archive, Report 2016/702 (2016)
44. Patarin, J.: Personal communication (2017)
45. Patarin, J., Montreuil, A.: Benes and butterfly schemes revisited. In: Won and Kim [49], pp. 92–116 (2009)
46. Shibutani, K., Isobe, T., Hiwatari, H., Mitsuda, A., Akishita, T., Shirai, T.: *Piccolo*: an ultra-lightweight blockcipher. In: Preneel, B., Takagi, T. (eds.) CHES 2011. LNCS, vol. 6917, pp. 342–357. Springer, Heidelberg (2011). doi:10.1007/978-3-642-23951-9_23
47. Stam, A.J.: Distance between sampling with and without replacement. Stat. Neerl. **32**(2), 81–91 (1978)
48. Volte, E.: Miroirs, Cubes et Feistel Dissymétriques. (Mirrors, cubes and unbalanced Feistel schemes). Ph.D. thesis, Cergy-Pontoise University, France (2014)
49. Volte, E., Nachef, V., Marrière, N.: Automatic expectation and variance computing for attacks on Feistel schemes. Cryptology ePrint Archive, Report 2016/136 (2016)
50. Won, D.H., Kim, S. (eds.): ICISC 2005. LNCS, vol. 3935. Springer, Heidelberg (2006)
51. Wu, W., Zhang, L.: LBlock: a lightweight block cipher. In: Lopez, J., Tsudik, G. (eds.) ACNS 2011. LNCS, vol. 6715, pp. 327–344. Springer, Heidelberg (2011). doi:10.1007/978-3-642-21554-4_19

Real-World Crypto

A Formal Treatment of Multi-key Channels

Felix Günther(✉) and Sogol Mazaheri(✉)

Cryptoplexity, Technische Universität Darmstadt, Darmstadt, Germany
guenther@cs.tu-darmstadt.de, sogol.mazaheri@cryptoplexity.de

Abstract. Secure channel protocols protect data transmission over a network from being overheard or tampered with. In the common abstraction, cryptographic models for channels involve a single key for ensuring the central security notions of confidentiality and integrity. The currently developed next version of the Transport Layer Security protocol, TLS 1.3, however introduces a key updating mechanism in order to deploy a sequence of multiple, possibly independent encryption keys in its channel sub-protocol. This design aims at achieving forward security, protecting prior communication after long-term key corruption, as well as security of individual channel phases even if the key in other phases is leaked (a property we denote as phase-key insulation). Neither of these security aspects has been treated formally in the context of cryptographic channels so far, leading to a current lack of techniques to evaluate such channel designs cryptographically.

We approach this gap by introducing the first formal model of multi-key channels, where sender and receiver can update their shared secret key during the lifetime of the channel without interrupting the communication. We present modular, game-based notions for confidentiality and integrity, integrating forward security and phase-key insulation as two advanced security aspects. As we show, our framework of notions on the lower end of its hierarchy naturally connects to the existing notions of stateful encryption established for single-key channels. Like for classical channels, it further allows for generically composing chosen-ciphertext confidentiality from chosen-plaintext confidentiality and ciphertext integrity. We instantiate the strongest security notions in our model with a construction based on authenticated encryption with associated data and a pseudorandom function. Being comparatively close, our construction additionally enables us to discuss the TLS 1.3 record protocol design.

1 Introduction

Secure channel protocols are at the heart of today's communication infrastructure, protecting data in transit in countless connections each day. Major examples include the Transport Layer Security (TLS) protocol [22] securing the Web, the Secure Shell (SSH) protocol [48] enabling secure remote logins, and the Internet Protocol Security (IPsec) protocol [34] protecting, e.g., tunneled network-to-network connections.

J. Katz and H. Shacham (Eds.): CRYPTO 2017, Part III, LNCS 10403, pp. 587–618, 2017.
DOI: 10.1007/978-3-319-63697-9_20

1.1 Secure Cryptographic Channels

In the cryptographic realm, the established game-based abstraction of secure channels is that of *stateful encryption*, introduced by Bellare, Kohno, and Namprempre [9]. Stateful encryption first of all inherits the classical security requirements of (non-stateful) encryption: confidentiality and integrity. Confidentiality of encryption, first formalized by Goldwasser and Micali [31], intuitively demands that the content of transmitted messages remains secret. Integrity, in parts concurrently introduced by Katz and Yung [33], Bellare and Rogaway [11], and Bellare and Namprempre [10], in contrast ensures that an adversary cannot forge ciphertexts that, on decryption, lead to (meaningful) messages. In order to provide secure communication through a sequence of messages, stateful encryption schemes go beyond these standard requirements and moreover protect against reordering, dropping, and replays of messages transmitted in a channel. On a constructive level, channels to this extend incorporate authenticated encryption with associated data (AEAD) schemes [44] as an essential cryptographic building block, integrated with message-order and error handling.

Starting from and partially building upon the work by Bellare, Kohno, and Namprempre, various extensions and adaptations of (game-based) channel models have been proposed. For example, Kohno, Palacio, and Black [35] define a hierarchy of channels with varying resilience against replays, reordering, or message dropping. In order to capture potential padding of messages before encryption, Paterson, Ristenpart, and Shrimpton [42] introduce the notion of length-hiding authenticated encryption. Motivated by practical attacks due to implicit information leakage through different error messages or different timings of an error message, e.g., caused by either a MAC or a decryption failure, Boldyreva et al. [17] discuss decryption algorithms that distinguish more than a single error message. They also study the effects of multiple error messages on the generic relation between confidentiality and integrity established earlier by Bellare and Namprempre [10]. In order to capture fragmented delivery of ciphertexts as it arises in real-world attacks on secure channels (cf. [3]), Boldyreva et al. [16] and Albrecht et al. [2] consider stateful encryption with ciphertext fragmentation. Going one step further, Fischlin et al. [29] additionally study plaintext fragmentation to capture scenarios where channels are required to process a stream of data. Finally, protocols in practice usually establish a bi-directional communication channel, a setting whose security was recently studied by Marson and Poettering [39].

1.2 Multi-key Channels

In all cryptographic models of secure channels established so far, security originates from a single, symmetric key shared between the two endpoints of the channel. The upcoming version of the TLS protocol, TLS 1.3 [43], whose specification is currently being developed, however deviates from this paradigm and instead deploys a sequential series of multiple keys. The TLS 1.3 channel (the so-called record protocol) as usual begins with deriving an initial key for encryption and decryption of messages. As a novel component, both parties are further able to trigger key updates, leading to a key switch according to a pre-defined schedule while maintaining channel's operation. One particular motivation for this approach is that long-lived TLS connections may exhaust the cryptographic limits of some algorithms on how much data can be safely encrypted under a single key (cf. [43, Sect. 5.5], [38]).

A more general, major reason for refreshing the key used in a secure channel and specifically TLS 1.3 is *forward security*, a notion primarily known from and well-established in the context of key exchange protocols [19,23,32]. When using the same key throughout the lifetime of a channel, an attacker that learns this key (e.g., through cryptanalysis or even temporary break-in into the system) immediately compromises the confidentiality of previous and the integrity of future communication. In contrast, forward security demands that even if key material is leaked at some point, previous communication remains secure. Forward-secure symmetric encryption in the non-stateful setting is considered understood and in particular can be built from forward-secure pseudorandom bit generator [13] or, more generally, through re-keying [1]. In the context of secure channels, a formal treatment of forward security is however lacking so far.

Beyond forward security, a second security property arises for secure channels (in particular in the design of TLS 1.3) which we refer to as *phase-key insulation*. While forward security targets a full compromise (and prior security), phase-key insulation is concerned with the *temporary* compromise of a channel in the form of leaking the key used in a certain time period (phase), but not in others. Such temporary compromise might, e.g., result from differing strengths of key material used to derive some of the phase keys (as is the case for keys established in the TLS 1.3 key exchange [27,28,37]) or from storing the currently active key in less secure memory for efficiency reasons. A secure channel with phase-key insulation should then uphold confidentiality and integrity in uncompromised phases, even if the key of prior or later phases is revealed. Moreover, security should be retained even if the attacker learned a phase's key while that phase was still active.

As we will see, phase-key insulation orthogonally complements the notion of forward security, which is only concerned with a posteriori leakage of keys. Requiring it furthermore introduces new pitfalls in the design of secure channels. For example, the initial draft design of the TLS 1.3 record protocol with key updates enabled truncation attacks in non-compromised phases that would go unnoticed during the further execution of the protocol, as Fournet and the miTLS [40] team discovered [30]. We hence consider it being crucial to establish a formal understanding of channels using multiple keys, which is lacking at this point, in order to allow thorough analyses of proposed protocols and means for evaluating their provable security guarantees.

1.3 Our Contributions

In this work we initiate the study of channels that employ a sequence of multiple keys. To this end, we introduce a formalization of such *multi-key channels* and set up an according framework of game-based security notions. We then analyze the relations between our security notions as well as connections to the established notions for stateful encryption and finally provide a generic construction of a provably secure multi-key channel.

Following the game-based tradition in modeling channels, our formalism builds upon and extends that of Bellare, Kohno, and Namprempre [9] and Bellare and Yee [13]. More specifically, our notion of multi-key channels augments that of regular stateful encryption in three aspects. Obviously, we first of all consider a sequence of keys to be used for encryption and decryption. Secondly, switches between these keys are initiated through a specific key-update algorithm which makes the channel proceed from one phase to the next. Lastly, we separate two hierarchies of keys by additionally considering a level of master secret keys which, also evolving over time, are used to derive the channel key for each phase. As we will discuss, this carefully crafted syntax and key hierarchy in particular allows us to quite closely model the key schedule of the TLS 1.3 record protocol draft [43].

We then define security of multi-key channels via a a framework of notions. Beyond capturing the classical requirements of confidentiality and integrity, our notions modularly integrate the advanced security properties of forward security and phase-key insulation arising in the context of multi-key channels. The core technical challenge here is to appropriately capture the desired security properties while excluding trivial attacks in the stateful multi-key setting. We furthermore modularize the adversary's capability to proceed a channel to a next phase through key updates. Thereby, our framework elegantly also captures the single-key variants of our security notions, i.e., the cases where a multi-key channel only operates in a single phase.

Our single-key security notions enable us to provide a formal link to the established stateful-encryption notions for regular channels. We show that analogous notions in both models are essentially equivalent (modulo the differences in syntax) by providing natural, generic transforms between each pair of corresponding confidentiality and integrity notions. Furthermore, we establish separations that give rise to a hierarchy of our security notions and in particular establish forward security and phase-key insulation as independent security properties. To complete the picture of relations, we also translate the classical composition result for symmetric encryption by Bellare and Namprempre [10] to the setting of multi-key channels, showing that chosen-plaintext confidentiality combined with ciphertext integrity implies the stronger chosen-ciphertext notion of confidentiality.

Finally, we instantiate our model by providing a construction of a multi-key channel from a nonce-based authenticated encryption with associated data (AEAD) scheme and a pseudorandom function. To ensure both forward security and phase-key insulation, we match suitable techniques established for forward-secure key generation and for ensuring causal integrity. Leveraging our composition theorem, we then prove that our construction meets our strongest confidentiality and integrity notions for multi-key channels. Coming back to the initial motivation from real-world protocol design, we compare our construction with the draft design of the TLS 1.3 record protocol.

1.4 Related Work

Beyond the preceding works on secure channels discussed earlier, there has been substantial work on mostly the handshake but also the record protocol of the TLS 1.3 drafts; see Paterson and van der Merwe [41] for an overview. Badertscher et al. [4] analyze an early draft of the TLS 1.3 record protocol without key updates in the constructive cryptography setting. Bellare and Tackmann [12] analyze the multi-user security of the AES-GCM as authenticated-encryption building block of TLS 1.3. Bhargavan et al. [14,15] provide verified implementations of the TLS 1.3 record protocol.

Our notion of phase-key insulation is similar in spirit to, and hence borrows its name from, the notion of key insulation introduced in the public-key setting [24,25] and also transferred to (non-stateful) symmetric encryption [26]. Beyond treating (phase-)key insulation in the different context of secure channels, our notion permits more fine-grained corruption of keys. It thereby enables studying the interaction of forward secrecy and phase-key insulation in a single, modular framework.

2 Multi-key Channels

We begin with defining the syntax and correctness of multi-key channels, focusing on their functionality in this section; we will treat their security in Sect. 3. In Fig. 1 we exemplify the operations of a multi-key channel and already hint at their expected security.

Like a regular, single-key channel (abstractly modeled as stateful encryption [9]), a multi-key channel is used by a sender to transform a sequence of messages $m_1, m_2, \ldots \in \{0,1\}^*$ into a corresponding sequence of ciphertexts c_1, $c_2, \ldots \in \{0,1\}^*$ using a sending algorithm Send.[1] The receiver then sequentially uses a corresponding Recv algorithm on each transmitted ciphertext to recover the sent message sequence.

In addition to regular channels, both sender and receiver can decide to update their keys used for sending and receiving, thereby switching to the next *phase* of the multi-key channel. In our model, we consider a two-level hierarchy for key derivation. On the first level, the complete multi-key channel is bootstrapped from a single, initial *master secret key* generated upon initialization of the channel. Master secret keys are furthermore evolved when switching to the next phase, following a deterministic key schedule to derive the master secret key msk_{t+1} for phase $t+1$ from the master secret key msk_t of the previous phase. On the second

[1] In order to make explicit that a secure multi-key channel might only provide integrity but no confidentiality, we choose to make use of the more general terms "sending" and "receiving" instead of "encryption" and "decryption".

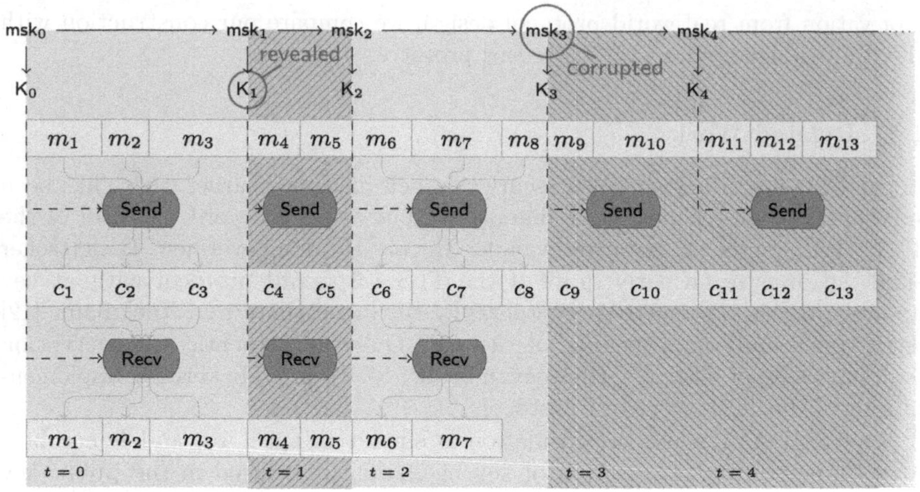

Fig. 1. Illustration of the behavior of a multi-key channel (cf. Definition 1). The beginning of a new phase t is indicated by the derivation of a phase key K_t from the corresponding master secret key msk_t. The phase key K_t is then used to send and receive in-order messages resp. ciphertexts via algorithms Send and Recv in this phase. In this example, the phase key K_1 of phase 1 is revealed and the master secret key msk_3 is corrupted. The affected phases 1 resp. 3 and following are marked in hatched-pattern red (with lines towards top right for the effects of the revealed K_1 and toward bottom right for the effects of the corrupted msk_3). For security (cf. Sect. 3), a forward-secure and phase-key–insulated multi-key channel is demanded to provide security in the non-affected phases 0 and 2, marked by non-hatched green areas. (Color figure online)

level, the actual *phase key* K_t used in the channel for sending and receiving messages in a phase t is derived (again deterministically) from that phase's master secret key msk_t.

Although Fig. 1 depicts only a single key schedule with the phase keys forwarded to both the Send and Recv algorithms of that phase, in a real execution of the channel, the key updates and derivations are invoked independently on the sending and receiving side. For correct functionality, the key updates need to be aligned in order to process sent and received ciphertexts under matching keys on both sides. In practice, key updates may be either delivered alongside of the messages transmitted in a channel (and hence potentially authenticated) or in an out-of-band manner, e.g., via a separate control channel, and with their position in the channel's ciphertext sequence not being explicitly authenticated.[2] In our abstraction of multi-key channels, we do not rely on the authenticity of the key-update signaling (in particular, we will later allow adversaries to tamper

[2] In the context of TLS 1.3, for example, both variants have been discussed. The current draft design [43] specifies that key update notifications are transmitted (and authenticated) within the data channel.

with the timing of key updates) but leave it up to the channel to ensure their correct position with respect to the transmitted ciphertexts.

We now define the syntax and correctness of multi-key channels capturing the given intuition.

Definition 1 (Syntax of multi-key channels). *A* multi-key channel $\mathsf{Ch} = (\mathsf{Init}, \mathsf{Send}, \mathsf{Recv}, \mathsf{Update})$ *with associated sending and receiving state space $\mathcal{S}_S$ resp. $\mathcal{S}_R$, master secret key space $\mathcal{MSK}$, phase key space $\mathcal{K}$, error space $\mathcal{E}$ with $\mathcal{E} \cap \{0,1\}^* = \emptyset$, and maximum number* $\mathsf{maxmsg} \in \mathbb{N} \cup \{\infty\}$ *of messages supported per phase consists of four efficient algorithms defined as follows.*

- $\mathsf{Init}(1^\lambda) \xrightarrow{\$} (\mathsf{msk}_0, \mathsf{K}_0, \mathsf{st}_{S,0}, \mathsf{st}_{R,0})$. *This probabilistic algorithm is composed of three algorithms:*
  - $\mathsf{MasterKeyGen}(1^\lambda) \xrightarrow{\$} \mathsf{msk}_0$. *On input security parameter 1^λ, this probabilistic algorithm outputs an initial master secret key $\mathsf{msk}_0 \in \mathcal{MSK}$.*
  - $\mathsf{KeyDerive}(\mathsf{msk}) \rightarrow \mathsf{K}$. *On input a master secret key* msk, *this deterministic algorithm outputs a phase key $\mathsf{K} \in \mathcal{K}$. The initial phase key is derived as $\mathsf{K}_0 \leftarrow \mathsf{KeyDerive}(\mathsf{msk}_0)$.*
  - $\mathsf{StateGen}(1^\lambda) \rightarrow (\mathsf{st}_{S,0}, \mathsf{st}_{R,0})$. *On input 1^λ, this deterministic algorithm outputs initial sending and receiving states $\mathsf{st}_{S,0} \in \mathcal{S}_S$ resp. $\mathsf{st}_{R,0} \in \mathcal{S}_R$.*
- $\mathsf{Send}(\mathsf{st}_{S,t}, \mathsf{K}_t, m) \xrightarrow{\$} (\mathsf{st}'_{S,t}, c)$. *On input of a sending state $\mathsf{st}_{S,t} \in \mathcal{S}_S$, a key $\mathsf{K}_t \in \mathcal{K}$, and a message $m \in \{0,1\}^*$, this (possibly) probabilistic algorithm outputs an updated state $\mathsf{st}'_{S,t} \in \mathcal{S}_S$ and a ciphertext (or error symbol) $c \in \{0,1\}^* \cup \mathcal{E}$.*
- $\mathsf{Recv}(\mathsf{st}_{R,t}, \mathsf{K}_t, c) \rightarrow (\mathsf{st}'_{R,t}, m)$. *On input of a receiving state $\mathsf{st}_{R,t} \in \mathcal{S}_R$, a key $\mathsf{K}_t \in \mathcal{K}$, and a ciphertext $c \in \{0,1\}^*$, this deterministic algorithm outputs an updated state $\mathsf{st}'_{R,t} \in \mathcal{S}_R$ and a message (or error symbol) $m \in \{0,1\}^* \cup \mathcal{E}$.*
- $\mathsf{Update}(\mathsf{msk}_t, \mathsf{st}_{S,t}/\mathsf{st}_{R,t}) \rightarrow (\mathsf{msk}_{t+1}, \mathsf{K}_{t+1}, \mathsf{st}_{S,t+1}/\mathsf{st}_{R,t+1})$. *This deterministic algorithm is composed of the following two algorithms:*
  - $\mathsf{MasterKeyUp}(\mathsf{msk}_t) \rightarrow \mathsf{msk}_{t+1}$. *On input of a master secret key $\mathsf{msk}_t \in \mathcal{MSK}$, this deterministic algorithm outputs a master secret key $\mathsf{msk}_{t+1} \in \mathcal{MSK}$ for the next phase.*
  - $\mathsf{StateUp}(\mathsf{st}_{S,t}/\mathsf{st}_{R,t}) \rightarrow \mathsf{st}_{S,t+1}/\mathsf{st}_{R,t+1}$. *On input of a sending or receiving state $\mathsf{st}_{S,t} \in \mathcal{S}_S$ resp. $\mathsf{st}_{R,t} \in \mathcal{S}_R$, this deterministic algorithm derives the next phase's state $\mathsf{st}_{S,t+1} \in \mathcal{S}_S$, resp. $\mathsf{st}_{R,t+1} \in \mathcal{S}_R$.*

  It further employs the (same) deterministic algorithm $\mathsf{KeyDerive}$ *as given for* Init *to derive an updated phase key $\mathsf{K}_{t+1} \in \mathcal{K}$ as $\mathsf{K}_{t+1} \leftarrow \mathsf{KeyDerive}(\mathsf{msk}_{t+1})$.*

We call a channel with a deterministic Send algorithm a *deterministic* multi-key channel.

Shorthand notation. Given a sending state $\mathsf{st}_S \in \mathcal{S}_S$, a phase key $\mathsf{K} \in \mathcal{K}$, an integer $\ell \geq 0$, and a vector of messages $\mathbf{m} = (m_1, \ldots, m_\ell) \in (\{0,1\}^*)^\ell$, let $(\mathsf{st}'_S, \mathbf{c}) \xleftarrow{\$} \mathsf{Send}(\mathsf{st}_S, \mathsf{K}, \mathbf{m})$ be shorthand for the sequential execution $(\mathsf{st}^1_S, c_1) \xleftarrow{\$} \mathsf{Send}(\mathsf{st}^0_S, \mathsf{K}, m_1), \ldots, (\mathsf{st}^\ell_S, c_\ell) \xleftarrow{\$} \mathsf{Send}(\mathsf{st}^{\ell-1}_S, \mathsf{K}, m_\ell)$ with $\mathbf{c} = (c_1, \ldots, c_\ell)$, $\mathsf{st}^0_S = \mathsf{st}_S$, and $\mathsf{st}'_S = \mathsf{st}^\ell_S$. For $\ell = 0$ we define $\mathbf{c}$ to be the empty vector and the final state $\mathsf{st}_S^\ell = \mathsf{st}'_S$ to be the initial state st_S. We use an analogous notation for the Recv algorithm.

Correctness of multi-key channels intuitively guarantees that if at the receiver side the keys are updated only after having received all messages sent in the previous phase, then the received messages are equal to those sent in the entire communication.

Definition 2 (Correctness of multi-key channels). *Let* $t \in \mathbb{N}$ *and* $(\mathsf{msk}_0, \mathsf{K}_0, \mathsf{st}_{S,0}, \mathsf{st}_{R,0}) \xleftarrow{\$} \mathsf{Init}(1^\lambda)$. *Let* $\mathbf{m}_0, \ldots, \mathbf{m}_t \in \{0,1\}^{**}$ *be* $t+1$ *vectors of messages of lengths* $|\mathbf{m}_i| \leq \mathsf{maxmsg}$ *(for* $i \in \{0, \ldots, t\}$*). Let* $\mathbf{c_0}, \ldots, \mathbf{c_t} \in \{0,1\}^{**}$ *be the corresponding ciphertext vectors output by* Send *given that* Update *is invoked between each sending of two subsequent message sequences, i.e., such that for* $k = 0, \ldots, t$, $(\mathsf{st}'_{S,k}, \mathbf{c_k}) \xleftarrow{\$} \mathsf{Send}(\mathsf{st}_{S,k}, \mathsf{K}_k, \mathbf{m}_k)$ *and for* $k = 0, \ldots, t-1$, $(\mathsf{msk}_{k+1}, \mathsf{K}_{k+1}, \mathsf{st}_{S,k+1}) \leftarrow \mathsf{Update}(\mathsf{msk}_k, \mathsf{st}'_{S,k})$.

Now let $\mathbf{m}'_0, \ldots, \mathbf{m}'_t \in \{0,1\}^{**}$ *be the results of receiving these ciphertexts with likewise interleaved* Update *invocations on the receiver's side, i.e., for* $k = 0, \ldots, t$, *let* $(\mathsf{st}'_{R,k}, \mathbf{m}'_k) \leftarrow \mathsf{Recv}(\mathsf{st}_{R,k}, \mathsf{K}_k, \mathbf{c_k})$ *and for* $k = 0, \ldots, t-1$, *let* $(\mathsf{msk}_{k+1}, \mathsf{K}_{k+1}, \mathsf{st}_{R,k+1}) \leftarrow \mathsf{Update}(\mathsf{msk}_k, \mathsf{st}'_{R,k})$.

We say that a multi-key channel Ch *is* correct *if for any choice of* t, $\mathbf{m}_0, \ldots, \mathbf{m}_t$, *and all choices of the randomness in the channel algorithm it holds that* $\mathbf{m}_0 = \mathbf{m}'_0, \ldots, \mathbf{m}_t = \mathbf{m}'_t$.

2.1 Syntax Rationale

The syntax of a cryptographic component defines its design space and also drives the security properties it may achieve. Before we continue with defining security for multi-key channels, let us pause to provide some rationale for our choices in the given syntax.

Probabilistic vs. deterministic Send. At first glance, the modeling of secure channels in form of stateful encryption [9] may appear as merely a stateful variant of authenticated encryption. For authenticated encryption (optionally with associated data), the established notion is a deterministic one [44], where encryption instead of fresh randomness takes a (unique) nonce. One major motivation for this approach is that (good) randomness may be hard to obtain in practice, e.g., due to design flaws or implementation bugs in random number generators, or limited system entropy available. Ideally, one hence bootstraps an encryption scheme from a (short) random key and then only relies on a unique nonce (e.g., a counter) for message encryption.[3]

The same argument in principle applies to secure channels, yielding the question whether the Send algorithm should be fixed as deterministic. As we will see next, our security model allows us to seamlessly capture the desired security properties for channels with probabilistic and deterministic Send at the same time. We hence decided to stay in line with previous formalizations of

[3] See the work originating from [46] on (nonce-misuse) resistance to non-unique nonces.

channels (including [9,16,29,42]) and use the more generic syntax with (possibly) probabilistic Send. Nevertheless, we deem a *deterministic* multi-key channel to be the more desirable variant in practice. Indeed, the generic construction we provide in Sect. 4 is deterministic.

Inputs to key updates. We define updates of master secret and phase keys (via MasterKeyUp and KeyDerive) to be deterministically derived from the initial master secret key msk_0. They are hence necessarily equivalent (in each phase) on the sender and receiver side.

A design alternative would be to also include the current state in the derivation, enabling keys to be influenced by, e.g., the message history. We however decided to focus on deterministic updates from msk_0, for mainly two reasons (besides significantly reducing the security model's complexity). First, this approach captures the concept of separating key derivation from message sending, in particular if master secrets are kept in more secure memory. Second, the syntax is compliant with both theoretical concepts for forward-secret encryption [13] as well as the practical key schedule employed in TLS 1.3 [43]. Note that, still, channels can for example take the message history into account within the Send and Recv algorithms.

3 Security Notions for Multi-key Channels

Classically, two security properties are expected from a secure channel. *Confidentiality* aims at protecting the content of transported messages from being read by eavesdroppers or active adversaries on the network. In contrast, *integrity* ensures that messages are received unmodified and in correct order, i.e., without messages being reordered or intermediate messages being dropped. We take up these notions in the context of multi-key channels and extend them to capture two more advanced security aspects arising in this scenario which we denote as *forward security* and *phase-key insulation*.

Forward security, as established also in other settings, is concerned with the effects of leaking a channel's master secret key on prior communication. The notion aims at situations where all key material of a communication partner becomes known to an attacker, e.g., through a break-in into a system or exfiltration of secrets. Following common terminology, we demand that a forward-secure multi-key channel upholds both confidentiality and integrity for messages sent in phases *before* corruption of a master secret key took place, even if one endpoint of the channel is still processing data in these phases when the corruption happens. Naturally, as the deterministic key schedule implies that the current and any future phase's key can be derived from a master secret key, we however cannot expect confidentiality or integrity for messages sent from the point of corruption on.

Phase-key insulation in contrast captures the selective leakage of some phases' keys while the master secret key remains uncompromised. Such leakage may be due to cryptanalysis of some of these keys, partial misuse of the key material, or temporary compromise. In particular, it reflects that the master secret key of a channel may be stored in more secure memory (e.g., trusted hardware) while the current phase key potentially resides in lesser secured memory for performance reasons. From a phase-key–insulated multi-key channel we demand, on a high level, that confidentiality and integrity in a certain phase is not endangered by the leakage of keys in prior or later phases.

3.1 Confidentiality

The established way of modeling confidentiality for channels is by demanding that the encryptions of two (left and right) sequences of messages are indistinguishable [9,31]. Formally, an adversary sequentially inputs pairs of messages m_0, m_1 of its choice to a sending oracle $\mathcal{O}_{\mathsf{Send}}$ and is given the encryption c_b of always either the first or the second message depending on an initially fixed, random challenge bit $b \xleftarrow{\$} \{0,1\}$. The adversary's task is to finally determine b. Hence, the corresponding security notion is established under the name of indistinguishability under chosen-plaintext attacks (IND-CPA). In the stronger setting of chosen-ciphertext attacks (IND-CCA), the adversary is additionally given a receiving oracle $\mathcal{O}_{\mathsf{Recv}}$ with the limitation that it may not query it on challenge ciphertexts, in a way to be defined later.

In the multi-key setting however, the advanced security aspects of forward security and particularly phase-key insulation render it impossible to use a single challenge bit throughout all phases. An adversary that adaptively learns keys for some phases is immediately able to learn whether the left or the right messages were encrypted in these phases. If this would be a fixed choice for all phases, the adversary could also tell which messages were encrypted in all other phases. In our formalization of multi-key confidentiality we hence deploy a separate challenge bit b_i for each phase i, chosen independently at random. This allows us to capture the expected insulation of phases against compromises in other phases and, ultimately, later corruption.

We define confidentiality in a modular notion s-IND-kATK through the experiment $\mathsf{Expt}^{s\text{-}\mathsf{IND}\text{-}k\mathsf{ATK}}_{\mathsf{Ch},\mathcal{A}}$ given in Fig. 2. The experiment is parameterized with s, k, and ATK.

- The parameter s specifies the advanced security aspects captured in the notion and can be either empty or take one of the values ki, fs, or fski. As expected, fs indicates that the notion ensures forward security and ki denotes that the notion demands phase-key insulation; for fski both properties are integrated. Forward security is modeled through allowing the adversary to corrupt the master secret key at some point through a corruption oracle $\mathcal{O}_{\mathsf{Corrupt}}$. When ensuring phase-key insulation, the adversary is given a reveal oracle $\mathcal{O}_{\mathsf{Reveal}}$ which allows it to selectively learn the keys of some phases.
- Via the parameter k, we capture both single-key (sk) and multi-key (mk) security notions in a single experiment. To model the single-key setting,

$\mathsf{Expt}^{s\text{-}\mathsf{IND}\text{-}k\mathsf{ATK}}_{\mathsf{Ch},\mathcal{A}}(1^\lambda)$:

$(\mathsf{msk}_0, \mathsf{K}_0, \mathsf{st}_S, \mathsf{st}_R) \xleftarrow{\$} \mathsf{Init}(1^\lambda)$
$t_S \leftarrow 0,\ t_R \leftarrow 0$
$b_0 \xleftarrow{\$} \{0,1\}$
$i_0 \leftarrow 0,\ j_0 \leftarrow 0$
$\mathsf{sync} \leftarrow 1$
$t_{corr} \leftarrow +\infty$
$Rev \leftarrow \emptyset$
$(t, b) \xleftarrow{\$} \mathcal{A}(1^\lambda)^{\mathcal{O}_{\mathsf{LoR}}, [\mathcal{O}_{\mathsf{Recv}}]_{\mathsf{ATK}=\mathsf{CCA}}, [\mathcal{O}_{\mathsf{Update}}]_{k=\mathsf{mk}}, [\mathcal{O}_{\mathsf{Reveal}}]_{s\in\{\mathsf{ki},\mathsf{fski}\}}, [\mathcal{O}_{\mathsf{Corrupt}}]_{s\in\{\mathsf{fs},\mathsf{fski}\}}}$
if $t > \max(t_S, t_R)$ then
  return 0
return $((b_t = b) \wedge (t \notin Rev) \wedge (t < t_{corr}))$

If $\mathcal{A}$ queries $\mathcal{O}_{\mathsf{LoR}}(m_0, m_1)$:
if $|m_0| \neq |m_1|$ then
  return $\lightning$
$i_{t_S} \leftarrow i_{t_S} + 1$
$(\mathsf{st}_S, \mathbf{C}[t_S][i_{t_S}]) \xleftarrow{\$} \mathsf{Send}(\mathsf{st}_S, \mathsf{K}_{t_S}, m_{b_{t_S}})$
if $t_R > t_S$ and $t_S \notin Rev$ then
  $\mathsf{sync} \leftarrow 0$
return $\mathbf{C}[t_S][i_{t_S}]$

If $\mathcal{A}$ queries $\mathcal{O}_{\mathsf{Recv}}(c)$:
$j_{t_R} \leftarrow j_{t_R} + 1$
$(\mathsf{st}_R, m) \leftarrow \mathsf{Recv}(\mathsf{st}_R, \mathsf{K}_{t_R}, c)$
if $(t_R > t_S$ or $j_{t_R} > i_{t_R}$ or $c \neq \mathbf{C}[t_R][j_{t_R}])$ and $t_R \notin Rev$ then
  $\mathsf{sync} \leftarrow 0$
if $\mathsf{sync} = 0$ then
  return m
else
  return $\lightning$

If $\mathcal{A}$ queries $\mathcal{O}_{\mathsf{Update}}(role)$:
$(\mathsf{msk}_{t_{role}+1}, \mathsf{K}_{t_{role}+1}, \mathsf{st}_{role}) \leftarrow \mathsf{Update}(\mathsf{msk}_{t_{role}}, \mathsf{st}_{role})$
if $role = R$ and $t_S \geq t_R$ and $j_{t_R} < i_{t_R}$ and $t_R \notin Rev$ then
  $\mathsf{sync} \leftarrow 0$
$t_{role} \leftarrow t_{role} + 1$
$\mathsf{st}^{begin}_{role, t_{role}} \leftarrow \mathsf{st}_{role}$
if $role = S$ then
  $b_{t_S} \xleftarrow{\$} \{0,1\}$

If $\mathcal{A}$ queries $\mathcal{O}_{\mathsf{Reveal}}(t, role)$:
if $t > t_{role}$ then
  return $\lightning$
$Rev \leftarrow Rev \cup \{t\}$
return $(\mathsf{st}^{begin}_{role,t}, \mathsf{K}_t)$

If $\mathcal{A}$ queries $\mathcal{O}_{\mathsf{Corrupt}}(role)$:
if $t_{corr} < +\infty$ then
  return $(\mathsf{st}^{begin}_{role, t_{corr}}, \mathsf{msk}_{t_{corr}})$
$t_{corr} \leftarrow t_{role}$
return $(\mathsf{st}^{begin}_{role, t_{role}}, \mathsf{msk}_{t_{role}})$

Fig. 2. Security experiment for *confidentiality* (sIND-kATK) of a multi-key channel Ch. An adversary $\mathcal{A}$ has only access to an oracle $[\mathcal{O}_{\mathsf{X}}]_c$ if the condition c is satisfied.

we simply drop the adversary's capability to proceed to a next phase via an $\mathcal{O}_{\mathsf{Update}}$ oracle, essentially restricting it to a single phase (and hence key).

- Finally, the parameter ATK distinguishes between chosen-plaintext (ATK = CPA) and chosen-ciphertext (ATK = CCA) attacks. While the adversary always has access to a left-or-right encryption oracle $\mathcal{O}_{\mathsf{LoR}}$, the receiving oracle $\mathcal{O}_{\mathsf{Recv}}$ is only available for notions with CCA attacks.

The adversary finally has to output a phase t and a bit guess b and wins if the challenge bit used in phase t by the left-or-right oracle $\mathcal{O}_{\mathsf{LoR}}$ is equal to b and the targeted challenge phase t is neither revealed nor affected by corruption (i.e., $t < t_{corr}$, where t_{corr} is the corrupted phase, initialized to infinity).

In order to prevent trivial attacks, we have to restrict the output of adversarial queries to the receiving oracle $\mathcal{O}_{\mathsf{Recv}}$ in the setting of chosen-ciphertext attacks. Obviously, if $\mathcal{O}_{\mathsf{Recv}}$ outputs the message decrypted on input the unmodified challenge ciphertext sequence, the challenge bit used in $\mathcal{O}_{\mathsf{LoR}}$ would be immediately distinguishable. Still, as the Recv algorithm is stateful, we must allow the adversary to first make this algorithm proceed to a certain, potentially vulnerable state, before mounting its attack. For this purpose, we follow Bellare et al. [9] in suppressing the output of the Recv algorithm as long as the adversary's inputs to $\mathcal{O}_{\mathsf{Recv}}$ are *in sync* with the challenge ciphertext sequence output by $\mathcal{O}_{\mathsf{LoR}}$. As soon as synchronization is lost though, $\mathcal{O}_{\mathsf{Recv}}$ returns the output of the receiving algorithm Recv to the adversary.

Defining what it means to be in sync now becomes the crucial task in defining CCA security: we want to make the security notion as strong as possible without allowing trivial attacks. Intuitively, $\mathcal{O}_{\mathsf{Recv}}$ stays in sync (denoted by a flag $\mathsf{sync} = 1$) and decryptions are suppressed as long as the adversary forwards ciphertexts to $\mathcal{O}_{\mathsf{Recv}}$ that are obtained from $\mathcal{O}_{\mathsf{LoR}}$ in the same phase. So far, this is essentially a transcription of the stateful encryption definition of CCA security (IND-sfCCA [9]) to the multi-key setting with multiple phases. When targeting forward security and phase-key insulation, we however also need to consider how to define synchronization in phases where the adversary knows the key. Obviously, in such phases we cannot demand that a channel can strictly distinguish adversarial encryptions from the honest ciphertext sequence generated in $\mathcal{O}_{\mathsf{LoR}}$ as the adversary may simply replicate the latter's behavior. We accordingly do not consider synchronization to become lost in revealed phases. Still, we demand that a secure channel notices modifications later in uncompromised phases. Moreover, it should even detect truncations at the end of an uncompromised phase if the next phase's key is revealed, latest when the channel recovers from temporary compromise and enters the next, uncompromised phase.[4] We hence, additionally to the regular stateful encryption setting, define synchronization to be lost if the receiver proceeds from an uncompromised phase to the next phase without having received all sent ciphertexts, or if the sender issues a ciphertext in a phase when the receiver already proceeded to the next phase.

In the following we describe the functionality and purpose of the oracles in the multi-key confidentiality experiment in Fig. 2 in detail.

- The $\mathcal{O}_{\mathsf{LoR}}$ oracle can be queried with a pair of messages (m_0, m_1) of equal length. It responds with the output of Send on message $m_{b_{t_S}}$, where b_{t_S} is the challenge bit for the current sending phase t_S.

[4] Recall that we consider key updates to be unauthenticated, possibly transmitted out-of-band.

If the receiver already proceeded to a later phase, the sent message cannot be received correctly anymore. As long as the key of the sender's phase is unrevealed, we hence declare synchronization to be lost (setting $\mathsf{sync} \leftarrow 0$). The restriction to uncompromised phases is necessary to prevent trivial attacks where the adversary leverages the phase key to, e.g., make the receiver process more messages than sent earlier to cover up the mismatch.

- The $\mathcal{O}_{\mathsf{Recv}}$ oracle can only be queried if $\mathsf{ATK} = \mathsf{CCA}$. On input a ciphertext c, $\mathcal{O}_{\mathsf{Recv}}$ computes the corresponding messages obtained under Recv. In case the receiving oracle is ahead in phase, has received more messages than sent, or c deviates from the corresponding sent ciphertext, synchronization is lost (again, to ignore trivial forgeries, as long the receiver's current phase is unrevealed). Finally, if still in sync, $\mathcal{O}_{\mathsf{Recv}}$ suppresses the message output and returns an according flag $\lightning$ to the adversary $\mathcal{A}$. Otherwise it provides $\mathcal{A}$ with the obtained message m.
- The $\mathcal{O}_{\mathsf{Update}}$ oracle is only available if $k = \mathsf{mk}$. Using the oracle, the adversary can separately make both the sender or receiver proceed to the next phase, updating their master secret, phase key, and state. If the sender side is updated, a new challenge bit for the new phase is chosen at random. Moreover, the experiment goes out of sync if the receiver side is updated too soon, i.e., without having received all sent ciphertexts, and the receiver's phase is not revealed.
- The $\mathcal{O}_{\mathsf{Reveal}}$ oracle can be used by the adversary to obtain the key of any phase t (along with this phase's initial sender resp. receiver state) and is accessible if $s \in \{\mathsf{ki}, \mathsf{fski}\}$. Phase t is then added to a set of revealed phases Rev.
- The $\mathcal{O}_{\mathsf{Corrupt}}$ oracle is provided if $s \in \{\mathsf{fs}, \mathsf{fski}\}$. Upon the first call, the adversary obtains for a chosen role *role* the current phase's master secret key and initial state. This phase is then recorded as the phase of corruption t_{corr} for later comparison. If a corruption has already taken place (i.e., $t_{corr} < +\infty$), the adversary can obtain the other role's initial state in the corrupted phase via a further $\mathcal{O}_{\mathsf{Corrupt}}$ call. For simplicity, we assume the state to be empty in phases not yet entered. Observe that it suffices to consider a single point in time for corruption, as later master keys are deterministically derived from the corrupted one.

Definition 3 (s-IND-kATK Security). *Let* $\mathsf{Ch} = (\mathsf{Init}, \mathsf{Send}, \mathsf{Recv}, \mathsf{Update})$ *be a multi-key channel and experiment* $\mathsf{Expt}^{s\text{-}\mathsf{IND}\text{-}k\mathsf{ATK}}_{\mathsf{Ch},\mathcal{A}}(1^\lambda)$ *for an adversary* $\mathcal{A}$ *be defined as in Fig. 2.*

The security experiment is parameterized in three directions: s, k, *and* ATK. *The parameter* s *indicates the advanced security aspects and can take one of the values* ki *(phase-key–insulated),* fs *(forward-secure),* fski *(forward-secure and phase-key–insulated), or the empty string*[5] *(plain / neither forward-secure nor phase-key–insulated). The parameter* k *integrates both single-key* (sk) *and multi-key* (mk) *security notions in a single experiment. Finally, the parameter* ATK

[5] For legibility, we also drop the leading dash in a notion s-IND-kATK if s is the empty string and simply write IND-kATK in this case.

distinguishes between chosen-plaintext ($\mathsf{ATK} = \mathsf{CPA}$*) and chosen-ciphertext (*$\mathsf{ATK} = \mathsf{CCA}$*) security.*

Within the experiment the adversary $\mathcal{A}$ *always has access to a left-or-right sending oracle* $\mathcal{O}_{\mathsf{LoR}}$. *Moreover,* $\mathcal{A}$ *has access to a receiving oracle* $\mathcal{O}_{\mathsf{Recv}}$ *if* $\mathsf{ATK} = \mathsf{CCA}$, *an update oracle* $\mathcal{O}_{\mathsf{Update}}$ *if* $k = \mathsf{mk}$, *a key-reveal oracle* $\mathcal{O}_{\mathsf{Reveal}}$ *if* $s \in \{\mathsf{ki}, \mathsf{fski}\}$, *and finally a corruption oracle* $\mathcal{O}_{\mathsf{Corrupt}}$ *if* $s \in \{\mathsf{fs}, \mathsf{fski}\}$.

We say that the channel Ch *provides* indistinguishability under multi-key (resp. single-key) chosen-plaintext (resp. chosen-ciphertext) attacks *(*s-IND-$k\mathsf{CPA}$ *resp.* s-IND-$k\mathsf{CCA}$ *for* $k = \mathsf{mk}$ *resp.* $k = \mathsf{sk}$*), potentially* with forward security *(if* $s \in \{\mathsf{fs}, \mathsf{fski}\}$*)* and/or phase-key insulation *(if* $s \in \{\mathsf{ki}, \mathsf{fski}\}$*) if for all PPT adversaries* $\mathcal{A}$ *the following advantage function is negligible in the security parameter:*

$$\mathsf{Adv}^{s\text{-}\mathsf{IND}\text{-}k\mathsf{ATK}}_{\mathsf{Ch},\mathcal{A}}(\lambda) := \Pr\left[\mathsf{Expt}^{s\text{-}\mathsf{IND}\text{-}k\mathsf{ATK}}_{\mathsf{Ch},\mathcal{A}}(1^\lambda) = 1\right] - \frac{1}{2}.$$

Our generic confidentiality notion in Definition 3 captures as its weakest variant indistinguishability under single-key chosen-plaintext attacks (IND-skCPA) and as its strongest variant indistinguishability under multi-key chosen-ciphertext attacks with forward security and phase-key insulation (fski-IND-mkCCA). We discuss the relations among these notions in more detail in Sect. 3.4.

3.2 Integrity

Integrity is traditionally defined in two flavors: integrity of plaintexts (INT-PTXT) and integrity of ciphertexts (INT-CTXT) [10], with according stateful-encryption analogs INT-sfPTXT [18] and INT-sfCTXT [9]. Integrity of plaintexts intuitively ensures that no adversary is able to make the receiver output a valid message that differs from the previously sent (sequence of) messages. The stronger notion of ciphertext integrity ensures that no adversary can make the receiver output any valid, even recurring message by inputting a forged or modified ciphertext.

Similarly to confidentiality, we define a modular multi-key integrity notion s-INT-$k\mathsf{ATK}$, given through the experiment $\mathsf{Expt}^{s\text{-}\mathsf{INT}\text{-}k\mathsf{ATK}}_{\mathsf{Ch},\mathcal{A}}$ in Fig. 3. Again, the notion is parameterized to integrate forward security and phase-key insulation (via s), the single- and multi-key setting (via k), as well as the two attack targets, $\mathsf{ATK} = \mathsf{PTXT}$ and $\mathsf{ATK} = \mathsf{CTXT}$. An adversary $\mathcal{A}$ against the experiment $\mathsf{Expt}^{s\text{-}\mathsf{INT}\text{-}k\mathsf{ATK}}_{\mathsf{Ch},\mathcal{A}}$ has access to a sending oracle $\mathcal{O}_{\mathsf{Send}}$ (in contrast to confidentiality without left-or-right functionality), one of two receiving oracles $\mathcal{O}^{\mathsf{ATK}}_{\mathsf{Recv}}$ depending on ATK, and—depending on the advanced security properties and key setting captured—oracles $\mathcal{O}_{\mathsf{Update}}$ (without setting a new challenge bit), and $\mathcal{O}_{\mathsf{Reveal}}$ and $\mathcal{O}_{\mathsf{Corrupt}}$, identical to those for confidentiality. In the integrity experiment, the adversary does not provide a particular challenge output, but instead needs to trigger a winning flag win to be set within the experiment run.

Beyond the sending oracle $\mathcal{O}_{\mathsf{Send}}$ only taking and encrypting a single message, the major difference to the confidentiality setting lies in the definition of the $\mathcal{O}^{\mathsf{ATK}}_{\mathsf{Recv}}$

$\mathsf{Expt}^{s\text{-}\mathsf{INT}\text{-}k\mathsf{ATK}}_{\mathsf{Ch},\mathcal{A}}(1^\lambda)$:
$(\mathsf{msk}_0, \mathsf{K}_0, \mathsf{st}_S, \mathsf{st}_R) \xleftarrow{\$} \mathsf{Init}(1^\lambda)$
$t_S \leftarrow 0$, $t_R \leftarrow 0$
$i_0 \leftarrow 0$, $j_0 \leftarrow 0$
$\mathsf{sync} \leftarrow 1$
$\mathsf{win} \leftarrow 0$
$t_{corr} \leftarrow +\infty$
$Rev \leftarrow \emptyset$
$\mathcal{A}(1^\lambda)^{\mathcal{O}_{\mathsf{Send}}, \mathcal{O}^{\mathsf{ATK}}_{\mathsf{Recv}}, [\mathcal{O}_{\mathsf{Update}}]_{k=\mathsf{mk}}, [\mathcal{O}_{\mathsf{Reveal}}]_{s\in\{\mathsf{ki},\mathsf{fski}\}}, [\mathcal{O}_{\mathsf{Corrupt}}]_{s\in\{\mathsf{fs},\mathsf{fski}\}}}$
return win

If $\mathcal{A}$ queries $\mathcal{O}_{\mathsf{Send}}(m)$:
$i_{t_S} \leftarrow i_{t_S} + 1$
$(\mathsf{st}_S, \mathbf{C}[t_S][i_{t_S}]) \xleftarrow{\$} \mathsf{Send}(\mathsf{st}_S, \mathsf{K}_{t_S}, m)$
$\mathbf{M}[t_S][i_{t_S}] \leftarrow m$
if $t_R > t_S$ and $t_S \notin Rev$ then
  $\mathsf{sync} \leftarrow 0$
return $\mathbf{C}[t_S][i_{t_S}]$

If $\mathcal{A}$ queries $\mathcal{O}^{\mathsf{PTXT}}_{\mathsf{Recv}}(c)$:
$j_{t_R} \leftarrow j_{t_R} + 1$
$(\mathsf{st}_R, m) \leftarrow \mathsf{Recv}(\mathsf{st}_R, \mathsf{K}_{t_R}, c)$
if $m \neq \mathbf{M}[t_R][j_{t_R}]$ and $m \notin \mathcal{E}$
  and $t_R \notin Rev$
  and $t_R < t_{corr}$ then
  $\mathsf{win} \leftarrow 1$
return m

If $\mathcal{A}$ queries $\mathcal{O}^{\mathsf{CTXT}}_{\mathsf{Recv}}(c)$:
$j_{t_R} \leftarrow j_{t_R} + 1$
$(\mathsf{st}_R, m) \leftarrow \mathsf{Recv}(\mathsf{st}_R, \mathsf{K}_{t_R}, c)$
if $(t_R > t_S$ or $j_{t_R} > i_{t_R}$
  or $c \neq \mathbf{C}[t_R][j_{t_R}])$
  and $t_R \notin Rev$ then
  $\mathsf{sync} \leftarrow 0$
if $\mathsf{sync} = 0$ and $m \notin \mathcal{E}$
  and $t_R \notin Rev$
  and $t_R < t_{corr}$ then
  $\mathsf{win} \leftarrow 1$
return m

If $\mathcal{A}$ queries $\mathcal{O}_{\mathsf{Update}}(role)$:
$(\mathsf{msk}_{t_{role}+1}, \mathsf{K}_{t_{role}+1}, \mathsf{st}_{role}) \leftarrow$
  $\mathsf{Update}(\mathsf{msk}_{t_{role}}, \mathsf{st}_{role})$
if $role = R$ and $t_S \geq t_R$ and $j_{t_R} < i_{t_R}$
  and $t_R \notin Rev$ then
  $\mathsf{sync} \leftarrow 0$
$t_{role} \leftarrow t_{role} + 1$
$\mathsf{st}^{begin}_{role,t_{role}} \leftarrow \mathsf{st}_{role}$

If $\mathcal{A}$ queries $\mathcal{O}_{\mathsf{Reveal}}(t, role)$:
if $t > t_{role}$ then
  return $\lightning$
$Rev \leftarrow Rev \cup \{t\}$
return $(\mathsf{st}^{begin}_{role,t}, \mathsf{K}_t)$

If $\mathcal{A}$ queries $\mathcal{O}_{\mathsf{Corrupt}}(role)$:
if $t_{corr} < +\infty$ then
  return $(\mathsf{st}^{begin}_{role,t_{corr}}, \mathsf{msk}_{t_{corr}})$
$t_{corr} \leftarrow t_{role}$
return $(\mathsf{st}^{begin}_{role,t_{role}}, \mathsf{msk}_{t_{role}})$

Fig. 3. Security experiment for *integrity* (sINT-kATK) of a multi-key channel Ch. An adversary $\mathcal{A}$ has only access to an oracle $[\mathcal{O}_{\mathsf{X}}]_c$ if the condition c is satisfied.

oracle, which in particular comprises the winning condition check. Depending on the attack target, the adversary has access to either the $\mathcal{O}^{\mathsf{PTXT}}_{\mathsf{Recv}}$ or the $\mathcal{O}^{\mathsf{CTXT}}_{\mathsf{Recv}}$ variant of the receiving oracle. Both oracles first of all obtain a ciphertext c and provide the adversary $\mathcal{A}$ with the decrypted message m output by Recv on that ciphertext. Beyond this, they differ in assessing whether $\mathcal{A}$ has succeeded in breaking plaintext resp. ciphertext integrity (in which case they set $\mathsf{win} \leftarrow 1$):

- The $\mathcal{O}^{\mathsf{PTXT}}_{\mathsf{Recv}}$ oracle declares the adversary successful if the received message m differs from the corresponding sent message in this phase and position, given that the current receiving phase is neither revealed nor corrupted.
- The $\mathcal{O}^{\mathsf{CTXT}}_{\mathsf{Recv}}$ in contrast for winning requires that, on input an out-of-sync ciphertext in a phase neither revealed nor corrupted, Recv outputs a valid message m, i.e., $m \notin \mathcal{E}$ is not an error message.

  In the same way as for confidentiality, synchronization is considered to be lost on an $\mathcal{O}_{\mathsf{Recv}}$ oracle call if the receiving oracle, in a non-revealed phase, is ahead of the sending oracle in phase or message count, or if c deviates from the corresponding sent message. Furthermore, synchronization may be lost by non-aligned key updates on both sides of the channel, captured in $\mathcal{O}_{\mathsf{Send}}$ and $\mathcal{O}_{\mathsf{Update}}$ as in the confidentiality experiment (cf. Fig. 2).

Definition 4 (s-INT-kATK Security). *Let* $\mathsf{Ch} = (\mathsf{Init}, \mathsf{Send}, \mathsf{Recv}, \mathsf{Update})$ *be a multi-key channel and experiment* $\mathsf{Expt}^{s\text{-}\mathsf{INT}\text{-}k\mathsf{ATK}}_{\mathsf{Ch},\mathcal{A}}(1^\lambda)$ *for an adversary* $\mathcal{A}$ *be defined as in Fig. 3. The security experiment is parameterized via* s, k, *and* ATK. *Parameters* s *and* k *are as for confidentiality in Definition 3. The parameter* ATK *distinguishes between plaintext integrity (*$\mathsf{ATK} = \mathsf{PTXT}$*) and ciphertext integrity (*$\mathsf{ATK} = \mathsf{CTXT}$*).*

Within the experiment the adversary $\mathcal{A}$ *has always access to a sending oracle* $\mathcal{O}_{\mathsf{Send}}$ *and a receiving oracle* $\mathcal{O}^{\mathsf{ATK}}_{\mathsf{Recv}}$ *(the latter differs depending on* ATK*). Moreover,* $\mathcal{A}$ *has access to an update oracle* $\mathcal{O}_{\mathsf{Update}}$ *if* $k = \mathsf{mk}$, *a key-reveal oracle* $\mathcal{O}_{\mathsf{Reveal}}$ *if* $s \in \{\mathsf{ki}, \mathsf{fski}\}$, *and finally a corruption oracle* $\mathcal{O}_{\mathsf{Corrupt}}$ *if* $s \in \{\mathsf{fs}, \mathsf{fski}\}$.

We say that Ch *provides* multi-key (resp. single-key) integrity of plaintexts (resp. ciphertexts) *(*s-INT-kPTXT *resp.* s-INT-kCTXT *for* $k = \mathsf{mk}$ *resp.* $k = \mathsf{sk}$*), potentially* with forward security *(if* $s \in \{\mathsf{fs}, \mathsf{fski}\}$*)* and/or phase-key insulation *(if* $s \in \{\mathsf{ki}, \mathsf{fski}\}$*) if for all PPT adversaries* $\mathcal{A}$ *the following advantage function is negligible in the security parameter:*

$$\mathsf{Adv}^{s\text{-}\mathsf{INT}\text{-}k\mathsf{ATK}}_{\mathsf{Ch},\mathcal{A}}(\lambda) := \Pr\left[\mathsf{Expt}^{s\text{-}\mathsf{INT}\text{-}k\mathsf{ATK}}_{\mathsf{Ch},\mathcal{A}}(1^\lambda) = 1\right].$$

Remark 1. Note that the advanced properties of forward security and phase-key insulation are only reasonable to consider in the multi-key setting ($k = \mathsf{mk}$). Indeed, for the single-key setting ($k = \mathsf{sk}$), the plain, fs, ki, and fski flavors of each notion collapse to being equivalent. For this, observe that an adversary in the single-key setting, lacking access to the $\mathcal{O}_{\mathsf{Update}}$ oracle, is restricted to the initial phase $t_S = t_R = 0$. At the same time, in order to win in this phase (by outputting a confidentiality guess resp. breaking integrity), it must neither reveal nor corrupt either of the parties. Hence, it effectively cannot make use of the $\mathcal{O}_{\mathsf{Reveal}}$ and $\mathcal{O}_{\mathsf{Corrupt}}$ queries, rendering both non-effective. Consequently, we can focus on only the plain version of our single-key security notions.

3.3 Modeling Rationale

As for the definition of syntax, there are choices to make when defining security for multi-key channels. Before further studying the relations among the confidentiality and integrity notions just set up, let us hence provide some rationale for aspects of our security model.

LoR vs. IND$. In our confidentiality experiment, the adversary is challenged to (be unable to) distinguish encryptions of left-or-right (LoR) messages. In the stateless authenticated-encryption setting particularly for AEAD schemes [44], the established notion for defining confidentiality instead is the stronger indistinguishability from random strings (IND$) [45].[6]

It might seem natural to adopt the strong IND$ confidentiality for channels from its common building block AEAD. On second thought, however, this notion turns out to be inappropriate for secure channels. While AEAD is an invaluable building block, a channel is a higher-layer object in a more complex setting, aiming not only at confidentiality and integrity, but also at replay and reordering protection [9,35] as well as further aspects such as data processing [16,29]. For this purpose, channel protocols regularly include header information like length or content type fields within the output ciphertexts, rendering them clearly distinguishable from random strings. In our security definition, we hence stick to the left-or-right indistinguishability notion rightfully established through previous channel models including [9,16,29,42].

Multiple challenge bits. As pointed out earlier, using a single challenge bit across all phases in the confidentiality experiment is infeasible: an adaptive Reveal query for some phase would in this case also disclose the challenge phase's (same) bit. We hence deploy multiple, independent challenge bits for each phase.

Alternative options would be to employ a single challenge bit in one phase and provide regular (non–LoR) encryption oracles for all other phases, or to have the adversary choose whether to compromise a phase at its beginning. We however deem these approaches not only more complex, but most importantly less adaptive, as they prevent the adversary from retrospectively choosing (non-)challenge phases.

3.4 Relations Between Multi- and Single-Key Notions

The modularity of our notions for multi-key confidentiality and integrity, parameterized by forward security and phase-key insulation, leads to a set of notions of varying strength. In the following, we establish that forward security and phase-key insulation are orthogonal properties; expectedly both adding to the strength of a security notion. Furthermore, we show that without forward

[6] A third variant, real-or-random (RoR) indistinguishability is equivalent to LoR indistinguishability [8]. See also Barwell et al. [5] for an (historical) overview of the security notions established for authenticated encryption.

security and phase-key insulation the single-key security notions of our framework are essentially equivalent to the respective established stateful encryption notions: we give generic, pure syntactical transforms to translate secure single-key schemes between the two realms. Figure 4 illustrates the relations we establish.

Trivial Implications. First of all, let us observe the trivial implications between the security notions of our framework, indicated by solid arrows in Fig. 4. Those implications arise by restricting the access to one (or multiple) oracles in the security experiments: a notion with access to a certain oracle immediately implies an otherwise identical notion without this oracle access. For instance, a fski-IND-mkCPA-secure channel is also ki-IND-mkCPA-secure, since if no adversary can distinguish left-or-right ciphertexts when being able to corrupt

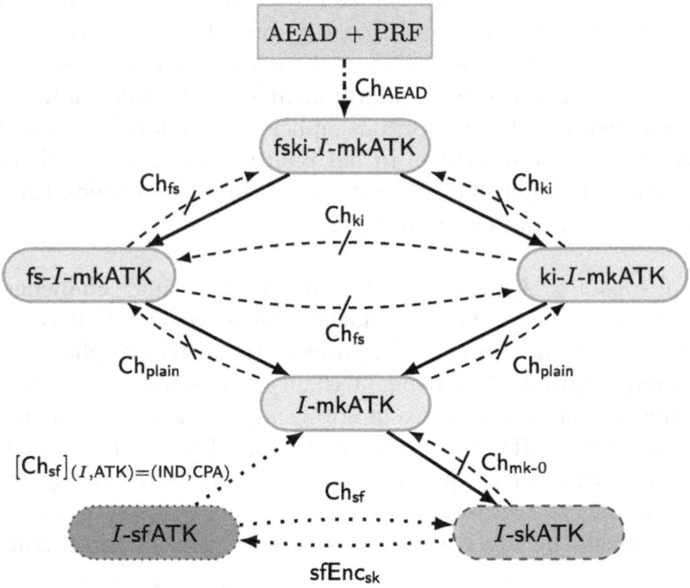

Fig. 4. Illustration of the relations between different flavors of confidentiality and integrity in our multi-key and single-key settings as well as for stateful encryption [9]. The variables I and ATK are placeholders for confidentiality notions (I = IND with ATK = CPA/CCA) and integrity notions (I = INT with ATK = PTXT/CTXT). Rounded rectangles indicate multi-key (solid-line, green), single-key (dashed-line, blue), or stateful-encryption notions (dotted-line, purple); regular (orange) rectangles indicate building blocks. Solid arrows indicate trivial implications. Dashed, stroke-out arrows indicate separations and dotted arrows generic transforms we establish, both provided in Sect. 3.4. The dash-dotted arrow indicates the generic construction we provide in Sect. 4. Labels refer to the respective construction, with brackets $[\mathsf{X}]_c$ restricting a relation to condition c.

the master secret key, then doing so does not become easier when corruption is not a possibility.

Separations. We discuss the separations between notions possibly providing forward security and phase-key insulation starting from a multi-key channel that provides both properties at the example of indistinguishability under chosen-plaintext attacks. The cases of integrity and indistinguishability under chosen-ciphertext attacks are analogous. More precisely, let $\mathsf{Ch}_{\mathsf{fski}} := (\mathsf{Init}_{\mathsf{fski}}, \mathsf{Send}_{\mathsf{fski}}, \mathsf{Recv}_{\mathsf{fski}}, \mathsf{Update}_{\mathsf{fski}})$ be a multi-key channel which provides fski-IND-mkCPA security. Recall that master secret and phase keys are computed using two deterministic sub-algorithms $\mathsf{MasterKeyUp}_{\mathsf{fski}}$ and $\mathsf{KeyDerive}_{\mathsf{fski}}$, respectively.

Now we construct a new channel $\mathsf{Ch}_{\mathsf{fs}}$ which differs from $\mathsf{Ch}_{\mathsf{fski}}$ only in its key derivation algorithm, which we replace by the identity function, i.e., we define $\mathsf{KeyDerive}_{\mathsf{fs}}(\mathsf{msk}_i) := \mathsf{msk}_i$ for all phases $i \in \mathbb{N}$. As MasterKeyUp remains unmodified, $\mathsf{Ch}_{\mathsf{fs}}$ inherits the forward security of $\mathsf{Ch}_{\mathsf{fski}}$. Furthermore, observe that a revealed phase key (equal to the master secret key $\mathsf{K}_i = \mathsf{msk}_i$) can be iteratively used to compute the next master secret keys $\mathsf{msk}_{i+1} = \mathsf{MasterKeyUp}_{\mathsf{fs}}(\mathsf{msk}_i)$ and therefore also the next phase keys $\mathsf{K}_{i+1} = \mathsf{KeyDerive}_{\mathsf{fs}}(\mathsf{msk}_{i+1})$. As a result, $\mathsf{Ch}_{\mathsf{fs}}$ has dependent phase keys and hence only provides fs-IND-mkCPA security, but not fski-IND-mkCPA security, separating the two notions.

Next we build a channel $\mathsf{Ch}_{\mathsf{ki}}$ from $\mathsf{Ch}_{\mathsf{fski}}$ which has a master secret key space $\mathcal{MSK}_{\mathsf{ki}} = \mathcal{MSK}^*_{\mathsf{fski}}$ and updates its master secret keys using a function $\mathsf{MasterKeyUp}_{\mathsf{ki}}(\mathbf{msk}_i) := (\mathbf{msk}_i, \mathsf{MasterKeyUp}_{\mathsf{fski}}(\mathbf{msk}_i[i]))$, where $\mathbf{msk}_0 = (\mathsf{MasterKeyGen}_{\mathsf{fski}}(1^\lambda))$. In other words, $\mathsf{Ch}_{\mathsf{ki}}$ keeps a copy of all master secret keys generated so far in the current master secret key, and uses the last entry to derive the next master secret key. The phase keys are then derived from the last master secret key entry, i.e., we define $\mathsf{KeyDerive}_{\mathsf{ki}}(\mathbf{msk}_i) := \mathsf{KeyDerive}_{\mathsf{fski}}(\mathbf{msk}_i[i])$. While $\mathsf{Ch}_{\mathsf{ki}}$ provides the phase-key insulation of $\mathsf{Ch}_{\mathsf{fski}}$, forward security is lost. On corruption in any phase, all previous master secret keys are leaked, allowing an adversary to derive any previous phase key. Therefore $\mathsf{Ch}_{\mathsf{ki}}$ only provides ki-IND-mkCPA security, but not fski-IND-mkCPA security.

Combining the two modifications above leads to a channel $\mathsf{Ch}_{\mathsf{plain}}$ which only satisfies plain IND-mkCPA security, but neither ki-IND-mkCPA nor fs-IND-mkCPA security.

Finally, we consider the separation between the single-key notions and their corresponding multi-key notions, both without forward security and phase-key insulation. Again, we only discuss the notions IND-skCPA and IND-mkCPA as an example; the other cases follow identically. We build from an IND-skCPA secure single-key channel $\mathsf{Ch}_{\mathsf{sk}}$ a multi-key channel $\mathsf{Ch}_{\mathsf{mk\text{-}0}}$ which uses the single-key channel's key for the initial phase both as master secret and phase key. As the master secret key for the second and all following phases it then uses the zero-string, i.e., $\mathsf{MasterKeyUp}_{\mathsf{mk}}(\mathsf{msk}_i) := 0^\lambda$. Clearly the security is not preserved by $\mathsf{Ch}_{\mathsf{mk\text{-}0}}$ in any phase other than the initial one, in which it behaves exactly like $\mathsf{Ch}_{\mathsf{sk}}$. Hence, $\mathsf{Ch}_{\mathsf{mk\text{-}0}}$ is IND-skCPA-secure, but not IND-mkCPA-secure.

Generic Transforms Between Stateful Encryption and Multi-key Channels. To complete the picture, we finally study the relations between the established notions for secure channels, stateful authenticated encryption, and our notion of multi-key channels.

For this purpose, let us first briefly recall the notation for stateful encryption schemes as introduced by Bellare, Kohno, and Namprempre [9]. A stateful encryption scheme $\mathsf{sfEnc} = (\mathsf{KGen}, \mathsf{Enc}, \mathsf{Dec})$ consists of the following three efficient algorithms. The randomized key generation algorithm $\mathsf{KGen}(1^\lambda) \xrightarrow{\$} (K, \mathsf{st_E}, \mathsf{st_D})$ outputs a key $K \in \mathcal{K}$ and initial encryption and decryption states $\mathsf{st_E}$, $\mathsf{st_D}$. The randomized, stateful encryption algorithm $\mathsf{Enc}(\mathsf{st_E}, K, m) \xrightarrow{\$} (\mathsf{st_E}', c)$ takes state, key, and a message m and outputs an updated state and ciphertext c. The deterministic, stateful decryption algorithm $\mathsf{Dec}(\mathsf{st_D}, K, c) \xrightarrow{\$} (\mathsf{st_D}', m)$ conversely maps state, key, and a ciphertext to an updated state and either a message or special error symbol $\bot$.

Clearly, stateful encryption does not aim at achieving the advanced security properties we consider in this work, forward security and phase-key insulation. In the comparison, we hence focus on the plain confidentiality and integrity notions, i.e., IND-kATK and INT-kATK (for both $k \in \{\mathsf{mk}, \mathsf{sk}\}$ and variants $\mathsf{ATK} \in \{\mathsf{CPA}, \mathsf{CCA}\}$ resp. $\mathsf{ATK} \in \{\mathsf{PTXT}, \mathsf{CTXT}\}$) in our framework as well as the stateful-encryption notions IND-sfCPA resp. IND-sfCCA and INT-sfPTXT resp. INT-sfCTXT.

The relations we establish are twofold. First, our single-key security notions which allow an adversary to access a multi-key channel only in its initial phase are indeed equivalent in strength to the corresponding stateful-encryption notions, beyond syntactical differences. For this, consider the following natural and generic transforms for constructing a multi-key channel $\mathsf{Ch_{sf}}$ from any stateful encryption scheme sfEnc and, conversely, a stateful encryption scheme $\mathsf{sfEnc_{sk}}$ from any multi-key channel with single-entry error space $\mathcal{E} = \{\bot\}$.

- $\mathsf{Ch_{sf}}(\mathsf{Init_{sf}}, \mathsf{Send_{sf}}, \mathsf{Recv_{sf}}, \mathsf{Update_{sf}})$.

  For initialization, derive $(K, \mathsf{st_E}, \mathsf{st_D}) \xleftarrow{\$} \mathsf{KGen}(1^\lambda)$ and set $\mathsf{msk}_0 = \mathsf{K}_0 = K$, $\mathsf{st}_{S,0} = \mathsf{st_E}$, and $\mathsf{st}_{R,0} = \mathsf{st_D}$. For sending and receiving, use Enc and Dec as direct replacements. Finally, the Update algorithm does nothing; i.e., StateUp, MasterKeyUp, and KeyDerive are defined to be the identity function.

- $\mathsf{sfEnc_{sk}}(\mathsf{KGen_{sk}}, \mathsf{Enc_{sk}}, \mathsf{Dec_{sk}})$.

  For key generation, derive $(\mathsf{msk}_0, \mathsf{K}_0, \mathsf{st}_{S,0}, \mathsf{st}_{R,0}) \xleftarrow{\$} \mathsf{Init}(1^\lambda)$ and set $K = \mathsf{msk}_0$, $\mathsf{st_E} = \mathsf{st}_{S,0}$, and $\mathsf{st_D} = \mathsf{st}_{R,0}$. Encryption and decryption is directly replaced by Send resp. Recv.

Careful inspection of the single-key ($k = \mathsf{sk}$) notions in our framework and those defined for stateful encryption [9,18][7] readily establishes that each two

[7] As a technical side-remark, we here consider a slight variant of stateful integrity where the adversary in the decryption oracle is given the decrypted message instead of only a bit telling whether decryption resulted in an error or not.

corresponding notions (i.e., I-skATK and I-sfATK for same I and ATK) are preserved by the generic transforms given above. That is, if the underlying stateful encryption scheme sfEnc achieves, e.g., IND-sfCCA security then the transformed multi-key channel $\mathsf{Ch}_{\mathsf{sf}}$ satisfies the corresponding IND-skCCA notion.

Finally, and perhaps surprisingly at first glance, our generic transform $\mathsf{Ch}_{\mathsf{sf}}$ of a stateful encryption scheme into a multi-key channel also achieves (plain) multi-key IND-mkCPA security. The reason for this is that the degenerated Update algorithm does not alter the key which hence also makes the $\mathcal{O}_{\mathsf{Send}}$ oracle not alter its behavior across different phases. On the other hand, the message resp. ciphertext vectors $\mathbf{M}$ resp. $\mathbf{C}$ in the $\mathcal{O}_{\mathsf{Recv}}$ oracle can be easily set out-of-sync by invoking Update at different positions in the ciphertext sequence on the sender and receiver side. As a result, an adversary can make challenge ciphertexts to be considered as valid forgery in a "different" phase (in the multi-key integrity game) or force challenge messages to be output by $\mathcal{O}_{\mathsf{Recv}}$ (in the IND-mkCCA game). Hence, $\mathsf{Ch}_{\mathsf{sf}}$ achieves neither IND-mkCCA nor INT-mkPTXT or INT-mkCTXT security.

3.5 Generic Composition

We round up the discussion of our framework of multi-key security notions by lifting the classical composition theorem by Bellare and Namprempre [10] for symmetric encryption, namely that IND-CPA and INT-CTXT security imply IND-CCA security, to the setting of multi-key channels. As noted by Boldyreva et al. [17], this result is not directly applicable in settings where the decryption algorithm may output multiple, distinguishable errors, an observation that also applies to our setting. Boldyreva et al. re-establish composition in the multiple-error setting by requiring that with overwhelming probability an adversary is only able to produce a single error (a notion they call *error invariance*). Here, we instead make use of the more versatile approach introduced as *error predictability* in the context of stream-based channels by Fischlin et al. [29]. Error predictability roughly requires that there exists an efficient *predictor* algorithm Pred that, given the ciphertexts sent and received so far, can with overwhelming probability predict the error message caused by receiving a certain next ciphertext (if that ciphertext produces at all an error).

In comparison, error predictability is a milder assumption than error invariance [17] as it allows for channels outputting multiple distinguishable and non-negligible errors. For stateless authenticated encryption, Barwell et al. [5] considered the alternative notion of *error simulatability* in which error leakage is simulated under an independent key. Their notion seems incomparable to error predictability in the stateful setting, where the history of ciphertexts needs to be taken into account and it is less clear how to define an independent receiver's internal state.

We translate the notion of error predictability to the multi-key setting, parameterized as s-kERR-PRE with forward security and phase-key insulation, and in a single- and multi-key variant. This enables us to show the following composition result: for any advanced security property $s \in \{\varepsilon, \mathsf{fs}, \mathsf{ki}, \mathsf{fski}\}$ and key setting $k \in \{\mathsf{sk}, \mathsf{mk}\}$, if a multi-key channel provides the according notion of

$\mathsf{Expt}^{s\text{-}k\mathsf{ERR\text{-}PRE}}_{\mathsf{Ch},\mathsf{Pred},\mathcal{A}}(1^\lambda)$:

$(\mathsf{msk}_0, \mathsf{K}_0, \mathsf{st}_S, \mathsf{st}_R) \xleftarrow{\$} \mathsf{Init}(1^\lambda)$
$t_S \leftarrow 0,\ t_R \leftarrow 0$
$i_0 \leftarrow 0,\ j_0 \leftarrow 0$
$\mathcal{A}(1^\lambda)^{\mathcal{O}_{\mathsf{Send}}, \mathcal{O}_{\mathsf{Recv}}, [\mathcal{O}_{\mathsf{Update}}]_{k=\mathsf{mk}}, [\mathcal{O}_{\mathsf{Reveal}}]_{s\in\{\mathsf{ki},\mathsf{fski}\}}, [\mathcal{O}_{\mathsf{Corrupt}}]_{s\in\{\mathsf{fs},\mathsf{fski}\}}}$
return win

If $\mathcal{A}$ queries $\mathcal{O}_{\mathsf{Send}}(m)$:
$i_{t_S} \leftarrow i_{t_S} + 1$
$(\mathsf{st}_S, \mathbf{C}_S[t_S][i_{t_S}]) \xleftarrow{\$} \mathsf{Send}(\mathsf{st}_S, \mathsf{K}_{t_S}, m)$
return $\mathbf{C}_S[t_S][i_{t_S}]$

If $\mathcal{A}$ queries $\mathcal{O}_{\mathsf{Recv}}(c)$:
$j_{t_R} \leftarrow j_{t_R} + 1$
$(\mathsf{st}_R, m) \leftarrow \mathsf{Recv}(\mathsf{st}_R, \mathsf{K}_{t_R}, c)$
if $m \in \mathcal{E}$ and $m \neq \mathsf{Pred}(\mathbf{C}_S, \mathbf{C}_R, c)$ then
  $\mathsf{win} \leftarrow 1$
$\mathbf{C}_R[t_R][j_{t_R}] \leftarrow c$
return m to $\mathcal{A}$

If $\mathcal{A}$ queries $\mathcal{O}_{\mathsf{Update}}(role)$:
$(\mathsf{msk}_{t_{role}+1}, \mathsf{K}_{t_{role}+1}, \mathsf{st}_{role}) \leftarrow \mathsf{Update}(\mathsf{msk}_{t_{role}}, \mathsf{st}_{role})$
$t_{role} \leftarrow t_{role} + 1$
$\mathsf{st}^{begin}_{role,t_{role}} \leftarrow \mathsf{st}_{role}$

If $\mathcal{A}$ queries $\mathcal{O}_{\mathsf{Reveal}}(t, role)$:
if $t > t_{role}$ then
  return $\lightning$
return $(\mathsf{st}^{begin}_{role,t}, \mathsf{K}_t)$

If $\mathcal{A}$ queries $\mathcal{O}_{\mathsf{Corrupt}}(role)$:
return $(\mathsf{st}^{begin}_{role,t_{role}}, \mathsf{msk}_{t_{role}})$

Fig. 5. Security experiment for *error predictability* (s-kERR-PRE) with respect to error predictor Pred of a multi-key channel Ch. An adversary $\mathcal{A}$ has only access to an oracle $[\mathcal{O}_X]_c$ if the condition c is satisfied.

ciphertext integrity (s-INT-kCTXT), chosen-plaintext confidentiality (s-IND-kCPA), and error predictability (s-kERR-PRE), then it also provides chosen-ciphertext confidentiality (s-IND-kCCA).

We formalize the parameterized, multi-key version of error predictability, s-kERR-PRE, in Definition 5 below through the experiment $\mathsf{Expt}^{s\text{-}k\mathsf{ERR\text{-}PRE}}_{\mathsf{Ch},\mathcal{A}}$ in Fig. 5. An adversary wins against this experiment if it can ever cause the Recv algorithm to output an error message that differs from the output of the predictor algorithm. Meanwhile, when forward security or phase-key insulation is demanded, the adversary is even allowed to corrupt the master secret key resp. reveal phase keys at will.

Definition 5 (Error predictability of multi-key channels (s-kERR-PRE)). *Let* Ch = (Init, Send, Recv, Update) *be a multi-key channel with error space* $\mathcal{E}$, *advanced security aspects* $s \in \{\varepsilon, \mathsf{fs}, \mathsf{ki}, \mathsf{fski}\}$ *and key setting* $k \in \{\mathsf{sk}, \mathsf{mk}\}$. *We say that* Ch *provides* error predictability *(s-kERR-PRE) with respect to an efficient probabilistic algorithm* $\mathsf{Pred}\colon \{0,1\}^{**} \times \{0,1\}^{**} \times \{0,1\}^{*} \xrightarrow{\$} \mathcal{E}$, *called the* error predictor, *if, for every PPT adversary* $\mathcal{A}$ *playing in the experiment* s-kERR-PRE *defined in Fig. 5 against channel* Ch, *the following advantage function is negligible:*

$$\mathsf{Adv}^{s\text{-}k\mathsf{ERR\text{-}PRE}}_{\mathsf{Ch},\mathsf{Pred},\mathcal{A}}(\lambda) := \Pr\left[\mathsf{Expt}^{s\text{-}k\mathsf{ERR\text{-}PRE}}_{\mathsf{Ch},\mathsf{Pred},\mathcal{A}}(1^\lambda) = 1\right].$$

We are now ready to state our generic composition theorem for the setting of multi-key channels. The proof of the multi-key composition theorem follows along the lines of the classical result [10] adapted to the stateful setting and making use of the error predictor in the simulation of multiple errors in the receiving oracle as in [17,29]. Due to space limitations, we provide the proof in the full version of this work.

Theorem 1 (s-INT-$k\mathsf{CTXT} \wedge s$-IND-$k\mathsf{CPA} \wedge s$-$k\mathsf{ERR}$-$\mathsf{PRE} \implies s$-IND-$k\mathsf{CCA}$)**.** *Let* $\mathsf{Ch} = (\mathsf{Init}, \mathsf{Send}, \mathsf{Recv}, \mathsf{Update})$ *be a correct multi-key channel with error space* $\mathcal{E}$*. If* Ch *provides indistinguishability under chosen-plaintext attacks, integrity of ciphertexts, and error predictability (wrt. some predictor* Pred*) with advanced security aspects* $s \in \{\varepsilon, \mathsf{fs}, \mathsf{ki}, \mathsf{fski}\}$ *for a key setting* $k \in \{\mathsf{sk}, \mathsf{mk}\}$*, then it also provides indistinguishability under chosen-ciphertext attacks for* s *and* k*. Formally, for every efficient* s-IND-$k\mathsf{CCA}$ *adversary* $\mathcal{A}$ *there exist an efficient* s-INT-$k\mathsf{CTXT}$ *adversary* $\mathcal{B}_1$*,* s-$k\mathsf{ERR}$-PRE *adversary* $\mathcal{B}_2$*, and* s-IND-$k\mathsf{CPA}$ *adversary* $\mathcal{B}_3$ *such that*

$$\mathsf{Adv}^{s\text{-}\mathsf{IND}\text{-}k\mathsf{CCA}}_{\mathsf{Ch},\mathcal{A}} \leq \mathsf{Adv}^{s\text{-}\mathsf{INT}\text{-}k\mathsf{CTXT}}_{\mathsf{Ch},\mathcal{B}_1} + \mathsf{Adv}^{s\text{-}k\mathsf{ERR}\text{-}\mathsf{PRE}}_{\mathsf{Ch},\mathsf{Pred},\mathcal{B}_2} + \mathsf{Adv}^{s\text{-}\mathsf{IND}\text{-}k\mathsf{CPA}}_{\mathsf{Ch},\mathcal{B}_3}.$$

4 AEAD-Based Construction of a Multi-key Channel

In this section we generically construct a (deterministic) multi-key channel $\mathsf{Ch}_{\mathsf{AEAD}}$ from on a nonce-based AEAD scheme AEAD and a pseudorandom function f. We then prove that our construction provides the strongest security notions for both confidentiality and integrity in our model, namely indistinguishability under multi-key chosen-ciphertext attacks and multi-key integrity of ciphertexts, both with forward security and phase-key insulation (fski-IND-mkCCA and fski-INT-mkCTXT).

Our generic construction $\mathsf{Ch}_{\mathsf{AEAD}} = (\mathsf{Init}, \mathsf{Send}, \mathsf{Recv}, \mathsf{Update})$ is defined via the algorithms given in Fig. 6. It uses a nonce-based AEAD scheme $\mathsf{AEAD} = (\mathsf{Enc}, \mathsf{Dec})$ with key space $\mathcal{K} = \{0,1\}^\lambda$, message and ciphertext space $\{0,1\}^*$, nonce space $\{0,1\}^n$, associated data space $\{0,1\}^*$, and an error symbol $\perp$. Furthermore, it employs a pseudorandom function $f\colon \{0,1\}^\lambda \times \{0,1\} \rightarrow \{0,1\}^\lambda$. The deterministic AEAD encryption algorithm maps a key $K \in \{0,1\}^\lambda$ (which we write in subscript), a nonce $N \in \{0,1\}^n$, an associated data value $ad \in \{0,1\}^*$, and a message $m \in \{0,1\}^*$ to a ciphertext $c \in \{0,1\}^*$. The deterministic decryption algorithm conversely maps a key, nonce, associated data value, and ciphertext to either a message or the error symbol $\perp$.

Our construction supports a maximum number of $\mathsf{maxmsg} = 2^n$ messages per phase, where n is the AEAD nonce length. The master-secret-key and phase-key space in our construction are equal to the AEAD and PRF key space, $\mathcal{MSK} = \mathcal{K} = \{0,1\}^\lambda$. The error space $\{\perp, \perp'\}$ consists of the error symbol $\perp$ of the AEAD scheme and a second symbol $\perp'$ indicating exceedance of maxmsg. The sending and receiving state space is $\mathcal{S}_S = \mathcal{S}_R = \mathbb{N} \times \mathbb{N}^* \times \{0,1\}$, encoding a message sequence number, a list of the message counts in all previous phases, and a failure flag indicating a previously occurred error.

Init(1^λ):
1 $(\mathsf{st}_{S,0}, \mathsf{st}_{R,0}) \leftarrow$ StateGen(1^λ)
2 $\mathsf{msk}_0 \xleftarrow{\$}$ MasterKeyGen(1^λ)
3 $K_0 \leftarrow$ KeyDerive(msk_0)
4 return $(\mathsf{msk}_0, K_0, \mathsf{st}_{S,0}, \mathsf{st}_{R,0})$

Send(st_S, K, m):
5 parse st_S as (seqno, prevnos, fail)
6 if seqno $=$ maxmsg or fail $= 1$ then
7   fail $\leftarrow 1$
8      $\mathsf{st}_S \leftarrow$ (seqno, prevnos, fail)
9   return $(\mathsf{st}_S, \perp')$
10 seqno $\leftarrow$ seqno $+ 1$
11 $c \leftarrow$ Enc$_K$(seqno, prevnos, m)
12 $\mathsf{st}_S \leftarrow$ (seqno, prevnos)
13 return (st_S, c)

Recv(st_R, K, c):
14 parse st_R as (seqno, prevnos, fail)
15 if fail $= 1$ then
16   return $(\mathsf{st}_R, \perp)$
17 seqno $\leftarrow$ seqno $+ 1$
18 $m \leftarrow$ Dec$_K$(seqno, prevnos, c)
19 if $m = \perp$ then
20   fail $\leftarrow 1$
21     $\mathsf{st}_R \leftarrow$ (seqno, prevnos, fail)
22 return (st_R, m)

StateGen(1^λ):
23 $\mathsf{st}_{S,0} = (0, (), 0)$
24 $\mathsf{st}_{R,0} = (0, (), 0)$
25 return $(\mathsf{st}_{S,0}, \mathsf{st}_{R,0})$

MasterKeyGen(1^λ):
26 $\mathsf{msk}_0 \xleftarrow{\$} \{0, 1\}^\lambda$
27 return msk_0

KeyDerive(msk):
28 return $f(\mathsf{msk}, 1)$

Update($\mathsf{msk}, \mathsf{st}$):
29 $\mathsf{msk} \leftarrow$ MasterKeyUp(msk)
30 $K \leftarrow$ KeyDerive(msk)
31 $\mathsf{st} \leftarrow$ StateUp(st)
32 return $(\mathsf{msk}, K, \mathsf{st})$

StateUp(st):
33 parse st as (seqno, prevnos, fail)
34 $\mathsf{st} \leftarrow (0, (\text{prevnos}, \text{seqno}), \text{fail})$
35 return st

MasterKeyUp(msk):
36 return $f(\mathsf{msk}, 0)$

Fig. 6. Our generic construction of a deterministic multi-key channel Ch$_{\mathsf{AEAD}}$.

On a high level, Ch$_{\mathsf{AEAD}}$ derives master secret and phase keys via the (domain-separated) PRF f, an established technique ensuring forward security and separation of the keys derived; see, e.g., [13]. For encryption, it ensures reorder protection via a sequence number used as nonce. It further authenticates the number of messages seen in previous phases via the associated data field, borrowing established concepts from distributed computing to ensure causality.[8] In detail, our construction operates as follows.

– The Init algorithm uses StateGen to initialize the sending and receiving states as tuples containing a message sequence number seqno $= 0$, a list of the

---

[8] Note that, for a more efficient construction, one can get similar authenticity guarantees by storing a chained hash value of the number of messages received in previous phases using a collision-resistant hash function. For the sake of simplicity we omit this hash-chain optimization here and focus on demonstrating the feasibility of our security notions.

number of messages sent in all previous phases $\mathsf{prevnos} = ()$, and a failure flag $\mathsf{fail} = 0$. Via MasterKeyGen, the Init algorithm then samples an initial master secret key $\mathsf{msk}_0 \xleftarrow{\$} \{0,1\}^\lambda$ uniformly at random. Finally it derives the initial phase key $\mathsf{K}_0 \leftarrow f(\mathsf{msk}_0, 1)$ via KeyDerive as the output of the PRF f keyed with the initial master secret key and on input 1.

- The Send algorithm immediately outputs an error $\perp'$ in case the maximum number $\mathsf{maxmsg} = 2^n$ of messages has been reached in this or a prior call (indicated by $\mathsf{fail} = 1$). Otherwise, it increases the message sequence number in its state by one. It then invokes the deterministic AEAD encryption algorithm on the message m to obtain the ciphertext c. Here, the sequence number is used as the nonce $N = \mathsf{seqno}$ and the previous phases' message count as the associated data $ad = \mathsf{prevnos}$. The output of Send is the new state and the ciphertext c.
- The Recv algorithm immediately outputs an error $\perp$ in case the failure flag has been set ($\mathsf{fail} = 1$) in an earlier invocation, indicating that a previous AEAD decryption algorithm has failed. Otherwise it increases the message sequence number contained in the receiving state by one. It then uses the nonce $N = \mathsf{seqno}$ and associated data $\mathsf{prevnos}$ in the AEAD decryption algorithm on the ciphertext c to obtain m. In case the decryption fails and $m = \perp$, the failure flag is set to 1. The output of Recv is the new state and the message (or error) m.
- The Update algorithm uses StateUp to reset the new message sequence number to 0, and appends the previous message sequence number to the list of previous phases' message counts, i.e., $\mathsf{prevnos} \leftarrow (\mathsf{prevnos}, \mathsf{seqno})$. Then it invokes MasterKeyUp to derive a new master secret key as the output of f keyed with the previous master secret key and on input 0. Finally, it uses KeyDerive to compute a new phase key from the new master secret key.

Correctness. Correctness of our $\mathsf{Ch}_{\mathsf{AEAD}}$ construction follows immediately from correctness of the underlying AEAD scheme. In particular, observe that both receiver and sender compute their master secret and phase keys via the same, deterministic key schedule. Moreover, whenever both sides process the same number—not exceeding maxmsg—of messages per phase (as is a precondition in the correctness definition), they will also use the same associated data values for encryption and decryption, thus rendering the receiver to derive the correct messages as required.

Remark 2. At first glance, it might seem counter-intuitive that the sequence number in our $\mathsf{Ch}_{\mathsf{AEAD}}$ construction is reset to 0 at the start of a new phase. Would it not be more natural to have the sequence number running over all phases in order to ensure at the start of a phase that all messages of the previous phase were received, and to prevent reordering of messages across phases?

As surfaced by Fournet and the miTLS [40] team in the discussion around TLS 1.3 [30], this approach would however enable truncation attacks if the leakage of phase keys is considered in the security definition, as we do for phase-key insulation.[9] If sequence numbers are continued, an adversary holding the key of some phase t can truncate a prefix of the messages (with sequence numbers $i, \ldots, i+j$) in phase $t+1$ by providing the receiver with $j+1$ self-generated messages at the end of t. Dropping the first $j+1$ messages in phase $t+1$, the receiver's sequence number matches again the one of the sender (for message $i+j+1$), so the truncation would go unnoticed. Resetting the sequence numbers to 0 when switching phases prevents this attack, though additional care needs to be taken to prevent suffix truncation at the end of a phase. In our construction, we ensure the latter through authenticating the number of messages sent in all previous phases. We note that this mechanism would even allow to not reset the sequence number, but we decided to keep the reset in order to stay closer to the channel design of TLS 1.3 (cf. the discussion in Sect. 4.2).

4.1 Security Analysis

We now show that our generic $\mathsf{Ch}_{\mathsf{AEAD}}$ construction achieves the strongest multi-key security notions for confidentiality and integrity, namely forward-secure and phase-key–insulated indistinguishability under multi-key chosen-ciphertext attacks (fski-IND-mkCCA) and integrity of ciphertexts (fski-INT-mkCTXT). For proving the former notion we proceed via first showing the corresponding CPA confidentiality variant as well as that our construction provides error predictability (for multiple keys and with forward security and phase-key insulation), and then leverage our generic composition theorem (Theorem 1). Our results hold under the assumption that the underlying nonce-based AEAD scheme AEAD provides confidentiality in the sense of IND-CPA security and integrity in terms of AUTH security as defined by Rogaway [44][10], as well as that the employed pseudorandom function f meets the standard notion of PRF security.

We begin with stating the multi-key chosen-plaintext confidentiality with forward security and phase-key insulation. The according proof, provided in the full version, proceeds in three steps. First, we guess the challenge phase t the adversary will select, introducing a loss of n_t. Second, we gradually replace all master secret keys up to msk_{t+1} and phase keys up to K_t with independent random values, bounding the advantage difference by n_t times the PRF security of f via a hybrid argument. In the last step, we show that the remaining advantage can be bounded by reducing the challenge phase's operations to the IND-CPA security of the employed AEAD scheme.

Theorem 2 ($\mathsf{Ch}_{\mathsf{AEAD}}$ is fski-IND-mkCPA-secure). *The $\mathsf{Ch}_{\mathsf{AEAD}}$ construction from Fig. 6 provides forward-secure and phase-key–insulated indistinguishability under multi-key chosen-plaintext attacks (*fski-IND-mkCPA*) if the employed*

---

[9] In our framework, the weakest integrity property broken through this attack is phase-key–insulated integrity of plaintexts (ki-INT-mkPTXT).

[10] While Rogaway defines confidentiality via the stronger IND$-CPA notion, it suffices for our result that AEAD provides regular indistinguishability of encryptions.

authenticated encryption with associated data scheme AEAD *provides indistinguishability under chosen-plaintext attacks (*IND-CPA*) and the employed pseudorandom function f is* PRF*-secure.*

Formally, for every efficient fski-IND-mkCPA *adversary $\mathcal{A}$ against* $\mathsf{Ch}_{\mathsf{AEAD}}$ *there exists efficient algorithms $\mathcal{B}_1$ and $\mathcal{B}_2$ such that*

$$\mathsf{Adv}^{\mathsf{fski\text{-}IND\text{-}mkCPA}}_{\mathsf{Ch}_{\mathsf{AEAD}},\mathcal{A}}(\lambda) \leq n_t \cdot \left(n_t \cdot \mathsf{Adv}^{\mathsf{PRF}}_{f,\mathcal{B}_1}(\lambda) + \mathsf{Adv}^{\mathsf{IND\text{-}CPA}}_{\mathsf{AEAD},\mathcal{B}_2}(\lambda)\right),$$

where $n_t = \max(t_S, t_R) + 1$ is the maximum number of phases active in the fski-IND-mkCPA *experiment.*

We now turn to the multi-key integrity of ciphertexts with forward security and phase-key insulation of $\mathsf{Ch}_{\mathsf{AEAD}}$. In the proof, the first two steps follow closely the proof of fski-IND-mkCPA security. For the last step, a careful case analysis of the situations where synchronization is lost in the integrity experiment and how this is reflected in the $\mathsf{Ch}_{\mathsf{AEAD}}$ construction establishes the reduction to the underlying AEAD scheme's authenticity. We provide the proof of integrity for our $\mathsf{Ch}_{\mathsf{AEAD}}$ construction in the full version.

Theorem 3 ($\mathsf{Ch}_{\mathsf{AEAD}}$ is fski-INT-mkCTXT-secure). *The* $\mathsf{Ch}_{\mathsf{AEAD}}$ *construction from Fig. 6 provides forward-secure and phase-key–insulated multi-key integrity of ciphertexts (*fski-INT-mkCTXT*) if the employed authenticated encryption with associated data scheme* AEAD *provides authenticity (*AUTH*) and the employed pseudorandom function f is* PRF*-secure.*

Formally, for every efficient fski-INT-mkCTXT *adversary $\mathcal{A}$ against* $\mathsf{Ch}_{\mathsf{AEAD}}$ *there exists efficient algorithms $\mathcal{B}_1$ and $\mathcal{B}_2$ such that*

$$\mathsf{Adv}^{\mathsf{fski\text{-}INT\text{-}mkCTXT}}_{\mathsf{Ch}_{\mathsf{AEAD}},\mathcal{A}}(\lambda) \leq n_t \cdot \left(n_t \cdot \mathsf{Adv}^{\mathsf{PRF}}_{f,\mathcal{B}_1}(\lambda) + \mathsf{Adv}^{\mathsf{AUTH}}_{\mathsf{AEAD},\mathcal{B}_2}(\lambda)\right),$$

where $n_t = \max(t_S, t_R) + 1$ is the maximum number of phases active in the fski-INT-mkCTXT *experiment.*

Finally, in the full version, we show that our $\mathsf{Ch}_{\mathsf{AEAD}}$ provides multi-key error predictability with forward security and phase-key insulation (fski-mkERR-PRE). We can then conclude from Theorem 1 that it also achieves strong fski-IND-mkCCA confidentiality.

4.2 Comparison to the TLS 1.3 Record Protocol

Our notion of multi-key channels is particularly inspired by the ongoing developments of the upcoming Transport Layer Security (TLS) protocol version 1.3 [43]. It is hence insightful to compare our generic construction with the design of the TLS 1.3 record protocol (cf. [43, Sect. 5]).

First of all note that, in contrast to previous TLS versions, TLS 1.3 mandates the use of AEAD schemes as encryption and authentication mechanisms for the record protocol. It follows the basic secure-channel design principle to include a sequence number for protecting against reordering attacks; as in our construction. Both in TLS 1.3 and our construction, the sequence number enters the AEAD's nonce field and is reset to 0 at the start of each new phase. Also identically to our construction, the TLS 1.3 record protocol keys are derived via a deterministic key schedule in which, starting from an initial master secret key (denoted `client/server_traffic_secret_0` in TLS 1.3) the current phase's key as well as the next phase's master secret key are derived via independent applications of a pseudorandom function (TLS 1.3 uses HMAC [7,36] for this purpose). Beyond enabling key switches to allow secure encryption of large amounts of data, the TLS 1.3 design in particular names forward security (combined with insulation of phase keys) as a security goal [43, Appendix E.2]. In this sense, our generic $\mathsf{Ch}_{\mathsf{AEAD}}$ construction is comparatively close to the internal channel design of the TLS 1.3 record protocol in both techniques and security goals.

Still, there are some notable differences between the two designs, both in technical details as well as in the practically achieved security and its underlying assumptions. On the technical side, the TLS 1.3 record protocol additionally includes a content-type field in ciphertexts to enable multiplexing of messages from multiple sources. Furthermore, TLS 1.3 does not explicitly authenticate the numbers of seen ciphertexts in previous phases (as our construction does via the $\mathsf{prevnos}$ field), but instead relies on the authenticated transmission of key update messages. To be precise, key update messages are encoded as a specific control ("post-handshake") message and sent within the data channel. Thereby associated with a sequence number, they serve as an authenticated "end-of-phase indicator" that allows the record protocol to infer in unrevealed phases that all messages in a phase have been correctly received when the key update message arrives.

In contrast, our model does not rely on the authenticity of key updates but captures more generic settings where key update notifications may be send out-of-band and without being authenticated. Our construction hence cannot rely on key updates as indicators that a phase was gracefully completed, but instead needs to leverage the next uncompromised phase to detect truncations in an earlier phase. Nevertheless, our generic $\mathsf{Ch}_{\mathsf{AEAD}}$ scheme serves as proof-of-concept construction that strong confidentiality and integrity can be achieved in the multi-key setting with forward security and phase-key insulation even with unauthenticated, out-of-band key updates.

5 Conclusions and Future Work

In this work we initiate the study of multi-key channels, providing a game-based formalization, a framework of security notions and their relations, as well as a provably secure construction based on authenticated encryption with associated data and a pseudorandom function. Motivated by the channel design of the upcoming version 1.3 of the Transport Layer Security (TLS) protocol involving key updates and thus multiple keys, our work casts a formal light on the design criteria for multi-key channels and their achievable security guarantees.

Being a first step towards the understanding of, in particular, real-world designs of multi-key channels, our work also gives rise to further research questions. A natural next step is to analyze the exact security guarantees achieved by the multi-key TLS 1.3 record protocol. In this context, a question of independent interest lies in analyzing the trade-offs between relying on authenticated key updates versus not authenticating them, both with respect to the security properties achievable as well as potential functional and efficiency impacts. In a different direction, Fischlin et al. [29] observed that TLS and other channels deviate on the API level from the classical cryptographic abstraction of channels by providing a streaming interface rather than an atomic-message interface. Hence, their notion of stream-based channels is a natural candidate to blend with our multi-key notions in order to investigate the interplay of discrete key updates with a non-discrete stream of message data. Finally, it would be interesting to extend the notion of multi-key channels to capture more complex, non-deterministic key schedules, e.g., those employed in secure messaging protocols like Signal [47] aiming at extended security properties [6,20,21].

Acknowledgments. We thank Giorgia Azzurra Marson for helpful discussions in the early phase of this work. We furthermore thank the anonymous reviewers of EUROCRYPT 2017 and CRYPTO 2017 for their valuable comments. This work has been funded by the DFG as part of projects P2, S4 within the CRC 1119 CROSSING.

References

1. Abdalla, M., Bellare, M.: Increasing the lifetime of a key: a comparative analysis of the security of re-keying techniques. In: Okamoto, T. (ed.) ASIACRYPT 2000. LNCS, vol. 1976, pp. 546–559. Springer, Heidelberg (2000). doi:10.1007/3-540-44448-3_42
2. Albrecht, M.R., Degabriele, J.P., Hansen, T.B., Paterson, K.G.: A surfeit of SSH cipher suites. In: Weippl, E.R., Katzenbeisser, S., Kruegel, C., Myers, A.C., Halevi, S. (eds.) ACM CCS 2016, pp. 1480–1491. ACM Press, October 2016
3. Albrecht, M.R., Paterson, K.G., Watson, G.J.: Plaintext recovery attacks against SSH. In: 2009 IEEE Symposium on Security and Privacy, pp. 16–26. IEEE Computer Society Press, May 2009
4. Badertscher, C., Matt, C., Maurer, U., Rogaway, P., Tackmann, B.: Augmented secure channels and the goal of the TLS 1.3 record layer. In: Au, M.-H., Miyaji, A. (eds.) ProvSec 2015. LNCS, vol. 9451, pp. 85–104. Springer, Cham (2015). doi:10.1007/978-3-319-26059-4_5
5. Barwell, G., Page, D., Stam, M.: Rogue decryption failures: reconciling AE robustness notions. In: Groth, J. (ed.) IMACC 2015. LNCS, vol. 9496, pp. 94–111. Springer, Cham (2015). doi:10.1007/978-3-319-27239-9_6
6. Bellare, M., Camper Singh, A., Jaeger, J., Nyayapati, M., Stepanovs, I.: Ratcheted encryption and key exchange: the security of messaging. In: Katz, J., Shacham, H. (eds.) CRYPTO 2017, Part III. LNCS, vol. 10403, pp. 619–650. Springer, Cham (2017)
7. Bellare, M., Canetti, R., Krawczyk, H.: Keying hash functions for message authentication. In: Koblitz, N. (ed.) CRYPTO 1996. LNCS, vol. 1109, pp. 1–15. Springer, Heidelberg (1996). doi:10.1007/3-540-68697-5_1

8. Bellare, M., Desai, A., Jokipii, E., Rogaway, P.: A concrete security treatment of symmetric encryption. In: 38th FOCS, pp. 394–403. IEEE Computer Society Press, October 1997
9. Bellare, M., Kohno, T., Namprempre, C.: Breaking and provably repairing the SSH authenticated encryption scheme: a case study of the encode-then-encrypt-and-MAC paradigm. ACM Trans. Inf. Syst. Secur. **7**(2), 206–241 (2004)
10. Bellare, M., Namprempre, C.: Authenticated encryption: relations among notions and analysis of the generic composition paradigm. In: Okamoto, T. (ed.) ASIACRYPT 2000. LNCS, vol. 1976, pp. 531–545. Springer, Heidelberg (2000). doi:10.1007/3-540-44448-3_41
11. Bellare, M., Rogaway, P.: Encode-then-encipher encryption: how to exploit nonces or redundancy in plaintexts for efficient cryptography. In: Okamoto, T. (ed.) ASIACRYPT 2000. LNCS, vol. 1976, pp. 317–330. Springer, Heidelberg (2000). doi:10.1007/3-540-44448-3_24
12. Bellare, M., Tackmann, B.: The multi-user security of authenticated encryption: AES-GCM in TLS 1.3. In: Robshaw, M., Katz, J. (eds.) CRYPTO 2016. LNCS, vol. 9814, pp. 247–276. Springer, Heidelberg (2016). doi:10.1007/978-3-662-53018-4_10
13. Bellare, M., Yee, B.: Forward-security in private-key cryptography. In: Joye, M. (ed.) CT-RSA 2003. LNCS, vol. 2612, pp. 1–18. Springer, Heidelberg (2003). doi:10.1007/3-540-36563-X_1
14. Bhargavan, K., Blanchet, B., Kobeissi, N.: Verified models and reference implementations for the TLS 1.3 standard candidate. In: 2017 IEEE Symposium on Security and Privacy (S&P 2017), pp. 483–503. IEEE, May 2017
15. Bhargavan, K., Delignat-Lavaud, A., Fournet, C., Kohlweiss, M., Pan, J., Protzenko, J., Rastogi, A., Swamy, N., Zanella-Béguelin, S., Zinzindohoué, J.K.: Implementing and proving the TLS 1.3 record layer. In: 2017 IEEE Symposium on Security and Privacy (S&P 2017) (2017)
16. Boldyreva, A., Degabriele, J.P., Paterson, K.G., Stam, M.: Security of symmetric encryption in the presence of ciphertext fragmentation. In: Pointcheval, D., Johansson, T. (eds.) EUROCRYPT 2012. LNCS, vol. 7237, pp. 682–699. Springer, Heidelberg (2012). doi:10.1007/978-3-642-29011-4_40
17. Boldyreva, A., Degabriele, J.P., Paterson, K.G., Stam, M.: On symmetric encryption with distinguishable decryption failures. In: Moriai, S. (ed.) FSE 2013. LNCS, vol. 8424, pp. 367–390. Springer, Heidelberg (2014). doi:10.1007/978-3-662-43933-3_19
18. Brzuska, C., Smart, N.P., Warinschi, B., Watson, G.J.: An analysis of the EMV channel establishment protocol. In: Sadeghi, A.R., Gligor, V.D., Yung, M. (eds.) ACM CCS 2013, pp. 373–386. ACM Press, November 2013
19. Canetti, R., Krawczyk, H.: Analysis of key-exchange protocols and their use for building secure channels. In: Pfitzmann, B. (ed.) EUROCRYPT 2001. LNCS, vol. 2045, pp. 453–474. Springer, Heidelberg (2001). doi:10.1007/3-540-44987-6_28
20. Cohn-Gordon, K., Cremers, C., Dowling, B., Garratt, L., Stebila, D.: A formal security analysis of the Signal messaging protocol. In: 2017 IEEE European Symposium on Security and Privacy (EuroS&P 2017). IEEE, April 2017
21. Cohn-Gordon, K., Cremers, C.J.F., Garratt, L.: On post-compromise security. In: IEEE 29th Computer Security Foundations Symposium (CSF 2016), pp. 164–178 (2016)
22. Dierks, T., Rescorla, E.: The Transport Layer Security (TLS) Protocol Version 1.2. RFC 5246 (Proposed Standard). http://www.ietf.org/rfc/rfc5246.txt. Updated by RFCs 5746, 5878, 6176

23. Diffie, W., Van Oorschot, P.C., Wiener, M.J.: Authentication and authenticated key exchanges. Des. Codes Cryptogr. **2**(2), 107–125 (1992)
24. Dodis, Y., Katz, J., Xu, S., Yung, M.: Key-insulated public key cryptosystems. In: Knudsen, L.R. (ed.) EUROCRYPT 2002. LNCS, vol. 2332, pp. 65–82. Springer, Heidelberg (2002). doi:10.1007/3-540-46035-7_5
25. Dodis, Y., Katz, J., Xu, S., Yung, M.: Strong key-insulated signature schemes. In: Desmedt, Y.G. (ed.) PKC 2003. LNCS, vol. 2567, pp. 130–144. Springer, Heidelberg (2003). doi:10.1007/3-540-36288-6_10
26. Dodis, Y., Luo, W., Xu, S., Yung, M.: Key-insulated symmetric key cryptography and mitigating attacks against cryptographic cloud software. In: Youm, H.Y., Won, Y. (eds.) ASIACCS 2012, pp. 57–58. ACM Press, May 2012
27. Dowling, B., Fischlin, M., Günther, F., Stebila, D.: A cryptographic analysis of the TLS 1.3 handshake protocol candidates. In: Ray, I., Li, N., Kruegel, C. (eds.) ACM CCS 2015, pp. 1197–1210. ACM Press, October 2015
28. Fischlin, M., Günther, F.: Replay attacks on zero round-trip time: the case of the TLS 1.3 handshake candidates. In: 2017 IEEE European Symposium on Security and Privacy. IEEE, April 2017
29. Fischlin, M., Günther, F., Marson, G.A., Paterson, K.G.: Data is a stream: security of stream-based channels. In: Gennaro, R., Robshaw, M. (eds.) CRYPTO 2015. LNCS, vol. 9216, pp. 545–564. Springer, Heidelberg (2015). doi:10.1007/978-3-662-48000-7_27
30. Fournet, C.: Re: [TLS] [tls13-spec] resetting the sequence number to zero for each record key (#379). https://mailarchive.ietf.org/arch/msg/tls/extoO9ETJLnEm3MRDTO23x70DFM
31. Goldwasser, S., Micali, S.: Probabilistic encryption. J. Comput. Syst. Sci. **28**(2), 270–299 (1984)
32. Günther, C.G.: An identity-based key-exchange protocol. In: Quisquater, J.-J., Vandewalle, J. (eds.) EUROCRYPT 1989. LNCS, vol. 434, pp. 29–37. Springer, Heidelberg (1990). doi:10.1007/3-540-46885-4_5
33. Katz, J., Yung, M.: Unforgeable encryption and chosen ciphertext secure modes of operation. In: Goos, G., Hartmanis, J., Leeuwen, J., Schneier, B. (eds.) FSE 2000. LNCS, vol. 1978, pp. 284–299. Springer, Heidelberg (2001). doi:10.1007/3-540-44706-7_20
34. Kent, S., Seo, K.: Security Architecture for the Internet Protocol. RFC 4301 (Proposed Standard). http://www.ietf.org/rfc/rfc4301.txt. Updated by RFC 6040
35. Kohno, T., Palacio, A., Black, J.: Building secure cryptographic transforms, or how to encrypt and MAC. Cryptology ePrint Archive, Report 2003/177 (2003). http://eprint.iacr.org/2003/177
36. Krawczyk, H., Bellare, M., Canetti, R.: HMAC: Keyed-Hashing for Message Authentication. RFC 2104 (Informational). http://www.ietf.org/rfc/rfc2104.txt. Updated by RFC 6151
37. Krawczyk, H., Wee, H.: The OPTLS protocol and TLS 1.3. In: 2016 IEEE European Symposium on Security and Privacy, pp. 81–96. IEEE, March 2016
38. Luykx, A., Paterson, K.: Limits on authenticated encryption use in TLS (2016). http://www.isg.rhul.ac.uk/~kp/TLS-AEbounds.pdf
39. Marson, G.A., Poettering, B.: Security notions for bidirectional channels. IACR Trans. Symm. Cryptol. **2017**(1), 405–426 (2017)
40. miTLS: A Verified Reference Implementation of TLS. http://mitls.org/
41. Paterson, K.G., Merwe, T.: Reactive and proactive standardisation of TLS. In: Chen, L., McGrew, D., Mitchell, C. (eds.) SSR 2016. LNCS, vol. 10074, pp. 160–186. Springer, Cham (2016). doi:10.1007/978-3-319-49100-4_7

42. Paterson, K.G., Ristenpart, T., Shrimpton, T.: Tag size *Does* matter: attacks and proofs for the TLS record protocol. In: Lee, D.H., Wang, X. (eds.) ASIACRYPT 2011. LNCS, vol. 7073, pp. 372–389. Springer, Heidelberg (2011). doi:10.1007/978-3-642-25385-0_20
43. Rescorla, E.: The Transport Layer Security (TLS) Protocol Version 1.3 - draft-ietf-tls-tls13-20. https://tools.ietf.org/html/draft-ietf-tls-tls13-20
44. Rogaway, P.: Authenticated-encryption with associated-data. In: Atluri, V. (ed.) ACM CCS 2002, pp. 98–107. ACM Press, November 2002
45. Rogaway, P., Bellare, M., Black, J., Krovetz, T.: OCB: a block-cipher mode of operation for efficient authenticated encryption. In: ACM CCS 2001, pp. 196–205. ACM Press, November 2001
46. Rogaway, P., Shrimpton, T.: A provable-security treatment of the key-wrap problem. In: Vaudenay, S. (ed.) EUROCRYPT 2006. LNCS, vol. 4004, pp. 373–390. Springer, Heidelberg (2006). doi:10.1007/11761679_23
47. Signal protocol: Advanced cryptographic ratcheting. https://whispersystems.org/blog/advanced-ratcheting/
48. Ylonen, T., Lonvick, C.: The Secure Shell (SSH) Protocol Architecture. RFC 4251 (Proposed Standard). http://www.ietf.org/rfc/rfc4251.txt

Ratcheted Encryption and Key Exchange: The Security of Messaging

Mihir Bellare[1(✉)], Asha Camper Singh[2], Joseph Jaeger[1], Maya Nyayapati[2], and Igors Stepanovs[1]

[1] Department of Computer Science and Engineering, University of California, San Diego, USA
{mihir,jsjaeger,istepano}@eng.ucsd.edu
[2] Salesforce, San Francisco, USA

Abstract. We aim to understand, formalize and provably achieve the goals underlying the core key-ratcheting technique of Borisov, Goldberg and Brewer, extensions of which are now used in secure messaging systems. We give syntax and security definitions for ratcheted encryption and key-exchange. We give a proven-secure protocol for ratcheted key exchange. We then show how to generically obtain ratcheted encryption from ratcheted key-exchange and standard encryption.

1 Introduction

The classical view of cryptography was that the endpoints (Alice and Bob) are secure and the adversary is on the communication channel. The prevalence of malware and system vulnerabilities however makes endpoint compromise a serious and immediate threat. In their highly influential OTR (Off the Record) communication system, Borisov, Goldberg and Brewer (BGB) [10] attempt to mitigate the damage from endpoint compromise by regularly updating (ratcheting) the encryption key. (They do not call it ratcheting, this term originating later with Langley [19].) Ratcheting was then used by Open Whisper Systems in their Signal protocol [22], which in turn is used by WhatsApp and other secure messaging systems.

This widespread usage —WhatsApp alone reports handling 42 billion text messages *per day*— motivates an understanding and analysis of ratcheting: what is it aiming to accomplish, and does it succeed? The answer to this question does not seem clear. Indeed, in their SOK (Systemization of Knowledge) paper on secure messaging, UDBFPGS [25] survey many of the systems that existed at the time and attempt to classify them in terms of security, noting that security claims about ratcheting in different places include "forward-secrecy," "backward-secrecy," "self-healing" and "future secrecy," and concluding that *"The terms are controversial and vague in the literature"* [25, Section 2.D].

In this paper, we aim to formalize the goals that ratcheting appears to be targeting. We give definitions for ratcheted encryption and ratcheted key-exchange. We then give protocols (based on ones in use but not identical to them) to provably achieve the goals.

J. Katz and H. Shacham (Eds.): CRYPTO 2017, Part III, LNCS 10403, pp. 619–650, 2017.
DOI: 10.1007/978-3-319-63697-9_21

Our work aims to be selective rather than comprehensive. Our intent is to formalize and understand the simplest form of ratcheting that captures the essence of the goal, which is single, one-sided ratcheting. This (as we will see) is already complex enough. Extended forms of ratcheting are left as future work.

Ratcheting. The setting we consider is that sender Alice and receiver Bob hold keys $K_s = (k, \ldots)$ and $K_r = (k, \ldots)$, respectively, k representing a shared symmetric key and the ellipses indicating there may be more key information that may be party dependent. In practice, these keys are the result of a session-key exchange protocol that is authenticated either via the parties' certificates (TLS) or out-of-band (secure messaging), but ratcheting is about how these keys are used and updated, not about how they are obtained, and so we will not be concerned with the distribution method, instead viewing the initial keys as created and distributed by a trusted process.

In TLS, all data is secured under the shared key k with an authenticated encryption scheme. Under ratcheting, the key is constantly changing. As per BGB [10] it works roughly like this:

$$B \rightarrow A\colon g^{b_1} \;;\; A \rightarrow B\colon g^{a_1}, \mathcal{E}(k_1, M_1) \;;\; B \rightarrow A\colon g^{b_2}, \mathcal{E}(k_2, M_2) \;;\; \ldots \qquad (1)$$

Here a_i and b_i are random exponents picked by A and B respectively; $k_1 = H(k, g^{b_1 a_1})$, $k_2 = H(k_1, g^{a_1 b_2})$, ...; H is a hash function; $\mathcal{E}$ is an encryption function taking key and message to return a ciphertext; and g is the generator of an underlying group. Each party deletes its exponents and keys once they are no longer needed for encryption or decryption.

Contributions. This paper aims to lift ratcheting from a technique to a cryptographic primitive, with a precise syntax and formally-defined security goals. Once this is done, we specify and prove secure some protocols that are closely related to the in-use ones.

If ratcheting is to be a primitive, a syntax is the first requirement. As employed, the ratcheting technique is used within a larger protocol, and one has to ask what it might mean in isolation. To allow a modular treatment, we decouple the creation of keys from their use, defining two primitives, ratcheted key exchange and ratcheted encryption. For each, we give a syntax. While ratcheting in apps is typically per message, our model is general and flexible, allowing the sender to ratchet the key at any time and encrypt as many messages as it likes under a given key before ratcheting again.

Next we give formal, game-based definitions of security for both ratcheted key exchange and ratcheted encryption. At the highest level, the requirement is that compromise (exposure in our model) revealing a party's current key and state should have only a local and temporary effect on security: a small hiccup, not compromising prior communications and after whose passage *both* privacy and integrity are somehow restored. This covers forward security (prior keys or communications remain secure) and backward security (future keys and communications remain secure). Amongst the issues in formalizing this is that following exposure there is some (necessary) time lag before security is regained, and that privacy and integrity are related. For ratcheted key exchange, unexposed keys are required to be indistinguishable from random in the spirit of [5] —rather than merely, say, hard to recover— to allow them to be later securely used. For ratcheted encryption, the requirement is in the spirit of nonce-based authenticated encryption [23], so that authenticity in particular is provided.

The definitions are chosen to allow a modular approach to constructions. We exemplify by showing how to build ratcheted encryption generically from ratcheted key-exchange and multi-user-secure nonce-based encryption [8]. This allows us to focus on ratcheted key exchange.

We give a protocol for ratcheted key exchange that is based on DH key exchanges. The core technique is the same as in [10] and the in-use protocols, but there are small but important differences, including MAC-based authentication of the key-update values and the way keys are derived. We prove that our protocol meets our definition of ratcheted key exchange under the SCDH (Strong Computational Diffie-Hellman) assumption [1] in the random oracle model (ROM) [4]. The proof is obtained in two steps. The first is a standard-model reduction to an assumption we call ODHE (Oracle Diffie-Hellman with Exposures). The second is a validation of ODHE under SCDH in the ROM.

Model and syntax. Our syntax specifies a scheme RKE for ratcheted key exchange via three algorithms: initial key generation RKE.IKg, sender key generation RKE.SKg and receiver key generation RKE.RKg. See Fig. 3 for an illustration. The parties maintain output keys (representing the keys they are producing for an overlying application like ratcheted encryption) and session keys (local state for their internal use). At any time, the sender A can run RKE.SKg on its current keys to get update information *upd* that it sends to the receiver, as well as updated keys for itself. The receiver B correspondingly will run RKE.RKg on received update information and its current keys to get updated keys, transmitting nothing. RKE.IKg provides initial keys for the parties, what we called K_s and K_r above, that in particular contain an initial output key k (the same for both parties) and initial session keys. A ratcheted encryption scheme RE maintains the same three key-generation algorithms, now denoted RE.IKg, RE.SKg and RE.RKg, and adds an encryption algorithm RE.Enc for the sender —in the nonce-based vein [23], taking a key, nonce, message and header to deterministically return a ciphertext— and a corresponding decryption algorithm RE.Dec for the receiver. The key for encryption and decryption is what ratcheted key exchange referred to as the output key.

Besides a natural correctness requirement, we have a robustness requirement: if the receiver receives an update that it rejects, it maintains its state and will still accept a subsequent correct update. This prevents a denial-of-service attack in which a single incorrect update sent to the receiver results in all future communications being rejected.

Security. In the spirit of BR [5] we give the adversary complete control of communication. Our definition of security for ratcheted key exchange in Sect. 4.2 is via a game KIND. After (trusted) initial key-generation, the game gives the adversary oracles to invoke either sender or receiver key generation and also to expose sender keys (both output and session). Roughly the requirement is that un-exposed keys be indistinguishable from random. The delicate issue is that this is true only under some conditions. Thus, exposure in one session will compromise the next session. Also, a post-expose active attack on the receiver (in which the adversary supplies the update information) can result in continued violation of integrity. Our game makes the necessary restrictions to capture these and other situations. For ratcheted encryption, the game RAE we give in Sect. 5 captures ratcheted authenticated encryption with nonce-based security. The additional oracles for the adversary are encryption and decryption. The requirement is that, for un-exposed and properly restricted keys, the adversary cannot distinguish whether its encryption and decryption oracles are real, or return random ciphertexts and $\perp$ respectively.

Schemes. Our ratcheted key exchange scheme in Sect. 4.3 is simple and efficient and uses the same basic DH technique as ratcheting in OTR [10] or WhatsApp, but analysis is quite involved. The sender's initial key includes g^b where b is part of the receiver's initial key, these quantities remaining static. Sender key generation algorithm RKE.SKg picks a random a and sends the update upd consisting of g^a *together with a mac under the prior session key* that is crucial to security. The output and next session key are derived via a hash function applied to g^{ab}. Theorem 1 establishes that the scheme meets our stringent notion of security for ratcheted key exchange. The proof uses a game sequence that includes a hybrid argument to reduce the security of the ratcheted key exchange to our ODHE (Oracle Diffie-Hellman with Exposures) assumption. The latter is an extension of the ODH assumption of [1] and, like the latter, can be validated in the ROM under the SCDH assumption of [1] (which in turn is a variant of the Gap-DH assumption of [21]). We show this in [7]. Ultimately, this yields a proof of security for our ratcheted key exchange protocol under the SCDH assumption in the ROM.

Our construction of a ratcheted encryption scheme in Sect. 5 is a generic combination of any ratcheted key exchange scheme (meeting our definition of security) and any nonce-based authenticated encryption scheme. Theorem 2 establishes that the scheme meets our notion of security for ratcheted encryption. The analysis is facilitated by assuming multi-user security for the base nonce-based encryption scheme as defined in [8], but a hybrid argument reduces this to the standard single-user security defined in [23]. Encryption schemes meeting this notion are readily available.

Setting and discussion. There are many variants of ratcheting. What we treat is one-sided ratcheting. This means one party (Alice) is a sender and the other (Bob) a receiver, rather than both playing both roles. In our model, compromises (exposures) are allowed only on the sender, not on the receiver. In particular the receiver has a static secret key whose compromise will immediately violate privacy of our schemes, regardless of updates. From the application perspective, our model and schemes are suitable for settings where the sender (for example a smartphone) is vulnerable to compromise but the receiver (for example a server with hardware-protected storage) can keep keys safely. In two-sided ratcheting, both the sender and the receiver may be compromised. Another dimension is single (what we treat) versus double ratcheting. In the latter, keys are also locally ratcheted via a forward-secure pseudorandom generator [9]. Conceptually, we decided to focus on the single, one-sided case to keep definitions (already quite complex) as simple as possible while capturing the essence of the goal and method. But we note that what Signal implements, and what is thus actually used, is double, two-sided ratcheting. Treating this does not seem like a simple extension of what we do and is left as future work.

Secure Internet communication protocols (both TLS and messaging) start with a session-key exchange that provides session keys, K_s for the sender and K_r for the receiver. These are our initial keys, the starting points for ratcheting. These keys are not to be confused with higher-level, long-lived signing or other keys that are certified either explicitly (TLS) or out-of-band (messaging) and used for authentication in the session-key exchange.

Messaging sessions tend to be longer lived than typical TLS sessions, with conversations that are on-going for months. This is part of why messaging security seeks, via ratcheting, fine-grained forward and backward security. Still, exactly what threat ratcheting prevents in practice needs careful consideration. If the threat is malware on a communicant's phone that can directly exfiltrate text of conversations, ratcheting will not help. Ratcheting will be of more help when users delete old messages, when the malware is exfiltrating keys rather than text, and when its presence on the phone is limited through software security.

Related work. In concurrent and independent work, Cohn-Gordon, Cremers, Dowling, Garratt and Stebila (CCDGS) [11] give a formal analysis of the Signal protocol. The protocol they analyze includes ratcheting steps but stops at key distribution: unlike us, they do not consider, define or achieve ratcheted encryption. They treat Signal as a multi-stage session-key exchange protocol [18] in the tradition of authenticated session-key exchange [3,5], with multiple parties and sessions. We instead consider ratcheted key exchange as a two-party protocol based on a trusted initial key distribution. This isolates ratcheted key exchange from the session key exchange used to produce the initial keys and allows a more modular treatment. They prove security (like us, in the ROM) under the Gap-DH [21] assumption while we prove it under the weaker SCDH [1] assumption. Ultimately their work and ours have somewhat different goals. Theirs is to analyze the particular Signal protocol. Ours is to isolate the core ratcheting method (as one of the more novel elements of the protocol) and formalize primitives reflecting its goals in the simplest possible way.

Cohn-Gordon, Cremers and Garratt (CCG) [12] study and compare different kinds of post-compromise security in contexts including authenticated key exchange. They mention ratcheting as a technique for maintaining security in the face of compromise.

Key-insulated cryptography [13–15] also targets forward and backward security but in a model where there is a trusted helper and an assumed-secure channel from helper to user that is employed to update keys. Implementing the secure channel is problematic due to the exposures [2]. Ratcheting in contrast works in a model where all communication is under adversary control.

2 Preliminaries

Notation and conventions. Let $\mathbb{N} = \{0, 1, 2, \ldots\}$ be the set of non-negative integers. Let ε denote the empty string. If $x \in \{0,1\}^*$ is a string then $|x|$ denotes its length, $x[i]$ denotes its i-th bit, and $x[i..j] = x[i] \ldots x[j]$ for $1 \leq i \leq j \leq |x|$. If mem is a table, we use $\mathsf{mem}[p]$ to denote the element of the table that is indexed by p. By $x \parallel y$ we denote a uniquely decodable concatenation of strings x and y (if lengths of x and y are fixed then $x \parallel y$ can be implemented using standard string concatenation). If X is a finite set, we let $x \leftarrow\!\!\$\, X$ denote picking an element of X uniformly at random and assigning it to x. We use a special symbol $\bot$ to denote an empty table position, and we also return it as an error code indicating an invalid input; we assume that adversaries never pass $\bot$ as input to their oracles.

Algorithms may be randomized unless otherwise indicated. Running time is worst case. If A is an algorithm, we let $y \leftarrow A(x_1, \ldots; r)$ denote running A with random coins r on inputs $x_1, \ldots$ and assigning the output to y. We let $y \leftarrow\!\!\$\, A(x_1, \ldots)$ be the result of picking r at random and letting $y \leftarrow A(x_1, \ldots; r)$. We let $[A(x_1, \ldots)]$ denote the set of all possible outputs of A when invoked with inputs $x_1, \ldots$. Adversaries are algorithms.

We use the code based game playing framework of [6]. (See Fig. 2 for an example.) We let Pr[G] denote the probability that game G returns true. In code, uninitialized integers are assumed to be initialized to 0, Booleans to false, strings to the empty string, sets to the empty set, and tables are initially empty.

Function families. A family of functions F specifies a deterministic algorithm F.Ev. Associated to F is a key length $\mathsf{F.kl} \in \mathbb{N}$, an input set F.In, and an output length F.ol. Evaluation algorithm F.Ev takes $fk \in \{0,1\}^{\mathsf{F.kl}}$ and an input $x \in \mathsf{F.In}$ to return an output $y \in \{0,1\}^{\mathsf{F.ol}}$.

Strong unforgeability under chosen message attack. Consider game SUFCMA of Fig. 1, associated to a function family F and an adversary $\mathcal{F}$. In order to win the game, adversary $\mathcal{F}$ has to produce a valid tag σ_{forge} for any message m_{forge}, satisfying the following requirement. The requirement is that $\mathcal{F}$ did not previously receive σ_{forge} as a result of calling its TAG oracle with m_{forge} as input. The advantage of $\mathcal{F}$ in breaking the SUFCMA security of F is defined as $\mathsf{Adv}^{\mathsf{sufcma}}_{\mathsf{F},\mathcal{F}} = \Pr[\mathrm{SUFCMA}^{\mathcal{F}}_{\mathsf{F}}]$. If no adversaries can achieve a high advantage in breaking the SUFCMA security of F while using only bounded resources, we refer to F as a MAC algorithm and we refer to its key fk as a MAC key.

Symmetric encryption schemes. A symmetric encryption scheme SE specifies deterministic algorithms SE.Enc and SE.Dec. Associated to SE is a key length $\mathsf{SE.kl} \in \mathbb{N}$, a nonce space SE.NS, and a ciphertext length function $\mathsf{SE.cl}\colon \mathbb{N} \to \mathbb{N}$.

Game $\text{SUFCMA}_{\mathsf{F}}^{\mathcal{F}}$	Game $\text{MAE}_{\mathsf{SE}}^{\mathcal{N}}$
$fk \leftarrow_{\$} \{0,1\}^{\mathsf{F.kl}}$ $\mathsf{win} \leftarrow \mathsf{false}$ $\mathcal{F}^{\text{TAG},\text{VERIFY}}$ Return win <u>$\text{TAG}(m)$</u> $\sigma \leftarrow \mathsf{F.Ev}(fk, m)$ $S \leftarrow S \cup \{(m, \sigma)\}$ Return σ <u>$\text{VERIFY}(m, \sigma)$</u> $\sigma' \leftarrow \mathsf{F.Ev}(fk, m)$ If $(\sigma = \sigma')$ and $((m, \sigma) \notin S)$ then $\mathsf{win} \leftarrow \mathsf{true}$ Return $(\sigma = \sigma')$	$b \leftarrow \{0,1\}$; $v \leftarrow 0$ $b' \leftarrow_{\$} \mathcal{N}^{\text{NEW},\text{ENC},\text{DEC}}$; Return $(b' = b)$ <u>NEW</u> $v \leftarrow v + 1$; $\mathsf{sk}[v] \leftarrow_{\$} \{0,1\}^{\mathsf{SE.kl}}$ <u>$\text{ENC}(i, n, m, h)$</u> If not $(1 \leq i \leq v)$ then return $\perp$ If $(i, n) \in U$ then return $\perp$ $c_1 \leftarrow \mathsf{SE.Enc}(\mathsf{sk}[i], n, m, h)$; $c_0 \leftarrow_{\$} \{0,1\}^{\mathsf{SE.cl}(\lvert m \rvert)}$ $U \leftarrow U \cup \{(i, n)\}$; $S \leftarrow S \cup \{(i, n, c_b, h)\}$ Return c_b <u>$\text{DEC}(i, n, c, h)$</u> If not $(1 \leq i \leq v)$ then return $\perp$ If $(i, n, c, h) \in S$ then return $\perp$ $m \leftarrow \mathsf{SE.Dec}(\mathsf{sk}[i], n, c, h)$ If $b = 1$ then return m else return $\perp$

Fig. 1. Games defining strong unforgeability of function family F under chosen message attack, and multi-user authenticated encryption security of SE.

Encryption algorithm SE.Enc takes $sk \in \{0,1\}^{\mathsf{SE.kl}}$, a nonce $n \in \mathsf{SE.NS}$, a message $m \in \{0,1\}^*$ and a header $h \in \{0,1\}^*$ to return a ciphertext $c \in \{0,1\}^{\mathsf{SE.cl}(|m|)}$. Decryption algorithm SE.Dec takes sk, n, c, h to return message $m \in \{0,1\}^* \cup \{\perp\}$, where $\perp$ denotes incorrect decryption. Decryption correctness requires that $\mathsf{SE.Dec}(sk, n, \mathsf{SE.Enc}(sk, n, m, h), h) = m$ for all $sk \in \{0,1\}^{\mathsf{SE.kl}}$, all $n \in \mathsf{SE.NS}$, all $m \in \{0,1\}^*$, and all $h \in \{0,1\}^*$. Nonce-based symmetric encryption was introduced in [24], whereas [23] also considers it in the setting with associated data. In this work we consider only *nonce-based* symmetric encryption schemes *with associated data*; we omit repeating these qualifiers throughout the text, instead referring simply to "symmetric encryption schemes".

<u>Multi-user authenticated encryption.</u> Consider game MAE of Fig. 1, associated to a symmetric encryption scheme SE and an adversary $\mathcal{N}$. It extends the definition of *authenticated encryption with associated data* for nonce-based schemes [23] to the multi-user setting, first formalized in [8]. The adversary is given access to oracles NEW, ENC and DEC. It can increase the number of users by calling oracle NEW, which generates a new (secret) user key. For any of the user keys, the adversary can request encryptions of plaintext messages by calling oracle ENC and decryptions of ciphertexts by calling oracle DEC. In the real world (when $b = 1$), oracles ENC and DEC provide correct encryptions and decryptions. In the random world (when $b = 0$), oracle ENC returns uniformly random ciphertexts and oracle DEC returns the incorrect decryption symbol $\perp$. The goal of the adversary is to distinguish between these two cases. In order to avoid trivial

attacks, $\mathcal{N}$ is not allowed to call DEC with ciphertexts that were returned by ENC. Likewise, we allow $\mathcal{N}$ to call ENC only once for every unique user-nonce pair (i, n). This can be strengthened to allow queries with repeated (i, n) and instead not allow queries with repeated (i, n, m, h), but the stronger requirement is satisfied by fewer schemes. The advantage of $\mathcal{N}$ in breaking the MAE security of SE is defined as $\mathsf{Adv}^{\mathsf{mae}}_{\mathsf{SE},\mathcal{N}} = 2\Pr[\mathrm{MAE}^{\mathcal{N}}_{\mathsf{SE}}] - 1$.

3 Oracle Diffie-Hellman with Exposures

The Oracle Diffie-Hellman (ODH) assumption [1] in a cyclic group requires that it is hard to distinguish between a random string and a hash function H applied to g^{xy}, even given g^x, g^y and an access to an oracle that returns $H(X^y)$ for arbitrary X (excluding $X = g^x$). We extend this assumption for multiple queries, based on a fixed g^y and arbitrarily many $g^{x[0]}, g^{x[1]}, \ldots$. For each index v we allow either to expose $x[v]$, or to get a challenge value; the challenge value is either a random string, or H applied to $g^{x[v]\cdot y}$. We also extend the hash function oracle to take a broader class of inputs.

Oracle Diffie-Hellman with Exposures assumption. Let $\mathbb{G}$ be a cyclic group of order $p \in \mathbb{N}$, and let $\mathbb{G}^*$ denote the set of its generators. Let H be a function family such that $\mathsf{H.In} = \{0,1\}^*$. Consider game ODHE of Fig. 2 associated to $\mathbb{G}, \mathsf{H}$ and an adversary $\mathcal{O}$, where $\mathcal{O}$ is required to call oracle UP at least once prior

Game $\mathrm{ODHE}^{\mathcal{O}}_{\mathbb{G},\mathsf{H}}$

$b \leftarrow_{\$} \{0,1\}$; $hk \leftarrow_{\$} \{0,1\}^{\mathsf{H.kl}}$; $g \leftarrow_{\$} \mathbb{G}^*$; $y \leftarrow_{\$} \mathbb{Z}_p$; $v \leftarrow -1$
$b' \leftarrow_{\$} \mathcal{O}^{\text{UP,CH,EXP,HASH}}(hk, g, g^y)$; Return $(b' = b)$

UP

$\mathsf{op} \leftarrow \varepsilon$; $v \leftarrow v + 1$; $x[v] \leftarrow_{\$} \mathbb{Z}_p$; Return $g^{x[v]}$

CH(s)

If (op = "exp") or $((v, s, g^{x[v]}) \in S_{\mathsf{hash}})$ then return $\perp$
$\mathsf{op} \leftarrow$ "ch" ; $S_{\mathsf{ch}} \leftarrow S_{\mathsf{ch}} \cup \{(v, s, g^{x[v]})\}$; $e \leftarrow g^{x[v]\cdot y}$
If $\mathsf{mem}[v, s, e] = \perp$ then $\mathsf{mem}[v, s, e] \leftarrow_{\$} \{0,1\}^{\mathsf{H.ol}}$
$r_1 \leftarrow \mathsf{H.Ev}(hk, v \,\|\, s \,\|\, e)$; $r_0 \leftarrow \mathsf{mem}[v, s, e]$; Return r_b

EXP

If op = "ch" then return $\perp$
$\mathsf{op} \leftarrow$ "exp" ; Return $x[v]$

HASH(i, s, X)

If $(i, s, X) \in S_{\mathsf{ch}}$ then return $\perp$
If $i = v$ then $S_{\mathsf{hash}} \leftarrow S_{\mathsf{hash}} \cup \{(i, s, X)\}$
Return $\mathsf{H.Ev}(hk, i \,\|\, s \,\|\, X^y)$

Fig. 2. Game defining Oracle Diffie-Hellman with Exposures assumption for $\mathbb{G}, \mathsf{H}$.

to making any oracle queries to CH and EXP. The game starts by sampling a function key hk, a group generator g and a secret exponent y. The adversary is given hk, g, g^y and it has access to oracles UP, CH, EXP, HASH. Oracle UP generates a new challenge exponent $x[v]$ and returns $g^{x[v]}$, where v is an integer counter that denotes the number of the current challenge exponent (indexed from 0) and is incremented by 1 at the start of every call to oracle UP. Oracle HASH takes an arbitrary integer i, an arbitrary string s and a group element X to return $\mathsf{H.Ev}(hk, i \,\|\, s \,\|\, X^y)$. For each counter value v, the adversary can choose to either call oracle EXP to get the value of $x[v]$ or call oracle CH with input s to get a challenge value that is generated as follows. In the real world (when $b = 1$) oracle CH returns $\mathsf{H.Ev}(hk, v \,\|\, s \,\|\, g^{x[v] \cdot y})$ and in the random world (when $b = 0$) it returns a uniformly random element from $\{0, 1\}^{\mathsf{H.ol}}$. The goal of the adversary is to distinguish between these two cases. Oracle CH can be called multiple times per challenge exponent, and it returns consistent outputs regardless of the challenge bit's value. The advantage of $\mathcal{O}$ in breaking the ODHE security of $\mathbb{G}, \mathsf{H}$ is defined as $\mathsf{Adv}^{\mathsf{odhe}}_{\mathbb{G},\mathsf{H},\mathcal{O}} = 2\Pr[\mathrm{ODHE}^{\mathcal{O}}_{\mathbb{G},\mathsf{H}}] - 1$.

In order to avoid trivial attacks, $\mathcal{O}$ is not allowed to query oracle HASH on input (i, s, X) if $X = g^{x[i]}$ and if oracle CH was already called with input s when the counter value was $v = i$. Note that adversary is allowed to win the game if it happens to guess a future challenge exponent x and query it to oracle HASH ahead of time; the corresponding triple (i, s, X) will not be added to the set of inputs S_{hash} that are not allowed to be made to oracle CH. Finally, recall that the string concatenation operator $\|$ is defined to produce uniquely decodable strings, which helps to avoid trivial string padding attacks.

Plausibility of the ODHE assumption. We do not know of any group $\mathbb{G}$ and function family H that can be shown to achieve ODHE in the standard model. The original ODH assumption of [1] was justified by a reduction in the random oracle model to the Strong Computational Diffie-Hellman (SCDH) assumption. The latter was defined in [1] and is a weaker version of the Gap Diffie-Hellman assumption from [21]. In [7] we give a definition for the SCDH assumption and prove that it also implies the ODHE assumption in the random oracle model.

We provide this result as a corollary of two lemmas. The lemmas use the Strong Computational Diffie-Hellman with Exposures (SCDHE) assumption as an intermediate step, where SCDHE is a novel assumption that extends SCDH to allow multiple challenge queries, and to allow exposures. To formalize our result, we define the Oracle Diffie-Hellman with Exposures in ROM (ODHER) assumption that is equivalent to the ODHE assumption in the random oracle model.

The first lemma establishes that SCDHE implies ODHE in the random oracle model, by a reduction from ODHER to SCDHE. The proof of this lemma emulates the ODH to SCDH reduction of [1]. In their reduction, the SCDH adversary simulates the random oracle and the hash oracle for the ODH adversary; it uses its own decisional-DH oracle to check whether the ODH adversary feeds g^{xy} for the challenge values of x and y, and to maintain consistency between simulated oracle outputs. This consistency maintenance is the main source of complexity in our reduction because —in addition to the oracles mentioned above— we must also ensure that the simulated challenge oracle is consistent.

The second lemma is a standard model reduction from SCDHE to SCDH. This reduction is a standard "guess the index" reduction in which our SCDH adversary guesses which query the SCDHE adversary will attack. The SCDH adversary replaces the answer to this query with the challenge values it was given and replaces all other oracle queries with challenges that it has generated itself. As usual, this results in a multiplicative loss of security, so the final theorem (combining both lemmas) has a bound of the form $\mathsf{Adv}^{\mathsf{odher}}_{\mathbb{G},\mathsf{H},\mathcal{O}} \leq q_{\mathrm{UP}} \cdot \mathsf{Adv}^{\mathsf{scdh}}_{\mathbb{G},\mathcal{S}}$, where $\mathcal{S}$ is the SCDH adversary and q_{UP} is the number of UP queries made by ODHER adversary $\mathcal{O}$.

Because of the multiplicative loss of security caused by the second lemma we also examine the possibility of using Diffie-Hellman self-reducibility techniques to obtain a tighter bound on the reduction from SCDHE to SCDH. The possibility of exposures in SCDHE makes this much more difficult than one might immediately realize. We present a reduction that succeeds despite these difficulties, by using significantly more complicated methods than in our first example of this deduction. Specifically we build an SCDH adversary that makes guesses about the future behavior of the SCDHE adversary it was given, and "rewinds" this adversary whenever its guess was incorrect. Thus we ultimately obtain the much tighter bound of $\mathsf{Adv}^{\mathsf{odher}}_{\mathbb{G},\mathsf{H},\mathcal{O}} \leq \mathsf{Adv}^{\mathsf{scdh}}_{\mathbb{G},\mathcal{S}_u} + q_{\mathrm{UP}} \cdot 2^{-u}$. Here $\mathcal{S}_u$ is the SCDH adversary that is defined for any parameter $u \in \mathbb{N}$ that bounds its worst case running time, and q_{UP} is the number of UP queries made by ODHER adversary $\mathcal{O}$.

4 Ratcheted Key Exchange

Ratcheted key exchange allows users to agree on shared secret keys while providing very strong security guarantees. In this work we consider a setting that encompasses two parties, and we assume that only one of them sends key agreement messages. We call this party a sender, and the other party a receiver. This model enables us to make the first steps towards capturing the schemes that are used in the real world messaging applications. Future work could extend our model to allow both parties to send key agreement messages, and to consider the group chat setting where multiple users engage in shared conversations.

4.1 Definition of Ratcheted Key Exchange

Consider Fig. 3 for an overview of algorithms that constitute a racheted key exchange scheme RKE, and the interaction between them. The algorithms are RKE.IKg, RKE.SKg and RKE.RKg. We will first provide an informal description of their functionality, and then formalize their syntax and correctness requirements.

Initial key generation algorithm RKE.IKg generates and distributes the following keys: $k, stk_s, stk_r, sek_s, sek_r$. Output key k is the initial shared secret key that can be used by both parties for any purpose such as running a symmetric encryption scheme. Static keys stk_s and stk_r are long-term keys that will not get

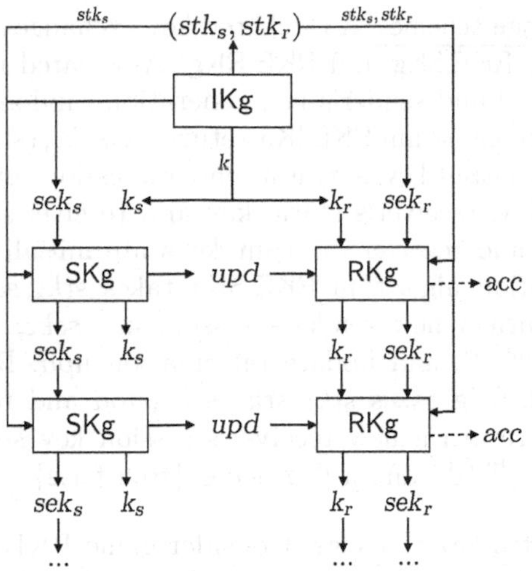

Fig. 3. The interaction between ratcheted key exchange algorithms.

updated over time. It is assumed that stk_s is known to all parties, whereas stk_r contains potentially secret information and will be known only by the receiver. Session keys sek_s and sek_r contain secret information that is required for future key exchanges, such as MAC keys (to ensure the authenticity of key exchange) and temporary secrets (that could be used for the generation of the next output keys). As a result of running RKE.IKg, the sender gets stk_s, sek_s, k_s and the receiver gets stk_s, stk_r, sek_r, k_r, where $k_s = k_r = k$. We use "s" and "r" as subscripts for output keys and session keys, to indicate that the particular key is owned by the sender or by the receiver, respectively. Note that normally both parties will have the same output key (i.e. $k_s = k_r$), but this might not be true if an attacker succeeds to tamper with the protocol.

Next we define sender's and receiver's key generation algorithms RKE.SKg and RKE.RKg. These algorithms model the key ratcheting process that generates new session keys and output keys while deleting the corresponding old keys.

Sender's key generation algorithm RKE.SKg is run whenever the sender wants to produce a new shared secret key. It takes the sender's static key stk_s and the sender's session key sek_s. It returns an updated sender's session key sek_s, a new output key k_s, and update information *upd*. The update information is used by the receiver to generate the same output key.

Receiver's key generation algorithm RKE.RKg takes sender's static key stk_s, receiver's static key stk_r, receiver's session key sek_r, update information *upd* (received from the sender) and the current shared output key k_r. It returns receiver's session key sek_r, output key k_r, and a Boolean flag *acc* indicating whether the new keys were generated succesfully. Setting $acc = \mathsf{false}$ will generally mean that the received update information was rejected; our correctness definition will require that in such case the receiver's output key k_r and the receiver's session key sek_r should remain unchanged. This requirement is the reason why RKE.RKg takes the old value of k_r as one of its inputs.

Ratcheted key exchange schemes. A ratcheted key exchange scheme RKE specifies algorithms $\mathsf{RKE.IKg}$, $\mathsf{RKE.SKg}$ and $\mathsf{RKE.RKg}$. Associated to RKE is an output key length $\mathsf{RKE.kl} \in \mathbb{N}$ and sender's key generation randomness space $\mathsf{RKE.RS}$. Initial key generation algorithm $\mathsf{RKE.IKg}$ returns $k, sek_s, (stk_s, stk_r, sek_r)$, where $k \in \{0,1\}^{\mathsf{RKE.kl}}$ is an output key, sek_s is a sender's session key, and stk_s, stk_r, sek_r are sender's static key, receiver's static key and receiver's session key, respectively. The sender's and receiver's output keys are initialized to $k_s = k_r = k$. Sender's key generation algorithm $\mathsf{RKE.SKg}$ takes stk_s, sek_s and randomness $r \in \mathsf{RKE.RS}$ to return a new sender's session key sek_s, a new sender's output key $k_s \in \{0,1\}^{\mathsf{RKE.kl}}$, and update information upd. Receiver's key generation algorithm $\mathsf{RKE.RKg}$ takes stk_s, stk_r, sek_r, upd and receiver's output key $k_r \in \{0,1\}^{\mathsf{RKE.kl}}$ to return a new receiver's session key sek_r, a new receiver's output key $k_r \in \{0,1\}^{\mathsf{RKE.kl}}$, and a flag $acc \in \{\mathsf{true}, \mathsf{false}\}$.

Correctness of ratcheted key exchange. Consider game RKE-COR of Fig. 4 associated to a ratcheted key exchange scheme R and an adversary $\mathcal{C}$, where $\mathcal{C}$ is provided with an access to oracles UP and RATREC.

Oracle UP runs algorithm $\mathsf{R.SKg}$ to generate a new sender's output key k_s along with the corresponding update information upd; it then runs $\mathsf{R.RKg}$ with upd as input to generate a new receiver's output key k_r. It is required that $acc = \mathsf{true}$ and $k_s = k_r$ at the end of every UP call. This means that if the receiver uses update information received from the sender (in the correct order), it is guaranteed to successfully generate the same output keys as the sender.

Game $\text{RKE-COR}_{\mathsf{R}}^{\mathcal{C}}$	Game $\text{RE-COR}_{\mathsf{R}}^{\mathcal{C}}$
$\mathsf{bad} \leftarrow \mathsf{false}$	$\mathsf{bad} \leftarrow \mathsf{false}$
$(k, sek_s, (stk_s, stk_r, sek_r)) \leftarrow \mathsf{R.IKg}$	$(k, sek_s, (stk_s, stk_r, sek_r)) \leftarrow \mathsf{R.IKg}$
$k_s \leftarrow k$; $k_r \leftarrow k$	$k_s \leftarrow k$; $k_r \leftarrow k$
$\mathcal{C}^{\text{UP},\text{RATREC}}$; Return $(\mathsf{bad} = \mathsf{false})$	$\mathcal{C}^{\text{UP},\text{RATREC},\text{ENC}}$; Return $(\mathsf{bad} = \mathsf{false})$

UP

$r \leftarrow\$ \mathsf{R.RS}$; $(sek_s, k_s, upd) \leftarrow \mathsf{R.SKg}(stk_s, sek_s; r)$

$(sek_r, k_r, acc) \leftarrow\$ \mathsf{R.RKg}(stk_s, stk_r, sek_r, upd, k_r)$

If not $((acc = \mathsf{true})$ and $(k_s = k_r))$ then $\mathsf{bad} \leftarrow \mathsf{true}$

RATREC(upd)

$(sek_r', k_r', acc) \leftarrow\$ \mathsf{R.RKg}(stk_s, stk_r, sek_r, upd, k_r)$

If $(acc = \mathsf{false})$ and not $((k_r' = k_r)$ and $(sek_r' = sek_r))$ then $\mathsf{bad} \leftarrow \mathsf{true}$

ENC(n, m, h)

$c \leftarrow \mathsf{R.Enc}(k_s, n, m, h)$; $m' \leftarrow \mathsf{R.Dec}(k_r, n, c, h)$; If $(m' \neq m)$ then $\mathsf{bad} \leftarrow \mathsf{true}$

Fig. 4. Game RKE-COR defining correctness of ratcheted key exchange scheme R, and game RE-COR defining correctness of ratcheted encryption scheme R. Oracles UP and RATREC are used in both games, whereas oracle ENC is only used in game RE-COR.

Oracle RATREC takes update information *upd* of adversary's choice and attempts to run R.RKg with *upd* (and current receiver's keys) as input. The correctness requires that if the receiver's key update fails (meaning $acc = \mathsf{false}$) then the receiver's keys k_r, sek_r remain unchanged. This means that if receiver's attempt to generate new keys is not successful (e.g. if the update information is corrupted in transition), then the receiver's key generation algorithm should not corrupt the receiver's current keys. This is a usability property that requires that it is possible to recover from failures, meaning that the receiver can later re-run its key generation algorithm with the correct update information to successfully produce its next pair of (session and output) keys.

We consider an unbounded adversary and allow it to call its oracles in any order. The advantage of $\mathcal{C}$ breaking the correctness of R is defined as $\mathsf{Adv}^{\mathsf{rkecor}}_{\mathsf{R},\mathcal{C}} = 1 - \Pr[\text{RKE-COR}^{\mathcal{C}}_{\mathsf{R}}]$. Correctness property requires that $\mathsf{Adv}^{\mathsf{rkecor}}_{\mathsf{R},\mathcal{C}} = 0$ for all unbounded adversaries $\mathcal{C}$. Note that our definition of the correctness game with an unbounded adversary is equivalent to a more common correctness definition that would instead explicitly quantify over all randomness choices of all algorithms. We stress that our correctness definition does *not* require any security properties. In particular, it does not require that the update information is authenticated because oracle RATREC considers only the case when R.RKg sets $acc = \mathsf{false}$.

Our definition requires *perfect* correctness. However, it can be relaxed by requiring that adversary $\mathcal{C}$ can only make a bounded number of calls to its oracles, and further requiring that its advantage of winning the game is negligible.

4.2 Security of Ratcheted Key Exchange

Ratcheted key exchange attempts to provide strong security guarantees even in the presence of an attacker that can steal the secrets stored by the sender. Specifically, we consider an active attacker that is able to intercept and modify any update information sent from the sender to the receiver. The goal is that the attacker cannot distinguish the produced output keys from random strings, and cannot make the two parties agree on output keys that do not match. Furthermore, we desire certain stronger security properties to hold even if the attacker manages to steal secrets stored by the sender, which we refer to as forward security and backward security. Forward security requires that such an attacker cannot distinguish prior keys from random. Backward security requires that the knowledge of sender's secrets at the current time period can not be used to distinguish keys generated (at some near point) in the future from random strings. Recall that our model is intentionally one-sided; exposure of receiver's secrets is not allowed. In particular, compromise of all of the receiver's secrets will permanently compromise security.

It is clear that if an attacker steals the secret information of the sender, then it can create its own update information resulting in the receiver agreeing on a "secret" key that is known by the attacker. It can be difficult to say what restrictions should be placed on the keys that the attacker makes the receiver agree to. Is it a further breach of security if the attacker then later causes the sender and the receiver to agree on the same secret key? What should happen if the attacker later forwards update information that was generated by the sender to the receiver?

In our security model we choose to insist on two straightforward policies in this scenario. The first is that whenever update information not generated by the sender is accepted by the receiver, even full knowledge of the key that the receiver has generated should not leak any information about other correctly generated keys. The second is that at any fixed point in time, if update information generated by the sender is accepted by the receiver then the receiver should agree with the sender on what the corresponding output key is, and the adversary should not be able to distinguish the shared output key from random.

Key indistinguishability of ratcheted key exchange schemes. Consider game KIND on the left side of Fig. 5 associated to a ratcheted key exchange scheme RKE and an adversary $\mathcal{D}$. The advantage of $\mathcal{D}$ in breaking the KIND security of RKE is defined as $\mathsf{Adv}^{\mathsf{kind}}_{\mathsf{RKE},\mathcal{D}} = 2\Pr[\mathrm{KIND}^{\mathcal{D}}_{\mathsf{RKE}}] - 1$.

The adversary is given the sender's static key stk_s as well as access to oracles RatSend, RatRec, Exp, ChSend, and ChRec. It can call oracle RatSend to receive update information *upd* from the sender, and it can call oracle RatRec to pass arbitrary update information to the receiver. Oracle Exp returns the current secrets sek_s, k_s possessed by the sender as well as the random seed r that was used to create the most recent *upd* in RatSend. Note that according to our notation convention from Sect. 2, integer variable r is assumed to be initialized to 0 at the beginning of the security game; this value will be returned if adversary calls Exp prior to RatSend.

The challenge oracles ChSend and ChRec provide the adversary with keys k_s and k_r in the real world (when $b = 1$), or with uniformly random bit strings in the random world (when $b = 0$). The goal of the adversary is to distinguish between these two worlds. To disallow trivial attacks the game makes use of tables op and auth (initialized as empty) as well as a boolean flag restricted (initialized as false). Specifically, op keeps track of the oracle calls made by the adversary and is used to ensure that it can not trivially win the game by calling oracle Exp to get secrets that were used for one of the challenge queries. Table auth keeps track of the update information *upd* generated by RatSend so that we can set the flag restricted whenever the adversary has taken advantage of an Exp query to send maliciouly generated *upd* to RatRec. In this case we do not expect the receiver's key k_r to look random or match the sender's key k_s so ChRec is "restricted" and will return k_r in both the real and random worlds.

Authenticity of key exchange. Our security definition implicitly requires the authenticity of key exchange. Specifically, assume that an adversary can violate the authenticity in a non-trivial way, meaning without using Exp oracle to acquire the relevant secrets. This means that the adversary can construct malicious update information *upd** that is accepted by the receiver, while not setting the restricted flag to true. By making the receiver accept *upd**, the adversary achieves the situation when the sender and the receiver produce different

<u>Game $\text{KIND}^{\mathcal{D}}_{\mathsf{RKE}}$</u>

$b \leftarrow\$ \{0,1\}$; $i_s \leftarrow 0$; $i_r \leftarrow 0$
$(k, sek_s, (stk_s, stk_r, sek_r)) \leftarrow\$ \mathsf{RKE.IKg}$
$k_s \leftarrow k$; $k_r \leftarrow k$
$b' \leftarrow\$ \mathcal{D}^{\text{RatSend},\text{RatRec},\text{Exp},\text{ChSend},\text{ChRec}}(stk_s)$
Return $(b' = b)$

<u>RatSend</u>

$r \leftarrow\$ \mathsf{RKE.RS}$
$(sek_s, k_s, upd) \leftarrow \mathsf{RKE.SKg}(stk_s, sek_s; r)$
$\mathsf{auth}[i_s] \leftarrow upd$; $i_s \leftarrow i_s + 1$
Return upd

<u>RatRec(upd)</u>

$z \leftarrow\$ \mathsf{RKE.RKg}(stk_s, stk_r, sek_r, upd, k_r)$
$(sek_r, k_r, acc) \leftarrow z$
If not acc then return false
If $\mathsf{op}[i_r] =$ "exp" then restricted $\leftarrow$ true
If $upd = \mathsf{auth}[i_r]$ then restricted $\leftarrow$ false
$i_r \leftarrow i_r + 1$; Return true

<u>Exp</u>

If $\mathsf{op}[i_s] =$ "ch" then return $\bot$
$\mathsf{op}[i_s] \leftarrow$ "exp" ; Return (r, sek_s, k_s)

<u>ChSend</u>

If $\mathsf{op}[i_s] =$ "exp" then return $\bot$
$\mathsf{op}[i_s] \leftarrow$ "ch"
If $\mathsf{rkey}[i_s] = \bot$ then $\mathsf{rkey}[i_s] \leftarrow\$ \{0,1\}^{\mathsf{RKE.kl}}$
If $b = 1$ then return k_s else return $\mathsf{rkey}[i_s]$

<u>ChRec</u>

If restricted then return k_r
If $\mathsf{op}[i_r] =$ "exp" then return $\bot$
$\mathsf{op}[i_r] \leftarrow$ "ch"
If $\mathsf{rkey}[i_r] = \bot$ then $\mathsf{rkey}[i_r] \leftarrow\$ \{0,1\}^{\mathsf{RKE.kl}}$
If $b = 1$ then return k_r else return $\mathsf{rkey}[i_r]$

<u>Game $\text{RAE}^{\mathcal{A}}_{\mathsf{RE}}$</u>

$b \leftarrow\$ \{0,1\}$; $i_s \leftarrow 0$; $i_r \leftarrow 0$
$(k, sek_s, (stk_s, stk_r, sek_r)) \leftarrow\$ \mathsf{RE.IKg}$
$k_s \leftarrow k$; $k_r \leftarrow k$
$b' \leftarrow\$ \mathcal{A}^{\text{RatSend},\text{RatRec},\text{Exp},\text{Enc},\text{Dec}}(stk_s)$
Return $(b' = b)$

<u>RatSend</u>

$r \leftarrow\$ \mathsf{RE.RS}$
$(sek_s, k_s, upd) \leftarrow \mathsf{RE.SKg}(stk_s, sek_s; r)$
$\mathsf{auth}[i_s] \leftarrow upd$; $i_s \leftarrow i_s + 1$
Return upd

<u>RatRec(upd)</u>

$z \leftarrow\$ \mathsf{RE.RKg}(stk_s, stk_r, sek_r, upd, k_r)$
$(sek_r, k_r, acc) \leftarrow z$
If not acc then return false
If $\mathsf{op}[i_r] =$ "exp" then restricted $\leftarrow$ true
If $upd = \mathsf{auth}[i_r]$ then restricted $\leftarrow$ false
$i_r \leftarrow i_r + 1$; Return true

<u>Exp</u>

If $\mathsf{op}[i_s] =$ "ch" then return $\bot$
$\mathsf{op}[i_s] \leftarrow$ "exp" ; Return (r, sek_s, k_s)

<u>Enc(n, m, h)</u>

If $\mathsf{op}[i_s] =$ "exp" then return $\bot$
$\mathsf{op}[i_s] \leftarrow$ "ch"
If $(i_s, n) \in U$ then return $\bot$
$c_1 \leftarrow \mathsf{RE.Enc}(k_s, n, m, h)$
$c_0 \leftarrow\$ \{0,1\}^{\mathsf{RE.cl}(|m|)}$; $U \leftarrow U \cup \{(i_s, n)\}$
$S \leftarrow S \cup \{(i_s, n, c_b, h)\}$
Return c_b

<u>Dec(n, c, h)</u>

If restricted then
  Return $\mathsf{RE.Dec}(k_r, n, c, h)$
If $\mathsf{op}[i_r] =$ "exp" then return $\bot$
$\mathsf{op}[i_r] \leftarrow$ "ch"
If $(i_r, n, c, h) \in S$ then return $\bot$
$m \leftarrow \mathsf{RE.Dec}(k_r, n, c, h)$
If $b = 1$ then return m else return $\bot$

Fig. 5. Games defining key indistinguishability of ratcheted key exchange scheme RKE, and authenticated encryption security of ratcheted encryption scheme RE.

output keys $k_s \neq k_r$. Now adversary can call oracles ChSend and ChRec to get both keys and compare them to win the game. In the real world ($b = 1$) the returned keys will be different, whereas in the random world ($b = 0$) they will be the same. We formalize this attack in [7].

Allowing recovery from failures. Consider a situation when an attacker steals all sender's secrets, and hence has an ability to impersonate the sender. It can drop all further packets sent by the sender and instead use the exposed secrets to agree on its own shared secret keys with the receiver. In the security game this corresponds to the case when the adversary calls Exp and then starts calling oracle RatRec with maliciously generated update information *upd*. This sets the restricted flag to true, making the ChRec oracle always return the real receiver's key k_r regardless of the value of game's challenge bit b. The design decision at this point is – do we want to allow the game to recover from this state, meaning should the restricted flag be ever set back to false?

Our decision on this matter was determined by the two "policies" discussed above. As long as the adversary keeps sending maliciously generated update information *upd*, the restricted flag will remain true. In this case, the real receiver's key k_r returned from ChRec should be of no help in distinguishing the real sender's key k_s from random, as desired from the first policy. To match the second policy, the next time adversary forwards the *upd* generated by the sender (i.e. $upd = \mathsf{auth}[i_r]$) to RatRec, if *upd* is accepted by the receiver then the restricted flag is set back to false. This makes the output of ChRec again depend on the challenge bit, thus requiring k_r to be equal to k_s and indistinguishable from random.

Alternative treatment of restricted flag. Our security definition of KIND can be strengthened by making it never reset the restricted flag back to false. Instead, the game could require that if the adversary exposes sender's secrets and uses them to agree on its own shared output key with the receiver, then all the communication between the sender and the receiver should be disrupted. Meaning that any future attempt to simply forward sender's update information *upd* to the receiver should result in RatRec rejecting it. Otherwise adversary would be defined to win the game. This can be formalized in a number of ways. Our construction of ratcheted key exchange from Sect. 4.3 should be secure for a stronger definition like that, but would likely require stronger assumptions to prove.

4.3 Construction of a Ratcheted Key Exchange Scheme

In this section we construct a ratcheted key exchange scheme, and discuss some design considerations by presenting a number of attacks that our scheme manages to evade. In Sect. 4.4 we will deduce a bound on the success of any adversary attacking the KIND security of our scheme. The idea of our construction is as follows. We let the sender and the receiver perform the Diffie-Hellman key exchange. The receiver's static key contains a secret DH exponent $stk_r = y$ and the sender's static key contains the corresponding public value

$stk_s = g^y$ (working in some cyclic group with generator g). In order to generate a new shared secret key, the sender picks its own secret exponent x and computes the output key (roughly) as $k_s = H(stk_s^x) = H(g^{xy})$, where H is some hash function. The sender then sends update information containing g^x to the receiver, enabling the latter to compute the same output key. In order to ensure the security of the key exchange, both parties use a shared MAC key, meaning the update information also includes a tag of g^x.

Note that the used MAC key should be regularly renewed in order to ensure that the scheme provides backward security against exposures. As a result, the output of applying the hash function on g^{xy} is also used to derive a new MAC key. The initial key generation provides both parties with a shared MAC key and a shared secret key that are sampled uniformly at random. The formal definition of our key exchange scheme is as follows.

Ratcheted key exchange scheme RATCHET-KE. Let $\mathbb{G}$ be a cyclic group of order $p \in \mathbb{N}$, and let $\mathbb{G}^*$ denote the set of its generators. Let F be a function family such that $\mathsf{F.In} = \mathbb{G}$. Let H be a function family such that $\mathsf{H.In} = \{0,1\}^*$ and $\mathsf{H.ol} > \mathsf{F.kl}$. We build a ratcheted key exchange scheme $\mathsf{RKE} = \mathsf{RATCHET\text{-}KE}[\mathbb{G}, \mathsf{F}, \mathsf{H}]$ as defined in Fig. 6, with $\mathsf{RKE.kl} = \mathsf{H.ol} - \mathsf{F.kl}$ and $\mathsf{RKE.RS} = \mathbb{Z}_p$.

Algorithm RKE.IKg	Algorithm $\mathsf{RKE.SKg}((hk, g, Y), (i_s, fk_s); r)$
$k \leftarrow_\$ \{0,1\}^{\mathsf{RKE.kl}}$ $fk \leftarrow_\$ \{0,1\}^{\mathsf{F.kl}}$ $hk \leftarrow_\$ \{0,1\}^{\mathsf{H.kl}}$ $g \leftarrow_\$ \mathbb{G}^*$; $y \leftarrow_\$ \mathbb{Z}_p$ $stk_s \leftarrow (hk, g, g^y)$; $stk_r \leftarrow y$ $sek_s \leftarrow (0, fk)$ $sek_r \leftarrow (0, fk)$ $z \leftarrow (k, sek_s, (stk_s, stk_r, sek_r))$ Return z	$x \leftarrow r$; $X \leftarrow g^x$; $\sigma \leftarrow \mathsf{F.Ev}(fk_s, X)$ $s \leftarrow \mathsf{H.Ev}(hk, i_s \,\|\, \sigma \,\|\, X \,\|\, Y^x)$; $k_s \leftarrow s[1 \ldots \mathsf{RKE.kl}]$ $fk_s \leftarrow s[\mathsf{RKE.kl}+1 \ldots \mathsf{RKE.kl}+\mathsf{F.kl}]$ Return $((i_s+1, fk_s), k_s, (X, \sigma))$ Algorithm $\mathsf{RKE.RKg}((hk, g, Y), y, (i_r, fk_r), (X, \sigma), k_r)$ $acc \leftarrow (\sigma = \mathsf{F.Ev}(fk_r, X))$ If not acc then return $((i_r, fk_r), k_r, acc)$ $s \leftarrow \mathsf{H.Ev}(hk, i_r \,\|\, \sigma \,\|\, X \,\|\, X^y)$; $k_r \leftarrow s[1 \ldots \mathsf{RKE.kl}]$ $fk_r \leftarrow s[\mathsf{RKE.kl}+1 \ldots \mathsf{RKE.kl}+\mathsf{F.kl}]$ Return $((i_r+1, fk_r), k_r, acc)$

Fig. 6. Ratcheted key exchange scheme $\mathsf{RKE} = \mathsf{RATCHET\text{-}KE}[\mathbb{G}, \mathsf{F}, \mathsf{H}]$.

Design considerations. We will examine some of the design decisions of RKE by considering several ratcheted key exchange schemes that are weakened versions of RKE, and corresponding adversaries that are able to successfully attack these schemes. The first two will omit the use of a MAC and thus be vulnerable to attacks where the adversary sends its own update information to RatRec without having called Exp first (though the second will have to make an expose query afterwards). In the latter two examples we consider variations of RKE that use fewer inputs to the hash function. Our adversaries against these schemes thereby justify the choices we made for the input to the hash function. For the

Adversary $\mathcal{D}_1(stk_s)$

$(hk, g, Y) \leftarrow stk_s$
$x \leftarrow_{\$} \mathbb{Z}_p$; $\textsc{RatRec}(g^x)$
$k_r \leftarrow \textsc{ChRec}$
$k_r' \leftarrow \mathsf{H.Ev}(hk, Y^x)$
If $k_r' = k_r$ then return 1
Else return 0

Adversary $\mathcal{D}_2(stk_s)$

$(hk, g, Y) \leftarrow stk_s$
$x \leftarrow_{\$} \mathbb{Z}_p$; $\textsc{RatRec}(g^x)$
$k_r \leftarrow \textsc{ChRec}$
$(r, fk_s, k_s) \leftarrow \textsc{Exp}$
$k \,\|\, fk \leftarrow \mathsf{H.Ev}(hk, fk_s \,\|\, Y^x)$
If $k = k_r$ then return 1
Else return 0

Adversary $\mathcal{D}_3(stk_s)$

$upd_0 \leftarrow \textsc{RatSend}$; $\textsc{RatRec}(upd_0)$; $k_s \leftarrow \textsc{ChSend}$
$upd_1 \leftarrow \textsc{RatSend}$; $\textsc{RatRec}(upd_1)$
$(r, fk_s, k_s) \leftarrow \textsc{Exp}$; $(X_0, \sigma_0) \leftarrow upd_0$
$\sigma \leftarrow \mathsf{F.Ev}(fk_s, X_0)$; $upd_2 \leftarrow (X_0, \sigma)$
$\textsc{RatRec}(upd_2)$; $k_r \leftarrow \textsc{ChRec}$
If $k_s = k_r$ then return 1 else return 0

Adversary $\mathcal{D}_4(stk_s)$

$(r, sek_s, k_s) \leftarrow \textsc{Exp}$
$((i_s^*, fk_s^*), k_s^*, upd^*) \leftarrow_{\$} \mathsf{RKE.SKg}(stk_s, sek_s)$
$upd_0 \leftarrow \textsc{RatSend}$; $\textsc{RatRec}(upd^*)$
$upd_1 \leftarrow \textsc{RatSend}$; $(X, \sigma) \leftarrow upd_1$
$\sigma^* \leftarrow \mathsf{F.Ev}(fk_s^*, X)$; $upd^* \leftarrow (X, \sigma^*)$; $\textsc{RatRec}(upd^*)$
$k_s \leftarrow \textsc{ChSend}$; $k_r \leftarrow \textsc{ChRec}$
If $k_s = k_r$ then return 1 else return 0

Fig. 7. Attacks against insecure variants of $\mathsf{RKE} = \mathsf{RATCHET\text{-}KE}[\mathbb{G}, \mathsf{F}, \mathsf{H}]$.

sake of compactness we omit showing that the constructed KIND adversaries have access to oracles RatSend, RatRec, Exp, ChSend, ChRec, and we omit showing that oracle calls return any output whenever this output is not used by the adversary.

Schemes without a MAC. First let us consider changing RKE to not use its MAC F and instead simply use an unauthenticated g^x as its update information. For simplicity we will additionally assume that the only input to H is a group element g^{xy}. Consider adversary $\mathcal{D}_1$ shown in Fig. 7. It makes a RatRec query with a g^x of its own choice, then calls oracle ChRec and checks whether the key it received was real or random by comparing it to $\mathsf{H}(hk, Y^x)$. Referring to this weakened scheme as RKE_1, it is clear that $\mathsf{Adv}^{\mathsf{kind}}_{\mathsf{RKE}_1, \mathcal{D}_1} = 1 - 2^{-\mathsf{RKE.kl}}$.

Besides using a MAC, another way to prevent the specific attack given above would be to put a shared secret key fk into the hash function along with g^{xy} for every update. Let RKE_2 denote a version of RKE that still does not use a MAC but updates its keys with the hash function via $k \,\|\, fk \leftarrow \mathsf{H.Ev}(hk, fk \,\|\, g^{xy})$. An adversary like $\mathcal{D}_1$ will not work against RKE_2 because computing the new value of k requires knowing the secret value fk. But there is still a simple attack against RKE_2. Consider adversary $\mathcal{D}_2$ shown in Fig. 7. It works in the same way as $\mathcal{D}_1$ except it needs to make an expose query to obtain fk_s before it can compute k using the hash function. One subtle point to notice is that it is important that $\mathcal{D}_2$ calls Exp *after* its call to RatRec. Otherwise the restricted flag in KIND would have been set to true and ChRec would always return the real key (instead of returning a randomly chosen key when the challenge bit in KIND is set to 0). Having noticed this it is clear that $\mathsf{Adv}^{\mathsf{kind}}_{\mathsf{RKE}_2, \mathcal{D}_2} = 1 - 2^{-\mathsf{RKE.kl}}$.

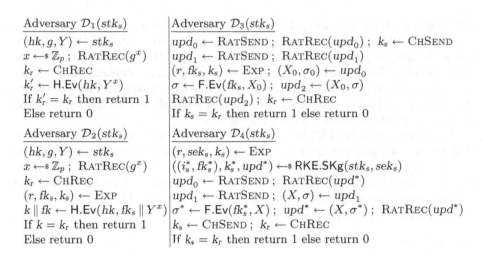

In [7] we give an attack against *any* ratcheted encryption scheme, showing that if it is possible for an adversary to generate its own *upd* that the receiver will accept, than the adversary can use this ability to successfully attack the ratcheted encryption scheme. This proves that some sort of authentication is required for the update information if we want a scheme to be secure.

Authenticating the update information in the Double Ratchet algorithm. The default version of the Double Ratchet algorithm [16,20] — which is used in the Signal protocol [22] — does not authenticate the update information. A single, one-sided version of this algorithm would evolve its keys in a way that is vaguely similar to the RKE_2 scheme discussed above, so it would not meet our security definition. This does not immediately lead to any real-world attacks, and could mean that our security definition is stronger than necessary. Furthermore, [16] describes the header encryption variant of the Double Ratchet algorithm. A single, one-sided version of this algorithm provides some form of authentication for update information and might meet our security definition.

Necessity of inputs to H. In the construction of RATCHET-KE, function $\mathsf{H}(hk, \cdot)$ takes a string $w = i \,\|\, \sigma_i \,\|\, g^{x_i} \,\|\, g^{x_i y}$ as input. The most straightforward part of w is $g^{x_i y}$, which provides unpredictability to ensure that the generated keys are indistinguishable from uniformly random strings. String w also includes the counter i, and the corresponding update information $upd_i = (g^{x_i}, \sigma_i)$. The inclusion of counter i in w ensures that an attacker cannot perform a "key-reuse" attack to make the receiver generate an output key that was already used before; we provide an example of such attack below. We also describe a "key-collision" attack against the KIND security of the scheme that is prevented by including upd_i in w. Finally, note that our concatenation operator $\|$ is defined to produce uniquely decodable strings, so the mapping of $(i, \sigma_i, g^{x_i}, g^{x_i y})$ into string w is injective; this helps to avoid attacks that take advantage of malleable encodings.

Key-reuse attack. Game KIND makes sure that if challenge keys are acquired from the sender and the receiver for the same value of i (i.e. $i_s = i_r$), then these keys are consistent even if they are picked randomly. Otherwise it would be trivial to attack any ratcheted key exchange scheme. However, the game does not maintain such consistency between different values of i. Let RKE_3 denote RKE if it was changed to use only g^{xy} as input to the hash function. Consider the "key-reuse" attack $\mathcal{D}_3$ shown in Fig. 7 that exploits the above as follows. Adversary $\mathcal{D}_3$ starts by calling RATSEND, RATREC and CHSEND to get a sender's challenge key k_s. Note that if the challenge bit is $b = 1$ in game KIND, then k_s equals to $\mathsf{H.Ev}(hk, Y^x)$ for some exponent x generated during RATSEND. Next, the adversary calls both RATSEND and RATREC to ratchet the key forward, in order to be able to make EXP queries. It calls EXP to get fk_s so that it can re-authenticate the same value of $X = g^x$ that was used for the sender's challenge query. Then it sends X and its new MAC tag σ to the receiver, which sets the restricted flag true. The latter means that calling CHREC results in getting the receiver's real output key regardless of the challenge bit. If this key is equal to the previously learned sender's challenge key then it is highly likely that the challenge bit b equals 1, otherwise it must be 0. This gives the advantage of $\mathsf{Adv}^{\mathsf{kind}}_{\mathsf{RKE}_3, \mathcal{D}_3} = 1 - 2^{-\mathsf{RKE.kl}}$.

Key-collision attacks. We now describe the final attack idea that does not work against our construction but would have been possible if the update information $upd = (g^{x_i}, \sigma)$ was not included in the hash function. Consider changing $\mathsf{RATCHET\text{-}KE}[\mathbb{G}, \mathsf{F}, \mathsf{H}]$ to have $\mathsf{H}(hk, \cdot)$ take inputs of the form $w = i \parallel g^{x_i y}$. Call this scheme RKE_4. This enables the following attack, as defined by the adversary $\mathcal{D}_4$ in Fig. 7. Assume that an attacker compromises the sender's keys k_s and fk_s and immediately uses the compromised authenticity to establish new keys k_s^* and fk_s^*, shared between the attacker and the receiver. Now let $upd = (X, \sigma)$ be the next update information produced by the sender. The attacker can construct malicious update information $upd^* = (X, \sigma^*)$, where $\sigma^* = \mathsf{F.Ev}(fk_s^*, X)$, and send it to the receiver. The receiver would accept upd^* and use the output of $\mathsf{H.Ev}(hk, i \parallel X^y)$ as new key material, resulting in the same keys as those generated by the sender. Now the receiver and the sender share an output key, while the $\mathsf{restricted}$ flag is set true, so checking whether the output of the two challenge oracles is the same yields a good attack.

We will not give the exact advantage of $\mathcal{D}_4$. If σ^* and σ happen to be exactly the same, then the $\mathsf{restricted}$ flag would be set back to false and the attack would fail because the two keys received from the sender's and the reciever's challenge oracles would be the same regardless of game's challenge bit. But if $\sigma^* = \sigma$ was likely to occur then the ratcheted key exchange scheme would be insecure for other reasons. One could formalize this by building a second adversary against RKE_4 to show that one of the two adversaries must have a high advantage. For the purpose of this section we simply note that this event is extremely unlikely to occur for any typical choice of hash function and MAC.

4.4 Security Proof for Our Ratcheted Key Exchange Scheme

In previous section we showed that several variations of our ratcheted key exchange scheme $\mathsf{RKE} = \mathsf{RATCHET\text{-}KE}[\mathbb{G}, \mathsf{F}, \mathsf{H}]$ are insecure. In this section we will prove that our scheme is secure. We now present our theorem bounding the advantage of an adversary breaking the KIND-security of RKE to the SUFCMA-security of F and to the ODHE-security of $\mathbb{G}, \mathsf{H}$.

Theorem 1. *Let $\mathbb{G}$ be a cyclic group of order $p \in \mathbb{N}$, and let $\mathbb{G}^*$ denote the set of its generators. Let F be a function family such that $\mathsf{F.In} = \mathbb{G}$. Let H be a function family such that $\mathsf{H.In} = \{0,1\}^*$ and $\mathsf{H.ol} > \mathsf{F.kl}$. Let $\mathsf{RKE} = \mathsf{RATCHET\text{-}KE}[\mathbb{G}, \mathsf{F}, \mathsf{H}]$. Let $\mathcal{D}$ be an adversary attacking the KIND-security of RKE that makes q_{RatSend} queries to its RatSend oracle, q_{RatRec} queries to its RatRec oracle, q_{Exp} queries to its Exp oracle, q_{ChSend} queries to its ChSend oracle, and q_{ChRec} queries to its ChRec oracle. Then there is an adversary $\mathcal{F}$ attacking the SUFCMA-security of F, and adversaries $\mathcal{O}_1, \mathcal{O}_2$ attacking the ODHE-security of $\mathbb{G}, \mathsf{H}$, such that*

$$\mathsf{Adv}^{\mathsf{kind}}_{\mathsf{RKE},\mathcal{D}} \leq 2 \cdot (q_{\text{RatSend}} + 1) \cdot \mathsf{Adv}^{\mathsf{sufcma}}_{\mathsf{F},\mathcal{F}} + 2 \cdot q_{\text{RatSend}} \cdot \mathsf{Adv}^{\mathsf{odhe}}_{\mathbb{G},\mathsf{H},\mathcal{O}_1} + 2 \cdot \mathsf{Adv}^{\mathsf{odhe}}_{\mathbb{G},\mathsf{H},\mathcal{O}_2}.$$

Adversary $\mathcal{F}$ makes at most q_{RatSend} queries to its Tag oracle and q_{RatRec} queries to its Verify oracle. Adversary $\mathcal{O}_1$ makes at most q_{RatSend} queries to *its* UP *oracle,* 2 *queries to its* CH *oracle,* q_{EXP} *queries to its* EXP *oracle, and* $q_{\text{RATSEND}} + q_{\text{RATREC}} - 2$ *queries to its* HASH *oracle. Adversary* $\mathcal{O}_2$ *makes at most* q_{RATSEND} *queries to its* UP *oracle,* $q_{\text{RATSEND}} + q_{\text{RATREC}}$ *queries to its* CH *oracle,* q_{EXP} *queries to its* EXP *oracle, and* $q_{\text{RATREC}} + q_{\text{EXP}}$ *queries to its* HASH *oracle. Each of* $\mathcal{F}$*,* $\mathcal{O}_1$*,* $\mathcal{O}_2$ *has a running time approximately that of* $\mathcal{D}$*.*

The proof requires careful attention to detail due to subtleties. The most natural proof method may be to proceed one RATSEND query at a time, first replacing the output of the hash function with random bits (unless an expose happens) and then using the security of the MAC to argue that the adversary cannot produce any modified update information that will be accepted by the receiver without exposing. But there is a subtle flaw with this proof technique. The adversary may attempt to create a forged *upd* before it has decided whether to expose. In this case we need to check the validity of their forgery with a MAC key, before we know whether it should be random or a valid output of the hash function.

To avoid this problem we first use a hybrid argument to show that no such forgery is possible before replacing all non-exposed keys with random. We proceed one RATSEND query at a time, showing that we can temporarily replace the key with random when checking the sort of attempted forgery described above. This then allows us to use the security of the MAC to assume that the forgery attempt failed without us having to commit to a key to verify with. We thus are able to show one step at a time that all such forgery attempts can be assumed to fail without having to check.

Once this is done, we are never forced to use a key before the adversary has committed to whether it will perform a relevant exposure of the secret state. As such we can safely delay our decision of whether or not the key should be replaced by random values until it is known whether an expose will happen. This allows us to use the ODHE security of H and $\mathbb{G}$ to argue that we can replace all of the generated keys with randomness, only using H to generate the real keys at the last moment whenever an expose query is made.

Some explanation has been removed from the proof below due to lack of space. A more detailed proof is available in the full version of the paper [7].

Proof (Theorem 1). Consider the sequence of games shown in Fig. 8. Lines not annotated with comments are common to all games. $G_{0,0}$ is identical to $\text{KIND}_{\mathsf{RKE}}^{\mathcal{D}}$ with the code of RKE inserted. Additionally, a flag unchanged has been added. This flag keeps track of whether the most recent update information was passed unchanged from the sender to the receiver and thus the keys k_r and fk_r should be indistinguishable from random to adversary $\mathcal{D}$. In this case, the adversary should not be able to create update information *upd* that is accepted by RATREC unless it calls EXP or forwards along the *upd* generated by the sender. We prove this with a hybrid argument over the games $G_{0,0}, \ldots, G_{0,q_{\text{RATSEND}}+1}$. Game $G_{0,j}$ assumes forgery attempts fail for the first j keys, sets a bad flag if $\mathcal{D}$ is successful at forging against the $(j+1)$-th key, and performs normally for all following keys. Game $G^*_{0,j}$ is the same except it also acts as if $\mathcal{D}$ failed to forge even when the bad flag is set. Thus, from the perspective of an adversary $G^*_{0,j}$ is simply assumping that forgery attempts fail for the first $j+1$ keys, making it equivalent to $\mathrm{G}_{0,j+1}$. Thus for all $j \in \{0,\ldots,q_{\text{RATSEND}}\}$,

$$\Pr[\mathrm{G}_{0,0}] = \Pr[\mathrm{KIND}^{\mathcal{D}}_{\mathsf{RKE}}] \quad \text{and} \quad \Pr[\mathrm{G}^*_{0,j}] = \Pr[\mathrm{G}_{0,j+1}].$$

Furthermore, for all $j \in \{1,\ldots,q_{\text{RATSEND}}\}$, games $\mathrm{G}_{0,j}$ and $\mathrm{G}^*_{0,j}$ are identical until bad, so the fundamental lemma of game playing [6] gives:

$$\Pr[\mathrm{G}_{0,j}] - \Pr[\mathrm{G}^*_{0,j}] \leq \Pr[\mathsf{bad}^{\mathrm{G}^*_{0,j}}],$$

where $\Pr[\mathsf{bad}^{\mathsf{Q}}]$ denotes the probability of setting the bad flag in game Q.

We cannot directly bound $\Pr[\mathsf{bad}^{\mathrm{G}^*_{0,j}}]$ using the security of F because the key being used for F is chosen as output from H instead of uniformly at random, consider the relationship between games $\mathrm{G}^*_{0,j}$ and I_j (the latter also shown in Fig. 8). Game I_j is identical to $\mathrm{G}^*_{0,j}$, except that in I_j the output of hash function H is replaced with a uniformly random string whenever $i+1=j$ (thus the key used to check whether bad should be set when $i=j$ is uniformly random).

Note that when $j=0$ the games $\mathrm{G}^*_{0,0}$ and I_0 are identical so $\Pr[\mathsf{bad}^{\mathrm{G}^*_{0,0}}] = \Pr[\mathsf{bad}^{\mathrm{I}_0}]$. For other values of j we relate the probability that these games set bad to the advantage of the oracle Diffie-Hellman adversary $\mathcal{O}_1$ that is defined in Fig. 10. Adversary $\mathcal{O}_1$ picks j' at random and then uses its oracles to simulate $\mathrm{G}^*_{0,j}$ or I_j. Then if the bad flag is set it sets a bit b' equal to 1. This bit is ultimately returned by $\mathcal{O}$. Thus the probability that $\mathcal{O}$ outputs 1 is exactly the probability that the bad flag would be set in the game it is simulating.

Let b_{odhe} denote the challenge bit in game $\mathrm{ODHE}^{\mathcal{O}_1}_{\mathbb{G},\mathsf{H}}$, and let b' denote the corresponding guess made by the adversary $\mathcal{O}_1$. Let j' be the value sampled in the first step of $\mathcal{O}_1$. For each choice of j', adversary $\mathcal{O}_1$ perfectly simulates the view of $\mathcal{D}$ in either $\mathrm{G}^*_{0,j'}$ or $\mathrm{I}_{j'}$ depending on whether its CH oracle is returning real output of the hash function or a random value. If $\mathcal{D}$ performs an action that would prevent bad from being set (such as calling EXP when $i_s = j'$) then $\mathcal{O}_1$ no longer perfectly simulates the view of $\mathcal{D}$, but it does not matter for our analysis because we already know bad (and thus b') will not be set. So for all $j \in \{1,\ldots,q_{\text{RATSEND}}\}$, we have

$$\Pr[\mathsf{bad}^{\mathrm{G}^*_{0,j}}] = \Pr[\, b'=1 \mid b_{\mathsf{odhe}}=1, j'=j\,],$$
$$\Pr[\mathsf{bad}^{\mathrm{I}_j}] = \Pr[\, b'=1 \mid b_{\mathsf{odhe}}=0, j'=j\,].$$

Combining the above for all values of j (using $\Pr[\mathsf{bad}^{\mathrm{G}^*_{0,0}}] = \Pr[\mathsf{bad}^{\mathrm{G}_{i_s}}]$) gives

$$\begin{aligned}\mathsf{Adv}^{\mathsf{odhe}}_{\mathbb{G},\mathsf{H},\mathcal{O}_1} &= \Pr[\, b'=1 \mid b_{\mathsf{odhe}}=1\,] - \Pr[\, b'=1 \mid b_{\mathsf{odhe}}=0\,] \\ &= \sum_{j=1}^{q_{\text{RATSEND}}} \Pr[j=j'](\Pr[\mathsf{bad}^{\mathrm{G}^*_{0,j}}] - \Pr[\mathsf{bad}^{\mathrm{I}_j}]) = \sum_{j=0}^{q_{\text{RATSEND}}} \frac{\Pr[\mathsf{bad}^{\mathrm{G}^*_{0,j}}] - \Pr[\mathsf{bad}^{\mathrm{I}_j}]}{q_{\text{RATSEND}}}.\end{aligned}$$

Note that we were able to change the starting index of j for that last summation because $\Pr[\mathsf{bad}^{\mathrm{G}^*_{0,0}}] = \Pr[\mathsf{bad}^{\mathrm{I}_0}]$, as we noted before.

<u>Games $G_{0,j}$, $G^*_{0,j}$, I_j</u>

$b \leftarrow\$ \{0,1\}$; $i_s \leftarrow 0$; $i_r \leftarrow 0$; $\mathsf{unchanged} \leftarrow \mathsf{true}$; $rand \leftarrow\$ \{0,1\}^{\mathsf{H.ol}}$
$k_s \leftarrow\$ \{0,1\}^{\mathsf{RKE.kl}}$; $k_r \leftarrow k_s$; $fk_s \leftarrow\$ \{0,1\}^{\mathsf{F.kl}}$; $fk_r \leftarrow fk_s$
$hk \leftarrow\$ \{0,1\}^{\mathsf{H.kl}}$; $g \leftarrow\$ \mathbb{G}^*$; $y \leftarrow\$ \mathbb{Z}_p$; $stk_s \leftarrow (hk, g, g^y)$
$b' \leftarrow\$ \mathcal{D}^{\text{RatSend,RatRec,Exp,ChSend,ChRec}}(stk_s)$; Return $(b' = b)$

<u>RatSend</u>

If $\mathsf{op}[i_s] = \bot$ then $\mathsf{op}[i_s] \leftarrow$ "ch"
$x \leftarrow\$ \mathbb{Z}_p$; $\sigma \leftarrow \mathsf{F.Ev}(fk_s, g^x)$; $upd \leftarrow (g^x, \sigma)$
$s \leftarrow \mathsf{H.Ev}(hk, i_s \,\|\, \sigma \,\|\, g^x \,\|\, g^{xy})$
If $i_s + 1 = j$ then $s \leftarrow rand$ // I_j
$\mathsf{auth}[i_s] \leftarrow upd$; $i_s \leftarrow i_s + 1$; $k_s \leftarrow s[1 \ldots \mathsf{RKE.kl}]$
$fk_s \leftarrow s[\mathsf{RKE.kl}+1 \ldots \mathsf{RKE.kl}+\mathsf{F.kl}]$; Return upd

<u>RatRec(upd)</u>

$(X, \sigma) \leftarrow upd$
If $\mathsf{unchanged}$ and ($\mathsf{op}[i_r] \neq$ "exp") and ($upd \neq \mathsf{auth}[i_r]$) then
  If $i_r < j$ then return false
  If $i_r = j$ then
    If $\sigma \neq \mathsf{F.Ev}(fk_r, X)$ then return false
    $\mathsf{bad} \leftarrow \mathsf{true}$
    Return false // $G^*_{0,j}$, I_j
If $\sigma \neq \mathsf{F.Ev}(fk_r, X)$ then return false
If $\mathsf{op}[i_r]$ = "exp" then $\mathsf{restricted} \leftarrow \mathsf{true}$
If $upd = \mathsf{auth}[i_r]$ then
  $\mathsf{unchanged} \leftarrow \mathsf{true}$; $\mathsf{restricted} \leftarrow \mathsf{false}$
Else
  $\mathsf{unchanged} \leftarrow \mathsf{false}$
$s \leftarrow \mathsf{H.Ev}(hk, i_r \,\|\, \sigma \,\|\, X \,\|\, X^y)$
If $i_r + 1 = j$ then $s \leftarrow rand$ // I_j
$i_r \leftarrow i_r + 1$; $k_r \leftarrow s[1 \ldots \mathsf{RKE.kl}]$
$fk_r \leftarrow s[\mathsf{RKE.kl}+1 \ldots \mathsf{RKE.kl}+\mathsf{F.kl}]$; Return true

<u>Exp</u>

If $\mathsf{op}[i_s]$ = "ch" then return $\bot$
$\mathsf{op}[i_s] \leftarrow$ "exp" ; Return $(x, (i_s, fk_s), k_s)$

<u>ChSend</u>

If $\mathsf{op}[i_s]$ = "exp" then return $\bot$
$\mathsf{op}[i_s] \leftarrow$ "ch"
If $\mathsf{rkey}[i_s] = \bot$ then $\mathsf{rkey}[i_s] \leftarrow\$ \{0,1\}^{\mathsf{RKE.kl}}$
If $b = 1$ then return k_s else return $\mathsf{rkey}[i_s]$

<u>ChRec</u>

If $\mathsf{restricted}$ then return k_r
If $\mathsf{op}[i_r]$ = "exp" then return $\bot$
$\mathsf{op}[i_r] \leftarrow$ "ch"
If $\mathsf{rkey}[i_r] = \bot$ then $\mathsf{rkey}[i_r] \leftarrow\$ \{0,1\}^{\mathsf{RKE.kl}}$
If $b = 1$ then return k_r else return $\mathsf{rkey}[i_r]$

Fig. 8. Games $G_{0,j}$, $G^*_{0,j}$, I_j for proof of Theorem 1.

```
Games G1–G2
b ←$ {0,1} ; i_s ← 0 ; i_r ← 0 ; unchanged ← true
k_s[0] ←$ {0,1}^RKE.kl ; k_r ← k_s[0] ; fk_s[0] ←$ {0,1}^F.kl ; fk_r ← fk_s[0]
hk ←$ {0,1}^H.kl ; g ←$ G* ; y ←$ Z_p ; stk_s ← (hk, g, g^y)
b' ←$ D^{RatSend,RatRec,Exp,ChSend,ChRec}(stk_s) ; Return (b' = b)

RatSend
If op[i_s] = ⊥ then op[i_s] ← "ch"
x ←$ Z_p ; σ ← F.Ev(fk_s[i_s], g^x) ; upd ← (g^x, σ)
s ← H.Ev(hk, i_s ‖ σ ‖ g^x ‖ g^{xy})                          // G1
s ←$ {0,1}^H.ol                                               // G2
auth[i_s] ← upd ; i_s ← i_s + 1 ; k_s[i_s] ← s[1 ... RKE.kl]
fk_s[i_s] ← s[RKE.kl + 1 ... RKE.kl + F.kl] ; Return upd

RatRec(upd)
(X, σ) ← upd
If unchanged and (op[i_r] ≠ "exp") and (upd ≠ auth[i_r]) then
   Return false
If unchanged then fk_r ← fk_s[i_r]
If (σ ≠ F.Ev(fk_r, X)) then return false
If op[i_r] = "exp" then restricted ← true
If upd = auth[i_r]
   unchanged ← true ; restricted ← false ; i_r ← i_r + 1
Else
   unchanged ← false
   s ← H.Ev(hk, i_r ‖ σ ‖ X ‖ X^y)
   i_r ← i_r + 1 ; k_r ← s[1 ... RKE.kl]
   fk_r ← s[RKE.kl + 1 ... RKE.kl + F.kl]
Return true

Exp
If op[i_s] = "ch" then return ⊥
op[i_s] ← "exp" ; (X, σ) ← auth[i_s − 1]
s ← H.Ev(hk, (i_s − 1) ‖ σ ‖ X ‖ X^y) ; k_s[i_s] ← s[1 ... RKE.kl]
fk_s[i_s] ← s[RKE.kl + 1 ... RKE.kl + F.kl]
Return (x, (i_s, fk_s[i_s]), k_s[i_s])

ChSend
If op[i_s] = "exp" then return ⊥
op[i_s] ← "ch"
If rkey[i_s] = ⊥ then rkey[i_s] ←$ {0,1}^RKE.kl
If b = 1 then return k_s[i_s] else return rkey[i_s]

ChRec
If restricted then return k_r
If op[i_r] = "exp" then return ⊥
op[i_r] ← "ch"
If rkey[i_r] = ⊥ then rkey[i_r] ←$ {0,1}^RKE.kl
If unchanged then k_r ← k_s[i_r]
If b = 1 then return k_r else return rkey[i_r]
```

Fig. 9. Games G_1, G_2 for proof of Theorem 1.

Adversary $\mathcal{O}_1^{\text{UP,CH,EXP,HASH}}(hk, g, Y)$

$j' \leftarrow_\$ \{1, \ldots, q_{\text{RATSEND}}\}$; $b \leftarrow_\$ \{0,1\}$; $b' \leftarrow 0$
$i_s \leftarrow 0$; $i_r \leftarrow 0$; unchanged $\leftarrow$ true
$k_s \leftarrow_\$ \{0,1\}^{\text{RKE.kl}}$; $k_r \leftarrow k_s$
$fk_s \leftarrow_\$ \{0,1\}^{\text{F.kl}}$; $fk_r \leftarrow fk_s$; $stk_s \leftarrow (hk, g, Y)$
$\mathcal{D}^{\text{RATSENDSIM,RATRECSIM,EXPSIM,CHSENDSIM,CHRECSIM}}(stk_s)$
Return b'

RATRECSIM(upd)

$(X, \sigma) \leftarrow upd$
forge $\leftarrow$ ((op[i_r] $\neq$ "exp") $\wedge$ ($upd \neq$ auth[i_r]))
If unchanged and forge then
  If $i_r < j'$ then return false
  If $i_r = j'$ then
    If $\sigma \neq$ F.Ev(fk_r, X) then return false
    bad $\leftarrow$ true ; $b' \leftarrow 1$; Return false
If $\sigma \neq$ F.Ev(fk_r, X) then return false
If op[i_r] = "exp" then restricted $\leftarrow$ true
If upd = auth[i_r] then
  unchanged $\leftarrow$ true ; restricted $\leftarrow$ false
Else unchanged $\leftarrow$ false
If $i_r + 1 \neq j'$ then $s \leftarrow$ HASH($i_r, \sigma \| X, X$)
Else $s \leftarrow$ CH($\sigma \| X$)
$i_r \leftarrow i_r + 1$; $k_r \leftarrow s[1 \ldots \text{RKE.kl}]$
$fk_r \leftarrow s[\text{RKE.kl}+1 \ldots \text{RKE.kl}+\text{F.kl}]$
Return true

EXPSIM

If op[i_s] = "ch" then return $\perp$
op[i_s] $\leftarrow$ "exp" ; $x \leftarrow$ EXP
Return $(x, (i_s, fk_s), k_s)$

RATSENDSIM

If op[i_s] = $\perp$ then op[i_s] $\leftarrow$ "ch"
$X \leftarrow$ UP ; $\sigma \leftarrow$ F.Ev(fk_s, X)
$upd \leftarrow (X, \sigma)$
If $i_s + 1 \neq j'$ then
  $s \leftarrow$ HASH($i_s, \sigma \| X, X$)
Else
  $s \leftarrow$ CH($\sigma \| X$)
auth[i_s] $\leftarrow upd$; $i_s \leftarrow i_s + 1$
$k_s \leftarrow s[1 \ldots \text{RKE.kl}]$
$fk_s \leftarrow s[\text{RKE.kl}+1 \ldots \text{RKE.kl}+\text{F.kl}]$
Return upd

CHSENDSIM

If op[i_s] = "exp" then return $\perp$
op[i_s] $\leftarrow$ "ch"
If rkey[i_s] $=\perp$ then
  rkey[i_s] $\leftarrow_\$ \{0,1\}^{\text{RKE.kl}}$
If $b = 1$ then return k_s
Else return rkey[i_s]

CHRECSIM

If restricted then return k_r
If op[i_r] = "exp" then return $\perp$
op[i_r] $\leftarrow$ "ch"
If rkey[i_r] $=\perp$ then
  rkey[i_r] $\leftarrow_\$ \{0,1\}^{\text{RKE.kl}}$
If $b = 1$ then return k_r
Else return rkey[i_r]

Fig. 10. Adversary $\mathcal{O}_1$ for proof of Theorem 1.

To complete the hybrid argument part of the proof, we bound the probability that bad gets set true in I_j. Adversary $\mathcal{F}$ (shown in Fig. 11) guesses when $\mathcal{D}$ will first create a forgery and uses that to create its own forgery. Thus for $j \in \{0, \ldots, q_{\text{RATSEND}}\}$, $\Pr[\text{bad}^{\text{I}_j}] \leq \Pr[\,\text{SUFCMA}_{\mathsf{F}}^{\mathcal{F}} \mid j' = j\,]$ which gives $\mathsf{Adv}_{\mathsf{F},\mathcal{F}}^{\mathsf{sufcma}} \geq (1/(q_{\text{RATREC}}+1)) \sum_{j=0}^{q_{\text{RATREC}}} \Pr[\text{bad}^{\text{I}_j}]$.

The above work allows us to transition to game $\text{G}_{0,q_{\text{RATSEND}}+1}$ as shown in the following equations. From there we will move to games G_1, G_2 shown in Fig. 9. All of the summations below are from $j = 0$ to $j = q_{\text{RATSEND}}$.

```
Adversary F^{Tag,Verify}
j' ←$ {0, ..., q_RatSend} ; b ←$ {0,1}
i_s ← 0 ; i_r ← 0 ; unchanged ← true
rand ←$ {0,1}^{H.ol} ; k_s ←$ {0,1}^{RKE.kl} ; k_r ← k_s
fk_s ←$ {0,1}^{F.kl} ; fk_r ← fk_s ; hk ←$ {0,1}^{H.kl}
g ←$ G* ; y ←$ Z_p ; stk_s ← (hk, g, g^y)
D^{RatSendSim,RatRecSim,ExpSim,ChSendSim,ChRecSim}(stk_s)

RatRecSim(upd)
(X, σ) ← upd
forge ← ((op[i_r] ≠ "exp") ∧ (upd ≠ auth[i_r]))
If unchanged and forge then
   If i_r < j' then return false
   If i_r = j' then
      If not Verify(X, σ) then return false
      bad ← true
      Return false
If (i_r = j') then
   If not Verify(X, σ) then return false
Else
   If σ ≠ F.Ev(fk_r, X) then return false
If op[i_r] = "exp" then restricted ← true
If upd = auth[i_r] then
   unchanged ← true ; restricted ← false
Else
   unchanged ← false
s ← H.Ev(hk, i_r || σ || X || X^y)
If i_r + 1 = j then s ← rand
i_r ← i_r + 1 ; k_r ← s[1 ... RKE.kl]
fk_r ← s[RKE.kl + 1 ... RKE.kl + F.kl]
Return true

RatSendSim
If op[i_s] = ⊥ then op[i_s] ← "ch"
x ←$ Z_p
If i_s = j' then σ ← Tag(g^x)
Else σ ← F.Ev(fk_s, g^x)
s ← H.Ev(hk, i_s || σ || g^x || g^{xy})
If i_s + 1 = j then s ← rand
upd ← (g^x, σ) ; auth[i_s] ← upd
i_s ← i_s + 1 ; k_s ← s[1 ... RKE.kl]
fk_s ← s[RKE.kl + 1 ... RKE.kl + F.kl]
Return upd

ExpSim
If op[i_s] = "ch" then return ⊥
op[i_s] ← "exp"
Return (x, (i_s, fk_s), k_s)

ChSendSim
If op[i_s] = "exp" then return ⊥
op[i_s] ← "ch"
If rkey[i_s] = ⊥ then
   rkey[i_s] ←$ {0,1}^{RKE.kl}
If b = 1 then return k_s
Else return rkey[i_s]

ChRecSim
If restricted then return k_r
If op[i_r] = "exp" then return ⊥
op[i_r] ← "ch"
If rkey[i_r] = ⊥ then
   rkey[i_r] ←$ {0,1}^{RKE.kl}
If b = 1 then return k_r
Else return rkey[i_r]
```

Fig. 11. Adversary $\mathcal{F}$ for proof of Theorem 1.

$$
\begin{aligned}
\Pr[\mathrm{KIND}^{\mathcal{D}}_{\mathsf{RKE}}] &= \Pr[\mathrm{G}_{0,0}] = \Pr[\mathrm{G}_{1,q_{\mathrm{RatSend}}}] + \textstyle\sum_j \Pr[\mathrm{G}_{0,j}] - \Pr[\mathrm{G}^*_{0,j}] \\
&\leq \Pr[\mathrm{G}_{1,q_{\mathrm{RatSend}}}] + \textstyle\sum_j \Pr[\mathsf{bad}^{\mathrm{G}^*_{0,j}}] \\
&= \Pr[\mathrm{G}_{1,q_{\mathrm{RatSend}}}] + q_{\mathrm{RatSend}} \cdot \mathsf{Adv}^{\mathsf{odhe}}_{\mathbb{G},\mathsf{H},\mathcal{O}_1} + \textstyle\sum_j \Pr[\mathsf{bad}^{\mathrm{I}_j}] \\
&\leq q_{\mathrm{RatSend}} \cdot \mathsf{Adv}^{\mathsf{odhe}}_{\mathbb{G},\mathsf{H},\mathcal{O}_1} + (q_{\mathrm{RatSend}} + 1) \cdot \mathsf{Adv}^{\mathsf{sufcma}}_{\mathsf{F},\mathcal{F}} + \Pr[\mathrm{G}_{1,q_{\mathrm{RatSend}}}].
\end{aligned}
$$

Game G_1 is identical to $\mathrm{G}_{0,q_{\mathrm{RatSend}}+1}$, but has been rewritten to allow make the final game transition of our proof easier to follow. The complicated, nested if-condition at the beginning of RatRec has been simplified because $i_r < q_{\mathrm{RatSend}} + 1$ always holds when unchanged is true. Additionally, when unchanged is true (and thus *upd* has been directly forwarded between RatSend and RatRec without being modified) we delay setting k_r, fk_r until they are

```
Adversary O_2^{Up,Ch,Exp,Hash}(hk, g, Y)
b ←$ {0,1} ; i_s ← 0 ; i_r ← 0 ; unchanged ← true
k_s[0] ←$ {0,1}^{RKE.kl} ; k_r ← k_s[0]
fk_s[0] ←$ {0,1}^{F.kl} ; fk_r ← fk_s[0] ; hk ←$ {0,1}^{H.kl}
g ←$ G* ; y ←$ Z_p ; stk_s ← (hk, g, Y)
b' ←$ D^{RatSendSim,RatRecSim,ExpSim,ChSendSim,ChRecSim}(stk_s)
If (b' = b) then return 1 else return 0

RatSendSim
If op[i_s] = ⊥ then
   op[i_s] ← "ch"
   If i_s ≠ 0 then
      (X, σ) ← auth[i_s − 1] ; s ← Ch(σ||X)
      SaveKeys(i_s, s)
X ← Up ; σ ← F.Ev(fk_s[i_s], X) ; upd ← (X, σ)
auth[i_s] ← upd ; i_s ← i_s + 1 ; Return upd

RatRecSim(upd)
(X, σ) ← upd
forge ← ((op[i_r] ≠ "exp") ∧ (upd ≠ auth[i_r]))
If unchanged and forge then return false
If unchanged then fk_r ← fk_s[i_r]
If (σ ≠ F.Ev(fk_r, X)) then return false
If op[i_r] = "exp" then restricted ← true
If upd = auth[i_r]
   unchanged ← true ; restricted ← false ; i_r ← i_r + 1
Else
   unchanged ← false ; s ← Hash(i_r, σ||X, X)
   i_r ← i_r + 1 ; k_r ← s[1 ... RKE.kl]
   fk_r ← s[RKE.kl + 1 ... RKE.kl + F.kl]
Return true

SaveKeys(i, s)
k_s[i] ← s[1 ... RKE.kl]
fk_s[i] ← s[RKE.kl + 1 ... RKE.kl + F.kl]
```

```
ExpSim
If op[i_s] = "ch" then return ⊥
If (op[i_s] =⊥) and (i_s ≠ 0) then
   x ← Exp
   (X, σ) ← auth[i_s − 1]
   s ← Hash(i_s − 1, σ||X, X)
   SaveKeys(i_s, s)
op[i_s] ← "exp"
Return (x, (i_s, fk_s[i_s]), k_s[i_s])

ChSendSim
If op[i_s] = "exp" then return ⊥
If (op[i_s] =⊥) and (i_s ≠ 0) then
   (X, σ) ← auth[i_s − 1]
   s ← Ch(σ||X)
   SaveKeys(i_s, s)
op[i_s] ← "ch"
If rkey[i_s] =⊥ then
   rkey[i_s] ←$ {0,1}^{RKE.kl}
If b = 1 then return k_s[i_s]
Else return rkey[i_s]

ChRecSim
If restricted then return k_r
If op[i_r] = "exp" then return ⊥
If (op[i_r] =⊥) and (i_r ≠ 0) then
   (X, σ) ← auth[i_r − 1]
   s ← Ch(σ||X)
   SaveKeys(i_r, s)
op[i_r] ← "ch"
If rkey[i_r] =⊥ then
   rkey[i_r] ←$ {0,1}^{RKE.kl}
If unchanged then k_r ← k_s[i_r]
If b = 1 then return k_r
Else return rkey[i_r]
```

Fig. 12. Adversary $\mathcal{O}_2$ for proof of Theorem 1.

about to be used, at which point they are set to match the appropriate k_s, fk_s that have been stored in a table. We have $\Pr[G_{0,q_{\text{RATSEND}}+1}] = \Pr[G_1]$.

Games G_1 and G_2 differ only in that, in G_2, values of k_0 and fk_s are chosen at random instead of as the output of H (unless EXP is called in which case we reset them to the correct output of H). We bound the difference between $\Pr[G_1]$ and $\Pr[G_2]$ by the advantage of the Diffie-Hellman adversary $\mathcal{O}_2$ that is defined in Fig. 12. Specifically, we have $\mathsf{Adv}^{\mathsf{odhe}}_{\mathbb{G},\mathsf{H},\mathcal{O}_2} = \Pr[G_1] - \Pr[G_2]$. As a result of the above and our previous sequence of inequalities, we get:

$$\Pr[\text{KIND}^{\mathcal{D}}_{\mathsf{RKE}}] \le q_{\text{RATSEND}} \cdot \mathsf{Adv}^{\mathsf{odhe}}_{\mathbb{G},\mathsf{H},\mathcal{O}_1} + (q_{\text{RATSEND}} + 1) \cdot \mathsf{Adv}^{\mathsf{sufcma}}_{\mathsf{F},\mathcal{F}} + \Pr[\mathrm{G}_1]$$
$$= q_{\text{RATSEND}} \cdot \mathsf{Adv}^{\mathsf{odhe}}_{\mathbb{G},\mathsf{H},\mathcal{O}_1} + (q_{\text{RATSEND}} + 1) \cdot \mathsf{Adv}^{\mathsf{sufcma}}_{\mathsf{F},\mathcal{F}} + \mathsf{Adv}^{\mathsf{odhe}}_{\mathbb{G},\mathsf{H},\mathcal{O}_2} + \Pr[\mathrm{G}_2].$$

Finally, $\Pr[\mathrm{G}_2] = 1/2$ because the view of $\mathcal{D}$ is independent of b in G_2. This yields the claimed bound on the advantage of $\mathcal{D}$. The bounds on the number of oracle queries made by the adversaries are obtained by examining their code. □

5 Ratcheted Encryption

In this section we define ratcheted encryption schemes, and show how to construct them by composing ratcheted key exchange with symmetric encryption. This serves as a starting point for discussing ratcheted encryption, and we also discuss possible extensions.

Ratcheted encryption schemes. Our definition of ratcheted encryption extends the definition of ratcheted key exchange by adding encryption and decryption algorithms. Ratcheted encryption schemes inherit the key generation algorithms from ratcheted key exchange schemes, and use the resulting shared keys as symmetric encryption keys. In line with our definition for ratcheted key exchange, we only consider one-sided ratcheted encryption, meaning that the sender uses its key only for encryption, and the receiver uses its key only for decryption.

A ratcheted encryption scheme RE specifies algorithms $\mathsf{RE.IKg}$, $\mathsf{RE.SKg}$, $\mathsf{RE.RKg}$, $\mathsf{RE.Enc}$ and $\mathsf{RE.Dec}$, where $\mathsf{RE.Enc}$ and $\mathsf{RE.Dec}$ are deterministic. Associated to RE is a nonce space $\mathsf{RE.NS}$, sender's key generation randomness space $\mathsf{RE.RS}$, and a ciphertext length function $\mathsf{RE.cl}\colon \mathbb{N} \to \mathbb{N}$. Initial key generation algorithm $\mathsf{RE.IKg}$ returns $k, sek_s, (stk_s, stk_r, sek_r)$, where k is an encryption key, stk_s, sek_s are a sender's static key and session key, and stk_r, sek_r are receiver's static key and receiver's session key, respectively. The sender's and receiver's (symmetric) encryption keys are initialized to $k_s = k_r = k$. Sender's key generation algorithm $\mathsf{RE.SKg}$ takes stk_s, sek_s and randomness $r \in \mathsf{RE.RS}$ to return a new sender's session key sek_s, a new sender's encryption key k_s, and update information upd. Receiver's key generation algorithm $\mathsf{RE.RKg}$ takes stk_s, stk_r, sek_r, upd and receiver's encryption key k_r to return a new receiver's session key sek_r, a new receiver's encryption key k_r, and a flag $acc \in \{\mathsf{true}, \mathsf{false}\}$. Encryption algorithm $\mathsf{RE.Enc}$ takes k_s, a nonce $n \in \mathsf{RE.NS}$, a plaintext message $m \in \{0,1\}^*$ and a header $h \in \{0,1\}^*$ to return a ciphertext $c \in \{0,1\}^{\mathsf{RE.cl}(|m|)}$. Decryption algorithm $\mathsf{RE.Dec}$ takes k_r, n, c, h to return $m \in \{0,1\}^* \cup \{\bot\}$.

Correctness of ratcheted encryption. Correctness of ratcheted encryption extends that of ratcheted key exchange. It requires that messages encrypted using sender's key should correctly decrypt using the corresponding receiver's key.

Consider game RE-COR of Fig. 4 associated to a ratcheted encryption scheme R and an adversary $\mathcal{C}$, where $\mathcal{C}$ is provided with an access to oracles UP, RATREC and ENC. The advantage of $\mathcal{C}$ breaking the correctness of R is defined as $\mathsf{Adv}^{\mathsf{recor}}_{\mathsf{R},\mathcal{C}} = 1 - \Pr[\text{RE-COR}^{\mathcal{C}}_{\mathsf{R}}]$. Correctness property requires that $\mathsf{Adv}^{\mathsf{recor}}_{\mathsf{R},\mathcal{C}} = 0$

for all unbounded adversaries $\mathcal{C}$. Compared to the correctness game for ratcheted key exchange, the new element is that adversary $\mathcal{C}$ also gets access to an encryption oracle ENC, which can be queried to test the decryption correctness.

Ratcheted authenticated encryption. Consider game RAE on the right side of Fig. 5 associated to a ratcheted encryption scheme RE and an adversary $\mathcal{A}$. It extends the security definition of ratcheted key exchange (as defined in game KIND on the left side of Fig. 5) by replacing oracles CHSEND and CHREC with oracles ENC and DEC. Oracles RATSEND, RATREC and EXP are the same in both games. Oracles ENC and DEC are defined as follows. In the real world (when $b = 1$) oracle ENC encrypts messages under the sender's key, and oracle DEC decrypts ciphertexts under the receiver's key. In the random world (when $b = 0$) oracle ENC returns uniformly random strings, and oracle DEC always returns an incorrect decryption symbol $\perp$. The goal of the adversary is to distinguish between the two cases. The advantage of $\mathcal{A}$ in breaking the RAE security of RE is defined as $\mathsf{Adv}^{\mathsf{rae}}_{\mathsf{RE},\mathcal{A}} = 2\Pr[\mathrm{RAE}^{\mathcal{A}}_{\mathsf{RE}}] - 1$.

We note that the adversary is only allowed to get a single encryption for each unique pair of (i_s, n). This restriction stems from the fact that most known nonce-based encryption schemes are not resistant to *nonce-misuse*. Our definition can be relaxed to only prevent queries where (i_s, n, m) — or even (i_s, n, m, h) — are repeated, but it would increasingly limit the choice of the underlying symmetric schemes that can be used for this purpose (fewer schemes would satisfy stronger security definitions of multi-user authenticated encryption).

Revisiting the treatment of the restricted flag. Similar to the definition of KIND, one could consider strengthening the definition of RAE by never resetting the restricted flag back to false (as discussed in Sect. 4.2). There would seem to be a more clear motivation to use the stronger definition in the case of encryption. Namely, our current security definition allows adversary to comprimse the sender, use the exposed secrets to communicate with the receiver, and then restore the initial conversation link between the sender and the receiver. This represents an ability to stealthily insert arbitrary messages in the middle of someone's conversation, without ultimately disrupting the conversation. However, note that even a stonger definition (one that does not reset the restricted flag) appears to allow such attack, because the adversary might be able to compromise the sender and insert the messages before the next time the key ratcheting happens. The success of such attack would depend on how often the keys are being ratcheted.

Ratcheted encryption scheme RATCHET-ENC. We build a ratcheted encryption scheme by combining a ratcheted key exchange scheme with a symmetric encryption scheme. In our composition the output keys of the ratcheted key exchange scheme are used as encryption keys for the symmetric encryption scheme.

Let RKE be a ratcheted key exchange scheme. Let SE be a symmetric encryption scheme such that SE.kl = RKE.kl. We build a ratcheted encryption scheme RE = RATCHET-ENC[RKE, SE] with RE.NS = SE.NS, RE.RS = RKE.RS and $\mathsf{RE.cl} = \mathsf{SE.cl}$ as follows. Let $\mathsf{RE.IKg} = \mathsf{RKE.IKg}$, $\mathsf{RE.SKg} = \mathsf{RKE.SKg}$, $\mathsf{RE.RKg} = \mathsf{RKE.RKg}$, $\mathsf{RE.Enc} = \mathsf{SE.Enc}$, and $\mathsf{RE.Dec} = \mathsf{SE.Dec}$. Thus RE is directly using RKE for key generation and SE for encryption.

Security of ratcheted encryption scheme RATCHET-ENC. The following says that the RAE security of ratcheted encryption scheme $\mathsf{RE} = \mathsf{RATCHET\text{-}ENC}[\mathsf{RKE}, \mathsf{SE}]$ can be reduced to the KIND security of the ratcheted key exchange scheme RKE and MAE security of the symmetric encryption scheme SE. The proof is in [7].

Theorem 2. *Let* RKE *be a ratcheted key exchange scheme. Let* SE *be a symmetric encryption scheme such that* $\mathsf{SE.kl} = \mathsf{RKE.kl}$. *Let* $\mathsf{RE} = \mathsf{RATCHET\text{-}ENC}[\mathsf{RKE}, \mathsf{SE}]$. *Let* $\mathcal{A}$ *be an adversary attacking the* RAE*-security of* RE *that makes* q_{RATSEND} *queries to its* RATSEND *oracle,* q_{RATREC} *queries to its* RATREC *oracle,* q_{EXP} *queries to its* EXP *oracle,* q_{ENC} *queries to its* ENC *oracle, and* q_{DEC} *queries to its* DEC *oracle. Then there is an adversary* $\mathcal{D}$ *attacking the* KIND*-security of* RKE *and an adversary* $\mathcal{N}$ *attacking the* MAE*-security of* SE *such that*

$$\mathsf{Adv}^{\mathsf{rae}}_{\mathsf{RE},\mathcal{A}} \leq 2 \cdot \mathsf{Adv}^{\mathsf{kind}}_{\mathsf{RKE},\mathcal{D}} + \mathsf{Adv}^{\mathsf{mae}}_{\mathsf{SE},\mathcal{N}}.$$

Adversary $\mathcal{D}$ *makes at most* q_{EXP} *queries to its* EXP *oracle,* q_{ENC} *queries to its* CHSEND *oracle,* q_{DEC} *queries to its* CHREC *oracle, and the same number of queries as* $\mathcal{A}$ *to oracles* RATSEND, RATREC. *Adversary* $\mathcal{N}$ *makes at most* $\max(q_{\text{RATSEND}}, q_{\text{RATREC}})$ *queries to its* NEW *oracle,* q_{ENC} *queries to its* ENC *oracle, and* q_{DEC} *queries to its* DEC *oracle. Each of* $\mathcal{D}$, $\mathcal{N}$ *has a running time approximately that of* $\mathcal{A}$.

Extensions. We defined our encryption schemes to be one-sided in both communication (meaning that the messages are assumed to be sent only in one direction, from the sender to the receiver), and in security (only protecting against the exposure of the sender's secrets). It would be useful to consider *two-sided* communication (but still one-sided security). In our model the sender and the receiver already share the same key, but one would need to update the security game to allow using either key for encryption and decryption.

An important goal in studying ratcheted encryption is to model the *Double Ratchet algorithm* [16, 20] used in multiple real-world messaging applications, such as in WhatsApp [26] and in the Secret Conversations mode of Facebook Messenger [17]. This work models the asymmetric layer of key ratcheting, whereas the real-world applications also have a second layer of key ratcheting that happens in a symmetric setting. In our model, this can be possibly achieved by using the output keys of ratcheted key exchange to initialize a *forward-secure* symmetric encryption scheme. We do not capture this possibility; both the syntax and the security definitions would need to be significantly extended.

Acknowledgments. We thank the EUROCRYPT 2017 and CRYPTO 2017 reviewers for their comments. Bellare, Jaeger and Stepanovs were supported in part by NSF grants CNS-1526801 and CNS-1228890, ERC Project ERCC FP7/615074 and a gift from Microsoft.

References

1. Abdalla, M., Bellare, M., Rogaway, P.: The oracle diffie-hellman assumptions and an analysis of DHIES. In: Naccache, D. (ed.) CT-RSA 2001. LNCS, vol. 2020, pp. 143–158. Springer, Heidelberg (2001). doi:10.1007/3-540-45353-9_12
2. Bellare, M., Duan, S., Palacio, A.: Key insulation and intrusion resilience over a public channel. In: Fischlin, M. (ed.) CT-RSA 2009. LNCS, vol. 5473, pp. 84–99. Springer, Heidelberg (2009). doi:10.1007/978-3-642-00862-7_6
3. Bellare, M., Pointcheval, D., Rogaway, P.: Authenticated key exchange secure against dictionary attacks. In: Preneel, B. (ed.) EUROCRYPT 2000. LNCS, vol. 1807, pp. 139–155. Springer, Heidelberg (2000). doi:10.1007/3-540-45539-6_11
4. Bellare, M., Rogaway, P.: Random oracles are practical: a paradigm for designing efficient protocols. In: ACM CCS 1993 (1993)
5. Bellare, M., Rogaway, P.: Entity authentication and key distribution. In: Stinson, D.R. (ed.) CRYPTO 1993. LNCS, vol. 773, pp. 232–249. Springer, Heidelberg (1994). doi:10.1007/3-540-48329-2_21
6. Bellare, M., Rogaway, P.: The security of triple encryption and a framework for code-based game-playing proofs. In: Vaudenay, S. (ed.) EUROCRYPT 2006. LNCS, vol. 4004, pp. 409–426. Springer, Heidelberg (2006). doi:10.1007/11761679_25
7. Bellare, M., Singh, A.C., Jaeger, J., Nyayapati, M., Stepanovs, I.: Ratcheted encryption and key exchange: the security of messaging. Cryptology ePrint Archive, Report 2016/1028 (2016)
8. Bellare, M., Tackmann, B.: The multi-user security of authenticated encryption: AES-GCM in TLS 1.3. In: Robshaw, M., Katz, J. (eds.) CRYPTO 2016. LNCS, vol. 9814, pp. 247–276. Springer, Heidelberg (2016). doi:10.1007/978-3-662-53018-4_10
9. Bellare, M., Yee, B.: Forward-security in private-key cryptography. In: Joye, M. (ed.) CT-RSA 2003. LNCS, vol. 2612, pp. 1–18. Springer, Heidelberg (2003). doi:10.1007/3-540-36563-X_1
10. Borisov, N., Goldberg, I., Brewer, E.: Off-the-record communication, or, why not to use pgp. In: Proceedings of the ACM Workshop on Privacy in the Electronic Society (WPES) (2004)
11. Cohn-Gordon, K., Cremers, C., Dowling, B., Garratt, L., Stebila, D.: A formal security analysis of the Signal messaging protocol. In: Proceedings of IEEE European Symposium on Security and Privacy (EuroS&P) (2017)
12. Cohn-Gordon, K., Cremers, C., Garratt, L.: On post-compromise security. In: IEEE 29th Computer Security Foundations Symposium (CSF) (2016)
13. Dodis, Y., Katz, J., Xu, S., Yung, M.: Key-insulated public key cryptosystems. In: Knudsen, L.R. (ed.) EUROCRYPT 2002. LNCS, vol. 2332, pp. 65–82. Springer, Heidelberg (2002). doi:10.1007/3-540-46035-7_5
14. Dodis, Y., Katz, J., Xu, S., Yung, M.: Strong key-insulated signature schemes. In: Desmedt, Y.G. (ed.) PKC 2003. LNCS, vol. 2567, pp. 130–144. Springer, Heidelberg (2003). doi:10.1007/3-540-36288-6_10
15. Dodis, Y., Luo, W., Xu, S., Yung, M.: Key-insulated symmetric key cryptography and mitigating attacks against cryptographic cloud software. In: ASIACCS 2012
16. Perrin, T., Marlinspike, M. (ed.): The double ratchet algorithm, 20 November 2016. https://whispersystems.org/docs/specifications/doubleratchet/
17. Facebook: Messenger secret conversations technical whitepaper. Technical whitepaper, 8 July 2016. https://fbnewsroomus.files.wordpress.com/2016/07/secret_conversations_whitepaper-1.pdf

18. Fischlin, M., Günther, F.: Multi-stage key exchange and the case of Google's QUIC protocol. In: ACM CCS 2014 (2014)
19. Langley, A.: Pond. GitHub repository, README.md (2012). https://github.com/agl/pond/commit/7bb06244b9aa121d367a6d556867992d1481f0c8
20. Marlinspike, M.: Advanced cryptographic ratcheting, 26 November 2013. https://whispersystems.org/blog/advanced-ratcheting/
21. Okamoto, T., Pointcheval, D.: The gap-problems: a new class of problems for the security of cryptographic schemes. In: Kim, K. (ed.) PKC 2001. LNCS, vol. 1992, pp. 104–118. Springer, Heidelberg (2001). doi:10.1007/3-540-44586-2_8
22. Open Whisper Systems: Signal protocol library for java/android. GitHub repository (2017). https://github.com/WhisperSystems/libsignal-protocol-java
23. Rogaway, P.: Authenticated-encryption with associated-data. In: ACM CCS 2002 (2002)
24. Rogaway, P.: Nonce-based symmetric encryption. In: Roy, B., Meier, W. (eds.) FSE 2004. LNCS, vol. 3017, pp. 348–358. Springer, Heidelberg (2004). doi:10.1007/978-3-540-25937-4_22
25. Unger, N., Dechand, S., Bonneau, J., Fahl, S., Perl, H., Goldberg, I., Smith, M.: SoK: secure messaging. In: IEEE Symposium on Security and Privacy (2015)
26. WhatsApp: Whatsapp encryption overview. Technical white paper, April 4 2016. https://www.whatsapp.com/security/WhatsApp-Security-Whitepaper.pdf

PRF-ODH: Relations, Instantiations, and Impossibility Results

Jacqueline Brendel(✉), Marc Fischlin, Felix Günther, and Christian Janson

Cryptoplexity, Technische Universität Darmstadt, Darmstadt, Germany
{jacqueline.brendel,marc.fischlin,felix.guenther, christian.janson}@cryptoplexity.de

Abstract. The pseudorandom-function oracle-Diffie–Hellman (PRF-ODH) assumption has been introduced recently to analyze a variety of DH-based key exchange protocols, including TLS 1.2 and the TLS 1.3 candidates, as well as the extended access control (EAC) protocol. Remarkably, the assumption comes in different flavors in these settings and none of them has been scrutinized comprehensively yet. In this paper here we therefore present a systematic study of the different PRF-ODH variants in the literature. In particular, we analyze their strengths relative to each other, carving out that the variants form a hierarchy. We further investigate the boundaries between instantiating the assumptions in the standard model and the random oracle model. While we show that even the strongest variant is achievable in the random oracle model under the strong Diffie–Hellman assumption, we provide a negative result showing that it is implausible to instantiate even the weaker variants in the standard model via algebraic black-box reductions to common cryptographic problems.

1 Introduction

Proposing new cryptographic assumptions is a valid strategy to analyze or design protocols which escape a formal treatment so far. Yet, the analysis of the protocol, usually carried out via a reduction to the new assumption, is only the first step. Only the evaluation of the new assumption completes the analysis and yields a meaningful security claim.

1.1 The PRF-ODH Assumption

In the context of key exchange protocols, a new assumption, called the pseudorandom-function oracle-Diffie–Hellman (PRF-ODH) assumption has recently been put forward by Jager et al. [23] for the analysis of TLS 1.2. It is a variant of the oracle-Diffie–Hellman assumption introduced by Abdalla et al. [1] in the context of the encryption scheme DHIES. The PRF-ODH assumption basically says that the function value $\mathsf{PRF}(g^{uv}, x^\star)$ for a DH key g^{uv} looks random, even if given g^u and g^v and if seeing related values $\mathsf{PRF}(S^u, x)$ and/or $\mathsf{PRF}(T^v, x)$ for chosen values S, T, and x.

J. Katz and H. Shacham (Eds.): CRYPTO 2017, Part III, LNCS 10403, pp. 651–681, 2017.
DOI: 10.1007/978-3-319-63697-9_22

The PRF-ODH appears to be a natural assumption for any DH-based key exchange protocol, aiming at security against man-in-the-middle attacks (see Fig. 1). In DH-based protocols both parties, the client and the server, exchange values g^u, g^v and locally compute the session key by applying a key derivation (or pseudorandom) function to the key g^{uv} and usually some parts of the transcript. The man-in-the-middle adversary can now try to attack the server's session key $\mathsf{PRF}(g^{uv}, \dots)$ by submitting a modified value S instead of g^v to the client, yielding a related key $\mathsf{PRF}(S^u, \dots)$ on the client's side. The PRF-ODH assumption guarantees now that the server's key is still fresh.

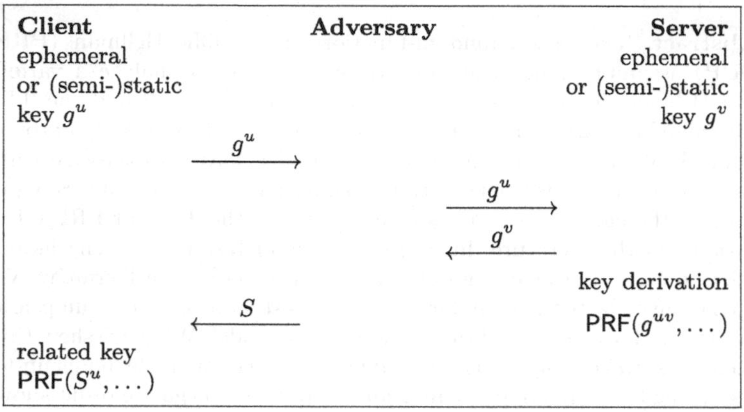

Fig. 1. Origin of the PRF-ODH assumption: Man-in-the-middle attack on DH-based key exchange protocol.

Note that simple authentication of transmissions does not provide a remedy against the above problem. The adversary could act under a different, corrupt server identity towards the client, and only re-use the Diffie–Hellman data, authenticated under the corrupt server's key. Then the Diffie–Hellman keys in the executions would still be non-trivially related. This happens especially if keys are used in multiple sessions. Another problem is that some protocols may derive keys early, before applying signatures, e.g., such as for handshake encryption as well as in the post-handshake authentication mechanism in TLS 1.3 [36].

It therefore comes as no surprise that the PRF-ODH assumption has been used in different protocols for the security analysis, including the analysis of the TLS 1.2 [13] ephemeral and static Diffie–Hellman handshake modes [8,23,29], the TLS 1.3 [36] Diffie–Hellman-based and resumption handshake candidates [14–16] as well as 0-RTT handshake candidates [18], and a 0-RTT extension of the extended access control (EAC) protocol [10], for the original EAC protocol listed, for example, in Document 9303 of the International Civil Aviation Organization [22]. Notably, these scientific works use different versions of the PRF-ODH assumption, due to the different usages of the key shares g^u, g^v. These key shares can be ephemeral (for a single session), semi-static (for a small number of sessions), or static (for multiple sessions). Therefore, the man-in-the middle adversary may ask to see no related key for either key share, a single related key, or multiple related keys. For instance, while Jager et al. [23] required only security against a single query for one of the two key shares, Krawczyk et al. [29] modify the original PRF-ODH assumption because they require security against multiple oracle queries against this key share. In [18] an extra query to the other key share has been added, and [10] require multiple queries to both key shares.

1.2 Evaluating the PRF-ODH Assumptions

Consequently, and to capture all of the above assumptions simultaneously, we generally speak of the lrPRF-ODH assumption, allowing the adversary no ($\mathsf{l}, \mathsf{r} = \mathsf{n}$), a single ($\mathsf{l}, \mathsf{r} = \mathsf{s}$), or multiple ($\mathsf{l}, \mathsf{r} = \mathsf{m}$) related key queries, for the "left" key g^u or the "right" key g^v. Such queries are handled by oracles ODH_u and ODH_v, returning the corresponding pseudorandom function value. This results in nine variants, for each combination $\mathsf{l}, \mathsf{r} \in \{\mathsf{n}, \mathsf{s}, \mathsf{m}\}$. We also discuss some more fine-grained distinctions, e.g., if the adversary learns both keys g^u, g^v before choosing the input $x^\star$ for the challenge value $\mathsf{PRF}(g^{uv}, x^\star)$, or if $x^\star$ can only depend on g^u.

To evaluate the strengths of the different types of lrPRF-ODH assumptions one can ask how the variants relate to each other. Another important aspect is the question whether, and if so, to which (well investigated) Diffie–Hellman problem it possibly relates to, e.g., the computational Diffie–Hellman (CDH), the decisional Diffie–Hellman (DDH), the strong Diffie–Hellman (StDH), or the even more general Gap-Diffie–Hellman (GapDH) problem. While the answer to this question may rely on the random oracle model, the final issue would be to check if (any version of) the assumption can be instantiated in the standard model.

Especially the question whether the PRF-ODH assumption (or which variant) can be instantiated in the standard model is of utmost interest. Some of the aforementioned works refer to the(ir) PRF-ODH assumption as a standard-model assumption, since there is no immediate reference to a random oracle. This would not only apply to the schemes analyzed with respect to the PRF-ODH assumption, but potentially also to other works where the Gap-DH or related assumptions in the random oracle have been used for the analysis, yet where the PRF-ODH assumption is a promising alternative for carrying out a proof. Examples include the QUIC protocol [17,32] and OPTLS [30] which forms the base for TLS 1.3.

1.3 Our Results

Figure 2 gives an overview over our results. We explain the details next.

Instantiations. Our first contribution is to discuss instantiation possibilities of the PRF-ODH variants. We stress that some of these results mainly confirm the expectation: the nnPRF-ODH assumption where no oracle queries are allowed can be based upon the decisional Diffie–Hellman assumption DDH, and the one-sided

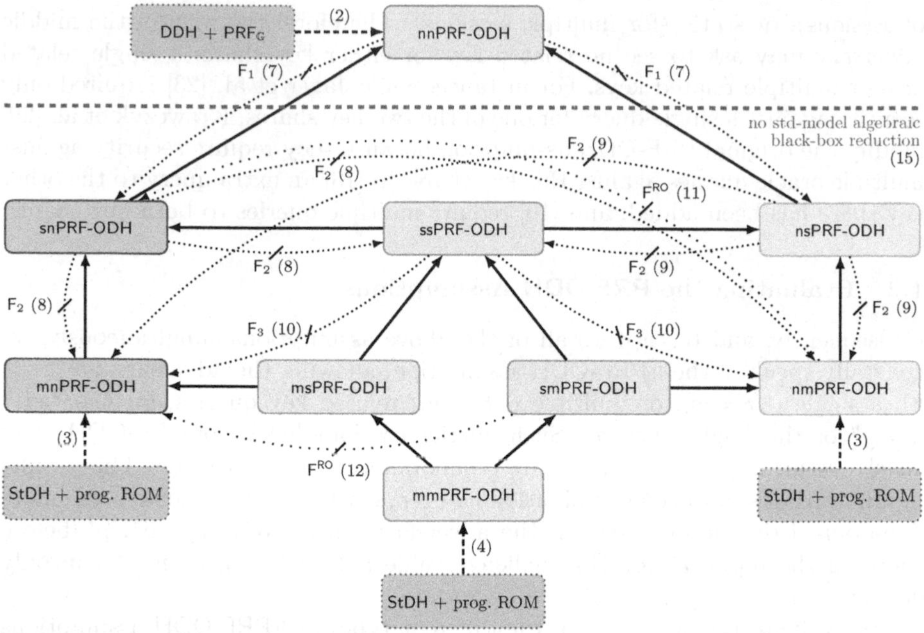

Fig. 2. Relations between the different PRF-ODH variants (in solid-line rounded rectangles) from Definition 1 and other assumptions (in dotted-line rounded rectangles). Solid arrows indicate the trivial implications between PRF-ODH variants, dashed arrows indicate implications we establish. Struck-out, densely dotted arrows indicate separations in the standard model via the indicated function $\mathsf{F}_n \in \mathcal{F}$ (cf. Definition 5). Struck-out, sparsely dotted arrows indicated separations in the random-oracle model. The dashed horizontal line demarcates the boundary below which our impossibility result for standard-model algebraic black-box reductions from Section 5 holds. Numbers in parentheses indicate the respective propositions and theorems.

assumptions mnPRF-ODH and nmPRF-ODH where the adversary has (multiple) access to either oracle ODH_u or ODH_v can be based on the strong Diffie–Hellman assumption in the random oracle model. The strong DH assumption (StDH) demands that the adversary solves the computational problem of computing g^{uv} from g^u, g^v, but having access to a decisional oracle $\mathsf{DDH}(g^u, \cdot, \cdot)$ checking for DH tuples. Such checks are necessary to provide consistency when simulating the random oracle through lazy sampling, i.e., in the case that random values are only sampled on their first explicit usage. The proofs for mnPRF-ODH and nmPRF-ODH appear already implicitly in previous work about key exchange, e.g., [12,17,26,30–32,37], but where the reduction to the StDH problem in the random oracle model has been carried out by dragging along all the steps of the key exchange protocols.

Our final instantiation result for the strongest notion mmPRF-ODH holds in the random oracle model under the strong DH (StDH) assumption. Surprisingly, the proof is less straightforward than one would expect, since the availability of both oracles ODH_u and ODH_v imposes the need for further consistency checks between cross-over calls for the two oracles in the simulation. We show that such consistency checks can indeed be implemented assuming StDH, but causing a square-root loss in the security reduction to StDH. This loss is due to the fact that in an intermediate step we go through the square-DH problem SqDH (given g, g^v compute g^{v^2}) to which CDH reduces by making two calls to the square-DH problem adversary (see, e.g., [24]), effectively squaring the success probability.

The instantiations are shown through the boxes with dotted surrounding lines in Fig. 2. We also discuss briefly the relationship to related-key security for pseudorandom functions, where the adversary can ask to see values for transformed keys $\phi(K)$. While similar in spirit at first glance, it seems to us that the notions differ in technical details which makes it hard to relate them.

Relations. The instantiation results give a sort of general method to achieve any PRF-ODH notion, leaving open the possibility that one notion may be actually easier to achieve. This is even more relevant in light of the fact that previous works used different notions. In order to support a better comparison between the various notions we relate them in terms of strength of the assumption. Some of these relationships, especially implications, are easy to establish. For example, since the adversary in the mmPRF-ODH game can always forgo using its ODH_v oracle, this immediately implies mnPRF-ODH security. All implications are marked by solid arrows in Fig. 2.

As for separations we are able to rule out a number of implications unconditionally. By this we mean that we only make the minimal assumption that a secure instantiation exists, and then build one still satisfying this notion but not the stronger one. These separations are displayed in Fig. 2 through dotted arrows.

We are also able to separate further notions conditionally, using random oracles and a plausible number-theoretic assumption. Namely, under these assumptions, the notion of snPRF-ODH (with a single call to ODH_u) is strictly stronger than the nmPRF-ODH notion where the adversary can ask the ODH_v oracle multiple times but does not get access to the ODH_u oracle. With a similar strategy we can also separate mnPRF-ODH with multiple ODH_u queries from smPRF-ODH, where the adversary can now make one extra call to ODH_u on top of the ODH_v queries.

The conditional separations are not symmetric in the sense that they apply to the other oracle as well. The reason is that these results exploit that the adversary receives g^u before g^v, such that the converse does not simply follow. Besides these opposite cases there are also some other cases where we could not provide a separation, e.g., from mmPRF-ODH to msPRF-ODH. We give more insights within.

Impossibility Result. The third important contribution is our impossibility result. We show that proving security of even the mild snPRF-ODH or nsPRF-ODH notions based on general cryptographic problems is hard. Besides the common assumption that the reduction uses the adversary only as a black box, we also assume that the reduction is algebraic. This means that whenever the reduction passes a group element A to the outside, it knows a representation $(\alpha_1, \alpha_2, \dots)$ such that $A = \prod g_i^{\alpha_i}$ for the reduction's input values $g_1, g_2, \dots$. This notion of algebraic reductions has been used in other separation works before, e.g., [9,20,35]. Unlike generic reductions, algebraic reductions can take advantage of the representation of group elements.

In detail, we then show via a meta-reduction technique [9,21,35], that one cannot prove security of the snPRF-ODH or nsPRF-ODH assumption via algebraic black-box reductions to a class of cryptographic problems. The problems we rule out are quite general, saying that the adversary receives some input, can interact multiple times with a challenger in an arbitrary way, and should then provide a solution. We remark that we also need to augment this problem by a Diffie–Hellman problem in order to give a reference point for the algebraicity of the reduction. Our result also requires that the decisional square-DH problem is hard, i.e., that g, g^v, g^{v^2} is indistinguishable from g, g^v, g^z for random v, z.[1]

In a sense, our negative result, displayed by the dashed horizontal line on top in Fig. 2, is optimal in terms of the relation of PRF-ODH assumptions, as it rules out exactly the notions "one above" the nnPRF-ODH notion with a standard model instantiation. We still note that the restrictions on the reduction, and the additional assumption, may allow to bypass our result. This also means that our implications and separations between the different notions, established earlier, are not moot.

Implications for Practical Key Derivation Functions. Since the PRF-ODH assumptions have been used in connection with applied protocols like TLS, we finally address the question which security guarantees we get for practical key derivation functions used in such protocols. We are especially interested in HMAC [25] on which the key derivation function HKDF [27,28] is based upon. Our instantiation results in the random oracle so far treat the key derivation function as a monolithic random oracle, whereas key derivation functions like HMAC have an iterative structure. At the same time, our impossibility result tells us that giving a standard-model proof for HMAC, based on say collision-resistance of the compression function, may be elusive. We thus make the assumption that the compression function is a random oracle.

We show that HMAC provides the strong notion of mmPRF-ODH security, assuming StDH and that the compression function is a random oracle. We note that Coron et al. [11] show that a variant of HMAC is indifferentiable from a random oracle, and Krawczyk [27] briefly remarks that the result would carry over to the actual HMAC construction. However, in HKDF the HMAC function is applied in a special mode in which the key part is hashed first, and it is therefore unclear if our result for the monolithic random oracle immediately applies. But based on the techniques used in the instantiation part we can give a direct proof of the security of (the general mode of) HMAC.

---

1 While the computational version of the square-DH problem is known to be equivalent to the CDH problem, it is unclear if the decisional version follows from DDH.

2 PRF-ODH Definition

Different variants of the new PRF oracle-Diffie–Hellman (PRF-ODH) assumption have been introduced and used in the literature in the context of key exchange protocols. In this section we first provide a generic PRF-ODH assumption definition capturing all different flavors and discuss its relation to previous occurrences [10,15,16,18,23,29].

Definition 1 (Generic PRF-ODH assumption). *Let $\mathbb{G}$ be a cyclic group of order q with generator g. Let $\mathsf{PRF}\colon \mathbb{G} \times \{0,1\}^* \to \{0,1\}^\lambda$ be a pseudorandom function that takes a key $K \in \mathbb{G}$ and a label $x \in \{0,1\}^*$ as input and outputs a value $y \in \{0,1\}^\lambda$, i.e., $y \leftarrow \mathsf{PRF}(K, x)$.*

We define a generic security notion lrPRF-ODH which is parameterized by $\mathsf{l}, \mathsf{r} \in \{\mathsf{n}, \mathsf{s}, \mathsf{m}\}$ indicating how often the adversary is allowed to query a certain "left" resp. "right" oracle (ODH_u resp. ODH_v) where n indicates that no query is allowed, s that a single query is allowed, and m that multiple (polynomially many) queries are allowed to the respective side. Consider the following security game $\mathsf{Game}^{\mathsf{lrPRF\text{-}ODH}}_{\mathsf{PRF},\mathcal{A}}$ between a challenger $\mathcal{C}$ and a probabilistic polynomial-time (PPT) adversary $\mathcal{A}$.

1. *The challenger $\mathcal{C}$ samples $u \xleftarrow{\$} \mathbb{Z}_q$ and provides $\mathbb{G}, g$, and g^u to the adversary $\mathcal{A}$.*
2. *If $\mathsf{l} = \mathsf{m}$, $\mathcal{A}$ can issue arbitrarily many queries to the following oracle ODH_u.*
   ODH_u **oracle.** *On a query of the form (S, x), the challenger first checks if $S \notin \mathbb{G}$ and returns $\perp$ if this is the case. Otherwise, it computes $y \leftarrow \mathsf{PRF}(S^u, x)$ and returns y.*
3. *Eventually, $\mathcal{A}$ issues a challenge query $x^\star$. On this query, $\mathcal{C}$ samples $v \xleftarrow{\$} \mathbb{Z}_q$ and a bit $b \xleftarrow{\$} \{0,1\}$ uniformly at random. It then computes $y_0^\star = \mathsf{PRF}(g^{uv}, x^\star)$ and samples $y_1^\star \xleftarrow{\$} \{0,1\}^\lambda$ uniformly random. The challenger returns $(g^v, y_b^\star)$ to $\mathcal{A}$.*
4. *Next, $\mathcal{A}$ may issue (arbitrarily interleaved) queries to the following oracles ODH_u and ODH_v (depending on l and r).*
   ODH_u **oracle.** *The adversary $\mathcal{A}$ may ask no ($\mathsf{l} = \mathsf{n}$), a single ($\mathsf{l} = \mathsf{s}$), or arbitrarily many ($\mathsf{l} = \mathsf{m}$) queries to this oracle. On a query of the form (S, x), the challenger first checks if $S \notin \mathbb{G}$ or $(S, x) = (g^v, x^\star)$ and returns $\perp$ if this is the case. Otherwise, it computes $y \leftarrow \mathsf{PRF}(S^u, x)$ and returns y.*
   ODH_v **oracle.** *The adversary $\mathcal{A}$ may ask no ($\mathsf{r} = \mathsf{n}$), a single ($\mathsf{r} = \mathsf{s}$), or arbitrarily many ($\mathsf{r} = \mathsf{m}$) queries to this oracle. On a query of the form (T, x), the challenger first checks if $T \notin \mathbb{G}$ or $(T, x) = (g^u, x^\star)$ and returns $\perp$ if this is the case. Otherwise, it computes $y \leftarrow \mathsf{PRF}(T^v, x)$ and returns y.*
5. *At some point, $\mathcal{A}$ stops and outputs a guess $b' \in \{0,1\}$.*

We say that the adversary wins the lrPRF-ODH game if $b' = b$ and define the advantage function

$$\mathsf{Adv}^{\mathsf{lrPRF\text{-}ODH}}_{\mathsf{PRF},\mathcal{A}}(\lambda) := 2 \cdot \left(\Pr[b' = b] - \frac{1}{2}\right)$$

and, assuming a sequence of groups in dependency of the security parameter, we say that a pseudorandom function PRF *with keys from* $(\mathbb{G}_\lambda)_\lambda$ *provides* $\mathsf{lrPRF\text{-}ODH}$ *security (for* $\mathsf{l}, \mathsf{r} \in \{\mathsf{n}, \mathsf{s}, \mathsf{m}\}$*) if for any* $\mathcal{A}$ *the advantage* $\mathsf{Adv}^{\mathsf{lrPRF\text{-}ODH}}_{\mathsf{PRF},\mathcal{A}}(\lambda)$ *is negligible in the security parameter* λ.

In the following, if clear from the context, we will omit the group $\mathbb{G}$ and sometimes its generator g as explicit inputs to the adversary.

Relations to Previous PRF-ODH *Assumptions.* The above generic and parameterized lrPRF-ODH definition captures different variants of the PRF-ODH assumption present in the literature. The PRF-ODH formulation put forward by Jager et al. [23] is captured by ours in case the parameters are set to $\mathsf{l} = \mathsf{s}$ and $\mathsf{r} = \mathsf{n}$ meaning that only the "left" oracle (querying the DH share g^u) can be queried once. Note that Step 2 is only required if $\mathsf{l} = \mathsf{m}$, capturing that Jager et al. first request their challenge before issuing an oracle query. The same variant, snPRF-ODH, was also used by Dowling et al. [16]. Krawczyk et al. [29] modified the PRF-ODH formulation of Jager et al. since they require security against multiple ("left") oracle queries against the DH key share. Thus, their variant is captured by ours through setting the parameters to $\mathsf{l} = \mathsf{m}$ and $\mathsf{r} = \mathsf{n}$, and thus making use of Step 2. Recent works further introduced an additional query to the other DH key share, due to the fact that the keys are static or semi-static, respectively. In more detail, Fischlin and Günther [18] require an extra single ("right") oracle query while still requesting polynomial many queries to the "left" oracle. This is captured by our definition through setting the parameters to $\mathsf{l} = \mathsf{m}$ and $\mathsf{r} = \mathsf{s}$. Lastly, Brendel and Fischlin [10] require to query both key shares multiple times, which our definition captures as well by choosing the parameters as $\mathsf{l} = \mathsf{m}$ and $\mathsf{r} = \mathsf{m}$.

Design Options. The above generic definition can be refined further, e.g., by enabling the challenger to provide the value g^v to the adversary at the outset in Step 1. This variant was used in the analysis of earlier TLS 1.3 draft handshakes by Dowling et al. [15]. Such change would be accompanied by giving the adversary in Step 2 also access to the ODH_v oracle in case $\mathsf{r} = \mathsf{m}$. Another reasonable change could encompass enabling the adversary in multi-query variants (i.e., $\mathsf{l} = \mathsf{m}$ or $\mathsf{r} = \mathsf{m}$) to also issue *multiple* challenge queries in Step 3, for the same value g^v or even freshly chosen values g^{v_i} in each call. However, one can show via a standard hybrid argument that both notions (i.e., single challenge query and multiple challenge query) are polynomially equivalent.

In this work, we focus on the common structure of previously studied PRF-ODH notions [10,16,18,23,29] which are captured by our generic definition above. Additionally, in Sect. 4 we briefly discuss the impact of such changes regarding the analysis of the relations between the different variants of the assumption.

3 Instantiating the PRF-ODH Assumption

We next turn to the question how to instantiate the PRF-ODH assumption. Concretely, we provide instantiations of the two notions that mark both ends of the strength spectrum of the PRF-ODH variants. First, we show that the weakest PRF-ODH variant, nnPRF-ODH, can be instantiated in the standard model under well-established assumptions, namely the Decisional Diffie–Hellman (DDH) assumption and (ordinary) PRF security in a group $\mathbb{G}$. Second, we establish that, in the (programmable) random oracle model, both the strongest *one-sided* PRF-ODH variants, mnPRF-ODH and nmPRF-ODH, as well as the most general mmPRF-ODH assumption can be instantiated from the strong Diffie–Hellman assumption (StDH). We define all these number-theoretic assumptions when discussing the security notions. Furthermore, we discuss the relation of the PRF-ODH notion to that of PRF security under related-key attacks.

3.1 Standard-Model Instantiation of nnPRF-ODH

We begin with instantiating the nnPRF-ODH assumption in the standard model. For this we speak of a function $\mathsf{F}\colon \mathbb{G} \times \{0,1\}^* \to \{0,1\}^\lambda$ to be $\mathsf{PRF}_\mathbb{G}$-secure if no efficient adversary which, upon querying x, gets to see either the function value $\mathsf{F}(K,x)$ for a then chosen random key $K \xleftarrow{\$} \mathbb{G}$, or a random value, can distinguish the two cases. As in the other games before, the choice of answering genuinely or randomly is made at random, and we let $\mathsf{Adv}_{\mathsf{F},\mathcal{A}}^{\mathsf{PRF}_\mathbb{G}}$ denote the advantage of algorithm $\mathcal{A}$. Here, we normalize again the advantage by subtracting the guessing probability of $\frac{1}{2}$ and multiplying the result by a factor of 2. Note that the difference to the nnPRF-ODH assumption is that the adversary does not get to see a pair g^u, g^v from which the key is generated.

The underlying DDH assumption says that one cannot efficiently distinguish tuples (g, g^u, g^v, g^{uv}) from tuples (g, g^u, g^v, g^z) for random $u, v, z \in \mathbb{Z}_q$. More formally, for an adversary $\mathcal{B}$ we define $\mathsf{Adv}_{\mathbb{G},\mathcal{B}}^{\mathsf{DDH}}$ to be the probability of $\mathcal{B}$ predicting a random bit b, when given g, g^u, g^v, g^{uv} for $b = 0$ and g, g^u, g^v, g^z for $b = 1$, with the usual normalization as above. Alternatively, one may define $\mathsf{Adv}_{\mathbb{G},\mathcal{B}}^{\mathsf{DDH}}$ to be the advantage in the nnPRF-ODH game for the function $\mathsf{F}(K,x) = K$.

Theorem 2 (DDH + $\mathsf{PRF}_\mathbb{G} \implies$ nnPRF-ODH). *If a function* $\mathsf{F}\colon \mathbb{G}\times\{0,1\}^* \to \{0,1\}^\lambda$ *is* $\mathsf{PRF}_\mathbb{G}$*-secure and the* DDH *assumption holds in* $\mathbb{G}$*, then* F *is also* nnPRF-ODH*-secure. More precisely, for any efficient adversary* $\mathcal{A}$ *against the* nnPRF-ODH *security of* F*, there exist efficient algorithms* $\mathcal{B}_1$ *and* $\mathcal{B}_2$ *such that*

$$\mathsf{Adv}_{\mathsf{F},\mathcal{A}}^{\mathsf{nnPRF\text{-}ODH}} \le 2 \cdot \mathsf{Adv}_{\mathbb{G},\mathcal{B}_1}^{\mathsf{DDH}} + 2 \cdot \mathsf{Adv}_{\mathsf{F},\mathcal{B}_2}^{\mathsf{PRF}_\mathbb{G}}.$$

We note that the factor 2 is the common loss due to the game-hopping technique, when switching from indistinguishability for two fixed games to choosing one of the games at random. The proof appears in the full version of this paper.

3.2 Random-Oracle Instantiation of mnPRF-ODH and nmPRF-ODH

Abdalla et al. [1] proved that the oracle DH assumption ODH is implied by the strong Diffie–Hellman assumption in the random oracle model. Here, we show that our strongest *one-sided* PRF-ODH variants, mnPRF-ODH and nmPRF-ODH, can be instantiated under the strong Diffie–Hellman assumption StDH. The assumption says that, given g, g^u, g^v and access to a decisional DH oracle for fixed value g^u, i.e., $\mathsf{DDH}(g^u, \cdot, \cdot)$, it is infeasible to compute g^{uv}. Observe that this assumption is implied by the GapDH assumption, where the adversary can choose the first group element freely, too. Let $\mathsf{Adv}^{\mathsf{StDH}}_{\mathbb{G},\mathcal{B}}$ denote the probability of algorithm $\mathcal{B}^{\mathsf{DDH}(g^u,\cdot,\cdot)}(g, g^u, g^v)$ outputting g^{uv}.

Theorem 3. *In the random oracle model,* StDH *implies* mnPRF-ODH *security and* nmPRF-ODH *security of* $\mathsf{F}(K, x) = \mathsf{RO}(K, x)$ *for random oracle* RO. *More precisely, for any efficient adversary* $\mathcal{A}$ *against the* mnPRF-ODH *or* nmPRF-ODH *security of* F, *there exists an efficient algorithms* $\mathcal{B}$ *such that*

$$\mathsf{Adv}^{\mathsf{mnPRF\text{-}ODH}}_{\mathsf{F},\mathcal{A}} \leq \mathsf{Adv}^{\mathsf{StDH}}_{\mathbb{G},\mathcal{B}} \quad \text{and} \quad \mathsf{Adv}^{\mathsf{nmPRF\text{-}ODH}}_{\mathsf{F},\mathcal{A}} \leq \mathsf{Adv}^{\mathsf{StDH}}_{\mathbb{G},\mathcal{B}}.$$

The proof appears in the full version. It follows previous proofs in the context of key exchange protocols. The crucial aspect here is that one programs the random oracle for ODH_u queries (S, x) by returning random values. This implicitly defines the random oracle value for (unknown) key S^u and x, but such that one later needs to check for consistency if the adversary makes a random oracle query about key $K = S^u$ and x and one simulates the answer. This verification can be performed via the oracle $\mathsf{DDH}(g^u, \cdot, \cdot)$ by checking if $\mathsf{DDH}(g^u, S, K) = 1$ for any previous ODH_u query (S, x). Vice versa, one also needs to check for ODH_u queries (S, x) if the random oracle value for (S^u, x) has already been set. This can be done again via the $\mathsf{DDH}(g^u, \cdot, \cdot)$ oracle.

If a consistent simulation is enforced then the only possibility for the adversary to distinguish a real or random challenge $y^\star$ is to ask the random oracle about the DH key $K = g^{uv}$ at some point. This is again easy to detect by checking if $\mathsf{DDH}(g^u, g^v, K) = 1$ for any such query K, in which case we solve the StDH problem.

3.3 Random-Oracle Instantiation of mmPRF-ODH

We next look at the case that the adversary can make queries to both oracles, ODH_u and ODH_v. Interestingly, this does not follow straightforwardly from the StDH assumption as above. The reason is that, there, we have used the DDH-oracle with fixed element g^u to check for consistency of ODH_u queries with random oracle queries. In the most general mmPRF-ODH case, however, we would also need to check consistency across ODH_u and ODH_v queries. In particular, a simulator would need to be able to check for queries (S, x) to ODH_u and (T, x) to ODH_v if they result in the same key $S^u = K = T^v$, but the simulator is given only S, T, g, g^u, and g^v. Such a test cannot be immediately performed with the $\mathsf{DDH}(g^u, \cdot, \cdot)$ oracle as in the StDH case, and not even with the more liberal $\mathsf{DDH}(\cdot, \cdot, \cdot)$ oracle as in the GapDH case.

Suppose that we take the StDH problem and augment it by another oracle which allows to check for "claws" S, T with $S^u = T^v$. Call this the claw-verifying oracle Claw and the problem the ClawStDH problem. For pairing-friendly groups

$\mathbb{G}$ we get this oracle for free via the bilinear map e as $\mathsf{Claw}(S,T) = [e(g^u, S) = e(g^v, T)?]$. Next, we show that for general groups the claw-verifying oracle can be implemented in the StDH game, too, but at the cost of a loose security reduction to StDH.

The idea of representing the oracle Claw is as follows. Suppose that, in addition to g, g^u and g^v we would also receive the value $g^{u/v}$ (where we assume here and in the following that $v \neq 0$, since the case $v = 0$ is trivial to deal with). Then we can run the check for claws via the stronger DDH oracle by calling $\mathsf{DDH}(g^{u/v}, S, T)$, checking that $S^{u/v} = T$ and therefore $S^u = T^v$. The question remains if the computational problem of computing g^{uv} given $g^{u/v}$ (in the presence of a DDH oracle) becomes significantly easier, and if we can relax the requirement to a $\mathsf{DDH}(g^u, \cdot, \cdot)$ oracle. Switching to the square DH problem in an intermediate step, we show that this is not the case, although the intermediate step causes a loose security relationship.

Assume that we have an algorithm $\mathcal{A}$ which (given oracle access to $\mathsf{DDH}(g^u, \cdot, \cdot)$, $\mathsf{DDH}(g^v, \cdot, \cdot)$, and the claw-verifying oracle Claw) on input (g, g^u, g^v) is able to compute g^{uv}. Then we show that we can use this algorithm to build an algorithm $\mathcal{B}$ for the square-DH problem (given g, g^v compute g^{v^2}) relative to a $\mathsf{DDH}(g^v, \cdot, \cdot)$ oracle. For this, algorithm $\mathcal{B}$ for input g, g^v picks $r \xleftarrow{\$} \mathbb{Z}_q$ and sets $g^u = (g^v)^r$. With this choice, $g^{u/v} = g^r$ can be easily computed with the knowledge of r, allowing to implement the claw-verifying oracle for free. Similarly, we have $\mathsf{DDH}(g^u, \cdot, \cdot) = \mathsf{DDH}(g^v, (\cdot)^r, \cdot)$, giving us the "mirrored" oracle for free. Algorithm $\mathcal{B}$ now runs $\mathcal{A}$ on input (g, g^u, g^v) and answers all oracle requests of $\mathcal{A}$ during the computation with the help of its $\mathsf{DDH}(g^v, \cdot, \cdot)$ oracle. Suppose that the adversary $\mathcal{A}$ eventually outputs K. Then, $\mathcal{B}$ returns $K^{1/r}$ which equals g^{v^2} for a correct answer $K = g^{uv} = g^{rv^2}$ of $\mathcal{A}$.

Next, we show that from a solver for the square-DH problem (with $\mathsf{DDH}(g^v, \cdot, \cdot)$ oracle) we can build a solver for the StDH problem. Going from the square-DH problem to the CDH problem is already known. Interestingly, though, the common strategies in the literature [2,19,33] require three calls to the square-DH solver, basically to compute the square $g^{(u+v)^2} = g^{u^2+2uv+v^2}$ and then to divide out g^{u^2} and g^{v^2}. Fortunately, two calls are sufficient, see for example [24], yielding a tighter security bound.

So suppose we have a square-DH algorithm (with oracle $\mathsf{DDH}(g^v, \cdot, \cdot)$) then we call this algorithm once on g, g^{u+v} and once on $g, g^{r(u-v)}$ for randomizer $r \xleftarrow{\$} \mathbb{Z}_q$. Since both inputs are random and independent, we get two valid answers $g^{u^2+2uv+v^2}$ and $g^{r^2(u^2-2uv+v^2)}$ with the product of the square-DH algorithm's success probability. Note that these two executions at most double the number of oracle queries to the DDH oracle. Dividing out the exponent r^2 from the second term by raising it to the power $1/r^2$, and then dividing the two group elements we obtain g^{4uv} from which we can easily compute g^{uv}.

Overall, we can show that solving the problem in presence of the decisional oracles for g^u and g^v, and an additional claw-verifying oracle, is implied by the StDH assumption, albeit with a security loss. More precisely, for any efficient adversary $\mathcal{A}$ against ClawStDH we get an efficient adversary $\mathcal{B}$ (making at most twice as many calls to its StDH oracle as $\mathcal{A}$) such that

$$\mathsf{Adv}^{\mathsf{ClawStDH}}_{\mathbb{G},\mathcal{A}} \leq \sqrt{\mathsf{Adv}^{\mathsf{StDH}}_{\mathbb{G},\mathcal{B}}}.$$

We can now give our security proof for mmPRF-ODH, implying also security of msPRF-ODH and smPRF-ODH, of course:

Theorem 4. *In the random oracle model,* ClawStDH *(resp.* StDH*) implies* mmPRF-ODH *security of* $\mathsf{F}(K,x) = \mathsf{RO}(K,x)$ *for random oracle* RO. *More precisely, for any efficient adversary* $\mathcal{A}$ *against the* mmPRF-ODH *security of* F, *there exist efficient algorithms* $\mathcal{B}_1, \mathcal{B}_2$ *such that*

$$\mathsf{Adv}^{\mathsf{mmPRF\text{-}ODH}}_{\mathsf{F},\mathcal{A}} \leq \mathsf{Adv}^{\mathsf{ClawStDH}}_{\mathbb{G},\mathcal{B}_1} \leq \sqrt{\mathsf{Adv}^{\mathsf{StDH}}_{\mathbb{G},\mathcal{B}_2}}$$

The proof is almost identical to the one for mnPRF-ODH, only that we here simulate the other oracle ODH_v as the oracle ODH_u, and for each query to either of the oracles also check via the help of Claw consistency between ODH_u and ODH_v evaluations. This provides a sound simulation of the random oracle. It follows as before that the adversary $\mathcal{A}$ can only distinguish genuine $y^\star$ from random ones if it queries the random oracle about g^{uv} (in the sound simulation), in which case $\mathcal{B}_1$ finds this value in the list of queries.

3.4 On the Relation Between PRF-ODH and Security Against Related-Key Attacks

The PRF-ODH assumption demands the output of a PRF to be indistinguishable from random even when given access to PRF evaluations under a related (group-element) key, sharing (at least) one exponent of the challenge key. On a high level, this setting resembles the concept of *related-key attack (RKA) security* for pseudorandom functions as introduced by Bellare and Kohno [4]. This raises the question if the PRF-ODH assumption can be instantiated from RKA-secure PRFs (or vice versa).

Related-key attack security of a PRF $f\colon \mathcal{K}\times\mathcal{D}\to\mathcal{R}$ with respect to a set Φ of related-key-deriving (RKD) functions is defined as the indistinguishability of two oracles $F_{(\cdot,K)}(\cdot)$ and $G_{(\cdot,K)}(\cdot)$ for a randomly chosen key $K \xleftarrow{\$} \mathcal{K}$. The distinguishing adversary $\mathcal{A}$ may query the oracles on inputs $(\phi, x) \in \Phi\times\mathcal{D}$ on which the oracles respond as $F_{(\phi,K)}(x) := f(\phi(K), x)$ and $G_{(\phi,K)}(x) := g(\phi(K), x)$ for a function g drawn uniformly at random from the set $\mathcal{FF}(\mathcal{K},\mathcal{D},\mathcal{R})$ of all functions $\mathcal{K}\times\mathcal{D}\to\mathcal{R}$. Formally, the advantage of $\mathcal{A}$ against the RKA-PRF security of f with respect to set Φ is defined as

$$\begin{aligned}\mathsf{Adv}^{\mathsf{RKA\text{-}PRF},\Phi}_{f,\mathcal{A}} := \; & \Pr\left[\mathcal{A}^{F_{(\cdot,K)}(\cdot)} = 1 \mid K \xleftarrow{\$} \mathcal{K}\right] \\ & - \Pr\left[\mathcal{A}^{G_{(\cdot,K)}(\cdot)} = 1 \mid K \xleftarrow{\$} \mathcal{K}, g \xleftarrow{\$} \mathcal{FF}(\mathcal{K},\mathcal{D},\mathcal{R})\right].\end{aligned}$$

Intuitively, one should now be able to relate RKA-PRF security to PRF-ODH security by considering two correlated sets of RKD functions corresponding to the PRF-ODH oracles ODH_u and ODH_v with respect to a group $\mathbb{G}$ with generator g and two exponents $u, v \in \mathbb{Z}_q$:

$$\Phi_{\mathsf{ODH}_u} := \{\phi_{\mathsf{ODH}_u,S} \mid S \in \mathbb{G} \setminus \{g^v\}\} \qquad \text{where } \phi_{\mathsf{ODH}_u,S}(K) := (K^{1/v})^{\log_g(S)},$$
$$\Phi_{\mathsf{ODH}_v} := \{\phi_{\mathsf{ODH}_v,T} \mid T \in \mathbb{G} \setminus \{g^u\}\} \qquad \text{where } \phi_{\mathsf{ODH}_v,T}(K) := (K^{1/u})^{\log_g(T)}.$$

Insurmountable hurdles however seem to remain when trying to relate PRF-ODH notions and RKA-PRF security (for according sets Φ) via implications. In the one direction, the adversary in the PRF-ODH setting is provided with the DH shares g^u and g^v forming the (challenge) PRF key while such side information on the key is not given in the RKA-PRF setting. Hence, in a reduction of PRF-ODH security to some RKA-PRF notion, even for an appropriate RKD function set a simulation always lacks means to provide the PRF-ODH adversary with these shares. In the other direction, the RKA-PRF challenge can be issued on any related key $\phi(K)$ for an admissible RKD function ϕ while the PRF-ODH challenge is, for the case of the real PRF response, always computed on the key g^{uv}. A reduction would hence need to map the RKA-PRF challenge for an arbitrary, related key onto the fixed PRF-ODH challenge key.

Though on a high level capturing a relatively similar idea, the relation between PRF-ODH and RKA-PRF security hence remains an open question.

4 PRF-ODH Relations

In this section we study the relations of different PRF-ODH variants spanned by our generic Definition 1. The relationships are also illustrated in Fig. 2.

Let us start with observing the trivial implications (indicated by solid arrows in Fig. 2) which are induced by restricting the adversary's capabilities in our definition. That is, by restricting the access to one of the oracles ODH_u and ODH_v (from multiple queries to a single query or from a single query to no query) for a notion from Definition 1, we obtain a trivially weaker variant. The more interesting question is which of these implications are strict, i.e., for which of two PRF-ODH variant pairs one notion is *strictly* stronger than the other. For a majority of these cases we can give separations which only require the assumption that the underlying primitive exists at all, for some separations we rely on the random oracle model (and a plausible number-theoretic assumption).

4.1 Separations in the Standard Model

For our standard model separations we introduce the following family of functions $\mathcal{F}$.

Definition 5 (Separating function family $\mathcal{F}$). *Let* $\mathsf{G}\colon \mathbb{G}\times\{0,1\}^* \to \{0,1\}^\lambda$. *We define the family of functions* $\mathcal{F} = \{\mathsf{F}_n\}_{n\in\mathbb{N}}$ *with* $\mathsf{F}_n\colon \mathbb{G} \times \{0,1\}^* \to \{0,1\}^\lambda$ *as follows:*

$$\mathsf{F}_n(K,x) := \begin{cases} \mathsf{G}(K,1) \oplus \ldots \oplus \mathsf{G}(K,n) & \text{if } x = 0 \\ \mathsf{G}(K,x) & \text{otherwise.} \end{cases}$$

As a warm-up, let us first consider the (in)security of functions $\mathsf{F}_n \in \mathcal{F}$ in the standard PRF setting. It is easy to see that no function $\mathsf{F}_n \in \mathcal{F}$ can satisfy the (regular) security notion for pseudorandom functions: for any function F_n, querying the PRF oracle on $x_0 = 0, \ldots, x_n = n$ yields responses $y_0, \ldots, y_n$ for which the combined XOR value $y = y_0 \oplus \ldots \oplus y_n$, in case the oracle computes the real function F_n, is always 0 whereas otherwise it is 0 only with probability $2^{-\lambda}$. However, in a restricted setting where the PRF adversary $\mathcal{A}$ is allowed to query the oracle only a limited number of times (at most n queries for function F_n), we can indeed establish the following, restricted PRF security for functions $\mathsf{F}_n \in \mathcal{F}$.

Proposition 6 ($\mathcal{F}$ is restricted-PRF-secure). *If G is an (ordinary) secure pseudorandom function, then each $\mathsf{F}_n \in \mathcal{F}$ from Definition 5 is an n-restricted secure pseudorandom function in the sense that it provides PRF security against any adversary that is allowed to query the PRF oracle at most n times.*

Proof (informal). Fix a function $\mathsf{F}_n \in \mathcal{F}$. First, we replace G in the definition of F_n by a truly random function G'. The introduced advantage difference for adversary $\mathcal{A}$ by this step can be bounded by the advantage of an adversary $\mathcal{B}$ against the PRF security of G, simulating the (restricted) PRF game for $\mathcal{A}$ using its own PRF oracle for G.

After this change, the output values of F_n on inputs $x > 1$ are independent random values and the output on $x = 0$ is the XOR of the outputs on $x = 1, \ldots, n$. In contrast, for a truly random function, the outputs on all inputs (incl. $x = 0$) are independent and random. However, any adversary $\mathcal{A}$ that is allowed to query the PRF oracle on at most n inputs cannot distinguish these two cases, bounding its success probability at this point by 0. □

Let us now turn to the more involved PRF-ODH setting. Equipped with the function family $\mathcal{F}$, we can establish separations between various PRF-ODH variants, as illustrated in Fig. 2. The key insight for these separations is similar to the one in the standard PRF setting: an adversary with a limited number of n queries (including the challenge query in the PRF-ODH setting) cannot distinguish (a challenge under) F_n from (a challenge under) a truly random function. As subsequent propositions establish, this allows us to separate the notion nnPRF-ODH (with only one challenge query) from snPRF-ODH and nsPRF-ODH (with two queries, the challenge and one to an ODH oracle) via function F_1. Furthermore, the notions snPRF-ODH and nsPRF-ODH (with two queries) are separated from mnPRF-ODH, ssPRF-ODH, and nmPRF-ODH (with three or polynomially many queries) via F_2. Finally, we establish that the notion ssPRF-ODH (three queries) can be separated from mnPRF-ODH and nmPRF-ODH (multiple queries) using function F_3. Note that functions $\mathsf{F}_n \in \mathcal{F}$ cannot provide a separation between two notions that both allow polynomially many queries (e.g., mnPRF-ODH and msPRF-ODH). To keep the propositions compact, the given separations constitute the minimal spanning set; recall that if a notion A implies another notion B, separating a notion C from B also separates C from A.

We begin with separating nnPRF-ODH from snPRF-ODH and nsPRF-ODH security.

Proposition 7 (nnPRF-ODH $\not\Rightarrow$ snPRF-ODH, nsPRF-ODH). *If* G *from Definition 5 is* nnPRF-ODH*-secure, then* $\mathsf{F}_1 \in \mathcal{F}$ *is* nnPRF-ODH*-secure, but neither* snPRF-ODH- *nor* snPRF-ODH*-secure. More precisely, for any efficient adversary* $\mathcal{A}$ *against the* nnPRF-ODH *security of* F_1*, there exists an efficient algorithm* $\mathcal{B}$ *such that*

$$\mathsf{Adv}^{\mathsf{nnPRF\text{-}ODH}}_{\mathsf{F}_1,\mathcal{A}} \leq \mathsf{Adv}^{\mathsf{nnPRF\text{-}ODH}}_{\mathsf{G},\mathcal{B}},$$

but there exist algorithms $\mathcal{A}_1$*,* $\mathcal{A}_2$ *with non-negligible advantage* $\mathsf{Adv}^{\mathsf{snPRF\text{-}ODH}}_{\mathsf{F}_1,\mathcal{A}_1} = \mathsf{Adv}^{\mathsf{nsPRF\text{-}ODH}}_{\mathsf{F}_1,\mathcal{A}_2} = 1 - 2^{-\lambda}$.

Proof. First, observe the following snPRF-ODH-adversary $\mathcal{A}_1$ and nsPRF-ODH-adversary $\mathcal{A}_2$ are successful (except with negligible probability). Both first challenge F_1 on $x^\star = 0$ (obtaining as $y^\star$ either $y_0^\star = \mathsf{G}(g^{uv}, 1)$ or $y_1^\star \xleftarrow{\$} \{0,1\}^\lambda$), then query $(g^v, 1)$ resp. $(g^u, 1)$ to their ODH_u resp. ODH_v oracle, obtaining a value $y = \mathsf{G}(g^{uv}, 1)$. They distinguish the challenge by outputting 0 if $y^\star = y$ and 1 otherwise and win except if coincidentally $y_1^\star = y$, which happens with probability $2^{-\lambda}$.

To see that F_1 is nnPRF-ODH-secure if G is, consider an algorithm $\mathcal{B}$ that simply relays its obtained value g^u to $\mathcal{A}$ and the challenge query of $\mathcal{A}$ to its challenger unmodified if $x^\star \neq 0$, but for $x^\star = 0$ asks its challenge query on 1. Forwarding the response and outputting the same bit b' as $\mathcal{A}$ outputs, $\mathcal{B}$ provides a correct simulation for $\mathcal{A}$ and, moreover, wins if $\mathcal{A}$ does. □

We continue with three further separations:

- snPRF-ODH from mnPRF-ODH, ssPRF-ODH, and nmPRF-ODH;
- nsPRF-ODH from mnPRF-ODH, ssPRF-ODH, and nmPRF-ODH; and
- ssPRF-ODH from mnPRF-ODH and nmPRF-ODH.

Due to space restrictions, we only state the respective propositions and defer the proofs to the full version. Note that the proofs follow the same underlying idea as the one of Proposition 7, namely that an adversary being allowed to query a PRF oracle only n times cannot distinguish F_n from a truly random function (given the internal function G satisfies pseudorandomness properties we specify).

Proposition 8 (snPRF-ODH $\not\Rightarrow$ mnPRF-ODH, ssPRF-ODH, nmPRF-ODH). *If* G *from Definition 5 is* mnPRF-ODH*-secure, then* $\mathsf{F}_2 \in \mathcal{F}$ *is* snPRF-ODH*-secure, but neither* mnPRF-ODH-*, nor* ssPRF-ODH-*, nor* nmPRF-ODH*-secure. More precisely, for any efficient adversary* $\mathcal{A}$ *against the* snPRF-ODH *security of* F_2*, there exist efficient algorithms* $\mathcal{B}_1, \ldots, \mathcal{B}_4$ *such that*

$$\begin{aligned}\mathsf{Adv}^{\mathsf{snPRF\text{-}ODH}}_{\mathsf{F}_2,\mathcal{A}} \leq\ & \mathsf{Adv}^{\mathsf{mnPRF\text{-}ODH}}_{\mathsf{G},\mathcal{B}_1} + 4 \cdot \mathsf{Adv}^{\mathsf{mnPRF\text{-}ODH}}_{\mathsf{G},\mathcal{B}_2} \\ & + 4 \cdot \mathsf{Adv}^{\mathsf{mnPRF\text{-}ODH}}_{\mathsf{G},\mathcal{B}_3} + \mathsf{Adv}^{\mathsf{mnPRF\text{-}ODH}}_{\mathsf{G},\mathcal{B}_4},\end{aligned}$$

but there exist algorithms $\mathcal{A}_1, \ldots, \mathcal{A}_3$ *with non-negligible advantage* $\mathsf{Adv}^{\mathsf{mnPRF\text{-}ODH}}_{\mathsf{F}_2,\mathcal{A}_1} = \mathsf{Adv}^{\mathsf{ssPRF\text{-}ODH}}_{\mathsf{F}_2,\mathcal{A}_2} = \mathsf{Adv}^{\mathsf{nmPRF\text{-}ODH}}_{\mathsf{F}_2,\mathcal{A}_3} = 1 - 2^{-\lambda}$.

Proposition 9 (nsPRF-ODH $\not\Rightarrow$ mnPRF-ODH, ssPRF-ODH, nmPRF-ODH). *If* G *from Definition 5 is* nmPRF-ODH*-secure, then* $\mathsf{F}_2 \in \mathcal{F}$ *is* nsPRF-ODH*-secure, but neither* mnPRF-ODH-*, nor* ssPRF-ODH-*, nor* nmPRF-ODH*-secure. More precisely, for any efficient adversary* $\mathcal{A}$ *against the* nsPRF-ODH *security of* F_2*, there exist efficient algorithms* $\mathcal{B}_1, \ldots, \mathcal{B}_4$ *such that*

$$\begin{aligned}\mathsf{Adv}^{\mathsf{nsPRF\text{-}ODH}}_{\mathsf{F}_2,\mathcal{A}} \leq\ & \mathsf{Adv}^{\mathsf{nmPRF\text{-}ODH}}_{\mathsf{G},\mathcal{B}_1} + 4 \cdot \mathsf{Adv}^{\mathsf{nmPRF\text{-}ODH}}_{\mathsf{G},\mathcal{B}_2} \\ & + 4 \cdot \mathsf{Adv}^{\mathsf{nmPRF\text{-}ODH}}_{\mathsf{G},\mathcal{B}_3} + \mathsf{Adv}^{\mathsf{nmPRF\text{-}ODH}}_{\mathsf{G},\mathcal{B}_4},\end{aligned}$$

but there exist algorithms $\mathcal{A}_1, \ldots, \mathcal{A}_3$ *with non-negligible advantage* $\mathsf{Adv}^{\mathsf{mnPRF\text{-}ODH}}_{\mathsf{F}_2,\mathcal{A}_1} = \mathsf{Adv}^{\mathsf{ssPRF\text{-}ODH}}_{\mathsf{F}_2,\mathcal{A}_2} = \mathsf{Adv}^{\mathsf{nmPRF\text{-}ODH}}_{\mathsf{F}_2,\mathcal{A}_3} = 1 - 2^{-\lambda}$.

Proposition 10 (ssPRF-ODH $\not\Rightarrow$ mnPRF-ODH, nmPRF-ODH). *If* G *from Definition 5 is* msPRF-ODH*-secure, then* $\mathsf{F}_3 \in \mathcal{F}$ *is* ssPRF-ODH*-secure, but neither* mnPRF-ODH- *nor* nmPRF-ODH*-secure. More precisely, for any efficient adversary* $\mathcal{A}$ *against the* ssPRF-ODH *security of* F_3*, there exist efficient algorithms* $\mathcal{B}_1, \ldots, \mathcal{B}_5$ *such that*

$$\begin{aligned}\mathsf{Adv}^{\mathsf{ssPRF\text{-}ODH}}_{\mathsf{F}_3,\mathcal{A}} \leq\ & \mathsf{Adv}^{\mathsf{msPRF\text{-}ODH}}_{\mathsf{G},\mathcal{B}_1} + 3 \cdot \mathsf{Adv}^{\mathsf{msPRF\text{-}ODH}}_{\mathsf{G},\mathcal{B}_2} + 3 \cdot \mathsf{Adv}^{\mathsf{msPRF\text{-}ODH}}_{\mathsf{G},\mathcal{B}_3} \\ & + 3 \cdot \mathsf{Adv}^{\mathsf{msPRF\text{-}ODH}}_{\mathsf{G},\mathcal{B}_4} + \mathsf{Adv}^{\mathsf{msPRF\text{-}ODH}}_{\mathsf{G},\mathcal{B}_5},\end{aligned}$$

but there exist algorithms $\mathcal{A}_1, \mathcal{A}_2$ *with non-negligible advantage* $\mathsf{Adv}^{\mathsf{mnPRF\text{-}ODH}}_{\mathsf{F}_3,\mathcal{A}_1} = \mathsf{Adv}^{\mathsf{nmPRF\text{-}ODH}}_{\mathsf{F}_3,\mathcal{A}_2} = 1 - 2^{-\lambda}$.

4.2 Separations in the Random Oracle Model

In the following we use the following problem of computing non-trivial v-th roots in $\mathbb{G}$ for implicitly given v. That is, consider an algorithm $\mathcal{A}$ which outputs some group element $x \in \mathbb{G}$ with $x \neq 1$ (and some state information), then receives g^v for random $v \xleftarrow{\$} \mathbb{Z}_q$, and finally outputs y given g^v and the state information, such that $y^v = x$. Denote by $\mathsf{Adv}^{\mathsf{iiDH}}_{\mathbb{G},\mathcal{A}}$ the probability that $\mathcal{A}$ succeeds in this *interactive inversion* DH problem.

Note that the problem would be trivial if $x = 1$ was allowed (in which case $y = 1$ would provide a solution), or if x can be chosen after having seen g^v (in which case $x = g^v$ and $y = g$ would trivially work). Excluding these trivial cases, in terms of generic or algebraic hardness the problem is equivalent to the CDH problem. Namely, assume $\mathcal{A}$ "knows" $\alpha \in \mathbb{Z}_q$ such that $x = g^\alpha$. Since x is chosen before seeing g^v the adversary can only compute it as a power of g and, in addition, $x \neq 1$ implies $\alpha \neq 0$. Therefore, for any valid solution y the value $y^{1/\alpha}$ would be a v-th root of g, because $(y^{1/\alpha})^v = x^{1/\alpha} = g$. This problem of computing $g^{1/v}$ from g, g^v, however, is known as the inversion-DH (iDH) problem; it is equivalent to the CDH problem with a loose reduction [2].

For our separation result we still need a slightly stronger version here where, in the second phase, the adversary also gets access to a decision oracle which, on input two group elements $A, B \in \mathbb{G}$ outputs 1 if and only if $A^v = B$. We call this the strong interactive-inversion DH problem and denote it by siiDH.

Note that for example for a pairing-based group such an oracle is given for free, while computing a v-th root of g (or, equivalently, solving the DH problem may still be hard).

Proposition 11 (nmPRF-ODH $\not\Rightarrow$ snPRF-ODH). *In the random oracle model, and assuming* StDH *and* siiDH*, there exists a function* F^{RO} *which is* nmPRF-ODH*-secure but not* snPRF-ODH*-secure. More precisely, for any efficient adversary* $\mathcal{A}^{\mathsf{RO}}$ *against the* nmPRF-ODH *security of* F^{RO}*, there exist efficient algorithms* $\mathcal{B}_1, \mathcal{B}_2$*, such that*

$$\mathsf{Adv}^{\mathsf{nmPRF\text{-}ODH}}_{\mathsf{F}^{\mathsf{RO}},\mathcal{A}^{\mathsf{RO}}} \leq \mathsf{Adv}^{\mathsf{StDH}}_{\mathbb{G},\mathcal{B}_1} + h \cdot \mathsf{Adv}^{\mathsf{siiDH}}_{\mathbb{G},\mathcal{B}_2} + \frac{h}{q} + 2^{-\lambda},$$

for the at most h *queries to the random oracle, but there exists an algorithm* $\mathcal{A}^{\mathsf{RO}}$ *with non-negligible advantage* $\mathsf{Adv}^{\mathsf{snPRF\text{-}ODH}}_{\mathsf{F}^{\mathsf{RO}},\mathcal{A}} \geq 1 - 2^{-\lambda+1}$.

The idea is to use the following function:

$$\mathsf{F}^{\mathsf{RO}}(K,(x,y)) = \begin{cases} y & \text{if } \mathsf{RO}(Kx^{-1},(x,0^\lambda)) = y \text{ and } x \neq 1 \\ \mathsf{RO}(K,(x,y)) & \text{else} \end{cases}$$

For this function it is easy for an adversary to check for the challenge value $x^\star = (g^u, 0^\lambda)$ if the reply $y^\star$ is real or random, by making an ODH_u query about $(g^{v+1}, (g^u, y^\star))$. With high probability this will trigger the exceptional case of F^{RO} for $\mathsf{RO}(g^{u(v+1)}g^{-u}, g^u, 0^\lambda) = y^\star$ if and only if $y^\star$ is the correct function value. On the other hand, any adversary with oracle access to ODH_v only, will not be able to take advantage of this special evaluation mode for the key g^{uv} and challenge value $x^\star = (x, y)$, since this would mean that such a query (T, x) to the ODH_v oracle implies that $x = (Tg^{-u})^v$, i.e., that the adversary can compute a v-th root of x, which is chosen before learning the value g^v. This, however, would contradict the siiDH assumption. Moreover, the adversary will not ask the random oracle about the key g^{uv} either, or else we get a contradiction to the StDH assumption (with a loose reduction). But then the challenge value still looks perfectly random to the adversary. The complete proof following this idea appears in the full version.

The idea can now be transferred to the case that we still allow one oracle query to ODH_u, basically by "secret sharing" the reply in the exceptional case among two queries:

Proposition 12 (smPRF-ODH $\not\Rightarrow$ mnPRF-ODH). *In the random oracle model, and assuming* StDH *and* siiDH*, there exists a function* F^{RO} *which is* smPRF-ODH*-secure but not* mnPRF-ODH*-secure. More precisely, for any efficient adversary* $\mathcal{A}^{\mathsf{RO}}$ *against the* smPRF-ODH *security of* F^{RO}*, there exist efficient algorithms* $\mathcal{B}_1, \mathcal{B}_2$*, such that*

$$\mathsf{Adv}^{\mathsf{smPRF\text{-}ODH}}_{\mathsf{F}^{\mathsf{RO}},\mathcal{A}^{\mathsf{RO}}} \leq \sqrt{\mathsf{Adv}^{\mathsf{StDH}}_{\mathbb{G},\mathcal{B}_1}} + h \cdot \mathsf{Adv}^{\mathsf{siiDH}}_{\mathbb{G},\mathcal{B}_2} + \frac{h}{q} + 2^{-\lambda},$$

for the at most h *queries to the random oracle, but there exists an algorithm* $\mathcal{A}^{\mathsf{RO}}$ *with non-negligible advantage* $\mathsf{Adv}^{\mathsf{mnPRF\text{-}ODH}}_{\mathsf{F}^{\mathsf{RO}},\mathcal{A}^{\mathsf{RO}}} \geq 1 - 2^{-\lambda+1}$.

In fact, in the negative result for mnPRF-ODH the adversary only needs to ask two queries to the ODH_u oracle *after* receiving the challenge query. Since the function is still secure for a single ODH_u query, this is optimal in this regard. The proof appears in the full version.

4.3 Discussion

Let us close this section with some remarks about the separations.

Remark 13. Our separating function family (cf. Definition 5) establishes quite a number of separations, but cannot be used in order to separate the remaining variants. This is due to the fact that our function family cannot separate between notions that both allow polynomial many queries as for example nmPRF-ODH and smPRF-ODH. Thus, we have turned to the random oracle model to establish further separations. Using this model is alleviated by the result about the implausibility of instantiating the PRF-ODH assumption in the standard model.

In the random oracle model we have shown that it is crucial if the adversary has access to the ODH_u oracle or not (or how many times). This uses some asymmetry in the two oracles, namely, that g^u is given before the challenge query, and g^v only after. Our separations take advantage of this difference, visualized via the interactive-inversion DH problem which is only hard if $x^\star$ is chosen before receiving g^v.

It is currently open if the other notions are separable. Beyond the asymmetry that g^u is already available before the challenge, it is unclear how to "encode" other distinctive information into the input to the "memoryless" PRF which one oracle can exploit but the other one cannot.

Remark 14. In case our generic PRF-ODH assumption (cf. Definition 1) would provide the adversary additionally with the share g^v in the initialization phase (cf. step 1) then Fig. 2 would symmetrically "collapse" along the vertical axis in the middle. In other words, this would result in equivalences of the notions snPRF-ODH and nsPRF-ODH, mnPRF-ODH and nmPRF-ODH, as well as msPRF-ODH and smPRF-ODH. Note that this is not a contradiction to our separation results among those notions, as they only work if (and exploit that) g^v is not given in advance.

5 On the Impossibility of Instantiating PRF-ODH in the Standard Model

In this section we show that there is no *algebraic* black-box reduction $\mathcal{R}$ which reduces the snPRF-ODH assumption (and analogously the nsPRF-ODH assumption) to a class of hard cryptographic problems, called DDH-augmented abstract problems. With these problems one captures reductions to the DDH problem or to some general, abstract problem like collision resistance of hash functions.

5.1 Overview

The idea is to use the meta-reduction technique. Assume that we have an algebraic reduction $\mathcal{R}$ from the snPRF-ODH assumption which turns any black-box adversary into a solver for a DDH-augmented problem. Then we in particular consider an inefficient adversary $\mathcal{A}_\infty$ which successfully breaks the snPRF-ODH assumption with constant probability. The reduction, with black-box access to $\mathcal{A}_\infty$, must then solve the DDH-augmented problem. For this it can then either not take any advantage of the infinite power of $\mathcal{A}_\infty$—in which case we can already break the DDH-augmented problem—or it tries to elicit some useful information from $\mathcal{A}_\infty$. In the latter case we build our meta-reduction by simulating $\mathcal{A}_\infty$ *efficiently.* This is accomplished by exploiting the algebraic property of the reduction and "peeking" at the internals of the reduction's group element choices. Our meta-reduction will then solve the decisional square-DH problem, saying that (g, g^a, g^{a^2}) is indistinguishable from (g, g^a, g^b) from random a, b.

Our impossibility result works for pseudorandom functions PRF, which take as input arbitrary bit strings and maps them to λ bits. We stick with this convention here, but remark that our negative result also holds if the input length is 1 only, and the output length is super-logarithmic in λ. Similarly, we assume that PRF is a nnPRF-ODH, although it suffices for our negative result that the function PRF for a random group element (and some fixed input, say 1) is pseudorandom, i.e., that $\mathsf{PRF}(X, 1)$ is indistinguishable from random for a uniformly chosen group element $X \xleftarrow{\$} \mathbb{G}$ (without giving any "Diffie–Hellman decomposition" of X).

Theorem 15. *Assume that there is an efficient algebraic black-box reduction $\mathcal{R}$ from the* snPRF-ODH *(or* nsPRF-ODH*) assumption to a DDH-augmented problem. Then either the DDH-augmented problem is not hard, or the decisional square-DH problem is not hard.*

If one assumes vice versa that both the underlying augmented-DDH problem and decisional square-DH problem are hard, then this means that there cannot be a reduction as in the theorem to show security of the nsPRF-ODH or snPRF-ODH assumption.

5.2 DDH-augmented Cryptographic Problems

DDH-augmented problems are cryptographic problems in which the adversary either solves a DDH problem or some abstract (and independent) problem in which it receives some instance inst, can make oracle queries about this instance, and then generates a potential solution sol. The adversary can decide on the fly which of the two problems to solve. In terms of our setting here we build a reduction against such DDH-augmented problems, capturing for example the case that one aims to show security of the PRF-ODH assumption by assembling a scheme out of several primitives, including the DDH assumption, and giving reductions to each of them.

We next define cryptographic problems in a general way, where it is convenient to use the threshold of $\frac{1}{2}$ for decisional games to measure the adversary's advantage. We note that we can "lift" common computational games where the threshold is the constant 0 by outputting 1 if the adversary succeeds or if an independent coin flip lands on 1. Formally, a cryptographic problem consists of three probabilistic polynomial-time algorithms $\mathsf{P} = (\mathsf{P.Gen}, \mathsf{P.Ch}, \mathsf{P.Vf})$ such that for any probabilistic polynomial-time algorithm $\mathcal{A}$ we have

$$\mathsf{Adv}^{\mathsf{Prob}}_{\mathsf{P},\mathcal{A}}(\lambda) := 2 \cdot \left(\mathrm{Prob}\left[\mathsf{P.Vf}(\mathsf{secret}, \mathsf{sol}) = 1 : \begin{array}{l} (\mathsf{inst}, \mathsf{secret}) \xleftarrow{\$} \mathsf{P.Gen}(1^\lambda), \\ \mathsf{sol} \xleftarrow{\$} \mathcal{A}^{\mathsf{P.Ch}(\mathsf{secret}, \cdot)}(1^\lambda, \mathsf{inst}) \end{array} \right] - \frac{1}{2} \right)$$

is negligible.

A DDH-augmented cryptographic problem $\mathsf{P}^{\mathrm{DDH}}$ for some group $\mathbb{G}$ (or, more precisely, for some sequence of groups) based on a problem P, consists of the following algorithms:

- $\mathsf{P.Gen}^{\mathrm{DDH}}(1^\lambda)$ runs $(\mathsf{inst}, \mathsf{secret}) \xleftarrow{\$} \mathsf{P.Gen}(1^\lambda)$, picks $x, y, z \xleftarrow{\$} \mathbb{Z}_q$ and $b \xleftarrow{\$} \{0,1\}$, and outputs $\mathsf{inst}^{\mathrm{DDH}} = (g^x, g^y, g^{xy+bz}, \mathsf{inst})$ and $\mathsf{secret}^{\mathrm{DDH}} = (b, \mathsf{secret})$.
- $\mathsf{P.Ch}^{\mathrm{DDH}}(\mathsf{secret}^{\mathrm{DDH}}, \cdot)$ runs $\mathsf{P.Ch}(\mathsf{secret}, \cdot)$.
- $\mathsf{P.Vf}^{\mathrm{DDH}}(\mathsf{secret}^{\mathrm{DDH}}, \mathsf{sol}^{\mathrm{DDH}})$ checks if $\mathsf{sol}^{\mathrm{DDH}} = (\text{"DDH"}, b')$ and, if so, outputs 1 if and only if $b = b'$ for bit b in $\mathsf{secret}^{\mathrm{DDH}}$. If $\mathsf{sol}^{\mathrm{DDH}} = (\text{"P"}, \mathsf{sol})$ then the algorithm here outputs $\mathsf{P.Vf}(\mathsf{secret}, \mathsf{sol})$. In any other case it returns 0.

5.3 Algebraic Reductions for the snPRF-ODH Assumption

Algebraic reductions have been considered in [9] and abstractly defined in [35]. The idea is that the reduction can only perform group operations in the predefined way, e.g., by multiplying given elements. As a consequence, whenever the reduction on input group elements $g_1, g_2, \ldots$ generates a group element $A \in \mathbb{G}$ one can output a representation $(\alpha_1, \alpha_2, \ldots)$ such that $A = \prod g_i^{\alpha_i}$. In [35] this is formalized by assuming the existence of an algorithm which, when receiving the reduction's input and random tape, can output the representation in addition to A.

In order to simplify the presentation here, we simply assume that the reduction, when forwarding some group element to the adversary, outputs the representation itself. The base elements $g_1, g_2, \ldots$ for the representation are those which the reduction has received so far, as part of the DDH-part of the input or from the interaction with the adversary. The representation is hidden from the adversary in the simulation, of course, but our meta-reduction may exploit this information.

We consider (algebraic) reductions $\mathcal{R}$ which use the adversary $\mathcal{A}$ in a black-box way. The reduction may invoke multiple copies of the adversary, possibly rewinding copies. We use the common technique of derandomizing our (unbounded) adversary in question by assuming that it internally calls a truly random function on the communication so far, when it needs to generate some randomness. Note that the truly random function is an integral part of the adversary, and that we view the adversary being picked randomly from all adversaries with such an embedded function. Since the reduction is supposed to work for all successful adversaries, it must also work for such randomly chosen adversaries.

It is now convenient to enumerate the adversary's instances which the reduction invokes as $\mathcal{A}_i$ for $i = 1, 2, \ldots$. Since our adversary in question is deterministic we can assume that the reduction "abandons" a copy $\mathcal{A}_i$ forever, if it starts the next copy $\mathcal{A}_{i+1}$. This is without loss of generality because the reduction can re-run a fresh copy to the state where it has left the previous instance. This also means that the reduction can effectively re-set executions with the adversary.

The reduction receives as input a triple (g^x, g^y, g^z) and some instance inst and should decide if $g^z = g^{xy}$ or g^z is random, or provide a solution sol to inst with the help of oracle $\mathsf{P.Ch}$. We stress that the reduction is algebraic with respect the DDH-part of the DDH-augmented problem. In particular, encasing a PRF-ODH-like assumption into the general P problem and providing a trivial reduction to the problem itself is not admissible. The group elements (and their representations) handed to the adversary in the reduction are determined by the DDH-part of the input. Finally, we note that we only need that, if $\mathcal{R}$ interacts with an adversary against snPRF-ODH with advantage $1 - 2^{-\lambda}$, then $\mathcal{R}$ solves the DDH-augmented problem with a non-negligible advantage.

5.4 Outline of Steps

Our negative result proceeds in three main steps:

1. We first define an all-powerful adversary $\mathcal{A}_\infty$ which breaks the snPRF-ODH assumption by using its infinite power. This adversary will, besides receiving the challenge at point $x^\star = 0$, ask the ODH_u oracle to get the value at $(S, 1)$ for random $S = g^s$, where the random value s is generated via the integral random function. It then uses its power to compute the Diffie–Hellman key g^{uv}, verifies the answer of oracle ODH_u with the help of s, and only if this one is valid, gives the correct answer concerning the challenge query. In any other case, the adversary aborts.
2. We then show that the algebraic reduction $\mathcal{R}$, potentially spawning many black-box copies of our adversary $\mathcal{A}_\infty$, must answer correctly to the ODH_u query in one copy and use the input values g^x, g^y, g^z non-trivially, or else we can already break the underlying DDH-augmented problem efficiently.
3. Next we show that, if the reduction answers correctly and non-trivially in one of the copies, then we can—using the algebraic nature of the reduction—replace the adversary $\mathcal{A}_\infty$ by an efficient algorithm, the meta-reduction $\mathcal{M}$, and either break the decisional square-DH assumption or refute the pseudorandomness of PRF for a fresh random group element.

The decisional square-DH assumption says that it is infeasible to distinguish (g, g^a, g^{a^2}) from (g, g^a, g^b) for random a, b. It implies the DDH assumption, but is only known to be equivalent to classical DH problem in the computational case

[2]. More formally, we will use the following variation: $(g, g^a, g^{a^2}, g^{a^2b}, g^b, g^{ab})$ is indistinguishable from $(g, g^a, g^{a^2}, g^{a^2b}, g^b, g^c)$ for random a, b, c.

We briefly argue that the above decision problem follows from the decisional square-DH assumption. The latter assumption implies that we can replace g^{a^2} and g^{a^2b} in these tuples by group elements g^d, g^{db} for random d, using knowledge of b to compute the other elements. Then, by the DDH assumption, we can replace g^{ab} in such tuples by a random group element g^c, using knowledge of d to compute the other group elements g^d, g^{bd}. In the last step we can re-substitute g^d, g^{db} again by g^{a^2} and g^{a^2b}, using knowledge of b and c to create the other group elements.

5.5 Defining the All-Powerful Adversary

Let us define our adversary $\mathcal{A}_\infty$ (with an internal random function $f : \{0,1\}^* \rightarrow \mathbb{Z}_q$) against snPRF-ODH formally:

1. Adversary $\mathcal{A}_\infty$ receives g, g^u as input.
2. It then asks the challenge oracle about $x^\star = 0$ to receive $y^\star$ and g^v. We call this the challenge step.
3. It computes $s = f(g^u, g^v, y^\star)$ and $S = g^s$ and asks the ODH_u oracle about $(S, 1)$ to get some y_t. We call this the test step.
4. It computes $S^u = (g^u)^s$ and, using its unbounded computational power, also g^{uv}.
5. If $y_t \neq \mathsf{PRF}(S^u, 1)$ then $\mathcal{A}_\infty$ aborts.
6. Else, $\mathcal{A}_\infty$ outputs 0 if and only if $y^\star = \mathsf{PRF}(g^{uv}, 0)$, and 1 otherwise.

Note that the probability that $\mathcal{A}_\infty$ outputs the correct answer in an actual attack is $1 - 2^{-\lambda}$ and thus optimal; the small error of $2^{-\lambda}$ is due to the case that the random $y^\star$ may accidentally hit the value of the PRF function.

5.6 Reductions Without Help

Ideally we would now first like to conclude that any reduction which does not provide a correct answer for the test step in any of the copies, never exploits the adversary's unlimited power and would thus essentially need to immediately succeed, without the help of $\mathcal{A}_\infty$. We can indeed make this argument formal, simulating $\mathcal{A}_\infty$ efficiently by using lazy sampling techniques for the generation of s and always aborting in Step 5 if reaching this point. However, we need something slightly stronger here.

Assume that the reduction provides some g^u in one of the copies for which it knows the discrete logarithm u, i.e., it is not a non-trivial combination of the input values g^x, g^y, g^z for unknown logarithms. Then the reduction can of course answer the adversary's test query $(S, 1)$ successfully by computing S^u and $\mathsf{PRF}(S^u, 1)$. Yet, in such executions it can also compute the reply to the challenge query itself, even if it does not know the discrete logarithm of g^v. In this sense the reduction cannot gain any knowledge about its DDH input, and we also dismiss such cases as useless.

Formally, we call the j-th run of one of the adversary's copies *useless* if either the instance aborts in (or before) Step 5, or if the representation of the adversary's input g^u in this copy in the given group elements g, g^x, g^y, g^z and the challenge query values $S_1, S_2, \ldots, S_{j-1}$ so far, i.e.,

$$g^u = (g^x)^\alpha (g^y)^\beta (g^z)^\gamma g^\delta \cdot \prod_{i<j} S_i^{\sigma_i},$$

satisfies $x\alpha + y\beta + z\gamma = 0 \bmod q$. Note that the reduction may form g^u with respect to all externally provided group elements, including the S_i's, such that we also need to account for those elements. We will, however, always set all of them to $S_i = g^{s_i}$ for some known s_i, such that we are only interested in the question if combination of the DDH input values g^x, g^y, g^z vanishes.

Let $\mathsf{useless}_j$ be the event that the j-th instance is useless in the above sense. For such a useless copy we can efficiently simulate adversary $\mathcal{A}_\infty$, because it either aborts early enough, or the algebraic reduction outputs some g^u with its representation from which we can compute the discrete logarithm $u = \delta + \sum_{i<j} s_i\sigma_i \bmod q$ and thus execute the decision and test steps of $\mathcal{A}_\infty$. Let $\mathsf{useless}$ be the event that all executions of $\mathcal{A}_\infty$ of the reduction are useless. We next argue that, if the event $\mathsf{useless}$ happens with overwhelming probability, then we can solve the DDH-augmented problem immediately.

The claim holds as we can emulate the all-powerful adversary $\mathcal{A}_\infty$ easily, if the reduction essentially always forgoes to run the adversary till the very end or uses only trivial values g^u. Let $(g^x, g^y, g^z, \mathsf{inst})$ be our input and pass this to the reduction. We simply emulate *all* the copies of the adversary efficiently by:

- using lazy sampling to emulate the random function f,
- for each invocation check at the beginning that $(g^x)^\alpha(g^y)^\beta(g^z)^\gamma = 1$ for the representation received with the input g^u for that instance, in which case we can use the discrete logarithm $u = \delta + \sum_{i<j} s_i\sigma_i \bmod q$ to run this copy of $\mathcal{A}_\infty$, and
- else always abort after having received y in Step 3.

Denote this way of simulating each copy by adversary $\mathcal{A}_{\mathrm{ppt}}$ (even though, technically, the copies share state for the lazy sampling technique and should be thus considered as one big simulated adversary). Then

$$\mathrm{Prob}\left[\mathsf{P.Vf}(\mathsf{secret},\mathsf{sol}) = 1 : \begin{array}{l}(\mathsf{inst},\mathsf{secret}) \xleftarrow{\$} \mathsf{P.Gen}(1^\lambda),\\ \mathsf{sol} \xleftarrow{\$} \mathcal{R}^{\mathsf{P.Ch}(\mathsf{secret},\cdot),\mathcal{A}_\infty}(1^\lambda,\mathsf{inst})\end{array}\right]$$

$$\leq \mathrm{Prob}\left[\mathsf{P.Vf}(\mathsf{secret},\mathsf{sol}) = 1 : \begin{array}{l}(\mathsf{inst},\mathsf{secret}) \xleftarrow{\$} \mathsf{P.Gen}(1^\lambda),\\ \mathsf{sol} \xleftarrow{\$} \mathcal{R}^{\mathsf{P.Ch}(\mathsf{secret},\cdot),\mathcal{A}_{\mathrm{ppt}}}(1^\lambda,\mathsf{inst})\end{array}\right] + \mathrm{Prob}\left[\overline{\mathsf{useless}}\right]$$

The latter probability for event $\overline{\mathsf{useless}}$ is negligible by assumption. We therefore get an efficient algorithm $\mathcal{R}^{\mathcal{A}_{\mathrm{ppt}}}$ which breaks the DDH-augmented problem with non-negligible advantage.

5.7 Our Meta-reduction

We may from now on thus assume that Prob $\boxed{\textsf{useless}} \not\approx 0$ is non-negligible. This implies that the reduction answers at least in one copy of $\mathcal{A}_\infty$ of the at most polynomial number $q(\lambda)$ in the test queries in Step 3 with the correct value y_t for some non-trivial input g^u, with non-negligible probability. Our meta-reduction will try to guess the first execution k where this happens and to "inject" its input $g^a, g^{a^2}, g^{a^2b}, g^b, g^c$ into that execution in a useful way. More precisely, it will insert these values into g^x, g^y, g^z and S_k such that the expected key K for evaluating PRF for the test query equals a function of g^{ab} if $g^c = g^{ab}$, but is random if g^c is random. In the latter case predicting y is infeasible for the reduction, though, because the PRF is evaluated on a fresh and random key. This allows to distinguish the two cases.

The meta-reduction's injection strategy captures two possible choices of the reduction concerning the equation $x\alpha + y\beta + z\gamma \neq 0 \bmod q$ in the (hopefully correctly guessed) k-th execution. One is for the case that $x\alpha + y\beta \neq 0 \bmod q$, the other one is for the case that $x\alpha + y\beta = 0 \bmod q$ and thus $z\gamma \neq 0 \bmod q$ according to the assumption $x\alpha + y\beta + z\gamma \neq 0 \bmod q$. The meta-reduction will try to predict (via a random bit e) which case will happen and inject the values differently for the cases. This is necessary since the g^z-value, if it is not random, should contain the DH value of the other two elements.

Our meta-reduction $\mathcal{M}$ works as follows:

1. The meta-reduction receives $g^a, g^{a^2}, g^{a^2b}, g^b, g^c$ as input and should decide if $g^c = g^{ab}$. If $a = 0$ then we can decide easily, such that we assume that $a \neq 0$ from now on.
2. The meta-reduction picks an index $k \xleftarrow{\$} \{1, 2, \dots, q(\lambda)\}$ for the polynomial bound $q(\lambda)$ of adversarial copies the reduction $\mathcal{R}$ runs with $\mathcal{A}_\infty$. It also picks $x', y', z' \xleftarrow{\$} \mathbb{Z}_q^*$, $s_1, \dots, s_{k-1} \xleftarrow{\$} \mathbb{Z}_q$, $e, d \xleftarrow{\$} \{0, 1\}$, and samples $(\textsf{inst}, \textsf{secret}) \xleftarrow{\$} \textsf{P.Gen}(1^\lambda)$.
3. For the first injection strategy, $e = 0$, it sets
$$g^x = (g^a)^{x'}, g^y = (g^a)^{y'}, g^z = (g^{a^2})^{x'y'} \text{ for } d = 0 = \text{ resp. } g^z = (g^{a^2})^{z'} \text{ for } d = 1.$$
For the other injection strategy, $e = 1$, it sets
$$g^x = (g^a)^{x'}, \quad g^y = g^{y'}, \quad g^z = (g^a)^{x'y'} \text{ for } d = 0 \text{ resp. } g^z = g^{az'} \text{ for } d = 1.$$
4. It invokes the reduction $\mathcal{R}$ on input g^x, g^y, g^z as well as $\textsf{inst}$.
5. The meta-reduction simulates the interactions of $\mathcal{R}$ with $\textsf{P.Ch}$ and $\mathcal{A}_\infty$ as follows:
   - Each oracle query to $\textsf{P.Ch}$ is answered by running the original algorithm $\textsf{P.Ch}$ for $\textsf{secret}$.
   - Use lazy sampling to emulate the random function f.
   - For each of the first $j < k$ invocations of $\mathcal{A}_\infty$ check at the beginning that $(g^x)^{\alpha_j}(g^y)^{\beta_j}(g^z)^{\gamma_j} = 1$ for the representation received with the input g^{u_j} for that instance, in which case $\mathcal{M}$ can use the discrete logarithm $u_j = \delta_j + \sum_{i<j} s_i\sigma_i \bmod q$ to efficiently run this copy of $\mathcal{A}_\infty$, using $S_j = g^{s_j}$ for the test query.

   - Otherwise, if $(g^x)^{\alpha_j}(g^y)^{\beta_j}(g^z)^{\gamma_j} \neq 1$, for the j-th invocation of an adversarial copy of $\mathcal{A}_\infty$ for $j < k$, up to Step 3, efficiently simulate $\mathcal{A}_\infty$ using $S_j = g^{s_j}$ for the test query, and immediately abort after this step.

6. For the k-th invocation simulate $\mathcal{A}_\infty$ by using $S_k = g^b$. If $\mathcal{M}$ receives a reply y_t from $\mathcal{R}$, do the following. Let g^{u_k} be the input value of this adversary's copy. Since the reduction is algebraic it has also output values $\alpha_k, \beta_k, \gamma_k, \delta_k, \sigma_1, \ldots, \sigma_{k-1} \in \mathbb{Z}_q$ such that

$$g^{u_k} = (g^x)^{\alpha_k}(g^y)^{\beta_k}(g^z)^{\gamma_k} g^{\delta_k} \cdot \prod_{i<k} S_i^{\sigma_i}.$$

   Note that all the base elements, up to this point, only depend on g, g^a (and g^{a^2} in case of strategy $e = 0$) of $\mathcal{M}$'s inputs $g^a, g^{a^2}, g^{a^2 b}, g^b, g^c$, because g^{u_k} is output before seeing $S_k = g^b$.[2]

7. If strategy $e = 0$ is used and we have $a(x'\alpha_k + y'\beta_k) \neq 0 \bmod q$ (which can be checked for $a \neq 0$ by consulting the known values $x', \alpha_k, y', \beta_k$), then the meta-reduction decides as follows. From the value $g^{a^2 b}$ it can compute $g^{bz\gamma_k} = (g^{a^2 b})^{x'y'\gamma_k}$ resp. $(g^{a^2 b})^{z'\gamma}$ for both cases $d \in \{0, 1\}$ and can then set

$$K = (g^c)^{x'\alpha_k + y'\beta_k} g^{bz\gamma_k} (g^b)^{\delta_k + \sum_{i<k} s_i \sigma_i}.$$

   It immediately outputs 0 if $y_t = \mathsf{PRF}(K, 1)$, else it continues.

8. If strategy $e = 1$ is used and we have $ax'\alpha_k + y'\beta_k = 0 \bmod q$ (which can be checked by verifying that $(g^a)^{x'\alpha_k} g^{y'\beta_k} = 1$), then the meta-reduction computes the key as

$$K = \begin{cases} (g^c)^{x'y'\gamma_k}(g^b)^{\delta_k + \sum_{i<k} s_i\sigma_i} & \text{for } d = 0 \text{ and} \\ (g^c)^{z'\gamma_k}(g^b)^{\delta_k + \sum_{i<k} s_i\sigma_i} & \text{for } d = 1 \end{cases}$$

   and immediately outputs 0 if $y_t = \mathsf{PRF}(K, 1)$; else it continues.

9. In any other case, if the reduction aborts prematurely or if the insertion strategy has been false, i.e., the choice of e does not match the condition on $x'\alpha_k + y'\beta_k \neq 0 \bmod q$, then output a random bit.

5.8 Analysis

For the analysis assume for the moment that our meta-reduction has actually chosen the index k of the first correct and non-trivial answer y_t, i.e., where $x\alpha_k + y\beta_k + z\gamma_k \neq 0 \bmod q$. Additionally, assume that $(x\alpha_k + y\beta_k) \neq 0 \bmod q$. Then $e = 0$ with probability at least $\frac{1}{2}$. This holds since the reduction remains perfectly oblivious about the choice of e, because all values in the interaction have the same distributions in both cases for e. Then the actual key for answering the test query is

$$(g^{u_k})^b = (g^{ab})^{x'\alpha_k + y'\beta_k}(g^{bz})^{\gamma_k}(g^b)^{\delta_k + \sum_{i<k} s_i\sigma_i}.$$

[2] The same is true for g^{v_k} generated in the challenge query before, such that the result applies to the $\mathsf{nsPRF\text{-}ODH}$ assumption accordingly.

This implies that the meta-reduction's input g^c yields the same key K if $g^c = g^{ab}$ and hence equality for the PRF value. Yet, it yields a random value if g^c is random (since the exponent $x'\alpha_k + y'\beta_k$ does not vanish). In the latter case, since the value g^c is at no point used in the simulation before the reduction outputs y_t, the probability that y_t predicts $\mathsf{PRF}(K, 1)$ for the fresh random key, is negligible. This final step in the argument can be formalized straightforwardly.

Assume next that, besides the correct prediction of index k, we have $e = 1$ and $ax'\alpha_k + y'\beta_k = 0 \bmod q$. Then, since $ax'\alpha_k + y'\beta_k + z\gamma_k \neq 0 \bmod q$, we must have that $z\gamma_k \neq 0 \bmod q$ and therefore also $x'y'\gamma_k \neq 0 \bmod q$ for $d = 0$ resp. $z'\gamma_k \neq 0 \bmod q$ for $d = 1$. The same argument as in the previous case applies now. Namely, for $g^c = g^{ab}$ the meta-reduction computes the expected key, whereas for random g^c the contribution to the computed value K is for a non-zero exponent, such that equality for the PRF value only holds with negligible probability.

Putting the pieces together, for $g^c = g^{ab}$ our algorithm correctly outputs 0 if the reduction uses the adversary's help (with non-negligible probability $\mathrm{Prob}\left[\boxed{\mathsf{useless}}\right]$), if the prediction k is correct (with non-negligible probability $\frac{1}{q(\lambda)}$), and if the insertion strategy is correct (with probability at least $\frac{1}{2}$). Let

$$\epsilon(\lambda) \geq \frac{1}{2q(\lambda)} \cdot \mathrm{Prob}\left[\boxed{\mathsf{useless}}\right]$$

denote the non-negligible probability that the meta-reduction outputs 0 early. It also outputs 0 with probability $\frac{1}{2}$ in any other case, such that the probability of outputting 0 for $g^c = g^{ab}$ is at least

$$\epsilon(\lambda) + \frac{1}{2} \cdot (1 - \epsilon(\lambda)) \geq \frac{1}{2} + \frac{\epsilon(\lambda)}{2}.$$

In case that g^c is random, our meta-reduction only outputs 0 if the PRF value matches y_t for the random key K, or if the final randomly chosen bit equals 0. The probability of this happening is only negligibly larger than $\frac{1}{2}$. This conversely means that the meta-reduction correctly outputs 1 in this case with probability at least $\frac{1}{2} - \mathrm{negl}(\lambda)$ for some negligible function $\mathrm{negl}(\lambda)$.

Overall, the probability of distinguishing the cases is at least

$$\frac{1}{2} \cdot \left(\frac{1}{2} + \frac{\epsilon(\lambda)}{2}\right) + \frac{1}{2} \cdot \left(\frac{1}{2} - \mathrm{negl}(\lambda)\right) \geq \frac{1}{2} + \frac{\epsilon(\lambda)}{4} - \frac{\mathrm{negl}(\lambda)}{2},$$

which is non-negligibly larger than $\frac{1}{2}$ for non-negligible $\epsilon(\lambda)$.

6 PRF-ODH Security of HMAC

In this section we briefly discuss the PRF-ODH security of HMAC [25], augmenting previous results on the PRF security of HMAC [5,11,27]. We show that $\mathsf{HMAC}(K, X)$ as well as its dual-PRF [3] usage $\mathsf{HMAC}(X, K)$, as encountered in

TLS 1.3, are mmPRF-ODH secure, which is our strongest notion of PRF-ODH security. For a complete treatment see the full version.

Recall that HMAC is usually based on a Merkle-Damgård hash function H, using a compression function $h : \{0,1\}^c \times \{0,1\}^b \to \{0,1\}^c$. The function HMAC is then defined as

$$\mathsf{HMAC}(K, X) := H(K \oplus \mathsf{opad} || H(K \oplus \mathsf{ipad} || X)),$$

for key $K \in \{0,1\}^b$ and label X, HMAC, where opad and ipad are fixed (distinct) constants in $\{0,1\}^b$. In terms of the iterated compression function we have

$$\mathsf{HMAC}(K, X) = h^*(\mathsf{IV}, K \oplus \mathsf{opad} || h^*(\mathsf{IV}, K \oplus \mathsf{ipad} || X || \mathsf{padding}) || \mathsf{padding}).$$

Keys which are shorter than b bits are padded first, and longer keys K are first hashed down to $H(K) \in \{0,1\}^c$ and then padded.

In the full version we show the following security property of HMAC, independently of whether the key $K \in \mathbb{G}$ is longer or shorter than the block length b:

Theorem 16. *Assume that the underlying compression function $h : \{0,1\}^c \times \{0,1\}^b \to \{0,1\}^c$ of* HMAC *is a random oracle. Then* HMAC *is* mmPRF-ODH-*secure under the* StDH *assumption. More precisely, for any efficient adversary $\mathcal{A}$ against the* mmPRF-ODH *security of* HMAC, *there exists an efficient algorithm $\mathcal{B}$ such that*

$$\mathsf{Adv}^{\mathsf{mmPRF\text{-}ODH}}_{\mathsf{HMAC},\mathcal{A}} \leq \sqrt{\mathsf{Adv}^{\mathsf{StDH}}_{\mathbb{G},\mathcal{B}}} + (q_{\mathsf{RO}} + (q_{\mathsf{ODH}_u} + q_{\mathsf{ODH}_v}) \cdot \ell_{\mathsf{ODH}} + 1)^2 \cdot 2^{-c}$$

where q with the respective index denotes the maximal number of the according oracle queries, and ℓ_{ODH} the maximal number of oracle calls to h in each evaluation of any ODH *oracle call.*

As mentioned earlier, one specific use case of the PRF-ODH assumption arises in the setting of TLS 1.3. Here, the HKDF scheme [27,28] is adapted for key derivation. In particular, the function HKDF.Extract is used to derive an internal key K' as

$$K' \leftarrow \mathsf{HKDF.Extract}(X, K) := \mathsf{HMAC}(X, K),$$

where an adversarially known value X is used as the HMAC key while the secret randomness source in the form of a DH shared secret $K = g^{uv}$ is used as the label. At a first glance, this swapping of inputs may seem odd. However, the specified purpose of HKDF.Extract is to extract uniform randomness from its *second* component.

One way to prove that K' is indeed a random key (as long as g^{uv} is not revealed to the adversary) is to model $\mathsf{HKDF.Extract}(X, \cdot)$ as a random oracle. An alternative approach is pursued in [15,16,18] where the authors prove the statement under the assumption that $\mathsf{HKDF.Extract}(XTS, IKM) = \mathsf{HMAC}(XTS, IKM)$ is PRF-ODH secure when understood as a PRF keyed with $IKM \in \mathbb{G}$ (i.e., when the key is the *second* input). In this light, it is beneficial to show that $\mathsf{HMAC}(X, K)$ remains PRF-ODH secure for key $K \in \mathbb{G}$

and $X \in \{0,1\}^\star$.[3] Fortunately, our general treatment of $\mathsf{HMAC}(K, X)$ in Theorem 16 with arbitrarily long keys allows us to conclude the analogous result for $\mathsf{HMAC}(X, K)$ with swapped key and label. This is formally stated in the full version.

In recent developments initiated by the NIST hash function competition it has been established that sponge-based constructions can be used to build cryptographic hash functions. We are confident that the proof of Theorem 16 can be adapted to achieve the same result for HMAC if the underlying cryptographic hash function H is replaced by a sponge-based construction such as SHA-3 with the random permutation π modeled as a random oracle.[4] This proof can also be established along the lines of Bertoni et al. [7] who provide results showing that the sponge construction is indifferentiable from a random oracle when being used with a random transformation or a random permutation.

7 Conclusion

To the best of our knowledge, this is the first systematic study of the relations between different variants of the PRF-ODH assumption which is prominently being used in the realm of analyzing major real-world key exchange protocols. We provide a generic definition of the PRF-ODH assumption subsuming those different variants and show separations between most of the variants. Our results give strong indications that instantiating the PRF-ODH assumption without relying on the random oracle methodology is a challenging task, even though it can be formalized in the standard model. In particular, we show that it is implausible to instantiate the assumption in the standard model via algebraic black-box reductions to DDH-augmented problems.

Despite our negative result, we emphasize that using the PRF-ODH assumption still provides some advantage over the StDH assumption in the random oracle model. Namely, it supports a modular approach to proving key exchange protocols to be secure, shifting the heavy machinery of random-oracle reductions to StDH in the context of complex key exchange protocols to a much simpler assumption. As the PRF-ODH naturally appears in such protocols and enables simpler proofs, it is still worthwhile to use the assumption directly.

Acknowledgments. We thank the anonymous reviewers for valuable comments. This work has been co-funded by the DFG as part of project S4 within the CRC 1119 CROSSING and as part of project D.2 within the RTG 2050 "Privacy and Trust for Mobile Users".

[3] Though formally defined for arbitrary length, recall that the minimal recommended length is c bits.

[4] SHA-3 is part of the Keccak sponge function family [6]. It has been standardized in the FIPS Publication 202 [34], wherein it is explicitly approved for usage in HMAC.

References

1. Abdalla, M., Bellare, M., Rogaway, P.: The oracle Diffie-Hellman assumptions and an analysis of DHIES. In: Naccache, D. (ed.) CT-RSA 2001. LNCS, vol. 2020, pp. 143–158. Springer, Heidelberg (2001). doi:10.1007/3-540-45353-9_12
2. Bao, F., Deng, R.H., Zhu, H.F.: Variations of Diffie-Hellman problem. In: Qing, S., Gollmann, D., Zhou, J. (eds.) ICICS 2003. LNCS, vol. 2836, pp. 301–312. Springer, Heidelberg (2003). doi:10.1007/978-3-540-39927-8_28
3. Bellare, M.: New proofs for NMAC and HMAC: security without collision-resistance. In: Dwork, C. (ed.) CRYPTO 2006. LNCS, vol. 4117, pp. 602–619. Springer, Heidelberg (2006). doi:10.1007/11818175_36
4. Bellare, M., Kohno, T.: A theoretical treatment of related-key attacks: RKA-PRPs, RKA-PRFs, and applications. In: Biham, E. (ed.) EUROCRYPT 2003. LNCS, vol. 2656, pp. 491–506. Springer, Heidelberg (2003). doi:10.1007/3-540-39200-9_31
5. Bellare, M., Lysyanskaya, A.: Symmetric and dual PRFs from standard assumptions: a generic validation of an HMAC assumption. Cryptology ePrint Archive, Report 2015/1198 (2015). http://eprint.iacr.org/2015/1198
6. Bertoni, G., Daemen, J., Peeters, M., Assche, G.V.: The Keccak SHA-3 submission. Submission to NIST (Round 3) (2011). http://keccak.noekeon.org/Keccak-submission-3.pdf
7. Bertoni, G., Daemen, J., Peeters, M., Assche, G.: On the indifferentiability of the sponge construction. In: Smart, N. (ed.) EUROCRYPT 2008. LNCS, vol. 4965, pp. 181–197. Springer, Heidelberg (2008). doi:10.1007/978-3-540-78967-3_11
8. Bhargavan, K., Fournet, C., Kohlweiss, M., Pironti, A., Strub, P.-Y., Zanella-Béguelin, S.: Proving the TLS handshake secure (as it is). In: Garay, J.A., Gennaro, R. (eds.) CRYPTO 2014. LNCS, vol. 8617, pp. 235–255. Springer, Heidelberg (2014). doi:10.1007/978-3-662-44381-1_14
9. Boneh, D., Venkatesan, R.: Breaking RSA may not be equivalent to factoring. In: Nyberg, K. (ed.) EUROCRYPT 1998. LNCS, vol. 1403, pp. 59–71. Springer, Heidelberg (1998). doi:10.1007/BFb0054117
10. Brendel, J., Fischlin, M.: Zero round-trip time for the extended access control protocol. Cryptology ePrint Archive, Report 2017/060 (2017). http://eprint.iacr.org/2017/060
11. Coron, J.-S., Dodis, Y., Malinaud, C., Puniya, P.: Merkle-Damgård revisited: how to construct a hash function. In: Shoup, V. (ed.) CRYPTO 2005. LNCS, vol. 3621, pp. 430–448. Springer, Heidelberg (2005). doi:10.1007/11535218_26
12. Dagdelen, Ö., Fischlin, M.: Security analysis of the extended access control protocol for machine readable travel documents. In: Burmester, M., Tsudik, G., Magliveras, S., Ilić, I. (eds.) ISC 2010. LNCS, vol. 6531, pp. 54–68. Springer, Heidelberg (2011). doi:10.1007/978-3-642-18178-8_6
13. Dierks, T., Rescorla, E.: The transport layer security (TLS) protocol version 1.2. RFC 5246 (proposed standard), August 2008. http://www.ietf.org/rfc/rfc5246.txt. Updated by RFCs 5746, 5878, 6176, 7465, 7507, 7568, 7627, 7685, 7905, 7919
14. Dowling, B., Fischlin, M., Günther, F., Stebila, D.: A cryptographic analysis of the TLS 1.3 handshake protocol candidates. In: Ray, I., Li, N., Kruegel: C. (eds.) ACM CCS 2015, pp. 1197–1210. ACM Press, October 2015
15. Dowling, B., Fischlin, M., Günther, F., Stebila, D.: A cryptographic analysis of the TLS 1.3 handshake protocol candidates. Cryptology ePrint Archive, Report 2015/914 (2015). http://eprint.iacr.org/2015/914

16. Dowling, B., Fischlin, M., Günther, F., Stebila, D.: A cryptographic analysis of the TLS 1.3 draft-10 full and pre-shared key handshake protocol. Cryptology ePrint Archive, Report 2016/081 (2016). http://eprint.iacr.org/2016/081
17. Fischlin, M., Günther, F.: Multi-stage key exchange and the case of Google's QUIC protocol. In: Ahn, G.J., Yung, M., Li, N. (eds.) ACM CCS 2014, pp. 1193–1204. ACM Press, November 2014
18. Fischlin, M., Günther, F.: Replay attacks on zero round-trip time: the case of the TLS 1.3 handshake candidates. In: 2017 IEEE European Symposium on Security and Privacy. IEEE, April 2017
19. Galbraith, S.D.: Mathematics of Public Key Cryptography. Cambridge University Press, Cambridge (2012)
20. Garg, S., Bhaskar, R., Lokam, S.V.: Improved bounds on security reductions for discrete log based signatures. In: Wagner, D. (ed.) CRYPTO 2008. LNCS, vol. 5157, pp. 93–107. Springer, Heidelberg (2008). doi:10.1007/978-3-540-85174-5_6
21. Goldwasser, S., Micali, S., Rivest, R.L.: A digital signature scheme secure against adaptive chosen-message attacks. SIAM J. Comput. **17**(2), 281–308 (1988)
22. International Civil Aviation Organization (ICAO): Machine Readable Travel Documents, Part 11, Security Mechanisms for MRTDs, 7th edn. Doc 9303 (2015)
23. Jager, T., Kohlar, F., Schäge, S., Schwenk, J.: On the security of TLS-DHE in the standard model. In: Safavi-Naini, R., Canetti, R. (eds.) CRYPTO 2012. LNCS, vol. 7417, pp. 273–293. Springer, Heidelberg (2012). doi:10.1007/978-3-642-32009-5_17
24. Kiltz, E.: A tool box of cryptographic functions related to the Diffie-Hellman function. In: Rangan, C.P., Ding, C. (eds.) INDOCRYPT 2001. LNCS, vol. 2247, pp. 339–349. Springer, Heidelberg (2001). doi:10.1007/3-540-45311-3_32
25. Krawczyk, H., Bellare, M., Canetti, R.: HMAC: keyed-hashing for message authentication. RFC 2104 (Informational), February 1997. http://www.ietf.org/rfc/rfc2104.txt. Updated by RFC 6151
26. Krawczyk, H.: HMQV: a high-performance secure Diffie-Hellman protocol. In: Shoup, V. (ed.) CRYPTO 2005. LNCS, vol. 3621, pp. 546–566. Springer, Heidelberg (2005). doi:10.1007/11535218_33
27. Krawczyk, H.: Cryptographic extraction and key derivation: the HKDF scheme. In: Rabin, T. (ed.) CRYPTO 2010. LNCS, vol. 6223, pp. 631–648. Springer, Heidelberg (2010). doi:10.1007/978-3-642-14623-7_34
28. Krawczyk, H., Eronen, P.: HMAC-based extract-and-expand key derivation function (HKDF). RFC 5869 (Informational), May 2010. https://rfc-editor.org/rfc/rfc5869.txt
29. Krawczyk, H., Paterson, K.G., Wee, H.: On the security of the TLS protocol: a systematic analysis. In: Canetti, R., Garay, J.A. (eds.) CRYPTO 2013. LNCS, vol. 8042, pp. 429–448. Springer, Heidelberg (2013). doi:10.1007/978-3-642-40041-4_24
30. Krawczyk, H., Wee, H.: The OPTLS protocol and TLS 1.3. In: 2016 IEEE European Symposium on Security and Privacy, pp. 81–96. IEEE, March 2016
31. Li, X., Xu, J., Zhang, Z., Feng, D., Hu, H.: Multiple handshakes security of TLS 1.3 candidates. In: IEEE Symposium on Security and Privacy, SP 2016, San Jose, CA, USA, 22–26 May 2016, pp. 486–505. IEEE Computer Society (2016)
32. Lychev, R., Jero, S., Boldyreva, A., Nita-Rotaru, C.: How secure and quick is QUIC? Provable security and performance analyses. In: 2015 IEEE Symposium on Security and Privacy, pp. 214–231. IEEE Computer Society Press, May 2015
33. Maurer, U.M., Wolf, S.: Diffie-Hellman oracles. In: Koblitz, N. (ed.) CRYPTO 1996. LNCS, vol. 1109, pp. 268–282. Springer, Heidelberg (1996). doi:10.1007/3-540-68697-5_21

34. NIST: Federal Information Processing Standard 202, SHA-3 Standard: Permutation-based hash and extendable-output functions, August 2015. http://dx.doi.org/10.6028/NIST.FIPS.202
35. Paillier, P., Vergnaud, D.: Discrete-log-based signatures may not be equivalent to discrete log. In: Roy, B. (ed.) ASIACRYPT 2005. LNCS, vol. 3788, pp. 1–20. Springer, Heidelberg (2005). doi:10.1007/11593447_1
36. Rescorla, E.: The transport layer security (TLS) protocol version 1.3 - draft-ietf-tls-tls13-20, April 2017. https://tools.ietf.org/html/draft-ietf-tls-tls13-20
37. Ustaoglu, B.: Obtaining a secure and efficient key agreement protocol from (H)MQV and NAXOS. Des. Codes Cryptography **46**(3), 329–342 (2008)

A New Distribution-Sensitive Secure Sketch and Popularity-Proportional Hashing

Joanne Woodage[1(✉)], Rahul Chatterjee[2], Yevgeniy Dodis[3], Ari Juels[2], and Thomas Ristenpart[2]

[1] Royal Holloway, University of London, Egham, England
joanne.woodage.2014@rhul.ac.uk
[2] Cornell Tech, New York City, USA
[3] New York University, New York City, USA

Abstract. Motivated by typo correction in password authentication, we investigate cryptographic error-correction of secrets in settings where the distribution of secrets is a priori (approximately) known. We refer to this as the distribution-sensitive setting.

We design a new secure sketch called the layer-hiding hash (LHH) that offers the best security to date. Roughly speaking, we show that LHH saves an additional $\log H_0(W)$ bits of entropy compared to the recent layered sketch construction due to Fuller, Reyzin, and Smith (FRS). Here $H_0(W)$ is the size of the support of the distribution W. When supports are large, as with passwords, our new construction offers a substantial security improvement.

We provide two new constructions of typo-tolerant password-based authentication schemes. The first combines a LHH or FRS sketch with a standard slow-to-compute hash function, and the second avoids secure sketches entirely, correcting typos instead by checking all nearby passwords. Unlike the previous such brute-force-checking construction, due to Chatterjee et al., our new construction uses a hash function whose runtime is proportional to the popularity of the password (forcing a longer hashing time on more popular, lower entropy passwords). We refer to this as popularity-proportional hashing (PPH). We then introduce a framework for comparing different typo-tolerant authentication approaches. We show that PPH always offers a better time / security trade-off than the LHH and FRS constructions, and for certain distributions outperforms the Chatterjee et al. construction. Elsewhere, this latter construction offers the best trade-off. In aggregate our results suggest that the best known secure sketches are still inferior to simpler brute-force based approaches.

1 Introduction

In many settings, secrets needed for cryptography are measured in a noisy fashion. Biometrics such as fingerprints [31,35], keystroke dynamics [23,24], voice [22], and iris scans [31] are examples — each physical measurement produces slight variants of one another. A long line of work has built ad hoc solutions

J. Katz and H. Shacham (Eds.): CRYPTO 2017, Part III, LNCS 10403, pp. 682–710, 2017.
DOI: 10.1007/978-3-319-63697-9_23

for various cryptographic settings [17,22–24], while another line of work starting with Dodis, Ostrovsky, Reyzin and Smith [13] explored a general primitive, called a fuzzy extractor, that can reproducibly derive secret keys given noisy measurements. The canonical fuzzy extractor construction combines a traditional key-derivation function (KDF) with a secure sketch, the latter serving as an error-correction code that additionally leaks a bounded amount of information about the secret.

In this work, we explore error correction for noisy secrets in the distribution-sensitive setting, in which one knows the distribution of secrets while designing cryptographic mechanisms. We ground our investigations in an important running case study: typo-tolerant password checking [12,20], and ultimately offer a number of improvements, both theoretical and practical, on cryptographic error-tolerance in general and the design of typo-tolerant password hardening systems in particular.

Typo-Tolerant Password Checking. Recent work by Chatterjee et al. [12] revealed that users suffer from a high rate of typographical errors (typos), with even a handful of simple-to-correct typos (such as caps lock or other capitalization errors) occurring in 10% of all login attempts at Dropbox. They offered a usability improvement called "brute-force checking": enumerate probable corrections of the submitted (incorrect) password, and check each of them using a previously stored slow-to-compute cryptographic hash of the correct password (e.g., scrypt [26], argon2 [6], or the PKCS#5 hashes [18,27]). They also show empirically that this relaxed checking approach does not noticeably degrade security, assuming careful selection of the typos to correct.

To maintain performance, however, one must limit the runtime of password checking. One can at most handle approximately $b = \mathsf{RT}/\mathsf{c}$ errors given a runtime budget RT and cryptographic hash function that takes time c to compute.[1] Given that c should be slow — in order to prevent brute-force attacks — the size b of the ball, or set of potential corrections around an incorrect password, must be fairly small. Extending to larger numbers of errors — for example we would like to handle the most frequent 64 typos, which would account for approximately 50% of all typos seen in measurement studies — would appear to force c to be too low to ensure security in the face of attackers that obtain the password hash and mount dictionary attacks.

An existing alternative approach to brute-force ball search is to store, along with the password hash, a small bit of information to help in correcting errors. Because we want to maintain security in the case of compromise of a password database, we must ensure that this helper information does not unduly speed up brute-force cracking attacks. We therefore turn to secure sketches [13].

Secure Sketches. Introduced by Dodis, Ostrovsky, Reyzin and Smith [13], sketches allow correction of errors together with bounds on the information leaked about the original secret to an attacker. Traditionally, sketch security is measured by the conditional min-entropy $\tilde{\mathrm{H}}_\infty(W|s)$ of the secret W given the

[1] This ignores parallelism, but the point remains should one consider it.

sketch s against unbounded adversaries. Fuller, Reyzin, and Smith (FRS) [15] show that the best one can hope for when achieving correction error at most δ is $\tilde{\mathrm{H}}_\infty(W|s) \geq \mathrm{H}^{\mathrm{fuzz}}_{t,\infty}(W) - \log(1-\delta)$, where $\mathrm{H}^{\mathrm{fuzz}}_{t,\infty}(W)$ is called the fuzzy min-entropy of the distribution and captures the worst-case cumulative weight of all points in a ball.

FRS give a clever construction, called layered hashing, that almost achieves the optimal result. They prove that

$$\tilde{\mathrm{H}}_\infty(W|s) \geq \mathrm{H}^{\mathrm{fuzz}}_{t,\infty}(W) - \log(1/\delta) - \log \mathrm{H}_0(W) - 1 .$$

Here $\mathrm{H}_0(W)$ is the Hartley entropy, defined to be the logarithm of the size of the distribution's support. The FRS construction provides better bounds than any prior secure sketch construction (and, by the usual construction, the best known fuzzy extractor [13]). The construction works by splitting possible secrets into different layers according to their probability in the distribution W, and then applying a universal hash of a specific length based on a message's layer. Both the layer identifier and the resulting hash value are output. Intuitively, the idea is to tune hash lengths to balance error correction with entropy loss: more probable points are grouped into layers that have much shorter hash values, with less probable points grouped into layers with longer hashes.

The layered sketch works only in (what we call) the distribution-sensitive setting, meaning that the distribution of messages must be known at the time one designs the sketching algorithm. As another potential limitation, correcting an error using the sketch takes time linear in the size of the ball around the point, meaning the construction is only computationally efficient should balls be efficiently enumerable. That said, both conditions are satisfied in some settings, including typo-tolerant password checking: password leaks allow accurate characterization of password distributions [7,19,21,33] when constructing sketches, and as mentioned above, the ball of errors required to cover most observed typos is small and fast to enumerate.

Our Contributions. In this work, we explore the open question above: How can we securely correct more errors than Chatterjee et al. in [12]? We offer two new approaches. The first uses secure sketching, and we give a new scheme, called the layer-hiding hash (LHH), and prove that it leaks less information than prior constructions. Perhaps counter-intuitively, LHH does so by actually lengthening, rather than shortening, the output of the sketch as compared to the FRS construction. Our second approach is a new distribution-sensitive brute-force based technique called popularity-proportional hashing (PPH), in which the time required to hash a password is tuned based on its popularity: The more probable the password is, the longer the hashing should take.

Finally, we offer a framework for comparing various approaches, and show that PPH offers a better time / security trade-off than LHH and FRS. For certain error settings, PPH allows us to correct more errors securely than Chatterjee et al.'s brute-force checking. Elsewhere their brute-force checking offers a better trade-off still. In fact, we conjecture that for many distributions no sketch will beat brute-force based approaches.

The Layer-Hiding Hash Sketch. Our first contribution is to provide a new sketch that we call the layer-hiding hash (LHH) sketch. We prove that LHH enjoys an upper bound of $\tilde{\mathrm{H}}_\infty(W|s) \geq \mathrm{H}^{\mathrm{fuzz}}_{t,\infty}(W) - \log(1/\delta) - 1$, yielding a substantial saving of $\log \mathrm{H}_0(W)$ bits of entropy over FRS. The LHH starts with the same general approach as FRS, that of putting passwords into layers based on their probability. The key insight is that one can, as the name implies, hide the layer of the password underlying a sketch. To do so, the construction takes the output of applying a layer-specific strongly universal hash to the password and pads it to a carefully chosen maximum length with random bits. During recovery, one looks for a matching prefix of the sketch value when applying (differing length) strongly universal hashes. Hiding the level intuitively avoids leaking additional information to the adversary, but, counterintuitively, the proof of security does not require any properties of the hash functions used. Rather, the proof only uses that the length of hash outputs is bounded plus the fact that (unlike in the FRS construction) sketches from different layers can collide. The proof of correctness relies on the strong universality of the underlying hashes.

LHH's bound improves over FRS (and, consequently, all other known constructions) because it removes the $\log \mathrm{H}_0(W)$ term. The improvement in the bound can be significant. Assuming W places non-zero probability on all passwords from the RockYou password leak [29] already makes $\log \mathrm{H}_0(W) \geq 3$. The min-entropy (let alone fuzzy min-entropy) of common password distributions is commonly measured to be only about 7 bits, making a loss of 3 bits significant. Of course, as pointed out by FRS, the loss due to $\log(1/\delta)$ — which LHH also suffers — is likely to be even more problematic since we'd like δ to be small. An important question left open by our work is whether one can build a sketch that replaces $\log(1/\delta)$ with the optimal $\log(1-\delta)$.

Sketch-Based Typo-Tolerant Checking. A seemingly attractive way of building a typo-tolerant password-based authentication scheme is to store a sketch of the password along with a slow-to-compute hash of the password. To later authenticate a submitted string, one first checks it with the slow hash and, if that fails, uses the sketch to error correct, and checks the result with the slow hash. In terms of security, we are primarily concerned about attackers that obtain (e.g., by system compromise) the sketch and slow hash value and mount offline brute-force dictionary attacks. The sketch will leak some information useful to the attacker.

The first challenge that arises in security analysis is that the traditional sketch security measure, conditional min-entropy $\tilde{\mathrm{H}}_\infty(W|s)$, does *not* provide good bounds when adversaries can make many guesses. The reason is that it measures the worst-case probability of guessing the message given the sketch in a single attempt, and for non-flat distributions the success probability of subsequent guesses after the first will be much lower. We therefore introduce a more general conditional q-min-entropy notion, denoted $\tilde{\mathrm{H}}^q_\infty(W|s)$. It is the worst-case aggregate probability of a message being any of q values, conditioned on the sketch. We revisit secure sketches in this new regime and analyze the q-min-entropy for the FRS and LHH constructions. These results are actually strictly more general since they cover the $q = 1$ bounds as well, and so in the body we start with the more general treatment and show the $q = 1$ results mentioned above as corollaries.

Popularity-Proportional Hashing. We also offer a new distribution-sensitive variant of brute-force checking called popularity-proportional hashing. Recall that brute-force checking uses the same slow hash function for all passwords. In popularity-proportional hashing, we use knowledge of the distribution of passwords to tune the time required to hash each password. The more popular a password, equivalently the more probable, the longer the hash computation.

In typo-tolerant hashing this has a nice effect for certain distributions: the ball of possible passwords around a submitted string will consist of a mix of lower- and higher-probability points, making the aggregate time required to check all of them lower than in brute-force checking. Timing side-channels can be avoided by fixing an upper bound on this aggregate time, and setting the hashing costs of the scheme such that every password can be checked within this time. The checking algorithm is then implemented to process each password for this maximum time, and accordingly its run time reveals nothing about the password being checked. This serves to "smooth" the distribution from the point of view of a brute-force attacker, who must choose between checking a popular password versus lower-cost checks of less probable passwords. We shall ultimately see that PPH offers a better time / security trade-off than sketch-based checking using both FRS and LHH. We note that the benefits of population-proportional hashing appear to be specific to the typo-tolerant setting; in exact checking schemes one would want to hash passwords with the maximum cost allowed by the runtime of the scheme, regardless of their weight.

Comparing the Approaches. We use the following methodology to compare the time / security trade-offs of the various approaches to error-tolerant authentication. First, one fixes an error setting, such as choosing a set of 64 frequently made typos, as well as a runtime budget RT for authentication. Then, one compares the brute-force attack security of various constructions that operate in time at most RT and correct the specified errors. So for brute-force checking, for example, one must pick a slow hash function that takes $\mathsf{RT}/64$ time to compute, and for secure sketches one can use a slow hash of time $\mathsf{RT}/2$ (where for simplicity we ignore the sketch cost, which is in practice negligible relative to RT). For popularity-proportional hashing one picks hash speeds so that the ball whose passwords have the highest aggregate probability can be checked in time RT.

With this framework in place, we prove that PPH provides a better time / security trade-off than both FRS-assisted and LHH-assisted checking. The proofs require lower-bounding the security of the FRS and LHH constructions in the face of a computationally efficient attacker whose runtime constraint affords him q slow hash queries (equivalently q guesses at the underlying password). The attack is simple: enumerate probable passwords, check which match the sketch, and output the heaviest q that match. It may not be obvious that this is efficient, we will argue so in the body.

To analyze the attacker's success, we use a proof strategy which at a high level proceeds as follows. We first model the hash underlying the sketch as a random oracle. This is conservative as it can only make the adversary's task harder. We then transform the analysis of the attacker's success probability to a type of balls-in-bins analysis that differs slightly based on the construction. For the FRS case, which is simpler, balls of differing sizes represent passwords of differing weights, and bins represent individual sketch values within a layer. The random oracle 'throws' the balls into the bins; the compromise of a sketch and subsequent guessing attack is captured by sampling a bin and allowing the attacker to choose q balls from it. As such computing a lower bound on the q-conditional min-entropy is reduced to computing the expected (over the random oracle coins) aggregate weight of the q heaviest balls across all bins.

Instead of tackling analysis of this expectation directly, we instead form direct comparison with PPH by showing that with overwhelming probability the set of points queried by an optimal brute-force adversary running in the same time against PPH will be included in the set of points that the adversary against FRS chooses. As such a brute-force attacker against FRS-assisted checking will always either match or (more often) beat attacks against PPH. We derive a similar result for LHH-assisted checking via a modified balls-in-bins experiment.

With the improvement of PPH over sketch-assisted checking established, we next compare PPH and brute-force checking. We quantify precisely the conditions which determine whether PPH or brute-force checking represents the better trade-off for a given error setting, and show that for certain error settings PPH allows us to correct many more errors securely than brute-force checking.

While PPH can be shown to improve on sketch-assisted checking for any distribution, the same is not true for brute-force checking — indeed there exist settings in which brute-force checking will lead to a dramatic reduction in security — and in general comparing the brute-force and sketch-assisted approaches directly appears technically challenging. However by combining the above results, we show that for certain error settings (including passwords) the seemingly simplest brute-force checking approach provides the best trade-off of all — first by invoking the result showing PPH outperforms sketch-assisted checking, and then by showing that brute-force checking offers an even better trade-off than PPH. As such for any given error setting, our results can be used to determine how many errors can be tolerated, and whether PPH or brute-force checking offers the better approach to typo-tolerance.

Extensions and Open Problems. We frame our results in the context of typo-tolerant password hashing and (reflecting the majority of in-use password hashing functions) primarily measure hashing cost in terms of time. We will in Sect. 7 briefly discuss how our results may be extended to incorporate memory-hard functions [1–3,6,26] and indicate other cryptographic applications, such as authenticated encryption and fuzzy extraction, in which they are applicable. Finally we will discuss the key open problem — can *any* distribution-sensitive secure sketch offer a better time / security trade-off than brute-force based approaches? We conjecture that for a large class of error settings no sketch can perform better. We offer some intuition to this end, and highlight it as an interesting direction for future research.

2 Definitions and Preliminaries

Notation. The set of binary strings of length n is denoted by $\{0,1\}^n$. We use $\perp$ to represent the null symbol. We write $x||y$ to denote the concatenation of two binary strings x and y, and $[y]_1^j$ to denote the binary string y truncated to the lowest order j bits. We let $[j]$ denote the set of integers from 1 to j inclusive, and $[j_1, j_2]$ the set of integers between j_1 and j_2 inclusive. The notation $x \xleftarrow{\$} \mathcal{X}$ denotes sampling an element uniformly at random from the set $\mathcal{X}$, and we let $x \xleftarrow{W} \mathcal{X}$ denote sampling an element from the set $\mathcal{X}$ according to the distribution W. All logs are to base 2, and e denotes Euler's constant. For a given distribution W where $\mathcal{M} = \text{supp}(W)$, we let $w_1, \ldots, w_{|\mathcal{M}|}$ denote the points in the support of W in order of descending probability, with associated probabilities $p_1, \ldots, p_{|\mathcal{M}|}$.

Hash Functions. Here we recall the definitions of universal and strongly universal hash function families.

Definition 1. *A family of hash functions* $\mathsf{F} : \mathcal{S} \times \{0,1\}^\ell \rightarrow \{0,1\}^d$ *is said to be universal if for all* $w \neq w' \in \mathcal{S}$, *it holds that*

$$\Pr\left[\mathsf{F}(w;\mathsf{sa}) = \mathsf{F}(w';\mathsf{sa}) \ : \ \mathsf{sa} \xleftarrow{\$} \{0,1\}^\ell\right] = 2^{-d}\,.$$

Definition 2. *A family of hash functions* $\mathsf{F} : \mathcal{S} \times \{0,1\}^\ell \rightarrow \{0,1\}^d$ *is said to be strongly universal if for all* $w \neq w' \in \mathcal{S}$, *and* $y, y' \in \{0,1\}^d$, *it holds that*

$$\Pr\left[\mathsf{F}(w;\mathsf{sa}) = y \ : \ \mathsf{sa} \xleftarrow{\$} \{0,1\}^\ell\right] = 2^{-d}\,, \text{ and}$$

$$\Pr\left[\mathsf{F}(w;\mathsf{sa}) = y \wedge \mathsf{F}(w';\mathsf{sa}) = y' \ : \ \mathsf{sa} \xleftarrow{\$} \{0,1\}^\ell\right] \leq 2^{-2d}\,.$$

Error Settings and Typos. Let $\mathcal{S}$ be a set with associated distance function $\mathsf{dist} : \mathcal{S} \times \mathcal{S} \rightarrow \mathbb{R}^{\geq 0}$. If dist is a metric over $\mathcal{S}$ — that is to say that dist is non-negative, symmetric, and for all $x, y, z \in \mathcal{S}$, it holds that $\mathsf{dist}(x,z) \leq \mathsf{dist}(x,y) + \mathsf{dist}(y,z)$ — then we say that the pair $(\mathcal{S}, \mathsf{dist})$ is a metric space. We can assign to $\mathcal{S}$ a distribution W, and let $\mathcal{M}$ denote the set of possible messages, $\mathcal{M} = \text{supp}(W)$. We set an error threshold t, denoting the maximum distance between points $w, \tilde{w}$ for which will consider $\tilde{w}$ an error of w. Together these components, $(\mathcal{S}, W, \mathsf{dist}, t)$ define an *error setting.*

For an error setting $\mathsf{E} = (\mathcal{S}, W, \mathsf{dist}, t)$, the (closed) ball of size t around $\tilde{w} \in \mathcal{S}$ is the set of all points $w' \in \text{supp}(W)$ such that $\mathsf{dist}(w', \tilde{w}) \leq t$, that is $B_t(\tilde{w}) = \{w' \in \text{supp}(W) \mid \mathsf{dist}(w', \tilde{w}) \leq t\}$. We let $\beta_{\max}$ denote the size of the largest ball in the error setting; that is to say $\beta_{\max} = \max_{\tilde{w}} |B_t(\tilde{w})|$. In this work, we shall be especially interested in error settings for which balls are *efficiently enumerable*, a property which we formalize below.

Definition 3. *Let* $\mathsf{E} = (\mathcal{S}, W, \mathsf{dist}, t)$ *be an error setting with maximum ball size* $\beta_{\max}$. *We say* E *has efficiently enumerable balls, if there exists an algorithm* Enum *which takes as input a point* $\tilde{w} \in \mathcal{S}$, *and outputs a set of points* $\mathcal{L}$ *such that for all* $\tilde{w} \in \mathcal{S}$ *it holds that*

$$\Pr\left[\mathcal{L} = B_t(\tilde{w}) \ : \ \mathcal{L} \xleftarrow{\$} \mathsf{Enum}(\tilde{w})\right] = 1 ,$$

and Enum *runs in time polynomial in* $\beta_{\max}$.

Entropy. We now discuss several notions of entropy which capture the maximum success probability of an attacker who attempts to guess a point sampled from a given distribution. Traditionally these notions only consider the case in which the adversary gets one guess. However in subsequent work, when we wish to capture the success rate of an adversary attempting to perform a brute-force attack, it will be useful to generalize these entropy notions to capture the maximum success probability of an adversary who may output a vector of q guesses. We define these notions below generalized to the multi-guess setting; one can easily extract the familiar definitions by setting $q = 1$.

Definition 4. *Let* W *and* Z *be distributions. We define the q-min-entropy of* W, *denoted* $\mathrm{H}^q_\infty(W)$ *to be,*

$$\mathrm{H}^q_\infty(W) = -\log\left(\max_{w_1,\ldots,w_q} \sum_{i=1}^{q} \Pr\left[\,W = w_i\,\right]\right),$$

where $w_1, \ldots, w_q$ *are distinct elements of* $\mathcal{S}$. *The conditional q-min-entropy of* W *conditioned on* Z, *denoted* $\tilde{\mathrm{H}}^q_\infty(W|Z)$, *is defined to be,*

$$\tilde{\mathrm{H}}^q_\infty(W|Z) = -\log\left(\sum_z \max_{w_1,\ldots,w_q} \sum_{i=1}^{q} \Pr\left[\,W = w_i \mid Z = z\,\right] \cdot \Pr\left[\,Z = z\,\right]\right);$$

and the q-min-entropy of W *joint with* Z, *denoted* $\mathrm{H}^q_\infty(W, Z)$, *is defined,*

$$\mathrm{H}^q_\infty(W, Z) = -\log\left(\max_{\substack{w_1,\ldots,w_q \\ z_1,\ldots,z_q}} \sum_{i=1}^{q} \Pr\left[\,W = w_i \wedge Z = z_i\,\right]\right),$$

where the $w_1, \ldots, w_q$ *and* $z_1, \ldots, z_q$ *are distinct elements of the supports of* W *and* Z *respectively. The Hartley entropy of* W, *denoted* $\mathrm{H}_0(W)$, *is defined to be,*

$$\mathrm{H}_0(W) = \log|\mathrm{supp}(W)| .$$

For an example which surfaces the usefulness of extending min-entropy definitions beyond one guess, consider a pair of distributions W_1 and W_2, such that W_1 is flat with $2^{-\mathrm{H}_\infty(W)} = 2^{-\mu}$ and W_2 consists of one point of probability $2^{-\mu}$ and $2^{2\mu} - 2^{\mu}$ points of probability $2^{-2\mu}$. While $\mathrm{H}^1_\infty(W_1) = \mathrm{H}^1_\infty(W_2) = \mu$, the two distributions are clearly very different, and in particular an attacker given some

$q > 1$ guesses to predict a value sampled from each of the distributions is going to have a much easier time with W_1. This difference is highlighted when considering the q-min-entropy, with $\mathrm{H}^q_\infty(W_1) = q{\cdot}2^{-\mu}$, whereas $\mathrm{H}^q_\infty(W_2) = 2^{-\mu}{+}(q{-}1){\cdot}2^{-2\mu}$.

In the $q = 1$ case, the conditional min-entropy and Hartley entropy are linked via the chain rule for conditional min-entropy [13]. It is straightforward to see that this result extends to the multi-guess setting; for completeness we include a proof in the full version.

Lemma 1. *Let W, Z be distributions. Then*

$$\tilde{\mathrm{H}}^q_\infty(W|Z) \geq \mathrm{H}^q_\infty(W, Z) - \mathrm{H}_0(Z) .$$

Secure Sketches. Let $\mathsf{E} = (\mathcal{S}, W, \mathsf{dist}, t)$ be an error setting. Secure sketches, introduced by Dodis et al. in [13], allow reconstruction of a message which may be input with noise, while preserving as much of the min-entropy of the original message as possible.

In this work we focus on sketches in the distribution-sensitive setting, in which the distribution of secrets is precisely known at the time of designing the sketch. While distribution-sensitivity may not always be feasible, in the case of passwords there is a long line of work on accurately modeling the distribution of human-chosen passwords. Primarily motivated by password cracking, modeling techniques such as hidden Markov models (HMM) [11], probabilistic context free grammars (PCFG) [32,33], or neural networks [21] use the plethora of real password leaks (e.g., [9]) to learn good estimates of W. See [19] for a detailed discussion of these approaches. Of course, estimates may be wrong. A discussion on the effect of transferring our results to a setting in which the distribution is only approximately known is included in the full version. We recall the formal definition of secure sketches below.

Definition 5. *Let $\mathsf{E} = (\mathcal{S}, W, \mathsf{dist}, t)$ be an error setting. A secure sketch for E is a pair of algorithms $\mathsf{S} = (\mathsf{SS}, \mathsf{Rec})$ defined as follows:*

- SS *is a randomized algorithm which takes as input $w \in \mathcal{S}$, and outputs a bit string $s \in \{0,1\}^*$.*
- Rec *is an algorithm, possibly randomized, which takes as input $\tilde{w} \in \mathcal{S}$ and $s \in \{0,1\}^*$, and outputs $w' \in B_t(\tilde{w}) \cup \{\perp\}$.*

We note that we slightly modify the definition of [15] so that Rec on input $\tilde{w}$ always outputs $w' \in B_t(\tilde{w}) \cup \{\perp\}$, as opposed to $w' \in \mathcal{S} \cup \{\perp\}$. As we shall see in the following definition, we only require Rec to return the correct point if that point lies in $B_t(\tilde{w})$. As such this is mainly a syntactic change, and all pre-existing sketch constructions discussed in this work already adhere to the condition. In the following definition, we generalize the security requirement to the multi-guess setting in the natural way; the usual definition (e.g. [13,15]) is obtained by setting $q = 1$.

Definition 6. *A sketch $\mathsf{S} = (\mathsf{SS}, \mathsf{Rec})$ is an $((\mathcal{S}, W, \mathsf{dist}, t), \bar{\mu}_q, \delta)$*-secure sketch *if:*

1. (Correctness) *For all* $w, \tilde{w} \in \mathcal{S}$ *for which* $\mathsf{dist}(w, \tilde{w}) \leq t$, *it holds that*

$$\Pr\left[\, w = w' \ :\ w' \leftarrow \mathsf{Rec}(\tilde{w}, \mathsf{SS}(w)) \,\right] \geq 1 - \delta \ ,$$

where the probability is taken over the coins used by SS *and* Rec.

2. (Security) *The q-min-entropy of W conditioned on* $\mathsf{SS}(W)$ *is such that,*

$$\tilde{\mathrm{H}}^{q}_{\infty}(W | \mathsf{SS}(W)) \geq \bar{\mu}_q \ .$$

Since the help string s is public any party — including the adversary — can query $\mathsf{Rec}(\cdot, s)$ on $\tilde{w} \in \mathcal{S}$. In an ideal secure sketch, knowledge of s would offer no greater advantage than that gained via oracle access to $\mathsf{Rec}(\cdot, s)$. In this case, an adversary challenged to guess the original value $w \in \mathcal{S}$ is forced to guess some $\tilde{w}$ such that $\mathsf{dist}(w, \tilde{w}) \leq t$. To capture this notion of ideal secure sketch security, Fuller et al. [15] introduce the notion of fuzzy min-entropy, which we generalize to the multi-guess setting in the natural way.

Definition 7. *Let* $\mathsf{E} = (\mathcal{S}, W, \mathsf{dist}, t)$ *be an error setting. The q-fuzzy min-entropy of W is defined to be,*

$$\mathrm{H}^{q,\mathrm{fuzz}}_{t,\infty}(W) = -\log\left(\max_{\tilde{w}_1, \ldots, \tilde{w}_q} \sum_{w' \in \cup_{i=1}^{q} B_t(\tilde{w}_i)} \Pr\left[\, W = w' \,\right] \right),$$

where $\tilde{w}_1, \ldots, \tilde{w}_q$ *are distinct elements of* $\mathcal{S}$.

3 New Bounds for FRS Sketches

In this section we describe and analyze two constructions of secure sketches due to Fuller, Reyzin, and Smith [15]. The FRS sketches have a number of attractive properties. The first is that these are the only secure sketches (to our knowledge) that can be utilized with *any* choice of distance function dist. We would like this flexibility so that ultimately we can tailor the distance function used to the context of correcting password typos for which, being non-symmetric, traditional metrics such as edit distance are not best suited [12].

Even if edit distance were appropriate, we know of no constructions which provide sufficient security when used with parameters typical to password distributions. Constructions in [13,14] either embed the edit metric into the Hamming or set distance metrics using a low distortion embedding of Ostrovsky and Rabani [25], or use a novel c-shingling technique.

As pointed out in [12], when applied to typical password distributions which have a large alphabet of 96 ASCII characters, then even if we only attempt to correct edit distance one errors, these constructions incur entropy loss ≈ 91 bits and ≈ 31 bits respectively. Given that password distributions typically have at most 8 bits of min-entropy [8], it is clear these constructions are unsuitable for our purposes.

Most importantly, the FRS constructions achieve almost optimal security in the $q = 1$ case. It was shown in [15] that high fuzzy min-entropy is a necessary condition for the existence of a good secure sketch or fuzzy extractor for a given error setting, surfacing a lower bound on the security of such schemes. We recall the result in the lemma below, which we extend to the multi-guess setting. The proof is given in the full version.

Lemma 2. *Let* $\mathsf{E} = (\mathcal{S}, W, \mathsf{dist}, t)$ *be an error setting, and let* $\mathsf{S} = (\mathsf{SS}, \mathsf{Rec})$ *be an* $((\mathcal{S}, W, \mathsf{dist}, t), \bar{\mu}_q, \delta), \bar{\mu}_q, \delta)$*-secure-sketch. Then* $\bar{\mu}_q \leq \mathrm{H}^{q,\mathrm{fuzz}}_{t,\infty}(W) - \log(1 - \delta)$.

FRS showed that in the distribution-sensitive setting, in which the precise distribution is known at the time of building the sketch, high fuzzy min-entropy also implies the existence of a good secure sketch for that distribution. We recall their constructions, and prove new results about them.

3.1 Secure Sketches for Flat Distributions

FRS describe a secure sketch which is nearly optimal for error settings $\mathsf{E} = (\mathcal{S}, W, \mathsf{dist}, t)$ such that W is flat, which we recall in Fig. 1. We refer to this construction as $\mathsf{FRS1} = (\mathsf{FRS1\text{-}SS}, \mathsf{FRS1\text{-}Rec})$.

The construction is built from a universal hash function family with output length $\log(\beta_{\max}) + \log(1/\delta)$ bits, where $\beta_{\max}$ denotes the size of the largest ball in the error setting. $\mathsf{FRS1\text{-}SS}$ chooses a salt $\mathsf{sa} \overset{\$}{\leftarrow} \{0,1\}^\ell$, computes $y = \mathsf{F}(w; \mathsf{sa})$, and outputs $s = (y, \mathsf{sa})$. On input $\tilde{w} \in \mathcal{S}$ and s, Rec searches in $B_t(\tilde{w})$ for a point w' such that $\mathsf{F}(w'; \mathsf{sa}) = y$, returning the first match which it finds. The authors note that the construction is not novel, with universal hash functions representing a commonly used tool for information reconciliation (e.g., [5,28,30]). Correctness follows from a straightforward application of Markov's Inequality. In the following lemma we extend analysis to cover the q-conditional min-entropy. The proof is given in the full version.

Lemma 3. *Let* $\mathsf{E} = (\mathcal{S}, W, \mathsf{dist}, t)$ *be an error setting for which* W *is flat, and let* $\beta_{\max}$ *denote the size of the largest ball. Let* $\mathsf{FRS1} = (\mathsf{FRS1\text{-}SS}, \mathsf{FRS1\text{-}Rec})$ *be as described in Fig. 1, and let* $\mathsf{F} : \mathcal{S} \times \{0,1\}^\ell \rightarrow \{0,1\}^{\log(\beta_{\max})+\log(1/\delta)}$ *be a family of universal hash functions where* $0 < \delta < 1$*. Then* $\mathsf{FRS1}$ *is a* $((\mathcal{S}, W, \mathsf{dist}, t), \bar{\mu}_q, \delta), \bar{\mu}_q, \delta)$*-secure sketch, where*

$$\bar{\mu}_q \geq \mathrm{H}^{\mathrm{fuzz}}_{t,\infty}(W) - \log(q) - \log(1/\delta) .$$

3.2 Layered Hashing for Non-flat Distributions

The above construction may be significantly less secure in settings where the distribution in question is non-flat. In this case, having high fuzzy min-entropy does not exclude the possibility that the distribution contains a dense ball consisting of many low probability points. Disambiguating between points in this

FRS1-SS(w) :	FRS1-Rec($\tilde{w}, s$) :
$\mathsf{sa} \xleftarrow{\$} \{0,1\}^{\ell}$	$(y, \mathsf{sa}) \leftarrow s$
$y \leftarrow \mathsf{F}(w; \mathsf{sa})$	for $w' \in B_t(\tilde{w})$
$s \leftarrow (y, \mathsf{sa})$	if $\mathsf{F}(w'; \mathsf{sa}) = y$
Ret s	Ret w'
	Ret $\perp$

Fig. 1. Construction of a secure sketch $\mathsf{FRS1} = (\mathsf{FRS1\text{-}SS}, \mathsf{FRS1\text{-}Rec})$ for an error setting $\mathsf{E} = (\mathcal{S}, W, \mathsf{dist}, t)$ from a universal hash function family $\mathsf{F} : \mathcal{S} \times \{0,1\}^{\ell} \rightarrow \{0,1\}^{\log(\beta_{\max})+\log(1/\delta)}$. Here $\beta_{\max}$ denotes the size of the largest ball in the error setting.

dense ball forces a hash function with a large range to be used, which leaks more information to adversaries.

The key idea is to split the support of the distribution into nearly flat layers; the layer in which a point lies is determined by its probability, and the layers are defined such that the probabilities of points in any given layer differ by at most a factor of two. We include the index of the layer in which a point lies as part of its sketch, and then apply the secure sketch for flat distributions of Lemma 3 tuned to the parameters of the appropriate layer. Revealing the layer in which a point lies degrades security; in an attempt to limit the damage, the number of layers is restricted so the extra loss amounts to $\log \mathrm{H}_0(W) + 1$ bits; for full details of the proof see [15].

For simplicity of exposition, we assume the existence of an efficient algorithm L which takes as input a point $w \in \mathcal{S}$ and outputs the index $j \in \mathcal{J}$ of the layer in which it lies. We note that the parameters required to compute the cut-off points between layers are readily obtained from the password model, so computing the partitions is straightforward in practice; provided we can efficiently look up the weights of points in the password model, the algorithm L will be efficient also. The full construction is given in Fig. 2.

FRS2-SS(w) :	FRS2-Rec($\tilde{w}, s$) :	FRS2-Layer(W) :
$j \leftarrow \mathsf{L}(w)$	$(y, \mathsf{sa}, j) \leftarrow s$	$\lambda \leftarrow \mathrm{H}_{\infty}(W) + \lfloor \mathrm{H}_0(W) - 1 \rfloor$
if $j = \lambda$	If $j = \lambda$	for $j = \mu, \ldots, \lambda - 1$
$s \leftarrow (w, \perp, \lambda)$	Ret y	$L_j \leftarrow (2^{-(j+1)}, 2^{-j}]$
else	for $w' \in B_t(\tilde{w}) \cap L_j$	$L_{\lambda} \leftarrow (0, 2^{-\lambda}]$
$\mathsf{sa} \xleftarrow{\$} \{0,1\}^{\ell_j}$	if $\mathsf{F}_j(w'; \mathsf{sa}) = y$	Ret $\{L_j : j \in [\mu, \lambda]\}$
$y \leftarrow \mathsf{F}_j(w; \mathsf{sa})$	Ret w'	
$s \leftarrow (y, \mathsf{sa}, j)$	Ret $\perp$	
Ret s		

Fig. 2. Secure sketch $\mathsf{FRS2} = (\mathsf{FRS2\text{-}SS}, \mathsf{FRS2\text{-}Rec})$ for an error setting $\mathsf{E} = (\mathcal{S}, W, \mathsf{dist}, t)$ from a set of universal hash function families $\mathsf{F}_j : \mathcal{S} \times \{0,1\}^{\ell_j} \rightarrow \{0,1\}^{j - \mathrm{H}^{\mathrm{fuzz}}_{t,\infty}(W) + \log(1/\delta) + 1}$ for $j \in [\mu, \lambda]$, utilizing layering FRS2-Layer.

Theorem 1 [15]. *Let* $\mathsf{E} = (\mathcal{S}, W, \mathsf{dist}, t)$ *be an error setting. Let* $\mathsf{F}_j : \mathcal{S} \times \{0,1\}^{\ell_j} \to \{0,1\}^{j-\mathrm{H}^{\mathrm{fuzz}}_{t,\infty}(W)+\log(1/\delta)+1}$ *be a family of universal hash functions, where* $0 < \delta \le \frac{1}{2}$. *Consider* $\mathsf{FRS2} = (\mathsf{FRS2\text{-}SS}, \mathsf{FRS2\text{-}Rec})$ *with layering* FRS2-Layer *as defined in Fig. 2. Then* FRS2 *is a* $((\mathcal{S}, W, \mathsf{dist}, t), \tilde{\mu}_1, \delta)$*-secure sketch where*

$$\tilde{\mu}_1 = \mathrm{H}^{\mathrm{fuzz}}_{t,\infty}(W) - \log \mathrm{H}_0(W) - \log(1/\delta) - 1.$$

In the following theorem, we provide an analysis for FRS2 in the q-min-entropy setting. Our analysis also provides a tighter bound in the case that $q = 1$. The full proof is given in the full version.

Theorem 2. *Let* $\mathsf{E} = (\mathcal{S}, W, \mathsf{dist}, t)$ *be an error setting, where* $\mathrm{H}^{\mathrm{fuzz}}_{t,\infty}(W) = \tilde{\mu}$. *Let* $\mathsf{F}_j : \mathcal{S} \times \{0,1\}^{\ell_j} \to \{0,1\}^{j-\mathrm{H}^{\mathrm{fuzz}}_{t,\infty}(W)+\log(1/\delta)+1}$ *be a family of universal hash functions, where* $0 < \delta \le \frac{1}{2}$. *Consider* $\mathsf{FRS2} = (\mathsf{FRS2\text{-}SS}, \mathsf{FRS2\text{-}Rec})$ *with layering* FRS2-Layer *as defined in Fig. 2. Then* FRS2 *is a* $((\mathcal{S}, W, \mathsf{dist}, t), \tilde{\mu}_q, \delta)$*-secure sketch for,*

$$2^{-\tilde{\mu}_q} \le \Pr[W \in L_\lambda] + \sum_{j=\mu}^{\lambda-1} \Pr[W \in L_j(q \cdot |R_j|)].$$

Here $L_j(q')$ *denotes the set of the* $\min\{q', |L_j|\}$ *heaviest points in layer* L_j. *We let* $R_j = range(\mathsf{F}_j)$ *and let* $L_\lambda = \{w \in W : \Pr[W = w] < 2^{-\lambda}\}$ *where* $\lambda = \mathrm{H}_\infty(W) + \lfloor \mathrm{H}_0(W) - 1 \rfloor$.

We note that the additional tightness in the bound is especially beneficial when considering distributions with many sparsely populated or empty layers. To give a concrete example of a distribution for which the tightness in the bound makes a significant difference, consider an error setting for which W contains 2^{99} points of weight 2^{-100}, and 2^{199} points of weight 2^{-200}, and the case that $q = 1$. Since $\mathrm{H}_0(W) \approx 199$, the bound of Theorem 1 implies that $\tilde{\mathrm{H}}_\infty(W|\mathsf{FRS2\text{-}SS}(W)) \ge \mathrm{H}^{\mathrm{fuzz}}_{t,\infty}(W) - \log(1/\delta) - 8.64$. In contrast applying the new bound of Theorem 2 implies that $\tilde{\mathrm{H}}_\infty(W|\mathsf{FRS2\text{-}SS}(W)) \ge \mathrm{H}^{\mathrm{fuzz}}_{t,\infty}(W) - \log(1/\delta) - 2$, (since $\Pr[W \in L_j(|R_j|)] \le 2^{-\mathrm{H}^{\mathrm{fuzz}}_{t,\infty}(W)+\log(1/\delta)+1}$ for $j = 100, 200$, and 0 otherwise). This results in a saving of over 6.6 bits of entropy.

4 A New Construction: Layer Hiding Hash

In this section we present a new construction which yields a substantial increase in security over FRS2, while enjoying the same degree of correctness. The construction, which we call layer hiding hash and denote LHH = (LHH-SS, LHH-Rec) is similar to FRS2, but crucially does not explicitly reveal the layer in which a point lies as part of the sketch.

First we split the distribution into layers as shown in Fig. 3. Note that this layering is slightly different to that used in FRS2. We now require a family of *strongly* universal hash functions, which we use to hash points $w \in \mathcal{M}$ to a fixed length which is a parameter of the scheme, and then truncate this hash to various lengths depending on the layer in which the point lies (in turn creating a family of strongly universal hash functions for each layer). The strong universality of the hash is required for the proof of correctness in which we bound the probability that the hash of a point w collides with a given string; this represents a recovery error and the lengths of the truncated hashes are chosen such that the probability this event occurs is at most δ.

The twist that enables the security savings is that rather than outputting this truncated hash as is and revealing the layer in which a point lies, we now view this hash as a *prefix*. The sketch is then computed by choosing a string at random from the set of all strings of a given length (a parameter of the scheme) which share that prefix. This is done efficiently by padding the hash with the appropriate number of random bits. The effect of this is to nearly flatten the joint distribution of W and $\mathsf{SS}(W)$ such that for all $w \in \mathcal{M}$ and $s \in \text{supp}(\mathsf{SS}(W))$, it holds that $\Pr[W = w \wedge \mathsf{SS}(W) = s] \leq 2^{-(\gamma+\ell)}$ (where γ indexes the layer of least probable points, and ℓ denotes the length of the salt) *regardless* of the layer in which the point lies. During recovery, the sketch searches in the ball of the input for a point whose truncated hash matches the prefix of the sketch value, and outputs the first match it finds. The full construction is shown in Fig. 3.

$\underline{\mathsf{LHH\text{-}SS}(w):}$	$\underline{\mathsf{LHH\text{-}Rec}(\tilde{w}, s):}$	$\underline{\mathsf{LHH\text{-}Layer}(W):}$
$\mathsf{sa} \xleftarrow{\$} \{0,1\}^\ell$	$(y, \mathsf{sa}) \leftarrow s$	$\gamma \leftarrow \left\lfloor -\log\left(\min_{w \in W} \Pr[W = w]\right)\right\rfloor$
$j \leftarrow \mathsf{L}(w)$	for $w' \in B_t(\tilde{w})$	for $j = \mu, \ldots, \gamma$
$y_1 \leftarrow [\mathsf{F}(w; \mathsf{sa})]_1^{j-\tilde{\mu}+\log(\frac{1}{\delta})+1}$	$\quad j' \leftarrow \mathsf{L}(w')$	$\quad L_j \leftarrow (2^{-(j+1)}, 2^{-j}]$
$y_2 \xleftarrow{\$} \{0,1\}^{\gamma-j}$	$\quad y' \leftarrow [\mathsf{F}(w'; \mathsf{sa})]_1^{j'-\tilde{\mu}+\log(\frac{1}{\delta})+1}$	Ret $\{L_j \ : \ j \in [\mu, \gamma]\}$
$y \leftarrow y_1 \| y_2$	$\quad$ if $y' = [y]_1^{j'-\tilde{\mu}+\log(\frac{1}{\delta})+1}$	
$s \leftarrow (y, \mathsf{sa})$	$\qquad$ Ret w'	
Ret s	Ret $\perp$	

Fig. 3. Construction of secure sketch $\mathsf{LHH} = (\mathsf{LHH\text{-}SS}, \mathsf{LHH\text{-}Rec})$ for an error setting $\mathsf{E} = (\mathcal{S}, W, \mathsf{dist}, t)$ with $\tilde{\mu} = \mathrm{H}^{\mathrm{fuzz}}_{t,\infty}(W)$, from a family of strongly universal hash functions $\mathsf{F} : \mathcal{S} \times \{0,1\}^\ell \rightarrow \{0,1\}^{\gamma-\tilde{\mu}+\log(\frac{1}{\delta})+1}$, utilizing layering $\mathsf{LHH\text{-}Layer}$.

In the following theorem we analyze the correctness and security of LHH, and emphasize the substantial entropy saving in the $q = 1$ case of $\log \mathrm{H}_0(W)$ bits in comparison to $\mathsf{FRS2}$. The proof is given in the full version.

Theorem 3. *Let* $\mathsf{E} = (\mathcal{S}, W, \mathsf{dist}, t)$ *be an error setting. Let* $\mathsf{F} : \mathcal{S} \times \{0,1\}^\ell \rightarrow \{0,1\}^{\gamma-\mathrm{H}^{\mathrm{fuzz}}_{t,\infty}(W)+\log(1/\delta)+1}$ *be a family of strongly universal hash functions where* $0 < \delta < 1$. *Let* $\mathsf{LHH} = (\mathsf{LHH\text{-}SS}, \mathsf{LHH\text{-}Rec})$ *be as shown in Fig. 3 with layering* $\mathsf{LHH\text{-}Layer}$. *Then* LHH *is a* $((\mathcal{S}, W, \mathsf{dist}, t), \bar{\mu}_q, \delta), \bar{\mu}_q, \delta)$*-secure sketch, where,*

$$\bar{\mu}_q = \mathrm{H}^{q \cdot \eta}_\infty(W') \ .$$

Here $\eta = 2^{\gamma-\mathrm{H}^{\mathrm{fuzz}}_{t,\infty}(W)+\log(1/\delta)+1}$, *and* W' *is the distribution constructed by taking each point* $w \in \mathcal{M}$ *and replacing it with* $2^{(\gamma-j)}$ *points, each of weight*

$\Pr[W = w] \cdot 2^{-(\gamma - j)}$, *where* $w \in L_j$. *In particular in the case where* $q = 1$, *this gives,*

$$\bar{\mu}_1 \geq \mathrm{H}^{\mathrm{fuzz}}_{t,\infty}(W) - \log(1/\delta) - 1 .$$

5 Typo-Tolerant Password-Based Key Derivation

In this section we consider the application of secure sketches to typo-tolerant password-based key-derivation functions (PBKDF). PBKDFs are used in a number of settings, for example in password-based authentication during login and password-based encryption. PBKDFs are designed to slow attackers that mount brute-force attacks, by incorporating a computationally slow and / or memory-consuming task.

We begin by treating password-based authentication schemes (PBAS). We discuss how to extend to other PBKDF settings in Sect. 7. Roughly speaking, our results will apply in any situation in which the PBKDF-derived key is used in a cryptographically strong authentication setting, including notably password-based authenticated encryption. We will use an oracle model to capture computational slowness, analogous to prior treatments of PBKDFs in the random oracle model (ROM) [4,34]. We will denote by $\mathbf{H}$ the oracle, and assume it behaves as a random oracle mapping arbitrary length strings to randomly chosen strings of a fixed length ℓ_H. We let $\mathbf{H}$ take an additional input c representing the unit cost of querying $\mathbf{H}$. We formalize such schemes below, following [12].

Definition 8. *A PBAS is a pair of algorithms* $\mathsf{PBAS} = (\mathrm{Reg}, \mathrm{Chk})$ *defined as follows:*

- $\mathrm{Reg}^{\mathbf{H}}$ *is a randomized algorithm which takes as input a password* $w \in \mathcal{M}$ *and returns a string* h.
- $\mathrm{Chk}^{\mathbf{H}}$ *is a (possibly randomized) algorithm which takes as input* $\tilde{w} \in \mathcal{S}$ *and string* h, *and returns either true or false.*

Both algorithms have access to oracle $\mathbf{H}(\cdot;\cdot,\mathsf{c}) : \{0,1\}^* \times \{0,1\}^{\ell_{\mathsf{sa}}} \rightarrow \{0,1\}^{\ell_H}$ *where* c *denotes the unit cost of calling* $\mathbf{H}$.

$\mathrm{MR}^{\mathcal{A}}_{\mathsf{PBAS},\mathsf{E}}$
$w \xleftarrow{W} \mathcal{S}$
$h \xleftarrow{\$} \mathrm{Reg}(w)$
$w' \leftarrow_{\$} \mathcal{A}^{\mathbf{H}}(h)$
$\mathrm{Ret}\ (w' = w)$

Fig. 4. Security game for password recovery in an offline brute-force cracking attack for a PBAS $\mathsf{PBAS} = (\mathrm{Reg}, \mathrm{Chk})$ and error setting $\mathsf{E} = (\mathcal{S}, W, \mathsf{dist}, t)$.

The canonical scheme $\mathsf{PBAS} = (\mathrm{Reg}, \mathrm{Chk})$, used widely in practice, has $\mathrm{Reg}^{\mathbf{H}}$ choose a random salt sa and output $(\mathsf{sa}, \mathbf{H}(w; \mathsf{sa}, \mathsf{c}))$. Then, $\mathrm{Chk}^{\mathbf{H}}(\tilde{w}, (\mathsf{sa}, h))$ computes $h' = \mathbf{H}(\tilde{w}; \mathsf{sa}, \mathsf{c})$ and outputs $h' \stackrel{?}{=} h$. The runtime is c, the cost of one query to $\mathbf{H}$. Typically PBKDF $\mathbf{H}$ will be the c-fold iteration $\mathbf{H}(\cdot; \cdot, \mathsf{c}) = H^{\mathsf{c}}(\cdot; \cdot)$ of some cryptographic hash function $H : \{0,1\}^* \times \{0,1\}^{\ell_{\mathsf{sa}}} \rightarrow \{0,1\}^{\ell_H}$ which we model as a random oracle. We will, in general, ignore the cost of other operations (e.g., the comparison $h = h'$) as they will be dominated by c. For example if $\mathbf{H}$ consists of 10,000 iterations of a hash function such as SHA-256 then c would be the cost of 10,000 computations of SHA-256.

We do not yet consider memory-hardness, and leave a proper treatment of it to future work (see Sect. 7).

Security Against Cracking Attacks. We will focus primarily on security against offline cracking attacks. Should an adversary obtain access to the output of Reg, we want that it should be computationally difficult — in terms of the number of oracle calls to $\mathbf{H}$ — to recover the password w. We formalize this in game MR shown in Fig. 4, a close relative of existing security notions capturing brute-force attacks against passwords (e.g. [4,16]). For an error setting $\mathsf{E} = (\mathcal{S}, W, \mathsf{dist}, t)$, we define the advantage of an adversary $\mathcal{A}$ against a scheme PBAS by

$$\mathbf{Adv}^{\mathrm{mr}}_{\mathsf{PBAS},\mathsf{E}}(\mathcal{A}) = \Pr\left[\,\mathrm{MR}^{\mathcal{A}}_{\mathsf{PBAS},\mathsf{E}} \Rightarrow \mathsf{true}\,\right].$$

The probability is over the coins used in the game and those of the adversary. We assume that the adversary $\mathcal{A}$ has exact knowledge of the error setting E. The number of queries $\mathcal{A}$ may make to oracle $\mathbf{H}$ is determined by its run time T and the cost c of querying $\mathbf{H}$, and for simplicity all other computations are assumed to be free. For example if $\mathbf{H}$ has cost c, then an adversary $\mathcal{A}$ running in time T may make $q = T/\mathsf{c}$ queries to $\mathbf{H}$.

5.1 Brute-Force Checkers

To improve the usability of a given $\mathsf{PBAS} = (\mathrm{Reg}, \mathrm{Chk})$ for some error setting $\mathsf{E} = (\mathcal{S}, W, \mathsf{dist}, t)$, Chatterjee et al. [12] advocate retaining the original Reg algorithm but modify the Chk algorithm to a 'relaxed checker' that loosens the requirement that a password be entered exactly. They define the (what we will call) brute-force error correction scheme $\mathsf{PBAS\text{-}BF} = (\mathrm{Reg}, \mathrm{Chk\text{-}BF})$ as follows.

Definition 9. *Let* $\mathsf{PBAS} = (\mathrm{Reg}, \mathrm{Chk})$, *and let* $\mathsf{E} = (\mathcal{S}, W, \mathsf{dist}, t)$ *be an error-setting. Let* $\mathbf{H}(\cdot; \cdot, \mathsf{c}_{\mathsf{bf}})$ *be a random oracle. Then the brute-force error-correction scheme* $\mathsf{PBAS\text{-}BF} = (\mathrm{Reg}, \mathrm{Chk\text{-}BF})$ *is defined as follows,*

- $\mathrm{Reg}(w)$ *chooses a salt* sa *at random, and outputs* $(\mathsf{sa}, \mathbf{H}(w; \mathsf{sa}, \mathsf{c}_{\mathsf{bf}}))$.
- $\mathrm{Chk\text{-}BF}(\tilde{w}, (\mathsf{sa}, h))$ *checks whether* $h = \mathbf{H}(\tilde{w}; \mathsf{sa}, \mathsf{c}_{\mathsf{bf}})$ *or* $h = \mathbf{H}(w'; \mathsf{sa}, \mathsf{c}_{\mathsf{bf}})$ *for each* $w' \in B_t(\tilde{w})$. *If it finds a match, it returns true, and otherwise returns false.*

Since $\mathsf{c_{bf}}$ denotes the unit cost of running $\mathbf{H}$, it follows that the runtime RT of this algorithm is the unit cost of $\mathbf{H}$ times the worst case ball size, i.e., $\mathsf{RT} = \mathsf{c_{bf}} \cdot \beta_{\max}$, where $\beta_{\max} = \max_{\tilde{w}} |B_t(\tilde{w})|$. To avoid potential side-channels, one may want to always compute $\mathbf{H}$ the same number of times, making the run time always RT.

An adversary $\mathcal{A}$ running in time at most T in game MR can make at most $q_{\mathrm{bf}} = T/\mathsf{c_{bf}}$ queries to $\mathbf{H}$. It is straightforward to see that $\mathcal{A}$'s optimal strategy is to query the q_{bf} most probable points in W to $\mathbf{H}$, and so $\mathbf{Adv}^{\mathrm{mr}}_{\mathsf{PBAS\text{-}BF,E}}(\mathcal{A}) \leq 2^{-\mathrm{H}^{q_{\mathrm{bf}}}_{\infty}(W)}$. This value is precisely the q-success rate of Boztas [10], and is a standard measure of the predictability of a password distribution.

Empirical analysis in [12] finds that when we only attempt to correct a very small number of errors per password (e.g. balls of size at most four) then the brute-force checker yields a noticeable increase in usability for a small reduction in security. However the above security bound highlights a potential limitation of the brute-force checker; if we wish to correct balls with larger numbers of points, we either need to accept an impractically long run time, or reduce $\mathsf{c_{bf}}$ to a level which for some error settings may result in significant security loss. This is an important consideration in the context of password typos where the large alphabet (of up to 96 ASCII characters depending on the password creation policy) means that the set of points within edit distance one of a six character string $\tilde{w} \in \mathcal{S}$ contains well over 1000 points. This raises the question of whether secure sketches can be employed to achieve a better time / security trade-off.

5.2 Typo-Tolerant PBAS Using Secure Sketches

The error-correcting properties of secure sketches (see Sect. 2) make them a natural candidate to build typo-tolerant PBAS schemes. We now describe how to compose a secure sketch with any existing PBAS scheme to create a typo-tolerant PBAS. The construction is so simple it is essentially folklore. See also a discussion by Dodis et al. [13]. Our contribution here is merely to formalize it so that we can provide a full security analysis in our computational setting.

Definition 10. *Let* $\mathsf{S} = (\mathsf{SS}, \mathsf{Rec})$ *be an secure-sketch for error setting* $\mathsf{E} = (\mathcal{S}, W, \mathsf{dist}, t)$. *Let* $\mathbf{H}(\cdot; \cdot, \mathsf{c_{ss}})$ *be a random oracle. Then we define the scheme* $\mathsf{PBAS\text{-}SS[S]} = (\text{Reg-SS}, \text{Chk-SS})$ *as follows:*

- Reg-SS(w) *runs* $\mathsf{SS}(w)$ *to obtain a sketch* s. *It additionally chooses a salt* sa *at random, and outputs* $(s, \mathsf{sa}, \mathbf{H}(w; \mathsf{sa}, \mathsf{c_{ss}}))$.
- Chk-SS$(\tilde{w}, (s, \mathsf{sa}, h))$ *first runs* $w' \leftarrow\!\!\$\ \mathsf{Rec}(s, \tilde{w})$. *It then checks whether* $h = \mathbf{H}(\tilde{w}; \mathsf{sa}, \mathsf{c_{ss}})$ *or* $h = \mathbf{H}(w'; \mathsf{sa}, \mathsf{c_{ss}})$. *If either matches, it returns true, and otherwise returns false.*

As written the run time of checking is always two calls[2] to $\mathbf{H}$ with unit cost $\mathsf{c_{ss}}$; it follows that $\mathsf{RT} = 2 \cdot \mathsf{c_{ss}}$. One could short-circuit checking by first checking

[2] If S is perfectly correct, it would be sufficient to simply run $w' \leftarrow \mathsf{Rec}(s, \tilde{w})$ and check if $h = \mathbf{H}(w'; \mathsf{sa}, \mathsf{c_{ss}})$, reducing the number of calls to $\mathbf{H}$ to one.

$\tilde{w}$ and only computing the secure sketch if authentication fails, however side-channels would now reveal when a user makes a typo. We would not want to short-circuit the calculations of $\mathbf{H}$ on the sketch outputs, as this could reveal even more information about w to a side-channel adversary.

An adversary $\mathcal{B}$ running in time at most T in game MR can make at most $q_{ss} = T/\mathsf{c}_{ss}$ queries to $\mathbf{H}$. It is clear that $\mathcal{B}$'s optimal strategy on input $(s, \mathsf{sa}, \mathbf{H}(w; \mathsf{sa}, \mathsf{c}_{ss}))$ is to query the q_{ss} heaviest points when ordered in terms of $\Pr[W = w \mid \mathsf{SS}(W) = s]$ to $\mathbf{H}(\cdot; \mathsf{sa}, \mathsf{c}_{ss})$. As such for a given $\mathsf{S} = (\mathsf{SS}, \mathsf{Rec})$ and error setting E, the definition of q-conditional min-entropy implies that $\mathbf{Adv}^{\mathrm{mr}}_{\mathsf{PBAS\text{-}SS[S],E}}(\mathcal{B}) \leq 2^{-\tilde{\mathrm{H}}^{q_{ss}}_{\infty}(W|\mathsf{SS}(W))}$.

5.3 Popularity-Proportional Hashing

We now describe a new distribution-sensitive variant of brute-force checking — popularity-proportional hashing (PPH). We shall see in Sect. 6 that for certain error settings and cracking attack run times, PPH allows us to correct more password errors securely than brute-force checking. For all other error settings, it serves as a useful stepping stone to show that brute-force checking provides a superior time / security trade-off than sketch-based typo-tolerant PBAS based on FRS and LHH.

The key idea is to partition the points in the error setting into layers based upon their probability (as done in LHH), then have the hashing cost vary across the layers. This is accomplished by having the PBKDF $\mathbf{H}$ take as input a different iteration count for each layer. Formally, for a distribution W with $\mathrm{H}^{\mathrm{fuzz}}_{t,\infty}(W) = \tilde{\mu}$, if a password w is such that $\Pr[W = w] \in (2^{-(j+1)}, 2^{-j}]$, then hashing w incurs a cost of $\mathsf{c}^j_{\mathrm{PPH}} = \mathsf{c}_{\mathrm{PPH}} \cdot 2^{\tilde{\mu}-(j+1)}$, where $\mathsf{c}_{\mathrm{PPH}}$ is a parameter of the scheme. By making it more computationally intensive for an attacker to hash popular passwords, the boost to an attacker's success probability resulting from querying a likely password is offset by the greater cost incurred to compute the relevant PBKDF output. We provide full details of the scheme in Fig. 5. In the following lemma, we show how to set the parameter $\mathsf{c}_{\mathrm{PPH}}$ to achieve a desired checking run time RT.

Lemma 4. *Let* $\mathsf{E} = (\mathcal{S}, W, \mathsf{dist}, t)$ *be an error setting. Let* PBAS-PPH *be as shown in Fig. 5 using random oracle* $\mathbf{H}$*. Then setting* $\mathsf{c}_{\mathrm{PPH}} = \mathsf{RT}$ *implies that*

$$\mathsf{RT}(\text{Chk-PPH}, \mathsf{c}_{\mathrm{PPH}}) \leq \mathsf{RT}\ ,$$

where $\mathsf{RT}(\text{Chk-PPH}, \mathsf{c}_{\mathrm{PPH}})$ *denotes the maximum run time of* Chk-PPH *with cost parameter* $\mathsf{c}_{\mathrm{PPH}}$ *on any input* $\tilde{w} \in \mathcal{S}$.

Proof. Fix any point $\tilde{w} \in \mathcal{S}$. Then if W is such that $\mathrm{H}^{\mathrm{fuzz}}_{t,\infty}(W) = \tilde{\mu}$, and recalling that $w \in L_j$ implies that $\Pr[W = w] > 2^{-(j+1)}$ it follows that

$$2^{-\tilde{\mu}} \geq \Pr[W \in B_t(\tilde{w})] > \sum_{j=\mu}^{\gamma} |B_t(\tilde{w}) \cap L_j| 2^{-(j+1)}\ .$$

Reg-PPH(w) :	Chk-PPH$(\tilde{w}, (\mathsf{sa}, h))$:	PPH-Layer(W) :
$\mathsf{sa} \xleftarrow{\$} \{0,1\}^{\ell_{\mathsf{sa}}}$	for $w' \in B_t(\tilde{w})$	$\gamma \leftarrow \left\lfloor -\log \left(\min_{w \in \mathcal{M}} \Pr\left[W = w \right] \right) \right\rfloor$
$j \leftarrow \mathsf{L}(w)$	$\quad j' \leftarrow \mathsf{L}(w')$	for $j = \mu, \ldots, \gamma$
$h \leftarrow \mathbf{H}(w; \mathsf{sa}, c_{\mathrm{PPH}}^{j})$	$\quad$ if $\mathbf{H}(w'; \mathsf{sa}, c_{\mathrm{PPH}}^{j'}) = y$	$\quad L_j \leftarrow (2^{-(j+1)}, 2^{-j}]$
Ret (sa, h)	$\quad\quad$ Ret true	Ret $\{ L_j \; : \; j \in [\mu, \gamma] \}$
	Ret false	

Fig. 5. The popularity-proportional hashing PBAS scheme PBAS-PPH $=$ (Reg-PPH, Chk-PPH), from a PBKDF $\mathbf{H}$ such that $\mathbf{H}(\cdot; \cdot, c_{\mathrm{PPH}}^{j})$ costs $c_{\mathrm{PPH}}^{j} = c_{\mathrm{PPH}} \cdot 2^{\tilde{\mu}-(j+1)}$ to compute where c_{PPH} is a parameter of the scheme, and $\mathrm{H}_{t,\infty}^{\mathrm{fuzz}}(W) = \tilde{\mu}$. The scheme uses layering PPH-Layer.

Multiplying both sides by $c_{\mathrm{PPH}} \cdot 2^{\tilde{\mu}}$ and recalling that $c_{\mathrm{PPH}} = \mathsf{RT}$ and $c_{\mathrm{PPH}}^{j} = c_{\mathrm{PPH}} \cdot 2^{\tilde{\mu}-(j+1)}$ gives

$$\mathsf{RT} > \sum_{j=\mu}^{\gamma} |B_t(\tilde{w}) \cap L_j| c_{\mathrm{PPH}} \cdot 2^{\tilde{\mu}-(j+1)} = \sum_{j=\mu}^{\gamma} |B_t(\tilde{w}) \cap L_j| c_{\mathrm{PPH}}^{j} ,$$

where the right hand side is precisely the run time of Chk-PPH on input $\tilde{w}$. Since the choice of $\tilde{w}$ was arbitrary, it follows that the run time of Chk-PPH on any input $\tilde{w} \in \mathcal{S}$ is at most RT, proving the claim. ∎

6 Comparing the PBAS Approaches

In the last section we saw three different ways to provide typo-tolerant password-based authentication. Now we dig deeper into the trade-offs incurred by the different schemes, in an attempt to determine which provides the best time / security trade-off. We are most interested in the following question:

> *When balls are efficiently enumerable, can PBAS-SS ever provide a better time / security trade-off compared to PBAS-BF/PBAS-PPH?*

We will answer this question, in the negative, for the cases of using FRS or LHH. To do so, we will fix an error setting E with computationally enumerable balls (Definition 3), fix the time allotted to authentication, and show that for *any* error setting the popularity-proportional hashing PBAS PBAS-PPH provably provides better security than both PBAS-SS[FRS2] or PBAS-SS[LHH]. We will then discuss the conditions on error settings and attacker run time under which PBAS-BF offers a better trade-off still.

An incorrect interpretation of our results would be that sketches are useless. This would be the wrong takeaway for several reasons. First, our analysis will only be for specific sketches, not all sketches in general, and so answering our question in full generality remains an interesting open question (see Sect. 7). Second, even if the answer to our main question is negative, it only considers computationally enumerable balls, and many of the error correction settings motivating secure sketches have balls too large to be efficiently enumerated. Potential examples include high-entropy biometrics such as iris scans and fingerprints. Another reason is that we only consider settings where one can check that a correction is in fact correct, which allows the brute-force ball search. Finally, and most broadly, we do not consider information theoretic security — the original setting of most sketch constructions.

With these caveats in place, we turn to setting up a framework by which we can make apples-to-apples comparisons between the different PBAS schemes.

Qualities of Typo-Tolerant PBAS. There are three key axes upon which we compare efficacy of typo-tolerant PBAS schemes; correctness, security and run time. Correctness is readily assessed — it is straightforward to see that for any error setting E and δ-correct sketch $\mathsf{S} = (\mathsf{SS}, \mathsf{Rec})$, $\mathsf{PBAS\text{-}SS[S]}$ inherits the δ-correctness of underlying sketch. On the other hand, the two brute-force correction schemes, $\mathsf{PBAS\text{-}BF}$ and $\mathsf{PBAS\text{-}PPH}$ are perfectly correct. This highlights a bonus of the brute-force approach — if the correct password lies in the ball around a typo, these schemes will *always* recover the correct point.

The comparison between the time / security trade-offs incurred by the different approaches is less immediate. For a given PBAS, this trade-off is primarily dictated by the computational cost c we assign to $\mathbf{H}$ (corresponding, in practice, to picking larger security parameters for the slow hashing scheme). In order to compare different approaches, we fix a runtime budget RT for checking passwords, set each of the schemes' parameters to achieve maximal security subject to the run time constraint RT, and compare the security as measured by the message recovery game of Fig. 4.

6.1 PBAS-BF versus FRS1 for Flat Distributions

As a warm up, we discuss the trade-off between $\mathsf{PBAS\text{-}BF}$ and $\mathsf{PBAS[FRS1]}$ where $\mathsf{FRS1} = (\mathsf{FRS1\text{-}SS}, \mathsf{FRS1\text{-}Rec})$ (Lemma 3).

Let $\mathsf{E} = (\mathcal{S}, W, \mathsf{dist}, t)$ be an error setting, such that W is flat with $\mathrm{H}_\infty(W) = \mu$ and maximum ball size $\beta_{\max}$. For a given run time budget RT, setting $\mathsf{c}_{\mathrm{ss}} = \mathsf{RT}/2$ and $\mathsf{c}_{\mathrm{bf}} = \mathsf{c}_{\mathrm{ss}} \cdot \frac{2}{\beta_{\max}}$ ensures both schemes have equal run times. Let $\mathcal{A}$ be an adversary in game MR running in time at most T. Letting $q_{\mathrm{ss}} = T/\mathsf{c}_{\mathrm{ss}}$, it follows that,

$$\mathbf{Adv}^{\mathrm{mr}}_{\mathsf{PBAS\text{-}BF},\mathsf{E}}(\mathcal{A}) = \left(q_{\mathrm{ss}} \cdot \frac{\beta_{\max}}{2}\right) 2^{-\mu} \ ; \text{ and}$$

$$\mathbf{Adv}^{\mathrm{mr}}_{\mathsf{PBAS\text{-}SS[FRS1]},\mathsf{E}}(\mathcal{A}) \leq \left(q_{\mathrm{ss}} \cdot \frac{\beta_{\max}}{\delta}\right) 2^{-\mu} .$$

The first statement arises since $\mathcal{A}$ can query at most $T/\mathsf{c}_{\mathrm{bf}} = q_{\mathrm{ss}} \cdot \frac{\beta_{\max}}{2}$ points in time T, each of which contributes weight $2^{-\mu}$ to its success probability. The latter follows since $\mathcal{B}$ can query at most $q_{\mathrm{ss}} = T/\mathsf{c}_{\mathrm{ss}}$ points in time T; substituting this into the bound on q-conditional min-entropy given in Lemma 3 yields the claim. Since $0 < \delta < 1$ (and since δ represents the error probability of the sketch, in practice we would like δ to be small), this clearly illustrates that in terms of existing upper bounds PBAS-BF offers a significantly better time / security trade-off than PBAS-SS[FRS1]. However, this does not rule out tighter upper bounds being found. To conclusively show that PBAS-BF offers the best performance, we would like to reverse the inequality sign in the above statement, and prove a *lower* bound on security for PBAS-SS[FRS1] that is larger than the upper bound on security for PBAS-BF.

Let's unpick what this means. Let $\mathcal{B}$ be the optimal attacker in game MR against PBAS-SS[FRS1]. We model the universal hash function family $\mathsf{F} : \mathcal{S} \times \{0,1\}^\ell \rightarrow \{0,1\}^{\log(\beta_{\max})+\log(1/\delta)}$ utilized by FRS1 as a family of random oracles $\mathcal{H} = \{\mathsf{h}\}$; rather than including $\mathsf{sa} \xleftarrow{\$} \{0,1\}^\ell$ as part of the sketch, we now give access to the chosen random oracle $\mathsf{h} \xleftarrow{\$} \{\mathcal{H}\}$. We note that this modeling is conservative, since it can only make the attacker's job harder. With this in place, we may lower bound $\mathbf{Adv}^{\mathrm{mr}}_{\mathsf{PBAS\text{-}SS[FRS1]},\mathsf{E}}(\mathcal{A})$ via a balls-in-bins experiment. We represent each point $w \in \mathcal{M} = \mathrm{supp}(W)$ by a ball of weight $2^{-\mu}$, and associate each of the $2^{\log(\beta_{\max})+\log(1/\delta)} = \frac{\beta_{\max}}{\delta}$ points $y \in \mathrm{range}(\mathcal{H})$ with a bin. The choice of oracle $\mathsf{h} \xleftarrow{\$} \mathcal{H}$ fixes a 'throwing' of the balls into the bins, and the adversary's success probability is equal to the expected weight accrued when they are allowed to choose up to q_{ss} balls from each bin where $q_{\mathsf{ss}} = T/\mathsf{c}_{\mathsf{ss}}$. The advantage is then calculated by taking the expectation of this total over the coins of the random oracle.

With this in place, all we must do is show that with overwhelming probability when we are allowed to choose at most q_{ss} balls from each bin, the resulting set contains at least $q_{\mathsf{ss}} \cdot \frac{\beta_{\max}}{2}$ balls. Intuitively this must be the case. We would *expect* each bin to contain $\frac{\delta \cdot |\mathrm{supp}(W)|}{\beta_{\max}}$ balls, and this value must be much larger than q_{ss} or the attack would be trivial. As such to *not* hit our total, a very high proportion of the bins must contain a number of balls which has diverged wildly from the mean. However, formalizing this intuition is non-trivial. A theorem statement to this end can be easily derived as a special case of those of Theorem 4; we defer the formal statement and analysis to the full version.

6.2 PPH versus FRS2 and LHH

In this section, we show that PBAS-PPH offers a better time / security trade-off than PBAS-SS implemented with the FRS and LHH sketch constructions of Sect. 3.

To facilitate the comparison, we first set the hashing cost parameter $\mathsf{c}_{\mathsf{PPH}}$ such that PBAS-PPH achieves the same runtime as PBAS-SS with associated hashing cost c_{ss}. With this parameter setting, PBAS-SS has checking run time $\mathsf{RT} = 2 \cdot \mathsf{c}_{\mathsf{ss}}$, so Lemma 4 implies that setting $\mathsf{c}_{\mathsf{PPH}} = 2 \cdot \mathsf{c}_{\mathsf{ss}}$ ensures PBAS-PPH achieves run time RT also. With this in place, we now upper-bound the success probability of an optimal attacker against PBAS-PPH with these parameters; the proof is given in the full version.

Lemma 5. *Let* $\mathsf{E} = (\mathcal{S}, W, \mathsf{dist}, t)$ *be an error setting, where* $\mathrm{H}^{\mathrm{fuzz}}_{t,\infty}(W) = \tilde{\mu}$. *Let* PBAS-PPH *be the population-proportional hashing scheme where random oracle* $\mathbf{H}$ *has associated cost* $\mathsf{c}_{\mathsf{PPH}} = 2\cdot\mathsf{c}_{\mathsf{ss}}$. *Let* $\mathcal{A}$ *be an adversary in game* $\mathrm{MR}^{\mathcal{A}}_{\mathsf{PBAS\text{-}PPH,E}}$ *running in time at most* T. *Then,*

$$\mathbf{Adv}^{\mathrm{mr}}_{\mathsf{PBAS\text{-}PPH,E}}(\mathcal{A}) \le q_{\mathrm{ss}} \cdot 2^{-\tilde{\mu}} .$$

where $q_{\mathrm{ss}} = T/\mathsf{c}_{\mathsf{ss}}$.

To give the above term some context, consider the equivalent upper bounds on success probability for sketch-based schemes PBAS-SS[FRS2], and PBAS-SS[LHH] (which are derived by substituting the parameters of the error setting into Theorems 1 and 3 respectively).[3] For any adversary $\mathcal{B}$ running in time at most T it holds that,

$$\mathbf{Adv}^{\mathrm{mr}}_{\mathsf{PBAS\text{-}SS[FRS2],E}}(\mathcal{B}) \le q_{\mathrm{ss}} \cdot \frac{\mathrm{H}_0(W)\cdot 2^{-(\tilde{\mu}-1)}}{\delta} \text{ , and}$$

$$\mathbf{Adv}^{\mathrm{mr}}_{\mathsf{PBAS\text{-}SS[LHH],E}}(\mathcal{B}) \le q_{\mathrm{ss}} \cdot \frac{2^{-(\tilde{\mu}-1)}}{\delta} .$$

By comparison with Lemma 5, it is immediately clear that PBAS-PPH enjoys better security upper bounds than either construction. Of course it could be that the upper bounds on the sketches can be improved.

We therefore, in the following theorem, lower bound the success probability of an optimal attack against PBAS-SS[FRS2] and PBAS-SS[LHH] in terms of the advantage of any adversary against PBAS-PPH. This rules out improving the upper bounds enough to make the sketch-based schemes better than PBAS-PPH. We first state the theorem, then discuss its significance.

Theorem 4. *Let* $\mathsf{E} = (\mathcal{S}, W, \mathsf{dist}, t)$ *be an error setting with* $\mathrm{H}^{\mathrm{fuzz}}_{t,\infty}(W) = \tilde{\mu}$. *Let* $\Pi\text{-}\mathsf{S} = (\Pi\text{-}\mathsf{SS}, \Pi\text{-}\mathsf{Rec})$ *be the secure sketch for the same error setting where* $\Pi \in \{\mathsf{FRS2}, \mathsf{LHH}\}$, *achieving* $1-\delta$ *correctness for some* $0 < \delta < 1$. *We model the (strongly) universal hash functions used by the sketch as random oracles. Let* PBAS-SS[Π-S] *be the sketch-assisted* PBAS *built from* Π-S, *using random oracle* $\mathbf{H}$ *with associated cost* c_{ss}. *Let* PBAS-PPH *be the popularity-proportional hashing* PBAS *for this error setting, with random oracle* $\mathbf{H}'$ *with associated cost* $\mathsf{c}_{\mathsf{PPH}}$ *set such that* $\mathsf{RT}(\text{Chk-SS}, \mathsf{c}_{\mathsf{ss}}) \ge \mathsf{RT}(\text{Chk-PPH}, \mathsf{c}_{\mathsf{PPH}})$. *Then for any adversary* $\mathcal{A}$ *against* PBAS-PPH *running in time at most* T, *there exists an adversary* $\mathcal{B}$ *against* PBAS-SS[Π-S] *such that*

$$\mathbf{Adv}^{\mathrm{mr}}_{\mathsf{PBAS\text{-}PPH,E}}(\mathcal{A}) \le \mathbf{Adv}^{\mathrm{mr}}_{\mathsf{PBAS\text{-}SS[\Pi\text{-}S],E}}(\mathcal{B}) + \left(\frac{e\cdot\delta}{2}\right)^{q_{\mathrm{ss}}}$$

and, moreover, $\mathcal{B}$ *runs in time* T *and so can make at most* $q_{\mathrm{ss}} = T/\mathsf{c}_{\mathsf{ss}}$ *queries.*

[3] Since they are stated in terms of $\tilde{\mu}$, we use the (looser) upper bounds here for ease of comparison. It is straightforward to derive similar statements showing the tighter bound are poorer too; see the proof of Theorem 4.

We have stated the theorem in the form of a reduction to highlight that PBAS-PPH provides at least as good a time / security trade-off as the seemingly more sophisticated sketch-based scheme. Given that q_{ss} will be large (this is the number of hash computations an attacker can make), then, provided that $\delta < 2/e \approx 0.736$ the second term in the bound is infinitesimally far from zero. Since δ represents the error rate of the sketch, in practice any useable sketch will require δ much smaller than .736.

The proof of the theorem proceeds by specifying a concrete adversary $\mathcal{B}$ against PBAS-SS[Π-SS] for $\Pi \in \{\mathsf{FRS2}, \mathsf{LHH}\}$, where the underlying (strongly) universal hash function family is modeled as a family of random oracles $\mathcal{H} = \{\mathsf{h}\}$. It works as one would expect: the adversary is given some sketch s and access to the oracle h used in the computation of the sketch. The attack queries the q_{ss} heaviest points in the preimage set

$$\mathcal{X}_s = \{w \in \text{supp}(W) \ : \ \Pr\left[W = w \wedge \Pi\text{-}\mathsf{SS}^{\mathsf{h}}(W) = s\right] > 0\}$$

to the PBKDF $\mathbf{H}$, where $q_{ss} = T/\mathsf{c}_{ss}$. This is the optimal attack.

We note that $\mathcal{B}$ need not compute the entire preimage set before submitting his guesses to the oracle $\mathbf{H}$ — rather his most efficient strategy is to compute the hashes of candidate points under h in descending order of weight, looking for points which lie in the preimage set. Intuitively this will be efficient because, assuming the sketch behaves uniformly, we would expect to find preimage set points at fairly regular intervals. For example, if (for simplicity) the sketch was simply $\mathsf{h}(w) = y$, then the expected run time for $\mathcal{B}$ to find q_{ss} matches (over the coins of h) is $q_{ss} \cdot |y|$ computations of h.

The proof then must show a lower bound on the success of $\mathcal{B}$. This analysis turns out to be quite tricky, involving a nuanced balls-in-bins argument. We make things easier by targeting only a rather loose lower bound that suffices to show the desired relationship with PBAS-PPH. We believe that better lower bounds can be found. Better lower bounds would signify an even bigger gap between the security of PBAS-PPH and PBAS-SS, making PBAS-PPH look even better in comparison.

We note that while the above result shows that PBAS-PPH always offers a better time / security trade-off than sketch-based schemes using FRS or LHH, the same cannot be shown to hold for PBAS-BF. For example, consider an error setting such that W consists of 2^{49} points of weight 2^{-50} and 2^{99} points of weight 2^{-100}, for which all balls contain a single point, except for one large ball containing 2^{20} of the lower weight points. As such $\mathrm{H}^{\text{fuzz}}_{t,\infty}(W) = 50$, and so by Theorems 2 and 3 it is easy to see that the security of the sketch-based schemes will degrade linearly and gracefully as T grows. On the other hand, the huge ball of 2^{20} points means that for matching run-times we must set $\mathsf{c}_{bf} = 2^{-19} \cdot \mathsf{c}_{ss}$ — so low that security for PBAS-BF (at least initially; see Sect. 6.3) degrades dramatically compared to PBAS-SS.

This counterexample may be contrived, but for more realistic distributions there remains a technical challenge in comparing PBAS-BF and PBAS-SS for FRS and LHH directly. The fact that the latter schemes are parameterized by

$\tilde{\mu} = \mathrm{H}^{\mathrm{fuzz}}_{t,\infty}(W)$ means that the natural derived security bounds are in terms of $\tilde{\mu}$ also, whereas for PBAS-BF, security is dictated by the sum of the weights of the points at the head of the distribution. Therefore any balls-in-bins analysis of the form described above involves a complicated comparison between two somewhat orthogonal terms. To overcome this, we can use PPH (whose success probability is also a function of $\tilde{\mu}$) as a bridge, first invoking Theorem 4 to show that PBAS-PPH offers a better time / security trade-off than the sketch-based PBAS and then assessing, using results in Sect. 6.3, whether PBAS-BF offers a better trade-off still.

6.3 Brute-Force Checking versus PPH

In the following theorem, we quantify precisely the conditions on an error setting E under which PBAS-PPH represents a better time / security trade-off than PBAS-BF. We fix a run time RT for the checking algorithms of both schemes, and set the associated hashing cost c_{bf} and hashing cost parameter c_{PPH} in a way that ensures both schemes work within this run time. We then consider the success probabilities of optimal adversaries attacking the schemes, both running in some time T.

The following theorem formally captures our comparison of the two schemes. Roughly speaking, the result indicates that there exists a crossover point: for T smaller than this point, PBAS-PPH provides better security than PBAS-BF, and for T larger than this point, the inverse is true. The crossover point is dictated by the error setting. As we discuss in more detail below, the crossover point for typical error distributions seen with human-chosen passwords is actually pretty small, meaning that PBAS-BF would appear to dominate for distributions of practical interest. Whether PBAS-PPH can be improved is an open question.

Theorem 5. *Let* $\mathsf{E} = (\mathcal{S}, W, \mathsf{dist}, t)$ *be an error setting, where* $\mathrm{H}^{\mathrm{fuzz}}_{t,\infty}(W) = \tilde{\mu}$ *and the largest ball is of size* $\beta_{\max}$. *Let* PBAS-BF = (Reg, Chk-BF) *be the brute-force* PBAS *for this error setting, using oracle* $\mathbf{H}$ *with associated cost* c_{bf} *and run time budget* RT. *Let* PBAS-PPH = (Reg-PPH, Chk-PPH) *be the popularity-proportional hashing* PBAS *for this error setting using an oracle* $\mathbf{H}'$ *with associated cost parameter* c_{PPH} *set such that* $\mathsf{RT}(\text{Chk-BF}, c_{\mathrm{bf}}) \geq \mathsf{RT}(\text{Chk-PPH}, c_{\mathrm{PPH}})$. *Let* $\mathcal{A}$ *and* $\mathcal{B}$ *be optimal attackers in games* $\mathrm{MR}^{\mathcal{A}}_{\mathsf{PBAS\text{-}PPH,E}}$ *and* $\mathrm{MR}^{\mathcal{B}}_{\mathsf{PBAS\text{-}BF,E}}$ *respectively running in time* T. *Let* $q_{\mathrm{bf}} = T/c_{\mathrm{bf}} = T \cdot \beta_{\max}/\mathsf{RT}$. *Then if* T *is such that*

$$T \leq \left(2^{-\mathrm{H}^{q_{\mathrm{bf}}}_{\infty}(W)} \cdot 2^{(\tilde{\mu}-1)}\right) \cdot \mathsf{RT}\,,$$

it holds that $\mathbf{Adv}^{\mathrm{mr}}_{\mathsf{PBAS\text{-}PPH,E}}(\mathcal{A}) \leq \mathbf{Adv}^{\mathrm{mr}}_{\mathsf{PBAS\text{-}BF,E}}(\mathcal{B})$. *For all error settings such that,*

$$T \geq \left(2^{-\mathrm{H}^{q_{\mathrm{bf}}}_{\infty}(W)} \cdot 2^{\tilde{\mu}} + 1\right) \cdot \mathsf{RT}\,,$$

it holds that $\mathbf{Adv}^{\mathrm{mr}}_{\mathsf{PBAS\text{-}BF,E}}(\mathcal{B}) \leq \mathbf{Adv}^{\mathrm{mr}}_{\mathsf{PBAS\text{-}PPH,E}}(\mathcal{A})$.

The proof works by upper and lower bounding the success probability of an optimal attacker against PPH, and comparing this to the success probability of an optimal attacker against the brute-force checker. The proof is given in the full version.

At a high level, the first bound in the theorem shows that PBAS-PPH favors error settings for which the weight of points decreases slowly (relative to the attack run time) as we move down through the distribution starting from the heaviest point. In such error settings PBAS-PPH allows us to securely correct larger balls — and accordingly more errors — than brute-force checking, provided balls are constructed such that the fuzzy min-entropy is high. This latter requirement is not much of a restriction, since a well designed error setting will seek to maximize the utility for a given level of security by defining balls to have many points but low aggregate mass. For most such error settings, while there will be a point after which PBAS-BF offers the better time / security trade-off, this will be for an attack run time too large to be of concern. This class of distributions includes those described in Sect. 6.2 for which brute-force checking degrades security dramatically.

On the other hand, the second bound shows that if the weight of points decreases quickly as we move down through the distribution, then PBAS-BF offers the better time / security trade-off. Intuitively this is because, as the weight of points decreases, the gap between the (higher) hashing cost under PPH decreases until it is, in fact, lower than the hashing cost used with PBAS-BF. As such the crossover point after which brute-force checking offers the better trade-off falls within the attack run times of concern. Since password distributions are typically very 'top-heavy', with the weights of points decreasing rapidly to leave a long tail, they fall into the class for which brute-force checking offers the better time / security trade-off.

The theorem gives both upper and lower bounds on T, with a small gap between them, meaning the crossover point is not precisely pinned down. This is due to a small amount of slack in upper and lower bounding the success probability of an optimal attacker against PBAS-PPH for general error settings. For specific error settings, one can sharpen the analysis.

7 Conclusion

In this work we investigated error correction for cryptographic secrets in the known-distribution setting. Using typo-tolerant password checking as a guiding case study, we provided several improvements on both theory and practice. On the theory side, we introduced a new information-theoretic security goal for secure sketches that better matches the needs of applications that may allow an attacker to make multiple guesses about the secret. While for high-entropy settings the distinction is moot, for passwords it is critical. We then provided analysis of the best known schemes in this setting, due to Fuller et al. [15].

Our first main contribution was the design and analysis of a new secure sketch construction, the layer-hiding hash (LHH). We proved that it provides better security than prior schemes. We then introduced a new distribution-sensitive brute-force based technique called property-proportional hashing (PPH) that, unlike the prior brute-force checking approach of Chatterjee et al. [12], varies the run time of the hash function according to the popularity of the password being hashed.

We gave a framework for comparing different approaches to typo-tolerant authentication, and used it to show that PPH outperforms sketch-based solutions to typo-tolerance, even when using the layer-hiding hash sketch. We determine the conditions under which PPH improves on the brute-force checking approach of Chatterjee et al. [12], along with the conditions under which their simpler brute-force checking offers a better trade-off. Put all together, our results indicate that brute-force based approaches perform better than the best known secure sketches. We now finish with a few important points and open questions.

Complexity Beyond Time. Most in-use slow hashes only target extending the time required for a single hash computation. Increasingly, however, practitioners are transitioning to slow hashing that targets memory-hardness [1–3,6,26], meaning that computing a hash requires that the space-time complexity (the product of memory and time utilized) is lower bounded. Our constructions work with memory-hard hash functions as well, though our comparisons of different approaches currently only considers time complexity. Future work may also consider parallel computation models, which could be useful when a password checking system can use multiple cores to simultaneously check multiple possible corrections.

Additional Applications. While we motivated and used as a running example the setting of password-based authentication, our constructions are generic. They hold for any distribution-sensitive setting in which one has efficiently enumerable balls (the same general setting considered by FRS). The FRS, LHH, and PPH approaches will not work for error settings with large balls, such as attempting to correct large Hamming or edit distances. In these contexts, existing secure sketch constructions [13,14] seem to be the only solution. We note that their entropy loss is significantly worse than the FRS or LHH constructions, and so they would not seem useful for passwords.

We have focused on authentication, but our results and comparisons are applicable to any cryptographic application in which noisy secrets are used to derive a key for which one can efficiently test correctness. This includes at least all authentication primitives, such as message authentication codes and authenticated encryption. Similarly, our new sketch constructions can also be used to build a fuzzy extractor using the construction from [13], which inherits the security improvement over the fuzzy extractor from FRS.

Secure Sketches in the Multi-guess Setting. In the previous section, we proved that PBAS-SS never offers a better time / security trade-off than PBAS-PPH/PBAS-BF when implemented with the FRS sketches, and the new — and nearly optimal, in the single-guess setting — LHH sketch. The key open question is whether *any* distribution-sensitive secure sketch can perform better in this context. The challenge is to design a sketch which preserves much of the min-entropy of the underlying distribution in the face of an attacker who can make q guesses for varying and large values of q. This is an important requirement in many practical settings, yet has been overlooked in existing literature.

Intuitively, the correctness requirement means that the sketch must include sufficient information to disambiguate between points in the heaviest ball(s). As such any efficiently-computable sketch — (we disregard those which, for example, solve an NP-hard problem to create an optimal arrangement of points into sketch preimage sets) — is likely to leak more information than is strictly necessary for correctness in less heavy balls. This additional leakage can then be exploited by an attacker. More generally we would expect that the larger q is, the wider the gap between the security of a sketch $\mathsf{S} = (\mathsf{SS}, \mathsf{Rec})$ for that error setting $\tilde{\mathrm{H}}^q_\infty(W|\mathsf{SS}(W))$, and the theoretical best case security bound $\mathrm{H}^{q,\mathrm{fuzz}}_{t,\infty}(W) - \log(1-\delta)$.

We conjecture that for a significant class of error-settings — especially those such as passwords, which inherently contain large balls — no efficient distribution sensitive secure sketch can offer a better time / security trade-off than brute-force based approaches. Indeed it seems likely that any intuition leading to an improvement in secure sketch performance over LHH may also be utilized to create a brute-force approach which improves on PBAS-PPH (similar to the way in which the same layered approach is used by both LHH and PPH, with better performance in the latter). Refining and improving upon the brute-force based approaches described here is an interesting open problem.

Acknowledgements. This work was supported in part by NSF grants 1619158, 1319051, 1314568, 1514163, United States Army Research Office (ARO) grant W911NF-16-1-0145, EPSRC and UK government grant EP/K035584/1, and gifts from VMware Labs, Google, and Microsoft.

References

1. Alwen, J., Blocki, J.: Efficiently computing data-independent memory-hard functions. In: Robshaw, M., Katz, J. (eds.) CRYPTO 2016. LNCS, vol. 9815, pp. 241–271. Springer, Heidelberg (2016). doi:10.1007/978-3-662-53008-5_9
2. Alwen, J., Chen, B., Kamath, C., Kolmogorov, V., Pietrzak, K., Tessaro, S.: On the complexity of scrypt and proofs of space in the parallel random oracle model. In: Fischlin, M., Coron, J.-S. (eds.) EUROCRYPT 2016. LNCS, vol. 9666, pp. 358–387. Springer, Heidelberg (2016). doi:10.1007/978-3-662-49896-5_13
3. Alwen, J., Chen, B., Kamath, C., Kolmogorov, V., Pietrzak, K., Tessaro, S.: On the complexity of scrypt and proofs of space in the parallel random oracle model. In: Fischlin, M., Coron, J.-S. (eds.) EUROCRYPT 2016. LNCS, vol. 9666, pp. 358–387. Springer, Heidelberg (2016). doi:10.1007/978-3-662-49896-5_13
4. Bellare, M., Ristenpart, T., Tessaro, S.: Multi-instance security and its application to password-based cryptography. In: Safavi-Naini, R., Canetti, R. (eds.) CRYPTO 2012. LNCS, vol. 7417, pp. 312–329. Springer, Heidelberg (2012). doi:10.1007/978-3-642-32009-5_19

5. Bennett, C.H., Brassard, G., Robert, J.M.: Privacy amplification by public discussion. SIAM J. Comput. **17**(2), 210–229 (1988)
6. Biryukov, A., Dinu, D., Khovratovich, D.: Argon and argon2: password hashing scheme. Technical report (2015)
7. Bonneau, J.: Guessing human-chosen secrets. Ph.D. thesis, University of Cambridge. http://www.cl.cam.ac.uk/jcb82/doc/2012-jbonneau-phd_thesis.pdf
8. Bonneau, J.: The science of guessing: analyzing an anonymized corpus of 70 million passwords. In: IEEE Symposium on Security and Privacy (SP), pp. 538–552. IEEE (2012)
9. Bowes, R.: Skull Security, Passwords. https://wiki.skullsecurity.org/Passwords
10. Boztas, S.: Entropies, guessing, and cryptography. Department of Mathematics, Royal Melbourne Institute of Technology. Technical report, vol. 6, pp. 2–3 (1999)
11. Castelluccia, C., Dürmuth, M., Perito, D.: Adaptive password-strength meters from markov models. In: NDSS (2012)
12. Chatterjee, R., Athalye, A., Akhawe, D., Juels, A., Ristenpart, T.: pASSWORD tYPOS and how to correct them securely. In: 2015 IEEE Symposium on Security and Privacy (SP (2016)
13. Dodis, Y., Reyzin, L., Smith, A.: Fuzzy extractors: how to generate strong keys from biometrics and other noisy data. In: Cachin, C., Camenisch, J.L. (eds.) EUROCRYPT 2004. LNCS, vol. 3027, pp. 523–540. Springer, Heidelberg (2004). doi:10.1007/978-3-540-24676-3_31
14. Dodis, Y., Reyzin, L., Smith, A.: Fuzzy extractors. In: Tuyls, P., Skoric, B., Kevenaar, T. (eds.) Security with Noisy Data, pp. 79–99. Springer, London (2007)
15. Fuller, B., Reyzin, L., Smith, A.: When are fuzzy extractors possible? In: Cheon, J.H., Takagi, T. (eds.) ASIACRYPT 2016. LNCS, vol. 10031, pp. 277–306. Springer, Heidelberg (2016). doi:10.1007/978-3-662-53887-6_10
16. Juels, A., Ristenpart, T.: Honey encryption: security beyond the brute-force bound. In: Nguyen, P.Q., Oswald, E. (eds.) EUROCRYPT 2014. LNCS, vol. 8441, pp. 293–310. Springer, Heidelberg (2014). doi:10.1007/978-3-642-55220-5_17
17. Juels, A., Wattenberg, M.: A fuzzy commitment scheme. In: Tsudik, G. (ed.) Sixth ACM Conference on Computer and Communications Security, pp. 28–36. ACM Press (1999)
18. Kaliski, B.: PKCS #5: password-based cryptography specification version 2.0, rFC 2289 (2000)
19. Ma, J., Yang, W., Luo, M., Li, N.: A study of probabilistic password models. In: 2014 IEEE Symposium on Security and Privacy (SP), pp. 689–704. IEEE (2014)
20. Mehler, A., Skiena, S.: Improving usability through password-corrective hashing. In: Crestani, F., Ferragina, P., Sanderson, M. (eds.) SPIRE 2006. LNCS, vol. 4209, pp. 193–204. Springer, Heidelberg (2006). doi:10.1007/11880561_16
21. Melicher, W., Ur, B., Segreti, S.M., Komanduri, S., Bauer, L., Christin, N., Cranor, L.F.: Fast, lean and accurate: modeling password guessability using neural networks. In: Proceedings of USENIX Security (2016)
22. Monrose, F., Reiter, M.K., Li, Q., Wetzel, S.: Cryptographic key generation from voice. In: Proceedings of 2001 IEEE Symposium on Security and Privacy. S&P 2001, pp. 202–213. IEEE (2001)
23. Monrose, F., Rubin, A.: Authentication via keystroke dynamics. In: Proceedings of the 4th ACM conference on Computer and Communications Security, pp. 48–56. ACM (1997)
24. Monrose, F., Rubin, A.D.: Keystroke dynamics as a biometric for authentication. Future Gener. Comput. Syst. **16**(4), 351–359 (2000)

25. Ostrovsky, R., Rabani, Y.: Low distortion embeddings for edit distance. J. ACM (JACM) **54**(5), 23 (2007)
26. Percival, C., Josefsson, S.: The scrypt password-based key derivation function. Technical report (2016)
27. PKCS #5: Password-based cryptography standard (RFC 2898). RSA Data Security, Inc., version 2.0, September 2000
28. Renner, R., Wolf, S.: The exact price for unconditionally secure asymmetric cryptography. In: Cachin, C., Camenisch, J.L. (eds.) EUROCRYPT 2004. LNCS, vol. 3027, pp. 109–125. Springer, Heidelberg (2004). doi:10.1007/978-3-540-24676-3_7
29. Siegler, M.: One Of the 32 Million With A RockYou Account? You May Want To Change All Your Passwords. Like Now. Tech Crunch, 14 December 2009
30. Škoric, B., Tuyls, P.: An efficient fuzzy extractor for limited noise. In: Symposium on Information Theory in the Benelux, pp. 193–200 (2009)
31. Wadhwa, T.: Why Your Next Phone Will Include Fingerprint, Facial, and Voice Recognition. Forbes, New York (2013)
32. Weir, M., Aggarwal, S., de Medeiros, B., Glodek, B.: Password cracking using probabilistic context-free grammars. In: IEEE Symposium on Security and Privacy (SP), pp. 162–175 (2009)
33. Wheeler, D.L.: zxcvbn: low-budget password strength estimation. In: Proceedings of USENIX Security (2016)
34. Yao, F.F., Yin, Y.L.: Design and analysis of password-based key derivation functions. In: Menezes, A. (ed.) CT-RSA 2005. LNCS, vol. 3376, pp. 245–261. Springer, Heidelberg (2005). doi:10.1007/978-3-540-30574-3_17
35. Zhao, Q., Liu, F., Zhang, L., Zhang, D.: A comparative study on quality assessment of high resolution fingerprint images. In: International Conference on Image Processing (ICIP), pp. 3089–3092 (2010)

Author Index